THE CAMBRIDGE HISTORY OF

RUSSIA

The second volume of *The Cambridge History of Russia* covers the imperial period (1689–1917). It encompasses political, economic, social, cultural, diplomatic and military history. All the major Russian social groups have separate chapters and the volume also includes surveys on the non-Russian peoples and the government's policies towards them. It addresses themes such as women, law, the Orthodox Church, the police and the revolutionary movement. The volume's seven chapters on diplomatic and military history, and on Russia's evolution as a great power, make it the most detailed study of these issues available in English. The contributors come from the USA, UK, Russia and Germany: most are internationally recognised as leading scholars in their fields, and some emerging younger academics engaged in a cutting-edge research have also been included. No other single volume in any language offers so comprehensive, expert and up-to-date an analysis of Russian history in this period.

DOMINIC LIEVEN is Professor of Russian Government at the London School of Economics and Political Science. His books include *Russia's Rulers under the Old Regime* (1989) and *Empire: The Russian Empire and its Rivals* (2000).

THE CAMBRIDGE HISTORY OF

RUSSIA

This is a definitive new history of Russia from early Rus' to the successor states that emerged after the collapse of the Soviet Union. Volume I encompasses developments before the reign of Peter I; volume II covers the 'imperial era', from Peter's time to the fall of the monarchy in March 1917; and volume III continues the story through to the end of the twentieth century. At the core of all three volumes are the Russians, the lands which they have inhabited and the polities that ruled them while other peoples and territories have also been give generous coverage for the periods when they came under Riurikid, Romanov and Soviet rule. The distinct voices of individual contributors provide a multitude of perspectives on Russia's diverse and controversial millennial history.

Volumes in the series

Volume I
From Early Rus' to 1689
Edited by Maureen Perrie

Volume II
Imperial Russia, 1689–1917
Edited by Dominic Lieven

Volume III
The Twentieth Century
Edited by Ronald Grigor Suny

THE CAMBRIDGE HISTORY OF RUSSIA

★

VOLUME II
Imperial Russia, 1689–1917

★

Edited by
DOMINIC LIEVEN
London School of Economics and Political Science

CAMBRIDGE
UNIVERSITY PRESS

University Printing House, Cambridge CB2 8BS, United Kingdom

Cambridge University Press is part of the University of Cambridge.

It furthers the University's mission by disseminating knowledge in the pursuit of education, learning and research at the highest international levels of excellence.

www.cambridge.org
Information on this title: www.cambridge.org/9781107639416

First published 2006
Reprinted 2010
First paperback edition 2015

A catalogue record for this publication is available from the British Library

ISBN 978-0-521-81529-1 Hardback
ISBN 978-1-107-63941-6 Paperback

Contents

List of plates ix
List of maps xi
Notes on contributors xii
Acknowledgements xvi
Note on the text xvii
List of abbreviations in notes and bibliography xviii
Chronology xx

Introduction *1*
DOMINIC LIEVEN

PART I
EMPIRE

1 · Russia as empire and periphery *9*
DOMINIC LIEVEN

2 · Managing empire: tsarist nationalities policy *27*
THEODORE R. WEEKS

3 · Geographies of imperial identity *45*
MARK BASSIN

PART II
CULTURE, IDEAS, IDENTITTIES

4 · Russian culture in the eighteenth century *67*
LINDSEY HUGHES

5 · Russian culture: 1801–1917 92
ROSAMUND BARTLETT

6 · Russian political thought: 1700–1917 116
GARY M. HAMBURG

7 · Russia and the legacy of 1812 145
ALEXANDER M. MARTIN

PART III
NON-RUSSIAN NATIONALITIES

8 · Ukrainians and Poles 165
TIMOTHY SNYDER

9 · Jews 184
BENJAMIN NATHANS

10 · Islam in the Russian Empire 202
VLADIMIR BOBROVNIKOV

PART IV
RUSSIAN SOCIETY, LAW AND ECONOMY

11 · The elites 227
DOMINIC LIEVEN

12 · The groups between: *raznochintsy*, intelligentsia, professionals 245
ELISE KIMERLING WIRTSCHAFTER

13 · Nizhnii Novgorod in the nineteenth century: portrait of a city 264
CATHERINE EVTUHOV

14 · Russian Orthodoxy: Church, people and politics in Imperial Russia 284
GREGORY L. FREEZE

15 · Women, the family and public life 306
BARBARA ALPERN ENGEL

16 · Gender and the legal order in Imperial Russia *326*
MICHELLE LAMARCHE MARRESE

17 · Law, the judicial system and the legal profession *344*
JORG BABEROWSKI

18 · Peasants and agriculture *369*
DAVID MOON

19 · The Russian economy and banking system *394*
BORIS ANANICH

PART V
GOVERNMENT

20 · Central government *429*
ZHAND P. SHAKIBI

21 · Provincial and local government *449*
JANET M. HARTLEY

22 · State finances *468*
PETER WALDRON

PART VI
FOREIGN POLICY AND THE ARMED FORCES

23 · Peter the Great and the Northern War *489*
PAUL BUSHKOVITCH

24 · Russian foreign policy, 1725–1815 *504*
HUGH RAGSDALE

25 · The imperial army *530*
WILLIAM C. FULLER, JR

26 · Russian foreign policy, 1815–1917 *554*
DAVID SCHIMMELPENNINCK VAN DER OYE

27 · The navy in 1900: imperialism, technology and class war 575
NIKOLAI AFONIN

PART VII
REFORM, WAR AND REVOLUTION

28 · The reign of Alexander II: a watershed? 593
LARISA ZAKHAROVA

29 · Russian workers and revolution 617
REGINALD E. ZELNIK

30 · Police and revolutionaries 637
JONATHAN W. DALY

31 · War and revolution, 1914–1917 655
ERIC LOHR

Bibliography 670
Index 711

Plates

The plates will be found between pages 420 and 421.

1 Imperial mythology: Peter the Great examines young Russians returning from study abroad. From *Russkii voennyi flot*, St Petersburg, 1908.
2 Imperial grandeur: the Great Palace (Catherine Palace) at Tsarskoe Selo. Author's collection.
3 Alexander I: the victor over Napoleon. From *Russkii voennyi flot*, St Petersburg, 1908.
4 Alexander II addresses the Moscow nobility on the emancipation of the serfs. Reproduced courtesy of John Massey Stewart Picture Library.
5 Mikhail Lomonosov: the grandfather of modern Russian culture. Reproduced courtesy of John Massey Stewart Picture Library.
6 Gavril Derzhavin; poet and minister. Reproduced courtesy of John Massey Stewart Picture Library.
7 Sergei Rachmaninov: Russian music conquers the world. Reproduced courtesy of John Massey Stewart Picture Library.
8 The Conservatoire in St Petersburg. Author's collection.
9 Count Muravev (Amurskii): imperial pro-consul. By A.V. Makovskii (1869–1922). Reproduced courtesy of John Massey Stewart Picture Library and Irkutsk Fine Arts Museum.
10 Imperial statuary: the monument to Khmel'nitskii in Kiev. Reproduced courtesy of John Massey Stewart Picture Library.
11 Tiflis: Russia in Asia? Reproduced courtesy of John Massey Stewart Picture Library.
12 Nizhnii Novgorod: a key centre of Russian commerce. Reproduced courtesy of John Massey Stewart Picture Library.
13 Rural life: an aristocratic country mansion. Author's collection.
14 Rural life: a central Russian village scene. Author's collection.
15 Rural life: the northern forest zone. Author's collection.
16 Rural life: the Steppe. Author's collection.
17 Naval ratings: the *narod* in uniform. From *Russkii voennyi flot*, St Petersburg, 1908.
18 Sinews of power? Naval officers in the St Petersburg shipyards. *Russkii voennyi flot*, St Petersburg, 1908.
19 The battleship *Potemkin* fitting out. *Russkii voennyi flot*, St Petersburg, 1908.

20 Baku: the empire's capital of oil and crime. Reproduced courtesy of John Massey Stewart Picture Library.
21 Alexander III: the monarchy turns 'national'. From *Russkii voennyi flot*, St Petersburg, 1908.
22 The coronation of Nicholas II. Reproduced courtesy of John Massey Stewart Picture Library.
23 A different view of Russia's last emperor. Reproduced courtesy of John Massey Stewart Picture Library.
24 Nicholas II during the First World War. Author's collection.

Maps

1 The provinces and population of Russia in 1724. Used with permission from *The Routledge Atlas of Russian History* by Martin Gilbert. xxiv

2 Serfs in 1860. Used with permission from *The Routledge Atlas of Russian History* by Martin Gilbert. xxv

3 Russian industry by 1900. Used with permission from *The Routledge Atlas of Russian History* by Martin Gilbert. xxvi

4 The provinces and population of European Russia in 1900. Used with permission from *The Routledge Atlas of Russian History* by Martin Gilbert. xxvii

5 The Russian Empire (1913). From Archie Brown, Michael Kaser and G. S. Smith (eds.) *Cambridge Encyclopedia of Russia* (1982). xxviii

Notes on contributors

NIKOLAI AFONIN is a former Soviet naval officer and an expert on naval technology and naval history. He has contributed many articles to journals on these subjects.

BORIS ANANICH is an Academician and a Senior Research Fellow at the Saint Petersburg Institute of History of the Russian Academy of Sciences, as well as a Professor of Saint Petersburg State University. His works include *Rossiia i mezhdunarodnyi kapital, 1897–1914* (1970) and *Bankirskie doma v Rossii. 1860–1914. Ocherki istorii chastnogo predprinimatel'stva* (1991).

JORG BABEROWSKI is Professor of East European History at the Humboldt University in Berlin. His books include *Der Feind ist Uberall. Stalinismus im Kaukasus* (2003) and *Der Rote Terror. Die Geschichte des Stalinismus* (2004).

ROSAMUND BARTLETT is Reader in Russian at the University of Durham. Her books include *Wagner and Russia* (1995) and *Chekhov: Scenes from a Life* (2004).

MARK BASSIN is Reader in Cultural and Political Geography at University College London. He is the author of *Imperial Visions: Nationalist Imagination and Geographical Expansion in the Russian Far East 1840–1865* (1999) and the editor of *Geografiia i identichnosti post-sovetskoi Rossii* (2003).

VLADIMIR BOBROVNIKOV is a Research Fellow at the Institute for Oriental Studies in Moscow. He is the author of *Musul'mane severnogo Kavkaza: obychai, pravo, nasilie* (2002) and 'Rural Muslim Nationalism in the Post-Soviet Caucasus: The Case of Daghestan', in M. Gammer (ed.), *The Caspian Region*, Vol. II: *The Caucasus* (2004).

PAUL BUSHKOVITCH is Professor of History at Yale University. His books include *Peter the Great: The Struggle for Power 1671–1725* (2001) and *Religion and Society in Russia: The Sixteenth and Seventeenth Centuries* (1992).

JONATHAN W. DALY is Assistant Professor of History at the University of Illinois at Chicago. His works include *Autocracy under Siege: Security Police and Opposition in Russia 1866–1905* (1998).

BARBARA ALPEN ENGEL is a Professor at the University of Colorado, Boulder. Her works include *Between the Fields and the City: Women, Work and Family in Russia, 1861–1914* (1994) and *Women in Russia: 1700–2000* (2004).

CATHERINE EVTUHOV is Associate Professor at Georgetown University. Her books include *The Cross and the Sickle: Sergei Bulgakov and the Fate of Russian Religious Philosophy, 1890–1920* (1997) and (with Richard Stites) *A History of Russia: Peoples, Legends, Events, Forces* (2004).

GREGORY L. FREEZE is Victor and Gwendolyn Beinfield Professor of History at Brandeis University. His books include *The Russian Levites: Parish Clergy in the Eighteenth Century* (1997) and *the Parish Clergy in Nineteenth-Century Russia* (1983).

WILLIAM C. FULLER, JR is Professor of Strategy at the Naval War College and the author of *Civil–Military Conflict in Imperial Russia, 1881–1914* (1985) and *Strategy and Power in Russia 1600–1914* (1992).

GARY M. HAMBURG is Otho M. Behr Professor of History at Claremont McKenna College and the author of *Boris Chicherin and Early Russian Liberalism* (1992) and, with Thomas Sanders and Ernest Tucker, of *Russian–Muslim Confrontation in the Caucasus: Alternative Visions of the Conflict between Imam Shamil and the Russians, 1830–1859* (2004).

JANET M. HARTLEY is Professor of International History at the London School of Economics and Political Science. Her books include *A Social History of the Russian Empire 1650–1825* (1999) and *Charles Whitworth: Diplomat in the Age of Peter the Great* (2002).

LINDSEY HUGHES is Professor of Russian History in the School of Slavonic and East European Studies, University College London. Her books include *Russia in the Age of Peter the Great* (1998) and *Peter the Great: A Biography* (2002).

DOMINIC LIEVEN is Professor of Russian Government at the London School of Economics and Political Science. His books include *Russia's Rulers under the Old Regime* (1989) and *Empire: The Russian Empire and its Rivals* (2000).

ERIC LOHR is Assistant Professor of History, American University. He is the author of *Nationalizing the Russian Empire: The Campaign against Enemy Aliens during World War I* (2003) and the co-editor (with Marshall Poe) of *The Military and Society in Russia 1450–1917* (2002).

MICHELLE LAMARCHE MARRESE is Assistant Professor at the University of Toronto and the author of *A Woman's Kingdom: Noblewomen and the Control of Property in Russia, 1700–1861* (2001).

ALEXANDER M. MARTIN is Associate Professor of History at Oglethorpe University and the author of *Romantics, Reformers, Reactionaries: Russian Conservative Thought and Politics in the Reign of Alexander I* (1997) and the editor and translator of *Provincial Russia in the Age of Enlightenment: The Memoirs of a Priest's Son* by Dmitri I. Rostislavov (2002).

DAVID MOON is Reader in Modern European History at the University of Durham. His books include *The Russian Peasantry 1600–1930: The World the Peasants Made* (1999) and *The Abolition of Serfdom in Russia, 1762–1907* (2001).

BENJAMIN NATHANS is Associate Professor of History at the University of Pennsylvania and the author of *Beyond the Pale: The Jewish Encounter with Late Imperial Russia* (2002) and editor of the Russian-language *Research Guide to Materials on the History of Russian Jewry (Nineteenth and Early Twentieth Centuries) in Selected Archives of the Former Soviet Union* (1994).

HUGH RAGSDALE is Professor Emeritus, University of Alabama, and is the editor of *Imperial Russian Foreign Policy* (1993). His authored books include *The Soviets, the Munich Crisis, and the Coming of World War II* (2004).

DAVID SCHIMMELPENNINCK VAN DER OYE is Associate Professor of History at Brock University. He is the author of *Toward the Rising Sun: Russian Ideologies of Empire and the Path to War with Japan* (2001) and co-editor (with Bruce Menning) of *Reforming the Tsar's Army: Military Innovation in Imperial Russia from Peter the Great to the Revolution* (2004).

ZHAND P. SHAKIBI is a Fellow at the London School of Economics and Political Science and the author of *The King, The Tsar, The Shah and the Making of Revolution in France, Russia, and Iran* (2006).

TIMOTHY SNYDER is Associate Professor of History at Yale University and the author of *Nationalism, Marxism and Modern Central Europe: A Biography of Kazimierz Kelles-Krauz* (1998) and *The Reconstruction of Nations: Poland, Ukraine, Lithuania, Belarus, 1569–1999* (2003).

PETER WALDRON is Professor of History at the University of Sunderland and the author of *Between Two Revolutions: Stolypin and the Politics of Renewal in Russia* (1998) and *The End of Imperial Russia* (1997).

THEODORE R. WEEKS is Associate Professor of History at Southern Illinois University at Carbondale. He is the author of *Nation and State in Late Imperial Russia* (1996) and *From Assimilation to Antisemitism: The 'Jewish Question' in Poland, 1850–1914* (2006).

ELISE KIMERLING WIRTSCHAFTER is Professor of History at California State Polytechnic University in Pomona and the author most recently of *The Play of Ideas in Russian Enlightenment Theater* (2003) and *Social Identity in Imperial Russia* (1997).

LARISA ZAKHAROVA is Professor of History at Moscow Lomonosov State University. She is the author of *Samoderzhavie i otmena krepostnogo prava* (1984) and the editor (with Ben Eklof and John Bushnell) of *Russia's Great Reforms, 1855–1881* (1994).

REGINALD E. ZELNIK was Professor of History at the University of California at Berkeley. His books included *Labor and Society in Tsarist Russia: The Factory Workers of St Petersburg, 1855–1870* (1971) and he was also the editor and translator of *A Radical Worker in Tsarist Russia: The Autobiography of Semen Ivanovich Kanatchikov* (1986).

Acknowledgements

I cannot pretend that editing this volume and simultaneously serving as head of a large and complicated department has always been a joy. Matters were not improved by a variety of ailments which often made it impossible to spend any time at a computer screen. I owe much to Isabel Crowhurst and Minna Salminen: without the latter the bibliography might never have happened. My successor, George Philip, and Nicole Boyce provided funds to find me an assistant at one moment of true emergency: for this too, many thanks. The volume's contributors responded very kindly to appeals for information and minor changes, sometimes of an entirely trivial and infuriating nature. Jacqueline French and Auriol Griffith-Jones coped splendidly with the huge jobs respectively of copy-editing the text and compiling the index. John Massey Stewart spent hours showing me his splendid collection of postcards and slides: I only regret that due to strict limitations on space I was able to reproduce just a few of them in this volume. All maps are taken, by permission, from *The Routledge Atlas of Russian History* by Sir Martin Gilbert. Isabelle Dambricourt at Cambridge University Press had to spend too much time listening to me wailing in emails. When editing a volume of this scale and running the department got too exciting, my family also spent a good deal of effort trying to keep me happy, or at least sane. My thanks to everyone for their patience.

This volume is dedicated to the memory of Professor Petr Andreevich Zaionchkovskii (1904–83).

Note on the text

The system of transliteration from Cyrillic used in this volume is that of the Library of Congress, without diacritics. The soft sign is denoted by an apostrophe but is omitted from place-names (unless they appear in transliterated titles or quotations); English forms of the most common place-names are used (e.g. Moscow, St Petersburg, Yalta, Sebastopol, Archangel). In a number of cases (e.g. St Petersburg-Petrograd-Leningrad-St Petersburg) the names of cities have been changed to suit political circumstances. On occasion this has meant substituting one ethnic group's name for a city for a name in another language (e.g. Vilna-Vilnius-Wilno). No attempt has been made to impose a single version on contributors but wherever doubts might arise as to the identity of a place alternative versions have been put in brackets. The same is true as regards the transliteration of surnames: for example, on occasion names are rendered in their Ukrainian version with a Russian or Polish version in brackets. Where surnames are of obvious Central or West European origin then they have generally been rendered in their original form (e.g. Lieven rather than the Russian Liven). Anglicised name-forms are used for tsars (thus 'Alexander I') and a small number of well-known figures retain their established Western spellings (e.g. Fedor Dostoevsky, Leo Tolstoy, Alexander Herzen), even though this may lead to inconsistencies. Russian versions of first names have generally been preferred for people other than monarchs, though some freedom has been allowed to contributors in this case too. Translations within the text are those of the individual contributors to this volume unless a printed source is quoted. All dates are rendered in the Julian calendar, which was in force in the Russian Empire until its demise in 1917. The only exceptions occur in chapters where the European context is vital (e.g. when discussing Russian foreign policy). In these cases dates are often rendered in both the Julian and the Gregorian forms. The Gregorian calendar was eleven days ahead in the eighteenth century, twelve days in the nineteenth and thirteen days in the twentieth.

Abbreviations in notes and bibliography

ARCHIVE COLLECTIONS AND VOLUMES OF LAWS

GARF — Gosudarstvennyi arkhiv Rossiisko Federatsii (State Archive of the Russian Federation)
GIAgM — Gosudarstvennyi istoricheskii arkhiv gorod Moskvy (Moscow State Historical Archive)
OR RGB — Otdel rukopisei: Rossiiskaia gosudarstvennaia biblioteka (Manuscript section: Russian State Library)
OPI GIM — Otdel pis'mennikh istochnikov: gosudarstvennyi istoricheskii muzei (Manuscript section: State Historical Museum)
PSZ — *Pol'noe sobranie zakonov Rossiiskoi Imperii* (Complete Collection of Laws of the Russian Empire)
RGADA — Russkii gosudarstvennyi arkhiv drevnikh aktov (Russian State Archive of Ancient Acts)
RGAVMF — Rossiiskii gosudarstvennyi arkhiv voenno-morskogo flota (Russian State Naval Archive)
RGIA — Rossiiskii gosudarstvennyi istoricheskii arkhiv (Russian State Historical Archive)
RGVIA — Rossiiskii gosudarstvennyi voenno-istoricheskii arkhiv (Russian State Military-Historical Archive)
SZ — *Svod zakonov Rossiiskoi Imperii* (Code of Laws of the Russian Empire)

JOURNALS

AHR — *American Historical Review*
CASS — *Canadian American Slavic Studies*
CMRS — *Cahiers du Monde Russe et Sovietique*
IZ — *Istoricheskie zapiski*

JfGO	*Jahrbücher fur Geschichte Osteuropas*
JMH	*Journal of Modern History*
JSH	*Journal of Social History*
KA	*Krasnyi arkhiv*
RH	*Russian History*
RR	*Russian Review*
SEER	*Slavonic and East European Review*
SR	*Slavic Review*
VI	*Voprosy istorii*
ZGUP	*Zhurnal grazhdanskogo ugolovnogo prava*
ZMI	*Zhurnal Ministerstva Iustitsii*

OTHER ABBREVIATIONS

AN	Akademiia nauk
ch.	chast' (part)
d.	delo (file)
ed. khr.	edinitsa khraneniia (storage unit)
Izd.	Izdatel'stvo
l. / ll.	list/list'ia (folio/s)
LGU	Leningrad State University
MGU	Moscow State University
ob.	oboroto (verso)
op.	opis' (inventory)
otd.	otdel (section)
SGECR	Study Group on Eighteenth-Century Russia
SpbU	St Petersburg State University
SSSR	USSR
st.	stat'ia (article)
Tip.	Tipografiia

Chronology

1689	overthrow of regency of Tsarevna Sophia
1697–8	Peter I in Western Europe
1700	Great Northern War begins with Sweden
1703	foundation of Saint Petersburg
1709	Battle of Poltava: defeat of Swedes and Ukrainian Hetman Mazepa
1711	establishment of Senate
1717	formation of administrative colleges
1721	foundation of the Holy Synod: disappearance of the patriarchate
1721	Treaty of Nystadt ends Great Northern War: Baltic provinces gained
1722	creation of Table of Ranks
1725	foundation of Academy of Sciences
1725	death of Peter I. Accession of Catherine I
1727	death of Catherine I. Accession of Peter II
1730	death of Peter II. Accession of Anna. Failed attempt to limit autocracy
1740	death of Anna. Accession of Ivan VI
1741	overthrow of Ivan VI. Accession of Elizabeth
1753	abolition of internal customs duties
1754	foundation of Moscow University
1755	outbreak of Seven Years War
1761	death of Elizabeth. Accession of Peter III
1762	'emancipation' of the nobility from compulsory state service
1762	overthrow of Peter III. Accession of Catherine II
1765	death of Lomonosov
1767	Catherine II's *Nakaz* (Instruction) and Legislative Commission

1768	war with Ottoman Empire
1773	beginning of Pugachev revolt
1774	Treaty of Kuchuk-Kainardji: victory over Ottomans
1775	reform of provincial administration
1783	annexation of Crimea
1785	charter of the nobility
1790	publication of Radishchev's *Journey from St Petersburg to Moscow*
1795	final partition of Poland
1796	death of Catherine II. Accession of Paul I
1797	new succession law: male primogeniture established
1801	overthrow of Paul I. Accession of Alexander I
1802	creation of ministries
1804	university statute
1807	Treaty of Tilsit
1810	creation of State Council
1811	Karamzin's 'Memoir on Ancient and Modern Russia'
1812	defeat of Napoleon's invasion
1814	Russian army enters Paris
1815	constitution for Russian Kingdom of Poland issued
1825	death of Alexander I. Accession of Nicholas I. Decembrist revolt
1826	foundation of Third Section
1830–1	rebellion in Poland
1833	Code of Laws (*Svod zakonov*) issued
1836	first performance of Glinka's *A Life for the Tsar*
1836	Chaadaev's *First Philosophical Letter*
1837	death of Pushkin
1847–52	publication of Turgenev's *Zapiski okhotnika* (A *Huntsman's Sketches*)
1854	French, British and Ottomans invade Crimea
1855	death of Nicholas I. Accession of Alexander II
1856	Treaty of Paris ends Crimean War
1861	emancipation of the serfs
1862	foundation of Saint Petersburg Conservatoire
1863	rebellion in Poland
1864	local government (*zemstvo*) and judicial reforms introduced
1865–6	publication begins of Tolstoy's *Voina i mir* (*War and Peace*)
1866	Karakozov's attempt to assassinate Alexander II

1866	foundation of Moscow Conservatoire
1866	publication of Dostoevsky's *Prestuplenie i nakazanie* (*Crime and Punishment*)
1874	introduction of universal military service
1874	first performance of Mussorgsky's *Boris Godunov*
1875	the 'To the People' movement goes on trial
1877–8	war with Ottoman Empire. Treaty of Berlin
1878	formation of 'Land and Freedom' revolutionary group
1880	Loris-Melikov appointed to head government
1880	publication of Dostoevsky's *Brat'ia Karamazovy* (*The Brothers Karamazov*)
1881	assassination of Alexander II. Accession of Alexander III
1881	introduction of law on 'states of emergency'
1884	Plekhanov publishes *Nashi raznoglasiia* (Our Differences)
1889	introduction of Land Captains
1891	construction of Trans-Siberian railway begins
1894	Franco-Russian alliance ratified
1894	death of Alexander III. Accession of Nicholas II
1898	first congress of the Social Democratic party
1899	foundation of journal *Mir iskusstva* (World of Art)
1901	formation of the Socialist Revolutionary party
1902	Lenin publishes *Chto delat'?* (*What Is to Be Done?*)
1903	Kishinev pogrom
1904	outbreak of war with Japan
1904	assassination of Plehve: Sviatopolk-Mirsky's 'thaw' begins
1905	'Bloody Sunday' ushers in two years of revolution
1905	defeats at battles of Mukden and Tsushima
1905	Treaty of Portsmouth (September) ends war with Japan
1905	October 17 Manifesto promises a constitution
1906	First Duma (parliament) meets and is dissolved
1906	Stolypin heads government: agrarian reforms begin
1907	entente with Britain
1907–12	Third Duma in session
1910	death of L. N. Tolstoy
1911	Western Zemstvo crisis
1911	assassination of Stolypin
1912	Lena goldfields shootings: worker radicalism re-emerges
1913	first performance of Stravinsky's *Rite of Spring*
1914	outbreak of First World War

1915	Nicholas II assumes supreme command and dismisses 'liberal' ministers
1916	first performance of Rachmaninov's Vespers (*vsenochnaia*)
1916	Brusilov offensive
1917	overthrow of monarchy in 'February Revolution'

Map 1. The provinces and population of Russia in 1724. Used with permission from *The Routledge Atlas of Russian History* by Martin Gilbert.

Map 2. Serfs in 1860. Used with permission from *The Routledge Atlas of Russian History* by Martin Gilbert.

Map 3. Russian industry by 1900. Used with permission from *The Routledge Atlas of Russian History* by Martin Gilbert.

Map 4. The provinces and population of European Russia in 1900. Used with permission from *The Routledge Atlas of Russian History* by Martin Gilbert.

Map 5. The Russian Empire (1913). From Archie Brown, Michael Kaser, and G. S. Smith (eds.) *Cambridge Encyclopedia of Russia* 1982.

Introduction

DOMINIC LIEVEN

The second volume of the *Cambridge History of Russia* covers the 'imperial era', in other words the years between Peter I's assumption of power and the revolution of 1917.

As is true of almost all attempts at periodisation in history, this division has its problems. For example, peasants were the overwhelming majority of the empire's population in 1917, as in 1689. The history of the Russian peasantry obviously neither began in 1689 nor ended in 1917. The enserfment of the peasantry was largely concluded in the century before Peter's accession. The destruction of the peasant world as it had existed in the imperial era came less in the revolution of 1917 than during Stalin's era of collectivisation and ruthless industrialisation.

Nevertheless, if one is to divide up Russian history into three volumes then defining the dates of volume two as 1689 to 1917 is much the best option. In formal terms, this volume's title (*Imperial Russia*) accurately defines the period between Russia's proclamation as an empire under Peter I and the fall of the Romanov dynasty and empire in March 1917. More importantly, this era is united by a number of crucial common characteristics. Of these, the most significant were probably the empire's emergence as a core member of the European concert of great powers and the full-scale Westernisation of the country's ruling elites. These two themes are the great clichés of modern Russian history-writing: like most such clichés they are broadly true in my opinion.

In editing this volume, I have made only a limited effort to impose my own conception of Russian history on the volume's shape, let alone on how individual contributors approach their topics. Readers who wish to gain a sense of my own overall understanding of the imperial era will find this in chapter 1, on Russia as empire and European periphery. They will be wise to remember that, like most academics, I see my own myopic obsessions – currently empire and peripherality – as the key to understanding the whole period to which this volume and my scholarly life has been devoted.

As editor, however, my key belief has been that a Cambridge History must be both comprehensive and diverse. The Russian Empire between 1689 and 1917 was a very diverse and complex society, which can and should be understood and studied from a great many different angles. To take but one example: it is in the nature of the Cambridge History as fundamentally a work of reference that most of its chapters have to be broad surveys of key themes in Russian history. But in some ways the micro-history of a single Great Russian village in a single year in the eighteenth century would provide more insights into crucial aspects of Russian history than a handful of general chapters, however well informed.

Even more important than diversity is comprehensiveness. I have tried to edit a volume from which the teacher of an MA programme in Russian history and her or his students can draw a rich and detailed understanding of Russian history in the imperial era. Very few people will read this volume as a whole and at one 'sitting'. But they will need to find within it detailed, scholarly coverage of a very broad range of themes. 'Coherence', though important, is therefore less of an issue than comprehensiveness. This volume covers politics and government: foreign policy and military history; economic and financial affairs; the history of all the key social groups in Russia, as well as of women and of the empire's non-Russian minorities; the legal and judicial system, the police and the revolutionary movement; Russian intellectual history and the history of Russian high culture.

To fit all this into a single volume has not been easy but in my view it has been essential. For example: in order to concentrate more space on other issues, I was urged at one point to drop the two chapters on Russian cultural history on the grounds that this subject is amply covered in histories of Russian literature, music and art. It seemed to me, however, that this volume would approach these subjects from a different angle to the ones most common in histories of Russian literature or the arts. Moreover, in some respects the vast and unexpected contribution made to European and world culture by Russian writers, musicians and artists is the most significant and exciting element in the history of Imperial Russia. To ignore it would therefore be a touch bizarre. In addition, Russians' understanding of themselves and their place in Europe, the world and the cosmos was so totally intertwined with literature, music and art that to leave out these themes would seriously distort the history of Imperial Russia.

In my opinion, the only way to address the requirements of the Cambridge History given the 228 years covered by this volume and the nature of the existing literature was thematic. Most chapters in this volume are therefore broad thematic surveys. To cover the vast range of necessary topics and do justice to the existing literature, in most cases I was only able to allow contributors roughly 7,000 words each. It is immensely difficult for scholars who have devoted their lives to detailed study of topics to compress a lifetime's insights into so short a space. I was very grateful to contributors for their willingness to do this and vastly impressed by the outstanding skill with which they addressed this challenge.

Most themes chose themselves. To take the most obvious examples, you cannot have a history of Russia without a chapter on the Orthodox Church or the peasantry. A generation ago you not only could but would have had a volume without a chapter on Russian women. Barbara Engel's splendidly comprehensive and thought-provoking piece on a vast subject which is very difficult to define or confine shows just how much genuine progress has been made in this area over the last thirty years.

But if I have exercised some editorial influence in the selection of chapters it has been on the whole in what many will consider a conservative sense. This volume is based overwhelmingly on American and British scholarship. For all its excellence, this scholarship has tended at times to concentrate on a narrow range of fashionable topics. Traditional core topics such as foreign policy or the history of Russia's economy, financial, fiscal and military systems have been extremely unfashionable among Anglophone historians in recent decades. For example, there are no standard histories of Russian foreign policy or of the empire's fiscal and financial systems written in the last thirty years which one could confidently assign to Anglophone graduate students. This volume gives what I conceive to be appropriate weight to these crucial but unfashionable topics. This is of course a matter of my own judgement and responsibility. But my sense that this was necessary was strengthened by talking to Russian historians of Russia. In my view, to justify the work that goes into a volume of the Cambridge History that volume must be respected and legitimate in Russian eyes, as well as those of the Anglophone academic community.

Although the thematic structure of this book is in my view essential and inevitable, it does create some problems as regards chronology and the integration of the various themes. Ideally, two volumes on this period would have allowed one to concentrate on periods and another on thematic topics. Given the requirement of one volume, I have concentrated on themes but included a number of chapters either on overall contexts (for instance chapters 3 and 1 by Mark Bassin and myself respectively) or on specific periods (the chapters by Paul Bushkovitch, Larisa Zakharova and Eric Lohr).

As already noted, historical truths and insights come from many different angles. Had space permitted, I would have indulged my commitment to micro-history more fully. I have, however, sought to lace the volume's survey chapters with a small number of much narrower and more detailed vignettes. These are in a sense almost literally verbal illustrations attached to groups of thematic chapters. Thus Catherine Evtuhov's chapter on Nizhnii Novgorod is designed to complement and illustrate the chapters on Russia's 'middle classes', economy and Church: Michelle Marrese's chapter links but also illustrates the survey chapters on law and women by Jorg Baberowski and Barbara Engel, not least by showing graphically that for all its imperfections law made a hugely important impact on eighteenth-century Russian life; Alex Martin's chapter on 1812's impact on Russian identities encapsulates a key theme in the broader chapters on Russian culture and political thinking; Nikolai Afonin's chapter on the navy in 1900 plays the same role in linking the chapters on Russian empire and power to themes of economic development and revolution. If these vignettes have allowed the inclusion of younger scholars among the contributors to the *Cambridge History*, that is an additional bonus.

Although, as noted above, I expect only the occasional martyr to read this book from cover to cover, I have nevertheless conceived of it as a coherent whole. Perhaps more significantly, I see the book as comprising a number of groups of chapters which can profitably be read together at a single sitting. The table of contents shows how I see these groupings to work.

The first three chapters introduce the overarching theme of empire from different perspectives: in comparative and geopolitical perspective (Lieven), as it managed the minority peoples (Weeks) and as empire affected Russian conceptions of their own identity and that of their polity (Bassin). The next four chapters are all linked to Mark Bassin's theme of Russian perceptions of their nation and its ideals. They are followed by three chapters on the non-Russians (Poles and Ukrainians; Jews; Muslims), which ought to be read in conjunction with Theodore Weeks's Chapter 2. After this come nine chapters on Russian society, three on domestic government (Shakibi, Hartley, Waldron) and five on diplomatic and military affairs. Larisa Zakharova's excellent chapter illustrates the close link between failure in war and radical domestic political change in the mid-nineteenth century. This leads logically to the volume's last three chapters, which tell the story of the regime's struggle with revolution and the empire's ultimate collapse in the midst of global war.

A word is needed about the bibliography. This has been a major nightmare for me since in principle it could have been longer than the rest of the volume. The first section of the bibliography is a very limited guide to the most important published 'official histories', primary sources, collections of documents and guides to archival holdings. The rest of the bibliography covers secondary sources. I have divided this into themes in order to make the book more friendly to teachers and students. I have also given strong priority to books over articles. I did this partly because I needed some principle which would allow me to confine the bibliography to manageable limits and partly because the majority of these books themselves contain bibliographies which will provide the reader with a guide to further reading. I have included no memoirs in the bibliography, because this would open the floodgates, but draw readers' attention to Petr Zaionchkovsii's exceptionally valuable multi-volume guide to memoirs which is listed in Section one. Given this volume's readership, it seemed sensible to give priority firstly to books in English and then to works in the Russian language.

Two final points are required in this introduction.

Shortly after writing his chapter for this volume Professor Reggie Zelnik was killed in an accident. The community of historians of Russia thereby lost not only a fine scholar but also a human being of great generosity and warm-heartedness. These qualities are recalled not only by his books but also in the memory of his friends and his former students.

For technical and financial reasons, this volume is based overwhelmingly on Anglophone scholarship. This is in no way an assertion that this scholarship is superior to that of our continental European or Russian comrades-in-arms and colleagues. One of the great joys of travelling to Russia at present is that one meets a wide range of excellent and enthusiastic young Russian historians. Given the frequent poverty and material challenges that these young people face, their commitment and enthusiasm is humbling. Even more humbling is recollection of the courage and integrity with which the best Russian scholars of the older generations sustained academic standards amidst the frustrations, dangers and temptations of the Soviet era. By dedicating this volume to Professor Petr Zaionchkovskii of Moscow University I wish to pay tribute not just to an outstanding scholar and human being but also to the many other Russian historians during the Soviet era to whom our profession owes a great debt.

PART I

*

EMPIRE

I

Russia as empire and periphery

DOMINIC LIEVEN

Empire is one of the most common types of polity in history.[1] It existed from ancient times into the twentieth century. Among its core characteristics were rule over many peoples and huge territories, the latter being a great challenge in the era of pre-modern communications. Military power was crucial to the creation and maintenance of empire but long-term survival also required effective political institutions.[2] Most empires were ruled by some combination of a theoretically autocratic monarch and a warrior-aristocratic class, though in some cases large and sophisticated bureaucracies greatly enhanced an empire's strength and durability.[3] In the long term the most interesting and important empires were those linked to the spread of some great high culture or universal religion.

Tsarist Russia was a worthy member of this imperial 'club'. If its long-term historical significance seems somewhat less than that of Rome, of the Han Chinese empire or of the Islamic tradition of empire, its achievements were nevertheless formidable. This is even more the case when one remembers Russia's relatively unfavourable location, far from the great trade routes and the traditional centres of global wealth and civilisation.[4] The tsarist regime directed one of the most successful examples of territorial expansion in history. Until the emergence of Japan in the twentieth century, it was the only example of a non-Western polity which had challenged effectively the might of the

1 For a historical survey of types of empire within a comparative study of polities see S. Finer, *A History of Government*, 3 vols. (Oxford: Oxford University Press, 1997). Also M. Duverger (ed.), *Le Concept d'Empire*, (Paris: Presses universitaires de France, 1980). D. Lieven, *Empire: The Russian Empire and its Rivals* (London: John Murray, 2000) discusses many of the themes of this chapter at length and contains a full bibliographical essay.

2 On 'bureaucratic thresholds' and the institutionalisation of empire, see e.g. M. Doyle, *Empires* (Ithaca: Cornell University Press, 1986), especially chapter 5.

3 S. N. Eisenstadt, *The Political System of Empires*, new edn (New Brunswick and London: Transaction Publishers, 1992).

4 J. Abu-Lughod, *Before European Hegemony: The World System AD 1250–1350* (New York: Oxford University Press, 1989), pp. 156–7. Russia earns one paragraph in a book devoted to the world system of the thirteenth and fourteenth centuries.

European great powers. Moreover, in the nineteenth century, this empire's ruling elites spawned a musical and literary high culture which made an immense contribution to global civilisation.

Tsarist history belongs not just to the overall history of empire but also, more specifically, to the modern story of the expansion of Europe. To a great extent Russian expansion depended on imported European institutions, technologies and even cadres, both military and civil. Its 'victims', often nomadic and Islamic, had many similarities with the peoples conquered by other European empires. Increasingly the ideology which justified expansion was that of European civilising mission. In this sense matters did not even change after 1917. Marxism was a Western, racially blind but culturally arrogant theory of historical development whose optimism and commitment to one unilinear path of development had much in common with Macaulay and nineteenth-century liberal champions of empire.

As is true of most empires, the tsarist empire was made up of radically differing lands and peoples which it acquired and used for a variety of purposes. Initially it was furs which drew the Russians into Siberia, the early period of Russian empire beyond the Urals thereby having something in common with the French fur-based empire in Canada. The cotton-based empire in late nineteenth-century Central Asia had parallels with the cotton economy of British Egypt, though central Asia (like Egypt) had also been acquired as part of the Anglo-Russian struggle for geopolitical advantage in Asia. Finland was annexed to enhance the security of St Petersburg, and military and geopolitical factors were also behind the initial Russian decision to jump the Caucasus range and incorporate Georgia into the empire.

The three most crucial acquisitions in the imperial era were the Baltic provinces, Ukraine and Poland. The first was vital because it opened up direct trade routes to Europe, which contributed greatly to the growth of the eighteenth-century economy. By the end of the nineteenth century 'New Russia' and the southern steppe territories were the core of Russian agriculture and of its coal and metallurgical industries: without them Russia would cease to be a great power. Expansion into Ukraine and the 'empty' steppe was Russia's equivalent to the 'New Worlds' conquered and colonised by the British and Spanish empires. Odessa, founded in 1794, had a population of 630,000 by 1914 and was one of the world's great grain-exporting ports. Mark Twain commented that it 'looked just like an American city'.[5] Of all Russia's

5 P. Herlihy, *Odessa: A History 1794–1914* (Cambridge, Mass.: Harvard University Press, 1986), p. 13.

imperial acquisitions, Poland proved to be the biggest thorn in Petersburg's flesh in the nineteenth century, though it made a considerable contribution to the imperial economy and its territory was a useful glacis against invasion from the West. Poland's initial division between Russia, Austria and Prussia had something in common with the 'Scramble for Africa' a century later. It was a product of great-power rivalry and bargaining, a convenient compromise which aggrandised the great powers and lessened tensions between them at the expense of weaker polities.

Being recognised as the rulers of a European great power and empire (to a considerable extent the two concepts were seen as identical) was central to the Romanovs' self-esteem and identity, not to mention to the raison d'être and legitimacy of their regime. At the same time, in the eighteenth and nineteenth centuries there were excellent objective reasons for wishing to be a great power and an empire. In an era when a small group of predator states – Britain, France, Spain, the United States and (later) Germany – were subjecting most of the globe to their direct or indirect dominion, the alternative to being a great imperial power was unappetising.

Russia was a more successful European great power in the first half of the imperial period than in the second. The obvious dividing line was the Crimean War of 1854–6, though the reasons for failure in that war could be traced back two generations at least.

From 1700 until 1815, the key to being a European great power, apart from having the basic human and economic resources, was the creation of an effective military and fiscal state apparatus. This Peter I and his successors achieved. Without belittling the achievement of two outstanding monarchs and their lieutenants in 'catching up with Louis XIV', they did enjoy certain advantages. A key impediment to maximising the effectiveness of the European absolutist military-fiscal state was the various territorial and corporate institutions and privileges inherited from the feudal era. These had never been so deeply rooted in the Muscovite frontier lands of Europe, and where they had existed they were uprooted by tsars in the late fifteenth and sixteenth centuries. Moreover, Russia like Prussia, belonging to the second wave of European absolutist state-building, was not lumbered by outdated and venal fiscal and administrative institutions, and the vested interests which grew around them.[6] The tsarist

6 See e.g. chapter 1 of T. Ertman, *Birth of the Leviathan: Building States and Regimes in Medieval and Early Modern Europe* (Cambridge: Cambridge University Press, 1997) and chapter 11 by Richard Bonney, 'The Eighteenth Century II: The Struggle for Great Power Status and the End of the Old Fiscal Regime', in R. Bonney (ed.), *Economic Systems and State Finance* (Oxford: Clarendon Press, 1995).

autocracy and its alliance with a serf-owning nobility was an exceptionally effective (and ruthless) mechanism for mobilising resources from a vast and pre-modern realm which lacked European assets such as a university-trained bureaucracy until well into the nineteenth century.

By the mid-nineteenth century a professional bureaucratic elite was being created, but by then the factors of power in Europe were changing to Russia's disadvantage. Above all this stemmed from the onset of the Industrial Revolution in Western Europe, and its extension to Germany in the second half of the nineteenth century. Though Nicholas I's government in his thirty-year reign before 1855 might have done a little more to speed Russian economic development, the basic geographical pattern of industrialisation in Europe was way beyond the means of any Russian government to change. Russia's economic backwardness was cruelly evident during the Crimean conflict. The British and French fought and moved with the technology of the industrial era, for instance travelling to the theatre of operations more quickly by steamship and railway from Western Europe than Russian troops could reach Crimea on foot. Meanwhile Russian finances collapsed under the strains of war, and a military system rooted in serfdom could not provide the armed forces with sufficient reserves of trained manpower.

The Crimean War made it clear that modernisation, social and governmental as well as economic, was essential if Russia was to survive as a great power. In 1863 the threat of Anglo-French intervention in support of the Polish rebellion rammed this point home. So too did Prussia's subsequent defeat of Austria and France by skilful use of railways, trained and educated reservists, and a sophisticated modern system of general staff planning, management and co-ordination. In response the tsarist regime did embark on radical policies of economic, administrative and social modernisation. By 1914 Russia was much more modern than she had been in 1856, but in relative terms she was still well behind Germany or Britain. Moreover, the price of very rapid forced modernisation was acute class and ethnic conflict.

The regime's relative failure in war and diplomacy between 1856 and 1914 itself greatly contributed to its declining legitimacy. At the same time internal conflict and tsarism's reduced domestic legitimacy were major factors undermining its position as a great power. It was the threat of revolution at home as much as military reverses which determined the regime to accept unequivocal defeat and sue for peace in 1905 with Japan. By January 1917 Russia's military and economic performance in the Great War had in most ways been deeply impressive, and much better than anyone had a right to expect.[7] With American intervention looming on the horizon, a place among the war's victors was a near certainty. Revolution and the collapse of the home front destroyed this prospect.

Although the onset of the Industrial Revolution was the key factor determining Russia's declining success as a great power after 1815, relationships between the European great powers were also crucial. In the eighteenth century fortune tended to favour Russia. Her three immediate rivals in Eastern Europe – the Ottomans, Swedes and Poles – were all in decline, as was their patron, France. From 1689 until 1815 Anglo-French rivalry was a fixed point in European international relations. In attempting to dismantle the French-backed international status quo in Eastern Europe Russia could usually reckon on British benevolent neutrality, and sometimes on active financial and other support. Even more important was the emergence of rival Germanic powers in central Europe. The Habsburgs and Hohenzollerns were almost inveterate rivals, both of them looking to Russia for support. This was, for example, an important factor in Catherine II's ability to smash the Ottoman Empire and extend Russia's territory to the Black Sea without European intervention.

In the nineteenth century matters changed very much to Russia's disadvantage. After 1815 automatic Anglo-French rivalry could not be taken for granted. The Crimean War illustrated the great vulnerability of Russia's enormous coastline to combined British and French naval and military power. By 1856 even Petersburg itself was in danger from the Royal Navy. To defend these coasts Russia was forced to sustain two (Baltic and Black Sea) fleets, to which by the twentieth century Pacific rivalries and the rise of Japan had added a third. Navies and the infrastructure to sustain them are always at the cutting edge of technology and are exceptionally expensive to sustain. For a relatively poor country to run three separate fleets at different ends of the earth and with immense difficulties as regards mutual reinforcement was crippling. Since in the case of the nineteenth-century Black Sea and twentieth-century Pacific these fleets and bases had to be sustained at the end of immensely long and difficult communications they were not only expensive but also vulnerable. In both the Crimean and Japanese wars this resulted in enemy amphibious operations capturing both the fleet and its base.[8]

7 D. R. Jones, 'Imperial Russia's Forces at War', in A. R. Millett and W. Murray (eds.), *Military Effectiveness*, 3 vols., vol. I: *The First World War* (Boston: Allen and Unwin, 1988, pp. 249–328. O. R. Ayrapetov (ed.), *Poslednaia voina imperatorskoi Rossii* (Moscow: Tri Kvadrata, 2002).

8 On dilemmas of Russian naval power: F. N. Gromov, *Tri veka rossiiskogo flota*, 3 vols. (St Petersburg: Logos, 1996).

Even more threatening was the situation in Central Europe after 1871. German unification established Europe's leading military and economic power on Russia's western border, within striking distance of the empire's economic and political heartland. The Austro-German alliance of 1879 ended the rivalry between Habsburgs and Hohenzollerns from which Russia had benefited for so long. To some extent Germany now backed Austria in the Balkans, where Russian and Austrian interests had long been in conflict. By the end of the nineteenth century, as was the case with the British and Americans, the German and Austrian relationship was more than a question of realpolitik. A certain solidarity of culture, values and ethnicity also existed, most importantly among the elites, but also more deeply in society too.

Some members of the Russian elite began to see the coming century as impending a 'clash of civilisations', and although this was a dangerously self-fulfilling idea, it was not entirely wrong. In the twentieth century Russia was to ruin itself in competition firstly with a Germanic bloc and its clients, and then with the Anglo-Americans. Russia's answer to this challenge by 1900 was the alliance with France and the Slav bloc. The latter was always weakened, however, by rivalries between the Slav peoples, to many of whom tsarism in any case seemed a very unattractive model. The French alliance was a surer source of security, though one rooted only in realpolitik and not at all in cultural, let alone ideological, solidarity. In addition, alliance with France always entailed the risk that it would incite the Germans to use force to break out of perceived 'encirclement'. As the events of 1914–17 showed, for Russia to stand in the way of Germany's bid for global power could be fatal. On the other hand, as Stalin discovered in 1939–41, to stand aside from European balance-of-power politics and allow Germany to defeat France and establish a Napoleonic degree of hegemony on the continent could also prove catastrophic.

Much of the history of tsarist empire can usefully be viewed through the prism of its position on the periphery of the European continent, in other words in direct contact with the polities whose power grew enormously during the period 1700–1914 and came to dominate the globe. For Russia, Europe was neither a devastating sudden apparition as for the native Americans, nor a faraway object of interest and nuisance as for the eighteenth-century Chinese and Japanese. On the contrary, it was throughout the imperial period the crucial source of models, emulation and challenges.

Russia's closest imperial equivalent was the Ottoman Empire, another great power on Europe's periphery. On the whole, in terms of empire's essence and raison d'être, which is power, Russia comes well out of this comparison. In 1600 Europeans regarded the Ottoman Empire as a very great power and a major threat. Muscovy by comparison, was a minor peripheral polity, as barbaric but far less important. Three centuries later the situation was totally reversed. The tsar ruled over a European great power extending from Germany to the Pacific and containing 170 million subjects. The Ottoman sultan ruled perhaps 33 million subjects and his empire's survival depended on the 'goodwill' of the Christian powers, in other words on the mutual jealousies which meant that none of them was willing to see a rival empire annex Ottoman territory.[9]

Geopolitics was one explanation for tsarist success and Ottoman failure. With the collapse of the Mongol Empire and its heirs, a vast vacuum of power opened up between the Urals and the Pacific which Russia easily filled. Part of that vacuum, for example, became the Urals metallurgical region, the key to Russia's position as Europe's premier iron producer for much of the eighteenth century. In the Ottomans' case, the power vacuum to their east was filled by the Safavids, who not merely blocked eastward expansion but also established a very dangerous second front with which Ottoman rulers engaged in war in Europe always had to reckon. By 1600 the Ottomans had in any case reached the geopolitical and logistical limits to possible expansion. This had implications for the legitimacy and finances of an empire whose previous prosperity had partly lain in the proceeds of territorial conquest. Meanwhile Russia was able to move southwards out of the forest zone and into the fertile steppe, in the process enabling the huge expansion of its economy and population, and legitimising the alliance between autocratic tsar and serf-owning nobility. It was much easier for the Russians to deploy their power in this region, than for the Ottomans to block them so far north of the Black Sea. Moreover Russian victory owed much to the shift in the military balance away from the nomadic warrior-cavalryman and towards the massed firepower of the European infantry-based army, in other words the military model which the tsars had adopted.

Other factors were also important. At its peak in the sixteenth century the Ottoman system of government was both more efficient and more just than was ever the case in serf-owning Russia. But the system of close bureaucratic regulation of society was hard to sustain over the generations, especially given the immense area of the empire. As the Ching dynasty also discovered in China's bureaucratic empire, the system relied in part on exceptionally able

9 There is a vast literature on the decline of the Ottoman Empire: for a suitably non-committal overview, see D. Quataert, *The Ottoman Empire* (Cambridge: Cambridge University Press, 2000), chapters 1 and 2; also R. Mantran (ed.), *Histoire de l'Empire Ottoman* (Paris: Fayard, 1989). For a specifically military angle: R. Murphey, *Ottoman Warfare 1500–1700* (London: University College London Press, 1999).

and diligent monarchs who were able to impose their authority on court and bureaucratic factions.[10] The Russian alliance between autocratic tsar and serf-owning mini-autocratic noble landlord allowed far greater exploitation of the peasantry than existed when the Ottoman system worked properly. But the Russian system of linking central power to a property-owning hereditary provincial nobility was more robust and more easily sustainable. The eighteenth-century Ottoman situation in which local satraps remitted minimal resources to the centre and obeyed its orders when they chose was fatal to imperial power and inconceivable in the tsarist context.

Tsarist success was also owed to willingness to import and utilise European institutions, ideas and cadres, of whom the German noble and professional classes of the Baltic provinces were the most prominent. In the fifteenth century the Ottomans had been equally open, for example creating a navy from scratch and packing it with Christian officers. From the sixteenth century, openness began to decline, however, partly as a result of the Ottomans' newly won position as ruler of the Arab lands and Holy Places, and defender of Sunni orthodoxy against the Shia dissident regime in Persia and its potential Shia fifth-column allies under Ottoman rule. Perhaps too there is a banal but important reason for the two empires' different trajectories. Past success had given the Ottomans few reasons to question traditional ways and institutions. Not until the catastrophic defeats in 1768–74 was the necessity of radical change and borrowing self-evident. By contrast, Russia in the seventeenth century was self-evidently weak and vulnerable, having barely escaped with its independent statehood from the Time of Troubles.

Whatever its causes, the Ottomans' failure to sustain their power had disastrous consequences for millions of their Muslim subjects. At its height, the Ottoman Empire provided security for Muslims from the north Caucasus, through Crimea and the Balkans, to the Arab lands of the Levant and north Africa. The empire's decline and fall resulted in the expulsion of the great majority of the Muslim population from the empire's European provinces, amidst extreme levels of suffering and murder. It also resulted in Christian and Jewish colonisation of Algeria and Palestine, and indeed an attempt in 1919–22 to deprive the Turks of part of their Anatolian homeland.

At least tsarist power protected the Russian people from such a fate. It also provided the essential military backing for their colonisation of the rich steppe lands of south-east Europe and south-western Siberia. But the tsarist

10 See in particular B. S. Bartlett, *Monarchs and Ministers: The Grand Council in mid Ch'ing China* (Berkeley: California University Press, 1991).

regime achieved this at a great price in terms of economic exploitation and the denial of rights and freedoms. As noted above, the key differences between tsarist and Ottoman empire can partly be seen as the greater effectiveness with which tsarism's military-fiscal apparatus exploited its subjects, and the greater openness of its social elites to Westernisation. For this the regime and the elites themselves paid a heavy price in 1917. Among the key factors behind the exceptionally bitter social revolution in 1917–21 were memories of serfdom and its legacy, and the wide cultural gap between European elites and Russian masses. On Europe's periphery one paid a high price for both power and powerlessness.

Comparisons with the maritime empires at Europe's western periphery are in some ways less useful. Trans-oceanic empire differed from any land empire in several key ways. So long as one exercised maritime hegemony, as the British did for a century after 1815, one's metropolis and colonies enjoyed a security which no land empire could easily obtain. But the loss of maritime power could bring rapid disaster. By the late eighteenth century, roughly 40 per cent of Madrid's revenues came from the Americas in one form or another. The interdiction of Spanish trade by the British navy after 1795 bankrupted the Spanish government, played a major role in encouraging revolution in Latin America and led to the definitive loss of Spain's status as a great power. It contributed too to a massive financial and political crisis in metropolitan Spain which lasted for a generation or more.[11]

Colonists in a trans-oceanic empire were likely to feel removed from a metropolis to which few of them would ever return. The ocean voyage itself marked a clear break. For Russian colonists migrating across the Eurasian steppe it was far less obvious that they had left their motherland. Even so, geography was only one factor in the emergence of separate colonial identities in the maritime empires. Self-governing institutions in the British colonies were crucial in the creation of colonial political identity, and elected elites who defined and defended separate colonial interests. Self-government in this explicit sense did not exist in Spanish America but provincial institutions packed with Creole elites, who had often bought their offices, played a not dissimilar role.

In seventeenth- and eighteenth-century Russia the cultural and 'ideological' gap between Cossack frontiersman and Petersburg aristocratic elite was

11 On this see chapter 5 in D. Ringrose, *Spain, Europe and the 'Spanish Miracle' 1700–1900* (Cambridge: Cambridge University Press, 1996); chapter 9 in J. Lynch, *Bourbon Spain. 1700–1808* (Oxford: Basil Blackwell, 1989); and chapters 1, 2 and 3 of C. J. Esdaile, *Spain in the Liberal Age* (Oxford: Basil Blackwell, 2000).

much greater than that between Virginian and English gentlemen. Siberian regionalists in the nineteenth century proclaimed a sense of separate identity rooted in the rugged frontier experience and even in intermarriage with the natives. A flood of colonists from European Russia on the Trans-Siberian railway in the late nineteenth century helped to dilute regional separatism but so too did tsarist policy as regards both Siberians and Cossacks. The regime was very careful to deny the autonomous political institutions around which dangerous identities might crystallise, and to crush any vestige of separatism at birth. It succeeded in turning Cossack frontier rebels into loyal servants of the autocratic state.

There were good reasons why Europe's peripheral powers founded its greatest empires. It was far easier to expand outside Europe than at the continent's core, where rival great powers could unite and intervene to block one's efforts. A comparison between the Romanov and Habsburg empires illustrates this point. Russia in the eighteenth century was able to conquer Ukraine and demolish its separate political institutions and identity. The latter could survive only if Ukrainian leaders received support from Russia's great-power rivals. Partly because of Ukraine's geographical inaccessibility this was not a realistic danger between Charles XII's defeat at Poltava and the German protectorate established in Ukraine in 1918 after the Russian Empire's dissolution. By contrast the Habsburgs never succeeded in imposing central authoritarian rule for long in Hungary, and by 1914 were paying a heavy political and military price for this failure. Hungarian intransigence was a key cause for Habsburg failure, but so too was the fact that at vital moments in the Habsburg relationship with Hungary, Magyar rebels received decisive support from the Ottomans or Prussia.

Common peripherality both united and divided Britain and Russia. At times both empires tried to steer clear of European entanglements, but faced by a real threat of French or German hegemony in Europe, they were in the end likely to unite against the common danger, mobilising the resources of their non-European territories to help them in the struggle. Their resources and their relative geopolitical invulnerability were the crucial reasons why no universal empire was ever established in nineteenth- or twentieth-century Europe. On the other hand, when Europe was stabilised and no immediate threat of hegemony existed, nineteenth-century Britain and Russia became rivals for hegemony in Eurasia. To some extent the same happened in the second 'Great Game', otherwise known as the Cold War, though by then the United States had replaced Britain as the leading player in the Anglophone bloc.

Before the middle of the nineteenth century almost all empires had been federations of aristocratic elites. The political weight of the usually illiterate peasant masses was very limited. The eighteenth-century British Empire in Ireland illustrates this point and its implications for empire's security. British elites believed that their rule was illegitimate in the eyes of the Irish Catholic masses, but they were confident that by expropriating the native land-owning class and denying positions in government or the professions to Catholics, they had made successful revolt impossible by depriving it of possible leaders, unless Ireland was invaded by large French armies. In the eighteenth century this calculation proved correct but nineteenth-century developments made it redundant. Above all this was because of the growth of mass literacy and a Catholic middle class, of democratic and nationalist ideology, and of a vibrant Catholic civil society whose members were also politicised by the existence of an increasingly democratic political system.[12]

From the middle of the nineteenth century not just the British in Ireland but, to varying degrees, all European empires were beginning to experience what one might define as the dilemma of modern empire. One aspect of this dilemma was the growing consensus that the future belonged to polities of a continental scale, with resources to match. Even in the first half of the nineteenth century, Herzen and de Tocqueville had predicted that for this reason the next century would belong to Russia and the United States. By the second half of the nineteenth century such predictions were commonplace, partly being inspired by the success of modern technology and communications in opening up continental heartlands to colonisation and development. Continental scale, however, almost inevitably entailed multiethnicity. In an era when democratic and nationalist ideologies were gaining ever-greater strength and legitimacy, how were such polities to be legitimised and made effective? At the very least, socioeconomic modernisation meant that the traditional policy of alliance with peripheral aristocracies would not suffice to hold an empire together. Moreover, as government itself intervened more deeply in society to respond to the demands of modernity, new and sensitive issues emerged, especially as regards questions of language, state employment and education.[13]

The implications of this dilemma took a century or more to come to full fruition. Empire in Europe, including British rule in most of Ireland, did

12 On eighteenth-century British calculations see S. J. Connolly, *Religion, Law and Power: The Making of Protestant Ireland 1660–1760* (Oxford: Oxford University Press, 1992), pp. 249–50. On the evolution of a nationalist civil society in nineteenth-century Ireland see W. Kissane, *Explaining Irish Democracy* (Dublin: University College Dublin Press, 2002).

13 Lieven, *Empire*, pp. 50–1.

not long survive the First World War. Two more generations passed before empire's demise in Asia and Africa. Modernity came to different empires, and their very different provinces, at varying speeds. In principle, however, there were a number of strategies which an empire could adopt to face this challenge, though in practice empires might adopt a mix of strategies from time to time and from province to province.

Most Victorian-era empires sought to identify themselves with progress, modernity and the triumph of civilisation,[14] though it was not easy for traditional dynastic empires to do this with the same confidence and consistency as was trumpeted by the United States or, later, the Soviet Union. An entirely modern, supra-ethnic identity which could trump or at least weaken the political salience of ethnicity was beyond the possibility or even the imagination of Victorian empire. Much more conceivable was the attempt to preserve traditional supra-ethnic sources of identity and loyalty. To some extent all empires did this by exploiting popular monarchism. The most thoroughgoing and potentially successful strategy to utilise pre-modern supra-ethnic identities was pursued by Abdul Hamid II, who attempted to unite Turks, Arabs and Kurds by mobilising Islam to legitimise Ottoman rule.[15] Catholicism in the Habsburg Empire had played a similar role well into the eighteenth century but by 1900 had lost much political ground to modern, secular liberal and nationalist loyalties. By 1900 Russian Orthodoxy was too inherently national to offer much hope of matching Islam's role as supra-ethnic legitimiser of empire.

The most common imperial strategy was to attempt to consolidate as much as possible of the empire into a core ethno-national bloc. This was *inter alia* to recognise the unstoppable force of nationalism and to seek to harness majority nationalism to the cause of imperial and conservative elites. Both the Russians and the Magyars attempted to do this in the decades before 1914. During the First World War the Turkish nationalist leadership pursued the same goal in Anatolia by the most terrible possible means, namely genocide. Though its tactics were totally different, British Empire Federalism had the same final goal, namely the creation of a Greater British nation and polity, combining the United Kingdom and the White colonies. British imperialists hoped that the security, prosperity and great civilisation represented by the

14 Even, for example, the Ottomans, whom Europeans saw as the epitome of incivility and reaction: see S. Deringil, *The Well-Protected Domains: Ideology and the Legitimation of Power in the Ottoman Empire 1876–1909* (London: I. B. Tauris, 1998).

15 See in particular: K. H. Karpat, *The Politicization of Islam: Reconstructing Identity, State, Faith and Community in the Late Ottoman State* (Oxford: Oxford University Press, 2001), especially chapters 7 and 8.

British Empire would hold the loyalty of non-Whites too but by 1900 it was widely recognised that Britain's long-term hopes of remaining a great power rested on the maintenance of a Greater British identity and loyalty in the White colonies.

A final possible strategy was the one adopted, initially more by *force majeure* than by intention, in the Austrian half of the Habsburg Empire. This entailed a move from traditional authoritarian empire towards multiethnic federalism, in the process developing many policies and constitutional guarantees designed to protect the civil, political and cultural rights of ethnic minorities. These, for example, included the right of minorities to education in their own language, as well as protection through the courts and the police against harassment and discrimination. They also included the recognition that sensitive issues concerning ethno-national rights and identities must be settled by negotiation between communities, not by majority or state diktat.[16]

In many ways Habsburg Austria stood out for its civilised management of empire's dilemmas, not only in comparison with Russia and Hungary but also when measured against Britain's White colonies and the United States, where indigenous and non-White peoples were not merely denied civil and cultural rights but also subjected to murderous pogroms to which government turned a blind eye. But, however relatively civilised, the Austrian 'solution' to empire's dilemmas by no means ended ethnic tensions, while contributing to the weakening of the state's armed forces and external might. Without nationalist enthusiasm it was difficult to persuade parliaments to accept high peacetime military budgets or to motivate millions of conscripts to die for the state in time of war. Given traditional tsarist priorities, this fact alone would have damned the Austrian model in Russian official eyes.

Until the middle of the nineteenth century the tsarist polity was more a dynastic and aristocratic empire, than an ethnic Russian one.[17] As was quite often the case in pre-modern empires, the core Russian population was in some respects worse exploited than peripheral ethnic minorities. Very obviously, Baltic German, Ukrainian, Georgian and other aristocrats gained far more from empire than was the case with the enserfed Russian masses. Incorporating non-Russian aristocracies into the Russian imperial elite, whose own identity

16 See above all S. Stourzh, 'Die Gleichberechtigung der Volkstamme als Verfassungsprinzip 1848–1918', in A. Wandruszka (ed.), *Die Habsburger Monarchie 1848–1918*, vol. III / ii (Vienna: Verlag der Osterreichischen Akademie der Wissenschaften, 1980), pp. 975–1206.

17 In this discussion my debt to Andreas Kappeler is obvious: see A. Kappeler, *Russland als Vielvolkerreich* (Munich: C. H. Beck, 1993).

was in any case being transformed by Westernisation, was a vital and very successful element in the creation and maintenance of empire.

The tsarist regime never entirely abandoned this policy. In the twentieth century, fear of social revolution often strengthened the mutual dependence of regime and non-Russian land-owning elites. Nor, very sensibly, did the regime ever have a single, 'coherent' strategy for dealing with the non-Russians. An empire whose rulers attempted to govern Balts, Kyrgyz and Ukrainians in similar fashion would not have lasted long. Nevertheless, the old overall strategy of alliance with local aristocracies was clearly inadequate in a modernising empire. This first became evident in Poland, where most of the local elite refused to be co-opted in traditional tsarist fashion and led rebellions in 1831 and 1863. The traditional strategy also came under attack from Russian society, where influential voices began to call for a closer identification of the regime and empire with ethnic Russians' interests and values. In most European states in the second half of the nineteenth century, conservative elites adopted a more nationalist hue in order to mobilise support against their liberal and socialist enemies: Bismarck and Disraeli set the trend but Russia was no exception.

In any case, nationalism and the attempted preservation of empire could easily overlap. Consolidating a sense of Russian nationhood in as large as possible a core population made obvious sense to most of the tsarist ruling elite, regardless of whether they considered themselves Russian nationalists. Above all, this meant ensuring that no separate sense of Ukrainian nationhood emerged, which Petersburg tried to do by blocking the evolution of a distinct Ukrainian literary language and high culture.[18] In 1897 only 44 per cent of the empire's population were Great Russians: define Ukrainians and Belorussians as Russians who merely spoke a local dialect, and a much more comforting message emerged for those committed to the empire's preservation. Two-thirds of the population were now of the core nationality. In typical Victorian style, tsarist elites tended to regard nomads and Central Asian Muslims as too backward to be politically threatening, while the smaller Christian peoples were seen as too weak to sustain a separate high culture, let alone political independence. It was on calculations such as these that a relatively optimistic view of the empire's viability could be based even in 1914.

In reality, by the eve of the First World War tsarism was very far from having solved the dilemmas of empire, though to do the regime justice the same was true in other empires and some of empire's key problems were in fact

18 For an excellent recent discussion of these issues see: A. I. Miller, *'Ukrainskii vopros' v politike vlastei i russkom obshchestvennom mnenii (vtoraia polovina XIXv)* (St Petersburg: Aleteiiya, 2000).

insoluble. In the Russian case, the management of multiethnicity was bound to get more difficult as even the limited freedom of the constitutional era allowed nationalists to organise and put down roots in society, and as modernisation came to previously isolated and illiterate sections of the community, making them potentially more accessible to the nationalist message. Nevertheless, in 1914 minority nationalism was no immediate threat to the regime. Most non-Russians were still peasants and nomads, and usually still beyond the reach of nationalist politicians. Many of the tsar's subjects regarded empire in general and the Russian Empire in particular as inescapable realities in an imperialist age. A great many of them by no means preferred the kaiser or the Ottoman sultan to the tsar. In a centralised empire such as Russia, power was in any case concentrated in the Russian capitals, Petersburg and Moscow. In the last resort a government which controlled them and the railway network could reassert its power in the periphery, as tsarism did in 1905–7 and the Bolsheviks in 1918–23. Non-Russian nationalism would only become a major danger if Russia entered a European war or revolt erupted in the Russian heartland. This of course happened in 1914–17.

It is useful to view political instability even in Great Russia through the prism of peripherality. Russia had always been peripheral in Europe but the Industrial Revolution sharpened this reality. A gap had emerged by 1900 between on the one hand a European 'First World' made up of a north-western group of states which encompassed Britain, France, the Low Countries and Germany, and on the other the 'Second World' countries of Europe's southern and eastern periphery. The fact that the First World was largely Protestant and the Second was overwhelmingly Catholic or Orthodox sharpened this distinction. The states of the Second World were poorer and politically less stable than the core. Constant comparisons with the core themselves contributed to a sense of their regimes' failure and illegitimacy. Dependence on foreign loans and investment worsened resentment. Even without the problems of extreme multiethnicity which plagued Hungary, let alone Russia, creating a nation was much harder in Italy and Spain than in France or Britain. Whether one measures a government's nation-building potential in terms of prestige, money or effective administration, the European periphery was poor by the core's standards.

Empire itself was part of the problem. Building a political nation in Britain, France and Germany had owed much to the reserves of patriotism and collective pride accumulated by victory in war and the struggle for empire. Defeat in 1898 increased the Spanish right's propensity to compare the degenerate present to a previous golden age. Defeat in Morocco in 1923 finally destroyed the liberal Restoration regime.[19] The same nearly happened in Italy after the catastrophe of Adowa in 1896, itself the product of Crispi's search for military glory to legitimise the liberal regime and assuage a desperate thirst for recognition as a great power.[20] Russia was a great power but not one with many victories to its name in the decades before 1914. Partly for that reason, the nationalist newspaper *Novoe vremia* greeted the new year in 1914 with a reminder to all of Russia's 'still terrible thirst for greatness'.[21] Defeat against Japan had indeed been tsarism's equivalent of Adowa and Anual, and had even more dramatic domestic consequences. Of course, the British and French too sometimes suffered colonial disasters. On Europe's periphery, however, weakness made colonial disasters both more likely and more politically dangerous.

In general, political stability in Russia was even more under threat in 1914 than in the other major states of the periphery, Hungary, Spain and Italy. The sheer size and multiethnic complexity of Russia contributed to this. So too did the fact that tsarism had made fewer concessions to liberalism than the regimes in power in Hungary, Spain and Italy. Civil rights were therefore less secure in Russia than elsewhere, much to the fury of many members of the upper and middle classes.[22] Another aspect of the survival of the Old Regime was that the dynastic state was less under the control of social elites in Russia than was the case elsewhere in the periphery, which added to the sense of distrust and alienation from authority, even in circles which were natural supporters of conservatism.

The survival of a 'pure' Old Regime meant that trade union rights were even less secure and the working class even more militant in Russia on the eve of the war than was the case in Spain and Italy. Meanwhile the attempt at a conservative strategy of agrarian modernisation in Russia had led to the preservation of the peasant commune as a barrier against landlessness and immiseration in the countryside. Though in many ways this strategy embodied a vision of social justice which was attractive in comparison to the

19 On the impact of Spain's loss of her 'second' empire see: S. Balfour, *The End of the Spanish Empire 1898–1923* (Oxford: Clarendon Press, 1997). Compare this e.g. to the much less traumatic response to the much greater loss of the 'first' empire in the early nineteenth century: see M. P. Costeloe, *Responses to Revolution: Imperial Spain and the Spanish American Revolution 1810–1840* (Cambridge: Cambridge University Press, 1986).

20 C. Duggan, *Francesco Crispi: From Nation to Nationalism* (Oxford: Oxford University Press, 2002), especially pp. 670–709.

21 Cited in D. Lieven, *Russia and the Origins of the First World War* (London: Macmillan, 1983), p. 132.

22 See the very revealing comparisons of the status of civil rights in various pre-1914 European states: N. Bermeo and P. Nord (eds.), *Civil Society before Democracy* (Lanham: Rowman and Littlefield, 2000).

impact of economic liberalism in the Italian and Spanish countrysides, the sense of peasant solidarity it encouraged in Russia's villages rebounded on the regime in 1905 and 1917. Add to all this the fact that the Orthodox Church was much weaker politically than its Catholic counterpart in Spain and Italy, and Russia's vulnerability to social revolution is further confirmed.

The point of course is, that although Hungary, Spain and Italy were less vulnerable than Russia, their path after 1914 was also to be anything but smooth. Nowhere did one see liberalism's survival and mutation, British-style, into liberal democracy. Especially in Spain and Italy fragmentation within the ruling liberal group was a factor here. More important was the growing threat of revolutionary socialist movements in the towns and, still worse, of agrarian revolution. In Hungary as in Russia, the aftermath of the First World War saw the coming to power of a communist dictatorship, which in the Hungarian case was overthrown by foreign intervention. In Italy the liberal order had very limited legitimacy by 1921 and many of its erstwhile supporters turned with relief to fascism as a bulwark against socialist revolution and a means to gain for Italy the status she 'deserved' among the Great Powers but supposedly had been denied by the Versailles settlement. After the collapse of the monarchy in 1931, Spain entered a period not altogether unlike the Russian experience in 1917. Political polarisation along ideological, class and regional lines proved too extreme to be contained by peaceful means. Civil war was the result, in Spain as in Russia. In the Spanish case it was the right that won. This was partly because foreign intervention was much more purposeful than in the Russian civil war, partly because the elite of the peacetime Spanish army spearheaded the counter-revolution, whereas its closest Russian equivalent had been wiped out on the eastern front. But the right's victory was also owed to the strength of the Roman Catholic Church and of the conservative small-holding peasantry of northern Spain.

Putting Russia in the context of Europe's Second World periphery does not therefore incline one to optimism about its likely political fate in the twentieth century. On the other hand, looking at Russia's pre-communist history as empire and periphery from the perspective of 2004 can inspire some hope for the future. The obvious conclusion from this chapter has to be that empire has been a huge burden on the Russian people, albeit one which in the past there were often very good reasons to sustain. This is true whether one sees empire primarily in terms of great military power, or in terms of managing a vast and multiethnic polity. Historically, the Russians had to devote a catastrophic share of their meagre wealth to military power, and the autocratic regime required to mobilise these resources was inevitably highly repressive and unlikely to develop a sense of citizenship in its subjects. Meanwhile, merging with many other peoples into a huge imperial conglomerate complicated the definition of Russian identity and the creation of a Russian nation of citizens. Despite the immediate difficulties of the post-imperial 1990s, shedding the Soviet empire and living in an era when traditional empires in any case are redundant opens up more hopeful perspectives for Russia's future.[23]

If Europe's Second World has now disappeared, that is partly because the continent's southern periphery has been absorbed into its core. In the decades after 1945, a benign international context, the discrediting of authoritarianism of the right and the left, and massive economic growth all contributed to this. In 1900 north-west European Protestants were much inclined to believe that economic modernity and democratic stability were beyond the genius of the benighted Catholics of Europe's southern periphery. They proved to be wrong. There is no reason in principle why the same should not be true as regards Russia.

23 These are central themes in G. Hosking, *Russia: People and Empire* (London: Harper Collins, 1997).

2

Managing empire: tsarist nationalities policy

THEODORE R. WEEKS

Almost from its inception, Russia has been a multinational state. Long before anyone spoke of the 'Russian Empire' (*Rossiiskaia Imperiia*), a designation that dates from the latter part of Peter I's reign, a variety of ethnic groups lived in territories claimed by the Muscovite tsar. However, the very concepts of nations and nationality, now considered a central element of human identity, were largely absent in Imperial Russia, at least until the later nineteenth century. Rather, religion played a far more central role in defining what was 'foreign' than language or 'ethnicity,' a slippery concept at best. The role of the Orthodox religion (*Pravoslavie*) for Russian identity cannot be overstated. Thus a 'Catholic Russian' or 'Muslim Russian' even today are conceptually difficult for many Russians to accept.

In Russian – unlike English – one can differentiate between Russian as a cultural-ethnic category (*russkii*) and Russian as a political-geographical designation (*rossiiskii*). In practice, however, the distinction was never made consistently in the imperial period, not even by officials who should have known better. Even more inconsistent, perhaps, is the use of the term 'Russification' both at the time and in subsequent historiography. The Russian Empire did not 'embrace diversity' – such an idea would have seemed absurd to the tsars and their servitors. They took for granted the predominance of Russian culture (including language) and the Russian Orthodox religion within the empire. But Imperial Russia also lacked the resources and even will to carry out consistent and activist programmes of national assimilation or 'ethnic cleansing' whether through education or more violent methods. Tsarist 'nationalities policy' was not, in fact, one single policy. Rather, there were very different measures taken in, say, the Caucasus, Poland or Central Asia, at different times. Typically an activist, often violent period in which non-Russians would be actively persecuted would be followed by years in which a more passive, though seldom benevolent policy was followed.

Nationalities before Peter

When Peter the Great came to the throne, the Russian Empire already stretched from the White Sea and Pskov in the west all the way to the Pacific Ocean. While some small Finnic tribes lived in Muscovite territory from an early date, the real beginning of Russia as a multinational empire can be dated rather precisely in the years 1552–6. At this point Ivan IV ('the terrible') seized the Volga khanates of Kazan and Astrakhan, bringing at a stroke thousands of Muslim Tatars under Muscovite rule. The conquest of Kazan and Astrakhan also opened the way for further Russian expansion to the east, into Siberia. On the whole, Moscow allowed the Tatar elite to retain its status and property demanding, however, loyalty to the Russian centre. Only in the eighteenth century did Peter and, with less consistency, his successors press Muslim landowners to accept Russian Orthodoxy or give up their estates. Here again the key issue was not ethnicity or national culture but religion. The baptised Tatar landowners did not soon give up their ethnic and cultural distinctiveness.

Having gained power over the Volga Muslim khanates but stymied in their attempts to seize territory to the west and south, the natural direction of expansion lay to the east. To be sure, Russian traders – in particular the Stroganov family – had even earlier ventured beyond the Urals, but consistent exploration leading to permanent territorial claims began only in the late sixteenth century. Conquest of Siberia is usually connected with the Stroganov family and in particular the Cossack commander in their employ, Ermak, who helped defeat the Muslim overlords of western Siberia in the 1580s, opening the way to Russian conquest of the entire sparsely-populated expanse of territory between the Ural mountains and the Pacific. The city of Tobolsk was founded in 1587, Tomsk in 1604 and Okhotsk on the Pacific Ocean in 1648. Russian expansion over this huge area proceeded slowly but without encountering serious obstacles. The local peoples, a hugely various collection of linguistic, cultural and religious groups, were seldom in a position to oppose the better-armed and organised Russians. Nor did Russian rule particularly impinge on their everyday lives. On the whole, Moscow had no particular interest in direct rule, but was ruthless in enforcing a tribute paid in furs, the *yasak*. Certain groups, most notably the nomadic Kalmyks, did oppose accepting Muscovite rule (and the *yasak*), but their raids could not prevent the steady Russian march to the east over the seventeenth century. This process of territorial expansion was capped by the Treaty of Nerchinsk in 1689, which set down the Sino-Russian border that would not change for nearly two centuries.[1]

Expansion in the eighteenth century and nationality

Conquest of the Baltic under Peter

Peter the Great was the true founder of the Russian Empire. Indeed, it was he who insisted on a change in the Russian state's nomenclature to *Rossiiskaia Imperiia*, a change only gradually accepted by the other European powers. More important than the name change were territorial gains. After his crushing victory over Charles X of Sweden at Poltava (summer 1709), the fate of Sweden's erstwhile Baltic provinces was sealed. In the course of the following year the region from Riga to Vyborg (Viipuri) came under Russian rule. Peter was careful not to alienate the ruling classes in this strategic area. The cities of Riga and Reval (Tallinn) retained their customary privileges, including the use of German language and a great deal of autonomy. Similarly the Livonian nobility (of mainly German ethnicity) continued to exercise its traditional rights and even gained back considerable lands previously lost to the Swedish crown. Religious freedom was guaranteed, though Orthodox churches were also introduced. Thus the transfer of sovereign power from Stockholm to St Petersburg changed little in the everyday workings of these provinces. The mainly German nobility and middle class continued to exercise almost total control over the economy and social life of the region, also profiting from the opening of the Russian market to their agricultural products. Furthermore, the Baltic German nobility was to play an inordinately important role as officers, officials and ambassadors of the Russian Empire. Typically for the age, the peasant masses of Estonian and Latvian ethnicity did not play a role in St Petersburg's political calculations.

Peter's victory at Poltava also sealed the fate of Ukraine as an independent entity. The Ukrainian leader Mazepa's alliance with the Swedes spelled his downfall; in the eighteenth century Russia tightened its grip on left-bank

1 The best overview of Russia as a multinational state is A. Kappeler, *The Russian Empire: A Multiethnic History* (New York: Pearson Education, 2001). On Russia's 'first (minority) nationalities' – primary among them the Volga Tatars – see A. Kappeler, *Russlands erste Nationalitäten: das Zarenreich und die Völker der Mittleren Wolga vom 16. bis 19. Jahrhundert* (Cologne: Böhlau 1982). The struggles of the Kalmyks against the expanding Muscovite / Russian state are explored in Michael Khodarkovsky, *Where Two Worlds Met: The Russian State and the Kalmyk Nomads, 1600–1917* (Ithaca: Cornell University Press, 1992).

(east of the Dnieper) Ukraine which it had gained in the Treaty of Andrusovo (1654). However, significant territories of present-day Ukraine remained under Ottoman and Polish rule until later in the century.

Ukraine under Catherine

Catherine the Great (reigned 1762–96) continued Peter's work of imperial expansion. During her reign the empire expanded to the Black Sea in the south and the Vistula river in the west, taking over territory relinquished by two declining states, Poland and the Ottoman Empire. Russian military victories on land and sea forced the Sultan to agree to the Treaty of Küçük Kaynarca early in 1774. The terms of this treaty gave Russia a foothold on the Black Sea (between the Dniester and Bug rivers); two decades later Russian rule extended over the entire northern Black Sea littoral from the Dniester eastward. This territory was sparsely populated and the government quickly put in place programmes to entice new settlers to what they called 'New Russia'. On the site of a Turkish fort called Yeni Dunai ('New World') the city of Odessa was founded in 1794, soon to become one of the most ethnically mixed and cosmopolitan cities in the empire.

Partitions of Poland

Even more than the conquest of Ottoman territories, Catherine's legacy has been marked by her participation in the dismemberment of Poland. For Poles, the German-born Russian empress represents a despised and much reviled figure. In his *Books of the Polish Pilgrimage* the national poet Adam Mickiewicz described her as 'The most debauched of women, a shameless Venus proclaiming herself a pure virgin.' Catherine did not initiate the actual partitions – that role belonged to King Frederick II ('the Great') of Prussia. But certainly Catherine did everything she could to contribute to the weakening of the Polish state which resulted in its ultimate demise in 1795. In the three partitions, Russia gained considerable territories in what is now Belarus, Ukraine and Lithuania. Unlike Prussia and Austria, Russia did not take over ethnically Polish territory in the partitions. However, in the vast eastern lands of the erstwhile Polish-Lithuanian Commonwealth, the nobility (*szlachta* to use the Polish term) was generally Polish by language and culture, and Catholic in religion. The peasantry was Lithuanian, Belarusian and Ukrainian by ethnicity, and Catholic, Orthodox or Uniate by religion. Thus, with the partitions, Russia took on not one, but several potential 'national problems', leaving aside for a moment the most troubling one of all: the Jewish question.

With the destruction of the Polish-Lithuanian Commonwealth and the incorporation of its eastern half by the Russian Empire, St Petersburg took on a very serious national challenge. As subsequent tsars were to discover, ruling over Poles was far more challenging than dividing up their ailing state. Poles differed from other national groups living within the empire in their long and distinguished history as a major power (Russians certainly did not forget the role of the Poles during the Time of Troubles of the late sixteenth century), their well-developed national culture (Copernicus was, after all, a Pole), the high level of national consciousness among the Polish nobility and their strong Catholicism. The Polish nobility had international connections, both to the Vatican and to their brethren in Prussia and Austria. Catherine's rather cynical and contemptuous attitude towards the Poles reflected her inability to appreciate the long-term ramifications – most of them negative – of the Partitions.[2] For the moment, however, Catherine's policy favoured the incorporation of the Polish nobility into the ruling elite of this region as long as these nobles expressed their loyalty to the Russian state, as many did.

Jewish question

With the partitions Russia acquired not only a sizeable class of potentially troublesome Poles but an even larger group of religious aliens: the Jews. Muscovy had never allowed Jews to reside within the state and even Peter the Great had not been free of judeophobic prejudice. When urged to consider the economic benefits of allowing Jewish merchants to trade in Russia, Peter's daughter Elizabeth I had replied 'I seek no gain from the hands of the enemies of Christ.' Now, mere decades later, some of the largest and oldest Jewish communities in Europe came under Russian rule.

Under Polish-Lithuanian rule, Jews had enjoyed considerable autonomy. In effect, the Jews had been considered a separate estate with its own rights and responsibilities, a not uncommon set-up in a pre-modern state. Initially Catherine proceeded cautiously, guaranteeing her new Jewish subjects in 1772 (after the first partition) the continuation of 'all freedoms relating to religion and property' that they had hitherto enjoyed. At the same time, Catherine needed to assign the Jews a place in the Russian estate (*soslovie*) system. Since they were obviously neither peasants nor nobles, Jews were assigned for the most part to the vague 'townspeople' (*meshchane*) category, to the considerable consternation of Christian townsfolk. But Russian policy toward the Jews

2 For more detail on Polish nationalism around the time of the partitions, see A. Walicki, *The Enlightenment and the Birth of Modern Nationhood: Polish Political Thought from Noble Republicanism to Tadeusz Kosciuszko* (Notre Dame: University of Notre Dame Press, 1989).

was contradictory. On the one hand, it attempted to integrate them into the Russian social and economic system. Simultaneously, St Petersburg showed great reluctance to grant Jews the rights allowed other urban dwellers. This contradiction would only worsen in the course of the nineteenth century.

The Jews' special status was codified in the Jewish statute of 1804. While retaining Jewish autonomy in the form of the *kahal*, this law made clear that the ultimate goal of Russian policy was to reduce the cultural gap between Jews and Christians. To this end Jewish schools were obliged to use either Russian, Polish or German as a language of instruction, a rule that was of course utterly divorced from the realities of the Jewish *heder* and subsequently ignored or circumvented. In order to make Jews – to use the contemporary language – 'more productive', Jewish participation in the liquor trade was to be forbidden starting in 1807. This measure caused considerable economic hardship for thousands of Jewish innkeepers. The 1804 statute also set down the official boundaries of the notorious 'Pale of Settlement', that is, those provinces in which Jews were permitted to reside. By defining the Pale, the law also made clear that St Petersburg regarded the Jews as a unique and particularly dangerous group that had to be restricted to one part of the empire.[3]

Policy under Alexander I and Nicholas I

Napoleonic period and Congress of Vienna

During the period of the Napoleonic wars Russia gained two important new provinces on its western frontier. The first, Finland, was annexed from Sweden in 1808/9. Already during Peter's Great Northern Wars there had been talk of incorporating Finland into the empire as had been done with the Baltic provinces. But actually annexation took place in the context of the Peace of Tilsit (1807) which allowed Alexander I to invade and occupy Finland. Finland became a part of the Russian Empire, but as a highly autonomous province with its own laws, currency and legislature. Later Finnish jurists were to argue that the Grand Duchy of Finland, as it was now styled, was linked with the Russian Empire only through the person of the Tsar who was *ex officio* the Grand Duke of Finland. While such an interpretation certainly overstates the province's autonomy, it is clear that Russia respected local rights – at least to

3 On the early history of Jews in the Russian Empire, see John D. Klier, *Russia Gathers Her Jews: The Origins of the 'Jewish Question' in Russia, 1772–1825* (DeKalb: Northern Illinois University Press, 1986).

the last decades of the century – and in so doing created a space for Finnish national institutions to develop. The only other major territorial acquisition of this period was Bessarabia, bordering on Ottoman territory (now Romania) in the south. The initially granted autonomy here did not last long. After 1828 Bessarabia was administered, with minor exceptions, like other 'Russian' provinces.

In the early morning hours of 12 June (24 June new style) 1812 Napoleon's *Grande Armée* crossed the Niemen (Nemunas) River into Russia, taking St Petersburg by surprise. Days later Napoleon entered Vilnius (Wilno) where the city's Polish residents welcomed him. As is well known, by September Napoleon's armies had advanced all the way to central Russia where they took Moscow – but without the city's occupants. The 'Great Fatherland War' of 1812 became a central myth in the Russian national pantheon, as novels like *War and Peace* and Tchaikovsky's '1812 Overture' testify. Napoleon's stay in Moscow was short, his army's retreat painful and humiliating, and in early 1814 Russian troops entered Paris, where they stayed rather longer than the *Grande Armée* in Russia. But more important than the military episode itself was its aftermath, in particular the creation of the Kingdom of Poland at the Congress of Vienna (1815).

From the start, the Kingdom of Poland (the 'Congress Kingdom' or 'Kongresówka') was a rather peculiar entity. Napoleon had created a 'Grand Duchy of Warsaw' out of Polish lands previously seized by Prussia and Austria; now this 'Grand Duchy', stripped of Poznania to the west and Kraków to the south, was handed over to Russia at the Congress of Vienna and renamed the Kingdom of Poland. Just as the Russian tsar was Grand Duke of Finland, he was also the King of Poland (*tsar' polskii*). Polish autonomy was even greater than Finnish, for the Poles not only had their own legislature (*sejm*), army, currency, school system and administration (all official business was to be conducted exclusively in Polish) but furthermore were granted a quite liberal constitution by Tsar Alexander I. Inevitably, the existence of a constitutional Polish entity within the autocratic Russian Empire led to strains between Warsaw and St Petersburg. As long as Alexander remained on the throne (to 1825) these differences did not have to mount into a crisis. Once Alexander was replaced by his younger and considerably more conservative brother Nicholas, however, tensions grew increasingly acute.

Nicholas ascended to the throne under the cloud of the Decembrist revolt and knew well of connections between Poles and Decembrists. The new tsar did not view the Poles with sympathy and certainly did not share his elder brother's 'guilty conscience' over the partitions. A man for whom duty and order were supreme, Nicholas did not openly abrogate the constitution and autonomy granted the Kingdom of Poland, but he did interpret this autonomy in the narrowest possible sense. In particular, Nicholas steadfastly rejected any attempts to extend Polish culture and influence into the so-called Western Provinces (today's Belarus, Lithuania and Western Ukraine). Anti-Russian conspiracies (as he saw it) at the mainly Polish university in Wilno (now Vilnius) in the later years of Alexander I's reign had further increased Nicholas's distrust of the Poles. The Polish uprising of November 1830 merely corroborated Nicholas's view of Poles as a politically unreliable and nationally hostile element. Without outside help, the insurrection had little chance of success and by autumn 1831 rebels had everywhere been captured, executed or forced to flee abroad. Polish nobles implicated in the uprising had their estates confiscated, universities in Warsaw and Wilno were shut down, and the Polish constitution was abrogated. Polish autonomy was replaced by an 'organic statute' (1832) emphasising the territory's status as a part of the Russian Empire. A Russian viceroy (to 1856, Prince Ivan Fedorovich Paskevich) replaced the sejm as the primary centre of power in the Kingdom.[4]

Nicholas I

Tsar Nicholas I (r. 1825–55) is perhaps best known for the tripartite formula 'Orthodoxy, Autocracy, Nationality' thought up by his minister of education, Sergei Uvarov. This formula is frequently cited as evidence for strong nationalist and Russifying tendencies under Nicholas. A closer look at the formula itself calls this interpretation into question. 'Nationality' (which in Russian is the considerably more nebulous *narodnost'*) is, after all, the *third* and last element here and in a sense derives from the first two. Certainly, Nicholas emphasised the importance of Russian culture (and the Orthodox religion) in the empire; for instance, he demanded that his bureaucrats write their reports in Russian and not, as had often previously been the case, in French. For many of the highest officials, this order must have been very difficult indeed to fulfil.

It was also during Nicholas's reign that the term *inorodtsy* (aliens) came to be applied to many of the empire's Asian subjects. The actual law establishing the inorodets category was part of Mikhail Speranskii's Siberian Reforms of

4 On Poland in the 'long' nineteenth century, see Piotr S.Wandycz, *The Lands of Partitioned Poland, 1795–1918* (Seattle: University of Washington Press, 1974). On the November 1830 rising, see R. F. Leslie, *Polish Politics and the Revolution of 1830* (London: Athlone Press, 1956).

1822.[5] As originally defined, the inorodtsy were non-Christian peoples living in Siberia, considered by the Russian government as living at a low level of civilisation. Most (but not all) inorodtsy did not live in sedentary communities, and the Russian government (like, it must be said, other imperial powers) felt ill at ease with nomadic peoples.[6] As the nineteenth century progressed, the inorodets category would be expanded to include a number of small (numerically) peoples of Siberia and the Far East, as well as Kyrgyz and – most remarkable – Jews. Typically for the Russian Empire, however, ethnicity and language played absolutely no role in determining whether one belonged to this legal category. By the later nineteenth century, however, in popular – and to some extent official – usage the term inorodets took on the connotation of 'non-Russian' and was even used to describe Christians such as Poles.

It would be a mistake, however, to ascribe overtly Russifying motives to Nicholas I – he was far too conservative a man for that. Rather, Nicholas aimed above all things at maintaining order and existing hierarchies. Finland's autonomy, for example, was not touched. And when the Slavophile Iurii Samarin dared to criticise imperial policy in the Baltic provinces as too favourable towards the Baltic German nobility in 1849, Nicholas I had him removed from his position and locked up (albeit briefly) in the Peter and Paul Fortress in St Petersburg. In a personal conversation with Samarin, Nicholas made clear to the young idealist (and Russian nationalist) that real threats to Romanov rule came not from the loyal Baltic Germans but from the ignorant Russian masses.[7]

In one instance, however, Nicholas did adopt a more activist policy towards non-Russians. His reign witnessed serious measures aimed at breaking down Jewish corporate structures. Under Nicholas, Jews were subjected to the military draft. More notoriously yet, under-age Jewish boys were drafted into so-called 'cantonist' units. At the same time, Nicholas's minister of education, Uvarov, elicited the help of the enlightened Jewish educator, Dr Max Lilienthal, to set up state Jewish schools. Though government-sponsored 'rabbinical institutes' were established in Wilno, Zhitomir and Warsaw, they ultimately failed to create the desired 'enlightened Jewish community' envisioned by

5 On this law and the further development of the *inorodets* category, see John W. Slocum, 'Who, and When, Were the *Inorodtsy*? The Evolution of the Category of "Aliens" in Imperial Russia', *RR* 57, 2 (April 1998): 173–90. The actual law was entitled 'Ustav ob Upravlenie inorodtsev' and dated 22 July 1822.

6 On one group of inorodtsy under tsarist and Soviet rule, see Yuri Slezkine, *Arctic Mirrors: Russia and the Small Peoples of the North* (Ithaca: Cornell University Press, 1994).

7 The best single source on Nicholas I remains Nicholas Riasanovsky, *Nicholas I and Official Nationality in Russia, 1825–1855* (Berkeley: University of California Press, 1967).

reformers. Another project aimed at increasing Jewish 'productiveness' was a programme to encourage Jews to take up farming, in particular in the sparsely populated region north of the Black Sea. Once again, the policy had at best limited effects. A more important change was Nicholas's abolition of the Jewish kahal (autonomous community) in 1844. Nonetheless, in matters of family life and religious practices, Russia's Jewish communities were only marginally affected by government policy even at the end of Nicholas's reign.[8]

Expansion in the Caucasus and Central Asia

Russia, as we have seen, had extended its rule into Asia (Siberia) already in the seventeenth century. By Alexander I's reign, Russian rule stretched all the way to the New World: Russian settlements in Kodiak and Sitka (Alaska) were founded in 1784 and 1799 respectively. In both Siberia and Alaska, Russia was primarily interested in furs and the actual Russian presence was quite sparse (some 800 Russians in Alaska, for example, in the 1830s).[9] It was from Siberia that Russia gradually extended its rule into what is now known as Central Asia. The 1840s saw skirmishes between Russian troops and Kazakhs, a nomadic Turkic people. But the real push into Central Asia was to come in the second half of the nineteenth century.[10]

In the eighteenth century Russia's southern frontier between the Caspian and Black seas had gradually reached the foothills of the Caucasus mountains. Indeed, Peter the Great had sent troops to the region to fight Persian and Ottoman forces. But real Russian control over the Caucasus was achieved only in the nineteenth century. In 1801 the Christian kingdom of Georgia was annexed to the empire and in the next few decades the Russian frontier extended southward to include the Armenian capital, Erevan. In both cases, the local Christian elites generally welcomed Russian rule. By mid-century a number of Muslim nationalities including Chechens and Daghestanis found themselves under Russian rule, despite their intense resistence. Hundreds of thousands of Muslims left their homeland, often pushed out by local Christians, and emigrated to the Ottoman Empire rather than live under Christian Russian

8 For more detail on Jews in the Russian Empire under Nicholas I, see Michael Stanislawski, *Tsar Nicholas I and the Jews: The Transformation of Jewish Society in Russia, 1825–1855* (Philadelphia: Jewish Publication Society of America, 1983).

9 A. Kappeler, *Russland als Vielvölkerreich. Enstehung-Geschichte-Zerfall* (Munich: C. H. Beck, 1992), p. 170.

10 On this early period of Russian-Central Asian contact, see Edward Allworth, 'Encounter', in E. Allworth (ed.), *Central Asia: 130 Years of Russian Dominance, A Historical Overview*, 3rd edn (Durham and London: Duke University Press, 1994), pp. 1–59.

rule. Even after their departure, the Caucasus remained one of the empire's most diverse in religion, language and ethnicity.[11]

After 1863: the birth of 'Russification'

Polish insurrection of 1863

Thus far we have spoken much more of imperial expansion than of 'nationalities policy' per se. In fact, it is difficult to discern any one consistent 'policy' towards the diverse assembly of non-Russian peoples during this period. St Petersburg was far more concerned while keeping order and collecting taxes than in effecting any major changes on the lands it had conquered. In a sense, this would always be the case: for major programmes of social and ethnic engineering, one must wait for the Soviet period. And yet, the inklings of a more activist nationalities policy do appear in the aftermath of the Polish January uprising of 1863. The uprising, taking place amidst the unsettled situation of the Great Reforms (serf emancipation had been announced two years earlier but had almost nowhere been put into effect), shook the imperial government, including Tsar Alexander II himself. Clearly, the Poles had not reconciled themselves to Russian rule. Nor had they given up the idea of Polish cultural hegemony in the Western Provinces. Tsarist policy in the post-1863 decades would aim to secure the Russian position (militarily and administratively) in the Kingdom of Poland, or as it was now officially called, the 'Vistula Land', while limiting Catholic and Polish influences in the Western Provinces. This policy, both in this region and throughout the empire, has been described as 'Russification'.

Birth of Russification

In an influential article, Edward C. Thaden described three types of Russification: 'unplanned, administrative, cultural'.[12] Unplanned Russification would be the more or less natural spread of Russian culture and language. Administrative Russification refers to the efforts of St Petersburg to enforce centralisation and the use of Russian language throughout the empire. Finally,

11 Muriel Atkin, 'Russian Expansion in the Caucasus to 1813', in Michael Rywkin (ed.), *Russian Colonial Expansion to 1917* (London: Mansell Publishing, 1988), pp. 139–87. For more detail on the two major Christian peoples of the Caucasus, see Ronald Grigor Suny, *Looking toward Ararat: Armenia in Modern History* (Bloomington: Indiana University Press, 1993) and *The Making of the Georgian Nation*, 2nd edn (Bloomington: Indiana University Press, 1994).

12 'Introduction' in Edward C. Thaden (ed.), *Russification in the Baltic Provinces and Finland, 1855–1914* (Princeton: Princeton University Press, 1981), pp. 8–9.

cultural Russification would be the attempt to assimilate non-Russian ethnic groups through government measures such as Russian-language schools, the army, prohibitions on speaking or publishing in certain languages and the like. After 1863, a push for more administrative and cultural centralisation certainly grew. Since *Russian* officials were pushing this centralisation, it was often tinged – at the very least – with Russifying elements. Even from a completely practical viewpoint, efforts to introduce reforms such as elected city governments and *zemstva* (rural organs of limited self-government) forced the issue of what language should be used in their deliberations. The same question arose when new schools were proposed. In areas of mixed nationality, none of these questions were easily answered and Russian officialdom often erred on the side of the 'reigning language', Russian. The development of modern means of communication only complicated matters further. In 1862 St Petersburg was linked to Warsaw by rail, thereby connecting the Russian railway network with that of the rest of Europe. What language to use in telegraph offices and the railroads? The 'logical' – or at least easiest – answer was Russian.

'Cultural Russification' is probably best exemplified by policy in the Western Provinces. The uprising of 1863 had convinced St Petersburg that the local Polish nobility and clergy could not be trusted. In the Western Provinces every effort was made to stymy the spread of Polish culture and to weaken the Polish land-owning class economically. Polish estates were saddled with a special tax and Poles could not acquire land here other than by inheritance. Meanwhile, Russian landowners and peasants were offered special incentives to settle here. There was even an effort to introduce Russian into certain Catholic churches in the Belarusian area. Government schools taught only in Russian, though a thriving 'underground' school net may have educated nearly as many youngsters in Polish literacy.

Ukrainians and Belarusians were not allowed schools in their native tongue, and censorship did not allow most publications in those languages. To quote the minister of the interior, Petr Valuev, in a notorious circular of 1863: 'A separate Little Russian [Ukrainian] language never existed, does not exist, and cannot exist.' No tsarist official could deny the existence of a separate Lithuanian language, but publishing in Lithuanian was also prohibited unless the Russian (Cyrillic) alphabet was used. Since a large percentage of literate Lithuanians were Catholic priests, such an alphabet reform could not be accepted. Instead, Lithuanian-language publications were smuggled in from neighbouring East Prussia. Poles continued to publish in their own language, but censorship was considerably stricter in Warsaw and the Western Provinces than elsewhere.

To get around this fact, a Polish weekly of conservative-liberal views, *Kraj*, was founded in St Petersburg in the 1880s, where it continued to be published well into the twentieth century.[13]

Just as Russifying policies were being applied to Russia's Western and Polish Provinces, Pan-Slav ideas were gaining popularity in Russian society. While Pan-Slavism had little direct influence on official policy, the government could not entirely ignore the popular desire for some kind of tutelary relationship between the Russian state and other Slavic peoples, in particular in the Balkans. Still, Pan-Slavism played little role in the formulation of domestic policy. Most officials (and the emperor himself) found the Pan-Slavs' effusions about Slavic brotherhood abstract, unreal and a bit silly in light of the undeniably Slavic Poles' recent anti-Russian behaviour.[14]

Baltic Provinces and Finland

The Baltic Provinces were also subject to various Russifying measures, in particular in the century's final decades. The ethnic situation here was complex: the German ruling classes found their position challenged by rising Latvian and Estonian peasant nationalism. Despite the loyalty of the Baltic Germans, St Petersburg could not ignore the national-cultural demands of Latvians and Estonians. Thus the use of Latvian and Estonian in schools and private organisations was far less circumscribed than, say, Polish. At the same time, Lutheran Estonians and Latvians were encouraged to convert to Orthodoxy and, once converted, found it impossible to return to their original faith. A desire to reduce local privileges while assuring Russian control over the Baltic Sea littoral led to the whittling away of German privileges in courts, administration and education. Most spectacularly, the German university in Dorpat (now Tartu) – whose founding pre-dated Russian rule there – was transformed in the 1890s into the Russian university of Iurev, as the city was renamed. In the end, Russifying efforts in the Baltic Provinces not only did not strengthen Russian culture there but alienated all affected nationalities – Germans, Estonians, Latvians – from tsarist rule. Similar, but far less justified, centralising policies were introduced in the Grand Duchy of Finland around the turn of the century. Particularly resented were the introduction of Russian as the language of official business and the attempt to subject Finns to the Russian

13 On Russification in the Kingdom of Poland and the Western Provinces after 1863, see Theodore R. Weeks, *Nation and State in Late Imperial Russia: Nationalism and Russification on the Western Frontier, 1863–1914* (DeKalb: Northern Illinois University Press, 1996).

14 On this movement see Michael Boro Petrovich, *The Emergence of Russian Panslavism 1856–1870* (New York: Columbia University Press, 1956).

military draft. St Petersburg's refusal to compromise despite considerable and well-organised Finnish resistance led in 1904 to the assassination of the Russian governor-general, N. I. Bobrikov, in Helsinki.[15]

Central Asia and Muslims

Russian rule in Central Asia differed in almost every particular from the situation in the west. On the one hand, from the 1860s to 1890s Russia extended its rule over huge territories including the cities of Tashkent, Khiva, Merv and Samarkand. Thus, by the 1890s, the Russian Empire abutted to the south on Persia and Afghanistan – to the considerable annoyance of the British in India. Economic motivations, in particular the cultivation of cotton, played a role in this expansion, but probably more important was the desire to prevent other powers from gaining a foothold in the region. By the early twentieth century, Russians had built railways that connected the major cities of the region to Russia. Another major construction project was the founding of Russian Tashkent, a European-style colonial city from which Russia ruled Turkestan. On the whole the Russian administrators in Central Asia avoided offending local sensibilities; in particular missionary activity among local Muslims was tightly circumscribed. Little attempt was made to bring Russian culture to the local population.[16] When the Russian authorities interfered with everyday life – usually in the context of public health and hygiene – their efforts were greatly resented and often actively resisted, as the cholera riots in Tashkent in 1892 show. But even greater anger was engendered by the opening of Turkestan to Russian settlement in 1907. The increasing numbers of Russian settlers in the southern Kazakh steppe would lead to a large-scale revolt against them and Russian rule in 1916.[17]

While the tsar's new Muslim subjects in Kokand, Merv and Bukhara remained for the most part untouched by Russian culture, a very different situation existed among the Volga Tatars. After all, this region had by now been under Russian rule for over three centuries and there had developed over that time significant numbers of Christian Tatars or *Kriashens*. A mixed Russian and Tatar city, Kazan also housed the empire's only university in a largely

15 Besides the excellent articles in the volume edited by Thaden cited above, see Heide W. Whelan, *Adapting to Modernity: Family, Caste and Capitalism among the Baltic German Nobility* (Cologne: Böhlau, 1999).

16 Nonetheless, at least at an elite level, Russian rule helped crystallise Muslim modernisers in the *jadid* movement. See Adeeb Khalid, *The Politics of Muslim Cultural Reform: Jadidism in Central Asia* (Berkeley: University of California Press, 1998).

17 On Central Asia after 1860, see the articles by Hélène Carrère d'Encausse in Allsworth (ed.), *Central Asia*, pp. 131–223.

Muslim region. From the late 1850s a new effort was inaugurated to strengthen the faith of the Christian Tatars (who were notorious backsliders into Muslim influences) and at the same time pave the way for broader knowledge of Russian. The pedagogue Nikolai I. Il'minskii pushed for a new type of missionary school using native languages written in Cyrillic script and where possible employing native teachers. By the 1870s, the 'Il'minskii system' was used in hundreds of schools in the Volga-Ural region but also in Siberia and Central Asia. Il'minskii was a sincere Russifier believing, however, that Russian identity derived primarily from Orthodoxy rather than language. Thus Il'minskii held that limiting the influence of Muslim Tatars was far more important than pressing the Russian language on local populations. Il'minskii's system was always controversial but enjoyed the support of central authorities at least during his lifetime (to the 1890s).[18]

The Caucasus

Aside from the Volga region and Central Asia, the Caucasus contained a large Muslim population. Here an extreme level of ethnic and religious diversity complicated Russian rule. Besides the Muslims (present-day Azeris, but at the time generally called simply 'Tatars'; Chechens, Daghestanis and others), there were Christian Armenians and Georgians. The region had been incorporated into the empire by the first decade of the nineteenth century but, as the stories of Mikhail Lermontov and Leo Tolstoy attest, the mountain peoples were not subdued until well past the middle of the century. The establishment of Russian rule was accompanied by the mass involuntary emigration of Muslims from the Caucasus (in particular over 300,000 Cherkessy in the 1860s and 1870s) across the border to the Ottoman Empire. The capture of the Muslim 'freedom fighter' Shamil, in 1859 may be seen as the beginning of the end for active armed resistence to Russian power.[19] The subdued territory was divided administratively into a half-dozen provinces under the leadership of the governor-general in Tiflis (Tbilisi).

Ironically it was a Christian group who came to be seen as the greatest threat to Russian rule in the Caucasus. From the 1880s Russian policy increasingly took on an anti-Armenian tone, beginning with efforts to force Armenian schools to adopt more use of Russian and, in effect, to Russify them. Armenians lived throughout the Caucasus both in towns and as peasants, but

18 On Il'minskii and his 'system', see Robert P. Geraci, *Window on the East: National and Imperial Identities in Late Tsarist Russia* (Ithaca: Cornell University Press, 2001).

19 On this process, see Austin Jersild, *Orientalism and Empire: North Caucasus Mountain People and the Georgian Frontier 1845–1917* (Montreal: McGill-Queen's University Press, 2002).

it was their urban presence that unsettled tsarist authorities. By the 1890s Russian officials identified Armenians with revolution, rather similarly to official Russia's attitudes towards the Jews. In particular the anti-Armenian governor-general Prince G. S. Golitsyn pressed for a hard line against Armenians and narrowly escaped assassination in 1904. The other large Christian nationality in the Caucasus, the Georgians, was seen as a lesser threat which in retrospect may seem ironic (J. Dzhugashvili was born in 1879).

The 1905 Revolution and after

The turmoil associated with Russia's poor military showing in Manchuria and against the Japanese navy unleashed severe civil unrest among Russia's ethnic minorities. In particular the Baltic region, Russian Poland and the Caucasus were convulsed with revolution. In effect, the government lost control of Warsaw, Riga, Baku and other major cities in 1905. While the October Manifesto of that year did not specifically mention non-Russians, it did promise basic civil rights and a legislature, the Duma. An earlier *ukaz* (decree) of 12 December 1904 had promised, among other things, 'to carry out a review of all existing decrees limiting the rights of non-Russians and natives of distant locations in the Empire [*inorodtsev i urozhentsev otdel'nykh mestnostei Imperii*] in order to leave in effect only those [laws] demanded by fundamental state interests and the obvious needs [*pol'za*] of the Russian [*russkii*] people'. Thus already before the October 1905 Manifesto, commissions were reviewing, for example, whether to allow teaching in Polish and whether restrictions on Jews should be mitigated.

The Duma election law was deeply undemocratic, based as it was on the Prussian model. Still, when the first Duma was convened in July 1906, among the delegates were dozens of Poles, dozens of Muslims and a smattering of other non-Russians. All in all, at least a third of the Duma's 490 delegates can be described as 'non-Russian'.[20] To be sure, the national question played but a small role in the quick demise of the first two Dumas, but St Petersburg and the tsar himself were deeply suspicious of the Jewish, Armenian, Polish and Muslim deputies' loyalties to Russia. The reactionary new electoral law of June 1907, pushed through by the dynamic new prime minister Peter A. Stolypin, specifically limited representation from borderland regions. The law contained a lengthy preamble with one sentence of prime importance for

20 Kappeler gives the figures 220 'non-Russians' to 270 Russians, but he apparently includes Ukrainians and Belarusians in the former number, which may not adequately reflect their own perceived identity. For details, see Kappeler, *Russland als Vielvölkerreich*, p. 278.

the tsar's non-Russian subjects: 'Created to strengthen the Russian [*rossiiskoe*] State, the State Duma must also be Russian [*russkoiu*] in spirit.' In the third Duma (1907–12) the number of Polish deputies dropped to less than a third of representation in the first Duma; there remained only nine Muslims and a single Jew.

At the same time, the Russian government pressed forward with policies to turn back the liberalisation that had occurred since 1904. Polish and Ukrainian cultural organisations and schools were shut down, Muslim activists were jailed and Finnish autonomy was attacked. St Petersburg's obsession with the 'Jewish menace' came out in the open in the grotesque Beilis trial. A Kiev worker, Mendel Beilis, was accused of ritually murdering a Christian lad. The minister of justice, I. V. Shcheglovitov, worked diligently behind the scenes for a conviction, but the government's case against Beilis was so weak that the mainly peasant jury acquitted him. The court's decision did, however, leave open the possibility – against all evidence – that the crime may indeed have been a ritual murder, only carried out by some other Jew.[21]

While the post-1907 period is characterised by more activist pro-Russian and Russifying policies, there is some reason to question whether the government would have continued along this line. Peter Stolypin, the architect of the 1907 electoral law and other Russian nationalist policies, was clearly on his way out when an assassin's bullet caught him in Kiev in September 1911. At the same time, nationalism in both cultural and political guises grew rapidly among non-Russians in the post-1907 period. Despite government harassment, private Polish and Armenian schools, Ukrainian and Yiddish newspapers, and Muslim political and cultural organisations flourished.

First World War

The outbreak of war in August 1914 utterly changed the dynamics of nationalities policy in the Russian Empire.[22] Suddenly it became crucial to woo the Poles and a decree of mid-August promised a reunited Poland under the tsar's sceptre at the end of the war. Germans, on the other hand, had their cultural organisations shut down and were even subjected to a prohibition from speaking German in public. The Ottoman Empire's decision to join the

21 A recent account of the Beilis trial is Albert Lindemann, *The Jew Accused: Three Anti-Semitic Affairs (Dreyfus, Beilis, Frank), 1894–1915* (Cambridge: Cambridge University Press, 1991).

22 Indeed, a recent book argues convincingly that the war allowed the Russian government to embark on hitherto-unseen 'nativising' policies: Eric Lohr, *Nationalizing the Russian Empire: The Campaign against Enemy Aliens during World War I* (Cambridge, Mass.: Harvard University Press, 2003).

Central Powers raised the fear of a Turkic-Muslim fifth column, but the only serious outburst of anti-government violence among Muslims was caused by St Petersburg's own policies in Central Asia. Strains that had long been building over Slavic colonisation exploded into a major rebellion when Russia unwisely attempted to draft local Muslims to do labour duties for the army (unlike Jews, Muslims were exempt from the military draft). Before this 1916 uprising was quelled, over 3,000 Russians and many more Muslims (mainly Kyrgyz and Kazakhs) had lost their lives.

It bears remembering that the First World War in the east was fought in non-Russian regions. As the front moved eastwards (Warsaw was lost to the Germans in mid-1915, Vil'na / Wilno that autumn), the military and civilian authorities pursued a brutal policy of forcibly displacing large numbers of local inhabitants, in particular Jews and Germans, but including many others.[23] As in other European countries, the war fuelled nationalist rhetoric but on the whole policy towards Russia's national minorities did not significantly change. The Russian Empire was fighting, after all, for its survival, a battle it ultimately lost in 1917. Whether more conciliatory and enlightened policies towards non-Russians could have prevented that defeat is a question that can be endlessly debated but not unambiguously supported or refuted.

23 For more on this tragic story, see Peter Gatrell, *A Whole Empire Walking: Refugees in Russia during World War I* (Bloomington: Indiana University Press, 1999).

3
Geographies of imperial identity

MARK BASSIN

Introduction

The problem of identity in modern Russia is commonly framed in terms of the elemental tension between the country's alternative embodiments as *empire* or *nation*.[1] Without any question, this has been a critical distinction for Russia, and the inability to negotiate it successfully must be seen as a key factor in the collapse of Soviet civilisation at the end of the twentieth century. At the same time, however, it may be argued that for earlier centuries the distinction was, if not less salient, then at least salient in a rather different way. This is neither to deny the emergence of a recognisably modern sense of nationhood in Russia by the late eighteenth or early nineteenth centuries, nor to discount its affective significance, at least for educated Russians. The fact remains, however, that national discourses in pre-revolutionary Russia stood not in contradistinction to an imperial identity, but rather were subsumed almost without exception within a broader and more fundamental geopolitical vision of Russia as an empire. Indeed, one must search very hard to find any significant subjective sense of mutual exclusivity between the two. Identity was of course problematic and contested, in Russia as everywhere. This contestation was not, however, expressed through the nation–empire juxtaposition, but rather through alternative visions of Russia as an empire. This chapter seeks to explore identity in pre-revolutionary Russia by examining three different configurations of the imperial vision.

Russia as a European empire

Upon the successful conclusion of Russia's protracted 21-year war with Sweden in 1721, an elaborate and somewhat theatrical ceremony was staged by the

1 G. Hosking, *Russia: People and Empire 1552–1917* (London: Fontana, 1997); V. Tolz, *Russia: Inventing the Nation* (London: Arnold, 2001)

Senate in St Petersburg, in the course of which a new designation was added to Peter I's already lengthy list of official titles. Henceforth, in addition to the traditional terms *tsar* and *samoderzhets* (autocrat), the Russian ruler would carry the title *imperator vse-rossiiskii*, or Emperor of all the Russias. The significance of the novel epithet lay not in its explicit attribution of an imperial character to the Russian state, for Russia had been an empire already for several centuries and indeed had a clear understanding of itself as such. What was significant, rather, was the resolution to formalise this status using the foreign Latin-based terms *imperiia* and *imperator*. The option to draw on a Western rather than a native Slavic lexicon for the purposes of this all-important characterisation was taken in the spirit of the so-called Europeanisation project launched during the Petrine period, and it indicated that the ambitions of this project involved recasting the very character of the Russian state itself. The notion of Russia as an empire may not have been new, but the imputation that it was a *European* empire certainly was. And in order to be truly European, Russia had now to appear to conform to the basic contours of the imperial states of the West.

The Europeanisation of Russia's imperial image involved many things, but among the most fundamental was the need for a basic perceptual rebounding and rebranding of its domestic geographical space, in order to bring it into better correspondence with the way space was organised and valorised within the European empires. Above all, this involved the clear differentiation within the imperial state between the space of the imperial centre or metropole on the one hand and that of the subject colonial realm on the other. Geographically, the closest European parallel to Russia was the Habsburg Empire with its contiguous continental-territorial dominions, and in the eighteenth century at least the Russians stressed this particular axis of affinity very strongly. At the same time, however, Russia's imperial pretensions were from the outset explicitly global, and this meant that it was not 'Austria' but rather the maritime colonial empires of the European West that would provide the most compelling model. Here, however, differences in geographical configuration represented a problem of the first order. In the West European empires the perceptual distinction between metropole and colony generally corresponded to a real physical–geographical separation by large bodies of water, and thus was obvious and straightforward. Because, however, Russia's imperial space was contiguous geographical space, the specific territorial differentiation between metropole and colony had always been obscure. In the West, moreover, the metropole–colony distinction was further reified by the circumstance that it corresponded to the natural–continental juxtaposition of Europe, Africa, Asia and the Americas, a juxtaposition which by the eighteenth century had developed extremely powerful overtones of relative cultural and social development. By virtue once again of Russia's territorial contiguity, however, the specific nature and location of the continental divide between Europe and Asia that notionally ran across its territory remained indeterminate. In so far as pre-Petrine Muscovy did not share the civilisational calculus which so favoured Europe, the lack of clarity regarding the continental boundary stirred no particular apprehension. It immediately became a major point of concern in Petrine Russia, however, for a clear continental divide would establish the objective natural-geographical framework necessary for the sort of perceptual revisioning of Russia's traditional imperial space that was implicit in the Europeanisation project.

In the event, the resolution of the problem came relatively quickly. In the decade following Peter's death in 1725, one of his chief ideologues, Vasilii Tatishchev, identified the Ural mountain chain as the proper natural-geographical boundary between the continents of Europe and Asia. Tatishchev's proposition rapidly gained general acceptance, and the division of the empire into 'European' and 'Asiatic' parts along the Urals which it established provided a new geographical map upon which the West European imperial model could be deployed. Effectively, this modest and low-lying mountain range took the place perceptually of an ocean, and the relationship between the territories on either side was characterised in European terms of continental and civilisational contrast, very much as if they were located on different parts of the globe. In this spirit, the absolute foreignness of the territories east of the Urals vis-à-vis European Russia in all regards – physiography, climate, flora, fauna, social organisation and cultural development – was insisted upon, in terms that corresponded quite precisely to the respective metropole–colony distinctions drawn by empires in the West. Indeed, it is not too much to say that for the eighteenth century at least, the Russians perceived their own imperial domains largely through the categories of Western imperialism. For Russia, as for the West, their colonial domains played the role of a constituting Other, which helped critically to stabilise the newly appropriated identity of 'European' Russia west of the Urals. The colonial populations were viewed with the same intense fascination as exotic and utterly foreign ethnographic material, and as in the West great efforts were expended in studying and cataloguing the empire's immense polyethnic diversity.[2] The extent to which Russians viewed their colonial domain through the lenses of

2 Y. Slezkine, 'Naturalists versus Nations: Eighteenth-Century Russian Scholars Confront Ethnic Diversity', in D. Bower and E. Lazzerini (eds.), *Russia's Orient. Imperial Borderlands and Peoples 1700–1917* (Bloomington: Indiana University Press, 1997), pp. 27–57.

West European colonialism is suggested by Lomonosov's enthusiastic comparisons of the Lena river to the Nile, or yet more pointedly by the common references to Siberia in the eighteenth and early nineteenth centuries as 'our Peru', 'our Mexico', a 'Russian Brazil', or indeed 'our little India'.[3]

A subtle but fundamental ambivalence was, however, built into the Petrine projection of a European identity upon Russia. Was Russia's Europeanness a reality of the present day, or was it rather a desired future aspiration? Was Russia in its present state really a *puissance Européenne*, as Catherine the Great had declared with solemn conviction in the preamble to her *Nakaz* (Instruction), or was this a rather over-confident claim already to be something which the country was more accurately striving to become?[4] In Russia, the Europeanisation project effectively subsumed both of these alternatives. This provided it with a certain useful elasticity but at the same time insured that the quality of Russia's Europeanness would remain subject to more-or-less constant uncertainty. This was apparent already in the eighteenth century, but with the crystallisation of a doctrine of Russian nationalism in the early nineteenth century the proliferating anxieties about Russia's status as a genuine part of European civilisation became arguably the central preoccupation and challenge for Russian identity overall. Russian nationalism responded to this challenge in very different ways, but a significant stream of nationalist sentiment remained faithful to the Petrine project of bringing Russia more fully into the European fold, and for this perspective the vision we have been considering of Russia as a European empire acquired a new significance. The vision itself had been founded on criteria that were supposed to be objective, most importantly the identification of a natural–geographical division between the continents of Europe and Asia. Once elaborated, however, elements of Russia's imperial identity were quickly pressed back into service in order now to reconfirm the original supposition, namely that Russia was indeed a European country in the first place. The paradox that this involved is evident, for the latter proposition – having been objectively demonstrated by geography – should in principle not have stood in question at all.

The most important element of this ideological inversion proved to be the civilisational juxtaposition between Europe and Asia. As we have noted,

3 Mikhail V. Lomonosov, 'Oda na den' vosshestviia na vserossiiskii prestol Ee Velichestva Gosudaryni Imperatritsy Elisavety Petrovny 1747 goda', in *Polnoe sobranie sochinenii* (Moscow and Leningrad, 1950–83 (orig. 1747)), vol. VIII, p. 203; M. Bassin, 'Inventing Siberia: Visions of the Russian East in the Early Nineteenth Century', *AHR* 96, 3 (1991): 770.

4 *Instruction de sa majesté impériale Catherine II* (St Petersburg: Académie des sciences, 1769), p. 3.

the Petrine imperial image incorporated and internalised this juxtaposition like the other European empires, and it understood it in the same way. The Russians developed their own elaborate ideology of 'Orientalism', which adopted the Western sense of the absolute superiority of Russia's notionally European culture and civilisation over the collective peoples of Asia and accepted the corresponding moral imperative to bring Western enlightenment and progress to these benighted masses.[5] As in Europe, the Russians typically understood this enterprise to be a providentially assigned mission, and as such it immediately became a matter of national destiny. Dmitrii Romanov, a government official involved in wresting the territorial concessions in the Far East from China that were codified in the Treaty of Peking in 1860, waxed enthusiastic at the prospect of the opening of the Middle Kingdom to Western influence. 'Fully one-third of the human race, which up to this point remained as if it were non-existent for the rest of the world, is now entering into contact with the advanced nations, and is becoming accessible for European civilization.' Romanov clearly saw Russia as a bearer of the latter, and spoke explicitly of the *evropeizm* or 'Europeanism' which his compatriots were now in a position to disseminate across East Asia.[6] The essential Europeanness of Russia's civilising mission, moreover, was not limited to such philanthropic concerns for ameliorating the public welfare of its Oriental minions, and could easily be appropriated for the purposes of an aggressively forward policy of imperial conquest and expansion. Here as well the essential similitude with European empires was stressed very heavily. It was in just these terms, for example, that the foreign minister, Alexander Gorchakov, justified to the rest of Europe Russia's thrust into Turkestan in the mid-1860s. As a fully developed Western country, he explained in a now-famous diplomatic circular, Russia shared in the general European responsibility of civilising the backward regions of the globe. Drawing explicit parallels with the United States' pacification of the indigenous population of North America, the French in Algeria and Britain in India, Gorchakov identified Russia's own 'special mission' as the bringing of an enlightened social and political order to those 'barbarous countries' and 'half-savage nomad populations' that it confronted in Central Asia.[7]

5 S. Layton, *Russian Literature and Empire: Conquest of the Caucasus from Pushkin to Tolstoy* (Cambridge: Cambridge University Press, 1994); A. L. Jersild, *Orientalism and Empire: North Caucasus Mountain Peoples and the Georgian Frontier, 1845–1917* (Montreal: McGill-Queen's University Press, 2002)

6 D. I. Romanov, *Poslednie sobytiia v Kitae i znachenie ikh dlia Rossii* (Irkutsk: Irkutskaia gubernskaia Tip. 1861), p. 3.

7 Quoted in Alexis Krausse, *Russia in Asia. A Record and a Study 1558–1899* (London: Grant Richards, 1899), pp. 224–5.

All of these declarations exuded a certain confidence in Russia's status as a full-fledged representative of European civilisation. Russia's imperial character could be invoked in a rather different spirit, however, which gave rather clearer expression to the ambivalences and insecurities that were embedded in its own self-image. In this alternative sense, 'European' Russia retained its superiority relative to its Asiatic colonies, but rather than standing at one with the West, Russia was seen instead to occupy an intermediary position between the two. Russia thus was not a European but more precisely a Europeanising country, clearly more advanced than Asia, but equally clearly lagging behind the West. By virtue of this intermediary positioning, a sort of dialectical relationship took shape between Russia's engagement in these two arenas, whereby activity in one direction had immediate implications for and an impact upon the other. Specifically, by exercising its imperial beneficence and civilising its Asiatic colonial realm, Russia would be able to enhance and develop in itself those qualities which would make it – Russia – genuinely European. The civilising mission was thus not merely, and not even primarily the pursuit of an altruistic God-given responsibility but rather a vital opportunity to realise the Petrine injunction to Europeanise Russia itself. An entirely special urgency attached to this, moreover, for Russia's colonial realm in Asia was seen by many not merely as another arena upon which the country could pursue its Westernising agenda but rather the very best arena, uniquely well suited for the task at hand. Mikhail Petrashevskii, banished for socialist agitation to remote Siberia in the 1850s and thus in a position to judge first-hand, recognised this special quality at once. 'Here [in Asiatic Russia] is the environment in which the moral and industrial strengths of Russia can manifest themselves freely and independently, with the least constraint.' In Siberia, he argued, Russia could find its most auspicious opportunity to ameliorate the quality of its own social and cultural development. 'Our present position in Asia, its strengthening or weakening may be considered an indication of the level of our social development, a general conclusion about our social life, a touchstone for the evaluation of the degree to which we have assimilated the principles of Europeanism, which are general principles of humanity.' Russian civilising activity in Siberia, he concluded, 'is destined to achieve for us a diploma with the title of a truly European nation!'[8]

8 Brd [Mikhail Petrashevskii], 'Neskol'ko myslei o Sibiri', *Irkutskie gubernskie vedomosti* 9 (11 June 1857): 3–4, 5.

Russia as an anti-European empire

There was an alternative response to the dilemmas thrown up by Russian nationalism regarding the quality of the country's identity vis-à-vis the West. This took the form of a wholesale reaction against the very principle of Europeanisation and an insistence upon the fact that differences of an essential and insurmountable character separated Russia from the West. Russia was not and had never been in any real sense European, and thus it should not seek in some artificial and forced manner to become so now. Rather, it represented an autonomous world unto itself, which possessed its own distinct cultural ethos and legacy of positive historical accomplishment. 'The East is not the West' lectured the nationalist historian Mikhail Pogodin, 'we have a different climate . . . , a different temperament, character, different blood, a different physiognomy, a different outlook, a different cast of mind, different beliefs, hopes, desires . . . . Everything is different.'[9] From this standpoint, Russia could not possibly be judged in Western terms but rather exclusively on the basis of its own distinctive national qualities and native virtues. Accordingly, the nationalists spent a great deal of energy elaborating precisely what these qualities and virtues were, and concepts such as *sobornost'* (social collectivity) and *dukhovnost'* (spirituality), which they identified, proved highly successful in sustaining the vision of fundamental Russian exclusivity and difference from the European West.

For all of their pointed hostility to the suggestion that Russia possessed or should strive to possess a European character, however, there was one fundamental aspect of the Europeanisation project which these Russo- or Slavophilic nationalists quite notably did not reject. Despite the vociferous criticism they directed towards the person of Peter the Great himself, the nationalists retained a principled and dedicated commitment to that particular vision of Russian empire born of his efforts. They not only accepted the eighteenth century imperial perspective we have been considering as an entirely natural expression of Russia's genuine character, but beyond this they critically enhanced its most important elements as they developed their own perspective. Thus, the vision of formal geopolitical bifurcation of the state territory into metropole and colonial realm was endorsed, as was essentially the same sense of a civilisational juxtaposition and essential differentiation between the two entities. Indeed, with remarkably few exceptions, the entire nationalist sense of Russia's

9 Quoted in W. Bruce Lincoln, *Nicholas I* (Bloomington: Indiana University Press, 1978) p. 251.

historical greatness and its importance on a broader international arena was founded squarely upon this particular image of imperial configuration and expansionist dynamism. It is entirely indicative that nationalists who were uncompromisingly hostile to the West and to Europeanisation as such figured among Russia's most enthusiastic and determined empire-builders in the nineteenth century and provided an activist core for the vanguard which led Russia's dramatic imperial advances across the century into the Caucasus, the Far East and Central Asia.

Along with this persistent commitment to the Petrine imperial model went a commitment to the belief in a Russian mission to civilise the Asiatic realms already under its jurisdiction, or destined in their eyes soon to be. The Russophilic nationalists, however, fundamentally rearranged the terms of this prospect as we have considered it up to this point, with the result that the civilisational juxtaposition upon which it was based was now mobilised *against* the West rather than in line with it. From this standpoint, Russia's civilising mission and its progressive accomplishments in its colonial realm demonstrated not Russia's commonality with Europe but rather its difference from it. The enlightenment of Asia was not really a responsibility shared among the colonial powers, but rather belonged most naturally and legitimately to Russia alone. Russia's natural prerogative in this regard came in the first instance from the facts of geography, which placed Russia in much closer physical proximity to the Asiatic realms in question, but also from historical circumstance, which from the very beginning had intimately linked Russia's destiny – unlike that of Europe – with the peoples of the East. 'The East belongs to us unalterably, naturally, historically, voluntarily', declared Aleksandr Balasoglo, a colleague of Petrashevskii's, in the late 1840s. 'It was bought with the blood of Russia already in the pre-historic struggles of the Slavs with the Finnish and Turkic tribes, it was suffered for at the hand of Asia in the form of the Mongol yoke, it has been welded to Russia by her Cossacks, and it has been earned from Europe by [the Russian] resistance to the Turks.'[10]

These proprietary claims to the spaces and peoples of Asia based on historical experience were much enhanced by the contrast which (so the nationalists claimed) distinguished their own present-day colonial activities from those of the European empires. The latter were not genuinely inspired by a philanthropic desire to assist the hapless populations of their Asiatic colonies but rather were motivated exclusively by their own predatory self-interest and a

10 V. A. Desnitskii (ed.), *Delo Petrashevtsev*, 3 vols. (Moscow: Izd. AN SSSR, 1937–51), vol. II, p. 44.

determiniation to maximise their own profit. Russia, by contrast, went about its God-given mission with no concerns beyond the welfare of its colonial subjects. The geographer Petr Semenov (later Semenov-Tian-Shanskii) reflected upon this profound contrast on the occasion of the Russian occupation and annexation of the Amur river basin in the 1850s. 'The Russians do not annihilate – either directly, like the Spanish at the time of the discovery of America, or indirectly, like the British in North America and Australia – the half-wild tribes of Central Asia and the Far East.' Indeed, the nationalist Semenov strove to disassociate his own country as fundamentally as possible from the brutal and bloody legacy left by the Europeans in the non-European world. Each new step of Russia into Asia, he concluded, was 'another peaceful and sure victory of human genius over the wild, still unbridled forces of Nature, of civilization over barbarism'.[11] No other European power, he clearly believed, could legitimately characterise their colonial presence in such confidently positive terms.

Russia's colonial dominions offered rather more to the nationalists than an opportunity to demonstrate their simple moral superiority over the West. The prospect of imperial activity in Asia could also be seen as a deliberate and radical turn away from Europe, as if the fact of Russia's intermediary physical-geographical location between Europe and Asia represented a sort of existential opportunity or indeed imperative to choose between the two. This particular sentiment was manifested most intensely at those moments when Russia's confrontation with the West appeared especially problematic and the prospect of a sort of escape to the East correspondingly offered its greatest appeal. One such moment was the Crimean War, when the Russians felt themselves to be under attack from a concert of hostile European countries. During the war, the historian Pogodin summoned his countrymen to renounce the West and to redirect their energies in the future to the East. 'Leaving Europe in peace in the expectation of better circumstances, we should turn all of our attention to Asia . . . Let the European peoples live as they know how and arrange themselves in their own countries as they wish, while half of Asia – China, Japan, Tibet, Bukhara, Khiva, Persia – belongs to us if we want.' This reorientation was to be accompanied by a dizzying programme of constructive actitity, which would stimulate Russia's national spirit and provide new meaning for it. 'Lay new roads into Asia or search out old ones, develop communications, if only in the tracks indicated by Alexander the

11 P. P. Semenov, 'Obozrenie Amura v fiziko-geograficheskom otnoshenii', *Vestnik imperatorskogo geograficheskogo obshchestva* 15, 6 (1855): 254.

Great and Napoleon, set up caravans, girdle Asiatic Russia with railroads, send steamships along all of its rivers and lakes . . . , and you will increase happiness and abundance across the entire globe.'[12]

Several decades later essentially the same sort of summons was repeated by the novelist Fedor Dostoevsky. In his message, however, we may begin to detect the same shift of emphasis observed in the musing of Petrashevskii, in the sense that the subject to be improved through this activity was not so much the indigenous colonial population as Russia itself. A refocusing of attention upon Asia, Dostoevsky insisted, 'will lift and resuscitate our spirit and our strengths . . . Our civilising mission there will give us spirit and draw us out, if only we would get on with it!' Like Pogodin, Dostoevsky envisioned an ambitious programme of construction and development. 'Build just two railroads, for a start – one into Siberia and the other into Central Asia – and you will see the results immediately.'[13] It seems obvious that the 'results' Dostoevsky refers to here had much more to do with the Russians themselves than with the latter's Asiatic colonies. Like Petrashevskii, Dostoevsky believed that Russia's efforts towards civilising its Asian colonies would have the far more important effect of enabling Russia to transform, indeed to civilise itself. Quite unlike Petrashevskii, however, Dostoevsky shared with Pogodin an ultimate aim which was not integration into the European fraternity but rather precisely the contrary, that is to say the ever-greater individualisation of Russia, its differentiation from the West and the advancement of its own special destiny.

Or was it? The fact that the vision of Russia as an anti-European empire continued to accept the civilisational distinction between Europe and Asia set out in the eighteenth century insured that it would remain encumbered with the fundamental nationalist dilemma regarding Russia's European identity. When confronting Europe directly, the nationalists we are considering could be confident in their unconditional disassociation from and rejection of it. This clear demarcation was undermined, however, precisely by the fact of Russia's colonial Asian realm. Russia's colonies beyond the Urals retained their function as a constituting Other for Russia itself, and the particular civilisational juxtaposition that this invoked dictated that Russia was by definition, and thus by necessity European. There simply was no alternative. Russian nationalism wrestled ceaselessly with the geographical illogic of this conundrum without

12 M. P. Pogodin, 'O russkoi politike na budushchee vremia', in *Istoriko-politicheskie pis'ma i zapiski v prodolzhenii Krymskoi voiny 1853–1856* (Moscow: V. M. Frish, 1874 (orig. 1854)), pp. 242–4.

13 F. M. Dostoevskii, 'Geok Tepe. Chto dlia nas Aziia', in *Polnoe sobranie sochinenii* (Leningrad: Nauka, 1972–90), vol. XXVII, p. 36.

ever being able fully to master it. Among other things, this failure insured that even the most vociferous nationalist insistence on Russia's non-European character was nearly always tempered by some degree or shade of lingering commitment to the original Petrine identification of Russia as a Western empire.

Thus we see that the same Pogodin who demanded that Russia turn its indignant back on a bellicose West could at the same time speak with the greatest warmth and conviction about Russia's essential affinities with Europe. Upon learning of the brutal Sepoy revolt against the British in India in 1857, for example, the image of a hostile competitor empire was immediately replaced by a sense of commonality and shared destiny. 'We forgot at once that the English were our enemy, and we saw in them only Europeans, Christians, sufferers. We saw in them an advanced nation which barbarism was threatening with destruction, and a general compassion and sympathy was expressed from all corners.'[14] The same point was made yet more emphatically by Dostoevsky, for as soon as he directed his attention away from the West and towards the Russian East, it became clear that the national transformation for which he was hoping had everything to do with Europe. Russia's imperial presence beyond the Urals, he argued, could allow the country finally and definitively to shed the stigma of backwardness and thereby become European. 'In Europe we are hangers-on and slaves, but in Asia we are masters,' he observed crisply. 'In Europe we are Tatars, but *in Asia we too are Europeans.*' This transformation would be brought about through Russia's progressive civilising activities, and the all-important point – as with Petrashevskii – was that the West itself should and would appreciate this. 'Europe is sly and clever,' he assured his compatriots, 'it is guessing what is going on and, believe, me, will begin to respect us immediately!'[15] Clearly, and paradoxically, the civilisation that Dostoevsky was hoping that its Asiatic colonies would provide for Russia was nothing other than Europeanisation itself.

Russia as a national empire

The late imperial period produced yet a third perspective on Russia's imperial identity. Like the others we have examined, this perspective was influenced decisively by impulses from the West. Now, however, these impulses came not so much from discourses about empire as from the growing preoccupation

14 M. P. Pogodin, 'Vtoroe pis'mo k Izdatel'iu gazety "Le Nord"', in *Stat'i politicheskie i pol'skii vopros* (Moscow: F. B. Miller, 1876 (orig. 1856)), p. 16.

15 Dostoevskii, 'Geok Tepe', pp. 36–8; emphasis added.

with the processes of nation-building and nation-state consolidation. In this spirit, the first priority was the principle of national unity, understood in a manner that went well beyond traditional Russian notions of centralisation within the autocratic state. Indeed, in a very real sense this new concern contravened the very principle of imperial bifurcation and heterogeneity which had been so carefully constructed and maintained in the Petrine vision of Imperial Russia. Now the challenge was rather to overcome internal differentiation by integrating and unifying the far-flung spaces of the empire economically, demographically and politically, with the ultimate goal of creating a single cohesive and homogeneous political-geographical corpus. It is highly significant in this regard that the thinking of Sergei Witte – minister of finance from 1892 to 1903 and one of the most powerful tsarist officials of the late empire – was heavily influenced by the apostle of German national consolidation Friedrich List.[16] Witte enthuastically embraced List's dogma of a consolidated and standardised 'national market', and the various projects of national development which he was to sponsor – notably the construction of the very railways across Asiatic Russia to the Pacific and into Central Asia that Pogodin and Dostoevsky had called for – were intended among other things to create the conditions for such an integrated national arena in Russia. The great chemist Dmitrii Mendeleev, who shared Witte's general perspective on national development, attempted to give graphic expression to this imperative of national consolidation by drafting an entirely new cartographic projection of the empire, which purported to depict more accurately than standard projections the natural physiographic coalescence of Russia's imperial spaces.[17]

The great ethnographic and geographical diversity of the empire, which had served as such an obvious and important marker of Russia's imperial identity, was of course not to be denied. The new perspective sought to reorganise and subsume this variety, however, within a uniform standardised framework of imperial civil order, or *grazhdanstvennost'*. The imperial population in its entirety was now characterised as a single civil society, in which each individual was a citizen endowed with the same fundamental array of privileges and duties.[18] This sort of vision of civil society had been developing in Russia since the late eighteenth century, but it gained public momentum only in the 1860s as part of the Great Reforms. The first target for this programme of radical

16 S. Iu. Vitte, *Po povodu natsionalizma. Natsional'naia ekonomiia i Fridrikh List*, 2nd edn (St Petersburg: Brokgauz and Efron, 1912 (orig. 1889)).
17 D. I. Mendeleev, *K poznaniiu Rossii* (Munich: Izd. Molavida, 1924; (orig. 1906)).
18 D. Yaroshevski, 'Empire and Citizenship', in Brower and Lazzerini (eds.) *Russia's Orient*, pp. 58–79.

social and political inclusion had been the newly emancipated serfs, but the scope was broadened in subsequent decades to include the indigenous non-Russian populations of the colonial periphery as well. To be sure, the new principle of grazhdanstvennost' incorporated many of the traditional imperial concerns and attitudes. Thus, the extension of imperial citizenship to the empire's colonial subjects was intended to help consolidate and strengthen centralised tsarist authority in non-Russian regions where it was perceived to be tenuous, and to facilitate their administrative incorporation into the imperial framework. Moreover, the commitment to equal enfranchisement was very much driven by the same convictions we have noted earlier regarding the superiority of European-Russian civilisation (Russian language, Russian Orthodoxy and so on), the latter's civilising mission and the imperative that the empire's colonial subjects eventually adopt the Russian cultural ethos. Indeed, it was ultimately this ethos which was to provide the cement for imperial unity *in toto*.

At the same time, however, the new perspective approached this process in a manner very different from the other visions of empire that we have considered. The adoption of the Russian ethos would not be achieved through diktat and forced imposition, but rather naturally and voluntarily, through peaceful exposure to the superior Russian example. These alternative nuances were captured in the distinction between the terms *russifikatsiia* (Russification) and *obrusenie* (Russianisation).[19] Moreover, in stark contrast to the view of the empire's non-Russian subjects as an 'essentially' foreign ethnographic Other, the project of Russianisation took the national homogenisation of the entire imperial population entirely seriously and looked forward confidently to the complete assimilation of non-Russian elements into the dominant Russian core. This process would not necessarily lead to the complete dissolution of traditional non-Russian ethnic or tribal attachments, but the primordial particularism of the latter would be emphatically – and willingly – subordinated to a new common identity defined in terms of imperial citizenship. Again, the critical contrast with the other perspectives we have examined was the eventual prospect of assimilation: ethno-cultural differences were no longer essentialised as immutable realities which needed to be managed but rather tended to be seen as obstacles to the cohesion of the modern state which could and would be overcome. In this spirit, terms such as *sblizhenie* (rapprochement) and *sliianie* (blending or merging) – familiar to us today

19 D. Brower, *Turkestan and the Fate of the Russian Empire* (London: RoutledgeCurzon, 2003), pp. 65–6, 68.

from their later deployment in the tortured lexicon of Soviet nationality policy – were already in active use to characterise the interactive dynamics of the empire's many nationalities.[20]

In all of this, empire-building was clearly crossing lines with nation-building, and the emphasis on unity and homogeneity within the imperial framework led to a further blurring of the distinction between empire and nation in Russia. Effectively, policies intended to consolidate and strengthen the former were at the very same time supposed to foster the latter as well. It should be noted that this particular paradox was by no means Russia's alone, for other European empires also struggled in this period to balance the enhancement of empire with the increasingly irresistible imperative towards national consolidation, and for them as well the simple conflation of the two could represent the most appealing way of achieving this. This at any rate was the option urged by the historian and ideologist of British imperialism J. R. Seeley, who wrote in the 1880s that 'our Empire is not an empire at all in the ordinary sense of the word. It does not consist of a congeries of nations held together by force, but in the main of one nation, as much as if it were no Empire but an ordinary [national] state.' To be sure, Seeley was discerning enough to appreciate that ethnographic distinctions could not credibly be written out of the calculus of nationhood in the modern world, and thus his sweeping conclusion that 'our Empire is a vast English nation' was drawn only with the careful stipulation that 'we exclude India from consideration'.[21] This sort of general perspective found a powerful resonance in Russia, notably among the liberal elite assembled in the Constitutional-Democratic or Kadet party. In 1914 Petr Struve declared Russia to be a 'nation-state empire', in which all the nationalities already had or would eventually assimilate to the dominant Russian ethos.[22] This view was echoed three years later on the eve of the revolution by Struve's colleague Boris Nolde, who characterised the empire in a similar spirit as a 'Russian national state (*russkoe gosudarstvo*)'.[23] The striking difference with Seeley was that the notion of imperial-national unity as affirmed by these Russians demonstratively failed to grant his concession to the ethnographic dimension of nationhood, in which spirit, for example, the Briton's exclusion of India might have been matched in the case of Russia by Turkestan. The vision of Russia as a national empire, however, imbued Russian nationality

20 Brower, *Turkestan*, p. 19.

21 J. Seeley, *The Expansion of England: Two Courses of Lectures* (London: Macmillan, 1883), pp. 51, 75.

22 Quoted in Dominic Lieven, 'Dilemmas of Empire 1850–1918: Power, Territory, Identity', *Journal of Contemporary History* 34, 2 (1999): 179.

23 Quoted in Tolz, *Russia*, pp. 173–4.

with a distinctly imperial quality that enabled it to be at once multiethnic and supra-ethnic. It was founded upon affinities that effectively both absorbed and superseded mere racial and ethnographic criteria. This line of thinking in late imperial Russia provided a direct link with nationality debates and policies throughout the Soviet Union and indeed down to the present day.

The national assimilation of its non-Russian populations, however, was only one means by which the empire was to be 'Russianised'. Along with it went a heightened awareness of the pervasiveness of ethnic Russian settlement itself across the remote imperial expanses, an awareness that was apparent above all in a new historiographical emphasis on the factors of resettlement and colonisation in Russian history. The groundwork for such a perspective had been laid in the early 1840s, in the theories of the Moscow historian Sergei Solov'ev about the genesis of the Russian nation. Anticipating a theme that later in the century would figure prominently in nationalist historiography in many countries, Solov'ev argued that the Russian nation had been formed by a primordial process of movement across and settlement of vast geographical spaces. His attention was fixed upon Russia's earliest history, and the geographical realm he had in mind was correspondingly limited, but after the middle of the century his ideas were generalised into the prospect of a single colonising moment which ran throughout all of Russia's historical experience from its origins down to the present, and which included the full geographical scope of all Russia's vast imperial domains.[24] This was a view of Russia as a nation 'colonising itself', as Solov'ev's successor at Moscow University, Vasilii Kliuchevskii, famously put it, in which resettlement and colonisation were 'the basic facts of [its] history'.[25] With varying emphases, this perspective was developed in subsequent decades by numerous historians, including A. P. Shchapov, M. K. Liubavskii, G. I. Vernadskii and many others.

Indeed, its appeal extended far beyond the university lecture hall, and it gave rise to a teleological vision of inexorable movement eastwards 'against the sun' that ran throughout the entire historical life of the Russian nation – effectively a sort of Russian Manifest Destiny.[26] Like the American prototype, this prospect bequeathed new meaning and rationale both to the Russian historical chronicle as well as to Russia's imperial spaces themselves, and it

24 S. K. Frank, *Imperiale Aneignung. Diskursive Strategien der Kolonisation Sibiriens durch die russische Kultur* (Habilitationschrift, University of Konstanz, 2003) pp. 108–23.

25 V. O. Kliuchevskii, *Sochineniia v deviati tomakh*, 9 vols. (Moscow: Mysl', 1987), vol. I, pp. 50–1.

26 G. I. Vernadskii, 'Protiv solntsa. Rasprostranenie russkogo gosudarstva k Vostoku', *Russkaia mysl'* 1 (1914): 56–79; Georgii Vernadskii, 'O dvizhenii russkikh na vostok', *Nauchnyi istoricheskii zhurnal* 1, 2 (1913): 52–61.

additionally served as a convenient rationalisation and justification for the expansionist activities of the present day. Once again the geographer Semenov gave voice to this perspective, linking Russia's contemporary advances on the Manchurian frontier to a deeper geo-historical thrust in the life of the nation. 'The occupation and colonization of the Amur brilliantly brings to an end the remarkable movement of the Slavic tribe, which began in the sixteenth century and which pressed . . . in a direction diametrically opposed to all [other] national migrations: namely from the west to the east, from the shores of the Volga to the coasts of the Pacific Ocean.' The history of the exploration and settlement of all Siberia, he concluded, 'clearly demonstrates that the entire Slavic migration from the west to the east was a natural phenomenon, which flowed gradually out of the life of the Russian nation'.[27]

This emphasis on movement and colonisation as intrinsic aspects of Russia's historical experience had substantial implications for the articulation of the vision of the empire as consolidated national space. It indicated on the one hand that the Russians historically had had a physical presence right across the empire, which in turn meant that the manifest ethno-cultural contrasts between Russian and non-Russian within the empire were no longer necessarily reflected geographically in the contrast between regions that were 'essentially' European (and thus native Russian) and those that were 'essentially' Asian (and hence colonial and foreign). Precisely this distinction, of course, had been a foundational element of the Petrine vision of empire, and even a partial readjustment of it involved a reconceptualisation of the differentiation of imperial space in its entirety into organic Russian as opposed to non-Russian parts – the very differentiation, that is to say, between metropole and colony. It is perhaps not too much to speak of a perceptual revolution in this regard, which was manifested most clearly in regard to Russia's oldest, largest and in many senses most important colony, namely Siberia. With the new insistence on the unbroken and organic continuity of the process of Russian settlement across the ages, Siberia began to be seen not only as the exotic foreign colony envisioned in the eighteenth century, clearly distinguished from Russia proper – i.e. 'European' Russia west of the Urals – in terms of geography and ethnography. Beyond this, it was revisioned as a sort of geographical extension of Russia itself and thus an organic part of it, with a long historical tradition of settlement by populations that were ethnically Russian. Indeed, this latter point had been noted since the early decades of the

27 Quoted in Mark Bassin, *Imperial Visions: Nationalist Imagination and Geographical Expansion in the Russian Far East, 1840–1865* (Cambridge: Cambridge University Press, 1999), p. 269.

century by Russian nationalists, who delighted in the fact that native Russian folkways and traditions long vanished in European parts of the empire could still be found in Russian society east of the Urals. From this standpoint, Siberia could not legitimately be characterised as a colony at all, for it represented not imperial space but rather the space of the Russian nation.[28]

The appeal of this vision of the Russian empire as cohesive national space was not limited to the Europhilic tendency of Russian nationalism as represented by Westernisers such as Witte, Struve or Nolde. Very much to the contrary, it was embraced by the nationalist anti-Western camp as well; indeed, in formulations such as those offered by the Pan-Slav Nikolai Danilevskii in his manifesto *Russia and Europe* (1871) it received what was perhaps its fullest and most radical expression. Danilevskii concurred with the emphasis on national unity as the necessary foundation of all forms of statehood that we have already noted. 'Nationality [*narodnost'*] represents . . . the essential basis for the state, the very rationale for its existence. The principal goal of the state is precisely the preservation of the nation.' He went even further, insisting that the state–nation correspondence must be based on an absolute exclusivity, in the sense that only 'a single nation may form any one state'. Pluralistic states in which a 'haphazard mixture of nations [*sluchainaia smes' narodnostei*]' were assembled within a common political space violated this principle, thereby insuring their own instability and ineffectiveness.[29] The Russian state, he argued, had historically represented the former model in that it was based upon a single Russian nation.

Danilevskii did not believe that this fact was undermined or contradicted by the poly-ethnic diversity of the imperial body politic. The tribal or ethnographic identifications which this diversity represented related only to the lowest and most primitive forms of social association, and did not interfere with the principle of modern nationality, which was historically more advanced and took clear precedence. Over the centuries, the Russians had naturally absorbed into their own national ethos the various peoples they encountered, and Danilevskii's consistent option for the term *assimiliatsiia* (assimilation) to describe this process – rather than the more mutualistic and even-handed *sblizhenie* or *sliianie* – left no doubt as to the absolute pre-eminence of Russian nationality in this process. On this latter point he was most emphatic, stressing

28 Mark Bassin, 'Imperialer Raum/Nationaler Raum: Sibirien auf der kognitiven Landkarte Rußlands im 19. Jahrhundert', *Geschichte und Gesellschaft: Zeitschrift für Historische Sozialwissenschaft* 28, 3 (2002): 378–403.

29 N. Ia. Danilevskii, *Rossiia i Evropa. Vzgliad na kul'turniye i politicheskie otnosheniia Slavianskogo mira k Germano-Romanskomu* (Moscow: Kniga, 1991 (orig. 1871)), p. 222.

the 'assimilating power' (*upodobitel'naia sila*) of the Russian ethos that rendered it capable of 'converting' or 'turning' (*pretvorit'*) the non-Russian nationalities of the empire quite literally into 'its own flesh and blood' (*v svoiu plot' i krov'*).[30] In the most fundamental and absolute sense, therefore, Danilevskii believed that the imperial population already represented the Russian nation, to a significant extent at least.

Danilevskii embellished his argument regarding the essential unity and homogeneity of the empire with an impassioned attempt to revise the Petrine vision of Russia's geographical bifurcation between two continents. In the early pages of his work, he devoted considerable energy to deconstructing the very continental boundary which had been so carefully constructed in the early eighteenth century and which provided the foundation for the other imperial perspectives we have considered. The Urals, he insisted, were a thoroughly minor physiographic feature which could hardly represent a continental boundary, and there was moreover no satisfactory alternative to them to serve as a boundary between Europe and Asia across Russian space. The simple fact was that, rather than being geographically bifurcated in any way, the entirety of Russia's imperial realm represented a unified 'natural region' (*estestvennaia oblast'*) as organically cohesive as the geographical space of the French nation, for example, if on a larger scale.[31] This natural-geographical cohesiveness, plus the lack of a Europe–Asia boundary, set the basis for Danilevskii's radical reconfiguration of the traditional bipartite civilisational contrast between Europe and Asia into a tripartite juxtaposition. Imperial Russia represented a third world, equally distinct from Europe and Asia and no less significant in world-historical terms than either. Danilevskii's tentative thoughts along this line were systematised some years later by his fellow Pan-Slav Vladimir Lamanskii in a study entitled *The Three Worlds of the Euro-Asiatic Continent*, and after the revolution were developed much further by a group of émigrés – including Vernadskii himself and a former acolyte of Struve, Petr Savitskii – into the doctrines of Eurasianism.[32]

In stark contrast to European territorial expansion – always associated with violence and brutality – the historical expansion of Russia to occupy its 'natural region' was in Danilevskii's view an organic and benign process. The edifice

30 Danilevskii, *Rossiia*, p. 486.
31 Danilevskii, *Rossiia*, pp. 56–7.
32 V. I. Lamanskii, *Tri mira Aziiskogo-Evropeiskogo materika*, 2nd edn (Petrograd: Novoe Vremia, 1916 (orig. 1892)); N. V. Riasanovsky, 'The Emergence of Eurasianism', *California Slavic Studies* 4 (1967): 39–72; M. Laruelle, *L'Idéologie eurasiste russe, ou comment penser l'empire* (Paris: L'Harmattan, 1999).

of the Russian state that it produced was 'not built on the bones of trampled nations' but rather represented a harmonious and voluntaristic entity.[33] Danilevskii endorsed the notion of Manifest Destiny with the teleological argument that these open continental spaces were truly 'predestined' for Russian occupation and assimilation. The clear implication was that Russia possessed no colonies or foreign territories at all, only contiguous national spaces, and on this point Danilevskii finally made explicit the revision of the status of Russia's Siberian 'colony'. Russian settlements beyond the Urals, he declared, 'do not represent new [and disassociated] centres of Russian life, but rather only serve to broaden Russsia's unified, indivisible sphere'. The historical and ethnographic unity of Russian settlement, from the western borderlands to the Pacific, was quite complete and corresponded moreover to the essential physiographic unity of the landmass it covered. 'Russia never possessed colonies' he concluded, 'and it is entirely mistaken [*ves'ma oshibochno*] to regard Siberia as an example of one, as many do.'[34] With this, the fundamental innovation upon which the other visions of Russia as a European empire were founded had been undone, and the reformulation of Russia's imperial image had come full circle.

33 Danilevskii, *Rossiia,* pp. 24–5.
34 Danilevskii, *Rossiia*, p. 485.

PART II

★

CULTURE, IDEAS, IDENTITIES

4

Russian culture in the eighteenth century

LINDSEY HUGHES

Russia and the West: 'catching up'

Two edicts issued within a few weeks of each other offer a foretaste of the trajectory of Russian culture in the eighteenth century. At the end of December 1699 Peter I replaced the Byzantine practice of counting years from the creation of mankind with numbering from the birth of Christ, 'in the manner of European Christian nations'. Henceforth the year would begin in January, not September.[1] On 4 January 1700 townsmen were ordered to adopt Western dress, a decree that was extended later in the year to women.[2] In both cases, Peter's potentially recalcitrant subjects were provided with visual aids: examples of New Year festive greenery and mannequins wearing 'French and Hungarian' dress were displayed in public places to prevent anyone 'feigning ignorance' about what was required. Both these measures presupposed 'Christian Europe' as Russia's model. Both offended Orthodox sensibilities. Traditionalists protested that Peter was tampering with Divine time and that the 'German' dress and the clean-shaven faces imposed on men a few years earlier were ungodly. Elite Russians in Western fashions entered a Western time scale, while the mass of the traditionally clad population, who had little need to know what year it was, continued to live by the cyclical calendar of feasts and saint's days. Historians agree that these and subsequent reforms widened the gap between high and low culture: the elite 'caught up' with the West, while the lower classes 'lagged behind'.

With this in mind and with a focus on high culture, we shall examine developments in architecture, the figurative arts, theatre, music and literature

1 *PSZ*, 3rd series, no. 1735, pp. 680–1, no. 1736, pp. 681–2.

2 *PSZ*, 4th series, no. 1741, p. 1. On calendar and dress reform, see L. Hughes, *Russia in the Age of Peter the Great* (New Haven and London: Yale University Press, 1998) and 'From Caftans into Corsets: The Sartorial Transformation of Women during the Reign of Peter the Great', in P. Barta (ed.), *Gender and Sexuality in Russian Civilization* (London: Routledge, 2001), pp. 17–32.

from the late seventeenth century to the end of the eighteenth. Exploring these topics within the framework of individual reigns reflects the fact that Russian high culture was overwhelmingly dependent on initiative and funding from the sovereigns and their circle. From the 1690s to the 1790s the dominant trend was the assimilation of the devices of classicism in its various guises – baroque, rococo, neoclassicism. The sources of inspiration shifted over time, as Polish-Ukrainian influences were replaced by German and French, with a phase of 'Anglophilia' in Catherine II's reign, but the basic process remained one of imitation and apprenticeship. Often Russia's eighteenth century has been presented as a means to an end, the end being the internationally recognised achievements of Russian literature, music and, eventually, the visual arts in the nineteenth and early twentieth centuries. The century justified its existence by producing the poet Alexander Pushkin (born 1799). Even Soviet nationalist historians, who eulogised several key figures of the Russian Enlightenment, were uncomfortable with the 'century of apprenticeship' and the debt that Russian culture owed to foreign models. In this chapter I hope to put these issues into perspective.

The reign of Peter I (1682–1725)

Elite Russian culture at the beginning of the eighteenth century developed in a peculiar hot-house environment, show-cased in St Petersburg. The new capital's creator, Peter I, summoned foreign architects to construct palaces, and foreign artists to fill them with pictures. He instructed agents abroad to purchase what could not be produced at home.[3] Once seen as revolutionary, Peter's cultural programme is best regarded as an intensification and acceleration of innovations that occurred less ostentatiously in the seventeenth century. Peter's father Alexis (1629–76) is the first Russian ruler of whom we have more or less authentic painted likenesses and the first to maintain a court theatre and a court poet. Alexis's daughter Sophia (1657–1704) was the first Russian woman to be the subject of secular portraiture. Poets praised her wisdom in syllabic verse.[4]

Such developments derived from two main cultural strands that continued into Peter's reign and beyond. Firstly, there was Latinate Orthodox culture

3 See N. V. Kaliazina and G. N. Komelova, *Russkoe iskusstvo Petrovskoi epokhi* (Leningrad: Khudozhnik, 1990); M. V. Piotrovskii (ed.), *Osnovateliu Peterburga. Katalog vystavki* (St Petersburg: Ermitazh, 2003).

4 See L. Hughes, *Sophia, Regent of Russia* (New Haven and London: Yale University Press, 1990) and my chapter in volume I of *The Cambridge History of Russia*.

filtered through Ukraine and Belarus and propagated by the Slavonic-Greek-Latin (Moscow) Academy, established in 1687 on the model of the Kiev Academy.[5] Its teachers, pupils and artists produced syllabic verses, allegorical engravings, school drama and programmes for parades and firework displays, employing the devices of the Polish Renaissance and baroque. Secondly, Western craftsmen entered the tsars' service, many employed in the Kremlin Armoury workshops. The Moscow Academy and the Armoury catered to many of Peter's cultural needs both before and after his first visit to the West (1697–8). In the 1690s, for example, Armoury artists painted pictures of 'troops going by sea' copied from German engravings and decorated the ships that Peter built at Voronezh.[6] In 1696 the Academy organised a programme of classical architectural devices, allegorical paintings and sculptures on triumphal gates for a victory parade to celebrate the capture of Azov from the Turks.[7] Such parades, inspired by Imperial Rome, continued to be held in Moscow and later St Petersburg to celebrate Russia's successes against the Swedes in the Great Northern War (1700–21).

Only after his major victories in 1709–10 could Peter devote attention to the construction of St Petersburg. The city was to be designed according to a regular plan (never fully implemented), in contrast to Moscow's haphazard maze of streets. Unlike in Moscow, where the tsars' court mainly operated within the constricted, walled space of the Kremlin, with men and women segregated, in St Petersburg a number of riverbank sites accommodated Peter's mixed-sex parties and masquerades, parades and regattas. Key landmarks were constructed of brick, stuccoed and painted in bright colours and decorated with bands of flat white pilasters and window surrounds. Characteristic touches in interiors were the use of blue and white Delft tiles, carved wooden panelling and allegorical frescoes. Some historians apply the all-purpose term 'Petrine Baroque' to the architecture of early St Petersburg, although in fact there was no attempt to impose a uniform style beyond achieving a generally Western look.

5 R. Lucas, 'Dutch and Polish Influences in Russian Architecture 1660–1725', *Study Group on Eighteenth-Century Russia Newsletter* (hereafter, *SGECRN*) 8 (1980): 23–7; M. Okenfuss, *The Rise and Fall of Latin Humanism in Early Modern Russia* (Leiden and New York: Brill, 1995); N. Chrissides, 'Creating the New Educational Elite. Learning and Faith in Moscow's Slavo-Greco-Latin Academy, 1685–1694', unpublished PhD thesis, Yale University (2000).

6 See Hughes, *Russia in the Age*, pp. 12–20, and 'The Moscow Armoury and Innovations in 17th-century Muscovite Art', *CASS* 13 (1979): 204–23.

7 See details in Richard Wortman, *Scenarios of Power. Myth and Ceremony in Russian Monarchy*, 2 vols. (Princeton: Princeton University Press, 1995), vol. I, pp. 42–4.

The supervisor of many projects was the Swiss-Italian Domenico Trezzini (1670–1734), whom Peter hired to build the Peter and Paul fortress.[8] In 1710 Trezzini designed Peter's modest Summer Palace, with relief sculpture by the German Andreas Schlüter (1665–1714) and Dutch formal gardens. Across the river the boldest point on the skyline was Trezzini's cathedral of saints Peter and Paul (1712–33), with its tall golden spire. The basilical structure departed radically from the centralised Greek cross of Russo-Byzantine church architecture, while the gilded iconostasis resembled a triumphal arch. The churches in Trezzini's St Alexander Nevsky monastery were more traditional in style. Significantly, this was to be the only monastery in early St Petersburg, located well away from the centre of the growing city.

For a while the French architect Jean Baptiste Le Blond (1679–1719) looked like eclipsing Trezzini, but he died after spending only three years in Russia. His activity was centred at the grand palaces at Peterhof and Strel'na on the Gulf of Finland, Peter's versions of Versailles, with extensive formal gardens, terraces, fountains and sculptures. Peterhof also owed a great deal to Johann Friedrich Braunstein, in Russia 1714–28. Among his several pavilions in the grounds was Peter's favourite retreat, the small Mon Plaisir palace, which housed what was probably Russia's first art gallery. Gottfried Johann Schädel (1680–1752) from Hamburg worked mainly for Peter's favourite, Aleksandr Menshikov (1673–1729), building the prince's impressive Italianate residences at Oranienbaum (1713–25) and on Vasilevskii island (1713–27). The only extant building by Georg Johann Mattarnovy (died 1719) is the Kunstkamera, which housed Peter's notorious collection of 'monsters' and other curiosities.

Among the Russian architects who received their initial training from these foreigners were Mikhail Zemtsov, Peter Eropkin and Ivan Korobov, who only began to take on major commissions in the late 1720s. Peter's painters were nearly all foreigners, too, as was the case at most European courts.[9] The most prolific court painters were Louis Caravaque (1684–1754) and Gottfried

8 On architects and architecture, see J. Cracraft, *The Petrine Revolution in Russian Architecture* (Chicago: University of Chicago Press, 1990); W. Brumfield, *A History of Russian Architecture* (Cambridge: Cambridge University Press, 1994); Iu. V. Artem'eva and S. A. Prokhvatikova (eds.), *Zodchie Sankt-Peterburga. XVIII vek* (St Petersburg: Lenizdat, 1997); L. Hughes, 'German Specialists in Petrine Russia: Architects, Painters and Thespians', in R. Bartlett and K. Schönwälder (eds.), *The German Lands and Eastern Europe* (Basingstoke: Macmillan, 1999), pp. 72–90.

9 J. Cracraft, *The Petrine Revolution in Russian Imagery* (Chicago: University of Chicago Press, 1997); S. O. Androsov, 'Painting and Sculpture in the Petrine Era', in A. G. Cross (ed.), *Russia in the Reign of Peter the Great: Old and New Perspectives* (hereafter, *RRP*) (Cambridge: SGECR, 1998), pp. 161–72; L. Hughes, 'Images of Greatness: Portraits of Peter I', in L. Hughes (ed.), *Peter the Great and the West: New Perspectives* (Basingstoke: Palgrave, 2000), pp. 250–70.

Dannhauer (Tannhauer, 1680–1733/7). In addition to painting portraits and battle scenes (both produced versions of Peter at Poltava), their prime task was to record and celebrate the newly Westernised men and women of the court. Caravaque also introduced feminine-erotic elements into Russian art, as in his double portrait of Peter's daughters, Anna and Elizabeth (1717), which depicts the two girls as personifications of youth, beauty and fruitfulness. Such portraits often hung in rooms decorated with half-naked Dianas and Aphrodites. The allegorical female nude was a daring novelty in Russia, where classical conventions were still poorly understood and even 'seemly' portraits of women were a recent innovation.[10] Peter's taste was more for marine and battle scenes, but he also purchased the work of Old Masters.

Foreign artists taught their craft to Russian pupils, nearly all of whom started out as icon-painters. One such apprentice was Ivan Nikitin (*c*. 1680 till after 1742), whom Peter later sent to study in Italy. Nikitin's reputation was to some extent a Soviet invention. His biographers claimed that the Russian approached painting not as a 'pupil', but boldly and creatively, outstripping all the foreign artists working in Russia, whose works seemed 'inept and naïve' in comparison.[11] A deathbed portrait of Peter I attributed to Nikitin was said to display a 'patriotic, purely Russian understanding of the image, a grief of loss which could be conveyed only by a Russian artist', whereas a canvas on the same theme by the German Dannhauer was dismissed as 'devoid of feeling'.[12] Nikitin's most recent biographer takes a more balanced approach.[13] Some paintings once attributed to Nikitin, who left only two signed canvases, are the subject of further investigation, for example the splendid portrait once erroneously entitled *The Field Hetman*. Russian art historians are now at liberty to acknowledge and research the foreign originals on which many Petrine images were based.[14] The work of foreign artists in Russia awaits thorough investigation, however.

The making of prints and engraving was supervised by foreign masters such as Adriaan Schoenebeck and Peter Picart, who superimposed Russian subjects on Western templates, for example siege and battle scenes from the Northern

10 See L. Hughes, 'Women and the Arts at the Russian Court from the Sixteenth to the Eighteenth Century', in J. Pomeroy and R. Gray (eds.), *An Imperial Collection. Women Artists from the State Hermitage* (Washington DC: National Museum of Women in the Arts, 2003), pp. 19–49.

11 See, for example, A. Savinov, *Ivan Nikitin 1688–1741* (Moscow: Iskusstvo, 1945).

12 T. A. Lebedeva, *Ivan Nikitin* (Moscow: Iskusstvo, 1975), p. 88.

13 S. O. Androsov, *Zhivopisets Ivan Nikitin* (St Petersburg: Dmitrii Bulanin, 1998), p. 24.

14 See, for example, Julia Gerasimova, 'Western Prints and the Panels of the Peter and Paul Cathedral Iconostasis in St Petersburg', in J. Klein and S. Dixon (eds.), *Reflections on Russia in the Eighteenth Century* (Cologne, Weimar and Vienna: Böhlau, 2001), pp. 204–17.

War. To them and to the Russian engravers Ivan (1677–1743) and Aleksei Zubov (1682–1751) we owe a good part of our visual impression of the Petrine era.[15] A major subject was St Petersburg itself, as, for example, in Aleksei Zubov's city panorama (1716). Much-reproduced prints depict the dwarfs' wedding staged by Peter in 1710 and the wedding feast of Peter and his second wife Catherine in 1712.[16]

Unlike engraving, which was used in Muscovy for religious subjects, stone and metal sculpture in the round was completely new to most Russians, having long been stigmatised by the Orthodox Church as the art of graven images. Peter's chief sculptor was the Italian Carlo Bartolomeo Rastrelli (1675?–1744), whose bronze bust of Peter (1723–30), with its dynamic metal draperies, remains one of the key images of the tsar. Rastrelli failed to establish a school of Russian sculptors, however. Russian artists were more comfortable working with wooden relief carving, little of which has survived. The bulk of the statues for St Petersburg's gardens and residences had to be imported, mainly from Italy, where agents purchased both antique and contemporary pieces.[17]

Another Western novelty was instrumental music. Peter probably heard his first Western-style music in Moscow's Foreign Quarter and experienced opera and ballet on his first trip abroad. He preferred choral singing and drumming, both of which he practised vigorously, but he acknowledged the importance of courtly musical entertainments. In St Petersburg, guests at court functions were invariably entertained by musicians, who, like painters and foreign chefs, became an elite fashion accessory, especially after the Law on Assemblies of 1718 encouraged home entertainments. Foreign dance masters were in demand to teach Russians the latest steps.[18] The Dutch painter Cornelius de Bruyn thought the orchestra he heard in Menshikov's Moscow residence sounded 'just like in our countries: violins, basses, trumpets, oboes, flutes'.[19]

The use of musical instruments, including the organ, was still banned in church, but sacred music for the human voice was adapted for the new era. Parades celebrating military victories featured not only fanfares, but also choirs

15 See M. A. Alekseeva, *Graviura Petrovskogo vremeni* (Leningrad: Iskusstvo, 1990), and *Aleksei Fedorovich Zubov. Katalog vystavki* (Leningrad: Gos. Russkii muzei, 1988).

16 See L. Hughes, 'Peter the Great's Two Weddings: Changing Images of Women in a Transitional Age', in R. Marsh (ed.), *Women in Russia and Ukraine* (Cambridge: Cambridge University Press, 1996), pp. 31–44.

17 S. O. Androsov, *Ital'ianskaia skul'ptura v sobranii Petra Velikogo* (St Petersburg: Ermitazh, 1999).

18 See N. Zozulina, 'Vremia peterburgskoi tantsemaniii', *Peterburgskii teatral'nyi zhurnal* (2003), no. 7: 16–32.

19 I. V. Saverkina and Iu. N. Semenov, 'Orkestr i khor A. D. Menshikova', *Pamiatniki kul'tury. Novye Otkrytiia, 1989* (1990): 161–6.

singing panegyric verses and cants. The seventeenth-century choral tradition was harnessed to the needs of the state and the rich expansiveness of the Russian unaccompanied choral music in church lived on into the new age, under the influence of both Russian native composers and foreigners, as did folk-song. Menshikov, for example, kept a choir of Russian and Ukrainian singers alongside his foreign instrumentalists. All three strands were to continue into the great age of Russian music more than a century later, although Soviet musical historians were obliged to stress the importance of secular music and to underplay sacred works.[20]

It is unlikely that Peter had any memory of his father's court theatre, which closed in 1676. His own adult experience of the theatre probably began in the Dutch Republic in August 1697, where he saw a 'play about Cupid'.[21] Peter was probably indifferent to serious theatre, but he understood that theatre, like music, was an integral part of the Western cultural scene that he sought to emulate. In 1702 a troupe led by the German Johann-Christian Kunst duly arrived in Moscow to perform in a playhouse built in the Kremlin. The first plays were all in German, but Kunst and his successor Otto Fürst took on Russian pupils and from 1705 plays in Russian (all translations) were staged. The repertoire consisted mainly of comic low-brow material from German and Dutch originals and bowdlerised versions of such plays as Molière's *Le Médecin malgré lui*. Despite its impressive scenery and costumes, the theatre was poorly attended and soon ceased functioning altogether.[22] Peter's ill-fated public theatre was only part of the story. The Moscow Academy staged school dramas featuring characters personifying virtues and vices, while plays such as *Russia's Glory* celebrated current events. Plays were also staged at the Moscow Medical School.[23] In Rostov, Bishop Dmitrii established a theatre and staged his own plays, including *The Nativity Play*, with thrilling scenes of the slaughter of the innocents and Herod in hell.[24] Peter's sister Natalia and his sister-in-law

20 See O. Dolskaya-Ackerly, 'Choral Music in the Petrine Era', *RRP*, pp. 173–86; O. Dolskaya-Ackerly, 'From Titov to Teplov: The Origins of the Russian Art Song', in L. Hughes and M. di Salvo (eds.), *A Window on Russia. Papers from the Fifth International Conference of SGECR* (hereafter, *WOR*) (Rome: La Fenice edizioni, 1996), pp. 197–213.

21 *Pis'ma i bumagi Petra Velikogo*, 13 vols. to date, vol. I (Moscow, 1887), p. 186.

22 See P. O. Morozov, 'Russkii teatr pri Petre Velikom', *Ezhegodnik imperatorskikh teatrov. 1893–1894* (St Petersburg, 1894), book 1, pp. 52–80; S. Karlinsky, *Russian Drama from its Beginnings to the Age of Pushkin* (Berkeley: University of California Press, 1985). Some texts are published in A. S. Eleonskaia (ed.), *P'esy stolichnykh i provintsial'nykh teatrov pervoi poloviny XVIII v.* (Moscow: Nauka, 1975).

23 'Slava Rossiiskaia', in *P'esy shkol'nykh teatrov Moskvy* (Moscow: Nauka, 1972); Morozov, 'Russkii teatr', p. 72.

24 'Rozhdestvenskaia drama': see Eleonskaia, *P'esy*, p. 9; O. A. Derzhavina (ed.), *Russkaia dramaturgiia poslednei chetverti XVII–nachala XVIII v.* (Moscow: Nauka, 1972), pp. 220–74.

Tsaritsa Praskovia organised amateur dramatics, the Bible and lives of saints providing material for *Play about the Holy Martyr Evdokia* and *Comedy of the Prophet Daniel*.[25]

Historians often speak of a virtual absence of Petrine 'literature', on the grounds that scarcely any fiction, poetry or drama appeared in print.[26] Generally this shortage is explained by the practical priorities of government-sponsored publishing (no Russian presses were in private hands until the 1780s) and by a lack of leisure for private reading among Russia's small, literate (but still not very cultured) elite. Modern anthologies tend to highlight publicistic writings by churchmen such as Feofan Prokopovich (1681–1736), who praised Russia's progress through the literary forms of panegyric verse and sermons. Prokopovich's oration at Peter's funeral remains one of the best-known works of the era still in print.[27] If, however, we consider texts available in manuscript, including popular religious works, a livelier picture of literary culture emerges. Readers continued to enjoy the lives of saints, tales of roguery, picaresque stories and romances inherited from the previous century.[28] The two best-known examples of manuscript fiction assigned to the Petrine era, the tales of the Russian sailor Vasilii Koriotskii and the valiant Russian cavalier Alexander, continue this tradition, although neither of these texts can be reliably dated. Both fuse travellers' tales, love interest and exotic detail with contemporary elements. Alexander, for example, longs 'to enjoy foreign states with his own eyes' and to study their 'polite manners'.[29]

With regard to non-fiction, historians have identified a 'print revolution' in Peter's reign. Between 1700 and 1725 one hundred times more printed material was produced in Russia than in the whole of the previous century. Instructions

25 Eleonskaia, *P'esy*, p. 12; L. Hughes, 'Between Two Worlds: Tsarevna Natal'ia Alekseevna and the "Emancipation" of Petrine Women', in *WOR*, pp. 29–36.

26 See Gary Marker, *Publishing, Printing, and the Origins of Intellectual Life in Russia, 1700–1800* (Princeton: Princeton University Press, 1985), and 'Publishing and Print Culture', *RRP*, pp. 119–32. S. P. Luppov, *Kniga v Rossii v pervoi chetverti XVIII v.* (Leningrad: Nauka, 1973). Generally on Russian literature, see H. B. Segal (ed.), *The Literature of Eighteenth-Century Russia*, 2 vols. (New York: E. P. Dixon, 1967); C. Drage, *Russian Literature in the Eighteenth Century* (London: published by author, 1978); W. E. Brown, *A History of Eighteenth-Century Russian Literature* (Ann Arbor: Ardis, 1980); W. Gareth Jones, 'Literature in the Eighteenth Century', in N. Cornwell (ed.), *The Routledge Companion to Russian Literature* (London and New York: Routledge, 2000), pp. 25–35. In Russian, some of the best literary scholarship has appeared in *XVIII vek: sbornik* (Leningrad/St Peterburg: Nauka), 22 vols. so far. See also *SGECRN*, 33 vols. so far.

27 Text in Segal, *The Literature of Eighteenth-Century Russia*, vol. I, pp. 141–8.

28 See M. A. Morris, *The Literature of Roguery in Seventeenth- and Eighteenth-Century Russia* (Evanston: Northwestern University Press, 2000).

29 Texts in G. Moiseeva (ed.), *Russkie povesti pervoi treti XVIII veka* (Moscow and Leningrad, 1965), pp. 191–210, 211–94.

issued in February 1700 to an Amsterdam publisher set the tone: 'to print European, Asian and American land and sea maps and charts and all manner of prints and portraits and books in the Slavonic and Dutch languages . . . for the glory of the great sovereign and his tsardom [and] for the general usefulness and profit of the nation and instruction in various crafts'.[30] From 1703 Russia's first newspaper, *Vedomosti* (Gazette), carried information about military and diplomatic affairs. Analysis of the subject matter of 1,312 titles published in Russia in 1700–25 indicates that laws and regulations accounted for 44%, official notices – 14.6%, religion – 23.5%, military affairs – 7.9%, calendars – 1.8%, *Vedomosti* – 1.8%, primers and language – 1.7%, history and geography – 1.5%, technology and science – 1.1%, secular philosophy – 0.5% and belles-lettres – 0.2%.[31] The demand for new books was uneven and many remained unsold. There are no reliable statistics for literacy rates in Peter's reign, but estimates for 1797 of 6.9% in the population as a whole suggest low figures indeed for the early 1700s.[32] Even so, state- and church-sponsored projects, such as the Moscow School of Mathematics and Navigation, educated new readers and the reading primer *First Lesson to Youths* (1720) by Prokopovich was a bestseller.[33]

A publishing landmark was the introduction of a new typeface, the so-called civil script (*grazhdanskii shrift*). After several revisions through 1708–10, thirty-eight Cyrillic letters based on modern designs for Latin characters were approved, with redundant letters from church script (*kirillitsa*) excluded.[34] The first schedule of new books (1710) included works on letter-writing, geometry, artillery, the capture of Troy and descriptions of triumphal gates. The first books actually to be printed in the revised typeface were translations from Ernst-Friedrich Borgsdorf's works on siege warfare and fortification. Despite such evidence of secular trends, one should treat with caution the notion of the secularisation of publishing in Peter's reign. Civil script did not replace church script. Religious literature published in the latter still accounted for over 40 per cent of volumes (as opposed to titles) published, in fact, *more*

30 *PSZ*, 4th series, no. 1751, pp. 6–8.
31 Figures in Marker, *Publishing*, pp. 30–1.
32 B. Mironov, 'Gramotnost' v Rossii 1797–1917 godov', *Istoriia SSSR* (1985), no. 4: 149. (Figures for urban males: 28%, urban females: 12%; all urban: 21%).
33 M. Okenfuss, 'The Jesuit Origins of Petrine Education', in J. Garrard (ed.), *The Eighteenth Century in Russia* (Oxford: Oxford University Press, 1973), pp. 106–30; M. Okenfuss, *The Discovery of Childhood in Russia: The Evidence of the Slavic Primer* (Newtonville: Academic International Press, 1980).
34 A. G. Shitsgal (ed.), *Grazhdanskii shrift pervoi chetverti XVIII veka 1708–1725* (Moscow: Kniga, 1981); Gary Marker, 'The Petrine "Civil Primer" reconsidered', *Solanus*, 1989: 25–39.

religious books were published in Peter's reign than in the seventeenth century. At the same time, a third of the titles printed in church script were secular in content, for example laws and manifestos.[35] It is hard to agree that the two 'opposing' typefaces were 'linked with the opposition of two cultures, Petrine and anti-Petrine' in an entirely consistent way.[36] It is also misleading to make a sharp distinction between the secular ('progressive') and the sacred ('unprogressive') printed word. Religious literature and writers also served the state. Sermons, prayers of thanksgiving, allegorical prints combining biblical and mythological motifs provided the essential theological underpinnings of autocracy. Prokopovich's play *Vladimir* (1705), about the christianisation of Rus in the tenth century, features a group of ignorant pagan priests, whose resistance to the new religion mimics that of Peter's unenlightened opponents. Even an apparently 'secular' work like the behaviour book *The Honourable Mirror of Youth* (1717) emphasised faith, piety and obedience.[37] The Church retained considerable control over the printed word. In February 1721 most presses were placed under the direction of the Holy Synod.[38]

The new culture was very unevenly distributed. Concentration of the cultural experiment in St Petersburg reduced the availability of craftsmen and materials for the rest of Russia, where there was little attempt to impose foreign styles. For important buildings outside the capital the 'Moscow Baroque' style remained popular for several decades, while for routine construction, even in the back streets of St Petersburg, wood remained the standard material. The spectacular wooden church of the Transfiguration at Kizhi was completed in 1714 as Trezzini's thoroughly Western Peter and Paul cathedral got under way. Everywhere icons, in both traditional and 'Italianate' styles, were in far greater demand than portraits, as were *lubok* wood prints, sold on the streets by vendors. Several *lubki* have themselves become 'icons' of the Petrine era, notably the print of a scissors-wielding barber attacking an Old Believer's beard, and 'The Mice Bury the Cat', a seventeenth-century subject that became associated with opponents' jubilation at Peter's death. Popular icon subjects also appeared on *lubki*.[39]

35 Figures in Marker, *Publishing*, passim.

36 V. M. Zhivov, 'Azbuchnaia reforma Petra I kak semioticheskoe preobrazovanie', *Uchenye zapiski Tartuskogo gos. universiteta* 720 (1986): 56, 60–1.

37 See L. Hughes, '"The Crown of Maidenly Honour and Virtue": Redefining Femininity in Peter I's Russia', in W. Rosslyn (ed.), *Women and Gender in Eighteenth-century Russia* (London: Ashgate, 2002), pp. 35–49.

38 S. P. Luppov, *Kniga v Rossii v pervoi chetvertoi XVIII v.* (Leningrad: Nauka, 1973) p. 69.

39 See D. A. Rovinskii, *Russkie narodnye kartinki*, 5 vols. (St Petersburg, 1881), vol. IV, pp. 322–9; vol. V, pp. 159–61; E. A. Mishina, *Russkaia graviura na dereve XVII–XVIII vekov* (St Petersburg: Dmitrii Bulanin, 2000), pp. 106–7, 126.

Private initiatives in high art remained weak. Local artists and architects fully trained in the Western manner were slow to appear, as was a whole range of subject matter in art, including free-standing landscapes, still life, history painting and domestic genre. These anomalies have been explained by the dearth of independent patrons with a taste for secular art, the limited opportunities for Russian artists to assimilate new subject matter, clients' preference for prestigious foreign originals, even by the theory that certain genres were too 'frivolous' for war-focused Russia.[40] There was as yet no academy or school for the arts, although the Academy of Sciences, whose charter Peter issued shortly before his death, sponsored artistic activities. Even nobles, harnessed to state service and absent from their homes for long periods, had few opportunities for collecting and connoisseurship.[41] The typical country manor house was a glorified wooden cabin, perhaps topped with a rustic pediment and with a couple of family portraits in 'parsuna' style inside.[42]

Resistance or indifference undoubtedly slowed the reception of certain arts, for example sculpture and theatre. The men and women of Peter's circle had little choice about Westernising, but further afield things were different. Grass-roots protesters, both urban and rural, were liable to identify portraits of Peter with the goddess Minerva as the 'icons of Antichrist' and the tsar's German boots as the Devil's hooves. In 1713 the vice-governor of Archangel complained that local people were still wearing old-style clothes and refusing to shave. 'Truly, lord', he wrote to Peter, 'such boorishness must be stopped and these heathen customs of dress rooted out.'[43] Some observers predicted that once Peter's iron hand was removed, there would be a general return to Muscovite beards and even to Moscow itself. That this proved not to be the case testifies to the foundations that Westernised culture had laid among Russia's upper classes and to the dedication of Peter's successors to his cultural programme.

From Catherine I to Peter III: 1725–1762

Historians once neglected the period between Peter I's death and the accession to the throne of his self-styled 'spiritual daughter' Catherine II. Catherine I

40 See O. S. Evangulova, 'Portret petrovskogo vremeni i problemy skhodstva', *Vestnik MGU*. Seriia 8. Istoriia, no. 5 (1979): 69–82, and 'K probleme stilia v iskusstve petrovskogo vremeni', ibid., no. 4 (1974): 67–84.

41 On a rare exception, see N. V. Kaliazina, and I. V. Saverkina, 'Zhivopisnoe sobranie A. D. Menshikova', in *Russkaia kul'tura pervoi chetverti XVIII veka. Dvorets Menshikova* (St Petersburg: Ermitazh, 1992).

42 On parsuna portraits, see my chapter in volume I of the *Cambridge History of Russia*.

43 *Pis'ma i bumagi imperatora petra velikogo*, vol. XIII (i) (repr. St Petersburg: Nauka, 1992), p. 374.

(1725–7) and Peter III (1761–2) reigned too briefly and Peter II (1727–30) and Ivan VI (1740–1) died too young to make much personal impression on the cultural scene. At the same time, standard historiography castigated Anna (1730–40) for her over-reliance on German favourites and Elizabeth (1741–61) for her extravagance. Only recently has it been possible for Russian historians to acknowledge that German influence under Anna was not overwhelming and that Elizabeth's extravagance served its purpose in the positive presentation of monarchy.[44]

While the nobles were still tied to obligatory state service (to 1762), the elite culture of the imperial court in St Petersburg remained disproportionately influential. For a time Peter II's aristocratic entourage threatened to restore Moscow to pre-eminence, but his successor Anna preferred to consolidate her power in the setting of her uncle, Peter I's, capital. In her reign a more or less regular royal household was established, where the luxury and outward display were said to emulate the court of France. Little of Anna's architectural programme survives today, however. Indeed, visitors to St Petersburg during her reign spoke of a mixture of magnificence and squalor, with many buildings left unfinished.[45]

The 1730s saw the launch of the career of mid-eighteenth-century Russia's most successful architect, Bartolomeo Francesco Rastrelli (1700–71). In 1732–5 Rastrelli constructed the wooden Winter Palace, the third on the site. He owed his lasting fame to his projects for Elizabeth, however, whose court required ever more generous architectural spaces, linked series of rooms for promenading and grand halls with high ceilings for balls and banquets. Her pageants, parades and festivals celebrated a monarch who served the good of her fortunate subjects. In particular, Elizabeth, who owned thousands of costly outfits, loved transvestite masquerades. To cater to such tastes, in the 1740s–50s Rastrelli built the grand Catherine Palace at Tsarskoe Selo, an amazing confection of vast length, its turquoise blue walls set off by white stone and gilded ornamentation and ornate plasterwork. Inside, guests progressed through a series of gilt-embellished rooms, full of rare furniture and porcelain, mirrors and chandeliers. The Winter Palace in St Petersburg, completed in 1762, was, in Rastrelli's words, created 'solely for the glory of Russia'. Its

44 See E. V. Anisimov, 'Anna Ivanovna', and V. P. Naumov, 'Elizaveta Petrovna', in *Russian Studies in History* 32, 4 (1994): 37–72 and 8–38; E. V. Anisimov, *Empress Elizabeth: Her Reign and Her Russia*, ed. and trans. John T. Alexander (Gulf Breeze: Academic International Press, 1995).

45 See Maria di Salvo, 'What did Algarotti see in Moscow?' in R. Bartlett and L. Hughes (eds.), *Russian Society and Culture in the Long Eighteenth Century: Essays in Honour of Anthony G. Cross* (Munster: Litverlag, 2004), pp. 72–81.

facade was formed of seemingly endlessly repeated units of white columns framing ornate window-surrounds, all with gilded details. The whole effect was like a grand theatrical backdrop. Rastrelli's blue and white five-domed cathedral for Smolnii convent reflected Elizabeth's preference for Orthodox conventions in church architecture, embellished with Italianate decoration.[46]

As palaces proliferated, pictures were required by the square metre. Foreign artists were aided, then succeeded by their Russian pupils, such as Ivan Vishniakov (1699–1761) and Aleksei Antropov (1716–95). Andrei Matveev (1701/4–39), who trained in Italy and the Netherlands, is credited with the first Russian easel painting on an allegorical subject, *Allegory of Painting* (1725). Another of Matveev's works, generally identified as a self-portrait of the artist and his wife (1729), is the first known double portrait by a Russian artist. The assimilation of new subject matter was aided by the founding in 1757 of the St Petersburg Academy of the Three Fine Arts on the initiative of Elizabeth's favourite, Ivan Shuvalov. Initially reliant on foreign teachers (the Frenchmen N. F. Gillet and J. L. De Velly were the first professors of sculpture and painting), it admitted Russians of any social class, occasionally even serfs. Few nobles, however, contemplated a career in architecture, painting or sculpture, which continued to be regarded as high-grade trades. Students followed a course that included the study of history and mythology and copying from engravings, classical sculpture and life models. Successful graduates were sent abroad for further training.

Music, singing and dancing were important at both Anna's and Elizabeth's courts. In the late 1730s the French ballet master Jean-Baptiste Landé opened the first ballet school in St Petersburg. The first opera performance in Russia (Ristori's *Calandro*) was staged in Moscow in 1731. Five years later audiences in St Petersburg saw *La Forza del'amor e del'odio* by Francesco Araja (1700–67/70), who served as *maestro di capella* at the court from 1735 to 1759. He and his successor Hermann Raupach were the first in a long line of foreign *maestri* in the imperial household. Foreign masters wrote new works for the court orchestra, composed mainly of Italian and French musicians, and directed operatic and ballet spectacles involving lavish costumes and intricate scenery, sound and lighting effects.[47] Theatricals and the staged life of the court intermingled.

In literature the 1730s–40s witnessed some of the first fruits of Westernisation, even though *belles-lettres* still occupied an insignificant place in

46 There is no major study of Rastrelli in English. See Iu. V. Artem'eva and S. A. Prokhvatikova (eds.), *Zodchie Sankt-Peterburga. XVIII vek* (St Petersburg: Lenizdab, 1997), pp. 217–90.

47 See G. Seaman, *A History of Russian Music, Vol. I. From its Origins to Dargomyzhsky* (Oxford: Blackwell, 1967).

publishing schedules.[48] Writers subsequently included in the literary canon were unpublished in their lifetime. This was true of Antiokh Kantemir (1708–44), whose satires in verse, written between 1729 and 1731, heaped scorn upon detractors of Peter's reforms and opponents of science and learning. All his works were self-confessed exercises in classical and Western genres, the satires, for example, drawing on Horace, Juvenal and Nicholas Boileau. The writings of Vasilii Trediakovskii (1703–69), who studied for a time in The Hague and Paris, likewise consciously imitated and sometimes translated French and German writers. Both he and Mikhail Lomonosov (1711–65), who was famed as a scientist and co-founder of Moscow University (1755), wrote panegyric verses and speeches to celebrate imperial achievements.

It was individuals like Trediakovskii and Lomonosov who laid the groundwork for professional literary culture by absorbing and experimenting with Western literary genres and acquiring foreign languages. They were pioneers of literary theory and poetic metre, advocating and demonstrating the use of syllabo-tonic versification, which ousted syllabic verse.[49] Trediakovskii's *A Method for Composing Russian Verse* (1752) summarised the achievements of the reform. Lomonosov's influential work *On the Usefulness of the Church Books* (1757) promoted the use of three styles or registers of literary language: the higher the style, the more Church Slavonic included, the lower, the more vernacular. Even so, a Russian literary language easily comprehensible to today's readers took several more decades to evolve. The readership for new works expanded with the growth of educational institutions, such as the St Petersburg Cadet Corps for noblemen, founded in 1731. Literary circles developed along with literary journals, for example, Lomonosov's *Monthly Compositions* (1755).

In the 1740s–50s Russians began to write seriously for the theatre, which was revived after the failures of earlier experiments. In 1747 'Russia's Racine', Aleksandr Sumarokov (1717–77), wrote *Khorev*, the first Russian classical tragedy, which warned against tyranny, excessive favouritism and succumbing to passions. It played alongside an adaptation of Shakespeare's *Hamlet* (1748) in Sumarokov's translation, which was followed by three more neoclassical tragedies based on Racine and Corneille. In 1750 the court repertoire featured eighteen French comedies, fourteen Russian tragedies and comedies, four Italian and German interludes. In 1756 Elizabeth appointed Sumarokov as the first director of the Imperial Theatre, which was based in a professional company of Russian actors under the direction of the actor-manager Fedor Volkov (1729–63).

48 See note 26 above.
49 Jones, 'Literature', p. 28.

The developments reviewed so far were overwhelmingly for the court and the nobility. Beyond these circles literacy rates remained low, opportunities for schooling few. And as long as nobles continued to be bound to the crown by service, even their scope for independent cultural activity were limited. The most notable act of the last ruler of this period, Peter III, who himself played the violin and enjoyed the theatre, was to free the nobility from compulsory service. In so doing, he unwittingly released time and energies that allowed hundreds of Russian nobles to travel abroad and also promoted the blossoming of noble culture in the Russian provinces, creating a so-called 'golden age' that continued into the first decades of the nineteenth century.

Catherine the Great: 1762–1796

To quote from Sir Joshua Reynolds, to whom she once sent an expensive snuffbox, Catherine II was 'a sovereign to whom all the Poets, Philosophes and Artists of the time have done homage'.[50] Catherine had a passion for architecture and landscape gardening; she was an indefatigable author, of plays as well as legislation, and an insatiable collector.[51] Among her tally of acquisitions were approximately 4,000 Old Masters, which included 225 paintings offered to Catherine after Frederick the Great could not afford to buy them and the eight Rembrandts, six Van Dycks, three Rubens and one Raphael in the Pierre Crozat collection. Catherine also bought coins and medals, *objets de vertu*, applied art and porcelain, of which one of the most spectacular examples was the 944-piece Green Frog Service, 1773–4 by Josiah Wedgwood, featuring British scenes.

Like most European monarchs of her time, Catherine embraced neoclassicism in architecture. Space and proportion, not ornament, were the watchwords and Rastrelli's baroque did not outlive Elizabeth. A fine example of Russian neoclassical architecture is the Tauride palace, built in 1783–9 by the architect Ivan Starov (1745–1808) for Catherine's favourite, Grigorii Potemkin,

50 Quoted in Simon Dixon, *Catherine the Great* (London: Longman, 2001), p. 103. On Catherine as patron, see A. McConnell, 'Catherine the Great and the Fine Arts', in E. Mendelsohn (ed.), *Imperial Russia 1700–1917. Essays in Honour of Marc Raeff* (DeKalb: Northern Illinois University Press, 1988); I. Forbes (ed.), *Catherine the Great. Treasures of Imperial Russia* (Dallas and St Petersburg: State Hermitage, 1990).

51 On architecture and gardens, see A. G. Cross, 'Catherine the Great and the English Garden', in J. Norman (ed.), *New Perspectives on Russian and Soviet Artistic Culture* (Basingstoke: Macmillan, 1994), pp. 17–24; on Catherine as writer, see Dixon, *Catherine*, pp. 94–8; as collector, R. P. Gray, *Russian Genre Painting in the Nineteenth Century* (Oxford: Clarendon Press, 2000), pp. 14–19; G. Norman, *The Hermitage: The Biography of a Great Museum* (London: Jonathan Cape, 1997), pp. 21–46.

himself a lavish patron of the arts.[52] The interior was sumptuously decorated, but the exterior was modestly plain, redolent of 'antique elegance'. One of Catherine's favourite architects and designers, the Scot Charles Cameron (1746–1812), built her a gallery addition to the Catherine Palace at Tsarskoe Selo in the shape of a Greek temple for the display of her collection of antique busts. Nearby Pavlovsk, a summer residence built by Cameron in 1782–6 for Grand Duke Paul and his wife, was set in a picturesquely landscaped park dotted with Greek temples and rotundas. The main palace reflected the popularity in Russia of the Palladian style.[53] Another of Catherine's favourite architects was Giacomo Quarenghi (1744–1817), who surmounted his Academy of Sciences (1783–9) with the plainest of porticoes. Inspired by British examples, Catherine's tastes also extended to neo-Gothic details applied to classical proportions, as, for example, in the church and palace at Chesme (by G.-F. Velden [Felten], 1770s). However, the Gothic palace at Tsaritsyno designed by Vasilii Bazhenov (1737–99) was not completed.

Neoclassical principles were not only applied to Catherine's personal projects. Restructuring the built environment was part of her plan to inculcate civic pride in her subjects, and classical St Petersburg stamped a more or less uniform blueprint over the empire, giving visual expression to notions of antique harmony and order. A planning model devised in 1763 by the Commission of Masonry Construction for the reconstruction of Tver was adapted for other towns. It incorporated columned trading arcades around a central square with a radiating street plan. Subsequently, each town designated as a 'capital' in the Provincial Statute of 1775 was supposed to build a governor's or chief official's house and other civic buildings. In Moscow the new premises for the university (1782–93) and the Noble Assembly (1793–1801) by Matvei Kazakov (1738–1813) underlined the city's role as a centre of learning and the nobility's participation in the empress's projects.

Nobles began to transform pockets of the Russian landscape on the basis of these new ideals. Gracious private dwellings sprang up, still often built of wood, but of a regular classical design.[54] Landscaped gardens in the 'natural' English style were popular, with artificial water features and temples to Friendship and the Muses. Such landscapes suggested historical, allegorical and

52 See Simon Sebag Montfiore, *Prince of Princes: The Life of Potemkin* (London: Weidenfeld and Nicolson, 2000).

53 See D. O. Shvidkovskii, *The Empress and the Architect: British Gardens and Follies in St. Petersburg, 1750–1830* (New Haven: Yale University Press, 1996).

54 See Priscilla Roosevelt, *Life on the Russian Country Estate: A Social and Cultural History* (New Haven: Yale University Press, 1995); Iu. M. Lotman, *Besedy o russkoi kul'ture: byt i traditsii russkogo dvorianstva (XVIII–nachalo XIX veka)* (St Petersburg: Iskusstvo-SPb, 1994).

philosophical themes for strollers to enjoy and contemplate. On the grander country estates serfs contributed to the upsurge of cultural life outside the capital. Some performed collectively in choirs, theatrical and dance troupes or horn bands, while individuals who showed promise were trained as actors, master craftsmen, painters and architects. The estates at Kuskovo and Ostankino outside Moscow, for example, both owned by members of the wealthy Sheremetev clan, were built and furnished by serfs, including several generations of Argunovs.

The Academy of Arts would remain the virtually unchallenged centre and arbiter of the figurative arts in Russia until the middle of the nineteenth century. In 1764 a charter placed the academy directly under the sovereign's patronage and in the same year its grand new neoclassical building, the first in St Petersburg, was begun. Foreign artists continued to play a prominent role in court portraiture – the Danish artist Vigilius Eriksen and the Swede Alexander Roslin, for example, left striking portraits of Empress Catherine – but local artists competed with them. The first Russian professor of history painting was Anton Losenko (1737–73). His *Vladimir and Rogneda* (1770) was the first Russian history painting on a national theme, while *Hector Taking Leave of Andromache* (1773) treats a classical subject, emphasising the virtues of civic duty and moral heroism.[55]

The most accomplished artist of the period was the Ukrainian Dmitrii Levitskii (1735–1822), who painted most of the leading figures of his time. His best-known works are the several versions of *Catherine in the Temple of Justice*, in which a sculpture of Justice and a plaque of a Roman lawgiver underpin the central image of the empress sacrificing her youth and strength on an altar in the service of Russia. In Levitskii's seven canvases (1770s) depicting students of the Smolnii Institute for Noble Girls, the subjects sing, dance, act in a school play and, in one case, operate a scientific instrument.[56] Many of the paintings of Vladimir Borovikovskii (1735–1825) feature young women clad in fashionable empire-line garments and set against outdoor greenery in the manner of the English portraitists. His 1794 painting of Catherine walking her dog in the gardens at Tsarskoe Selo contrasts the empress's informal appearance with a reminder of her military victories in the monument in the background.

55 There are no major studies of later eighteenth-century Russian painting in English. For information on artists mentioned here, see Alan Bird, *A History of Russian Painting* (Oxford: Phaidon, 1987).

56 A recent study is S. Kuznetsov, *Neizvestnyi Levitskii: portretnoe iskusstvo zhivopistsa v kontekste peterburgskogo mifa* (St Petersburg: Logo SPb, 1996).

All the leading artists of the period made their names with portraits and history painting. 'Domestic' landscapes and genre subjects from everyday life evidently were not popular with buyers, who preferred Italian and classical vistas to scenes of the humble Russian rural landscape.[57] No Russian artist produced images of appealing peasant children to evoke pleasurable feelings of compassion among well-off audiences in the manner of, for example, Thomas Gainsborough in England. In Russia, perhaps even more than elsewhere in Europe and North America, the style and content of elite art and architecture were filtered through the prism of neoclassicism, which privileged the beautiful and the idealised over the ugly and everyday. Even serfs trained in a Western idiom were expected to discard vestiges of 'rustic' aesthetics. In *Portrait of an Unknown Woman in Russian Dress* (1784) by the serf artist Ivan Argunov (1729–1802), it is unclear whether the attractive subject is a peasant in her Sunday outfit (perhaps a wet nurse) or a noblewoman in fancy dress. Only a few academic paintings of real peasants have survived. These include studies of a peasant wedding and a peasant meal by the serf Mikhail Shibanov (?– after 1789), both of which have an ethnographic emphasis.

Among the peasantry, meanwhile, traditional crafts such as woodwork, brassware, embroidery and lace-making flourished. Everyday objects like distaffs and boxes were elaborately carved and painted. *Lubki* with lurid illustrations and minimal texts could be shared by readers and non-readers alike and were a part of both the rural and the urban scenes. Popular subjects included exotic, foreign ones, such as 'The Cat-Man of Barcelona' and 'The Mighty Elephant Beast'. The images were often crude and bawdy, with depictions of and/or textual references to defecation and urination, sex and nudity, all, of course, highly stylised. Cheap paper prints of such images were sold alongside religious subjects. Icons were always in demand.

Towards the end of the century, under the influence of Western trends some members of the elite began to appreciate selected elements of folk culture. For example, there was an interest in folklore, that developed further in the nineteenth century.[58] The folk-songs collected by Nikolai L'vov (1751–1803), himself a notable poet and architect, and Ivan Prach became popular at musical evenings. Naturally classical music predominated at Catherine's court, despite the fact that the empress claimed to be tone deaf. As before, foreign composers and musicians set the tone, but native composers such as D. S. Bortnianskii

57 For background, see Christopher Ely, *This Meager Nature: Landscape and National Identity in Imperial Russia* (DeKalb: Northern Illinois University Press, 2002).

58 See Faith Wigzell, 'Folklore and Russian Literature', in Cornwell, *The Routledge Companion*, pp. 36–48.

(1751–1825) and the violinist Ivan Khandoshkin (1747–1804) laid the foundations of the great Russian classical music traditions of the nineteenth and twentieth centuries. Catherine sponsored music and the performing arts through the Imperial Theatre Administration, run until 1779 by Ivan Elagin (1725–94) and then by a series of successors.[59] The budget, frequently overspent, maintained theatrical troupes, orchestras and a ballet and opera company, which put on performances in St Petersburg and suburban palaces. During certain seasons of the year performances alternated with masquerades. On stage a repertoire of foreign and Russian plays was developed, including Catherine's own works, such as *O These Times!* (1772), and *Mrs Grumbler's Nameday*, satires about meanness, gossip and superstition, and her lavish historical pageant *The Beginning of Oleg's Reign* (1790). She was the author of some twenty-five plays, all of them adaptations of foreign authors, including Shakespeare.[60] In 1783–6 the Hermitage theatre (by Quarenghi) was built next to the Winter Palace and in 1785 the public Bolshoi Theatre opened in St Petersburg. Ballet reached a wider public through the work of the Italian dancer Filippo Baccari, who in the 1770s–80s trained dancers to perform in the Znamenskii and Petrovskii theatres in Moscow. The latter, built by the English impresario Michael Maddox, held two thousand spectators. The Bolshoi Ballet Company dates its origins from these enterprises.

It has been argued that theatre made a substantial contribution to the 'civilising' mission of the Russian Enlightenment. Theatre for paying audiences helped to create 'a sphere of civic activity' and sociability, which was largely lacking outside the court.[61] The major trend in drama was didactic and moralising, laced with comedy, with virtuous Dobronravs and Pravdins confronting villainous Chuzhekhvats and Krivosudovs. Denis Fonvizin (1745–92) created a gallery of such characters in his comedies of manners *The Brigadier* (first performed in 1769) and *The Minor* (1783). The latter work poked fun at such trends as excessive adulation of French fashions and rude rustic manners. Plays could satirise foibles and abuses of the system, but not the system itself. Iakov Kniazhnin's *Misfortune over a Carriage* (1779), for example, lampoons cruel and thoughtless serf owners who subvert the marriage plans of their serfs for their

59 See Victor Borovsky, 'The Emergence of Russian Theatre, 1763–1800', in R. Leach and V. Borovsky (eds.), *A History of Russian Theatre* (Cambridge: Cambridge University Press, 1999).

60 See Lurana O'Malley, *Two Comedies by Catherine the Great, Empress of Russia: Oh, These Times! and The Siberian Shaman* (Amsterdam: Harwood Academic, 1998) and 'How Great *Was* Catherine?: Checkpoints at the Border of Russian Theater', *Slavonic and East European Journal* 43 (1999): 33–48.

61 E. K. Wirtschafter, *The Play of Ideas in Russian Enlightenment Theater* (DeKalb: Northern Illinois University Press, 2003), p. 13.

own selfish interests in a plot where all ends well. Rustic plots were popular with noble audiences. One of the best-loved comic operas, Aleksandr Ablesimov's *The Miller who was Wizard, Cheat and Matchmaker* (1779), hinges on a quarrel between peasant parents over whether their daughter should marry a peasant or a nobleman. Some classical tragedies were also Russified, for example Kniazhnin's *Vadim of Novgorod* (1789).

In poetry and prose fiction we see the appearance of Russia's first more or less independent talents. It must be borne in mind, however, that in Russia, as elsewhere, talent was still measured largely by the skill with which authors handled set genres, rather than by innovative genius. Practically all the literature in Russian at the disposal of educated readers, a mere handful of the population, was borrowed from foreign models, with translations from the French accounting for one in four of all books published in the second half of the eighteenth century. Translations of novels by British and French writers were popular, providing models for the first Russian novelists, such as F. A. Emin (1735–70), who wrote about twenty-five books, and M. D. Chulkov (1743–92), whose *Comely Cook* (1770) was a particularly successful example of the tales of sexual adventures that readers enjoyed.[62] Eighteenth-century Russian erotic and pornographic literature of a stronger sort, especially the works of Ivan Barkov, fell victim to the much more draconian censorship of later tsarist and Soviet regimes.[63] For much of Catherine's reign there was a remarkably free press, without a central censorship authority, with prohibitions confined to heresy, blasphemy and pornography. In 1783 private individuals were given permission to run printing presses.

An important vehicle for literature and literary-philosophical debate were journals, of which 500 or so existed in the 1780s, subscribed to overwhelmingly by nobles. In 1769 the first issue of *About This and That* appeared, containing anonymous articles by Catherine herself. It sparked a debate about the nature of satire, whether it should be aimed at human vices in general, as the empress believed, or against named persons. One of the participants was Nikolai Novikov (1743–1820), whose own journals such as *The Painter* and *The Drone* took the debate further. In the 1790s Novikov's Freemasonry activities and writings earned him Catherine's disfavour and a spell of imprisonment.[64]

62 D. Gasperetti, *The Rise of the Russian Novel: Carnival, Stylization and the Mockery of the West* (DeKalb: Northern Illinois University Press, 1998).

63 M. Levitt, et al. (eds.), *Eros and Pornography in Russian Culture, Eros i pornografiia v russkoi kul'ture* (Moscow: Ladomir, 1999).

64 See W. Gareth Jones, *Nikolay Novikov: Enlightener of Russia* (Cambridge: Cambridge University Press, 1984).

Eighteenth-century Russia's finest poet was Gavrila Derzhavin (1743–1816), who first won favour with 'Felitsa' (1782), a mock ode in praise of Catherine. Derzhavin took a flexible approach to genre, injecting a strong personal element into his work. His philosophical poems 'The Waterfall' and 'God' and lighter subjects such as 'Life at Zvanki' are among the most original works of eighteenth-century Russian literature. Derzhavin was at the heart of an extended literary circle frequented by most of the leading figures of his day, including Anna Bunina (1774–1829), Russia's first professional woman writer. A number of women wrote and even published poetry, albeit usually with the support of male mentors.[65] The popularity of 'light' genres at the end of the century and the vogue for Sentimentalism, for example the work of M. N. Murav'ev (1757–1807), have been associated with the increase in female readership. Russia's most successful man of letters, Nikolai Karamzin (1766–1826), was a leading voice in Russian Sentimentalism and one of the creators of the modern Russian literary language. His story 'Poor Liza' (1792), about a peasant girl who drowns herself after being abandoned by her noble suitor, remains one of the best-known works of all eighteenth-century Russian literature. Karamzin's *Letters of a Russian Traveller* (1791–7) and *History of the Russian State*, written in the 1810s–20s after he became official historiographer, also enjoyed great success.[66]

In the Soviet canon it was not Derzhavin or Karamzin, but Aleksandr Radishchev (1749–1802) who earned the loudest accolades. His novel in letters *A Journey from St Petersburg to Moscow*, published privately in about six hundred copies in 1790, became notorious for its advocation of emancipation and revolution.[67] 'The purpose of this book is clear on every page: its author, infected with . . . the French madness, is trying in every possible way to break down respect for authority, to stir up the people's indignation against their superiors and against the government,' wrote Catherine. As she famously jotted in the margin of her copy: 'He is a rebel worse than Pugachev.' Only thirty copies of the *Journey* reached readers before the print run was confiscated. Radishchev

65 S. Shaw, '"Parnassian sisters" of Derzhavin's acquaintance', in *WOR*, pp. 249–56; Catriona Kelly (ed. and trans.), *An Anthology of Russian Women's Writing, 1777–1992* (Oxford: Oxford University Press, 1994). W. Rosslyn, *Feats of Agreeable Usefulness: Translations by Russian Women 1763–1825* (Fichtenwalde: Verlag F. K. Gopfert, 2000); W. Rosslyn, *Women and Gender*, pp. 1–14, for an excellent bibliography.

66 A. G. Cross, *N. M. Karamzin: A Study of his Literary Career, 1783–1803* (Carbondale: Southern Illinois University Press, 1971); A. Kahn, (ed.), *Nikolai Karamzin: Letters of a Russian Traveller A translation, with an Essay on Karamzin's Discourses of Enlightenment* (Oxford: Voltaire Foundation, 2003).

67 See Andrew Kahn, 'Sense and Sensibility in Radishchev's *Puteshestvie iz Peterburga v Moskvu*: Dialogism and the moral spectator', *Oxford Slavonic Papers*, NS, 30 (1997): 40–66.

was sentenced to death, commuted to ten years of exile to Siberia. Later he was hailed as the forerunner of the Russian intelligentsia, but it is misleading to speak of an eighteenth-century 'intelligentsia' in the nineteenth-century sense of a body of privileged, radical opponents of the system. By and large, the small, literate, largely noble public shared the empress's belief in a combination of autocracy 'without despotism' and serfdom 'without cruelty', adorned with Westernisation. It had no time for alternative systems or values, still less for revolution. Rather, in the spirit of German Enlightenment, it favoured rational improvement of the *status quo*. Opposition, when it occurred, tended to come from conservatives, who believed that Westernisation had gone too far. For example, in an unpublished work Prince Mikhail Shcherbatov (1733–90) lamented the corruption of morals among the Russian nobility, when 'man's natural voluptuousness and luxury' (encouraged by the bad example of the imperial court) led to dissipation and the ruination of families.[68]

Conclusion

The 'dilemma' of eighteenth-century Russian culture was succinctly expressed by Karamzin. A fervent admirer of Peter I in his youth, later in life Karamzin was influenced by new thinking about national identity and spirit. In his view, without Peter, Russia would have needed 600 years to catch up with Western Europe, but accelerated 'progress', he believed, had been bought at a high price: 'We became citizens of the world, but ceased in certain respects to be citizens of Russia.'[69] In this, of course, Russia was not as an aberration, but only a late-comer, its cultural development conforming with the general pattern throughout eighteenth-century Europe and North America, where a small educated elite 'kept up' with international trends, and technical brilliance was more prized than brilliant originality. All the same, eighteenth-century Russian culture was more a follower than a leader and languished in the shadow of later national achievements. Almost the only eighteenth-century Russian play to remain in the repertoire is Fonvizin's *The Minor*. Hardly any eighteenth-century Russian novels are still read today. No eighteenth-century Russian painters, writers or composers are much known outside Russia.

The international character of eighteenth-century culture and Russia's 'junior' status in the cultural pecking order created a particular headache

68 M.M. Shcherbatov, *On the Corruption of Morals in Russia*, ed. and trans. Antony Lentin (London: Cambridge University Press, 1969).

69 R. Pipes (ed.), *Karamzin's Memoir on Ancient and Modern Russia* (New York: Atheneum, 1966), pp. 123–4.

for Soviet scholars obliged to emphasise national originality (*samobytnost'*). Some took comfort in the discourse that Russians 'selected only the best' from Western culture, discarding anything alien to indigenous tastes. Foreign prototypes were ignored or glossed over.[70] The lack of comparative perspectives was caused not only by ideological constraints, but also by restricted access to Western scholarship and texts, so that sometimes simple ignorance lay behind the exaggeration of Russian 'originality'. Western histories of European culture, on the other hand, were apt to omit Russia from the picture altogether.

The limited social range of the eighteenth-century Russian public and the overarching influence of the court also seemed to distinguish Russia from more developed Western societies. Some writers observed that true culture was incompatible with despotic government and that the arts could never flourish if 'enforced by the knout'.[71] In the realm of high culture there were few opportunities for independent literary or cultural activity outside the provisions made by the state. If you were a writer, the only place you could publish was with state presses, apart from a brief period in the 1780s–90s. And the potential readership was tiny. For aspiring architects, painters and sculptors the only institution that offered rigorous training, including study trips abroad, was the Imperial Academy of Arts, which also oversaw commissions. This is not to say that the imperial establishment deliberately set out to restrict, censor and repress, rather that a significant private commercially oriented sector failed to develop much beyond the nobility. As has often been observed, the bourgeoisie was missing. And there were few dissenting voices. By and large, when Russian writers praised monarchs, painters and sculptors flattered them and architects provided grandiose backdrops for their ceremonies, it was because of a genuine commitment to the values they represented. From the 1760s the doctrines of Enlightened Absolutism provided a theoretical and philosophical underpinning to such support.

Such alarming events as the Pugachev revolt periodically reminded the consumers of high culture that their alien ways could provoke popular wrath, but such instances of the violent polarisation of the 'two Russias' were the exception rather than the rule. The binary models developed by the Tartu school of semioticians has proved exceptionally fruitful for exploring the

70 For late Soviet examples, see B. I. Krasnobaev (ed.), *Ocherki istorii russkoi kul'tury vosemnadtsatogo veka* (Moscow: Izd. MGU, 1972) and *Ocherki russkoi kul'tury XVIII veka* (Moscow: Izd. MGU, 1985).

71 See Gianluigi Goggi, 'The Philosophes and the Debate over Russian Civilization', in *WOR*, pp. 299–305.

tension between 'old' and 'new', 'west' and 'east' in Russian culture,[72] but the distinctness of elite and popular, urban and rural culture should not be exaggerated. Peasants as a social group were not confined to the countryside, as Peter I recognised when he imposed a fine of half a kopeck on bearded peasants entering towns, while Russian nobles raised by peasant servants and resident on their country estates in summer could hardly avoid contact with the 'other Russia'.[73] In towns, puppet theatres, peep-shows and fairgrounds attracted diverse audiences. Russian traditions of church singing provided common ground for all classes, while the scores of Russian comic operas were based on folk songs orchestrated in a classical idiom. All social classes had access to handwritten literature, often on topics or genres on which Westernisation had made little impact, such as lives of saints, popular tales, riddles, songs and devotional works. Noblewomen and merchants' wives alike enjoyed books on fortune-telling and the interpretation of dreams.[74] Although Western fashions remained de rigueur for everyday wear for the elite, Catherine II introduced a style of female court dress based on loose-fitting traditional Russian robes. Conversely, popular art absorbed motifs from high art. Ladies and gentlemen, even peasants in Western dress appear in popular wood prints; neoclassical ornaments mingle with traditional ones on carved and painted wooden objects.

As regards the impact of Westernisation, for every Karamzin who mourned his country's loss of national identity, there were several foreigners ready with an Orientalist discourse. Many travellers perceived (or were programmed to expect) something non-European about Russia, even in St Petersburg. The Reverend William Coxe wrote in the 1780s: 'The richness and splendour of the Russian court surpasses description. It retains many traces of its ancient Asiatic pomp, blended with European refinement.'[75] Armies of serf retainers, people from the Russian East, the sheer lavishness of clothes and jewellery helped to create this impression, as did the continuing high profile of Orthodox art and ritual. Religious culture was one of the 'blind spots' of both Soviet and Western scholars, who generally underestimated the role of the Church

72 For a seminal work, see Iu. M. Lotman and B. A. Uspenskii, 'Binary Models in the Dynamic of Russian Culture to the End of the Eighteenth Century', in A. D. Nakhimovsky and A. S. Nakhimovsky (eds.), *The Semiotics of Russian Cultural History* (Ithaca: Cornell University Press, 1985), pp. 30–66.

73 This argument provides the thread of Orlando Figes, *Natasha's Dance: A Cultural History of Russia* (London: Allen Lane, 2002).

74 See Faith Wigzell, *Reading Russian Fortunes: Print Culture, Magic and Divination in Russia from 1765* (Cambridge: Cambridge University Press, 1998).

75 W. Coxe, *Travels in Poland, Russia, Sweden, and Denmark*, 2 vols. (London: J. Nichols, 1784), vol. II, p. 84.

and religious belief in eighteenth-century Russia, favouring 'the story of the progressive emancipation of culture from the stiffening control of established religion', beginning with Peter's alleged 'secularisation' of Russian culture.[76] But Russia's eighteenth-century rulers and their supporters could not do without Orthodox ritual, churches and icons. Nearly all the leading artists started their careers painting icons and frescoes and continued to do so simultaneously with undertaking secular commissions. There was far more demand for icons than for portraits. Orthodox scruples about 'graven images' hampered the development of Russian sculpture. The equestrian statue to Peter I in St Petersburg (1782, Etienne Falconet and Marie Collot) was, amazingly, the first public monument to be erected in Russia.[77] The interdependence of religious and secular art awaits a full investigation.

In the first decade of the twenty-first century the cultural history of eighteenth-century Russia is still being written. Russian scholars have seized new opportunities to explore foreign influences and religious culture. The Marxist-Leninist ideological framework that prioritised the search for motifs of dissent and a 'serf intelligentsia' has largely been abandoned, while topics once off-limits or subject to ideological disapproval, such as imperial court ceremonial and noble estate culture, are being studied.[78] Work has been published in both East and West on once taboo figures, such as Potemkin, and the first studies of Catherine II's life for over a hundred years have appeared in Russian, giving due credit to her massive contribution to Russian culture. Even the once despised empresses Anna and Elizabeth are beginning to be acknowledged as patrons of the arts. Eighteenth-century Russian culture may never appeal to Western audiences as much as what preceded it and came after, but there is at least the prospect that we shall understand it better.

76 G. Florovsky, 'The Problem of Old Russian Culture', *SR* 21 (1962): 3.

77 See L. Hughes, 'Restoring Religion to Russian Art', in G. Hosking and R. Service (eds.), *Reinterpreting Russia* (London: Arnold, 1999), pp. 40–53; V. Zhivov, 'Religious Reform and the Emergence of the Individual in Russian Seventeenth-Century Literature', in S. Baron and N. S. Kollmann (eds.), *Religion and Culture in Early Modern Russia and Ukraine* (DeKalb: Northern Illinois University Press, 1997), pp. 184–98, and 'Kul'turnye reformy v sisteme preobrazovaniia Petra I', in A. Koshelev (ed.), *Iz istorii russkoi kul'tury. Tom III (XVII–nachalo XVIII veka)* (Moscow: Iazyki russkoi kul'tury, 1996), pp. 528–83.

78 See, for example, O. Ageeva, *Velichaishii i slavneishii bolee svekh gradov v svete: grad Sviatogo Petra* (St Petersburg: Blits, 1999); E. Pogosian, *Petr I – arkhitektor rossiiskoi istorii* (St Petersburg: Iskusstvo-SPb, 2001) (on court ceremonial).

5
Russian culture: 1801–1917

ROSAMUND BARTLETT

Russian culture comes of age

To gain a sense of the achievements of Russian culture during this period, it is instructive to compare the comments made on the subject by Petr Chaadaev in a 'Philosophical Letter' he published in 1836 with the sentiments expressed by a critic reviewing an exhibition in 1909. Chaadaev felt that Russia under Nicholas I simply had no cultural achievements it could be proud of. In his opinion, Russia was neither part of the continuum of European or Asian civilisation, nor did it have any civilisation of its own – and he did not mince his words about his nation's many defects, which, significantly, were written in French rather than Russian:

> At first brutal barbarism, then crude superstition, then cruel and degrading foreign domination, the spirit of which was inherited by our national rulers – such is the sad history of our youth . . . Now I ask you, where are our sages, our thinkers? Who has ever done the thinking for us? Who thinks for us today? And yet, situated between the two great divisions of the world, between East and West, with one elbow resting on China and the other on Germany, we ought to have united in us the two principles of intellectual life, imagination and reason, and brought together in our civilization the history of the entire globe. But this was not the part Providence assigned to us. Far from it; she seems to have taken no interest in our destiny . . . You would think, looking at us, that the general law of humanity has been revoked in our case. Alone in the world, we have given nothing to the world, taught the world nothing; we have not added a single idea to the fund of human ideas; we have contributed nothing to the progress of the human spirit, and we have disfigured everything we have taken of that progress . . . We have never taken the trouble to invent anything ourselves, while from the inventions of others we have adopted only the deceptive appearances and useless luxuries.[1]

1 P. Chaadaev, 'Letters on the Philosophy of History', quoted in W. J. Leatherbarrow and D. C. Offord (trans. and eds.), *A Documentary History of Russian Thought From the Enlightenment to Marxism* (Ann Arbor: Ardis, 1987), pp. 68, 72–3.

The critic reviewing the Russian section of an architecture and design exhibition in Vienna in 1909, by contrast, felt quite differently. If anything, Russia's very backwardness, in his view, had made a crucial contribution to its new position of cultural pre-eminence:

> A very short while ago it was a saying that if one scratched a Russian, one discovered a barbarian . . . A few years ago Western art had to acknowledge the invasion of the Japanese. Last spring at our architectural exhibition the Russians spoke, and everyone's attention was attracted. We were made to envy them for the remains of barbarism which they have managed to preserve. The West has become a common meeting ground, invaded by distant and foreign peoples as in the last days of the Roman Empire, and while they wish to learn from us, it turns out that they are our teachers.[2]

Indeed, Russian artists were now increasingly assuming positions at the forefront of the European avant-garde, their achievements equal to anything produced by their counterparts in Western Europe. This was spectacularly demonstrated when Sergei Diaghilev began his triumphant export of Russian culture to Paris at the beginning of the twentieth century: the legendary *Saisons russes* showcased the brightest talents of Russian ballet, art and music, culminating in the epochal premiere of Stravinsky's *The Rite of Spring* in 1913. Back in Moscow, Stanislavsky had founded an innovatory acting technique and a world-class repertory theatre which championed the plays of Chekhov, soon to be recognised as one of the greatest of modern dramatists. And once the novels of Tolstoy and Dostoevsky had begun to reach international audiences via translations, it was not long before writers like Virginia Woolf were proclaiming Russian literature to be the best in the world.[3] By the time of the 1917 Revolution, it was no longer possible to claim that Russia had merely borrowed from other cultures, and contributed nothing original of its own. In the space of a hundred years, the country's artistic life had been transformed beyond recognition, as the feelings of inferiority which were the residue of Russia's brusque Europeanisation in the eighteenth century gave way to a pride in national achievements. The subsequent discovery of Russian culture, combined with the constraints imposed by the constant threat of censorship, had ultimately galvanised Russian artists, writers and musicians into forging a cultural identity that was distinctive precisely for its strong national character. As soon as

2 L. Gewaesi, 'V mire iskusstva', *Zolotoe runo*, 2/3 (1909): 119–20, quoted in Camilla Gray, *The Russian Experiment in Art, 1863–1922*, revised and enlarged edition by Marian Burleigh-Motley (London: Thames and Hudson, 1986), p. 119.

3 See Virginia Woolf, 'The Russian Point of View', in *The Common Reader* (London: Hogarth Press, 1925), p. 180.

Russian creativity was given the conditions to flourish in the nineteenth and early twentieth centuries, a profusion of novels, symphonies, paintings and operas poured forth which were of a calibre never encountered either before or after.

Russian culture under Alexander I (1801–1825) and Nicholas I (1825–1855)

Exactly how accurate was the pessimistic diagnosis of Russian culture set forth in Chaadaev's 'Philosophical Letters'? Born in 1794, Chaadaev had come of age during the Napoleonic campaigns, in which he served as an officer. He had then resigned his commission and spent three years in Western Europe, which probably saved him from the brutal punishments meted out to his friends and fellow liberals who had taken part in the Decembrist uprising in 1825. Nicholas I's chief of police, Count Benckendorff, proclaimed triumphantly: 'Russia's past is admirable; her present situation is more than wonderful; as for her future, this exceeds even the boldest expectations',[4] but Chaadaev had grounds for possessing a jaundiced view of Russia. Like the Decembrists, who had been profoundly shocked when they returned home after observing Western liberty in action when they occupied Paris at the end of the war with Napoleon, Chaadaev had come to the conclusion that the source of Russia's 'unhealthy atmosphere and paralysis' was the iniquitous institution of serfdom.[5] This challenged the nationalist feelings inspired by 1812. But modernisation was out of the question under a tsar terrified of further rebellion, and in 1833 his minister of education, Sergei Uvarov, formulated an official state ideology based on 'Orthodoxy, autocracy and nationality' which was to set the course for cultural policy throughout Nicholas's reign.[6] Accordingly, the teachers and students at the St Petersburg Academy of Arts were uniformed civil servants who were enjoined to uphold the techniques and artistic ideals of classical antiquity. In music, there simply was no institution yet for the professional training of native composers and performers, and the already low prestige of Russian music was soon to be further undermined when an Italian opera company was installed in St Petersburg's main opera house

4 A. Walicki, *A History of Russian Thought from the Enlightenment to Marxism* (Stanford: Stanford University Press, 1979), p. 88.
5 Leatherbarrow and Offord, *A Documentary History of Russian Thought*, p. 87.
6 See Maureen Perrie, 'Narodnost': Notions of National Identity', in C. Kelly and D. Shepherd (eds.), *Constructing Russian Culture in the Age of Revolution: 1881–1940* (Oxford: Oxford University Press, 1998), pp. 28–36.

in 1843.[7] The Russian literary canon, meanwhile, was still so small that in Pushkin's story *The Queen of Spades* (*Pikovaia dama*), set in 1833, the old countess could express surprise that there are any novels written in Russian.[8]

But it was in the 1820s and 1830s that Peter the Great's secularising reforms began to bring forth fruit in terms of native works of art of outstanding originality. Pushkin published the first great Russian novel (in verse), *Eugene Onegin*, in 1823–31. The following year Russia's first professional critic, Vissarion Belinsky, made his debut with an article which the literary historian D. S. Mirsky memorably called the 'manifesto of a new era in the history of Russian civilization'.[9] In 1833 too Karl Briullov completed his mammoth canvas *The Last Day of Pompeii*, described by Gogol as a 'complete universal creation' and celebrated by Sir Walter Scott, Bulwer Lytton and countless Italian academicians.[10] Two other cultural landmarks were to follow in 1836, the year in which Chaadaev's 'First Philosophical Letter' was published: Gogol's play *The Government Inspector* (*Revizor*) and Glinka's opera *A Life for the Tsar.* This was also the year in which Pushkin launched *The Contemporary* (*Sovremennik*), which was destined to become Russia's most famous literary journal in the nineteenth century and in which Orest Kiprensky, one of Russia's finest Romantic painters, died. Other important artists of the first half of the nineteenth century who were not products of the Imperial Academy, and who treated Russian themes, include Aleksei Venetsianov, who received no formal training, and Vasili Tropinin, a gifted serf given his freedom only at the age of forty-seven. Both excelled in depicting scenes from daily life.

The central figure of what is now referred to as the 'Golden Age' of Russian poetry was Pushkin of whose work David Bethea has written: 'It engages prominent foreign and domestic precursors (Derzhavin, Karamzin, Byron, Shakespeare, Scott) as confident equal, defines issues of history and national destiny (Time of Troubles, legacy of Peter, Pugachev Rebellion) without taking sides, provides a gallery of character types for later writers . . . and expands the boundaries of genre . . . in an intoxicating variety that earned him the name of Proteus.'[11] Pushkin's work alone undermines Chaadaev's theory of Russian cultural stagnation.

7 See Richard Taruskin, *'Ital'yanshchina'*, in *Defining Russia Musically: Historical and Hermeneutical Essays* (Princeton: Princeton University Press, 1997), pp. 186–236.

8 A. S. Pushkin, *Complete Prose Fiction*, trans., intro. and notes Paul Debreczeny (Stanford: Stanford University Press, 1983), p. 215.

9 D. S. Mirsky, *A History of Russian Literature from its Beginnings to 1900*, ed. Francis J. Whitfield (New York: Vintage, 1958), p. 75.

10 A. Bird, *A History of Russian Painting* (Oxford: Phaidon, 1987), pp. 78–9.

11 D. Bethea, 'Literature', in N. Rzhevsky (ed.), *The Cambridge Companion to Modern Russian Culture* (Cambridge: Cambridge University Press, 1998), p. 177.

Pushkin was one of the first Russian writers to earn his living through his literary works, and the last to have to suffer the dubious privilege of having them personally scrutinised by the tsar, who appointed himself as the poet's personal censor when graciously allowing his subject to return from exile in the south. Pushkin's career exemplifies the growing rift that was opening up between artists and the state in Russia, as the nascent *intelligentsia* increasingly came to define itself by its opposition to the Government. The fate of Chaadaev's 'Philosophical Letter', meanwhile, exemplifies the cultural atmosphere under Nicholas I as a whole: its author was pronounced insane and placed under house arrest, the man who failed to censor the article was sacked, the journal in which it was published was shut down, and its editor exiled. It is not surprising, under these circumstances, that culture, and in particular literature, became so politically charged during the reign of Nicholas I. The headstrong young poet and hussar Mikhail Lermontov was courtmartialled for writing an outspoken poem condemning the society which allowed a genius like Pushkin to be killed in a duel.[12] Lermontov's career was also cut short: he died in a duel in the Caucasus in 1841 at the age of twenty-seven, leaving behind a corpus of remarkable lyrical poetry (representing the apex of Russian literary Romanticism) and a justly celebrated novel, *A Hero of our Time* (*Geroi nashego vremeni*), whose 'superfluous' hero is clearly the successor to Pushkin's Onegin.

Not all Russian artists wished to antagonise the regime in the 1830s and 1840s. Glinka's patriotic opera *A Life for the Tsar*, the first full-length Russian opera, is also a celebration of the official ideology of nationality propagated by Sergei Uvarov. For that reason it was enthusiastically endorsed by Nicholas I, but then became a problematic work for the nationalist composers who came to prominence in the 1870s. Gogol too was an ardent monarchist, whose political outlook grew more rather than less conservative as he grew older. Epitomising the new breed of non-noble *raznochinets*, Belinsky, by contrast, forged his career by championing new literary talent in Russia and promoting a radical social agenda. In his preoccupation with civic content, he was largely immune to Gogol's stylistic brilliance in works such as the first part of his novel *Dead Souls* (*Mertvye dushi*, 1842). His dismay with the writer's preoccupation with moral rather than social values culminated in a vituperative 'Letter to N. V. Gogol' following the publication of the latter's reactionary *Selected Passages from Correspondence with Friends* (1847). Gogol's defence of serfdom provoked Belinsky to furious rhetoric. Russia did not need sermons and prayers or an encouragement in the shameless trafficking of human beings, he thundered,

12 L. Kelly, *Lermontov: Tragedy in the Caucasus* (London: Robin Clark, 1883), pp. 59–65.

but 'rights and laws compatible with good sense and justice'. Fresh forces were 'seething and trying to break through' in Russian society, he continued; 'but crushed by the weight of oppression they can find no release and produce only despondency, anguish and apathy. Only in literature is there life and forward movement, despite the Tatar censorship.'[13]

Such an incendiary document could not be published in Russia but it circulated widely in manuscript. A reading of Belinsky's letter to Gogol at a meeting of the Petrashevsky Circle in St Petersburg in 1849 brought about Dostoevsky's exile to Siberia. The young Turgenev, who also began his literary career in the 1840s, was exiled to his estate for over a year in 1852 for praising Gogol in an obituary. Belinsky himself did not live long enough to witness the publication that year of Turgenev's *A Huntsman's Sketches* (*Zapiski okhotnika*), in which peasants were sympathetically depicted for the first time in Russian literature as human beings and individuals. Turgenev shared Belinsky's Westernising sympathies, and so *A Huntsman's Sketches* was welcomed by progressive circles who seized upon its veiled attack on serfdom, but the stories were also praised by the Slavophile community for the dignified way in which the peasant characters were depicted.

Of the three great Russian novelists who began their literary careers in the latter part of Nicholas I's reign, Tolstoy was the last to make his debut. By this time, the era of poetry had long given way to one of prose, and Tolstoy's essentially autobiographical novella *Childhood* (*Detstvo*, 1852) is written in the realist style which would dominate Russian literature for the ensuing decades. This trend is also evident in the genre paintings of Pavel Fedotov (e.g. 'The Major's Marriage Proposal', 1848), often seen as one of the best satirists of contemporary Russian life. At the same time, however, artists representative of the 'second wave' of Romanticism were tackling large-scale, monumental themes (e.g. Aleksandr Ivanov's 'Appearance of Christ to the People', 1857).

Russian culture under Alexander II (1855–1881)

During Alexander II's reign Russian culture flourished. The spirit of optimism encouraged by the 'Great Reforms', together with the relaxation of censorship and other restrictions unleashed an unprecedented creative energy among artists, musicians and writers. The dramatic change of mood can be seen by comparing the two generations depicted in Turgenev's novel *Fathers and Sons* (*Ottsy i deti*, 1861). There is a stark contrast between the urbane and

13 Leatherbarrow and Offord, *A Documentary History of Russian Thought*, pp. 131–2.

unashamedly romantic older gentlemen of the 1840s with the brash young 'men of the 1860s', a new breed typified by the hero Bazarov, who rejects art and religion in favour of science and practical activity. Compare also the static first part of Goncharov's *Oblomov*, written in the 1840s, with the rest of his novel, completed later and published in 1859, in which an impoverished nobleman attempts to abandon his supremely indolent lifestyle and enter the real world. The rich legacy of symbolism inherited from the Russian Orthodox Church and deeply embedded in the writings of all the great nineteenth-century novelists, is nowhere more apparent than in the character of Oblomov, whose rejection of modern Western ideas and slow decline back into his former state of inertia is prophetic of Russia's path in the 1860s and 1870s as the programme of reform faltered, and censorship was once again tightened.

What is also remarkable about Russian culture under Alexander II is the way in which all the arts were now dominated by nationalist concerns. Peter the Great's Europeanisation of Russia had engendered ambivalence towards native culture amongst the Russian aristocracy which persisted until the middle of the nineteenth century. It had been responsible, for example, for the derision which greeted Pushkin's attempts to write folk tales in the early 1830s. Pushkin had recognised the enormous potential of fairytales for the creation of a truly national culture (he was so adept at imparting a Russian spirit to his verse imitations of Western legends that works such as *The Tale of Tsar Saltan* and *The Golden Cockerel*[14] soon became part of Russian folklore), but his snobbish critics had considered the oral folk tradition fit only for peasant consumption. That situation changed with the publication of Alexander Afanasiev's pioneering collection of Russian folk tales, the first volume of which appeared in 1855, the year of Alexander II's accession. Afanasiev's 640 tales represent the Russian equivalent of the famous anthology published by the Brothers Grimm at the beginning of the nineteenth century,[15] and were to have a huge influence on composers, writers and painters alike, stimulating further interest in Russian native culture.

The new sense of national pride felt by Russian artists was not always inspired by identical motivations. The transformation of Russian musical life brought about by the virtuoso pianist Anton Rubinstein, for example, was occasioned by his consternation at the lack of respect Russian musicians were

14 Their original plots in fact came from the pen of the American writer Washington Irving, whose 1832 collection of tales *The Alhambra* was inspired by a sojourn in a Moorish palace in Spain.

15 See Roman Jakobson's commentary, *'On Russian Folk Tales'*, *Russian Fairy Tales Collected by Aleksandr Afanasiev*, trans. Norbert Guterman (New York: Pantheon, 1945), pp. 631–56.

paid in their own country (this was another legacy of the Europeanisation of the elites in the eighteenth century). Rubinstein had studied and frequently performed in Germany, and could not but be struck by how revered musicians were there. In Russia, a country where one's position in society was still determined by the Table of Ranks, musicians had no professional status, nor could they benefit from any institutionalised training. Rubinstein determined to raise the prestige of Russian musicians first by setting up the Russian Musical Society in 1859, with the help of Grand Duchess Elena Pavlovna's patronage. It was the first organisation in Russia to hold orchestral concerts throughout the winter season. Next Rubinstein succeeded in founding the St Petersburg Conservatoire in 1862. Tchaikovsky was one of its first graduates three years later, and he went on to teach at the Moscow Conservatoire founded in 1866 by Anton Rubinstein's brother Nikolai. Because Rubinstein had based the Conservatoire curriculum on the German model he revered, and because he was of Jewish extraction, charges of lack of patriotism were often levelled at him by other musicians who were sometimes jealous of his success. 'The time has come to stop transplanting foreign institutions to our country and to give some thought to what would really be beneficial and suitable to *our* soil and *our* national character', wrote the critic Vladimir Stasov in 1861, for example.[16] It was Stasov, a full-time employee of the Imperial Public Library in St Petersburg, and an ardent Slavophile, who played a leading role in promoting a group of five nationalist composers which formed at this time led by Mily Balakirev (another piano virtuoso), and who coined their nickname 'the mighty handful'. Neither Balakirev, Borodin, Rimsky-Korsakov, Mussorgsky nor Cui had received professional training, and all combined writing music with other careers (in Borodin's case, teaching chemistry at St Petersburg University). In defiant opposition to the Conservatoire and its 'academic' methods, Balakirev founded a Free Music School in 1862 aimed at educating the general public.

Stasov also waged a vigorous campaign on behalf of the nationalist and 'anti-academic' cause in the Russian art world at this time. His criticism of the conservatism of the Academy of Arts, which continued to adhere rigidly to its classical ideals, spurred on some of its students to action. In 1863, fourteen of them finally rebelled against the academy's failure to engage with the pressing problems of the day when they were set 'The Entry of Wotan into Valhalla' as the assignment for the Gold Medal; after the jury refused to change the

16 V. Stasov, *Selected Essays on Music*, trans. Florence Jonas, intro. Gerald Abraham (London: Barrie and Rockliff, 1968), p. 83.

assignment, the students simply walked out. Stasov retained a close association with the Free Artists' Co-operative set up that year by the leader of the protest, Ivan Kramskoi. Another key figure during this period was the radical critic and novelist Nikolai Chernyshevsky, who assumed Belinsky's mantle when the latter died in 1848 in championing the cause of literature as a weapon for social reform, and came, like him, from a lowly provincial background. Chernyshevsky's pivotal essay *The Aesthetic Relations of Art to Reality*, published in 1855, set a strongly pro-realist agenda for all of Russian art in the late 1850s and 1860s, and ensured that debates were always highly charged. Proclaiming art to be inferior to science, and declaring that 'beauty is life',[17] it was the first of many assaults on the old idealist aesthetics. Chernyshevsky's active involvement in subversive politics resulted in his arrest in 1862, but his subsequent imprisonment enabled him to sketch out his socialist vision for the future in his influential novel *What Is to Be Done?* (*Chto delat'?*, 1863) before being exiled to Siberia.

Chernyshevsky's utilitarian view of art, his theories of rational self-interest and his atheism in turn came under attack from Dostoevsky when he returned from exile in 1859. Indeed, beginning with *Notes from Underground* (*Zapiski iz podpol'ia*, 1864), Dostoevsky's mature work may be seen as a sustained polemic against the ideology of Chernyshevsky and his followers. Tolstoy retained an Olympian distance from the ideological battles in the capital, both intellectually and physically, having retired to his country estate following his marriage in 1862. His first great novel, *War and Peace* (*Voina i mir*), written between 1863 and 1869, was unusual for fiction written at this time in not having a contemporary theme (as *Anna Karenina*, by contrast, would) but was typical in its Russocentrism, and in its generic challenge to Western convention. As Tolstoy himself put it in one of his draft prefaces, 'in the modern period of Russian literature there is not one work of art in prose even slightly better than average that could fully fit into the form of a novel, epic or story'.[18]

Against the background of Russian Populism, the lengthy realist novel of ideas remained the dominant literary form during the turbulent years of Alexander II's reign. The realist mood also pervaded music written in the 1860s and 1870s, as in Mussorgsky's song cycle *The Nursery* (1870), in which the composer imitates the speech of a child and his nurse, and Tchaikovsky's opera *Eugene Onegin* (1878), based on Pushkin's novel in verse set in the

17 Walicki, *History of Russian Thought*, p. 200.
18 D. Fanger, 'The Russianness of the Nineteenth-Century Novel', in T. G. Stavrou (ed.), *Art and Culture in Nineteenth-Century Russia* (Bloomington: Indiana University Press, 1983), p. 45.

Russian provinces. Despite major differences in their artistic sensibilities, both Tchaikovsky and Mussorgsky considered themselves to be 'realists' (an anomaly that is matched by Tolstoy, Dostoevsky and Turgenev, who also saw themselves in the same light, despite the wide gulf which separates each of their writing styles). Both composers also sought to establish their careers as opera composers, which became more feasible after the opening in 1860 of the St Petersburg Mariinsky Theatre, the new home for the beleaguered Russian Opera. The world premiere in 1862 of Verdi's *La forza del destino*, commissioned at great cost by the Imperial Theatres, marked the apogee of the Italian Opera's prestige in Russia and partly explains the ambivalent response to Mussorgsky's unconventional operatic writing when he first presented the score of *Boris Godunov* for performance in 1869 (the premiere took place in 1874 after substantial revisions). *Khovanshchina*, begun in 1872 and incomplete at his death in 1881, was another innovative large-scale historical opera, focusing this time on events prior to the accession of Peter the Great. Its subject was suggested by the indefatigable Stasov, who also inspired Borodin in 1869 to start work on *Prince Igor*, a re-working of a classic of medieval Russian literature. The intense interest in the forces of Russian history seen in these operas is partnered by a similar trend in painting of the time, particularly in the work of Vasily Surikov, which includes his *Morning of the Execution of the Streltsy* (1881).

As in the other arts, narrative content also tended to prevail over purely formal qualities in painting at this time. By 1870, the young rebels who had broken away from the Academy of Arts had founded a Society of Wandering Exhibitions in order to engage more directly with contemporary life and exhibit work outside Moscow and St Petersburg.[19] The so-called Wanderers were influential on the early career of the prolific Ilya Repin, best known for his socially tendentious canvas entitled *The Volga Barge-Haulers* (1873). Stasov continued to champion the cause of the Wanderers in St Petersburg, but the group had also acquired a powerful new ally in Moscow: a merchant called Pavel Tretiakov. One result of the Great Reforms was Russia's belated modernisation, and it was Moscow's merchant entrepreneurs who became its chief beneficiaries. Moscow had always been the country's commercial capital, but could never compete with the sophistication of St Petersburg. As its industrialists began to make immense fortunes from the building of railways and factories in the 1870s, however, the city began to lose its image as

19 See E. K. Valkenier, *Russian Realist Art, the State, and Society: The Peredvizhniki and Their Tradition* (New York: Columbia University Press, 1989).

a provincial backwater, and soon became the centre of the National movement in Russian art. Tretiakov, who came from a family of textile magnates, was one of the first Moscow merchants to become a patron of the arts, and one of the first to purchase paintings by the Wanderers, before their work became fashionable. As a passionate Slavophile, Tretiakov's aim was also to exhibit his increasingly large collection of Russian art, and work was begun in 1872 to build a new gallery to house it. With national identity the burning issue of the day, it is not surprising that Russian landscape painting, which first emerged as a distinct genre at this time, featured strongly in Tretiakov's collection. Under the inspiration of works of literature such as Lermontov's poem 'Motherland' 'Rodina', 1841) and the famous passage in chapter 11 of the first part of Gogol's *Dead Souls*, which were among the first to celebrate the humble features of the Russian landscape, painters began also to see their intrinsic beauty. They now became a powerful national symbol, to be revered precisely for their lack of similarity to the more immediately appealing vistas of Western Europe (as in Polenov's *Moscow Courtyard*, 1878). Ivan Shishkin executed countless detailed paintings of Russian trees (such as *In the Depths of the Forest*, 1872), for example, not because he lacked inspiration to paint anything else, but because he took pride in the grandeur of his country's natural state and felt that Russia was primarily a country of landscape. A pivotal and symbolic canvas was Aleksei Savrasov's 'The Rooks Have Arrived', exhibited at the first Wanderers' exhibition in 1871.[20]

The unveiling of the Pushkin statue in Moscow in 1880 was a public event of great significance. Since this was the first monument to a literary figure to be put up in a prominent location in Russia, the festivities lasted three days, with speeches from Dostoevsky and Turgenev. Embarrassed by the circumstances of Pushkin's death, the government had been reluctant to commission a statue in the capital, despite the writer's now iconic status as the undisputed national poet, and the statue had been funded by public subscription over two decades.[21] A year later the mood of celebration abruptly ended: not only was Alexander II assassinated, but Dostoevsky and Mussorgsky died, thus symbolically bringing to a close a remarkable era. Tolstoy, meanwhile, decided (temporarily, at least) to place fiction-writing second to the fighting of moral causes – such as vainly appealing for clemency to be granted to Alexander II's assassins.

20 See Christopher Ely, *This Meager Nature: Landscape and National Identity in Imperial Russia* (DeKalb: Northern Illinois University Press, 2002).

21 See Marcus Levitt, *Russian Literary Politics and the Pushkin Celebration of 1880* (Ithaca: Cornell University Press, 1989).

Russian culture under Alexander III (1881–1894)

Alexander III reacted to the violent circumstances of his father's death by introducing repressive measures which actually attempted to undo some of the 1860s reforms, and by increasing censorship: it should not be forgotten that Russian writers after 1804 had to endure the humiliation of submitting their work to the censor, and then complying with whatever demands were made. Russian culture had already begun to undergo significant change by the time of Alexander II's death, as non-conformists and former radicals amongst the artistic community gradually began to become part of the establishment: Rimsky-Korsakov was appointed to teach at the St Petersburg Conservatoire in 1871, and members of the Wanderers group had begun to take up professorships at the Academy of Arts. Under Alexander III, nationalist Russian culture was for the first time supported by the state and thus could no longer be seen as 'progressive'. Alexander's reactionary policies caused widespread despondency amongst the liberal educated population, who came to see this period as a sterile era of 'small deeds'. The government's closure of the country's leading literary journal in 1884, due to its allegiance to 'dangerous' (i.e. Populist) political ideas, was a further blow to morale; *Notes of the Fatherland* had been a mouthpiece of liberal thought for forty-five years. This was the year in which the Holy Synod assumed control of Russian primary schools, and universities lost their autonomy. It was also the year in which Alexander presented his wife with the first exquisitely crafted Easter egg commissioned from the court jeweller Carl Fabergé, and so began an annual tradition which was continued by his heir Nicholas II.

Konstantin Pobedonostsev, appointed procurator of the Holy Synod in 1880, was as much responsible as Alexander III for the atmosphere of gloom and paranoia during his reign. The lay head of the Russian Orthodox Church (this was a civil appointment, made by the emperor), he was a staunch defender of autocracy and an implacable opponent of reform. Pobedonostsev had licence to intervene in questions of censorship as well as in matters of national education and religious freedom, and his edicts were so unpopular in educated circles that they won him the nickname of 'The Grand Inquisitor' after a character in *The Brothers Karamazov* (*Brat'ia Karamazovy*; Dostoevsky, who had consulted him during the writing of his last novel, published in 1880, had been one of this dour man's few close friends). It is thus no coincidence that the voluminous, soul-searching novels of the 1860s and 1870s now gave way to short stories. The apathy and disillusionment of the period is captured well in the short stories of Chekhov, whose unambitious, melancholy characters indicate the diminution of the intelligentsia's hopes and dreams following the era of the great reforms.

Chekhov, now renowned as the master of the genre, stands out as almost the only writer of international calibre to emerge from Russia's literary doldrums of the 1880s and early 1890s, and the manner in which he established his reputation says a great deal about how much the Russian literary world had changed since the times when the great novelists had begun their careers. The son of a bankrupted shopkeeper, Chekhov came from an impoverished provincial background and wrote comic stories to supplement the family income while studying medicine at Moscow University. The lightweight comic journals which published his work flourished due to the burgeoning and increasingly literate lower classes in Russian cities and soon brought him the attention of newspaper editors. Finally, in 1887, when he was twenty-seven, Chekhov was invited to submit a story to one of Russia's prestigious literary journals. After the publication of *The Steppe* early the following year in *The Northern Messenger*, Chekhov's career was meteoric; it was quite unprecedented for a writer to begin a literary career in such an unpretentious way. The absence of any didacticism in his writing was a reaction to the preaching of moral ideas in the work of his elder contemporaries, and was severely criticised by those who saw his lack of ideological engagement as a flaw. In its gentle lyricism, Chekhov's work looks towards the modernist period, as do the landscape paintings of his friend Isaak Levitan, Russia's greatest landscape painter – a good example is his *Quiet Haven* (1890).

There was one aspect to Alexander III's notorious Russification policies which had positive consequences, namely his active promotion of native culture, including the 'revivalist' neo-Muscovite architecture which now became popular. The first major public building project of Alexander's reign was the onion-domed Church of the Resurrection, begun in 1882. Built on the spot where his father was assassinated, its pastiche of medieval Russian styles provides a stark contrast with the neoclassical architecture which surrounds it, and which had been specifically designed to emulate the European style and make a deliberate break with Muscovite tradition. This sort of retrogressive orientation was closely allied to Alexander III's reactionary and Slavophile political beliefs. Of far greater value was his decision to found the first state museum of Russian art, to which end he became an assiduous collector. The Russian Museum opened in 1898, six years after Tretiakov handed over his collection to the city of Moscow. But perhaps of even greater value were Alexander III's services to Russian performing arts. Alexander's decision to end the monopoly on theatrical production held by the Imperial Theatres in 1882, and to close down the Italian Opera in 1885 were to have far-reaching consequences for the further development of Russian culture.

The new freedom enabled entrepreneurs to found privately run theatres, which had hitherto been outlawed. Not surprisingly, Moscow took the lead here, and one of the first such ventures was the theatre founded by the lawyer Fyodor Korsh, who commissioned Chekhov's *Ivanov*, the play with which he made his stage debut in 1887. Another was the Private Opera founded in 1885 by the railway tycoon Savva Mamontov. It was a venture which brought together all his activities in the artistic sphere. Like Tretiakov, Mamontov was a passionate advocate of Russian art, a cause which he took up actively after purchasing Abramtsevo, a country estate outside Moscow, in 1870 and founding an artists' colony there. The survival of traditional peasant crafts was now under threat as a result of industrialisation, and Mamontov and his wife set up workshops to revive and study them, partly under the influence of the European Arts and Crafts movement. At the same time, Abramtsevo was hospitable to new trends, and it is for this reason that it has come to be known as the 'cradle of the modern movement in Russian art'.[22] Many of Russia's best-known artists working in the late nineteenth century spent time at Abramtsevo, including Repin, Antokolskii, the Vasnetsov brothers, Polenov, Vrubel, Serov, Nesterov and Korovin. These artists worked on a variety of subjects and in various media, including landscape, Russian history and legend, portraits, icons and frescoes, architecture and applied art. When Mamontov started producing and directing plays and operas, many of these artists designed sets and costumes, which was an unprecedented theatrical innovation in a theatrical culture still dominated by the ossified traditions of the state-run Imperial Theatres, whose scenery and props were perfunctory and unimaginative. But staging operas was a costly exercise even for a tycoon like Mamontov, and in 1892 he decided to call a temporary halt to productions.

The Imperial Theatres were well-funded. As the main opera company in St Petersburg, the Russian Opera at last started to prosper now that funds were no longer being wasted on the Italian troupe, and the Mariinsky became the nation's premier stage (with the old Bolshoi Theatre, former home to the Italian Opera, demolished to make way for the new building of the St Petersburg Conservatoire). Tchaikovsky was one of the first composers to benefit: his penultimate opera *The Queen of Spades* was commissioned and lavishly produced by the Imperial Theatres in December 1890, the same month in which Borodin's posthumously completed *Prince Igor* was premiered there.

22 Gray, *The Russian Experiment in Art, 1863–1922*, p. 9.

Unlike most of his peers, Tchaikovsky was a loyal and patriotic subject of Alexander III (he was the composer of a Coronation Cantata, performed in the Kremlin in 1883), but as a professional artist, he saw himself as a European as much as he saw himself as a Russian, and his music expresses his embrace of both traditions. He was also unashamed about pursuing beauty in an age which scorned too much emphasis on aesthetic considerations. In 1876 Tchaikovsky had acquired the patronage of Nadezhda von Meck, the widow of a wealthy railway builder, which released him from his onerous teaching responsibilities, and in 1884 he received an imperial decoration, and an annual pension from the tsar. Once he had more time to compose, his career began to take off, and it was during this time that some of his best-known works were written and first performed, including the *Rococo Variations* (1877), the *Violin Concerto* (1881), the *Piano Trio* (1882), and the Fourth, Fifth and Sixth Symphonies (1878, 1888 and 1893). Tchaikovsky was the first Russian composer to achieve fame abroad (he undertook several concert tours in Europe and also visited America), but it was only after his death in 1893 that the significance of his legacy was properly understood, particularly in the sphere of ballet music, which he transformed from being a mere accompaniment into a serious genre in its own right. The Russian aristocracy's love of ballet had led to Tchaikovsky's first commission to write the music for *Swan Lake*, first performed in Moscow at the Bolshoi Theatre in 1877. Tchaikovsky willingly conformed to the dictates of the Imperial Theatres and enjoyed in particular a fruitful relationship with Ivan Vsevolozhsky, who was appointed director in 1881 and commissioned Tchaikovsky to collaborate with the distinguished choreographer Marius Petipa to write a score for *Sleeping Beauty* in 1889. *The Nutcracker* followed in 1892.

Tchaikovsky also made a serious contribution to the renewal of Russian church music, which had stagnated ever since Dmitry Bortnianskii had acquired a monopoly on its composition and performance for the Imperial Court Chapel while serving as its director in the late eighteenth century. Tchaikovsky had won the right to publish his *Liturgy of St John Chrysostom* (1878) from the church censor, but the ecclesiastical authorities later banned it from being performed in a church after it was sung at a public concert. Undeterred, Tchaikovsky wrote an *All-Night Vigil* (1881–2) after serious study of Slavonic chant, and in 1884 was commissioned by Alexander III to write nine sacred pieces.[23] Other composers soon followed Tchaikovsky's example and helped to revive the sacred musical tradition in Russia.

23 See Francis Maes, *A History of Russian Music From Kamarinskaya to Babi Yar* (Berkeley: University of California Press, 2002), pp. 142–4.

Russian concert life was also in need of renewal by the time of Alexander III's accession. The main symphony concert series, which had been inaugurated by the Russian Musical Society in 1859, had become increasingly reliant on the classical repertoire by the 1880s and was beginning to lack freshness. The wealthy merchant patron Mitrofan Beliaev promoted contemporary composers at the concert series he founded in St Petersburg in 1885, but the repertoire was exclusively Russian and conservative stylistically. The 'Russian Symphony Concerts' were of inestimable value in consolidating a national musical tradition which was now well and truly established, but they did not explore new territory: composers like Arensky, Liadov and Glazunov hardly belonged to the avant-garde. The Russian school had hitherto prided itself on its anti-establishment stance, but the Beliaev concerts ironically succeeded in truly institutionalising it.[24] As a bastion of the musical establishment, and now the *éminence grise* of the St Petersburg Conservatoire, where he had been professor since 1882, Rimsky-Korsakov certainly did not use his position as Beliaev's main advisor to change its orientation. Several of his own works were written for the 'Russian Symphony Concerts', including his celebrated symphonic suite *Sheherazade* (1888), whose 'oriental' theme is a feature of many Russian musical compositions of the nineteenth century. In his 1882 overview 'Twenty-Five Years of Russian Art', indeed, Stasov defined it as one of the distinguishing features of music of the 'new Russian school', that is to say, the composers who originally made up the 'mighty handful'. Nowhere in his article does he draw a link, however, between the 'orientalism' of Russian music and Russian imperial expansion into Asia, which lies behind the aggressive nationalism of Borodin's *Prince Igor*, for example.[25]

Russian Culture Under Nicholas II (1894–1917)

Alexander's successor Nicholas II, was hardly less reactionary than his father, but it was during his reign that an explosion of creative talent took place across all the arts which produced what is now rightly regarded as a kind of Russian 'Renaissance'. For the first time Russian culture also became an international commodity as the great novels began to be translated into other languages, and performers, composers and artists began to acquire reputations abroad. By the end of the nineteenth century, St Petersburg could match any other European capital for elegance and refinement. Its cultural life was greatly enriched by

24 See Stephen Walsh, *Stravinsky: A Creative Spring, Russia and France 1882–1934* (London: Jonathan Cape, 1999), p. 65.

25 See Taruskin, 'Entoiling the Falconet', in *Defining Russia Musically*, pp. 152–85.

contact with Paris, Vienna and Berlin, cities to which there were fast train connections, and Russian society was to open up still further following the 1905 Revolution, which led to an easing in censorship. The ascendancy at this time of the Mariinsky Theatre, which could now be counted amongst the world's leading opera houses, with appearances by singers and conductors from abroad and a superb native company, is emblematic. Moscow, meanwhile, could boast Russia's most distinguished new theatre company, and a Conservatoire which could now more than hold its own with its sister institution in St Petersburg (Rachmaninov and Scriabin both graduated with Gold Medals as pianists in 1892). From 1910 onwards the city became a centre for the avant-garde – a dynamic, bustling metropolis where the most daring art exhibitions were held.

The cultural revival that was instigated at the beginning of the twentieth century was prompted to a certain extent by a desire to escape from a depressing political reality which was clearly going to worsen, but also partly by the simple and inevitable need to strike out in a new direction. Signs of the dawning of a new age in the arts had come with the production of Tchaikovsky's *The Queen of Spades*, which simultaneously represents the apotheosis of the Russian 'imperial style', and is also a work whose hallucinatory subject matter, nostalgic mood and stylistic pastiche align it with the preoccupations of the new generation of artists who emerged in the closing years of the nineteenth century. The rebellion against old forms and championing of the new saw Russian artists for the first time becoming leaders of the European avant-garde in the early years of the twentieth century, and, in the case of Stravinsky, Kandinsky and Malevich, changing the very language of art. Music was the last art form to be affected by the winds of change which now began to sweep through Russian cultural life, but it was ironically music which – through the agency of Stravinsky – was to make perhaps Russia's most significant contribution to the modernist movement in Europe.

The Russian avant-garde's rejection of rationality and concrete reality in favour of the world of the imagination can only partly be seen as a reaction to the superannuated realist movement. At a more fundamental level it was a reaction to the disintegration of moral and ethical values, religious beliefs and existing social structures which took place under the impact of Darwin's theories of evolution, the effects of capitalism and industrialisation and the ideas of such crucial figures as Nietzsche and Freud. The feelings of alienation, anxiety and loss of control which we associate with modern culture were particularly acute in *fin de siècle* Russia, where chaos and revolution loomed, but they nevertheless provided the stimulus for a cultural era of unprecedented richness and creativity, which came to a peak on the eve of the First World War.

In 1896 Mamontov relaunched his Private Opera company in Moscow. From the beginning, he had championed Russian opera, and he now began to focus on the works of Rimsky-Korsakov, many of which (beginning with *Sadko*, in 1898) received their premiere at his theatre. Like Mussorgsky and Borodin, Rimsky-Korsakov believed that the quickest path to creating a native musical tradition was through opera, and also chose to write on almost exclusively Russian subjects: twelve of his fifteen operas are based on Russian themes. Whereas Mussorgsky and Borodin concentrated largely on historical topics, Rimsky-Korsakov was attracted to the more exotic world of Russian fairy tales, and his operas now began to occupy a firm foothold in the repertoire. Mamontov's other major contribution in the field of Russian opera during this second phase was to launch the career of the legendary bass Fedor Chaliapin, who made his debut at the Private Opera in 1896, singing the role of Susanin in Glinka's *A Life for the Tsar*. In 1898 the company undertook a triumphant tour to St Petersburg, with Chaliapin performing the title role in *Boris Godunov*, which helped to reverse that opera's fortunes following neglect by the Imperial Theatres.

Two new ventures which were to have a lasting impact on Russian cultural life were launched in 1898, one in Moscow and the other in St Petersburg. The Moscow Art Theatre, founded by Konstantin Stanislavsky and Vladimir Nemirovich-Danchenko, was to revolutionise Russian theatre and achieved its greatest renown through its productions of Chekhov's four last plays. The amateur actor and director Stanislavsky, scion of one of the great merchant families in Moscow, made a good team with the drama teacher and playwright Nemirovich-Danchenko. Picking up on the new approach to the stage that had first started with Wagner, Stanislavsky and Nemirovich-Danchenko elevated drama to high art, investing it with the capacity not only to uplift but to transform and enlighten its audiences. Initially the educational aspect of their activities was emphasised in the word 'accessible' being part of the company's original title, but was later dropped. The word 'artistic' (typically contracted in English to 'art') remained, however, serving as a reminder of the idealistic goals nurtured by the theatre's founders. Going to the theatre suddenly became a serious business; lights were no longer kept burning during performances so that audience members could inspect each other; they were dimmed, forcing spectators to concentrate on what was unfolding on stage in pitch blackness. The décor of the auditorium was similarly austere – a marked change to the gilt and velvet of traditional theatres. Productions were properly rehearsed, and a production method pioneered which placed the emphasis on ensemble work. For the first time in the Russian theatre, stagings were conceptual, their style and atmosphere determined by a director. Chekhov's *The Seagull* (*Chaika*), first performed on 17 December 1898, was the Moscow Art Theatre's sixth production, and its success saved the theatre from plummeting to financial disaster in its first season. After a scandalous first production of the play by the Imperial Theatres in St Petersburg in 1896, Chekhov had been reluctant for it to be turned into a travesty a second time round, but in the end had no cause to regret giving his agreement after Nemirovich-Danchenko had pleaded with him on two occasions. *Uncle Vanya*, completed in 1895, was performed by the Moscow Art Theatre in 1899, and Chekhov's last two plays, *The Three Sisters* (*Tri sestry*, 1901) and *The Cherry Orchard* (*Vishnevy sad*, 1904), were written specifically for the Moscow Art Theatre. Another dramatist who enjoyed success at the Moscow Art Theatre was Maxim Gorky, whose *Lower Depths* (*Ha dne*) was staged in 1902. Gorky's gritty indictment of contemporary society was better suited to the hyper-realist style that was Stanislavsky's trademark, and which was ironically inappropriate for Chekhov's subtle theatre of mood. Thanks to Savva Morozov, the merchant millionaire who was its chief patron, in 1902 the Moscow Art Theatre was able to move into a new building designed for the company by Russia's finest avant-garde architect Fedor Shekhtel, who also built opulent Art Nouveau mansions for Mamontov in 1897, and for Stepan Ryabushinskii, another wealthy industrialist, in 1900–2.

Just as the Moscow Art Theatre could not survive without the patronage of Morozov, the arts journal founded in St Petersburg in 1898 also depended on substantial financial backing. *The World of Art* was edited by a group of cosmopolitan and eclectic young aesthetes led by the flamboyant figure of Sergei Diaghilev, a key figure in the history of Russian Modernism, who was also expert at raising money. This came principally from Princess Maria Tenisheva, who had founded another important artists' colony at her estate in Talashkino in the 1890s (Mamontov had offered support, but his arrest in 1899 led to his bankruptcy). No Russian magazine had even been so beautifully or so carefully produced, and the *World of Art*'s physical appearance, together with its all-encompassing title, say much about the priority of purely aesthetic categories. Indeed, the members of the highly eclectic *World of Art* group whose members included Aleksandr Benois, Leon Bakst, Konstantin Somov and Ivan Bilibin were torchbearers for the artistic movement which had begun to liberate Russian culture from the earnest utilitarianism that had dominated all the arts in the preceding period. In particular, they provided one of the first platforms for the poets who called themselves Symbolists. Led initially by Valerii

Briusov and Konstantin Balmont, who drew their inspiration from French writers such as Baudelaire and Verlaine, the Symbolists were quickly condemned as decadents. Their detractors deplored the fact that the Symbolists jettisoned a concern with ideology in favour of individual emotional experience and a quest for beauty, which was expressed at first in small, lyrical forms rather than the grand canvases of the Realist period. And they condemned the Symbolists' cultivation of amorality and the occult, which was an expression of the escape from the stifling Victorian mores of the 1880s in the aftermath of Nietzsche and the 'death' of God. In St Petersburg the leader of the new movement was the writer Dmitrii Merezhkovskii, who had published an influential article in 1893 which pinned the blame for the general decline in literary quality at the time on the didacticism of the Populist age and called for culture to be revived through a concern with metaphysical idealism and spiritual experience. The *World of Art* embraced music as well as literature and art, and here too Diaghilev and his colleagues had eclectic tastes. They were the first to create a Tchaikovsky cult, but they were also the first non-musicians in Russia to champion Wagner on the pages of their journal, regarding him as a founder of the Modernist movement in Russia as he had been elsewhere. The *World of Art* group played a key role in revitalising Russian culture, exchanging the narrow domestic focus of so much of what was produced earlier for a new cosmopolitan outlook which was consonant with the spirit of the modern city in which they lived.

Diaghilev had initially hoped to pursue a career as a musician but soon turned his energies to art: his cultural activities had begun with an exhibition of English and German watercolours in 1897. Convinced that the quality of modern Russian art was now equal to that of Western Europe, Diaghilev next decided to organise a series of international exhibitions beginning in 1898, which the aging Stasov predictably condemned as decadent. Diaghilev had anticipated this reaction. When soliciting work for his first exhibition, he had addressed the problem directly: 'Russian art at the moment is in a state of transition', he wrote to prospective exhibitors; 'History places any emerging trend in this position when the principles of the older generation clash and struggle with the newly developing demands of youth.'[26] After several more successful exhibitions, and a spell as editor of the Imperial Theatres annual, into which he breathed new life (even impressing Nicholas II), Diaghilev then began triumphantly to export Russia's cultural legacy to the West. He started

26 V. Kamensky (ed.), *The World of Art Movement in Early Twentieth-Century Russia*, (Leningrad: Avrora, 1991), p. 20.

with music. If Russian composers had fought a hard battle for recognition in their own country, conquering Europe presented an even greater challenge, since their music was still largely unknown. The five concerts of the first *Saisons russes*, which took place in Paris in 1907, were a great success, however. Chaliapin, Rimsky-Korsakov and Rachmaninov were amongst the musicians who travelled to Paris to help showcase some of the masterpieces of their native repertoire. In 1908, Diaghilev exported opera to Paris. The triumphant production of *Boris Godunov* now launched Chaliapin's career as an international soloist. In 1909, it was the turn of ballet. With stars like Anna Pavlova and Vaslav Nijinsky, and revolutionary choreography by Michel Fokine, the legendary Ballets Russes company which Diaghilev formed in 1910 was to transform Western attitudes to ballet as an art form. In 1910 Diaghilev also commissioned the unknown Igor Stravinsky to write a score for a new ballet called *The Firebird*. It was followed in 1911 by *Petrushka*, and in 1913 by *The Rite of Spring*. All three scores drew from and transformed the Russian background Stravinsky had been brought up in. Benois, Goncharova and Bakst were amongst the many gifted artists whose vibrant sets and costumes contributed significantly to the success and originality of the Ballets Russes.

It was Diaghilev's genius to perceive that native style was an essential ingredient if Russia was to come into its own and contribute something new to world culture, if made part of a modernist aesthetics. Native style was a vital factor in the creation of the Ballets Russes, in whose success Stravinsky was to become such a lynchpin, and, after his first commission to write the score to *The Firebird*, it inspired the development of a neo-nationalist orientation in his music which would later explode with *The Rite of Spring*. In that work Stravinsky presented Russian folk life with a greater authenticity than any other composer before him. It was the apotheosis of the neo-nationalist style cultivated by the artists and aesthetes of the *World of Art* group and it captivated Western audiences. The neo-nationalism of the Russian avant-garde may have begun in the 1870s as a desire to preserve native crafts in the face of encroaching capitalism and urbanisation. Soon, however, particularly at Princess Tenisheva's artists' colony in Talashkino, folklore came to be seen more as a stylistic resource with which to regenerate art, and infuse it with a vigour and energy that was commonly felt to have been lost. Both Stravinsky and the artist Nikolai Rerikh (who designed *The Rite of Spring*) spent time at Talashkino. Ethnographic colour as artistic content had been the cornerstone of nationalist aesthetics of the 1870s but had come by this point to be regarded as distinctly outmoded. Stravinsky was the first Russian composer to turn to folklore as a source for stylistic renewal and experimentation. In so doing he moved abruptly away from the 'academic' and 'de-nationalised' style of composition that characterised so much Russian music written at that time.[27]

Stravinsky's first commission for the Ballets Russes was not the only significant event in Russian culture in 1910. It was the year in which Tolstoy died at the age of eighty-two, and in which Symbolism lost coherence as a literary movement (although its three greatest second-generation representatives Aleksandr Blok, Andrei Bely and Viacheslav Ivanov had some of their most important work still ahead of them). The year 1910 was also a watershed for the Russian avant-garde. An exhibition provocatively entitled 'The Jack of Diamonds' opened in Moscow, and the bright colours and unconventional subject matter of the paintings provoked furious debates. Amongst the artists represented were painters like Nataliia Goncharova, Mikhail Larionov, Vasili Kandinsky and Kazimir Malevich, all of whom shared Stravinsky's interest in drawing inspiration from native traditions for their own work. Goncharova, for example, who along with Larionov headed the Neo-Primitivist movement which emerged at this time, was inspired by peasant woodcuts and icons. In 1910 she painted four imposing *Evangelists*, which were condemned as blasphemous and removed by the police when exhibited at the equally controversial 'Donkey's Tail' exhibition in 1912. 'We can no longer be satisfied with a simple organic copy of nature', wrote Aleksandr Shevchenko about Neo-Primitivism in 1913; 'We are striving to seek new paths for our art . . . For the point of departure in our art we take the *lubok* and the icon, since we find in them the most acute, the most direct perception of life.'[28] The appreciation of Russian icons as works of art rather than as exclusively religious artefacts was a relatively recent phenomenon and had come about as a result of painstaking conservation work. The removal of layers of accumulated soot and over-painting in the early years of the twentieth century had made people in Russia aware for the first time that they too had a precious artistic legacy which went back hundreds of years.

It was also in 1910 that Scriabin and Kandinsky began to forge new artistic languages in their respective fields: the first abstract paintings for Kandinsky, the first abandonment of traditional tonality for Scriabin in his last orchestral work *Prometheus*. The dissatisfaction with 'mere' representation which the Russian avant-garde experienced at the beginning of the twentieth century

27 See Richard Taruskin, *Stravinsky and the Russian Traditions* (Oxford: Oxford University Press, 1996), vol. I, pp. 497–502 for a discussion of the process of denationalisation in Russian music.

28 *Russian Art of the Avant-Garde: Theory and Criticism*, ed. J. E. Bowlt, rev. edn (London: Thames and Hudson, 1988), pp. 45–6.

inspired a relentless experimentation with new forms which would eventually change the face of twentieth-century culture. When in the early 1900s Andrei Bely, for example, found conventional imagery inadequate to the task of giving expression to the deeper realities which he believed underlay everyday life, and which he was interested in exploring in his fiction, he began pushing the very boundaries of language to create new theories of semantic structure in literature, as in his novel *Petersburg* (1916). Scriabin's artistic imagination, meanwhile, led him to contemplate the very disappearance of the physical plane of consciousness as the inevitable consequence of the world cataclysm which would accompany the performance of the *Mysterium*, a planned synaesthetic musical work combining religion and philosophy, designed to transport all participants into a state of supreme final ecstasy. Scriabin's new harmonic system with its mystical chord of superimposed fourths led to the dissolution of a sense of time. At the same time, Kandinsky was turning to signs, colours and shapes for symbolising abstract ideas and intangible states in his paintings as he searched to free art from its ties to material reality. Kandinsky had always been interested in spirituality, in the unconscious and in the subjective world like other Russian Modernists. He now dissolved conventional form by rejecting traditional subject matter to explore instead abstract ideas, thereby releasing what he thought was the inner sound of colour, seeking to make visible an otherwise inaccessible world through the liberation of colours and harmonies from their traditional structures. For him moving away from representational depictions in his canvases was the first step towards the complete dissolution of matter.

If Scriabin and Kandinsky turned their gaze inwards (as Kandinsky wrote in his seminal work *On the Spiritual in Art*, 1912), another section of the Russian avant-garde did the opposite by taking their art into the streets. There was a strong link between Neo-Primitivism and Futurism, the movement which arose in Russia in 1912, and which blurred the boundaries between literature and painting. Like the Neo-Primitivists, the Futurists wanted art to be revolutionary, and both their work and their behaviour was deliberately shocking (the exuberant Vladimir Mayakovsky wore a yellow waistcoat and painted his face). Following the publication of their manifesto, *A Slap in the Face of Public Taste* in 1912, the Futurists sought to dispense with all of past culture and create a new world. In December 1913, the year in which the Romanov dynasty celebrated its three hundredth annniversary, the world's first Futurist opera, *Victory Over the Sun*, was first performed in St Petersburg. Its two brief acts are set in an indefinite time and place, the cast is all male, none of the characters have proper names or developed personalities, their speech and actions seem completely absurd, and there is no recognisable plot beyond the capture of the sun by strong men of the future. The production was designed by Malevich, whose abstract Cubo-Futurist sets and costumes were the most radical ever seen on the stage at that time anywhere in the world. Firmly convinced that the external world was exhausted as a source of inspiration, in 1915 Malevich went on to form his own movement, Suprematism, which he saw as a natural development of Cubism and Futurism. With its exclusive exploration of non-objective geometric forms and pure aesthetic feeling, it is regarded as the first systematic school of abstract painting. When Malevich's most famous canvas, *Black Square* was first exhibited in 1915, it was hung in a way that deliberately alluded to the so-called 'red corner' where icons were traditionally to be found in people's homes.

Malevich's iconic *Black Square* symbolised both an end and a beginning, and was the extreme point of the Russian artistic avant-garde's relentless journey into new territories (as Stravinsky's scores were in music and Bely's novels in literature). But to gain an accurate picture of Russia's remarkably vibrant cultural life on the eve of the 1917 Revolution (given that the country was then at war), Malevich's, Stravinsky's and Bely's works must be considered alongside Boris Kustodiev's colourful and nostalgic paintings of Moscow merchant life such as *Shrovetide* (1916), Ivan Bunin's elegant but traditional prose (as in 'The Gentleman from San Francisco', 1915), Gorky's trenchant autobiographical masterpieces *Childhood (Detstvo)*, *In the World* (*V liudiakh*) and *My Universities* (*Moi universitety*, 1913–15), the radical stage director Vsevelod Meyerhold's stylised theatre productions (his Studio made its official public debut in 1915) and Rachmaninov's *All-Night Vigil* (1915), the work which marked the apex of the revival of Russian sacred music initiated by Tchaikovsky. Together they make up a richly patterned and intricate mosaic of a quality and intensity which Russian artists have never been able to match since.

6

Russian political thought, 1700–1917

GARY M. HAMBURG

From Muscovy to the Early Enlightenment: the problem of resistance to ungodly rulers

Muscovites almost universally regarded the grand prince as anointed by God and thus as deserving obedience, or even reverence, but the obligation to obey him was contingent on his adherence to moral law and on his respect for an unwritten compact that was felt to constitute the foundation of government. Political actors and churchmen had the duty to render sound advice to the grand prince and to reprove him when his conduct departed from well-established Christian norms; the grand prince's reciprocal obligations were to seek wise counsel and heed justified reproofs. When the grand prince stubbornly turned against godly ways, Christians were conscience-bound to disobey his spiritually inimical decrees. On this point there was strong consensus. Iosif Volotskii (1439–1515), usually classified as a supporter of princely absolutism, warned Christians not to obey an unrighteous ruler. The archpriest Avvakum (1620–82), who had once enjoyed a cordial personal relationship with Tsar Alexis Mikhailovich, instructed his flock, on becoming convinced of Alexis's support for 'heretical' church reforms: 'Place not your hope in princes, in a son of man, in whom there is no help.'[1] As a rule, Muscovite thinkers stopped short of calling for active resistance to the government. The customary recourse for morally outraged Christians was to flee from Muscovy or at least from areas under an evil grand prince's immediate control. In the correspondence attributed to Prince Andrei Mikhailovich Kurbskii (d. 1583) and Tsar Ivan IV, the Kurbskii letters justified not only flight from Muscovy but service to the rival Lithuanian commonwealth. However, during the seventeenth-century controversy over new religious rituals, Old Believer monks at Solovetskii Monastery moved

1 *La vie de l'archiprêtre Avvakum écrite par lui-meme*, trans. Pierre Pascal (Paris: Gallimard, 1938) p. 137.

beyond flight, taking up arms in self-defence against the government. They justified their act on the grounds that Tsar Alexis had supported 'diabolical' liturgical innovations. Avvakum apparently approved the armed resistance at Solovki. Thus, if Muscovite political literature generally lacked a formal doctrine of active resistance to an unrighteous ruler, Muscovites had the functional equivalent.

Under Peter the political opposition often justified itself in traditional Christian terms. Vasilii Sokovnin, arrested in 1697 on charges of conspiracy to kill the tsar, told interrogators that Peter 'has ruined everyone, and for that reason it is permissible to kill him, and it will not be sinful'.[2] In March 1712 Stefan Iavorskii (1658–1722), criticised Peter's comportment from the pulpit, the sermon being an archetypal vehicle for conveyance of 'good advice' to an errant sovereign. Iavorskii's sermon later helped inspire Crown Prince Alexis to resist Peter's policies. The tsarevich's conduct in 1716–18 – flight from Russia, passive resistance to an ungodly tsar, then tacit support for active resistance – followed to the letter the Muscovite script for legitimate opposition.

Peter's allies deployed religious and secular arguments to counter this traditionalist Christian opposition. In his 1716 historical essay on the rebellions against Peter 'Opisanie v sovremennom ispytaniem i podlinnym izvestiem o smutnom vremeni' (A True Account of the Time of Troubles), Andrei Artamonovich Matveev (1666–1728) attributed the resistance to 'fratricidal and ineradicable hatred rooted in human nature'.[3] Rejecting the notion that opposition might be justified in Christian terms, Matveev suggested that Peter's opponents had learned the art of rebellion from the Ottoman janissaries, whose 'insidious designs and actions' were based on the 'lawless Quran'. The issue of opposition to Peter was also raised in Petr Pavlovich Shafirov's *Rassuzhdenie* (Discourse) of 1716 on the Swedish war, a book to which the tsar contributed several pages. Shafirov (1669–1739) accused the Swedes of 'stirring up His Majesty's subjects to rebellion', and he implied that Crown Prince Alexis had treasonously undermined the Russian campaign against Sweden. Shafirov's *Discourse* explained Russia's conduct in the war as consistent with contemporary European thinking on international law and sovereignty, citing texts from Grotius and Pufendorf. Yet Shafirov also quoted biblical texts in support of Peter's conduct, and called the Swedes 'infidels' for violating

2 Quoted in P. Bushkovitch, *Peter the Great: The Struggle for Power, 1671–1725* (Cambridge: Cambridge University Press, 2001), p. 194.

3 *Zapiski Andreia Artamonovicha Grafa Matveeva,* in *Zapiski russkikh liudei sobytiia vremen Petra Velikogo* (St Peterburg: Tip. Moskovskogo Universiteta, 1841) p. 2.

'the custom of all civilized and Christian nations' by spreading of sedition in Russia.[4]

Archbishop Feofan Prokopovich (1618–1736) categorically attacked Peter's opponents for disobeying anointed authority. In *Slovo o vlasti i chesti tsarskoi* (Sermon on Royal Power and Honor, 1718), written during the affair of Tsarevich Alexis, Prokopovich warned Christians that to disobey sovereign authority 'is a sin against God warranting not only temporal but eternal punishment'.[5] He rejected interpretations of the Bible purporting to justify resistance to ungodly magistrates on the ground that the Scriptures order obedience not only to righteous authorities, but to perverse and faithless ones. Later, Prokopovich propounded a secular defence of undivided sovereignty and royal absolutism in the tract *Pravda o voli monarshei* (Truth Concerning the Monarch's Will, 1722). Here he added historical and philosophical justification for hereditary monarchy from Grotius, Pufendorf and Hobbes.

Peter's death in 1725 and the absence of able successors shook the stability of the system he had fostered and led to further debate over the legitimacy of resistance to the crown. In *Proizvol'noe i soglasnoe razsuzhdenie i mnenie sobravshagosia shliakhtsva russkago o pravlenii gosudarstvennom* (Personal and Collective Discourse and Opinion of the Russian Landed Nobility on Royal Government, 1730), Vasilii Nikitich Tatishchev (1686–1750) defended legally unrestricted monarchy. Accepting Aristotle's prejudice that monarchy is the best form of government, he argued that Russia had flourished under undivided monarchical rule. In his horror of divided sovereignty, Tatishchev showed the influence of Pufendorf, Hobbes and Prokopovich. Although Tatishchev has most often been read as a secularist thinker, he demanded that the tsar pay attention to close advisors lest dismissing their wisdom provoke divine punishment. In his dialogue *Razgovor dvukh priiatelei o pol'ze nauk i uchilishch* (Conversation of Two Friends on the Utility of the Sciences and of Schools, 1733), he portrayed religion as a shaper of human will and statutory law. In *Istoriia rossiiskaia* (Russian History, 1768–84) Tatishchev predicted all peoples in the empire would embrace the Russian language and Russian Orthodoxy.

From the late 1730s to 1762 Russian thinkers redefined the ideal of the virtuous tsar. The polymath Mikhail Vasil'evich Lomonosov (1711–65) asserted that an ideal ruler should protect Russia from foreign aggression and expand its

4 'A Discourse Concerning the Just Reasons Which his Czarist Majesty, Peter I, Had for Beginning the War against the King of Sweden, Charles XII', in P. P. Shafirov, *A Discourse Concerning the Just Causes of the War between Sweden and Russia: 1700–1721*, ed. W. Butler, (Dobbs Ferry, NY: Oceana Publications, 1973) p. 321.

5 F. Prokopovich, *Sochineniia* (Moscow: Izd. AN SSSR, 1961) pp. 77–8.

borders at its neighbours' expense. Domestically, an ideal ruler should promote useful enterprises and should display moral discernment and 'self-restraint'. Lomonosov's portrait of the ideal ruler resembled Prokopovich's image of Peter as the energetic warrior tsar and simultaneously recalled the Muscovite image of the pious sovereign.

The playwright Aleksandr Petrovich Sumarokov (1717–77) looked forward to a society of patriotic, dutiful, virtuous nobles governed by an equally patriotic, dutiful and virtuous legislator tsar. His play *Sinav i Truvor* (Sinav and Truvor, 1750) suggested that a morally irreproachable private life is a precondition of just rulership. That private virtue was not a sufficient condition for social justice was demonstrated by his drama *Pustynnik* (The Hermit, 1769), which observed that service to God can sometimes harm one's family and society as a whole.

Enlightenment and Counter-Enlightenment: civic virtue, absolutism and liberty

The most consequential thinker of the Russian Enlightenment was Catherine the Great (1727–96), whose *Nakaz* (Instruction, 1767) treated liberty as a crucial ingredient of just rule. The *Instruction* was not without a substantial conservative component. The first article cited the Christian imperative 'to do mutual good to one another as much as we possibly can'.[6] The section on education called on parents to inculcate into children 'all those duties which God demands of us in the Ten Commandments and our Orthodox Eastern Greek religion'.[7] Furthermore, the *Instruction* insisted that Russia's sovereign power 'must rest in the hands of an absolute ruler', for there 'is no other authority . . . that can act with a vigour proportionate to the extent of such a vast domain'.[8] Meanwhile, Catherine defended 'natural liberty', by which she meant the innate human desire to improve social conditions. She also defended political liberty, defined as 'the right of doing what the laws allow'. Catherine seemed not to notice that, by equating political liberty with specific legal obligations, she contradicted her subjects' natural liberty to the degree that their own impulses for social improvement ran in different directions from

6 F. W. Reddaway (ed.), *The Instructions to the Commissioners for Composing a New Code of Laws, Documents of Catherine the Great* (Cambridge: Cambridge University Press, 1931) p. 215.
7 Reddaway, *Instructions*, p. 272.
8 Reddaway, *Instructions*, p. 216.

her own. For subsequent thinkers Catherine's *Instruction* legitimated concepts such as the legislator monarch, civic virtue, and liberty under law.

Among the leaders of the Russian Enlightenment were Denis Ivanovich Fonvizin (1744–92), Nikolai Ivanovich Novikov (1744–1818) and Aleksandr Nikolaevich Radishchev (1749–1802).

Fonvizin and Novikov were supporters of Catherine who became disillusioned by her policies. Fonvizin's satirical plays *Brigadir* (The Brigadier, 1769) and *Nedorosl'* (The Adolescent, 1781) pilloried the equation of high service rank with virtue and attacked the adoption by Russian noblemen of foppish French fashions – both by-products of Catherine's service system. In his *Rassuzhdenie o nepremennykh gosudarstvennykh zakonakh* (Discourse on Indispensable State Laws, 1784) Fonvizin argued for the adoption in Russia of fundamental laws. The *Discourse* depicted the monarch as 'the soul of society'. 'If the monarch is proud, arrogant, crafty, greedy, a sensualist, shameless or lazy, then . . . all these vices will spread to the court, the capital and finally to the nation at large.'[9] Clearly preferable was a monarch who was 'righteous' and 'gentle', who understood that 'between sovereign and subjects exist mutual obligations'. In Fonvizin's opinion, subjects owed the crown obedience when policy was based on legal principle (*pravo*), but, in turn, the crown owed respect to the nation's political liberty, defined as the right of each subject 'to do what he / she wishes, and not to be forced to do what he / she may not desire to do'. Fonvizin departed from Catherine's *Instruction* by criticising serfdom as an illegitimate property system wherein 'each person is either a tyrant or victim'.

Novikov's satirical journals – *Truten'* (The Drone, 1769), *Pustomel'* (The Tattler, 1770), *Zhivopisets* (The Painter, 1772) and *Koshelek* (The Bag, 1774) – were inspired by Addison and Steele's *Spectator* but also by Catherine's own *Vsiakaia vsiachina* (All Sorts, 1769), with which Novikov conducted cautious polemics. In these journals he praised the empress's person but pointed to the moral flaws of her court and of the nobility. Yet in '*Otryvok puteshestviia v*** I*** T****' (Excerpt of a Journey to N by I***T***, 1772), he blamed village poverty on a 'cruel tyrant who robs the peasants of daily bread and their last measure of tranquility'.[10] In the journal *Utrennyi svet* (Morning Light, 1777–80), he preached Masonic ideals of ethical perfection and philanthropy. Although Novikov saw no contradiction between Masonry and Orthodoxy, Catherine ordered his publications investigated on suspicion of their undermining Christian values. In 1791 she had him arrested for sedition.

9 D. I. Fonvizin, *Sobranie sochinenii v dvukh tomakh* (Moscow and Leningrad: Gos. izd. khudozhestvennoi literatury, 1959), vol. II, p. 256.

10 *Satiricheskie zhurnaly N. I. Novikova* (Moscow and Leningrad: Izd. AN SSSR, 1951), p. 296.

Radishchev was the most radical figure of the Russian Enlightenment. His book *Puteshestvie iz S. Peterburga v Moskvu* (Journey from St Petersburg to Moscow, 1790) alerted Russians to the ways in which discharging conventional social roles perpetrates injustice, in particular, toward the peasantry. Among serfdom's costs he numbered: the destruction of natural equality under God, the 'crime' of destroying natural liberty, the diminution of economic growth and of the peasant population, the destruction of peasants' individual dignity, and the spread of arrogance among serf owners. In Radishchev's opinion, serfdom, being a departure from the natural human order, was bound to end badly, probably in a terrible uprising.

Radishchev argued that a just political system must be based on individual and collective virtue. The keys to such virtue were productive physical labour, the labour of the heart (exercising compassion) and mental labour (using reason to achieve self control). Not every society manages to construct a just political order, because custom, law and virtue often contradict one another. In his view, a virtuous citizen should respect custom in so far as custom is consistent with law, 'the lynchpin of society'. He saw law as universal in application, so that, if a monarch violated it, a citizen would be justified in disobeying the sovereign. In his 'Ode to Liberty' in *Journey*, Radishchev called freedom 'the source of all great deeds'. He bitterly attacked censorship, accusing the censors of keeping knowledge from the poor to the detriment of society as a whole. He saw no justifiable religious ground for maintaining censorship, and labelled the Church's role in its maintenance as 'shameful'. Although Radishchev was inspired by Masonry and by Voltairean Deism, his rhetoric was often biblical in inspiration. Indeed, his moral vocabulary owed as much to Orthodoxy as to secular sources.

Mikhail Mikhailovich Shcherbatov (1733–90) has sometimes been classified as eighteenth-century Russia's only Counter-Enlightenment thinker. In part, his reputation as a reactionary derived from his outspokenness at the 1767 Legislative Commission where he warned the government not to tamper with serf owners' privileges. The principal reason for his reputation has been the misreading of two extraordinary texts: *Puteshestvie v zemliu Ofirskuiu* (Journey to the Land of Ophir, written 1777–84) and *O povrezhdenii nravov v Rossii* (On Corruption of Morals in Russia, written 1786–7). *Journey to the Land of Ophir* described an ideal society strictly divided into classes or estates (*sosloviia*) – nobles serving the state, merchants dedicated to commerce, artisans pursuing crafts and peasants ploughing the land. Each estate enjoyed a system of schools delivering basic literacy, numeracy and the virtues appropriate to all subjects of the realm: self-discipline, compassion for others and respect for the law. At the heart of the ideal social order Shcherbatov placed the nobility, whom he imagined as officer-soldiers and state officials but also as elected representatives from each province. He projected legislative 'general meetings' of these representatives at the national level. The head of state was an emperor 'bound by the laws' and chastened by fear that, should he commit crimes in office, posterity would remember him ill. In *On Corruption of Morals in Russia* Shcherbatov used Muscovy as a yardstick for measuring contemporary Russia's moral dissolution. According to his account, the Muscovite grand prince had set the tone for society by personifying contempt for sensual pleasure (*slastoliubie*) – so that Muscovite court life was admirably austere. Peter the Great and his successors had abandoned virtue in favour of sensualism, so that by Catherine's time high society had been corrupted. Shcherbatov feared that 'corruption of the heart' would lead to 'corruption of reason' – to disastrous wars and ill-considered domestic policies. Although Shcherbatov referred repeatedly to the laws of God in his plea for virtue, he was less a Christian than a classical moralist, attracted to an impersonal code of virtues. An advocate of abstract virtue, he was closer in spirit to Fonvizin and Novikov than to later-day conservatives.

In the French Revolution's shadow: conservatism, constitutionalism and republicanism

Between 1789 and the early 1830s a distinctively Russian variant of conservatism began to emerge. A pivotal figure in its formation was the belletrist and historian Nikolai Mikhailovich Karamzin (1766–1826), a man called not only Russia's first conservative but its first political scientist as well. His most important political tract was *Zapiska o drevnei i novoi Rossii* (Memorandum on Ancient and Modern Russia, 1811), a document intended to dissuade Alexander I from instituting a Russian version of the *Code de Napoléon* and from abolishing serfdom. In it Karamzin contended that 'Russia was founded by military victories and by unitary government; it perished from division of authority and was saved by wise autocracy.'[11] He claimed that autocracy had long ago earned popular support, that the people 'felt no regrets for the ancient *veche* or for the dignitaries who tried to restrain the sovereign's authority'. During Ivan IV's tyranny, he asserted, 'neither the boiars nor the people had presumed to plot against him', proof that 'Russian virtue did not even hesitate in choosing between death and resistance.'[12] In identifying obedience and virtue,

11 R. Pipes (ed.), *Karamzin's Memoir on Ancient and Modern Russia: A Translation and Analysis* (New York: Atheneum, 1969) p. 110.

12 Pipes, *Karamzin's Memoir*, p. 113.

Karamzin attempted to delegitimise resistance to ungodly magistrates – a position that ignored the Muscovite moral consensus he purported to admire. In current circumstances, Karamzin advised Alexander to reject foreign-inspired reforms, particularly any division of sovereign authority between the tsar and State Council. He rejected serf emancipation on the ground that 'it is safer to enslave men than to give them freedom prematurely'.

Three other Aleksandrine conservatives were Aleksandr Semenovich Shishkov (1754–1841), Sergei Nikolaevich Glinka (1776–1847) and Aleksandr Skarlatovich Sturdza (1791–1854).

Shishkov's *Razsuzhdenie o starom i novom sloge rossiiskago iazyka* (Comments on the Ancient and Modern Style of the Russian Language, 1803) contended that Russian peasant dialects were rooted in ancient Church Slavonic and that the proximity to the old liturgical language tended to preserve among the common people Orthodox customs. He decried the modern Russian language spoken by the nobility, for it had been corrupted by foreign, irreligious influences that fostered vice among the social elites. In his *Razsuzhdenie o liubvi otechestva* (Treatise on Love of Fatherland, 1811–12), he rooted Russian national pride in Orthodoxy, in love of Russia's language and literature, and in civic education conducted not by foreigners but by Russians. Shishkov's conservatism, therefore, rested on linguistic nationalism, Orthodoxy and xenophobia.

Glinka's journal *Russkoi vestnik* (Russian Messenger) saluted pre-Petrine Russia for honouring 'its ancestral customs, its fatherland, its tsar and God', and it called on contemporary Russians to do the same. His *Zerkalo novago Parizha* (Mirror of Modern Paris, 1809) attributed the French Revolution to declining morals in the French court and among the provincial *noblesse.* It ascribed French decadence to an absence of Christian self-discipline and to a consequent fatal indulgence in worldly passions. By reminding educated Russians of Russia's glorious past and of the dangers of irreligion, Glinka encouraged them to abandon foreign vices for Orthodox virtues.

Sturdza was an adherent of Orthodoxy who attributed Europe's two great ills, despotism and liberalism, to Catholicism and Protestantism, respectively, but who called for a consortium of Christian confessions led by the Orthodox to prevent the spread of revolution across Europe. His ideal state was a Christian polity in which a strong monarch received wise advice from an advisory body of vigilant officials – something like the harmonious balance that had allegedly existed between Orthodox sovereign and his Muscovite subjects, with the key difference that Sturdza opposed resistance, passive or active, to an ungodly magistrate.

The task of generalising conservative ideas into a single political platform fell to Sergei Semenovich Uvarov (1786–1855), whose 1832 memorandum on Moscow University contained the formula: Orthodoxy, Autocracy, Nationality. Uvarov was a paradoxical figure who accepted the Enlightenment notions of historical progress and representative government, but who also understood liberty, equality and brotherhood as gifts from God that would appear gradually through organic evolution rather than through revolutionary change. He considered government's purpose to be provision of a secure environment for educating the people in religious virtue and the fruits of civilisation. To spread the wisdom of the ages, he thought, was to collaborate with Providence; to embrace false philosophy was to rebel against God, to shake the foundations of society and temporarily to reverse the ordained direction of history.

Aside from provoking a conservative reaction in Russia, the French Revolution engendered plans for reform from above. In 1809, Mikhail Mikhailovich Speranskii (1772–1839) prepared a series of memoranda on political reform, the most important of which was a draft introduction to a projected Russian law code. Although he carefully avoided describing the draft introduction as a constitution, that was its unmistakable purpose. In it Speranskii argued for a division of government into three branches: executive, judicial and legislative. He called for a multi-level, elective system of representation in which volosts, districts, provinces and the empire as a whole would select delegates to exercise oversight over the administrators of their respective jurisdictions. At the imperial level a State Duma (elected assembly) would be empowered to discuss laws proposed by the State Council. In discussing the prerogatives of citizens, Speranskii limited political rights to property owners, but made civil rights common to all Russian subjects. He called serfdom a violation of human nature and asked for its gradual abolition.

In 1818 Alexander ordered Nikolai Nikolaevich Novosil'tsev (1761–1836) to prepare a constitutional charter for Russia to be based partly on the Polish experience. Novosil'tsev's proposal, which underwent three redactions by the tsar, was entitled 'La Charte constitutionelle de l'Empire russe' (1820). Like Speranskii's plan, it divided the functions of government among three branches, and it also projected a legislature incorporating elected delegates from the various regions of Russia. Novosil'tsev proclaimed that all citizens would receive equal protection under the law, and his plan forbade arbitrary arrests and administrative punishments. His plan neither extended civil rights to the peasantry nor raised the prospect of abolishing serfdom. Novosil'tsev's plan differed from Speranskii's in two other respects. First, it contemplated a federal arrangement dividing the empire into vice regencies (*namestnichestva*) each with its own viceroy and vice-regal council. Second, it declared Orthodoxy the 'dominant faith of the empire' but promised not to oppress members of other creeds except for the Jews. The federalist element, nod toward religious toleration and the Jewish exclusion clause were part of Novosil'tsev's effort to contend with the empire's diversity.

Between Napoleon's defeat and Nicholas I's accession to the throne in December 1825 there developed a movement among patriotic army officers and nobles seeking to create in Russia a new active citizenry and a representative political order. In its first stages the movement focused on the inculcation of civic virtue through education and philanthropy; in its later stages it concentrated on political revolution. In the so-called Northern Society the most interesting thinker was Nikita Mikhailovich Murav'ev (1796–1843), the author of a *Proekt konstitutsii* (Draft Constitution, 1821–22) envisaging Russia as a federal republic. Murav'ev claimed that 'autocratic government is ruinous', and that 'it is incompatible with our holy religion's commandments and with common sense'.[13] He called for a division of Russia into thirteen states (*derzhavy*), each of which would elect state governments by ballot of property holders. At the national level there would be three branches of government, including a bicameral assembly with the right to pass laws over the emperor's veto. Murav'ev's constitution was influenced by the American constitution but also by his admiration for the Old Russian *veche* (popular assembly). In a short essay he handed to Karamzin himself, Murav'ev accused the conservative historian of preaching political quietism in the face of political evil. Murav'ev's answer to autocracy's imperfections was 'eternal struggle' against errors and vice.

In the Southern Society the dominant figure was Colonel Pavel Ivanovich Pestel' (1793–1826), whose constitutional plan *Russkaia Pravda* (Russian Law, 1824) was the most radical platform to appear in Russia before 1861. A fervent republican and great admirer of the French Jacobins, Pestel' was also an exclusivist Christian who treated the New Testament as the natural law foundation of a just society. In *Russian Law*, he proposed the elimination of social privileges based on property, abolition of serfdom, destruction of the monarchy, and institution of a 'provisional' dictatorship that would prepare the country for a republic. He also demanded the prohibition of any acts by non-Christian faiths 'contrary to the spirit of Christian law'. Although he declared himself willing to tolerate Islam and Judaism under certain conditions, he exhorted the revolutionary regime to proselytise Muslims to convert to Christianity.

13 *Izbrannye sotsial'no-politicheskie i filosofskie proizvedeniia dekabristov v trekh tomakh* (Moscow: Gos. izd. politicheskoi literatury, 1951), vol. I, p. 295.

He also warned Jews that, if they did not surrender their 'privileged' status, the government would 'assist' them to establish their own state 'somewhere in Asia Minor'.[14] Pestel' has often been called a forerunner of later-day egalitarian republicans, but it could be said with equal justice that he anticipated twentieth-century ethnic cleansers.

The Westerniser–Slavophile Debate

After the turn of the century but especially between 1826 and 1855 Russian intellectuals focused on the historical, religious and philosophical problem of Russian national identity. The reasons behind this shift of focus are complicated: on the one hand, strict censorship made it more difficult openly to debate contemporary policy, for even a hint of opposition to the government could result in unpleasant consequences for its critics; on the other hand, the parlous condition of the Holy Alliance in the wake of the Greek war for independence in the 1820s lent urgency to the process of redefining Russia's place in the universal political order. Aside from these external factors, Russian thinkers struggled to assimilate recent trends in Western European scholarship, especially the renascence of religious traditionalism and the ascendancy of philosophical idealism. Yet the most crucial immediate stimulus for rethinking the Russian question was the challenge to Russia's pride by Petr Iakovlevich Chaadaev (1794–1856) in his eight *Lettres philosophiques* (written 1828–31).

Stripped to its essentials, Chaadaev's view was that Russia had never been a historically significant community. In the 'First Philosophical Letter' he famously described Russians as rootless 'orphans with one foot in the air'. He attributed this anomie partly to Kievan barbarism, to Tatar cruelty, to Muscovite severity. In the 'Second Philosophical Letter' he criticised the Orthodox Church for permitting the perpetuation of serfdom, an institution that fatally divided Russians into masters and bondsmen. His main point, however, was that Russia had cut itself off from the Roman Catholic Church, which, in his opinion, had constructed in the West a genuine multinational community based on a deeply traditional, but also rational value system. In Chaadaev's opinion, the Catholic Church could be credited with eliminating serfdom in the West and with developing law codes recognising human dignity, but its largest achievement was the construction of a vital civilisation from which individuals and nations derived a shared identity.

14 M. Raeff, *The Decembrist Movement* (Englewood Cliffs: Prentice-Hall, 1966), pp. 145–6.

The most forceful response to Chaadaev came from the Slavophiles Aleksei Stepanovich Khomiakov (1804–60), Ivan Vasil'evich Kireevskii (1806–56) and Konstantin Sergeevich Aksakov (1817–60). Khomiakov's initial reaction to Chaadaev in the article, 'O starom i novom' (On the Old and the New, 1838), was to acknowledge the dark spots of early Russian history but also to note that Old Russian life 'had not been alien to human truth'. He claimed: 'the laws of justice and mutual love had served as the foundation of its almost patriarchal social order'.[15] In his remarkable short book, *Tserkov' odna* (The Church Is One, written 1844–5), Khomiakov depicted the Eastern Church as the community of all Christians – past, present and future – joined by divine grace and immune from doctrinal error. Aside from right teaching, the Eastern Church was sustained by an inner spirit, 'the living spirit of Christ', which did not inhabit the 'schismatic' confessions of the West. He held the Roman Church guilty of the 'pride of reason and of illegitimate power', and he ridiculed Protestants for their rationalism and liberalism. Thus, Khomiakov blunted Chaadaev's charges against Russia by arguing that the real, historically significant community had been constituted not in the West but in the East.

Kireevskii's clearest response to Chaadaev was his article,'O kharaktere prosveshcheniia Evropy i o ego otnoshenii k prosveshcheniiu Rossii' (On the Character of Europe's Enlightenment and Its Relationship to Russia's Enlightenment, 1852). In it he asserted that European thought's main consequence was 'virtually universal dissatisfaction and dashed hope'.[16] Western rationalism had fostered selfish individualism, the desire for conquest, a society divided into political factions, classes at war with one another and revolutionary destruction. Meanwhile, Russian life had been guided by the Eastern Church's harmonious outlook, by a search for 'inner rectitude', by a sense of 'natural proportion, dignity and humility testifying to spiritual balance and to depth and integrity of moral conscience'. Kireevskii believed Russian society, based on selflessness, mutual aid and Christian justice, to be immune from social revolution.

Aksakov's two essays titled 'Osnovnye nachala russkoi istorii' (Fundamental Principles of Russian History, 1860) argued that Russia was superior to the West. Whereas Western polities had been created by violent conquest, the Slavs had invited the Varangians to 'come and rule over us'; ever after the Russians had rightly regarded government as no better than a 'necessary evil'.

15 A. S. Khomiakov, *Polnoe sobranie sochinenii* (Moscow: Tip. Moskovskogo Universiteta, 1900), vol. III, pp. 28–9.
16 *Polnoe sobranie sochinenii I. V. Kireevskago v dvukh tomakh* (Moscow: Tip. T. Sakharova, 1911), vol. I, p. 176.

When Russia's rulers had behaved tyrannically, the Russian people had never rebelled against them, choosing instead to adhere silently to the inner truth of Christian humility. At times, Russia's rulers had received sage advice from the people gathered in assemblies of the land (*zemskie sobory*). Aksakov called on contemporary Russians to abandon inferior Western ways, to embrace again principles of Christian harmony that had animated Old Russia.

The Slavophiles' chief adversaries were the so-called Westernisers, a loose-knit network of intellectuals usually thought to include the literary critic Vissarion Grigor'evich Belinsky (1811–48), the historians Timofei Nikolaevich Granovskii (1813–55) and Sergei Mikhailovich Solov'ev (1820–79), the jurist Konstantin Dmitrievich Kavelin (1818–85), and the radical writers Alexander Ivanovich Herzen (1812–70) and Mikhail Aleksandrovich Bakunin (1814–76). Although the Westernisers recognised the distinctiveness of Russia's past, they still regarded Russia as a member of the European commonwealth, and therefore they insisted that its fate was bound to Europe.

Belinsky's article,'Rossiia do Petra Velikogo' (Russia before Peter the Great, 1842), argued that, among all existing cultures, only Europe had grown beyond the primitive stage of 'natural immediacy' into a fully conscious, 'world-historical civilisation'. The key to this startling development was the productive tension stemming from collisions among its various peoples and from its disparate cultural elements: for example, the clash between classical philosophy and Christianity had led to significant intellectual advances. Elsewhere the absence of dialectical tension had favoured stagnation rather than progress. Russia itself had escaped stasis only through the intervention of Peter the Great, 'a god who breathed a living soul into the colossal, sleeping body of ancient Russia'.[17] By so doing, Peter had bound Russia to European civilisation but had also made it possible for a distinctively Russian national identity (*natsional'nost'*) to emerge. Although the article stopped short of making political demands, Belinsky's criticism of Muscovy as a site of enforced slavery, segregation of women, violence, legal corruption and popular ignorance made clear his hopes for Europeanised Russia. Later, in his famous 'Pis'mo k Gogoliu' ('Letter to Gogol', 1847), he decried religious obscurantism and seigneurial oppression of serfs. By depicting Jesus as a rebel against social injustice, he strongly implied that serfs had the moral right to throw off their oppressors.

Granovskii, Kavelin and Solov'ev followed Belinsky in admiring Peter the Great and in regarding the Petrine reforms as a moment of convergence

17 V. G. Belinskii, *Polnoe sobranie sochinenii* (Moscow: Izd. AN SSSR, 1954), vol. V, p. 93.

between Russia and Europe. All predicted that, in the future, the enlightenment of the heretofore-benighted Russian people would enable individuals to join the educated classes and to enjoy the prospect of intellectual self-determination. Granovskii called this process of education the 'decomposition of the masses' into free, conscious individuals. Kavelin's long essay, 'Vzgliad na iuridicheskii byt drevnei Rossii' (Analysis of Juridical Life in Ancient Russia, 1847) argued that Russia had moved from a society based on varying degrees of blood ties (the tribe, clan or family) into a society organised on abstract legal principles (duty to the state, citizenship, status defined by law). The end of the process, in Russia as in Europe, would be the complete development of individuality (*lichnost'*). Kavelin implied that the abolition of serfdom and the establishment of representative government in Russia were inevitable. In his multi-volume *Istoriia Rossii s drevneishikh vremen* (History of Russia from Ancient Times, 1851–79) Solov'ev argued that Russia had evolved from a loose association of tribes into a modern state, based on shared religious and civic values and ruled by an enlightened government. Since Peter's reign, he contended, Russia had moved rapidly toward the same historical goals as Western Europeans. He did not subscribe to Belinskii's opinion that violence in the name of social progress was morally justified, rather he treated Russia's transformation as a case study in gradual evolution.

Herzen and Bakunin constituted the radical wing of the Westerniser movement. Herzen's essays, 'Diletantizm v nauke' (Dilettantism in Scholarship, 1843) and 'Pis'ma ob izuchenii prirody' (Letters on the Study of Nature, 1845) made the case that modern society stood on the verge of a new epoch in which the tyranny of abstractions that had characterised the Christian era would be displaced by a new philosophical synthesis between philosophical idealism and materialism: idealism would protect human beings against the demoralising impact of soulless science, and materialism would save individuals from slavery to monstrous dogmas. In his *Pis'ma iz Frantsii i Italii* (Letters from France and Italy, 1847–52) Herzen asserted that the new era could not begin until all Europe had been plunged into revolutionary destruction. He wrote: 'the contemporary political order along with its *civilisation* will perish; they will be *liquidated*'.[18] In the book *O razvitii revoliutsionnykh idei v Rossii* (On the Development of Revolutionary Ideas in Russia, 1851) he noted that Europeans, being wealthy, feared revolution, whereas Russians were 'freer of the past, because our own past is empty, poor and limited. Things like Muscovite

18 A. I. Gertsen, 'Pis'ma iz Italii i Frantsii', in *Sochineniia* (Moscow: Gos. izd. khudozhestvennoi literatury, 1956), vol. III, p. 221.

tsarism or the Petersburg emperorship it is impossible to love.'[19] He argued that Russians, with their love for bold experiments, might well lead the world toward socialism.

Bakunin's article, 'Die Reaktion in Deutschland' (The Reaction in Germany, 1842), claimed that the age of unfreedom would soon come to an end when the 'eternal spirit' of history finally destroyed the old European order. He rejected traditional Christianity in the name of a new 'religion of humanity', which, by expressing justice and love through liberty, would fulfill the highest commandment of Christ. Bakunin's pamphlet, *Vozzvanie k slavianam* (Appeal to the Slavs, 1848) demanded the Central European Slavs seek their independence from the Austrian empire. To liberate themselves from the German yoke, the Slavs would have either to wring concessions from the erstwhile masters or annihilate them as oppressors. In 1848–9 he began to suggest that the Russian people themselves lived under a 'German' yoke in the form of the Romanov dynasty. He forecast in Russia a popular revolution patterned on the Pugachev rebellion that would sweep away the 'German monarchy'. In *Ispoved'* (Confession, 1851), written in prison to Tsar Nicholas I, Bakunin admitted that he hoped to provoke 'A Slav war, a war of free, united Slavs against the Russian Emperor.'[20] The simultaneous emancipation of Slavs everywhere in Europe would make possible a Slavic confederation consisting of Russia, Poland, South Slavs and West Slavs.

In retrospect, the Westernisers shared love of liberty, but they did not define it in the same way. The moderates associated liberty with representative government and with virtually unfettered self-determination in the private sphere, while the radicals thought it the absence of all oppression – a definition that logically entailed the disappearance of government itself.

National identity, representative government and the market

The Great Reforms so altered Russian social and civil life as to radically affect subsequent political debates. As the long-standing discussion over ancient and modern Russia soon lost much of its salience, other questions quickly became urgent: whether the edifice of the Great Reforms would be 'crowned' by the addition of a European-style representative government at the imperial

19 A. I. Gertsen, *O razvitii revoliutsionnykh idei v Rossii*, in *Sochineniia* (Moscow: Gos. izd. khudozhestvennoi literatury, 1956), vol. III, p. 491.

20 *The Confession of Mikhail Bakunin*, trans. Robert C. Howes (Ithaca: Cornell University Press, 1977) p. 57.

level; whether Russia's economic transformation from serfdom to a market economy should be hastened by the abolition of the peasant commune and the creation of an urban working class on the English model; and whether in the political and economic realms the Russian ethnos should be privileged over non-Russian elements or whether the empire should be rebuilt on an egalitarian, multinational footing.

In the reform period Russian thinkers developed a range of political ideas that, at least superficially, resembled the right-to-left spectrum existing in continental Western European countries. Conservative thought built on Uvarov's formula – Orthodoxy, Autocracy, Nationality – but, under the threat of social instability, became more aggressive in its attitude toward non-Russian nationalities. Russian liberalism was, generally speaking, closer in spirit to European social liberalism than to classical liberalism, so most Russian liberals identified with the left rather than the centre or right. On the left populists, anarchists and social democrats vied for ascendancy.

The leading conservative thinkers of the post-reform period were the jurist Konstantin Petrovich Pobedonostsev (1827–1907), the journalist Mikhail Nikiforovich Katkov (1818–87), the Pan-Slav theoretician Nikolai Iakovlevich Danilevskii (1822–85), the diplomat Konstantin Nikolaevich Leont'ev (1831–91) and the novelist Fedor Mikhailovich Dostoevsky (1821–81).

Among Russian officials the most assertive conservative was Pobedonostsev, who tutored the last two Romanov tsars and served as procurator of the Holy Synod from 1880 to 1905. He was a critic of Western representative government and the Enlightenment whose antidote to those evils was strong central government and an assertive established Church. In an anthology entitled *Moskovskii sbornik* (Moscow Anthology) (1896), he described Rousseau's notion of popular sovereignty as 'the falsest of political principles'.[21] In practice, he contended, parliamentary institutions constituted the 'triumph of egoism': they were bodies that promised to represent the will of the people but which actually did the bidding of a handful of wilful leaders and served as pliant instruments of political factions. Western public opinion was ruled not by reason but by lying journalists who manipulated an idle public characterised 'by base and despicable hankering for idle amusement'.[22]

Outside the government the dominant conservative of the early reform era was Katkov whose journals *Russkii vestnik* (Russian Courier), *Sovremmennaia letopis'* (Contemporary Chronicle) and *Moskovskie vedomosti* (Moscow Courier)

21 K. P. Pobedonostsev, *Reflections of a Russian Statesman* (Ann Arbor: University of Michigan Press, 1965), p. 32.

22 Ibid., pp. 65–6.

strongly influenced state policy. Katkov made his reputation as patriot during the Polish uprising of 1863–4, when he demanded the military suppression of the Poles on the ground that 'any retreat . . . would be a death certificate for the Russian people'.[23] He described the political monopoly of Russians within the empire 'not as coercion . . . but a law of life and logic'.[24] In 1867, he called for the introduction of Russian language into schools in Estonia and for the elimination of traditional Baltic German privileges in the area – a harbinger of the Russification policies pursued by Alexander III after 1881. In foreign policy Katkov was a Realpolitiker, who sometimes raised the banner of Pan-Slavism against Germany and Austria, but who always made it clear that Russian interests took priority over those of other Slavic peoples.

In *Rossiia i Evropa* (Russia and Europe, 1869) Danilevskii elaborated a theory of historical types claiming that ten distinctive civilisations had appeared in the past. He considered the European or 'Germano-Romanic' civilisation as the latest to reach world dominance, but he regarded the industrial stage into which that civilisation had evolved as proof of its decline. He predicted that Slavdom would constitute the eleventh great civilisation in world history. The Slavic peoples would be brought together by Russia, through the conquest of Istanbul and the destruction of Austro-German power in Europe. To achieve these objectives, Russians would have to subordinate themselves to the centralised state, for only by the merciless execution of the state's divine mission would the past bloodshed of Russian history be redeemed.

In a remarkable book, *Vizantizm i slavianstvo* (Byzantinism and Slavdom, 1873), Leont'ev defined the earmarks of Byzantinism as: autocracy, Orthodoxy, a disinclination to overvalue the individual, an inclination to disparage the ideal of earthly happiness, rejection of the notion that human beings can achieve moral perfection on earth, and rejection of the hope that the universal welfare of all peoples can be attained. He argued that the historic vitality of Russia was directly related to Russians' loyalty to autocracy, faith in Orthodoxy, and acceptance of earthly inequality – all 'Byzantine' traits. He celebrated Peter the Great and Catherine the Great precisely because their reforms increased social inequality, thereby making possible the flowering of a creative, 'aristocratic' culture among the nobility. He warned that modern-day Russians faced a crucial choice: either to maintain their distinctive, hierarchically based national culture; or to 'subordinate themselves to Europe in the pursuit of [material]

23 Quoted in K. Durman, *The Time of the Thunderer: Mikhail Katkov, Russian Nationalist Extremism and the Failure of the Bismarckian System, 1871–1887* (Boulder: Columbia University Press, 1988), p. 56.

24 Durman, *Time of the Thunderer*, p. 62.

progress'. To follow the second option would be disastrous, for it would risk Russia's survival for the false religion of human felicity on earth. Although Leont'ev recognised the tribal connections between Russians and other Slavs, he did not think common blood or similarity of languages to be adequate foundations for Slavic political unity. In view of his scepticism toward the other Slavs, Leont'ev cannot be regarded as a Pan-Slav of the Danilevskii type.

Dostoevsky's conservatism was predicated on opposition to Western liberalism and socialism, on hostility to individualism and capitalism, on rejection of Catholicism and religious authoritarianism in any form, on opposition to movements inimical to Russia – nihilism, Polish nationalism, Jewish separatism and feminist radicalism. In his fiction he balanced his many antipathies by applauding the religiosity of common Russian people, the wisdom of saintly monastic elders and the fabled capacity of Russians from every social stratum to embrace suffering. Although Dostoevsky the novelist was self-evidently an anti-nihilist, a conservative nationalist, a partisan of Orthodoxy and the Great Russian ethnos, his fictional politics were less programmatic than the positions taken by his publishers, Katkov and the gentry reactionary Prince Vladimir Petrovich Meshcherskii (1839–1914). However, Dostoevsky's journalistic writing, particularly his *Dnevnik pisatelia* (*Diary of a Writer*, 1873–81), was lamentably clear. In March 1877, for example, he predicted: 'Sooner or later Constantinople will be ours.'[25] That same month, in a series of articles on the Jewish question, he accused the Jews of material greed, of hostility toward Russians, of constituting themselves a 'state within a state'. Later, in his June 1880 speech at the Pushkin monument in Moscow, he issued a call for 'universal human brotherhood' based on Russians' disposition to 'bring about universal unity with all tribes of the great Aryan race'.[26] Although his auditors received the speech well, sober readers found his messianic nationalism and religious exclusivism disturbing.

Among Russian liberals the four most interesting thinkers were the classical liberal Boris Nikolaevich Chicherin (1828–1904), the philosopher Vladimir Sergeevich Solov'ev (1853–1900), the social liberal Pavel Nikolaevich Miliukov (1859–1943) and the right liberal Petr Berngardovich Struve (1870–1944).

Chicherin began his intellectual career as a moderate Westerniser. In his earliest political writing, the article 'Sovremmennye zadachi russkoi zhizni' (Contemporary Tasks of Russian Life, 1856), he championed the abolition

25 F. M. Dostoevskii, 'Eshche raz o tom, chto Konstantinopol', rano li, pozdno li, a dolzhen byt' nash', *Dnevnik pisatelia za 1877 god*, in *Polnoe sobranie sochinenii* (Leningrad: Nauka, 1983), vol. XXVI, pp. 65–6.

26 F. M. Dostoevskii, 'Pushkin', *Polnoe sobranie sochinenii*, vol. XXVI, p. 147.

of serfdom and the introduction of civil liberties (freedoms of conscience, of speech and press, academic freedom, public judicial proceedings, publicity of all governmental activities) in Russia. In his book, *O narodnom predstavitel'stve* (On Popular Representation, 1866), however, he explained why he thought Russia was yet unprepared for constitutional government. Pointing to the practical flaws of representative institutions and the falsity of Rousseau's theory of popular sovereignty, he argued that representative governments are workable only in 'healthy' societies with some experience of civil liberties, and only when the voting franchise is limited to educated property owners. This sharp distinction between civil and political liberties was a hallmark of Chicherin's thinking.

In the late 1870s Chicherin undertook a systematic study of German socialism. His trenchant critique of Marx's *Das Kapital* was a cardinal contribution to Russian social thought, a rare defence of free markets against their increasingly vociferous enemies. His book, *Sobstvennost' i gosudarstvo* (Property and the State, 1882–3), was nineteenth-century Russia's most erudite attempt to identify entrepreneurial freedom as an essential civil liberty. In the book Chicherin pointed to the incommensurability of individual liberty with social equality. He warned contemporaries against the danger of 'a new monster', – namely, intrusive society, which threatened to 'swallow both the state and the private sphere'.[27] His book, *Filosofiia prava* (Philosophy of Law, 1900), criticised legal theories that, in the name of morality or utility, would take away individual rights for some appealing social end. Chicherin's philosophical legacy was his conception of individual freedom from constraint by others, in so far as that liberty is compatible with others' freedom, as the sole and original right that belongs to every human being by virtue of his or her humanity. His political legacy can be found in the anonymous pamphlet, *Rossiia nakanune dvadtsatogo stoletiia* (Russia on the Eve of the Twentieth Century, 1900), in which he predicted the imminent end of Russian absolutism and demanded the addition of elected delegates to the imperial State Council. Miliukov called Chicherin's proposal 'the minimum demand of Russian liberalism'.

Solov'ev began his intellectual life as a religious philosopher in the Slavophile tradition, yet he made two signal contributions to liberalism. First, in his remarkable *Natsional'nyi vopros v Rossii* (National Question in Russia, 1883–91), he made the case for setting nationality policy on a genuinely Christian foundation. He demanded that state officials take seriously the moral duties of Russia toward non-Russian groups by making a voluntary act of 'national

27 B. N. Chicherin, *Sobstvennost' i gosudarstvo* (Moscow, 1882), vol. I, pp. xix–xx.

self-denial' – that is, by renouncing the dangerous principle of Russian exclusivity and dominance over others. This self-renunciation would require Russians not only to tolerate non-Orthodox peoples, but to build a community in which they were equal members. His irenic interpretation of Christianity provided a theoretical basis for pluralism and equality among the empire's peoples. Second, he insisted that Christianity requires recognition of the individual's right to a dignified material existence. In his system of ethics, *Opravdanie dobra* (Justification of the Good, 1897), he argued against classical liberalism that private property must never be assigned an absolute ethical value, that the exploitation of nature must be limited by 'love of nature for its own sake', and that the freedom of economic consumption must be subordinated to ethically defensible principles.

A distinguished historian and thoroughgoing positivist who accepted Auguste Comte's three-stage theory of human social development, Miliukov anticipated that the spread of science in Russia would mean the liberation of its people from religious prejudice and exclusive nationalism. His three-volume *Ocherki po istorii russkoi kul'tury* (Essays on the History of Russian Culture, 1896–1900) argued that critical social consciousness was gradually displacing national consciousness as the dominant force in Russia. The book implied that this historical evolution was creating the basis for popular representative government in the empire. Miliukov's political ideal was progressive social legislation and constitutional monarchy, wherein the monarch's authority would be balanced by an elected legislature. Under Russian conditions, he argued, that ideal might be attained through the practical co-operation of socialists and liberals. Repeatedly during the revolutionary crisis from 1904–7 he countenanced from the left 'direct action', including terrorism, for the sake of undermining the government. To counter Great Russian nationalism, he recommended the redrawing of internal administrative jurisdictions along ethnic borders, but he stopped short of advocating a federal solution to ethnic disputes. As his *Istoriia vtoroi russkoi revoliutsii* (History of the Second Russian Revolution, 1918–21) made clear, Miliukov lived to regret his alliance with the revolutionary left and also his attempts to encourage nationalist consciousness among minority peoples.

Not all Russian liberals in the duma period followed Miliukov's 'new liberalism' or his policy of 'no enemies to the left'. In the anti-revolutionary polemic *Vekhi* (Signposts, 1909), Struve posited that the revolutionary gospel had led in practice to 'licentiousness and demoralisation'. Once a social democrat, Struve joined the right wing of the Constitutional Democratic party, declaring himself a partisan of Chicherin's theory of individual rights. In internal politics he defended the equitable treatment of national minorities but under the proviso that Great Russians remain the empire's dominant ethnos. In foreign policy he supported expansion of Russian influence in the Balkans, for the empire's destiny as a great power was in the south. The irony of a Russian liberal assuming a 'Pan-Slav' perspective on nationality and foreign policy could not be more striking. Struve's grand design was to reconcile Russian liberalism to a strong centralised state and to an assertive international policy – that is, to pursue a policy of national liberalism not unlike that adopted by the German national liberals in the Bismarck period.

Among Russian socialists there were three main currents of political thinking: populism, built on hostility toward capitalism, on the idealisation of the urban guild (*artel'*) and of the peasant land commune (*obshchina* or *mir*); anarchism, focused on the abolition of state power; and social democracy, oriented toward the destruction of market relations and the eventual elimination of bourgeois democracy.

Among the populists the leading figures were the 'enlightener' (*prosvetitel'*) or 'nihilist' Nikolai Gavrilovich Chernyshevsky (1828–89), and the 'classical populists' Petr Lavrovich Lavrov (1823–1900), Nikolai Konstantinovich Mikhailovsii (1842–1904) and Petr Nikitich Tkachev (1844–86).

Chernyshevsky rejected traditional Christianity in the name of the new 'religion of humanity' that would establish earthly justice based on material equality and gender equity. His ethical system of 'rational egoism' judged the virtue of human actions according to the benefits they would bring not to the individual but to the majority of society. His novel, *Chto delat'?* (*What Is to Be Done?*, 1863), described the heroism of young people who, being rational egoists, emancipate themselves from slavery to social conventions. Superficially, the story was a narrative of consciousness-raising and women's liberation, but its meta-narrative posited a mysterious revolutionary elite whose sudden disappearances, commitments to outrageous actions (faked suicides, approval of euthanasia, vigilante justice) and deliberately obscure leadership hierarchy were meant to teach readers the ethics and modus operandi of revolutionary conspiracy. This elitism captured the imaginations of progressive readers, including the young Lenin, who confessed that the book 'ploughed a deep furrow' in him.

Lavrov's essay 'Ocherki teorii lichnosti' (Outlines of a Theory of Personality, 1859), contended that the most important aspect of human consciousness is free will, that critically thinking individuals express free will in society by seeking justice for all, and that social justice requires the abolition of property as an affront to human dignity. This ethical perspective constituted the skeleton of Lavrov's book, *Istoricheskie pis'ma* (Historical Letters, 1868–9), which identified the goal of history as 'the physical, intellectual, and moral development of the individual, and the incorporation of truth and justice in social institutions'.[28] Lavrov regretted that no existing society had fulfilled this formula, for everywhere critically thinking individuals were in a small minority, able to effect social change only on the margins. Even the existence of these few justice seekers had cost humanity dearly: 'Progress for a small minority was purchased at the price of enslaving the majority, depriving it of the chance to acquire the same bodily and mental skills which constituted the dignity of the representatives of civilization.'[29] Lavrov's argument that, in Russia, critically thinking individuals had a moral responsibility to the suffering masses helped mobilise 'repentant nobles' of the 1870s to join the socialist movement.

Mikhailovskii attacked Western industry for its dependence on specialised labour, which inhibited workers from developing all sides of their personality. In contrast, he noted, Russian communal peasants performed a variety of agricultural tasks, from sowing and reaping to constructing houses, in the process exercising their minds as well as bodies. Building on that simple juxtaposition, his article 'Chto takoe progress?' (What Is Progress?, 1869), elaborated his famous definition: 'Progress is the gradual approach to the integral individual, the fullest possible and most diversified division of labour among an individual's organs and the least possible division of labour among individuals.'[30] The article rejected Herbert Spencer's view that there is a positive correlation between modern technological sophistication and individual happiness, and it sided with Marx's moral critique of industrial specialisation and worker alienation.

The goal of annihilating individualism was at the centre of Tkachev's political agenda. His article 'Chto takoe partiia progressa?' (What Is the Party of Progress?, 1870), defined progress as 'the fullest possible equality of individuals' – that is, 'organic physiological equality stemming from the same education and from identical conditions of life'.[31] Because individual needs will vary and most societies are too impoverished to satisfy those needs, Tkachev advocated strict limitation of individual demands on material resources. In his socialist collective, there would be no adjustments in distribution of goods

28 P. Lavrov, *Historical Letters*, trans. James P. Scanlan (Berkeley and Los Angeles: University of California Press, 1967), p. 111.

29 Lavrov, *Historical Letters*, p. 133.

30 N. K. Mikhailovskii, *Polnoe sobranie sochinenii v desiati tomakh* (St Petersburg: Tip. M. M. Stasiulevicha, 1908), vol. I, p. 150.

31 P. N. Tkachev, *Sochineniia v dvukh tomakh* (Moscow: Izd. sotsial'no-ekonomicheskoi literatury, 1975), vol. I, p. 508.

to accommodate differences in age, gender, personality or occupation. In his journal *Nabat* (The Tocsin, 1875) Tkachev demanded that Russian radicals band together to launch an immediate revolution. Peasants would be led by determined conspirators, who would destroy 'the immediate enemies of the revolution', seize state power, then 'lay the basis for a new rational social life'. After the revolution Tkachev imagined a generation-long dictatorship that would construct anew 'all our economic, juridical, social, private, family relations, all our viewpoints and understandings, our ideals and our morality'.[32]

The populists hoped to avoid or curtail capitalist development in Russia. In 1859 Chernyshevsky raised the prospect that Russia, by studying the experience of more advanced Western societies, might be able to skip 'intermediate phases of development' between the communal order and socialism. He pleaded with Russians: 'Let us not dare attack the common use of the land.'[33] Tkachev's outlook on the question derived from reading Marx's *Zur Kritik der politischen Oekonomie*, from which he concluded that a socialist revolution could be made to occur in Russia either after capitalism had fully developed or before it had developed at all. In 1874, in his 'Otkrytoe pis'mo F. Engel'su' (Open Letter to F. Engels), he argued that the Russian bourgeoisie and capitalist relations were so weak that they could be easily eradicated. In 1877 Mikhailovskii rejected Marxist determinism on the grounds that it would compel Russians to accept 'the maiming of women and children' entailed by capitalism; it was morally preferable, he thought, to resist 'inevitable' capitalism in the hope that socialism could be built on the foundation of the commune.

The three principal anarchist thinkers were Mikhail Aleksandrovich Bakunin, Petr Kropotkin (1842–1921) and Lev Nikolaevich Tolstoy (1828–1911).

Bakunin's major anarchist writings were *Fédéralisme, socialisme et antithéologisme* (1868), *L'Empire knouto-germanique et la révolution sociale* (1870–1) and *Étatisme et anarchie* (1873). In the first text Bakunin attacked religion as a prop of the existing political order, rejected centralised government as inimical to liberty and defended a 'bottom-up' federalist organisation of society. Soon after writing it, he fell into rivalry with Marx over the control of the International Working Men's Association. In September 1868 Bakunin pronounced communism 'the negation of liberty . . . because communism concentrates and swallows up in itself for the benefit of the state all the forces in society'.[34]

32 Quoted in D. Hardy, *Petr Tkachev, the Critic as Jacobin* (Seattle: University of Washington Press, 1977) p. 275.

33 Quoted in A. Walicki, *The Controversy over Capitalism: Studies in the Social Philosophy of the Russian Populists* (Oxford: Clarendon Press, 1969), p. 19.

34 Quoted in E. H. Carr, *Michael Bakunin* (London: Macmillan, 1937), p. 341.

In his view, the Marxian principle 'from each according to his work, to each according to his need' would require an external mechanism of surveillance and distribution – a state apparatus – that would destroy liberty. In the name of liberating human beings from material want and establishing scientific socialism, Marx would set up a government that 'cannot fail to be impotent, ridiculous, inhuman, cruel, oppressive, exploiting, maleficent'.

In *The Knouto-Germanic Empire and the Social Revolution* Bakunin adopted Feuerbach's theory of God as a psychic projection of human virtues whose 'existence' impoverishes and enslaves human beings. According to Bakunin, the courage to dissent from God, to embrace materialism and therefore liberty, comes to human beings from our two highest faculties: the ability to think and the desire to rebel. He took the original rebel, Satan, as his literary inspiration. How did Bakunin expect 'Satanic' materialists to provoke a revolution in Christian Russia? Following Belinsky, he contended that the religiosity of Russian peasants was superficial, and he thought it could give way at any moment to the peasants' instinctive rebelliousness. The anarchists' task was to arouse within the peasantry the slumbering spirit of outlawry. He insisted that anarchists not *impose* revolution on the masses but *provoke* it, seeing in this policy a major difference with Marx.

Kropotkin sought a theoretical foundation for 'scientific anarchism'. In the revolutionary manifesto, *Dolzhny-li my zaniatsia rassmotreniem ideala budushchego stroia?* (Should We Devote Ourselves To Analysing the Ideal of the Future Order?, 1873), and in his major books *La Conquête du pain* (1892) and *Mutual Aid* (1904), he elaborated that theory. In the manifesto Kropotkin argued that social equality cannot be achieved if the means of production remain in private hands, nor can equality be reached if property falls under state control, for that would mean the tyranny of some self-appointed body over workers. The state apparatus would have to be destroyed and the power decentralised in local federations, each based on a network of communes and guilds. In *The Conquest of Bread*, Kropotkin argued against Marx that a just society must not be based on the principle, 'from each according to his work, to each according to his needs'. Taking the product of workers' labour would require the establishment of a supervisory body to monitor labour and confiscate the goods produced by it, to the detriment of liberty. In place of such a bureaucratic approach, Kropotkin projected a voluntary arrangement whereby workers would contribute five hours per day to satisfy collective needs, but would retain the right to do additional labour to produce luxury goods for themselves. Thus, his mature social philosophy entailed social ownership of the means of production, but not the elimination of all private property.

In *Mutual Aid* Kropotkin criticised those followers of Charles Darwin who saw competition as the motor of evolution. According to Kropotkin, animal species, including human beings, are less likely to survive through pitiless competition than through mutual aid. Early societies had been based on co-operation in the clan, commune, guild and free city, but unfortunately the rise of the state had destroyed those free institutions. Kropotkin now expected the peoples of Europe to overthrow centralised government, thus liberating the submerged principle of mutual aid.

The immediate cause of Tolstoy's conversion to anarchism was the decision, following his spiritual crisis from 1876 to 1878, to rethink his religious principles. In *Ispoved'* (Confession, 1879) he described his painful realisation that the simple Christian faith of the peasantry constituted a more viable world-view than the selfish rationalism to which he and his privileged peers had adhered. In *V chem moia vera?* (What I Believe), Tolstoy set out his own interpretation of Christianity, based on reading the evangelist Matthew's account of the Sermon on the Mount. He reduced Jesus's message to five commands: 'Do not be angry, do not commit adultery, do not swear oaths or judge your neighbors, do not resist evil by evil, and do not have enemies.' He interpreted the injunction against oaths as a justification for refusing to pledge loyalty to the tsar and state. He saw in the command to 'resist not evil' an ethical prohibition against state violence of any kind. The order not to have enemies he understood as a directive not to divide peoples into states. His book *Tsarstvo Bozhie vnutri vas* (The Kingdom of God Is Within You, 1893) rejected the term 'Christian state' as a contradiction, classified universal history as a 'pagan epoch' and spoke of human progress as 'the conscious assimilation of the Christian theory [of nonviolence]'.[35] He described the modern conscript army as a barbarous institution, and he held up modern patriotism as a vicious lie. His anarchism started with the ethical individual refusing to acknowledge the right to shed blood or use force.

Among social democrats the key political thinkers were the classical Marxist and Menshevik Georgii Valentinovich Plekhanov (1856–1918), the Legal Marxist Petr Berngardovich Struve (1870–1944), the internationalist Lev Davidovich Bronshtein (Trotsky) (1879–1940), the Bolshevik theoretician Vladimir Il'ich Ulianov (Lenin) (1870–1924) and the futurologist Aleksandr Aleksandrovich Malinovskii (Bogdanov) (1873–1928).

35 L. Tolstoy, *The Kingdom of God Is Within You: Christianity Not as a Mystic Religion But as a New Theory of Life*, trans. Constance Garnett (Lincoln and London: University of Nebraska Press, 1984) p. 247.

Plekhanov, the 'father of Russian Marxism', began his revolutionary career as a populist. In *Sotsializm i politicheskaia bor'ba* (Socialism and the Political Struggle, 1883) and *Nashi raznoglasiia* (Our Differences, 1885) he explained his break with that movement. Both books criticised Lavrov for not understanding that the overthrow of the Russian monarchy by a bourgeois constitutional regime would be a progressive step. They also criticised Tkachev for imagining that a revolutionary minority could initiate a socialist revolution in feudal Russia, and they warned that a premature socialist revolution would lead to monstrous dictatorship. For socialists the only realistic immediate goal was 'the conquest of free political institutions and making preparations for the formation of a future Russian workers' socialist party'.[36] Plekhanov assumed that skipping stages of historical development is impossible. Interpreting Marx as a historical determinist, he stressed the necessity of capitalism as a preliminary to socialism. Not surprisingly, he defined freedom as co-operation with the laws of history.

The Legal Marxists rejected Plekhanov's historical determinism and again unlike Plekhanov classified political freedoms as valuable in themselves, not just as stepping stones on the path to socialism. In the book *Kriticheskie zametki k voprosu ob ekonomicheskom razvitii Rossii* (Critical Observations on the Economic Development of Russia, 1894), Struve made the case against Marx's theory of the inevitable impoverishment of the working class and in favour of evolutionary socialism – a position that anticipated the conclusions of the German revisionists. In his article, 'Die Marxsche Theorie der sozialen Entwicklung' (Marx's Theory of Social Development, 1899), he endorsed Eduard Bernstein's idea that socialism may emerge from capitalism non-violently, by slow degrees. By the turn of the century, under pressure from Lenin, Struve had begun to turn away from Marxism. In his essay for the anthology *Problemy idealizma* (Problems of Idealism, 1902) Struve criticised social democrats for their simplistic historical determinism and dismissal of universal ethics – a conclusion that signalled his transition to liberalism.

Lenin came to Marxism under the influence of Chernyshevsky's elitism and Tkachev's Blanquism. These sources reinforced his innate wilfulness, contributing significantly to his subsequent historical voluntarism. In his earliest Marxist work Lenin attacked Struve's book on Russian economic development by insisting that Marxism is not just a sociological hypothesis but a theory of revolutionary struggle. In *Zadachi russkikh sotsial-demokratov* (Tasks

36 G. V. Plekhanov, *Sotsializm i politicheskaia bor'ba. Nashi raznoglasiia* (Moscow: OGIZ-Gos. izd. politicheskoi literatury, 1939), p. 65.

of Russian Social Democrats, 1898) he endorsed Plekhanov's strategy of making alliances with bourgeois opponents of the autocracy but emphasised that Social Democrats must take advantage of these alliances for their own purposes. He was impatient with Plekhanov's necessitarian Marxism, which linked social democracy too closely to the pursuit of bourgeois freedoms. His most important early book, *Razvitie kapitalizma v Rossii* (Development of Capitalism in Russia, 1899), argued that, in rural Russia, capitalism had already led to the social differentiation of the peasantry. That simple conclusion was both a blow against neo-populists, who imagined that Russia might still avoid capitalism, and a theoretical basis for a future revolutionary alliance between the proletariat and poor peasants against the bourgeoisie.

Lenin's pivotal book *Chto delat'?* (*What Is to Be Done?*, 1902), laid out his theory of the vanguard party. He stated: 'the history of all countries shows that the working class, exclusively by its own effort, is able to develop only trade-union consciousness'.[37] In his opinion, social democratic consciousness could only be brought to workers 'from without', by members of a tightly organised, centralised party of professional revolutionaries. Although other Marxists had advocated strong revolutionary leadership, Lenin was the first to contend that, absent the guidance of the revolutionary vanguard, the working class could develop only bourgeois consciousness. In the wake of *What Is to Be Done?*, Plekhanov accused Lenin of mocking Marx's belief in socialism's inevitability. Trotsky warned of the prospect that Lenin's theory of the party might lead Russia to permanent 'Jacobin' dictatorship: eventually, he wrote, the 'organization of the party takes the place of the party; the Central Committee takes the place of the organization; and finally the dictator takes the place of the Central Committee'.[38] Later it became clear that *What Is to Be Done?* was a first step toward a party ideocracy, a system of government in which the party, conceived as the source of historically privileged knowledge, imposed its will in all spheres of culture.

After he elaborated the theory of the vanguard party, Lenin developed two other crucial ideas. First, he moved toward a theory of nationality policy in which he opposed 'any attempt to influence national self-determination [among non-Russian peoples of the empire] from without by violence or coercion', and simultaneously limited the expression of the right to

37 V. I. Lenin, *What Is to Be Done? Burning Questions of Our Movement* (New York: International Publishers, 1969), p. 31.

38 Trotsky's prophecy, from his pamphlet *Our Political Tasks*, is discussed in Leszek Kolakowski, *Main Currents of Marxism, Vol. II: The Golden Age* (Oxford and New York: Oxford University Press, 1978), p. 408.

self-determination to those cases in which self-determination was in the interests of social democrats.[39] In effect, he made national self-determination contingent on permission from the party vanguard. Second, he incorporated into his own theory of socialist revolution Trotsky's idea of 'permanent revolution', which held that, due to the weakness of the Russian bourgeoisie, the Russian proletariat would have to lead the bourgeois revolution and that, therefore, the bourgeois revolution could be transformed into a socialist revolution in one continuous process. According to Trotsky, the Russian proletariat was numerically too weak to hold power for long unless it received assistance from the West, but he felt that the revolution in Russia might provide a 'spark' to ignite a general revolution in Western Europe. When combined with Lenin's idea of contingent national self-determination, Trotsky's idea of permanent revolution produced the curious result that Russia was both a subordinate part of a universal process of historical change and the director / initiator of that process. In other words, revolutionary Russia could be understood simultaneously as 'of Europe' and as 'apart from Europe'.

Lenin's crowning work was *Gosudarstvo i revoliutsiia* (State and Revolution, 1917). Taking the experience of the Paris Commune as his guide, Lenin asserted that a socialist revolution should entail the ruthless destruction of the old, bourgeois administrative machinery by the armed masses and the insertion in its place of a proletarian dictatorship. He imagined that, in the socialist state, workers themselves would execute most governmental functions, for simple 'bookkeeping' could be done by any literate person. For as long as the proletarian state remained in power it would exercise the strongest possible control over production and consumption and would maintain its vigilance over the remnants of the bourgeoisie. Only at the end of the socialist stage, after an equitable scheme of economic distribution had been established and after class antagonism had been annihilated, would the state begin to 'wither away', as Marx had predicted. Nowhere in *State and Revolution* did Lenin enumerate protections for individual liberty, for he was interested only in the workers' collective freedom from want.

It is valuable to compare Lenin's view of the socialist state to that of Bogdanov, the most prolific philosopher among the early Bolsheviks. In his science fiction novel *Krasnaia zvezda* (Red Star, 1908) Bogdanov imagined communism as a stateless order wherein individual workers would select their jobs based on statistical employment projections, and citizens would be clothed androgynously, be fed manufactured rations and be offered free medical care.

39 Quoted in Kolakowski, *Main Currents*, vol. II, p. 400.

Simultaneously, however, Bogdanov projected a desperate collective effort to keep social production ahead of population growth, technology ahead of nature, and the human spirit ahead of satiation and depression. He was suggesting that communism would not constitute the end of history after all. Moreover, *Red Star* depicted within 'stateless' communism a directorate of intellectuals, an exclusive group of scientific experts, who would make society's most crucial decisions. In Bogdanov's prophetic reckoning, the socialist state as a formal legal entity might dissolve only to re-emerge in a new, supralegal form.

7

Russia and the legacy of 1812

ALEXANDER M. MARTIN

Russia stood at a historical crossroads when it experienced the trauma of the 1812 Napoleonic invasion. Like Germany's 1813 *Befreiungskrieg* and Spain's 1808–14 *Guerra de independencia*, Russia's *Otechestvennaia voina* – War for the Fatherland – became the stuff of ambiguous patriotic legend.

Speaking for many who saw 1812 as a unique opportunity to transcend Russia's bitter internal divisions, Leo Tolstoy argued in *War and Peace* that the heroes of the war had been the Russians of all social classes whose deep roots in Russian culture and spirituality made them selflessly patriotic and intolerant of social injustice, but also generous towards their nation's defeated enemies. Tolstoy's villains, by contrast, were 'Westernised' aristocrats, cynical cowards whose shrill wartime xenophobia reflected the same spiritual rootlessness and disdain for their own people that had also conditioned their pre-war Francophilia. According to this vision, the 'War for the Fatherland' had proved the Russian people's civic maturity and ought to have been followed by Russia's transformation into a liberal nation-state. Tolstoy's original idea for the novel had actually centred on the liberal Decembrist uprising of 1825 against the autocracy, a blow for freedom that he and many others regarded as a natural outgrowth of 1812. Of course, that coup had failed, and Russia remained a dynastic, autocratic, serf-based empire; as collective memories, however, the war and the Decembrist revolt raised Russians' national consciousness and created an impetus to expand the realm of human freedom and dignity that was often suppressed but never snuffed out.

This liberal nationalist reading of the war contains an element of historical truth and is itself a part of history thanks to its place in Russian society's cultural consciousness, but it should not hide from view the more illiberal aspects of the legacy of 1812. Like the Second World War and the collapse of the Soviet

I thank Olavi Arens, Mariia Degtiareva, Janet Hartley, Deniel Klenbort, Dominic Lieven, Michael Melancon and Katya Vladimirov, for their helpful comments on an earlier version of this chapter.

system in the early 1990s, it gave Russians the heady sensation of witnessing a turning point in history, thereby encouraging a sense of empowerment and a long-term quest for emancipation. However, also like those other traumas, it too convinced many Russians of their own vulnerability in the face of vast, malevolent forces, and that only a stern, authoritarian order could shield them against foreign hostility and the brittleness of their own social order. This chapter will develop that argument by discussing the challenges Russia faced on the eve of the war; the war's contribution to a xenophobic and reactionary nationalism, a reflexive social conservatism, and what might be called (to borrow Richard Hofstadter's phrase) 'the paranoid style in Russian politics';[1] and the efforts to use an authoritarian religiosity and militarism as tools for post-war state-building and for closing the social fault lines exposed by the war.

Russian culture and society before 1812

At the turn of the century, Russian elite culture faced three main challenges.

One involved the meaning of 'Russianness'. Cultural Europeanisation had given the elite an identity separate from everyone else's; as Richard Wortman has argued, 'by displaying themselves as foreigners, or like foreigners, Russian monarchs and their servitors affirmed the permanence and inevitability of their separation from the population they ruled'.[2] The regime had also sketched out ambitious imperial projects, from Peter I's dream of making Russia *the* trade route between Europe and the Orient to Catherine II's 'Greek Project' of creating a Greco-Slavic empire that would give Russia hegemony in south-eastern Europe and – in a bold *non sequitur* – identify Russia, *qua* successor to Orthodox Byzantium, to be the true heir to pagan classical Greece and hence a senior member in the family of European cultures.[3] The Russian elite thus had to come to terms with both its own national identity *and* an ill-defined imperial destiny, issues that became all the more urgent once the French Revolution crystallised modern nationalism and shattered the old international system.

1 See. R. Hofstadter, *The Paranoid Style in American Politics and Other Essays* (New York: Knopf, 1965).

2 R. Wortman, *Scenarios of Power: Myth and Ceremony in Russian Monarchy*, 2 vols. (Princeton: Princeton University Press, 1995–2000), vol. I, p. 5.

3 L. Hughes, *Russia in the Age of Peter the Great* (New Haven and London: Yale University Press, 1998), p. 57; E. V. Anisimov, *Vremia petrovskikh reform* (Leningrad: Lenizdat, 1989), p. 418; A. Zorin, *Kormia dvuglavogo orla . . . Literatura i gosudarstvennaia ideologiia v Rossii v poslednei treti XVIII – pervoi treti XIX veka* (Moscow: Novoe literaturnoe obozrenie, 2001), pp. 35–8.

Furthermore, Russia's sociopolitical order was neither stable nor just. Sensitive, educated Russians worried that their vast empire, with its oppressive serfdom, corrupt officials and nouveaux riches aristocrats, represented – to borrow Robert Wiebe's description of the United States in the Gilded Age – 'a peculiarly inviting field for coarse leadership and crudely exercised power'.[4] The dynastic turmoil of the eighteenth century and the parade of unaccountable favourites who dominated court politics, together with the threat of popular revolts like the one led by the Cossack Emelian Pugachev in 1773–5, also rendered the system disturbingly unpredictable.

Lastly, the Russian elite faced conflicting cultural imperatives as they alternated schizophrenically between exercising untrammelled power on their estates and suffering the most pedantic regimentation in their own service as army officers or civilian officials. Religion and state service demanded ascetic self-discipline, while the fashionable 'Voltairean' scepticism of the Enlightenment, combined with the social pressure to flaunt one's wealth and the atmosphere of legal impunity created by serfdom, made it acceptable to indulge one's whims with little regard to the consequences. One manifestation of the conflicts this bred was a sexual morality torn between conservative modesty and unbridled hedonism, as we see in the pious noblewoman Anna Labzina's bitter tale of her marriage to the libertine Karamyshev.[5] Another was the quasi-suicidal propensity of many noblemen in state service for staking their well-being on a literal or figurative roll of the dice, for example, in high-stakes card games or lethal duels; thus wilfully abandoning one's fate to chance was also a form of rebellion against the stifling power of the regime.[6] Hesitating between conflicting models of individual conduct, Russian nobles remained deeply uncertain about what it meant to live a good and honourable life.

The 1812 war and Russian nationalism

To understand the war's psychological impact, it is important to recall the drama and speed with which it unfolded. Napoleon invaded Russia in June. By September, he was in Moscow. And by Christmas, his *Grande Armée* had been annihilated, at the cost to Russia of hundreds of thousands of lives and

4 R. H. Wiebe, *The Search for Order, 1877–1920* (New York: Hill and Wang, 1967), pp. 37–8.

5 *Days of a Russian Noblewoman: The Memories of Anna Labzina, 1758–1821*, ed. and trans. Gary Marker and Rachel May (DeKalb: Northern Illinois University Press, 2001), passim.

6 Iu. M. Lotman, *Besedy o russkoi kul'ture. Byt i traditsii russkogo dvorianstva (XVIII – nachalo XIX veka)* (St Petersburg: Iskusstvo-SPb, 1994), p. 163.

immense economic losses; in Moscow, the devastation and carnage were such that the sheer stench was unbearable even from miles away.[7] Countless nobles found themselves on the run as they fled east or south from the war zone. For many, this brought eye-opening new thoughts and experiences.

Not surprisingly, many conceived a bitter hatred for the French, but Napoleon's alliance with other states also led many to blame Europeans in general. The young aristocrat Mariia A. Volkova was typical in her outrage at the French 'cannibals' and their allies for daring to call the Russian people 'barbarians': 'Let those fools call Russia a barbarous country, when their civilisation has led them to submit voluntarily to the vilest of tyrants. Thank God that we are barbarians, if Austria, Prussia, and France are considered civilised.'[8] Aside from the fear and loathing spawned by the invasion itself, these comments reflected the agreeable discovery that lower-class and provincial Russians, whom the educated elite had traditionally despised and feared but among whom many noble refugees and army officers perforce now found themselves, were in fact capable of patriotism, humanity and good sense, even though – or more likely, to a generation reared on the ideas of Jean-Jacques Rousseau, *because* – they had been little exposed to European 'civilisation'.

Educated Russians' long-standing love–hate relationship with France had taken a turn for the worse in the decade preceding the war, when cultural Francophobia had become an all-purpose device for criticising the decadence of aristocratic mores, the liberal reform plans attributed to Alexander I's advisers (especially Mikhail M. Speranskii), and Russia's defeats in the Napoleonic Wars. Nationalistic writers and officials fostered a climate of opinion that regarded absolute monarchy, the old-regime social hierarchy, the Orthodox faith and cultural Russianness as the core of a national identity whose antithesis was post-revolutionary France.[9]

The only other country at which such venom was directed was Poland. Russia and Poland shared a complicated history, including a protracted struggle for hegemony in present-day Belarus and western Ukraine; Poland's intervention in Russia's Time of Troubles; Russia's part in the partitions of Poland and the extremely bloody suppression of its constitutionalist movement in 1794; and the 1812 war, when Russian eye-witnesses

7 'Griboedovskaia Moskva v pis'makh M. A. Volkovoi k V. I. Lanskoi, 1812–1818 gg.', *Vestnik Evropy* 9, 8 (August 1874): 613.

8 'Griboedovskaia Moskva', 608, 613, 616.

9 See A. M. Martin, *Romantics, Reformers, Reactionaries: Russian Conservative Thought and Politics in the Reign of Alexander I* (DeKalb: Northern Illinois University Press, 1997).

singled out Napoleon's Polish auxiliaries as having been especially brutal occupiers.[10]

In the hands of the nationalist writers associated with the influential Aleksandr S. Shishkov, as the historian Andrei Zorin argues, this painful past became raw material for a compelling mythopoesis of Russian national identity. Poland had all the attributes of both a national and an ideological enemy: it was an old religious rival; it was a traditional ally of France, and associated in Russian eyes with similar revolutionary attitudes; and the presence of many ethnic Poles in the Russian Empire created fears about a Polish 'fifth column'. After Napoleon's victories over Austria, Prussia, and Russia in 1805–7 had crushed Russian national pride and led to the creation of the irredentist and pro-Napoleonic Grand Duchy of Warsaw, even while the Polish patriot Prince Adam Czartoryski figured prominently among Alexander I's liberal advisers and Russia reluctantly allied itself with France, 'Shishkovist' writers took to celebrating the Time of Troubles – which, fortuitously, had occurred exactly two centuries earlier – in poetry and on stage. In so doing, Zorin contends, they initiated a fundamental shift in Imperial Russia's sense of history. Two hundred years earlier, they argued, a divided Russia had been conquered by Polish aggressors with the complicity of domestic traitors, but in the end the nobility and the people had come together under the aegis of the Orthodox Church, restored Russian liberty and freely invited the House of Romanov to rule over them. This patriotic, anti-Western movement 'from below' in 1612–13 – and not, as had been proclaimed in the eighteenth century, Peter I's Westernising reforms 'from above' – was the true founding moment for the Russian nation, whose essence lay not in a European destiny achieved by a Westernised nobility and emperor, but in the unity of the Orthodox under a traditional Russian tsar, and in their selfless struggle against foreign (especially Polish) invaders and vigilance against domestic traitors.[11]

The regime was slow to endorse these views. Alexander I's entourage remained as multiethnic as ever after the war, and his conception of Russia's imperial destiny had no strong ethnic component. Internationally, he sought to stabilise the post-war order (and Russia's dominant place in it) by uniting the monarchs of Europe in a cosmopolitan, ecumenical 'Holy Alliance'; and in cases where his domestic policies were innovative and liberal – as when

10 For examples, see A. M. Martin, 'The Response of the Population of Moscow to the Napoleonic Occupation of 1812', in E. Lohr and M. Poe (eds.), *The Military and Society in Russia, 1450–1917* (Leiden, Boston and Cologne: Brill, 2002), p. 477.

11 Zorin, *Kormia dvuglavogo orla*, pp. 159–86.

he issued constitutions to Finland and Poland or abolished serfdom in the Baltic Provinces – it was often in ways that privileged the empire's 'European' periphery relative to Russia proper. He disliked Moscow, the symbolic historic capital of the Great Russians, and while he enjoyed commemorating the campaigns of 1813–14 in Europe, he ignored sites and anniversaries associated with the 1812 war in Russia (when his own role had been considerably less heroic). However, Alexander's effort to impose a non-nationalist reading of the events of 1812–15 failed, and his post-war attempt to build a new European system and imperial culture on an ecumenical Christian basis crumbled within a few years under the weight of its own contradictions. Instead, the revival of elite interest in religion ultimately benefited Orthodoxy while Russian thinkers grew increasingly preoccupied with exploring the historical roots and ethnocultural specificity of the Great Russian nation. At the same time, the alliance with Berlin and Vienna increasingly derived its resilience not from the Christian faith but a shared pragmatic interest in preventing a restoration of Polish independence and a recurrence of the sort of international anarchy associated with the French Revolution and Napoleon.

By the 1830s, the regime and its supporters had clearly embraced the nationalist conception of history. Alexander's post-war attempt to reconcile Russians and Poles collapsed amidst the 1830–1 Polish revolt and the subsequent suppression of Polish autonomy; in 1833, Nicholas I's minister of education, Sergei S. Uvarov, famously defined the essence of Russian identity as being 'Orthodoxy, Autocracy, Nationality'; Mikhail I. Glinka's patriotic, anti-Polish opera *A Life for the Tsar*, set in the Time of Troubles, premiered in 1836; and in 1839, Aleksandr I. Mikhailovskii-Danilevskii published the official history of 1812, *An Account of the War for the Fatherland in 1812*, whose very title helped canonise the interpretation, and the name, of the conflict as a 'patriotic' war of the Russian nation. The notion of a centuries-old unity of altar, throne and Russian ethnos, adumbrated by writers after the defeats of 1805–7 and preached by regime and Church in 1812, had become official ideology by the 1830s and remained so until the end of the Romanovs.

Not all the implications of this theory enjoyed universal acclaim. The regime itself remained ambivalent about its anti-Western ramifications, while many educated Russians believed that, by defeating Napoleon's tyranny and upholding Russian independence, the nation in 1812 had won the right to a freer, less authoritarian sociopolitical order. Yet most accepted the nationalist conception's key propositions – the focus on Muscovite history and Russian ethnicity, the sense of Russian national uniqueness, the moral valorisation of the common folk and the importance attributed to their spiritual bond with the regime. Perhaps aided by the growth of the education system and the propaganda campaigns of the Napoleonic Wars, these views also reached the general population, as is apparent from the notebook into which the provincial goldsmith Dmitrii S. Volkov in the 1820s copied readings that were particularly meaningful to him: a patriotic, anti-French diatribe by the nationalist Fedor V. Rostopchin, a primer on how to behave in church, a sermon by an Orthodox Greek preacher and a text cataloguing Russia's monarchs from the legendary Riurik to Peter I.[12] 'Orthodoxy', 'Autocracy' and 'Nationality' were all represented.

The war and Russian political culture

Russians by 1800 had recently experienced two very different models of monarchy: Catherine II had presented herself as a consensus-builder who welcomed input from 'society' and favoured an embryonic form of electoral politics – exemplified by the Legislative Commission of 1767 and by her support for noble and municipal self-government – that pointed in the direction of political liberalism, while her son Paul I had favoured the opposite role of authoritarian, militaristic commander-in-chief. Alexander I was torn between these two options, but ultimately political liberalism suffered disastrous setbacks under his reign. Aside from the court politics of the time, this was due to the convergence of two forces whose growth was fatefully accelerated by the Napoleonic Wars. One was the nationalist conception of history that added a powerful layer of ideological armour to autocracy by depicting it as the indispensable corollary to Orthodoxy, Russianness and national unity. The other was the way in which the political culture was poisoned by the growing tendency to imagine politics as a succession of malicious conspiracies.

Because of the absence of a civil society and the vast power wielded by small, secretive groups of unaccountable individuals, conspiracy had long played an important role in Russian government. Conspiracies traditionally involved lower-class pretenders who claimed to be the 'true tsar', or else power struggles within the dynasty. However, the mischief by pretenders faded after the Pugachev revolt, and the last dynastic coup took place in 1801 when Paul I was assassinated and replaced with Alexander I. Instead, from the late 1780s onwards, conspiracy theories increasingly centred on ideologically or ethnically motivated opposition to the regime as such, especially by freemasons, liberals or socialists, and Poles or (later) Jews, often at the behest of Russophobic

12 OPI GIM, Fond 450, d. 835a.

foreigners. Two factors accounted for this. First, the upheavals of the era – Paul's capricious oppressiveness, Alexander's stabs at liberal reform and, of course, the shock waves radiating from France – made clear how much more was now at stake in politics than in the past. Second, it came to be widely believed across Europe that the upheavals that began in 1789 and continued far into the nineteenth century were caused by a conspiracy to overthrow monarchy, religion and the existing order everywhere.[13] This notion originated in the West, particularly France, and came to Russia largely through the influence of francophone conservatives such as abbé Augustin Barruel and Joseph de Maistre.

Fuelled by Russia's military defeats in the wars against Napoleon and by the fact that Alexander I's entourage – as opposed, for example, to Catherine II's – contained a conspicuous numbers of foreigners with agendas driven by the interests of their homelands, the Russian version of this conspiracy theory imagined traitors to be present at the very top of the regime. It focused on social and ethnic outsiders: Alexander's liberal adviser Mikhail Speranskii was attacked as a priest's son out to undermine noble rights, while the Baltic German Mikhail Barclay de Tolly (the hapless commander of the Russian army during its retreat in 1812) and the liberal Pole Czartoryski were presumed to be disloyal to Russia. 'In the Russian interpretation', Zorin points out, 'the anti-masonic mythology fused almost immediately with time-honoured notions of a secret conspiracy against Russia that was being hatched beyond its borders.'[14] The suspected wire-puller was Napoleon, whom – according to a verse making the rounds in 1813 – 'the first Mikhail (that is, Speranskii) summoned, the second Mikhail (Barclay) received, and the third Mikhail (Prince Kutuzov) drove out'.[15] To pacify public opinion, Alexander had to send Speranskii into ignominious exile and replace Barclay with the popular General Kutuzov, while Fedor Rostopchin, the governor-general of Moscow during the 1812 war, demonstratively deported foreign residents, purged freemasons from the bureaucracy and turned over the merchant's son Vereshchagin, accused of serving the masonic conspiracy, to a lynch mob. According to Zorin, whose chapter on this subject bears the chillingly evocative title 'The Enemy of the People', Rostopchin's real target had been Speranskii; only when that prize proved beyond his reach did he fall back on the wretched Vereshchagin as a

13 Douglas Smith, *Working the Rough Stone: Freemasonry and Society in Eighteenth-Century Russia* (DeKalb: Northern Illinois University Press, 1999), pp. 164–73; Zorin, *Kormia dvuglavogo orla*, pp. 204–5.

14 Zorin, *Kormia dvuglavogo orla*, pp. 206–7.

15 'Griboedovskaia Moskva', 625.

substitute scapegoat whose killing by the 'people' would symbolically restore the unity of the nation.[16]

After 1814, Alexander I and his entourage were convinced that the continuing troubles in Europe and subversion in Russia were co-ordinated by a nefarious 'comité directeur' based in Western Europe, while Alexander's conservative critics regarded his own beloved Russian Bible Society as part of an Anglo-masonic plot against Russian Orthodoxy. Meanwhile, ironically, no one took action against the *real* conspiracy that almost overthrew Alexander's successor in December 1825. Spooked by the Decembrist revolt and the European revolutions of 1830 and 1848, the regime of Nicholas I offered an even more inviting field for conspiracy theories; thus, it seems that the disgraced ex-official Mikhail Leont'evich Magnitskii, in a secret 1831 memorandum, was the first to claim that Jews and freemasons were collaborating in a grand anti-Russian plot.[17] By the 1860s, stereotypes of this sort were sufficiently entrenched to convince the satirist Mikhail E. Saltykov-Shchedrin that his hilarious 'history' of the town of Glupov – a ludicrous compilation of the clichés of eighteenth-century Russian society and politics set in the microcosm of an imaginary provincial backwater – required a few absurd 'Polish intrigues' to be complete.[18]

How deep into the population these fears reached is difficult to tell. However, the common Muscovites who lynched Vereshchagin apparently accepted Rostopchin's notion of a masonic plot; as for the longer-term impact, Vladimir Dal's authoritative dictionary of the late nineteenth century defines the popular colloquialism *farmazon* (freemason) as 'pejor. freethinker and atheist', and in Saltykov-Shchedrin's satirical novel, a Glupov craftsman declares with a kind of naïve cynicism that as a 'false priest' in the 'sect of *farmazony*', he is of course an atheist and adulterer. Maxim Gorky writes that his merchant grandfather around 1870 called an artisan whose craft he found disturbingly mysterious a 'worker in black magic' and a 'freemason',[19] and at least as late as 1938 – when, in the film adaptation of Gorky's book, the grandfather unselfconsciously uses *farmazon* as the rough equivalent of 'troublemaker' – Soviet audiences could evidently be expected to know the word's connotations.

16 Zorin, *Kormia dvuglavogo orla*, pp. 234–7.

17 A. Iu. Minakov, 'M. L. Magnitskii: K voprosu o biografii i mirovozzrenii predtechi russkikh pravoslavnykh konservatorov XIX veka', in *Konservatizm v Rossii i mire: proshloe i nastoiashchee. Sbornik nauchnykh trudov*, vyp. 1 (Voronezh: Izd. Voronezhskogo gos. universiteta, 2001), pp. 83–4.

18 M. E. Saltykov-Shchedrin, *Istoriia odnogo goroda: Skazki* (Moscow: Olimp, Izd. AST, 2002), pp. 44, 47, 49.

19 M. Gorky, *My Childhood*, trans. Ronald Wilks (Harmondsworth: Penguin Books, 1966), p. 116; Saltykov-Shchedrin, *Istoriia*, p. 37.

1812 and the problem of social stability

Concern about treason in high places reflected a deep-seated awareness of the brittleness of Russia's social order, which had faced no assault comparable to 1812 since the Time of Troubles. The army's failure to stop Napoleon's advance came as a shock and contributed to the proliferation of conspiracy theories, while upper-class Russians feared that the masses would now run riot or even, egged on by Napoleon, rise up in revolt. Forty years earlier, state authority had crumbled before the illiterate Cossack Pugachev's lightly armed rabble, whom the peasantry in some places had joined en masse. What, then, to expect from the most powerful army in European history, led by a brilliant general who advocated revolutionary ideas?

While the army was reeling, the stress on the administration was immense. As Janet Hartley has shown,

> although provincial government [in the war zone] continued to function throughout the period of invasion it proved impossible to carry out to the full all the demands made of it in respect of provision of supplies and the care of the sick and wounded. Furthermore, the administration was unable to prevent disorder from breaking out and ultimately could not protect the inhabitants from the ravages of war.[20]

In Moscow, government authority was maintained through the summer thanks to a clever if distasteful combination of demagogy and repression that culminated in the lynching of Vereshchagin, but collapsed once the army had withdrawn. Hordes of peasants then joined the *Grande Armée* in picking the abandoned city clean, while terrified Muscovites fleeing the city faced the prospect of crossing a possibly hostile and anarchic countryside. Cossacks looted some villages and burned others astride the invasion route, while the police (at least in Moscow) apparently enriched themselves on a grand scale while 'restoring order' after the French had left. Russian society appeared to be coming apart at the seams.

Yet, mysteriously, the empire held. Napoleon did not try to incite a popular revolt,[21] and the systematic pillaging and coarse anticlericalism practised by his multinational army deeply alienated the population, creating a lasting resentment against the 'twenty nations' (a phrase popularised by the

20 J. M. Hartley, 'Russia in 1812, Part II: The Russian Administration of Kaluga *Gubernija*', *JfGO* 38, 3 (1990): 416, and 'Russia and Napoleon: State, Society and the Nation', in M. Rowe (ed.), *Collaboration and Resistance in Napoleonic Europe: State-Formation in an Age of Upheaval*, c. *1800–1815* (Houndmills: Palgrave Macmillan, 2003), pp. 187–8.

21 See J. M. Hartley, 'Russia in 1812, Part I: The French Presence in the *Gubernii* of Smolensk and Mogilev', *JfGO* 38, 2 (1990): 182.

Orthodox hierarchy and repeated in many memoirs) that composed it. What Teodor Shanin has written of 1905 also applies to the year 1812: it was a 'moment of truth' that offered Russians 'a dramatic corrective to their understanding of the society in which they lived'.[22] Russia suffered an unexpected series of shocking setbacks, but even in the direst of circumstances, the army and administration held. Napoleon's huge army with its pan-European composition and revolutionary ideology – the quintessence of the West's aggressive rationalism – invaded Russia, abused its people and violated its shrines, but ultimately imploded under the pressure of its own indiscipline and overreaching. Vast numbers even of 'Europeanised' Russians, on the other hand, became implicated in a form of all-out warfare that they came to regard as distinctly Russian: abandoning or even burning their homes and possessions – as he had earlier with his Francophobic propaganda and anti-masonic campaign, Rostopchin again set an example by demonstratively burning both his own estate and (most likely) Moscow itself – peasants, urban people and nobles fought or fled rather than live under enemy occupation. They watched in awe as the primordial forces of Russian life – vengeful peasants and Cossacks, fire-prone cities, and the empire's vast spaces and unforgiving climate – ground up the presumptuous *Grande Armée*. All in all, it was a tremendous display of elemental 'Russianness' that confirmed, in the educated classes, a deep and increasingly proud sense of national uniqueness.

Patriotic pride notwithstanding, however, most found these experiences more terrifying than exhilarating, at least at the time when they occurred. As the noblewoman Karolina K. Pavlova later recalled, 'the news of the fire of Moscow struck us like lightning. It was fine for Pushkin to exclaim with poetic rapture, a dozen years later: "Burn, great Moscow!" But the general feeling while it was burning, as far as I know, was not enthusiastic at all.'[23] Nearer the other end of the social scale, the Moscow printer's widow Afim'ia P. Stepanova had this to say about 1812:

> Owing to my modest means and because my children and I were sick, I stayed in my house, but during the invasion by the enemy army all my possessions and my daughter's trousseau . . . they took all of it before my eyes, carried it away and smashed it, and while threatening to kill me as well as my children they beat and tormented [me], causing me and my whole family to fall ill for six months.

22 T. Shanin, *Russia, 1905–07: Revolution as a Moment of Truth*, vol. II: *The Roots of Otherness: Russia's Turn of Century* (New Haven and London: Yale University Press, 1986), p. xv.
23 K. Pavlova, 'Moi vospominaniia', *Russkii Arkhiv*, 4, 10 (1875): 224.

Yet she was among the lucky ones, for all members of her family had at least survived, as had (apparently) their house.[24] The scale of the misery, and the expectation at least among the urban population that the state would provide redress, is illustrated by the fact that in Moscow alone, over 18,000 households – a substantial majority of all Muscovites who were not serfs – filed such petitions for assistance.[25]

Michael Broers argues that in the lands of Napoleon's 'inner empire' – e.g. the Rhineland or northern Italy – where his rule had been comparatively long-lived and stable, 'the Napoleonic system left a powerful institutional heritage', and after 1815 '[the] restored governments were expected to meet French standards' on pain of losing the support of influential constituencies. By contrast, in the restless 'outer empire' of Spain, southern Italy and elsewhere, 'Napoleonic rule was traumatic and destabilizing. It was ephemeral, in that it left few institutional traces, yet profound in the aversion to the Napoleonic state it implanted at so many levels of society.'[26]

While Russia was never formally a part of the Napoleonic empire, its experience comes closest to that of the outer empire. Like the peoples of that region, common Russians' encounter with Napoleon's regime endowed them with little understanding of, let alone sympathy for, the revolutionary Enlightenment principles he supposedly represented. Instead, many viewed his invasion of Russia through a pre-modern religious and ideological lens that could inspire great kindness but also terrible cruelty. For example, a poor midwife in Orel reportedly took five prisoners of war from the *Grande Armée* into her home. After exhausting her own savings, she even went begging to feed the men. But when, at last, 'her' prisoners were removed by the authorities, 'this simple-hearted woman smashed all the crockery from which they had eaten and drunk at her home, because she believed these people – whom she had cared for so attentively and aided so selflessly – to be unclean heathens'. Educated Russians proudly seized on such episodes as evidence that their common people resembled the indomitable Spaniards in the emotional, combative patriotism and

24 Tsentral'nyi istoricheskii arkhiv Moskvy, Fond 20, op. 2, d. 2215, l. 12.

25 E. G. Boldina, 'O deiatel'nosti Komissii dlia rassmotreniia proshenii obyvatelei Moskovskoi stolitsy i gubernii, poterpevshikh razorenie ot nashestviia nepriiatel'skogo', in E. G. Boldina, A. S. Kiselev and L. N. Seliverstova (eds.), *Moskva v 1812 godu. Materialy nauchnoi konferentsii, posviashchennoi 180-letiiu Otechestvennoi voiny 1812 goda* (Moscow: Izd. ob'edineniia 'Mosgorarkhiv', 1997), p. 47.

26 M. Broers, *Europe Under Napoleon, 1799–1815* (London and New York: Arnold, 1996), pp. 266–7.

religiosity with which they resisted aggressors who claimed to represent a superior civilisation.[27]

A different interpretation that also took root among the people in 1812 and the succeeding decades recognised that Napoleon was a revolutionary but situated him, and the entire notion of 'republicanism', in the native tradition of anarchic *jacqueries* that many Russians had learned to fear. Thus, Gorky's grandfather recalled that Napoleon

> was a bold man who wanted to conquer the whole world and he wanted everyone to be equal – no lords or civil servants but simply a world without classes. Names would be different, but everyone would have the same rights. And the same faith. I don't have to tell you what nonsense that is . . . We've had our own Bonapartes – [the Cossack rebels] Razin, Pugachov [*sic*] – I'll tell you about them some other time.

A similar outlook shines through the recollections, also from the 1870s, of a former house serf who in 1812 had witnessed a riot behind Russian lines – 'they were all getting drunk, fighting, cursing', she recalled: 'it was a republic all right, absolutely a republic!'[28]

The legacy of the war

In Russia, as in the lands of the 'outer empire', Napoleon's regime thus enjoyed little support. Yet across Europe, his empire had aroused intense ideological partisanship, created a form of state that reached new heights of power while plumbing depths of aggression and exploitation, and encouraged a synthesis of militaristic elitism and popular mobilisation, imperialistic chauvinism and the romantic myth of the 'career open to talent' exemplified by the 'little Corsican' himself. Post-war society had to contend with this legacy, finding ways to replicate his regime's ability to integrate, control and mobilise the nation, but without contracting its socially egalitarian tendencies or its self-destructive imperialism.

One response was religious; it was centred in the masonic movement, pietist circles and the newly created Russian Bible Society, and drew heavily

27 Pavlova, 'Moi vospominaniia', 228; M. A. Dodelev, 'Rossiia i voina ispanskogo naroda za nezavisimost' (1808–1814 gg.)', *VI* (1972), no. 11: 33–44.

28 Gorky, *My Childhood*, pp. 86–7; 'Razkaz nabilkinskoi bogodelenki, Anny Andreevny Sozonovoi, byvshei krepostnoi Vasil'ia Titovicha Lepekhina', in 'Razkazy ochevidtsev o dvenadtsatom gode', *Russkii vestnik* 102 (November 1872): 291.

on German and British influences. It gained tremendous momentum from the seemingly miraculous manner of the destruction of Napoleon's army in 1812: 'The fire of Moscow lit up my soul', Alexander I would later explain, 'and the Lord's judgment on the ice fields filled my heart with a warmth of faith that it had never felt before. Now I came to know God as He is revealed by the Holy Scriptures.'[29] The manifestation of this ideology in foreign policy was the effort to unite Europe in the 'Holy Alliance', while domestically, a newly created Ministry of Spiritual Affairs and Popular Enlightenment was charged with reforming the moral tenor of Russian culture. The goal was to make Russians into ecumenically minded Christians in whom better education, Bibles in the vernacular (a controversial innovation) and participation in organised philanthropy would instil benevolence, self-discipline, a sense of social responsibility and a heightened civic consciousness. The state's authority over the people would henceforth be rooted in mutual respect, not fear, and Russia would become the kind of cohesive, authoritarian, mildly progressive polity that Napoleon had modelled, but at peace with others and without the socially explosive notion of 'careers open to talent'.

Its institutional armature allowed this ideology to reach Russians beyond the upper classes that had conceived it. Thus, Aleksandr V. Nikitenko, although legally still a serf at the time, became the secretary of the Bible Society's chapter in the town of Ostrogozhsk (Voronezh Province) and embraced its commitment to the 'religious truths that the Gospel had given us' and 'their salutary influence on the morals of individuals and society' with 'sincere enthusiasm and youthful ardor'; and the headmaster of the church school in Kasimov (Riazan Province) – a corrupt petty tyrant who prospered by exploiting the students and clergy under his power – also joined the Bible Society, though his motives were probably more careerist than idealistic.[30] By the mid-1820s, however, the effort to ground the culture and politics of Russia and Europe in a Bible-centred Christianity had fallen so far short of its goals, and generated resistance from so many quarters, that it was scaled back and the Orthodox Church's pre-eminence within Russia was restored. Yet in an Orthodox and more emphatically 'Russian' guise, the ideological linkage between the regime

29 N. K. Shil'der, *Imperator Aleksandr Pervyi. Ego zhizn' i tsarstvovanie*, 4 vols. (St Petersburg: A. S. Suvorin, 1904–5), vol. III, p. 378.

30 A. Nikitenko, *Up From Serfdom: My Childhood and Youth in Russia, 1804–1824*, trans. Helen Saltz Jacobson (New Haven and London: Yale University Press, 2001), pp. 180–1; D. I. Rostislavov, *Provincial Russia in the Age of Enlightenment: The Memoir of a Priest's Son*, trans. and ed. A. M. Martin (DeKalb: Northern Illinois University Press, 2002), pp. 134, 175–6.

and Christianity remained stronger in the nineteenth century than it had been before 1812.

A second emerging force that structured nineteenth-century Russian society was militarism, which, in Russia as in Napoleonic France, was associated with government that was hierarchical and centralised but also effective and inclined to social fairness. It acquired momentum under Paul I and touched broad social strata: 'My God!', exclaimed the merchant Nikolai F. Kotov in his reminiscences,

> from the very outset of Emperor Paul I's accession [in 1796], what strictness, what meekness, what a martial spirit began to rule in Moscow! From being arrogant and unapproachable, the nobles became humble, for the law was the same whether one was a noble or a merchant. Ostentatious luxury came under suspicion. And among the common people, there appeared a kind of terror and obedience before a sort of martial or enlightened-authoritarian spirit, for the strictness and obedience extended to all classes of people.[31]

Russia was at war almost continually from the 1790s to 1814. These wars entailed a vast mobilisation of people and created new role models for society, ranging from dashing hussars to female peasant guerrillas, who demonstrated Russians' capability for both heroism and cruelty, for co-operation between social classes and disciplined, organised action. The end of the war brought the return of newly self-confident and worldly veterans who changed the tone of society, whether by bringing a whiff of European humanism to stale provincial backwaters or by abusing Russian peasants and small-town notables like conquered enemy populations.[32]

While the wars themselves contributed to the militarisation of Russian life, Paul and his successors also saw militarism as a pedagogical tool for counteracting revolutionary ideology. However, while Napoleonic militarism had favoured meritocratic egalitarianism as a way to unite France's post-revolutionary polity and create a powerful fighting force to serve an imperialistic foreign policy, its Russian incarnation instead focused on symbolic elements that might instil respect for the social hierarchy: drill and pageantry were emphasised, cadet schools for noble boys were founded, uniforms became mandatory for university students, and even life at church academies was militarised;[33] while its actual combat readiness stagnated, the

31 OR RGB, Fond 54 (Vishniakov), ch. 8, 'Zapiski Nikolaia Fedorovicha Kotova o tsarst. Ekat. II i Pavla I 1785 po 1800 gg.,' l. 40–40 ob.
32 Nikitenko, *Up From Serfdom*, p. 135; Rostislavov, *Provincial Russia*, p. 180.
33 See, for example: D. I. Rostislavov, 'Peterburgskaia dukhovnaia akademiia pri grafe Protasove, 1836–1855 gg.', *Vestnik Evropy* 18 (July 1883): 158–62.

army became the preferred metaphor for a society that was orderly, disciplined and committed to the regime's vision of carefully controlled societal progress.

However, even while it suggested ways to stabilise society and strengthen the state, the Napoleonic experience had also disrupted traditional social patterns and created expectations that would prove troublesome to the regime in the future. There are indications that Russian peasants understood their 'liberation' from Napoleon to mean freedom from serfdom as well, and like Spain, though to a far lesser degree, Russia had peasant guerrillas who might become a threat to the regime once the French were gone. A more fateful parallel with Spain was the creation of secret societies of disillusioned officers who were committed to radical political change and would attempt to overthrow the autocracy in December 1825.[34] Nikitenko met some of them when he was still a serf in Ostrogozhsk:

> [p]articipants in world events, these officers were not figures engaged in fruitless debates, but men who . . . had acquired a special strength of character and determination in their views and aspirations. They stood in sharp contrast to the progressive people in our provincial community, who, for lack of real, sobering activity, inhabited a fantasy world and wasted their strength in petty, fruitless protest. The contact the officers had had with Western European civilization, their personal acquaintance with a more successful social system . . . , and, finally, the struggle for the grand principles of freedom and the Fatherland all left their mark of deep humanity on them. . . . In me they saw a victim of the order of things that they hated.[35]

Like the proponents of militarism and the Holy Alliance – who were, after all, their friends and relatives – the Decembrists saw an opportunity to resolve the problems outlined at the opening of this chapter. They proposed to place progressive military men, whose moral authority rested on a patriotism tested in battle, at the head of a cohesive and mighty Russian nation-state. By liberalising the social and political order to a degree that even Alexander I and Speranskii had never seriously contemplated, they meant to confront tyranny and social injustice. In adopting for themselves the persona of austere, dignified, outspoken, emphatically moral men of action committed to the public good, they offered their own answer to the crisis of spiritual meaning and of the norms of individual conduct that beset the nobility.[36] By creating 'secret

34 Isabel de Madariaga discusses this issue in 'Spain and the Decembrists', *European Studies Review* 3, 2 (1973): 141–56.

35 Nikitenko, *Up From Serfdom*, p. 135.

36 See the (by now classic) 'Dekabrist v povsednevnoi zhizni', in Lotman, *Besedy*, pp. 331–84.

societies' as a framework for political action, they acknowledged the same absence of a viable civil society that prompted Alexander I and Nicholas I to foster religious associations, bureaucracy and militarism. And in seeking to gain power through a *pronunciamiento*, they joined nationalistic officers from San Martín to Nasser in following in the footsteps of General Bonaparte's Brumaire coup, but they also helped to bring the violent, conspiratorial culture of eighteenth-century Russian politics into the ideologically polarised world of the nineteenth.

PART III

★

NON-RUSSIAN NATIONALITIES

8
Ukrainians and Poles

TIMOTHY SNYDER

Europe's road to Muscovy passed through Warsaw and Kyiv (Kiev). Despite what one reads in books, the Renaissance and Reformation did reach Muscovy, if by this most indirect route. In the middle of the seventeenth century, Orthodox clerics trained in the rhetoric and languages of the Polish Renaissance and Reformation settled in Moscow. As Muscovy's political power extended across eastern Ukraine and Kiev with Hetman Bohdan Khmelnyts'kyi's rebellion against Poland (1648–54) and the Treaty of Eternal Peace between Muscovy and Poland (1686), Orthodox clerics came to terms with their new position in a highly backward Orthodox state. Alexis Mikhailovich (r. 1645–76) saw them as people capable of improving Muscovite administration, and encouraged the emigration of learned Ukrainians. Iepifanii Slavynets'kyi was an early arrival, in 1649. Symeon Polots'kyi taught Alexis's children Latin and Polish. The occasional Polish Jesuit was allowed to dispute with the Orthodox, as did Andrzej Kwieczynski before he was sent to break rocks in Siberia in 1660. Disputation itself was an import from Poland, and at this time Polish and Latin were understood to be the languages of reason. Latin itself was learned from Polish translations, for example of Ovid's 'Metamorphoses'.

Ukrainian clerics such as Stepan Iavors'kyi and Teofan Prokopovych were indeed engaged in some fundamental transformations: of themselves as they reoriented Ruthenian Orthodoxy to Moscow, and of Moscow as they reoriented public life and political thought to the West. Such men introduced the baroque, not only in rhetoric, but in architecture, ceremonial and secular public displays. Stepan Chyzhevs'kyi, an alumnus of a Jesuit collegium, arranged Moscow's first theatrical production. Finding an absence of political thought, Ukrainian clerics formulated Muscovy's first theories of tsarist rule. Polots'kyi's 'Russian Eagle' was a baroque (in every sense of the word) apology for Muscovite rule of eastern Europe. Lazar Baranovych presented Alexis with his 'Spiritual Sword' (1666), which described the tsar as the protector of all Rus and the heir of Volodymyr – although in 1671 he concluded his massive

Polish-language *Apollo's Lute* with an appeal to the old Polish-Lithuanian fatherland. The *Sinopsis*, the first Russian history book, was produced in Kiev around 1674. Most famously, it presented an elaborate account of the transfer of legitimate rule from Kiev to Vladimir-on-the-Kliazma to Moscow. It described Rus as a larger nation embracing different groups of Orthodox believers, whose local traditions deserved respect.

Polish influence was perhaps greatest under Tsar Fedor (r. 1676–82), who married two women with Polish connections, and under the regency of Sophia (1682–9). Sophia's reign was the heyday of Jan Andrzej Bialoblocki, a Polish convert to Orthodoxy who led the Moscow Baroque and taught Latin to the boyars before setting out to negotiate with the Chinese (or their Jesuit envoys) at Nerchinsk. Not all of Sophia's foreign policy plans were crowned with success. She staked her rule on an alliance with the Polish-Lithuanian Commonwealth against the Ottoman Empire, and its failure in the Crimean campaigns brought her down. When she was succeeded by Peter (r. 1689–1725), Polish and Ukrainian churchmen had been at court and in Muscovy for two generations, and a certain kind of Westernisation was well under way.[1]

Ukrainian clerics, for example, all but controlled the Russian Orthodox Church. To be sure, Patriarch Iaokim managed to have the leading Latin Sil'vestr Medvedev executed, and the Jesuits expelled. Yet even as the possibility of a radical Latinisation of the Russian Orthodox Church disappeared, its fundamental Ukrainisation remained. Peter's church reforms involved his preferences for certain Ukrainian clerics over others. His agents, Teofan Prokopovych and Stefan Iavors'kyi, brought a group of Ukrainian clients to the heights of the Russian Church. When Iavors'kyi was discredited in the tsarevitch affair, the church leadership was replaced at the Synod of 1721. Again, the house-cleaning was carried out by Ukrainians, this time mainly by Prokopovych.

Ukrainian churchmen in left-bank Ukraine (east of the Dnieper River) lost any institutional distinctiveness but preserved regional differences. The Kiev metropolitanate was reduced to the Kiev region itself, and placed under the jurisdiction of the Moscow patriarchy. One by one, Kiev's former dioceses placed themselves directly under the protection of Moscow. The first to go was Lazar Baranovych and Chernihiv (Chernigov), although his Chernihiv school continued its baroque curriculum and he continued his work in the Polish language. Likewise, the Kiev Academy preserved a curriculum modelled on those of Jesuit academies, and served as a point of transmission of Polish

1 P. Bushkovitch, *Peter the Great: The Struggle for Power, 1671–1725* (New York: Cambridge University Press, 2001). See also Natalia Iakovenko, *Ukrains'ka shliakhta* (Kiev: Naukova dumka, 1993).

trends to Muscovy, even as Polish models themselves shifted from baroque to neoclassical. Latinate and classical motifs also appeared in Ukrainian religious art of the period, for example in the Pokrova icons placing the Cossack officer class under the mantle of the Mother of God.[2]

Although the alliance between Ukrainian Cossacks and Muscovy is dated from the agreement at Pereiaslav (1654), nothing like a Cossack state aligned with Moscow existed before Peter's time.[3] The Cossacks profited from Pereiaslav to free themselves and much of Ukraine from Poland, but then under Hetman Doroshenko aimed for an alliance with the Ottomans. Only when Moscow and Warsaw allied against the Ottomans in the Treaty of Eternal Peace (1686) did the situation stabilise somewhat. Henceforth Muscovy held the left bank and Kiev, while the right bank fell to Warsaw. The left-bank lands controlled by Cossack officers became the Hetmanate, the largest autonomous region of Muscovy. The Hetmanate did not include the Zaporihizian Sich and its free Cossacks, tied still more loosely to Muscovy. The Cossacks, like Ukrainian churchmen, had adopted Polish modes of thought, but this did not mean that they wished Polish rule for themselves. The Polish-Lithuanian Commonwealth under King Jan Sobieski failed to develop a sensible policy towards left-bank Ukraine, and the Cossacks feared that any return of Polish rule would mean a worsening of their position. After the Treaty of Eternal Peace (1686), they migrated in the tens of thousands from right-bank (Polish) to left-bank (Russian) Ukraine.[4]

In the 1690s, the Polish option remained, as a cultural model in Ukraine and as a potential ally for Muscovy. In the Hetmanate, nostalgia indeed increased with time. Cossack officers hazily recalled the Polish period as one of freedom, appropriating for themselves the liberties of Polish nobles. Cossacks accepted the myths of Sarmatian or Khazar origin now widespread among Polish nobles. The Hetmanate under Ivan Mazepa (r. 1686–1709) revealed that Polish cultural influence could increase as Polish political power waned. Mazepa himself studied in Warsaw and served King Jan Kazimierz of Poland. As Hetman he funded the reconstruction, in baroque style, of ancient Ukrainian churches at Chernihiv and Kiev. Mazepa enjoyed good relations with Peter, who for his

2 S. Plokhy, *Tsars and Cossacks: A Study in Iconography* (Cambridge, Mass.: Harvard University Press, 2001). See also F. E. Sysyn, *Between Poland and the Ukraine: The Dilemma of Adam Kysil, 1600–1653* (Cambridge, Mass.: Harvard University Press, 1985); D. A. Frick, *Meletij Smotryc'kyj* (Cambridge, Mass.: Harvard University Press, 1995).

3 An introduction to the Pereiaslav debate: John Basarab, *Pereiaslav 1654: A Historiographical Study* (Edmonton: CIUS, 1982).

4 S. Plokhy, *The Cossacks and Religion in Early Modern Ukraine* (Oxford: Oxford University Press, 2001).

part wished to make Poland his ally. Yet the alliance, when it came, reduced rather than increased the influence of Ukrainians and Poles in Moscow.[5]

Peter met King Augustus II of Poland at Rava Rus'ka in August 1698 and persuaded his new friend to join him in an attack on the Swedes. Together they plotted what became the Great Northern War, Muscovy's great triumph, Poland's great failure and Ukraine's last moment of choice. When Peter moved against Sweden, the Swedes responded by invading Poland and dethroning Augustus. A considerable part of the Polish nobility formed the Confederation of Sandomierz, which fought to restore Augustus and drive out the Swedes. Even though such confederations were a legitimate part of the Polish constitutional tradition, their emergence usually revealed internal division and civil strife. Although the Confederation of Sandomierz was ultimately successful, Poland itself fell into a state of civil war and was henceforth never again an important ally of Russia.[6]

The Polish collapse was also a fateful moment for the Cossacks. In October 1708 Hetman Mazepa allied with the Swedes, bringing along perhaps half of his men from the Hetmanate and most of the fighters of the Zaporizhian Sich. They were routed along with the Swedes at Poltava in June 1709, and Mazepa fled with King Charles of Sweden to Ottoman territory. Peter's response was milder than is generally remembered: he took it upon himself to appoint Hetman colonels, and only in 1721 tried to abolish the office of Hetman and place political authority with a Little Russian College. This experiment lasted only six years, for in 1727 Peter II allowed the return of the office of Hetman, and for the next forty years the Cossack State enjoyed considerable autonomy. In secular political thought, Hetman Bohdan Khmelnyts'kyi returned to symbolise the alliance with Moscow. Emperors and empresses, in particular Tsaritsa Elizabeth, began to appear in Pokrova icons, as leaders enjoying the protection and intercession of the Virgin Mary.

This was a Latin touch long since native in Ukraine, but alien to Moscow, although feminine protection of another kind played a role in relations between Muscovy and the Hetmanate. Elizabeth (r. 1741–61) consorted with the Ukrainian Cossack Oleksii Rozumovs'kyi, whose brother Kyrylo was elected Hetman in 1752. Kyrylo's rule gave the Hetmanate much of the appearance of a state. He was able to increase the formal powers of the Hetman, introduce standard uniforms for his Cossacks and restore the traditional Cossack

5 O. Subtelny, *Mazepists: Ukrainian Separatism in the Early Eighteenth Century* (New York: Columbia University Press, 1982).

6 For the immediate background see Antoni Kaminski, *Republic vs. Autocracy: Poland-Lithuania and Russia, 1686–1697* (Cambridge, Mass.: Harvard University Press, 1993).

capitals, Hlukhiv and Baturyn. The military organisation of the Cossacks became a form of civilian rule over the population. As the Hetman became a civilian ruler as well as a warlord, his officers took up duties such as tax collection. This capped a longer social transformation, in which the Cossack officer class became the new ruling class of left-bank Ukraine.

Most of them were arrivistes. Most of the native great nobility had been killed or forced to emigrate during the Khmelnyt'skyi rebellion. Although the Cossacks led that rebellion in the name of the people and profited from peasant rebellions, in times of peace they sought to establish themselves as the new nobility. Hetmans endorsed monarchy and opposed the tradition of election by their men. In good szlachta style, Cossack officers insisted on their own rights vis-à-vis the Hetman, but then sought to control territory and bind peasants to the land. In the 1760s, the Society of Notable Military Fellows became a closed estate at the summit of Cossackdom, including 2,400 but excluding about 350,000 Cossacks. These elite officers asked that the tsaritsa recognise their traditional rights, which they identified as the rights of Polish nobles.

Catherine II (r. 1762–96) had a different conception of the future of the Russian state. Whereas the Cossacks sought to garner for themselves rights that they regarded as traditional, Catherine set out to recreate Russia as a centralised political order. Both of these ideas could be understood as reform, but practice revealed their essential contradiction. In 1763, Cossack notables gathered in imitation of a Polish *sejm* (parliament/assembly), and planned a revival of ancient Polish and Lithuanian institutions. They imagined a separate legal system for themselves based upon the old Lithuanian Statutes, and a personal union of the Hetmanate with the Russian Empire. Catherine's response was rather severe. The following year she forced the resignation of Hetman Rozumovs'kyi and abolished the Hetmanate as such.[7]

A decision made by the greater power was discussed in an open forum, Catherine's legislative commission of 1767–8. Here the Cossacks' intellectual appropriation of the Polish system they themselves once militarily destroyed reached its logical extreme. The most articulate defender of Cossack rights, Hryhorii Poletyka, claimed that the Ukrainian leading classes always had rights, which he identified with the golden freedom of the Polish-Lithuanian Commonwealth. In his retelling, only religion had divided Ukraine from Poland, which otherwise shared a single social and political system. The idea of the

7 Z. Kohut, *Russian Centralism and Ukrainian Autonomy: Imperial Absorption of the Hetmanate 1760s–1830s* (Cambridge, Mass.: Harvard University Press, 1988).

traditional rights of nobles, invented or not, had always been alien to Muscovite traditions. Now it presented itself as a barrier to Catherine's ambitious plans.

Yet Catherine was able to win support for the elimination of the Hetmanate. Her military victories over the Ottomans and her annexation of the Crimea reduced the military importance of the Cossacks. The Zaporizhian Cossacks, free men living south and east of the Hetmanate, were simply eliminated by a Russian surprise attack in June 1775. In this situation the creation of Russian provinces in Ukraine from 1781 was accepted for lack of any practical alternative. This amounted to the elimination of real or imagined Ukrainian distinctiveness, as these provinces were part of a single centralised system. In 1786 the Ukrainian dioceses were secularised, as the Russian had been before them. The Kiev Academy, which taught a classical curriculum in Polish and Latin, was suddenly transformed into a theological school with Russian as the language of instruction. The introduction of conscription in 1789 ended any local particularities among fighting forces.

The Cossack elite accepted these fundamental transformations almost without resistance. Precisely because they defined themselves as a ruling class, they were able to accept local power on new terms. Russian reforms facilitated their claims to own land and peasants. Centralised administration opened new posts in provincial capitals. Forced to abandon the utopia of traditional Polish rights, the Cossacks happily accepted a new status as members of the Russian dvorianstvo (according to the 1785 Charter of the Nobility). The costs to Ukraine were greater, perhaps, than the costs to the Cossacks. Peasants became serfs, and the Jews were expelled from Kiev. Yet many Cossacks found that the end of traditional rights associated with Little Russia was amply compensated by the opening of new horizons in Great Russia.

Cossacks began imperial careers in Petersburg. The precedent for such a move had been set under Peter and Elizabeth, and in the 1770s and 1780s the Bezborod'ko, Zavodovs'kyi, Kochubei and Troshchyns'kyi families sent their most promising sons to the capital. In the 1790s a much larger group followed. They found a great empire with great needs. Ukrainians filled the ranks of the civil service, provided most of the notable educators, most of the (non-foreign) doctors, most of the composers, most of the journalists, and many of the great writers (Gogol arrived in 1828).

As had the clerics of the seventeenth century, the clerks of the nineteenth century brought with them historical schemes that explained their individual choices. Oleksandr Bezborod'ko was associated with the Little Russian idea of the plurality of Russian peoples, whereas Viktor Kochubei argued for a ruthless self-assimilation. Although these Ukrainians often knew Polish, the Polish political option collapsed along with the Hetmanate. The late eighteenth century was the period of the partitions of Poland, which important Ukrainians now observed from the heights of Petersburg. Petro Zavodovs'ky, the Ukrainian who served as the Russian Empire's education minister, captured the drama of the affair in 1794: 'Poland will cease to exist in Europe, like stars that have disappeared from the heavenly sphere.'[8]

The Polish-Lithuanian Commonwealth did indeed cease to exist the following year, partitioned between Prussia, Austria and Russia. Catherine was the main agent of Poland's destruction, although the final outcome was far from inevitable. She had supported her former lover, Stanislaw Poniatowski, in the 1764 royal elections. His victory heralded both reform and Russian influence, both of which were inimical to the conservative Polish-Lithuanian nobles united in the Confederation of Bar. About 100,000 nobles fought 500 engagements between 1768 and their final defeat in 1772, after which thousands of them, although Polish citizens, were exiled to Siberia. Poland was partitioned for the first time that same year.

The twenty-three years between the first and the final partitions are often seen as the final gasp of a decadent Polish political system, doomed to failure and awaiting only the proper stage for a final dramatic collapse. In fact, these were two decades of enthrallingly ambitious and successful social and political reform, led by a king who had to negotiate between the desires of his Russian patroness and the needs of his loyal subjects. Stanislaw August Poniatowski created a system of administration for the crownlands, created a state treasury from practically nothing, reformed the military and built a cadet school, rebuilt Warsaw as a proper European capital and sponsored translations of European scientific and philosophical literature.

The political classes and educated elites he essentially created in these twenty years took an interested part in the constitutional debate that began in 1789. Its culmination, the Constitution of 3 May 1791, was not only the first written constitution in Europe, it was a surprisingly progressive legal foundation for a renewed Polish political and social order. It would have transformed Poland into a constitutional monarchy, in which property rather than noble birth would determine voting rights. It replaced the traditional rights of nobles, easily manipulated by the great magnates and outside powers such as Russia, with civil rights clearly defined. Polish noble opponents announced the Targowica Confederations and invited the Russian army to restore the previous

8 D. Saunders, *The Ukrainian Impact on Russian Culture, 1750–1850* (Edmonton: CIUS, 1985).

order. After a few battles, the Polish parliament was forced to accept a second partition, in June 1793. In March 1794 Tadeusz Kosciuszko launched a massive national uprising, the last great military effort of the old Commonwealth. His troops were as many as 70,000, and he routed the local Targowicans and won victories against both Prussian and Russian forces. With a constitution and with an army, Poland was again a potential political and military rival to Russia, and Catherine initiated the third and final partition as soon as she could bring the necessary forces from the Ottoman front. Poland's last king, Stanislaw August Poniatowski, abdicated in November 1795.[9]

Russia gained about half of the territory of the extinct Polish-Lithuanian Commonwealth. But for the sliver of Ruthenian territory that Austria called eastern Galicia, it inherited all of the lands inhabited by eastern-rite believers. The way was open for a 'gathering in' of the 'Russian' peoples, including the Belarusians and Ukrainians. Russia also became the country with the largest population of Jews, replacing Poland in this role. Poland had provided Jews with a relatively tolerant haven for half a millennium, and Polish kings and nobles had elaborated a sophisticated and transparent system of communal toleration for the Jews.[10] Last but not least, Russia became the country in the world with the largest population of Poles, more than half of whom were Russian subjects after the territorial adjustments of the Congress of Vienna (1815). Poles represented not only a large native nobility with a long tradition of rights as an estate, but also a recent experiment in constitutionalism and experience (in Napoleon's Duchy of Warsaw) with new models of French civil law.[11]

Although about 30,000 Poles (and a third of the students of the university at Wilno) fought with Napoleon against Russia, Alexander (r. 1801–25) was rather patient. The Congress of Vienna created a Kingdom of Poland, usually known as the Congress Kingdom, which included Warsaw and some of central Poland. Its borders were those of Napoleon's Duchy of Warsaw, minus Cracow and Posen. Although it contained only one-seventh the territory and one-fifth the population of the pre-partition Commonwealth, it came to be seen as a Polish state. It was governed as a constitutional monarchy, with the tsar as monarch. Local legislative business was handled by a Sejm, the local language of administration was Polish, and the Congress Kingdom boasted a

9 A. Zamoyski, *The Last King of Poland* (New York: Hippocrene Books, 1992).

10 M. Rosman, *Founder of Hasidism: A Quest for the Historical Ba'al Shem Tov* (Berkeley: University of California Press, 1996); G. D. Hundert, *Jews in a Polish Private Town: The Case of Opatów in the Eighteenth Century* (Baltimore: Johns Hopkins Press, 1992).

11 E. C. Thaden, *Russia's Western Borderlands, 1710–1870* (Princeton: Princeton University Press, 1984).

separate schools system and (most fatefully) army. Lithuania was separated from Poland, although native institutions such as the school in Wilno, the law code and the local dietines were allowed to continue. Although Alexander took these arrangements seriously, disappointment with his suspicious and polonophobic successor, Nicholas (r. 1825–55), brought the November uprising of 1830.[12]

The end of the Polish-Lithuanian Commonwealth had transformed the masses of the landless gentry from conservatives (dependent on the support of rich nobles and so suspicious of the king and reforms) to radicals (protective of whatever rights were offered in the new system, and idealising the previous order). The uprising was fought to protect the constitution from Nicholas, and included in its rhetoric the Decembrists and all oppressed people of Europe. It began as a military conspiracy and seemed for some months to have a serious chance of success. Russian victory brought considerable reductions in local autonomy, codified by the 'Organic Statute' of 1832. To the east, historical legacies of Rus, Lithuania and the Commonwealth, such as the Uniate Church and the Lithuanian Statute, were undone by the Russian Empire. About 10,000 Poles (still a political notion, many of them were east Slavs and some were Jews) departed the empire, in the Great Emigration.

Beyond the frontiers of Russia, these Russian subjects established a vibrant and furiously contested world of émigré politics, centred in Paris. From without they hoped (mostly in vain) to influence the course of events within the empire. The main trends were monarchist (associated with Prince Adam Czartoryski, 1770–1861), republican (associated with the historian Joachim Lelewel, 1786–1891) and Romantic (associated with the poet Adam Mickiewicz, 1798–1855). It is worth noting that all of these trends were of political thought, rather than of ethnic identification. Czartoryski represented a great Lithuanian noble family, Lelewel's father was German and Mickiewicz was of Belarusian-Lithuanian (and perhaps Jewish) origin. Although they disagreed about much, all took for granted that the resuscitated Polish state would be a political project embodying political ideals.

Czartoryski's followers saw monarchism as a means to build a more modern social and political order. Karol Hoffman, for example, argued that a monarch was needed to build the cities and the middle classes. The monarchist 'Party of 3 May' associated itself with the Constitution of 1791, and argued that a true monarchy mediates between the nation and power. The tsar, in other words,

12 S. Kieniwicz, A. Zahorski and W. Zajewski, *Trzy powstania narodowe* (Warsaw: Książka i Wiedza, 1992).

was a false monarch. One of Czartoryski's followers, Józef Bem (1794–1850), was commander-in-chief of the revolutionary Hungarian forces in Transylvania in 1848. Monarchism was thus seen to be a progressive idea, although insufficiently so for Lelewel. His ideal was the native Slavic commune, whose pacific traditions remained alive in Poland and Ukraine, though they had long since been crushed by Muscovite despotism.

Romantic nationalism, as exemplified by Mickiewicz, also treated Russia rather as a political perversion than a national enemy, and emphasised not so much Polish national uniqueness as the Polish national mission. The 1830s and 1840s were the high tide of political Romanticism. Its lovely conceits are better remembered than the Germanic (even when written in Polish or French) Hegelianism of the Polish national philosophers. Yet the experience of disappointment with Russian rule and failure in rebellion led these men to rather interesting positions. They tended to be more open to German ideas than French philosophers, and vice versa; and more versed in both than the Russians of their day. August Cieszkowski, for example, was one of the most interesting of the Left Hegelians, known in his time for his Theory of Action. Like his colleagues, he sought to unite theory and practice, and wrote on matters of political economy and education.[13]

Yet these ideas were difficult to apply in Poland. To take a crucial example, the number of secondary school students in the Congess Kingdom declined by 50 per cent between 1829 and 1855. Even so, people of Polish education played a prominent part in the scientific life of the Russian Empire. Attainment in science or culture did not require national commitment, and indeed created some room for manoeuvre between nation and state. Some, such as Wincenty Wiszniewski (1797–1856), chose a realm of science in which national questions were transcended: he travelled the length and breadth of European Russia, choosing 273 points from which to chart the heavens. Poland had metaphorically 'disappeared like a star from the heavenly sphere', but a Pole used the vastness of Russia to chart the true locations of real stars.

The sublimated national energies of rebellious Poles with complicated careers served Russian science, as in the case of the Chodźko brothers. The younger brother, Aleksander (1804–91) took part in the national philosophic conspiracies of Wilno University, and had to leave the city. He studied eastern languages in Petersburg, became a Russian diplomat and wrote scholarly works on Persian and Kurdish languages and poetry. The elder brother, Józef

13 A. Walicki, *Philosophy and Romantic Nationalism: The Case of Poland* (Notre Dame: University of Notre Dame Press, 1982).

(1800–81), was also a Vilnius conspirator, and enlisted in the Russian army without breaking these ties. In 1830 he was asked to lead the insurrection in the Vilnius area, but his superiors had the wit to transfer him to Moldova. After another transfer in 1840, he became the leading topographer of the Caucasus. Another student conspirator provides further evidence of the pattern. Jan Prosper Witkiewicz (1808–39) was sentenced to death, had his sentence commuted to military service, learned eastern languages, became the adjutant of the governor-general of Orenburg and led secret missions to Kabul. He was a favourite guest of the Persian shah, a companion of Alexander Humboldt and, of course, the soul of the Polish community in Orenburg.

Others Poles chose Russian state service from conviction, and added to the intellectual elaboration of the Russian idea rather than to the development of intellectual life in Russia. Tadeusz Bulgarin (1789–1859) fought on both the French and the Russian sides in the Napoleonic Wars, settled in Petersburg in 1816 and published the popular Russian-language 'Northern Bee' from 1825. Though increasingly a Russian nationalist, he maintained good relations with Poles such as Mickiewicz. Józef Sękowski (1800–58), professor of oriental studies at Petersburg from 1822, played a similar role as editor of the popular 'Reader's Library'. He broke all contacts with Polishness after the failure of the November uprising. Both men helped their broad Russian readership consider the national mission of the enlarged empire, not least with respect to Ukraine.

The partitions of Poland brought right-bank Ukraine, lands west of the Dnieper, into the Russian Empire. These lands had been divided between Russia and Poland for the previous hundred years, and would continue on different trajectories within Russia for the next hundred. In left-bank Ukraine, the full integration of the old Hetmanate in the early nineteenth century was unsurprisingly softened by a sentimental remembrance of the old order. This took a sharper turn with the publication of the *Istoriia Rusov* in 1846, for this history (which had been circulating for twenty years) treated the Cossacks as the true people of Rus, and the empire as a usurper. Kharkov University (founded in 1805) was east of the old Hetmanate, and intended to anchor Ukraine in a new and more European Russia. In the event, it served to transmit a general European trend that emphasised local particularities: Romanticism. The greatest Ukrainian Romantic, Taras Shevchenko (1814–61), published his 'Kobzar' in 1840. Shevchenko composed in Russian as well as Ukrainian, and recent scholarship draws attention to the importance of Warsaw, Wilno and Polish Romanticism to his own poetic sensibility.

It is artificial to speak of a break of Ukrainian traditions with the downfall of the Hetmanate (which was never really a state, nor did it cover much of Ukraine), or of a renaissance of Ukrainian culture with Kharkiv Romanticism (which was founded only a generation after the dissolution of the Hetmanate, and beyond its former borders). Almost all culture in 'Ukraine', or 'Little Russia', or 'southern Russia' can be interpreted as consistent with Ukrainian political traditions or with Russian centralising trends. There was no inherent reason why cultured Ukrainians could not continue to provide Russian culture with a centre of gravity. The failure of Catherine's co-optation had political causes: the Crimean War (1856) and the perceived need for further state-building reform, and the Polish January uprising (1863).[14] Only at this rather late date did important connections emerge between left-bank and right-bank Ukraine, as, for example, when the populist Volodymyr Antonovych renounced right-bank principles in favour of an allegiance to the Ukrainian people in his 1862 'Confessions'.

What were these right-bank principles? Unlike left-bank Ukraine, right-bank Ukraine preserved its Polish upper and Jewish commercial classes. The political order that the left-bank Cossacks wished for in the eighteenth century actually survived in Poland, although of course the Poles ruled and the Ukrainians were almost entirely peasants. Under Russian rule this arrangement was challenged. In 1831 the Commission on National Education, which had organised schooling for Poles in the eastern partitioned territories, was closed. In 1833 the Polish lycée at Krzemeniec was shut down, and its priceless library of 34,000 volumes (including the collections of the Royal Palace in Warsaw) was transferred to Kiev. An 1845 order forbade nobles from providing Polish schooling for peasants. After 1831 about two-thirds of the local Roman Catholic monasteries were liquidated.

In 1840 the Lithuanian Statute was annulled, on the grounds that it was foreign to Russia. Ironically, this statute (written originally in Chancery Slavonic) represented an east Slavic legal tradition stretching back to Kievan Rus, broken only by the Russian Empire of the nineteenth century. The legal status of the bulk of the Polish nobility of right-bank Ukraine was attacked more directly. The policy of declassification of nobles, pursued consistently for two decades after 1831, deprived about 340,000 men of noble status, leaving only about 70,000. Ninety per cent of these possessed neither land nor serfs, meaning that right-bank Ukraine was left with about 7,000 great landholding Polish nobles. These in their turn exploited new laws on property to expel

14 P. Bushkovitch, 'The Ukraine in Russian Culture,' *JfGO*, 39, 3 (1991): 347–50.

their poorer noble brethren from the land they had tilled for generations or centuries.[15]

Polishness in west Ukraine, then, was represented by rich and often ruthless landowners. Antonovych, originally a Polish noble himself, was denouncing just this tradition when he joined the ranks of the Ukrainian populists. These landholders did, however, resist further incursions of the Russian state. They became, in a peculiar way, modernisers, exploiting Jews and Poles as their leasing agents and increasingly as the managers of their sugar-beet refineries. Petersburg attempted to counterbalance them by encouraging Russians to settle, but few Russians ever felt that they could join this society. Landholders circumvented legal restrictions on selling land to Poles by a variety of stratagems, including the leasing of land to Jews. Precisely this Polish predominance discouraged Petersburg from establishing local assemblies (*zemstva*) before 1911, for fear that they too would be controlled by Poles.

Petersburg and the Kiev governors thought to use the Ukrainian (or as they saw matters Russian) peasantry against the Polish landowners, but this was a double-edged sword. Peasants encouraged to revolt by imperial promises then had to be quelled by imperial soldiers. The land reform of 1861 raised the temperature everywhere, for peasants did not get enough land to prosper and found the (Russian-style) collective reallocation of land frustrating. Ukrainian peasants wished to know just where their individual plots were, and of course also wished to continue to use common lands to which they had enjoyed rights for centuries. Meanwhile, landless Polish nobles, abandoned by their more prosperous brethren and ignored by imperial law, also began to press their claims. Violence in right-bank Ukraine peaked in 1905–7, when 3,924 peasant uprisings were recorded. Although the declassification of nobles and the redistribution of land are usually seen as modernising steps, in the tsars' Volhynia, Podolia and Kiev provinces the Polish landlords remained atop a very traditional social order.

In central Poland (the Congress Kingdom) and in Lithuania (the Kovno, Vitebsk, Vilna, Grodno, Minsk and Mogilev provinces), modern politics emerged from the defeat of the January uprising of 1863.[16] Unlike the 1830

15 D. Beauvois, *Pouvoir russe et noblesse polonaise en Ukraine, 1793–1830* (Paris: CNRS editions, 2003); D. Beauvois, *Le Noble, le serf, et le revizor: La noblesse polonaise entre le tsarisme et les masses ukrainiennes (1831–1863)* (Paris: Editions des archives contemporaines, 1985); D. Beauvois, *La bataille de la terre en Ukraine, 1863–1914: Les polonais et les conflits socio-ethniques* (Lille: Presses universitaires de Lille, 1993).

16 T. Snyder, *The Reconstruction of Nations: Poland, Ukraine, Lithuania, Belarus, 1569–1999* (New Haven: Yale University Press, 2003); T. Weeks, *Nation and State in Late Imperial Russia: Nationalism and Russification on the Western Frontier, 1863–1914* (DeKalb: Northern Illinois University Press, 1996).

uprising, which began as a more or less organised military conspiracy, the 1863 uprising resulted from elevated hopes for political reform and lack of agreement between Poles themselves. The abolition of serfdom in the Russian Empire began furious debate in Poland on the land question, which soon became a more general discussion about the prospects for the resuscitation of local institutions. Andrzej Zamoyski was the leading voice in this debate, and was associated with the call for a 'moral revolution'. His political adversary, Aleksander Wielopolski, thought less of their countrymen, and believed that only a firm deal with Petersburg could create the foundation for reform. In this he had considerable successes: he gained the tsar's approval for land reform, a quasi-university in Warsaw and equality for the Jews.

Yet he was helpless to stem the expectations of conspiratorial radicals ('Reds'), who expected much more, and who gained support in the cities in 1861 and 1862. Wielopolski forced the issue by trying to conscript them, which led to a doomed revolt. Once military forces were in the field, moderates ('Whites') felt obliged to join the uprising, often against their better judgement. The short-lived National Government promised land to the peasants but had mixed success in their recruitment to the cause. The uprising was the high point of Polish–Jewish patriotic co-operation, as many Jews fought and died for the cause (although most Jews, like most Polish peasants, simply kept their heads down). Although many Russian radicals sympathised with the Poles, the dominant reaction in Petersburg was shock. The drastic Russifying measures that followed the uprising's defeat in 1864 forced the Warsaw intelligentsia (the term was popularised at this time) to reconsider their position in the empire.[17]

It was one of isolation, for Poland received very little international support. Warm words from Paris and hot declarations of the First International Workingmen's Congress hung in the air. Although Roman Catholicism was the religion of most Poles, the Vatican was not the ally of Poland in such moments. The Romantic messianism of Mickiewicz was popular among Poles but of course heresy for Popes. After the uprising the Roman Catholic Church within the Russian Empire was further humbled. By 1870 not a single bishop sitting in 1863 remained in his diocese. The Polish Church was subordinated to a Catholic College in Petersburg. The remnants of the Uniate Church (of Eastern rite but Western hierarchy) were absorbed by the Orthodox Church. By the turn of the century many Catholic parishes were unable to meet the

17 P. Wandycz, *The Lands of Partitioned Poland 1795–1918* (Seattle: University of Washington Press, 1974).

elementary spiritual and pastoral needs of their members. Nevertheless, the Roman Catholic Church was unchallenged in central Poland and retained 1359 churches beyond the boundaries of the old Congress Kingdom in 1914.

The main intellectual response to the catastrophe was a resolutely secular school of thought, known as Polish positivism.[18] The positivists drew the term from Comte but more of their ideas from Spencer. Their leading light was Aleksander Świętochowski (1849–1938), who spoke of 'internal independence'. Warsaw positivists hoped that society (a civic Polish nation) could be made to function like a self-sufficient organism, despite the fact that it lacked its own state. They counted on industrialisation to create a new Polish middle class, and on education to spread national culture as well as technique. Industrialisation was a reality. In the 1870s and 1880s certain parts of the Congress Kingdom became centres of the industrial revolution in Russia. Yet progress itself remained out of reach, no matter how committed intellectuals remained to science. Science itself was the new faith, and even if some of the miracles forecast in Bolesław Prus's great positivist novel *The Doll* were eerily achieved by Marie Curie (née Maria Skłodowska), technical achievements failed to end moral debates about the future of the nation.

The positivists' ambition to substitute scientific research for Romantic yearnings was realised in an extraordinarily direct manner by exiled rebels of 1863. Both Aleksander Czekanowski (1833–76) and Mikolaj Hartung (1835–83) made the journey to Siberia on foot, and collected and classified beetles along the way. Jan Czerski (1845–1915) explored Siberia for thirty years, describing dozens of unknown mammals. Michał Jankowski (1840–1912) explored the arctic on skis and in self-made boats, settled on Askold Island and ran the mine and meteorological station, then moved to the mainland and pioneered the acclimation of plants. A more literalised positivist hero is scarcely to be imagined, unless it is Adam Szymański (1852–1916), of a later generation and himself a positivist, who was sentenced to life in Yakutsk after a denunciation, and within three years had gained admission to the Russian Geographical Society for his scholarly work in geography.

Yet educated Poles of the positivist era made scientific careers in official institutions as well, without the mediation of deportation. Some of the most prominent of these served in the army, the institution that defeated the January uprising. Tomasz Augustynowicz (1809–91), the military doctor and syphilis researcher, assembled the empire's largest botanical collection. Jan Minkiewicz

18 J. Jedlicki, *A Suburb of Europe* (Budapest: Central European University Press, 1999); Stanislaus Blejwas, *Realism in Polish Politics* (New Haven: Yale Concilium on International and Area Studies, 1984).

(1826–92), head surgeon of the Caucasian Army, published 150 papers in geography and other fields, in one of them closing the circle of his many interests by comparing his own description of the river Rioni to that of Hippocrates. Leon Barszczewski (1849–1910), a colonel, won a gold medal at the 1895 Paris exposition for his photographs of minerals. Bronisław Grąbczewski, a general, discovered several minerals and insects. The greatest military entomologist of all was General Oktawiusz Radoszkowski (1820–95), president of the relevant imperial Society. While the Polish rebels (and entomologists) Czekanowski and Hartung walked to Siberia, their compatriot General Radoszkowski (entomologist) built Russian fortifications in Poland.[19] (By the way, a beetle was the crucial symbol in Prus's other great positivist novel, *Pharaoh*.) At all events, here nationality and scientific interests were no guide to political actions.

Positivists had counselled Poles to turn their gaze from 'the heavenly sphere' to the ground beneath their feet. Yet 'work at the foundations' might reinforce the state rather than build the nation, or it might have no social consequences at all. The modern Polish political activists of the 1880s and 1890s took science very seriously, but placed their faith rather in organised action. The National Democratic movement (usually dated from the founding of the National League in 1893) also used Spencerian ideas, but emphasised competition between groups rather than harmony within individual organisms.[20] Although their organisation was elitist and conspiratorial, they counted on educating the Polish-speaking masses to a proper Polish identity. Although both of the leading thinkers, Roman Dmowski and Zygmunt Balicki, were non-believers and former socialists, the movement came to be increasingly identified with the Roman Catholic faith. Jews were seen at first as difficult to assimilate, and then as essentially inassimilable. As the percentage of Jews in the lands of the Congress Kingdom grew from 9 per cent in 1827 to 15 per cent in 1909, and as Jews emigrated to Warsaw in the 1880s and 1890s, this question was impossible to avoid.

Socialists had a different answer. Polish Marxists agreed with nationalists that science could guide politics, and that science revealed a world of competition: but between classes rather than nations or races. Assimilated Jews could work as equals within the socialist movement, and nowhere else. Yet Polish Marxists disagreed among themselves about the central national question: should Poland be restored, or should Poles simply play their part

19 Notes on Polish scientists in the Russian Empire here and elsewhere drawn from Artur Kijas, *Polacy w Rosji od XVII wieku do 1917 roku: Slownik biograficzny* (Warsaw: Pax, 2000).

20 B. Porter, *When Nationalism Began to Hate: Imagining Modern Politics in Nineteenth-Century Poland* (New York: Oxford University Press, 2000).

in a world proletarian revolution? Rosa Luxemburg (1870–1919) argued that national questions distract the working class, while Kazimierz Kelles-Krauz (1872–1905) maintained that nation-states were a natural stage on the way to socialism. Luxemburg's Social Democrats were the smaller group, although they formed the core of the Communist Party of Poland formed after the First World War. The more patriotic Polish Socialist Party of Józef Pilsudski (1867–1935) was by far the more important organisation in the 1890s. During the revolution of 1905 his party split into two fractions, one counting on revolution and the other on armed conspiracy.[21]

Although socialism in Poland had to confront peculiarly Polish questions, in its origins it was in considerable measure a Russian import. The generation raised after the failure of 1863 had to grant that the Russian populists, and the socialists, were a model worthy of emulation. Interestingly, Russian populism also took a special national course in Ukraine. Many of the great students of Ukrainian culture were themselves populists, sometimes of Russian or Polish origin, who 'went to the people' and found the people to be Ukrainian. The 1876 ban on the publication of books in Ukrainian and other measures led to the emigration of Ukrainian scholars and activists from Kiev to Austrian Galicia, where their populist ideas filled the needs of an emerging Ukrainian national movement. Mykhailo Hrushevs'kyi (1866–1934) wrote his great synthesis of Ukrainian history as a professor in Lwów.

Ukrainian politics in Russia was forced towards the centre, but remained preoccupied with the peasant, who in Ukraine was or wished to be a farmer. Like a dozen or so national groups within the empire, Ukrainians exploited the occasion of 1905 to request a measure of decentralisation. Some activists pressed for an assembly in Kiev, very few had more radical hopes than federalism and socialism. Like many others, the Ukrainian neo-Kantian legal scholar Bohdan Kistiakovs'kyi (1868–1920) believed that a rule-of-law state was the best resolution of national questions. Most of the legal concessions granted by the Dumas were reversed by the end of 1907. One lasting change was Stolypin's agricultural reforms, which were greeted enthusiastically by peasants in right-bank Ukraine. Many finally got their land, and kept it until starved out by Stalin's collectivisation.

Polish ambitions during 1905 were exceptional. Two fairly mature political parties vied with each other to determine the revolution's national meaning. The Polish Socialist Party generally sought to exploit the occasion to win

21 T. Snyder, *Nationalism, Marxism, and Modern Central Europe: A Biography of Kazimierz Kelles-Krauz, 1872–1905* (Cambridge, Mass.: Harvard University Press, 1998); N. Naimark, *History of the 'Proletariat'* (Boulder: East European Monographs, 1981).

independence. The National Democrats, who in principle also wanted a Polish state, believed the situation should be allowed to mature. Piłsudski travelled to Tokyo to enlist the support of Japan against Russia; Dmowski travelled to Tokyo to thwart him. The greatest Polish statesmen of their day had a Japanese picnic. The National Democrats sought to exploit the Duma by passing legislation that supported Polish culture, but all their gains were reversed by 1907. The most pathetic moment was perhaps Stolypin's appeal to Dmowski that the latter 'admit that the greatest blessing is to be a Russian citizen'. Here was a great misunderstanding: Dmowski was willing to co-operate with the Russian state because he believed in that state's inevitable collapse.[22]

The deeper irony is that Poles played an indispensable role in the intellectual and physical construction of the Russian Empire. By this time about half a million Poles lived beyond the borders of the old Commonwealth, and notable Polish explorers and scientists pushed as far east as it was possible to go. Russia's fantastic borders were quite literally placed on maps by Poles: by geologists such as Karel Bohdanowicz (1864–1947), the most thorough explorer of Asian Russia, Leonard Jaczewski (1858–1916), who studied volcanic activity in eastern Siberia, and Józef Morozewicz (1865–1941), who described the Magnetic Mountain; or by sailors such as Józef Trzemeski (1879–1923), who spent a ten-month frozen winter north of the Arctic Circle and proved the existence of a legendary island, and Andrzej Wilkicki (1858–1913), the naval general who left the systems of signals and lamps that allowed those who followed to navigate the Arctic Sea. Poles also built the empire on land. Ksawery Skarzyński (1819–76) built the rail lines between Warsaw, Petersburg and Moscow, and then Andrzej Przenicki (1869–1941) designed bridges for the capital. Kazimierz Elżanowski (1875–1932) tunnelled through the Caucusus and also built the rail line from Samarkand to Tashkent. Tadeusz Niklewicz (1877–1956) built the port of Vladivostok.

As Russian and Ukrainian nationalism emerged in the early twentieth century, both placed the cradle of nationhood in Kiev. The Russian archeologist who studied Kiev's St Sofia, the spiritual centre of these national histories, was in fact a Polish architect, Karol Majewski (1824–97), whose major professional task was the design of modern state buildings in Petersburg and Moscow. Whether such work is understood as culture or civilisation, the sheer force of Polish achievement within the late Russian Empire is undeniable. Just as seventeenth-century Ukrainian clerics from Kiev adapted to new predicaments by conceiving for Muscovites a theory of rule that left a dignified place

22 E. Chmielewski, *The Polish Question in the Russian State Duma* (Knoxville: University of Tennessee Press, 1970).

for Ukraine, and eighteenth-century Cossacks turned the end of traditional rights into an honourable role in tsarist expansion by migrating to Petersburg, so nineteenth-century Polish men and women, responding to dilemmas of modernity, helped, directly or indirectly, to modernise Russia. The story is rarely told thus. The afterglow of a collapsed empire casts mainly shadows, and the Ukrainian and Polish questions are seen darkly in the fading light. Indeed, no Russian empire could survive without Ukraine, and no Russian state with European aspirations could avoid a challenge from Latin and Catholic Poland. Yet over the centuries, the main work of Ukrainians was constitutive, and the main direction of Polish activity was creative.

9
The Jews

BENJAMIN NATHANS

Let us begin with the end. It has not escaped attention that the execution of Tsar Nicholas II and his family on 17 July 1918 was directed by Yakov Moiseevich Sverdlov (1885–1919), the first chairman of the Soviet government. The image of a Jew administering the *coup de grâce* to the Romanov dynasty and to tsarist Russia was at one time emblematic of the striking role of Jews in the Russian Revolution, a source of one of the twentieth century's most potent controversies. Well before the Bolshevik seizure of power, however, Russian Jews had already imprinted themselves on world consciousness, not as regicides but as pogrom victims and impoverished refugees. During its final decades, over 2 million Jews fled the Romanov empire for points west (Europe and especially America) and, in far smaller but historically no less significant numbers, south (Ottoman Palestine). Among the enormous waves of human migration from Europe in the nineteenth and early twentieth centuries, in fact, only the Irish matched Russian Jews in the magnitude and permanence of their departure.

Many explanations have been offered for these remarkable phenomena, but one has tended to overshadow them all: that a deeply anti-Semitic Russia, alone among the European great powers at the end of the 'long nineteenth century' (1789–1914), had failed to emancipate its Jews.[1] In a display of what the historian Tómaš Masaryk called Russia's 'Christian medievalism', the tsarist autocracy confined its Jewish subjects to the 'Pale of Settlement' in the empire's western borderlands, at a safe distance from most ethnic Russians. In addition to territorial containment, a vast labyrinth of discriminatory laws – 'exceeding in volume the [entire] Code Napoleon', as a liberal Russian journal lamented in 1885 – restricted Jews' choice of career, their ability to own real estate, and countless other arenas of daily life.[2]

1 One other state, Rumania, also maintained official discrimination against Jews until after the First World War.
2 *Vestnik Evropy* (January 1885): 461.

The history of Russian Jewry has thus appeared as a self-reinforcing triad of discrimination, emigration and revolution, a turbulent reflection of the tsarist doctrine of 'Orthodoxy, Autocracy, and Nationality' inaugurated by Nicholas II's great-grandfather and namesake, Tsar Nicholas I. And yet, like that doctrine, the image of Russian Jewry as driven by state-sponsored repression to mass exodus or revolutionary struggle barely begins to capture the deeper structures of official policy, the forces at work within Jewish society and the dynamics of the Russian–Jewish encounter.

The present chapter explores these issues over the course of two and a half centuries, divided into three unequal periods. The first, a prologue, concerns the era prior to the partitions of Poland at the end of the eighteenth century, during which Jews were legally barred from Russia. The second, extending from the partitions to the Great Reforms of the middle of the nineteenth century, surveys the earliest efforts by the tsarist government to reform its newly acquired Jewish population as well as the currents of pietism and enlightenment that began to recast Jewish society from within. The third, extending from the Great Reforms to the First World War, traces the increasing presence of Jews in Russian society, the rise of independent Jewish political movements and the emergence of the so-called 'Jewish Question' at the heart of debates about modernity and empire in Russia.

The pre-partition period

By the year 1600 the majority of the world's Jews lived in the eastern half of Europe. Rising persecution in the West, including massacres by Crusaders, accusations of ritual murder and host desecration, and numerous expulsions from cities or entire countries, had driven hundreds of thousands of Jews eastwards, where leaders of relatively less urbanised (and more tolerant) lands promoted Jewish settlement in order to stimulate commercial activity and fiscal vigour. Russia's neighbours, the Polish-Lithuanian Commonwealth and the Ottoman Empire, dividing between them the East European corridor from the Baltic Sea in the north to the Black Sea in the south, were the principal recipients of this migration. They quickly became the demographic heartland of Jewish civilisation for much of the early modern period.

This historic migration from Western to Eastern Europe halted abruptly at the border of Muscovite Russia, whose rulers repeatedly banned Jewish settlement. Muscovy's long-standing fear of proselytising by foreign faiths had crystallised, in the Jewish case, during the so-called 'Judaisers' (*zhidovstvuiushchie*) controversy in the late fifteenth century. While it is by no means clear that the

'Judaisers' or their teachings bore any substantive relation to Judaism, their legacy was a strident Judeophobia among Muscovy's clerical and political elites. But not, apparently, among Russians at large: prior to the nineteenth century, Russian popular culture was largely free of references to Jews, if only because of the absence of sustained contact with them.[3] The occasional exceptions to the ban on Jews in Russia were typically granted at the behest of Christian merchants eager to buy and sell goods with Polish Jews at annual trade fairs in Riga, Kiev, Nezhin and elsewhere.

Under Peter the Great (r. 1689–1725), pragmatic considerations gained strength. While bans on Jewish settlement were not rescinded, neither were they renewed. Peter imported a number of Jewish converts from the Netherlands and employed them at various levels of government, from court jester to chief of police in the newly founded city of St Petersburg. His successors, however, quickly reverted to a hard line. In 1727, for example, Catherine I (r. 1725–7) extended the ban on Jews to the recently acquired Ukrainian territories. Empress Anna (r. 1730–40) renewed the ban, suggesting possible difficulties with its enforcement. Anna also presided over the public burning in St Petersburg of Baruch Leibov, a Jewish merchant accused of instigating the conversion to Judaism of a Russian naval captain as well as of torturing a Christian girl in order to obtain her blood for ritual purposes. Peter the Great's daughter Elizabeth I (r. 1741–61) inaugurated a campaign of forced conversion of Russia's non-Orthodox subjects, including Muslims and Jews, and reissued older decrees barring Jews from Russian soil. In response to a petition from Christian merchants in Riga requesting special permission for their Jewish counterparts to do business in the city, Elizabeth famously declared, 'I desire no mercenary profit from the enemies of Christ.'

Even as Jews were repeatedly barred from coming to Russia, however, Russia itself was coming to the Jews, an unintended consequence of its successful wars against the Polish and Ottoman states. The annexation of eastern Ukraine from Poland in 1667 brought thousands of Jews de facto under Russian rule. Conquests in the Baltic region (1721), the Crimean peninsula (1783) and the northern littoral of the Black Sea (1791) – the last two seized from the Ottoman Empire – similarly placed significant numbers of Jews under the dominion of the tsars. The most fateful recasting of borders came, however, with the three-stage partition of Poland (1772, 1792, 1795), as a result of which some half a million Jews – the largest Jewish population of any country in the world – were transformed into subjects of the Romanovs.

3 J. Klier, *Russia Gathers Her Jews: The Origins of the 'Jewish Question' in Russia, 1772–1825* (DeKalb: Northern Illinois University Press, 1986), p. 30.

Early encounters

Russia was by no means the only country to acquire its Jews unintentionally. Prussia and Austria, the other participants in the partitioning of Poland, found themselves in a similar situation, as had France two centuries earlier with the conquest of Alsace and Lorraine. But these countries had had prior (if not very happy) experience with Jews, and the Jewish communities they acquired as a result of annexation were relatively small. Half a million Polish Jews could not be dealt with by the traditional method of expulsion – at least not in the imagination of eighteenth-century rulers.

Under Polish rule, Jews had achieved a degree of collective autonomy unsurpassed in their European diaspora. They possessed their own languages – Hebrew for liturgical and scholarly purposes, Yiddish as the vernacular. Their forms of dress, especially for males, were distinctive. They were highly concentrated in certain occupations (as tavern-keepers, estate managers, merchants and artisans) and maintained a dense network of communal institutions whose task was to sustain religious traditions and to secure the basic needs of the poor. While intimately enmeshed in urban economies and networks of exchange between land-owning aristocrats and enserfed peasants, Polish Jews typically lived in segregated quarters. They benefited from numerous exemptions from general laws even as they suffered from multiple forms of legal discrimination. Most importantly, Polish Jews sustained a system of collective self-government (including internal taxation and administration of justice according to Jewish law) that made Judaism not just a religion but a social order. Though not formally part of the hierarchy of estates that composed Polish society, in practice the Jews functioned as one of the many corporate elements in a highly segmented population.

Catherine the Great (r. 1762–96), who presided over Russia's annexation of eastern Poland, was determined to order things differently. As part of her campaign to fashion a European-style society of hereditary estates, Catherine embarked on a programme of absorbing her newly acquired Jewish subjects into the Russian social hierarchy while gradually dismantling separate Jewish communal institutions. Henceforth, Jews were to enjoy the privileges and obligations of members of the urban estates – the *meshchanstvo* (artisans and petty traders) and *kupechestvo* (merchants). On paper, at least, Catherine granted terms of integration to her Jewish subjects that went beyond what any of Europe's old regimes had offered.

In reality, however, the old structures of Polish-Jewish life remained largely undisturbed. It was not simply a matter of Catherine's sudden loss of enthusiasm for Enlightenment ideas of order and utility in the wake of the French Revolution. Hostility in the imperial court, as well as among the clergy and segments of the Christian merchantry, deterred the tsarina from relaxing the inherited prohibition on Jews in the empire's Russian heartland. By confining her Jewish subjects to the former Polish and Ottoman territories annexed by St Petersburg, Catherine in effect perpetuated the *cordon sanitaire* established by her predecessors, laying the groundwork for what in 1835 formally became the 'Pale of Permanent Jewish Settlement' (*cherta postoiannoi evreiskoi osedlosti*), a territory extending from Kovno to Odessa, roughly the size of France.

Quite apart from pervasive anti-Jewish sentiment, Catherine's integrative agenda ran up against the fact that, from a strictly utilitarian viewpoint, the costs of dismantling Jewish corporative autonomy threatened to exceed the benefits. Who, if not the local Jewish communal governing board, the *kahal*, would collect Jewish taxes for the imperial treasury? Who would record Jewish births and deaths, censor books in Yiddish and Hebrew and render justice at the local level? Stretched to the limit by its recent imperial conquests, the tsarist regime lacked alternatives to the kahal as an instrument of fiscal and social control. A similar logic helped preserve, at least in the short term, a relatively high degree of communal autonomy among other recently conquered peoples such as Poles and Finns.

During the initial decades of tsarist rule, in fact, the most significant threat to the kahal's authority came from within Jewish society itself. By the beginning of the nineteenth century, the mystical-pietist movement known as Hasidism had fanned outwards from its birthplace in the Ukrainian province of Podolia as far north as Bialystok and as far south as Odessa. Investing new, person-centred meaning into traditional Jewish texts and practices, Hasidism offered its followers (the *Hasidim*) a kind of spiritual enfranchisement, making accessible the esoteric teachings of Jewish mysticism, or *kabbalah*. At the heart of the new movement was the figure of the *tsaddik* (holy man and wonder worker), whose charismatic authority contrasted with that of the traditional rabbi, the interpreter of Jewish law.[4] While the Hasidim – in contrast to Jewish religious reformers in Central Europe – remained strictly within the bounds of Jewish law and liturgy, the movement's radically new leadership structure posed an unprecedented challenge to traditional communal and rabbinic

4 For an excellent recent summary of scholarship on Hasidism and Polish-Jewish society on the eve of the partitions of Poland, see G. Hundert, *Jews in Poland-Lithuania in the Eighteenth Century: A Genealogy of Modernity* (Berkeley: University of California Press, 2004).

authority. Hasidism assumed the character of a large but diffuse sect (its precise dimensions remain unknown), with separate houses of worship, charitable institutions, and quasi-royal 'courts' centred around the tsaddikim. The resulting threat to established Jewish elites – whose coercive powers were limited to begin with – gave rise to numerous intramural conflicts, including instances in which rabbis appealed to tsarist officials for assistance in their struggle against Hasidic rivals – and vice versa.[5]

Relations with gentile powers-that-be were traditionally the exclusive prerogative of the kahal. To put it more theoretically: if, as Max Weber argued, the monopoly on the legitimate use of violence is the defining characteristic of the modern state, then the kahal's monopoly on legitimate *recourse* to the gentile state was the guiding principle of Jewish political behaviour and the sine qua non of Jewish autonomy.[6] It should be noted, however, that the challenge posed by Hasidism to the kahal's monopoly over access to tsarist authorities was an unintended consequence of the movement's growth, rather than part of some larger Hasidic plan to employ non-Jewish power in order to transform Jewish society. Most of the tsar's Jewish subjects at the time, Hasidic or not, wished above all to be left alone.

The same cannot be said for the followers of the Jewish Enlightenment (*Haskalah*), which during the early nineteenth century spread from its point of origin in Berlin to outposts in the Russian Empire such as Odessa, Riga, Shklov and Vilna. Like the larger European Enlightenment from which it derived, the Haskalah was less a coherent movement than a distinctive form of social criticism. It aimed to transform the Jews by recasting the way they were educated: stripping away accumulated superstitions, introducing secular subjects, replacing the corrupt Yiddish 'jargon' with German or Russian (along with revitalising the study of Hebrew) and steering Jews to productive labour, especially agriculture.[7] In contrast to inward-looking Hasidism, and because its followers were so few and so isolated, the Haskalah in Russia looked to the state as an ally for Jewish reform. Isaac Baer Levinson (1788–1860), for example, who served as a translator for Russian forces during the Napoleonic Wars, submitted numerous memoranda to the tsarist government urging reform of

5 G. M. Deych (ed.), *Tsarskoe pravitel'stvo i khasidskoe dvizhenie v Rossii. Arkhivnye dokumenty* (self-published, 1994).

6 E. Lederhendler, *The Road to Modern Jewish Politics: Political Tradition and Political Reconstruction in the Jewish Community of Tsarist Russia* (New York: Oxford University Press, 1989), pp. 3–13.

7 On the Haskalah in the Russian Empire see I. Etkes (ed.), *Ha-dat ve-hahaim: Tenu 'at ha-haskalah be-mizrakh eiropa* (Jerusalem: Merkaz Zalman Shazar, 1993) and M. Zalkin, *Ba- 'alot ha-shahar: Ha-haskalah ha-yehudit ba-imperyah ha-rusit ba-me 'ah ha-tesha- 'esreh* (Jerusalem: Hebrew University Magnes Press, 2000).

Jewish parochial schools and stricter supervision of Hebrew publishing. His major programmatic work, *Te'udah be-yisrael* (A Witness in Israel), publication of which was delayed for five years by Jewish opponents, bore the imprimatur of the Russian government.

Of course tsarist bureaucrats in the Petrine and Catherinian mould hardly needed Jewish dissidents to introduce them to Enlightenment ideas. In fits and starts, notions of economic utility and social engineering were beginning to compete with Muscovite Judeophobia to reshape government policies. The rhetoric of 'civic improvement' of the Jews, borrowed from earlier debates in Europe, was already present in the deliberations of various official 'Jewish Committees' under Alexander I (r. 1801–25), though with little or no effect on the ground. Real change began under Nicholas I (r. 1825–55), who gave Jews definitive evidence that the old (Polish) dispensation was gone. Like his predecessors, Nicholas sought to break down Jewish autonomy through state-sponsored 'merging' (*sliianie*) with the surrounding population. Unlike them, however, he took as his medium for accomplishing this aim not the embryonic hierarchy of urban estates but the imperial army. As part of his extension of compulsory military service to many of the groups inhabiting the formerly Polish territories, Nicholas decreed in 1827 that henceforth Jewish communities would no longer enjoy the privilege of paying extra taxes in lieu of sending recruits. Over the course of the next three decades, some 50,000 Jews served as soldiers in Russia's army, where the normal term of service was twenty-five years. Among them were thousands of 'cantonists', boys as young as eight or nine.

The introduction of compulsory military service produced what can arguably be called the first 'Russian' Jews. Many served outside the Pale, in Russia proper. Several thousand converted to Christianity. Most – including Yakov Sverdlov's grandfather – learned Russian and were exposed to Russian ways of life. But their integration was painfully incomplete: unless they converted, Jews were barred from advancing to the rank of officer, and veterans who survived the gruelling twenty-five years of service were forced to return to the Pale of Settlement, where once again they faced all the standard legal disabilities against Jews even as their former communities shunned them as outsiders. Those communities, too, were deeply shaken by the draft. The fact that the macabre job of selecting recruits was placed in the hands of communal authorities only deepened sectarian and class fault lines, producing numerous instances of rioting, kidnapping and denunciation. Although by mid-century some 50,000 Jews had been drafted, they were judged to have contributed little to the army's strength – certainly less than the value of the taxes Jews had previously paid for the privilege of exemption from military service.[8]

Other, less coercive strategies of 'merging' the Jews with the surrounding population were even less successful. Abolition of the kahal by imperial decree in 1844 stripped Jewish self-government of formal recognition by the tsarist state but hardly put an end to the institutions and practices of Jewish communal life.[9] In an effort to weaken the grip of Jewish religious education, the government's 'Jewish Committee' (1840–63; officially known as the 'Committee for the Determination of Measures for the Fundamental Transformation of the Jews in Russia') established a network of state-sponsored primary schools specifically for Jews. In the face of severe communal suspicion, however, only a few hundred boys enrolled annually. Similarly, when special agricultural colonies were set up in an effort to fashion a Jewish peasantry, only several hundred families took part, and many subsequently returned to their home communities. Like military service, neither secular schools nor agricultural labour gave 'merged' Jews rights equal to those of their Christian counterparts. Graduates of state-sponsored Jewish schools still required a gymnasium diploma in order to apply to an institution of higher education. Jewish agricultural colonists were kept carefully segregated from Christian peasants for fear that the former would revert to old habits and 'exploit' the labour of the latter.

For the time being, then, the tangible influence of Enlightenment notions of integration and social utility – whether championed by followers of the Haskalah or by tsarist bureaucrats – was slight at best. Until the second half of the nineteenth century, in fact, Russian Jewry as a whole was marginal – literally and figuratively – to imperial Russia's political and cultural life, the object of a minor species of Orientalism along with gypsies and other exotic 'Eastern' peoples.

This state of affairs was destined to change, however, for a variety of reasons. To begin with, the Jewish population was expanding at an exceptionally high rate over the course of the nineteenth century. By the time of the 1897 census, there were some 5.2 million Jews in the Russian Empire,

8 M. Stanislawski, *Tsar Nicholas I and the Jews: The Transformation of Jewish Society in Russia, 1825–1855* (Philadelphia: Jewish Publication Society, 1983), pp. 13–34; Y. Petrovsky-Shtern, *Evrei v russkoi armii 1827–1914* (Moscow: Novoe literaturnoe obozrenie, 2003), pp. 113–72.

9 A. Shochat, 'Ha-hanhaga be-kehilot rusiya im bitul ha-kahal', *Tsiyon* 42, 3/4 (1977): 143–233; I. Bartal, 'Responses to Modernity: Haskalah, Orthodoxy, and Nationalism in Eastern Europe', in S. Almog, J. Reinharz and A. Shapira (eds.), *Zionism and Religion* (Hanover, USA: University Press of New England, 1998), pp. 13–24.

an approximately tenfold increase over the course of a single century, nearly five times the growth rate of the ethnic Russian population. Jews became the empire's fifth largest – and the largest non-Slavic and non-Christian – ethnic group.[10] It is not that Jewish women bore markedly more children than others; nor was Jewish life-expectancy longer than that of most other ethnic groups. Rather, the key factors appear to have been a lower rate of infant mortality (possibly due to religiously prescribed hygienic practices and lower levels of alcohol consumption) along with dramatically higher rates of remarriage (as well as divorce), thus allowing individuals to create second families.[11]

Robust demographic growth produced a population both young and mobile. By the end of the nineteenth century over half the empire's Jews were under the age of twenty. Internal migration brought hundreds of thousands of Jews out of *shtetlakh* (small rural towns, sing. *shtetl*) into rapidly expanding cities. Never before had so many Jews lived in one country and never, since their expulsion from ancient Israel, had Jews formed such a high proportion of the local population: by 1897 over a tenth of the population of the Pale as a whole, a third or more in cities such as Warsaw, Odessa, Lodz and Vilna, and an absolute majority in dozens of large towns across the Pale. By century's end, half the Jewish population lived in urban settings, as compared with 16 per cent of ethnic Russians and Latvians and 23 per cent of ethnic Germans and Armenians.

Demographic expansion, an increasingly youthful population and significant geographic mobility only intensified the centrifugal forces that had begun to weaken Jewish communal authority from within. As the kahal gradually lost its monopoly on recourse to outside powers, and as the tsarist state began to accept input from other, internally unsanctioned sources, a contest for authority was unleashed within the Jewish world that would define much of Russian-Jewish history for the next century.

10 Jews outnumbered Estonians, Latvians and Lithuanians combined (4.1 million), Tatars (3.7 million), Kazaks (3.1 million), Georgians (1.4 million) and Armenians (1.2 million). While the empire's Muslims totalled some 14 million, they were divided into numerous ethnic and linguistic groups (e.g. Tatars, Kazaks, Bashkirs, Uzbeks). See H. Bauer et al. (eds.), *Die Nationalitäten des Russischen Reiches in der Volkszählung von 1897* (Stuttgart: F. Steiner, 1991), vol. II: *Ausgewählte Daten*, pp. 77–8.

11 C. Y. Freeze, *Jewish Marriage and Divorce in Imperial Russia* (Hanover, USA: University Press of New England, 2002), pp. 68–71; D. Ransel, 'The Ethno-Cultural Impact on Childbirth and Disease Among Women in Western Russia', *Jews in Eastern Europe* (Fall, 2001): 27–47.

Into the whirlwind

One of the first groups to rise to prominence in that contest was a cohort of Jewish merchants whose livelihoods brought them into frequent contact with tsarist officials and at the same time made them economically independent of Jewish communal authorities. By the middle of the nineteenth century, Jews had come to dominate commercial life in the empire's western borderlands; some 27,000 registered Jewish merchants constituted nearly three-quarters of the merchant estate in the territories of the Pale. Dozens of them built mini-empires of their own as tax-farmers in the liquor trade, collecting millions of roubles for the state treasury (which depended heavily on revenue from the sale of vodka) and amassing considerable fortunes for themselves. Foremost among them was Evzel Gintsburg (1812–78). Like a good number of his colleagues, Gintsburg shared the Haskalah's aspirations to reform Jewish society and to break down the barriers separating it from the surrounding population. Unlike men such as Levinsohn, however, Gintsburg had proved his utility to the tsarist state and had direct access to high officials in the imperial capital.

Sensing a change in the political winds following the death of Nicholas I, Jewish merchants began to submit what would become an extended series of petitions to the government's Jewish Committee. In essence, these proposals called for St Petersburg to return to the estate-based approach adopted by Catherine the Great, that is, to 'merge' Jews with the surrounding population by incorporating them into the appropriate estates. This time, however, rather than automatically assigning the entire Jewish population to the various urban estates, only certain groups of Jews who had demonstrated their usefulness to society at large would qualify, and having been formally recognised as merchants, artisans, soldiers, etc., they would receive the same rights and privileges as other members of the given estate. Chief among the rights sought by Gintsburg and other merchants was the freedom to live and work outside the Pale, in the empire's vast Russian interior. The potential economic gains, for the merchants themselves as well as for the imperial treasury, were considerable. But so, according to Gintsburg, were the civilising influences that would flow from exposure to 'native Russians', the empire's 'ruling' nationality, in contrast to the Poles, Lithuanians and 'little Russians' (Ukrainians and Belorussians) among whom Jews resided in the Pale.[12]

12 See the petition by Gintsburg and other Jewish merchants quoted in Benjamin Nathans, *Beyond the Pale: The Jewish Encounter with Late Imperial Russia* (Berkeley: University of California Press, 2002), pp. 50–1.

In effect, Gintsburg and his fellow merchants proposed a dramatic widening of social and legal distinctions within the Jewish population. Yet they had something far broader in mind than their own well-being. The granting of freedom of residence and other privileges only to 'useful' Jews was meant to serve as a powerful instrument in the Jewish elite's struggle to transform the Jewish masses, and thereby to chip away at the wall separating Jews from their neighbours. As Gintsburg's secretary, the Haskalah enthusiast Emanuel Levin, put it in an 1859 memorandum to his employer, 'We must gradually prepare our co-religionists for the great epoch, make them worthy and capable of apprehending the grand blessing whose arrival, especially under the new spirit of the current government, we have good reason to hope for.'[13]

In 1859, the tsarist government under Alexander II (r. 1855–81) granted to Jewish merchants of the first guild the rights and privileges of their Christian counterparts, including the freedom to reside with their families and employees outside the Pale. Over the course of the next decade, petitions streamed into the Jewish Committee from students, artisans, retired soldiers and other groups eager to translate their usefulness into expanded rights – often with the implicit endorsement of Evzel Gintsburg or his son Horace, who in the meantime had moved to St Petersburg and established the House of Gintsburg as the empire's largest private bank. The result was a series of laws that extended the rights and obligations associated with specific Russian estates – including residential rights – to Jewish graduates of Russian universities (1861), to certain categories of Jewish artisans who were in short supply outside the Pale (1865), to Jewish veterans of Nicholas I's army (1867) and finally to Jewish graduates of all Russian post-secondary educational institutions (1879).

The policy of selective Jewish integration was consistent with St Petersburg's general approach to ruling its non-Russian and non-Christian populations in the nineteenth century. In addition to serving as an instrument of social control within Russian society, the hierarchy of estates (*soslovіia*) also provided a technique of imperial management, allowing the government to assign privileges and obligations to corporate units within non-Russian ethnic groups, dividing the favoured from the unfavoured and binding the former to the imperial state. Prior to the Reform era, this practice was most visible at the top of the social ladder, as the tsarist state attempted to integrate non-Russian hereditary ruling elites (for example, among Poles, Baltic Germans, Georgians and Tatars) into the Russian nobility. Jews, however (along with Armenians, Old Believers and other minority groups), lacked such an elite, leading the

13 Nathans, *Beyond the Pale*, p. 52.

Reform-era government to focus instead on absorbing what it considered to be economically 'useful' elements of the Jewish population into the Russian estate hierarchy.

Russia's strategies of imperial rule were not the only model for the policy of selective Jewish integration. Indeed, in their public and private discussions of the subject, both tsarist officials and Jewish reformers were more likely to invoke the example of Jewish communities in Europe than that of other minority groups in the Russian Empire. Unlike Baltic Germans and Armenians, Jews were a truly pan-European minority. From the eve of the French Revolution to the aftermath of German unification, the so-called 'Jewish Question' had gained extraordinary prominence in European societies as the wave of Jewish emancipation swept across the continent from west to east – stopping abruptly, as had the Jews themselves in previous centuries, at the border of the Russian Empire. St Petersburg's Reform-era policy of selective Jewish integration can thus be understood as a cautious attempt to adapt European-style emancipation to the corporative structure of Russian society, which itself was not yet emancipated from the hierarchies of the old regime.

The results of selective integration were dramatic. By 1880, some 60,000 Jews were legally residing in the provinces of European Russia outside the Pale. By the time of the 1897 census, that number had risen to 128,343, while an additional 186,422 Jews were recorded as living in Siberia, Central Asia, the Caucasus and the Baltic provinces.[14] By century's end more than 314,000 Jews were thus living outside the Pale, with the largest single community in St Petersburg. 'It's apparent to everyone,' noted Dostoevsky in 1877 in his serialised *Writer's Diary* (*Dnevnik Pisatelia*), 'that their rights in choosing a place of residence have broadened immensely over the last twenty years. At least they have appeared in Russia in places where they weren't seen before.'[15] And, as contemporaries were quick to note, in institutions where they weren't seen before: above all those of higher education, the leading incubator of Russia's nascent civil society as well as of the revolutionary movement. By the 1880s Jews accounted for 10 per cent of gymnasium students and 15 per cent of university students across the Russian Empire. Inside and outside the Pale, Jewish beneficiaries of selective integration were becoming an unmistakeable presence in the worlds of banking and finance, journalism, and a host of

14 It is impossible, however, to determine how many of the latter group left the Pale thanks to selective integration and how many were descended from Jewish communities that had lived in these regions throughout the nineteenth century.

15 F. Dostoevsky, *A Writer's Diary*, trans. Kenneth Lantz (Evanston: Northwestern University Press, 1994), vol. II, p. 908.

white-collar professions whose ranks ballooned in the wake of the Great Reforms. Perhaps the most dramatic example was in the legal profession: by the 1880s, 13 per cent of the empire's lawyers and 20 per cent of apprentice lawyers were Jews. In cities such as Odessa, Warsaw and St Petersburg, the percentages were considerably higher.[16]

Jews also entered the ranks of virtually the entire spectrum of Russian revolutionary parties, from populists and terrorists to the multiple varieties of social democrats. In a handful of cases they were co-founders. Mark Natanson, a student at the Military-Medical Academy in St Petersburg, helped launch Land and Freedom, Russia's first revolutionary party, in 1878; six of the nine delegates to the founding congress of the Russian Social Democratic Workers' Party (RSDWP) in Minsk in 1898 were Jews; after 1903, the leader of the Menshevik fraction of the RSDWP was Iulii Martov (1873–1923), grandson of the Hebrew and Yiddish publisher Alexander Tsederbaum (1816–93). Contemporaries and historians have argued passionately about whether the presence of Jews in the revolutionary movement was a symptom of their assimilation to the Russian environment (the 'non-Jewish Jew' theory) or, on the contrary, of a modern Jewish propensity to rebellion (intellectual and political) against the gentile order.[17]

Selective integration began to transform Jewish society as well, imposing stark new forms of inequality. Graduates of Russian gymnasia and universities formed a new 'diploma intelligentsia' whose status, like that of Gintsburg and his cohort of merchants, rested on institutions outside the purview of Jewish communities. Some, like the lawyer and later Duma (parliament) deputy Joseph Gessen (1866–1943), used their independence to detach themselves from Jewish society, while others, like the ophthalmologist Max Mandelshtam (1839–1912), took an active role in communal and national affairs, often competing with rabbinic or plutocratic elites. There were, to be sure, instances of co-operation between Jewish intellectuals and wealthy notables: one of the most prominent was the Society for the Spread of Enlightenment among the Jews of Russia, established in St Petersburg in 1863. Initially conceived as a kind of headquarters for the Haskalah in Russia, the society's main achievement in its early decades was its massive subsidisation of scholarships for Jewish university students. Even more influential as a mouthpiece of the newly minted Jewish

16 See data in Nathans, *Beyond the Pale*, pp. 218, 343, 348 and 354.

17 Among noteworthy recent contributions to the debate are E. Haberer, *Jews and Revolution in Nineteenth-Century Russia* (Cambridge: Cambridge University Press, 1995); A. Solzhenitsyn, *Dvesti let vmeste (1795–1995)*, 2 vols. (Moscow: Russkii put', 2001–2); and Y. Slezkine, *The Jewish Century* (Princeton: Princeton University Press, 2004).

intelligentsia was the burgeoning Jewish press. The 1860s and 1870s witnessed the founding of nearly a dozen Jewish newspapers and journals in Russian, Hebrew, Yiddish and Polish, vehicles for (among other things) an explosion of Jewish literary creativity. The centres of the new Jewish print-culture included venerable cities such as Vilna and Warsaw but also newer communities based in Odessa and St Petersburg.[18] To an even greater extent than networks of rabbis or merchants, the periodical press brought far-flung Jewish communities into contact with one another, fostering for the first time in Russia a sustained public conversation on Jewish issues of the day.

In the Russian press, too, that conversation was increasingly audible, not to say shrill. By the late 1870s, in fact, selective integration had begun to produce a notable backlash. Even the modest easing of legal discrimination against Jews, coupled with a general increase in social mobility made possible by the Great Reforms, was presented as putting ethnic Russians at a disadvantage in their own empire. Jews, not alone but most prominently among various minority groups, were already disproportionately present in the professions that constituted the building blocks of an emerging imperial civil society. In this sense, selective integration and urbanisation produced effects strikingly similar to those that had followed legal emancipation elsewhere in Europe. Anti-Jewish riots, accusations of ritual murder, calls for scaling back Jewish rights – all these periodically surfaced in *fin-de-siècle* Russia as they did in the Austro-Hungarian Empire, Wilhelmine Germany, republican France and elsewhere.

Most striking in the Russian case were the outbursts of public violence against Jews. It is true that anti-Jewish riots had occurred sporadically well before the reform era, especially in southern cities like Odessa, where rapid Jewish in-migration stimulated ethnic hostility. But in the absence of a developed railroad network and means of mass communication, such incidents typically had been confined to a single town or city and were easily contained by police and military forces. By the 1880s this was no longer the case. The wave of anti-Jewish violence triggered by the assassination of Alexander II on

18 On the reform-era Jewish press, see J. Klier, *Imperial Russia's Jewish Question, 1855–1881* (Cambridge: Cambridge University Press, 1995), pp. 66–122; A. Orbach, *New Voices of Russian Jewry: A Study of the Russian-Jewish Press of Odessa in the Era of the Great Reforms, 1860–1871* (Leiden: Brill, 1980); and Y. Slutsky, *Ha-itonut ha-yehudit-rusit ba-me'ah ha-tesha'-esre* (Jerusalem: Mosad Bialik, 1970), pp. 9–55. On the rise of a modern literature in Jewish languages in the Russian Empire, see D. Miron, *A Traveler Disguised: A Study in the Rise of Modern Yiddish Fiction in the Nineteenth Century* (New York: Shocken Books, 1973), and Robert Alter, *The Invention of Hebrew Literature: Modern Fiction and the Language of Realism* (Seattle: University of Washington Press, 1988).

1 March 1881, for example, quickly spread to dozens of cities, and while individual pogroms rarely lasted more than a few days, attacks continued across southern provinces of the Pale for over three years, reaching hundreds of cities and towns and claiming dozens of lives along with millions of roubles worth of property.

Both the causes and the effects of the 1881–4 pogroms have been the subject of considerable controversy. Contemporary conspiracy theories, according to which tsarist officials instigated the violence to deflect popular discontent from an incompetent regime, or revolutionaries organised the riots as a prelude to a broader uprising, have now been laid to rest. Even the most common contemporary explanation – that the pogroms were the bitter harvest of Jewish exploitation of the peasantry – has failed to withstand scrutiny, given that little seems to have changed in relations between Jews and peasants that could account for the sudden outbursts of violence, and in any event the pogroms were almost exclusively urban. In fact, historians have yet to provide a satisfying explanation of the events beyond the undeniable but vague fact of widespread social and economic dislocation in the wake of the emancipation of the serfs and other Great Reforms.[19]

Much has been made of the pogroms' effects on Russia's Jews, and indeed on modern Jewish history as a whole. Episodes of violence – pogroms in the 1880s, the expulsion of some 15,000 Jews from Moscow in 1891 and far more violent pogroms in the period 1903–6 – were certainly an important stimulus for rising waves of Jewish emigration. Yet it would be a mistake to assume that violence was the sole or even primary cause of the exodus. Significant numbers of Jews had already begun to leave the Russian Empire in the 1870s as a consequence of widespread poverty, the decline of social control by communal authorities (most rabbis opposed emigration) and raised hopes regarding life in countries that had fully emancipated their Jews. Like these long-term factors, emigration swelled gradually over time, spiking in the aftermath of pogroms but never losing its own momentum. To the underlying long-range factors was added, following the pogroms of the 1880s, a marked shift in official policy. Convinced that the Jews themselves were to blame for the outburst of popular hostility against them, the tsarist government responded in 1882 by banning new Jewish settlements in rural areas *within* the Pale. Soon thereafter, quotas

19 H. Rogger, *Jewish Policies and Right-Wing Politics in Imperial Russia* (Berkeley: University of California Press, 1986); I. M. Aronson, *Troubled Waters: The Origins of the 1881 Anti-Jewish Pogroms in Russia* (Pittsburgh: University of Pittsburgh Press, 1990); J. Klier and S. Lambroza (eds.), *Anti-Jewish Violence in Modern Russian History* (Cambridge: Cambridge University Press, 1992).

were established on admission of Jews to gymnasia and institutions of higher education, the medical and legal professions, and many other arenas of Russia's rapidly modernising economy and society. Jews' right to vote and stand for office in municipal elections was also curtailed. In effect, Alexander III (r. 1881–94) froze the mechanisms of selective integration (as he did the Great Reforms) without reversing their effects.

The potent combination of rising pressure from without – whether in the form of popular violence or the official narrowing of the paths of integration – combined with growing ferment from within, sharply politicised Russian-Jewish life. One of the first manifestations was the emergence of the Zionist movement. A characteristic early leader of the movement, the physician Yehuda Leib (Lev) Pinsker (1821–91), had been an ardent integrationist, a prominent member of the Odessa branch of the Society for the Spread of Enlightenment among the Jews of Russia, until the pogroms forced a dramatic change of heart. In 1882, in the midst of plunder and assault, Pinsker published a searing pamphlet entitled *Autoemancipation!* in which he diagnosed anti-Semitism as an incurable psychosis and called on the Jews to put an end to their dispersion by settling en masse in a single territory – whether in Palestine or elsewhere.[20] Hundreds of Jewish students, declaring that 'we do not believe in the possibility of a bearable existence in Russia', enacted their own version of the Populists' 'going to the people' movement, visiting synagogues in cities across the Pale in an attempt to promote mass emigration to the ancient land of Israel.[21] Though largely unsuccessful in the short term, with time Zionism would become one of the leading political orientations among Russia's Jews, and Russia would supply the majority of the tens of thousands of Jewish immigrants to Ottoman Palestine prior to the First World War.

Zionism was the earliest and most radical but hardly the only expression of secular Jewish nationalism in late Imperial Russia. True, the Jewish labour movement, whose origins go back to a series of strikes in the 1870s and 1880s by Jewish workers in Vilna and other cities in the Pale, began in a manner that can fairly be characterised as 'Jewish in form, socialist in content'. Georgii Plekhanov (1856–1918), the leading Russian Marxist of the time, lauded Jewish

20 *Autoemancipation! Mahnruf an seine Stammesgenossen von einem russischen Juden* (Berlin: Commissions-verlag von W. Issleib, 1882). Pinsker's pamphlet was published anonymously and directed to Jewish leaders in Western Europe, whom he regarded as the sole possible organisers of mass Jewish emigration.

21 Quoted in Jonathan Frankel, *Prophecy and Politics: Socialism, Nationalism, and the Russian Jews, 1862–1917* (Cambridge: Cambridge University Press, 1981), p. 97.

strikers as 'the avant-garde of the workers' army of Russia'.[22] At its founding in 1897, the 'Bund' (the General Jewish Workers' Union (Bund) in Lithuania, Poland and Russia) was militantly internationalist in orientation, pressing for class struggle against the Jewish plutocracy in the name of a broader revolutionary assault on tsarism. Over time, however, the Bund's leaders came to doubt the willingness of 'all-Russian' social-democrats (including the Jews among them) to address specifically Jewish grievances. As the Bund zigzagged towards the demand for Jewish national autonomy within a post-revolutionary federal Russian state, its relations with Lenin's All-Russian Social Democratic Workers' Party oscillated between coalition (the Bund was declared an 'autonomous organisation' within the RSDWP at the latter's founding in 1898) and separatism (the Bund quit the RSDWP in 1903, only to grudgingly rejoin in 1906).

Even after the introduction of parliamentary politics in Russia in 1906, the Bund and the various Zionist parties (some socialist, others not) were less interested in gathering votes than in building alternative institutions on the Jewish street, from mutual aid funds and primary schools to paramilitary self-defence units. In this sense they resembled micro-societies in the making, secular alternatives to the dense network of traditional Jewish communal institutions that had governed life in the Pale for centuries. It was a sign of the far-reaching politicisation of Russian Jewry, moreover, that by 1911 even the representatives of tradition itself, namely the rabbinate, saw fit to band together in a self-styled 'Brotherhood of Israel' (Agudat Yisrael), bringing together leaders of Hasidism with their erstwhile orthodox opponents.

On the eve of the Great War, Russian Jewry thus presented a picture of tremendous ferment and fragmentation. It was not simply a matter of struggle between separatism and integration: the separatist camp itself was divided between traditional (religious) and modern (secular) variants, as well as between proponents and opponents of emigration, while integrationists were similarly split between those who aspired to join Russia's emerging civil society and those determined to reconstruct that society via revolution.

For Russian history, of course, it was the integrationists among the Jews – not just regicides like Sverdlovsk, but the larger ranks of literate, urbanised entrepreneurs, professionals, writers, artists and others – who ultimately mattered most. What began in the medieval and early imperial periods as an outright ban against Jews on Romanov soil had given way, by force of imperial expansion at the end of the eighteenth century, to territorial confinement

22 Quoted in Henry Tobias, *The Jewish Bund in Russia: From its Origins to 1905* (Stanford: Stanford University Press, 1972), p. 61.

in the empire's western borderlands. A century later, under the influence of Enlightenment notions of utility and imperial consolidation, territorial confinement had been tempered by a partial and highly uneven integration of Jews into Russia proper. In the process, Russia's Jews were transformed from a marginal people – literally and figuratively – to a hotbed of self-reinvention, a lightning rod for debates about winners and losers in the modernisation of Russia's multinational empire.

10

Islam in the Russian Empire

VLADIMIR BOBROVNIKOV

Islam in tsarist Russia has been studied in the Cambridge History for more than a century. Together with more recent scholarship in Russia and abroad, these works have produced a substantial body of literature focusing chiefly on the topics of Muslim resistance to Russian expansion, and controversies between Islamic 'reformism' (*jadidism*) and 'traditionalism' (*qadimism*).[1] Of course, these problems were of great importance for specific Muslim regions in limited historical periods. But they do not exhaust all the diversity of topics concerning Islam in the imperial context. Moreover, both themes used to be approached according to misleading nationalist and modernist conceptions. Taking Islam and the Russian empire for natural antagonists, such a vision relied on the Orientalist approach representing Islam as a homogeneous and timeless entity opposing all non-Muslim cultures. In reality, Islam and the empire seemed to have interacted with each other more often than they engaged in conflict.

Tsarist Russia brought under its control numerous diverse populations inhabiting traditionally Muslim lands in the Volga-Ural region, western Siberia, the North Caucasus and Central Asia. The Volga-Ural region was Islamised more than other Muslim lands of the empire. In the North Caucasus, Siberia and the Kazakh steppe a gradual Islamisation continued until the first half of the nineteenth century. The century and a half from the 1730s until the mid-1880s was a period of rapid growth and shift for both the polity and Muslim communities within it. At the end of the nineteenth century Russia housed a

I would like to thank Sergey Abashin, Dmitri Arapov, Allen Frank, Michael Kemper and Paul Werth, whose critical comments on earlier drafts of this survey improved the final version immeasurably. I am also very grateful to Dominic Lieven and Vera Prokhorova for the corrections of the English text.

1 Typical of this approach are A. Bennigsen, *Les Mouvements nationaux chez les musulmans de Russie: le 'Sultangalievisme' au Tatarstan* (Paris: Mouton, 1960); A. Rorlich, *The Volga Tatars: A Profile in National Resilience* (Stanford: Stanford University Press, 1986); R. G. Landa, *Islam v istorii Rossii* (Moscow: Vostochnaia literatura, 1995).

diverse population of some 14 million Muslims (out of a total population of 150 million subjects).

In response to the challenges of Russian rule local forms of Islam were changing. The history of Islam in Imperial Russia can be roughly divided into four periods. The first continued from Peter I's reign (1682–1725) until the late 1760s. While oscillating between relative toleration and missionary attacks against non-Orthodox confessions, the government had no distinct Muslim policy yet. The second period started under Catherine II (r. 1762–96) and finished in the middle of the nineteenth century. It resulted in the acknowledgement of Islam and the creation of official Islamic hierarchies. The third period was related to the Great Reforms and continued until the beginning of the twentieth century. The confessional policy became more complicated and contradictory. Different projects of constructing a Muslim clergy came into tension with one another. In the fourth period (1905–17) between the two Russian revolutions Islam acquired a new political dimension. It was a time of new fears and expectations of Islam both in the central government and in regional elites.

There were some constants characterising the position of Islam during the imperial period. Most of the Russian Muslims belonged to the *Hanafi* religious legal school in Sunni Islam. Historically, *Shafi'is* were dominant in Dagestan and Chechnia only. The majority of Muslims in Transcaucasia and a number of congregations in Central Asia belonged to *Shi'is*. Muslim identity was granted by membership in mosque congregations, which were mostly rural and often scattered among larger non-Muslim populations. Basic Islamic institutions included Friday and daily mosques, primary (*maktab*) and/or higher (*madrasa*) mosque schools, as well as Sufi lodges with their own schools or *khanaqahs* (holy places). All these institutions are often taken for granted. But in fact, they did not constitute a 'standard equipment' for a Muslim community, as Allen Frank has shown for the Volga-Ural region.[2] None of these institutions was funded by the state. Depending on private funding they disappeared if it stopped. *Waqf* foundations (property donated in perpetuity to a charitable purpose) were not widespread in Inner Russia and had no tax-exempt status.

Muslim congregations settled their own religious and to some extent judicial matters. Their autonomy was often taken for isolation from the outside non-Muslim world. Actually Muslim communities maintained regular connections throughout Russia and outside it, in particular with Islamic centres in

2 A. J. Frank, *Muslim Religious Institutions in Imperial Russia: The Islamic World of Novouzensk District and the Kazakh Inner Horde, 1780–1910* (Leiden: Brill, 2001), pp. 176–210, 278–91.

Transoxiana, Mogul India and the Middle East. Their main channels were pilgrimage and exchange of Muslim students and scholars. The religious leader of a community was the mullah (*imam*), known also as *khatib*. He conducted the five daily prayers, pronounced the Friday sermon (*khutba*) and ensured that the month of Ramadan and religious feasts were properly observed. In addition, he could teach in mosque school as *mudarris* and resolve disputes between community members as Muslim lawyer (*qadi*). But usually mullah and qadi were different religious figures. The highest office in the Muslim administration at the district (*uezd*) level was held by a specialist in *shari'a* law known as *akhund* (or *akhun*). He was elected by the community and then appointed by a Russian governor of the province.

Supervising the political loyalty of Muslim elites, the Russian administrators and central government did not meddle in the religious affairs of the Muslim communities. Peter I and his successors of the first half of the eighteenth century followed these principles of governance dating back to the reign of Ivan IV's son, Fedor Ioanovich (r. 1584–98). Adherents of all non-Orthodox faiths were granted a moderated toleration, if they were 'loyal subjects, good tax-payers and soldiers' of the empire. Members of the Muslim military elite (*mirzas*/*murzas*) had entered the Russian nobility (*dvorianstvo*) under Muscovite rule. Some noble families like the Tevkelevs and Enikeevs remained Muslims. In exchange for military and other services on the frontiers, the Bashkir troops retained noble status and a degree of internal self-government.

On the other hand, Muslims were viewed with suspicion. Though Islam had never been outlawed, conversion to Christianity was always encouraged. From the fifteenth century onwards it was common for the Muslim elites to convert to Orthodoxy and become Russian nobles (*boiare, dvoriane*). Godunovs, Iusupovs, Urusovs, Tenishevs and dozens of other Orthodox noble families were of Muslim origin. Muslims were attracted to Christianity by various material and legal benefits or a fear of loss of privileged status. Sometimes new converts received direct payment in money and goods. In return for baptism, Peter I offered a three-year tax break, freedom from the military draft and work in state factories. A decree of 1713 forced the Muslim nobility in Kazan and Azov provinces either to be deprived of their estates and Orthodox serfs or to convert to Christianity.

Given the absence of a specific code of laws relating to Muslims, state policy towards Islam was in flux. Campaigns of forceful conversion followed periods of toleration. The position of Russian Muslims worsened under Anna Ioanovna (r. 1730–40) and Elizabeth Petrovna (r. 1741–61), when a missionary campaign was launched in the Volga region. Beginning in 1731, with the establishment of the Commission for the Affairs of New Converts (*Komissiia novokreshchenykh del*), headed by the Priest Aleksei Raifsky, Orthodox missionaries baptised about 8,000 Muslims in Kazan and Nizhnii Novgorod provinces. In 1740–64 the Office for the Affairs of New Converts (*Novokreshchenaia kontora*) worked under the direction of Archbishop Luka Kanashevich of Kazan in the town of Sviiazhsk. Between 1740 and 1744 missionaries destroyed 418 of the 536 mosques in Kazan province.[3] Construction of new mosques was outlawed (1742). Since many baptised Muslims (*novokreshchenye*) continued practising Islam secretly, severe penalties were set up. For instance, in 1738 Orenburg governor and historian V. N. Tatishchev ordered Toigil'da Zhuliakov to be burned alive for 'having been seduced to Muhammedan law again'.

A new period in the history of Islam in Russia began under Catherine II. The empress continued Peter I's conquests along the Black and Caspian seashores. The most crucial acquisitions of her reign were Poland and Lithuania (1772, 1793, 1795), Crimea and the north-western Caucasus (1783), Dagestan's lowlands and eastern Transcaucasia (1796). These huge annexations introduced into the polity numerous Muslim subjects of the Ottoman Empire, the Crimean khanate, and the khanates and mountaineers' confederations in the North Caucasus and Transcaucasia, as well as from the Polish-Lithuanian Commonwealth. The authorities had to decide how to govern them.

Especially in the North Caucasus, Muslim elites loyal to the state encountered militant Islamic movements. Also, having been expelled from their lands which were occupied by Russian fortresses and Cossack settlements, some initially loyal Muslims turned against the Russians. In 1785–90 a Chechen named Ushurma, generally known as Sheikh or *Imam* Mansur ('Victorious'), defeated Russian troops in a number of battles. He used to be regarded as the first militant Naqshbandi Sufi sheikh in the region. However, as Anna Zelkina has shown, whether he was a Sufi or not, Mansur appealed to universal Sufi and Islamic principles in attempting to consolidate mountaineers' communities around the shari'a.[4] He headed the army of *ghazis* and sided with Ottoman troops operating by the Black Sea shore. In 1791 Ushurma was captured in Anapa, then sent to St Petersburg and imprisoned in the Shlisselburg fortress, where he died in 1794.

3 E. A. Malov, 'O tatarskikh mechetiakh v Rossii', *Pravoslavnyi sobesednik* (1867), no. 3: 297. See also *Polnoe sobranie postanovlenii i rasporiazhenii po vedomstvu pravoslavnogo ispovedaniia Rossiiskoi imperii*, 2nd series, vol. II (St Petersburg, 1872), no. 662.

4 A. Zelkina, *In Quest for God and Freedom: Sufis Responses to the Russian Advance in the North Caucasus* (London: Hurst, 2000), p. 67. See also: A. Bennigsen, 'Un mouvement populaire au Caucase au XVIIIe siècle. La 'Guerre Sainte' du *sheikh* Mansur (1785–1791), page mal connue et controversée des relations russo-turques', *CMRS* 5, 2 (1964): 175–9.

Given the importance of Islam as a means of Muslim political mobilisation, Catherine II changed the state's confessional policies. The empress launched a new policy of toleration of Islam and other non-Orthodox faiths. In 1773 her famous 'Toleration to All Faiths' edict became law. Its purpose was mainly to grant Islam legally recognised status. The construction of mosques was permitted all over Russia. The empress's Manifesto issued on 8 April 1783 confirmed a general trend towards the toleration of Islam. The state promised the Muslims of Crimea 'to protect and defend their lives, temples and natural faith'.[5] Later the same freedom was granted to other conquered Muslim populations, like Lithuanian Tatars in Poland in 1795.

The government moderated the militant activities of Orthodox missionaries. In 1764 the Office for the Affairs of New Converts was closed. Instead, the authorities attempted to attract Muslim military and religious elites to empire's cause. According to the edict of 1784, Muslim princes and murzas were granted noble status and privileges (except that they could not own Christian serfs) in exchange for military or civil service. The state was engaged in mosque construction. In 1769 Catherine II charged D. I. Chicherin, the governor of Siberia, with building mosques for Central Asian ('Bukharan') migrants. In 1782 a new, more ambitious programme was funded to build a series of mosques along the Kazakh steppe acquired by the empire between 1731 and 1743. Tatar mullahs were sent to propagate Islam among 'wild nomads' of the region. According to the empress's edict, the first Arabic version of the Koran was printed in 1787 under the supervision of the Tatar mullah Usman Ismail. Between 1789 and 1798 five successive editions of the Koran appeared, the last one in 3,600 copies. A Muslim state publishing house had been established in St Petersburg and later moved to the town of Kazan (1802).

Both the causes and the effects of this confessional policy were misunderstood by the nineteenth-century missionaries, who criticised it. Catherine II was held responsible for 'Islamisation' of Kazakhs and other 'animist' tribes. She was supposed to have overestimated the role of Islam in Russia's Orient.[6] But the Kazakh nomads became Muslim much earlier. Their Islamic institutions were less formal than among the sedentary populations, hence less comprehensible to the empire's functionaries and scholars. The empress was not fascinated with Islamic exotics. On the contrary, her policy was guided by

5 D. Iu. Arapov (ed.), *Islam v Rossiiskoi imperii. (Zakonodatel'nye akty, opisaniia, statistika)* (Moscow: Akademkniga, 2001), p. 47. See also pp. 45–6.

6 For instance, see E. A. Malov, 'O tatarskikh mechetiakh v Rossii', p. 22; I. Altynsarin, *Izbrannye sochineniia* (Alma-Ata: Izd. AN KSSR, 1957), pp. 315–27. A substantial critique of this stereotype is in Frank, *Muslim Religious Institutions*, pp. 274–313.

quite pragmatic concerns. As Catherine II confessed herself, she aimed 'not at introduction of Muhammedanism', but at using Islam as a 'bait to catch a fish with', in order to attach Muslim borderlands to Russia.

According to the Enlightenment's ideas, each faith was treated according to its utility to the state: the more it contributed to the maintenance of the empire, the more was the scope of toleration. The regime supported mostly 'enlightened' forms of religion, fighting against sectarians, 'superstition and other abuses'. Obligatory enrolment in a religious community brought almost all Russian subjects under state supervision. In principle all subjects by law had an ascribed confessional affiliation. In terms of the well-known Foucauldian approach, the turn to regulatory toleration under Catherine II can be treated as the transition to religious discipline using Islamic affiliation as the means of domination and projecting imperial power on its frontiers.[7]

Another important shift in confessional policy concerned the creation of an official Muslim hierarchy. The idea seemed to be conceived on the pattern of both the Holy Synod, and the modified *mufti* establishment in the Ottoman Empire. As Dmitri Arapov and Robert Crews argued, the Ottoman experience in administering Islam was seriously studied in tsarist Russia.[8] On 22 September 1788, the Orenburg Assembly (its full name was *Orenburgskoe magometanskoe dukhovnoe sobranie* or *OMDS*) was set up by a decree of Catherine II.[9] In non-official usage it was also called muftiate. Next year the office was opened in Ufa. In 1796 it moved to Orenburg but returned to Ufa in 1802. *OMDS* was responsible for opening and registration of mosque congregations in St Petersburg, Moscow, Inner Russia, the Volga-Ural region and Siberia. The Kazakh steppe was also placed under its jurisdiction in 1788–1868.

Based on both shari'a and imperial laws, the Orenburg Assembly worked as a kind of Muslim Supreme Court and issued legal decisions (*fatwas*) in matters of marriage and divorce, inheritance, burial, as well as appointments of imams

7 M. Foucault, *Discipline and Punish: The Birth of the Prison*, trans. Alan Sheridan (New York: Penguin, 1977). For a useful discussion of regulatory toleration in tsarist Russia after Catherine's reign, see R. Crews, 'Empire and Confessional State: Islam and Religious Politics in Nineteenth-Century Russia', *AHR* 108, 1 (2003): 50–83.

8 Crews, 'Empire and Confessional State', p. 57; D. Iu. Arapov, 'Imperskaia politika v oblasti gosudarsvennogo regulirovaniia islama na Severnom Kavkaze v XIX – nachale XX vv.', in I. L. Babich and L. T. Solov'eva (eds.), *Islam i pravo v Rossii* (Moscow: Izd. Rossiiskogo universiteta druzhby narodov, 2004), vol. I, p. 24. The tsarist Islamic hierarchy followed not so much Ottoman institutions, as their image constructed in the eighteenth-century Orthodox ecclesiology. See F. A. Emin, *Kratkoe opisanie drevnego i noveishego sostoianiia Ottomanskoi porty* (St Petersburg, 1769); *Sokrashchenie Magometanskoi very* (Moscow, 1784).

9 Arapov, *Islam v Rossiiskoi imperii*, pp. 50–3, 205–8. For a thorough study of this institution see D. D. Azamatov, *Orenburgskoe magometanskoe dukhovnoe sobranie v kontse XVIII–XIX vv.* (Ufa: Ufimskii nauch. tsentr RAN, 1999).

and mosque building. The assembly staff included a council of three qadis nominally headed by a mufti. In principle all members of the assembly were supposed to be elected, but in practice Ufa's governors appointed the mufti. So religious as well as legal practices of Muslims were placed under state control. Sufi networks were not legally recognised and hence not brought under the control of the *OMDS*. Mosques, madrasas and waqf properties were also beyond its direct authority and were regulated by the civil authorities in provinces.

A more regulated pattern of confessional policy, fashioned according to principles of the well-ordered police state (*Polizeistaat*),[10] was adopted under Alexander I (r. 1801–25) and Nicholas I (r. 1825–55). Following the consistorial pattern of Napoleonic France, Mikhail Speranskii, the influential adviser to Alexander I, created a Department of Spiritual Affairs in order to 'protect rites of all the Russian and foreign faiths'. In 1810 the Main Directorate of Religious Affairs of Foreign Confessions was set up and in 1832 turned into the *Departament dukhovnykh del inostrannykh ispovedanii* (*DDDII*) within the Ministry of Internal Affairs, the most important ministry in the imperial government. From the 1830s the ministry was responsible for maintaining the 'principle of religious toleration as far as this toleration corresponded to state interest'. Its third division was charged with supervision over the Orenburg Assembly. It is noteworthy that one petition from Orenburg mullahs in 1863 addressed the minister of the interior as the 'Minister of Interior and Muslim Religious Affairs'.[11]

While the administration provided new mechanisms of social control, the law reinforced dependence of Muslim religious elites on the imperial administration. Towards the end of Nicholas I's reign, laws and instructions as they concerned Islam were compiled into a single Muslim statute drafted as a part of the Statute of Religious Affairs of Foreign Confessions (*Ustav dukhovnykh del inostrannykh ispovedanii*). It was published soon after the emperor's death, in 1857. The application of Islamic law was limited. The use of corporal punishment for alcohol drinking, theft and adultery according to the shari'a criminal law (*al-hadd*) was abolished. Beginning in 1828, village and town imams were forced to compile registers (*metricheskie knigi*) of all marriage contracts, deaths and legitimate births which happened in their communities. These registers were used for tax rolls and were overseen by the Spiritual Assembly.

10 See M. Raeff, *The Well-Ordered Police State: Social and Institutional Change through Law in the Germanies and Russia, 1600–1800* (New Haven: Yale University Press, 1983).
11 *Materialy po istorii Tatarii vtoroi poloviny XIX veka: Agrarnyi vopros i krestianskoe dvizhenie 50–70-kh godov XIX v.* (Moscow and Leningrad: Izd. AN SSSR, 1936), p. 166.

Under Nicholas I, Polizeistaat laws attempted to manage even symbolic expressions of Islam. In 1829 Nicholas I himself approved a single design for all future mosques of Russia inspired by the contemporary Orthodox Church architecture. A decree of 1844 established mosques' obligatory plan and location. Mosques were to be constructed in settlements' squares at a distance of 100 *sazhen* from the nearest church. It was allowed to build one mosque per 200 male Muslims. The more liberal government of Alexander II abandoned obligatory model plans for mosques in 1862.

In the reign of Nicholas I the government became more anxious about an unprecedented degree of power concentrated in the hands of the new Muslim elites. In order to reduce the importance of the Orenburg Assembly, the second Tauride Directorate (*Tavricheskoe magometanskoe dukhovnoe pravlenie* or *TMDP*) was established. It had been envisaged in 1794 under Catherine II on the basis of the former Ottoman offices of mufti, qadi-asker, etc., but was finally set up only on 23 December 1831 in Simferopol' in Crimea.[12] This office had jurisdiction over the Muslim communities in Crimea, on the north shore of the Black Sea, and in the former Polish-Lithuanian Commonwealth (*Rech' Pospolitaia*).

The Tauride Directorate was designed along the lines of the Orenburg Assembly, following its main functions and personnel. It was headed by a mufti and included five district (uezd) qadis, and a mufti's assistant known under the title of *qadi-asker* dating back to the Crimean khanate rule. In the *TMDP* a more strict hierarchy of Muslim religious elites was set up. Village and town imams, known as khatibs and mullahs, were put under the control of the district qadi who in his turn obeyed the orders of the directorate. Contrary to the *OMDS*, sheikhs of Sufi lodges were also included in the Muslim elite. In Crimea *waqfs* were recognised and brought under the control of the directorate. Later they were put under the control of the state.

How did Muslim religious elites respond to the challenges of tsarist policy in the eighteenth and nineteenth centuries? The toleration laws and recognition of Islam brought about the blossoming of Muslim societies and their institutions, in particular the growth of mosques, Muslim schools and the appearance of a dynamic Muslim nobility and commercial bourgeoisie in the Volga-Ural region and western Siberia. In 1911, the official statistics counted 6,144 mosques in the *OMDS*'s jurisdiction and 845 mosques registered by the *TMDP*. Their staff included respectively 12,341 and 981 licensed qadis, mudarrises, mullahs and mu'adhdhins.[13] Only a few mosques were built or subsidised by the state.

12 Arapov, *Islam v Rossiiskoi imperii*, pp. 58, 197–205, 247–50.

13 M. F. Farkhshatov, 'Musul'manskoe dukhovenstvo', in S. M. Prozorov (ed.), *Islam na territorii byvshei Rossiiskoi imperii* (Moscow: Vostochnaia literatura, 1999), fasc. 2, p. 72.

Beginning in the eighteenth century and continuing until the early twentieth century, Muslim elites were involved in lively discussions, touching upon religious, social and political innovations affecting the Muslim communities at large. In these discussions modern imperial issues were referred to through traditional Islamic literary genres. The common Islamic learning was based on a network of local Islamic institutions. Michael Kemper has termed these kinds of debates 'Islamic discourse'.[14]

The crucial theme of Islamic discourse was the legitimacy of the Orenburg Assembly, which was not accepted by all the Volga-Ural *'ulama'*. Some of them, like Muhammedzhan Husainov, the first Orenburg mufti, supported a new Islamic hierarchy recognising the empire as the 'world of Islam' (*dar al-Islam*). The other Muslim scholars and Sufis considered the power of muftis 'unpermitted innovations' (*bida'*) from the Islamic point of view. An anti-mufti position was most strongly defended in the works of the Sufi Abd al-Rahman Utyz-Imani (or al-Bulghari, 1754–1835) and some Bashkir *abyz*es. The most prominent anti-mufti movement was the Vaisov brotherhood founded by a famous Tatar, Sufi Baha al-Din Vaisov (d. 1893) and later led by his son Inan al-Din (d. 1918). It is interesting that they called themselves the 'Blessed community' (*firqa-yi najiyya*) or 'Vaisov's Holy Regiment of the Old Believer Muslims' (*Vaisov bozhii polk musul'man-staroverov*) evoking the Old Belief that they praised for rejecting 'unpermitted innovations' in Orthodoxy.

From the middle of the nineteenth century a new period in the history of Islam in Russia began. The reign of Alexander II (r. 1855–81) was marked by vast annexations of Muslim lands. Russian conquests in the Muslim East had been completed by the mid-1880s. The end of the long Caucasian war (1864) brought mountaineers of the North Caucasus under Russian rule. The last acquisitions in western Armenia and southern Georgia (Muslim Lazistan) in Transcaucasia dated from the Russian-Ottoman war of 1877–8. Between 1862 and 1885 the Russians conquered Central Asia. The khanates of Kokand, Khiva and Bukhara were annexed. While the first was abolished, Khiva and Bukhara were turned into Russian protectorates.

Some peoples and rulers accepted the imposition of Russian rule, while others opposed the Russian presence in different ways. Forms of Muslim resistance in the borderlands included revolts, raids into Russian lands, as well as massive exodus to Iran and the Ottoman Empire. North-Caucasian 'ulama'

14 M. Kemper, *Sufis und Gelehrte in Tatarien und Baschkirien, 1789–1889. Der islamische Diskurs unter russischer Herrschaft* (Berlin: Klaus Schwarz Verlag, 1998), S. 473–75. On criticism by Tatar 'ulama' of the Orenburg Assembly within the regional Islamic discourse see pp. 50–61, 66–70, 290–9.

and the rulers of Bukhara and Kokand proclaimed 'holy war' (*ghazawat* as a form of *jihad*) against Russian conquerors. In Dagestan and Chechnia an *imamate* state emerged at the end of the 1820s. As Moshe Gammer and Michael Kemper have shown,[15] it was based on shari'a institutions and some changed Sufi principles, notably *murid-murshid* relations borrowed from Sufi practices and transformed into relations between a ruler and subjects in the jihad state. Three successive imams, the most prominent of whom was Shamil (r. 1834–59), involved village communities in the united administrative network, a principle that was continued by the imperial authorities after the defeat of the imamate in 1859. Shamil's activities greatly resembled those of the emir Abdelkader in French Algeria.

The imperial vision of Islam shifted once more. There appeared fears of an Islamic threat. Encountering Muslim resistance in the borderlands, the government became especially anxious about Sufism. The Russians mistakenly took the jihad state for a Sufi network. They regarded different Sufi orders and their lodges as branches of a 'single anti-Russian movement'. The Muslim resistance of the North Caucasian mountaineers against Russia became famous under the name of '*M'uridism*'.[16] Fears of Sufism provoked a number of anti-Sufi decrees and persecutions. In 1836 Nicholas I forbade granting Sufi sheikhs of 'Asian origin' Russian citizenship. They were prohibited to pass the Russian frontier.

Despite the pacifist character of his teaching, the Qadiri sheikh Kunta-hajji was arrested in Chechnia in 1863 and exiled to Nizhnii Novgorod province, where he died in 1867. His followers were dispersed by Russian troops in the village of Shali. Kunta-hajji's movement was labelled 'Zikrism' after the Sufi practice of loud prayer (*dhikr*) performed by his followers in contrast to 'silent *dhikr*' adopted in the North-Caucasian branch of the Naqshbandiyya order. In Inner Russia the Vaisov brotherhood was crushed in 1884. Its leader was put into a madhouse and some members sentenced to hard labour in Siberia.

Under Alexander II and Alexander III (r. 1881–94) new fears about Muslims emerged. There occurred a gradual re-evaluation of Islam. The earlier confessional policy reflected the government's indifference to knowledge of Islam. Oriental studies (*vostokovedenie*), which had been launched in Russia by Peter I and flourished from the reign of Catherine II, were confined

15 M. Gammer, *Muslim Resistance to the Tsar: Shamil and the Conquest of Chechnia and Dagestan* (London: Frank Cass, 1994), pp. 225–40; M. Kemper, 'Khalidiyya Networks in Daghestan and the Question of *Jihad*', *Die Welt des Islams* 42, 1 (2002): 41–71.

16 A discussion of this notion in imperial practice and modern scholarship is examined in V. O. Bobrovnikov, and M. Kemper, 'M'uridism', in M. S. Prozorov (ed.), *Islam na territorii byvshei Rossiiskoi imperii* (Moscow: Vostochnaia literatura, n.d.), fasc. 5.

mostly to the investigation of outside 'classic' Islam while neglecting its contemporary Russian forms. In the second half of the nineteenth century a closer co-operation between the state and Orientalists occurred. It resulted in the substantial growth of institutions and personnel familiar with Islam – universities, scientific societies and museums. The Russians paid more attention to foreign models of colonial governance over Muslims such as French Algeria, British India and Egypt. Knowledge of Islam, as has been argued in a number of recent excellent studies on this matter,[17] became an important tool of imperial governance.

At the forefront of this re-evaluation were missionaries and military officers. In this regard, Nikolai Il'minskii (1822–91), a professor of Turkic languages at Kazan University and the Anti-Muslim Missionary Division opened in the Kazan Ecclesiastical Academy in 1854, played a crucial role. Il'minskii, Evfimii Malov, Gordii Sablukov and their students faulted the authorities for their ignorance of the Islamic threat. They insisted on a meticulous study of Islam, to combat 'Muslim fanaticism' in the Russian Orient. To carry out this programme, eastern and especially indigenous languages as well as Islamic scholarship were introduced into curricula at the Anti-Muslim Missionary Division and the missionary schools. In 1870, under Il'minskii's influence, the government introduced a network of Russian Tatar schools for baptised Muslims, where teaching was in Tatar. The same year Russo-Kazakh schools were planned and soon opened to all Kazakhs.

There appeared a wave of Islamic literature and Orientalist criticism translated from different eastern and western languages. In 1845 A. K. Kazembeg, a professor at Kazan University and the future dean of the Oriental Faculty of St Petersburg University, published the shari'a compendium 'Mukhtasar al-wiqayat'. In 1850 Baron E. N. Tornau, a high official in Transcaucasia, compiled 'An Outline of the Principles of Muslim Legal Science' on French Orientalist models. In 1875 Malov translated the 'Critical Historical Introduction to the Koran' written by the German Orientalist G. Weil. The two first direct translations of the Koran from Arabic were made by Sablukov (1878) and General D. N. Boguslavskii (1871). In 1898 General N. I. Grodekov, the governor of Syrdaria province, ordered the translation of the famous legal treatise 'al-Hidaya'

17 R. D. Crews, 'Allies in God's Command: Muslim Communities and the State in Imperial Russia', unpublished PhD dissertation, Princeton University (1999); R. P. Geraci, *Window on the East: National and Imperial Identities in Late Tsarist Russia* (Ithaca: Cornell University Press, 2001); P. W. Werth, *At the Margins of Orthodoxy: Mission, Governance and Confessional Politics in Russia's Volga-Kama Region, 1827–1905* (Ithaca: Cornell University Press, 2002).

from its English version into Russian. These efforts fell perfectly into the category which Edward Said has called a 'philological Orientalism'.[18]

Orientalist activities played an important but not hegemonic role in late tsarist Russia. Influential liberal churchmen and officials had never accepted Il'minskii's ideas. In 1870, in the reign of Alexander II, the Anti-Muslim Missionary Division was even closed, though again restored in 1884 under the conservative Alexander III. New approaches to Islam were partly adopted by the Ministry of Internal Affairs. The staff of the *DDDII* was drawn from Orientalists of missionary or academic background. The department's leading consultant in the field of Islamic law was Kazembeg, a Dagestani Persian of Shi'i origin converted to Presbyterianism in his youth. He and other academic Orientalists, such as N. V. Khanykov, the eminent diplomat and high official in the Caucasian viceroyalty (*namestnichestvo*), shared fears of militant Islam.

Imperial officials were split into two factions. The first insisted on the co-option of Muslim religious elites into the state body. They argued for creating new muftiates in annexed Muslim regions. The opposite faction discouraged the creation of muftiates, pointing out the danger of concentrating power in the hands of 'anti-Russian fanatically minded mullahs', as the influential war minister D. A. Miliutin (1861–81) put it once.[19] The adherents of the second faction supported the hands-off policy requesting 'disregard of the local Muslim clergy'. The first approach was backed up by the powerful Ministry of Internal Affairs that attempted to spread its network through the *DDDII* over all the Muslims of the empire. The second approach was more popular in the War Ministry, which supervised Muslims in the borderlands. The situation actually was even more complicated. Both factions existed in each ministry and among different functionaries in provinces.

Officials from the Ministry of Internal Affairs launched an ambitious programme aiming to turn different groups of the Muslim religious elites ('ulama') into a unified imperial estate (*soslovie*). Given the absence of Church and clergy as such in Islam, imperial lawmakers 'invented' them in the framework of previously established muftiates. Mosque congregations were turned into 'parishes' (*prikhod*) modelled in the Orthodox fashion. Like Orthodox priests in the bureaucratised hierarchy of the Holy Synod, loyal Muslim 'ulama' were co-opted into the imperial administration at village, district and provincial levels, which granted them the privileged status of 'Muslim clergy'

18 E. Said, *Orientalism*, 2nd edn (London: Routledge and Kegan Paul, 1995), p. 285.

19 D. Iu. Arapov, 'D. A. Miliutin o "musul'manstve"', *Aktual'nye problemy gumanitarnykh, sotsial'nykh, ekonomicheskikh i tekhnicheskikh nauk*, vyp. 2, t. 2 (Moscow, 2003): 227.

(*musul'manskoe dukhovenstvo*). They were exempted from corporal punishment and military draft. Muslim religious titles were included in the Table of Ranks and divided into two separate groups. Mu'adhdhins and imams of daily and Friday mosques known as mullahs belonged to junior clerics. Muftis, qadis, akhunds and the qadi-asker in Crimea constituted the higher 'Muslim clergy'.

The position of the 'Muslim clergy' in the Orenburg Assembly differed from that in the Tauride Directorate. In Crimea the 'Muslim clergy' became a more closed estate group. Only male descendants of the local 'ulama' got access to it. In the Orenburg Assembly lower and higher clergy formed two separate groups. Junior clerics had no tax-exempt status and were ascribed to peasant and townsfolk (*meshchane*) estates like members of their community. Only senior clerics received a tax-free status. Their long service was rewarded by personal noble status. Akhunds and mufti were paid by the assembly. The status of a 'Muslim cleric' was available to every educated Muslim. A candidate had to travel to the town of Ufa to pass an examination which tested his knowledge of basic Islamic sciences and practices. Upon passing the exam candidates were granted a licence (*ukaz*), and became known as *ukaznoi mulla* or mu'adhdhin.

The number of regional Muslim hierarchies multiplied. Two more muftiates were created in Tiflis on 5 April 1872. These were the Shi'i and Sunni Transcaucasian Directorates (their full official titles were *Zakavkazskie magometanskie dukhovnye pravleniia shiitskogo i sunnitskogo uchenii* or *ZMDP*).[20] Like the other muftiates they were charged with religious, legal and educational affairs of Muslims. Contrary to the Orenburg Assembly, the *ZMDP* had a more hierarchically fashioned collegial organisation that established a clear chain of command running from the Russian viceroy to a local mosque. At the top of the hierarchy was a Spiritual Board, headed by a mufti for the Sunnis or a *sheikh-ul-Islam* among the Shi'is. They ruled over provincial *majlis*es, which in their turn supervised district (*uezd*) qadis, teachers and students. The lowest level of religious administration was a Sunni mullah (and a Shi'i *pish-namaz*) administering a Friday mosque, teaching in a Muslim school, if any, and composing communal registers (*metricheskie knigi*) of parishioners.

Religious personnel of the Sunni and Shi'i muftiates shared certain privileges and institutions. Only Sufi leaders and their adherents, who were supposed to share an anti-Russian position, did not receive privileged legal status and were ascribed to the 'lower classes'. The official status of the Caucasian Muslim

20 Arapov, *Islam v Rossiiskoi imperii*, pp. 165–9, 210–47. See also 'Instruktsiia o poriadke ispytaniia na vstuplenie v musul'manskoe dukhovenstvo' (1873), in Tsentral'nyi gos. arkhiv Respubliki Dagestana, Makhachkala, Fond 26, op. 2, d. 14, pp. 28–32.

clergy was much higher than in the Tauride Directorate, and in particular in the Orenburg Assembly. Likewise, they were divided into lower and higher clergies. 'Muslim clerics' and their children were exempted from corporal punishment, the military draft and tax payments. The senior clerics were paid by the Russian administration, while the lower ones were subsidised by their congregations. The Russian state covered all their travel costs and provided a daily allowance. Having served more than twenty years, senior clerics were granted personal noble status.

The emergence of the 'Muslim clergy' provided the state with able functionaries in different spheres of imperial governance. Their number grew quickly. In 1911 the official statistics counted 46,492 higher and lower Muslim clerics in the Russian Empire. Not all of them had legally defined status: 25,251 'clerics' from four Central Asian provinces were not included in the framework of officially recognised 'Muslim clergy'.[21] The latter existed only in the regions included in the jurisdiction of four muftiates.

In the second half of the nineteenth century 'Muslim clergy' were introduced into the Russian army and navy, where the number of Muslims was quickly growing, in particular after the establishment of compulsory military service in 1874. Muslims of the North Caucasus and Central Asia were exempt from conscription, but many of them served as volunteers in irregular Muslim regiments. To administer the military oath of allegiance and let Muslim soldiers and officers perform religious rites and duties prescribed by Islam, a hierarchy of 'Muhammedan clergy' was created. It included a number of officer and subaltern ranks from military Muhammedan mullah and mu'adhdhin to akhund. The highest position was held by a senior akhund of the Guards. Military Muslim officers were drawn overwhelmingly from junior and senior clerics attached to the Orenburg Assembly. The *OMDS* was also charged with supervision over the Muslim military clergy in the Siberian, Ural and Astrakhan Cossack Hosts.

The position of Muslim populations and elites in the Caucasus and Central Asia much depended on local military governors. In 1844 the Caucasian viceroyalty was created in the North Caucasus and Transcausasia. It was ruled by a viceroy reporting directly to the emperor. In 1856–62 this office was held by Prince A. I. Bariatinskii, the victor over the famous Imam Shamil and Alexander II's personal friend. His successor was Grand Duke Mikhail Nikolaevich (1862–81), the emperor's younger brother who had even more influence among the highest imperial elite in St Petersburg.

21 Farkhshatov, 'Musul'manskoe dukhovenstvo', p. 72.

In the Caucasus the so-called 'military communal administration' (*voenno-narodnoe upravlenie*) was planned by Bariatinskii and carried out by Mikhail Nikolaevich in the 1860s.[22] Muslim mountaineers were granted legal and administrative autonomy under the supervision of Russian military officers. They were allowed to preserve their customs (*'adat*), in particular village community and adat courts. Fearing Muslim resistance, Bariatinskii proposed to undermine the influence of Muridism in the North Caucasus by strengthening customary law at the expense of shari'a. Customary law courts under the direction of Russian military officers were designed. In practice, however, mixed oral and mountain courts (*mahkama*) were created that followed principles of 'adat, shari'a and partly imperial laws. Without abolishing 'old' Muslim religious elites, the authorities turned village imams into functionaries known as mullah or *efendi* and reduced their number to one per 200 people. Waqf properties and mosque schools became subject to state supervision.

A number of reasons, chiefly the massive exodus of Muslims to the Ottoman Empire, prevented the government from introducing this model all over the Caucasus. It was established only in the province of Dagestan, as well as in the districts of Zakataly, Sukhum, Batum and Kars in Transcaucasia. Elements of the military communal administration model were used in the north-western Caucasus and the Transcaspian Province (present Turkmenistan). As a rule the Caucasian experience did not fit to the conditions of Turkestan. For instance, in 1866 mixed *mehkeme* designed in the Caucasian manner and based on both Islamic and customary law were set up. But they failed to work and unofficial qadis' courts had to be restored.

The complicated system of Muslim administration in Central Asia is still basically unstudied with the exception of a thorough account by P. P. Litvinov on Turkestan.[23] Initially, Central Asian provinces were divided into the Turkestan and the Steppe regions, Transcaspian Province, and the khanates of Khiva and Bukhara, which were under a Russian protectorate. The Steppe governor-generalship had been formed from the former Siberian province and was subordinated directly to the Ministry of Internal Affairs. The war minister supervised the Turkestan governor-generalship.

In the governor-generalships of Central Asia 'disregard of the Muslim clergy' prevailed. In this region, as in the North Caucasus, Islam was not

22 I attempted to compare this regime with other types of indirect rule of Muslims as they were applied in the Ottoman Empire and French Algeria in V. O. Bobrovnikov, *Musul'mane Severnogo Kavkaza: obychai, pravo, nasilie* (Moscow: Vostochnaia literatura, 2002), pp. 147–75.

23 P. P. Litvinov, *Gosudarstvo i islam v russkom Turkestane (1865–1917)* (Elets: Elets gos. ped. instit., 1998).

institutionalised. In Turkestan, mullahs and other members of the Muslim religious elites were not recognised. Fearing possible Muslim uprisings, the authorities put waqf properties, holy places and Sufis under state control. Wandering dervishes were prohibited to preach and recite prayers (*dhikr*) in the towns. All practising Sufi masters, holy graves and mosque schools were registered and became the subject of police supervision. They had no legally defined status or privileges. When the Turkestan region became independent of the Orenburg Assembly in 1880, K. P. von Kaufmann, the Turkestan governor-general, ordered the expulsion of all mullahs with a licence issued in Orenburg (*ukaznye mully*).

The reaction of Muslim populations towards the new conceptions and methods of the imperial government was mixed. Their attitudes varied from open hostility to collaboration and to adaptation to imperial rule. As Paul Werth has shown for the Volga-Kama region, missionaries failed to prevent a return to Islam among baptised Muslims, although a segment of converts did embrace Orthodoxy and came to represent a distinct group known as 'kriasheny'.[24] In the Volga-Ural region, rejection of Orthodoxy continued, its peak being the 'Great Apostasy' of 1866.

Imposition of new rules as well as persecutions of Sufis provoked a number of local uprisings in the North Caucasus and Central Asia. In 1877 spontaneous revolts broke out throughout Dagestan and Chechnia. *Jihad* was declared and an Avar, Mohammed-Hajji, a son of the famous Naqshbandi sheikh Abd al-Rahman al-Sughuri (1792–1882), was elected to the office of imam. At Andijan in 1898 there was a revolt led by a Naqshbandi sheikh Mohammed Ali known as Dukchi *Ishan*. All these rebellions were defeated by Russian troops, while their leaders were sentenced to death or exile in Inner Russia. Though crushed, they strengthened Russian anxieties about Islam and especially Sufism.

Beginning in the last quarter of the nineteenth century and especially in the early twentieth century a 'Muslim question' confronted the tsarist regime. It complemented a long list of the many other 'alien (*inorodcheskii*) questions': Jewish, Balts, Polish, Ukrainian etc. Many conservatives considered a population of about 20 million Muslim subjects a particular threat to the stability and integrity of the vast empire.[25] The possibility of a Pan-Islamic uprising haunted the minds of top-level state officials such as K. P. Pobedonostsev, the

24 Werth, *At the Margins*, pp. 147–76.

25 A thorough account of the history of the 'Muslim question' in late tsarist Russia was made in E. I. Vorob'eva, 'Musul'manskii vopros v imperskoi politike Rossiiskogo samoderzhaviia: vtoraia polovina XIX veka – 1917 g.', Candidate dissertation, Institute of Russian History, St Petersburg, 1999.

procurator-general of the Holy Synod (1880–1905), and S. M. Dukhovskoi, the Turkestan governor-general (1898–1901).

From the 1860s until the 1910s, officials generated a great number of draft bills concerning new Islamic institutions, in particular muftiates in separate regions of the borderlands. M. G. Cherniaev, the Turkestan governor-general (1882–4), set up a commission to create a separate Turkestan Spiritual Board. In 1898 the Turkestan governor-general Dukhovskoi returned to this idea, attempting to bring mullahs, madrasas and *waqf* properties under state control. In 1889 the commander-in-chief in the Caucasus, Prince A. M. Dondukov-Korsakov (1882–90) sent to the War Ministry his project of a separate Muslim muftiate in Kuban and Terek provinces under his supervision. In 1906 the well-known anti-Muslim activist and conservative V. P. Cherevanskii submitted one more project for the Special Conference on the Religious Affairs of the Sunni Muslims (*Osoboe soveshchanie po delam very musul'man-sunnitov*). He proposed to divide the Orenburg Assembly into three districts (centred in St Petersburg, Ufa and Troitsk / Petropavlovsk) and to replace existing muftiates by eight new District Directorates in St Petersburg, Simferopol (Crimean), Tiflis (Caucasian), Troitsk or Petropavlovsk (Siberian), Orenburg, Ufa (Bashkir) and Akmolinsk (Steppe).

The impetus for a general shift in confessional policy grew considerably in the years immediately before the revolution of 1905–7. Numerous projects were submitted to the Ministry of Internal Affairs. Though none of them were carried out, they show well the existence of a substantial 'reformist idea' in the government whose development did not depend entirely on revolutionary pressure, as Rafael Ganelin has argued.[26] As early as 26 February 1903, Nicholas II promised 'to strengthen the steadfast observance by the authorities concerned with religious affairs of the guarantees of religious toleration contained in the fundamental laws of the Russian Empire'. A decree of 12 December 1904, raising a number of the future reform issues, called on the government 'to take now . . . appropriate measures for the elimination of all constraints on religious life not directly established by law'. At last, a decree of 17 April 1905 confirmed by the famous Manifesto of 17 October granted Muslims and other non-Orthodox religious communities 'freedom of conscience'.[27] Religious conviction was recognised as the foundation of a formal confessional status.

26 R. Sh. Ganelin, *Rossiiskoe samoderzhavie v 1905 godu: reformy i revoliutsiia* (St Petersburg, Dmitrii Bulanin, 1991).
27 *PSZ*, St Petersburg, 3rd series, vol. 23, no. 22581; ibid., vol. 24, no. 25495 and no. 26126.

For their part, Muslim intellectuals began to seek the improvement of the Muslims' position in the Russian Empire. From the 1880s the reform movement known as jadidism emerged first among the 'ulama' in Crimea and the Volga-Ural region and soon spread in many Muslim regions of Russia. In Russia it was initiated by the Crimean Tatar Ismail Bey Gasprinskii (Gaspraly, 1851–1914), who developed ideas of contemporary Muslim reformers from abroad, in particular those of the famous scholar and writer Jamal al-Din al-Afgani (1839–97). Russia's reformers also drew on the works of two prominent nineteenth-century scholars from the Volga-Ural region, namely Abu-l-Nasr al-Kursavi (1776/7–1812) and Shihab al-Din al-Marjani (1818–89).

The basic idea of the movement was to liberate Islam from Western domination by 'opening the door of interpretation' (*ijtihad*) closed in Islam by the eleventh century. This would make it possible to study modern sciences and languages, and to spread a new system of education among the Muslim youth (the Arab term *jadid* means 'new, modern'). The means of the campaign was the press and the schools. Gasprinsky's weekly newspaper *Tercuman* (Interpreter), founded in 1883, reached all parts of the empire. It was written in a literary Turkish that was clear to numerous Turkic-speaking peoples of Russia, and used the Arab alphabet.

Gasprinskii and his followers set up a network of reformed (*novometodnye*) schools, the first of which was opened in the town of Bakhchisarai in 1884. They competed both with traditional mosque schools as well as with the network of Russo-Tatar schools of the Il'minskii's model. On the primary (*maktab*) level of the jadid schools, a phonetic method of teaching the Arabic language was introduced. Teaching of Russian and modern European languages was initiated in the higher classes. Some secular subjects such as mathematics and geography, as well as Tatar history, were brought into the madrasa curriculum. Jadid schools became widespread in the first decades of the twentieth century. There were 5,000 reformed schools in the empire as a whole by 1916. Most were in the towns of Crimea and the Volga-Ural region.

The importance of jadidism and its role in creating the foundations of a Tatar national identity is often overestimated. A lot of traditionally Muslim regions like Transcaucasia remained out of the movement. Recent thorough studies of the movement, in particular an account by Adeeb Khalid on Central Asia,[28] have shown that it comprised actually a tiny intellectual stratum and had not touched the majority of the 'ulama'. Never very numerous, the Jadids

28 A. Khaleed, *The Politics of Muslim Cultural Reform: Jadidism in Central Asia* (Berkeley: University of California Press, 1998).

constituted not so much a group as a broad trend among schoolmasters, Sufis, lawyers and publicists. The driving force behind the jadid movement remained the 'ulama' in the town centres of Crimea and the Volga-Ural region. The Tatar incomers played a crucial role in establishing jadid schools and a local Islamic press in Central Asia.

Paradoxically, Russian conservatives and Muslim reformers shared the Orientalist critique of isolated and inward-looking Muslim communities in Russia.[29] Both sides insisted on improving the Muslim administration to make the empire more homogeneous. In reality, they proposed to transform the empire into a nation-state. But the background of such a state was sought in different 'national traditions' – either among the Turkic Muslims or among the Orthodox Great Russians. A new scenario of imperial power elaborated under the rules of Alexander III and Nicholas II (r. 1894–1917) projected the government as a unitary Russian master subjecting lesser peoples and promoting the spread of Russian Orthodox culture among non-Russian populations (*obrusenie*).

The outbreak of the 1905–7 Revolution gave Islam a new political dimension. Muslims were permitted to organise public gatherings and form political movements. Muslim elites were involved in the political struggle concerning elections to the Parliament (*Duma*) and the emergence of new political parties. The *jadid* movement was translated into a number of political bodies. In August 1905 in the town of Nizhnii Novgorod, the First All-Russian Muslim Congress set up *Ittifaq al-Muslimin* (Muslim Union), the first Muslim political party in Russia. This organisation was in the hands of Tatars and was close to the Russian Constitutional Democrats (*Kadety*). In April 1906 the party's leaders were elected to the Duma, where they formed a joint Muslim faction that worked in all the four successive Dumas until February 1917. Both Ittifaq al-Muslimin and the Muslim faction remained under the strong influence of jadidism, mostly of Volga-Ural origin. Some of their members came from the official clergy and Muslim elites of Crimea, Central Asia, the Caucasus and the Steppe governor-generalship. Politically, they continued to side with the liberal opposition headed by the Kadets, while some Muslim deputies belonging to the Muslim Labour Group and Labourists were drawn to the Socialist Revolutionary Party.

29 As Gasprinsky put it, traditional Muslim communities 'vegetate in the narrow, stifling realm of their old ideas and prejudices, as if isolated from the rest of humanity'. See Ismail Bei Gasprinsky, *Russkoe musul'manstvo: mysli, zametki i nabliudeniia musul'manina*, (Oxford: Oxford University Press, 1985), p. 29.

Gradually the party programme and organisation were designed in the second and third Muslim Congresses held in St Petersburg and Nizhnii Novgorod in January and August 1906. At the same time, the party submitted to the government a wide programme of religious reforms for the Russian Muslims. A new religious legislative body was drafted aiming to turn Russia into a modern secular state without an official religion. To minimise state control in administering Muslim communities, supervision over Islamic institutions would be moved from the Ministry of Internal Affairs to a new All-Russian Muslim Ministry whose manager (called *ra'is al-'ulama'*) would report directly to the emperor. A network of muftiates would become an elected hierarchy responsible for all religious, cultural and economic matters of the Muslims including mosque schools and waqf foundations. The Muslim faction in the Duma continued re-drafting this programme. Its new version was elaborated in the next Muslim Congress held in St Petersburg on the eve of the First World War, in June 1914. They claimed to broaden the rights of official Muslim administration and increase the state funding of Muslim clergy.

The defeat of the revolution prevented the carrying out of this ambitious programme. The government was dominated by Russian conservatives and P. A. Stolypin, the influential minister of internal affairs (1906–11), was more unfavourable towards Islam than Count S. Iu. Witte, the minister of finance (1892–1903) and later the chairman of the Council of Ministers (1905–6). Actually the authorities did not want to co-operate even with a legal political opposition based in the Duma. They were also alarmed by the international troubles that followed shortly after the first Russian Revolution, namely the Iranian revolution of 1907–11 and the Young-Turk revolution of 1908–9. Russian Muslims were regarded as possible supporters of anti-Russian religious movements from abroad. Islamophobia much increased. In 1910–11 the Special Conference of the Ministry of Internal Affairs elaborated a programme of measures designed to 'oppose Pan-Islamist and Pan-Turkist influence on the Muslim populations'. Reformed Muslim schools were to be brought under strict state control, exchanges between the Russian and Ottoman Muslims were to be hampered and Orthodox missionary activities received increasing support from the state.

Nevertheless, administrative measures failed to stop the politicisation of Islam. Some Muslim political leaders emigrated to revolutionary Iran and Turkey, while others began to draw nearer to socialists and nationalists. In the 1910s new Muslim parties emerged, some of which later headed the nationalist movements which emerged in the borderlands after the collapse of the tsarist regime in 1917. Among these were the *Musavat* (Equality) party in Azerbaijan in 1911, the movement *Alash Orda* (Loyalty) among the Kazakhs in the Steppe governor-generalship in 1912, and *Melli Firqa* (National Party) in Crimea. In the Central Asian khanates under the Russian protectorate political movements of the Young Bukharans and the Young Khivans appeared already in 1909 under the impact of *jadid* associations in Tashkent. None of these parties was 'nationalist' in the strict sense (except perhaps *Alash Orda*). Most of them sought emancipation for all Muslims within the imperial framework and under shari'a law. Even the Tatars did not claim territorial separation from Russia. Azeris, Kazakhs and Central Asians preferred a federal organisation of future Russia.

Most of the Muslim political groups in late tsarist Russia were created secretly. Some were closed by the authorities later. Much more influential appeared to be the Muslim press, which emerged in the post-1905 period especially in Kazan and Baku. As Dilara Usmanova has shown, it played a crucial role in politicising Muslims in the last decade of the tsarist regime.[30] Making their first appearance in 1904–5, Muslim journals and newspapers much contributed to the spread of secular and even anticlerical ideas among the Muslim intelligentsia. The majority of newspapers and journals such as *Azat*, *Din we-Magyshat*, *Din we-l-Edeb* in Kazan, and *Hayat*, *Irshad*, *Taraqqi*, *Fuyuzat* and *Molla Nasreddin* in Baku were published in Turkic and used the Arab alphabet. There was also an Arabic press such as the well-known *Jaridat Daghestan* printed in the town of Temir-Khan-Shura in 1913–19.[31] It is noteworthy that most of these periodicals abandoned the traditional Islamic discourse, while sharing modernist visions of tsarist Russia and Islam in it.

Meanwhile, the old regime was losing political control in certain regions. Serious disturbances occurred in the North Caucasus, Central Asia and the Steppe region. When in 1913 rumours spread that Russian notaries (*pisari*) would be introduced in Muslim oral courts in the North Caucasus, troubles known as the Anti-notary uprising spread all over Dagestan province. Another insurrection engulfed the Steppe and parts of Turkestan in 1916. The primary cause was the hardships imposed on the local populations (exempt from conscription during the First World War), especially the mobilisation of men between eighteen and forty-three years old for home-front work in other

30 D. M. Usmanova, 'Die tatarische Presse 1905–1918: Quellen, Entwicklungsetappen und quantitative Analyse', in A. von Kuegelgen, M. Kemper and A. J. Frank (eds), *Muslim Culture in Russia and Central Asia*, vol. I (Berlin: Klaus Schwarz Verlag), S 239–78; D. M. Usmanova, *Musul'manskaia fraktsiia i problemy 'svobody sovesti' v Gosudarstvennoi Dume Rossii (1906–1917)* (Kazan: Master Line 1999), especially pp. 48–64.

31 Some of these periodicals even survived the old regime. E.g. the just-mentioned Arabic newspaper *Jaridat Daghestan* was issued under the title of *Daghestan* in 1918–19 until the outbreak of the civil war in the Caucasus.

parts of the empire. Both revolts were severely suppressed, but stability was not completely re-established. In the Kazakh steppe troubles continued until the spring of 1917, when the whole imperial building disintegrated. Its collapse in 1917 caused the subsequent destruction of some basic Islamic institutions and practices like the official hierarchies of the Muslim clergy and Islamic discourse that had emerged in the imperial context and were unable to exist without the imperial framework.

In conclusion, the relationship between the tsarist state and Islam should be understood as involving interaction sooner than confrontation. Having recognised Islam at the end of the eighteenth century, the authorities constructed a complicated imperial network of Islamic institutions including Muslim clergy, parishes and four regional muftiates. The administration of Muslims differed in central Russia and the borderlands. In a number of frontier regions such as the North Caucasus and Central Asia, Islam had not been institutionalised even at the end of the old regime. New Muslim elites emerged in response to these new Islamic institutions, which were accepted by most Russian Muslims. Despite this long history of interaction, however, the crisis of the tsarist regime beginning in the last third of the nineteenth century generated new fears and trepidations concerning Islam among tsarist functionaries. And indeed Muslims were involved in the political opposition that finally crushed the imperial regime in 1917.

PART IV

★

RUSSIAN SOCIETY, LAW AND ECONOMY

11

The elites

DOMINIC LIEVEN

Throughout the imperial period Russia's political and social elites were drawn overwhelmingly from members of the hereditary noble estate (*soslovie*).[1] Even in 1914 the core of the social elite were members of great aristocratic land-owning families.[2] This group overlapped to a still considerable but ever decreasing degree with the political elite, whose core were senior civilian and military officials. The aristocrats were all from hereditary noble families, these families usually being both old and titled, as well as rich. Most of the military and bureaucratic elite were also by birth from the hereditary nobility, the majority still coming from well-established though not usually rich land-owning families of the provincial gentry, or sometimes from well-entrenched service noble 'dynasties'. The still relatively small minority of senior generals and bureaucrats who were not noble by birth had acquired this status automatically by reaching senior ranks in the civil and military service.[3]

There were really only two relatively minor exceptions to the rule that the imperial elite was made up of hereditary noblemen. During the whole period senior clerics of the Orthodox Church, all of them drawn from the celibate monastic clergy, played a significant role in tsarist government and society.[4] Since the Church was firmly subordinated to the secular ruling elite and enjoyed limited status in aristocratic society, perhaps the senior clergy is

1 On the soslovie/estate system: G. L. Freeze, 'The *Soslovie* (Estate) Paradigm in Russian Social History', *AHR* 91, (1986): 11–36.

2 In D. Lieven, *The Aristocracy in Europe 1815–1914* (London: Macmillan, 1992), pp. 49–50, I have tables listing the names of owners of over 50,000 desiatiny: these are derived from L. P. Minarik, *Ekonomicheskaia kharakteristika krupneishikh sobstvennikov Rossii kontsa XIX–nachala XX vek* (Moscow: Nauka, 1971).

3 On the official and military top elite, see D. Lieven, *Russia's Rulers under the Old Regime* (London: Yale University Press, 1989). On the senior bureaucracy as a whole, see D. Lieven, 'The Russian Civil Service under Nicholas II: Some Variations on the Bureaucratic Theme', *JfGO* 29, 3 (1981): 366–403. Much of this chapter is derived from my three publications cited in notes 2 and 3.

4 Between 1701 and 1763 most bishops were Ukrainian, many of whom claimed to be Polish nobles: I am grateful to Paul Bushkovitch for this information.

best defined as a sub-elite. The other non-noble sub-elite worth mentioning is the new Russian business class which had emerged since the middle of the nineteenth century and whose national centre was Moscow. Whereas before the 1850s most great business fortunes either were founded by the nobility or were absorbed into it by marriage or ennoblement,[5] this became much less true in the last three generations of Imperial Russia, when a distinctive Moscow business elite and subculture emerged and came to dominate Muscovite society. In 1914 this group was still of distinctly second-class status within the tsarist political and social world, and this was a source of weakness for the tsarist regime. By contrast, the Petersburg business and financial elite was less Russian than its Muscovite peers and its financial barons in the nineteenth and twentieth centuries were closely linked to the Ministry of Finance.

Although members of the imperial social and political elite were almost all hereditary nobles, the hereditary nobility as a group was not a class, let alone a ruling class. It was not a class above all because of its enormous heterogeneity in terms of wealth, culture, lifestyles, economic interests, ethno-national allegiances and careers. Even its aristocratic core was not a true ruling elite because it lacked the political institutions which would have allowed it to define and defend coherent policies and interests, choose its own leaders and control the government machine.[6] One way to illustrate these points is by reference to England, whose aristocracy and gentry in the eighteenth and nineteenth centuries were a ruling class in the full sense of the word. Through Parliament in the centre and the justices of the peace in the counties the English aristocracy and gentry itself governed the country and developed the skills and mentalities of a political ruling class. Though, except for the tiny group of peers, the English elites had no legally defined status or privileges, the English 'gentlemen' were far more coherent in values, culture, lifestyles and loyalties than the Russian hereditary nobility. This was because to acquire the values and live in the style of an English gentleman required a substantial income. By the nineteenth century almost all gentlemen shared a common experience of socialisation through the expensive Public School system.[7]

5 E. P. Karnovich, *Zamechatel'nye bogatstva chastnikh lits v Rossii* (St Petersburg: Izd. A. S. Suvorov, 1885): e.g. p. 18: 'almost all the wealth, originally created in our country in the sphere of commercial and industrial activity, became noble wealth'.

6 For a useful recent discussion of precisely these points in the context of the emancipation era, see I. A. Khristoforov, *'Aristokraticheskaia' oppozitsiia velikim reformam* (Moscow: Russkoe slovo, 2002).

7 My comparisons with English (and German) aristocracy are drawn from Lieven, *Aristocracy*.

The hereditary nobility was not a class nor a political elite but rather a group (estate / *soslovie*) defined by law whose members shared certain privileges and institutions. These were largely set out in legislation enacted under Peter I and Catherine II.[8] This legislation established who was or was not a noble, how one acquired nobility, what rights and obligations noble status entailed, and what common institutions united the nobility. The most famous piece of Petrine legislation was the 1722 Table of Ranks which stressed the link between service to the crown and noble privilege, and created the rule that officers and civil servants acquired noble status automatically upon reaching defined ranks. Peter's imposition of lifelong state service on male nobles was unique in European (and Russian) history and did not long survive his death. Nevertheless the service ethic remained very important. Until the middle of the nineteenth century even wealthy young nobles usually served some years in the army (or more rarely the bureaucracy) before retiring into a private life of marriage and estate-management.

The eighteenth-century legislation also confirmed the nobility as a property-owning class, with absolute possession of their estates and the subsoil, and exclusive rights to ownership of serfs. Catherine II's son, Paul I (1796–1801), attempted to infringe her Noble Charter of 1785 which had confirmed that noble property could under no circumstances be confiscated by the crown and that noble honour entailed an absolute exemption from corporal punishment. Paul's (actually rather limited) assault on the nobility's sense of its rights and dignity was a key factor in his overthrow and assassination by members of the Petersburg aristocracy.[9] Catherine II also established noble corporate institutions in each province (*guberniia*) and district (*uezd*). These gave shape and identity to the local nobility, and the elected provincial and district noble marshals became key figures in local government and society. Nevertheless these noble corporate bodies never enjoyed anything approaching the power of provincial estate institutions in Central and Western Europe and it was only after 1905 that the nobility was allowed to create a central overarching body (the Union of the United Nobility) through which it could unite and lobby the government in defence of its interests.

One fundamental point about the hereditary nobility was that it was a relatively small group when one considers the governing, modernising and

8 On Peter and Catherine's legislation, see respectively: S. M. Troitskii, *Russkii absoliutizm i dvorianstvo* (Moscow: Nauka, 1974) and I. de Madariaga, *Russia in the Age of Catherine the Great* (London: Weidenfeld; 1981).

9 On the conspiracy which overthrew Paul I, see H. Ragsdale (ed.), *Paul I: A Reassessment of his Life and Reign* (Pittsburgh: University of Pittsburgh Press, 1979).

civilising role which the state expected it to play in Russian government and society. According to Isabel de Madariaga in 1700 the (still not fully defined) nobility entitled to own estates and serfs came to little more than 15,000 men, 'who had to carry the whole military and administrative burden of the new empire'.[10] Over the next two centuries the hereditary nobility grew enormously in size, by 1897 numbering 1.2 million people, or roughly 1 per cent of the total population.[11] Though this sounds formidable, one has to remember that until well into the second half of the nineteenth century most of the professional class was in state service and thereby ennobled, as were almost all the leading businessmen. Even in 1897 there were two-thirds as many hereditary nobles as there were members of the non-noble professional, clerical and merchant estates combined. European comparisons underline the point that Russia's educated and ruling cadres remained small. In pre-partition Poland 8 per cent of the population was noble, in Hungary in 1820 the figure was 4 per cent. In pre-revolutionary France 1.5 per cent of the population was noble but in addition a large and relatively well-educated middle class also existed. When Russia confronted revolutionary and Napoleonic France its lack of educated cadres put it at a serious disadvantage. Even most officers in Russian infantry regiments of the line in 1812 were not much more than literate, whereas even the French royal army of the 1770s already required literacy of senior non-commissioned officers.[12] This helps to explain the warm welcome that the tsarist regime gave to foreigners willing to enter Russian service.

In Peter I's reign the nobility was very largely Russian in ethnic terms, though it included many assimilated (and now Orthodox) nobles of Tatar origin. In the course of the imperial era, however, the nobility became much more diverse. This was partly because both non-Russian subjects of the tsars and foreigners were ennobled in Russian military and civil service, though the families of very many of these servicemen became entirely statist in loyalty and Russian in culture and language. Numerically much more important and politically sometimes less reliable were the nobilities of regions conquered by Russia in the eighteenth and nineteenth centuries and incorporated into the

10 See I. de Madariaga, 'The Russian Nobility in the Seventeenth and Eighteenth Centuries', in H. M. Scott (ed.), *The European Nobilities in the Seventeenth and Eighteenth Centuries*, 2 vols., (London: Longman, 1995), vol. II, p. 249.

11 The fullest discussion of the size of the nobility and of the 1897 census is in A. P. Korelin, *Dvorianstvo v poreformennoi Rossii* (Moscow: Nauka, 1979), chapter 1.

12 On the Russian officer corps in 1812, see D. G. Tselerungo, *Ofitsery russkoi armii–uchastniki borodinskogo srazheniia* (Moscow: Kalita, 2002): on educational levels, see pp. 111–34. On the French army, see S. F. Scott, *The Response of the Royal Army to the French Revolution* (Oxford: Clarendon Press, 1978), pp. 15–16.

empire. In the 1897 census 53% of hereditary nobles defined their first language as Russian, 28.6% as Polish, 5.9% as Georgian, 5.3% as Turkic / Tatar and 2.04% as German.[13] In the senior ranks of the Russian military and civil service it was Germans, and above all members of the small group of Baltic gentry families, who made by far the biggest impact. Not surprisingly, for most of the imperial period Baltic noblemen in service were much appreciated by the Romanovs and often thoroughly disliked by Russian nobles with whom they were competing for jobs.

Much the most significant privilege possessed by all members of the hereditary nobility before 1861 was their exclusive right to own serfs. However, an ever-growing number of hereditary nobles were not serf owners. Even in 1700 the great majority of noble estates were very small. Subsequently they were partitioned among heirs, with daughters as well as sons increasingly taking a share of lands and serfs. For many men from established noble families, let alone for the growing number of ennobled servicemen, military and civil service became their career, and their source of income and identity. Of the Russian officers who fought at Borodino 77 per cent claimed neither to own estates themselves, nor to be heirs to estates.[14] Since this figure includes the Guards regiments, and since army officers were more noble than civil servants, the statistic is all the more striking. After 1861 the landless element within the nobility grew apace, partly because of the problems faced by Russian noble agriculture and partly because the growing size of the bureaucracy and armed forces resulted in ever more ennoblements through service. Between 1875 and 1895, for instance, 37,000 individuals acquired hereditary noble status. By 1905 only 30 per cent of the hereditary nobility owned any land.[15]

Given the immense degree of differentiation within the land-owning nobility even common ownership of land (or serfs) did little to create a common sense of interest or identity. In 1797, 83.8 per cent of serf owners possessed fewer than 100 serfs, their total ownership amounting to 11.1 per cent of the whole serf population. By contrast the 1.5 per cent of serf owners who possessed over 1,000 serfs owned 35.3 per cent of the serf population.[16] Wealth bought culture: radically differing levels of education, cosmopolitanism and civilisation differentiated the nobility even more than crude statistics of property-owning

13 Korelin, *Dvorianstvo*, pp. 48–9.

14 Tselerungo, *Ofitsery*, p. 102.

15 Korelin, *Dvorianstvo*, p. 67. But see Seymour Becker's discussion and statistics in Appendix C of S. Becker, *Nobility and Privilege in Late Imperial Russia* (DeKalb: Northern Illinois University Press, 1985), p. 188, where he states that 38–9 per cent of nobles belonged to land-owning families in 1905.

16 Madariaga, 'Russian Nobility', pp. 254–5.

suggest. Before the nineteenth century, education and culture in general had to be acquired privately, and were therefore largely the monopoly of the aristocratic elite. The tiny handful of state educational institutions usually provided only the most rudimentary education to a small minority of the run-of-the-mill provincial nobility. In the nineteenth century the overall cultural level of the nobility rose dramatically but economic differentiation within the land-owning class certainly did not decrease. Everywhere in Europe great aristocratic magnates found it far easier to survive in a capitalist economy than was the case with the land-owning gentry as a whole. Typically, in Russia between 1900 and 1914 the 155 individuals who owned over 50,000 *desiatiny* sold only 3 per cent of their land, the nobility as a whole over 20 per cent.[17] The differing interests of aristocratic magnates and provincial gentry made solidarity difficult, until of course all landowners were threatened by social revolution and expropriation in the twentieth century.

At the core of the hereditary nobility there existed what one can justifiably call an aristocracy. Before 1700 a Russian boyar aristocracy had existed for centuries. The eighteenth century saw it enlarged and enriched. A market for agricultural surpluses emerged, which made commercial agriculture profitable in some regions. Nobles founded a swathe of industrial enterprises on their estates, their monopoly in distilling proving especially valuable, though a small number of magnates also made great fortunes from sugar in the nineteenth century. Most profitable of all was the Urals metallurgical industry, which made Russia the world's leading iron producer by the last quarter of the eighteenth century. By 1800 the whole of this industry was in the hands of a small number of aristocratic families. Meanwhile the massive expansion of Russian territory had brought fertile grain-lands and many other resources into Russian possession. Much of eighteenth-century Russia's new wealth accrued to the crown, which re-distributed a large part of it to favourites and to leading military and civil officers. Most of the richest families of the nineteenth-century Russian aristocracy were descended from these individuals either in the direct male line, or through fortunate marriages with heiresses. By 1815 the fruits of the previous century's dramatic economic growth were largely in aristocratic hands and the aristocratic elite, which was to survive down to 1917, was fully formed.

The precise parameters of this group are impossible to draw. Unlike its German or English peers, borders were not defined by titles or by membership of upper houses in the legislature, though even in the British and German cases

17 Minarik, *Ekonomicheskaia*, p. 37.

the boundaries of the aristocracy were in reality much more blurred and porous than legal definitions might imply. What united and constituted the Russian aristocracy was membership of a small group of inter-married and usually titled families, all of them very wealthy and with a close historical relationship with the court and the Romanovs. Acceptance into this small circle was defined by marriage and by access to exclusive private salons and clubs (above all, in the nineteenth century the Yacht Club), and to the most aristocratic regiments of the Imperial Guard (Chevaliers Gardes, Horse Guards, Emperor's Life Guard Hussars, Preobrazhensky Guards Infantry Regiment). Since the officers of these regiments in the nineteenth century had the right to accept or reject candidates, this reinforced the principle that membership of the aristocracy was by then above all determined by the aristocrats themselves.[18]

Some families of the aristocracy were branches of the princely dynasties descended from Rurik and Gedymin. The list of Russia's greatest landowners in 1900 includes, for example, Golitsyns, Gagarins, Volkonskiis and Belosel'skii-Belozerskiis, some of whose members were huge Urals landowners. Other aristocratic families were descended from non-titled boyar families of the Muscovite court, of whom the Sheremetevs and Naryshkins were most prominent in court, society and government throughout the imperial era. Most of the remaining aristocratic families, such as the Shuvalovs, Vorontsovs and Orlovs, were from the lesser pre-Petrine nobility, whose ancestors had performed military service either in the Moscow or provincial cavalry units. Even in the eighteenth century it was very difficult for any Russian from outside these groups to come within range of imperial notice and largesse. A handful of non-nobles did achieve this, however, of whom the most famous was Prince Menshikov in the reign of Peter I. In addition, two famous Russian merchant families lived at the core of the aristocracy in the imperial era, the Stroganovs from its inception and the Demidovs by the nineteenth century.

Whatever their ultimate ethnic origin, all these families were ethnic Russians by the eighteenth century though the cosmopolitan and frequently French-speaking world of Petersburg high society was often seen as alien, even disloyal, by nineteenth-century Russian nationalists. Nevertheless it was one of the strengths of the tsarist regime that it was able to incorporate the aristocracies of most of its non-Russian peripheral regions into the imperial nobility and even into the Petersburg aristocracy. This was particularly crucial as regards the Ukraine. The raw Cossack elite of the Hetmanate may have regretted

18 On this, apart from Lieven, *Russia's Rulers*, see G. S. Chubardin, *Staraia gvardiia* (Orel: Izd. Veshnie vody, 2002).

some of the freedoms it lost upon assimilation into the empire, but the status, careers and privileges it acquired through membership of the Russian nobility made it easier to bow to the inevitable.[19] Some of the most famous names of eighteenth- and early nineteenth-century Russian political history (Razumovskii, Potemkin, Bezborodko, Kochubei) were minor nobles of the Western Borderlands transformed by imperial favour and their own ability into core members of the Petersburg elite.

The same process occurred with a few families of ultimately Tatar or non-Christian origin, for example the Yusupovs, but in these cases entry into the Russian aristocracy meant complete sundering of ancestral roots. This was true to a much lesser degree of the leading Georgian families, the Bagrations, Immeritinskiis, Orbelianis and Dadianis. The regime's relationship with the Polish aristocracy was more troubled, though for obvious reasons the great magnates were much less inclined to radical nationalism than was the case with the Polish gentry as a whole. The Baltic German gentry on the contrary was very loyal, at least until the 1880s when tsarist administrative centralisation and support for Russian nationalism began to alienate many of its members. Although Baltic noble agriculture flourished throughout the imperial era and countless Balts made outstanding careers in the Russian service, very few big Baltic landowners also acquired great estates in Russia or joined the Petersburg aristocracy. As Haxthausen noted, the list barely extended beyond the Lievens and Pahlens, though in the nineteenth century the Benckendorffs were also fully-fledged members of Petersburg aristocratic society.[20]

By the end of the first half of the imperial era (i.e. roughly 1815) these families and their peers had been consolidated into a relatively homogeneous aristocratic elite. Though this aristocratic core of the Russian nobility to a very great extent survived down to 1917, in the interim it had been forced to concede much of its political power and role in government to the rapidly expanding bureaucracy. This was an inevitable concomitant of the modernisation of state and society, and had its parallels throughout nineteenth-century

19 On the very important issue of the integration of Ukrainian elites, see Z. Kohut, *Russian Centralism and Ukrainian Autonomy* (Cambridge, Mass.: Harvard University Press, 1988) and D. Saunders, *The Ukrainian Impact on Russian Culture 1750–1850* (Edmonton: CIUS, 1988).

20 For example, 'scarcely any (Balts i.e. my addition) have acquired their fortunes in Russia. It would be easy to enumerate those who, like the Lievens and Pahlens, owe a part of them to the munificence of the tsars': A. von Haxthausen, *The Russian Empire: Its People, Institutions and Resources*, trans. R. Faire, 2 vols. (London: Frank Cass, 1968): here vol. II, p. 199. One branch of the Lievens, for example, held its main estates in Courland and Livonia but also owned land in Russia and possessed Yuzovka, the core of the Ukrainian mining industry.

Europe. Bureaucracies grew in scale and professionalism in order to regulate and modernise increasingly complex societies. No aristocracy could provide recruits for all the new posts and skills that an expanding bureaucracy required. Even had it done so, these recruits' professional skills and career experience would still have differentiated them from each other and from the bulk of the land-owning elite.

The Russian bureaucratic elite which developed in the nineteenth century drew some of its recruits from the aristocracy and many more from the sons of the provincial land-owning gentry. In its initial period of growth, and especially under Nicholas I (r. 1825–55), its senior ranks were often dominated by generals, very many of whom were also aristocrats. By the second half of the nineteenth century most ministers were former civil servants, though right down to 1917 almost all governors-general, many provincial governors and a few other senior officials of the Ministry of Internal Affairs were military officers. All officers of the Gendarmerie (i.e. the political police) had previously served in the army and still to some extent came under the jurisdiction of the Ministry of War.

By the reign of Nicholas II the army was dominated by military professionals, often of humble origin, who were usually graduates of the General Staff Academy. Senior officers serving in the Ministry of Internal Affairs, in the Ministry of the Imperial Court or as regional governors and governors-general on the contrary were usually former Guards officers from well-connected families who had often abandoned professional military careers at a relatively early age for more rapid and sometimes easier careers in the civil administration. Governors by definition were 'generalists' and in addition even in the twentieth century benefited from an ability to move comfortably in provincial land-owning society. Not at all surprisingly, and in a way that had many Prussian and English parallels, governorships were very frequently held by aristocrats and members of prominent gentry families. Some of these men were former Guards officers but even more had previously served as district and provincial marshals of the nobility.

If the Ministry of Internal Affairs, and in particular its top provincial official, remained gentry nests in the bureaucracy, the same was even more true of the Foreign Ministry and diplomatic service, which were packed with aristocrats. Once again, in this Russia followed the usual European pattern of the era. Indeed in a monarchical Europe where the political world and high society were still intertwined, it was relatively easy to justify the continuing domination of the Foreign Ministry by scions of the aristocracy and prominent gentry families.

The most spectacular examples of aristocratic military and naval officers who held key positions in government were some of the Romanov grand dukes, all of whom served in the armed forces but some of whom played important roles in domestic politics and administration even in the reign of the last emperor. The values, lifestyles and social circle of these men linked them much more closely to the aristocracy than to the professional civil servants who increasingly dominated the government, and for whom in general the Romanovs had little sympathy. On the other hand, most of the Romanov family, and above all the last two monarchs, also had no sympathy for aristocratic political pretensions. Nicholas II in particular was a populist who far preferred the peasants (or at least his own conception of the peasantry) to Petersburg high society, in which he (not to mention his wife) felt increasingly ill at ease. By January 1917 Nicholas II had succeeded in alienating himself from almost the entire Russian elite, whether aristocratic, bureaucratic or military.

The civil bureaucratic elite of the nineteenth century was mostly educated in one of four higher educational institutions: the Alexander Lycée and the School of Law, both exclusively noble boarding schools, and the universities of St Petersburg and Moscow. These institutions were on a par with the best schools and universities in Europe. As its name implies, the School of Law existed to train judicial officials, and most graduates of the two universities had also studied in their law faculties. The Alexander Lycée, on the other hand, offered a broader humanitarian curriculum. Its graduates packed the top ranks of Nicholas II's Foreign Ministry, just as graduates of the School of Law dominated the Ministry of Justice and the Senate. On the whole by the last quarter of the nineteenth century senior and middle-ranking officials in Petersburg were intelligent, incorruptible and professionally competent bureaucrats with a strong commitment to the state and to Russia. As in many bureaucracies, the ablest officials were often those serving in the key co-ordinating central institutions: in Russia's case that meant above all the State Chancellery and the Chancellery of the Committee of Ministers. Also very able were most officials of the Finance Ministry. Some top Finance Ministry officials by the twentieth century had considerable experience in running private investment banks. Although most senior officials saw themselves (by no means necessarily wrongly) as more competent than any other group to govern Russia, their authoritarian and paternalistic proclivities were often tempered by acute awareness of the state's need to hold the allegiance of key social elites, who in many cases remained their own friends and close relations.

Inevitably senior officials sometimes lacked political skills and were at sea after 1905 when forced to speak and propagandise for government policy in the *Duma* (parliament). In other respects they were sometimes all too political: since ministers were senior officials and no real barrier divided politics and administration, officials had to be sensitive to policy, and to ideological and factional conflict at court and among the ministers simply in order to survive. Making a successful career in some parts of the civil service required not just hard work and professional competence but also caution, and the ability to acquire powerful patrons and to keep one's nose to the current political wind. When they actually reached top ministerial positions, the free-wheeling political skills they had honed during bureaucratic careers could, however, often serve senior officials well. Traditionally tsarist bureaucracy has had a very bad press from Russian aristocratic, liberal and radical critics, not to mention from Anglo-American historians. But from the origins of the modern Russian civil bureaucracy in the 1800s under the wing of Mikhail Speranskii down to 1917, the civil service produced many outstanding statesmen. A bureaucratic elite whose last generation produced men as diverse, imaginative and effective as Serge Witte, Petr Stolypin, Petr Durnovo and Alexander Krivoshein was something more than a Gogolean farce.[21]

In the imperial era the Russian elites, both aristocratic and bureaucratic, were part of a broader European elite culture and society. This was more true in the nineteenth century than in the eighteenth, and it always tended to be most true the higher up the social ladder one travelled. By the last quarter of the eighteenth century the Petersburg and Moscow intellectual elite, inevitably drawn overwhelmingly from the wealthier nobility, was developing its own variation on the theme of modern European literary culture.[22] In the nineteenth century it was to produce some of Europe's greatest musicians, poets and novelists. In general, education had high prestige among the nineteenth-century Russian elites, including among their wives and daughters. Given the extent to which the Russian elites drew on European models for everything from literary culture to fashionable dress and administrative modernisation, it was inevitable that they would attach a very high value to European languages. In certain respects educated Russian elites in the nineteenth century were indeed more 'European' than many of their peers in western and central

21 The whole discussion of the bureaucratic elite is derived from Lieven, *Russia's Rulers*.

22 The classic work on the noble origins of the Russian intelligentsia remains M. Raeff, *Origins of the Russian Intelligentsia* (New York: Harcourt, Brace, 1966). See also chapter 1 of N. Marasinova, *Psikhologiia elity rossiiskogo dvorianstva poslednei tret'i XVIII veka* (Moscow: Rosspen, 1999).

Europe in that they were better equipped to look at European culture in total and without some of the national blinkers of the French, English or Germans.

In cultural terms the nineteenth-century Russian elites were obviously far closer to Europe than to Asia. In fact, even if one goes back to 1700 and compares socioeconomic and political structures rather than cultures, one comes to the same conclusion. One good way to situate Russia on the global map is to make brief comparisons with the two other great empires in Asia at that time, namely the Ottoman Empire and China's Ching dynasty. In very many ways, comparing these three land empires provides rewarding insights for a Russianist, but it also underlines how much closer to Europe than to Asia the Russian elites were even in the Petrine era.

If, for instance, one looks at the Ottoman ruling group, the slave elite which governed the Ottoman Empire at its apogee had much in common with other ruling systems in the Middle East and very little in common with Russia. Even after the abolition of the *devsirme* the Ottoman elite was far from being an hereditary, military, property-owning nobility on the European (or Russian) model. The absence of monogamy and the existence of the imperial harem strongly differentiated Russian and Ottoman patterns of inheritance and power relations. So too did the absence in the Ottoman Empire of secure property rights to land. Already in the seventeenth century Russia was borrowing ideas and techniques from Europe. Quite apart from anything else, overt borrowing from an Islamic state would have been very difficult.[23]

In the case of the Chinese imperial tradition, one might argue that Chinese elites' strong identification with state service had some similarities with Russia. But the highly refined and self-confident secular high culture of Chinese elites had no equivalent in Petrine Russia. Nor did the cultural and ideological hegemony of the civil bureaucracy, and the latter's contempt for the brutal craft of war. In imperial Russian elite culture and society, officers, and especially Guards officers, always enjoyed far higher respect than the despised bureaucracy. One can indeed make some interesting comparisons between Russian elites and the Manchu military aristocracy which shared the rule of Ching China, so long as one remembers that in terms of mutual cultural

23 As regards Russian and Ottoman elites and the contexts in which they operated, for example, compare Potemkin (see S. Sebag Montefiore, *Prince of Princes. The Life of Potemkin* (London: Weidenfeld and Nicolson, 2000)) and Ali Pasha of Ioannina (see K. E. Fleming, *The Muslim Bonaparte. Diplomacy and Orientalism in Ali Pasha's Greece* (Princeton: Princeton University Press, 1999)). On the politics of dynasty and court, L. P. Pierce, *The Imperial Harem: Women and Sovereignty in the Ottoman Empire* (Oxford: Oxford University Press, 1993). For general background see R. Mantran (ed.), *Histoire de l'Empire Ottoman* (Paris: Fayard, 1989).

awareness the two elites might as well have lived on separate planets. But even in structural-political terms, the position of an initially semi-nomadic conquest elite ruling over a culturally somewhat alien sedentary society has far more in common with the Mughal or Ottoman Empire than it does with tsarist Russia.[24]

If Russian elites belonged unequivocally to Europe rather than Asia, they were nevertheless a very specific variation on the European theme. In certain respects their position vis-à-vis the crown was much weaker than in most of the rest of Europe. One illustration of the Russian monarchy's power concerns the lands of the Church. In Catholic Europe the Church usually held on to its lands into the nineteenth century. In Protestant countries ecclesiastical land was usually acquired by the landed elites as a result of the Reformation. In the Russian case, however, the state took over the Church's lands and held on to them. That was one reason why on the eve of emancipation more Russian peasants 'belonged' to the state than to private landlords.

The absence of feudal traditions, or at least of traditions which survived into the eighteenth century, is often and correctly cited as one of the key weaknesses of the Russian aristocracy. At the core of feudalism was the contract mutually binding on monarch and aristocracy. In more concrete form feudalism bequeathed estate institutions which were the forebears of representative government and which operated on the principle that the king was subject to law and could not tax his subjects without their consent. Though the lack of such institutions and concepts did indeed make the Russian elites very vulnerable to an autocrat's whims, one should not, however, forget the other side of the picture. In 1763 the Russian bureaucracy was barely larger than the Prussian and far worse educated.[25] Most German princes governed states which were tiny by Russian standards and could employ a swathe of university-educated officials, many of whom studied courses in cameralism in educational institutions which had existed since medieval times. Russia's first university was founded in 1755. Even in 1800 the number of state high schools (*gymnazii*) was pitiful. Inevitably therefore the crown

24 In general on the early Ching, see W. J. Peterson (ed.), *The Cambridge History of China, Vol. IX, Part I: The Ching Dynasty to 1800* (Cambridge: Cambridge University Press, 2002). Specifically on court and ruling elite, see: E. S. Rawski, *The Last Emperors: A Social History of Qing Imperial Institutions* (Berkeley: University of California Press, 1998) and B. Bartlett, *Monarchs and Ministers: The Grand Council in mid Ch'ing China 1723–1820* (Berkeley: University of California Press, 1991). I made an amateur effort to compare the three imperial regimes in D. Lieven, *Empire: The Russian Empire and its Rivals* (London: John Murray, 2000).

25 R. E. Jones, *The Emancipation of the Russian Nobility 1762–1785* (Princeton: Princeton University Press, 1973) is the best introduction to this.

was very dependent on the provincial landowner, whom Paul I called the state's involuntary police chief and tax collector in the village. Moreover, as many eighteenth-century monarchs discovered, emperors who annoyed the Petersburg aristocracy were liable to be overthrown and murdered in palace coups.

The reign of Alexander I witnesses to some of the realities of this mutual dependence of crown and nobility. By 1801 a significant section of the Petersburg aristocratic elite was already beginning to hanker after English-style civil and political rights. Alexander's rejection of the claims of the so-called 'Senatorial Party' frustrated them. His failure after 1815 to deliver either on the abolition of serfdom or on constitutional reform infuriated the future Decembrists and led to plans for revolution and regicide. But Alexander too faced frustration. The evidence strongly suggests that his desire to end serfdom and introduce some sort of constitution was sincere. In the absence of support from at least a sizeable minority of the nobility, however, emancipation might easily lead both to his own assassination and to chaos in the state administration. The fiasco which resulted from his efforts to create military colonies does not suggest optimism about any attempt to rule the countryside directly through officialdom. Moreover, given both the political views and the low cultural level of the provincial landowners, one can at least understand why Alexander might believe that the cause of progress was best entrusted to unlimited autocratic power.[26]

The emergence of an effective bureaucracy during the nineteenth century changed the balance of power between crown and aristocracy. Tension between aristocracy and the growing bureaucratic state was common in Europe but in Russia took extreme forms. This was in part because the Russian bureaucracy was often peculiarly incompetent and intrusive. Relatively unconstrained by law, it was quite capable of trampling on the civil rights and dignity of noblemen. In addition, almost uniquely by 1900, Russia's social elites had no representative institutions through which they could exercise some degree of supervision over the bureaucratic state. It is not a complete coincidence that two of Europe's most famous anarchists were members of prominent Russian aristocratic (Petr Kropotkin) and gentry (Mikhail Bakunin) families. When the bureaucratic state imposed policies very unfavourable to noble interests

26 S. V. Mironenko, *Samoderzhavie i reformy. Politicheskaia bor'ba v Rossii v nachale XIXv.* (Moscow: Nauka, 1989) is realistic on Alexander's aspirations and some of the constraints under which he operated. So is Alexander Martin: see his 'The Russian Empire and the Napoleonic Wars', in P. G. Dwyer (ed.), *Napoleon and Europe* (London: Longman, 2001), pp. 243–63.

hostility threatened to turn into revolt. There were signs of this in the wake of the 1861 emancipation settlement. In 1900–5 the anger of noble landowners at Witte's policy of industrialisation was an important factor in the growing revolt of the elected local assemblies (*zemstva*) amidst a surge of gentry liberalism.

The landowners' anger has also, however, to be seen within the context of the economic difficulties faced by Russian nobles after 1861. Most noble-owned industrial enterprises collapsed since they could not operate profitably without serf labour and could not compete with modern, capitalist factories. Noble agriculture also faced huge difficulties, one result of which was that 43 per cent of all noble land was sold between 1862 and 1905. Traditionally the post-emancipation era has been seen as one of noble decline, a decline for which the nobles' own fecklessness was partly responsible.

Without in any way denying that fecklessness existed, the nobility's economic performance needs to be put in context. Everywhere in Europe, with the partial exception of Silesia, the aristocracy was pulling out of industrial leadership. In much of Russia it was virtually impossible to run big agricultural estates profitably, particularly after the influx of New World grain and meat into global markets which began in the 1870s. Everywhere in Europe noble agriculture faced varying shades of crisis. If the big East Anglian landowners, traditional paragons of agricultural enterprise and advanced technology, could not survive the Great Depression, it is not at all surprising that the same was true of many Russian landlords.[27]

In any case the picture of decline is only partly correct. Like their European peers, and very sensibly, many Russian nobles were withdrawing from direct industrial enterprise and moving into stocks and bonds. By 1910 some aristocrats had huge portfolios and 49 per cent of the 137,825 nobles residing in St Petersburg lived on income from securities. Between 1862 and 1912 noble land had increased in value by 443 per cent while diminishing in extent by more than half. No doubt many Russian nobles had made the sensible decision to cash in their land for a much more reliable source of income which enabled them to live snugly as urban rentiers. Of course by pursuing this strategy, the Russian nobility began to undermine their position as the dominant group in rural society and in rural government at district (uezd) and local levels. This is, however, an inevitable part of modernity, and one might argue that the Russians' strategy was healthier than the determination of the Prussian

27 I compare British, Russian and German responses to agricultural crisis in Lieven, *Aristocracy*, chapter 3.

junkers to preserve their increasingly anachronistic position as a rural ruling class through ruthless agrarian interest-group politics.[28]

The Russian situation in which the land-owning gentry suffered but aristocratic families became the core of a new industrial-era plutocracy was very common to Europe as a whole. On the eve of the First World War the ratio of debt to income among the Russian aristocracy was usually a good deal healthier than it had been a century before. Russia's richest aristocrats had incomes of between £100,000 and £200,000 per annum. Given their sometimes immense holdings of shares and urban land, there was every reason to expect these incomes to soar as the industrial economy took off, as had happened to some aristocratic incomes in England and Germany. Even the Urals aristocratic magnates, though temporarily falling on bad times, had much room for optimism in 1914. With bank capital and new railways on the point of linking the region's vast iron ore deposits to the coal of western Siberia, there was good reason to expect huge future profits from their still immense landholdings.

In the early twentieth century the biggest threat to the land-owning class was political rather than economic. In 1905 peasant looters tried to destroy many noble estates. In 1906–7 peasant deputies, who made up a majority in the first two Dumas, demanded the expropriation of all private large-scale land-owning in Russia. The revolution of 1905–6 in fact drove the regime and the nobility back into close alliance. The landowners understood that without the support of the tsarist police and army their estates would be forfeit. Meanwhile the government learned the dangers of isolation even from its natural supporters among Russia's elites. Relations between crown and landed nobility were much better after 1906 than they had been in the decade before 1905. Nevertheless tensions remained, often for reasons which were already familiar from Prussian developments. In Russia, as earlier in Prussia, the regime's response to near revolution had been to set up a parliament dominated by representatives of the land-owning elite, who for the first time were able to articulate programmes, unite to defend their group interests, and choose their own leaders. In time the Prussian agrarians became a formidable conservative lobby and a thorn in the side of the Berlin government. Their Russian equivalents strongly circumscribed Stolypin's reformist strategy because of their great influence in both the lower (Duma) and upper (State Council) houses of the newly established parliament.

28 Becker, *Nobility*, pp. 44, 53.

European comparisons suggest that in 1914 the Russian land-owning nobility was both not powerful enough and too powerful for its own good. In nineteenth-century England 7,000 individuals, mostly members of the aristocracy and gentry, owned over 80 per cent of the land. Prussian land-owning was never this aristocratic, but in some provinces the big estates covered more than half the land. Both upper classes controlled rural society with little difficulty. In the English tenant farmer and the Prussian 'big' peasant the nobles also had powerful allies in the defence of property and order. In 1848–9 the Prussian nobles could play off peasant and landless labourer in a way that was far harder in most of Russia, given the relative solidarity of the much more homogeneous communal peasantry. On the other hand, however, the Russian nobles had not yet succeeded in marginalising themselves in the manner of the west and south German nobilities. By 1914 the latter very seldom owned more than 5 per cent of the land in any province and were barely a worthwhile target for expropriation. By contrast, even in the Central Industrial region (admittedly in 1905) the Russian nobles still owned 13.7 per cent of the land. In the south and west German case, many generations had passed since the end of serfdom and the tensions it had caused. In addition, the growing power of urban and industrial lobbies was tending to create a common agrarian front, which in Catholic areas enjoyed the powerful support of the Church. None of this applied in Russia.[29]

For rather obvious reasons, between 1860 and 1945 political stability was more tenuous in the poorer 'Second World' periphery of Europe than in its richer First World core. Property was less secure against social revolution and large agrarian property least secure of all. If this was true *a fortiori* of Russia it was not much less true of Hungary, Italy, Spain or even Ireland. In the Irish case the uniquely wealthy English tax-payer bought out the landlords on generous terms, in the process probably weakening the Anglo-Irish union but killing any chance of social revolution.[30] This option was not available in the rest of peripheral Europe. In Italy in 1920–1 fascism made great strides by helping the landowners, especially of Tuscany and the Po valley, to crush agrarian radicalism. In Spain and Hungary it took full-scale military counter-revolution backed by formidable foreign intervention to save the land-owning aristocracy from probable destruction. In Russia in 1917 only the victory of military counter-revolution could have saved the big estates, which would have been

29 Lieven, *Aristocracy*, chapters 2 and 3.

30 W. Kissane, *Explaining Irish Democracy* (Dublin: University College of Dublin Press, 2002), chapter 4.

expropriated as certainly by a democratically elected parliament as they were in fact by peasant mobs and Bolshevik decrees. One could very legitimately see the regimes of General Franco or Admiral Horthy as a high price to pay for the survival of aristocracy. In the specific Russian case, however, the destruction of the traditional rural elite went along with the emergence of a Bolshevik regime whose leaders seldom had much sympathy for, or understanding of, agriculture or peasants. Under Stalin this regime was to mount an assault on the Russian peasantry which went well beyond anything conceivable to Horthy or Franco.[31]

31 The best comparative work on the politics of aristocratic landownership in Europe in the late nineteenth and early twentieth centuries is R. Gibson and M. Blinkhorn (eds.), *Landownership and Power in Modern Europe* (London: Harper Collins, 1991).

12

The groups between: *raznochintsy*, intelligentsia, professionals

ELISE KIMERLING WIRTSCHAFTER

Beginning in the eighteenth century, when regularised bureaucracy struck deep roots in imperial Russia, policy-makers struggled to visualise the middle layers of Russian society. The vast geographical reaches of the empire, the cultural diversity of its population and the absence of constituted political bodies made it difficult to define the social groups situated between the mass of peasant cultivators and the governing classes of noble landowners, civil servants and military officers. As early as the middle of the seventeenth century Muscovite officials codified the assignment of Russian subjects to legally defined ranks (*chiny*) that carried specific rights, privileges and obligations to the state. This practice continued in the eighteenth century, when agglomerated social categories (*sostoianiia* or *sosloviia*) took shape, and remained a key feature of Russian social organisation until the Bolshevik Revolution of 1917. Sometimes called 'estates' by modern-day historians, the Russian *sostoianiia* consisted of hereditary statuses that functioned both as tools of administration and as social communities.[1] The Russian categories did not play a political role equivalent to that of the French *États* or German *Stände*, but they did share important features with these groups. Like corporate groups in Western and Central Europe, Russian nobles, clergy and townspeople enjoyed distinctive hereditary privileges; however, in contrast to the European groups, their privileges were not historically constituted in the local law codes, institutions and offices of identifiable territories.[2] Indeed, at the Russian monarch's discretion, without the consent of any corporate institution, privileges could be granted or rescinded and obligations redefined.

1 The classic analysis remains, Gregory L. Freeze, 'The *Soslovie* (Estate) Paradigm in Russian Social History', *AHR* 91 (1986): 11–36.

2 There were exceptions in the Ukrainian, Polish, Baltic German and Finnish lands that were absorbed into the Russian Empire but allowed, in varying degrees, to preserve local laws and corporate institutions.

Alongside the primary categories of Russian society – the nobles, clergy, merchants, townspeople and peasants – the Russian government also erected a range of subgroups characterised by distinctive occupational functions, service obligations and legal privileges. Among the most significant and persistent of these subgroups, the category of the *raznochintsy* (literally 'people of various ranks' or 'people of diverse origins') appeared early in the eighteenth century and remained an officially recognised social status until the late nineteenth century. In some legal-administrative usages, the designation 'from the *raznochintsy*' referred to outsiders or non-members of a given social category or community – for example, non-nobles or town residents who were not registered members of the official urban community (the *posad*). In other applications, the raznochintsy represented an umbrella category encompassing a range of protoprofessionals and lesser servicemen: low-ranking civil servants and unranked administrative employees, retired soldiers, the children of senior military officers born before a father's ennoblement, the children of personal (non-hereditary) nobles, non-noble students in state schools and various specialists, scholars, artists and performers. Careful perusal of the relevant legislation suggests that the malleable contours of the raznochintsy derived from both positive definitions based on function and negative definitions based on exclusion.[3]

The multiplicity of economic, service and protoprofessional subgroups that made up the raznochintsy highlighted both the complicated structure of Russia's 'groups between' and the desire of the government to impose legal-administrative controls across society. Throughout the eighteenth and early nineteenth centuries, resource mobilisation, the regularisation and expansion of state service, and the spread of education gave rise to new social groups that, in accordance with the political thinking of the time, needed to be institutionalised as legally defined social categories. Because each category performed specific functions in society and polity, the various subgroups of raznochintsy tended to correspond to recognisable occupations. Yet as the composition of the raznochintsy also showed, the realities of everyday life – the ways in which people struggled to survive and thrive – were far too amorphous and changeable to be contained within prescribed social relationships.

For much of the imperial period, the raznochintsy included entrepreneurial and needy individuals whose economic relationships violated officially recognised social and geographic boundaries. Well into the nineteenth century, for

3 For full treatment, see E. K. Wirtschafter, *Structures of Society: Imperial Russia's 'People of Various Ranks'* (DeKalb: Northern Illinois University Press, 1994).

example, debt relations, private employment, and lost social identities allowed non-nobles to exploit serf labour, even though the possession of serfs had become an exclusive noble right in the 1750s.[4] Similarly, in violation of the 1649 Law Code (*Ulozhenie*) and much subsequent legislation, peasants continued to set up shop in the towns, a privilege theoretically restricted to registered members of the official urban community (the townspeople or *meshchane*). Notwithstanding legal prohibitions and cameralist policing, the Russian government appeared powerless to prevent the illicit pursuit of profit. Nor did it necessarily want to stymie the inventiveness of wayward subjects; when properly regulated through the sale of trading privileges, illicit economic ventures acquired official sanction and served the fiscal interests of the state. Thus, the ascribed (*pripisannyi*) or trading (*torguiushchii*) peasant of the eighteenth and early nineteenth centuries could legally reside in a town on condition that he pay taxes as both a peasant and a member of the urban community.[5] With the help of flexible legal definitions, including the various definitions of the raznochintsy, officials tolerated or only half-heartedly prosecuted enterprising subjects who usurped the economic privileges assigned by law to other social groups.

The category of the raznochintsy, by incorporating social and economic relationships that lay outside the framework of official 'society', at once facilitated and undermined governmental control. Prior to the abolition of serfdom in 1861, the pursuit of profit, the satisfaction of greed and the struggle to subsist frequently took the form of forbidden economic activity that the government sought to eradicate or co-opt. Moreover, because some productive, potentially beneficial economic ventures (subsequently regarded as legitimate entrepreneurship) remained illicit and informally organised, business fortunes also could be highly unstable. Thus, for over three decades, from 1813 until 1844, the serf entrepreneur Nikolai Shipov roamed the Russian Empire geographically and occupationally, by legal and illegal means, until finally he achieved emancipation and became a sutler in the Caucasus and Bessarabia.[6] As Shipov's experience illustrates, the Russian government's insistence that economic functions be based on social origin inevitably led ambitious and talented individuals to violate the law. The presence of successful entrepreneurs

4 E. K. Wirtschafter, 'Legal Identity and the Possession of Serfs in Imperial Russia', *JMH* 70 (1998): 561–87; Wirtschafter, *Structures of Society*, pp. 26–31, 76–85.

5 R. Hellie, 'The Stratification of Muscovite Society: The Townsmen', *RH* 5 (1978): 119–75; E. K. Wirtschafter, *Social Identity in Imperial Russia* (DeKalb: Northern Illinois University Press, 1997), pp. 130–4; Wirtschafter, *Structures of Society*, pp. 18–26, 31–4, 89.

6 Shipov's son graduated from the Kherson Gymnasium and became a teacher in Odessa. *V. N. Karpov, Vospominaniia – N. N. Shipov, Istoriia moei zhizni*, repr. (Moscow and Leningrad: Academia, 1933); Wirtschafter, *Structures of Society*, pp. 90–1.

among the raznochintsy revealed the skill with which ordinary Russians not only evaded state authority but also manipulated official social definitions in the interest of personal security and profit.

Try as it might to contain society's development within hereditary social categories, the imperial government's need to mobilise human and material resources also created legal opportunities for the crossing of social boundaries. The imposition of service obligations opened avenues of social mobility and spawned new subgroups of raznochintsy. When serfs, state peasants and registered townspeople were conscripted into the army, they became legally free from the authority of the landlord or local community; consequently, soldiers' wives and any children born to soldiers or their wives after the former entered service also attained legal freedom. Legal emancipation surely represented upward mobility, yet its realisation and consequences remained problematic. For while soldiers and their families enjoyed special economic and educational privileges, their actual lives did not always conform to official prescriptions. Soldiers' wives (*soldatki*) could obtain passports allowing them to engage in urban trades, and soldiers' sons (*soldatskie deti*) were required to enter military schools and eventually active service; however, local communities did not necessarily tolerate the presence of soldiers' wives, and soldiers' children, including female and illegitimate children, did not necessarily end up in the appropriate schools, institutions or occupational groups. By freeing lower-class people from local seignorial and community controls, the demands of military service produced a floating population, eligible for registration in a variety of service and economic groups, but not always living within the confines of their legal status.[7]

Whether historians focus attention on economic activities or state service, a dynamic relationship between governmental policy and spontaneous societal development underlies the phenomenon of the raznochintsy. Effective government required both trained personnel and a prosperous populace. But whereas the extraction of resources from society encouraged the imposition of ever-tighter social controls, the demand for educated servicemen loosened social restrictions and encouraged social mobility. Throughout the imperial period, commoners acquired education, benefited from the rewards of state service and rose into the hereditary nobility precisely because the state needed technically competent administrative and military personnel. At the higher levels of Russian society, the Table of Ranks institutionalised this process, which

7 E. K. Wirtschafter, 'Social Misfits: Veterans and Soldiers' Families in Servile Russia', *Journal of Military History* 59 (1995): 215–35.

included the creation of service-related raznochintsy. Established in 1722 by Peter the Great, the Table of Ranks regulated promotion and ennoblement in military, state and court service.[8] In state service, promotion to rank eight conferred hereditary nobility, whereas ranks nine to fourteen granted personal nobility. Personal nobles enjoyed all the rights and privileges of hereditary nobles, including the right to possess populated estates, but their non-noble children did not inherit these rights.[9] Thus children born to civil servants or military officers prior to hereditary ennoblement belonged to the raznochintsy, as did individual servicemen whose positions fell below the Table of Ranks and those whose ranks did not confer nobility (hereditary or personal). Adding to the complexity of these arrangements, a law of 1832 established the title 'honoured citizen', which granted noble-like privileges – exemption from conscription, the capitation and corporal punishment – in recognition of economic and cultural achievements.[10]

As the number of servicemen and educated non-nobles grew and as ennoblement occurred at ever-higher ranks, the significance of the raznochintsy moved beyond the realm of legal-administrative order into the realm of social consciousness. With the founding of Moscow University in 1755, the official boundaries of the raznochintsy had expanded to include all non-noble students at the university and preparatory gymnasia, many of whom would go on to serve in the army and bureaucracy.[11] Born of the government's need for scholars, artists, technical specialists and trained servicemen, the educated commoners became the most widely recognised subgroup of raznochintsy. In nineteenth-century literature, memoirs and journalism, and in much subsequent commentary and scholarship, the category of the raznochintsy referred to upwardly mobile educated commoners who belonged to a 'society' (*obshchestvo*) or 'public' (*publika*) of diverse social origins. This notion of 'society' as an abstract entity arose in the late eighteenth and early nineteenth centuries to indicate fashionable or polite society (*le grand monde*), 'the civil society

8 For recent treatment, see L. E. Shepelev, *Chinovnyi mir Rossii XVIII–nachalo XX v.* (St Petersburg: Iskusstvo-SPb, 1999). See also S. M. Troitskii, *Russkii absoliutizm i dvorianstvo v XVIII v.: Formirovanie biurokratii* (Moscow: Nauka, 1974); P. A. Zaionchkovskii, *Pravitel'stvennyi apparat samoderzhavnoi Rossii v XIX v.* (Moscow: Mysl', 1978).

9 Beginning in 1845 rank five conferred hereditary nobility; ranks nine through six, personal nobility; and ranks fourteen through ten, personal honoured citizenship. A decree of 1856 then raised the attainment of hereditary nobility to rank four. L. E. Shepelev, *Otmenennye istoriei – chiny, zvaniia tituly v Rossiiskoi imperii* (Leningrad: Nauka, 1977), pp. 11–16, 47–101.

10 Wirtschafter, *Structures of Society*, pp. 34, 76–7.

11 Of the two preparatory gymnasia attached to Moscow University, one was 'for nobles, and the other for *raznochintsy*, except serfs'. *PSZ*, 1st series: 1649–1825, 46 vols. (St Petersburg: Tip. II Otd., 1830), vol. 14, no. 10346. Quoted in Wirtschafter, *Structures of Society*, p. 22.

of the educated', or educated Russians who were 'neither agents of the government (*pravitel'stvo*) nor in the traditional sense its subjects (*narod*)'.[12] Organised around print culture and sites of polite sociability, 'society' originated in the educated service classes of the eighteenth century, which while overwhelmingly noble, also encompassed a sizeable contingent of non-noble raznochintsy.[13]

Almost from the outset, however, noble members of 'society' questioned the moral worthiness of the educated raznochintsy. Noble instructions to the Legislative Commission of 1767–8 defined the raznochintsy not simply as non-nobles, an established legal-administrative usage, but also as new service nobles in the derogatory sense of social upstarts. This derogatory usage acquired broad resonance in the nineteenth century, when major literary figures such as Nikolai Gogol and Ivan Turgenev depicted the raznochintsy as social and cultural inferiors. For P. D. Boborykin, a noble journalist prominent in the 1860s, the raznochintsy likewise represented social and cultural inferiors who nonetheless participated in the literary, theatrical and musical life of St Petersburg.[14] Whatever their contributions to the empire's military might and cultural glory, and these received recognition already in the eighteenth century, the raznochintsy in no way represented the best 'society'.

But the noble Boborykin also used the category raznochintsy in a more neutral sense to describe participants in a socially diverse urban cultural milieu. Out of this milieu there emerged in the middle of the nineteenth century an identifiable group of non-noble radical intellectuals enshrined in Russian cultural memory as 'the raznochintsy'. Associated with the likes of V. G. Belinsky, N. G. Chernyshevsky and N. A. Dobroliubov, the educated raznochintsy of the 1840s–70s combined literary careers with social radicalism and political opposition. As in the past, some members of Russian 'society' disdained the raznochintsy, seeing in their radical ideas and alternative lifestyle, a threat to morality and civilisation. To others, the raznochintsy represented a generation of 'new people' who would lead the country through a revolutionary transformation to a bright and joyous future. Regardless of how the raznochintsy were judged, their presence in the consciousness of Russia's educated

12 M. Raeff, 'Transfiguration and Modernization: The Paradoxes of Social Disciplining, Paedagogical Leadership, and the Enlightenment in Eighteenth-Century Russia', in H. Bödeker and E. Hinrichs (eds.), *Alteuropa – Ancien Régime – Frühe Neuzeit: Probleme und Methoden der Forschung* (Stuttgart, Bad Cannstatt: Fromann-Holzboog, 1991), p. 109. See also A. Netting, 'Russian Liberalism: The Years of Promise', unpublished PhD dissertation, Columbia University (1967), p. 20.

13 M. M. Shtrange, *Demokraticheskaia intelligentsiia Rossii v XVIII veke* (Moscow: Nauka, 1965).

14 Wirtschafter, *Structures of Society*, pp. 98–101.

classes contributed to the formation of another sociocultural identity, the intelligentsia, which has remained an 'institution' of Russian society to the present day.[15]

On-going scholarly research shows that the conceptual and historical reality of the intelligentsia, no less than that of the raznochintsy, cannot be subordinated to any single collective meaning.[16] Historians situate 'the origins of the Russian intelligentsia' in a variety of social milieus: the educated and increasingly disaffected service nobility of the eighteenth century; the idealist philosophical circles that formed around the universities, salons and 'thick' journals of the 1830s–40s; and finally, the radical raznochintsy and nihilist movement of the 1860s.[17] One historian counts over sixty definitions of the 'intelligentsia' in the scholarship of the former Soviet Union, the most common being a social group composed of individuals 'professionally employed in mental labour'. Echoing the official classifications of Soviet society, this definition equates the intelligentsia with the technically specialised professions of modern times.[18] Clearly, the possibilities for definition and redefinition are numerous. Suffice it to say that any effort to summarise or critically evaluate the massive historiography on the intelligentsia can hardly do justice to the complexity of the phenomenon or the diligence of its scholars.

15 On the continuity of the intelligentsia 'counterculture', see J. Burbank, 'Were the Russian *Intelligenty* Organic Intellectuals?' in L. Fink, S. T. Leonard and D. M. Reid (eds.), *Intellectuals and Public Life: Between Radicalism and Reform* (Ithaca: Cornell University Press, 1996), pp. 97–120.

16 As a collective term, intelligentsia appeared in Russia from the 1830s to the 1860s. Wirtschafter, *Structures of Society*, pp. 101–2, 125–33; O. Muller, *Intelligencija. Untersuchungen zur Geschichte eines politischen Schlagwortes* (Frankfurt: Athenaum, 1971); and most recently S. O. Shmidt, 'K istorii slova "intelligentsiia"', reprinted in *Obshchestvennoe samosoznanie rossiiskogo blagorodnogo sosloviia, XVII–pervaia tret' XIX veka* (Moscow: Nauka, 2002), pp. 300–9.

17 I provide here only a handful of references. M. Raeff, *Origins of the Russian Intelligentsia: The Eighteenth-Century Nobility* (New York: Harcourt, Brace and World, 1966); M. Malia, *Alexander Herzen and the Birth of Russian Socialism* (Cambridge, Mass.: Harvard University Press, 1961); D. Brower, 'The Problem of the Russian Intelligentsia', *SR* 26 (1967): 638–47; D. Brower, *Training the Nihilists: Education and Radicalism in Tsarist Russia* (Ithaca: Cornell University Press, 1975); A. Walicki, *A History of Russian Thought from the Enlightenment to Marxism*, trans. Hilda Andrews-Rusiecka (Stanford: Stanford University Press, 1979); V. Nahirny, 'The Russian Intelligentsia: From Men of Ideas to Men of Convictions', *Comparative Studies in Society and History* 4 (1962): 403–35; V. Nahirny, *The Russian Intelligentsia: From Torment to Silence* (New Brunswick: Transaction Books, 1983). For fuller historiographic treatment, see Wirtschafter, *Structures of Society*, pp. 93–150; Wirtschafter, *Social Identity*, pp. 86–99.

18 S. I. Khasanova, 'K voprosu ob izuchenii intelligentsii dorevoliutsionnoi Rossii', in G. N. Vul'fson (ed.), *Revoliutsionno-osvoboditel'noe dvizhenie v XIX–XX vv. v Povolzh'e i Priural'e* (Kazan: Izd. Kazanskogo universiteta, 1974), pp. 37–54; V. R. Leikina-Svirskaia, 'Formirovanie raznochinskoi intelligentsii v Rossii v 40-kh godakh XIX v.', *Istoriia SSSR* (1958) no. 1: 83–104; V. R. Leikina-Svirskaia, *Intelligentsiia v Rossii vo vtoroi polovine XIX veka* (Moscow: Mysl', 1971).

In current popular and scholarly usage, it often seems as if almost any educated or self-educated individual in Russia in the nineteenth or early twentieth century can be identified as an *intelligent* (pl. *intelligenty*), a member of the intelligentsia. But to warrant inclusion in the intelligentsia, a person also needed to possess a critical mind, a secular code of ethics, a commitment to social justice, a strong sense of individual dignity and cultural refinement or, as in the case of the nihilists of the 1860s, a distinctive lifestyle. An educated person who did not become a social radical or political oppositionist still could take an active interest in the reform of government and the welfare of the empire's population. Possessed of social conscience and political awareness, such a person might be called an *intelligent* and placed in the ranks of the intelligentsia. Membership in the intelligentsia is perhaps best represented as a sociocultural ideal or identity that encouraged the individual to define personal morality and personal interests in social terms. The *intelligent* worked for the betterment of society, whether or not this effort served the needs of his or her family and immediate community. To be an *intelligent* did not require adherence to any particular political movement, but it did imply a critical attitude toward conditions in society and government. Equally crucial, it implied a desire to change those conditions.[19]

Such an amorphous, value-laden definition of the intelligentsia can make concrete historical analysis difficult. A member of the intelligentsia could belong to or originate from a broad range of social, occupational and professional groups, including nobles and factory workers, officials and revolutionaries. He or she could embrace almost any political ideology or party, from monarchist to liberal to anarchist, and be a religious believer or an atheist, a nationalist or an internationalist. The *intelligent* also could represent almost any artistic movement or school of scholarly inquiry. Historians struggle valiantly to understand the intelligentsia in sociological, ideological and cultural terms. Not only do they seek to connect specific ideas to identifiable subcultures or social environments; their definitions also move back and forth between the intelligentsia as a 'subjective' state of mind and the intelligentsia as an 'objective' social stratum. Precisely because no single social circle, political movement or cultural current can contain the concept or reality of the intelligentsia, scholars end up distinguishing multiple intelligentsias: the noble intelligentsia, the 'democratic' (non-noble) intelligentsia, the liberal intelligentsia, the radical intelligentsia, the revolutionary intelligentsia,

19 M. Confino, 'On Intellectuals and Intellectual Traditions in Eighteenth- and Nineteenth-Century Russia', *Daedalus* 101 (1972): 117–49.

the worker intelligentsia, the peasant intelligentsia and so on. True to the very traditions of the Russian intelligentsia, historians are unable to avoid subjective judgements when trying to determine membership in the 'real' intelligentsia.[20]

Given the social and political diversity of the intelligentsia, even those historians who rely on subjective factors to define the group are reluctant to equate membership with a specific set of principles, beliefs or attitudes. Instead of compiling a laundry list of social, political and moral traits, they represent the intelligentsia as a form of individual or collective self-definition. Self-declared members of the intelligentsia assumed a déclassé position in Russian society by claiming to be above the interests and concerns of any particular social group or territorial community. Ironically, *intelligenty* propagated a myth of the intelligentsia that echoed the myth of the monarchy so many of them sought to oppose. Like the monarchy, members of the intelligentsia presented themselves as transcendent in the sense of being 'above class interests', though in contrast to the monarchy, they lacked concrete powers of intervention. Nor could the intelligentsia claim God-given or sacred authority; their moral authority remained strictly secular, sometimes even atheistic. Through education and personal behaviour, not election by God, individuals achieved social recognition as members of the intelligentsia.[21]

Whether one chooses to define the intelligentsia as myth, sociocultural self-image, political concept or sociological subculture, it remains necessary to explain how such a group arose in Russia and how it relates to the 'groups between'. Despite years of debate, argument and counter-argument, it is impossible to escape the conclusion that the Russian intelligentsia had its origins in the Enlightenment culture of the educated nobility or educated service classes of the late eighteenth century. By that time, elite Russia possessed all the trappings of European fashionable society, including a small commercialised print culture organised around private publishing, journalism, the book trade and public theatre (with permanent buildings and paid entry). The producers and promoters of this culture included eminent personages with close ties to the court and highest social circles, in addition to individuals from the foreign community and lesser service classes.[22] Among consumers – for example, public theatre audiences and purchasers of popular

20 Burbank, 'Russian *Intelligenty*', p. 101.

21 Like *raznochintsy*, intelligentsia also became a derogatory political label. See Muller, *Intelligencija*.

22 G. Marker, *Publishing, Printing, and the Origins of Intellectual Life in Russia, 1700–1800* (Princeton: Princeton University Press, 1985); G. Marker, 'The Creation of Journals and the Profession of Letters in the Eighteenth Century', in Deborah A. Martinsen (ed.),

prints and chapbooks – a humbler clientele also could be seen.[23] Consumers from the labouring, commercial and lesser service classes did not necessarily identify with Enlightenment ideas or become self-conscious creators of a literary product, but clearly they participated in a public culture where high and low forms of art, literature and sociability inevitably overlapped. Nobles purchased chapbooks, and Enlightenment themes entered 'popular' culture. Lower-class people (*chern'*) and petty bureaucrats attended the theatre, and among the authors of literary plays, one finds the serf M. A. Matinskii (1759–1829) alongside Empress Catherine the Great (r. 1762–96). In principle at least, to be a participant in the cosmopolitan, pan-European Enlightenment required not noble status, but noble behaviour.[24]

Ironically, however, the social diversity of Russia's lived Enlightenment did not produce a corresponding cultural or ideological pluralism. When compared with the educated classes of the nineteenth century, those of the eighteenth articulated a uniform brand of Enlightenment thought barely distinguishable from that of the court. Prior to 1800, Russia's governing classes, cultural luminaries and everyday consumers of print culture and the arts belonged overwhelmingly to the urban service milieu. In the nineteenth century, numerical growth and further social diversification produced educated classes of more varied ideological hues, yet the elite Enlightenment culture of the preceding century remained integral to the intelligentsia's understanding of justice, equality and progress. Despite the emergence of new cultural credos and organised political opposition, the government and educated classes continued to employ common categories of thought. Irrespective of political ideology, educated Russians defined themselves in relation to a contemporary European culture which they chose either to reject or to emulate. Perhaps more important, officials and self-proclaimed members of the intelligentsia, following the lead of the eighteenth-century educated service classes, also posed as carriers of civilisation and enlightenment to a presumably backward

Literary Journals in Imperial Russia (Cambridge: Cambridge University Press, 1997), pp. 11–33; E. K. Wirtschafter, *The Play of Ideas in Russian Enlightenment Theater* (DeKalb: Northern Illinois University Press, 2003), chapters 1–2. On the greater degree of commercialisation further west, see J. Brewer, *The Pleasures of the Imagination: English Culture in the Eighteenth Century* (New York: Farrar, Straus and Giroux, 1997); James Van Horn Melton, *The Rise of the Public in Enlightenment Europe* (Cambridge: Cambridge University Press, 2001).

23 On theatre audiences, see the brief treatment in Wirtschafter, *The Play of Ideas*, chapter 1. On the consumers of popular prints and chapbooks, see D. E. Farrell, 'Popular Prints in the Cultural History of Eighteenth-Century Russia', unpublished PhD dissertation, University of Wisconsin-Madison (1980), pp. 34–41.

24 In practice, most participants in the Russian Enlightenment originated from the nobility, but the principle of social pluralism remained.

and benighted Russian people.[25] In so far as nineteenth-century educated Russians identified with a broader 'society', they claimed to embody its essential aspirations and beliefs. Social progress corresponded to their understanding of social progress, and Russia's future became theirs to imagine.

That the eighteenth-century educated nobility or educated service classes represented the cultural origins of the Russian intelligentsia may help to explain why the intelligentsia so often can be seen as a creation or creature of the state. But clearly the concept of the intelligentsia, with its suggestion of morally autonomous political opposition and social criticism, did not simply represent an extension of enlightened bureaucracy or the societal obverse of the government.[26] The intelligentsia may have lacked strong ties to a broad audience or public, yet in social reach and influence it moved beyond the eighteenth-century educated classes. Indeed, early in the nineteenth century, a 'parting of ways' between the government and educated classes started to change the social and political landscape of Imperial Russia.[27] The self-conscious arrival of the intelligentsia in the 1860s showed that the 'parting of ways' had developed into ideological *and* social identity. In the concept of the intelligentsia, the educated classes resolutely declared their independence from the educated service classes at a time when social, professional and cultural elites in Russia still lacked the autonomous institutions of a politically organised civil society.

Across Europe, the modern concept of civil society has its origins in G. W. F. Hegel's definition of civil society as the realm of free market relations beyond the family and distinct from government. But prior to Hegel, theorists such as John Locke, Adam Ferguson, Adam Smith and various French Enlightenment figures concerned with the problem of making society civil used 'civil society' as a synonym for the political state.[28] Echoing this definition, historians of eighteenth-century Western and Central Europe see in the activities of constituted bodies – diets, provincial estates, *parlements*, Estates General and the English Parliament – the appearance of a 'new politics' of open contestation in

25 C. A. Frierson, *Peasant Icons: Representations of Rural People in Late Nineteenth-Century Russia* (New York: Oxford University Press, 1993).

26 W. B. Lincoln, *In the Vanguard of Reform: Russia's Enlightened Bureaucrats, 1825–1861* (DeKalb: Northern Illinois University Press, 1982); W. B. Lincoln, *The Great Reforms: Autocracy, Bureaucracy, and the Politics of Change in Imperial Russia* (DeKalb: Northern Illinois University Press, 1990); R. S. Wortman, *The Development of a Russian Legal Consciousness* (Chicago: University of Chicago Press, 1976).

27 N. Riasanovsky, *A Parting of Ways: Government and the Educated Public in Russia* (New York: Oxford University Press, 1976).

28 For an overview, see M. Riedel, 'Gesellschaft, bürgerliche', in O. Brunner, W. Conze and R. Koselleck (eds.), *Geschichtliche Grundbegriffe: Historisches Lexikon zur politisch-sozialen Sprache in Deutschland*, 8 vols. (Stuttgart: Ernst Klett, 1972–97), vol. II, pp. 719–800.

which the corporate institutions of 'absolute monarchy' became absorbed into an emergent 'public sphere' situated between the private sphere of the household and the sphere of public / political authority represented by the state.[29] In the public sphere, sometimes termed 'bourgeois' because of its roots in the capitalist market economy, the freedom and openness of relationships within the private household expanded into the arena of public / political authority. Through the development of autonomous civic organisations, the commercialisation of print culture, and the formation of communities structured around sites of sociability, the public sphere effectively limited the 'absolute' power of the state to the point where public / political authority became the common domain of society and government. The public sphere thus provided the setting for the emergence of a new kind of civil society organisationally independent of and more readily opposed to the political state.[30]

In broad outline, the development of Russian civil society followed the familiar European pattern. But in Russia, prior to the mid- or even the late nineteenth century, it would be misleading to speak of a politically organised civil society independent of the state. A realm of free market relations (Hegel's civil society) did exist, though often illicitly and without legal protections (remember the life of serf entrepreneur Nikolai Shipov), as did a pre-political literary public sphere grounded in print culture, learned and philanthropic societies, social clubs, commercial associations and masonic lodges. At the same time, however, the Russian reading public remained minuscule, and throughout the eighteenth century, Russian elites understood civic engagement as service in military and administrative bodies, including elective bodies and offices, which nevertheless were created, defined and regulated by state prescription. Nor did

29 With reference to the eighteenth century, 'absolutism' means not the 'absolute' power of a centralised state but a set of political institutions and relationships presided over by a monarch whose authority was assumed to be God-given and hence absolute. As the elected of God, the monarch presided over the implementation of God's laws in order to protect the people over whom he or she exercised sovereignty. Failure to live up to this obligation violated God's trust and already in the Middle Ages could be grounds for removal of the monarch. On these issues, see James Collins, *The State in Early Modern France* (Cambridge: Cambridge University Press, 1995); J. W. Merrick, *The Desacralization of the French Monarchy in the Eighteenth Century* (Baton Rouge: Louisiana State University Press, 1990); F. Kern, *Kingship and Law in the Middle Ages: I. The Divine Right of Kings and the Right of Resistance in the Early Middle Ages. II. Law and Constitution in the Middle Ages. Studies by Fritz Kern*, trans. S. B. Chrimes (Oxford: B. Blackwell, 1939).

30 On the 'public sphere', see J. Habermas, *The Structural Transformation of the Public Sphere: An Inquiry into a Category of Bourgeois Society*, trans. T. Burger and F. Lawrence (Cambridge, Mass.: MIT Press, 1989). On the 'new politics' of open contestation, see K. M. Baker, *Inventing the French Revolution: Essays on French Political Culture in the Eighteenth Century* (New York: Cambridge University Press, 1990). For recent discussion of the relationship between the 'new politics', the Habermasian public sphere and the emergence of civil society, see Melton, *Rise of the Public*.

the ownership of serfs and landed property carry legal-administrative authority beyond the family estate. When enlightened officials and educated Russians of the late eighteenth century called for civic engagement and worked to build civic institutions, they continued to equate social progress with personal moral reformation. Their calls for justice implied not open-ended social and political transformation but the restoration of God-given natural order. Only in the nineteenth century would their moral consciousness become a form of social identity to be affirmed by political means.

In Russia, the evolution from late-eighteenth-century 'civic society' to late-nineteenth-century 'civil society' can be traced through the provincial noble assemblies established in the reign of Catherine the Great. Although historians have devoted scant attention to these assemblies, there is no evidence to suggest that they played, or even aspired to play, a significant political role before the 1850s. On the contrary, the noble assemblies extended state administration into rural localities and provided a channel of communication between local nobles and the monarch in St Petersburg.[31] Governors appointed by the sovereign supervised the assemblies, and the cultural, educational and philanthropic activities they sponsored tended to result from official mandates. In general, judging from fragmentary and passing references, the assemblies served the social needs of local nobles by addressing genealogical, inheritance and welfare claims. Such a narrow particularistic orientation can hardly be equated with contested politics within an institutionalised public sphere.

But conditions changed in the era of the Great Reforms. Local nobles organised in provincial assemblies began to play a *translocal* political role not, as in the past, by serving in the army and bureaucracy, but by representing the interests of noble society in relation to the state and other social groups.[32] The turning point came in 1858, when at the behest of the central government, provincial committees met to draw up projects for the impending emancipation of the serfs.[33] The projects were locally conceived and generally non-political; however, the landed nobility appeared almost universally united in refusing to endorse the government's vision of the emancipation settlement. Not surprisingly, officials in St Petersburg roundly rejected the noble projects, a move that led some provincial assemblies to call for open debate and societal

31 How the noble assemblies used this channel of communication is a fascinating topic in need of study.

32 Based on local histories of 1812, I suspect that a shift may be discernible at the time of the Napoleonic invasion, though here too the formation of militias and the contribution of supplies and monies could have been imposed from above using administrative means.

33 T. Emmons, *The Russian Landed Gentry and the Peasant Emancipation of 1861* (Cambridge: Cambridge University Press, 1968).

representation in an on-going process of reform. The government had consulted with noble representatives on a matter of national importance but then completely ignored their views and silenced their voices, opting instead for emancipation by bureaucratic fiat.[34] Relations between the landed nobility and the monarchy would be changed forever. From this point onward, noble landowners would comprise a distinct social and political interest. Russia's pre-political literary public sphere, grounded in print culture and sociability, had evolved into a politically organised public sphere, grounded in legally and historically constituted institutions. The articulation of noble interests in opposition to official policy heralded the birth of Russian civil society independent of the state.

Of course, most Russian nobles remained loyal subjects of the monarchy. Still, the political and social agitation surrounding the peasant emancipation represented an early, if narrow, assertion of politically organised civil society. A more permanent locus of political action, one rooted in an institution of self-government rather than a particular policy decision, arose with the establishment of *zemstvo* (local elected council) assemblies in 1864.[35] Following the peasant emancipation, locally elected, multiclass zemstvos helped to fill the vacuum created by the removal of seignorial authority. The zemstvos enjoyed limited powers of taxation, which they used to finance meaningful social services, though always with the permission of the provincial governor or officials in St Petersburg. Local nobles dominated the ranks of private landowners and thus controlled the zemstvos; however, representatives of the peasant and urban classes also sat in the assemblies. Equally important for the development of a broad-based political society in Russia, zemstvo responsibility for infrastructure, education, public health and social welfare increasingly tied local self-government to the national political arena. Although Russia had no elected legislative body before 1906, zemstvo functions drew significant numbers of Russians into direct involvement with issues of empire-wide importance. This political experience, framed by an institution designed to meet the needs of diverse localities and social groups, provided a solid foundation for the emergence of modern civil society.

34 For the bureaucratic side of the story, see D. Field, *The End of Serfdom: Nobility and Bureaucracy in Russia, 1855–61* (Cambridge, Mass.: Harvard University Press, 1976).

35 On the zemstvos, see T. Emmons and W. S. Vucinich (eds.), *The Zemstvo in Russia: An Experiment in Local Self-Government* (New York: Cambridge University Press, 1982); N. M. Pirumova, *Zemskaia intelligentsiia i ee rol' v obshchestvennoi bor'be* (Moscow: Nauka, 1986); N. M. Pirumova, *Zemskoe liberal'noe dvizhenie: Sotsial'nye korni i evoliutsiia do nachala XX veka* (Moscow: Nauka, 1977); R. Robbins Jr., *Famine in Russia, 1891–1892: The Imperial Government Responds to a Crisis* (New York: Columbia University Press, 1975).

In functional and organisational terms, the zemstvo assemblies can be called institutions of the state *and* society. To a significant degree, the zemstvos, like the noble assemblies, represented an arm of government. They delivered public health services and elementary education, built roads and bridges and even provided famine relief. The zemstvos also remained subject to bureaucratic oversight, and they possessed no independent legislative authority. At the same time, however, the state–society relationship that the zemstvos made possible clearly contributed to the emergence of Russian civil society. If a politically organised civil society were to flourish in late Imperial Russia, the people of the empire needed to be incorporated into the everyday operations of government. They needed to be linked in a positive relationship to political authority. In contrast to what the intelligentsia ethos might suggest, effective civil societies limit the power of government not by disengaging from or opposing constituted authority but by sharing in its exercise, and if need be challenging specific policies, from a position of institutional autonomy. The zemstvos surely represented this potential, embodying both society's struggle for independent authority within the Russian polity and the integration of politically organised society into institutions of government.

If the raznochintsy revealed the capacity of ordinary Russians to fashion economic and social relationships outside official controls, and if identification with the intelligentsia effectively distinguished the educated classes from the educated service classes, the professions created a social environment in which the educated classes became connected to the needs of everyday life and ordinary people. Given the absence of autonomous guild structures in Russia, the professions originated in government-directed occupational training and specialisation.[36] Traditionally, teachers, physicians, midwives, medical orderlies, statisticians, agronomists, veterinarians, architects and engineers worked as state servicemen under military or civil administration. Yet as in so many areas of Russian life, conditions changed following the peasant emancipation. The establishment of the zemstvos allowed a significant number of professionals to find employment outside state institutions. This relative autonomy encouraged them to see in professional work a form of service to the nation rather than the government. Armed with scientific knowledge and technical expertise, professionals began to claim authority over the organisation of training and services. A small group of activists – a group that straddled the intelligentsia – joined professional organisations and became socially delineated from their rank-and-file colleagues. When the government disappointed

36 This discussion of the professions is adapted from Wirtschafter, *Social Identity*, pp. 86–96.

the expectations of these activists, denying them a role as expert consultants to policy-makers, they joined zemstvo and business leaders in open political opposition.[37]

The experience of public sector physicians (in the late nineteenth century about three-quarters of all physicians) illustrates the pattern.[38] Prior to the Great Reforms, physicians belonged to an official medical soslovie educated and employed by the state; however, beginning in the 1860s, the establishment of medical organisations and the articulation of a service ethic heralded the emergence of a distinct professional identity. Increasingly, physicians claimed authority over public health, and increasingly they felt frustrated by bureaucratic interference *and* popular indifference. By 1902, physicians and other medical professionals entered the political opposition with demands for social reform and broad civil rights. But like other professionals and paraprofessionals in the revolutionary era, physicians proved unable to sustain a unified political challenge or achieve control over licensing, medical ethics, education, employment and association. Lacking significant social recognition, the politicised among them joined the liberal or radical intelligentsia, while the majority lapsed into political apathy or avoided politics altogether.

When a national political movement appeared among professionals in August 1903, leading to the formation of a Union of Unions in early 1905, an activist minority became involved in the organisation of local unions and all-Russian congresses that demanded social and political change. Still, throughout the revolutionary crisis of 1905–7, political oppositionists never predominated in any of the professions. At the height of its influence in 1905–6, the All-Russian Teachers Union had no more than 14,000 members, and many of these neglected to pay their dues. Membership in the Union of All-Russian Medical Personnel peaked in August 1905 with a total of no more than 25,000 members out of close to 79,000 certified medical practitioners.[39] Geographic

37 For broad treatment that includes a range of professional groups, see H. Balzer (ed.), *Russia's Missing Middle Class: The Professions in Russian History* (Armonk: M. E. Sharpe, 1996); E. Clowes, S. Kassow and J. L. West (eds.), *Between Tsar and People: Educated Society and the Quest for Public Identity in Late Imperial Russia* (Princeton: Princeton University Press, 1991); Leikina-Svirskaia, *Intelligentsiia v Rossii.*

38 N. M. Frieden, *Russian Physicians in an Era of Reform and Revolution, 1856–1905* (Princeton: Princeton University Press, 1981).

39 Wirtschafter, *Social Identity*, pp. 91–2. The data on union membership come from S. Seregny, *Russian Teachers and Peasant Revolution: The Politics of Education in 1905* (Bloomington: Indiana University Press, 1989); J. F. Hutchinson, 'Society, Corporation, or Union? Russian Physicians and the Struggle for Professional Unity (1890–1913)', *JfGO* 30 (1982): 37–53.

distance, inadequate communications and outright poverty made it difficult for rural schoolteachers and medical practitioners – groups that directly served the Russian people – to maintain translocal organisational ties or provide basic professional services. The lack of professional unity, at the very moment when concessions from the monarchy allowed activists to organise in an unprecedented manner, provided telling evidence of the social and political fragmentation in Russian educated society.

Political repression surely played a role in weakening organisational ties, even after 1905; however, the fragility of professional bonds also resulted from the gap between highly educated, socially elite professionals on the one hand and uncertified protoprofessionals or less educated paraprofessionals on the other. In the most visible professions of the late nineteenth century – medicine, teaching and law – non-politicised and less educated specialists, working in local communities, could be difficult to distinguish from the populations they served. Over the objections of activist elites, these rank-and-file professionals were also more likely to co-operate with uncertified practitioners, a relationship that blurred the boundary between professional and non-professional services. Such practices generated conflict among professionals and between the professions and the government; however, they are most noteworthy for exposing popular disregard for the enlightened guardianship and expert knowledge that professionals (and officials) sought to deliver to ordinary people. Indeed, the widely recognised achievements of late imperial public health, education and justice would have been far less effective without the mediation of protoprofessional and paraprofessional groups.

Following the judicial reforms of 1864, the most autonomous and institutionally secure Russian professionals were the university-educated sworn attorneys organised in formal bar associations. In 1874, when the government suspended the establishment of new bar councils for thirty years, only three had come into existence – in Moscow, St Petersburg and Kharkov. Russia's modern legal profession, the pride and joy of Westernised liberal reformers, occupied a narrow field of action. But the limited social reach of the sworn attorneys is deceiving. Russians from all walks of life had participated in formal judicial proceedings since Muscovite times, and after 1861 the impact of official courts, including peasant courts, became massive.[40] How did a broad-based legal culture encompassing nearly the whole of Russian society flourish when

40 J. Burbank, 'Legal Culture, Citizenship, and Peasant Jurisprudence: Perspectives from the Early Twentieth Century', in P. H. Solomon Jr. (ed.), *Reforming Justice in Russia, 1864–1996* (Armonk: M. E. Sharpe, 1997), pp. 82–106; J. Burbank, 'A Question of Dignity: Peasant Legal Culture in Late Imperial Russia', *Continuity and Change* 10 (1995): 391–404.

the legal profession remained so small and the liberal judicial reforms only partially implemented?

An answer can be found in traditional forms of advocacy which effectively absorbed Russia's new legal profession. Prior to the Great Reforms, any subject of the empire, not expressly forbidden to do so by law, had the right to represent clients in court. The unofficial 'street advocates' who operated in the post-reform period thus belonged to a tradition of legal practitioners dating back to the reign of Peter the Great. Generally of low birth, the street advocates nevertheless included in their ranks nobles with higher education and, after 1864, qualified attorneys who chose not to join the bar.[41] In 1874 the government adopted measures that should have eliminated the illicit practitioners. 'Private attorneys', regardless of education, became eligible to practise law by purchasing licenses and registering with local courts; however, lax enforcement meant that registered attorneys continued to work with unregistered street advocates. Private and sworn attorneys pleaded cases in court for the street advocates and relied on them in return to refer clients. Although accused of corruption and incompetence, the street advocates not only survived but also provided a crucial link between formal judicial institutions and ordinary people.

In the fields of education and medicine, uncertified specialists performed a similar social function. The central government and local elites did not commit significant resources to universal primary education before the mid-1890s, yet already in the seventeenth century and continuing throughout the imperial period, unofficial schools taught basic literacy to ordinary people. In 1882, limited funding, a shortage of teachers and the tendency of peasants to leave school after acquiring minimal literacy and numeracy led to the legalisation of village schools where uncertified teachers taught reading, writing and counting.[42] By adapting education to the needs and expectations of peasant parents, less-educated rural schoolteachers, many of whom came from the peasantry, provided a meaningful link between the countryside and translocal civil society. Medical orderlies (*fel'dshery*) did likewise by working with traditional village healers to deliver methods of treatment acceptable to peasants. In the process, they also carried scientific knowledge to the countryside. Although formally trained physicians denounced the orderlies and other

41 W. E. Pomeranz, 'Justice from the Underground: The History of the Underground *Advokatura*', *RR* 52 (1993): 321–40.

42 J. Brooks, 'The Zemstvo and the Education of the People', in Emmons and Vucinich, *The Zemstvo in Russia*, pp. 243–78; B. Eklof, *Russian Peasant Schools: Officialdom, Village Culture, and Popular Pedagogy, 1861–1914* (Berkeley: University of California Press, 1986).

practitioners for performing illegal operations and prescribing inappropriate treatments – services for which they were not properly trained – they nonetheless relied on their less-educated associates to offset shortages of funding and certified personnel.[43] Once again, the much-maligned protoprofessionals and paraprofessionals connected the general population to the elite world of Russia's modern professions.

Of course, qualified professionals became dismayed when labouring people failed to distinguish street advocates from registered attorneys or physicians from witches, sorcerers and faith healers. They were likewise angered by the lack of political and organisational freedom before 1905 and by continuing governmental hostility and bureaucratic interference after the introduction of constitutional monarchy in 1906. Their frustrations, their dual alienation from the people and the government, pushed an activist minority into political opposition and identification with the intelligentsia. It was not, however, the ideologically articulate professional elites who represented the development of a politically effective Russian civil society. In contrast to the intelligentsia, whose condescension toward 'the people' and identification with the methods, if not the policies, of the state continues to this day, rank-and-file professionals together with their paraprofessional and uncertified associates served the everyday needs of real Russians.[44] Aside from the obvious practical benefits that accrued, their relationships with ordinary people linked local communities to translocal society without the mediation of government. In these independent relationships and in the independent relationships of the capitalist market economy, not in the identities and ideological movements of the intelligentsia, a Russian civil society distinct from official society came to life.

43 S. C. Ramer, 'The Zemstvo and Public Health', in Emmons and Vucinich, *The Zemstvo in Russia*, pp. 280–95; S. C. Ramer, 'The Transformation of the Russian Feldsher', in E. Mendelsohn and M. S. Shatz (eds.), *Imperial Russia, 1700–1917: State, Society, Opposition. Essays in Honor of Marc Raeff* (DeKalb: Northern Illinois University Press, 1988), pp. 136–60.

44 For a recent account that stresses the necessity of intelligentsia and state leadership, see B. N. Mironov, *Sotsial'naia istoriia Rossii perioda imperii (XVIII–nachalo XX v.): Genezis lichnosti, demokraticheskoi sem'i, grazhdanskogo obshchestva i pravovogo gosudarstva*, 2 vols. (St Petersburg: Dmitrii Bulanin, 1999), vol. II, pp. 196–373.

13

Nizhnii Novgorod in the nineteenth century: portrait of a city

CATHERINE EVTUHOV

To the present-day observer, standing on the mansion-lined embankment overlooking the confluence of the Volga and Oka rivers, or wandering through the restored and freshly painted central streets of the city, Nizhnii Novgorod does not look so different from the provincial town it was a century ago. The massive automobile factory, the military installations and large-scale industry of the Soviet city of Gorky – all of which closed the area to foreigners until 1991 – sprouted around the edges while leaving the city centre intact. Only the cupolas which once studded the streets like points of gold have vanished, victims of the 1929 eradication of churches. Nizhnii Novgorod boasts all the features of the most lovely of Russian provincial towns: perched picturesquely atop a network of ravines, it nevertheless follows a strictly Petersburgian layout with the three straight avenues radiating from the central kremlin. The above-mentioned observer can walk to the edge of the promenade to look out over the Oka at the old fairgrounds and the massive nineteenth-century Alexander Nevsky cathedral on the promontory. Across the Volga, in the meantime, forests still stretch north as far as one can see, past the pilgrimage site of Lake Svetloiar, whose depths conceal the lost city of Kitezh, and the historical refuge of the Old Belief.

Topography

The comfortable provincial ease with which Nizhnii Novgorod straddles bluffs and ravines was in fact the product of a concerted effort involving the central government, local authorities and the town population itself. The history of urban planning for Nizhnii Novgorod as for many Russian cities begins with Catherine the Great's 1785 Charter to the Towns, which not only bestowed certain privileges upon town dwellers, but converted frontier outposts and administrative centres into 'proper' imperial cities with regular street plans and municipal institutions.[1] Yet Catherine's quest for the well-ordered city had achieved only partial realisation at the time of Nicholas I's visit to Nizhnii Novgorod in 1834 – an event that immediately entered local lore and whose story continues to be told to this day. Stopping in Nizhnii on his tour of the realm, the tsar expressed horror and dismay at how little it resembled a real city. In defiance of the regularised city plan on paper, the buildings along even the main streets jutted out unevenly and at irregular intervals, resembling an assemblage of manors (*usad'by*) merely more tightly spaced than they would have been in the countryside. Not only had residents obliviously built their houses along the lovely Volga embankment with their backs to the river, but they used the gentle slope of the bluff itself as a garbage dump. Nicholas's solution both typified his mania for discipline (one of his passions was the planning of prison buildings) and his desire to bring the vast imperial reaches under central control.[2] An 1836 decree gave property owners three years to erect a wooden house on any vacant lots in the city centre, or five for a stone one, under the supervision of an architectural commission that was in turn subject to the Department of Military Colonies in St Petersburg. Non-compliance meant simply that the empty lot would be auctioned off.[3] The riverbank houses were turned around. In this fashion the central government enlisted the co-operation of the town residents, twisting their arms into conforming to its vision.[4] At the end of the nineteenth century, though, a glance at detailed street plans reveals that Nizhnii's streets remained lined not with single buildings as in a European or American city, but with whole manors: a main house and several outbuildings grouped around a courtyard – much as Belinsky had described Moscow at mid-century.[5]

The regular city plan required a victory not only over the undisciplined residents, but over nature itself. The meandering, slow-flowing Russian rivers

1 See Albert J. Schmidt, 'A New Face for Provincial Russia: Classical Planning and Building under Catherine II and Alexander I', forthcoming.

2 V. Kostkin, 'Poseshchenie Nizhnego Novgoroda Imperatorom Nikolaem I i ego zaboty po blagoustroistvu goroda', in *Deistviia nizhegorodskoi gubernskoi uchenoi arkhivnoi kommissii (NGUAK)* (Nizhnii Novgorod (henceforth NN): Tip. gubernskogo pravleniia, 1994), vol. XVII:1, pp. 1–14.

3 'Polozhenie ob ustroistve gubernskogo goroda', *PSZ*, 2nd series, 55 vols. (St Petersburg: 1830–84), 1836 no. 9149. Parallel decrees were issued, in this period, for many other cities, including Elizavetgrad, Kaluga, Yaroslavl, Saratov, Kharkov, Vladimir, Archangel, Tver, Kazan, Orel, Tiflis, Uman.

4 For particular cases, see RGVIA, Fond 405, op. 4 (1826–59): *Departament voennykh poselenii: khoziaistvennoe otdelenie (1835–1843); otdelenie voennykh poselenii (1843–1857)*.

5 B. Belinsky, 'Peterburg i Moskva', repr. in D. K. Burlak (ed.), *Moskva-Peterburg: pro et contra* (St Petersburg: Izd. Russkogo Khristianskogo gumanitarnogo instituta, 2000), pp. 185–214, p. 190.

almost inevitably have one high bank (the right) and one low one; the nineteenth-century naturalist Karl Baehr explained this phenomenon by relating the current of longitudinal rivers to the earth's rotation. The central part of Nizhnii Novgorod was located on the quite substantial hill that was created by the intersecting currents of the Oka and the Volga. Yet another feature of central Eurasian ecology, however, was the fragility and volatility of the topsoils – once upon a time ground down and eroded by the great Scandinavian-Russian glacier. Provincial residents were tormented by ravines, which a single rainfall could initiate, and which had been known to traverse paved roads, or agricultural plots, entirely within the space of a year. The construction of Nizhnii Novgorod involved a combination of careful coexistence with, and struggle against, the ravines: some were preserved and lined with houses, while others, including in the very centre of the city, had to be filled in or bridged with dams.

In about 1860, Nizhnii Novgorod was divided into four sections, each with a distinctive flavour and way of life. Atop the bluff lay the two Kremlin Sections, radiating out from the fifteenth-century kremlin situated exactly at the intersection of the two rivers. The formidable fortress, constructed as Muscovy's defence against the Tatars, eventually served as the jumping-off point for the conquest of Kazan in 1551. Nizhnii Novgorod witnessed military action only once, when a stray Tatar murza's bullet aimed at the walls landed along the Oka embankment and was commemorated by the construction of a small church which, curiously, the Soviet era merely concealed behind a prestigious apartment building bearing the slogan, 'Peace to the World!' (*Miru – mir!*). The expansive square around the kremlin accommodated the city's most majestic institutions: the Church of the Annunciation (currently a park), the Theological Seminary, the city duma (representative assembly, council) and, just behind, the Alexander Boys' High School.

Pokrovskaia street, universally known as Pokrovka, was Nizhnii's answer to Petersburg's Nevsky Prospect. Walking up the busy shop-lined thoroughfare from the kremlin, one would pass the houses of the most distinguished citizens, soon reaching the city theatre – for many years the sole focus of local cultural life, the governor's residence, and the National Bank. Perhaps more intriguing was the quieter Pecherskaia street, or Pechorka, just behind the Volga embankment. In the 1840s, the ethnographer and lexicographer Vladimir Dal' and Pavel Ivanovich Melnikov, who immortalised the Nizhnii Novgorod region in his magisterial diptych, *In the Forests* and *On the Hills*, lived next door to each other. Dal' drew heavily on local materials for the Dictionary, while Melnikov's pseudonym Andrei Pecherskii was taken from the street name. The pedantic record-keeping of the nineteenth century makes it possible to trace owners of every house until 1917. The documents show that, on the one hand, the social status of residents declined with distance from the centre; on the other, the social composition of the street gradually shifted from primarily gentry inhabitants in 1850 to a greater mix, including merchants and *meshchane* (urban lower-middle class), by 1900.[6] The richest merchants built their elaborate stucco-embellished mansions just in front of Pechorka, overlooking the Volga. A third, radial, street, Il'inka, attracted well-to-do merchants and housed the stock exchange. The city's limits were symbolically marked by the whitewashed building, rather charming to the contemporary eye, of the municipal prison.

Yet, while the typical provincial town would stop there, multifaceted Nizhnii Novgorod boasted two more neighbourhoods. The Makariev Section was perhaps the most dynamic part of the city. Nestled under the Oka bluff, it was Nizhnii's true commercial heart: here was the wharf, where goods from ships and barges coming from as far as Astrakhan or as close as Rybinsk or Kostroma were unloaded; here was a second 'main street' with its wholesale warehouses and commercial enterprises; here was the fantastically ornate eighteenth-century Rozhdestvenskaia church, a remarkable example of Naryshkin baroque. Finally, the Fair Section across the river – there was no permanent bridge until the 1890s – displayed the immense permanent Fair House, constructed in the 1820s, the temporary 'rows' (*riady*) of retail outlets and the exquisite Alexandrine Fair Cathedral (now serving as Nizhnii's primary house of worship), which, replete with Grail motifs, pyramids with all-seeing eyes, and a Pantheon-like vault, resembles a Masonic temple as much as a church. The Kunavino suburb outside the fairgrounds completed the ensemble.

Rhythms

Nizhnii Novgorod was the capital of a province quite diverse in its ecology and economy. In the northern districts beyond the Volga, agriculture was virtually non-existent; the sparse population farmed the rivers and the abundant forests instead of the sandy, rocky soil, exporting fish, timber and the famed Semenov wooden spoons. The black soil of the south-east corner provided the rest of the province with the grain it could not produce itself. The districts around the city itself – Nizhnii Novgorod, Gorbatov, Balakhna, Arzamas, Ardatov – had a mixed economy, combining agriculture with industrial production. Boris

6 GANO (Gos. arkhiv nizhegorodskoi oblasti), Fond. 27, op. 638, d. 1046, 1332, 3158, 3888.

Mironov has recently suggested that the separation between city and countryside in Russia remained partial even up to the early nineteenth century.[7] Life in Nizhnii Novgorod pulsed to the rhythms of the surrounding countryside, as well as the rhythms of commercial enterprise and those created by the religious calendar. In a climate that school geography textbooks described as 'sharply continental', trade, transport, agriculture and industrial production were all subject to dramatic seasonal variations. The last days of winter witnessed an influx of migrants in search of work on the steamships and barges that plied the Volga. Carpenters and masons followed in springtime, hiring themselves out as collectives to do the building that could only be accomplished in the summer months. Stevedores and porters were in high demand throughout the ice-free season. The onset of winter in October, and the first sleigh-roads in the snow, brought droves of *izvozchiki* (cobmen); as many as 800 operated out of the city.[8] Nizhnii Novgorod functioned as a magnet for the thousands of artisans, most of them doubling as farmers, working throughout the province: the leather manufacturers of Bol'shoe Murashkino came here to buy their sheepskins; farmers from the distant district of Sergach came to market their grain and tobacco; and the city provided the first major market for such locally renowned goods as Kniaginin caps and Vorsma locks. Still, it is interesting to note that much local or internal trade bypassed the city itself: the major river ports for grain exchange, for example, were located downriver at Lyskovo, upriver at Gorodets, and at Vorotyn. Nor did the city have a monopoly on factory production. Its two shipbuilding factories (one owned by a merchant, the other by a British citizen), salt-processing plant, sawmill and tobacco factory did well but ceded first place to establishments such as the renowned steel and iron manufacturers at Pavlovo (nicknamed the 'Russian Sheffield'), the enormous Sormovo ship-building plant, or the venerable leather producers in Arzamas.[9]

For two months every summer, Nizhnii Novgorod metamorphosed from a relatively quiet provincial town into a major international centre – the largest trade fair in Europe (bigger than Leipzig), and a unique meeting place of East and West, where traders from China, Persia, Bukhara and Armenia rubbed shoulders with Astrakhan fishmongers, Moscow entrepreneurs, Baltic merchants and itinerant Old Believer icon peddlers. The fair had a yearly turnover

7 B. N. Mironov, *Sotsial'naia istoriia Rossii*, 2 vols. (St Petersburg: Dmitrii Bulanin, 1999), vol. I, p. 299.

8 *Pamiatnaia knizhka nizhegorodskoi gubernii na 1865 god* (NN: Izdanie nizhegorodskogo gubernskogo statisticheskogo komiteta, 1864), p. 48.

9 NB these data are from the 1860s.

of 200 million roubles, and an attendance of 1.5 million;[10] the greatest volume of trade was in tea, cotton, fish and metal.[11] But aggregate trade statistics capture only a fraction of the life of the Nizhnii Novgorod Fair, which had moved upriver from its old site at Makariev following a fire there in 1817.[12] No stock exchange existed until late in the century, so that – in stark contrast to the commodities market in Chicago, for example (in some ways Nizhnii Novgorod's American equivalent) – goods had to be physically transported in order to be saleable.[13] Transactions took place, again until a new generation took over, through an elaborate informal network of friendships, marriages and deals sealed in smoky riverfront taverns. In his history of the daily life of the Fair, A. P. Melnikov describes the Madeira-lubricated rituals by which a debtor, unable to meet his obligations, appeases his creditor.[14] An 1877 guidebook directs the visitor towards the Siberian wharf, where he can sample teas for hours; the multi million rouble Iron Line; the odorous Greben' wharf, piled high with dried fish; and the Grain wharf. Paperweights made from Urals minerals, silver pistols from the Caucasus, exquisite Ferghana and Khorasan rugs, Tula samovars, books typeset in Old Russian, icons, crosses, gingerbread, sheepskin coats, felt boots, lace and Tatar soap vied for the visitor's attention. Equally usefully, the guidebook counsels him to avoid the pseudo-Asian ornamentation of the Chinese Row, where no one from China had ever traded; the Fashion Lane housing a number of brand-name establishments including the 'inevitable' Salzfisch; and the variety of theatres, circuses, zoos and freak shows that held no surprises for the sophisticated Western traveller.[15]

The Nizhnii Novgorod Fair functioned as an irreplaceable stimulus to the local economy as well. Where else could local sheepskin processors have bought Persian *merlushka* (lambskin) and Riga *ovchina* (sheepskin) – the top of the line for sheepskin manufacture[16]; local spoon-makers have bought palm

10 A. P. Melnikov, *Ocherki bytovoi istorii nizhegorodskoi iarmarki (1817–1917)* (repr. NN: Izd. AO 'Nizhegorodskii komp'iuternyi tsentr pol'zovatelei', 1993), p. 108.

11 *Vsepoddanneishii otchet Nachal'nika Nizhegorodskoi gubernii za 1871 god* (manuscript), Rossiiskaia istoricheskaia biblioteka, Moscow.

12 Rumours of arson abounded.

13 Melnikov, *Ocherki*, p. 64.

14 Melnikov, *Ocherki*, pp. 97–101. His father, Melnikov-Pecherskii, imparts a similar flavour in the negotiations between Smolokurov and the fish merchants, in *Na gorakh*, as the former, privy to information from St Petersburg on seal prices, tries to outwit his colleagues.

15 A. S. Gatsiskii, *Nizhegorodka* (NN: Tip. gubernskogo pravleniia, 1877), pp. 190–5.

16 'Promysly sela Bol'shogo Murashkina', in 'Kustarnye promysly nizhegorodskoi gubernii: Kniaginskii uezd,' *Nizhegorodskii sbornik* (NN: Tip. nizhegorodskogo gubernskogo pravleniia, 1890), vol. IX, pp. 242–3.

and maple to make the most exquisite spoons[17]; or Kniaginin hat-makers have bought Popov, Singer or Blok sewing machines?[18] Conversely, Pavlovo locks, knives, razors and surgical instruments, fine 'Russia-leather' gloves from Krasnaia Ramen' and even local jams (known inexplicably as 'Kievan') and pickles found their way to Moscow, Petersburg and European consumers via the fair.[19] Residents of Kunavino by the fairgrounds made good money by renting out their property for use as hotels, restaurants and taverns.[20]

Economic and religious rhythms overlapped to a large extent, as must be the case where the church calendar is the most reliable tool for calculating the passage of time. The two major trade congresses in Nizhnii Novgorod – one for the wood products which were one of the province's staples, and the other a big horse fair – were timed to coincide with Epiphany (6–7 January) and St John's (24 June), respectively. Artisans' work seasons often began and ended on religious holidays; wheel-makers, for example, ended their labours on the Feast of the Protection, when they returned to the land. The seven-week Lenten season regularly wreaked disaster in the lives of small-scale producers and factory workers, leaving them without employ and thus severing the fine thread that linked them to solvency.[21] No major event, from the yearly opening of the Fair to visits of royalty, was conceivable without the presence of the local hierarchy, with the bishop at its head. The actual moment of peasant emancipation, as everywhere throughout the empire, was as much a religious as a social phenomenon. The townspeople experienced Emancipation day, for Nizhnii Novgorod 12 March 1861, as one big religious procession: responding to pealing church-bells at ten o'clock in the morning, the gentry, merchantry and honorary citizenry gathered in the diocesan cathedral to hear, together with the crowd packing the kremlin grounds, the first words of the manifesto as read by the proto-deacon in full ceremonial dress. A liturgy of thanksgiving, led by Bishop Nektarii, was followed by the reading of the manifesto itself outside, on the central square, by Chief of Police Khval'kovskii, accompanied by Governor Muravev and Prince Shakhovskoi who had brought the manifesto from St Petersburg, as well as by the vice-governor, marshal of the nobility and others.[22]

17 L. Borisovskii, 'Lozhkarstvo v Semenovskom uezde', *Trudy kommissii po issledovaniiu kustarnoi promyshlennosti v Rossii*, issue 2 (St Petersburg: Tip. V. Kirshbauma, 1897), p. 14.

18 'Shapochnyi i kuznechnyi promysly v g. Kniaginine i okruzhaiushchikh ego slobodakh,' in 'Kustarnye promysly nizhegorodskoi gubernii: Kniagininskii uezd', p. 185.

19 *Pamiatnaia knizhka 1865*, pp. 63, 52, 49.

20 *Pamiatnaia knizhka 1865*, p. 48.

21 'Promysly sela Bol'shogo Murashkina', p. 234.

22 A. I. Zvezdin, 'K 50-letiiu ob'iavleniia manifesta 19 fevralia 1861 goda v Nizhegorodskoi gubernii', in *Deistviia NGUAK*, vol. X, p. 66.

Not all religious celebrations, of course, were linked to economic or social events. Nizhnii Novgorod counted fifteen major processions every year, on holidays. Religious feasts and even the Sunday liturgy had an unusual intensity in Nizhnii Novgorod: the bishop's reports, submitted annually to the Holy Synod, complained if anything of the excessive piety of local parishioners, who celebrated fervently and constantly (church attendance records were very high), while at the same time refusing to take communion even the obligatory one time a year, at Easter.[23] The bishops attributed this reluctance to make a definitive commitment to the Orthodox Church to 'infection' with the Old Belief.

People

At mid-century, Nizhnii Novgorod boasted a population of 41,543. The number included 5,085 gentry (1,838 of them hereditary), 1,627 clergy, 16,014 townspeople (merchants, honorary citizens, meshchane), 7,431 peasants, 10,397 military, 207 foreigners and 782 others.[24] The ethnic composition of the province as a whole was, characteristically for the Middle Volga region, quite diverse, and included Tatars, Mordvinians and Cheremis. However, it was mostly the Old Believers who gave the region its distinctive character. In the 1840s P. I. Melnikov counted 170,506 (as opposed to the mere 20,000 in the official governor's report) Old Believers in the province.[25] A breakdown of the town's residents by religion yields the following picture: 39,784 Orthodox, 136 *edinovertsy* (members of *Edinoverie*, a group which combined aspects of Orthodoxy and Old Belief), 260 Old Believers, 1 Armenian-Gregorian, 471 Catholic, 364 Protestant, 354 Jewish, 173 Muslim. They worshiped at forty-seven Orthodox churches and chapels; two major monasteries, Pecherskii and Blagoveshchenskii, both dating back to the thirteenth century, provided an important focal point for local religious life. Two *edinovercheskie* churches and one each Armenian-Gregorian, Catholic and Protestant, and one mosque, brought the total number of houses of worship to fifty-five.[26] At fairtime, the population swelled to at least double its normal size, placing Nizhnii Novgorod temporarily in the ranks of the most populous of Russian cities. By the time of the 1897 census, the town's year-round population had risen to 95,000, and proportions had shifted: the petty bourgeoisie (33 per cent) and peasants (48 per cent) together constituted the

23 RGIA, Fond 796, d. 60, l. 8, 15.

24 *Pamiatnaia knizhka 1865*, Statistical table #1, p. 116. Both genders are included in the count.

25 P. I. Melnikov, *Otchet o sovremennom sostoianii raskola P. I. Melnikova, 1854 goda*, in *Deistviia NGUAK*, vol. IX, p. 3.

26 *Pamiatnaia knizhka 1865*, Statistical table #8, p. 158.

bulk of urban residents.[27] In comparison with other cities, there may have been more merchants in Nizhnii Novgorod, or perhaps they merely wielded more power and influence.

Both the fair and the annual influx of impoverished labourers in search of employment created an underclass of beggars, wanderers, the homeless and the diseased, whose numbers evaded the *soslovie* (estate)-based categories of nineteenth-century statisticians. The dormitories and homeless shelters erected, in the Makariev Section in particular, bear ample witness to their presence. Cholera epidemics regularly spread up the Volga from Astrakhan, most devastatingly in 1892 and 1893 when the disease ravaged the working population of the fair.[28]

Aggregate statistics leave much to be desired if one is trying to capture the atmosphere of provincial society, for two reasons. First, one or two outstanding individuals could have an enormous influence on local development. Two such individuals in Nizhnii Novgorod were Pavel Ivanovich Melnikov (1819–83) and Aleksandr Serafimovich Gatsiskii (1838–93). Melnikov, the son of a minor landowner in the remote and densely forested Semenov district, made his mark as editor of the recently established Provincial Messenger (*Gubernskie vedomosti*), which he transformed from a terse purveyor of governmental directives into a vibrant annal of local life and history; and as an ethnographer who, while occupying a series of positions in the state bureaucracy, compiled an abundance of materials on the region's inhabitants and particularly the Old Believers. Eventually, these researches bore fruit in the extraordinarily rich and basically sympathetic fictional account of Old Believer life, *In the Forests* and *On the Hills*, composed under the pseudonym Andrei Pecherskii. Apparently, Melnikov's saga originated in the tales he recounted to the subsequently deceased heir to the throne, Nicholas, in the course of a voyage down the Volga in 1861.[29]

Gatsiskii, who came to Nizhnii from Riazan at the age of nine, dedicated his life to things local – as he jokingly put it, to *nizhegorodovedenie* and *nizhegorododelanie* from the moment of his return from a brief stint at St Petersburg University in the crucial year, 1861. Gatsiskii's curriculum vitae is a whirlwind of local activity: founder of the local statistical committee and editor of

27 K. Küntzel, *Von Niznij Novgorod zu Gor'kij: Metamorphosen einer russischen Provinzstadt: die Entwicklung der Stadt von der 1890er bis zu den 1930er Jahren* (Stuttgart: F. Steiner Verlag, 2001), p. 42, who gets this from D. Smirnov, *Nizhegorodskaia starina* (1948; repr. NN: Nizhegorodskaia iarmarka, 1995).

28 Melnikov, *Ocherki*, pp. 209–14.

29 'Melnikov, Pavel Ivanovich', in F. A. Brokgauz and I. A. Efron, *Entsiklopedicheskii slovar'* (repr. Moscow: Terra, 1992).

its papers, president of the local provincial archival commission, member of the *zemstvo* (elective district council)(at moments when he was able to meet the property qualification) and at one time its president, author of some 400 articles on local history, popular religion, archeology, ethnography and statistics. Gatsiskii never became a nationally known figure on the same scale as Melnikov; but he did enter the national limelight in the 1870s as the defender of the 'provincial idea' – the notion, in part inspired by Shchapov's regionalism (*oblastnichestvo*), that Russia's provinces had a crucial role to play in national development.[30]

Besides these two, a number of other key figures appear inevitably on the pages of any historical account of the city of Nizhnii Novgorod in the nineteenth century. The extremely active marshal of the nobility Prince Gruzinskii dispensed justice and charity in the first quarter of the century.[31] Merchants and Maecenases Nikolai Bugrov and Fedor Blinov (both millers) were famous for their municipal involvement and charitable deeds as well as their wealth.[32] The priest Ioann Vinogradov, from whose illustrious family the radical and poet Nikolai Dobroliubov came, managed a prestigious apartment house in the centre of town.[33] Ivan Kulibin gained national fame as the inventor of the steam engine; while the renown of the merchant of Greek origin and owner of the Sormovo shipyards D. E. Benardaki rested on his commercial achievements.[34]

Aggregate statistics prove inadequate for a second reason: they also fail to capture the dramatic changes in social composition experienced by many Russian cities, Nizhnii Novgorod among them, in the last third of the nineteenth century. In adhering to the traditional soslovie categories, information-gatherers ignored the emergence of significant new social groups, most notably middle classes and workers. To give the statisticians some credit, the perpetual flux of post-emancipation society, in which, for example, the same person could be the employee of a sheepskin manufacturer, an independent entrepreneur in

30 For more on this see C. Evtuhov, 'The Provincial Intelligentsia and Social Values in Nizhnii Novgorod, 1838–1891', *Slavica Lundensia*, forthcoming.

31 See Melnikov, *Ocherki*, pp. 33–7. The name, 'Gruzinskii,' was carried by descendants of the Georgian monarchs; the Nizhnii Novgorod line descended from Vakhtang VI, whose son Bakar (d. 1750) emigrated to Russia in 1724.

32 Galina Ulianova, 'Entrepreneurs and Philanthropy in Nizhnii Novgorod, from the Nineteenth Century to the Beginning of the Twentieth Century', in W. Brumfield, B. Anan'ich and Iu. Petrov (eds.), *Commerce in Russian Urban Culture, 1861–1914* (Washington/Baltimore: Woodrow Wilson Center Press/Johns Hopkins University Press, 2001), pp. 98–9, 100–4.

33 T. P. Vinogradova, *Nizhegorodskaia intelligentsiia vokrug N. A. Dobroliubova* (NN: Volgo-Viatskoe knizhnoe izd., 1992), pp. 47–50.

34 See Smirnov, *Nizhegorodskaia*, pp. 377–81, 430–3.

that same line of business and an agricultural labourer in the course of a single year, made it virtually impossible to measure status, occupation and class; the geographical location and employ of many provincial inhabitants was subject to change. The Sormovo shipbuilding plant, dating back to the 1840s and one of the earliest working-class communities in Russia, alone employed 10,748 workers in 1899 (up from 2,000 only five years earlier).[35]

Even more elusive are the middle classes. Fortunately, we can turn to the eye of contemporaries who, if they did not count, caught members of Nizhnii Novgorod society on paper or on film: Aleksandr Gatsiskii's fondest project, in fulfilment of his belief that 'history should take as its task the detailed biography of each and every person on the earth without exception',[36] was the compilation of quantities of biographies of local citizens; in combination with the exquisitely posed portraits by the local photographer A. O. Karelin, we can get a satisfying impression, if not quantification, of Nizhnii's middle class.[37] Through Gatsiskii's materials, we learn of Anna Nikolaevna Shmidt, the eccentric journalist of petty gentry background who created a theology which she called the Third Testament, and was 'adopted' by various Silver Age cultural figures, Zinaïda Gippius in particular; of Petr Bankal'skii, the *meshchanin* and small businessman who eventually opened a bar, then a hotel near the fairgrounds, in the meantime writing treatises that sought to reconcile science and religion;[38] of the much-admired local historian Stepan Eshevskii (1829–65);[39] of A. V. Stupin (1776–1861), founder of a well-known icon-painting school in the wilds of Nizhnii Novgorod province; of Liubov' Kositskaia (1829–68), beloved local actress.[40] Karelin, in the meantime, went inside the bourgeois household with his camera (1870s–90s) to portray families, loving couples, girls in exotic dress – in short, the whole panoply of Victorian photographic repertoire. Whether verbal or visual, the portraits are unmistakably middle-class. The middle class might perfectly well contain people officially classified as gentry, merchants, clergy (namely in the Dobroliubov family's apartment building), meshchane, and even peasants (who continued to be counted as such even if – as happened in Old Believer circles – they happened to be

35 Küntzel, *Von Niznij*, p. 94.
36 Gatsiskii, *Liudi nizhegorodskogo povolzh'ia* (NN: Tip. nizhegorodskogo gubernskogo pravleniia, 1887), p. vii.
37 See A. A. Semenov and M. M. Khorev (eds.), *A. O. Karelin: tvorcheskoe nasledie* (NN: Volgo-Viatskoe knizhnoe izd., 1990).
38 On these two figures, see C. Evtuhov, 'Voices from the Provinces: Living and Writing in Nizhnii Novgorod, 1870–1905', *Journal of Popular Culture* 31, 4 (Spring 1998): 33–48.
39 Gatsiskii, *Nizhegorodka*, pp. 235–47.
40 On Kositskaia, see Toby Clyman and Judith Vowles (eds.), *Russia through Women's Eyes: Autobiographies from Tsarist Russia* (New Haven: Yale University Press, 1996), chapter 4.

millionaires). Donald Raleigh estimated for another provincial town, Saratov, that the professional and commercial middle classes made up 25 per cent of the urban population.[41]

Administration and institutions

Since at least the local government reform of Catherine II, the provincial capital (*gubernskii gorod*) signified the extension, down to the provincial level, of the state administrative apparatus.[42] By definition, the provincial and district capitals were distinguished from other types of settlements by the presence of governmental offices – even though the non-administrative (*zashtatnyi*) town, the Cossack village (*stanitsa*), or the industrial village might have a larger population and every appearance of a city. The administration and institutions of every provincial capital were thus very nearly identical. Before the 1860s, these were limited to the governor and his staff, the Gentry Assembly, and the Merchant Guilds; the post office, the local Statistical Committee (1840s) and tax and customs officials completed the picture. The Great Reforms wrought deep and immediate changes in provincial administration, creating a new institution, the zemstvo, conceived by the monarchy (it was originally Nicholas I's idea) essentially as an organ for the more efficient collection and disbursement of taxes;[43] setting up a court system; and granting the provincial capitals a city council (1870). In the last third of the century, Nizhnii Novgorod housed the provincial zemstvo, the district zemstvo, the city duma and various offices of the government bureaucracy. Overlapping jurisdictions provoked frequent complaints.

Yet the importance of these institutions lies above all in the uses to which they were put, locally. Nizhnii Novgorod had a tradition of liberal governors that included Mikhail Urusov (1843–55), the ex-Decembrist Alexander Muravev (1856–61) and the beloved Aleksei Odintsov, whose illustrious governorship (1861–73) set the tone for the reform era in Nizhnii Novgorod. Odintsov, who, in a humorous farewell speech in 1873, characterised his tenure as

41 D. Raleigh, 'The Impact of World War I on Saratov and its revolutionary movement', in Rex Wade and Scott Seregny (eds.), *Politics and Society in Provincial Russia: Saratov, 1590–1917* (Columbus: Ohio State University Press, 1989), p. 258.

42 The central government's arm reached one level further, to the province's districts, and stopped there. The introduction of the zemskii nachal'nik in 1889 signalled the government's first intrusion into local jurisdiction.

43 See M. Polievktov, *Nikolai I: biografiia i obzor tsarstvovaniia* (Moscow: Izd. M. i S. Sabashnikovykh, 1918), pp. 212–13. Special commmittees set up in 1827, 1842 and 1847 raised the possibility of satisfying local needs by both collecting and spending taxes locally.

'proof – and this is my main achievement – that the province could do perfectly well without a governor for ten years',[44] in fact presided over the elections of the first zemstvo and the municipal duma, and managed the peaceful transition to new landlord-peasant relations. The conservative politics of his successor, Count Pavel Kutaisov (great-grandson of one of Paul I's henchmen) sat so ill with local society that they managed to squeeze him out of power and replace him briefly with the local marshal of the nobility, S. S. Zybin, until the appointment of a new and once again liberal governor, Nikolai Baranov, in 1882. One of the most potentially influential posts one could have on the governor's staff was that of 'official for special assignments' (*chinovnik osobykh poruchenii*): both P. I. Melnikov and A. S. Gatsiskii held this position, compiling some of their most important statistical and ethnographic studies under its auspices.

The Nizhnii Novgorod provincial zemstvo was one of the most dynamic among the thirty-four such institutions. In the first elections to the district zemstvos, the delegates numbered 402: 189 representing the landlords, 38 city-dwellers and 175 from the peasant communes. The zemstvos had a dual mandate: the 'obligatory' functions included oversight of peasant affairs, land redistribution, local administration (police, courts, statistics), transportation, and property taxes; and 'non-obligatory' responsibility for medicine, veterinary medicine, education, pensions, railways, commerce, welfare, agricultural credit and insurance. The 1864 law gave the zemstvos the right to collect and spend their own taxes; a good deal of decision-making power thus devolved on to this local institution. The Nizhnii Novgorod zemstvo built schools, hospitals, roads, sanitation, lighting, and provided fire insurance. Some of its most significant initiatives included an ultimately unsuccessful bid for the Trans-Siberian railroad, 'restoring the old natural route through Nizhnii Novgorod province to Siberia and Central Asia';[45] a constant struggle against the epidemics that periodically wound their way up the Volga; and an extremely sophisticated local cadaster (1880s–90s), funded by the zemstvo and executed by scientists from St Petersburg, intended to create an absolutely equitable system of land taxation and distribution.[46]

44 V. G. Korolenko, 'Pamiati A. S. Gatsiskogo', in K. D. Aleksandrov (ed.), *A. S. Gatsiskii, 1838–1938: sbornik posviashchennyi pamiati A. S. Gatsiskogo* (Gorky: Gor'kovskoe oblastnoe izd., 1939), p. 10.

45 *Sbornik postanovlenii nizhegorodskogo zemstva, 1865–1886* (NN: Tip. I. Sokolenkova, 1888), p. 490. The Moscow–Nizhnii line was one of the earliest in Russia, constructed in accordance with an 1857 decree.

46 See N. F. Annenskii, 'Zemskii kadastr i zemskaia statistika', *Trudy podsektsii statistiki IX s'ezda russkikh estestvoïspytatelei i vrachei* (Chernigov: Tip. gubernskogo zemstva, 1894), pp. 17–44.

The city duma was dominated by local merchants.[47] The influential mayor's post attracted some of the most visible municipal figures. Fedor Blinov, in the 1860s, became a sort of shadow mayor: elected by an overwhelming majority, he nevertheless, as an Old Believer, could not officially occupy the position.[48] If, prior to 1870, participation in municipal government was considered an onerous duty to be avoided by all available means – medical excuses, declaration of capital in other cities, or, in one case, serving a twenty-day prison term, the council, whose mandate was basically to ensure the absence of basic disorder, managed to achieve some limited goals. It was their decision that resulted in the construction of a water-supply system in 1847.[49] The reformed duma of 1870, headed by Mayor A. M. Gubin, included members of all estates but still a preponderance of merchants. Apart from routine management, they continued to make improvements in the water supply and initiated measures to institute gas lighting.

Secular regional administration functioned alongside a parallel ecclesiastical administration. Nizhnii Novgorod diocesan history was linked from the beginning (1672) with the struggle against Old Belief. Peter I's appointee Pitirim (1719–38) became renowned for his merciless campaigns against the regime's opponents.[50] In Catherine II's reign, Ioann Damaskin (1783–94) made his reputation in a different fashion, making converts among the Finnic and Turkic peoples of the region and compiling grammars of Mordvinian and other local languages. Catherine's secularisation of church lands had a profound effect on landholding patterns: the two major monasteries on the outskirts of the city, as well as Makariev monastery downriver, monasteries and a convent in Arzamas, all lost substantial holdings in the region. The ecclesiastical hierarchy extended down to the parish level, where local initiative had, until the 1880s, a means for expression through the elected blagochinnye. The Nizhnii Novgorod Seminary was one of the most visible and active institutions in the city landscape, situated just across the square from the kremlin and the Alma Mater of Nikolai Dobroliubov and other less iconoclastic priests' sons. The effort to increase 'bottom-up' participation emblematised by the *Gubernskie vedomosti* found an echo in the *Eparkhial'nye vedomosti*, established

47 A. Savelev, *Stoletie gorodskogo samoupravleniia v Nizhnem Novgorode, 1785–1885* (NN: Tip. Roiskogo i Dushina, 1885), p. 31.

48 Savelev, *Stoletie*, p. 24.

49 Savelev, *Stoletie*, p. 24.

50 Compare the policies of his near-contemporary: Georg Michels, 'Rescuing the Orthodox: The Church Policies of Archbishop Afanasii of Kholmogory, 1682–1702', in Robert Geraci and Michael Khodarkovsky (eds.), *Of Religion and Empire: Missions, Conversion, and Tolerance in Tsarist Russia* (Ithaca: Cornell University Press, 2001), pp. 19–37.

throughout the empire in the 1860s and in 1864 in Nizhnii Novgorod. In general, the 1860s witnessed remarkable social activism in clerical circles – the founding of rural schools, sometimes with just a few students; clerical participation in various scientific observations and educational experiments; and the centrally engineered effort, in the wake of the Emancipation which after all was to a large degree implemented by the Church, to add inspirational sermons to the highly ritualised liturgy. Ironically, this last effort backfired significantly in Nizhnii Novgorod, where parishioners complained that they came to church to hear the eternal wisdom of the Fathers of the Church, not some kind of off-the-cuff musings by their local priest.[51] In the 1880s, as Konstantin Pobedonostsev increasingly took the parish-school movement under his wing, the activities of the Nizhnii Novgorod Brotherhood of Saint Gurii (modelled after the seventeenth-century Ukrainian religious brotherhoods) intensified in the promotion of ecclesiastically sponsored education.

This 'official' religious life found a constant shadow and counterpoint across the river, in the sketes and communities of the Old Belief. This universe, where priests were a rarity and needed, if at all, to be imported from Old Believer communities at Belaia Krinitsa in Austria, was run by powerful female religious figures and funded by wealthy male merchants. Hundreds of thousands of faithful, from merchants' daughters sent to the sketes for a convent education to peddlers of icons and 'old-print' (i.e. Slavonic) books, found a home or a touchstone in the powerful communities, even after Nicholas I's (with Melnikov's critical help) massive campaign shut many of them down in the 1850s. Melnikov's unforgettable portrayal of this universe inspired a whole movement in art, music and literature, including Nikolai Rimsky-Korsakov's *Invisible City of Kitezh*, Modest Mussorgsky's *Khovanshchina*, Mikhail Nesterov's *Taking the Veil*, and Andrei Bely's *Silver Dove*.

Civic and cultural life

As in many provincial towns, cultural life in the first half of the nineteenth century revolved around a very small number of institutions: apart from the domestic living room and an occasional ball or concert, the Gentry Assembly and above all the town theatre provided a venue for social gatherings and entertainment. For a few days in 1847, the local *Gubernskie vedomosti* engaged in a debate over whether there was, in fact, anything to do in Nizhnii, or not. The newspaper's contributor A. P. Avdeev took a Gogolian tone, lamenting the

51 RGIA, diocesan reports, Fond 796, d. 60, l. 14.

boredom and limitations of provincial life ('You cannot imagine how difficult is the situation of a person taking up his pen to write the chronicle of a city, when there are decidedly no events in this city that could possibly deserve attention').[52] Finally, mimicking Gogol directly, he decided to describe theatre-goers as they left a performance. The editor, P. I. Melnikov, responding with local patriotism, insisted that Nizhnii Novgorod with its gentry elections, balls, masquerades, plays and religious processions, was better than most other places,[53] and exalted the physical beauty and architecture of the city. The Nizhnii Novgorod theatre provided the focal point of cultural life. It originated in the immensely successful serf troupe of the landowner Prince Shakhovskoi which, transported to an ugly and unwieldy but permanent building on the Pecherskaia Street in 1811, metamorphosed into a public institution.[54] Performances took place thrice weekly, and daily in holiday season; a second theatre on the fairgrounds played daily in the summer months.[55] A Russian and European repertoire – Griboedov, Ostrovsky, Tolstoy, alongside Shakespeare, Calderon and Kotzebue – attracted local audiences and foreign visitors, among them Baron Haxthausen who in 1843 pronounced the performance of the opera, 'Askold's Grave', not bad ('passablement bon').[56]

One of the key moments in Nizhnii's cultural and intellectual life took place outside the city and even the province: the founding of Kazan University in 1804 provided a regional centripetal focus and helped to create a local intelligentsia that was able to complete its education without travelling to the capitals, or abroad. Such figures as Stepan Eshevskii, Konstantin Bestuzhev-Riumin, and Melnikov wended their way downriver to study at Kazan, attending lectures by Shchapov, Lobachevskii and other more or less illustrious professors, subsequently returning to teach history, ethnography, mathematics and other subjects to students at the Nizhnii Novgorod gymnasium. When Eshevskii finally removed to Moscow in 1862, his first course of lectures there surveyed the provinces of the Roman Empire, proposing as its central thesis the retention of local culture – in the form of language, custom, religion and even social organisation – in the face of the centralising aims of the Roman state. An interesting early product of the Nizhnii Novgorod gymnasium is the *Statistical Description of Nizhnii Novgorod Province* written by the senior instructor, Mikhail Dukhovskii, and published under the auspices of the Kazan

52 *Nizhegorodskie gubernskie vedomosti* (NN) 1847, #37, p. 145.
53 *NGV* 1847, #39, p. 154.
54 A. S. Gatsiskii, *Nizhegorodskii teatr (1798–1867)* (NN: Tip. nizhegorodskogo gubernskogo pravleniia, 1867), p. 15.
55 Gatsiskii, *Nizhegorodskii teatr*, p. 21.
56 Gatsiskii, *Nizhegorodskii teatr*, p. 24.

University Press in 1827. Although the pamphlet bears little resemblance to our notion of statistics, it comprises a sober breakdown of types of industry and agriculture, population, architecture, ethnicity (which noted, among other things, the virtually complete assimilation of indigenous populations), religion, a detailed district-by-district survey, and a good deal of data and also colour on the Nizhnii Novgorod Fair.[57] An added, if serendipitous, impetus, to local cultural activity resulted from the temporary exile of Moscow literary circles specifically to the city in the wake of Napoleon's invasion in 1812. Nikolai Karamzin, S. N. Glinka and Konstantin Batiushkov found temporary refuge in Nizhnii's wilds, where their salons and gatherings doubtless fuelled the proverbial 'mixture of French with Nizhegorodian'.[58] Finally, the above-mentioned *Gubernskie vedomosti* – established by decree throughout European Russia beginning in 1838 – became itself a crucial agent in stimulating local historical, scientific and aesthetic interests. Particularly under Melnikov's editorship in 1845–50, the *Vedomosti* became an organ for the construction of a local, non-state-centred, narrative of Russian history, as well as for conveying useful local meteorological, statistical and ethnographic material.[59]

Still, the blossoming of provincial culture and civic life unquestionably belongs to the post-reform period. The new institutions – the zemstvo, the courts, the municipal duma – as well as some old ones – merchant guilds, corporations, the gentry assembly – were invested with real power to make decisions on a local level. Elections to the zemstvos, controversial court cases and important decisions on urban infrastructure – electric lighting, sanitation, transportation – became the stuff of animated public discussion. Nine full-fledged lawyers resided in town in 1877, as well as twenty-five persons authorised to intervene for other parties in the circuit or communal courts. Private societies and brotherhoods operating in the city in the 1870s included: a commercial club, a military club, a hunting society, societies for co-operation with industry and trade, a mutual insurance fund in case of shipwreck, a mutual aid society for the private service sector, a literacy society, a local physicians' society, a branch of the Russian Musical Society, the brotherhood of Cyril and Methodius, and the ubiquitous all-estate club; there were twenty in all. As the

57 Marie-Noëlle Bourguet also notes the descriptive nature of the 'statistics' of the Napoleonic period. M.-N. Bourguet, *Déchiffrer la France: la statistique départementale à l'époque napoléonienne* (Paris: Editions des archives contemporaines, 1989), p. 12.

58 See Smirnov, *Nizhegorodskie*, pp. 390–4 and probably also N. Khramtsovskii, *Kratkii ocherk istorii i opisanie Nizhnego Novgoroda* (NN: Izd. V. K. Michurina, 1857–59).

59 C. Evtuhov, 'The *Gubernskie vedomosti* and Local Culture, 1838–1860', paper presented at American Association for the Advancement of Slavic Studies, Seattle, 1997 (unpublished manuscript).

century drew to an end, the old soslovie organisations – merchant guilds and the meshchanstvo society in particular – began to function as corporations, providing social standing to small-scale entrepreneurs and creating a forum for commercial transactions. Some of the most prosperous merchants became known for their service to charity, among them Nikolai Bugrov (1837–1911), major industrialist and banker who became famous for his aid to Old Believer communities and for founding a homeless shelter (1880) that made it onto the pages of Maxim Gorky's novels.[60]

If, until the 1870s, the *Gubernskie vedomosti* had been the sole legal periodical publication in the Russian provinces, lifting the ban resulted in an explosion of provincial publishing. The questions of the potential civic role of the provincial press triggered a nationwide debate in the mid-1870s, that raised much deeper issues of the relation of the centre and the provinces. In response to the claim of the Petersburg publicist, D. L. Mordovtsev, that the capitals necessarily exercised a gravitational pull, extracting all true talent from the provinces, Aleksandr Gatsiskii argued that the centre could only be as strong as its constituent parts. The same year, a Kazan-based publication, *Pervyi shag*, brought together provincial authors to demonstrate the provinces' literary power. (One of the stories later provided material for one of the first Russian feature movies, *Merchant Bashkirov's Daughter*, 1913.) Already in 1880, Nizhnii Novgorod had two major daily newspapers (*Volgar'* and the *Vedomosti*), as well as the *Iarmorochnyi Listok* which came out in fairtime. Other publications came and went. Six private printing presses, three photographic studios, two bookstores and a public library provided the literary infrastructure.

Provincial residents read a good deal. An 1894 survey found that residents subscribed to 110 Russian journals and newspapers, or 4,198 copies. Adolf Marx's illustrated weekly, *Niva*, accounted for more than a quarter of all publications purchased. Judging by *Niva*'s popularity, as well as by the illustrated journals that followed it on the list (*Rodina, Zhivopisnoe obozrenie, Sever, Nov', Vokrug Sveta, Sem'ia, Vsemirnaia Illiustratsiia, Lug, Priroda i Liudi*), people wanted to read about, and see images of, exotic travels, family life, art and nature. *Russkaia mysl'* was by far the most widely read of the national thick journals, followed by *Russkoe bogatstvo* and *Vestnik Evropy*. Residents subscribed to national daily newspapers as well: *Svet, Novoe vremia* and *Russkie vedomosti* by the 1890s displaced the once-dominant *Syn Otechestva*.

Nizhegorodians had a particular penchant for music and science. In the 1840s the violinist and musicologist (and member of the local nobility) Aleksandr Uly-

60 Ulianova, 'Entrepreneurs', p. 102.

byshev – author of a two-volume biography of Mozart published in Leipzig – founded a musical circle at his house at the intersection of Bol'shaia and Malaia Pokrovka, playing chamber music, and importing musicians for a symphony orchestra from Moscow. The musical environment proved sufficiently rich to nurture Milii Balakirev (1837–1910) up to the age of sixteen, when, Ulybyshev's recommendation in hand, he travelled to Moscow to study with Glinka, and eventually to become a founder of the 'Mighty Five'. In the second half of the century, the musical tradition continued with the founding of a branch of Anton Rubinstein's Russian Musical Society through the efforts of V. I. Villuan, who came to the town in 1873. Concerts and charitable recitals formed an integral part of cultural life, and musical instruction was available to students at the local schools and institutes. The region also nourished a strong tradition of choral singing, most notably in the knife- and lock-producing area around Pavlovo.

Observation of the heavens was another local passion. If, in the 1840s, the pages of the *Gubernskie vedomosti* were already filled with the meteorological notes of local priests and teachers, by 1893 a province-wide network of meteorological stations was established (there were forty-seven by 1912); they drew on the efforts of the rural intelligentsia to chart average temperatures, precipitation rates, cloud movements, the behaviour of snow masses on the ground and so on. The Circle of Amateurs of Physics and Astronomy was founded in 1888 and flourished up to the First World War. They proudly proclaimed Camille Flammarion as one of their honorary members (he actually condescended to send them a letter acknowledging this honour), and counted some 150 real members, including Konstantin Tsiolkovskii, then a resident of Kaluga, by the turn of the century. The circle conducted meteorological observations of their own (here, peasants and clergy were their most dedicated contributors), as well as holding lectures and readings, conducting an active correspondence with learned societies in the capitals and abroad, and collecting a very respectable library of scientific works in French and German as well as Russian.

If one were to speak of a 'provincial culture' distinct from that of the capitals, one of the key loci for its emergence was the museum. For residents of provincial Russia, the notion of a museum evoked not so much an art collection, as an assemblage of historical, ethnographic, or natural-scientific artefacts. One of the first natural-historical museums was founded in Nizhnii Novgorod in 1888 by the soil scientist Vasilii Dokuchaev; its aim was not only the display of soil types, meteorological tables, examples of handicrafts, but also the education of visitors. Eventually, a network of such museums became a means for the dissemination of information and creation of a local consciousness throughout Russia. The major instrument for fostering historical consciousness became the Provincial Archival Commissions, established (like the *Gubernskie vedomosti* fifty years earlier) by decree from the central government in 1883.[61] Not only did the Archival Commissions (*NGUAK*) undertake the daunting task of sifting through mountains of ancient documents accumulated in one of the kremlin towers (in the process, incidentally, destroying a significant amount of materials that did not interest them), but they also launched a plethora of research expeditions, festivals and historical preservation efforts. Thus a tiny house where Peter the Great had stayed a few days became a museum; Nizhegorodians gathered in 1889 to celebrate the birthday of the city's legendary founder, Prince Georgii Vsevolodovich (1189–1238); and preparations were already well under way in the 1890s for the eventual jubilee of the rescue of Moscow from the Poles, projected to be celebrated in 1912. The Archival Commissions had published eighteen volumes (46 issues) of historical materials by 1914, including contributions by Sergei Platonov who kept up an active correspondence with commission members as part of his research on the Time of Troubles.

* * *

Two themes emerge from the above discussion. First, it is clear that there was nothing 'typical' or 'representative' about Nizhnii Novgorod in the nineteenth century. Like every other provincial town, it pulsated to its own rhythms, drawing on a richness of local environmental and social circumstances to create an individual personality. A thriving commercial life, the civic prominence of the merchant estate, the distinct cultural flavour of the Old Belief were but some of the particular characteristics of 'Russia's pocket' – as popular wisdom dubbed Nizhnii. A second theme is the importance of the Great Reforms for provincial Russia. A demographic upsurge, the creation of entirely new institutions like the zemstvo and the infusion of new energy into old ones, and a burgeoning press and musical, scientific, and historical societies marked the last third of the nineteenth century. The All-Russian Fair, held in Nizhnii Novgorod in 1896, presented to the public not only the products of Russian industry, commerce and agriculture, but a bustling and growing city poised to enter the twentieth century with considerable pride, optimism, and energy.

61 On the Archival Commissions, see V. P. Makarikhin, *Gubernskie uchenye arkhivnye komissii Rossii* (NN: Volgo-Viatskoe knizhnoe izd., 1991).

14

Russian Orthodoxy: Church, people and politics in Imperial Russia

GREGORY L. FREEZE

The Orthodox Church, which had possessed enormous property and power in medieval Russia, underwent profound change in Imperial Russia. It was not, as traditional historiography would have it, merely a matter of the Petrine reforms which purportedly turned the Church into a state agency and subservient 'handmaiden'. The Church's history did not end in 1721; it did, however, inaugurate a new age – one that brought fundamental changes in its status, clergy, resources, relationship to laity, and role in social and political questions. All this reflected the impact of new forces (and the Church's response): state-building, territorial expansion, growth and transformation of society, and the challenges posed by secularisation and religious pluralism.[1] Like the ancien régime itself, Russian Orthodoxy faced an acute crisis by the early twentieth century, affecting both its capacity to conduct internal reforms and its relationship to the regime and society. The Church thus faced revolution not only in state and society, but within its own walls – profoundly affecting its capacity (and desire) to defend the ancien régime.

Institutionalising Orthodoxy

Although the medieval Russian Church had constructed an administration to exercise its broad spiritual and temporal authority, it exhibited the same organisational backwardness as did the secular regime. The patriarchate, established in 1589, presided over a vast realm called the 'patriarchal region' (*patriarshaia oblast'*) and nominally supervised a handful of surrounding dioceses. Despite the resolutions of church councils and the patriarch, the Church had no centralised administration to formulate and implement a standardised policy. Attempts to do so, like the liturgical reforms of the 1650s, provoked resistance

1 For a comparative perspective (and summary of the recent critique of the secularisation thesis), see Hugh McLeod, *Secularisation in Western Europe, 1848–1914* (New York: St Martin's Press, 2000).

and precipitated schism and the Old Belief. At the diocesan level, ecclesiastical governance was nominal; Russian bishops simply could not exercise the kind of control found in Reformation and post-Reformation Europe.

These shortcomings in ecclesiastical administration, compounded by the sharp conflict between the tsar and patriarch, provided the primary impetus for the church reforms of Peter the Great.[2] When the conservative patriarch, Ioakim, died in 1700, Peter left the position vacant and appointed a *locum tenens* as acting head of the Church. Faced with the fierce exigencies of the Northern War, Peter was more interested in the Church's material resources and promptly re-established, in 1701, the 'Monastery Office' (*monastyrskii prikaz*) to siphon off income from monastic estates. That order was followed by others imposing new levies and restrictions on the Church and clergy. Only when the Northern War abated did Peter turn his attention to ecclesiastical administration and, in 1718, included the Church in his design for a new system of administrative colleges (*kollegii*), then deemed the model of efficient administration. For the Church, that meant replacing the patriarchate with a 'spiritual college' of bishops (later renamed the 'Holy Synod'). In 1721 Peter issued the 'Spiritual Regulation' (with a supplement in 1722) to serve as its governing charter and to set the agenda for ecclesiastical and religious reform. In 1722 he also established the office of chief procurator to serve as his 'eyes and ears' in ecclesiastical affairs. Peter also issued a plethora of other decrees, such as those restricting the construction of churches and limiting the number of monastic and secular clergy. But his death in 1725 came during the initial stages of implementation; his immediate successors either deferred or dismantled further reform.

From the 1740s, however, the project of 'church-building' (the ecclesiastical counterpart to state-building) and religious reform was once again underway. To improve diocesan administration, the Synod tightened its oversight and reorganised the mammoth Patriarchal (now 'Synodal') Region into several smaller, more manageable dioceses.[3] This process gained new impetus under Catherine the Great (r. 1762–96), who first vented ecclesiastical questions in the Legislative Question of 1767–8[4] and made a systematic reorganisation of dioceses in the 1780s (an ecclesiastical counterpoint to her provincial reform

2 The classic study is P. V. Verkhovskoi, *Uchrezhdenie Dukhovnoi kollegii i dukhovnyi reglament*, 2 vols. (Rostov-on-Don, 1916; Farnborough: Gregg, 1972).

3 *Polnoe sobranie postanovlenii i rasporiazhenii po vedomstvu pravoslavnogo ispovedaniia. Tsarstvovanie Ekateriny Petrovny*, 4 vols. (St Petersburg, 1899–1911), vol. I, p. 660 (Synodal resolution of 18 July 1744).

4 See the discussion and references in G. L. Freeze, 'Church, State and Society in Catherinian Russia: The Synodal Instruction to the Legislative Commission' in Eberhard

of 1775).[5] The new dioceses, operating under strict oversight of the Synod,[6] not only administered smaller territories and populations but also acquired new administrative organs – above all, the dean (*blagochinnyi*) as overseer for ten to fifteen parish churches. As a result, the bishop could now collect systematic information and tighten control over the clergy and, increasingly, the believers themselves.[7] At the same time, the Church expanded its network of seminaries to train clergy. Although mandated by Peter the Great, these existed only on paper until the Catherinean era and now steadily increased their enrolments and developed a full curriculum based on Latin.[8]

Reforms in the first half of the nineteenth century brought further institution-building. This included the formation of a 'system' of ecclesiastical schools in 1808–14, publication of the Charter of Ecclesiastical Consistories in 1841 (to direct diocesan administration)[9] and the introduction of annual diocesan reports in 1847.[10] All this brought tangible results – for example, in the Church's growing capacity to regulate marriage and divorce (which, in contrast to most of Western Europe, remained entirely in its hands). The Church used its new power to prevent and detect illegal marriages (those which violated canon or state law) and to thwart divorce. As a result, by the middle of the nineteenth century, marital dissolution – which had once been easy and informal – had become virtually impossible.[11]

The pre-reform era also marked an unprecedented expansion in the role of the chief procurator, above all, during the tenure of Count N. A. Protasov (1836–55). Protasov established his own chancellery (parallel to that of the Synod[12]) and used the diocesan secretary (the main lay official assisting the bishop) as his own agent in diocesan administration. Protasov even assumed a decisive role

Müller (ed.), '. . . *aus der anmuthigen Gelehrsamkeit*'. *Tübinger Studien zum 18. Jahrhundert* (Tübingen: Attempto Verlag, 1988), pp. 155–68.

5 I. M. Pokrovskii, *Russkie eparkhii v XVI–XIX vv.*, 2 vols. (Kazan, 1913), vol. II, appendix, pp. 55–8.

6 By the 1760s and 1770s, the Synod demanded – and received – systematic data on a wide variety of matters; see RGIA, Fond 796, op. 48, g. 1767, d. 301; op. 55, g. 1774, d. 534, ll. 9–10 ob. Previously, as the chief procurator (I. Melissino) complained to the Synod on 31 October 1764, such reporting was sporadic or non-existent (op. 45, g. 1764, d. 335, l. 1–1 ob.)

7 See G. L. Freeze, *The Russian Levites* (Cambridge, Mass.: Harvard University Press, 1977), pp. 46–77.

8 Ibid., pp. 78–106.

9 *Ustav dukhovnykh konsistorii* (St Petersburg: Sinodal'naia tip., 1841).

10 On the standardised annual reports (*otchety*), essential for the chief procurator's own annual reports, see: RGIA, Fond 797, op. 14, g. 1844, d. 33752, ll. 1–54.

11 G. L. Freeze, 'Bringing Order to the Russian Family: Marriage and Divorce in Imperial Russia, 1760–1860', *JMH* 62 (1990): 709–48.

12 For the establishment of the chancellery, see RGIA, Fond 797, op. 2, d. 6122, ll. 1–18.

in setting the Synod's agenda, framing its resolutions, and controlling their implementation. Nevertheless the bishops deeply resented the intrusion, the spirit of ill-will steadily mounting during his decades as chief procurator.[13]

The 'Great Reforms' under Alexander II (r. 1855–81) also included the Church and sought to transform the basic institutions of the Church – its administration, education, judiciary, censorship and parish. The reforms, largely undertaken at state initiative, applied the general principles and policies of the secular reforms to the Church. Above all, that meant measures to encourage society to help plan, finance and implement reform. In the case of the Church, this entailed a limited 'democratisation' (for example, by allowing priests to elect deans and hold diocesan assemblies) and even 'laicisation' (by allowing the laity to assume a greater role in parish affairs). The hope was to revitalise the Church and to bring it into greater accord with society and state.

These hopes were soon dashed. The 'democratisation' elicited strong criticism, chiefly on the grounds that the dean was now the agent of the clergy, not the bishop, and therefore lax and lenient in the face of grievous misdeeds and malfeasance. Nor did the diocesan assemblies perform as hoped, partly because of the bishops' hostility, partly because of the clergy's own shortcomings. In any case these changes failed to solve the needs of the clergy and seminary and to provide a forum for pastoral interaction and co-operation. The parish reforms were no less disappointing. The 1864 statute (establishing parish councils to raise funds for charity, schools, clergy and the parish church) ran into a wall of popular indifference: few parishes availed themselves of the opportunity to establish a council and, of those that did, they raised scant funds (which, for the most part, went mainly to renovate and beautify their church). By 1869 the reform resorted to an older strategy of 'reorganising parishes', i.e. merging them into larger units and reducing resident clerical staffs, with the expectation that a higher parishioner:priest ratio would enable more ample material support. That too failed: parishioners resisted and withheld support (by cutting the voluntary gratuities), while the clergy found that they had to serve many more parishioners for the same income.

Reform in ecclesiastical administration and judiciary failed even to pass from draft to law. Already the butt of lay criticism for red tape and corruption, ecclesiastical administration suffered from hyper-centralisation at the top and under-institutionalisation at the base. And time did not stand still: the workload rose sharply in the post-reform period, making the deficiencies

13 The classic critique came in A. N. Murav'ev, 'O vliianii svetskoi vlasti na dela tserkovnye' (RGIA, Fond 796, op. 205, d. 643).

of diocesan rule increasingly evident. The critical dynamic was the deluge of marital and divorce cases, which increased exponentially in sheer numbers and became ever more complex – so that, by century's end, they were completely overwhelming diocesan and Synodal administration.[14] Indeed, it is not wholly unfair to describe the final decades, marked by a gradual breakdown of ecclesiastical administration, as an incremental de-institutionalisation – a reversal of the process launched by the Petrine reforms in the early eighteenth century.

That was compounded by a sharp deterioration in Church–State relations in the years before the 1905 Revolution. One impetus was K. P. Pobedonostsev, the chief procurator (1880–1905) who engineered 'counter-reforms' (to dismantle the reforms of the 1860s) in an abrasive, imperious way that put a severe strain on Church–State relations.[15] Matters deteriorated further with the accession of Nicholas II to the throne in 1894: to an unprecedented degree, he personally intervened in strictly spiritual matters. Partly out of conviction, partly out of his own (and others') desire to 'resacralise' autocracy, Nicholas launched an inquiry into the moral and religious condition of monasteries, sought to shield 'popular' icon-painting from commercialisation and mass production, and personally sponsored the canonisation of a popular religious figure, Serafim Sarovskii, in 1903.[16] This unprecedented intrusion offended hierarchs and did little to resacralise autocracy. Particularly ominous was the February Manifesto of 1903 ('Plans for the Improvement of the State Order') with hints of further concessions to religious minorities that posed a direct challenge to the Church's privileged position. By 1905 clergy, lay activists and conservative prelates had come to demand an end to state tutelage, realisation of 'conciliarism' (*sobornost'*), even re-establishment of the patriarchate.

The clergy

The 'clerical estate' (*dukhovnoe soslovie*) that served the Church consisted of three categories: the ruling episcopate, celibate monastic clergy and married secular clergy. All underwent profound changes, some positive and some negative, that significantly recast their profile and *mentalité*.

14 See G. L. Freeze, 'Matrimonial Sacrament and Profane Stories: Class, Gender, Confession and the Politics of Divorce in Late Imperial Russia', in M. Steinberg and H. Coleman (eds.), *Sacred Stories* (forthcoming).

15 See G. L. Freeze, *The Parish Clergy in Nineteenth-Century Russia* (Princeton: Princeton University Press, 1983), pp. 409–48; A. Iu. Polunov, *Pod vlast'iu ober-prokurora* (Moscow: Aero-XX, 1995).

16 See G. L. Freeze, 'Subversive Piety: Religion and the Political Crisis in Late Imperial Russia', *JMH* 68 (1996): 308–50.

Episcopate

The hierarchy (comprised of three descending ranks – metropolitan, archbishop and bishop) still came exclusively from the ranks of monks but exhibited substantial change in the imperial era. The total size increased steadily, rising from 26 prelates under Peter the Great to 147 by 1917, partly through the establishment of additional dioceses but mainly through the appointment of suffragan bishops to assist in larger, less manageable dioceses. There were equally striking changes in their social and education profile.[17] To overcome opposition from tradition-bound Russian prelates, Peter chose prelates from Ukraine, not because of their ethnicity, but because of their superior education (often in Catholic institutions in the West), which, he presumed, would incline them to support his reforms. From the middle of the eighteenth century, however, prelates came primarily from central Russia, partly because of suspicion of Ukrainian prelates, but chiefly because of the growing network of seminaries in central dioceses (which could now supply qualified Russian candidates). The social origin of bishops also changed: whereas only half of the Petrine prelates came from the clerical estate, by the nineteenth century this quotient had climbed to more than 90 per cent. Bishops from other groups, notably the nobility, virtually disappeared. The critical factor here was education: elevation to the episcopate required a higher ecclesiastical education which was only accessible to members of the clerical estate. Indeed, most bishops held advanced degrees, published extensively and earned the sobriquet of 'learned monks'. Education also shaped their careers prior to consecration: many served as rectors in seminaries and academies, earning their spurs as scholars and administrators, and then rising quickly – at an early age – to choice episcopal appointments. Only in the late imperial era did this career-line change, chiefly because fewer students in the elite ecclesiastical academies were willing to take monastic vows. As a result, by the early twentieth century over half of the new prelates had come from non-academic careers in the secular clergy (widowed priests who had taken monastic vows) and in missions. They too, however, were of clerical origin and held a higher academic degree.[18]

After consecration, an episcopal career proved highly volatile, with bishops moving rapidly up (or down) the diocesan hierarchy, as their merits and luck

17 For details see Jan Plamper, 'The Russian Orthodox Episcopate, 1721–1917: A Prosopography', *Journal of Social History* 60 (2001): 5–24.

18 See G. L. Freeze, 'L'episcopato nella chiesa ortodossa russa: crisis politica e religiosa alla fine dell'ancien régime', in Adalberto Marinardi (ed.), *La grande vigilia* (Magnano: Comunita Monastica di Bose, 1998), pp. 30–4.

would have it. The rate of transfers steadily accelerated; under Alexander III the average tenure in a given diocese shrank to a mere 2.4 years. In theory, mobility gave prelates a broader, national perspective and a strong incentive for zealous performance. But rapid turnover also denied them a chance to develop spiritual bonds with local clergy and laity; it also generated accusations that prelates were careerists with no real interest in the spiritual needs of their flock. Tensions between prelates and priests, while hardly new or unique to Russia, increased markedly in post-reform Russia as priests and parishioners became ever more aggressive in asserting their rights and prerogatives. This challenge from below, compounded by the pressure from the secular state, made prelates increasingly protective of canons (and their prerogatives), deepening the divide within the clergy itself.

Monastic ('black') clergy

The monastic clergy became the object of a full-scale onslaught in the eighteenth century.[19] In medieval Russia they had been the backbone of Orthodoxy, monopolising high religious culture, attracting large numbers to take vows and acquiring vast tracts of populated land. Those material assets, long a temptation for the resource-starved state, became an irresistible target for Peter the Great as he desperately searched for the wherewithal to wage the Northern War. In 1701 he therefore re-established the 'Monastery Office' (*monastyrskii prikaz*), so unpopular with churchmen in the seventeenth century, to administer monasteries and divert their revenues to the state. After Peter, policy fluctuated between retreat and renewed attack, yet always short of fateful secularisation until an abortive attempt by Peter III in 1762. Catherine at first retreated, but in 1764 carried through the long-sought secularisation. Seeking primarily to pad state coffers (but also to end the mounting unrest among the Church's peasants), Catherine justified sequestration for liberating the Church from worldly cares so that it could focus upon its spiritual mission.[20] The state not only confiscated lands and peasants: it also closed two-thirds of the monasteries and forbade the tonsure of new males and females until the existing surfeit disappeared.[21] Once the surplus monks and nuns were eliminated, the Church found it difficult to attract new recruits; by the 1780s the

19 For overviews see Igor Smolitsch, *Russisches Mönchtum: Entstehung, Entwicklung und Wesen 988–1917* (Würzburg: Augustinus-Verlag, 1953); P. N. Zyrianov, *Russkie monastyri i monashestvo v XIX i nachale XX veka* (Moscow: Verbum-M, 2002).

20 See A. Zav'ialov, *Vopros o tserkovnykh imeniiakh pri Imp. Ekateriny II* (St Petersburg, 1900); A. I. Komissarenko, 'Votchinnoe khoziaistvo dukhovenstva i sekuliarizatsionnaia reforma v Rossii (20–60-gg. XVIII v.), unpublished PhD dissertation, Moscow (1984).

21 See RGIA, Fond 796, op. 55, g. 1774, d. 62.

surfeit had turned into a general shortage of monks and nuns.[22] As a result, by 1825 the number of monks, nuns, and novices (11,080) was less than half its size a century earlier (25,207).

By the second quarter of the nineteenth century, that crisis gave way to a renaissance of monasticism.[23] Most obvious was the sheer increase in the number of monasteries, as the state approved their establishment if they had sufficient financing and, especially, if they could bolster Orthodoxy in minority areas. Hence the number of monasteries, which had fallen to 476 by 1825, climbed to nearly 1,000 by 1914; resident monks, nuns and novices rose about 8.5 times (from 11,080 to 94,629).[24] New recruits came from increasingly diverse social backgrounds, especially in the case of women. No less important was the spiritual renaissance in the monastery, above all, the emergence of elderhood (*starchestvo*) as the quintessence of Orthodox religiosity.[25]

But the most remarkable feature of the monastic renaissance was the growing predominance of women. Once a minority, by the early twentieth century nuns and female novices had come to constitute a majority of the monastic clergy (77.5 per cent). This process was hardly unique to Russia, occurring as well in the contemporary West. The key factors in the Russian case included a heightened (and ascribed) sense of religiosity among women, breakdown of the patriarchal family (giving women greater autonomy and freedom of choice), the positive role of female cloisters (as hospitals, schools and homes for the elderly) and the Church's growing recognition of women's potential role in combatting dissent and de-christianisation.

Although monasticism was regaining its erstwhile status (and much property as well), it also elicited growing criticism. It was a favourite target of anticlericals, who accused it of harbouring indolence and gluttony, failing to perform useful worldly service, and associating with right-wing forces. Such criticism was also to be heard within the Church, especially among parish clergy, who resented the monastic monopoly of power in the episcopate and ecclesiastical schools. Even among the laity, despite the popular veneration of the monastery's religious significance, there was mounting resentment over monastic landholding amidst the 'land hunger' of late Imperial Russia.

22 RGIA, Fond 796, op. 63, g. 1782, d. 285, l. 4.
23 For a case study, with attention to the larger context, see Scott Kenworthy, 'The Revival of Monasticism in Modern Russia: The Trinity-Sergius Lavra, 1825–1921', unpublished PhD dissertation, Brandeis University (2002).
24 *Pravoslavnaia entsiklopediia: Russkaia pravoslavnaia tserkov'* (Moscow, 1998), p. 132.
25 See Robert L. Nichols, 'The Orthodox Elder *(Startsy)* of Imperial Russia', *Modern Greek Studies Yearbook* 1 (1985): 1–30.

Secular ('white') clergy

The secular clergy served primarily in parish churches, but they also staffed cathedrals, institutional churches, cemetery chapels and the like. The secular clergy consisted of two distinct groups: ordained clergy (*sviashchennosluzhiteli*) and sacristans (*tserkovnosluzhiteli*). The former included mainly priests (a small number of whom held the honorific title of archpriest) and deacons (*d'iakony*); only the priest could conduct the liturgy and dispense sacraments. If funding permitted, a parish preferred as well to have the optional deacon, prized for his voice and role in enriching the aesthetics of the liturgy. More numerous were the unordained sacristans (earlier *diachok* and *ponomar'*, retitled *psalomshchik* in 1869), who assisted the priest in performing rites and rituals, read the divine liturgy, and helped maintain the church and keep order during services.

The secular clergy increased in the eighteenth and nineteenth centuries, but at a far slower pace than the population. Thus, although the number of clergy more than doubled between 1722 and 1914 (from 61,111 in 1722 to 117,915), the population of Orthodox believers grew nearly tenfold (from 10 to 98 million). That meant, of course, a substantial rise in the ratio of parishioners to secular clergy, from 1,008 in 1824 to 1,925 in 1914. In many cases, the situation was actually worse: rural parishes often embraced numerous hamlets scattered over a broad, untraversable area, while some urban parishes swelled to gargantuan size (with tens of thousands of 'parishioners'). While this process also affected Western churches, especially Protestants, it had particularly negative consequences for Russian Orthodoxy: because the priest had to perform myriad daily rites, he found it exceedingly difficult to perform the new duties of pastor and preacher, not merely dispense various rituals and sacraments.

Yet those newer duties gained steadily in importance and underlay the Church's drive to educate and 'professionalise' the clergy. Whereas earlier priests had lacked formal education, the new educational network – which took root and expanded steadily after the middle of the eighteenth century – soon made formal seminary study and, later, a full seminary degree a sine qua non for the priesthood. Thus, 15 per cent of the priests had a seminary degree in 1805, but that quotient had jumped to 83 per cent in 1860 and reached 97 per cent by 1880. That superior education also generated growing emphasis on a pastoral, not just liturgical, role.[26] But this 'educational revolution' applied only to priests, not deacons and especially sacristans, who had scant formal

26 Handbooks on pastoral service became commonplace, following the seminal volume by Parfenii (Sopkovskii) and Georgii (Konisskii), *O dolzhnostiakh presviterov prikhodskikh* (St Petersburg: Sinodal'naia tip., 1776).

schooling. As the bishop of Saratov observed in 1850, the priests are well educated, but 'the deacons and sacristans, almost without exception, do not know the catechism'.[27] That educational gap, compounded by disputes over the sharing of parish revenues, was a ubiquitous bane of parish life.[28]

Education also played a role in transforming the secular clergy into a hereditary social estate (*dukhovnoe soslovie*). Whereas the Church in Muscovy had no educational barriers to the appointment of clergy (who were chosen by parishioners and merely confirmed and ordained by the bishops), educational requirements became a major obstacle to choosing clergy from other social groups: first, because the seminary was open only to the sons of clergy (to avoid wasting the Church's scarce resources on those who would not serve); and, second, because the bishop insisted that the best students (regardless of parish wish) receive appointments. A further obstacle to outsiders was the new poll tax: since the clergy had a privileged exemption, the state was loath to release poll-tax registrants (peasants and townspeople) to the clergy and thus diminish its revenues. While exceptions were possible (if the registrant's community agreed to pay the poll tax), that became increasingly rare after the middle of the eighteenth century.[29] A final factor was the vested interest of the clergy, who preferred to have kinsmen in the same parish. That was partly to avoid the presence of outsiders (deemed more likely to report misconduct or malfeasance), partly to ensure positions for relatives, and partly to provide dowries for daughters and support for elderly clergy (the new cleric agreeing to support his retiring predecessor). Although the Church tenaciously resisted kinship ties within the same parish, these nevertheless persisted and appear frequently in the clerical service registers (*klirovye vedomosti*).[30]

The formation of a closed estate was fraught with significant consequences. First, it had a negative impact on the quality of pastors and their ties to the laity. On the one hand, the hereditary order ensured a sufficient number (indeed surfeit) of candidates, but not necessarily zealous, committed servitors.

27 RGIA, Fond 796, op. 132, g. 1851, d. 2357, l. 311 (Saratov annual report for 1850). Such assessments figure frequently in the parish service records (*klirovye vedomosti*); see, for example, the disparaging assessments from Kursk in 1840 in Gos. arkhiv Kurskoi oblasti, Fond 20, op. 2, d. 10, ll. 2–2 ob., 7 ob.–8.

28 See, for example, the disparaging comments by I. S. Belliustin in his *Description of the Rural Clergy*, ed. G. L. Freeze (Ithaca: Cornell University Press, 1985).

29 In 1784, only 667 of the 86,671 clergy in the Russian Empire had come from poll-tax origins (0.8 per cent). See RGIA, Fond 796, op. 65, g. 1784, d. 443, ll. 71–85.

30 For example, see similar records from Moscow in 1854 (GIAgM, Fond 203, op. 772, d. 279), 1861 (op. 766, d. 241), and 1880 (op. 766, d. 229), Tver in 1830 (Gos. arkhiv Tverskoi oblasti, Fond 160, op. 1, d. 1672), Irkutsk in 1830 (Gos. arkhiv Irkutskoi oblasti, Fond 50, op. 1, d. 3840), and Kiev in 1830 (Tsentral'nyi derzhavnyi istorichnyi arkhiv Ukrainy, Fond 127, op. 1009, d. 275).

Critics argued that ordinands simply followed in their father's footsteps and lacked real commitment or vocation. On the other hand, the hereditary estate weakened the ties between priest and parishioner. That meant, in the first instance, few kinship ties: given that marriage into the disprivileged poll-tax population was undesirable, the clergy predictably showed a strong propensity for endogamous marriages. That endogamy was compounded by a growing cultural rift between the seminary-educated priest and the mass of illiterate parishioners. Not only did the priest find it difficult to communicate with his flock, but parishioners resented the diversion of scarce parish revenues to finance seminaries serving only the clergy's offspring.

The second problem was demographic imbalance. Given the slow rate of expansion in parishes and their personnel, the clerical estate simply produced far more progeny than the ecclesiastical domain could absorb. While the regime did 'harvest' the clerical estate periodically (through conscript of 'idle' sons into the army and enticement of seminarians into the civil service), these outlets proved insufficient. The result was a surfeit of unplaced clerical sons, including large numbers of seminary graduates, who became the focus of growing concern by the middle of the nineteenth century. This backlog of 'idle' seminary graduates steadily increased, rising from 430 in 1830 to 2,178 in 1850. Thus by mid-century – within the span of two or three generations – the Church had gone from a chronic shortage of educated candidates to a chronic surplus.[31]

In one important respect, however, the secular clergy experienced little change: in the form and amount of their material support. Financially, the parish was an autonomous unit: it provided land (for the clergy to cultivate themselves) and voluntary gratuities from various rites (such as baptism, weddings and burials) and holiday processions.[32] With the exception of a few prosperous parishes, support was marginal and left the clergy poor if not destitute; predictably, it was difficult to find candidates willing to come – and especially stay – in the poorer parishes. Even worse than the penury was the pernicious form of the support. Cultivating the parish plot, complained the priests, inevitably distracted them from spiritual duties, rendered the advanced

31 Complaints of a surfeit appeared as early as a report from Riazan in 1826 (Fond 796, op. 107, g. 1826, d. 460, ll. 87–88 ob.); by mid-century, they were ubiquitous. For example, in 1850 the bishop of Tula reported that 672 students had left diocesan schools (251 graduates; 421 with incomplete education), but that the diocese had no new openings (RGIA, Fond 796, op. 132, g. 1851, d. 2357, ll. 191 ob.–192).

32 In rare cases, the clergy derived income from other sources – such as a stipend (*ruga*) from a local magnate, salary from an institutional chapel, rental income from real estate, and the like.

education irrelevant, and diminished their status in the eyes of the privileged (and perhaps even the disprivileged). The 'voluntary' gratuities were even more problematic: they left the clergy feeling like beggars and triggered constant disputes, as the two sides haggled over the fee – with such disputes often ending in charges of 'extortion'.

Although the Petrine reform raised the question of clerical support, it had other priorities and left the problem unresolved. About all that the eighteenth-century state could do was to ensure that the parish staff had a full allotment (33 *desiatiny*) and to set guidelines for gratuities in 1765. The first to take concrete measures was Nicholas I, first by providing a small budget to subsidise clergy in the 'poorest' parishes (1829) and then by attempting to prescribe parish obligations (land and labour dues) and provide small subsidies in the politically sensitive western provinces (1842). But these measures did not apply to the mass of parish clergy, their economy remaining unchanged from pre-Petrine times – even as their expenses, above all, for educating sons, rose dramatically.

The ecclesiastical 'Great Reforms' sought to address the issues of the hereditary order and material support, but without success. As noted above, the parish reforms of the 1860s aimed at improving the clergy's material support – first by establishing parish councils, then by the reorganisation of parishes and reduction of parish staffs, but neither measure proved effective in alleviating the clergy's financial needs. Dismantling the hereditary estate also proved difficult. The reforms did abolish hereditary claims to positions (1867), assigned clerical offspring a secular legal status (1871) and opened ecclesiastical schools to outsiders, but the results proved very disappointing. By 1914 only 3 per cent of the secular clergy came from other social estates. And that 3 per cent came at a high cost. Abolition of family claims to positions simply eliminated the traditional form of social security; alternative schemes for pensions proved ineffective, forcing elderly clergy to remain in service and doomed retirees to destitution. Opening diocesan schools proved counterproductive: not only did few outsiders choose to matriculate (hardly surprising, given the failure to improve clerical income), but many of the clergy's sons used their right of exit to flee to secular careers. Hence the Church – after decades of a surfeit of candidates – suddenly faced a dearth of qualified candidates. To fill vacancies, bishops had to ordain inferior candidates and, increasingly, even those without a seminary degree. The result was a decline in the clergy's educational standards, with the proportion of priests with a seminary degree plummeting from 97 per cent in 1880 to 64 per cent in 1904.

Disenchantment with the reforms was intense and universal. The ostensible beneficiaries, the parish clergy, came to loathe the very word 'reform' – which promised so much and gave so little. Little wonder that some proved increasingly receptive to 'clerical liberalism' and even revolutionary causes.[33] Conservatives were no less disenchanted. That dim view of the reforms propelled Pobedonostsev's 'counter-reforms', including a reversal of parish reorganisation as well as measures to limit the matriculation of outsiders and to impede the 'flight' of seminarians from church service.[34] By the 1890s the failure to improve the clergy's material and legal status, compounded by the attempt to imprison sons in church service, only fuelled growing discontent within the secular clergy.

Believers

'Christianisation' was not an event in 988, but a complex, incremental process that slowly worked its way across the great Eurasian plain. Given the dispersion of population, the heterogeneity of local cultures, and the institutional backwardness of the medieval Church, Russian Orthodoxy was actually Russian Heterodoxy, with kaleidoscopic variations in local customs, superstitions and religious practice. In the sixteenth and seventeenth centuries the Church undertook to standardise and purify popular religious practice, but as yet lacked the instrumentalities to make a fundamental 'reformation' in popular religious practice.[35]

It was only in the eighteenth century that the Church launched a full-scale campaign to reshape popular Orthodoxy. The Petrine reform fired the initial salvo, but a sustained effort began only in the middle of the eighteenth century.[36] The issue was not disbelief, but deviant belief – the welter of unauthorised, sometimes heretical customs and practices that pervaded local religious life, such as sorcery and black magic, unofficial saints and relics, and 'miracle-working icons'. A further concern was the Old Belief, especially from the early nineteenth century, as the number of registered 'schismatics' – and, reports of 'semi-schismatics' (*poluraskol'niki*) – steadily increased.[37]

33 Freeze, *Parish Clergy*, pp. 389–97.

34 By 1900 the Synod limited outsiders (youths from non-clerical estates) to 10 per cent (RGIA, Fond 179, g. 1898, d. 415).

35 See, for example, '1651 g. oktiabria 20. Ustavnaia gramota temnikovskogo sobora protopopu o proizvodstve suda i tserkovnoi rasprave', *Izvestiia Tambovskoi uchenoi arkhivnoi komissii* 8 (1886): 71–6.

36 A. S. Lavrov, *Koldovstvo i religiia v Rossii* (Moscow: Drevlekharnilishche, 2000); G. L. Freeze, 'Policing Piety: The Church and Popular Religion in Russia, 1750–1850', in David L. Ransel and Jane Burbank (eds.), *Rethinking Imperial Russia* (Bloomington: Indiana University Press, 1998), pp. 210–49.

37 Official data, notorious for understating the number of Old Believers, none the less showed a steady increase – from 84,150 (1800) to 273,289 (1825) to 648,359 (1850). RGIA,

This 'reformation from above' had a twofold thrust. One was traditional: repression. Peter's *Spiritual Regulation* specified the superstitious and deviant behaviour that the clergy were to combat, and subsequent decrees continued the attack. In the 1740s the campaign was broadened to include behaviour in the Church and the performance of religious rites; the Church also took the first steps toward creating a new official to ensure this 'good order'. The second thrust was 'enlightenment' – the attempt to inculcate a basic understanding of Orthodoxy by requiring priests to catechise and preach, not merely perform rites. This broader pastoral vision, to be sure, was slow to take effect. Despite the dissemination of printed sermons,[38] parish priests found it difficult to comply, with most offering a sermon three or four times per year (if at all).[39] They proved more energetic about catechisation;[40] by the middle of the nineteenth century, a small but growing number of priests – especially in urban parishes – offered some form of catechism instruction.[41] With the initial campaign to open village schools (first by the Ministry of State Domains in 1838[42] and later by the Church itself), the clergy had yet another venue to teach religious fundamentals. The Church also expanded its publication of religious literature for the laity, which was initially aimed at the educated but later targeted at a less privileged readership. The result was a gradual confessionalisation that sought to make the folk more cognitively Orthodox, to be not only 'right-praising' but also 'right-believing'.

Church policy toward popular Orthodoxy underwent a significant shift in the middle of the nineteenth century. Although the Church continued to

Fond 138, g. 1857, d. 549, ll. 4–5; Fond 797, op. 25, otd. 2, st. 1, d. 105, ll. 16 ob., 23 ob. By mid-century prelates warned increasingly of the 'semi-schismatics', who, while nominally Orthodox, in fact simultaneously observed the Old Belief.

38 To encourage and facilitate such preaching, the Church published and distributed model sermons that parish priests (few of whom, until the early nineteenth century, had formal schooling) could simply read aloud to parishioners. For the fundamental three-volume collection, compiled by Platon (Levshin) and Gavriil (Petrov), *Sobranie raznykh pouchenii na vse voskresnye i prazdnichnye dni*, 3 vols. (Moscow: Sinodal'naia tip., 1776). The publication came at the direct initiative of Catherine II; see the memorandum from the chief procurator, 15 March 1772, in RGIA, Fond 796, op. 53, g. 1772, d. 19, l. 1–1 ob.

39 The rarity of sermons is evident from the service records; see, for example, the Kursk files in Gos. arkhiv Kurskoi oblasti, Fond 20, op. 2, d. 10, ll. 2–2 ob., 10 ob.–11, 18 ob.–19.

40 For the development of catechism texts, see Peter Hauptmann, *Die Katechismen der Russisch-Orthodoxen Kirche. Entstehungsgeschichte und Lehrgehalt* (Göttingen, 1971).

41 Stung by reports that few parishes offered catechism instruction, in the mid-1840s the Synod collected systematic data that showed a modest, but rising, percentage of churches giving catechism instruction: 7.8 per cent in 1847, 8.7 per cent in 1850 and 11.6 per cent in 1855 (G. L. Freeze, 'The Rechristianization of Russia: The Church and Popular Religion, 1750–1850', *Studia Slavica Finlandensia* 7 (1990): 109–10). Compliance varied considerably – from 12 parishes in Vladimir to 504 in Podolia (RGIA, Fond 797, op. 14, d. 33764, ll. 94–6).

42 For the ministry's appeal for clerical participation, see the 1838 memorandum in RGIA, Fond 796, op. 119, g. 1838, d. 1178.

intensify the clergy's didactic role (*uchitel'stvo*), it began to revise its view of popular Orthodoxy and now endeavoured to incorporate, not repress, lay religious practice. That meant, for example, a new view of icon processions; earlier derogated as useless and even harmful, the Church now tended to encourage such public displays of piety – both to satisfy the demands of believers and to demonstrate the power of Orthodoxy.[43] As one dean in Volhynia diocese explained: 'Such icon processions develop in the people a feeling of religious sensibility, arouse a profound reverence toward things sacred, instil piety in the souls, and protect them from superstition.'[44] The Church also sought to involve the laity directly in religious life, not only through the parish councils described above, but also through the development of choirs[45] and religious associations, such as societies of believers who bore religious banners during processions.[46]

To be sure, the Church had to fight an uphill battle against forces inimical to traditional religious life, not so much the intellectual challenges of disbelief and science, as the urbanisation and industrialisation that uprooted people from their community and its embedded traditions and beliefs. But it was not only 'sociological de-christianisation' that threatened Orthodoxy; the Church also faced serious challenges from religious pluralism – from the Old Believers, sectarians and other confessions seeking to convert the Orthodox. In the face of all this, did the Russian Church, like its peers in the West, experience a decline in religious observance?

That is a complex issue, but one conventional measure of religious practice is the data on confession and communion.[47] Significantly, especially when compared with Western Europe, observance among the Russian Orthodox remained extraordinarily high, with relatively modest fluctuations over the course of the entire nineteenth century (see Table 14.1). In 1900, on the eve of the revolutionary upsurge, Church data show that 87 per cent of the male and 91 per cent of the female believers performed their 'spiritual duty' of confession

43 For a typical application, which still required Synodal approval, see 1872 files from Riazan and Suzdal in RGIA, Fond 796, f. 153, g. 1872, dd. 601 and 707.

44 Derzhavnyi arkhiv Zhitomirskoi oblasti, f. f-1, op. 30, d. 423, l. 31 (dean's report from 1902).

45 For measures in 1886 to improve church singing, see RGIA, Fond 797, op. 56, otd. 2, st. 3, d. 11).

46 For a typical file, which involves the establishment of a society of banner-bearers (*khorugvenostsy*) in Vladimir in 1903 (with the charter specifying the duties to ensure good order during processions and in the church itself), see Gos. arkhiv Vladimirskoi oblasti, Fond 556, op. 1, d. 4366.

47 Measuring 'piety' is, at best, a perilous undertaking; data on confession and communion do, however, provide hard numbers on rates of religious *practice* and the laity's fervour or, at least, desire to uphold tradition or willingness to conform.

Table 14.1. *Confession and communion observance: Russian Empire (in per cent)*

					Neither confession nor communion			
	Confession and communion		Confession only		Excused		Indifference	
Year	Male	Female	Male	Female	Male	Female	Male	Female
1797	85.25	86.31	9.03	8.22	1.33	1.24	1.43	1.37
1818	85.07	86.76	8.09	8.13	0.47	0.12	5.38	4.72
1835	83.70	86.17	6.78	6.23	0.53	0.10	8.99	7.50
1850	84.18	85.84	5.98	6.06	2.33	1.09	7.51	7.01
1900	87.03	91.03	0.52	0.45	5.76	2.58	6.69	5.94

and communion.[48] Little wonder that, before the 1905 Revolution, the bishops' annual reports to the Holy Synod routinely exuded such complacency and confidence about popular piety. The data do, however, also reveal a darker side. Whereas the non-compliants had consisted primarily of semi-confessors in 1797 (i.e. people who made confession, but not received communion), that category all but disappeared in the nineteenth century. As local archival materials show, they did so for various reasons: some because they fell ill or encountered other impediments, others because they simply lacked the zeal to return for communion, and still others because of 'the counsel of their spiritual father' (for failing to observe the Lenten requirements of abstinence, especially from sexual intercourse). In lieu of the semi-observants, there emerged a larger pool of non-compliants who were either 'excused' (mainly because of absenteeism associated with trade or migrant labour) or 'unexcused' (for 'indifference'). In short, Russia showed signs of religious differentiation: an overwhelming mass of the population remained observant, while a tiny but distinct minority neglected or outright rejected their 'spiritual duty'.

Significantly, in the late nineteenth century church authorities were more inclined to complain about the parishioners' assertiveness, not their indifference. Ever since the Petrine reform, ecclesiastical authorities had increasingly violated traditional parish prerogatives, above all, in the appointment of clergy and expenditure of parish funds. The latter was particularly sensitive: the earnings from the sale of votive candles, a prime source of parish revenues, were diverted to finance the ecclesiastical schools open only to the clergy's

48 The data include a large number who missed confession and communion because they were too young (under age seven); these have been omitted from the calculations here.

offspring. In the post-emancipation era, parishioners increasingly sought to assert their rights over both the local clergy and the local revenues, an aspiration that erupted into full view as revolution shattered authority and emboldened parishioners to reclaim their rights.[49]

Worldly teachings: from 'reciprocity' to social Orthodoxy

Parallel with the 're-christianisation' of the folk, the Church began to develop and articulate its social and political teachings. To be sure, it reaffirmed the traditional teaching that the existing order was divinely ordained (applying that principle even to the Mongol suzerainty in the thirteenth to fifteenth centuries) and that 'subordinates' should obey their superiors – a paradigm that applied to ruler and ruled, masters and serfs, husbands and wives. But, under the influence of Western thought, the 'enlightened prelates' of Catherinean Russia added an important theme of 'reciprocity': duties and responsibilities were bilateral, not reducible to a mere commandment to 'obey and submit'. Power and wealth conveyed responsibilities, not merely the right to demand obedience; the superior had a moral obligation to care for those in his charge. In turn, subordinates were not only to obey, but to perform their duties faithfully and energetically. Hence the existing order was a kind of divinely ordained social contract, entailing hierarchy but also reciprocity in social relationships.[50]

The Church also applied that precept to serfdom.[51] Although formally excluded from 'meddling' in matters of the secular domain, prelates and priests none the less sought to apply the reciprocity principle, both to protect sacraments like marriage from violation and to uphold the Ten Commandments (broadly construed). Such injunctions were explicit in sermons and other writings that admonished squires to fulfil their responsibilities and, specifically, to attend to the spiritual needs of their serfs.[52] Some turned to deeds, not words,

49 See G. L. Freeze, '"All Power to the Parish"? The Problem and Politics of Church Reform in Late Imperial Russia', in Madhavan Palat (ed.), *Social Identities in Revolutionary Russia* (London: Macmillan, 2001), pp. 174–208.

50 For a classic statement, see the discussion of the 'fifth commandment' (and its extrapolation to masters and slaves, husbands and wives in the 'Short Catechism' (*Sokrashchennyi katekhizis*) appended to the three-volume Synodal collection of sermons distributed to clergy throughout the empire: Gavriil and Platon, *Sobranie raznykh poucheneniia*, vol. III, folio 147–47 verso.

51 For a discussion of the clerical attitudes and role with respect to serfdom, see G. L. Freeze, 'The Orthodox Church and Serfdom in Pre-Reform Russia', *SR* 48 (1989): 361–87.

52 See, for example, the work of a prelate later canonised: Tikhon (Zadonskii), *Nastavlenie o sobstvennykh vsiakogo khristianina dolzhnostiakh* (St Petersburg: Sinodal'naia tip., 1789), pp. 10–12. By 1870, this work had been reprinted forty-eight times.

and became embroiled in social unrest – most dramatically in the Pugachev rebellion of 1773–5,[53] but on a regular basis in villages in the first half of the nineteenth century.[54]

Significantly, by the 1840s and 1850s even some prelates, more accountable and conservative, came to disparage serfdom not only for its abuses, but for the harm it dealt to the serfs' spiritual needs. Whereas bishops had earlier counted on nobles to provide parish churches and ensure peasant religious observance, some prelates began to send reports chastising the squires for neglecting this duty. Indeed, in the Western Provinces, where the squire was non-Orthodox, bishops suspected the non-Orthodox squires of deliberately subverting religious practice: 'The chief cause [of the serfs' unsatisfactory religious condition] is the indifference of the Roman Catholic squires, who, because of their hostility toward Orthodoxy, are unconcerned about the spiritual benefit of the peasants and even try to disseminate religious indifference among them.'[55] That accusation gained momentum and even began to penetrate the reports from central dioceses. The bishop of Penza, for example, attributed the serfs' religious ignorance to the 'excessive use of serf labour during fasts and sometimes holidays'.[56]

By the 1850s, the clergy openly came to espouse the need to engage temporal questions. In part, that derived from the impending emancipation of serfs – who would need the active assistance and guidance of their parish priest in navigating the rights and perils of citizenship. Theology helped legitimise the engagement, as new currents in Christology counselled the Church to 'enter into the world', just as Christ had done, and underlined the connection between Orthodoxy and contemporaneity.[57] The profusion of new clerical periodicals, with their close attention to secular issues, reinforced the new engagement. Drawing on earlier practices (which encouraged priests to disseminate 'useful'

53 For the large complex of files on clerical involvement in the Pugachev rebellion, see the 'secret section' of the Synodal archive (RGIA, Fond 796, op. 205, dd. 76–99); for a Soviet summary of these files, see I. Z. Kadson, 'Krest'ianskaia voina 1773–5 gg. i tserkov'', unpublished candidate dissertation, Leningradskoe otdelenie instituta istorii (1963).

54 See Freeze, 'Orthodox Church and Serfdom', 375–8.

55 RGIA, Fond 796, op. 127, g. 1846, d. 1881, l. 15 ob. (1847 annual report from the bishop of Polotsk). For the famous case of the Baltic provinces in the 1840s, when diocesan authorities battled Lutheran squires over the serfs' religious needs, see G. L. Freeze, 'Lutheranism and Orthodoxy in Russia: A Critical Reassessment', in Hans Medick and P. Schmidt (eds.), *Luther zwischen Kulturen* (Göttingen: Vandenhoeck and Ruprecht, 2004), pp. 297–317.

56 RGIA, Fond 796, op. 137, g. 1856, d. 2398, l. 68 ob. (annual report for 1855).

57 G. L. Freeze, 'Die Laisierung des Archimandriten Feodor (Buchaev) und ihre kirchenpolitischen Hintergründe', *Kirche im Osten* 38 (1985): 26–52; G. L. Freeze, 'A Social Mission for Russian Orthodoxy' in Marshall Shatz and Ezra Mendelsohn (eds.) *Imperial Russia, 1700–1917* (DeKalb: Northern Illinois University Press, 1988), pp. 115–35.

knowledge about agriculture and medicine),[58] liberal clergy now redoubled and diversified such efforts. The seminary also played an important role; it not only produced a disproportionate number of radicals[59] but also had a significant impact on younger clergy.

The result was a 'social Orthodoxy' which emphasised the Church's responsibility to address key social ills. Sermons not only became a regular feature of parish services, but came to address a broad range of worldly problems, from spouse abuse to alcoholism. The religious press, similarly, gave growing attention to temporal issues. In practical terms too, post-reform clergy sought to tackle social problems like poverty and prostitution, encouraged parishes and monasteries to open almshouses and medical clinics, and generally endeavoured to bring the Church into the world.

Orthodoxy in the Russian prerevolution

The revolution of 1905–7 had a profound impact on Russian Orthodoxy. Most dramatically, it unleashed the pent-up discontent long percolating among the parish clergy, who, individually and collectively, embraced a range of liberal and even radical movements. To the horror of state officials, priests all across the empire proved receptive to the calls of the 'Liberation Movement' and used the occasion to press their own demands – for better material support, for the right of self-organisation, for a reduction in 'episcopal rule' and a greater role in diocesan administration. But others took up the needs of the disprivileged. Thus the clergy of one deanship in Viatka diocese, for example, urged the State Duma (parliament) to resolve 'the agrarian question according to the wishes of the people'.[60] And in numerous cases the local priest, whether from fear or conviction, became embroiled in the revolution itself, delivered incendiary sermons, performed requiems for fallen revolutionaries, and in sundry other ways supported his rebellious parishioners.[61]

58 For a typical statement, praising the parish clergy for 'endeavoring to give [the peasants] agricultural instruction' and encouraging 'the simple people, in case of dangerous diseases, to seek the assistance of doctors' (and eschew the traditional fatalism), see the 1851 annual report by the bishop of Riazan in RGIA, Fond 796, op. 132, g. 1851, d. 2363, l. 200.

59 See the overview in B. V. Titlinov, *Molodezh' i revoliutsiia* (Leningrad: Gosizdat, 1924). For typical reports on seminary disorders, which proliferate from the 1880s, see the cases from 1904 in RGIA, Fond 796, op. 185, g. 1904, dd. 225, 247–9, 382, 543, 553, 557.

60 Telegram of 21 June 1906 in RGIA, Fond 796, op. 187, g. 1906, d. 6809, l. 16.

61 See G. L. Freeze, 'Church and Politics in Late Imperial Russia', in Anna Geifman (ed.), *Russia under the Last Tsar* (Oxford: Blackwell, 1999), pp. 269–97; John H. M. Geekie, 'The Church and Politics in Russia, 1905–17', unpublished PhD dissertation, University of East Anglia (1976); Argyrios Pisiotis, 'Orthodoxy versus Autocracy: The Orthodox

It was not only a matter of radical priests: conservative prelates found themselves locked in a struggle with a regime fighting for survival. The decisive trigger to Church–State conflict was the emperor's Manifesto on the Freedom of Conscience (17 April 1905), an attempt to mollify disaffected religious and ethnic minorities by decriminalising apostasy and legalising conversion *from* Orthodoxy. The result, as the prelates feared, was a tidal wave of declarations to leave the Church.[62] The manifesto did not reconcile minorities, of course, but it did enrage churchmen – who saw it as a crass betrayal of the Church's vital interests.

Like the rest of Russian society, the clergy responded to the revolutionary crisis by pressing for reform. Their principal goal was to convene a church council – the first in more than two centuries – to address the Church's many problems and needs. And such seemed a realisable dream, as the regime acquiesced and authorised preparations for a church council. After first collecting the opinions of diocesan authorities, the Synod created a special pre-conciliar commission to analyse the opinions and draft proposals which bore the liberal stamp of these revolutionary ears. All that, however, came to naught: as the revolution receded, the emperor decided to defer the church council until more 'propitious' times.

The 'Duma Monarchy' of the inter-revolutionary years – that marked by the Third (1907–12) and Fourth (1912–17) Dumas – did nothing to solve problems or reduce tensions. At the very minimum, church authorities were aghast at the prospect of the multi-confessional Duma intervening in church affairs, as indeed soon became the case (with respect to salaries for the clergy, parish schools and a host of other issues).[63] Apart from seeking to influence from within (by promoting the election of clerical deputies),[64] the Church adamantly rejected the Duma's competence in most ecclesiastical affairs. Thus, in 1908, the chief procurator conveyed the Synod's rejection of attempts by the Duma (as a 'non-confessional legislative institution') to meddle in church business and to sponsor new laws on religious tolerance.[65] Similar sentiments were later voiced at a conference of prelates from central Russian dioceses, who

Church and Clerical Political Dissent in Late Imperial Russia, 1905–14', unpublished PhD dissertation, Georgetown University (2000).

62 For data on 1905–9, see RGIA, Fond 797, op. 79, otd. 2, st. 3, d. 494, ll. 36–8.

63 For the fullest account, though based only on printed sources, see Vladimir Rozhkov, *Tserkovnye voprosy v Gosudarstvennoi Dume* (Rome: Pontificium inst. orient. Studiorum, 1975).

64 See, for example, the Synod decree of 14 July 1912 urging active clerical involvement in elections to the Fourth Duma, in RGIA, Fond 796, op. 194, g. 1912, d. 1207, l. 10–10 ob.

65 See the chief procurator's memorandum to the Council of Ministers (dated 10.9.1908) in RGIA, Fond 797, op. 78, otd. 2, st. 3, d. 122/b, l. 53.

demanded the 'complete removal of church legislation from the purview of a non-confessional State Duma'.[66] Archbishop Stefan of Kursk expressed prevailing sentiment in the episcopate when he wrote that 'it is an empty and idle dream to count on the bureaucrats renouncing their coercion of the Church. It is a vain, futile hope to count on the Duma giving us the opportunity to free ourselves from the enslavement and to build the Church on "conciliar principles" as the canons require.'[67]

All this unfolded against the backdrop of growing anxiety about the moral-religious state of the Church. Among the folk themselves, piety seemed to be recovering, with high rates of religious observance, but it was clear that the 'simple folk' were no longer so simple: patterns of religious observance were complex, driven not so much by dissent and apostasy as by broader patterns of social and cultural change (migrant labour, the rebellion of youth and the like).[68] Publicly, the Church suffered enormously from the infamous 'Rasputinshchina', as Grigorii Rasputin, the self-appointed lay 'elder' (*starets*), gained extraordinary influence and compromised crown and altar in the process. Although public perception greatly exaggerated Rasputin's role, he nonetheless elicited fierce enmity among the ranking churchmen, especially after Rasputin's influence became public in 1912. As a police report from 1912 attested: 'According to public opinion, the ecclesiastical domain experienced a kind of revolutionary movement in 1912.'[69] Even extreme conservatives like Archbishop Antonii (Khrapovitskii) waxed indignant about the cancerous influences on the Church.[70]

The First World War inspired the Church, like most of Russia, to respond with patriotic support for what would quickly prove an unmitigated military catastrophe. The Church itself mobilised substantial resources to assist in the war, converted facilities to serve as military hospitals, raised funds for the war victims and campaigned to sustain the fighting morale of the troops and the home front. In that respect, it differed little from churches of the other combatants. But the context was different: far sooner than elsewhere, the Russian Empire was swept by an intense tide of anti-war sentiment. Hence the Church's identification with the 'imperialist war' did much to create a young generation of anti-religious veterans, the future Red Army men who would

66 RGIA, Fond 796, op. 189, d. 2229/b, l. 271.
67 RGIA, Fond 1101, op. 1, d. 1111, l. 3.
68 See G. L. Freeze, 'A Pious Folk? Religious Observance in Vladimir Diocese 1900–14', *JfGO*, 52 (2004): 323–40.
69 RGIA, Fond 1101, op. 1, d. 1111, l. 1.
70 'V tserkovnykh krugakh', *KA* 31 (1928): 204–13.

be particularly hostile to the Church. But the Church itself had grievances,[71] suffered mightily from the inflation and dislocation of war and had grown increasingly alienated from a crown irreparably besmirched by Rasputinism. Indeed, amidst the military crisis of 1915, with the country reeling from defeat, the Church suffered yet another scandal associated with Rasputin, as his protégé, the bishop of Tobolsk, conducted a hasty canonisation against the express orders of the Synod. The public resonance could hardly have been greater, and the damage to the Synod more ruinous. Little wonder that, when the autocracy appealed to the Church for support on 27 February 1917, in its critical hour, even the conservative Synod summarily refused.[72]

Russian Orthodoxy did not vanish after the Petrine reforms, but it certainly changed. Most striking was the resilience of popular faith; while the prerevolution brought and accelerated undeniable anti-religious tendencies, the vast majority remained faithful and, indeed, demanded a greater role for the Church and for themselves in the Church. But Orthodoxy was no longer part of the infamous 'Orthodoxy, Autocracy, Nationality' trilogy of official politics; it had excised the middle term and, increasingly, identified with the people, not with a secular state that had plundered its assets and failed to protect its vital interests.

71 See, for example, the collective statement of clerical deputies to the State Duma in August 1915 (at the very height of a political crisis), detailing all the Church's woes and how so little had been resolved, in 'Pechat' i dukhovenstvo', *Missionerskoe obozrenie* 11 (November 1915): 286–90.

72 A. V. Kartashev, 'Revoliutsiia i sobor 1917–1918 gg.', *Bogoslovskaia mysl'* 4 (1942): 75–101.

15
Women, the family and public life

BARBARA ALPERN ENGEL

It is difficult to generalise about the women of Russia, so much did their identity and experience vary according to their legally defined social status, religion and ethnicity, among other variables. To be sure, gender shaped key aspects of women's lives. Until well into the nineteenth century, if not later, most shared virtually an identical lot in life: learning women's duties at their mother's knee, a marriage arranged by others, then childbearing, childrearing and the labour of maintaining the home and provisioning the family. Changes that began in the reign of Peter the Great nevertheless affected the ways that women understood and fulfilled those family responsibilities; while developments in the final decades of the nineteenth century challenged the family order that governed most women's lives, and expanded and diversified alternative ways of living. Even so, beneath the developments traced in this chapter, fundamental continuities remained.

The Petrine revolution and its consequences

The period properly begins with the reign of Peter the Great, who brought a thoroughgoing revolution to aristocratic women's lives and initiated economic, social and legal changes that touched the lives of many of the rest. As part of his Westernising project, and in order to mobilise his subjects to suit his needs, Peter the Great endeavoured to transform Russia's traditional family regime. From the elites, he required new women, suitable consorts for the new men of the service elite and likewise modelled along Western lines. 'Upper-class Muscovite women were driven from the seclusion of the *terem*, or women's quarters, divested of their old-fashioned robes, squeezed into Western corsets and low-cut gowns and transformed into suitable companions for their "decent beardless" spouses.'[1] Only elite women were required to

1 L. Hughes, 'Peter the Great's Two Weddings: Changing Images of Women in a Transitional Age', in R. Marsh (ed.), *Women in Russia and the Ukraine* (Cambridge: Cambridge University Press, 1996), p. 31.

appear at social gatherings and display the requisite social skills; however, even women lower down on the social hierarchy became subject to the requirement that Russian women don European dress. The law of 1701 mandating German clothes, hats and footwear applied to the wives and children of men of all ranks of the service nobility, as well as of leading merchants, military personnel and inhabitants of Moscow and others towns; only clergy and peasants were exempted. Henceforward, such women who failed to wear dresses, German overskirts, petticoats and shoes risked a fine.[2]

Westernisation of elites began in the new capital, St Petersburg, and proceeded only gradually elsewhere. In the decades following Peter's death, increasing numbers of noble families sought to provide their daughters with at least a rudimentary education, and some aspired to more, hiring foreign governesses and tutors to instruct their daughters at home. In addition to a good dowry, a virtuous and submissive character, and competence in household management, educated men increasingly sought brides who could read and write and converse in foreign tongues. The well-educated Anna and Alexandra Panina, renowned for their knowledge and intelligence at mid-century, had no difficulty making excellent marriages.[3] During the reign of Elizabeth a few private boarding schools opened; such schools proliferated in the reign of Catherine the Great. By the close of the eighteenth century, there were over a dozen in Moscow and St Petersburg and more in provincial cities, invariably run by foreigners. Catherine made noblewomen's education the responsibility of the state. Her goal: to further the Westernisation of Russia's manners and morals by training mothers to become the moral educators of their young. In 1764, Catherine established Russia's first school for noble girls. Called the Society for the Training of Well-Born Girls (better known as Smolnyi Institute), the school admitted primarily daughters of servitors from the elite as well as middling-level ranks of military and civil service. The school graduated 70 students in its first year and about 900 women altogether during Catherine's reign. About twenty other institutes, organised along lines similar to Smolnyi, were opened in Russia's major cities and towns in the years after its founding.[4] Whether acquired at school or at home, the impact of education on elite women's literacy rates was substantial by the end of the century: Michelle Marrese has calculated that in the middle of the eighteenth century, only a

2 The decree is translated in J. Cracraft (ed.), *Major Problems in the History of Imperial Russia* (Lexington: D. C. Heath and Co., 1994), pp. 110–11.

3 B. Meehan-Waters, *Autocracy and Aristocracy: The Russian Service Elite of* 1730 (New Brunswick: Rutgers University Press, 1982), p. 113.

4 J. L. Black, 'Educating Women in Eighteenth-Century Russia: Myths and Realities', *Canadian Slavonic Papers* 20, 1 (1978): 23–43.

small fraction (4 to 26 per cent) of noblewomen dwelling in the provinces were literate; a quarter of a century later, the proportion was closer to half. Thereafter, women's literacy rates rose dramatically, to roughly 92 per cent at the start of the nineteenth century.[5]

By then, cultivation characterised women of the cream of Russia's elite. Judging by the women's dress, their hairdos, the dances that they performed and the language that they spoke – almost invariably French – they were virtually indistinguishable from their Western European counterparts. The artist Elisabeth Vigée Lebrun, who visited Russia in the 1790s, returned to Paris impressed by what she saw: 'There were innumerable balls, concerts and theatrical performances and I thoroughly enjoyed these gatherings, where I found all the urbanity, all the grace of French company.' She believed, in particular, that it would be impossible 'to exceed Russian ladies in the urbanities of good society'.[6] Some of these cultivated women also developed independent intellectual interests and enthusiastically pursued them; the erudition of a few rivalled that of their European counterparts. Catherine the Great herself was an enormously prolific writer, founding Russia's first satirical journal and authoring works in a wide variety of genres. Princess Catherine Dashkova (1743–1810), née Vorontsova, wrote numerous plays and articles and in 1783 became one of the first Russians to edit a journal, *The Companion of Lovers of the Russian Word*. That same year, Dashkova became one of the first women in Europe to hold public office, appointed by Catherine the Great as Director of the Academy of Sciences. Increasing numbers of women found their way into print, translating from foreign languages or writing prose and, more commonly, poetry of their own.[7]

Peter also attempted to transform private life, reforming marriage practices and bringing the state more intimately than ever before into the lives of his subjects. The aim was to raise the birth-rate by enhancing conjugal felicity, but also to weaken the ability of elite parents or elders to use marital alliances for political purposes. A decree of 1702 altered the Muscovite custom wherein marriages were contracted by the parents, or if they were dead, by close relatives of the bride and groom, who usually saw each other for the first time only after the wedding ceremony. The decree required a six-week betrothal period before the wedding, enabling the couple to meet and get to know one

5 M. L. Marrese, *A Woman's Kingdom: Noblewomen and the Control of Property in Russia, 1700–1861* (Ithaca: Cornell University Press, 2002), pp. 213–15.

6 Quoted in Judith Vowles, 'The "Feminization" of Russian Literature: Women, Language, and Literature in Eighteenth-Century Russia', in Toby W. Clyman and Diana Greene (eds.), *Women Writers in Russian Literature* (Westport: Praeger, 1994), p. 42.

7 Quoted in Vowles, 'The "Feminization" of Russian Literature', pp. 45–7.

another. Should they decide against marriage, either party gained the right to terminate the engagement, the betrothed as well as their parents. A decree of 1722 (rescinded in 1775) explicitly forbade forced marriages, including those arranged for 'slaves' by their masters, and required both bride and groom to take an oath indicating that they consented freely to their union. The two decrees may also have reflected Peter's own, more individualised, attitude towards conjugal life, which differed substantially from the official morality of his time, shaped by Russian Orthodoxy. The Church regarded the goal of marriage as reproduction and social stability, and condemned sexual enjoyment as sinful. Peter's second marriage to a woman he loved passionately and deeply introduced a new conjugal ideal that affirmed individual affection and the pleasures of life on earth. It was celebrated in public and disseminated in portraits of Peter, Catherine and their children.[8]

The fundamentally patriarchal character of Russian society nevertheless remained unaltered. Grounds for divorce did not include wife-beating; in Peter's day, husbands could rid themselves of unwanted wives by depositing them in a nunnery, as Peter did with his first wife Evdoksia. For the crime of adultery, wives were sentenced to forced labour, whereas men who killed their wives were merely flogged with the knout. Making it more difficult for women to avoid family life by entering a convent, in 1722 Peter raised the age at which women could take the veil to sixty.[9] Developments after Peter's death further buttressed the patriarchal family. The laws governing marriage permitted husbands and fathers to exercise virtually unlimited power over other family members, and required a wife to submit to her husband as head of the household and to live with him in love, respect and 'unlimited obedience'.[10] The strictures on marital dissolution tightened. Over the course of the eighteenth century, the Russian Orthodox Church steadily increased its authority over marriage and divorce, emphasising more than ever before the sacramental and indissoluble nature of marriage. The Church made divorce virtually inaccessible to the Russian Orthodox faithful, the majority of the population. Grounds for annulling a marriage also narrowed and were even more narrowly applied.[11] It became much more difficult for a woman to escape

8 N. S. Kollman, '"What's Love Got to Do With It?": Changing Models of Masculinity in Muscovite and Petrine Russia', in Barbara Clements, Rebecca Friedman and Dan Healey (eds.), *Russian Masculinities in History and Culture* (New York: Palgrave, 2002), pp. 15–32.

9 L. Hughes, *Russia in the Age of Peter the Great* (New Haven: Yale University Press, 1998), pp. 199–200.

10 *SZ* (St Petersburg, 1857) x, pt. 1, article 106.

11 G. L. Freeze, 'Bringing Order to the Russian Family: Marriage and Divorce in Imperial Russia, 1760–1860', *JMH* 62 (1990): 709–46.

an abusive or unsatisfactory marriage by obtaining a divorce; the law strictly forbade marital separation.

Yet in the final decades of the eighteenth century, literature imported from the West introduced new ways of thinking about marriage and the family. Conduct books and education manuals celebrated motherhood's sanctity, and instructed mothers to be the moral and spiritual guides of their children.[12] Sentimental literature elevated woman's role, presenting her as sensitive and emotional, a friend to the man whom she married.[13] Even Russian Orthodox views of marriage were affected by these trends: the Church placed new emphasis on the affective ties of spouses and their reciprocal responsibilities towards one another, while downplaying – although not eradicating – the patriarchal and misogynist elements of its previous stance.[14] In the reign of Nicholas I, a modified patriarchal ideal became the model of imperial rule. The private life of the tsar was staged so as to portray him as a loving and devoted husband and caring father, while the empress provided a model of maternal love and tenderness – a family idyll that was disseminated in paintings and engravings to a broad audience as well as to the elite. The new imagery dramatised a 'sharp division of sexual spheres' that mirrored developments in other European courts.[15]

Although arranged marriages continued to be the norm well into the nineteenth century, there is evidence that by the reign of Nicholas I, a portion of the nobility had embraced the new affective ideal of marriage and come to value intimate and loving family relations. 'Can a marriage be stable and happy, when it is not based on feelings of mutual respect and the most tender love?' rhetorically inquired the governor of Nizhegorod province in 1828.[16] However, it is questionable whether Nicholas's ideology of separate spheres had a broad popular basis in Russia, as it had in Great Britain and France.[17] While the

12 Diana Greene, 'Mid-Nineteenth Century Domestic Ideology in Russia', in Rosalind Marsh (ed.), *Women and Russian Culture* (Cambridge: Cambridge University Press, 1998), pp. 84–7; C. Kelly, *Refining Russia: Advice Literature, Polite Culture and Gender from Catherine to Yeltsin* (Oxford: Oxford University Press, 2001), p. 28.

13 O. E. Glagoleva, 'Dream and Reality of Russian Provincial Young Ladies, 1700–1850', *The Carl Beck Papers*, no. 1405, p. 44.

14 W. Wagner, *Marriage, Property and Law in Late Imperial Russia* (Oxford: Oxford University Press, 1994), p. 76.

15 R. Wortman, *Scenarios of Power: Myth and Ceremony in Russian Monarchy*, 2 vols. (Princeton: Princeton University Press, 1995), vol. I, p. 261.

16 GARF, Tret'e otdelenie sobstvennoi ego imperatorskogo velichestva kantseliarii, 1826–1880, Fond 109, 2aia ekspeditsiia, 1828, op. 58, ed. khr. 199, ll. 1–19; Mary Wells Cavendar, 'Nests of the Gentry: Family, Estate and Local Loyalties in Provincial Tver, 1820–1860,' unpublished PhD dissertation, University of Michigan (1997), p. 29.

17 M. Perrot, 'The Family Triumphant', in Michelle Perrot (ed.), *A History of Private Life: From the Fires of Revolution to the Great War*, 5 vols. (Cambridge, Mass.: Harvard University

'domestic' was defined as women's proper sphere, as it was elsewhere, for Russian noblewomen the domestic extended well beyond the confines of home and housekeeping. Women's subordinate status in law coexisted, sometimes uneasily, with their legal right to own and manage immovable property, which Russian wives, as well as single women and widows, enjoyed. Even married women could buy and sell and enter contracts, a status that was unique in Europe. Noblewomen's activities as property managers often took precedence over childrearing and brought such women into contact with local and central authorities and with the legal process.[18] Given the lawlessness of provincial life and noblewomen's control of human chattel, estate management could require determination, even ruthlessness, rather than the gentleness usually associated with domesticity.

Outside the circle of privilege

The changes introduced by Peter and his eighteenth-century successors affected women of Russia's tax-paying population, townspeople as well as peasants, primarily in negative ways. The most significant change derived from the practice of conscription that Peter introduced. Conscription created a new social category, the soldier's wife (*soldatka*). If a peasant, conscription put the *soldatka* in the most marginal position by freeing her and her children from serfdom, thereby depriving her of her husband's share of the communal land and other benefits. Because they represented an extra mouth to feed and a potential threat to the other women of the household and community, *soldatki* might be driven from the village. Such women became highly vulnerable. The cities to which many migrated offered them little in the way of respectable employment and large numbers of men prepared to pay for sexual companionship. Some women took up petty trade, many more hired out as domestic servants. However, enough turned to prostitution as a temporary or permanent expedient that soldiers' wives acquired an unsavory reputation. They also figured prominently among the mothers of illegitimate children. In the course of the eighteenth century, illegitimacy and infanticide became much more visible than they had been previously, and perhaps more commonplace as well. These social problems moved the state to action. Initially, concern to increase the population prompted Peter the Great to establish hospitals where mothers could deposit their illegitimate children in secret (in 1712, and again

Press, 1990), vol. IV, pp. 134–5; Catherine Hall, 'The Sweet Delights of Home', in Perrot, *A History*, p. 49.

18 Marrese, *A Woman's Kingdom*.

in 1714 and 1715). After his death, the shelters were dismantled. In the reign of Catherine the Great, foundling homes were established in Moscow (in 1764) and St Petersburg (1771), with the aim not only of preserving the lives of illegitimate children, but equally important, of creating an enlightened citizenry, capable of promoting the welfare of the country. The homes failed to achieve these goals.[19]

At the same time, the state moved to exert greater control over women's sexuality. A decree of 26 July 1721 stated that women and girls convicted of 'loose behaviour' were to be handed over to the College of Mines and Manufactures and given as workers to industrialists or sent to Moscow. In 1736 Empress Anna ordered all 'debauched' women to be beaten with a cat-of-nine-tails and thrown out of their homes. In 1762 Catherine the Great designated a hospital in St Petersburg for the confinement of women of 'debauched behaviour'. In 1800 Emperor Paul I sentenced to forced labour in Siberian factories all women who 'have turned to drunkenness, indecency and a dissolute life'.[20] The law also enjoined the police to pick up 'vagrant maids' of dubious character who belonged to 'the poorest and most disreputable classes' if they might be harbouring venereal disease.[21] Finally, in 1843, following the example of the French, the Russians moved to subject prostitutes to regulation. Illicit sexual behaviour would henceforward be tolerated, but only within the boundaries set by the state. A woman who 'traded in vice' could either enter a licensed brothel or register as an independent prostitute, carrying a 'yellow' ticket that attested to the state of her health. Both were required to undergo regular examinations for venereal disease. The policy clearly targeted lower-class women who lived outside the boundaries of the patriarchal family.

In many ways, the new emphasis on culture and education increased differences between elites and others. Only a tiny minority of non-elite women enjoyed access to education. Attached to Smolnyi institute was a school that admitted daughters of townsmen, although by 1791 nobles so inundated it that they outnumbered commoners. In 1786 Catherine established state primary and high schools that admitted girls and educated them for free. Alexander I extended her work, establishing parish schools at the base of the educational system. Some non-elite parents came to value education for daughters. During his childhood, recalled the clergyman Dmitrii Rostislavov, born in a provincial

19 D. Ransel, *Mothers of Misery: Child Abandonment in Russia* (Princeton: Princeton University Press, 1988), pp. 31–83, 154–8.

20 Laurie Bernstein, *Sonia's Daughters: Prostitutes and Their Regulation in Imperial Russia* (Berkeley: University of California Press, 1995), pp. 13–15.

21 Quoted in Laura Engelstein, 'Gender and the Juridical Subject: Prostitution and Rape in Nineteenth Century Criminal Codes', *JMH* 60 (September 1988): 485.

town in 1809, 'many clergymen, townspeople, and even rich peasants saw a need to teach reading . . . to their daughters'.[22] A few were even willing to pay: in Anna Virt's private school in Moscow, daughters of townsmen and a priest studied together with the offspring of officials, military officers and foreigners in 1818–20. Some merchants sent their daughters to school; Old Believers encouraged the literacy of daughters as well as sons. The overall number of women students remained tiny, however. Altogether, there were 1,178 female pupils in Russia by 1792, and 2,007 by 1802 (of a total of 24,064 pupils). In 1824, it was calculated that there were 338 girls in district schools and 3,420 in private schools; most female students undoubtedly derived from the nobility.[23] Literacy rates for Russia's population remained very low: in 1834, only 1 of 208 Russians could read and write; in 1856, 1 of 143, the overwhelming majority of them male. In response to clerical concerns about lagging behind educated society and complaints about uneducated wives, in 1843 the Russian Orthodox Church opened a special school for daughters of the clergy, with the goal of preparing them for marriage.[24] While accessible to only a few, education and culture had become another measure of elite status for women as well as men.

The reform era

Women's subordinate social status became a burning issue in the middle of the nineteenth century, as educated Russians began to subject every traditional institution to re-evaluation, the patriarchal family included.[25] In the opinion of those on the left of Russia's emergent political spectrum, authoritarian family relations reproduced and reinforced the social and political hierarchy. In order to foster the democratisation of society, family relations would have to be democratised, too. Social critics intended women to play a vital role in creating a new social order, but they disagreed about the character of that role. Was women's primary responsibility to devote themselves to the family and to appropriate mothering of future citizens? Or did the broader society need women's energies, too? As substantial numbers of women and men sought

22 D. I. Rostislavov, *Provincial Russia in the Age of Enlightenment: The Memoir of a Priest's Son*, ed. and trans. Alexander Martin (DeKalb: University of Northern Illinois Press, 2002), p. 40.

23 Janet Hartley, *A Social History of the Russian Empire* (London and New York: Longman, 1999), p. 142.

24 Quoted in G. L. Freeze, *The Parish Clergy in Nineteenth Century Russia* (Princeton: Princeton University Press, 1983), p. 178.

25 R. Stites, *The Women's Liberation Movement in Russia: Feminism, Nihilism and Bolshevism, 1860–1930* (Princeton: Princeton University Press, 1978), pp. 29–64.

to answer these questions for themselves and others, the 'woman question' emerged as one of the central issues of the day.

The debate unfolded in 1856, when Nikolai Pirogov (1810–81), the surgeon and educator, published an essay entitled 'Questions of Life' that posed explicitly the question of women's social role. Pirogov had just returned from the Crimean War (1854–6), where he had supervised some one hundred and sixty women who had volunteered as nurses. The women had served without pay and working right at the front, faced many of the same dangers and hardships as soldiers. To Pirogov, the women's exemplary work demonstrated that 'up to now, we have completely ignored the marvelous gifts of our women'.[26] To his mind, those gifts were mainly applicable in the family. To prepare women better to perform the role of mother to future male citizens and true companion to their husbands, capable of sharing fully in men's concerns and struggles, Pirogov advocated improvements in women's education.[27]

This was a goal that the new tsar could also embrace. In 1858 Alexander II approved a proposal for secondary schools for girls. The purpose: to improve the quality of public life by providing that 'religious, moral and mental education which is required of every woman, and especially, of future mothers'.[28] The new schools, called *gimnaziia*, were to be day schools, offering a six-year course of study that included Russian language, religion, arithmetic and a smattering of science. *Progimnazia* were opened the same year, offering a three-year course of training and a similar curriculum, exclusive of science. The schools were only partially subsidised; to cover the remaining costs, they depended on public support, which emerged only slowly. By 1865 there were 29 *gimnazia* and 75 *progimnaziia* in all of Russia; by 1883, there were 100 and 185 of each respectively, with an enrolment of roughly 50,000 students. Open to girls of all estates, *gimnaziia* and *progimnaziia* helped to encourage a blurring of social boundaries: over the next forty years, the proportion of well-born female students diminished, while that of peasants and townspeople grew.[29] In 1876 a supplementary year of pedagogical training became available to *gimnazia* students, qualifying graduates for employment as a domestic teacher or tutor, and as a teacher in elementary schools and the first four classes of girls' secondary schools.

26 Quoted in John S. Curtiss, 'Russian Sisters of Mercy in the Crimea, 1854–55', *SR* 25, 1 (March 1966): 106.

27 Barbara Alpern Engel, *Mothers and Daughters: Women of the Intelligentsia in Nineteenth Century Russia* (New York: Cambridge University Press, 1983), p. 52.

28 Ibid., p. 50.

29 C. Johanson, *Women's Struggle for Higher Education in Russia, 1855–1900* (Kingston and Montreal: McGill-Queens University Press, 1987), pp. 30–1.

Some social critics adopted a more radical approach to the 'woman question'. For the critic Nikolai Dobroliubov, writing in 1856, the family was a 'Realm of Darkness', in which 'despotism' bore most heavily on women. Although his essay by that title focused on the merchant milieu as depicted by the playwright Alexander Ostrovskii, in Dobroliubov's view family despotism was more widespread. Almost everywhere, he contended, 'women have about as much value as parasites'.[30] A new concern with women's rights in the family prompted critiques of the patriarchal character of family law. There can be no true Christian love or hatred of vice in a family where despotism, arbitrariness and coercion reign and 'wives are given over in slavery to their husband' contended the liberal jurist Mikhail Filippov in 1861.[31] The emancipation of the serfs added an economic dimension to the woman question, depriving many nobles of their livelihood and forcing their daughters to support themselves. Equally important, young people of this era who espoused 'new ideas' rejected the elite culture that they associated with serfdom – a life of idleness and luxury, supported by the toil of others. For some women, even dependence on a husband became unacceptable. The more radical were convinced that whether married or single, a woman must never 'hang on the neck of a man'.[32]

Encouraged by the attention of the press, elite women began to express their shared interest and identity as women. In 1859 noblewomen in the province of Vologda established separate meetings at gatherings of the provincial nobility. To minimise distinctions of wealth, they required participants to wear simple dress.[33] That same year, Russia's first woman-oriented association emerged, the Society for Inexpensive Lodgings, with the goal of providing decent housing and otherwise assisting needy gentlewomen. Three well-educated women from elite backgrounds took the lead: Anna Filosofova (1837–1912), the wife of a high-ranking bureaucrat; Nadezhda Stasova (1822–?), the daughter of a court architect and godchild of Alexander I, and Maria Trubnikova, (1835–97), the daughter of an exiled Decembrist (Vasilii Ivashev). To the charitable activities that had long comprised part of propertied women's role, the three brought the democratic spirit of the new era, providing employment for the residents of their housing, daycare for the children and a communal kitchen to prepare meals. Thus began a movement for expanding the rights of women.

30 Quoted in Barbara Alpern Engel, 'Women as Revolutionaries: The Case of the Russian Populists', in Renate Bridenthal and Claudia Koonz (eds.), *Becoming Visible: Women in European History* (Boston: Houghton-Mifflin, 1977), p. 349.
31 Quoted in Wagner, *Marriage, Property and Law*, p. 106.
32 Engel, *Mothers and Daughters*, p. 80.
33 Quoted in Engel, 'Women as Revolutionaries', p. 350.

Other women took action on their own behalf. In 1859 women began to audit university lectures, which had just been reopened to the public. Within a year, women's presence during university lectures had become almost commonplace. In 1861 several scientists at the St Peterburg Medical Surgery Academy opened their laboratories to women. Among those who audited medical lectures was Nadezhda Suslova, the daughter of a serf. Suslova completed her medical studies in Zurich, where she earned the degree of Doctor of Medicine in 1867, the first woman to receive such a degree from a European university. Her success inspired hundreds of other women to follow her example. In the cities, some young women openly flouted conventional gender expectations. They cropped their hair, dispensed with crinolines and simplified their dress; they smoked in public, went about the streets without an escort, and wore blue-tinted glasses. A few even donned the clothing of men in order to enjoy greater freedom. Young rebels became known to their critics as nihilists (*nigilistki*) because of their rejection of 'the stagnant past and all tradition'. Some came to regard intimate relations and family life as an obstacle to women's freedom and sought to reject them altogether. Their views can be heard in the credo of Lelenka, the heroine of Nadezhda Khvoshchinskaia's novella *The Boarding School Girl* (published 1860). Lelenka proclaims that she 'will never fall in love, never . . . On the contrary, I say to everyone, do as I have done. Liberate yourselves, all you people with hands and a strong will! Live alone. Work, knowledge, freedom – that's what life is all about.'[34]

Nikolai Chernyshevsky's enormously influential novel, *What Is to Be Done?* (*Chto delat'?* 1862), offered a different solution to the 'woman question', one that sought to create a balance between public and private life and granted men a central role. Freed from an oppressive family situation by marriage to a medical student, a 'new man', the heroine, Vera Pavlovna, enjoys a room of her own and the freedom to love another, as well as meaningful, socially useful work. She organises a sewing workshop according to collective principles; eventually, she becomes a physician, each stage of her development facilitated by her husband. By depicting the personal and productive relations that would constitute the socialist future, Chernyshevsky's novel linked women's liberation with the more sweeping goals of social transformation and revolution. The book became a key work in shaping the outlook of this and subsequent generations.

Among conservative officials, however, the radical implications of women's liberation aroused concern about threats to the political order. Although few

34 Engel, *Mothers and Daughters*, pp. 69, 113.

women were involved, conservatives connected women students with the student unrest of the early 1860s. In July 1863, the Ministry of Education closed university doors to women. A year later, the Medical Surgery Academy expelled women, too. Conservative fears complicated but failed to halt efforts by advocates of women's rights to expand their educational opportunities. Advanced secondary courses for women opened in 1869 (the Alarchinskii courses), as did university preparatory courses (the Liubianskii courses); three years later, courses that prepared women for secondary-school teaching became available (the Guerrier courses). Thanks to the support of Dmitrii Miliutin, minister of war, that same year the government established Courses for Learned Midwives in St Petersburg. In 1876 an additional year was added to the four-year programme and the courses renamed Women's Medical Courses, qualifying graduates to work as physicians. That same year, the government sanctioned the opening of 'higher courses' for women, essentially, women's universities that awarded no degree. Kazan University became the first to take advantage of the opportunity; in 1878, Kiev and St Petersburg followed. The St Petersburg courses, known as the Bestuzhev courses, became the most well-known and long-lasting. Graduates of women's courses found employment as midwives, medical assistants (*fel'dshery*), pharmacists, physicians, journalists and most commonly of all, teachers. The profession of teaching became increasingly feminised: the proportion of women teaching in rural schools in European Russia almost doubled between 1880 and 1894, growing from 20.6 to 38.6 per cent of the total. By 1911 women constituted well over half rural teachers. Initially drawn primarily from among the privileged, by the pre-war period over 40 per cent of women teachers in rural schools derived from the peasantry or were townswomen; indeed, the most striking fact about such teachers was their social diversity.[35]

A minority of educated women, however, viewed Russia's social inequities as far more important than educational or career opportunities. Precisely as conservative officials had feared, some women students came to oppose the social and political order. Hundreds of young women, most of privileged background, became involved in the populist movement of the 1870s and went 'to the people' to educate or rouse them to revolution. Many wound up in prison. In January 1878, Vera Zasulich, the daughter of an impoverished noble family, initiated the terrorist phase of the populist movement by shooting General Trepov, the city governor of St Petersburg, before a room full of

35 Ben Eklof, *Russian Peasant Schools: Officialdom, Village Culture and Popular Pedagogy, 1861–1914* (Berkeley: University of California Press, 1986), pp. 186, 189.

witnesses in retaliation for his beating of a radical prisoner. A jury acquitted her. Women played a prominent role in the People's Will, the organisation that emerged when the populist movement divided over the use of violence. On 1 March 1881, Sofia Perovskaia, the daughter of a former governor-general of St Petersburg, directed the successful assault on Tsar Alexander II, becoming the first Russian woman to be executed for a political crime.

The death of Tsar Alexander II at the hands of populist terrorists and the ascension to the throne of his son, Alexander III (r. 1881–94) brought significant efforts to restore the pre-reform gender order. Blaming higher education for women's political radicalism, conservative officials attempted to render it off limits. In 1882 the Women's Medical Courses ceased to accept new students, and in 1887 ceased operation. Admissions to all other women's courses ended in 1886, while the government pondered its next moves. Although the Bestuzhev courses were permitted to continue, their programmes were narrowed and enrolment was restricted, with a 3 per cent quota for non-Christians (meaning Jews). At the same time, the government sought to reinforce the patriarchal family. Regarding his own family as a 'sacred personal sphere' and himself as the 'guardian of the sanctity and steadfastness of the family principle', Tsar Alexander III strove to secure the inviolability of the marital bond.[36] The efforts of liberal jurists to reform Russia's patriarchal marital laws foundered on the rock of conservative resistance, led by Konstantin Pobedonostsev and the Russian Orthodox Church.

Nevertheless, reactionaries failed to turn back the clock, in large part because of the modernising changes that the government itself unleashed, which affected even some peasant women, although to a lesser extent than men. Between 1856 and 1896, the number of pupils in primary schools grew from roughly 450,000 to approximately 3.8 million, while the proportion of girls among them increased from 8.2 to 21.3 per cent.[37] While less than 10 per cent of peasant women were considered literate at the close of the nineteenth century according to the minimal standards of tsarist census-takers, even this low rate represented an advance over earlier years, and rates were rising among the younger age groups. Women's access to secondary education grew as well. During the reign of Alexander III, girls' *gymnaziia* almost doubled in number. Pressures to expand higher education for women intensified after his death.

36 Quoted in Richard Wortman, *Scenarios of Power: Myth and Ceremony in Russian Monarchy*, 2 vols. (Princeton: Princeton University Press, 2000), vol. II, p. 176; S. N. Pisarev, *Uchrezhdenie po priniatiiu i napravleniiu proshenii i zhalob, prinosimykh na Vysochaishee imia, 1810–1910 gg. Istoricheskii ocherk* (St Petersburg: Tovarishchestvo P. Golike i A. Vil'borg, 1909), p. 163.

37 Eklof, *Russian Peasant Schools*, pp. 309–13.

In 1895 the new tsar Nicholas II approved the St Petersburg Women's Medical Institute. Enrolment in the Bestuzhev courses expanded and the Moscow Higher Women's Courses (the Guerrier courses) re-opened in 1900–1. In 1903 a special pedagogical institute for women opened in Odessa, enrolling 600 hundred students in the first two years. Over time, the social background of students in higher educational institutions grew more diverse. Although impoverished students were far the less likely to complete the courses, in lecture halls and reading rooms, young women from clerical, merchant and artisan, even peasant backgrounds took their places beside the daughters of privileged elites.[38]

Economic developments in the post-reform period had somewhat broader repercussions for peasant women. The expansion of the cash economy affected their consumption patterns. Manufactured clothing and urban-style fashion increasingly became a mark of prestige in the countryside. But long-standing peasant practices often mediated women's interaction with the marketplace. Frequently, men rather than women took advantage of opportunities to earn money elsewhere, leaving women and the aged to tend the land. If a household needed the cash, women were more likely to labour at home. Offering a limitless reserve of inexpensive labour, in the hinterlands of Moscow tens of thousands wound cotton thread on bobbins for a factory or sewed kid gloves or rolled hollow tubes for cigarettes from materials distributed by an entrepreneur, who paid them for their work and sold the finished product. Their modest financial contributions did little to enhance women's status at home.[39] Connected to the market by virtue of their income-producing activities, women nevertheless worked within the traditional patriarchal household. Many of the tens of thousands of peasant women who earned wages in nearby factories likewise acted as members of a family economy rather than as independent labourers. Women moved in and out of the labour force in response to their household's needs.

Other circumstances narrowed the horizons of the growing numbers of women who laboured far from home. As industrialisation proceeded, women's proportion in the burgeoning factory labour force grew: from about one in every five workers in 1885 to about one in every three by 1914. Still larger numbers of migrant women found positions in domestic service. Although

38 Johanson, *Women's Struggle*, pp. 74–5, 99–101; *Sankt-Peterburgskie vysshie zhenskie kursy. Slushatel'nitsy kursov. Po dannym perepisi (ankety), vypolnennoi statisticheskim seminarom v noiabre 1909 g.* (St Petersburg, 1912), p. 4. S. Morrissey, *Heralds of Revolution: Russian Students and the Mythologies of Radicalism* (Berkeley: University of California Press, 1998), p. 161.

39 R. Glickman, *Russian Factory Women: Workplace and Society, 1880–1914* (Berkeley: University of California Press, 1984), pp. 34–52.

spinsters and widows, the first to migrate, often left for good, marriageable women usually migrated temporarily, in order to feed themselves, assemble a trousseau and, if possible, contribute to their family economy. Most migrant women experienced demoralising working and living conditions. They lived in factory dormitories, where dozens crowded together in a single large room, or they rented a corner just big enough for their bed in an apartment shared with others. Domestic servants often lacked even the modest room of their own available to their servant sisters to the West. The servant's wage was low, her position generally insecure and work never-ending. Women factory workers had lower rates of literacy than men and received a fraction of men's wages. Earning barely enough for subsistence, many survived on a diet of bread and cucumbers. Their gender barred women from the drinking establishments where men socialised and exchanged ideas. Domestic servants, who enjoyed little or no free time, were even more isolated and vulnerable than the woman worker. Perhaps as a result, domestic servants were disproportionately represented among both registered prostitutes and the 8–9,000 women who abandoned their illegitimate children to foundling homes every year in Moscow and St Petersburg.[40]

Even so, cities offered opportunities to women migrants. Wage in hand, women could extend their horizons and alter their fates in a manner unthinkable in the village. Aspiring to emulate the appearance of their social betters, single women workers sometimes spent their wages on urban-style fashions, skimping on food in order to afford a pair of boots or an attractive dress. In their free time, they found inexpensive entertainments at urban fairs and pleasure gardens or in the amateur workers' theatres, all of which proliferated at the end of the nineteenth century. By enabling migrant women to dress and amuse themselves in ways similar to women of other classes, city life could erode social boundaries and make social distinctions seem both less relevant and more burdensome.

The burgeoning marketplace also fostered such trends, by encouraging the desire for individual pleasure and gratification. Advertising enticed women of all classes to consume the items displayed in department store windows and on the pages of popular magazines and to employ beauty aides to decorate the self. Advice books on appropriate dress and deportment proliferated. New pastimes such as bicycling enhanced women's mobility and personal independence. Consumer culture tended to promote individual indulgence over family values.

40 Barbara Alpern Engel, *Between the Fields and the City: Women, Work, and Family in Russia, 1861–1914* (New York: Cambridge University Press, 1994), pp. 126–66.

Anastasia Vial'tseva vividly personified the new trend. Born a peasant in 1871, at the turn of the century Vial'tseva sang bitter-sweet romances about sexual desire, attracting hordes of worshipping fans and earning fabulous sums of money, which she spent lavishly and conspicuously on herself.[41]

As the century drew to a close, women assumed more visible roles in public life. Particularly in rural areas, women's religious communities provided charity to the poor, education to the young and care to the sick even during the worst of the reaction, and the number of such communities expanded dramatically towards the end of the century, part of a broader religious revival.[42] As restrictions eased in the early 1890s, unprecedented opportunities became available for women to contribute to and define the public welfare. In 1894 Municipal Guardianships for the poor, a form of welfare organisation, were established in all major cities. Private charitable organisations proliferated, offering a broad range of services. Women directed charitable organisations, served on governing and advisory boards, and worked for charitable establishments either as volunteers or as salaried employees, influencing their goals and orientation. Interestingly, Russia's charitable organisations eschewed the maternalist and domestic-oriented discourse that dominated such endeavours in the West, emphasising instead the importance of childcare institutions such as nurseries and asylums, and the role of women as workers.[43]

Women's new opportunities and enhanced sense of self left many dissatisfied with the limitations on their lives. When in a decree of 1897, the St Petersburg city government forbade women teachers to marry, women teachers protested. The marriage ban limited their personal freedom, argued Nadezhda Rumiantseva at a conference of teachers.[44] Responding to condescending treatment by university officials and male students, at the turn of the century women students increasingly framed their demands for change 'in terms of the individual right to self-expression and self-determination'.[45] By 1904 roughly a thousand working women had joined the separate women's

41 Louise McReynolds, 'The "Incomparable" Vial'steva and the Culture of Personality', in Helena Goscilo and Beth Holmgren (eds.), *Russia. Women. Culture* (Bloomington: Indiana University Press, 1996), pp. 273–91.

42 Adele Lindenmeyr, 'Public Life, Private Virtues: Women in Russian Charity, 1762–1914', *Signs* 18, 3 (Spring 1993): 574–8; B. Meehan-Waters, 'From Contemplative Practice to Charitable Activity: Russian Women's Religious Communities and the Development of Charitable Work, 1861–1917', in Kathleen McCarthy (ed.), *Lady Bountiful Revisited: Women, Philanthropy and Power* (New Brunswick: Rutgers University Press, 1990), pp. 142–56.

43 A. Lindenmeyr, 'Maternalism and Child Welfare in Late Imperial Russia', *Journal of Women's History* 5 (Fall 1993): 119–20.

44 C. Ruane, *Gender, Class and the Professionalization of Russian City Teachers, 1860–1914* (Pittsburgh: University of Pittsburgh Press, 1994), pp. 73, 76–81, 115.

45 Morrissey, *Heralds*, p. 84.

section of Gapon's Assembly of Russian Factory Workers that Vera Karelina organised in St Petersburg. Karelina's most effective organising tool was a story that she read aloud, describing the humiliating body searches by male personnel that women workers were forced to undergo.[46]

1905 and after

During the revolution of 1905, women across the social spectrum mobilised in enormous numbers to demand an expansion of political rights and greater social justice. Women industrial workers, clerical workers, pharmacists, professionals, even domestic servants, joined unions and walked off their jobs to attend mass meetings and demonstrations that called for an end to autocracy and a representative form of government. Labouring women often participated in the burgeoning strike movement in ways connected to their family roles. In factories where women predominated, the textile industry in particular, strike demands clearly reflected their presence. Factory after factory demanded day care, maternity leave, nursing breaks and protection of women workers. Even as they demonstrated new assertiveness, such demands reinforced a gender division of labour by touching on women's role as mother and not on their actual working conditions. Peasant women also participated actively in rural unrest primarily in their family roles.[47] However, the intense politicisation and pervasive use of a language of rights stimulated other women, primarily the educated, to speak on their own behalf and to claim their place in the expanding public sphere.

Feminist organisations emerged to promote women's interests. The most significant and the first to try to speak on behalf of all of Russia's women was the All-Russian Union for Women's Equality (Women's Union). The union's platform, adopted in May 1905, called for the equality of the sexes before the law; equal rights to the land for peasant women; laws providing for the welfare, protection and insurance of women workers; the abolition of regulated prostitution; co-education at all levels of schooling; and women's suffrage. Although its membership was primarily middle class, the Women's Union worked to forge alliances across the social divide and encourage lower-class women to speak for themselves, inviting 'women of the toiling classes' to

46 Glickman, *Russian Factory Women*, pp. 184–6.

47 Glickman, *Russian Factory Women*, pp. 190–4; Barbara Alpern Engel, 'Women, Men, and the Languages of Peasant Resistance, 1870–1907', in Stephen P. Frank and Mark D. Steinberg (eds.), *Cultures in Flux: Lower-Class Values, Practices, and Resistance* (Princeton: Princeton University Press, 1994), pp. 34–53.

formulate their own demands and pledging to support them.[48] Feminists also tried to reach out to peasant women, joining the Peasant Union, and convincing it to adopt the plank of women's suffrage.[49] Feminist efforts to expand their social base bore some fruit. Women domestic servants in Moscow and St Petersburg joined feminist-organised unions; they attended feminist-sponsored clubs. Women workers added their signatures to petitions favouring women's suffrage. A number of peasant women's groups were formed and some petitions signed by peasant men took up the demand for women's suffrage.

Nevertheless, 1905 brought feminists very little in the way of measurable gains. To be sure, the granting of civil liberties, however limited, allowed more scope for organising. The revolution also marked a watershed in the history of women's education. The curriculum of women's higher courses expanded and between 1906 and 1910, new women's courses opened in many provincial cities. In addition, a number of private co-educational universities were established, offering new curricula and electives. The enrolment of women students increased exponentially: in 1900–1, there were 2,588 women students enrolled in higher education in Russia; by 1915–16, the number was 44,017. Nevertheless, the status of women's education remained insecure and career options limited, leaving an enormous gap between education and employment opportunities.[50]

Moreover, the October Manifesto enfranchised only men. The liberal Kadet party divided over the issue of women's suffrage, while parties to the left, although staunch advocates of women's rights, were with the exception of the Trudovik party suspicious of and reluctant to support 'bourgeois feminism'. Further, the evidence suggests that working-class and peasant women felt more affinity with the men of their class than they did with middle-class feminists. Even when feminists succeeded in organising women workers, they had trouble retaining their loyalty. As one feminist lamented, it was relatively easy to establish circles among labouring women, but as soon as their political consciousness was raised, they wanted to work with the men of their class. As a result, the Women's Union 'acted as a kind of preparation for party work'.[51] The social divisions that weakened opposition to autocracy divided the women's movement as well. After 1907, membership in the

48 GIAgM, Fond 516, op. 1, ed. khr. 5, ll. 45–50.
49 L. H. Edmondson, *Feminism in Russia, 1900–1917* (Stanford: Stanford University Press, 1984), pp. 38–47.
50 Morrissey, *Heralds*, p. 161.
51 GIAgM, Fond 516, op. 1, ed. khr. 5, p. 73. Report of the Third Congress, 22 May 1906.

women's movement sharply declined, as it did in radical political parties in general.

In the aftermath of 1905, other issues, especially 'the sexual question', absorbed the public's attention. Commercial culture flourished. Advertisements encouraged women to develop more beautiful busts; they offered cures for sexual troubles; they touted contraceptives. On the back pages of newspapers, 'models' boasting 'attractive bodies' offered to pose for a fee.[52] The 'new woman' symbolised the new era. Freed from the constraints of conventional morality, she dominated the imagination of the reading public. The immensely popular boulevard novel, Anastasia Verbitskaia's *The Keys to Happiness* (*Kliuchi schast'ia*, published 1908–13) was one of the bestselling works of the time. The novel addressed women of all classes who felt stifled by societal and professional restraints, and emphasised their right to sexual adventure and professional achievement.[53] Non-readers might encounter the 'new woman' on the silver screen.

Yet more restrictive ways of regarding women continued, and drew new life from the fears that revolution evoked. This can be seen in the debate over abortion, which Russian law penalised as a form of murder. Supposedly, its incidence had escalated dramatically following the revolution of 1905. Progressive physicians sought, unsuccessfully, to decriminalise the procedure and at professional meetings, women physicians spoke vociferously on behalf of reproductive freedom. Among the most vocal was the feminist physician Maria Pokrovskaia, who denounced Russia's punitive abortion laws as unwarranted restrictions on female autonomy. Invoking the concept of voluntary motherhood, she claimed that only women were in a position to know their own needs. To proponents of decriminalisation such as she, abortion symbolised women's autonomy. To others, however, abortion symbolised women's sexual licence and underscored the dangerous aspects of women's emancipation. Even those who approved of women's freedom from legal and career restraints condemned women's sexual liberation.[54]

However controversial she might be, by the outbreak of the First World War, the 'new woman' had apparently come to stay. She was very much a product of the changes that had swept Russia in the latter part of the nineteenth century. The expansion of women's education, the growth of the market economy and

52 Laura Engelstein, *The Keys to Happiness: Sex and the Search for Modernity in Fin-de-siècle Russia* (Ithaca: Cornell University Press, 1992), p. 360.

53 Anastasya Verbitskaya, *Keys to Happiness*, ed. and trans. Beth Holmgren and Helena Goscilo (Bloomington: Indiana University Press, 1999), p. xiii.

54 Engelstein, *Keys*, pp. 341–4.

the increased emphasis on the self and its gratification contributed more to undermining the patriarchal family than had the radical critiques of the 1860s. Significantly, wifehood and motherhood played a minimal role in the woman-related discourse of the early twentieth century, although those themes gained more prominence following 1905. Yet the 'new woman' remained a minority phenomenon, swimming against a conservative tide. Patriarchal relations continued to serve as both metaphor and model for Russia's political order, upheld by the law and by the institutions and economies of the peasantry, still the vast majority of Russia's population. Wifehood and motherhood, not the pleasures and freedoms of new womanhood, remained the aspiration of countless numbers of Russia's women. Although the nature of social divides had changed, they remained almost as unbridgeable on the eve of the First World War as they had been 200 years before.

16

Gender and the legal order in Imperial Russia

MICHELLE LAMARCHE MARRESE

This chapter will explore a single but significant dimension of women's experience in Imperial Russia: the transformation of their legal status from the Petrine reforms to the eve of the 1917 Revolution. It has become a truism among scholars that law codes both mirror and produce gender difference and hierarchies.[1] In this regard, Russian legal culture proved no exception: normative law drew marked distinctions between women and men, as well as distinguishing between individuals on the basis of social standing. When applied to women, the juridical system in Imperial Russia was also noteworthy for tensions and inconsistencies that intensified with the elaboration of women's status in written law. This essay will investigate the origins of competing definitions of gender in the realms of property, family and criminal law. In the pre-reform era, the clarification of women's civil status elevated noblewomen's standing in the patriarchal family by extending their rights over property, yet simultaneously institutionalised their subordination to their husbands. The legal regime that emerged after the Great Reforms of the 1860s placed a novel emphasis on female vulnerability and the assignment of women to the domestic sphere, at the very moment that unprecedented numbers of peasant women were making their way into the urban marketplace.[2] As I will argue in the following pages, if the legal order in eighteenth-century Russia minimised sexual difference in many respects, nineteenth-century

I would like to thank Barbara Alpern Engel, John Bushnell and Dominic Lieven for their thoughtful comments, which have greatly improved this essay.

1 Laurie Bernstein, *Sonia's Daughters: Prostitutes and their Regulation in Imperial Russia* (Berkeley: University of California Press, 1995), p. 3; A. M. Schrader, *Languages of the Lash: Corporal Punishment and Identity in Imperial Russia* (DeKalb: Northern Illinois University Press, 2002), p. 6; W. G. Wagner, *Marriage, Property, and Law in Late Imperial Russia* (Oxford: Clarendon Press, 1994), p. 3.

2 B. A. Engel, *Between the Fields and the City: Women, Work, and Family in Russia, 1861–1914* (New York: Cambridge University Press, 1994), pp. 64–99; R. L. Glickman, *Russian Factory Women: Workplace and Society, 1880–1914* (Berkeley: University of California Press, 1984), pp. 59–104.

innovations in the law highlighted gender distinctions to an unprecedented degree.

Noblewomen, inheritance, and the control of property

The pre-Petrine law of property was characterised by unequal inheritance for sons and daughters and limitations on women's use and control of landed estates. For all that Muscovite law codes allowed women a surprising degree of independence in matters judicial,[3] elite Russian women shared many legal disabilities with their European counterparts. The reforms of Peter the Great, however, initiated an era of profound cultural and legal change for Russian noblewomen. Most notably, the eighteenth century witnessed the gradual expansion of women's rights to property. Innovations in female inheritance were less dramatic than advances in women's control of their fortunes, yet the elevation of women's inheritance rights and married women's acquisition of the right to manage and alienate their estates were emblematic of a larger process of legal change: the trend toward individualised rather than familial property rights among the nobility in the eighteenth century, and the efforts of the elite to clarify their standing in the law of property in relation to other family members and the state. Significantly, noblewomen took active part in the extension of their property rights and went on to make ample use of their legal prerogatives.[4]

From the middle of the nineteenth century, inspired by debates over the 'woman question', Russian historians and jurists wrote extensively on the topic of women's property rights. Russian scholars issued extravagant pronouncements about the legal status of their female compatriots, declaring them the most fortunate women in Europe with regard to control of property but the most disadvantaged in the domain of inheritance.[5] Both generalisations were overstated, yet it cannot be denied that from the eighteenth century the evolution of Russian women's legal status diverged significantly from that of their

3 N. S. Kollmann, 'Women's Honor in Early Modern Russia', in Barbara E. Clements, Barbara Alpern Engel and Christine D. Worobec (eds.), *Russia's Women: Accommodation, Resistance, Transformation* (Berkeley: University of California Press, 1991), pp. 60–73.

4 On women's role in the expansion of their property rights, see M. L. Marrese, *A Woman's Kingdom: Noblewomen and the Control of Property in Russia, 1700–1861* (Ithaca: Cornell University Press, 2002), pp. 28–39, 56–9.

5 Anna Evreinova, 'Ob uravnenii prav zhenshchin pri nasledovanii', *Drug zhenshchin* (November 1883), no. 11: 62; I. V. Gessen, 'Vliianie zakonodatel'stva na polozhenie zhenshchin', *Pravo* (1908), no. 51: col. 2837; A. Liubavskii, 'Ob uravnenii nasledstvennykh prav muzhchin i zhenshchin', *ZMI* 20, book 2 (May 1864): 412.

European equivalents. In Western Europe, differential control of property sharply distinguished the sexes, associating men with real estate and women with personality, while – as often as not – subjecting married women's property to control of their husbands.[6]

In regard to female inheritance, Russian law displayed only marginal superiority over European legal codes. The post-Petrine law of inheritance continued to favour male heirs, while failing to elucidate the claims of married daughters and the legal status of the dowry vis-à-vis inheritance. After decades of debate, imperial legislators guaranteed daughters, regardless of marital status, a statutory share of one-fourteenth, or 7 per cent, of their parents' immoveable property, as well as one-eighth of their personal assets, after which their brothers received equal shares of the estate. When no male offspring survived, daughters divided their parents' holdings equally. By the nineteenth century, intestate inheritance law was in dire need of revision, as European states began to equalise the inheritance rights of sons and daughters. Nonetheless, the revised rules of succession at the end of the eighteenth century represented a genuine achievement for noblewomen, who had won greater security in the law of inheritance and the right to litigate for a statutory share of family assets.[7]

It was in the realm of control of property, however, that Russian noblewomen made their most striking advance vis-à-vis their European counterparts. From 1753 Russian noblewomen enjoyed the right to alienate and manage their property during marriage.[8] Noblewomen's control of their assets, whether acquired as dowry, purchased or inherited, inspired foreign observers to remark on this curious exception to Russian women's legal servitude. 'You must know that every Woman has the right over her Fortune totally independent of her Husband and he is as independent of his wife', Catherine Wilmot marvelled in a letter from Russia to her sister Harriet in 1806. 'Marriage therefore is no union of interests whatsoever, and the Wife if she has a large Estate and happens to marry a poor man is still consider'd rich . . . This gives a curious sort of hue to the conversations of the Russian Matrons which to a meek English Woman appears prodigious independence in the midst of a Despotic Government!'[9] In his account of Russia in the 1840s, August von Haxthausen

6 A vast literature exists on the topic of women and property. For a detailed overview of this literature, see Marrese, *A Woman's Kingdom*.

7 M. L. Marrese, 'From Maintenance to Entitlement: Defining the Dowry in Eighteenth-Century Russia', in W. Rosslyn (ed.), *Women and Gender in Eighteenth-Century Russia* (Aldershot: Ashgate, 2003), pp. 209–26.

8 *PSZ*, vol. 13, no. 10.111 (14.06.1753). M. L. Marrese, 'The Enigma of Married Women's Control of Property in Eighteenth-Century Russia', *RR* 58, 3 (July 1999): 380–95.

9 Martha Wilmot, *The Russian Journals of Martha and Catherine Wilmot, 1803–1808*, ed. and intro. Marchioness of Londonderry and H. M. Hyde (London: Macmillan, 1935), p. 234.

also observed, 'In Russia the female sex occupies a different position from its counterpart in the rest of Europe.' He went on to relate that 'A large part of the real estate is . . . in the hands of women', adding that 'it is easy to understand what a great influence women enjoy in society as a result'.[10]

Noblewomen's control of their estates was, moreover, an active concept, rather than a mere legal convention in many families. Greater equality in the law of property translated into women's acquisition of estates and into striking similarities between women and men in regard to use of their assets: noblewomen became enthusiastic participants in the market for land and serfs, as well as urban real estate. Women as a group engaged in the same range of property transactions as men, and the size of women's estates was commensurate with that of their male counterparts. Indeed, the scale of women's holdings grew dramatically from the middle of the eighteenth century: by the nineteenth century, noblewomen controlled as much as one-third of the land and serfs in private hands. The presence of married women as both sellers and investors in property after 1750 increased steadily, while the participation of widows and unmarried women dwindled.[11] Married women engaged in business in their own names, were present at property transactions and assumed responsibility for managing the family estate. Noblewomen's legal and economic autonomy, coupled with the frequent absences of their husbands on state service, ensured that significant numbers of women in Imperial Russia were as likely to concern themselves with investment decisions and large-scale management as with the supervision of house serfs and other domestic tasks.

Gender conventions and the law of property in the eighteenth century

Russian law-makers stopped short of establishing complete parity between the sexes in regard to property, particularly in their failure to equalise inheritance rights. Yet the contention of this work is that, for noblewomen, from the middle of the eighteenth century, gender difference in Russia was muted in the law of property.[12] Once law-makers granted women the right to control their

10 A. von Haxthausen, *Studies on the Interior of Russia*, ed. S. Frederick Starr and trans. E. Schmidt (Chicago: University of Chicago Press), pp. 21–3.

11 On women's economic activities, see Marrese, *A Woman's Kingdom*, p. 109.

12 Over time, the right to control property was extended to women of the merchant and urban estates. Among the peasantry, customary law also protected women's dowries. Yet property rights among the peasantry remained collective until the twentieth century, as did the rights of merchants in many respects. B. A. Engel, *Women in Russia, 1700–2000* (New York: Cambridge University Press, 2004), p. 60; C. Worobec, *Peasant Russia: Family*

fortunes, they gradually withdrew legal provisions designed to protect wives from husbands who tried to defraud them of their assets. Far from being afforded special treatment, property-owning women assumed all the responsibilities of male proprietors. They were expected to defend their holdings against the encroachments of husbands, kin and neighbouring proprietors. Nor were noblewomen absolved of responsibility for their own, or their children's, financial affairs by virtue of their sex. Writing early in the nineteenth century, the memoirist F. F. Vigel criticised Princess Gargarina for neglecting her estate: 'Like all the nobility in our country, not only women, but also men, she did not think about her business affairs, which were in a sorry state.'[13] Like many of his contemporaries, Vigel all but prescribed an active role for women in estate administration.

With the extension of noblewomen's property rights, however, a fundamental contradiction characterised married women's legal status in Russia. At the heart of this contradiction lay the tension between married women's station in family law and their standing in the law of property. Custom, family law and religious ideology unanimously prescribed women's personal subjugation to their husbands. At the same time, from 1753 the law of property defined married women as autonomous agents and guaranteed them full control over any property in their possession. It should come as no surprise that these principles could clash, and often at the expense of female autonomy. Or, as one observer of Russian social customs remarked, 'Tho a married Woman has compleat power over her Fortune she has not over her person.'[14]

The tension between property and family law was an eighteenth-century innovation. Although Russian law acknowledged separate property and married women's ownership of the dowry long before 1753, the administration of marital property was traditionally a joint venture[15] and married women sold or mortgaged their estates only with their husbands' consent, if not at their behest.[16] Yet as rights of property came to be invested in (noble) individuals, rather than families, and women gained control of their estates, maintaining the boundary between the property of husband and wife created a host of dilemmas for Russian legal authorities. In particular, determining serf ownership when peasants who belonged to spouses married and produced children

and Community in the Post-Emancipation Period (Princeton: Princeton University Press, 1991); Wagner, *Marriage, Property, and Law*, p. 371.

13 F. F. Vigel, *Zapiski* (Moscow: 1928), p. 26.

14 Bradford, *The Russian Journals*, p. 232.

15 *Akty iuridicheskie, ili sobranie form starinnogo deloproizvodstva* (St Petersburg: 1838), no. 71, X; no. 357.

16 Marrese, *A Woman's Kingdom*, pp. 52–4.

repeatedly drew the attention of the courts. The debates over serf ownership exemplify the problems inherent in maintaining separate estates in marriage on a day-to-day basis. A series of legal conventions, including the registration of dowry villages in the name of the bride, made husbands and wives acutely aware of the separation of their assets and undermined marriage, in the words of Catherine Wilmot, as a 'union of interests'. To be sure, many noblewomen trusted their husbands to administer their holdings for their mutual benefit, as well as in the interests of their children. Yet this arrangement by no means worked to the advantage of women or their heirs if the presumption of common interests broke down. Women's failure to keep close watch on their holdings could lead to considerable loss for themselves or, if they predeceased their husbands and the latter remarried, for their children.[17] In order to reap the benefits of separate property, noblewomen were compelled to patrol the legal boundaries between their own estates and those of their husbands.

Serf women, particularly house serfs, comprised an important part of a Russian bride's dowry, along with other goods she would need to set up her household. As a result, marriages frequently took place between serfs belonging to married couples. Such arrangements disturbed no one while the serf owners' marriage endured; when one spouse died, however, a serious complication arose. The *Ulozhenie*, or Law Code, of 1649 forbade serf owners to separate wives from their husbands. Since married serfs could not be parted, the surviving serf owner confronted an awkward dilemma: which spouse was the owner of the serf couple and their offspring?

The widow Akulina Voeikova insisted that she was the rightful owner when she brought a suit before the Land College in 1737. Following her husband's death in 1735, Voeikova entered into a lengthy inheritance dispute with her son-in-law, Prince Nikanor Meshcherskii. Voeikova did not contest her daughter's right to inherit her father's estate, but she insisted on her full widow's entitlement of one-seventh of her husband's immoveable property, as well as the return of her dowry. According to Voeikova, Meshcherskii had left her with less than one-tenth of her husband's assets, and included in her daughter's share all of Voeikova's serf women, whom her husband had married to peasants in his own villages.

Voeikova pursued her case to the Senate in 1744, after the Land College ruled that her dowry serfs would be returned to her, but their husbands and children would be considered part of her entitlement, thus diminishing the portion she would inherit from her husband's estate. In contrast, the Senate found that

17 See, for example, RGIA, Fond 1330, op. 4, ed. khr. 262, ll. 2–3, 35.

the ruling of the Land College contradicted an article in the Ulozhenie, which stipulated that when a woman died without issue, her serf women should be returned to her natal family. If these serfs had been given in marriage, the husbands must accompany their wives, regardless of their original ownership. Voeikova therefore was entitled to claim her serf women and their families as part of her original dowry, the Senate decreed, in addition to her statutory share of one-seventh of her husband's property.[18]

Similar disputes over the inheritance of married serfs recurred throughout the eighteenth century.[19] Until mid-century, noble widows clearly benefited from the courts' assertion of their right to reclaim their serf women, along with their families. This state of affairs proved much less satisfactory to men who felt they or their heirs had been short-changed. In 1767 noble deputies to the Legislative Commission brought their complaints to the attention of Catherine II, arguing that under the present rules men suffered a loss in serf ownership and that the proprietor of the serf husband, rather than the owner of the wife, should claim the entire family when a division of property took place.[20]

Members of the Senate echoed the logic of the nobility in subsequent rulings on inheritance. During the second half of the eighteenth century, as law-makers revised their conception of women's relation to property, they also withdrew much of the protection they had previously offered propertied wives. Legal authorities acknowledged that, despite the formal separation of property in marriage before 1753, in practice married men made no distinction between their own and their wives' property. Thus, a decree in 1740 allowed for recruits to be levied from the villages of an officer's wife as well as from his own, 'since husbands use their wives' villages as they use their own, and for this reason they are required, upon retirement, to declare openly their own as well as their wives' villages'.[21] Having invested women with full rights of ownership in 1753, however, the Senate acknowledged the necessity of re-examining the problem of serf ownership by married couples.

As it reviewed a case presented in 1799, the General Session of the Senate discussed the principles that guided previous decisions on serf ownership in 1744 and 1762. The Senate had ruled in favour of the wife in 1744 because

18 *PSZ*, vol. 12, no. 9.095 (19.12.1744).

19 RGADA, Fond 1209, op. 79, ed. khr. 167, ll. 11–12; ed. khr. 365, lines 86–90; Fond 1209, op. 84, ch. 14, ed. khr. 1507, ll. 1–2.

20 *Sbornik imperatorskogo russkogo istoricheskogo obshchestva* (henceforth *SIRIO*), 148 vols. (St Petersburg, 1869), vol. IV, pp. 419, 424; (1871), vol. VIII, pp. 539–40.

21 Quoted in A. S. Paramonov, *O zakonodatel'stve Anny Ioannovny* (St Petersburg, 1904), pp. 161–2.

'in previous times the dowry estate was registered not only in the name of the woman who was marrying, but in the name of her husband, and for this reason the husband, considering himself the owner of his wife's estate, could give her women serfs in marriage to his serfs'. To prevent the loss of property to the wife and her clan, the Senate had decreed that serf women and their offspring were to be returned to the wife and her family. But after 1744, the Senate continued, new customs governed the registration of dowries. Men could no longer appropriate their wives' estates now that officials registered the dowry in the name of the wife alone and women administered their property without their husbands' permission. Consequently, the Senate argued, it was unjust to replace one serf woman with an entire family, and they offered new guidelines to regulate the future division of assets. When husbands and wives agreed to marry their serfs to one another, the following principle was to apply: henceforth, the serf family belonged to the owner of the serf husband. If a husband married his serf women to his wife's peasants, the wife would be considered the owner, and vice versa.[22] Yet in their discussion the Senate failed to acknowledge that brides were far more likely to bring serf women to marriage, thus placing female proprietors at a disadvantage. In short, once women acquired the right to control their estates, they also took on the burden – willingly or not – of protecting their fortunes from their husbands.

Transactions between husband and wife

Determining serf ownership was not the only quandary the courts confronted in regulating property relations between husband and wife. In keeping with the convenient assumption that women could now determine how they would use their assets, law-makers gradually withdrew the protection they had once extended to wives who were coerced to part with their fortunes. Having spelled out the consequences for spouses who chose to marry their serfs to one another, the courts then struggled with the question of whether spouses might sell and mortgage property to each other. Their dilemma derived from women's obligation to obey their husbands – a duty that was originally a tenet of ecclesiastical law and later articulated as well in civil codes. With good reason the courts initially expressed apprehension that husbands would exploit their wives' weakness and force the latter to part with their assets on unfavourable terms. By the nineteenth century, however, official solicitude for vulnerable

22 *PSZ*, vol. 26, no. 19.250 (19.01.1800).

wives gave way to a firm conviction that married women were responsible for the defence of their property rights.

Since the Muscovite era, the courts had been sensitive to the potential for forced sales of land by abused wives. In order to minimise this danger, sellers of both sexes were examined in court when they executed deeds of purchase, mortgaged property or registered wills.[23] Yet it was not until the second half of the eighteenth century, after noblewomen had gained control of their assets, that the legality of transactions between spouses loomed large in debates within the Senate. The first debate in the Senate on transactions between spouses took place in 1763. The summary of the case dwelled primarily on the right of members of one clan to sell property to another; however, the Senate finally ruled that conveyances between husband and wife were unacceptable on the basis of a 1748 edict which forbade spouses to claim their entitlement of one-seventh of the other's estate during the other's lifetime. The sale of property by wives to husbands was more objectionable still, the senators reasoned, since a woman could not dispute her husband's decision and might relinquish her property at his insistence.[24]

In subsequent rulings legislators focused at times on the murky legal status of property transactions between spouses, while on other occasions they highlighted the necessity of protecting wives from greedy husbands.[25] As the Senate debated the legal niceties of allowing spouses to engage in business, however, sales and mortgages continued to take place between husbands and wives. Finding it impossible to stop the practice, the Senate reversed its earlier decisions on the grounds that the resolution of the 1763 dispute represented a ruling on a particular case, not a general principle. The final debate took place in the Senate in 1825 between the minister of justice and members of the Committee on the Codification of Law. In their discussion, most of the senators skirted the problem of men's authority over their wives altogether and focused on the status of the 1763 edict. The minister of justice argued that the Land College had set forth its opinion in 1763 as a guide for ruling on future transactions between spouses. Committee members countered the minister's reservations with their own interpretation: the issue was not, they maintained, whether the sale of property between spouses was beneficial or harmful to the parties involved, but whether any principle in Russian law existed to prohibit these transactions. Having reviewed the regulations in the *Ulozhenie* and the 1785 Charter to the Nobility, the committee concluded that no rationale

23 *PSZ*, vol. 2, no. 763 (19.06.1679); vol. 2, no. 909 (05.04.1682).

24 *PSZ*, vol. 16, no. 11.764 (26.02.1763).

25 *PSZ*, vol. 20, no. 15.022 (25.06.1763); *PSZ*, vol. 27, no. 21.926 (30.09.1805).

could be found for preventing the transfer of property between spouses. After lengthy debate, with virtually no reference to feminine vulnerability, three of the four senators at the General Session agreed that transactions between husbands and wives should be permitted.[26]

Keeping in mind that previous decisions had rested, at least in part, on the conviction that propertied wives should be protected from abusive husbands, this was an ironic conclusion. As divorce petitions reveal, noblewomen continued to be the victims of beatings by husbands who wished to seize control of their estates.[27] Yet the ruling was consistent with the general tone of Russian property law in extending minimal protection to women. From the middle of the eighteenth century the law made few distinctions between men and women's use of their assets. Placing an equal burden on both sexes to safeguard their interests was the logical corollary of equalising women's status in the law of property. Thus, in the early nineteenth century Russian officials confronted a paradox that bedevils law-makers to this day: gender neutrality in the law by no means translated into a guarantee that women could fully realise their legal rights.

Unlimited obedience: women and family law

During the decades when Russian lawmakers elevated noblewomen's standing in the law of property, two noteworthy trends emerged in ecclesiastical and family law. First, from the middle of the eighteenth century, grounds for dissolving marriage in the Orthodox Church dwindled dramatically, making divorce virtually impossible. Second, although wives had always been expected to be subservient to their husbands, a woman's responsibility to obey her husband was for the first time articulated in civil law, in Catherine II's Statute on Public Order (*Ustav blagochiniia*) of 1782 and transformed into an obligation to demonstrate 'unlimited obedience' in the 1832 Digest of Laws (*Svod zakonov Rossiiskoi imperii*). The contradiction between women's economic liberty and their personal dependence soon drew the attention of legal scholars and became the subject of on-going controversy in the nineteenth century.

During the first half of the eighteenth century, laymen and parish priests 'made and unmade marriage' with relative ease.[28] The tenuous nature of

26 *PSZ*, vol. 37, no. 30.472 (31.08.1825).

27 RGIA, Fond 796 (*Kantseliariia Sinoda*), op. 39, ed. khr. 71, l. 1 (1758); Fond 796, op. 52, ed. khr. 278a, ll. 1–2 (1771); Fond 796, op. 58, ed. khr. 261, ll. 1–2 (1777); Fond 796, op. 61, ed. khr. 216, l. 1 (1780); Fond 796, op. 78, ed. khr. 440, l. 2 (1797).

28 G. L. Freeze, 'Bringing Order to the Russian Family: Marriage and Divorce in Imperial Russia, 1760–1860', *JMH* 62, 4 (December 1990): 714.

matrimonial vows before mid-century was also a feature of the pre-Petrine era:[29] not only did the Orthodox Church in early-modern Russia lack the means to enforce its authority over marriage, but ecclesiastical authorities accepted a broad range of grounds for divorce. Until 1730, parish priests granted divorce certificates when spouses agreed to separate – and despite the prohibition on voluntary divorce after 1730, the practice continued until the middle of the eighteenth century.[30] In subsequent decades, however, the Church not only stepped up its supervision of clergy and laity, but imposed far more rigid regulations for the dissolution of marriage.

Even as the grounds for divorce contracted, unhappy spouses continued to petition the Holy Synod for permission to end their union. Overwhelmingly, both sexes appealed in vain, since the Orthodox Church was reluctant to accept adultery as grounds for divorce and rejected severe physical mistreatment as sufficient reason for terminating marriage. Indeed, by and large the Church sanctioned divorce only when separation had, de facto, taken place: namely, in cases of desertion and Siberian exile.[31] Ironically, although ecclesiastical courts refused to grant women divorce even when extreme physical abuse could not be denied, the civil courts displayed far less tolerance for husbands who sold their wives' property or spent their dowry funds. Noblewomen thus discovered that crimes against their property were more likely to elicit the sympathy of the courts than violations against their persons.[32]

While the bonds of matrimony tightened in the late eighteenth and early nineteenth centuries, women's subservience to their husbands became the subject of civil law. The rules for conduct in marriage, articulated in the 1782 Statute on Public Order, instructed husbands to live with their wives in love and harmony, to protect them, forgive their shortcomings, sustain them in their infirmity and provide for their support. For their part, wives were to abide with their husbands in love, respect and obedience.[33] The emphasis on affective ties and feminine frailty in these strictures, as well as the demarcation of male and female responsibilities, betrayed the growing influence of Western domestic ideals on Russian gender conventions.[34] The impact of the

29 E. Levin, *Sex and Society in the World of the Orthodox Slavs, 900–1700* (Ithaca: Cornell University Press, 1989), pp. 114–26.

30 A. Lebedev, 'O brachnykh razvodakh po arkhivnym dokumentam Khar'kovskoi i Kurskoi dukhovnykh konsistorii', in *Chteniia v Imperatorskom obshchestve istorii i drevnostei rossiiskikh*, 2/1 (Moscow, 1887), pp. 27–9.

31 Freeze, 'Bringing Order to the Russian Family,' pp. 709–46.

32 Marrese, *A Woman's Kingdom*, pp. 86–97.

33 *PSZ*, vol. 21, no. 15.379 (08.04.1782), st. 41, otd. VIII, IX.

34 For a discussion of the impact of separate-spheres ideology on Russian gender conventions, see Marrese, *A Woman's Kingdom*, pp. 171–204.

Church on civil law was also apparent in an 1819 State Council ruling,[35] which prohibited spouses from living apart.[36] While this ruling did not put an end to informal separations, it prevented women – who relied on their husbands to obtain a passport, which was necessary for residence or employment – from fleeing an abusive or unhappy marriage without the latter's collusion.

Legal specialists hotly debated whether women's economic privileges ameliorated their submission to their husbands, or if the constraint of 'unlimited obedience' effectively undermined their rights as proprietors. The statutes that drew the ire of proponents of women's property rights were contained in the 1832 Digest of Laws, the first Russian law code since the Ulozhenie of 1649. The task of legal codification had eluded eighteenth-century monarchs, despite their sporadic efforts to rationalise the law. It was only in 1830 that Nicholas I successfully appointed a commission to collect all decrees issued after the Ulozhenie, to reconcile their contradictions and produce a new legal code. Among the articles in Volume X were a series of regulations governing marriage which were clearly at variance with women's economic autonomy. Article 103 codified the obligation of spouses to live together and decreed that wives must follow their husbands in cases of resettlement or when they embarked on state service. Article 107 expanded upon the 1782 instructions to wives, stating that 'A wife shall obey her husband as the head of the family, abide with him in love, respect and unlimited obedience (*v neogranichennom poslushanii*) and render him every satisfaction and affection as the mistress of the house.' The following article added that a wife's submission to her husband's will did not free her from her obligations to her parents. The Statute on Public Order also provided the foundation for Article 106, which set forth the duties of husbands: 'A husband shall love his wife as his own body and live with her in harmony; he shall respect and protect her, forgive her shortcomings, and ease her infirmities. He shall provide his wife nourishment and support to the best of his ability.'[37] Thus, the articles of the Digest of Laws not only institutionalised feminine weakness and reinforced gender hierarchies, but 'dramatized the sharp division of sexual spheres, between the public and the private, that was underway in Europe in these years'.[38]

The articles of the Digest of Laws graphically illustrated the tension between noblewomen's proprietary power and their subservient role in the patriarchal

35 See chapter 20 of this volume for discussion of the State Council's foundation and role.
36 Wagner, *Marriage, Property, and Law*, p. 71.
37 *SZ*, tomy VIII, ch. II–XI, ch. 1, arts. 103, 106–108 (St Petersburg, 1900).
38 R. S. Wortman, *Scenarios of Power: Myth and Ceremony in Russian Monarchy*, 2 vols. (Princeton: Princeton University Press, 1995), vol. I, p. 261.

family. The publication of the new code also initiated lively debate over women's ability to realise their economic prerogatives. The historian Nikolai Karamzin maintained that foreign influence had inspired the new emphasis on women's subjugation in Russian law, and accused the statesman Mikhail Speranskii of imitating the Napoleonic Code when he introduced the provision on wives' obedience in the Digest of Laws.[39] Writing in the second half of the nineteenth century, the scholar N. V. Reingardt declared that since the authority of husbands over wives was unlimited, women's economic independence was 'only a fiction'.[40] Similarly, K. D. Kavelin believed that the article mandating feminine obedience was not a mere recommendation but carried the force of law.[41]

By contrast, in his influential survey M. F. Vladimirskii-Budanov argued that eighteenth-century Russian law was noteworthy precisely for the absence of statutes concerning the relation of husband to wife, which belonged to the realm of religious ideology. He remarked that the 1782 Statute on Public Order was the first ruling to prescribe feminine obedience in civil law; furthermore, it was only in 1830 that the compilers of the Digest of Laws specified that women's obedience to their husbands must be unlimited. If this provision were implemented, he concluded, it would impinge not only upon women's financial autonomy but also on the prerogative of wives to file suit against their husbands. At no time, however, had Russian law restricted women's rights in this regard. In fact, Vladimirskii-Budanov observed, the 'recognition of equal rights for men and women' was 'the distinguishing feature of Russian law'.[42]

The glaring discrepancy between married women's personal and property rights in Russian law failed to recede as the imperial era drew to a close. Members of a commission for a new codification of Russian law in the 1880s discussed the troubling contradictions in women's legal status at length, and the majority spoke in favour of limiting the authority of husbands over their wives. According to one participant, marriage in Russia was still governed by the oppressive principles laid out in the *Domostroi* in the sixteenth century, which precluded married women's active control over their property. Another member of the commission maintained that although property law

39 V. I. Sinaiskii, *Lichnoe i imushchestvennoe polozhenie zamuzhnei zhenshchiny v grazhdanskom prave* (Iurev, 1910), pp. 116–17, 124, 158, 162, 185–7; G. A. Tishkin, *Zhenskii vopros v Rossii 50–60-e gody XIX v.* (Leningrad, 1984), p. 29.

40 N. V. Reingardt, *O lichnykh i imushchestvennykh pravakh zhenshchin po russkomu zakonu* (Kazan: Tip. gubernskogo pravlenia, 1885), pp. 7, 11–12.

41 K. D. Kavelin, *Sobranie sochinenii*, 4 vols. (St Petersburg, 1900), vol. IV, p. 1063.

42 M. F. Vladimirskii-Budanov, *Obzor istorii russkogo prava*, 6th edn (St Petersburg, 1909), pp. 445–6, 374.

guaranteed women independent ownership of their fortunes, when disputes between spouses arose, it was not uncommon for legal authorities to distort the law and declare that husbands were the custodians of their wives' dowry during marriage.[43] Despite ample archival evidence that the courts upheld the property rights of women across the social spectrum,[44] the prevailing view among legal scholars and officials was that married women stood little chance of administering their assets unless their husbands permitted them to do so.

Gender in criminal law

Criminal law, as well as the law of property, made few concessions to female weakness in the eighteenth century. Indeed, in cases of adultery or spousal murder, the law displayed far less leniency for women than for men.[45] Over the course of the nineteenth century, however, as Russian legal reformers became increasingly familiar with Western European law, notions of sexual difference intensified. The progressive legal order that evolved after 1861 emphasised female dependence and associated women with the domestic sphere to an extent never before witnessed in Russian law. As Laura Engelstein argues, although women could be tried in court and were subject to the rule of law, as late as 1903 they 'remained the objects of . . . custodial solicitude . . . Like children and the mentally incompetent, women continued to be marked by special disabilities in relation to the law.'[46]

Throughout the eighteenth and early nineteenth centuries, legal authorities made virtually no distinctions between women and men, meting out similar punishments regardless of sex. Prompted by the confession of a fourteen-year-old peasant girl to the axe-murder of two children, a decree of 1742 set the age of criminal accountability at seventeen years for offenders of both sexes, making them liable to exile, corporal punishment, and the death penalty.[47] Women were flogged in public and subject to torture under interrogation, sometimes so severely that they died in the process.[48] Nor were noblewomen exempt from brutal treatment when they dabbled in political intrigue: Empress

43 *Zamechaniia o nedostatkakh deistvuiushchikh grazhdanskikh zakonov* (St Petersburg, 1891), no. 109.

44 Marrese, *A Woman's Kingdom*, pp. 84–97; Worobec, *Peasant Russia*, p. 64.

45 Engel, *Women in Russia, 1700–2000*, p. 13.

46 L. Engelstein, *The Keys to Happiness: Sex and the Search for Modernity in Fin-de-Siècle Russia* (Ithaca: Cornell University Press, 1992), pp. 71–2.

47 *PSZ*, vol. 11, no. 8.601 (23.08.1742). Children under seventeen years of age could be whipped in public and sent to a monastery for fifteen years of hard labour.

48 E. Anisimov, *Dyba i knut: Politicheskii sysk i russkoe obshchestvo v XVIII veke* (Moscow: Novoe literaturnoe obozrenie, 1999), pp. 399, 405, 409, 411.

Elizabeth ordered Countess Natalia Lopukhina to have her tongue cut out and then exiled to Siberia when she indulged in subversive gossip.[49] Peter the Great took the step of exempting pregnant women from torture until giving birth – for the sake of the child, however, rather than the accused. The sole advantage female convicts enjoyed after 1754 was freedom from being branded and having their nostrils slit when transported to hard labour. Empress Elizabeth and the Senate did not revise the law on grounds of female weakness, however, but because they believed that women were less likely to flee exile than men.[50]

By the second quarter of the nineteenth century, in keeping with the European 'discovery of the sexes',[51] legal authorities demonstrated new concern with sexual difference in the context of criminal law. The growing significance of motherhood in official and public discourse prompted officials to spare pregnant women and nursing mothers from corporal punishment until their children could be weaned. In the 1830s, the Senate decreed that children should not be separated from exiled mothers. Special arrangements were to be made for mothers during transport to exile or who were in prison.[52] For their part, contemporaries greeted these innovations with approbation, singling out for praise provisions that made allowances for the 'sensitivity' of the female sex.[53]

Well into the nineteenth century, exemption from corporal punishment hinged on social rank and standing in the family, rather than gender: thus, noblewomen, along with their husbands, were freed from corporal punishment in the 1785 Charter to the Nobility; wives of merchants of the first and second guilds received similar immunity in Catherine II's Charter to the Towns.[54] The wives and widows of priests and deacons were granted exemption in 1808, seven years after their husbands received this privilege, while their children gained immunity only in 1835.[55] By the middle of the nineteenth century, however, appeals were heard in the Senate that all women should be spared corporal punishment by virtue of their weakness, both physical and mental, relative to men. These arguments portrayed women as infirm and passive, hence incapable of bearing severe floggings. Moreover, critics of corporal

49 *The Memoirs of Catherine the Great*, trans. Moura Budberg (London: Hamish Hamilton, 1955), p. 62; E. Anisimov, *Elizaveta Petrovna* (Moscow: Molodaia gvardia, 1999), p. 128.

50 Schrader, *Languages of the Lash*, pp. 125–7, 135.

51 T. Laqueur, *Making Sex: Body and Gender from the Greeks to Freud* (Cambridge, Mass.: Harvard University Press, 1990), pp. 149–92.

52 Schrader, *Languages of the Lash*, pp. 128–30.

53 I. V. Vasil'ev, 'O preimushchestvakh zhenshchin v Rossii po delam ugolovnym', *Damskii zhurnal* (1827), no. 11: 242–3.

54 *PSZ*, vol. 22, no. 16.187 (21.04.1785), otd. A, arts. 5, 6, 15; otd. Zh., art. 107; otd. Z, art. 113.

55 B. Mironov (with Ben Eklof), *A Social History of Imperial Russia, 1700–1917*, 2 vols. (Boulder: Westview Press, 2000), vol. I, p. 92.

punishment argued that women were incapable of governing their emotions and thus less accountable than men for the crimes they committed. Some authorities objected to the display of women's naked bodies being flogged in public: the sight of a woman naked and bleeding evoked sympathy in witnesses to her ordeal and was potentially subversive of the social order. According to other reformers, because women were inherently more virtuous than men, they were less likely to commit crimes in general and they suffered more than the men from the public display of their humiliation.

Ultimately, the significance of sexual difference was accentuated to a new extreme in criminal law. Women were portrayed as fragile, passionate, and even prone to insanity, yet with a highly developed sense of virtue lacking in their male counterparts.[56] Officials also reaffirmed the bond between women and the domestic sphere, arguing that the subjection of women to corporal punishment violated female modesty and subverted the familial order and pointing out that the vast majority of crimes committed by women – infanticide, homicide and prostitution – took place in the private realm.[57] Conversely, criminal law depicted men not only as capable of bearing physical suffering, but also able to govern their emotions and assume accountability for their actions.

An edict in 1863 finally pronounced all women, with the exception of female exiles, exempt from corporal punishment. Female exiles waited until 1893 for immunity from floggings, while male peasants remained subject to beatings as late as 1904.[58] Legal reformers, along with the educated public, perceived the end of corporal punishment for women as a symptom of progress, since 'respect' for the female sex was the hallmark of 'every educated society'.[59] Women's liberation from physical punishment was not, however, necessarily a mark of special favour. As Engelstein observes, 'The edict of 1863 did not mean that peasant women had been admitted to a higher status than men of their class . . . Women's exemption functioned, in fact, as a mark of the peasant male's improved standing, constituting the family as his inviolable domain and reinforcing the wife's 'private' status.'[60] The intrusion of Western European

56 Schrader, *Languages of the Lash*, pp. 157–61.

57 S. P. Frank, 'Women and Crime in Imperial Russia, 1834–1913: Representing Realities', in M. L. Arnot and C. Usborne (eds.), *Gender and Crime in Modern Europe* (London: University College London Press, 1999), p. 95. As Frank points out, however, although women represented a small percentage of accused felons, they were accused of the same range of crimes as men.

58 Engelstein, *The Keys to Happiness*, p. 74.

59 B. F. Adams, *The Politics of Punishment: Prison Reform in Russia, 1863–1917* (DeKalb: Northern Illinois University Press, 1996), p. 27.

60 Engelstein, *The Keys to Happiness*, p. 74.

legal norms and gender conventions thus laid the foundation in Russia for a social order that prescribed increasingly rigid gender roles for both sexes and intensified male domination in the family.[61]

In short, by exempting women from corporal punishment, authorities deemed them incapable of responsibility for their actions and, by implication, undermined their potential for full citizenship. Although reformers acted out of a genuine desire to protect women from abuse, they also deprived women of agency, reinforcing their subordination to their husbands and excluding them from the civic order. By contrast, a far more even-handed and inclusive approach to gender difference persisted in the law of property. During debates over the introduction of the income tax at the turn of the century, members of the State Council argued that women, as owners of property and wage earners, should be taxed along with their male counterparts. Taxation, by treating women as individuals, would serve as their 'introduction to civic life'.[62]

Conclusion

Over the course of the imperial era, Russian women's legal status continued to be distinguished far more by disabilities than privileges. In the law of property, women's standing remained secure. Lawmakers persevered in their defence of women's control of their fortunes, insisting that 'not only does the property of a wife not become the property of her husband, but he does not even acquire through marriage the right to use or manage it'. Yet gender neutrality proved an elusive goal even in property law. Early in the twentieth century, members of a commission for a new codification of the law reiterated the responsibility of men to provide for their wives, while stating that a wife 'is not obligated to seek independent earnings to support [her] husband'. Legal reformers also fell short of granting women equal inheritance rights in the revised law of succession in 1912.[63] In other respects as well, the position of women failed to improve or even deteriorated. Until 1917 women remained personally subject to male authority: the Orthodox Church resisted attempts on the part of the state to introduce more liberal divorce legislation, although growing numbers of women gained separation from their husbands through the office of the

61 For an account of changing gender relations in Western Europe, see Isabel Hull, *Sexuality, State, and Civil Society in Germany, 1700–1815* (Ithaca: Cornell University Press, 1996).

62 Y. Kotsonis, '"Face-to-Face": The State, the Individual, and the Citizen in Russian Taxation, 1863–1917', *SR* 63, 2 (2004): 231.

63 Wagner, *Marriage, Property, and Law*, pp. 207, 164, 364–71.

Imperial Chancellery for the Receipt of Petitions, which granted separate passports to women at the emperor's discretion.[64]

Most striking, however, was the trend in legal codes to highlight gender difference and to locate women firmly in the domestic sphere. Although legislators did not succeed completely in abolishing sexual asymmetry in property relations, the distinction between women and men in the law of property remained minimal. Women continued to control their fortunes independently, to litigate against kin and neighbours, and were afforded little protection on the grounds of 'feminine weakness'. At the same time, gender hierarchies in family and criminal law became increasingly pronounced. From the end of the eighteenth century, women's 'unlimited obedience' to their husbands was enshrined in written law, while women's dependence on their husbands for the right to work or travel and for sustenance was articulated in legal codes. Even the willingness of legal reformers to support marital separation was predicated on the 'presumed natural weakness of a wife', since the courts made separation contingent upon a husband's failure to fulfil his marital obligations.[65] Finally, criminal law accentuated sexual difference to the greatest degree, making concessions to female frailty, but at the same time situating women on the margins of civic life. In short, far from fostering women's equality with men, the efforts of imperial authorities to create a more progressive legal order served only to underscore women's precarious standing in the law.

64 Freeze, 'Bringing Order to the Russian Family', p. 744.
65 Wagner, *Marriage, Property, and the Law*, pp. 217–20.

17

Law, the judicial system and the legal profession

JORG BABEROWSKI

Reform

The 1864 judicial reform created Russia's first constitution. When Alexander II signed the decree for the introduction of the judicial reform in November 1864, he delivered the death-blow to the autocracy. Although the tsar did not immediately recognise these consequences, educated public opinion certainly entertained no doubts in this regard. The judicial reform limited the authority of the monarch, since it separated the judiciary from the legislative and executive institutions, and confirmed the principle of judicial independence and tenure as a matter of law. But the reform of course went even further. It broke with the estate-based system of justice, as it had been promulgated by Catharine II at the end of the eighteenth century and set forth the equality of all subjects before the law. At least *de jure*, Russia was transformed into a state under the rule of law on the European model. For nothing remained either of the secret and inquisitorial methods which had been practised by lay judges in the estate-based courts.[1] The long-familiar practices of Western Europe now came to Russia as well. No one was any longer to be punished for an action which the Criminal Code did not identify as a crime ('*nullum crimen sine lege*'), and in civil proceedings, the principle of 'where there is no plaintiff, neither shall there be a judge' thenceforth applied.

Not the least of the evils of the old system of justice was the secret and inquisitorial procedure which accorded no rights to the accused. The judges delivered

1 On the justice system before the reforms, see N. M. Kolmakov, 'Staryi sud', *Russkaia Starina* 52, 12 (1886): 511–44; V. Bochkarev, 'Doreformennyi sud', in N. V. Davydov, and N. N. Polianskii (eds.), *Sudebnaia reforma* (Moscow: Ob'edinenie, 1915), vol. I, pp. 205–41; I. A. Blinov, 'Sudebnyi stroi i sudebnye poriadki pered reformoi 1864 goda', in *Sudebnye ustavy 20 noiabria 1864 g, za piat'desiat let* (Petrograd, 1914), vol. I, pp. 3–101; J. LeDonne, 'The Judicial Reform of 1775 in Central Russia', *JfGO* 21 (1973): 29–45; J. Baberowski, *Autokratie und Justiz. Zum Verhältnis von Rückständigkeit und Rechtsstaatlichkeit im ausgehenden Zarenreich 1864–1914* (Frankfurt: Vittorio Klostermann, 1996), pp. 11–38; F. B. Kaiser, *Die Russische Justizreform von 1864. Zur Geschichte der russischen Justiz von Katharina II bis 1917* (Leiden: Brill, 1972), pp. 1–89.

their verdicts on the basis of police investigation files and in the absence of the defendant. And because the official evidentiary proceedings demanded that confessions be forced, the police could use physical and emotional pressure at their own discretion. Winning in civil proceedings depended on the ability to bribe the chambers clerks who drew up the final verdicts and presented them to the judges for their signatures. In order to remedy this evil, the reformed rules of procedure stipulated oral argumentation and public trials. What the police had determined in their inquiries had to be proven once more in open court. The burden of proof no longer lay with the defendant but with the state prosecutor, who had to publicly prove the correctness of his accusations. Thus was the criminal proceeding transformed from a dialogue between the police and the judges into a dispute between the prosecutor and the defendant. This conflict had to be decided by an impartial court, for the protection of society from crime could only succeed if the rights of the individuals who constituted society were not violated. In the Judiciary Statutes the reformers therefore not only confirmed the independence of the judges, but also introduced the participation of lawyers into criminal and civil proceedings.

In the view of the reformers, the reformed court was primarily a societal court in which not only the judges of the Crown, but also the subjects decided on the application of law. For this reason, they introduced the office of justice of the peace (*mirovoi sud'ia*) on the British model, for the trial of trivial offences. This officer was elected by the local self-government for the duration of three years. The declared belief in 'democratic' justice was demonstrated by the adoption of trial by jury as the standard procedure in the District Court, in other words the first judicial instance (*okruzhnyi sud*), and the participation of estate representatives (*soslovnye predstaviteli*) in proceedings against 'state criminals', which were conducted in the Judicial Chambers (*sudebnaia palata*). Verdicts of the justices of the peace and the district jury courts were final, for the voice of the people was to have the last word in judgement. Such verdicts could only be contested by way of a complaint to the Cassation Department of the Senate. The Senate then ruled not on the essence of the matter at issue, but only examined the verdicts of the first instance for procedural errors. If the senators found such errors, they referred the civil or criminal case back to the court of first instance.

The symbolic meaning of these innovations could hardly have been greater, for when had there ever before been an attempt in Russia not only to protect subjects from the arbitrariness of the authorities, but also to let them decide on their own destiny? Unlike in some European states, the principle of the separation of powers did not regulate only the relationship between the judiciary and the administration. It was even established within the judiciary itself: judges were freed from the influence of the minister of justice, and lawyers were given a self-administration of their own, independent of the courts.

With the judicial reforms, the functions of the prosecuting attorney's office, the 'eyes and ears of the Tsar', also changed. As officials of the Ministry of Justice, the public prosecutors (*prokurory*) lost their directive authority over judges and attorneys but received control over the preliminary proceedings of the police. The law nevertheless did not restrict the activity of the public prosecutors to the presentation of the charges. It also assigned to them the legal supervision over the administration; the Ministry of Justice thus grew into the role of a supervisory authority which monitored the compliance of the ministries with the laws of the empire. At least *de jure*, the autocracy had gone out of existence.[2] Contemporaries, too, now understood that the court statutes of 1864 were more than an attempt to replace the system of estate-based justice by modern methods of jurisprudence. The culture within which rulers and subjects operated was shaken. No one saw this more clearly than the liberal jurist Vladimir Nabokov, when in 1914 he recalled the beginnings of the judicial reform. Nowhere in Europe, he wrote, had the discussion about the legal system kindled such passions as in Russia. While some had idolised the legislation, others had abhorred it.[3] Admittedly such passions could only be ignited because supporters and opponents of the judicial reform alike held an instrumental attitude towards the law. For them, the law was primarily an instrument of social and cultural change. What issued from the courts was, in their view, not only justice, but also the 'spirit of the people'. And since the omnipotence of the tsar had not formally been limited, the courts assumed the function of substitute parliaments, in which liberals and conservatives debated Russia's political future.[4]

However, the reformed judicial system was not only a political anomaly; it was a stillbirth, because it expressed neither the executive needs of the

2 For the text of the judiciary statutes (*sudebnye ustavy*), see B. V. Vilenskii (ed.), *Sudebnaia reforma. Rossiiskoe zakonodatel'stvo X–XX vekov* (Moscow: Iuridicheskaia literatura, 1991), vol. IX. For the results of the judicial reform, see Baberowski, *Autokratie*, pp. 61–93; I. Ia. Foinitskii, *Kurs ugolovnogo sudoproizvodstva* (St Petersburg: Al'fa, 1996; orig. St Petersburg 1910), vol. I, pp. 59–44; F. Gredinger, 'Prokurorskii nadzor za piat'desiat let, istekshikh so vremeni ego preobrazovaniia po Sudebnym Ustavam Imperatora Aleksandra II', in *Sudebnye ustavy*, vol. II, pp. 197–249; S. M. Kazantsev, *Istoriia tsarskoi prokuratury* (St Petersburg: Izd. SPbu, 1993).

3 V. Nabokov, 'Raboty po sostavleniiu sudebnykh organov', in Davydov and Polianskii, *Sudebnaia reforma*, pp. 344–5.

4 Perceptive contemporaries already observed this: B. Kistiakovskii, 'V zashchitu prava', in *Vekhi. Sbornik statei o russkoi intelligentsii* (Moscow: Sablin, 1909), pp. 125–55.

administration nor the feeling of justice of the population. Certainly, Zarudnyi and other reformers referred continually to 'Russian' traditions and the will of the autocrat, in order to convince the political elite of their plans for restructuring the judicial system. Viewed by daylight, however, the 'traditions' also drew upon the imaginations of a Europeanised elite which, while it spoke constantly of the will of the people, had no idea what that will might be. The reformed judicial system and the spirit from which it emerged were rooted in the realm of the European enlightenment, where the reformers dwelt, but their subjects did not. In this realm, faith in the power of reason held sway.[5]

The old system of justice had reflected the heterogeneity of the empire; the new one was designed to overcome it. To this end, the reformers took the latest achievements of European jurisprudence and its application techniques, in order to achieve by procedural means what reality would not deliver. 'A reasonable law can never cause evil' – so spoke the *spiritus rector* of judicial reform, Zarudnyi.[6] For the reform commission of the State Chancellery, which was appointed by the tsar in October 1861 to reorganise the judicial system, it thus remained only to design such laws as corresponded to the reasoned concepts of enlightened officials. This is also the reason why the reformers needed only a few months to complete their legislative draft. Once they had convinced the tsar of the necessity of the reform, there was no one left who could have impeded the fulfilment of their plans.[7]

The task of the judicial reform was to make universal the legal consciousness of the enlightened officials. Another way of putting it would be: the European rule of law as the reformers understood it amounted to the levelling of the empire and its cultures. It was to transform a multiethnic society based on estates into a society of European citizens, and to transform peasants into law-abiding subjects. Europe's present was to be Russia's future. And as a late-comer, the empire could learn from the mistakes of Europe.[8]

5 A. F. Koni, *Ottsy i deti sudebnoi reformy. K piatidesiatiletiiu sudebnykh ustavov* (Moscow: Sytin, 1914); R. Wortman, *The Development of a Russian Legal Consciousness* (Chicago: University of Chicago Press, 1976), pp. 197–234; W. B. Lincoln, *In the Vanguard of Reform: Russia's Enlightened Bureaucrats 1825–1861* (DeKalb: Northern Illinois University Press, 1982), pp. 102–38.

6 RGIA, Fond 1149, op. 6 (1865), d. 42, l. 19.

7 On the judicial reform, see Baberowski, *Autokratie*, pp. 39–60; Kaiser, *Die russische Justizreform*, pp. 269–406; I. V. Gessen, *Sudebnaia reforma* (St Petersburg: Izd. P. P. Gershunina, 1905), pp. 31–129; Nabokov, *'Raboty po sostavleniiu'*, pp. 303–53; I. A. Blinov, 'Khod sudebnoi reformy', in *Sudebnye ustavy*, vol. I, pp. 102–232.

8 J. Baberowski, 'Auf der Suche nach Eindeutigkeit: Kolonialismus und zivilisatorische Mission im Zarenreich und in der Sowjetunion', *JfGO* 47 (1999): 482–504; D. Yaroshevsky, 'Empire and Citizenship', in D. Brower and E. Lazzerini (eds.), *Russia's Orient: Imperial Borderlands and Peoples, 1700–1917* (Bloomington: Indiana University Press, 1997), pp. 58–79.

In matters of law, in its institutions and in symbolic remarks, the tsarist elites represented themselves as conquerors arriving from afar and forcing a strange culture of discourse upon the people. However, the striving for homogeneity under the law was to remain an unfulfilled ideal. Justice which does not arise by consensus can be imposed, but it cannot be permanently installed. Russian law was imported from abroad, with no consideration taken for home-grown traditions. Its concepts addressed judges and officials, but not the population, for whom the law was either unattainable or impossible to understand. What the reformers considered modern was, in the experience of the population, a negation of their habits. It was deadly. To persist, under these circumstances, in maintaining the validity of standards which could not be fulfilled meant to undermine respect for the law.[9]

The judicial reform reinforced the legal dualism which separated the elites from their subjects, rather than overcoming it, as the programme of the reformers had intended. Why? Because it was unable to produce any uniform system of laws. For the ordering function of law consists in imparting knowledge of what one can expect of others and of oneself, and which expectations will win societal support and which will not. As Niklas Luhmann has put it, uncertainty of expectation is much more unbearable than the experience of surprises.[10] Wherever the state's writ runs, its standards must be unconditionally accessible and enforceable; the legal claims of the state and the expectations of justice on the part of the population must converge, for justice to prevail. If the law is no longer respected or implemented, it will be replaced by immediate forms of confidence confirmation. And so it was everywhere in the empire, wherever varying possibilities of providing meaning for one's life did not come into touch with one another, wherever the state's law and its system of justice either were not articulated or else were rejected. In short, the judicial reform met the expectations of the urban upper strata but had nothing to say to the lower classes of the empire.

The reformed judicial system and the peasants

The creators of the judicial reform believed in the power of institutions. There was no doubt that good institutions would develop the appreciation of law

9 C. Schmidt, *Sozialkontrolle in Moskau. Justiz, Kriminalität und Leibeigenschaft 1649–1785* (Stuttgart: Steiner Verlag, 1996), pp. 394–406; R. Wortman, *Scenarios of Power: Myth and Ceremony in Russian Monarchy*, vol. I: *From Peter the Great to Nicholas I* (Princeton: Princeton University Press, 1995), pp. 42–83.

10 N. Luhmann, *Das Recht der Gesellschaft* (Frankfurt: Suhrkamp, 1995), pp. 131–2, 151.

and order in the people. No institution embodied the hopes of the reformers as thoroughly as did trial by jury (*sud prisiazhnykh*). The jury court was, they believed, a characteristic of 'civilised nations', an 'ornament' (*ukrashenie*) of the court system. It was the 'palladium of the personal liberty and political independence of the people', as the legal scholar Ivan Foinitskii formulated it in his textbook on the law of criminal proceedings published in 1910.[11] The Russian reformers too had devoted themselves to this ideal of political liberalism. The jury court was, they believed, a vehicle for the political mobilisation of the subjects. Wherever citizens sat in judgement over their peers, they set limits to the capriciousness of the absolutist state. Jury courts and democracy were synonymous. In Russia, however, the jury court was primarily an instrument for educating and civilising the peasants. The reformers dreamt of overcoming the cultural dualism which characterised the system of serfdom. Now, former serfs should not only share the jury box with their former lords, they were to be allowed to sit in judgement over them in court as well. 'All were to serve a common cause, both the poor and the rich': thus Senator Berendts recalled the first steps of the new courts. Anatolii Koni, Russia's most well-known jurist, saw the jury court as a place where the upper strata would not only come into contact with the peasants, that 'mysterious unknown', but where the peasants too would learn to respect the rights of their fellow men and the laws of the state.[12] This was primarily of importance because the government had left the handling of trivial civil and criminal cases in the hands of rural village justice. The reformers hoped that the juryman would carry enlightened justice even to the village, and so contribute to the disappearance of legal dualism from Russian reality. In short: the ideal of the jury court, like that of the conscript army, was to turn peasants into citizens.

At first, the expectations of the reformers seemed to be fulfilled in the large towns, not least perhaps because the urban population actually did assemble in the jury boxes. However, beyond the major cities, the peasants remained among their peers, because the educated and those of means declined civic duties. For being called to jury duty meant being present in court until the end of the proceeding, which might drag on for as long as two weeks. However, by

11 Foinitskii, *Kurs*, vol. I, p. 359; J. Baberowski, 'Europa in Russland: Justizreformen im ausgehenden Zarenreich am Beispiel der Geschworenengerichte 1864–1914', in D. Beyrau and M. Stolleis (eds.), *Reformen im Russland des 19. und 20. Jahrhunderts. Westliche Modelle und russische Erfahrungen* (Frankfurt: Vittorio Klostermann, 1996), pp. 151–74.

12 A. F. Koni, *Za poslednye gody* (St Petersburg: Suvorin, 1898), p. 337; E. N. Berendts, 'Vliianie sudebnoi reforme 1864 g. na gosudarstvennyi i obshchestvennyi byt' Rossii', in *Sudebnye ustavy*, vol. II, pp. 728–30; I. G. Shcheglovitov, 'Novyia popytki izmenit' postanovku prisiazhnago suda v zapadnoi Evrope', in *Sudebnye ustavy*, vol. II, p. 162.

holding its sessions in remote provincial towns, in dilapidated buildings with unbearable hygienic conditions, the court placed an unreasonable imposition on members of the higher strata, which they tried to escape at all costs. Such shirking of duty was admittedly only possible because the autonomous local administration did not prevent it. On the contrary: the *zemstvo* (local elected assembly) commissions responsible for drawing up the jury registers released many privileged persons from the rosters, while others were not entered on them in the first place. The zemstvo usually left the preparation of the lists to the clerks of the marshals of the nobility. These did their best to 'free, as far as possible, the most highly developed and most educated persons from the practice of jury duty', as Minister of Justice Dmitrii Nabokov reported indignantly to the State Council in 1884.[13] Thus it came about that numerous mentally ill people, 'dead souls', blind men, deaf-mutes and foreigners appeared in the juror lists in the District of St Petersburg at the end of the 1870s. In one district of Tver, the autonomous local administration did not even shrink from entering persons onto the lists who had already died in 1858, eight years before the opening of the first courts. And because the privileged classes turned a deaf ear to the call of the courts, the peasants were forced to shoulder the entire burden of this civic duty. In the rural regions, the jury courts became peasant assemblies, with 85 per cent of the jurors illiterate. To hope for an 'enlightening effect' of jurisprudence was in effect to trust in the peasants to 'civilise' themselves in the courts.[14]

Yet to be called to jury duty was to be pressed into corvée service – or so at any rate it seemed to the peasants, who were unable to escape the civic duty which the reformers demanded of them. Although the district courts 'travelled' from one district town to another to reduce the sizes of the areas covered, this was cold comfort for the peasants, who still had to trudge as much as 50 kilometres, or even more, to reach the town where the court was located. There, their real problems started, for the impoverished peasants could usually pay neither for their accommodation nor for their food. In some places, they would take jobs as woodcutters, construction workers or gardeners during court session recesses, they would beg in the streets for alms, and if the judges did not provide them with accommodations, sleep in the open. Often judges were forced to release emaciated jurors

13 RGIA, Fond 1149, op. 10 (1884), d. 58, l. 10; S. S. Khrulev, 'O sposobe i poriadke sostavleniia spiskov prisiazhnykh zasedatelei', *Iuridicheskii vestnik* 16, 5/6 (1884): 212.

14 RGIA, Fond 1405, op. 73, delo 3655b, l. 15, d. 3656a, ll. 23, 189; A. F. Koni, 'Prisiazhnye zasedateli', in A. F. Koni, *Sobranie sochinenii* (Moscow: Iuridicheskaia literatura, 1966), vol. I, p. 334.

from their duties, especially if the sessions of the court coincided with harvest time.[15]

But it was not only the poverty of the peasants which was a heavy burden on the jury courts. Different worlds met in court – that of the jury and that of the jurists. Public prosecutors, lawyers and judges spoke a language which the rural jury did not understand. They understood nothing, and yet were to decide everything: not only the question of whether the defendant had committed the deed, but also whether he was to be found guilty as charged. The public prosecutor of the Kherson District Court complained about this as early as 1869, immediately after the introduction of the reformed judicial system in that province. The jurors, he wrote, were not only incapable of judging the evidence, they could not even understand 'what was going on in their presence before the court'.[16] As a result, rural juries acquitted defendants if they were unsure whether they had understood the facts correctly, or if they had fallen asleep in the courtroom from exhaustion. And where they had to share the jury box with members of the privileged classes, they usually did what these asked of them. At the Moscow District Court, a professor regularly forced the rural jurors with whom he sat in the jury box to find the defendants guilty; otherwise, he threatened the peasants, the court would inflict 'terrible punishments' on them. The rural jurors stated that they had 'been afraid of the uniformed jurists and of the gentlemen' who had sat in the jury box with them. They had, a municipal juror recalled, viewed the call of the court not as a service of honour, but as forced recruitment.[17]

Wherever the peasants composed the entire jury, rural customary law prevailed. From the jury boxes of the tsarist courts, the rural jurors waged a legal battle against the law of the state. They not only rejected the written laws and thus paralysed the execution of jurisprudence, but also raised customary law to the level of the standard of justice. The state laws, to them, expressed an understanding of conflict resolution of a strange world to which they did not want to submit. The law of the peasants was personalised, not abstract; it referred to the morals, not to the deeds, of the perpetrator. The social status of a perpetrator, his past and its way of life often were of greater importance

15 N. Timofeev, *Sud prisiazhnykh v Rossii* (Moscow, 1881), pp. 134–5, 152–5; N. I. Astrov, *Vospominaniia* (Paris: Panin, 1940), pp. 211–12; S. P. Mokrinskii, 'Sud prisiazhnykh', in *Sudebnye ustavy*, vol. II, p. 136; V. R. Zavadskii, 'V zale zasedanii s prisiazhnymi zasedateliami. Iz otchetov revizora', *ZMI* 2, 3 (1896): 114.

16 *Svod zamechanii o priminenii na praktike sudebnykh ustavov* (1869–70), pp. 22–3.

17 Timofeev, *Sud prisiazhnykh*, pp. 86, 301–8; N. Tsukhanov, 'O nedostatkakh nashego suda prisiazhnykh', *ZGUP* 11, 2 (1882): 94, 99–100; Zavadskii, 'V zale', 120–1, 125–7; V. F. Deitrikh, 'O sude prisiazhnykh', *ZMI* 1, 6 (1895): 3–4, 7; Mokrinskii, 'Sud prisiazhnykh', p. 148.

to the peasants than the crime itself. In judging an offence, they distinguished between sins, for which only God's punishment would apply, and crimes. Thus the takeover of manor land which was not cultivated by its owners was a sin; theft of peasant property however, was a crime. Where state law punished such sins, it met with disapproval in the villages. Peasants and officials perceived different crimes; hence they also had different concepts of law. It was also important in the village to mete out punishment in such a manner that victims and perpetrators could continue to live together. Rural common law was therefore oriented towards compensation, whereas the state required punishment. The village communities usually did not even approve of state sanctions if they were convinced that a criminal offence required punishment. They hid the criminal offences from the state's investigating magistrates whenever possible and administered punishment on their own, informally, by beatings or other forms of humiliation. Ultimately, the reintegration of the perpetrator was always the ultimate goal, for who in the community ultimately really had an interest in throwing indispensable workers into prison? The peasants only turned to extreme measures when criminals threatened their existence – if robbers, arsonists or horse thieves attacked their villages and took their personal belongings. In some areas, such as in Siberia, gangs of runaway prisoners terrorised the population without the police authorities' being able to put a stop to them. And because the authorities could not control crime, and the regular justice system punished robbery and theft with relatively mild sentences, the peasants turned to lynch-law for robbers and horse thieves. If the local state authorities learned of people thus taking the law into their own hands, they would have the ringleaders arrested and brought to trial. Obviously, this destroyed any respect for state law, which was thus proven to be a blunt sword against robbers and professional criminals, but an uncompromisingly tough weapon against the peasants' informal justice.[18]

That, too was the case of violent village crime, which in the perception of educated public opinion gained in intensity after the end of the nineteenth century, because it became visible to the elites with the immigration of peasants to the large cities. The seasonal workers from the villages were crowded together in the small spaces of the workers' barracks, factories and bars, which

18 S. P. Frank, *Crime, Cultural Conflict, and Justice in Rural Russia, 1856–1914* (Berkeley: University of California Press, 1999), pp. 115–44, 243–75; C. Frierson, 'Crime and Punishment in the Russian Village: Rural Concepts of Criminality at the End of the Nineteenth Century', *SR* 46 (1987): 55–69; C. D. Worobec, 'Horse Thieves and Peasant Justice in Post-Emancipation Russia', *JSH* 21 (1987): 281–93; P. Czap, 'Peasant Class Courts and Peasant Customary Justice in Russia, 1861–1912', *JSH* 1, 2 (1967): 149–78; V. V. Tenishev, *Pravosudie v russkom krest'ianskom bytu* (Briansk, 1907), pp. 47–54.

became the scenes of a kind of violent crime which was unknown to the educated citydwellers: ritualised mass fights, brawls between drunken peasants, rape and manslaughter – all that was being brought in from the village to the city. Where there were no hospitals, doctors, police or civil servants, the village and the urban workers' housing estates were left to their own devices. Violence became a cultural resource available to all. Moreover, belief in witches and magicians, miracles and conspiracies also survived in this environment. How else could murderous deeds have been justified by the claim that the victim was a witch or a magician, if the peasants had not been convinced that supernatural forces ruled their lives? In short, the violent exorcism of devils from human bodies, the killing of horse thieves, robbers and witches, the theft of property and the everyday practice of physical violence was, in the view of the peasants, not criminal, at least as long as such acts could be fitted into their view of the world.[19] And it was the jury courts which lent expression to this situation of legal turmoil which separated the elites and the people from one another.

The jury courts did not overcome the traditional legal dualism; they proclaimed it. The peasants in any event had no concept of the enlightened legal ideas of the judicial officers, and their decisions as jury-members of the state courts were no different than they would have been at a village assembly. Thus, while sectarians, blasphemers or robbers and thieves who had stolen peasant property could hope for no mercy from such juries, killers, rapists, hooligans and those accused by the authorities of having cut wood in the forests of the nobility or resisted the orders of state authorities were acquitted in a large numbers, sometimes even after they had confessed their guilt. In no other country did juries acquit more frequently than in Russia. In 1883, 45.5 per cent of all defendants brought before jury courts in the tsarist empire were acquitted; in the juridical districts of Odessa and Kherson, the figure for that year was 55 per cent.[20] And since the defendant's fate depended on the venue and social composition of the jury, the capriciousness which had been believed to have been overcome returned to the justice system. Jury verdicts were final, no appeal was possible. They could only be contested through a cassation

19 A. A. Levenstim, *Sueverie i ugolovnoe pravo* (St Petersburg, 1899), pp. 36–7; E. I. Iakushkin, 'Zametki o vliianii religioznykh verovanii i predrassudkov na narodnye iuridicheskie obychai i poniatiia', *Etnograficheskoe obozrenie* (1891), no. 2: 1–19.

20 RGIA, Fond 1405, op. 82, d. 372, l. 70; N. S. Kapustin, *Statistika suda prisiazhnykh. Sbornik pravovedeniia i obshchestvennykh znanii* (St Petersburg, 1894), vol. III, p. 250; A. K. Fon-Rezon, 'O nashem sude prisiazhnykh', *Russkii Vestnik* 182, 3 (1886): 58; E. N. Tarnovskii, 'Otnoshenie chisla opravdannykh k chislu podsudimykh v evropeiskoi Rossii za 1889–1893 gg. Sravnitel'no-statisticheskii ocherk', *ZMI* 3, 9 (1897): 172.

complaint at the Criminal Cassation Department of the Senate, if the public prosecutor or the attorney claimed that procedural errors had occurred.[21]

This popular justice contradicted the elites' concept of justice. The reformers who dreamt of a self-civilising process of the peasantry in the jury box could not ignore this fact. 'Instead of a state court with participation by representatives of the people, we have got a people's court with participation by representatives of the state.' Thus the public prosecutor of the St Petersburg Judicial Chamber, V. F. Deitrikh, described the dilemma of the Russian judicial reform.[22]

Like the jury courts, the justices of the peace too were to have been an example to the peasants. Justices of the peace were officials elected by the local self-administration. As such, they served not only state law, but also the interests of the 'society' in whose name they administered justice. For the reformers, it was important that the local justice system impose mild punishments and issue verdicts in civilian and criminal proceedings which fitted in with the common law of the rural population. For this reason, the legislation also therefore assigned to the justices of the peace the authority to solve conflicts by an arbitration procedure.[23] In the cities, the justices of the peace quickly won the confidence of the population by adjudicating in a way which publicly demonstrated their indispensability. The first justices of the peace came from the ranks of the reformers and conveyed a feeling of legal fairness to the municipal population without which society cannot continue to function.[24] In the rural regions, however, the reformers failed to achieve their goal of changing the legal consciousness of the peasants through the institution of the justice of the peace. Although the number of the trials rose steadily, too, in the provinces, and although wherever urban fashions and attitudes enriched rural life the institution of local justice was no longer suspected of

21 Uchrezhdenie sudebnykh ustanovlenii, §§ 81–102; Ustav ugolovnogo sudoproizvodstva, §§ 646–915; Foinitskii, *Kurs*, vol. II, pp. 547–57; S. F. Mal'tsev, 'Kassatsiia opravdatel'nykh prigovorov', *ZMI* 5, 10 (1989): 122–41.

22 Deitrikh, 'O sude prisiazhnykh', 18.

23 M. I. Brun, 'Mirovoi sud po sudebnym ustavam Aleksandra II', in *Vybornyi mirovoi sud. Sbornik statei* (St Petersburg, 1898), pp. 1–18; S. P. Mokrinskii, 'Vybornyi mirovoi sud', in *Sudebnye ustavy*, vol. II, pp. 1–64; N. N. Polianskii, 'Mirovoi sud', in Davydov and Polianskii, *Sudebnaia reforma*, vol. II, pp. 172–291; Foinitskii, *Kurs*, vol. I, pp. 207–339; V. A. Maklakov, 'Local Justice in Russia', *RR* 2 (1913): 127–62; Baberowski, *Autokratie*, pp. 247–53; T. Pearson, 'Russian Law and Rural Justice: Activity and Problems of the Russian Justices of the Peace', *JfGO* 32 (1984): 52–71.

24 A. E. Nos', *Mirovoi sud v Moskve. Ocherki razbiratel'stva u mirovykh sudei* (Moscow: Izd. Cherkesova, 1869), vol. I; V. Volodimirov, 'Mirovoi sud v Peterburge', *ZGUP* 14, 5 (1884): 1–58; *Petrogradskii mirovoi sud za piat'desiat let 1866–1916*, 2 vols. (Petrograd, 1916); Koni, 'Novyi sud', 288–304.

being an instrument of state arrogation of power, the peasants nonetheless usually avoided the justice of the peace. As elected officials of the local self-administration, justices of the peace were considered to represent the will of the majority group in the zemstvo, and thus to serve the interests of influential landowners. However, local justice was not only at the service of influential interest groups in the province. It often remained unapproachable to the peasants, at least in the larger provinces, because its venue was generally located in the district town. The originally planned deformalisation of the proceedings, too, remained nothing more than an unredeemed promise. It could not be realised, simply because the legal constitution not only allowed appeals or cassation complaints against verdicts of the justices of the peace at the Assembly of Justices of the Peace (*s"ezd mirovykh sudei*), but also assigned to the Senate the competence of ruling on cassation complaints against verdicts of the assemblies in the last instance. In this way, the rights of the subjects were to be protected, the capriciousness of the judges restricted. But cassation presupposed that the justices of the peace observed the formal regulations and kept court records of all stages of the proceedings. Complying with the formal procedures was the only way to win such an appeal. One had to justify the complaint, in writing and with reference to the legal stipulations upon which it was based. However, the peasants were hardly ever capable of doing so. They had to call on the help of so-called 'underground lawyers' (*podpol'nye advokaty*) who formulated complaints in their names, and also substantiated them. However, the peasants only seldom gained from such services. It was on the contrary the underground lawyers who profited from the written-complaint-based system. They persuaded the peasants to make hopeless complaints and had themselves paid princely sums for their 'help'.[25]

With the separation of powers, which was thoroughly implemented even at the local level, competing state offices mushroomed in the districts and battled each other for influence. The peasants, of course, had no idea what the concept of separation of powers meant. They were sure it meant no protection of their rights, but rather a weakening of those authorities who knew how to

25 *Vysochaishe uchrezhdennaia komissiia dlia peresmotra zakonopolozhenii po sudebnoi chasti. Podgotovitel'nye materialy* (St Petersburg, 1895), vol. X, pp. 1–9, 19–25; V. K. Sluchevskii, 'Iz pervykh let zhizni sudebnykh ustavov', *ZMI* 20, 2 (1914): 181–233; P. N. Obninskii, 'Mirovoi institut. Sudebno-bytovoi ocherk', *Iuridicheskii vestnik* 20, 2 (1888): 400–15; I. P. Zakrevskii, 'O zhelatel'nykh izmeneniiakh v sudebnykh ustavakh', *ZGUP* 11, 2 (1882): 17–57; Mokrinskii, 'Vybornii mirovoi sud', pp. 20–30; Polianskii, 'Mirovoi sud', pp. 218–25; V. Fuks, *Sud i politsiia* (Moscow: Universitetskaia tipografiia, 1889), vol. II, pp. 100–3; M. V. Krasovskii, 'O nedostatkakh nyneshnago ustroistva mirovykh sudebnykh ustanovlenii', *ZGUP* 18, 4 (1888): 30–57; W. E. Pomeranz, 'Justice from Underground: The History of the Underground Advokatura', *RR* 52 (1993): 321–40.

ensure them those rights. Nobody respected a judge who might be able to deliver a verdict, but could neither arrest nor punish, and whose verdicts might be annulled by a higher authority. For the peasants, the important thing was that their complaints be accepted and decided upon at one place and by one person. That fact provided the basis for Minister of the Interior Dmitrii Tolstoi's argument, in 1887, before the State Council, to abolish the institution of justice of the peace.[26] If a peasant had something he or she wanted to get done, the peasant called on the 'powers' for help. Those 'powers' included the local police chief (*ispravnik*), the landowners and the governors, but not the justices of the peace. And even the emperor in far-off St Petersburg received petitions from all regions of the empire in which peasants requested the help of their ruler. In view of the conditions under which the villagers lived, this behaviour was rational. But that did not help the reputation of the judicial system.

Justice and empire

The administrative and judicial reforms of the 1860s years were based on the conviction that the modern state under the rule of law would remain incomplete without a generally binding system of laws. It was therefore only logical for it to spread rapidly beyond European Russia to encompass the peripheral regions. Initially, the new institutions were established only in the central Russian regions of the empire. They were introduced in 1866 in the districts of the Moscow and St Petersburg Judicial Chambers, and between 1867 and 1871 in the equivalent judicial districts of Kharkov, Tiflis, Odessa, Kazan and Saratov. The judicial reform also came to Poland in 1875, and the government opened court chambers in Kiev and Vilna between 1880 and 1883, and in the Baltic provinces in 1889. In the Asian regions of the empire the reformed courts were set up only later. Although they were already established in Transcaucasia in 1867, they did not spread to Siberia, to the steppe regions or to Turkestan until the 1890s. With the opening of a Judicial Chamber in Tashkent in 1899, the introduction of the reformed judicial system was completed in the empire.[27]

The judicial reform was an ambitious attempt to subject the empire to a uniform system of laws and thus to remove all estate-based and special religious law systems which still existed. That happened in the 1880s for the first time, when the judicial reform was introduced in right-bank Ukraine,

26 RGIA, Fond 1149, op. 11 (1889), d. 44a, l. 11.
27 Baberowski, *Autokratie*, pp. 64–5, 339–427.

Poland, Lithuania and the Baltic provinces. But the new courts, the separation of powers and the public and verbal proceedings were not only a death knell for the old estate-based judicial system, the reformed judicial system also expanded the rights of the rural population vis-à-vis the land-owning and urban elites, and broke the supremacy of the Baltic-German and Polish elites in the western areas of the empire. Along with the courts and Russian law, Russian judges and judicial officials also came to the western periphery, primarily lawyers and their assistants who settled in the larger towns in Poland and the Baltic region. And because a complaint in court now required knowledge of the Russian language and of Russian law, the services of the jurists brought in from the outside became indispensable. For the native elites, these changes brought loss of control and power which could not be compensated even if they returned as trained jurists to the judicial offices. For the new judges were in the service of the law and did not issue judgements in the name of the estate to which they belonged. Thus, the former elites were transformed into mere ethnic minorities.[28]

Jury courts were established only in the judicial district of Kiev, but the government refrained from instituting the participation of the people in the judicial system in Poland and the Baltic provinces. The introduction of the jury courts in the Western Provinces was hampered not only by the general ignorance of the Russian language, but also because it was feared that ethnic conflicts might be carried out before the jury courts.[29] The central government wanted to avoid this at all costs.

Similar problems arose in the Caucasus, where the judicial reform had already been introduced in 1867, and in Siberia and Turkestan. The courts followed the Russian settlers into the Asian parts of the empire as they emigrated to Siberia and Turkestan in large numbers at the end of the nineteenth century. But the new courts were only established in the larger towns and the junctions where the railroads brought people from distant regions together. Under these circumstances, jury courts could not be introduced even where the population could speak the administrative language, as in Siberia. Extreme distances and a low population density, and especially in Turkestan the multiethnicity

28 RGIA, Fond 1149, op. 9 (1882), d. 81, ll. 2–9; N. Reinke, 'Obshchiia sudebnyia uchrezhdeniia v tsarstve Pol'skom. Zametki', *ZGUP* 8, 11 (1882): 1–10; A. G. Gasman, 'Sudebnaia reforma v pribaltiiskikh guberniiakh', *ZMI* 20, 9 (1914): 146–69; M. Haltzel, *Der Abbau der deutschen ständischen Selbstverwaltung in den Ostseeprovinzen Russlands* (Marburg: Herder Institut, 1977).

29 *Vysochaishe uchrezhdennaia komissiia dlia peresmotra zakonopolozhenii po sudebnoi chasti. Trudy*, 9 vol. (St Petersburg, 1895–9), vol. I, pp. 1–4; RGIA, Fond 1405, op. 515, d. 199, ll. 7–11.

of the population, gave the reformers little room for action. Here justices of the peace were appointed by the minister of justice, because there was no local self-government which might have elected them, and the functions of justices of the peace and of the examining magistrate were combined. These were, of course, not the only obstacles which the justice system faced in the Asian periphery. A major one was the unwillingness of talented jurists to serve in Tashkent, Ashkhabad or the crime capital Baku, where they might expect nothing but deprivation.[30]

As in Poland and the Baltic provinces, the judicial reform forced the local elites out of their administrative functions. With the jurists from the centre, new laws and procedures came to the periphery, which were displayed in an alien language and in alien symbols. Russian law could be mediated neither linguistically nor symbolically in the Muslim regions, and, because the judges were primarily from European Russia, could only be expressed at all via interpreters. Even in Tiflis and Baku, the melting-pots of the Caucasus, judges and examining magistrates could express themselves only in Russian. Thus neither the defendants nor the judges understood what the other really wanted. This reflected not only linguistic and symbolic misunderstandings.

As the chief procurator of the Senate, Reinke, who was sent to inspect judicial institutions in Tiflis in 1910, put it, proceedings in the courts in Central Asia and in Caucasus were like 'a cultural drama'. In trials before the Caucasian courts, 'two civilisations, two world-views, which were mutually exclusive', collided.[31] For Russian law punished what was not seen as criminal in the view of the natives: the bearing of daggers and guns, or murder and manslaughter arising from a blood feud. Where nomads stole the cattle of a clan with whom they were quarrelling to force negotiations about a dispute, tsarist justice imposed prison sentences against the robbers, and in so doing prevented a reconciliation between the parties to the quarrel in a way which would have reflected their own legal traditions. It criminalised what nomads considered the law.[32]

30 RGIA, Fond 1149, op. 6 (1866), d. 101, ll. 109–12; RGIA, Fond 1149, op. 12 (1896), d. 63; 'O sudebnoi reforme v Turkestanskom krae i Stepnykh oblastiakh', *ZMI* 5, 2 (1899): 63–110; 'Sudebnaia reforma v Sibirii', *ZMI* 2, 6 (1896): 145–60.

31 RGIA, Fond 1485, op. 1, d. 2, l. 44; M. E. Gegidze, 'K voprosu o reforme ugolovnogo sudoproizvodstva v Zakavkazskom krae', *ZMI* 2, 8 (1896): 37–61; B. I. Okolovich, 'Ob usloviiakh sledstvennoi sluzhby v okruge Bakinskago suda', *ZMI* 19, 8 (1913): 147–76.

32 N. A. Dingel'shtedt, 'Musul'manskii sud i sud'i', *ZMI* 4, 6 (1898): 58–81; G. M. Tumanov, *Razboi i reforma suda na kavkaze* (St Petersburg, 1903); V. Martin, 'Barimta: Nomadic Custom, Imperial Crime', in Brower and Lazzerini, *Russia's Orient*, pp. 249–70; J. Baberowski, *Der Feind ist überall. Stalinismus im Kaukasus* (Munich: Deutsche Verlags-Anstalt, 2003), pp. 41–4.

Under these circumstances, however, there could be no rapprochement between the two legal spheres. The natives boycotted the Russian courts: by targeted false testimony, designed primarily to lead the examining magistrates astray, and by violent resistance. If they resorted to the Russian courts at all, they instrumentalised them for their own purposes without respecting their authority. In the Caucasus and also in Turkestan, there were de facto two systems of laws which were not connected with each other. At least in Turkestan and in the steppe areas, the government therefore moved away from its plan to subject the population completely to its laws. Although the law stipulated the responsibility of Russian courts in cases of murder, homicide and serious robbery, it left all other cases to the jurisdiction of the local tribal or *sharia* courts. In Transcaucasia, however, where the administration insisted on imposing its laws but could not in fact do so, the courts succeeded in completely destroying their own authority. As a result, the governors ultimately fell back on the stipulations of the Emergency Laws enacted in 1881, which permitted them to punish by administrative measures what they considered deviant behaviour. As the governor-general of the Caucasus, Dondukov-Korsakov, wrote in 1890, the 'wildness of the customs' left the authorities no choice but to use military justice against the natives.[33] To sum up, the idea of the European rule of law was led *ad absurdum* under the conditions of the multiethnic empire, because it set the indigenous elites against the Russian administration without ensuring any homogenisation or 'civilisation' of legal views. There was no mediation of ruling power.

The reform of the reform

From its inception, the reformed judicial system was showered with harsh criticism. The conservative *Moskovskie vedomosti* and its editor-in-chief Mikhail Katkov described the ministers of justice as 'prime ministers of the judicial republic'. Conservative writers slandered the jury courts as 'mob justice', some even demanded the restoration of the obsolete estate-based system of justice. But it was not only conservative ideologues who criticised the justice system. At the beginning of the 1880s, the conclusion that the reform would not survive without in turn being reformed grew, even among jurists. These included, prominently, the chief procurator of the Holy Synod and mentor of Alexander III, Pobedonostsev, who had once been on the side of the liberal

33 RGIA, Fond 932, op. 1, d. 319, l. 43; Baberowski, *Der Feind*, pp. 42–4.

judicial reformers.[34] During the late 1880s, this led ministers of justice to propose several amendments to the law, designed primarily to cure the disfunctionality of the jury courts. They reformed the jury roster system, subordinating it to the control of the public prosecutors, and forbade the authorities to enter illiterates on to the rosters. Still, the abolition of lay participation in court judgements, which conservative critics had recommended with reference to the German and Italian experience, was not carried out. The jury courts lasted until the end of Imperial Russia, although none of the expectations which the reformers had once placed in them were fulfilled, even after the turn of the century. Not even the independence of the judiciary and of the bar, or the public and verbal nature of the proceedings, were ever really called into question. This was demonstrated in the disciplinary proceedings for judges introduced in 1885 by Minister of Justice Dmitrii Nabokov, which confirmed the liberal principle of judicial independence.[35]

The conservatives in the government were able to score only one victory, when they succeeded in 1889 with the support of the emperor in abolishing the justices of the peace and substituting for them so-called land captains (*zemskie nachal'niki*), against the resistance of the ministry of justice and its jurists. The land captains were usually recruited from the same circles as the justices of the peace had been, but combined administrative and judicative functions in one hand. Although the land captains deformalised and simplified procedures, they had a bad reputation among liberal jurists, who considered them uncontrollable despots who made no contribution to the 'civilisation' of the peasants but rather removed them from the blessings of justice under the rule of law instead of bringing them closer to it. In 1912 the government not only returned to justice-of-the-peace

34 I. V. Gessen, *Advokatura, obshchestvo i gosudarstvo 1864–1914. Istoriia russkoi advokatury* (Moscow, 1914), vol. I, p. 276; V. P. Meshcherskii, *Moi vospominaniia* (St Petersburg, 1912), vol. III, pp. 253–6; A. E. Nolde, 'Otnosheniia mezhdu sudebnoi i administrativnoi vlastiami i sud'ba osnovnykh nachal' sudebnykh ustavov v pozdneishem zakonodatel'stve', in *Sudebnye ustavy*, vol. II, pp. 613–16; *K. P. Pobedonostsev i ego korrespondenty. Pis'ma i zapiski* (Moscow: Gosizdat, 1923), vol. I, pp. 508–15; H. Whelan, *Alexander III and the State Council: Bureaucracy and Counter-reform in Late Imperial Russia* (New Brunswick: Rutgers University Press, 1982), pp. 100–1.

35 RGIA, Fond 1149, op. 11 (1889), d. 44a; Whelan, *Alexander III*, pp. 178–82; T. Pearson, *Russian Officialdom in Crisis. Autocracy and Local Self-Government, 1861–1900* (Cambridge: Cambridge University Press, 1989), pp. 164–209; G. Yaney, *The Urge to Mobilize. Agrarian Reform in Russia, 1861–1930* (Urbana: University of Illinois Press, 1982), pp. 68–96; V. M. Gessen, 'Genezis instituta zemskikh nachal'nikov', *Pravo* (1903), no. 52: 2941–54; A. Parenago, 'Krest'ianskii sud i sudebno-administrativnye uchrezhdeniia', in Davydov and Polianskii, *Sudebnaia reforma*, vol. II, pp. 81–171; V. I. Kriukovskii, 'Sushchestvennyia cherty preobrazovaniia mestnogo suda po zakonu 15 iiuniia 1912 goda', *ZMI* 20, 5 (1914): 117–42.

adjudication, it also combined it with the *volost* system of peasant justice in one procedural instance.[36]

The fact that the core of the reformed judicial system remained unchanged, although Alexander III detested the 'jurist blatherers' like 'castor oil', was to no small extent due to the growing influence of jurists in the higher echelons of the administration. For during the 1870s, jurists had conquered the key positions of power in the tsarist bureaucracy: they occupied the most important positions in the State Council and in the State Chancellery, and had moved into the Ministries of the Interior and Finance. There were even jurists in the secret police, the *okhrana*, and after the 1880s, former public prosecutors occupied the leading positions in the St Petersburg police department. Jurists monopolised the drafting and interpretation of the laws, for they had abilities which made them irreplaceable. This is also the reason that the ministers of justice gradually grew into the role of supervisors who oversaw the legality of the administration. All ministers of justice, even the conservative Ivan Shcheglovitov (1906–15), considered themselves proponents of the concepts of an independent judiciary and of the rule of law. They therefore resisted any proposals for implementing changes which would have called their own indispensability into question. Even such an uncompromising advocate of autocracy as Alexander III ultimately had to submit to the practical constraints which the bureaucracy imposed on him.[37] This was shown in the inability of the monarch to find a minister of justice who would submit to his will. The ministers of justice Dmitrii Nabokov (1879–85) and Nikolai Manasein (1885–94) were dismissed because they would not bow to Alexander's desire to rein in the justice system. Even with the conservative minister Nikolai Murav'ev, who remained in office until 1905, the monarchy failed to find happiness. In 1894 Alexander III directed him to form a commission which would place the system of justice on a new basis and homogenise it, but would above all abolish the independence of the judiciary. Murav'ev failed, because he neither fulfilled the desire of the conservatives to end the independence of the judges and abolish the jury courts, nor that of the liberals to expand the competence of the independent judiciary. No one, however, suffered a greater defeat than

36 Baberowski, *Autokratie*, pp. 206–34, 722–9.

37 A. A. Polovtsov, *Dnevnik (1883–1892)*, 2 vols. (Moscow: Nauka, 1966), vol. I, pp. 347–8, vol. II, p. 336; Koni, *Ottsy i deti*, pp. 156–72; D. Lieven, *Russia's Rulers under the Old Regime* (New Haven: Yale University Press, 1989), pp. 177–85; J. Daly, *Autocracy under Siege: Security Police and Opposition in Russia 1866–1905* (DeKalb: Northern Illinois University Press, 1998), p. 29; A. G. Zviagintsev and Ju. G. Orlov, *V epokhu potriasenii i reform. Rossiiskie prokurory 1906–1907* (Moscow: Rosspen, 1996), pp. 7–96.

the monarchs themselves, who ultimately had to capitulate to the power of the jurists.[38]

The justice system as a substitute constitution

The judicial reform embodied the impetuousness and the fresh-start atmosphere of the 1860s. It was the symbol of the attempt to change radically and to Europeanise the legal system. The rule of law was a bill of exchange on a liberal constitution and a forerunner of modern democracy – that was the view of the reformers and their disciples inside and outside the state bureaucracy. Judges and lawyers had embarked on a crusade for the fulfilment of their ideals of a state under the rule of law. 'It was an activity which seized the soul, a calling, a mission', wrote Koni in his recollections of those years. The Judicial Statutes were therefore his 'first love'. During the 1860s and 1870s, court proceedings were celebrated like 'sacred rituals', for here, not only was justice delivered, but the political maturity of the subjects was demonstrated. In these trials, judges and public prosecutors presented themselves to society as incorruptible guardians and advocates of the law, who brought light to the benighted provinces. To the educated public, they no longer appeared as representatives of the regime, but as advocates of society. Those with reputations as liberal critics of autocracy chose the judge's profession, for to be a judge meant no longer to have to obey the orders of the state administration. The study of law came into fashion primarily for those who recognised the political significance of the legal professions. These jurists of the 1860s were the ones who turned the courts into strongholds of liberalism. That was the real dilemma of the autocratic reforms: that with the reorganisation of the state, they at the same time brought an opposition into being.[39]

No profession had a greater share in this than did the bar. Attorneys not only enjoyed their own self-administration, the Council of Sworn Attorneys (*sovet prisiazhnykh poverennykh*) which independently and without state supervision handled all questions regarding the education and discipline of the advocates. In court, they had the privilege of free speech, to which no one else in the empire was entitled. The free, self-administered bar was an anomaly in a country

38 Baberowski, *Autokratie*, pp. 429–80.

39 Koni, A. F. 'Novyi sud', in Koni, *Sobranie sochinenii*, vol. I, p. 400; G. Dzhanshiev, *Epokha velikikh reform* (St Petersburg, 1907), pp. 428–50; M. F. Gromnitskii, 'Iz proshlago (Po lichnym vospominaniiam)', *Russkaia mysl'* (1899), no. 2: 49–71; no. 3: 68–88; no. 6: 1–33; no. 9: 210–50; no. 12: 51–68; V. S. Chevazhevskii, 'Iz vospominanii o sluzhbe po sudebnomu vedomstvu', *Russkaia starina* 167, 7 (1916): 71–80; Sluchevskii, 'Iz pervykh let', 185; Nol'de, 'Otnosheniia', 492–531.

which was formally still ruled by an autocrat. No one saw this more clearly than the lawyers themselves. They were, wrote the prominent lawyer M. M. Vinaver about the bar, members of a 'sacred order', charged with fulfilling a 'sacred mission'. The first lawyers considered themselves spokesman of society and defenders of liberty. *Advocatus Miles* – 'lawyer-soldiers' – was the title of a textbook for defence counsels published in 1911, and no slogan could more clearly have epitomised the self-conception of most attorneys.[40] However, not only liberals moved into the legal profession. From the outset, it also attracted radical opponents of the tsarist order, and after the turn of the century, leftist extremists. It was surely no coincidence that such revolutionaries as Kerenskii and Lenin had started their political career as lawyers. The extremists among the attorneys tried to change the profession into an association of political struggle, and in some towns they even managed, during the revolution of 1905, to seize power in the bar associations. For the radical political defence counsellors, the courtroom was primarily a platform for the proclamation of the revolutionary world-view. Not only the defendant's rights, but also his views were defended here. Such attorneys no longer had any conception of law and its function.[41]

The uncompromising attitude of some lawyers was not due only to the political possibilities which their profession opened up for them. Jurists who came into conflict with the state had no other path open to them but to become courtroom attorneys. And no other alternatives were open, either, to the numerous Jewish jurists, because the government did not allow them into the civil service or on to the bench. Thus, the profession of trial lawyer ultimately became an asylum for unemployed Jewish jurists. Their number increased so dramatically that the government in 1889 introduced a quota system into the legal profession as well. Jewish 'candidate lawyers' (*pomoshchniki prisiazhnykh poverennykh*) could henceforth be admitted to the profession of sworn attorneys

40 N. P. Karabchevskii, *Chto glaza moi videli* (Berlin: Izd. Ol'gi D'iakovoi, 1921), vol. II, p. 15; M. M. Vinaver, *Ocherki ob advokature* (St Petersburg: Tip M. M. Stasiulevich, 1902), p. 3; L. E. Vladimirov, *Advocatus Miles. Posobie dlia ugolovnoi zashchity* (St Petersburg: Zakonovedenie, 1911); J. Baberowski, 'Rechtsanwälte in Russland, 1866–1914', in C. McClelland and S. Merl (eds.), *Professionen im modernen Europa* (Berlin: Duncker and Humblot, 1995), pp. 29–59.

41 Kistiakovskii, 'V zashchitu prava', pp. 125–55; G. B. Sliozberg, *Dela minuvshikh dnei* (Paris: Imprimerie Pascal, 1933), vol. I, pp. 203–12; N. N. Polianskii, 'Zashchita i obvinenie po delam o gosudarstvennykh prestupleniiakh', *Pravo* (1910), no. 36: 2125; Gessen, *Advokatura*, pp. 385–426; Karabchevskii, *Chto glaza moi videli*, pp. 52–3; M. L. Mandel'shtam, *1905 god v politicheskikh protsessakh. Zapiski zashchitnika* (Moscow: Izd. Vsesoiuznogo obshchestva politkatorzhan, 1931); I. Moshinskii, 'Politicheskaia zashchita v dorevoliutsionnykh sudakh', in V. V. Vilenskii (ed.), *Deviatyi val. K desiatiletiiu osvobozhdeniia iz tsarskoi katorgi i ssylki* (Moscow: 1927), pp. 44–71.

only with the consent of the minister of justice. And since the ministers gave their consent in only a few cases before 1905, most Jewish jurists remained in the status of candidates. Is it any wonder under such circumstances, that numerous Jewish candidates became spokesmen of the radical defence counsels who argued against the autocratic order in the political trials after the turn of the century? One might say that circumstances threw them into the political opposition. At the same time, these circumstances were responsible for the fact that when there was nothing to defend, lawyers turned into blatant profiteers. For lawyers who saw the law merely as an instrument of struggle had no sufficient concept of its formal significance.[42]

Although the professional standards of the bar deteriorated from the 1880s, and the political conflicts between the attorneys and the administration gained in intensity, the government undertook only moderate interventions. After 1875 the Ministry of Justice refused the authorisation of additional bar associations and assigned the disciplinary oversight of the attorneys in newly established judicial districts to the courts. But in 1904, the government moved away from this position again as well. In view of the radicalism which lawyers exhibited during the political trials during the first Russian revolution, it was undoubtedly strange for the government to impose such a constraining structure upon itself.[43]

The conflicts caused by the anomaly of an independent judiciary in an autocratic state already appeared immediately after the introduction of the new courts, when judges contested the right of police officers and governors to interfere in judicial matters and went so far as to publicly express their disdain for the power of the state. When political cases were tried, there was open dispute between judges and the administration. This happened for the first time in 1871, when in the trial of the anarchist Sergei Nechaev, the St Petersburg Judicial Chamber acquitted numerous defendants, although the police and the minister of the interior had insisted that all those accused be convicted.[44] The presiding judge of the Judicial Chamber, who had not suppressed the political speeches of the lawyers in the courtroom, remained in office, but the emperor forced the minister of justice to turn over the prosecution

42 J. Baberowski, 'Juden und Antisemiten in der russischen Rechtsanwaltschaft 1864–1917', *JfGO* 43 (1995): 493–518.

43 *Ministerstvo iustitsii za sto let 1802–1902* (St Petersburg: Senatskaia tip., 1902), pp. 133–4; Gessen, *Advokatura*, p. 229, pp. 442–7; J. Burbank, 'Discipline and Punish in the Moscow Bar Association', *RR* 54 (1995): 44–64.

44 *Nechaev i Nechaevtsy, Sbornik materialov* (Moscow and Leningrad, 1931), pp. 159–86; N. A. Troitskii, *Tsarskie sudy protiv revoliutsionnoi Rossii* (Saratov: Izd. Saratovskogo universiteta, 1976), pp. 129–32; V. D. Spasovich, *Sochineniia*, 10 vols. (St Petersburg: Knizhnyi Magazin brat'ev Rymovich, 1889–1902), vol. V, pp. 136–9, 148–54, 186.

of political crimes to the Special Tribunal of the Senate (*Osoboe Prisutstvie*) in future. The conservatives in the government hoped for more severe verdicts from it. This hope seemed justified at first. Several dozen revolutionary students who had participated in the 'Going to the People' to provoke a peasants' uprising were sentenced to long prison sentences. But even in the Senate, spectacular cases of dropping of charges and of acquittals occurred at the end of the 1870s, primarily in the so-called 'Trial of the 193', when the senators refused to comply with government demands for severe punishments. More than half of the accused students were acquitted by the senators in January 1877. The political dispute between the justice system and the administration reached its climax when the jury of the St Petersburg District Court acquitted the revolutionary Vera Zasulich, who had shot the city governor (*Gradonachal'nik*) Trepov and injured him seriously. In this case, too, Presiding Judge Koni remained in office, but the government transferred the trial venue for terrorist crimes of violence to military courts which, since they administered justice on the basis of the Military Criminal Code, could impose death sentences against terrorists. The military courts made use of this power on several occasions during the early 1880s, although the military jurists who sat on these courts obeyed the government demand for the penalty only reluctantly.[45]

In August 1881, several months after the murder of Alexander II by terrorists of the *Narodnaia Volia* (People's Will), the government issued an ordinance for the protection of state order which enabled it to declare a state of emergency and to impose administrative punishments against troublemakers in the areas where this state of emergency had been established. There were two variants of the state of emergency: 'reinforced protection' (*usilennaia okhrana*), and 'extraordinary protection' (*chrezvychainaia okhrana*). 'Reinforced protection' made it possible for the governors to issue decrees for the maintenance of public order and to keep persons who opposed these orders in custody for up to three months. In regions where the Committee of Ministers had imposed 'extraordinary protection', governors-general were appointed, who received the right to remove office-holders from their positions and to hand terrorists over to courts martial. Above all, the emergency laws made it possible for the state administration to mete out extrajudicial punishment. It gave the governors-general the right to have troublemakers expelled from the area, or

45 A. Iakimova, 'Bol'shoi protsess ili protsess 193-kh', *Katorga i ssylka* 37, 8 (1927): 7–31; N. S. Tagantsev, *Perezhitoe* (Petrograd: CTOS tip., 1919), vol. II, pp. 134–51; A. F. Koni, 'Vospominaniia o dele Very Zasulich', in Koni, *Sobranie sochinenii*, vol. II, pp. 24–252; RGIA, Fond 1405, op. 76, d. 7352, l. 1–6; N. A. Troitskii, *'Narodnaia volia' pered tsarskim sudom 1880–1894* (Saratov: Izd. Saratovskogo universiteta, 1983); Baberowski, *Autokratie*, pp. 671–722.

exiled to Siberia for up to five years. A 'Special Committee' (*osoboe soveshchanie*) of the Committee of Ministers, consisting of two representatives each of the ministries of justice and the interior, made the final decision on exile. Unlike penal offenders sentenced by civil courts, these administrative exiles were not deprived of their rights. This made it possible for them to lead a normal life at their places of exile. Thus, lawyers who had been banished to Siberia by the 'Special Committee' could continue to practise their professions in exile. To prevent this, the civil courts would have had not only to deprive them of their civil rights, but also to sentence them to more severe punishments in such cases. In this way the authorities avoided a disproportionality of punishment in political cases during states of emergency, which was provided by the Criminal Code.[46]

Originally the Emergency Laws of 1881 were to apply only for a period of three years, but they were repeatedly extended after expiry, and thus remained in force until the Revolution. They attained real significance during 1905–7, when the government declared a state of emergency in the entire empire to check terrorism and violence. Between the summer of 1906 and the beginning of 1907, Prime Minister Stolypin used the powers which the Emergency Laws gave him to have more than one thousand terrorists sentenced to death by drumhead courts martial (*voennye polevye sudy*).[47]

This, however, did not exhaust the possibilities of the state of emergency. It gave the administration the instruments it needed to assert itself against hooligans, pogrom instigators, bands of robbers and rebellious peasants. It was no coincidence that they were first used against peasants and workers in 1882 who had participated in pogroms against the Jews in the province of Ekaterinoslav. The justice system was powerless in such cases, because its task was to prove individual guilt. It could not safeguard public order. The Emergency Laws gave the administration the ability to take vigorous action quickly against troublemakers without having to impose the severe punishments in every case which the Criminal Code provided. In Asian regions

46 V. M. Gessen, *Iskliuchitel'noe polozhenie* (St Petersburg: Pravo, 1908); W. Nabokow, 'Das aussergerichtliche Strafverfahren', in J. Melnik (ed.), *Russen über Russland. Ein Sammelwerk* (Frankfurt: Rutten and Loening, 1906), pp. 297–315; A. A. Lopukhin, *Nastoiashchee i budushchee russkoi politsii* (Moscow: Tip. v. Sablina, 1907); D. Rawson, 'The Death Penalty in Late Tsarist Russia', *RH* 11 (1984): 29–58; Baberowski, *Autokratie*, pp. 702–7; Daly, *Autocracy*, pp. 33–40.

47 N. N. Polianskii, *Epopeia voenno-polevykh sudov 1906–1907 gg.* (Moscow: Izd. Vsesoiuznogo obshchestra politkatorzhan, 1934); W. C. Fuller, *Civil–Military Conflict in Late Imperial Russia 1881–1914* (Princeton: Princeton University Press, 1984); N. I. Faleev, 'Shest'mesiatsev voenno-polevoi iustitsii. Ocherk', *Byloe* (1907), no. 14: 43–81.

of the empire, where the government was waging war against robbers and rebellious tribes, they replaced the regular justice system.

An imperial decree of 12 December 1904 re-established the jurisdiction of the civil justice system in cases of political crimes. Between May 1905 and March 1906, a 'Special Commission' met in St Petersburg under the chairmanship of Count A. P. Ignat'ev to consider the fate of the Emergency Laws in constitutional Russia. It resolved in favour of the restoration of the regular procedures of criminal justice. However, it did not advocate the abolition of the Emergency Laws, stating that the state must be given the possibility of maintaining order at all times and at all costs. If 'special dangers' threatened, it must be able to repel them. To this end, the authority of the state must be provided with 'extraordinary powers', such as those with which 'Western states' were also for the most part provided.[48] The case could be made that the Emergency Laws were all that made possible the very survival of the reformed judicial system in the first place, for there is no system of order which can be applied to a state of chaos. It may seem paradoxical, but the Emergency Laws were an indication of the transformation towards the rule of law which had by then been effected in the tsarist empire. The government needed a law to suspend the existing legal order, and it mandated itself and its subordinate authorities to observe the procedural rules. It could not simply ignore the system of laws and justify itself by invoking the will of the monarch. Thus, what happened in August 1881 would have been inconceivable without the changes which the judicial reform of 1864 had introduced into Russia.

The government held fast to the principles of judicial reform and saw no reason to revise its attitude, even in 1905, when the judiciary openly took sides against the regime's power. It renewed its adherence to the principle of the separation of powers after 1905, and it also reaffirmed the independence of the bench and the bar and defended the jury courts against their conservative critics to the end. How can such an attitude be explained? The ministers and higher officials of the emperor were convinced that only a state under the rule of law by European standards was modern, even if its implications might have the effect of destroying order. On the other hand, after 1905, the debate over Russia's political future shifted from the courts to other public platforms: the parliament, the parties and the press. No one any longer needed a courtroom to proclaim his world-views. At that time, the atmosphere changed among the jurists, too. With the constitution of 1906, judges and liberal lawyers

48 RGIA, Fond 1239, op. 16, prilozhenie, d. 1, l. 627; Daly, *Autocracy*, pp. 36–40; Baberowski, *Autokratie*, pp. 767–76.

had achieved what they had argued for. They lost interest in fundamental radical changes and made their peace with the new order, which had after all protected them from the anger of the people during the revolution. The legal professions 'normalised' themselves and became a mirror of 'society'. Conservatives were now to be found both among the judges and among the attorneys who wanted nothing more to do with the liberalism of earlier years. This normalisation also improved the relationship between the judicial authorities and the government. In brief, the system of laws of the late tsarist empire met the demands of the elites and the urban public for procedures in accordance with the rule of law. Therefore, nobody ever questioned it. But this system of laws remained nothing more than an unredeemed promise until the end of the empire, because it did not know how to communicate with the 'other Russia', the lower classes of the centre and the periphery. The rule of law, local self-government and parliamentarism remained a phenomenon of the cities in the European part of the multiethnic empire. They did not strike any roots outside this civil biotope. The bureaucracy tried to dominate the country with instruments which did not correspond to the realities of Russia. All it therefore achieved was that power remained unmediated. The revolution of 1917 was a revolt of the lower classes against the programme for a modern system of order of the tsarist elites. And, as Nikolai Sukhanov recalled in his notes about the revolution, what had been built over the course of three centuries disappeared within 'three days'.[49]

49 N. Sukhanov, *Zapiski o revoliutsii* (Moscow: Izd. politicheskoi literatury, 1991), vol. I, p. 126.

18

Peasants and agriculture

DAVID MOON

Imperial Russia had an overwhelmingly peasant population and its economy was largely agricultural. The Russian Empire was not able to compete economically and militarily with the more 'developed' states of north-western Europe, North America and Japan in the last few decades of its existence. Over the preceding two or three centuries, however, Russia's autocratic state had been able successfully to exploit its peasant population and agricultural economy to generate the resources, in particular tax revenues and military conscripts, to consolidate and maintain its power at home and build a vast empire that came to dominate eastern Europe and northern Asia. Imperial Russia's peasants were, thus, at the bottom of an exploitative social order. For much of the period, moreover, between a third and a half were the serfs of noble landowners in a system of bonded labour that emerged in the late sixteenth century and lasted until its abolition in 1861. Most of the rest of the peasantry lived on state lands and were subjected to slightly less onerous restrictions and demands. The subordinate and exploited status of all Imperial Russia's peasants is one of the wider contexts in which their ways of life can be examined. Another wider context is the natural environment in which they lived and worked. In the northern half of Russia, which was covered in forests, the soils were not very fertile, and the winters long and cold. In the southern half, in contrast, the black earth of the steppes was very fertile, the climate warmer, but the rainfall was low and unreliable. In spite of the burdens imposed by exploitation and the constraints as well as opportunities afforded by the environment, the numbers of peasants in the Russian Empire grew considerably between the late seventeenth and early twentieth centuries. This was the result of both natural increase and the acquisition of new territories with peasant populations. This chapter will seek to explain the endurance of the peasantry of Imperial Russia in these wider contexts by examining their ways of life, to wit: their largely, but not exclusively, agricultural economy; the ways they managed their labour and land in their households and village communities; and their attempts to reduce the demands made on them through protest.

The practices and customs that made up the peasantry's ways of life varied over time and by region. The time covered in this chapter will be divided into three periods. It is necessary to pay some attention to the hundred years prior to the late seventeenth century. This earlier period saw the consolidation of the autocracy (interrupted by the Time of Troubles of 1598–1613), corresponding increases in the state's demands on the peasantry for taxes and conscripts, and the emergence and consolidation of serfdom. The main focus of this chapter, however, is on the period between the late seventeenth and late nineteenth centuries. This second period was the high-point of Imperial Russia and its autocratic government. It was in these two centuries, moreover, that exploitation of the peasantry by the state and nobles reached its zenith. It is significant that it was in this period that the ways of life of much of the Russian peasantry had what are often assumed to be their 'classic', or even timeless, forms: the three-field system of arable farming; large, extended households; and communal land tenure. The third period covered in this chapter is the last decades of Imperial Russia in the late nineteenth and early twentieth centuries. In these decades the peasantry's relationship with the state and nobles was transformed by a series of 'Great Reforms', including the abolition of serfdom and major changes in conscription and taxation. These reforms led in time to a reduction in exploitation. Over the same period, peasants were affected by, and took part in, the social, economic, cultural and eventually political changes that were beginning to transform many aspects of life in Imperial Russia.

The ways of life of the peasantry of Imperial Russia also varied by region. The main focus of this chapter is on the approximate territory of the Russian state in the middle of the seventeenth century, prior to the annexations of Ukraine, Belorussia and the Baltic region in the west, and before the later imperial conquests in the Caucasus, Central Asia and the Far East. The territory of the Russian state at this time contained significant groups of Finnic and Tatar peasants in the north, east and south-east, some other Slavs in the west and south-west, but the largest part of the peasant population of this territory was Russian. This territory can be divided in two ways. The first division is between the central regions (Central Non-Black Earth, North-west, Central Black Earth and Mid-Volga) and outlying regions (the North, Northern and Southern Urals, Lower-Volga and Don, and Siberia). This division reflects the degree of control and exploitation of the peasantry by the state and nobles, which were greater in the centre than the periphery, and the centre of gravity of the population, most of whom lived in the central regions. Over the period, both the power of the state and nobility and the peasant population spread from the centre into outlying regions. The second division of the main territory covered in this chapter reflects differences in the environment between the less fertile, forested lands of north-central and northern Russia (Central Non-Black Earth, North-west, the North, Northern Urals and most of Siberia) and the more fertile, black-earth regions of the transitional forest-steppe and open steppe of south-central and south-eastern Russia (Central Black Earth, Mid-Volga, Lower-Volga and Don, Southern Urals and a small part of southern Siberia).[1]

* * *

The peasants' ways of life evolved in the different regions and over the three time periods in processes of interaction with the nobles and state authorities that exploited them and the environments in which they lived. The peasants' ways of life were also affected by the size and growth of the population, especially in relation to the land.

Exploitation was a major influence on the peasants' ways of life. Peasants owed obligations to the owners of the land they lived on. Over the two or two and half centuries prior to 1861, between a third and a half of the peasantry lived on nobles' estates as serfs. Their obligations took the forms of labour (*barshchina*) or cash or kind (*obrok*). Serfdom had originated in the central regions in the late sixteenth century and later spread to some parts of the outlying regions (but not Siberia). The legislation of 1861 set in motion a gradual process of abolishing serfdom, during which the freed serfs' obligations to the nobles were, in time, converted into 'redemption payments' for part of the land. Most of the rest of the peasantry lived on state lands, but some lived on the estates of the tsars' family and, until they were taken over by the state in 1762–4, the Russian Orthodox Church. By the nineteenth century most non-serf peasants paid their dues to their landowners in cash. In the late nineteenth century, like the freed serfs, these dues were converted into payments for their land.

All peasants had further obligations to the state. Until the middle of the seventeenth century, the main direct tax was a land tax. The amount peasants paid varied with the quantity and quality of land they cultivated (and were unable to conceal from the tax assessors). In 1645–78 the unit of assessment was changed in two stages from land to households, and households were charged a fixed rate. Peter the Great replaced the household tax with a poll tax

1 D. Moon, 'Peasant Migration and the Settlement of Russia's Frontiers 1550–1897', *Historical Journal*, 30 (1997): 859–93.

in 1719–24, which was levied at a single rate on all males of the lower orders, of which the peasantry was by far the largest part. The poll tax lasted until the 1880s. In addition, the state demanded men for its armed forces. Levies of conscripts were raised from the lower orders for short-term service in wartime in the seventeenth century. Peter the Great reformed and intensified the obligation by introducing annual levies for lifetime service from 1705. The term of service was reduced to twenty-five years in 1793, and levies were not always raised in peacetime. Nevertheless, conscription was a heavy burden on the peasantry. Between 1720 and 1867 over 7 million men were conscripted, the overwhelming majority of whom were peasants.[2] The burden was reduced by the military service reform of 1874. It is important to note that peasant communities were held jointly responsible for all their obligations to their landowners and the state. If some peasants or households failed to fulfil their share, then their neighbours were expected to make up the shortfall. Joint responsibility had its origins in pre-Petrine Russia and lasted until 1903.

Peasants did not passively accept their subordinate and exploited status, but sought to reduce the burdens imposed on them by a variety of forms of protest. Nevertheless, the level of exploitation by landowners and the state combined was very high. From the early eighteenth to the mid-nineteenth century, it is likely that Russian peasants were compelled to hand over around half of the product of their labour. State peasants may have had slightly lower burdens than serfs. In both the earlier and later periods, peasants' total obligations were lower. Levels of exploitation also varied in the short term and were highest during Imperial Russia's frequent wars. In addition, there were regional variations: peasants' obligations were higher in the central than outlying regions.[3] The peasantry's relationship with the state and nobles was a reciprocal one. In return for their obligations, peasants received access to allotments of land, and some assistance in times of dearth. The balance of exchange was uneven, however, and peasants' obligations far outweighed what they received in return.

A further influence on the ways peasants organised their lives was the environment. From the point of view of peasant agriculture, the important variables were soil fertility, heat and moisture. Forest soils, which were not very fertile, predominated in northern and north-central Russia. In the forested-steppe and open-steppe regions of south-central and south-eastern Russia,

2 See L. G. Beskrovnyi, *Russkaia armiia i flot v XVIII veke* (Moscow: Voennoe izd. Ministerstva oborony SSSR, 1958), pp. 26–9, 33–7, 294–7; L. G. Beskrovnyi, *Russkaia armiia i flot v XIX veke* (Moscow: Nauka, 1973), pp. 71–9, 86.

3 See D. Moon, *The Russian Peasantry, 1600–1930* (London and New York: Addison Wesley Longman, 1999), pp. 87–8, 115.

however, the soil was very fertile black earth (*chernozem*). To the north and north-east, the winters were long and harsh, leaving a short growing season of only four to five months. The growing season was longer to the south and south-east as the winters were shorter and milder. The available moisture, however, decreased from the north-west to the south-east, and the steppe regions suffered from periodic droughts. Thus, and this was of crucial importance for peasant agriculture, adequate and reliable heat and moisture coincided with fertile soils only on the forest-steppe of south-central Russia (the Central Black Earth and Mid-Volga regions), where they created very good conditions for farming. Peasants in much of the rest of Russia had to struggle with poor soil, long winters and the threat of untimely frosts, or with fertile soil, low rainfall and prospect of drought.

Many historians have stressed the impact of the environment on the Russian peasantry, in particular on the majority who, into the nineteenth century, lived in north-central and northern Russia. A recent study, which followed in the 'environmental-determinist' tradition of nineteenth-century historians such as Solov'ev and Kliuchevskii, argued that due to the 'perfidious role of our step-mother nature' the peasants of the non-black earth regions were condemned to backbreaking labour in their struggle to extract a meagre living from the land. It was further argued that the 'low surplus product' of agriculture in such conditions gave rise to 'compensatory mechanisms of survival', in particular the village commune, serfdom and the autocracy, and also caused the late development of capitalism and industry in Russia.[4] The relationship between peasants and the environment, however, was not just one way. Peasants also had an impact on the environment. Over the centuries, they chopped down or burned enormous swathes of forest and cleared vast areas of steppe grasses to prepare land for cultivation. The destruction of the natural vegetation cover exacerbated the problem of soil erosion and, it was believed by some scientists, led to climate change, making the rainfall in the steppe regions even less reliable.[5]

A third factor influencing the ways of life of the Russian peasantry was the size and growth of the peasant population. The numbers of peasants grew considerably over the whole period, especially from the middle of the eighteenth century, and most quickly in the last decades of Imperial Russia. Inside the borders of the Russian state of the middle of the seventeenth century,

4 L.V. Milov, *Velikorusskii pakhar' i osobennosti rossiiskogo istoricheskogo protsessa* (Moscow: Rosspen, 1998).

5 A.V. Dulov, *Geograficheskaia sreda i istoriia Rossii: konets XV–seredina XIX v.* (Moscow: Nauka, 1983), esp. pp. 50–87, 164–83.

the peasant population, both male and female, grew from around 9 million in 1678 to over 20 million in 1795, 32 million in 1857 and, most dramatically, to over 90 million by 1914–17. This was a result of natural increase, not territorial expansion or immigration. The growth of the peasant population of Imperial Russia as a whole was even greater due to the annexation of large territories to the west inhabited by Ukrainian, Belorussian and Baltic peasants. The total population of the expanding empire, 80–90 per cent of whom were peasants, increased from around 11 million in 1678 to almost 172 million in 1917.[6]

The natural increase in the peasant population was a direct result of practices, in particular near-universal and early marriage, which were encouraged by peasant households and communities in order to promote high birth-rates. Peasants did this for a number of reasons. One of the most important was the need to compensate for the very high death-rates, especially infant and childhood mortality, so that they could ensure new generations of labourers for their households and villages. Noble landowners also encouraged high fertility to increase the numbers of serfs they owned.[7] A further reason to promote high birth-rates was the abundance of land, relative to the population, that was available for cultivation in much of Russia until at least the late eighteenth century, but thereafter only in more outlying regions. Parallel to population growth was peasant migration. For the most part, peasants seem to have preferred to increase agricultural production to feed their growing numbers by extensification, i.e. bringing new land into cultivation, rather than intensifying production by adopting new methods. The main direction of migration from the early seventeenth century was south and south-east from the non-black-earth regions of north-central Russia to the more fertile, black-earth regions of the forest-steppe and, from the middle of the eighteenth century, to the open steppe. Peasants in time largely displaced the nomadic pastoralists who had lived on the steppe for millennia. In addition, growing numbers of peasants moved east, across the Ural mountains, to Siberia and, from the late nineteenth century, to parts of Central Asia and the Far East. From the middle of the nineteenth century, moreover, peasants moved in increasing numbers to the empire's growing cities. Migration to outlying areas throughout the period

6 See Moon, *Russian Peasantry*, p. 21; Ia. E. Vodarskii, *Naselenie Rossii v kontse XVII–nachale XVIII veka* (Moscow: Nauka, 1977), p. 192; V. M. Kabuzan, 'O dostovernosti ucheta naseleniia Rossii (1858–1917 gg.)', in *Istochnikovedenie otechestvennoi istorii 1981 g.* (Moscow: Nauka, 1982), p. 115.

7 P. Czap, 'Marriage and the Peasant Joint Family in the Era of Serfdom', in D. L. Ransel (ed.), *The Family in Imperial Russia* (Urbana: University of Illinois Press, 1978), pp. 103–23; B. N. Mironov, 'Traditsionnoe demograficheskoe povedenie krest'ian v XIX–nachale XX v.' in A.G. Vishnevskii (ed.), *Brachnost', rozhdaemost', smertnost' v Rossii i v SSSR* (Moscow: Statistika, 1977), pp. 83–105.

and to urban areas towards the end siphoned off only part of the growth in the peasant population. The ever-increasing numbers of peasants in the central regions put ever more pressure on the land.[8]

In order to support their growing numbers, cope with the environmental conditions and meet the demands of the state and landowners, Russia's peasants, sometimes in collaboration with landowners or the state authorities, developed practices and customs to ensure their subsistence and livelihoods in the present and the foreseeable future. The following discussion will consider, in turn, the peasantry's ways of life in: central Russia in the hundred years prior to the late seventeenth century; central Russia between the late seventeenth and late nineteenth centuries; the outlying regions over this second period; and Russia as a whole in the late nineteenth and early twentieth centuries.

* * *

Peasants in much of central Russia in the first period engaged in a variety of economic activities that were suitable for the environment of the non-black earth regions of north-central Russia where the majority still lived. The mainstay of the peasant economy was arable farming. The main crops were rye and oats: cereals that could grow in the forest soils and were hardy enough to survive all but the most extreme fluctuations in the climate. Peasants began to adopt the three-field system of crop rotation in the fifteenth and sixteenth centuries, but many still used two-field rotations or long-fallow systems, such as 'slash and burn' farming in the vast forests. Half the land farmed under two-field rotations was left uncultivated each year to allow it to recover its fertility. In long-fallow systems, fields were cleared and cultivated for a few years before being abandoned for longer periods. Peasants thus made very extensive use of land which, due to the relatively low population, was still in abundance in central Russia in the sixteenth and seventeenth centuries. Extensive systems of farming the forested and later steppe lands of the outlying regions, where population densities remained low, were widespread in the eighteenth and nineteenth centuries. The harvests achieved by peasant-farmers in central Russia in the earlier period fluctuated dramatically. In bad years, for example 1601–3, cold, wet summers and frosts in the late spring and early autumn destroyed the crops, leading to famine. At the other extreme, grain sown in the ashes of trees which had been 'slashed and burned' could yield bumper harvests for a year or two. On average, however, harvests returned about three times the amount of seed sown. As well as arable farming, peasants kept

8 See Moon, 'Peasant Migration'.

livestock, which they grazed on pastures and in the woods in the summer, and fed on hay and oats over the long winters. Rearing animals required around ten times as much land to produce the same quantity of food, measured in calories, as growing grain. Owing to the relatively low population densities, it played a large part in the peasant economy in central Russia before the late seventeenth century and in more outlying regions in later centuries. Peasants supplemented their diets by hunting game and gathering nuts, berries and mushrooms in the forests that surrounded their villages. Peasants were also involved in small-scale handicraft production, especially items made from wood, and in trade. But, the peasant economy in this early period was largely self-sufficient, and geared towards subsistence and meeting unavoidable obligations to landowners and the state.[9]

The basic unit of the peasant economy, and indeed peasant life as a whole, was the household. Investigations into tax registers have suggested that many peasant households in central Russia prior to the middle of the seventeenth century were small in size, typically five or six members, and simple in structure, i.e. they were nuclear families. This was because most sons left their parents' households and set up on their own when or shortly after they married. From the point of view of analysing household structures, the important point is that the typical pattern for household divisions was that sons left their natal households before the deaths of their fathers. Most young women left their parents' households to live with their husbands when they married. Almost all peasants married, moreover, and most did so in their late teens or very early twenties. As a result of these practices, there were large proportions of small, simple households.[10] Not all historians agree that small, simple households were prevalent in Russia in this period. Private deeds and legislative documents indicate that there were also larger households with more complex structures.[11] To the extent that small, simple households did prevail, it suggests either that heads of households could see no reason to prevent their adult children from breaking away, or that they lacked the means to keep young adults under their control in their households. There were similar customs regarding marriage and household divisions in many outlying regions, for example Siberia, throughout the seventeenth, eighteenth and nineteenth

9 See R. E. F. Smith, *Peasant Farming in Muscovy* (Cambridge: Cambridge University Press, 1977).

10 V. A. Aleksandrov, *Obychnoe pravo krepostnoi derevni Rossii: XVIII–nachalo XIX v.* (Moscow: Nauka, 1984), pp. 50–3; A. L. Shapiro (ed.), *Agrarnaia istoriia Severo-Zapada Rossii XVII veka* (Leningrad: Nauka, 1989), p. 56.

11 L. V. Danilova, *Sel'skaia obshchina v srednevekovoi Rusi* (Moscow: Nauka, 1994), pp. 262–3.

centuries, and consequently many small, simple households. There were also some larger households.[12]

Most peasant households were grouped in villages. Village communities organised themselves to manage relations between their members and with the outside world. In this period, village communes in central Russia did not generally hold their arable land in common, as became widespread in the later period, but it was held by individual households. When heads of households died, all their property, including the land, was divided up between their heirs. Male heirs usually took precedence, but widows and daughters could inherit property. The customs of household land tenure and partible inheritance, and the possibility of women inheriting property, persisted in many outlying regions well into the nineteenth century. There seems to have been a connection between the practice of holding land in household tenure and the relatively low levels of exploitation and population density in central Russia in the earlier period and in outlying regions in the subsequent two centuries.

A fourth aspect of the strategies peasants adopted was occasional acts of protest against the landowners and state authorities who oppressed and exploited them. Some peasants who engaged in protest in the central regions before the late seventeenth century were prepared to use extreme methods, including mass violence. Some, moreover, seem to have had radical objectives. Peasants fled in large numbers from the central regions, where serfdom was developing and the control and demands of the state were increasing, to seek better and freer lives in the borderlands, where serfdom was absent and state control limited. Many fugitives joined the Cossack communities that lived along and beyond the southern frontier. From the late seventeenth and early eighteenth centuries, however, large-scale peasant flight continued only from peripheral parts of the central regions and from outlying regions further from the centre of noble and state power. There was a religious dimension to some peasant flight. Peasants who rejected the reforms of the Russian Orthodox Church of the 1650s–60s, and became known as Old Believers, sought refuge from persecution in outlying regions.[13] Some peasants resorted to more active forms of protest. Russian peasants took part in four great revolts in the seventeenth and eighteenth centuries. Many of the rebels articulated their aims by

12 N. A. Minenko, *Russkaia krest'ianskaia sem'ia v Zapadnoi Sibiri (XVIII–pervoi poloviny XIX veka)* (Novosibirsk: Nauka, 1979).

13 See T. I. Smirnova, 'Pobegi krest'ian nakanune vystupleniia S.T. Razina', *VI* (1956), no. 6: 129–31; N. V. Kozlova, *Pobegi krest'ian v Rossii v pervoi treti XVIII veka* (Moscow: Izd. MGU, 1983).

claiming to support a 'good' tsar or a pretender, who claimed to be on the side of the oppressed and exploited.[14] The revolts began in outlying areas among Cossack communities and also involved townspeople and non-Russians. Each successive revolt, however, began further from the centre of Russia, and rebel activities were increasingly restricted to outlying regions. In 1606–7 the rebels led by Bolotnikov (among whom there were few peasants) reached Moscow, but this was the last time the old capital was threatened by a revolt from outside the city. There were peasant uprisings and mass murder of noble landowners in the mid-Volga region, 400 miles east of Moscow, during final stages of the Razin and Pugachev revolts in 1670–1 and 1773–4. The Don Cossack rebellion led by Bulavin in 1707–8 sparked off some peasant revolts in adjoining parts of southern Russia, but was mostly a Cossack affair. Old Believers who lived in outlying regions figured among the rebels under Razin, Bulavin and Pugachev. Ukrainian peasants also joined with Cossacks in massive revolts in 1648 and 1768. All the revolts, especially that lead by Pugachev, provoked considerable alarm and panic among the nobility and state authorities, but all were put down by military force and mass repression. By the end of the seventeenth century, and certainly after the suppression of the Pugachev revolt, most peasants in central Russia recognised the futility of mass violence.[15]

The practices and customs employed by peasants in the central regions in the period prior to the late seventeenth century were developed in the contexts of population densities and levels of exploitation that were lower than those in much of central Russia in the subsequent two centuries, and in the environment of the non-black-earth forested regions where most Russian peasants lived. Some of these practices and customs continued in the eighteenth and nineteenth centuries in more outlying regions, where population densities and levels of exploitation remained relatively low.

* * *

The ways of life of the peasants of central Russia began slowly to change, leading to the emergence of new customs and practices that persisted until the late nineteenth century and beyond. Between the late sixteenth and early eighteenth centuries, peasants altered or replaced the practices and customs

14 See M. Perrie, 'Popular Monarchism: The Myth of the Ruler from Ivan the Terrible to Stalin', in G. Hosking and R. Service (eds), *Reinterpreting Russia* (London: Arnold, 1999), pp. 156–69.

15 See P. Avrich, *Russian Rebels, 1600–1800* (New York: Norton, 1972); M. Khodarkovsky, 'The Stepan Razin Uprising: Was it a "Peasant War"?', *JfGO*, 42 (1994): 1–19; M. Raeff, 'Pugachev's Rebellion', in R. Forster and J. P. Greene (eds.), *Preconditions of Revolution in Early Modern Europe* (Baltimore: Johns Hopkins Press, 1970), pp. 169–202; V. A. Markina and V. V. Krizhanovskaia, 'Krest'iane Pravoberezhnoi Ukraine v bor'be za zemliu i voliu (vtoraia polovina XVII–XVIII v.)', *VI* (1992), no.1: 156–60.

that had been used by previous generations to ensure their subsistence and livelihoods. This was the period when many peasants in central Russia adopted the practices of farming using the three-field crop rotation, living in large, complex households, and holding their land in communal and repartitional land tenure. Most peasants, moreover, resorted only to limited forms of protest. It seems likely that peasants in central Russia developed and adopted these practices in response to the growing restrictions and demands made on them as a result of the development of serfdom and the state's increasing demands, which Peter the Great consolidated into the poll tax and regular levies of conscripts in the early eighteenth century. The increase in exploitation was most marked in central Russia where landowner and state control over the peasants was greatest. From the middle of the eighteenth century, moreover, the growing peasant population began to put pressure on the land in the central regions. As before, the natural environment influenced the strategies peasants devised. Regional variations became more pronounced as ever larger numbers of peasants migrated to the fertile black-earth regions of south-central Russia.

Agriculture, especially growing grain, remained the mainstay of the peasant economy in much of central Russia throughout the period between the late seventeenth and late nineteenth centuries. Already prior to the late seventeenth century, peasants in the central regions had begun to adopt the three-field system of crop rotation. In the 'textbook' version of the system, the arable land around a village was divided into three fields. Peasants sowed a winter grain, usually rye, in the first field, a spring crop, often oats or wheat, in the second field, and left the third field fallow to recover its fertility. The next year, the crops were rotated, thus the first field was sown with spring grain and so on in a three-year cycle of winter crop, spring crop, fallow in each field. In comparison with the two-field and long-fallow systems it supplanted, the three-field system made more intensive use of the land. It was adopted to make the land more productive partly in response to increased demands on peasants. Indeed, landowners sometimes initiated the transition to the three-field system to enable their peasants to produce more to meet higher obligations. The new system was introduced also partly as a reaction to the pressure of population increase that rendered more extensive and less productive systems obsolete.[16] The spread of the 'textbook' three-field system may have been exaggerated. It

16 See R. A. French, 'The Introduction of the Three-Field Agricultural System', in J. H. Bater and R. A. French (eds.), *Studies in Russian Historical Geography*, 2 vols. (London: Academic Press, 1983), vol. I, pp. 65–81; M. Confino, *Systèmes agraires et progrès agricole: l'assolement triennal en Russie aux XVIIIe–XIXe siècles* (Paris and The Hague: Mouton, 1969), pp. 59–88.

is likely that it coexisted with older two-field and long-fallow systems in parts of central Russia into the late eighteenth and early nineteenth centuries. In the forested regions of north-central Russia, many peasants practised a combination of the three-field and long-fallow systems. Fields were periodically left fallow not for one year, which was insufficient to allow the forest soil to recover its fertility, but for several years. The abandoned fields were replaced in the crop rotation with new fields cleared from the forests, which still existed in large enough quantities in the vicinity of many villages into the late eighteenth century. In the fertile black-earth regions of south-central Russia, where the main problem for arable farmers was the struggle with weeds rather than soil exhaustion, some peasants practised a four-field rotation: virgin land, spring grain, winter grain, short or long fallow.[17]

Peasants in central Russia between the late seventeenth and late nineteenth centuries engaged in other economic activities. Most kept some livestock for meat and dairy produce, as well as draught power to pull their ploughs and to produce manure for fertiliser. The livestock kept by Russian peasants tended to be small and thin. In comparison with Russian cattle, one observer noted, English cows 'looked like elephants'.[18] But, animal husbandry declined in importance relative to arable farming in the central regions as more land was ploughed up to grow grain to feed the rising population. Peasants continued to hunt and gather in the forests and grow vegetables and other crops in their household plots. Non-agricultural activities, such as forestry, handicraft production, trade, and migrant labour, became more important as sources of income for peasant households. From the middle of the eighteenth century, a degree of regional specialisation developed between the non-black-earth forested regions, where peasants devoted increasing resources to non-agricultural activities, and the fertile black-earth regions, where agriculture predominated. This, in turn, led to an expansion in interregional trade. Production for sale became a more important, if still secondary, motive for peasants' economic ventures in the vicinity of urban centres or transport arteries such as rivers. The growth in the market created more opportunities for peasants to make a living, or to supplement farming, by trade and wage labour.[19]

17 Milov, *Velikorusskii pakhar'*, pp. 17–27.

18 A. K. Smith, 'Peasant Agriculture in Pre-Reform Kostroma and Kazan' Provinces', *RH*, 26 (1999): 410.

19 See V. A. Fedorov, *Pomeshchich'i krest'iane tsentral'no-promyshlennogo raiona Rossii: kontsa XVIII–pervoi poloviny XIX v.* (Moscow: Izd. MGU, 1974); K. Gestwa, *Proto-Industrialisierung in Russland: Wirtschaft, Herrschaft und Kultur in Ivanovo und Pavlovo, 1741–1932* (Göttingen: Vandenhoeck und Ruprecht, 1999).

Despite the development of opportunities for market-orientated production for peasants in some areas, most Russian peasants seem generally to have been disinclined to maximise their production and incomes, or to adopt new methods of tilling the land. Many were averse to the drudgery of the extra labour entailed, because of the limited opportunities in many areas to sell surplus produce at the market, and the likelihood that most of any increases in production would be taken away from them in increased obligations by the state and landowners. For many peasants, producing enough food to subsist by relying on tried-and-trusted methods was more important than experimenting with new crops or agricultural techniques, which may have been more productive but may also have been more risky. Reducing risk was also one of the reasons why peasants engaged in different types of farming, and in both agricultural and non-agricultural activities. If one part of a household's activities failed, it could be compensated for by others.

It is usually argued that peasant agriculture in Russia was not very productive due to the low level of technology employed by peasants and the environmental conditions in which they farmed. Various sources, including figures reported by many provincial governors in the late eighteenth and first half of the nineteenth centuries, suggest that peasants in the central regions harvested around three or three-and-a-half times as much grain as they sowed.[20] There is evidence, however, for example data collected by the Free Economic Society and the records of some noble estates, that some peasants attained higher average yields, around five and six times the seed, especially in the fertile black-earth regions of the forest-steppe in south-central Russia.[21] Average yields conceal the main trend, which was considerable year-to-year fluctuations caused largely by the vagaries of the climate. There were periodic bad harvests in parts of central Russia between the late seventeenth and late nineteenth centuries.

The needs of the peasant economy, in particular agriculture, influenced the practices and customs peasants adopted in their households and village communities to manage their labour and land. Peasant households continued to farm their land individually, even after their villages began to hold their arable land in common, and household heads sought to ensure that they had a sufficient numbers of labourers under their roofs to support their members. As in the earlier period, household heads insisted on near-universal and early marriage to ensure high birth rates. From the late seventeenth century,

20 Milov, *Velikorusskii pakhar'*, pp. 162–89.

21 See N. L. Rubinshtein, *Sel'skoe khoziaistvo Rossii vo vtoroi polovine XVIII v.* (Moscow: Gospolitizdat, 1957), pp. 353–63; S. L. Hoch, *Serfdom and Social Control in Russia, Petrovskoe, a Village in Tambov* (Chicago: Chicago University Press, 1986), pp. 28–36.

moreover, many heads adopted a new practice regarding household divisions. Rather than allowing their sons to leave and set up their own households after they married, heads actively prevented their sons from breaking away. Instead, many adult sons, together with their wives and children, continued to live under the same roof as their parents until their fathers died. Married brothers and their families sometimes continued to live together afterwards. The prevalence of household divisions after the deaths of their heads in much of central Russia from the late seventeenth to the late nineteenth centuries meant that many village communities contained substantial proportions of households with large numbers of peasants and complex structures. Large and complex peasant households typically contained seven to ten or larger numbers of people, more than one married couple, and two or three generations. In contrast, the earlier practice of household divisions before the death of their heads had led to small, simple households. There were regional variations. Household divisions after the heads' death, resulting in large, complex households, were less widespread in forested regions where agriculture was less important.

There were several reasons for the development and spread of large, complex households. Between 1645 and 1678, the state switched from a tax assessed on land to a flat-rate household tax. By living in smaller numbers of larger households, therefore, peasants could reduce the amount of taxes they paid. The household tax was replaced by the poll tax in 1719–24, but large, complex households persisted for other reasons. They were an effective way of organising labour for agriculture and to meet the growing demands on peasants for obligations. Larger households were better able to meet the massive demands for labour at peak times in the agricultural calendar, in particular haymaking and harvesting. Large and complex households served as welfare institutions as their multi-generational structure meant they usually contained enough able-bodied adults to support the children, elderly and infirm, who were not able to work or look after themselves. Maintaining large and complex households was also a risk-averse strategy. Larger households with a number of adults and more than one married pair were better able than smaller households to cope with the premature deaths of adults or the conscription of a young man into the army.[22]

22 See Aleksandrov, *Obychnoe pravo*, pp. 42–69; P. Czap, '"A Large Family: The Peasant's Greatest Wealth": Serf Households in Mishino, Russia, 1814–1858', in R. Wall (ed.), *Family Forms in Historic Europe* (Cambridge: Cambridge University Press, 1983), pp. 105–51; R. Wall, 'The Perennial Multiple Family Household, Mishino, Russia 1782–1858', *Journal of Family History*, 7 (1982): 5–26; C. D. Worobec, *Peasant Russia: Family and Community in the Post-Emancipation Period* (Princeton: Princeton University Press, 1991).

Living in large and complex households may have been more viable than smaller, nuclear families, but it imposed constraints and burdens on their members. The younger generation of adults, male and female, lived under the authority of the older generation and bore the brunt of the burden of work in the household and on its land. The younger generation of women were subject both to their husbands and to their mothers-in-law, and sometimes had to fend off the advances of their fathers-in-law. Generation and gender were axes of tension and conflict inside large households, and led sometimes to demands from their younger members for household divisions.[23] It was not unusual for adult males to reach middle age before they became heads of their own households.

According to custom, there was a gendered division of labour inside households. The men were responsible for work in the arable fields, and usually did all the ploughing, harrowing and sowing. Men also looked after the horses. Women's customary roles, for which they had sole responsibility under the direction of the wife of the household head, were looking after the household, the children, the kitchen garden and small livestock. Women were required to enter the 'male domain' of the fields, however, to help out with the backbreaking tasks of haymaking and harvesting. Female peasants played a far larger role in field work, taking over this customary male role, if their menfolk were away for long periods as migrant labourers. Some villages in Kostroma province, in the Central Non-Black Earth region, became known as 'women's kingdoms' for this reason.[24]

Many village communes in central Russia, especially the Central Black Earth region, adopted a new form of land tenure over the seventeenth and early eighteenth centuries. In many villages, peasants began to hold their arable land in communal, rather than household, tenure and adopted one of the most famous practices of rural Russia: periodic redistribution of strips of arable land between households to take account of changes in their size. Households that increased in size, for example following the marriage of a son, were allocated more land at the expense of those that had got smaller, as a result, for example, of division or death. It is sometimes asserted that this practice reflected some communal ethos in the soul of the Russian people. Scholars who have delved more deeply into its origins have found practical motives. Village communes

23 Hoch, *Serfdom*, pp. 84–90; C. A. Frierson, 'Razdel: The Peasant Family Divided', *RR* 46 (1987): 35–51.

24 Smith, 'Peasant Agriculture', pp. 375–9; B. A. Engel, *Between the Fields and the City: Women, Work and Family in Russia, 1861–1914* (Cambridge: Cambridge University Press, 1994), pp. 34–63.

shared out the total burden of obligations demanded from them by landowners and the state, for which they were jointly responsible, between their member households. As these obligations increased over the seventeenth and early eighteenth centuries, it made practical sense for communes to try to ensure that households could support themselves without needing the assistance of their neighbours and, crucially, meet their shares of the communal obligations. One way to do this was to share out the land between households, as well as the obligations, and to make sure households' land allotments were roughly in conformance with their ability to work the land. When the sizes of households changed, moreover, it was necessary to adjust their land allotments accordingly. Communes also adopted the new system of land tenure in response to the growing pressure of population increase on the land. Rising obligations and population density are not the full explanation for the origins of communal and repartitional land tenure. The key to understanding the new system seems to be taxation. The introduction of the flat-rate tax on households in 1645–78 and, more importantly, the poll tax in 1719–24 were further reasons for communes to share out land fairly evenly to try to ensure that all households had the means to meet their shares of the communal obligations. Since the poll tax was periodically reassessed on the basis of new head counts of the numbers of tax-payers, moreover, it was expedient for communes to redistribute land to take account of changes in the numbers of peasants, i.e. tax-payers, inside households. The connection between the household and poll taxes and the origins of communal and repartitional land tenure is further suggested by the fact that this system of land tenure did not develop in Ukraine, Belorussia and the Baltic region, which had their own systems of serfdom and substantial populations, but where, crucially, the poll tax was introduced only in the late eighteenth century, in some cases long after they had been annexed to the Russian Empire. In all these western parts of the empire, individual household land tenure persisted. If households had more land than they could cultivate, they hired labourers from households that were short of land. Thus, in the west of the empire, as in most of the rest of Europe, labour, rather than land, moved around between households.[25]

Communal and repartitional land tenure have distracted the attention of historians from the other important functions of village communes. Although the land was farmed by individual households, communes oversaw the operation

25 See D. Atkinson, 'Egalitarianism and the Commune', in R. Bartlett (ed.), *Land Commune and Peasant Community in Russia* (Basingstoke and London: Macmillan, 1990), pp. 7–19; S. Hoch, 'The Serf Economy and the Social Order in Russia', in M. L. Bush (ed.), *Serfdom and Slavery* (London and New York: Longman, 1996), pp. 311–22.

of the three-field system, which required all households to observe the common crop rotation and not, for example, sow grain in their strips in the fallow field. In addition, communes organised assistance for households that were experiencing short-term difficulties, but were likely to recover and once again be able to make their contribution to the village's obligations. For example, a small household that had lost its only adult male to illness, but contained teenage boys, was a good bet for the future. Households that were persistently weak, for example due to alcohol abuse by their members, were not deemed worth supporting. In addition, communes mediated in disputes between households and maintained law and order in the villages. Communal elders, who were heads of their own households, backed each other up in maintaining their authority over the younger generation. Communes thus sought to support the system of large, complex households by trying to prevent younger peasants from breaking away. Household heads and elders of village communes found some coincidence of interests, moreover, with noble and state authorities. They all had a mutual interest in maintaining authority in the villages and ensuring that communes were able to meet their obligations, in which the largest part of the burden was borne by the young adults. The older generation used a variety of means to maintain their authority, ranging from public shaming and corporal punishment to exile from the village or selection of recalcitrant peasants as conscripts for the long term of military service from which few returned. The degrees of exploitation and social control, including maintenance of the complex household system, seem to have been at their greatest on magnate estates in the Central Black Earth region, where serfs performed onerous labour obligations, such as the Gagarin estate of Petrovskoe in Tambov province, in the late eighteenth and first half of the nineteenth centuries.[26]

Exploitation and oppression provoked some peasants to protest against the landowners and state authorities. In the central regions of Russia in the period between the late seventeenth and late nineteenth centuries, peasants mostly eschewed large-scale violent protests in favour of more limited forms of action. Open protests usually took the form of non-violent confrontations, often accompanied by the submission of petitions or complaints or the initiation of law suits. Peasants complained about and sought redress for specific grievances such as excessive exploitation, cruel treatment and rejections of requests for

26 See V. A. Aleksandrov, *Sel'skaia obshchina v Rossii (XVII–nachalo XIX v.)* (Moscow: Nauka, 1976); Hoch, *Serfdom*; E. Melton, 'Household Economies and Communal Conflicts on a Russian Serf Estate, 1800–1817', *JSH*, 26 (1993): 559–85; R. Bohac, 'The Mir and the Military Draft', *SR* 47 (1988): 652–66.

assistance in times of dearth. In addition, and as a matter of routine, peasants resorted to low-level 'weapons of the weak' of the type used by oppressed and exploited peoples in many societies. They worked badly on their landowners' land when performing their labour services, stole estate property, accidentally broke new machinery that threatened to make more work, paid less than the full amount of their cash dues late, feigned incomprehension of orders, hid in the woods for a few days to escape punishment, and a whole manner of similar tactics. In using limited forms of protest, however, peasants did not and could not hope to overturn the whole social system. Indeed, for most peasants, it is likely that such a notion existed only in the magical world of folklore and in the afterlife promised by the Christian religion. In the real world, peasants used their various tactics of protest to try to blunt the edges of their exploitation and carve out some living space for themselves. The trick was not to push the authorities too far and provoke a strong or violent response in which the peasants knew they were likely to be subjected to harsh repression.[27] Rather than engage in protest, many peasants, including the younger generation of men and women, seem grudgingly to have accepted their lot, worked hard to support their households and village communities, and to meet those obligations they were not able to evade or reduce. The daily grind of fieldwork from the early spring to the early autumn was punctuated by church and village festivals at which drink flowed freely and peasants could let off steam and, perhaps, imagine a better world.[28]

The living standards of most peasants in central Russia between the late seventeenth and late nineteenth centuries can certainly not be described as prosperous, but it would be a mistake to assume that the majority lived in grinding poverty. It seems safe to conclude that in most years and in many villages, the practices and customs peasants developed in the wider contexts of exploitation and the environmental conditions were adequate to support the growing numbers of peasants. There were variations in living standards. Some peasants were subjected to greater degrees of exploitation by their landowners than others. There were variations over time. Peasants ate best in the autumn, after the crops had been gathered in and livestock had been slaughtered. The weeks prior to the next harvest, on the other hand, could

27 See R. Bohac, 'Everyday Forms of Resistance: Serf Opposition to Gentry Exactions, 1800–1861', in E. Kingston-Mann and T. Mixter (eds.), *Peasant Economy, Culture, and Politics of European Russia, 1800–1921* (Princeton: Princeton University Press, 1991), pp. 236–60; P. Kolchin, *Unfree Labor: American Slavery and Russian Serfdom* (Cambridge, Mass.: Belknap Press, 1987), pp. 257–313; D. Moon, *Russian Peasants and Tsarist Legislation on the Eve of Reform, 1825–1855* (Basingstoke and London: Macmillan, 1992).

28 See M. M. Gromyko, *Mir russkoi derevni* (Moscow: Molodaia gvardiia, 1991).

be very difficult. Peasants were dependent also on fluctuations in agricultural production caused by the climate. Individual households' levels of prosperity were in part a function of their size and the ratio of able-bodied adults to all their members. Larger households and those with high proportions of members who could work hard seem to have been better off than smaller households and those with larger numbers of young or elderly peasants. Differences in living standards of this type would even out over the life-cycle of households as children grew up and married and older peasants died off. A few peasants were able to do well from trade, especially in parts of the Central Non-Black Earth region. In such areas, longer-term differences in living standards between the elites and poor of villages emerged. Factional politics inside villages also played a role; households of communal elders generally looked after their own interests at the expense of their neighbours.[29]

As a result of migration, ever larger numbers of peasants lived in the outlying regions of the north or south-east of European Russia and in Siberia. Peasants in these regions persisted long into the eighteenth and nineteenth centuries with the customs and practices that had been common in central Russia prior to the late seventeenth century. Thus, peasants in outlying regions continued to use more extensive systems of cultivation. Slash-and-burn agriculture remained widespread in the forested regions of the north and Siberia. The equivalent system on the open steppes was field-grass husbandry: peasants burned the steppe grasses, cultivated the very fertile, virgin black earth for a few years, before preparing new fields and leaving the old ones to return to the steppe. Change came, but only very late. On the steppes of the North Caucasus, for example, long-fallow systems were the norm as late as the 1880s, but the three-field system was making inroads by the end of the century. Livestock husbandry remained a large part of the rural economy in outlying regions, where pasture remained plentiful, throughout the eighteenth and nineteenth centuries.[30] Many peasants in outlying regions continued to live in small, simple households throughout the eighteenth and nineteenth centuries. As in central Russia, however, there was a trend towards larger households with more complex structures from the late seventeenth and early eighteenth

29 See R. E. F. Smith and D. Christian, *Bread and Salt: A Social and Economic History of Food and Drink in Russia* (Cambridge: Cambridge University Press, 1984), pp. 327–56; E. Melton, 'Proto-industrialization, Serf Agriculture and Agrarian Social Structure: Two Estates in Nineteenth-Century Russia', *Past and Present* 115 (1987): 69–106; E. Melton, 'Household Economies'.

30 See A. M. Anfimov (ed.), *Krest'ianstvo Severnogo Kavkaza i Dona v period kapitalizma* (Rostov-on-Don: Izd. Rostovskogo universiteta, 1990), p. 56; J. Pallot and D. J. B. Shaw, *Landscape and Settlement in Romanov Russia, 1613–1917* (Oxford: Clarendon Press, 1990), pp. 112–35.

centuries.[31] Peasant households in outlying regions continued to hold their land in household tenure. Indeed, this was compatible with the prevailing extensive systems of land use. Communal and repartitional land tenure spread only slowly to outlying regions, for example the North Caucasus and Western Siberia, only in the wake of the spread of the three-field system towards the end of the nineteenth century.[32] Thus, the newer practices and customs of peasant life spread little by little from the central to some outlying regions over the eighteenth and nineteenth centuries. Peasants in the more remote parts of Russia adopted more intensive ways of using the land and organising their labour in response to the increasing population density as a result of natural growth and, in particular, immigration, from central regions. Peasants altered the ways they did things in reaction also to the growing demands for obligations that spread outwards from the centre.

* * *

Peasants in Imperial Russia adapted and altered their customs and practices again in the late nineteenth and early twentieth centuries to cope with further changes. The legislation of 1861 that set in motion the abolition of serfdom was followed by similar reforms for the peasants who lived on the lands of the state and the tsar's family. By the end of the century, most peasants were buying their land allotments by paying instalments in 'redemption' schemes administered by the government. The state also reformed the main demands it made on the peasantry. The poll tax was phased out and replaced by taxes on sales and businesses in the 1880s. The system of military conscription was reformed in 1874. The maximum term of service was cut to seven years, and young men from all levels of society, not just the lower orders, were liable to serve. Conscripts were selected by ballot, moreover, not on the whim of local authorities. A much larger proportion of young men served in the army than before the reform. In marked contrast to the previous system, however, most conscripts came home and resumed their previous lives after a few years' service. The imperial government implemented other reforms. Elected district and provincial councils (*zemstva*), with peasant representatives, were set up in many provinces in the 1860s, and new local courts were established for peasants. These reforms were part of wider changes. There were improvements in transport with the construction of a national railway network, a national

31 See E. N. Baklanova, *Krest'ianskii dvor i obshchina na russkom severe: konets XVII–nachalo XVIII v.* (Moscow: Nauka, 1976), pp. 31–40; N. A. Minenko, *Russkaia krest'ianskaia sem'ia v Zapadnoi Sibiri*, pp. 42–76.

32 Anfimov, *Krest'ianstvo Severnogo Kavkaza*, p. 56; J. Channon, 'Regional Variation in the Commune: The Case of Siberia', in Bartlett, *Land Commune*, pp. 72–7.

market developed, industrialisation began to take off, and as a result there were more opportunities for wage labour in industry and commercial agriculture. Peasants became more mobile, migrating to the empire's rapidly growing cities as well as to Siberia and other far-flung regions. Peasants' horizons were broadened also by the growth of formal schooling and the spread of literacy in the villages. These processes should not be seen solely as changes from outside that were disrupting a 'traditional' way of life. Russian peasants were used to adapting to changes, and in late Imperial Russia they shaped the changing world they lived in just as much as they themselves were altered. A further development in this period was rapid population growth. Between 1857 and 1917, the number of peasants inside the mid-seventeenth-century borders of Russia increased three times, a rate of natural growth that to some extent prefigured the population explosion in the developing world in the latter part of the twentieth century.

Historians have debated whether peasants in late Imperial Russia were becoming more involved in and identifying with wider society. From the 1860s, more peasants than ever before came into contact with people, institutions and ideas from outside peasant life. The main areas of contact were the new local councils and courts, the reformed army, the growing cities and the new village schools. One line of interpretation has emphasised the extent to which peasants took over, or 'peasantised', many of these institutions (with the exception of the local councils) and transformed them in their image. It has been argued that customary norms of rural justice survived in spite of new courts, soldiers in the reformed army were simply 'peasants in uniform', the cities were swamped by migrants from the villages who brought their customs to urban areas, and peasants used schools to learn skills that they could use for their own purposes but sought to prevent their children from being socialised into an 'alien' culture. This view stressed the vitality, adaptability and endurance of peasant society and culture in Russia.[33] There is a great deal of evidence to support this view, at least in the short term. For example, peasants tried to subvert the Stolypin land reforms of 1906–11 that were intended to create a stratum of richer peasants who supported the tsarist regime.[34] There is another line of argument that, in the longer-term, peasant society and culture were changing rather more significantly, and peasants were becoming more involved in a wider, national society. The new courts, the reformed army, the

33 See B. Eklof and S. Frank (eds.), *The World of the Russian Peasant* (Boston, Mass: Unwin Hyman, 1990).

34 J. Pallot, *Land Reform in Russia 1906–1917* (Oxford: Clarendon Press, 1999).

growing cities, the schools and wider literacy were parts of this process of change, sites of cultural contact where new identities were formed. Towards the end of Imperial Russia, peasants seem to have been starting to construct newer, wider identities as they sought to adapt to and deal with the changing world of which they were a part.[35]

The older historiography of late Imperial Russia painted a picture of growing poverty in increasingly overcrowded villages as peasants, allegedly burdened with high payments and reduced land allotments by the terms of the abolition of serfdom, struggled to survive. The bad harvest and famine of 1891–2 and the rural revolutions of 1905–7 and 1917–18 were seen as the culminations of a growing crisis in rural Russia.[36] There is no doubt that many peasants believed that they should have been given all the land free of charge in 1861, nor that there was poverty in the villages. As radical intellectuals took a growing interest in the peasantry in the second half of the nineteenth century, moreover, educated Russians became acutely aware of the low living standards of their fellow Russians in rural areas. Contemporaries in the government and society blamed rural poverty on the peasants' 'backward' methods of cultivation, and believed that village communes and their communal practices were barriers to change. Furthermore, Russian scientists and agronomists became increasingly concerned about the impact of agriculture on the environment. Attention was concentrated on deforestation, soil erosion and climate change. In the 1870s, the Free Economic Society sponsored Vasilii Dokuchaev's pathbreaking study of the fertile black earth, which was one of Russia's greatest natural resources, but suffered from recurring poor harvests.[37] In the aftermath of the bad harvest of 1891, members of the society expressed concerns not only that Russian agricultural techniques were not able to cope with droughts in the steppe regions, but that they may have been contributing to changes in the environment that made droughts more likely.[38]

35 See G. Popkins, 'Peasant Experiences of the Late Tsarist State: District Congresses of Land Captains, Provincial Boards and the Legal Appeals Process, 1891–1917', *SEER* 78 (2000): 113–14; J. A. Sanborn, *Drafting the Russian Nation: Military Conscription, Total War, and Mass Politics, 1905–1925* (DeKalb: Northern Illinois University Press, 2003); J. Brooks, *When Russia Learned to Read: Literacy and Popular Literature, 1981–1917* (Princeton: Princeton University Press, 1985). See also C. J. Chulos, *Converging Worlds: Religion and Community in Peasant Russia, 1861–1917* (DeKalb: Northern Illinois University Press, 2003).

36 See G. T. Robinson, *Rural Russia under the Old Regime* (Berkeley: University of California Press, 1932), pp. 94–116.

37 V. V. Dokuchaev, *Russkii chernozem* (St Petersburg: Deklaron i Evdokimov, 1883).

38 'Besedy v i Otdelenii Imperatorskogo Vol'nogo Ekonomicheskogo Obshchestva po voprosu o prichinakh neurozhaia 1891 goda i merakh protiv povtoreniia podobykh urozhaev v budushchem', *Trudy Imperatorskogo Vol'nogo Ekonomicheskogo Obshchestva* (1892), no.1: 67–144.

There are other ways of looking at peasant living standards in late Imperial Russia. In spite of the views of contemporaries, peasants and radicals, it seems that the alleged negative aspects of the terms of the abolition of serfdom have been overstated. In time, the reforms of the 1860s–80s led to a reduction in the burden of exploitation on the peasantry. While the population was growing rapidly, so were opportunities for wage labour. In spite of periodic bad harvests, on average grain yields were increasing as some peasants did adopt new techniques, and some village communes actively promoted innovation.[39] The growth of the railway network, moreover, created new opportunities to produce for the market, and meant that grain could be moved to deficit areas in times in dearth. Over the late nineteenth and early twentieth centuries, grain production *per capita*, i.e. allowing for population growth, and after exports have been deducted, was also increasing. On average, therefore, it seems that there was a slow improvement in peasant standards of living in the last decades of Imperial Russia. New research into the physical stature of the population provides further evidence for improving living standards. This conclusion does not deny, however, that there were areas, such as the densely populated Central Black Earth region, where poverty was widespread, or that there were short-term crises, for example in 1891–3 and 1905–8.[40]

Finally, it remains to consider how peasants adapted or altered the customs and practices that made up their ways of life in the changing world of late Imperial Russia. A mixed picture emerges. Rather than undermining aspects of the peasants' ways of life, at least in the short term, some of the changes taking place reinforced practices that had evolved earlier in different circumstances and for other reasons. The complex household system persisted. Young male migrant workers and married men who were conscripted into the army left their wives and children with their parents while they were away, thus maintaining multi-generational households. Migrant workers sent part of their wages home to support these households. Peasants responded to the rapid

39 E. Kingston-Mann, 'Peasant Communes and Economic Innovation: A Preliminary Inquiry', in Kingston-Mann and Mixter, *Peasant Economy*, pp. 23–51. For contrasting views of 'backwardness', see D. Kerans, *Mind and Labor on the Farm in Black-Earth Russia, 1861–1914* (Budapest and New York: Central European University Press, 2001) and Y. Kotsonis, *Making Peasants Backward: Agricultural Cooperatives and the Agrarian Question in Russia, 1861–1914* (Basingstoke and London: Macmillan, 1999).

40 See S. L. Hoch, 'On Good Numbers and Bad: Malthus, Population Trends and Peasant Standard of Living in Late Imperial Russia', *SR* 53 (1994): 41–75; B. N. Mironov, 'New Approaches to Old Problems: The Well-Being of the Population of Russia from 1821 to 1910 as Measured by Physical Stature', *SR* 58 (1999): pp. 1–26; S. G. Wheatcroft, 'Crises and the Condition of the Peasantry in Late Imperial Russia', in Kingston-Mann and Mixter, *Peasant Economy*, pp. 128–72.

population increase that put pressure on the land by maintaining communal and repartitional land tenure, and introducing it in outlying regions, as a way of keeping households' land and labour resources in conformance.

On the other hand, the changes in wider society were also sowing seeds that led to changes in the ways peasants had organised their lives in central Russia since the late seventeenth and early eighteenth centuries. The reduction in the level of exploitation that followed the reforms, together with the removal of noble landowners from authority over their former serfs, led also to a reduction in the control exerted by household heads and village elders over the younger generation. The coincidence of interests between nobles and state officials and the elders of peasant society started to erode. The younger generation found greater independence for other reasons. The military service reform of 1874, with selection of conscripts by ballot for shorter terms of service, meant that village elders could no longer threaten to send, and send, recalcitrant young men to the army for twenty-five years. Younger peasants, both men and women, could find greater financial independence by working as wage labourers in the cities or on commercial farms. The growth of schooling and literacy gave younger peasants more access to ideas outside village culture. One result of these changes was the start of the breakdown of the complex household system in some areas, but later in the Central Black Earth region, as the younger generation sought to set up their own homes, independent of their parents' control. Many migrant workers and soldiers separated from their parents' households when they came home.[41] This was a reversion to the practices of household divisions before the deaths of the heads of households, and the consequent development of a large proportion of small, simple households, that seem to have been widespread in central Russia prior to the late seventeenth century.

There was another area in which peasants in late Imperial Russia reverted to practices that had disappeared in central Russia over the preceding period. The stresses and strains that accompanied the changes in society led to an increase in peasant discontent with their continued subordinate status. To the extent that some peasants were experiencing improvements in their living standards, dissatisfaction may have been fuelled by rising expectations, including hopes for a new land reform. Poverty among peasants who felt aggrieved by the land settlement of 1861 also caused disaffection. Over the same period, other groups in society, including the new middle classes and industrial workers, accumulated grievances. The authorities seem gradually to have been losing

41 See Frierson, 'Razdel'; Worobec, *Peasant Russia*, pp. 76–117.

their ability to keep control over society at home and to defend Imperial Russia's international status abroad. In 1905 and 1917, military defeats by Japan and Germany led to revolutions in the cities. On both occasions, peasants joined in and spread the revolutions to the villages with the aim of seizing the land still owned by non-peasants. Thus, in the early twentieth century, peasants resumed the earlier practice of open, direct protest with radical aims. The rural revolution of 1917–18 was marked by other elements of continuity. The peasants who seized land were continuing the practice of increasing production to feed more mouths by bringing more land into cultivation rather than adopting more intensive and productive methods. The revolution in the villages led also to the resurgence of traditional peasant institutions, especially the household and commune.[42] The elements of continuity were short-lived, however, as the peasantry's ways of life were shattered by Stalin's forced collectivisation of agriculture in 1930.

* * *

At both the beginning and end of the imperial period, Russia's population was made up overwhelmingly of peasants, most of whom devoted a large part of their energies to agriculture. Thus, the peasants and their ways of life endured. They were able to ensure their subsistence and livelihoods by their ability to adapt to change. By adapting and changing their practices and customs, moreover, Russia's peasants were able to cope with the demands of landowners and the state, feed their ever larger numbers and settle in parts of the outlying regions of the vast empire. While peasants were constrained to some extent by the natural environments in which they lived, they were able to adapt to support themselves in conditions as diverse as the forests of the north and Siberia, and the steppes of the south and south-east. In their struggles to meet the burden of exploitation and support the growing population, however, peasants transformed and degraded these environments, clearing vast areas of forest and steppe grasslands, thus sowing the seeds for the far greater human impact on the environment of Russia in the twentieth century.

42 See O. Figes, *Peasant Russia, Civil War: The Volga Countryside in Revolution (1917–1921)* (Oxford: Clarendon Press, 1989).

19

The Russian economy and banking system

BORIS ANANICH

Introduction

The beginning of the eighteenth century was a period of radical change in Russia's economy. These transformations are connected with the name Peter I, but they proved possible thanks to the development of trade and the accumulation of capital by the Muscovite government in the sixteenth and seventeenth centuries. The main sources of this capital growth were domestic and foreign trade, salt mines, fishing, payments to the treasury, customs duties and income from taverns. Capital was concentrated in the merchant class, the state and monasteries. Monasteries sold bread, salt and fish, and to a certain extent performed the functions of banks, undertaking credit transactions. Economically, Russia lagged behind the leading countries of Western Europe, where developed banking and stock markets already existed and where concepts such as bills of exchange and promissory notes were widespread.

In many ways, Peter I's transfer of the Russian capital to St Petersburg and his declaration of a Russian 'empire' predetermined the later development of the Russian government and economy. Peter's 'Europeanisation' of the country occurred during wars and was accompanied by the breakdown of old customs and societal structures. The foundation of the empire was an enormous financial burden on peasants and urban dwellers, and limited their freedom of movement as well. Peter I introduced a poll tax, military conscription and internal passport system. But the decisive role in Russia's economic development belonged to the government and state enterprises.

The 21-year war with Sweden greatly influenced Peter's commercial and industrial policies. Providing the army and navy with everything it needed required an intense development of industry and trade, all of which needed to occur in an extremely short period of time. Peter I went down in history as one of the founders of active government entrepreneurship.[1] As a result of the Petrine reforms there was a sharp jump in the development of manufacturing.[2] The state financed not only the construction of new factories but also founded new industrial districts. It owned industrial enterprises and enjoyed a monopoly over areas of foreign and domestic trade. In 1705 a state monopoly was introduced over salt and tobacco, products which brought state coffers significant revenues. The state also monopolised the right to sell key Russian exports. In 1706 yet another monopoly was introduced, this time on trade with China.

Peter I sought to turn his empire's capital city into a commercial and financial centre. He forcibly moved merchants from various Russian cities to St Petersburg, and when he opened a stock exchange in the city he forced merchants to appear and trade at the exchange at designated times.

Before the beginning of the eighteenth century, Russian foreign trade was conducted through the northern port of Archangel. In 1713 Peter broke with this tradition, declaring St Petersburg to be Russia's main trading port. Furthermore, delivering hemp, Russia leather (*iuft'*), potash and other exports to Archangel was prohibited. Despite these measures, however, the state's share of the export trade in Russia in the first quarter of the eighteenth century did not exceed 10–12 per cent.[3] Russian financial transactions in Western Europe were conducted during this time mainly through foreign financiers and merchants, while credit transactions in the country were carried out by administrative institutions.

By the end of the Great Northern War, Peter I's commercial-industrial policies had changed in certain respects. As a result of the reforms of 1719–24 the Mining, Manufacturing and Commercial College was created to manage trade and industry. In these same years a series of measures was approved to encourage private enterprise in trade and industry. Beginning in 1719 government monopolies were eliminated for almost all export goods. In the 1720s the transfer of state manufacturing enterprises into private hands became a relatively common occurrence.[4] If in the seventeenth century salt mines and

1 T. von Laue, *Sergei Witte and the Industrialisation of Russia* (New York and London: Columbia University Press, 1963). E. Anisimov, *Vremia petrovskikh reform* (Leningrad: Lenizdat, 1989).

2 E. Anisimov, *Gosudarstvennye preobrazovaniia i samoderzhavie Petra Velikogo v pervoi chetverti XVIII veka* (St Petersburg: Dmitrii Bulanin, 1997).

3 P. N. Miliukov, *Gosudarstvennoe khoziaistvo Rossii v pervoi chetverti XVIII veka i reforma Petra Velikogo,* 2nd edn (St Petersburg: Tip. M. M. Stasiulevicha, 1905), pp. 364, 485; N. I. Pavlenko, 'Torgovo-promyslennaia politika pravitel'stva Rossii v pervoi chetverti XVIII veka', *Istoriia SSSR* 3 (1958): 58–9.

4 Pavlenko, 'Torgovo-promyslennaia', 50–1.

trade in Siberia had been an important factor in capital accumulation, then in the first quarter of the eighteenth century government contracts, wine sales and tax farming had become the main sources of capital.[5] Peter the Great was an advocate of mercantilism. In 1724 a protectionist tariff was enacted to defend the interests of Russian merchants. The 1729 statute on promissory notes and bills of exchange, which was under preparation in Peter's lifetime, helped the development of international trade and financial ties.

The reforms of Peter I provided an impetus and new direction for economic development in Russia.[6] This new dynamic continued during the reign of Elizabeth Petrovna through the reforms of P. A. Shuvalov. Internal customs duties were eliminated while conditions for a freer development of trade were created.[7] Only in the middle of the eighteenth century did the creation of Russian banks to finance merchants and the nobility become possible. In 1754 the Loan Bank (Zaemnii Bank) was established. This was a mortgage institution (for long-term credit) and commercial institution (for short-term credit). In fact it was made up of two constituent banks: a Bank for the Nobility and a Bank for the Merchant Estate.

The Catherine system

The second half of the eighteenth century represented a new stage in the development of trade and banking in Russia.

The commercial-industrial and financial policy of Catherine II furthered the 'Europeanisation' of the Russian economy. The credit system created under her reign became known as the 'Catherine credit system', and lasted until the middle of the nineteenth century.[8]

Catherine II declared herself a supporter of the economic teachings of the Physiocrats. The customs tariffs of 1767 and 1782 were a further step towards free trade. For the first time, Russian state credit gained access to the international monetary market. The state's encouragement of trade promoted the intensification of foreign commerce, especially with England.[9] Reforms in the

5 Pavlenko, 'Torgovo-promyslennaia', 65–6.

6 See Anisimov. *Gosudarstvennye preobrazovaniia.*

7 E. V. Anisimov, 'Rossiia v "epokhu dvortsovykh perevorotov"', in B. V Anan'ich, et al. (eds.), *Vlast' i reformy. Ot samoderzhavnoi k sovetskoi Rossii* (St Petersburg: Dmitrii Bulanin, 1996), pp. 162–3.

8 More details in S. Ia. Borovoi, *Kredit i banki v Rossii (seredina XVII veka – 1861* (Moscow: Gosfinizdat, 1958); See 'Banki i bankiry. Ekaterinskaia sistema: 1760–1850e', in B. V. Anan'ich et al. (eds.), *Petersburg. Istoriia bankov* (St Petersburg: Tret'e Tysecheletie, 2001), pp. 34–108.

9 H. Kaplan, *Russian Overseas Commerce with Great Britain during the Reign of Catherine II* (Philadelphia: American Philosophical Society, 1995).

area of local government helped industrial development in the provinces. The accumulation of capital, as well as the improvement of banking and monetary circulation, created conditions for private credit and the expansion of industrial production.[10] The number of factories using hired labour increased to 2,000 during Catherine II's reign, a fourfold increase. Most of these hired workers were peasants on *obrok* (quit-rents).[11] However, these changes did not undermine the foundations of the serf system.

Wars and the growth of the empire exerted an enormous influence on the Russian economy, especially through the annexation of the economically developed areas of Poland and the Crimea. The expansion of the empire's borders proved hugely expensive but also promoted the development of industry and foreign trade. At the end of the eighteenth century, this development became very noticeable. Western European states gladly purchased inexpensive Russian raw materials. Russia in return imported cotton, wool, silk and colonial goods including tea, coffee, sugar and wines.[12]

A sharp budget deficit, worsened by expenditures on the 1769–74 war with Turkey, became one of the reasons for introducing paper money into circulation at the end of December 1768. Special banks were opened in Moscow and St Petersburg in 1769 for financial transactions with the new paper money. In 1786 these banks were united into a single State Paper Money (Assignat) Bank. From 1783 to 1790 a new building for the bank was built by the Italian architect Giacomo Quarenghi in St Petersburg, at the intersection of the Catherine canal and Sadovaia Street. Printed money was exchanged mainly for bronze coins. It was also traded for silver coinage, but in 1772 the exchange rate of paper money vis-à-vis silver began to drop, and further trading into silver became rare. The government used the resources of the Paper Money Bank to cover emergency expenditures, including war needs.

In 1786 Catherine II signed a manifesto transforming the Bank of the Nobility into a lending bank. This bank provided credit for real estate, including industrial enterprises and the construction of private stone houses. The bank offered 4 per cent interest rates to depositors and issued loans for a period of eight years, including to cities. The bank also opened an insurance company.

Besides banks, other institutions also conducted credit transactions, in particular the Moscow and Petersburg foundling homes. These organisations

10 V. Vitchevskii, *Torgovaia, tamozhennaia i promyshlennaia politika Rossii* (St Petersburg: Izdanie D. A. Kazitsina i Iu. D. Philipova, 1909), pp. 24–5.

11 See also R. Tugan Baranovskii, *Russkaia fabrika v proshlom i nastoiashchem* (Moscow: Moskovskii rabochii, 1922), pp. 41–2.

12 See Kaplan, *Russian Overseas Commerce.*

were directed by committees of 'guardians/trustees'. They paid interest on deposits, conducted money transfers between Moscow and St Petersburg and offered loans, accepting real estate and precious metals as collateral.

During Catherine II's reign the so-called 'court bankers' began to appear. These court bankers continued to exist in Russia until the 1860 reforms. As a rule, court bankers were foreign. In Russia they served both the private and state sectors. Amongst the court financiers of the second half of the eighteenth century was the English merchant William Gomm, who traded through Archangel, the Dutch merchant Fredericks, and Richard Sutherland, who became widely known as a court financier of Catherine II. A central function of the court bankers was to manage the government's foreign payments and search for international credit. During Catherine II's reign, Russia began to take out foreign loans regularly. In 1769 the government of Catherine, with Fredericks serving as the middleman, concluded its first major loan with the Amsterdam banking house Raymond and Theodore De Smeth. The money was used to cover military expenditures, specifically the upkeep of the Russian fleet in the Mediterranean Sea and to strengthen Russia's influence in Poland. The loan of 1769 marked the beginning of the growth of Russian foreign debt. Russia's main creditor became the Dutch banking house of Hope and Company. This firm financed Russia's military operations during the entire Russo-Turkish war of 1787–91. Russia took out eighteen loans from Hope and Company just between 1788 and 1793. Richard Sutherland was the intermediary between Hope and Company and the government of Catherine II until his death in 1791. In addition, three loans were taken in Genoa from the banking firm of Aimé Renny from 1791 to 1793. To help pay for the foreign debt, the tax on wine was increased.[13]

After Paul I's accession to the throne Russian debt to Dutch bankers was consolidated. The total was 8,833,000 guilders. This included the debt of the last Polish king and some private Polish debts. Paul I decreed in 1797 that a Special Committee for paying the debt be founded. The emperor reorganised the institute of court bankers. A royal decree of 4 March 1798 created the Office of Court Bankers and Commissioners (Vaught, Velho, Rally and Co.) to manage domestic and foreign financial operations. Their task was to maintain good relations with the Russian government's foreign contacts. Paul I intended to stop borrowing from abroad. However, in 1798 an agreement was concluded with the English government for a loan of £225,000 sterling plus £75,000 sterling

13 See B. V. Anan'ich and S. K. Lebedev, 'Kontora pridvornykh bankirov v Rossii i Evropeiskie denezhnye rynki (1798–1811)', in *Problemy sotsial'no-ekonomicheskoi istorii Rossii* (St Petersburg: Nauka, 1991), pp. 125–47.

monthly. This money was intended to finance a joint Anglo-Russian expedition in Holland and Russo-Austrian operations in northern Italy. Russia was to receive the money through the London banking house of Harman and Company. Many European banking houses, primarily from Hamburg, transferred money to the places of Russian troop deployment. London and Hamburg were the main centres through which Russian financial operations abroad took place. Through Harman and Company Russia received £815,000 in 1799, £545,494 in 1800, £250,000 in 1802, £63,000 in 1803 and £614,183 in 1807.[14] The court bankers also played a crucial role in financing Russian ground and sea military operations during the Napoleonic Wars (1805–14).

In 1801 Alexander I came to the throne. In 1802 a decree was issued to create ministries in Russia. In 1803 the Ministry of Finance set up an Office for Foreign Monetary Matters. Some of the court bankers' functions became the responsibility of this new unit. In 1811 the Office was formally closed, although it continued until 1816 to conduct limited money transfers abroad. In 1806 the Finance Committee was created. To a large extent, this committee determined the government's finance policies. After 1811 international financial operations were supervised by the Third Department of the Chancellery of the Ministry of Finance, which had been created to replace the Office for Foreign Monetary Matters. In 1824 it became the Credit Chancellery of the Finance Ministry and was subsequently again renamed as the Special Credit Chancellery of the Ministry of Finance. This chancellery controlled all foreign financial operations in pre-revolutionary Russia down to 1917.

The first minister of commerce, Count N. P. Rumiantsev, like Alexander I, was an advocate of free trade, which was fashionable in European intellectual circles at that time. But already by 1806 trade policy had become totally dependent on military affairs. In 1807 Alexander signed a treaty with Napoleon I at Tilsit. At France's insistence Russia joined the Continental System blockade against England, its main trading partner. The Continental System dealt a sharp blow to Russia's economy. But at the same time, it boosted the development of Russia's textile and sugar industries and furthered the development of trade relations in southern Russia. For example, Odessa's role as a major commercial port grew. Trade relations with England returned to normal only after the break with Napoleon I and the Grand Army's invasion of Russia. Under the influence of the 1815 Congress of Vienna, Russia introduced a customs tariff in 1816. This allowed much freedom for foreign trade. Soon after, the tariff of 1819 brought even lower duties on imported industrial

14 Anan'ich, 'Kontora pridvornykh', p. 136.

goods.[15] However, within two years the government had returned to the policy of protectionism. The tariff of 1822 prohibited the import of 300 types of goods and the export of 21.[16] This tariff lasted until 1841, when it was slightly relaxed, and remained in its revised form until 1851.[17] Despite the policy of protectionism the period of the 1820s–40s saw continued growth in Russia's foreign trade. Within twenty years the value of Russian exports almost doubled, from 55 to 100 million roubles; the value of imports did in fact double, from 40 to 80 million roubles. Seventy-five per cent of Russian exports were agricultural goods, 11 per cent were timber and commercial goods and 14 per cent were industrial goods.[18] Beginning in the 1830s, grain becomes an important Russian export as well. Sixty-two per cent of bread exports went through Odessa and other Mediterranean ports, 7 per cent through Archangel, 25 per cent through ports on the Baltic Sea and 6 per cent via land routes. The rise of bread prices on the European market further encouraged grain exports in the 1840s and the development of Russian factories specialising in agricultural equipment and tools.[19]

The 1840s also saw a growth in the development of Russian industry. In 1833 there were more than 5,500 factories and mills in Russia. By 1850 that number rose to 9,848, and the number of workers employed in them increased from 227,670 to 500,000.[20] Gradually, factories that employed serfs began to disappear. In 1839 Finance Minister E. F. Kankrin proposed to phase out factories with permanently assigned serf labour (*posessionnye*) forces.[21] In the first half of the nineteenth century, serf-labour factories slowly became capitalist, and the number of factories employing free labour grew greatly, their owners now sometimes being not only nobles and landowners, but also peasants.[22] Free labour was used, first of all, in the cotton industry. In the 1830s–50s, this industry experienced significant success. In these years railway construction also began in Russia. In 1837 the first railway was opened from St Petersburg to Tsarskoe Selo, and from 1843–51 a second rail line was built connecting Moscow and St Petersburg.

15 V. I. Pokrovskii, *Sbornik svedenii po istorii i statistike vneshnei torgovli Rossii* (St Petersburg: Departament Tamozhennykh Sborov, 1902), p. 30.
16 Vitchevskii, *Torgovaia*, p. 51.
17 A. S. Nifontov, *1848 v Rossii. Ocherki po istorii 40-kh godov* (Moscow and Leningrad: Sotsial'no economicheskoe izd. 1931), p. 15.
18 Nifontov, *1848*, pp. 16–17.
19 Nifontov, *1848*, pp. 19, 31.
20 Nifontov, *1848*, p. 34.
21 Vitchevskii, *Torgovaia*, p. 80.
22 Tugan-Baranovskii, *Russkaia fabrika*, pp. 80–3.

Despite these economic successes in the first half of the nineteenth century, Russia, devastated by the Continental System and the Napoleonic Wars, began to lag economically behind the West European powers, although its military prestige in Europe remained extremely high until the Crimean War. This economic backwardness was above all clear as regards the iron industry. In the first half of the eighteenth century Russia produced significantly more cast iron than England and until the end of the century it maintained a strong position in the world market. At the beginning of the nineteenth century, however, the export of iron from Russian began to decline rapidly as Russia lost its ability to compete with the economically developed European countries.

Beginning in this period, economic backwardness becomes a chronic phenomenon in Russia, and the government's commercial-industrial policy takes on a cyclical character. Periods of economic stagnation are followed by reformist activism aimed at catching up its European competitors and retaining Russia's influence in Europe.[23] Many Russian senior officials believed that the thirty years of stagnation during the reign of Nicholas I was the reason for Russia's economic backwardness.[24]

The Napoleonic Wars also disrupted the Russian monetary system and caused a budget deficit. To combat these ills, in 1839 Finance Minister E. F. Kankrin introduced monetary reform. A fixed exchange rate for paper money and silver was established, and then beginning 1 July 1841 it was announced that new banknotes would be introduced to replace the old paper money (assignats). By 1848 the old paper money had been fully exchanged into bank-notes (credit roubles) and the Paper Money Bank (Assignat Bank) was abolished. Bank-notes were also exchanged into silver, but with the beginning of the Crimean War this practice stopped.

In 1841 the emperor signed a decree creating savings banks. These were unique because they served all classes of society. The first savings bank opened in St Petersburg on 1 March 1842 on Bolshaia Kazanskaia Street. As industry and trade grew in the beginning of the nineteenth century, the question of commercial credit also became increasingly pressing. In January 1818 the Commercial Bank was established specifically to address this issue. One of the bank's main functions was inventorying bills of exchange. But by the middle of the nineteenth century, it became clear that the system of state banks had become obsolete. Indeed defeat in the Crimean War demonstrated the degree

23 T. Taranovskii (ed.), *Reform in Modern Russian History: Progress or Cycle?* (New York: Woodrow Wilson Centre Press and Cambridge University Press, 1995).
24 Ananich et al. (eds.), *Vlast'*, p. 423.

of Russia's overall backwardness. The lessons of defeat forced the government of Alexander II to embark on radical changes in Russia's economic and financial systems.

The era of Great Reforms

In the summer of 1859 advocates of radical change in the Finance Ministry prepared a monetary and credit reform. The decision was made to abolish state treasury banks. In that same year, Jewish merchants of the first guild were allowed to settle outside the Jewish Pale and the practice of accepting serfs, or 'living collateral', for credit to landowners was ended. On 26 December 1859 the Loan Bank no longer accepted deposits. The Commercial Bank accepted deposits until 1 July 1860. The supporters of financial and economic reforms in the Ministry of Finance were influenced by Western European economic theories, in particular, by the ideas of Saint-Simon on the all-powerful role of credit in industrial development. Relying on this theory, the famous bankers Isaac and Emile Pereire founded the major joint-stock bank Société Générale de Crédit Mobilier in 1852, which was closely connected with the government of Napoleon III. This new-generation financial enterprise actively engaged in railroad construction in France, Austria, Hungary, Switzerland, Spain and Russia. The extraordinary sweep of its operations drew attention, and the bank served as a model for similar institutions across Europe. The idea of credit's omnipotence conquered Russia as well and helped drive the development of private commercial credit, and later joint-stock credit.

On 31 May 1860 the State Bank was established, marking the beginning of a new banking system in Russia. The State Bank was located in St Petersburg, in the building of the old Paper Money Bank. The State Bank became a distinctive symbol of the empire's financial strength. Its basements housed Russia's gold reserves. From the moment of its creation, the State Bank was under the authority of the Ministry of Finance. Its resources were used for important state needs. It was supposed to promote the development of trade and monetary circulation. It was allowed to discount promissory notes and other obligations, to buy and sell gold, silver and state bonds, to accept deposits and give out loans. The State Bank quickly became the 'bank of banks', and allowed the government to influence the economy and banking. The State Bank was commercial, and not a bank of issue: new bank-notes were released only at the order of the Finance Ministry. The main source of income for the State Bank was deposits at a 4 per cent interest rate. The first director of the State Bank was Alexander Stieglitz, the last court banker.

The Stieglitz banking house grew up in the 1830s and early 1840s. In 1840 the Russian Finance Ministry took out a series of 4 per cent loans. The intermediary between the Russian government and the bankers of Amsterdam, London and Berlin was Ludwig Stieglitz, and after his death in 1843, Alexander Stieglitz. Alexander did much to make his banking house prosper. He established relations with the London banking house Baring Brothers and Co. and through them in 1849 a loan was secured to complete a railway from St Petersburg to Moscow. The most important loans during the Crimean War were also secured by Alexander Stieglitz.

Before the beginning of railway construction in Russia, foreign loans mainly were used to cover military expenditures and to support monetary circulation. Railway construction gave birth to a new category of loans. Railway companies' loans often were guaranteed by the state. In 1857 Alexander Stieglitz helped to found the Main Society of Russian Railways, which was formed to build and operate a planned 4,000 versts of railroad lines. These railway lines were supposed to connect Russia's farmlands with Petersburg, Moscow, Warsaw and the coasts of the Baltic and Black seas. Bankers from Warsaw, London, Amsterdam and Paris also helped to found the company.

The international financial crisis of 1858–9 disrupted monetary circulation in Russia. The Main Society of Railways was also affected. This, in turn, diminished the authority of Stieglitz. The banking and financial reforms of 1860 led to the liquidation of the Stieglitz banking house. But his appointment as head of the State Bank was, despite the criticisms against him in the press and the Ministry of Finance, a perfectly logical occurrence. Stieglitz continued to control all the threads of the empire's financial management. His transfer to the State Bank meant that many of the functions of the old court bankers now moved to the new financial structures. The State Bank was charged with managing Russia's international financial dealings. The bank kept this responsibility until 1866, as long as Stieglitz remained the head of the State Bank.

In his short time at the State Bank, Stieglitz brokered several foreign loans. In 1862 he helped to secure a loan of £15 million at 5 per cent interest for monetary reforms from the London- and Paris-based Rothschilds. In May 1862 it was announced that henceforth the State Bank would exchange gold and silver coins and bullion for paper money. However, the State Bank was forced to cease this practice by November 1863. The reform failed because of the Polish rebellion of January 1863. The rebellion led to a sharp budget deficit and panic on the Petersburg stock exchange. The free exchange of paper money into silver and gold had to be halted. A long period of paper money circulation began. Resources were needed to support the budget, and in 1864 and 1866 Stieglitz concluded two large loans at 5 per cent interest rates with the English and Dutch. These bailouts, brokered by Hope and Co. (Amsterdam) and Baring Brothers (London) were intended to stabilise Russia's financial situation. Other measures were taken as well, but this was not enough to overcome the fall of the exchange rate for the paper rouble. The State Bank raised its discount rate to 8.5 per cent, and Stieglitz was forced to resign. After his resignation, the Foreign Department of the Special Credit Chancellery of the Finance Ministry took control over concluding foreign loans.[25]

In the 1860–80s, a system of joint-stock banks of commercial credit emerged in Russia, as did mutual credit societies. St Petersburg and Moscow became large banking centres.

In 1864 in St Petersburg, the first joint-stock bank was founded, the Petersburg Private Bank. Soon after, several more banks opened in the capital: the Petersburg International Commercial Bank in 1869; the Volga-Kama Commercial Bank in 1870; and the Russian Bank for Foreign Trade in 1871. In 1899 the Siberian Bank transferred its board of directors from Ekaterinburg to St Petersburg and at the beginning of the twentieth century the Azov-Don Bank moved its headquarters from Taganrog to the Russian capital. This group of Petersburg banks began to play the leading role in the financial life of the empire.[26]

In contrast to the Petersburg banks, private banks in Moscow were connected to the government, foreign capital and European banking to a lesser degree. In Moscow capital was controlled largely by Old Believers, who were to a certain extent even anti-government. In 1866 the Merchant Bank was founded in Moscow; in 1869 the Moscow Merchant Society of Mutual Credit; and in 1870 the Moscow Discount (*Uchotnyi*) Bank and Moscow Commercial Bank. A number of other banks were founded in the 1870s but many of them quickly collapsed. Around the beginning of the twentieth century new influential banks appeared in Moscow, linked to L. S. Poliakov's banking house. Poliakov moved the headquarters of the Moscow-Riazan Bank from Riazan

25 For more on Stieglitz, see B. V. Anan'ich, 'Stiglitzty – Poslednie pridvornie bankiry v Rossii', in '*Bol'shoe budushchee'. Nemtsy v ekonomicheskoi zhizni Rossii* (Berlin, Bonn, Hessen and Moscow: Mercedes Druk, Berlin, 2000), pp. 196–201.

26 Anan'ich et al. (eds.), *Petersburg. Istoriia bankov*, pp. 120–207; Iu. A. Petrov, *Kommercheskie banky Moskvy. Konets XIX veka – 1914* (Moscow: Rosspen, 1998). Iu. A. Petrov, *Moskovskaia burzhuaziia v nachale XX veka: Predprinimatel'stvo i politika* (Moscow: Mosgorarchiv, 2002). For the Moscow bourgeoisie see also T. Owen, *Capitalism and Politics in Russia: A Social History of the Moscow Merchants 1855–1905* (Cambridge: Cambridge University Press, 1981); A. Rieber, *Merchants and Entrepreneurs in Imperial Russia* (Chapel Hill: University of North Carolina Press, 1982).

to Moscow, and later the bank became known as the Moscow International Commercial Bank. He also transferred the South-Russian Industrial Bank's main offices from Kiev to Moscow.

In the beginning of the 1860s a new system of mortgage credit was formed in Russia. In addition, societies of mutual land credit and several joint-stock land banks opened. Also, two state banks for mortgage credit were founded in the capital: the State Peasant Land Bank in 1883, and the State Noble Land Bank in 1885. The creation of state banks for mortgage credit further strengthened the Ministry of Finance's control over banking.

Banks in the capital and banking houses were closely connected to the government and many of them acted as conduits of state policy abroad. Among such banks at the end of the nineteenth and the very beginning of the twentieth century was the Saint Petersburg International Commercial Bank. In 1894 it acted jointly with a group of French banks to found the Russo-Chinese Bank. By the beginning of the Russo-Japanese War this bank became the main channel for moving capital from Russia to the Far East. The Discount-Loan Bank of Persia was created in Persia to benefit Russian investment and trade. In contrast to the Russo-Chinese Bank, the Discount-Loan Bank of Persia was not linked to foreign capital but instead issued credit at the expense of the State Bank and State Treasury. Hoping to break into markets in the Far East and Central Asia, the Finance Ministry also helped to create the short-lived Russo-Korean Bank.[27]

The Great Reforms of the late 1850s to early 1860s, especially the banking reform and emancipation of serfs, allowed the government to set a course for faster development of Russian industry. Beginning in the 1860s, the commercial-industrial policy of the tsarist government acquired a systematic character. The Russian government in the second half of the nineteenth century was often an imperfect machine. However the Ministry of Finance was a noteworthy exception. It was headed by distinguished statesmen: M. Kh. Reutern, N. Kh. Bunge, I. A. Vyshnegradskii and finally S. Iu. Witte were ministers of finance for long periods and key figures in government. Bunge and Vyshnegradsky were also scholars recognised worldwide.[28]

In his first years as finance minister, between 1866 and 1870, Reutern advocated encouraging private enterprise. With European countries increasingly

27 See B. V. Anan'ich, *Rossiiskoe samoderzhavie i vyzov kapitalov, 1895–1914* (Leningrad: Nauka, 1957); C. Dokkyu, *Rossiia v Koree, 1893–1905* (St Petersburg: Zero, 1996); S. K. Lebedev, *S-Peterburgskii mezhdunarodnii kommercheskii bank vo vtoroi polovine XIX veka* (Moscow: Rosspen, 2003).

28 P. A. Zaionchkovskii, *Pravitel'stvennyi aparat samoderzhavnoi Rossii v XIX veke* (Moscow: Mysl', 1978); L. E. Shepelev, *Tsarizm i burzhuaziia vo vtoroi polovine XIX veka. Problemy torgovo-promyshlennoi politiki* (Leningrad: Nauka, 1981).

allowing private enterprises to form without explicit government permission, Russian leaders understood that new legislation was needed to give more room for private initiative in the founding of joint-stock companies.[29] However, this idea remained unrealised. Possibly influenced by the 1873 stock-market crisis, Reutern ordered that work cease on the proposed legislation in 1874 and began to support restricting the foundation of joint-stock public enterprises.[30] In 1877 Reutern argued that the government should use its resources to combat speculation on the stock market, regulate the exchange rate of the rouble and bonds, and discourage free competition. It was this logic that started the practice of the government supporting, according to its own judgement, individual enterprises and banks by providing them special loans from the State Bank.[31] As a result, in the 1870s the state developed several methods to influence the country's economy.

In the 1870s the Russian government floated a series of railway bonds on European markets. From 1870 to 1884 the tsarist government produced seven issues of consolidated railroad bonds to replenish the special government fund for supporting railway companies. The first four bond issues, as well as the seventh, carried an interest rate of 5 per cent; the fifth issue offered 4.5 per cent, and the sixth issue – 4 per cent. The first five issues (two at £12 million, and the rest at £15 millions each) were sold through the Paris and London Rothschilds. The total sum of £15 million of the fourth bond issue was partly floated through the Rothschilds, the State Bank, and also through Hope and Co. as well as the Paris banking house Vernier. The active participation of German banks in Berlin, Hamburg and Frankfurt was significant in the sixth and seventh bond issues.

In the second half of the 1870s, because of the deterioration in Anglo-Russian relations due to competition in Central Asia, Russia's main creditor became Germany rather than England. By the beginning of the 1880s major German banks (Diskonto-Gesellschaft, Bleichroder, M. A. Rothschild, Mendelssohn, Warschauer, Berliner Handelsgesellschaft) formed the so-called Russian Syndicate for floating Russian loans. The Amsterdam banking house Lippmann and Rosenthal also closely worked with this syndicate.

Reutern's successors as finance minister generally shared his overall views on the government's role in economic policy. But this does not mean that Russia's economic policy after Reutern was unchanged. In many ways, economic

29 I. F. Gindin, *Gosudarstvennyi bank i aktsionernaia politika tsarskogo pravitel'stva (1861–1892)* (Moscow: Gosfinizdat, 1960), p. 45.

30 L. E. Shepelev, *Aktsionernye kompanii v Rossii* (Leningrad: Nauka, 1973), pp. 112, 116.

31 Gindin, *Gosudarstvennyi bank*, pp. 46–9.

policy depended on the general direction of politics and the personality of the minister. In this regard, the views and activities of N. Kh. Bunge as finance minister are quite revealing. Bunge was a distinguished professor and rector of the University of Saint Vladimir in Kiev and the author of numerous works on the history of finance and monetary circulation, trade and credit. He headed the Finance Ministry from February 1881. The appointment of a university professor to such a prestigious governmental post was very unusual. In part it can be explained by the fact that Bunge was well known to the Romanovs. In the beginning of the 1860s he taught financial law to Grand Duke Nicholas, the eldest son of Tsar Alexander II, and in the 1880s he taught the future Tsar Nicholas II. Bunge was very familiar with contemporary Western economic theory and could evaluate the experience of industrial development in Europe and the United States. In his academic writings Bunge devoted much effort to studying the relationship between private enterprise and state involvement in Russia's economic development.

As a teacher, Bunge tried to persuade the future emperor Nicholas II that he should avoid the extreme characteristics of Nicholas I's policies of state intervention in the economy. Bunge believed that the state should aid private initiative only when the state's interests made this truly necessary.[32] He was worried by the state's increasing role in the economic life of the empire. In the second half of the 1890s, in his famous 'Notes from the Afterlife', Bunge wrote that on the eve of the Crimean War, 'the private hand' in 'spiritual and material life' had been far too restricted.

> The disappointment felt by everyone during the Crimean War led to a domestic policy . . . which expected everything from private initiative, but this policy revealed itself sometimes in such deplorable forms that reasonable people began once again to cry out for governmental oversight and control, and even for replacing private with state activity. We are continuing in this direction even now, when people want the government to take over the grain trade and supply a population of a hundred million. It seems impossible to continue on in this direction unless you assume that the government should plow, sow and reap, and then publish all the newspapers and magazines, write stories and novels and make progress in the fields of art and science.[33]

Bunge believed that Russia lagged behind Western Europe in industrial development by a half-century. He argued that one reason for this was that

32 See N. I. Anan'ich, 'Materialy lektsionnykh kursov N. X. Bunge 60–80x godov XIX veka', *Arkheograficheskii Ezhegodnik za 1977 god.* (Moscow: Nauka, 1978), pp. 304–6.

33 A letter found in N. Kh. Bunge's papers, 1881–1894. RGIA, Fond 1622, op. I, d. 721, l. 52.

Russian lacked modern legislation regulating factories.[34] In the beginning of the 1880s, Bunge introduced new factory legislation. On 1 June 1882, a law was passed forbidding the employment of minors in factories. For adolescents aged 12–15 an eight-hour work day was established. In 1882 a Factory Inspectorate was established under the Ministry of Finance. On 3 June 1886 a law was published which regulated relations between factory owners and workers. The new Factory Inspectorate was charged with enforcing this law. Bunge also thought that workers should receive a share of an enterprise's profits, as this would relieve some social tensions. Bunge formulated his opinions on the workers question by relying on Western models: the Swiss government, for example, had built special workers quarters in Bern, and he often used the dye plants of Leclarke in England as an example of a model enterprise.[35]

Bunge developed and implemented a range of other economic reforms. One of his most important tax reforms was the elimination of the poll tax in 1886. This became an important step on the path to replacing estate-based taxation with property-based taxation. In the beginning of 1885 Bunge introduced an additional 3 per cent duty to the trade tax (*promyslovyi nalog*) and three years later a 5 per cent tax levy was added to incomes from monetary capital.[36] On 12 June 1886 the emperor authorised a law changing state peasants' obrok into payments towards purchasing their land. Thus, the opportunity arose for these peasants to become full landowners.[37] Bunge was a staunch opponent of the existing system of collective responsibility (*krugovaia poruka*) and of the passport system, because they hindered the free movement of the peasants.[38] At his initiative a passport reform was developed. However, following Bunge's resignation in December 1886, the reform got caught in bureaucratic red tape until the beginning of the 1890s.

The policy of forced industrial development

The poor harvests of 1883 and 1885 worsened an already unstable economic situation. Bunge's attempts to fix the budget deficit were unsuccessful. Advocates of a new course of state policy took advantage of this failure: The chief

34 L. E. Shepelev, *Tsarizm i burzhuaziia vo vtoroi polovine XIX veka* (Leningrad: Nauka 1981), pp. 138–9.

35 A letter found in N. Kh. Bunge's papers, l. 58 ob–59.

36 *PSZ*, 3rd series, vol. 5. no. 2961.

37 N. I. Anan'ich, 'K istorii otmeny podushnoi podati v Rossii', *Istoricheskie zapiski*, 94 (1974): 201.

38 For the connection between these two phenomena in the government policy of the 1880s–90s, see M. S. Simonova, 'Otmena krugovoi poruki', *IZ*, 83 (1969): 159–95.

procurator of the Synod K. P. Pobedonostsev, the editor of the newspaper *Moskovskie vedomosti* M. N. Katkov, and their supporters spoke out against the liberal reforms. They argued that 'a People's Autocracy' was a distinctive, natural form of rule for Russia. In their view, the Russian nobility should be the connecting link between the tsar and the people. Katkov's influence on Alexander III and state policy in the 1880s was so significant that in bureaucratic circles he and Pobedonostsev were seen as a second government alongside the legal one.[39] The central aim of Katkov and Pobedonostsev's economic programme was to strengthen autocratic power by developing domestic industry. They favoured protectionism, maintaining paper-money circulation, tight control over the stock market and private enterprise, using state monopolies (wine and tobacco) as a resource for taxation, and economic support for large landowners. The development of domestic industry was supposed to go together with the strengthening of communal landownership in the villages.

Pobedonostsev and Katkov began to campaign against Bunge in the press as early as autumn 1885. In January 1887 Bunge left the post of finance minister and was appointed to the prestigious but less influential position of chairman of the Committee of Ministers. I. A. Vyshnegradskii, who was close to Katkov, became the minister of finance. Vyshnegradskii was a former professor of mechanics, director of the Petersburg Technological Institute and also well known in the entrepreneurial world as a leading figure in the Petersburg Water Company and vice-chairman of the South-western Railways. But Katkov sought not only Bunge's resignation, but also that of the foreign affairs minister, N. K. Giers, and he hoped to replace the two 'Germans' with his own protégés, I. A. Vyshnegradskii and I. A. Zinovev respectively. But Katkov was not able to realise his plans fully: in the summer of 1887 the influential editor of *Moskovskie vedomosti* died.

I. A. Vyshnegradskii aligned himself with the *Moskovskie vedomosti* group long before his appointment to a ministerial post, and he actively supported Katkov's attacks on Bunge. In the middle of 1885, S. Iu. Witte, the young manager of the South-western Railways, joined the group. Vyshnegradskii set a goal – to eliminate the budget deficit. He quickly came to the conclusion that introducing a monopoly on tobacco was unrealistic and also decided against starting a monopoly on wine.

In March 1889 a Department of Railways was formed within the Ministry of Finance. It was headed by S. Iu. Witte. As a result of Vyshnegradskii's

39 V. A. Tvardovskaia, *Ideologiia poreformennogo samoderzhaviia (M.N. Katkov i ego izdaniia)* (Moscow: Nauka, 1978), pp. 225, 230, 235.

reforms, the state began buying up railways whereupon the income of the state railways rose, while expenditures on their upkeep declined.[40] Vyshnegradskii also believed that it was wise to develop large and profitable private railways.[41] In 1889 and 1890 import duties were raised and a new customs tariff was introduced. This was a severe protectionist measure and influenced the development of domestic industry.[42] Customs revenues steadily increased.[43] Beginning in 1889, despite resistance from landowners in central and western regions, Vyshnegradskii created a system of state regulation of bread prices. The tariff legislation of 1889 was further developed in 1893–7. During these years the state's role in the development of the grain trade increased. Vyshnegradskii also re-examined Bunge's legislation on workers. He removed officials from the Factory Inspectorate who were strongly disliked by the business community. The Factory Inspectorate now allowed minors to work on Sundays and holidays, and provincial factory inspectorates and governors could allow night employment for women and teenagers. As a result of these changes, the Factory Inspectorate, created by Bunge to enforce factory laws, lost its influence to a certain extent.

Vyshnegradskii's attempt to adapt Russia's economic policy to the general political doctrine of Alexander III was reflected not only in the increase of state intervention in the economy and the tightening of worker's legislation, but also in his support for a conservative agrarian policy. In 1886 a law was passed restricting the right of communal peasants to divide their land, and in 1889 the institution of the Land Captain (*zemskii nachal'nik*) was introduced. The 'Land Captain' assumed many functions of judges in the *mir* system. They appointed office-holders in villages and volost' administrations, as well as volost' judges.[44]

However, Vyshnegradskii did not blindly follow the economic programme of Katkov and Pobedonostsev. He rejected their idea of promoting paper-money circulation and continued with Bunge's course of trying to set Russia on the gold standard. In 1889 Vyshnegradskii tried to realise Bunge's plan of reconfiguring Russia's bond offers abroad. He sought to exchange current 5 and 6 per cent Russian bonds on European markets for new bonds that offered lower interest rates and longer maturation times. After the first group of new

40 P. P. Migulin, *Nasha noveishaia zheleznodorozhnaia politika i zheleznodorozhnie zaimy (1893–1902)* (Kharkov: Tipolitografiia 'Pechatnoe Delo' K. Gagarina, 1903), p. 17.

41 K. Akinori, 'Ekonomicheskaia programma dvoryanksoi reaktsii i politika I. A. Vyshegradskogo', *Journal of Asahikawa University* 5 (March 1977): 209.

42 *PSZ*, 3rd series, vol. 11. no. 7811.

43 Shepelev, *Tsarizm i burzhuaziia* (1981), p. 160.

44 P. A. Zaionchkovskii, *Rossiiskoe samoderzhavie v kontse XIX stoletiia* (Moscow: Mysl', 1970), p. 257.

Russian bonds were sold in 1889 Vyshnegradskii offered several more series in France. As a result, a significant part of Russian securities moved from German to French markets.

Vyshnegradskii's tenure as finance minister was marked by a sharp increase in exports. If under Bunge from 1882–6 the average yearly value of Russian exports was 574 million roubles, and imports were worth 508 million roubles, then under Vyshnegradskii from 1886–91 the numbers were 710.6 million roubles and 403.3 million roubles respectively. Grain represented the lion's share of Russian export. Bread exports rose from an annual average of 312 million roubles from 1882–6 to 441 million roubles from 1887–91. After abolishing the poll tax, Bunge had decided to forgive peasants' debt for unpaid poll-tax arrears from previous years. Vyshnegradskii believed otherwise, and from 1887 to 1888 was able to collect more than 16 million roubles in back taxes. Thanks to Vyshnegradskii's policies, the budget surplus between 1888 and 1891 reached the impressive figure of 209.4 million roubles. However, in the famine years of 1891 and 1892 the government was forced to spend 162.5 million roubles to aid the starving population.[45] These famine years and their destructive consequences proved to be a high price for Vyshnegradskii's aim to eliminate the budget deficit at any cost. Twenty-nine of Russia's ninety-seven provinces and oblasts suffered from the poor harvest, and more than 500,000 people died from famine and cholera.[46] Under these conditions, the failures of the 'Vyshnegradskii system' became obvious. In 1892 Vyshnegradskii became very ill and was forced to leave his post. S. Iu. Witte became the new finance minister. The famine of 1891–2 once again reminded the world of Russia's backwardness and of the necessity for radical changes not only in the economy, but also in the political system.

Alexander III died in 1894. The new emperor was Nicholas II. In his first public speech on 17 January 1894 at the Winter Palace, meeting with representatives of the *zemstvos* (elected district and provincial councils), Nicholas announced that he did not intend to change Russia's political system in any way. But this did not rule out economic reforms. They were needed to promote the autocracy and calm liberal elements of society. Consequently, Witte led a series of important economic reforms at the end of the 1890s.

45 See: Vitchevskii, *Torgovaia*, p. 128; P. A. Shvanebakh, *Nashe podatnoe delo* (St Petersburg: Tip. M. M. Stassiulevicha, 1903), p. 14.

46 See A. M. Anfimov, 'Prodovol'stvennye dolgi kak pokazatel' ekonomicheskogo polozheniia krest'ian dorevolutsionnoi Rossii (konets XIX – nachalo XX veka)', *Materialy po istorii sel'skogo khoziaistva i krest'ianstva SSSR* (Moscow: Nauka, 1960), p. 294.

As finance minister, Witte tried to continue the economic course of Katkov and Pobedonostsev. However, Witte soon began to move away from their ideas for reasons of pragmatism, and between 1896 and 1898, when Witte's policies began to be seen as a 'system', they were actually a compromise between the ideologists of the 1880s and the advocates of economic changes of the 1860s and 1870s. The year 1896 became a turning point for Witte's own ideology: formerly a staunch defender of communal landownership, he suddenly declared himself an ardent opponent of the idea. At the heart of Witte's strategy was speeding up the development of domestic industry. Until the mid-1880s, Witte was influenced by Slavophile ideology.[47] However at the end of the 1880s, his idol became the famous German economist and advocate of protectionism, Friedrich List. In 1889 Witte published a small brochure 'The National Economy and Friedrich List'. In it, Witte argued for rejecting cosmopolitan views and instead following the teachings of List, the prophet 'of Germany's greatness, which was created by Bismark on the basis of his [List's] theories'.[48]

It would seem that the tragedy of the 1892–3 famine should have had a sobering effect on the proponents of higher taxes. Nevertheless, Witte, like Vyshnegradskii, continued to use indirect taxation as an important source of replenishing the budget. From 1892 to 1901, revenues from indirect taxation increased by 50 per cent.[49] The spirits monopoly proved to be one of the most effective methods of raising capital. In 1894 Witte introduced the monopoly in four provinces (Perm, Orenburg, Ufa and Samara); later it was expanded throughout the country. Distilling remained in private hands, however the state gained control over sales. Purifying the spirit and producing vodka occurred in private factories but only to fill state orders and under the supervision of excise regulators. The sale of spirits, wine and vodka was under the sole purview of the state.

In the autumn of 1892 Witte tried to increase the amount of paper money in circulation by introducing a special 'Siberian' rouble to cover the costs of the Trans-Siberian railway. Evidently, Vyshnegradskii did not tell Witte about the Ministry of Finance's long preparations to introduce gold coinage in Russia. N. Kh. Bunge brought Witte's attention to the dangers of inflationary policy, and within a year the finance minister set about monetary reform in earnest. He

47 For Witte's economic views, see: Laue, *Sergei Witte*; A Korelin and S. Stepanov, *S. Iu. Vitte – Finansist, politik, diplomat* (Moscow: Terra, 1998); B. V. Anan'ich and P. Sh. Ganelin, *Serge Iulevich Vitte i ego vremiia* (St Petersburg: Dmitrii Bulanin, 2000).

48 Quoted in Korelin, *S. Iu. Vitte*, p. 314.

49 Shepelev, *Tsarizm i burzhuaziia* (1981), pp. 204–10; Shvanebakh, *Nashe podatnoe*, p. 16.

concluded the conversion operations begun by Vyshnegradskii and conducted a series of measures aimed at stabilising the rouble in a reform announced by the decree of 29 August 1897.[50] The amount of gold backing the rouble was reduced by one-third. Thus one paper rouble was worth 66.6 kopecks of gold. As a result of the reform the State Bank became an issuing institution and was given the right to issue bank-notes. All paper money in circulation, which totalled more than 300 million roubles, should have been backed in gold entirely. The introduction of the gold standard, on the one hand, opened new opportunities to obtain credit on European markets, but on the other hand, it required that the government constantly ensure that the rouble was backed by gold. Henceforth, the empire's loans were often needed not only for military expenditures, but to maintain the gold standard.

Foreign loans became one of the most important sources of finance for Witte's economic policies. He reorganised the system of commercial foreign agents within the Finance Ministry and by the beginning of 1894 he had opened agencies in Paris, London, Berlin and Washington, and later in Constantinople, Brussels, Yokohama and many other cities. In 1898 commercial agents were renamed agents of the Ministry of Finance and added to the ranks of Russian embassies and missions. As a result of this reform Witte was able to receive regular information about markets in Europe and other countries.

By the end of the 1890s, Witte began to advocate that Russia attract as much foreign investment as possible. This policy faced serious opposition, led by the Grand Duke Alexander Mikhailovich, who favoured limiting foreign capital investment in Russia, in particular in the oil industry.

Witte's programme of encouraging foreign investment accompanied protectionism, increasing indirect taxation and the raising of the commerce tax. This tax increase consisted of two parts: a main tax and an additional one. Businessmen paid the main tax by purchasing permits to operate their business. The tax burden was determined not by which guild the owners belonged to, as had been the case under previous legislation, but by the size of their business. The supplementary tax for joint-stock companies was divided into a tax on capital and a tax on a percentage of profit. It was levied only if profits exceeded 3 per cent of the fixed capital. The supplementary tax for non-public companies was divided into an arbitrary tax and a percentage tax on profits. The tax burden was determined by calculating the average profits of various enterprises.[51] Thus, a significant part of the commerce tax was based on an

50 *PSZ*, 3rd series, vol. 17, no. 14504.
51 *PSZ*, 3rd series, vol. 18, no. 15601.

archaic and primitive principle of apportioning taxation. Despite its imperfections, the new commerce tax increased state revenues. In 1898 collections from trade and commerce were 48.2 million roubles, and in 1899 – after the new commerce tax – 61.1 million roubles.[52]

By the end of the 1890s, Witte's economic programme had gained distinctive characteristics. The Finance Ministry's influence went far beyond its normal sphere of activity, and Witte had much influence on overall domestic politics. Witte linked Russia's economic development with a determined effort to gain access to markets in the East. In the second half of the 1890s, the Finance Ministry attempted the so-called peaceful economic penetration of Manchuria, Korea, Persia and Mongolia with the goal of preparing future markets for Russian industry. Banks played a central role in this policy: the Discount-Loan Bank of Persia, which was essentially a branch of the State Bank, and also the Russo-Chinese Bank, which dealt with both Russian and foreign capital. Aided by state and 'neutral' foreign capital, and through generous expenditures, the government planned on doing what the weak Russian private initiative still was incapable of undertaking. Witte hoped that within several years Russian industry would reach a rather high level of development. Russian goods would become competitive on the markets of Central Asia and the Far East, and this would allow 'the surplus from exports in Asia to pay the interest on capital obtained in Europe'.[53] From the very beginning of his tenure as Finance Minster, Witte regularly consulted with scholars. His assistants in important economics problems were D. I. Mendeleev and also the well-known economist I. I. Kaufman. Witte, perhaps more than any other minister, understood the value of science in developing the productive power of the country. This explains, in particular, his decision to create a network of polytechnic institutes in Russia.

Witte's programme to speed up the development of Russia's industry bore fruit. Industry grew particularly quickly in the mid-1890s. In the last forty years of the nineteenth century the volume of industrial production in Russia increased more than 700 per cent, while Germany's increased 500 per cent, France's 250 per cent and England's more than 200 per cent.[54] This great increase in the pace of industrial production is partially explained by Russia's relatively weak level of industrial development at the beginning of the 1860s. This was accompanied by relatively low productivity and low production of

52 S. Iu. Witte, *Konspekt lektsii o narodnom i gosudarstvennom khoziaistve* (St Petersburg: Fond 'Nachala', 1912), p. 485.
53 *Materialy po istorii SSSR*, vol. VI (Moskow: Nauka, 1959), pp. 167–8.
54 P. A. Khromov, *Ekonomicheskoe razvitie Rossii* (Moscow: Nauka, 1967), p. 283.

goods per capita as well. According to the Ministry of Finance's statistics, in 1898 cast-iron production per capita in Great Britain was 13.1 pood (old measurement in Russia = 16 kg), 9.8 pood in the United States, 9.0 pood in Belgium, 8.1 pood in Germany, 3.96 pood in France and 1.04 pood in Russia. Great Britain extracted 311.7 pood of coal, Belgium – 204, the United States – 162.4, Germany – 143.8, France – 50.7, and only 5.8 pood in Russia. This lag in production affected consumption and trade too. Russia's trade turnover, 1,286 million roubles in 1897, was less than a third of that in Germany and the United States, one-fifth of that in Great Britain, and was only equal to the turnover of Belgium.

In terms of capital, Russia was also poor. The total amount of capital in public companies, trade and industry, and also city and village credit was 11 billion roubles. About half of this amount came from abroad. At the same time, Germany's capital worth was 30 billion roubles, and England's was 60 billion.[55]

The development of industry promoted the growth of the working class and its consolidation. Data based on factory records, zemstvo documents and the 1897 census indicate that by the beginning of the twentieth century there were 14.5 million workers.[56] The development of industry also led to the growth of cities and urban populations. According to the 1897 census the population of both Moscow and St Petersburg was over one million. Cities gained an industrial feel and image as well. Petersburg turned into a capital for machine building. New areas of industry were being developed there: chemical and electrical industry. The Moscow industrial region remained the strongest in Russia. Besides old areas (the Central Industrial Region and the Urals) new areas arose: the coal-metallurgical district in the south and the oil district in Baku. The metallurgical factories in the south were built with foreign capital. They were equipped with the newest technologies and became noted for their high productivity. By the beginning of the 1890s, domestic production satisfied 93.7 per cent of the country's demand for cast-iron, 91.7 per cent of demand for iron and 97.1 per cent of demand for steel.[57] By the beginning of the twentieth century Russia became the world's leading extractor of oil. However, it was not able to keep this title and was overtaken by the United States.

55 'Vsepoddaneishii doklad S. Iu. Vitte "O polozhenii nashei promyshlennosti" Fevral' 1900', *Istorik-marksist*, 2/3 (1925).

56 L. M. Ivanov (ed.), *Istoriia rabochego klassa Rossii* (Moscow: Nauka, 1972), p. 18.

57 D. I. Mendeleev, 'Fabrichno-zavodskaia promyshlennost' i torgovlia Rossii', in D. I. Mendeleev, *Sochineniia* (Moscow: Izd. AN SSSR, 1952), vol. XXI, p. 190.

In post-1861 Russia there was an intensive railway-building campaign, especially between 1895 and 1899. Russia entered the twentieth century with the second longest track in the world, and 40 per cent of it had been laid in the 1890s.[58] At the end of the 1890s and beginning of the 1900s, Russian was one of the world's leading grain suppliers, competing with the United States. Russian grain exports in these years were nearly 500 million pood a year, about 20 per cent of its total grain harvest.[59]

A key financial characteristic of turn-of-the-century Russia was the extremely fast growth of the state budget. In 1867 revenues numbered only 415 million roubles. Thirty years later, they had increased to one billion roubles and by 1908 to two billion roubles. Five years later the budget reached 3 billion roubles. Over this whole period, however, the budget grew 2.4 times quicker than national revenue. Increased budgetary expenditure greatly depended on the income from the spirits monopoly.[60] As a result of the economic growth of the 1890s, Russia came closer to the level of industrially developed states, but did not reach it as Witte had planned.

By the 1880s the process of imperial expansion had ended. The expansion was noteworthy in its asymmetry from an economic point of view. Poland and Finland, Central Asia and Bukhara and the Caucasus clearly differed in their levels of economic development and business culture. Poland and Finland served as a bridge between Russian and European business culture. The economy of Poland and especially Finland enjoyed a certain degree of autonomy. For instance, Finland possessed its own customs system and currency. Finland also introduced gold money (*zolotaia marka*) twenty years before the gold standard was started in the empire. Finland independently concluded foreign loans, and during the First World War even acted as a creditor to the imperial government.[61] Areas where Islam was prevalent represented yet another level of economic development. Muslim entrepreneurship had its specific features. In these regions of the empire, even on the eve of the First World War, deals were concluded on the basis of *sharia*. The multinational and multi-confessional character of the empire affected the makeup of the Russian bourgeoisie and its disunity. For example, representatives of influential financial circles in Moscow,

58 A. N. Solov'eva, *Zheleznodorozhnii transport Rossii vo vtoroi polovine XIX veka* (Moscow: Nauka, 1975), p. 271.

59 T. M. Kitanina, *Khlebnaia torgovlia Rossii* (Moscow: Nauka, 1978), p. 275.

60 Iu. N. Shebaldin, 'Gosudarstvennii biudzhet tsarskoi Rossii v nachale XX veka (do pervoi mirovoi voiny)', *IZ*, 56 (1959): 165.

61 See K. Pravilova, 'Finliandiia i rossiiskaia imperia: politika i finansy', *IZ*, 124, 6 (2003): 180–240; B. V. Anan'ich, 'Zolotoi standart Finliandii i Rossii: finansovii aspect imperskoi politiki' in *Rossiia na rubezhe XIX–XX vekov. Materialy nauchnykh chtenii pamiati professora V.I. Bovykina, Moscow, 20 Jan. 1999* (Moscow: Nauka, 1999), pp. 115–24.

which were dominated by Old Believers, were very critical of their Petersburg counterparts. The Riabushinskiis, for example, believed Petersburg was a city of temptation, 'a frightening city', where 'market orgies' and 'unprincipled brokers' reigned.[62] This disunity would influence the Russian bourgeoisie's role in the political life of the country.

Financial and commercial policy at the beginning of the twentieth century

The world economic crisis at the beginning of the twentieth century and the ensuing depression brought serious harm to the Russian economy. The economy had not recovered when the country found itself locked in the Russo-Japanese War of 1904–5. In 1905 came revolution.

Witte's reforms did not pass these tests unscathed. During the war economic reforms were not possible. In addition, the Finance Ministry lost its special role in determining overall government policy after the creation in 1905 of the Council of Ministers, whose chairman was to play the role of prime minister. In the same year the Ministry of Trade and Industry was formed, and the Ministry of Agriculture was re-named and strengthened, thereby reducing the Ministry of Finance's previous domination of economic policy.

In 1903 Witte was forced to leave the Ministry of Finance. E. D. Pleske replaced him as minister. Pleske was an experienced and knowledgeable bureaucrat but was not connected with financial or scholarly circles. The same thing can be said of V. N. Kokovtsov, who headed the Ministry of Finance from 1904 to 1914, with a short break between 1905 and 1906. Until 1907, by Kokovstov's own admission, it was impossible even to think of any creative policies. His key concern was to maintain the gold standard, and then support P. A. Stolypin's land reforms.[63]

The revolutionary movement in Russia in November–December 1905 led to a massive outpouring of gold from savings banks. At the end of December 1905, the State Bank had almost exhausted its statutory lending limit. The fate of gold money in Russia depended on a large foreign loan. V. N. Kokovstov was sent to Paris on an emergency mission to conclude a deal. His trip coincided with the worsening of Franco-German relations over a conflict in Morocco. The Moroccan crisis was supposed to be solved at an international

62 B. V. Anan'ich, *Bankirskie doma v Rossii. 1860–1914. Ocherki istorii chastnogo predprinimatel'stva* (Leningrad: Nauka, 1991), p. 124.

63 V. S. Diakin, *Dengi dlia sel'skogo khoziaistva* (St Petersburg: St Petersburg University Press, 1997), pp. 191–206.

conference in Algeciras in January 1906. The French government repeatedly announced that it was counting on Russian support at Algeciras. Nicholas II ordered V. N. Kokovtsov to tell the French government in Paris that Russia was prepared to support France at Algeciras. In return, the French agreed to organise a small, and once the Algeciras conference was over, a large loan for Russia.

On 29 December 1905 / 11 January 1906 a contract was signed with French banks for a loan worth 100 million roubles. The situation was so critical in Petersburg that officials did not wait until the loan documents arrived from Paris by post and hurried to add 50 million roubles to the balance of the State Bank's foreign accounts.[64]

When on 18/31 March 1906 an agreement was finally reached in Algeciras, the French finance minister allowed the Russian ambassador in Paris, A. I. Nelidov, to begin negotiations with bankers for a larger loan. The Russian 5 per cent loan of 1906 was concluded on 9/22 April for a sum of 2,250 million francs, 1,200 million of which France paid, 330 million came from England, 165 million from Austria, 55 million from Holland and 500 million from Russian banks. The Russian government was unable to secure more international creditors for the loan: German, Italian, American and Swiss banks refused to participate.[65] The 1906 loan allowed the preservation of Witte's gold standard.

The trials to which the Russian financial system was subjected in the years of war and revolution motivated Kokovtsov to reject further forced development of domestic industry designed to catch up with the more economically developed countries of Western and Central Europe.

The world economic crisis of 1900–3 slowed the growth of Russian industry and resulted in more then 3,000 enterprise closures. In 1903 Russia boasted 23,000 industrial enterprises employing 2,200,000 workers.[66] In 1904 the rest of Europe experienced growth while the Russo-Japanese War and revolution led to the destabilisation of monetary circulation and a fall in industrial production in Russia. After a series of poor harvest years beginning in 1906, Russia finally produced a strong harvest in 1909. This immediately made an impact on the general economic health of the country. According to customs statistics, Russian exports were worth 1,300 million roubles in 1909, the highest figure of

64 B. A. Romanov, *Ocherki diplomaticheskoi istorii russko-iaponskoi voiny, 1895–1907* (Moscow and Leningrad: Izd. AN SSSR, 1955), p. 616.

65 B. V. Anan'ich, *Rossiia i mezhdunarodnii kapital. Ocherki istorii finansovykh otnoshenii* (Leningrad: Nauka, 1970), pp. 170–6.

66 Shepelev, *Tsarizm i burzhuaziia v 1904–1914* (Leningrad: Nauka, 1987), p. 15.

the decade by more than 325 million roubles. The trade surplus increased by 500 million roubles. This affected monetary circulation and increased Russia's gold reserves. By 1 January 1909 the gold reserve was 1,307 million roubles, and by the end of the year the sum had reached 1,708 million roubles, having increased by 401 million roubles.[67]

Russia's entrance into the Entente in 1907 strengthened Franco-Russia relations and coupled with renewed industrial growth promoted the development of co-operation between French and Russian banks. In particular, the French helped to improve the finances of the Petersburg private banks. In 1910 the Northern and Russo-Chinese Banks united. Together, they formed the new Russo-Asian Bank. During the years of economic growth before 1914 Franco-Russian financial groups were formed. From the Russian side, the main participating banks were: the Petersburg International, the Russian Commercial-Industrial, the Azov-Don, the Petersburg Discount-Loan, the Russian Foreign Trade, the Russo-French, and the Siberian Commercial Bank; and from the French side – Crédit Lyonnais, Comptoir National d'Escompte, Banque Française pour le Commerce et L'Industrie, Banque de L'Union Parisienne. French and Russian banks co-operated on railway projects in Siberia, Turkestan and the Caucusus and in joint operations in the Balkans.

The Franco-Russian financial co-operation did not end German influence in Russian banking, which continued to exist on the eve of the First World War. All the major Petersburg banks continued to work with banks in Berlin and Vienna. English capital became an important factor only immediately before the war. Petersburg banks undoubtedly played the central role in international banking connections. By 1914 the eight largest Petersburg banks controlled 61 per cent of the market share of joint-stock banks, which exceeded similar indicators of banking concentration in England and Germany.[68] On the eve of the First World War banks began to finance industrial enterprises more actively. Both Petersburg and Moscow banks played an important part in the development of industry in central Russia. The growing role of joint-stock banks affected their relationship with the State Bank. After the gold standard was introduced in Russia, the State Bank became the primary lending institution and commercial bank. It retained its status as the 'bank of banks', but by 1914 it nevertheless had less total financial strength than the joint-stock banks. Fifty joint-stock banks

67 Anan'ich, *Rossiia i mezhdunarodnyi*, p. 264.

68 On the participation of French banks in the Russian economy, see R. Girault, *Emprunts russes et investissements français en Russie. 1887–1914* (Paris: Armand Colin, 1973). V. I. Bovykin, *Frantsuzskie banki v Rossii. Konets XIX–nachalo XX vekov* (Moscow: Rosspen, 1999).

with 778 branches boasted balances of 6,285 million roubles compared to the State Bank's 4,624 million roubles.[69]

Banking houses also retained their influence in the economic life of the country, especially in St Petersburg and Moscow. By 1913 there were sixteen large banking houses in St Petersburg, including branches of Moscow firms. Among them were the banking houses: Zachary Zhdanov and Co., Kaftal, Handelman and Co., G. Lesin, A. I. Zeidman and Co., and I. E. Ginzburg. The Ginzburg banking house played an important role not just in the economy, but also in the cultural life of the capital at the beginning of the twentieth century. In Moscow, the banking house of Riabushinskii remained very influential. In 1912 it was reorganised by the Riabushinskii brothers into a large joint-stock commercial bank.

After the revolutionary events of 1905–7 the activity of political parties intensified, as did the consolidation of capital. These new party and business leaders took the initiative to formulate a programme for the development of Russia's productivity and industry. These problems were regularly discussed in St Petersburg at the meetings of the Council of Congresses of Representatives of Industry and Trade, where scholars and economists were invited to present research. In Moscow, the Riabushinskii banking house became a centre for such discussions, with debates on the economy taking place in P. P. Riabushinskii's apartment on Prechistinskii Boulevard. Famous historians, economists and law scholars took part in these discussions, including M. M. Kovalevskii, N. Kh. Ozerov, P. B. Struve and S. N. Bulgakov. Financial leaders' concern with the productivity of the country was reflected in a new series of commercial publications. In 1909–10 alone several newspapers and magazines appeared which were devoted to economics and finance: *Birzhevoi artel'shchik*, *Finansovoe obozrenie*, and the *Bankovskaia i torgovaia zhizn'*.

In 1911, at a meeting of the Congress of Representatives of Industry and Trade, V. V. Zhukovskii, a St Petersburg businessman and one of the leaders of the Council of Congresses defined the role of commercial-industrial circles in the following manner:

> We must think about the general situation of the country. We must take a systematic approach to solving the peoples' tasks, we must try to be a part of the very brains of the country, we cannot stop our ideological work. The wealth of the people is based not only on the land, but also in the factories; not only in money, but perhaps mainly in the people's moral foundations

69 See B. V. Anan'ich, S. V. Kalmykov and Iu. A. Petrov, *Glavnii bank Rossii. Ot gosudarstvennogo banka Rossiiskoi imperii k tsentral'nomu banku Rossiiskoi Federatsii. 1860–2000* (Moscow: TSPP TSB RPH, 2000), pp. 63–4.

Figure 1. Imperial mythology: Peter the Great examines young Russians returning from study abroad.

Figure 2. Imperial grandeur: the Great Palace (Catherine Palace) at Tsarskoe Selo.

Figure 3. Alexander I: the victor over Napoleon.

Figure 4. Alexander II addresses the Moscow nobility on the emancipation of the serfs.

Figure 5. Mikhail Lomonosov: the grandfather of modern Russian culture.

Figure 6. Gavril Derzhavin; poet and minister.

Figure 7. Sergi Rachmaninov: Russian music conquers the world.

Figure 8. The Conservatoire in St Petersburg.

Figure 9. Count Muravev (Amurskii): imperial pro-consul.

Figure 10. Imperial statuary: the monument to Khmel'nitskii in Kiev.

Figure 11. Tiflis: Russia in Asia?

Figure 12. Nizhnii Novgorod: a key centre of Russian commerce.

Figure 13. Rural life: an aristocratic country mansion.

Figure 14. Rural life: a central Russian village scene.

Figure 15. Rural life: the northern forest zone.

Figure 16. Rural life: the Steppe.

Figure 17. Naval ratings: the *narod* in uniform.

Figure 18. Sinews of power? Naval officers in the St Petersburg shipyards.

Figure 19. The battleship *Potemkin* fitting out.

Figure 20. Baku: the empire's capital of oil and crime.

Figure 21. Alexander III: the monarchy turns 'national'.

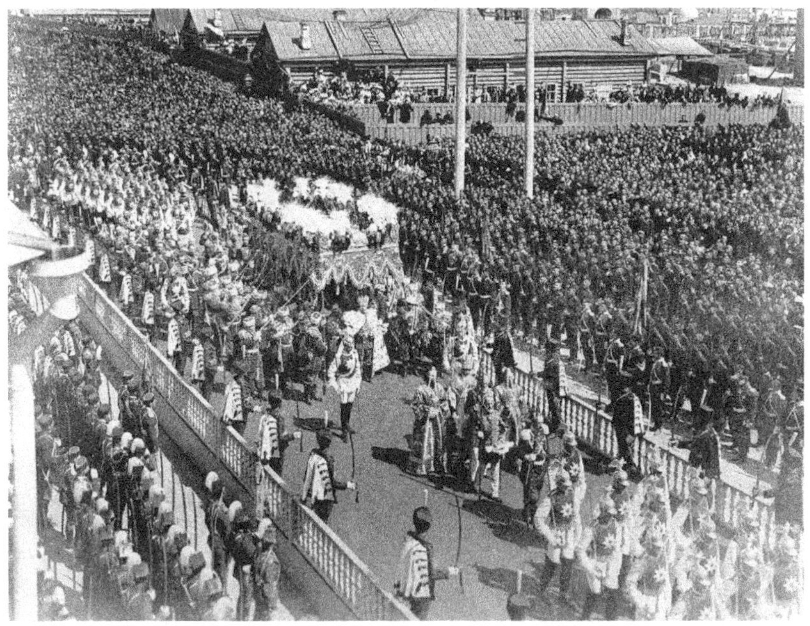

Figure 22. The coronation of Nicholas II.

Figure 23. A different view of Russia's last emperor.

Figure 24. Nicholas II during the First World War.

> and values. And in this regard the commercial-industrial class needs to show its work, its ideas, its conscience. And once we succeed in uniting, we will have the right to define and work towards a government programme which is drawn up from our commercial-industrial perspective and which is a synthesis of our practical interests and our ideological viewpoints.[70]

The growth of business organisations' influence in the financial life of Russia was linked to the new industrial growth in the country. However, at least until the beginning of the First World War, despite the co-operation of the state with representatives of financial circles, there were no signs of direct participation by business circles in the formulation of economic policy.

Industrial growth was very strong in 1910 and continued until 1914. By 1913 there were 29,315 industrial enterprises in Russia, employing 3,115,000 workers. The average yearly growth of industrial production was 8.8 per cent. Its value was 7,358 million roubles. Russia was second in the world in oil extraction, third in demand for cotton, fourth in steel production, fifth in coal extraction and sixth in iron ore.[71]

The grain harvest between 1909 and 1913 averaged 4,366.5 million pood yearly. This allowed Russia to increase its grain exports significantly, especially from 1909–10. However, already by 1914 the yield of almost all grain crops was dropping.[72]

On the eve of the First World War co-operation between Russian and French banks became even closer and more varied. The amalgamated railway loan of 1914 for 665 million francs, or 249 million roubles became an important event in Russo-French financial relations. Representatives of a large syndicate of powerful French banks helped float the loan, as did a small syndicate of provincial banks.

By 1914, seventy-one Russian industrial properties were listed on the Paris stock market. Their total value was 642 million roubles, and they included the stocks of fifteen of Russia's largest metallurgical factories, twelve oil and fifteen coal enterprises, and five banks. In Paris, stocks of Russian coal enterprises were traded that amounted to 60 per cent of the total money invested in these companies.[73] The French controlled 80 per cent of Russia's

70 I. Glivits, 'Politiko-ekonomicheskie vzglyady V. V. Zhukovskogo', *Promyshlennost' i torgovliia* (22 October 1916): 306–9.

71 Shepelev, *Tsarizm. 1904–1914*, p. 23.

72 S. G. Beliaev, *P.L. Bark i finansovaia politika Rossii 1914–1917* (St Petersburg: Izd. SPbu, 2002), p. 86.

73 B. A. Nikol'skii, *Frantsiia i Rossiia (k 25-letiu franko-russkogo soiuza)* (Petrograd: Red. Vestnik Finansov, 1917), p. 15.

foreign debts, and 35 per cent of foreign capital invested in Russia came from France.[74]

The Russian Empire entered the First World War with a significant state debt – more than 9 billion roubles. Of this, 4.3 billion roubles was foreign debt, more than twice the value of all foreign investment in the Russian economy. At the beginning of the twentieth century Russia had the second largest state debt, after France, but had the largest loan repayments. From 1904 to 1908, according to official statistics, Russia paid an average of 4.2 per cent interest on its foreign loans, and in the next 5 years paid 4.5 per cent annually, while France paid less than 3 per cent each year during the same period.[75]

Despite economic growth, Kokovtsov's policies became the object of sharp criticism in the press and by a series of influential opponents in government. Witte was one of the most uncompromising critics of Kokovtsov. He not only started a campaign against Kokovtsov in the press but also spoke out against him on 10/23 January 1914 at the State Council, accusing the minister of using the spirits monopoly not to fight alcoholism, but to 'pump out money from the people into state coffers'. 'The Russian people', said Witte, 'spend one billion roubles each year on vodka while the government spends only 160 million roubles on the Ministry of Education.'[76] The revenues from the sale of spirits occupied an important place in the budget not only in Russia, but in other countries as well. In the Russian budget, spirit sales were one of the most important sources of income. In 1895 the state received 16 million roubles from the sale of alcohol, and in 1913 – 675 million roubles. This was caused partly by the government's repeated increase of vodka prices.[77]

In January 1914, Kokovtsov was removed from office. I. L. Goremykin was appointed prime minister, and P. L. Bark was placed in charge of the Ministry of Finance. After Bark's appointment the government proclaimed a 'new course' in economic policy. However, the First World War destroyed their plans. After the war began, bread exports across European borders and the

74 P. Renouvin and J.-B. Duroselle, *Introduction à l'histoire des relations internationals* (Paris: Librairie A. Colin, 1964), p. 139.

75 See *Gosudarstvennaia duma. Stenograficheskie otchoty. Vtoraia sessiia*, ch. III (St Petersburg, 1914), column 1140.

76 Anan'ich and Ganelin, *Serge*, p. 371.

77 Beliaev, *P.L. Bark*, pp. 153–5. According to data collected by Beliaev, the average yearly income in roubles for an Englishman was 309 roubles, of which he spent 32 roubles on alcohol. A Frenchman spent 34 roubles of 256 on drink, while the average Russian citizen spent 6 roubles, 83 kopeks out of 63 roubles annually on alcohol. Beliaev calculated his figures based on the data in two books by M. I. Fridman: *Vinnaia monopoliia*, vol. I: *Vinnaia monopoliia v inostrannykh gosudarstvakh* (St Petersburg: Pravda, 1914.), vol. II: *Vinnaia monopoliia v Rossii* (Petrograd: Pravda, 1916).

Black Sea straits nearly halved (from 647.8 million pood to 374 million pood). Grain was Russia's main export, and Germany was an important trading partner. As a result, Russia lost its positive balance of trade as regards European commerce and a negative balance of trade developed across Asian borders as well. England became a key importer of Russian goods.[78] The war led to fewer joint-stock companies being founded. The abolition of the spirits monopoly at the beginning of war dealt a sharp blow to the budget. On 23 July / 5 August Nicholas II signed a decree prohibiting paper money to be exchanged for gold and expanding the State Bank's issuing authority.[79] I. L. Goremykin's government believed these would be temporary wartime measures. However, the gold standard proved incapable of surviving the First World War, not just in Russia, but throughout the world.

With the onset of the war, given state military orders, government control over industrial production inevitably increased.[80]

Conclusion

Russia did not enjoy total entrepreneurial freedom, even on the eve of the First World War, when political parties and bourgeois organisations had formed inside the country. Until 1917 Russia retained a system where joint-stock companies required state permission to incorporate. The tsar ignored suggestions from industrialists, bankers and scholars to tear down the barriers hampering the development of free enterprise. For example, Nicholas II did not react to a paper given to him on this topic by the famous economist Professor I. Kh. Ozerov. He drew the government's attention to the fact that Russian industrialists were starting their companies abroad, in France and England, where there were no legal obstacles. I. Kh. Ozerov tried to convince Nicholas II to eliminate restrictions for the European population of Russia, noting the United States' success as regards co-operation between people of different nationalities in the development of American productivity.[81] The idea of 'Americanising' the Russian economy was rather widespread in economic literature during the First World War. However, it cannot be said that it was universally accepted in

78 Beliaiev, *P.L. Bark*, p. 86.

79 On 27 July / 9 August this decree was discussed in the State Duma and State Council and became a law. See A. L. Sidorov, *Finansovoe polozhenie Rossii v gody pervoi mirovoi voiny. 1914–1917* (Moscow: Izd. AN SSSR, 1960), p. 109.

80 See I. F. Gindin, *Banki i ekonomicheskaia politika v Rossii (XIX–nachalo XX vekov). Ocherki istorii i tipologii russkikh bankov* (Moscow: Nauka, 1997), pp. 105–9; Beliaev, *P.L. Bark*, pp. 272–3.

81 Vsepoddanneishaia zapiska I.Kh. Ozerova, 2 Sentiabria 1914, RGIA, Fond 560, op. 38.

Russian financial circles. For example, the Riabushinskiis, leading representatives of Old-Believer enterprises, tied their hopes to a rebirth of Europe after the war and thus viewed the United States as a dangerous opponent.[82]

Just before the war, in July 1914, the Council of Congresses of the Representatives of Trade and Industry sent the Council of Ministers a memorandum arguing that a special meeting was needed to discuss measures to develop Russia's productivity. This question continued to be discussed in business circles during the war, along with the possibility of building wide-scale and 'cultured' capitalism in Russia.[83] But how should this 'cultured capitalism' look in Russia? The answer to this question is one of the complex riddles of history. Ruth Roosa, who dedicated many years to the study of bourgeois societal organisations in Russia, offered her theory on this mystery. She concluded that 'Russian society under the auspices of its business class in the twentieth century might well have had more in common with the moderate socialism of Scandinavia, the syndicalism of Italy in the 1920s, the authoritarian rule of Poland and the Baltic states between the wars, or the pattern of industrial organization that emerged in postwar Germany than with the open and competitive society that has been the American ideal.'[84] Whether or not this is true, one thing is certain: the government's role in Russia's economic development under any conditions would have been very significant given Russia's social and economic traditions, and the history of the formation of its entrepreneurial class.

The distinctive features of Russia's economic development and the degree of its backwardness have been a constant source of debate for historians. Until the beginning of the 1930s, Soviet historiography featured lively polemics on this subject, with a variety of viewpoints. At the end of the 1930s the Short History of the All-Union Communist Party was published. In it, pre-revolutionary Russia was described as a backward country dependent on foreign capital. This viewpoint became mandatory for all students of Russian economic history in the Soviet Union. After Stalin's death, at the end of the 1950s and beginning of the 1960s, a new polemic resurfaced on the distinctive features of Russia's economic development. Ultimately, the prevailing theory was one that said Russia belonged to the group of countries with a neither very advanced nor very backward level of economic development.[85] In Western historiography until the beginning of the 1980s Alexander Gerschenkron's theories dominated:

82 Anan'ich, *Bankirskie doma*, pp. 126–7.

83 M. V. Bernatskii, 'Pravitel'stvennyi nadzor nad kommercheskimi bankami', *Promyshlennost' i Torgovliia*, 19/221 (14 May, 1916).

84 R. Roosa, *Russian Industrialists in an Age of Revolution* (Armonk: M. E. Sharpe, 1997), p. 160.

85 K. N. Tarnovskii, *Sovetskaia istoriografiia rossiiskogo imperializma* (Moscow: Nauka, 1964).

he argued that Russia had been backward and the government's intervention in the economy had been exceptional. However, in later years his views have been revisited and revised.[86] In particular, Paul Gregory has suggested a new concept of the distinctive features of Russian economic development. He believes that Russia possessed a market economy on the eve of the war, that agriculture, 'despite serious institutional problems, grew just as quickly as in Europe', and that 'if Russia had remained on a market-oriented model of development after the war, its indicators of economic growth would have been no less than before the war': in other words, the pace of Russia's development would have surpassed the European average.[87]

86 A. Gerschenkron, *Europe in the Russian Mirror: Four Lectures in Economic History* (Cambridge: Cambridge University Press, 1970); *Economic Backwardness in Historical Perspective* (Cambridge, Mass.: Harvard University Press, 1962).

87 P. Gregory, *Ekonomicheskii rost Rossiiskoi imperii (konets XIX–nachala XX vekov)* (Moscow: Rosspen, 2003), pp. 248–9, trans. from the English (P. Gregory, *Economic Growth of the Russian Empire: New Estimates and Calculations*). Also see P. Gatrell, *The Tsarist Economy 1850–1917* (London: Macmillan, 1986).

PART V

*

GOVERNMENT

20

Central government

ZHAND P. SHAKIBI

Introduction

A study of the central government of the Russian Empire sheds light on three important issues in the imperial era. How well did the institutions handle the challenge of modernisation from above? How did the autocracy's and bureaucracy's view of their respective roles in society change over time? What were the major challenges related to effective governance from the centre and how did the monarchy and bureaucracy handle them? By extension a solid understanding of the workings of central government helps to determine the extent to which it and its personnel held responsibility for the collapse of the Romanov regime.

Peter the Great's reform of the central government marked the beginning of the imperial bureaucracy's evolution on two different but equally important and mutually linked levels. The ministerial bureaucracy from the early nineteenth century staffed the so-called subordinate organs (*podchinennye organy*), which at least theoretically handled activities in a designated field, such as finance or foreign affairs. The supreme organs (*verkhovnye organy*) had the responsibility to manage and co-ordinate the activities of the subordinate organs. The effectiveness of government depended on cadres at least as much as institutions. Indeed, Konstantin Pobedonostsev, well-known conservative and tutor to the last two emperors, Alexander III and Nicholas II, frequently stressed, 'Institutions are of no importance. Everything depends on individuals.'[1] Whilst his categorical rejection of the role of institutions is highly debatable, we do need to take into account the dynamic between institutions and human agents, the most important of whom was the emperor, in order

1 P. A. Zaionchkovskii (ed.), *Dnevnik gosudarstvennogo sekretaria A.A. Polovtsova*, 2 vols. (Moscow: Nauka, 1966) vol. I, p. 315.

to obtain a more coherent understanding of how the central organs actually functioned.[2]

Subordinate organs (*podchinennye organy*)

For most of his reign Peter the Great (1689–1725), occupied with transforming Russia into a great European power, relied primarily on the form of central government he had inherited. His predecessors, the first Romanovs, governed through some forty chancelleries (*prikazy*) which constituted the heart of the central governing organs. Noble servitors, often of boyar level, headed the prikazy: under them served non-noble cadres. Responsibilities and jurisdictions of the prikazy greatly overlapped and frequently contradicted each other, making difficult even relatively efficient government, including the extraction from society of resources needed to support Peter's military campaigns.

Peter, who had acquainted himself with the bureaucratic machines of some of the great powers of Europe, understood that this unwieldy structure could not help him realise his goal of making Russia a major European power. Like many of his fellow monarchs, Peter believed that more effective governing institutions provided the best mechanism for solving economic and societal ills. As a result, in the last seven years of his reign (1718–25) Peter set his sights on introducing radical change in Russia's central governing organs, a process which marked the end of the country's patrimonial state.

His plan on the one hand of founding a system of subordinate organs operating on rational concepts of administration similar to those of Western and Central Europe, and on the other hand of maintenance of the autocracy's establishment of the norms and rules for the bureaucracy remained a goal of Russia's monarchs until the end of the dynasty. However, as time would show, the concentration of absolute power in the hands of the emperor made realisation of this goal difficult. Peter's immediate concern was improvement of the government's taxing mechanism, establishment of budgetary controls and supervision over expenditures. Along with this came

2 For good basic reference texts see: A. Turgeva, *Vysshie organi gosudarstvennoi vlasti i upravleniia Rossii IX–XX vv.* (Moscow: S-ZAGS, 2000); D. N. Shilov, *Gosudarstvennie deiateli Rossiliskoi Imperii, 1802–1917* (St Petersburg: European University Press, 2003); O. Chustiakov (ed.), *Gosudarstvennii stroi Rossiiskoi Imperii nakanune krusheniia* (Moscow: Izd. MGU, 1995); J. LeDonne, *Ruling Russia: Politics and Administration in the Age of Absolutism, 1762–1796* (London: Princeton University Press, 1984); G. Mironov, *Istoriia gosudarstva rossiiskogo XIX vek* (Moscow: Nauka, 1995); M. Raeff, 'The Bureaucratic Phenomena of Imperial Russia', *AHR* 84 (1979); G. Yaney, *The Systematization of Russian Government* (Urbana: University of Indiana Press, 1973). P. A. Zaionchkovskii, *Pravitel'stvennii apparat samoderzhavnoi Rossii v XIX v.* (Moscow: Nauka, 1977).

greater centralisation of power and increased governmental penetration into society.

The heart of the system of subordinate organs was the colleges. Initially there were Foreign Affairs, War, Navy (which also looked after gun manufacture and the forests), Mining (which was also charged with the minting of money), Manufacture, Revenue, Control, State Expenditure, Commerce and Justice.[3] Each college was headed by a president chosen by Peter from his closest associates under whom in turn served a small group of ten to eleven trained officials who collectively took decisions within the college's purview.[4] A poor level of co-ordination between the individual college's various departments characterised the new system. However, the colleges were an improvement on the previous prikaz system. One of the major reasons for the emergence of the Russian Empire as a great power in the eighteenth century was this new administrative structure which proved effective in tax collection and military recruitment.[5] At the same time the Ottoman Empire's failure to copy such reforms played a large role in its decline.[6] But a great degree of overlapping remained. Frequently one area of activity fell under the jurisdiction of several colleges. That government was not divided into administrative, judicial, legislative and fiscal functions, but rather into blocks of activities helped create the conditions for institutional autonomous existence and also for poor responsiveness to co-ordination and integration from above.

During the remainder of the eighteenth century these centrifugal tendencies strengthened. Increasingly, individual heads of the colleges in private meetings with the monarch enacted policy in a haphazard manner. However the real power of the colleges and their ability to make policy were dependent to a large degree on the monarch and the influence of various groups around him or her. Not infrequently a college was charged with implementing policies which it had played no part in making. Whether the colleges made policy or the monarch and his or her closest servitors did so, overall co-ordination was poor. Catherine the Great (r. 1762–96) weakened the colleges with her Statute of Provincial Reforms of 1775 which transferred most of the their responsibilities to provincial governors. However, the central bureaucracy

3 Throughout the eighteenth century various colleges appeared and then were abolished according to the needs of the time.

4 Several small departments handling various aspects of a college's portfolio made up each college. Moreover, attached to each college was a chancellery which handled administrative issues.

5 L. Hughes, *Russia in the Age of Peter the Great* (New Haven: Yale University Press, 1998) pp. 133–5. However, Hughes adds: 'If the grand aim of the exercise was to impose order' and 'to make Russia better governed' Peter's reforms were not very successful.

6 D. Lieven, *Empire: The Russian Empire and Its Rivals* (London: John Murray, 2000), p. 140.

remained. During the eighteenth century its size increased in conjunction with a growing professionalism, thereby providing a springboard for the next major change in the subordinate organs under Alexander I.

Ministerial government

Alexander I (r.1801–25) established Russia's ministerial system which lasted until the collapse of the Romanov dynasty in February 1917.[7] The young emperor initially toyed with the idea of constitutional change but soon showed a preference for administrative reform which he saw as more essential for effective government and Russia's modernisation and less threatening to his autocratic power.

Alexander replaced what remained of Peter's collegiate system with ministries, a step which reinforced centralised power. He intended the ministries to be the highest subordinate organs headed by individual ministers who were appointed by and responsible to the emperor alone. The initial ministries were War, Navy, Foreign Affairs, Justice, Internal Affairs, Finance, Commerce, and Education. The number of ministries did not differ greatly until the beginning of the twentieth century. The founding of a ministerial system with its relatively clear responsibilities, specialised functions and internal structure represented an important step in the evolution of Russia's subordinate organs. Moreover, unlike the collegiate system where decisions were at least theoretically taken collectively within each college, a single minister directed a ministry, thereby increasing administrative efficiency.

Regular ministerial reports, written and oral, constituted the heart of the new system. Ministers met individually with the emperor to deliver oral reports and make policy decisions on matters at least theoretically directly related only to their own ministerial portfolio. The emperors preferred this arrangement for it provided them the opportunity to exercise direct personal influence over the administration of the empire. In addition, the emperors ensured for themselves a central and pivotal role in the running of government by ensuring they were the only ones privy to the activities and policies of all the ministries. Ministers also had the right to propose legislation and to participate in discussions over proposed laws.

The establishment of the ministerial system laid the groundwork for the emergence of a large and functionally differentiated bureaucratic apparatus. Alexander I and his successor, Nicholas I (r. 1825–55) also established universities and lycées to train future high-level bureaucrats, increasingly seen as

7 J. Hartley, *Alexander I* (London: Longman, 1994); S.V. Mironenko, *Samoderzhavie i reformy: politicheskaia bor'ba v Rossii v nachale XIX v.* (Moscow: Nauka, 1989).

the key to better government. Under Nicholas I and Alexander II (r. 1855–81) the bureaucratic machine grew immensely in size and became more professional, especially at the higher and middle ranks.[8] In 1847 Count S. S. Uvarov bemoaned that the bureaucracy as an institution had acquired a sovereignty of its own capable of rivalling that of the monarch. The increasing bureaucratisation had created a noble bureaucratic elite which the landed nobility viewed as a threat to its interests and its access to the monarch. As the nineteenth century progressed, much of the bureaucratic class came to regard the landed nobility as a relic of a bygone era and an obstacle to the further development of Russia. Beginning already during the reign of Catherine II and intensifying in the nineteenth century the landed nobility fought with the bureaucracy for influence over the emperor. At the same time, many of the senior officials came from land-owning families. Accompanying this process was increasing emphasis on the bureaucracy's role as catalyst for social and/or economic change, which began to take serious shape as a result of Catherine II's thoughts on enlightened despotism and gained irreversible momentum with the Emancipation of the Serfs and the Great Reforms under Alexander II. Consequently the bureaucracy's view of itself began to evolve. The bureaucrats of the seventeenth and eighteenth centuries regarded themselves as personal servitors of the tsar. By the last half of the nineteenth century the class of professional bureaucrats felt a genuine institutional loyalty, an *esprit de corps*. This institutional identity and the idea of service to the state as public officials began to compete with the person of the monarch for the bureaucracy's ultimate loyalty.

Modernisation from above, however, created administrative problems between the subordinate organs. Given the absence of public forums or parliamentary institutions, debates over the desirability and form of modernisation, and over how to handle its socioeconomic consequences took place within the bureaucratic structures, posing a challenge to bureaucratic efficiency.[9] The best-known cleavage emerged between the two most powerful subordinate organs, the Ministry of Finance and the Ministry of Internal Affairs. One of the greatest struggles between them dealt with labour issues around the turn of the twentieth century and had its origins in the priorities of the

8 See: W. B. Lincoln, *Nicholas I: Autocrat of All the Russias* (London: University of Indiana Press, 1977) and *The Great Reforms: Autocracy, Bureaucracy and the Politics of Change* (DeKalb: Northern Illinois University Press, 1990); L. N. Viskochov, *Imperator Nikolai I* (St Petersburg: Izd. SPbU, 2003).

9 H. W. Whelan, *Alexander III and The State Council* (New Brunswick: Rutgers University Press, 1982); D. T. Orlovsky, *The Limits of Reform: The Ministry of Internal Affairs in Imperial Russia, 1802–1881* (Cambridge, Mass.: Harvard University Press, 1982).

respective ministries. The prime responsibility of the Ministry of Internal Affairs was the maintenance of public order throughout the Empire. Moreover, many aristocrats, who believed that the autocracy had a responsibility to look after the wellbeing of the less fortunate in Russian society (namely the peasants and workers) staffed this ministry. They regarded worker disturbances, which became more frequent towards the end of the nineteenth century, as the logical consequence of the labourers' poor working conditions and pay, and therefore saw the factory owners as exploiters. While meeting striking workers with force, the Ministry of Interior supported policies which aimed at improving the lot of the worker at the expense of the emerging class of industrialists.

The Ministry of Finance's primary responsibility was the rapid industrialisation of Russia, which its head Sergei Witte regarded as essential if Russia was to avoid becoming a second-rate power and provider of natural resources to the great powers of Europe. To achieve this goal a Russian class of industrialists was needed, as was foreign investment. Witte regarded the Ministry of Internal Affairs' view on the labour problem as damaging for the realisation of the greater goal of industrialisation. The Ministry of Internal Affairs responded that the strikes derived from the workers' conditions and posed a serious political danger. In the absence of co-ordination from above these two ministries spent much time and energy either waging a bureaucratic struggle to gain control over the labour problem or following their respective and ultimately contradictory labour policies. One result of this administrative chaos was the large worker rebellions during the 1905 Revolution.

The conclusion can be reached that modernisation from above strengthened the process of atomisation of the ministries, each of which pursued its own policies, purpose and courses of action. This is not to say, however, that ministers were at each other's throats most of the time. Inevitably they understood the necessity of collaboration in most cases. A set of informal, unwritten procedures to regulate their relationship with each other emerged over time. In addition whenever a threat to overall ministerial integrity emerged, such as excessive influence of a figure outside of government, the bureaucratic *esprit de corps* worked to check it. The ministries had been established with the purpose of reorganising government into a single administrative system. By the last quarter of the nineteenth century the ministerial bureaucracy was capable of making and implementing policy but also had evolved into separate organisations, each with its own purpose which strengthened the need for stable and efficient supreme co-ordinating organs.

Supreme organs (*Verkhovnye organy*)

From the establishment of the collegiate system to the 1917 February Revolution, the imperial government faced the challenges of co-ordination, unity and supervision of the subordinate organs. Peter founded the Senate on 22 February 1711. His handwritten decree failed to enunciate clearly this supreme organ's responsibilities, save one. He charged the Senate with administering the empire when he absented himself from the capital to command troops in the field. That same day Russia declared war on the Ottoman Empire. A second decree dated March of that same year to a significant degree delineated the Senate's duties. In the period before the establishment of the collegiate system, the Senate was charged with increasing the amount of taxes collected, improving tax collecting organs, rooting out corruption, and supervision of the state's expenditure. It could issue its own directives which all institutions were required to obey. The Senate was indeed governing, exercising the executive, legislative and judicial powers of the monarch.

With the establishment of the collegiate system, the Senate lost administrative duties, such as tax collection, and received the responsibility of a supreme organ – co-ordination and supervision of the subordinate organs, the colleges. The Senate combined this with its role as a higher judicial body which was to provide a degree of conformity in the interpretation of the empire's laws. The presidents of the colleges were members of the Senate until 1722 when Peter came to the conclusion that having the heads of subordinate organs participate in the supreme organs whose responsibility was oversight of those same subordinate organs was counterproductive and discontinued the practice. The Senate's performance did not satisfy Peter, who eventually appointed a procurator-general who represented him in the Senate and was responsible to him alone. The procurator-general's role was supervisory, confirming the Senate's decrees and ensuring it carried out its duties and the emperor's will.

In the period between Peter's death in 1725 and the enthronement of Catherine II in 1762 the supreme organs existed in a state of great flux, reflecting a lack of institutionalisation and dependence on the attitudes of individual monarchs and high servitors. Under Catherine I (r. 1725–7) and Peter II (r. 1727–30) the Senate's role as a supreme organ diminished with the establishment of the Supreme Privy Council, the intended co-ordinating point of the subordinate organs. Anna Ivanovna (r. 1730–40), suspicious of the Supreme Privy Council given its members' attempt to limit her autocratic power at the beginning of her reign, in 1731 abolished it. The new focal point of the administration became Her Majesty's Cabinet. Elizabeth (r. 1741–62) abolished this body and restored many powers to the Senate, though real power of co-ordination remained in the hands of those close to the empress herself. Nonetheless, the Senate reviewed and approved most of the legislation of her reign. These changes in the supreme organs reflected a three-way battle for real power. One between the aristocracy and the bureaucratic bodies, one between the aristocracy and the autocracy, and another between the autocrat and the growing bureaucracy.

Catherine II was keen to reorganise the central organs which to her mind sorely lacked co-ordination and efficiency. Her adviser, Nikita Panin, stressed the need to found some form of imperial council capable of co-ordination and to establish an effective relationship between the monarch, the Senate and other governmental institutions. Taking into consideration Panin's views, the empress subordinated the Senate to the procurator-general once again, believing like Peter the Great before her, that a supervisor of the supervisory body would create the conditions for a more smooth and unified central government. Nevertheless by the end of her reign the continuous need for an effective mechanism capable of co-ordinating government was clear, especially given the growing tendency to see change in society as the responsibility of the government.

Co-ordination of the subordinate organs, the relationship between the supreme organs themselves and more specifically between them and the sovereign, were at the base of Alexander I's major administrative reforms. His decrees of 1801 and 1802 fundamentally changed the Senate's role. The body received the right of judicial review and supervision of the highest government organs, including the newly established ministries. Given his fleeting interest in constitutional change, Alexander gave senators the right to make remonstrances to the emperor and stipulated that no bill could become law without its approval. When the Senate exercised this right soon after, Alexander rescinded it. Clearly the supreme organs were to occupy themselves with co-ordination of the subordinate organs, not with infringement on the autocratic power. The founding of ministerial government and of the State Council (1810) led to the sidelining of the Senate in practice. For the remainder of the nineteenth century it was a High Court of Review and along with other institutions exercised a degree of administrative supervision.

Yet the problem of effective supreme organs remained. Count Mikhail M. Speranskii, Alexander's close adviser and regarded by many as the father of the modern imperial bureaucracy, argued that 'in the present system of government there is no institution for the general deliberation of governmental affairs from the point of view of their legislative aspect. The absence of such an institution leads to major disorders and confusion in all aspects of the administration.'[10] Recognising this, Alexander founded the State Council. On the day of its inauguration he drew attention to the reasons for taking this step:

> The order and uniformity of state affairs require that there be a single focal point for their general consideration. In the present structure of our administration, we do not have such an institution. In such a vast state as this, how can various parts of the administration function with harmony and success when each moves in its own direction and when these directions nowhere lead to a central focus? Given the great variety of state affairs, the personal activity of the supreme power alone cannot maintain this unity. Beyond this, individuals die and only institutions can survive and, in the course of centuries, preserve the basis of a state . . . The State Council will form the focal point of all affairs of the central administration.[11]

The intention was that the establishment of the State Council, which should be considered a major development in the history of the central government of the empire, was to end the search for a supreme co-ordinating organ begun some one hundred years previously under Peter I.

The emperor appointed the State Council's membership which consisted of sitting ministers and other high dignitaries. The body had no right to initiate legislation, which remained the prerogative of the autocrat and ministers, but it could make recommendations on legislation sent to it, which the emperor could accept or reject. In theory no legislative project could be presented to the emperor without the State Council's approval. Practice proved otherwise. At times the emperor and ministers chose or established alternative ways to push through legislation if the path through the State Council was considered too difficult. Nevertheless, the State Council did provide a forum for the debate, reformulation and preparation of legislation before its delivery to the emperor.

Russia's elite hoped the founding of the State Council would place the governmental and legislative process on some form of legal basis. With the State Council, Russia was to be an orderly autocratic state fixed on a foundation of law and legal process. But the continued existence of the autocracy undermined in practice this supreme organ. Alexander III (r. 1881–94), by a decree dated 5 November 1885, legalised what had been long going on in practice. According to the decree, all commands of the emperor carried the full force of legality. The State Council's role in the legislative process was fatally weakened. The upshot was the strengthening of the tendency on the part of ministers

10 Quoted in Whelan, *Alexander III*, p. 39.
11 Whelan, *Alexander III*, pp. 39–40.

to avoid seeking support amongst members of the supreme organs or fellow ministers and to rely on the emperor's support alone to obtain passage of legislation.

Alexander I, with two decrees dated 1802 and 1812, founded the Committee of Ministers. Its most important short-term responsibility was to govern the empire while he was at the front fighting Napoleon. The committee was charged with overall co-ordination of administrative issues as they emerged amongst the various subordinate organs and therefore could not become a supreme co-ordinating organ. A chairman headed the committee, a position which by the middle of the nineteenth century carried no great authority. When Sergei Witte was removed from his post as minister of finance in 1903 and made chairman he considered it a demotion. The emperor in theory could attend the committee, but almost never did so until its dissolution in 1906, thereby further weakening the committee's authority. Ministerial disunity and the committee's weak institutional authority limited its ability to have any real effect. In any case the available evidence does not show that Alexander even wanted the committee to play a cabinet-style role. On the one hand, he wished that ministers co-ordinate policies and consult each other before presenting bills for his consideration. But his continued practice of meeting in private with individual ministers undermined any moves in that direction. The committee did have the right to draw the monarch's attention to the need for a particular law or policy.

Alexander I initially showed a fair amount of interest in the Committee of Ministers, which enabled it to enjoy a relatively prominent role. However, in the final years of his reign he showed a decreasing inclination to rule, preferring to give greater authority to favourites. By deciding policy and making laws in meetings with individual ministers, Alexander or his current favourite greatly undercut the authority of the supreme institutions. Despite his intention to establish a degree of legality, routine and institutionalisation, Alexander followed in the footsteps of his illustrious predecessors, Peter I and Catherine II, and succumbed to the desire to rely primarily on personalities and pay less attention to institutions. Peter's legacy of 'institutional order as well as one of individual wilfulness' remained until the end of the empire.[12]

Nicholas I showed little trust for the supreme and subordinate organs established by Alexander. He preferred to govern the empire through ad hoc committees dedicated to specific issues and through His Majesty's Own Personal Chancellery which Paul I had founded in 1796. By placing the chancellery above

12 P. Dukes, *The Making of Russian Absolutism 1613–1801* (Longman: London, 1982). p. 122.

the supreme and subordinate organs and under his direct control, Nicholas further centralised power in his hands and in practice stripped the State Council, Senate and Committee of Ministers of their more significant functions. In the aftermath of the Decembrist revolt Nicholas believed he was fighting a two-front war. One was against the increasing penetration into Russia of Western ideas dangerous to the autocracy which required greater control over society. The other was against the enemy within the autocracy itself – the bureaucracy. As the bureaucracy increased in size, Russian monarchs struggled to maintain personal control over it and to overcome bureaucratic inertia which seemed increasingly to block the imperial will. Nicholas's response to this was the promotion of the chancellery, which to his mind provided for greater monarchical control over both the bureaucracy and society.

The chancellery's First Section prepared documents for the emperor's review and supervised the bureaucracy's personnel. The Second Section, under the administration of Speranskii, worked on the codification of the empire's laws. Between 1828 and 1830 Russia's laws, broadly defined and with some exceptions, were published. In 1832 a law code was published, which replaced the *Law Code of 1649*. At long last the government had written relatively coherent rules. The Fifth Section, established in 1836, studied the living conditions of state peasants and pursued reforms designed to improve them. Its research became a basis for the Emancipation of the Serfs in 1861 during the reign of Alexander II.

The Third Section became most well-known because of its police and supervisory functions that were equivalent to an internal intelligence service. It was a relatively effective state organ for the collection and analysis of information and for the implementation of the emperor's will. Five subsections handled wide-ranging duties, which included surveillance of society and rooting out of corruption in the state apparatus, censorship, investigation of political crimes and management of relations between landowner and peasant.

The autocracy's reliance on the chancellery lessened greatly with the start of Alexander II's reign. The problem of co-ordination of the subordinate organs became more acute with the continued growth in the size, tasks and complexity of the ministries, and once the new emperor decided to pursue the emancipation of the serfs and other reforms. The existing avenues for governing and co-ordination open to Alexander could not provide the mechanism needed for ministerial unity and co-ordination. The State Council was too large and unwieldy a body while the Committee of Ministers, itself also a large body, was bogged down in sorting out administrative detail. In 1857 Alexander founded the Council of Ministers which was to be the supreme organ capable of preparing and implementing reforms free of bureaucratic inertia, ensuring co-ordination of ministers and policy-making and thereby increasing the power of the emperor, under whose direct control the body existed.

No provisions were made for the post of a co-ordinating figure such as a first minister or chairman. That vital function the emperor himself was to fill. It was expected that the monarch would frequently himself chair the council's meetings. The purpose of this was twofold. Firstly, the emperor along with his ministers could consider legislation put forward by individual ministers before its submission to the State Council. This would create the conditions for greater policy co-ordination and coherence. Secondly, by obtaining collective council support for a measure, Alexander hoped to create ministerial unity behind policy decisions.

However, Alexander was not prepared to give up the great personal control afforded by the individual ministerial reports to him in private or to accept a first minister or chairman of the council. The ministers for their part understood that a guarantee of policy success was not obtained by discussion with colleagues in the Council of Ministers, but rather by going after the emperor's ear. This was the crux of the issue. Neither autocrat nor ministers wished in reality to see the full institutionalisation of the supreme organs which they correctly understood would lead to some limitation of their freedom of action. Consequently the Council of Ministers atrophied.

> The Council of Ministers could not become the co-ordinating point of governmental and ministerial activity . . . The unequal status of its members and the presence of the tsar exercising absolute power prevented this. This situation prevented the emergence of a collegiate organ and transformed it into a personal council of the tsar where collective discussion of questions was used to discover the position of the tsar himself. If we take into account that in practice the ministers continued to deliver reports to the tsar individually and privately, which should have been abandoned, it is easy to come to the conclusion that the last attempt before the Revolution of 1905–1906 to create in Russia a supreme collegiate organ failed and the central parts of governmental administration in the country remained disconnected.[13]

By the 1870s a dangerous political situation faced Alexander. Radicals stepped up their action against the monarchy, even attempting to assassinate the emperor himself. At the same time the government was losing moderate

13 S. V. Makarov, *Sovet Ministrov Rossisskoi Imperii 1857–1917* (St Petersburg: Izd. SPbU, 2000), p. 41.

public opinion due to the slowing pace of reform. Alexander understood that decisive action which required a united and co-ordinated government was needed to deal with the threat posed by the radicals and regain a degree of public support. In February 1880 Alexander made Count Loris-Melikov chief of the newly established Supreme Administrative Commission, a virtual dictator charged with co-ordination of government policies. Loris-Melikov quickly realised that full support of the emperor did not automatically give him the authority and real power to make the bureaucratic machine and its highest servants responsive to his wishes. Less than a month later he requested and received the portfolio of the Third Section. By the summer of 1880 this authority rooted in a bureaucratic entity was clearly not enough. Loris-Melikov disbanded the Supreme Commission and assumed stewardship of the most powerful bureaucratic institution, the Ministry of Internal Affairs. From this base, Loris-Melikov, with the open and full support of Alexander II, conducted a ministerial reshuffle to ensure all members of the Council of Ministers could be counted on for strong support.

During the eighteenth and early nineteenth century favourites had indeed ruled for and in the name of the monarch, but they did not have a political base in a particular bureaucratic institution, such as a ministry. By the second half of the nineteenth century the subordinate organs had become so large and unwieldy that when co-ordination of action and policy-making became necessary, the co-ordinating figure needed to have a base in a subordinate organ which provided real power. Alexander II had accidentally found a relatively effective way for establishing order among the subordinate organs. Alexander III and Nicholas II adopted this modus operandi, commonly alternating between the Ministry of Internal Affairs and the Ministry of Finance as the focal point of co-ordination of domestic policy. There was an additional benefit to this approach. It did not raise sensitivities over threats to the emperor's authority. A first minister or chairman of a ministerial council could prove a rival to the supreme monarchical power given his mediating role between the monarch and the ministers. The use of one 'strong' minister was one response to the recurring problem of co-ordination of the subordinate organs, policy direction and the preservation of the personal power of the autocracy. However, the unofficial status of a 'strong minister' combined with the absence of a first minister or chairman created conditions in which if the emperor did not play his designated co-ordinating role, supreme and then subordinate organs lost direction. It also meant that overall government policy could be excessively influenced by the perceptions of one ministry.

Autocrat and autocracy

Whatever the extent to which the subordinate organs improved in the imperial era, if the supreme organs failed to regulate the relationship between the highest members of the bureaucracy and to provide the means for relative unity in both policy-making and execution at the very top, governmental paralysis and disaster could ensue. Central to the issue of the supreme organs was the monarch, who appointed the highest members of the state apparatus and was ultimately responsible for co-ordinating and directing their actions. The importance of this role increased in the absence of a first minister. The monarch's modus operandi, views and opinions until the collapse of the Romanov state clearly exercised a vital impact on the subordinate and supreme organs' everyday operation and on the state's ability to act and react to the changing environment in which it found itself. Several years before the revolution of 1905 Witte summed up the situation for Nicholas II. 'These questions [i.e. key strategic issues – Z.S.] can only be properly solved if you yourself take the lead in the matter, surrounding yourself with people chosen for the job. . . . The bureaucracy itself cannot solve such matters on its own.'[14]

Autocracy was the form of government in Russia until 1905 when in theory a semi-constitutional monarchy was established. The official conception of the autocracy stressed that all political power and legitimacy emanated from the autocrat, who claimed to be God's representative on earth and responsible to Him alone. The autocracy was seen as uniquely Russian and the historical source of her greatness, indeed the only institution capable of mobilising and directing Russia's resources and of ensuring the empire's unity and modernisation. Therefore it was said that any diminution of its power, in theory or in practice, would have negative consequences for the future of Russia. The idea of union between the people and the autocratic tsar with strong paternalistic overtones constituted the base of the autocracy's ideology. Whilst carrying the title of emperor the tsar was also known as the 'little father' who according to apologists for the autocracy acted as the arbiter between the various self-interested groups in society, preventing exploitation and guaranteeing supreme truth and justice. The vast and relatively quick expansion of the bureaucracy in the nineteenth century made the emperors suspicious of its growing power and potential to infringe on the exercise of autocratic power. One result was a longing for a time when the tsar supposedly ruled his domains directly and maintained contact with his people. Consequently the monarch began to be portrayed as the defender of the people from his own bureaucracy. Nicholas

14 Quoted in D. Lieven, *Nicholas II* (London: John Murray, 1993), p. 84.

II took on this view to a much greater extent than any of his predecessors, which resulted in a behaviour that only created greater chaos in the central governing organs at a time of growing social and political problems.

The emperors and supporters of the autocratic principle understood that the growth of the bureaucracy, and specifically the functional specialisation and impersonalisation of government that accompanied it, was slowly and seemingly irreversibly eroding the practical extent to which the autocrat could exercise his power. At the same time the emperors recognised the need to instil order into the expanding system in order to improve co-ordination of governmental organs and policy-making and establish a form of legality and predictability. Their goal remained that the autocrat was to create laws and establish institutions which were to operate within the law whilst he would remain above the law, implementing absolute justice. Yet the systemisation of the governing organs eroded further the practical exercise of autocratic authority. Therefore the emperors whilst on the one hand attempting to introduce order into the system, at the same time undermined their own supreme organs, seeing in them a potential threat to their power. They established ad hoc committees or commissions to draw up decrees, supervise the execution of policy, or oversee the government of a territory. Alexander III's remark that he despised the administration and drank champagne to its destruction succinctly describes how Russia's emperors felt about the bureaucratic machine.

Even Alexander III, the embodiment of paternalist autocrat, clearly understood, however, that he could not govern without the bureaucracy. Even an intelligent and active monarch could not hope to govern the realm without the guidance, knowledge and administrative help of ministers. Ideally decisions were to be made within the supreme organs through the gathering of information and deliberation and analysis by experts. The reality of government then as always differed. Institutional and personal rivalries abounded, opinions differed sharply among ministers and top officials as regards both strategy and tactics. Of course, people seldom reach the top in politics without powerful egos and aggressive and ambitious personalities. The chief executive officer of any regime must ensure that such egos and squabbles do not paralyse the state's capacity to act and react. No Russian minister could formulate or execute any major policy without the explicit support of the monarch, who was therefore essentially the chief executive.

A successful minister had to retain the monarch's favour and consequently fortify and expand his power and influence with him by limiting the influence of, or discrediting fellow ministers. Consequently, a monarch could end up with a group of men who, rather than striving for a unified government, engaged in factional fighting and policy sabotage. This situation is attributable also to the absence of collective responsibility or of a common institutional or ideological loyalty (e.g. to a political party) amongst the ministers to balance departmental and personal conflicts. In the end most monarchs realised that a great degree of ministerial unity was needed if the government was to accomplish anything. That is particularly true as the bureaucratic apparatus grew in scale and specialisation and society became more complex.

However, one key question was who would fulfil the role of the co-ordinating centre? There was no reason in principle why a monarch himself could not fulfil the role of a first minister, engendering unity and co-ordinating the state's servants at the highest level. Louis XIV of France, Alexander III of Russia and Joseph II of Austria all governed in this way.[15] But to act as life-time chief executive officer and bear the burdens of head of state could easily break a twentieth-century monarch given the sheer complexity and scale of a modern government's activity. Alternatively, if the monarch recognised his unwillingness or inability to fulfil this role he could throw the full weight of the monarchy's power behind a chief minister. This would be done to ensure governmental unity in the absence of an active monarch. The relationships between Louis XIII and Cardinal Richelieu, Wilhelm I of Prussia/Germany and Otto von Bismarck, Alexander I and Count A. A. Arakcheev and Empress Maria-Teresa of Austria and Kaunitz are examples of this situation. Russian emperors could in extraordinary circumstances decide to appoint, perhaps temporarily, a Richelieu. Despite the growing size of the tsarist bureaucracy there was no reason one figure could not macro-manage it.[16] To entrust the job to a man who could be dismissed if too unpopular and who was not burdened with the job of chief executive officer for life made good sense. If, however, the monarch for any reason could not fulfil this co-ordinating role and refused to allow a capable first minister to do so, a hole in the centre of government emerged, fatally weakening its ability to act and react.

Russian emperors feared that a unified ministry would lead to 'ministerial despotism', whereby ministers would either limit the flow of information to the monarch or present a unified front on various policy decisions with the aim of obtaining imperial consent. Ministers did in fact have the opportunity to block both the flow of information to the monarch and the execution of policy since it was they who controlled to a great extent what the emperor did

15 T. C. W. Blanning, *Joseph II* (London: Longman, 1994); R. Hatton, *Louis XIV and Absolutism* (London: Macmillan, 1976); M. Deon (ed.), *Louis XIV par lui-même.* (Paris: Gallimard, 1991).
16 Yaney, *Systematization of Russian Government*, p. 307.

and did not see. Therefore the emperors adopted a form of divide and rule in a bid to protect monarchical power and the monarch's room for manoeuvre.

These were not problems or expedients unique to the Russian monarchy. A monarch's problems became more acute with the growth of the bureaucratic machinery of state. Not surprisingly, Imperial China, the first polity to develop a large and sophisticated bureaucracy, also provided some of the earliest and most spectacular examples of a monarch's efforts to struggle against bureaucratic encroachment on royal power. The Ming Emperor Wanli (1572–1620), disgusted with bureaucratic infighting, inertia and intransigence withdrew from governing altogether, refusing for years to meet with his top bureaucrats.[17] The first Ming emperor, T'ai-tsu, deeply suspicious of high-level bureaucrats, 'fractured bureaucratic institutions' in order to exercise real control and enable greater flow of information to himself. When his successors proved less competent or willing chief executives than the dynasty's founder this contributed greatly to the Ming regime's collapse.[18]

A more modern example of the chief executive's dilemma is provided by President Richard Nixon's building up of the National Security Council in order to make certain that various viewpoints could be heard and debated at the top, and clear policy choices thereby presented to him. Nixon wanted all differences of view to be 'identified and defended, rather than muted or buried'. Nixon stated that he did not want 'to be confronted with a bureaucratic consensus that leaves me no option but acceptance or rejection, and that gives me no way of knowing what alternatives exist'.[19]

The Russian emperors' response to the chief executive's dilemma was use of courtiers, unofficial advisers, or officials from outside the 'responsible' ministry's line-of-command to the great chagrin of their ministers. At times these figures constituted a useful alternative source of information and opinion. However, even when this was true, the co-ordination and consistency / execution of policy once a decision had been made had to be ensured, which often failed to happen under Nicholas II. Sometimes Nicholas would use such people to implement a policy which for some reason or another was not being followed by the responsible ministry. This happened as regards foreign policy in the Far East, with the Russo-Japanese War as its consequence:

17 J. Spence, *The Search for Modern China* (New York: Norton, 1990), p. 16. See also R. Huang, *1587. A Year of No Significance* (New Haven: Yale University Press, 1981).

18 J. Dull, 'The Evolution of Government in China', in P. Ropp (ed.), *The Heritage of China* (Berkeley: University of California Press, 1990). On Ming government see above all C. Hucker, 'Ming government', in D. Twitchett and F. Mote (eds.), *The Cambridge History of China*, vol. VIII, Part 2 (Cambridge: Cambridge University Press, 1996).

19 Quoted in J. McGregor Burns, *Leadership* (New York: Harper and Row, 1977), pp. 412–13.

another example was the establishment of the police trade unions, the remnants of which led the march to the Winter Palace on Bloody Sunday.

The last emperor was infamous for his suspicion of his ministers. During a meeting over foreign policy in the Far East, Minister of War Aleksei Kuropatkin, worried by Nicholas's tendency to listen to the counsel of unofficial advisors, complained that, '(your) confidence in me would only grow when I ceased to be a minister'. Nicholas responded, 'It is strange, you know, but perhaps that is psychologically correct.'[20] To do Nicholas justice, this was not a unique situation. Louis XV, frustrated by his foreign minister's failure to share his enthusiasm for Poland and Sweden, conducted a secret policy with these two countries, whilst George II of England sent secret agents to negotiate with Saxony and Austria in contradiction with his own government's policy.

Post 1905

As a result of the revolution of 1905 Russia became a semi-constitutional monarchy. The now half-elected State Council became the upper house of the parliamentary system. The Duma made up the lower house.[21]

The major change in the central governing organs was the prominence given to the Council of Ministers as the focal point of the administration and, more importantly, the emergence of the council's chairman. This figure held the responsibility of co-ordinating policy-making and ministerial activity and ensuring unity in the council. Many figures inside and outside of government came to the conclusion that the causes of the disasters of 1904–6 could be linked to the chaos and disunity of the subordinate organs resulting from faulty supreme organs. Particular blame was placed on Nicholas II who came to be regarded as unable to play the co-ordinating role demanded by the autocratic system. This drive for ministerial unity under the leadership of the chairman of the Council of Ministers predictably raised sensitivities concerning infringement on the emperor's real power and role. Nicholas II summed up his feeling in a telling comment. 'He (Peter A. Stolypin, chairman of the Council of Ministers, 1906–1911) dies in my service, true, but he was always so anxious to keep me in the background. Do you suppose that I liked always reading

20 'Dnevnik Kuropatina', *KA* 2 (1922): 57–8.

21 R. McKean, *The Russian Constitutional Monarchy, 1907–1917* (London: Macmillan, 1977); W. Mosse, 'Russian Bureaucracy at the end of the Ancien Regime: The Imperial State Council', *SR* (1980): 616–32; D. Macdonald, *United Government and Foreign Policy in Russia, 1900–1914* (Cambridge, Mass.: Harvard University Press, 1992); R. Sh. Ganelin, *Rossiiskoe Samoderzhavie v 1905 gody* (Leningrad: Nauka, 1991); A. P. Borodin, *Gosudarstvennii Sovet Rossii, 1906–1917* (Kirov: Vytka, 1999).

in the papers that the chairman of the council of ministers had done this . . . The chairman had done that? Don't I count? Am I nobody?'[22] For the rest of his reign Nicholas worked towards the emasculation of the chairman's power, which he considered a direct threat to his authority. However, he himself was unable to co-ordinate his government or provide astute political leadership – with disastrous consequences.

Nicholas's undermining of his own government was owed above all to his personality, though also to his conception of his role as patriarch of his people, and to the suspicion and contempt of bureaucracy widespread in Russian society.[23] Even Kaiser Wilhelm II of Germany, let alone Emperor Francis Joseph of Austria never undermined their chief ministers to the degree Nicholas sabotaged Stolypin and after him, Vladimir Kokovtsev. More importantly, the Hohenzollern and Habsburg monarchs did not see a fundamental difference between themselves and the policies followed by their governments.[24] Nicholas, however, regarded the Council of Ministers and the bureaucracy as direct threats to his power and worked to undermine them, which lead to paralysis of the central governing organs in the years before and during the First World War.

Modernisation from above

Inseparable from this discussion is the regime's institutional response to the challenges posed by modernisation from above. Unsurprisingly the achievement and maintenance of great power status, an essential plank in Romanov legitimacy, became a driving force behind the evolution of subordinate and supreme governing organs under Peter the Great and subsequently. Defeat in the Crimean War put on top of the agenda not only the necessity for major socioeconomic reform on a scale not seen since the time of Peter, such as the abolition of serfdom, inculcation of legal principles and industrialisation, but also the enlargement and improvement of the bureaucracy, whose responsibility now was transformation of a society regarded as backward in relation to the advanced powers of Europe.

22 V. Kokovtsev, *Iz moego proshlego* (Paris: priv. pub., 1933), pp. 282–3.

23 See e.g. R. Wortman, *Scenarios of Power* (Princeton: Princeton University Press, 2000), vol. II, part 3; Lieven, *Nicholas II*.

24 The literature on Wilhelm is immense; for guidance see C. Clark, *Kaiser Wilhelm II* (Harlow: Longman, 2000), pp. 262–5, J. C. G. Rohl, *The Kaiser and his Court: Wilhelm II and the Government of Germany* (Cambridge: Cambridge University Press, 1987); On Franz Josef, see e.g. S. Beller, *Francis Joseph* (Harlow: Longman, 1995) and J.-P. Bled, *Franz Joseph* (Oxford: Blackwell, 1992).

The Russian bureaucracy undertook one of the first programmes of modernisation from above, having been forced to play many roles which belonged to private groups in the economically advanced countries of Europe. The regime collapsed in 1917, but to deny the positive contributions of the bureaucratic system, despite all its faults, is difficult. Even if we just focus on the period from the Great Reforms to the Revolution the list of achievements is impressive: emancipation of the serfs, establishment of an independent judiciary system and local government (*zemstvos*), industrialisation, construction of a vast railway network, the beginnings of a constitutional form of government, Stolypin's land reforms, attempts at a genuine social welfare system and expansion of mass education. All of these required a fairly competent bureaucratic infrastructure as well as expertise and professionalism.[25] But the subordinate organs needed direction from above. In the absence of effective supreme organs, many times the ministries handled 'personal and particular problems, to the obvious detriment of larger, more important issues and unforeseen circumstances'.[26] In the end, Russia's subordinate organs in St Petersburg to a significant extent operated well, while the more serious problems of governing existed elsewhere in the supreme organs and in the modus operandi of the emperors and most especially of Nicholas II.

25 On senior late-imperial officials, see D. Lieven, *Russia's Rulers Under the Old Regime* (London: Yale, 1989): chapter 1 surveys the literature on the Russian bureaucracy.

26 A. Verner, *The Crisis of Russian Autocracy: Nicholas II and the 1905 Revolution* (Princeton: Princeton University Press, 1990), p. 46.

21
Provincial and local government

JANET M. HARTLEY

Introduction

A study of local government raises several important questions about the nature of the imperial Russian state, the level of development of provincial Russian society and the relationship between government and society in Russia. To what extent did the government allow or wish to encourage a genuine decentralisation or devolution of power to the provinces? Could local government institutions – either corporate institutions or 'all-class' institutions – flourish given both the pressures from the centre and the poor economic and cultural levels of rural Russia which inhibited the growth of an educated and politically conscious provincial society? To what extent can we even speak of a structure of local government when a significant proportion of the population – the peasants – were only rarely touched by it, at least until the Emancipation of 1861 and to some extent even thereafter? The status of local government – either as separate from the central bureaucracy or as an integral part of the government structure – was a major debate in Russia in the nineteenth century. At the root of these questions is the fundamental issue of the relationship between local government and the modernisation of the Russian state. On the one hand, local government was potentially a tool to stimulate corporate identity, urban self-confidence and economic and cultural progress across all sectors of society, including the peasantry after 1861. On the other hand, problems in local government could be interpreted as symbolic of the failure, or the unwillingness, of the tsarist regime to adapt to change and to establish an effective relationship between state and society. If the latter has some validity, then we have to ask in addition whether local government contributed to the downfall of the regime which created it.

Local government was a matter which concerned all the tsars but there were periods of particularly intensive and significant legislative activity, namely: (i) the reign of Peter I (1682–1725) when urban administration was reformed (in 1699 and more notably in 1721 when urban magistracies were established) and when, in 1718, the country was re-divided into *gubernii* (provinces), which were in turn subdivided into *provintsii* and *uezdy* (districts); (ii) the reign of Catherine II (1762–96) when three major laws were promulgated – the Statute of Provincial Administration of 1775 and the Charters to the Nobles and the Towns in 1785; (iii) the era of reforms in the decade which followed the Emancipation of the Serfs in 1861, which saw the introduction of the *zemstvos* (local elected assemblies) and the re-structuring of the legal system and reform of urban administration; (iv) the 1890s when many of the reforms of the 1860s were modified or curtailed. In addition, legislation which ostensibly only concerned central government – in particular the establishment of the Senate in 1711, the Ministry of Internal Affairs in 1802 and then the introduction of *national* representation in the State Duma (Parliament) in 1905 – had a significant impact on the functions of local institutions and their relationship with the centre. This chapter is concerned with *Russian* local administration but it should be noted that different structures, different traditions and even different law codes applied in many of the non-Russian parts of the empire until well into the nineteenth century and sometimes until 1917. These areas include the Baltic provinces, the lands of former Poland-Lithuania, the Ukraine, the Grand Duchy of Finland, the Caucasus and Central Asia.

The Centre and the provinces

Local government was an issue which spawned extensive, and lengthy, legislation over the whole imperial period (the 1775 Statute of Provincial Administration, for example, comprised 491 articles; the two statutes of 1864 and 1890 on the zemstvos comprised 120 and 138 articles respectively). The provenance and nature of this legislation reflect something of the relationship between the centre and the provinces. For the most part in the first two hundred years of this study, legislation was not stimulated by demands for its introduction from nobles or townspeople or by local officials. This does not mean, however, that these groups had no views on the matter. When they were asked for opinions – as they were in the Legislative Commission of 1767, by N. A. Miliutin in the 1840s in the context of municipal reform of St Petersburg, and in the formulation of what became the zemstvo legislation in the late 1850s and early 1860s – they were prepared to give them and to highlight the inadequacies of current local administration at the same time. But the timing and content of local government legislation was primarily determined by the tsars and their advisers and the institutional structures created were often based on Western models (which could be Swedish, Baltic, Prussian, French or English) rather than being drawn from analyses of local needs or the experiences of the provinces.

The 'dynamic, interventionist and coercive state', as Marc Raeff characterised Petrine Russia,[1] had always assumed that it had the power and the obligation to govern all aspects of the lives of its citizens. This belief was not, of course, unique to the Russian government, either in the eighteenth century or afterwards, but possibly featured most strongly in the Russian case because of the lack of balancing factors such as bodies representing estate interests, well-developed urban institutions or a powerful and independent Church hierarchy which existed elsewhere in Europe. A study of the legislation concerning local government, however, is not only central to the understanding of the intentions of central government but also exposes the weakness of the central government and the essential contradictions in tsarist policy. The government wanted to stimulate provincial and urban institutions of self-government and, by extension, stimulate the development of a provincial society, but it needed to control these institutions and ensure above all that they fulfilled state obligations as a greater priority than satisfying local needs. The potential for conflict between provinces and the centre was always there but became more acute after the establishment of the zemstvos in the 1860s. The government also needed the participation of elected, and poorly paid, officials from members of provincial noble and urban society (and also state peasants after 1775 and former serfs after 1864) to staff local institutions (in particular, the lower levels of courts) because it lacked the trained manpower and the financial resources to fill these posts with a professional bureaucracy appointed from the centre. At the same time it feared the independence of these officials and attempted to co-opt them to carry out government policies and subordinated them to appointed representatives of the government and to ministries in the capital.

These dilemmas of the central government can be seen both in the general scope of local government legislation and in relation to the functions given to particular institutions and individuals. The centre determined the boundaries of units of local administration (and re-drew them at various times either to increase efficiency or to incorporate new territorial acquisitions, often with a deliberate neglect of historical territorial division), defined, created and abolished towns (and designed their coats of arms and determined the layouts of

1 M. Raeff, *The Well-Ordered Police State: Social and Institutional Change through Law in the Germanies and Russia, 1600–1800* (New Haven: Yale University Press), p. 206.

the streets and the architectural styles to be employed),[2] decided the structure, social composition and areas of competence of all provincial and urban institutions, defined the membership and groupings of urban society, determined and altered the franchise for towns, noble assemblies and zemstvos, and set the fiscal and other obligations of all institutions, including taxation and billeting of troops in civilian houses (that is, *state* and not local needs). At the same time, local institutions from the time of Peter I were obliged to report and respond to 'local needs' and to stimulate the local economy.

The example of urban government in the eighteenth century will illustrate how government legislation could bear little relation to reality. Peter I and Catherine II tried to stimulate the corporate identity of townspeople and the economic development of Russian towns through legislation which deliberately attempted to incorporate 'Western' or 'European' practices. Both rulers attempted to introduce 'Western'-style craft guilds and passed regulations on their composition and on the training of apprentices (in 1785 Catherine even stipulated the hours of work for apprentices including the length of meal breaks!).[3] Both rulers defined the composition of urban society by law, and in addition divided the merchantry into groups according to their declared capital, and then used these groupings as a basis for the composition of an elaborate structure of urban institutions of self-government based on representatives from each group (six groups in the Charter to the Towns in 1785). These definitions were modified in the reigns of Alexander I and Nicholas I but not fundamentally altered.

This legislation, however, ignored the reality of eighteenth-century urban life. In practice, very few towns outside a few exceptional centres like St Petersburg and Moscow had a sufficiently developed economy or sufficiently wealthy merchants to fill all the social categories of townspeople as defined by Peter and Catherine. In 1786 it was reported that in the province of St Petersburg only the city of St Petersburg itself had representatives of all six urban groups and that only there were merchants divided into three guilds as Catherine had stipulated; the smaller district towns could not fill these social categories.[4] Urban government could never therefore function as the legislation envisaged

2 R. Jones, 'Urban Planning and Development of Provincial Towns in Russia during the Reign of Catherine II', in J. G. Garrard (ed.), *The Eighteenth Century in Russia* (Oxford: Clarendon Press, 1973), pp. 321–44.

3 *PSZ*, vol. 22, no. 16188, article 105, p. 378, The Charter to the Towns, 1785.

4 RGADA Moscow, Fond 16, d. 530, ll. 266–66ob, report by N. Saltykov to the Senate, 1786, also quoted in J. M. Hartley, *A Social History of the Russian Empire 1650–1825* (London and New York: Longman, 1999), p. 42. This theme is developed more fully in J. M. Hartley, 'Governing the City: St Petersburg and Catherine II's reforms', in A. Cross (ed.), *St Petersburg, 1703–1825* (London: Palgrave, 2003), pp. 99–118.

in the eighteenth century because representatives of some of the social groups on which the institutional structure was built simply did not exist. Furthermore, Russian towns in this period were overwhelmingly peasant in composition (state and serf) and these peasants were not only excluded from urban government but could also undercut urban guilds with their own home-made products. The attempt to revitalise urban life whist ignoring the peasant presence in the towns, the competition of peasant craft goods and the impossibility of separating the town from the countryside in an overwhelmingly rural economy made the import of Western-style institutions simply impractical. The dilemma facing local institutions of having to respond to local needs whilst carrying out their obligations to the state can also be seen in the weakness of eighteenth-century urban institutions. Service in urban institutions was unpopular and regarded as yet another state obligation – like billeting and conscription – imposed on a long-suffering and impoverished urban population. Urban institutions had only limited rights to impose taxation for local needs; their main function was to meet state fiscal obligations.

The ambiguity between local and national obligations is even more clearly illustrated by the zemstvos after 1864. Zemstvos were given considerable local rights, including the right to petition the governor directly on local concerns, to manage the local postal system, to have responsibility for local education and health, and to levy taxes for local as well as national needs. But these rights had only been granted after a ministerial struggle (in the centre, not in the provinces) over the merits of self-government versus central control. At the same time the governor was given the right to veto zemstvo activity if it conflicted with *state* interests. In practice, this meant inevitable conflict between zemstvos and local officials from the start and resulted in the curbing of the zemstvos' independent sphere of activities in 1890. This curb did nothing to ease relations between the zemstvo and the bureaucracy, and zemstvo radicalism increased after the accession of Nicholas II in 1894. Conflicts at the local level between zemstvo and governor were most heated over the zemstvos' right of taxation, particularly to raise income to provide education and healthcare, but more acute conflicts arose at the turn of the century between the zemstvos and officials in St Petersburg who by this stage not only opposed the rights of the zemstvo to claim much-needed taxation revenue but also had come to distrust every manifestation of what they regarded as elements of radical opposition to the regime.[5]

5 The relations between zemstvos and the centre are best described in T. Fallows, 'The Zemstvo and Bureaucracy', in T. Emmons and W. S. Vucinich (eds.), *The Zemstvo in*

The most serious conflict between the zemstvos and the central bureaucracy focused on the scope for inter-zemstvo contact and co-operation, a conflict which became part of the liberal opposition movement to the tsar up to and including the year 1905. Zemstvos were instructed to deal only with matters within the boundaries of their province and district. This restriction was based on the fear that the zemstvos, as representative bodies, albeit not democratic ones, would seek to expand their responsibilities upwards through co-operation with other provincial zemstvos and then ultimately in the 'crowning edifice' of a national body. The number of resolutions passed by zemstvos which included constitutional demands shows that this fear was not unfounded. This conflict was won by the zemstvos in the early twentieth century just as their political threat to the government diminished following the establishment of the State Duma and just as many of the provincial nobility who dominated the zemstvos were coming to renounce these liberal views. During the Russo-Japanese War of 1904–5, and again in the First World War, the government permitted the formation of an all-Russian union of zemstvos for the purpose of war relief.[6]

A further indication of the potential conflict in state-inspired local government can be seen in the relations between local and central officials. This was a dilemma from the start as Peter I attempted to reduce the influence of powerful *voevody* (military commanders) in the provinces by introducing governors in 1708. Governors always trod a difficult line, responsible for the conduct of local affairs whilst at the same time they were representatives of both the tsar and the central government. The sheer burden of work imposed by the centre – it has been estimated that governors had to sign over 100,000 papers per year by the 1840s[7] – meant that there were practical impediments to devoting time to local affairs. Marshals of the nobility, elected by their fellow nobles, also faced the problem of representing the interests of the provincial nobles whilst being weighed down with bureaucratic functions imposed by the governor and the state.[8] The provincial police force suffered from the same divided

Russia: An Experiment in Local Self-Government (Cambridge: Cambridge University Press, 1982), pp. 177–239. The rise of zemstvo radicalism is described in S. Galai, *The Liberation Movement in Russia 1900–1905* (Cambridge: Cambridge University Press, 1973), pp. 7–35.

6 T. E. Porter, *The Zemstvo and the Emergence of Civil Society in Late Imperial Russia 1864–1917* (San Francisco: Mellen Research University Press, 1991); these activities are described by a contemporary in T. J. Polner, *Russian Local Government during the War and the Union of Zemstvos* (New Haven: Yale University Press, 1930).

7 B. N. Mironov, 'Local Government in Russia in the First Half of the Nineteenth Century: Provincial Government and Estate Self-Government', *JfGO* 42 (1994): 165.

8 G. Hamburg, 'Portrait of an Elite: Russian Marshals of the Nobility 1861–1971', *SR* 40, 4 (1981): 585–602.

loyalties. A rural police officer (called the *zemskii komissar* in 1719 and the *zemskii ispravnik* after 1775) was elected from the nobility but was subordinated to the local regiment under Peter and then to the governor under Catherine, and was ultimately responsible to the central government. An urban police force was set up in 1782 whose responsibility extended beyond dealing with petty crimes to the preservation of the wellbeing and morals of the urban population (amongst other things the police had to ensure that the sexes were segregated in the bathhouses). But in 1802 the police force was subordinated to the Ministry of Internal Affairs (although land captains, or *zemskie nachal'niki*, remained responsible to the governor) and their relationship with local government thereby weakened. The establishment of the Third Department in 1826 in the reign of Nicholas I, made responsible for political security, added another layer of a secret police force which was entirely removed from local control.

On the other hand, the ability of the state to interfere in local administration was always curbed by two factors – the problem of communications in the vast empire, and poverty. Even in the middle of the nineteenth century it took forty-four days for a letter from Orenburg province to reach St Petersburg.[9] The situation improved only in the 1860s with the introduction of the telegraph. The poignancy and comic effect of Gogol's *Government Inspector* (*Revizor*, written in the 1830s) is based on the fact that inspectors so rarely visited the provinces in person so allowing local officials to act as they wished. Furthermore, the lawlessness of the Russian countryside – whether it be through bands of deserters or brigands or the spontaneous activities of individuals – militated against orderly government of any kind. Poverty meant that the state lacked the funds to staff the provinces in full or to offer high enough salaries to make elective posts attractive. The result was that Russia was seriously under-manned at all levels (with the possible exception of the peasant commune before 1861 which is outside the scope of this chapter). In 1763 Russia employed 16,500 officials in central and local government, while Prussia, with less than 1 per cent of Russia's land area employed some 14,000 civil servants.[10] It has been estimated that in 1796 there were only 6 administrators per 10,000 inhabitants; by 1857 this had only increased to 17 administrators per 10,000 inhabitants.[11] One estimate in 1897 was that there were just over

9 S. F. Starr, *Decentralization and Self-Government in Russia, 1830–1870* (Princeton: Princeton University Press, 1972), p. 45.

10 R. E. Jones, *The Emancipation of the Russian Nobility 1762–1785* (Princeton: Princeton University Press, 1973), p. 182.

11 Mironov, 'Local Government in Russia', 200.

100,000 officials with some police responsibility at all levels in Russia.[12] Despite the amount of legislation devoted to local administration the conclusion has to be that Russia was under- rather than over-governed throughout the imperial period.[13]

The operation of local administration

The problems outlined above made smooth and complete implementation of government legislation impossible to achieve. Local administration was further weakened by the exclusion of large sections of the population from its control. Before the reforms of the 1860s, many of the matters relating to the everyday concerns of peasants – state peasants and serfs – were dealt with by peasants themselves through the commune. The commune not only distributed state obligations such as taxation and the recruit levy but also acted as a peasant court of first instance, using customary law and 'peasant justice' for civil matters and minor criminal offences. The Statute of Administration of 1775 established a structure of courts for state peasants, but serfs only participated in the state legal system when they were accused of major criminal offences or when they were litigants in cases involving other social estates (which could happen in disputes in town courts involving so-called 'trading peasants'). After emancipation and the reforms of 1864, exclusively peasant institutions were retained, as in the case of the commune, or created, in the case of *volost'* peasant courts where customary law continued to be applied, so that peasants were deliberately treated differently from other members of society, separately and outside the reformed state court structure.[14] This suggested that the reforms of 1864, like those of 1775, were primarily *urban*, and were of relevance to towns but not to the countryside, where, of course, the majority of the population lived. Industrial workers before the 1860s in the

12 J. W. Daly, *Autocracy under Siege: Security Police and Opposition in Russia 1866–1905* (DeKalb: Northern Illinois University Press, 1998), p. 9. Weissman quotes a much lower figure of 47,866 police at the beginning of the twentieth century from a Police Department report: N. Weissman, 'Regular Police in Tsarist Russia, 1900–1914', *RR* 44, 1 (1985): 47. The figures are difficult to interpret as it is not clear whether several categories, such as night watchmen and other patrolmen, are included.

13 Velychenko has recently challenged the view that Russia was 'undergoverned' by arguing that valid comparisons should be made between the levels of staffing in Russia with European colonies rather than with West European states, but his argument, although stimulating, cannot disguise the serious undermanning of institutions and of police forces in European Russia or in towns in the empire which can legitimately be compared with towns elsewhere in Europe: S. Velychenko, 'The Size of the Imperial Russian Bureaucracy and Army in Comparative Perspective', *JfGO* 49, 3 (2001): 346–62.

14 S. F. Frank, *Crime, Cultural Conflict, and Justice in Rural Russia 1856–1914* (Berkeley: University of California Press, 1999), pp. 36–40.

large privately owned enterprises mainly comprised assigned, or possessional, serfs who were also outside the jurisdiction of local administration. The army, the clergy and several national and religious groups were also governed by a separate jurisdiction (although conflicts within towns between the Church and urban institutions, which was common in the seventeenth century, declined in the eighteenth century, particularly after the secularisation of Church land in 1764). These anomalies and the continuation of 'legal separateness' point to a fundamental problem in local administration, namely whether administration should be centred on *soslovie*, or social 'estate', reflecting corporate interests (such as urban institutions of self-government and noble assemblies), or whether administration should, or could be, 'all-class' or 'all-estate' (which was partly the case with some of the 1775 institutions, which excluded serfs but not state peasants, and fully the case with the zemstvos). An analysis of the functioning of both types of institution illustrates some of the dilemmas facing local administration during the imperial period.

Corporate institutions

The universal obligations of state service for individuals in Russia from the reign of Peter I – service for nobles (formal until 1762 and informal thereafter), dues and conscription for townspeople and peasants – combined with the government's deliberate choice of 'collective responsibility' as a means by which villages and towns (at least until the urban tax reform of 1775) met these obligations – inhibited the development of independent, corporate bodies which could defend the interests of their members against the government. This is not to say that corporate institutions could not become a pervasive and essential part of the life of the Russian people – the peasant commune for all categories of peasants is testimony to this – but it goes some way to explain the failure of the urban population or the nobility to develop powerful 'Western' or Central European-style corporate institutions.

The tsars – from Peter to Nicholas II – legislated at length on the structures of urban self-government and on the composition, responsibilities and privileges of the urban population. It has been seen above that government hoped through legislation to 'Westernise' or modernise Russian towns by the introduction of Western-style guilds, the creation, and then re-creation, of categories of urban citizens and the development of corporate institutions. The impracticability of this legislation in itself damaged the ability of corporate institutions to function in the way envisaged in the legislation, and only worsened from the late nineteenth century when the influx of new urban residents was not matched by an attempt to change the nature of urban representation. Further damage was inflicted by the inadequacies of the legislation itself, in particular: the confusion over administrative and judicial functions in Peter I's *ratushy* (town councils) in 1699 and *magistraty* or magistracies, established in 1721, which were not fully resolved by the re-definition of the magistracies as urban courts in Catherine II's legislation of 1775; the overlapping jurisdictions of the strata of town dumas established after 1775 and overlapping between the dumas and the urban courts and the urban police force; the ambiguous role of the governor in urban affairs (especially after the Municipal Statute of 1892); the relationship between urban government and the Ministry of Internal Affairs; the vast amount of paperwork which passed through institutions (Mironov has estimated that some 100, 000 documents passed through the St Petersburg city duma from 1838 to 1840);[15] the lack of clarity over the rights of the towns to raise local taxes for local needs; inadequate control over urban budgets, at least until the 1840s. The constant competition from an overwhelming peasant population in an overwhelmingly rural country in itself was always going to militate against the importance of towns and townspeople.

In the late eighteenth century there is some limited evidence to suggest that despite these inadequacies of legislation Catherine's 1785 Charter to the Towns did have some positive effects, quite possibly linked with the attempts in her reign to modernise and beautify towns by building schemes and town planning. The attempt to dignify urban office not only by financial rewards but by social recognition made at least the highest urban posts more attractive. Urban institutions began to play some part in the economic life of the cities which went beyond mere tax collectors for the state. Indeed, the physical inability of the centre to control the activities of local administrators enabled the towns to circumvent the legislation and make institutions more responsive to genuine urban needs. Urban posts became the preserve of a small number of prominent families, which, while it reflects poorly on the democratic nature of urban institutions, at least demonstrates that urban administration was considered to be of importance. In the first half of the nineteenth century, however, absenteeism increased in urban institutions while urban government became more chaotic and disorderly.

As the nineteenth century progressed, the large cities had to face far greater challenges in terms of housing, law and order, education, transport, health and sanitation as rural labourers flooded into the towns to seek employment in the

15 B. Mironov, 'Bureaucratic or Self-Government: The Early Nineteenth Century Russian City', *SR* 52, 2 (1993): 249.

newly established factories without an effective administration or adequate financial base. The need for more effective urban government which could address the economic, cultural and physical needs of the population had been partly recognised in the municipal reform of St Petersburg in 1846 and Moscow (and Odessa) in 1862, followed by the municipal statute of 1870, and seems to have encouraged the development of what can be termed a 'civil society' in the larger towns such as St Petersburg, Moscow and Odessa.[16] This development was, however, deliberately undermined by restrictions being placed on the urban franchise and on the independence of towns from the governor in the municipal statute of 1892. In Moscow, where there was a more established and stable urban class and where a sense of 'civic responsibility' seems to have developed, these issues were addressed to an extent. In St Petersburg, however, where the needs of the court, the central bureaucracy and the wealthy noble residents outweighed those of the merchantry and industrialists, these issues remained unresolved, with the inevitable consequence of the aggravation of social tensions within the city.[17] In Odessa, municipal government declined in effectiveness after the restrictions imposed on its activities in 1892 and lost the support of the professional classes,[18] whilst it deliberately neglected the needs of the new wave of urban poor employed in the factories. In this respect it can be said that corporate administration in the towns failed to respond to the needs of a rapidly changing urban population.

Catherine established the corporate institution for the nobility – noble assemblies – originally in 1766 to elect deputies for the Legislative Commission, although their functions were more fully defined in the Statute of Provincial Administration of 1775 and then in the Charter to the Nobles in 1785. The assemblies were supposed to fulfil state needs, namely to conduct the three-yearly election of nobles to posts in the new institutions of local administration established in 1775, but were also designed to stimulate a sense of local corporate responsibility by keeping records of nobles and to consider and act collectively to address local needs in the wake of the abolition of compulsory noble service to the state in 1762 and the beginnings of a settled provincial

16 Well described in M. F. Hamm (ed.), *The City in the Late Imperial Russia* (Bloomington: Indiana University Press, 1986), especially in the chapters on Kiev by Hamm and Odessa by F. W. Skinner. See also M. F. Hamm, *Kiev: A Portrait, 1800–1917* (Princeton University Press, 1993) and V. A. Nardova, 'Municipal Self-Government after the 1870 Reform', in B. Eklof, J. Bushnell and L. Zakharova, *Russia's Great Reforms, 1855–1881* (Bloomington: Indiana University Press, 1994), pp. 181–96.

17 J. H. Bater, 'Some Dimensions of Urbanization and the Response of Municipal Government: Moscow and St Petersburg', *RH* 5, 1 (1978): 46–63.

18 Skinner, 'Odessa and the Problem of Urban Modernization', in *The City in Late Imperial Russia*, p. 236.

noble society. Noble assembles, however, suffered from the same failure of the government to recognise the reality of provincial life which had adversely affected urban corporate institutions established by Peter I and Catherine II. In practice, the wealthy and most educated nobility preferred to live away from their estates, and in the remoter parts of Russia the resident nobility tended to be impoverished, to the extent that few met the qualifications (which were based on income and service rank) to vote or take elective office.[19]

Although the assemblies did serve to fill posts, which in turn provided some much needed income for some of the poorer provincial nobles, and although the elections generated equally welcome social activity which broke the tedium of life in the provincial backwaters, their significance for the development of a corporate mentality was limited. Even by the end of Catherine II's reign, absenteeism in assemblies at election time was rife. The prestige of the assemblies was undermined further by Paul I, who abolished assemblies at provincial level. Although Alexander I restored the provincial assemblies, the damage was done and the power of the governor grew over their conduct of affairs. The property qualifications for active participation – that is, voting – were further restricted in the reign of Nicholas I. Indeed, the noble assemblies were almost moribund when they were artificially revived during the debates on local administration in the wake of the Emancipation. This debate led to a not entirely welcome participation by the assemblies, in particular because six noble assemblies requested the establishment of a national parliament. The assemblies continued to coexist alongside the zemstvos after 1864. The intense political activity in the years 1904 to 1905 also affected the assemblies, although they tended to be more moderate than the zemstvos. There is no doubt that a corporate sense of shared interests and, not least, shared fears developed within the provincial gentry in the early years of the twentieth century as their land-ownership diminished. But the fact that this manifested itself far more within the zemstvos – that is, within 'all-estate' bodies – than within the noble assemblies was a reflection of the limited power and importance of this corporate institution for the nobility.

'All-estate' institutions

A limited attempt to create 'all-estate' institutions was made by Catherine II in 1775 when she established alongside the corporate institutions for the towns and nobles (her draft Charter for the State Peasantry was never promulgated)

19 The operation of noble assemblies is described in Hartley, *A Social History of the Russian Empire*, pp. 92–6.

an elaborate local government structure of courts and institutions for preserving law and order and for welfare in which members of three estates – nobles, townspeople and state peasants – participated, but which excluded serfs. Courts were segregated by the estate of the litigant in the first two instances and members of each of the three estates elected members of these courts (although state peasants only elected assessors and not the judges). But, at least in principle, nobles and state peasants sat together in the two institutions set up in 1775 whose functions are most imprecise: the conscience court (*sovestnyi sud*), a court which was set up to handle cases which fell outside the normal scope of civil and criminal offences (and which included a rather vague provision for habeus corpus, a concept acquired by Catherine from her reading of Blackstone in French translation);[20] the lower land court (*nizhnii zemskii sud*) whose activities are largely unrecorded, but which was supposed to handle rural police matters and petty crimes. All three estates also participated in the boards of social welfare (*prikazy obshchestvennogo prizreniia*) which were given an initial capital of 15,000 roubles each and which had responsibilities for a whole range of welfare institutions, including national schools, hospitals, almshouses, asylums, houses of correction, workhouses and orphanages. There is no record of the way in which representatives of different estates worked in this body. At least in some provinces the board was extremely active, although it was not always possible to set up the full range of institutions envisaged; reports in the 1780s found that the institutions were almost complete in the provinces of central Russia but that in Olonets province only a hospital had been opened.[21] Progress in establishing national schools was impressive given that the boards were operating almost from scratch; by 1792 there were 302 national schools teaching 16,322 boys and 1,178 girls.[22] Some boards also acted quite effectively as provincial banks by lending out its original capital at interest.[23]

A more comprehensive attempt to create an 'all-estate' institution occurred in 1864, with the establishment of zemstvos at the provincial and district level. This statute followed the Emancipation of the Serfs, and the consequent need

20 For the operation of this court see J. M. Hartley, 'Catherine's Conscience Court: An English Equity Court?', in A. Cross (ed.), *Russia and the West in the Eighteenth Century* (Newtonville, Mass.: Oriental Research Partners, 1983), pp. 306–18.

21 Sankt-Peterburg Filial Instituta russkoi istorii, St Petersburg, Fond 36, d. 478, f. 16, report by A. R. Vorontsov from Olonets guberniia; also cited in J. M. Hartley, 'Philanthropy in the Reign of Catherine the Great: Aims and Realities', in R. Bartlett and J. M. Hartley (eds.), *Russia in the Age of Enlightenment: Essays for Isabel de Madariaga* (Basingstoke: Macmillan, 1990), p. 181.

22 Hartley, *A Social History of Russia*, p. 138.

23 J. M. Hartley, 'The Boards of Social Welfare and the Financing of Catherine II's State Schools', *SEER* 67, 2 (1989): 211–27.

to create a substitute to handle the many administrative functions handled by the serf-owning nobleman, although the zemstvo legislation drew heavily on past experience of corporate institutions, including the peasant commune as much as urban and noble organs and the boards of social welfare.[24] Zemstvos at both levels had an assembly, to which nobles, townspeople and peasants' representatives were elected, and a board, with executive power, which was elected from the assemblies. But from the start the 'estate' nature of the elections to the assemblies were ambiguous, and the assumption that 'estates' were equal in any way was completely absent. In 1864 the three categories, or curia, were defined by their ownership of property – private landed, urban and collective land – rather than strictly by social estate (although merchants with 'certificates' were also eligible), which meant that peasants could participate in the first curia alongside nobles if they purchased sufficient land. The land qualification ensured that noble deputies would be in majority. In 1890, this principle of land-ownership as a franchise qualification was changed and became 'estate' based, with the peasants eligible to vote only in the third curia, a change inspired in part by the increase in land purchased by peasants at the expense of the rural nobility.[25] At the same time the rural property qualifications for nobles were lowered and certified merchants lost their automatic right to vote which served to increase the noble franchise at the expense of other social groups (including Jews and clergy). It also increased their representation on both district and provincial level assemblies, but most particularly at the district level (where it increased from 42.4 per cent in the period 1883–6 to 55.2 per cent in 1890)[26] and became even more prominent at the board level, which they had always dominated. In the last years of the imperial regime peasants regained some seats in the zemstvos, particularly at district level, as landowners but remained under-represented on zemstvo boards.

In addition, the zemstvo led to the employment of large numbers of zemstvo employees – teachers, agronomists, doctors, surveyors – of various social origins, which cut across the 'estate' character of the zemstvos. These white-collar workers were termed the 'Third Element' and became more politically minded and more radicalised than most zemstvo leaders. By the turn of the century the size and potential power of this group was a source of concern to the government; there were some 70,000 zemstvo employees in the thirty-four

24 S. F. Starr, 'Local Initiative in Russia before the Zemstvo', in Emmons and Vucinich, *The Zemstvo in Russia*, pp. 5–30.

25 A process most clearly described in K. E. McKenzie, 'Zemstvo Organization and Role within the Administrative Structure', in Emmons and Vucinich, *The Zemstvo in Russia*, pp. 31–78.

26 McKenzie, 'Zemstvo Organization', p. 44.

provinces where zemstvos had so far been set up, that is, some fifty members of the 'Third Element' to each elected member of the zemstvo board.[27]

The establishment of the zemstvos did not displace the existing corporate institutions. Urban institutions of self-government and noble assemblies continued to exist. Urban participation in the zemstvos was limited and did not diminish the significance of urban institutions of self-government. Peasants – both serf and state – had more direct experience, however, of self-government through the peasant communes than ordinary townspeople or the nobles collectively. Peasants continued to govern many of their own affairs outside the competence of the zemstvo, or any other institution, through the commune and the peasant, volost', courts, although the introduction of land captains (*zemskie nachal'niki*) in 1889, with the intention of imposing greater supervision over peasant institutions, created another link between the peasant village and provincial administration. Peasant experience of commune administration was reflected in their attitudes towards the zemstvo, which, along with the dominance of the nobles and the weakness of urban participation, inhibited the growth of any sense of the zemsvtos representing 'all-estate' interests. Peasants' resentment against the zemstvo paralleled their resentment of other state institutions and officials which oppressed them in return for few benefits. In particular peasants resented what they regarded as 'unnecessary' taxes imposed by the zemstvos, particularly tax on land which fell disproportionately on peasant allotment land, but they also shunned the, largely urban, welfare institutions – schools, hospitals, etc. – established by the zemstvos.[28] While other distinctive features of peasant obligation and non-privilege gradually came to an end – the poll tax, mutual responsibility for taxes, corporal punishment, etc. – peasant distinctiveness in local administration was retained. The increase in tax burdens by the zemstvo after 1890 as peasant representation declined only reinforced their negative perception of the 'all-estate' zemstvo as yet another burden imposed by the state and as an institution which served the interests of only one class, the nobility. The success of the provincial nobility in blocking Stolypin's attempts after 1907 to reform the zemstvos by increasing non-noble members only confirmed these views.

The zemstvos suffered from the same ambiguities in legislation as Petrine or Catherinian corporate institutions, which inhibited their opportunities to function effectively in the provinces. Some of this was due to ambiguous wording (such as 'participation' or 'co-operation' in certain activities) in some parts

27 Galai, *The Liberation Movement*, p. 32.

28 The relationship is described most fully in D. Atkinson, 'The Zemstvo and the Peasantry', in Emmons and Vucinich, *The Zemstvo in Russia*, pp. 79–132.

of 1864 statute.[29] More seriously, the areas of competence of the zemstvos potentially brought them into conflict with the governor, local officials, police and / or the central bureaucracy. Zemstvos (in the statutes of 1864 and 1890) had to address local needs (economic, administrative, educational, humanitarian) whilst implementing the demands of the local civil and military administration. It has already been noted that the main conflict of interest arose over the extent of the zemstvo rights to raise taxes for local needs as well as fulfilling state fiscal obligations – taxes, of course, which were largely paid by peasants and townspeople rather than by the nobles who dominated the zemstvo boards. Nevertheless, the zemstvos did make some advances in the provision of healthcare and primary education, which has been described as 'the area of greatest zemstvo achievement'[30] (by the turn of the century the zemstvo was supporting almost 20,000 elementary schools,[31] a number which had risen to over 40,000 by 1914),[32] and played some role in stimulating agricultural modernisation.[33] Zemstvos took over welfare functions which had previously been performed by the state through the boards of public welfare and, in the case of education, by the Church.

After 1890 the governor's powers to block zemstvo enactments and to supervise its operations were clarified and increased, but the zemstvos continued to provide and extend local services. But the conservative gentry reaction after the 1905 Revolution made the zemstvos far less receptive to reform; in their last decade zemstvos hindered the implementation of the Stolypin land reforms and blocked attempts to reform local administration, including the establishment of a zemstvo at the lowest, volost' level which was intended to make the peasants truly 'full members of Russian society'.[34] At the same time, the increase in state funding for primary schools at the expense of the zemstvos

29 McKenzie, 'Zemstvo Organization', p. 45.

30 J. Brooks, 'The Zemstvo and the Education of the People', in Emmons and Vucinich, *The Zemstvo in Russia*, p. 243.

31 N. B. Weissman, *Reform in Tsarist Russia. The State Bureacracy and Local Government, 1900–1914* (New Brunswick: Rutgers University Press, 1981), p. 32.

32 Brooks, 'The Zemstvo and the Education of the People', p. 249.

33 Recent research on one province has supported this view: G. Weldhen, 'The Zemstvo, Agricultural Societies and Agricultural Innovation in Viatka Guberniia in the 1890s and 1900s', in V. E. Musikhin (ed.), *Viatskomu Zemstvu 130 let. Materialy nauchnoi konferentsii* (Kirov, 1997), pp. 25–31.

34 This process is described by R. Manning in 'Zemstvo and Revolution: The Onset of Gentry Reaction, 1905–07' and R. D. MacNaughton and R. T. Manning, 'The Crisis of the Third of June System and Political Trends in the Zemstvos, 1907–14', in L. H. Haimson, *The Politics of Rural Russia 1905–1914* (Bloomington: Indiana University Press, 1979), pp. 30–66, 184–218. On the fate of Stolypin's proposed reforms after 1906 see P. Waldron, *Between Two Revolutions: Stolypin and the Politics of Renewal in Russia* (London: University College Press, 1998), pp. 77–99.

also meant an increase in state control over the operation of those schools even as their numbers rose. On the eve of war, the zemstvos had retreated from their 'all-estate' character and had become forums to reflect the views of the conservative provincial nobility.

A local bureaucracy?

Local administration suffered from the inability of the state to recruit men of quality. Local administration was never as prestigious, or as well rewarded, as service in St Petersburg or Moscow, and the civil service was never as highly regarded as military service. Young, provincial noble boys often entered the civil service only if they lacked the social connections or the physical ability to join a regiment. In the eighteenth century senior officials were frequently accused of corruption or ignorance. This was partly due to the lack of effective control exercised by the centre over distant provinces. It was also due to the paucity of institutions of higher education, and in particular to the slow development of legal training in Russia (the first *Russian* professor of law was S. A. Desnitskii, appointed in 1773 to Moscow University, who trained at Glasgow University),[35] to the poor salaries and to the unattractiveness of life in unsophisticated provincial backwaters. A high proportion of senior elective noble posts in the institutions set up in 1775 were occupied by nobles who had served in the army and had no civil training (in 1788 some 85 per cent of the presidents of the highest provincial courts were appointed directly from the army).[36] At the lower level, the clerical staff, who were mostly themselves the sons of clerks or sons of the clergy ('culled' or lured by the state from clerical seminaries), shifted vast amounts of paperwork around but were badly paid, badly educated and badly treated by their superiors. Police officers were underpaid, poorly trained and not respected. Bribery was endemic in Russian courts, and scarcely regarded as corrupt, at least at the lower levels.[37]

Although the corruption, greed and ignorance of local officials remained a theme in Russian literature in the nineteenth century, there is some evidence to

35 See A. H. Brown, 'S. E. Desnitsky, Adam Smith and the Nakaz of Catherine II', *Oxford Slavonic Papers*, NS, 7 (1974): 42–59.

36 R. D. Givens, 'Eighteenth-Century Nobiliary Career Patterns and Provincial Government', in W. M. Pintner and D. K. Rowney (eds.), *Russian Officialdom: The Bureaucratization of Russian Society from the Seventeenth to the Twentieth Century* (London: Macmillan, 1980), p. 122.

37 J. M. Hartley, 'Bribery and Justice in the Provinces in the Reign of Catherine II', in S. Lovell, A. Ledeneva and A. Rogachevskii (eds.), *Bribery and Blat in Russia. Negotiating Reciprocity from the Middle Ages to the 1990s* (Basingstoke: Macmillan, 2000), pp. 48–64.

suggest that a gradual professionalisation of the local bureaucracy was taking place during the century. Even in the late eighteenth century there were a small number of enlightened governors and senior provincial administrators who took their duties seriously and who developed a sense of what we might call 'a legal consciousness'.[38] Educational standards of senior officials rose after the introduction of formal examinations in 1809, and the reform of clerical schools and increase in numbers of state schools (at least in towns) led to a gradual increase of standards amongst junior staff (although salaries remained pitifully low). The number of direct transfers from the military to senior posts in the civil service declined in the first half of the nineteenth century. The proportion of nobles in the bureaucracy – local and central – fell as the century progressed. After the municipal statute of 1870 the levels of education amongst mayors and senior urban representatives rose. Land captains, despite the criticisms levelled at them at the time by peasants and St Petersburg officials alike, had respectable levels of education (some 30 per cent had higher education).[39] The most important change affected governors, who by the early twentieth century frequently had considerable experience of local government, either as marshals of the nobility or as vice-governors. They had become, as the historian Robbins states, 'experts' and 'specialists' who had a profound knowledge of local affairs (some 80 per cent of governors in 1913 had served in another capacity in the provinces).[40] The consequence of this, however, was that governors became less willing to implement government policy unquestioningly; after 1905 many governors blocked further attempts at local reform in order to preserve what they regarded as local interests.[41]

Epilogue

In times of crisis, local government institutions had performed valuable service. In 1812 noble assemblies and town dumas had collected considerable sums and foodstuffs which they contributed to the war effort.[42] The zemstvos (which by

38 See J. Keep, 'Light and Shade in the History of the Russian Administration', *Canadian Slavic Studies* 6, 1 (1972): 2–3 and Hartley, 'Bribery and Justice in the Provinces', pp. 55–62.

39 D. A. J. Macey, 'The Land Captains: A Note on the Social Composition 1889–1913', *RH* 16 (1989): 351.

40 R. G. Robbins, Jr, *The Tsar's Viceroys: Russian Provincial Governors in the Last Years of Empire* (Ithaca: Cornell University Press, 1987), p. 37.

41 R. G. Robbins, 'Choosing the Russian Governors: The Professionalisation of the Gubernatorial Corps', *SEER* 58, 4 (1980): 600.

42 See J. M. Hartley, 'Russia and Napoleon: State, Society and the Nation', in M. Rowe (ed.), *Collaboration and Resistance in Napoleonic Europe: State Formation in an Age of Upheaval, c. 1800–1815* (Basingstoke: Palgrave, 2003), pp. 186–202.

this time reflected predominantly noble interests) carried out important relief work during the Russo-Japanese War and the First World War. The All-Russian Union of Towns performed the same service in the First World War.[43] These were exceptional circumstances, but nevertheless, this activity demonstrated that there was some potential for local society to act collectively to address not only local but also national interests. By the early twentieth century there is some evidence that a corporate, or 'estate', identity had developed amongst the provincial nobility and at least in the merchant-dominated towns like Moscow. This was the type of identity which Peter I and Catherine II had tried to stimulate in the eighteenth century with very limited success. The tragedy was that by the time it had been achieved it was already anachronistic in the light of the very rapid social and economic changes which had taken place since the late nineteenth century. The exclusion of the most dissatisfied groups in society – peasants and workers – from all but the most limited participation in these institutions was symptomatic of a more general failure to recognise that society had changed and that local institutions should modernise to reflect the new economic and society reality. The fault lay not only with the government which established, and then modified, these institutions but also by the early twentieth century with the local institutions which blocked further reforms in defence of 'corporate' interests which no longer served the interests of the country.

43 Porter, *The Zemstvo and the Emergence of Civil Society*, p. 239.

22

State finances

PETER WALDRON

In 1898, Sergei Witte, the Russian minister of finance, wrote to Emperor Nicholas II:

> The French state budget is 1,260 million rubles for a population of 38 million; the Austrian budget is 1,100 million rubles for a population of 43 million. If our taxpayers were as prosperous as the French, our budget would be 4,200 million rubles instead of its current 1,400 million, and if we matched the Austrians, our budget would be 3,300 million rubles. Why can we not achieve this? The main reason is the poor condition of our peasantry.[1]

While the minister of finance bemoaned the poverty of the Russian population and the consequent low level of taxation that it produced, the Russian state's overall financial performance had proved to be relatively successful. Although it had faced financial difficulties, Russia had avoided the type of financial crisis that had made a major contribution to the collapse of the French monarchy at the end of the eighteenth century, and had given the Habsburg state such difficulties during the eighteenth and nineteenth centuries.[2] Witte's analysis identified low *per capita* yields from taxation as the fundamental weakness of the Russian state's financial system and he laid the blame for Russia's inability to generate a sufficiently large state budget firmly at the door of the peasantry. But Witte, Imperial Russia's most successful and influential finance minister, failed to recognise that the tsarist regime had proved adept at both avoiding fatal financial crises and at overcoming lesser problems. It had proved able to fight a multitude of wars and to expand the boundaries of its empire, as well as to make major internal reforms that had financial implications. This

I am very grateful for the financial support of the British Academy in carrying out the research for this chapter.

1 S. Iu. Vitte, *Vospominaniia. Memuary* (Moscow: AST, 2000), vol. I, p. 724.

2 See P. G. M. Dickson, *Finance and Government under Maria Theresa 1740–1780* (Oxford: Clarendon Press, 1987), vol II, chapters 1 & 2 for an account of Habsburg financial difficulties.

discussion of Russian state finances will examine the Russian government's chief elements of expenditure and revenue and analyse changes that took place during the eighteenth and nineteenth centuries. It will also analyse the impact of the government's taxation policies on the empire's population and the wider social consequences of fiscal policy.

The Russian state budget hardly warranted such an appellation until well into the nineteenth century. Troitskii describes the 'inadequate centralisation of financial administration, the lack of a central treasury, the secrecy of the budget, the unsatisfactory recording of business, the lack of accountability in agencies and the almost complete absence of state fiscal control of expenditure' that characterised Russian state finances during the first half of the eighteenth century.[3] Catherine the Great acknowledged the disarray of Russia's financial position at her accession to the throne in 1762: soldiers' wages were in arrears, customs duties had been farmed out for a tiny return to the state and the currency itself was of dubious worth.[4] While there were improvements during Catherine's reign, financial policy-making and the process of budget-making remained weak until the last decades of the nineteenth century. Even in 1879, a committee established to examine ways of reducing government expenditure reported that the Ministry of Finance could exert little influence over the process by which expenditure was determined and noted that, in effect, the Finance Ministry had proved unable to assert its authority over the spending ministries.[5] The process of budget-making was essentially driven by the demands of the spending ministries and the role of the Ministry of Finance was to raise the revenue that was demanded to meet the spending plans of each ministry. The absence of proper cabinet government in Russia until the first decade of the twentieth century also contributed to the lack of a clear direction in financial policy. Individual ministers had the right of access to the emperor and were able to plead the case for their own ministries' spending plans directly to the tsar, bypassing their fellow ministers. The inter-departmental Committee of Finances, designed to provide overall political direction for the empire's financial policies, played an inconsistent role. While it was the formal arena in which fiscal and monetary policy could be debated, its significance could depend on the level of interest that the emperor displayed in its affairs, as well

3 S. M. Troitskii, *Finansovaia politika russkogo absolutizma v XVIII veke* (Moscow: Nauka, 1966), p. 221.

4 I. de Madariaga, *Russia in the Age of Catherine the Great* (London: Weidenfeld and Nicolson, 1981), p. 470.

5 'Ob uchrezhdenii osoboi komissii o sokrashcheniem raskhodov', 30 December 1878, RGIA, Fond 560, op. 22, d. 160, ll. 12–13.

as in the political status of the Minister of Finance and on his place within the hierarchy of the empire's governing elite.

* * *

It was military expenditure that dominated Russia's state finances. During the eighteenth century, the army and navy consistently accounted for more than half of the Russian state's spending and, at times, more than 60 per cent of the budget was devoted to military expenditure.[6] This is hardly surprising, given Russia's persistent involvement in wars and the continuing impetus to extend the territorial boundaries of the empire. Military expenditure grew significantly during times of war, with sharp increases during the Napoleonic Wars, the Crimean War and the Russo-Turkish War of 1878–9.[7] There was also a considerable increase in military spending in the years preceding the First World War, with expenditure growing from 420 million roubles in 1900 to 820 million roubles in 1913.[8] Although this did not represent a significant increase in the proportion of the government's income devoted to military spending, since the state's budget was growing rapidly during this period, it was a much heavier burden than at first appears. By 1914, Russian military expenditure exceeded that of Britain, even though Britain's army and navy were needed to protect the security of its far-flung empire.[9] Throughout the nineteenth century, there were repeated efforts to restrain military expenditure and government committees regularly grappled with the problem of the cost of the Russian army and navy. A special committee met in 1818, followed by a review of military expenditure by A. A. Arakcheev in 1822, and a further attempt to rein in expenditure in 1835. This last review concluded that reductions in expenditure during the 1820s had had a negative impact on both Russia's military forces and on the overall national economy, as a reduced demand for materials by the army had resulted in an overall reduction in the prices of domestically produced goods and this had affected both manufacturers and the treasury, since the government suffered a consequent loss of tax revenues. The dominant place that Russia's military strength played in the government's

6 A. Kahan, *The Plow, the Hammer and the Knout* (Chicago: Chicago University Press, 1985), pp. 336–7; W. Pintner, 'The Burden of Defense in Imperial Russia, 1725–1914', *RR* 43 (1984): 248–9.

7 'Finansovaia politika v period 1861–1880 gg.', *Otechestvennye zapiski* (1882), no. 11, pp. 1–3.

8 A. P. Pogrebinskii, *Ocherki istorii finansov dorevoliutsionnoi Rossii (XIX–XX vv.)* (Moscow: Gosfinizdat, 1954), p. 176.

9 See P. Gatrell, *Government, Industry and Rearmament in Russia, 1900–1914: The Last Argument of Tsarism* (Cambridge: Cambridge University Press, 1994), pp. 152–5. Gatrell suggests that the proportion of Russia's national income devoted to military expenditure was almost twice as heavy as for the more economically developed countries of Britain, France and Germany.

thinking is reflected in the results of the 1835 review: the committee could only suggest 'housekeeping measures' to limit military spending and then only if both economic and military conditions continued to be stable.[10] A further attempt was made to reduce overall government expenditure in 1861 but, in the aftermath of the debacle in the Crimea, no serious attempt was made to constrain military spending.[11] The 1879 committee's work came at the end of the Russo-Turkish War, when it was again clearly impolitic to propose any major reductions in military spending. At the first hint of a proposed reduction in the army's budget, D. A. Miliutin, the minister of war, wrote to A. A. Abaza, the president of the State Council's economic department that 'any significant reduction in [military] expenditure would rapidly cause damage to the crucial matter of the state's readiness to support its political dignity'.[12] Abaza's committee had begun with the lofty ambition of moving beyond short-term solutions to the recurrent financial difficulties that faced the Russian government, and instead putting in place measures that would prevent ministries increasing their expenditure after their annual budget had been set. But by the middle of 1879, Abaza was compelled to admit that due to 'the alarming events of recent times', ministries had been unable to devote adequate attention to the work of his committee and that they had proved very tardy in providing the information he needed in order to proceed.[13] The Russian bureaucracy proved able to frustrate these plans; central authority was not yet well established enough to override the power of individual ministries.

Russia's military expenditure continued to grow in absolute terms, but other calls on the state's budget came to play a significant part in government spending. During the second half of the nineteenth century, the Russian government considerably extended its activities and, in particular, played a much greater direct role in the economy of the country. The government's recognition of the importance of the railway network in stimulating Russia's overall economic performance, together with the absence of other sources of investment capital, meant that the state itself took on much of the burden of financing Russia's railways. The Ministry of Communications accounted for

10 'Komitet o sokrashchenii raskhodov po ministerstvam: voennomu, morskomu, inostrannykh del i vedomstvam: pochtovomu, putei soobshchenii i dukhovnomu. 1835', RGIA, Fond 1172, op. 16, d. 1, ll. 54–7.

11 'Komitet finansov. Po zapiske Ministra Finansov o finansovykh merakh: uvelichenie dokhodov; sokrashchenie raskhodov; svod rospisi. 1861', RGIA, Fond 563, op. 2, d. 144, ll. 2–5. The War Ministry was able to suggest savings of only 881,000 roubles, out of a total annual budget of more than 90 million roubles.

12 D. A. Miliutin to A. A. Abaza, 29 May 1879, RGIA, Fond 1214, op. 1, d. 23, l. 1a.

13 'Doklad Predsedatelia Osoboi Komissii A. A. Abaza s kratkim otchetom o deiatel'nosti Osoboi Komissii', 11 June 1879, RGIA, Fond 1214, op. 1, d. 26, ll. 32–4.

only 2.5 per cent of the state budget in 1885, but by 1895 this had increased to 11 per cent and by 1908 to 20 per cent. The construction of the Trans-Siberian railway was an essential element in this development, and Witte was prepared to expend whatever resources were necessary in order to see the project realised. The government spent some 600 million roubles on its construction in the last decade of the nineteenth century, far above the original estimate of 320 million roubles, and further spending was needed after 1900, bringing the total cost for the railway to over 1,000 million roubles, at a time when Russia's annual budget was less than 1,500 million roubles.[14] The state also increased its direct involvement in another critical area of the Russian economy – the liquor trade. In 1863 the government abolished the system of tax farming that had generated revenue from the production and sale of vodka, but this was only a step on the road towards the state taking full control of the wholesale and retail trade in liquor. Between 1894 and 1901 the state became the only legal purchaser for the products of Russia's vodka distilleries and, while this proved an effective move in terms of safeguarding tax revenues from vodka, it did also involve the government in increased expenditure as it took direct control of the industry. By 1912, the state was expending nearly 200 million roubles annually to maintain the vodka monopoly.[15] Further strains were placed upon the Russian budget by the state's growing indebtedness and the need to service its loans. By 1899, 98 million roubles was required annually to pay interest on Russia's loans and Russia proved lucky in its ability to contain its expenditure in this area. Russian credit abroad had improved during the 1890s, especially with the signing of the Franco-Russian alliance in 1894, and this enabled the Russian government to reduce the level of interest it paid. Between 1891 and 1902, Russia was able to reduce its average rate of interest on its loans from 4.9 per cent to 3.86 per cent, thus allowing the state to borrow significantly more money, but without increasing the cost of servicing the public debt.[16]

The increasing social burdens that the Russian state assumed during the nineteenth century also had budgetary consequences. Judicial reform from the 1860s onwards made the legal system increasingly complex and easier access to justice resulted in a growing number of cases brought before the courts each year. The Ministry of Justice pressed for annual increases in its budget, emphasising that its expenditure was modest in comparison with that in other

14 Pogrebinskii, *Ocherki*, pp. 154–5.

15 M. Friedman, *Kazennaia vinnaia monopoliia*, 2 vols. (St Petersburg: Pravda, 1914), vol. II, p. 236.

16 O. Crisp, *Studies in the Russian Economy Before 1914* (London: Macmillan 1976), p. 109.

European states.[17] Education provision expanded rapidly at the end of the nineteenth century and the financial demands on the state grew significantly. In 1879 the central government budget had only contributed 11 per cent of total funding for rural schools, but this proportion increased to 45 per cent by 1911. The government spent 2 million roubles on primary education in 1895, but this increased very rapidly to 19 million roubles in 1907 and to more than 82 million in 1914. Total education expenditure accounted for 2.69 per cent of the state budget in 1881, but this had increased to 7.2 per cent in 1914.[18] There were growing pressures on Russia's budget from every side. The army and navy continued to take the largest single element of government spending as war and the threat of war remained ever-present. The state's expansion into both direct involvement in the national economy and into enhanced social provision meant that the government could not easily seek to compensate for increasing military expenditure by making significant reductions elsewhere. The result was that the overall Russian state budget grew as expenditure increased in nearly every area. The challenge for the state was to increase its revenues to match this additional spending.

* * *

The main component of government revenue during the eighteenth century was the poll tax. Peter the Great levied this tax on most of the male population, using it to replace the household tax that had been in force between 1678 and 1721. The rationale for the poll tax was straightforward: Peter needed a reliable source of income to support his military campaigns, while revenue from the household tax was falling as the population discovered that they could combine their households and thus evade the tax. The poll tax proved to be a highly successful means of raising money. Its collection presented no great difficulties: initially, military detachments collected the taxes from the regions in which they were stationed and then used the revenue to maintain themselves. After the end of Peter's wars, collection became the responsibility of the civil administration, and serf owners were given the prime responsibility for collecting the taxes from their serfs. The success of the poll tax was partly due, however, to the rise in the Russian population through the expansion of its frontiers and gradually decreasing mortality rates. Its relative ease of collection meant that the government felt able to increase poll-tax rates during the course of the century, increasing the burden on private serfs by one-third

17 'Zapiska o merakh, mogushchikh povesti k znachitel'nomu sokrashcheniiu raskhodov po vedomstvu Ministerstva Iustitsii', 1879, RGIA, Fond 1214, op. 1, d. 19, ll. 21–2.

18 B. Eklof, *Russian Peasant Schools. Officialdom, Village Culture and Popular Pedagogy, 1861–1914* (Berkeley: University of California Press, 1986), pp. 89–90.

across the period. Between 1726 and 1796, the amount collected from the poll tax increased from 4 million roubles to 10.4 million roubles.[19] After 1800, the poll tax played a less significant role in government revenues as other taxes contributed larger shares of the government's income. The emancipation of the serfs in the 1860s made the collection of the tax more difficult, while voices were heard suggesting that the tax burden should be more equally shared, rather than through the poll tax with its flat rate for each category of tax-payer.[20] The government remained undecided about the fate of the poll tax during the 1860s, recognising that it caused difficulties for some tax-payers, but also needing the revenue that it generated. Even at the end of the 1870s, the poll tax produced 59 million roubles annually.[21] It was the sense of growing crisis and peasant discontent that gripped the government in the late 1870s and early 1880s that propelled the Russian state towards a fundamental review of its taxation system and the abolition of the poll tax.[22]

Revenue also came from a variety of other sources. Indirect taxation formed an important part of the government revenues, even in the eighteenth century. The largest single source of indirect taxation was from liquor. Distilling was established as a monopoly of the nobility in 1754, and from 1767 revenue was collected through a system of tax farming in which a merchant obtained a concession to sell liquor and paid the government a fixed fee for the privilege; the Moscow and St Petersburg liquor farm for 1767–70 attracted a price of 2.1 million roubles annually. Revenue from the liquor trade made up an increasing proportion of the government's income during the eighteenth century: in 1724 only 11 per cent of the state's revenue came from liquor, but this jumped sharply, reaching a peak of 43 per cent of the total in 1780 and then falling back to 24 per cent in 1805.[23] During the nineteenth century, liquor revenue averaged 31 per cent of total government revenue. By the middle of the century, the government had developed sufficient bureaucratic capability to consider abolishing the system of tax farming and taking on itself the administration of the liquor trade. This was a highly significant development, since the state was now able to monopolise tax collection and thus gain much greater control over its fiscal affairs, without needing to take the tax farmers into account. In

19 Kahan, *The Plow*, p. 333.

20 See, for example, Iu. G. Gagemeister's 1856 report, 'O finansakh Rossii', in L. E. Shepelev (ed.), *Sud'by Rossii* (St Petersburg: Liki Rossii, 1999), p. 14.

21 L. Bowman, 'Russia's First Income Taxes: The Effects of Modernized Taxes on Commerce and Industry, 1885–1914', *SR* 52 (1993): 257.

22 N. I. Anan'ich, 'K istorii otmeny podushnoi podati v Rossii', *I Z* 94 (1974): 186–8.

23 J. P. LeDonne, 'Indirect Taxes in Catherine's Russia. II. The Liquor Monopoly', *JfGO* 24 (1976): 203. D. Christian, *Living Water: Vodka and Russian Society on the Eve of Emancipation* (Oxford: Clarendon Press, 1990), pp. 382–5.

1863, the tax farm was abolished. It not only signified the growing strength of the state's fiscal apparatus, but also resulted in an increase in the net revenue that the liquor trade brought in. Gross liquor revenues rose consistently after 1863, but the costs of collecting the new excise duties were consistently reduced. In the 1850s, some 18 per cent of gross liquor revenue was eaten up by the cost of collecting the taxation, but this was reduced to only 3 per cent by 1880. The risk that the state had taken in believing that its resources were strong enough to cope with this major change in its fiscal system proved to be justified. The introduction of a full government monopoly on the manufacture and sale of vodka brought significantly increased gross revenues to the treasury from liquor, reaching more than 950 million roubles in 1913, but this was offset by considerably higher costs, meaning that the net contribution to the state's budget from liquor remained steady after the 1894 reform.

In common with other states, the Russian government sought to raise revenue by taxing salt. Peter the Great introduced a state monopoly on salt in 1705 and the government took control of a vast enterprise to refine and distribute salt across the empire. This did not prove to be the same easy source of revenue as the liquor trade, since Russia's salt deposits were often located far away from the main centres of population and the costs involved in exploiting these resources proved to be very high. In 1762 the state spent one-third of its gross revenues from salt on production and distribution costs, leaving it with a net contribution to the budget of only 2.2 million roubles. Within twenty years, the net income had halved and, in 1791 the government made a loss on its salt operations for the first time.[24] In such a situation, the state had to act to protect its revenues. Even though the government raised the price of salt, this did not help in stabilising the situation and in 1818 the state gave up its monopoly on the sale of salt, eventually abolishing the salt tax completely in 1880.

The government also received income in its capacity as landowner from the peasants who lived on its land. In 1723 Peter the Great standardised the variety of labour service and other dues that were owed by state peasants and instead made them liable for cash payments (*obrok*) to the government. This produced a growing source of income and was one that the state believed it could exploit. During the eighteenth century, the rate of obrok payments increased by roughly twice the rate of inflation, although state peasants did pay significantly less than privately owned serfs. Discussions took place about

24 J. P. LeDonne, 'Indirect Taxes in Catherine's Russia. I. The Salt Code of 1781', *JfGO* 23 (1975): 188.

further increases in the rate of obrok in the 1840s alongside Kiselev's overall reforms of the state peasantry. The government was wary of demanding large additional sums from the peasants, believing that this 'would disturb the tranquillity of the population and have dangerous consequences'.[25] While obrok did offer some advantages to the government as it sought to increase its revenues, the government also recognised that by publicising its move away from the poll tax, it would be publicly demonstrating its problems in making an accurate census of the population. Kiselev did reform the system of obrok, but this question again raised its head when the emancipation of the state peasants was implemented in 1866. The government was reluctant to lose its income from obrok and was wary of making radical changes that might threaten the security of its revenues. Instead of moving immediately to a system of redemption payments, as with privately owned serfs, the government reformed the system of obrok, calculating peasants' liability not just by the value of the land they held, but by taking into account their total income. It was only in 1886 that state peasants' obrok payments were finally converted into redemption payments. This move resulted in a significant increase in revenues: the average total revenue from obrok between 1880 and 1885 was 32 million roubles annually, whereas in the period 1887 to 1890, income averaged 43 million roubles. The famine years of 1891 and 1892 witnessed a reduction in revenue from state peasants' redemption payments, but they then increased again, reaching 55 million roubles in 1895.[26]

As the Russian government looked for ways to curb its expenditure, it also sought to increase its revenues. This process, however, proved of equal difficulty. The 1841 committee that had rejected a large increase in obrok also found good reasons to turn down most other suggested methods of increasing the government's income. It avoided detailed discussion of the poll tax, preferring to wait for the Ministry of Finance to make its own proposals, argued that the government was already seeking ways to enhance the efficiency of the salt industry and thus enhance income from that source, and finally rejected any wholesale reform of the liquor industry.[27] The committee took a highly defensive tone towards criticism of the government's record on enhancing its own revenues, finding reasons to reject every suggestion for improvement. By the 1860s, the government's financial position was more precarious and attempts to find ways of raising additional revenues met with a more positive response.

25 'Osoboi komitet dlia pazsmotreniiu predstavlennogo Ego Velichestvu ot neizvestnogo obzora finansovoi chasti v Rossii, 1841', RGIA, Fond 1175, op. 16, d. 1. 118.

26 V. L. Stepanov, *N. Kh. Bunge. Sud'ba reformatora* (Moscow: Rosspen, 1998), p. 369.

27 RGIA, Fond 1175, op. 16, d. 1, ll. 17, 25 and 28–9.

This new attempt to increase revenues was also motivated by what proved to be a mistaken assumption; that the changes to the system of liquor taxation and the introduction of excise duties would lead to a fall in the government's income from that source. In 1861 the Committee of Finances proposed making small increases to both the poll tax levied on state peasants and to the level of obrok that they paid to produce an additional 3.2 million roubles of income annually. Alongside this, a rise in the salt tax was proposed, together with increases in customs duties and in postal charges. Altogether, the government calculated that these measures would bring in an extra 7.5 million roubles which would help to offset the expected decline in liquor revenues.[28] These proposals represented only adjustments to existing sources of taxation and did not involve any overall review of Russia's system of taxation.

From the mid-1860s, however, the government began to move towards a more radical approach to restructuring its sources of income. The motivation for this was complex. First, the emancipation of the serfs had consequences in the financial sphere, as in almost every other area of Russian life. The emancipation settlement itself had been significantly conditioned by the government's financial position which had led to the peasantry paying the full price for the land that they gained, without any government subsidy.[29] The perception of contemporaries was that redemption payments from the peasantry were thus set at a level which was on the edge of affordability for many of them. This view has been challenged by modern analyses[30] but in the 1870s and 1880s the tsarist state was deeply concerned about the potential threat that it faced from a discontented peasantry that was perceived to be downtrodden and impoverished. Changing the system of taxation to reduce the burden on the peasants and thus lessen the threat of discontent was an important reason for the tax reforms that took place in the 1880s. At the same time, the Russian government recognised that it could not hope to achieve significant increases in revenue from the existing taxation system and therefore needed to take more radical steps. During the nineteenth century, the government had faced a series of financial problems which had been resolved without making structural changes to either expenditure patterns or sources of revenue. By the last quarter of the century, officials were coming to realise that this strategy could not be sustained and that, especially at a time when the nature of the Russian

28 'Komitet finansov, zasedaniia 2, 13, 16, 20 & 23 dekabria 1861', RGIA, Fond 563, op. 2, d. 144, ll. 52–66.

29 S. L. Hoch, 'The Banking Crisis, Peasant Reform and Economic Development in Russia, 1857–1861', *AHR* 96 (1991): 796.

30 D. Moon, *The Russian Peasantry 1600–1930* (London: Longman, 1999), pp. 283–8 summarises the arguments.

economy was changing with the development of an industrial sector, new sources of revenue had to be found.

* * *

The crises that affected the Russian government's finances were mostly precipitated either by war or by the threat of war. War with Persia and with Turkey in the late 1820s placed stresses on the budget and, in late 1830, the Ministry of Finance indicated that the outbreak of further conflict would cause significant problems. Expenditure was already likely to rise due to a series of poor harvests and the outbreak of cholera in some parts of the empire and the Finance Ministry warned that further war could not be financed from ordinary expenditure: Kankrin, the minister of finance, had already reported to Nicholas I that the government would face severe difficulties in finding the additional resources needed for conflict. Kankrin's view was not, however, shared by the government as a whole and the Finance Committee argued that any difficulties could be overcome by printing money and by a number of measures that would enable the government to raise internal loans.[31] This approach to dealing with the financial pressures of war continued throughout the reign of Nicholas I. Discussions about managing the costs of the Crimean War in the mid-1850s resulted in the same measures being proposed. The Ministry of Finance issued more paper money as its first reaction to the increase in expenditure that was required by war, more than doubling the amount of paper money in circulation, but the Ministry did acknowledge that this solution was only sustainable if the war was short. It also recognised that this was a risky move to take, since the outcome of printing money would become clear only once the war was over: if the economy prospered, all would be well, but difficulties would arise if it weakened.[32]

The economic situation across Europe in the late 1850s was not propitious for a Russian recovery, and this was exacerbated by domestic conditions. A banking crisis, produced partly by a reduction in interest rates by the government, had effects that were felt right across the Russian economy. At the same time, the Ministry of Finance complained of a fall in exports as a result of both the war and poor domestic harvests. Combined with a growth in imports, this meant that Russia was suffering a net outflow of foreign capital and that government revenues were suffering. The national economy was facing serious difficulties,

31 'Ob otyskanii denezhnykh ressursov na sluchai voiny', 1830–1, RGIA, Fond 563, op. 2, d. 21, ll. 3–5 & 14.

32 'O sredstvakh k pokrytiiu raskhodov po sluchaiu voiny', February 1856, RGIA, Fond 563, op. 1, d. 6, ll. 2–6.

while the government's own financial position was looking increasingly precarious. Kniazhevich, the minister of finance, reported that the government had been using its traditional methods to deal with the budget deficit: loans and issuing paper money. But, by 1860, the situation was such that it was difficult to solve the burgeoning budget deficit in these ways. The government already owed very large sums to the banks, its debts having grown from 166 million roubles in 1845 to 441 million roubles in 1859. Over the same period, the amount of paper money in circulation had more than quadrupled, reaching 93 million roubles in 1859. Foreign debts had also increased, totalling 365 million roubles in 1859. Kniazhevich argued that while it would be possible, in an extreme case, to issue yet more paper money, this would threaten the whole financial system, since the population could easily lose confidence in the currency. The minister of finance was prepared to print money to finance one-off items of expenditure, but he argued that this method could no longer be used as a permanent means of monetary policy. Further loans, whether from domestic sources or from abroad, were unsustainable, given Russia's huge burden of debt. The government was faced with a growing budget deficit and the Finance Ministry could see no easy way of financing it.[33] This crisis demonstrated the weakness of the government's budget-setting process. The Ministry of Finance could only implore that expenditure be kept at its projected levels, and that any requests for additional spending must be communicated to the ministry before being sent for the emperor's approval. At the same time, ministries were presented with suggestions for reducing their expenditure, in one of the first examples of the Russian government as a whole taking responsibility for financial policy. Not surprisingly, ministries resented these attempts at central direction of their spending and argued fiercely against proposals that came from the Committee of Finances.[34]

The government was helped out of its immediate difficulties by the success of the new liquor taxation system in raising revenue but, without making any structural changes to the state's fiscal and spending systems, Russia's finances remained problematic. M. Kh. Reutern had been appointed as minister of

33 'Po predstavleniiu Ministra Finansov o khoziaistvennom i finansovom polozhenii Rossii, 30 ianvaria 1860', RGIA, Fond 563, op. 2, d. 115, ll. 6–13.

34 For example, it was suggested to the Ministry of the Imperial Court that its buildings department be abolished, that the ministry's Committee on St Isaac's Cathedral be disbanded, since the cathedral was now complete, and that the Imperial Theatres be placed in private hands. The ministry rejected all these proposals and argued that any expenditure on the court should remain outside audit and control by central government. RGIA, Fond 563, op. 2, d. 115, II, 13–16. 'Zhurnal Komiteta Finansov, 4, 11, 18 & 25 noiabria 1861'.

finance in 1862 and recognised that the issues raised by his predecessor Kniazhevich in 1860 had still not been solved. In 1866 Reutern wrote a lengthy report on the financial and economic condition of Russia that attracted the attention of Alexander II who presided at the meeting of the Committee of Finances in September 1866 where Reutern's report was considered. As his predecessors had done, Reutern identified a pressing need to cease using domestic loans as a means of covering government expenditure. He argued that it was now difficult for the government to raise money at home, as the financial markets were exhausted. But Reutern did recognise that he could not be over-prescriptive here, since the state had an urgent need to borrow to finance railway construction, and the long-term economic interests of the state over-rode these temporary financial difficulties. He was also prepared to use the state's slender credit resources to try to find a more permanent way out of Russia's financial difficulties, despite the risks that this presented. Reutern also wanted to protect the value of the rouble and proposed measures to stop the outflow of funds abroad. He wanted the government to stop making purchases abroad, and included the War Ministry and the Ministry of Communications in his strictures here, and was intent on stopping costly foreign visits by Russia's navy. Reutern argued that the budget deficit could be eliminated only by both raising additional revenue and by placing curbs on expenditure. As successive finance ministers had discovered, it was difficult to squeeze extra income from existing sources and the suggestion by P. A. Valuev that an income tax should be introduced was thus placed on the agenda for further investigation.[35] The government's good intention of relying less on loans could not be implemented immediately: in 1868 the Committee of Finance resolved that the only way in which it could finance a projected budget deficit for the year of 12.5 million roubles, as well as meet railway construction costs of more than 36 million roubles, was to take a loan from foreign bankers.[36]

Russia continued to run sizeable budget deficits. Between 1866 and 1888, the budget was in surplus for three years, and in balance for a further two. Deficits ranged from 1 million roubles in 1870 to 80 million roubles in 1881, with an average budgetary outcome across the period of 18 million roubles deficit annually. This did represent a considerable improvement on the pre-1861 period, when deficits averaged 45 million roubles annually in the thirty years after 1832, but it was only in the 1890s that the budget situation showed signs

35 'Zhurnal komiteta finansov, 29 sentiabria 1866', RGIA, Fond 560, op. 22, d. 120, ll. 23–5. Reutern's original report is published in Shepelev (ed.), *Sud'by Rossii*, pp. 114–59.

36 'Komitet finansov. O sredstvakh dlia pokrytiia defitsita po gosudarstvennoi rospisi na 1868g.', RGIA, Fond 563, op. 1, d. 16, l. 1.

of consistent improvement. This situation was short-lived, however, since the budget returned to deficit in eight of the years between 1900 and 1913, averaging a deficit of 44 million roubles annually. This situation, while equivalent in cash terms to the level of deficit between 1831 and 1861, represented some improvement on that period, since the overall level of government spending had increased more than tenfold by the beginning of the twentieth century and the largest deficit in this period – 386 million roubles in 1905 – represented 14 per cent of government revenue, in contrast to the average deficit of 16.8 per cent in the thirty pre-reform years. Improved performance during the 1890s came through significant increases in revenues, outstripping expenditure growth by 15 per cent over the decade. This reflected Russia's healthy overall economic situation during this period, as increased economic activity generated higher income from taxation. This was assisted by changes to the structure of the taxation system that were introduced during the 1880s.

The period of N. Kh. Bunge's tenure of the Ministry of Finance witnessed important shifts in the emphasis of the taxation system. The government shifted the balance of taxation away from direct levies and towards indirect taxation. The poll tax was gradually abolished between 1883 and 1886 but the government had to find other sources of income to compensate for the loss of the more than 50 million roubles of revenue that the poll tax generated annually at the beginning of the 1880s. Other direct taxes did not have sufficient potential to produce sufficient additional income. Revenue from the land tax barely grew during the 1880s and 1890s, remaining steady at some 6 million roubles each year. There was little scope to increase obrok significantly, although revenue from this source did increase from 33 million roubles in 1881 to 45 million roubles a decade later. Redemption payment revenue too remained steady at around 40 million roubles annually during the late 1880s and 1890s.[37] Attempts were made to increase the tax revenue from business by introducing an income tax, to add to the existing patent system of 1824 which gave merchants a licence to engage in a trade or industry in return for a fixed annual fee to the government.[38] In 1885 the government introduced a 3 per cent tax on business profits, increasing this to 5 per cent in 1893 and, in 1898, made the tax progressive. This proved to be an effective source of revenue, helping to more than double tax revenues from business between 1884 and 1895.[39]

The only other real opportunity for increasing revenue came from indirect taxation. The success of the government in gaining additional revenue from

37 Stepanov, *Bunge*, p. 369.
38 P. G. Ryndziunskii, 'Gil'deiskaia reforma Kankrina 1824 goda', *IZ* 40 (1952): 110–39.
39 Bowman, 'Russia's First Income Taxes', p. 277.

its alcohol monopoly has already been noted, but during the 1880s concerted efforts were made to enhance income from other sources. The existing taxes on tobacco and on sugar were increased, so that revenues from tobacco more than doubled between 1880 and 1895, while the income from taxing sugar showed a tenfold increase during this period. By 1895, taxes on sugar produced more than 47 million roubles annually, some 80 per cent of the revenue that the poll tax was producing in the last years before its abolition. The government also moved to introduce indirect taxes in new areas: oil and matches were both subject to new taxation from 1888, bringing in more than 27 million roubles annually by 1895. Stamp duties were also increased, resulting in a near-doubling of revenues from that source. The last area of indirect taxation where the government was able to increase its revenues was through customs duties. Tariffs produced close to 100 million roubles of revenue annually by 1880, but the government's policy of moving to increase duties on imported goods during the 1880s in order to stimulate domestic production resulted in an additional 40 million roubles of revenue by 1890. Bunge's successor as finance minister, I. A. Vyshnegradskii, put in place a major tariff reform in 1891 and this accelerated the growth of revenue from this source so that in 1894 the government collected more than 183 million roubles from customs duties. This development of indirect taxation made Russia much more dependent on these sources of income than any of the other European powers. By 1911, Russia gained 84 per cent of its revenues from indirect taxes, while indirect taxation in France accounted for 70 per cent of its budget and Britain's budget gained 59 per cent of its total revenue from this source.[40] This dependence on indirect taxation had serious consequences for Russia on the outbreak of war in 1914. In a fit of patriotic enthusiasm, the Russian government decided to introduce prohibition during wartime, but this brought about a severe and immediate reduction in the government's income, as it lost its income from liquor. Revenues in 1914 showed a reduction of more than 500 million roubles on the previous year, at the same time as the government was having to cope with severely increased expenditure to fight the First World War.

***

The impact of Russia's budgetary policies on its population was considerable. Since the overwhelming majority of Russia's population were peasants, it was inevitable that they would bear the greatest burden of taxation. Discussions over the effect of government taxation policies on the peasantry have centred

40 I. A. Mikhailov, *Gosudarstevennye dolgi i raskhody Rossii vo vremia voiny. Fakty i tsifry* (Petrograd: Pravda, 1917), p. 132.

on two periods: the early part of the eighteenth century, when Peter the Great introduced the poll tax, and the post-emancipation period. While the Russian government's need for revenue was acute, and its apparent authority over its population was very considerable, it had to act with considerable caution when calculating the impact of its taxation policies. The threat of peasant rebellion – whether real or merely perceived – was ever-present and the government was well aware that its control of the empire could easily be challenged by uprisings across its domains. The four great peasant revolts that Russia experienced after 1606, culminating in the Pugachev revolt in the 1770s, reinforced this belief and acted as a reminder of the power that the Russian peasant could exert. While the state had been able to deal with these rebellions and to reassert its own authority on each occasion, the government became wary of implementing policies that could provoke the peasants into further revolts. This was especially true in the mid- and late nineteenth century, when the interests of noble landowners had to be balanced against the needs of the peasantry in the construction of the 1861 emancipation settlement. An increase in the number of peasant revolts in the 1850s caused genuine alarm inside the government, and a nervousness about the potential power of the rural population played a significant part in the taxation reforms of the 1880s.

The impact of Peter the Great's introduction of the poll tax on the peasant has been widely debated. The emperor wanted to introduce a new and reliable source of revenue, but at the same time he was very conscious of the need not to antagonise the peasantry by making severe financial demands on them. Despite this, it has been argued, most notably by P. N. Miliukov in his writings before 1917, that the burden of taxation increased very substantially during Peter's reign and that, in particular, the poll tax generated 260 per cent more in revenue than the taxes that it replaced.[41] This argument is based on analysis of the total tax yield, rather than looking at the burden faced by each Russian household and does not take into account the increase in population over the period and has thus been challenged by more recent commentators. It has been argued that the state's tax revenues increased partly because there were more tax-payers, but that this was also due to inflation and that the real tax burden on individuals remained more or less steady. It has even been suggested that the introduction of the poll tax represented a reduction in the level of taxation, after the government's need to increase taxes to pay for the Great Northern War.[42] As has been widely acknowledged, however, there is insufficient evidence to

41 P. N. Miliukov, *Gosudarstvennoe khoziaistvo Rossii v pervoi chetverti XVIII stoletiia i reforma Petra Velikogo* (St Petersburg: Tip. M. M. Stasiulevicha, 1905), esp. pp. 471–91.

42 Kahan, *The Plow*, p. 332.

come to definitive judgements about the burdens of taxation in the early part of the eighteenth century. The Russian state did not have the bureaucratic capacity to maintain accurate records of its finances during this period and the budget-making process was still rudimentary. While complete evidence for the actual financial burdens faced by the peasantry during and immediately after Peter's reign is lacking, the perception produced by the introduction of the poll tax is much clearer. The population as a whole believed that the poll tax had resulted in significantly increased taxation. But this belief was related to the circumstances of the tax's introduction. The early 1720s were hard years for Russian farmers. Poor harvests and resulting high prices for grain helped to reduce the peasants' standard of living: many peasants were compelled to become purchasers of grain, rather than being able to sell their own produce. At the same time, the government moved to requisition grain, paying only very modest prices to the peasantry, to try to alleviate famine. The methods by which the new poll tax was collected also served to generate antagonism: the task of tax-collection was initially handed over to the army and the military sought to collect the new tax in cash. Previously, the work of tax-collection had been undertaken by landowners, and peasants had been able to negotiate to pay their taxes in kind or by performing additional labour services. The combination of the need for the peasants to produce cash to pay the new poll tax, together with the unbending attitude of the army during the process of collection, served to intensify the stress that the peasants were already feeling as a result of poor agricultural conditions. Even though the burden that the new tax represented may, overall, not have represented any substantial increase in the overall level of taxation demanded from the Russian peasants, their clear perception was that the poll tax did represent a considerable extra demand by the government.

The position of the peasantry in the second half of the nineteenth century was also complex. Emancipation had been introduced partly as a response to the apparent growth in peasant discontent during the 1850s. The terms of the settlement had been dictated as much by the Russian state's financial position as by the needs of either peasants or landowners. The government was extremely unsure of the likely peasant response to emancipation, both in the short term and as the real effects of the reform became clear. It was, therefore, very wary of making significant changes to the tax system until emancipation had bedded down. The system of redemption payments introduced a new financial burden for former serfs and, even though the state's need for extra revenue was considerable during the 1860s and 1870s, it was reluctant to embark on a radical restructuring of the tax system. The perception that gripped the Russian establishment after emancipation was that the peasantry were becoming more and more impoverished,[43] and that this was not unrelated to the growth in revolutionary activity in the 1870s, culminating in the assassination of Alexander II in 1881. The government came to believe that it needed to try to alleviate the financial situation of the peasant if it was to prevent widespread rebellion. Alongside this, in the last part of the nineteenth century the state wanted to promote industrial growth in Russia. As minister of finance, Bunge wanted to reduce the level of direct taxation on the peasantry, but the increases in indirect taxes in the 1880s and 1890s clearly had a significant impact on the rural population. The argument turns on the extent to which the reductions in direct taxation were balanced by increases in excise duties and other indirect levies. It has been suggested that in the first half of the 1880s the overall tax burden on the peasantry was reduced: even though indirect taxation increased by some 10 per cent, this was more than compensated for by significant reductions in direct taxes. Urban residents paid more in taxation during this period, but the rural population saw its overall tax burden reduced by some 8 per cent.[44] This analysis is short-sighted, since it considers only the first part of the 1880s and fails to take into account the new impositions that were levied during the late 1880s and 1890s. There has also been considerable debate over the overall standard of living that the Russian peasant enjoyed after emancipation, with historians arguing that the supposed 'crisis of Russian agriculture' at the end of the nineteenth century was a chimera.[45] The role that taxation played in the peasant economy has formed part of these discussions, with the increases in indirect taxation being taken as evidence to support the view that the peasant standard of living declined at the end of the nineteenth century. While indirect taxes do bear more heavily on lower-income groups, the peasantry could also purchase less of the taxed goods, should they find themselves in straitened circumstances. Even the excise duty on vodka could be avoided by the age-old practice of the peasantry distilling their own illegal spirits.

The increased revenues that the government received from indirect taxation at the end of the nineteenth century suggests that the population was sufficiently prosperous to continue to consume taxed goods, even as the tax on

43 See A. I. Engelgardt, *Letters from the Country, 1872–1887*, trans. C. A. Frierson (New York: Oxford University Press, 1993), for one of the main examples of this 'literature of social lament'.

44 See S. Plaggenborg, 'Tax Policy and the Question of Peasant Poverty in Tsarist Russia 1881–1905', *CMRS* 36, 1–2 (1995): 58.

45 J. Y. Simms, 'The Crisis of Russian Agriculture at the End of the Nineteenth Century', *SR* 36 (1977): 377–98 is the starting point for this discussion.

them rose. The preponderance of rural dwellers in the Russian Empire makes it improbable that it was townspeople who were the main purchasers of these goods and, in any case, significant numbers of the peasantry augmented their income from farming by wage labour in Russia's growing factories. It does appear as if the Russian peasant was, overall, well enough off to be able to continue to consume manufactured goods, even as the government increased the taxation on them. Witte's 1898 plaintive report to the emperor about the impoverishment of the peasantry and the effect this had on the state's budget is a reflection on the long-term relative poverty of the Russian peasant. The poor yields that Russian agriculture produced meant that the per capita income of Russia's farmers continued to be much lower than incomes elsewhere in Europe and thus, that the tax revenues that they could contribute were significantly lower than in Austria or France.

The challenge that the Russian state faced in framing its fiscal policies was how to enhance the overall prosperity of its population and thus increase the state's revenues. Although it was able to stave off the most serious financial crises, tsarist Russia faced a series of nevertheless persistent and significant budget difficulties. These were the product of the imperial Russian regime seeking to maintain a military profile equivalent to that of its Western neighbours and rivals from an economic base that was much less developed than its Great Power rivals. The tsarist state's expenditure was on the same level as that of its more prosperous rivals to the west, but its revenue-raising potential was much lower. The tsarist state had, therefore, to impose relatively high levels of taxation on its population to enable it to continue as a Great Power and it had to collect its revenues effectively and ruthlessly if it was to continue to be a credible military power.

PART VI

★

FOREIGN POLICY AND THE ARMED FORCES

23

Peter the Great and the Northern War

PAUL BUSHKOVITCH

From the end of the fifteenth century to Peter's time the main preoccupation of Russian foreign policy was the competition with Poland-Lithuania for territory and power on the East European plain. Poland was the hegemonic East European power for almost two centuries, and after initial success by 1514, Russia struggled in vain against its neighbour with few intervals of peace or goodwill. The long series of wars that resulted culminated in the war of 1653–67, which brought the Ukrainian Hetmanate into the Russian state and marked a decisive turn in Russia's favour. Relations with the Tatar khanates to the south and east were more complex. Russia had conquered Kazan and Astrakhan in 1552–6 but was unwilling to confront Crimea, whose overlord was the Ottoman Empire, western Eurasia's greatest power until the very end of the seventeenth century. The tsars preferred to build elaborate defences in the south, a line of forts and obstructions that stretched hundreds of miles from the Polish border to the Volga, and mobilise the army every spring rather than risk war with the Ottomans by pressing too hard on Crimea. The only area of relative security was the north-west, the Swedish border. The expansion of Sweden into Estonia in the 1570s and the capture of Ingria, ratified at Stolbovo in 1619, cut Russia off from the Baltic and placed an ever more powerful neighbour on Russia's frontier, but Sweden's main preoccupations were with Denmark, Germany and Poland, not Russia. In the seventeenth century Russia's relations with Sweden were good (apart from the war of 1656–8, a result of the Polish tangle) and the King of Sweden was the only European monarch to be allowed to send a resident emissary to Moscow, from 1630 until the outbreak of the Northern War. Thus it was not without reason that Peter's declaration of war on Sweden in 1700, in concert with Denmark and King Augustus II of Poland, came as a surprise in Stockholm.[1]

1 For more detailed discussion and a full bibliography see Paul Bushkovitch, *Peter the Great: the Struggle for Power 1671–1725* (Cambridge: Cambridge University Press, 2001) and Reinhard Wittram, *Peter der Grosse. Czar und Kaiser* (Göttingen: Vandenhoeck and Ruprecht, 1964).

Peter's new war was also a surprise because Russian foreign policy after 1667 had been preoccupied with the Ottoman Empire and its Crimean vassal. Russia's strategic situation had been radically altered by the acquisition of the Ukrainian Hetmanate, placing Russian troops in Kiev and other Ukrainian towns on the northern edge of the steppe, that is, of Crimean territory. The immediate result was the Chigirin War of 1677–81, the first in which Russian troops actually confronted Ottoman soldiers as well as the Crimeans. The outcome was a minor military defeat for Russia but also recognition of Russia's new border along the Dnieper. With their northern frontier secure, the Turks under Kara Mustafa pasha turned to Vienna but were defeated in 1683. The failed Turkish siege of Vienna led to the Habsburg reconquest of Hungary and the formation of the Holy League, consisting of the Empire, Poland, Venice and the Papacy. The regent Sophia, Russia's ruler in Peter's youth (1682–9) responded positively to an imperial invitation to join the Holy League, but such a step required a full reconciliation with Poland (1686), something that aroused doubts not only among Polish magnates but also in Moscow. The Naryshkin faction was against it, but Sofia and her favourite Prince V. V. Golitsyn persuaded the duma (council of Boyars) to go along and Russia joined in. Her contribution was to be the two Crimean campaigns of 1687 and 1689, both attempts to strike Crimea across the steppe, moving south from the Ukraine, and both ignominious failures. The failures led to the triumph of Peter and the Naryshkins, but the new government was not decisive enough either to break with the alliance or to continue the struggle. The war stagnated until the death of Peter's mother in 1694 put him wholly in charge for the first time. Late in that year, on his return from Archangel and his first sea voyage, Peter decided to move against the Turks and he did not consult the boyars about it. He followed the enthusiastic advice of his two foreign favourites, François Lefort of Geneva and the Scottish general Patrick Gordon, not that of his Naryshkin relatives. In the war Peter moved not against Crimea but against the Ottoman fort of Azak (Azov) at the mouth of the Don. The lack of a Russian navy caused the failure of the first siege, so over the following winter Peter built one at Voronezh and in 1696 took the fort. It seems that he intended to go on fighting the Turks, opening his way into the Black Sea, and talks with his allies were the diplomatic purpose of the famous trip to Europe in 1697–8. There he discovered that the Habsburgs in particular were weary of war and that Peter would himself have to make peace with Istanbul.

On the way home he met with Augustus II in Poland, who had a new idea: attack Sweden. If Peter went along it meant a break with the tsar's previous favourites, Lefort and Gordon, who continued to favour an anti-Ottoman policy, but both died early in 1699. He mourned their deaths, but for political support found two new favourites, Fedor Golovin, the scion of an old boyar family, and Aleksandr Menshikov, the son of one of the palace falconers. Peter moved quickly to make a treaty with Denmark, completing the circle of allies against Sweden. His method was characteristic, for he ordered the Danish envoy to Voronezh where he was inspecting the shipyards. There he met the Dane at night in a small house on the edge of town with only Fedor Golovin and a translator present, and together they wrote the treaty. Peter told the Dane to be sure to keep the matter secret from the Russian boyars. Complications with the Turkish peace put off the Swedish war until the autumn of 1700, but the new direction was now set.

The course of the war was full of surprises, for the political, military, economic and even demographic position of the warring powers was not what it seemed on the surface. Sweden had been the hegemonic power in northern Europe since the great victories of Gustavus Adolphus, having reduced Denmark in size and power and established itself not only in the Baltic provinces but in northern Germany. The performance of King Jan Sobieski's army before Vienna in 1683 seemed to suggest that Poland had recovered from its losses in the Russian-Ukrainian war. Contemporaries attributed great significance to Augustus II's success in Hungary as an imperial ally and commander, presuming that he, like Sobieski, could overcome the contentions of Polish magnates long enough to secure victory. Russia, in contrast, was still a marginal power, fighting with mixed success against the Turks and Tatars and apparently much less important than Poland.

In reality, the situation was quite different. Poland's problems extended beyond magnate quarrels with the king and with one another. The Cossack rebellion of 1648 and the subsequent wars had largely been fought on Polish territory, leading to economic catastrophe and demographic collapse. It did not regain its pre-1648 population (about 11 million) until the middle of the eighteenth century. Further, its crucial grain exports met increasing competition from improved farming techniques in Holland and England, its main markets. Polish cities stagnated after 1648, falling in population and prosperity. The most ruthless government would have raised revenue with difficulty in this situation, but revenue for the army was almost entirely at the will of the diet (Polish parliament) and the *szlachta* (nobility) served in the army as volunteer cavalry or on the wages of great magnates. A modern infantry army was an impossibility. The king also could not fully control Poland's Baltic ports (Danzig and Elbing) nor could he build a navy.

Sweden was in much better shape, but also had weaknesses under the surface. The new naval base at Karlskrona made it possible to check the Danish navy and control at least the northern Baltic, as long as England or Holland did not intervene. Sweden's army was the best trained and organised in the area, for the system of cantoning the army (*indelningsverk*) on particular districts preserved it as a fighting force even in peacetime. Sweden's state organisation, formed under Gustavus Adolphus and count Axel Oxenstierna, gave the country an efficiency that was the envy of Europe. The 1680 proclamation of absolutism by King Charles XI gave, it appeared, the flexibility to the execution of policy that the need to consult the *riksdag* (Swedish assembly of estates) thwarted. The return of royal lands (the *reduktion*) seemed to ensure revenue for the absolute king.

This impressive structure was built on sand. Under the Swedish crown was a population of only about 1.8 million in Sweden and Finland and a few hundred thousands in the Baltic provinces and other possessions. These numbers were too small to sustain large armies, and it was always necessary to recruit outside of Sweden. This meant money, and that was in short supply. Sweden was simply too poor to provide enough money, particularly in cash. For most of the seventeenth century the single largest item of cash income for the crown were the Riga tolls. Nothing in Sweden proper could compare. Gustavus Adolphus had pursued his wars by confiscating the tolls in Polish and Ducal Prussia and subsidies from France. The economic situation had not changed in any major way by the 1690s, and furthermore those years were ones of poor harvests and famine. Sweden could win a war only by carrying the fight to other lands, exploiting their wealth and attracting subsidies. The brilliance of Swedish organisation, civil and military, made such a strategy possible, but a long war could create immense obstacles.

Russia's strength lay under the surface and the initial underestimation of Peter's chances by allies and enemies alike was entirely understandable. Russia's army was in the process of modernisation, and previous experience demonstrated how difficult that was. The use of mercenaries in the Time of Troubles and the Smolensk War (1632–4) was a failure. Later on Tsar Alexis used European officers to train Russian soldiers, infantry and cavalry, in the new techniques of warfare, fighting in formation and using pikes to supplement musket fire. The change was not complete, however, and Peter had to start anew in the 1690s. Older elements remained, such as the Russian gentry cavalry, even operating in considerable numbers through the early years of the Northern War. The speed of change meant a great lack of trained officers, whom Peter recruited abroad, but that system had its own difficulties. Unless the modernisation was thorough and rapid, the changeover could create even greater confusion, as the first battle of Narva demonstrated.

No one had a clear idea of Russia's economic resources, but everyone knew the distances were vast and communications very poor. It did not have extensive iron production, artisanal or otherwise, and imported weapons in large numbers. Russia had to maintain an expensive permanent army on the southern frontier against the Crimeans. It had no navy, and thus no experienced officers and sailors when Peter built one. The tsar and great boyars were wealthy, but the country as a whole was poor (if not as poor as Sweden) and the administrative structure inadequate. In the provinces the administrative structure was especially limited, leaving the provincial governors with tiny staffs to administer areas the size of several French provinces. The central government in Moscow was slow and cumbersome, operating according to unwritten traditional procedures. Russia lacked not only trained officers but men with a whole series of technical skills necessary to warfare, modern fortification, shipbuilding, mathematically precise artillery. It had no engineers to drain swamps or build canals, rendering the communication problem even worse. Finally, most of the Russian elite lacked the general education on which to base the acquisition of these skills. In the terminology of the time, Russia lacked the arts and sciences and was thus 'barbaric'.

Nevertheless, Russia had some crucial advantages of which even her leaders may not have been fully aware. One important advantage was demographic. In Peter's time, from the 1670s to 1719, the population grew from some 11 million to about 15.5 million. In the sixteenth century, Russia and Poland-Lithuania had been similar in population (6 –7 million), probably with an advantage to Poland. After the middle of the seventeenth century Russia had decisively pulled ahead of Poland, and compared to Sweden, it was becoming a giant. This population growth had been rapid after the end of the Time of Troubles, and was accompanied by a shift in settlement away from the western frontier and the centre towards the east, the Urals and the south-east, the Volga and the steppe. This shift also meant that labour was available for the salt wells and iron mines of the north and the Urals, and that better, richer, land was coming under cultivation in the south. Thus grain prices remained stable over a century of population growth. Russia's foreign trade grew throughout the century, primarily through Archangel. As the terms of trade were in Russia's favour, Dutch and English merchants came to the Dvina with their ships ballasted with silver that flowed into the Russian treasury directly at Archangel and indirectly through Russian fairs and market towns. The importance of this trade lay not in any larger economic transformation – Russia remained firmly agrarian – but in the flow of cash which it produced. The tsar, unlike the King of Sweden, had a ready supply of silver coins, coming in from the sales tax and the vodka monopoly. The trade also provided the merchants with modest capital, part of which was invested in iron mines and metalworking shops that supplied the army. None of the favourable economic factors was strong enough to allow Russia to fight a war without difficulty, but all were sufficient to allow protracted conflicts without major crisis. The old Russian administration had been fairly good at procuring resources, and Peter's new methods were even better. He was able to take the war into the territory of his enemies and neighbours, and at the same time Russia's very size and poor communications were immense obstacles to any invader.

Thus Peter was by no means weak when he went to war, though he was probably no more aware of his advantages at first than other contemporaries. In his agreements with Augustus, he had demanded little, giving most of the Baltic provinces to Poland and asking only for a small coastal strip, basically Russia's pre-1617 territory. He had built a new army and navy, and was quickly learning how to mobilise resources, but he had only some experience of success and admired the alleged political and military skills of Augustus.The question that to some extent still eludes us is, however, what did he want to accomplish? The three wars of Peter's reign, the Azov Campaign, the Northern War and the Persian Campaign, were all different, but they had one thing in common, the desire for ports. This desire does not imply that Peter was trying to found a commercial empire, but it does seem to have been high on his priorities in all three cases.

The Azov Campaign is the most difficult to explain simply because of the character of record-keeping in seventeenth-century Russia. The Russian state kept detailed records of decrees, orders, military and tax rosters, diplomatic negotiations and judicial proceedings, but not of the discussions leading up to decisions. Thus we can only infer Peter's motives. In joining the Holy League, Sofia had demanded of the Ottomans access to the Black Sea at the Dnieper and Don and the destruction of the Crimean Khanate. Golitsyn's military strategy, a frontal attack on the peninsula, seems to vindicate the seriousness of these demands. After her overthrow, the Naryshkin government moderated these demands, requiring not the destruction of the Khanate but only a cessation of raids, and access to the Black Sea by the two rivers. The Naryshkins, however, were too indecisive to actually realise their presumed aims. Peter's military moves, a main blow at Azov with a secondary campaign on the Dnieper under Boris Sheremetev and Hetman Mazepa, fitted the Russian demands, which now gave priority to the river mouths. At the same time Russia's post-1667 borders had placed her in direct confrontation with the Ottomans. Not only were the Crimeans closer but from Kiev it was only a short journey across the steppe to the Ottoman forts at Bender and Khotin, the gates to the Balkans. The competition for power and territory was unavoidable, and in addition the religious factor is not to be discounted. Peter's propaganda and diplomacy stressed Christian solidarity against Islam, and given Peter's real if rather unconventional piety, as well as the culture of the age, these were serious motives. All this being said, we still have to infer Peter's reasons primarily from his actions.

The Northern War is another situation entirely, for there are many, if often imperfect, testimonies to Peter's motives. During the Great Embassy of 1697–8 a number of the Europeans who met Peter and his entourage recorded some discussion about acquiring a Baltic port, and diplomats back in Moscow picked up the same talk. We have nothing from Peter's hand that records this notion, but the envoy of Peter's new ally Augustus II, Georg Carl von Carlowitz, reported Peter's words, that the tsar felt that he was unjustly deprived of a Baltic port, both for his navy and for commerce, and wanted to revenge himself on Sweden. The latter remark may have referred to the insult Peter felt he had received at Riga in 1697 but also pointed to another issue that surfaced in the war and in Peter's private correspondence as well as public propaganda. The lands at the head of the Gulf of Finland, Ingria and the Kexholm province, had been part of Novgorod and then of Russia since the beginning of recorded history and were lost only in the Time of Troubles. The population remained to a large extent Orthodox (though most of it was probably Finnish speaking) after 1617. Thousands had left for Russian territory, fleeing Lutheran pastors and Swedish landlords, and new, Lutheran, settlers from the Finnish interior came to replace them in many areas. Of course the ethnic structure of the area per se was a matter of indifference in seventeenth-century Europe, but the whole story served as a reminder of the territory's Russian past. In the original treaty with Augustus II these territories were to be Russia's prize.

The problem with Ingria was that it had no port, so it is not surprising that once he declared war on Sweden in August 1700, Peter marched not into Ingria but towards Narva, in Estonia. This move disturbed Augustus II, since the treaty with Peter gave him all of Livonia and Estonia (including Narva) in the event of victory over Sweden. There was nothing Augustus could do, however, and the move did have a certain military logic, for Narva was more important a fortress than any of the small Swedish positions in Ingria. In the event Charles XII (with Anglo-Dutch naval help) knocked Denmark out of the war and turned towards Estonia. Peter's army suffered its greatest defeat before Narva on 19/30 November, an event that forced him to change direction, and in 1702–3 he captured Ingria, from the head of the Neva at Nöteborg (Oreshek, after 1703 Shlissel'burg) to Estonia, with the island of Retusaari in the gulf itself. At the mouth of the Neva Peter began to build St Petersburg, precisely the naval and commercial port he had wanted. Retusaari became Kronslot (Kronstadt), his main naval base in the Baltic. Peter's subsequent behaviour and statements underscored the centrality of the new city in his plans. During 1706–8 he made a number of overtures to Charles XII for a compromise peace. Though he had captured Narva and Dorpat in 1704, he offered to surrender all of his conquests with the exception of St Petersburg and its immediate vicinity. Charles rejected the offers, but they show what Peter considered absolutely essential. Nothing that Peter did or said after Poltava contradicts the priority given to the new port. Peter took Viborg in 1710 to provide a better defensive perimeter to the new city on the north-west, and the capture of Reval and Riga served the same aim, as well as expanding Russia's naval and commercial possibilities. Peter left Baltic society in the hands of the local nobility and encouraged the towns to act as ports for the empire as a whole. Similarly he had no interest in Finland west of Viborg, for the country was too poor, lacked good ports and significant commerce, and was not essential for the defence of Petersburg.

The priority given to the port was perhaps the basis of Peter's commitment to the war with Sweden, but it was not the only element. He seems to have really felt that the losses from the *Smuta* needed to be rectified. In 1716 he commissioned Shafirov to write a long defence of his policies in the war, which he personally edited and supplemented,[2] and had it translated into German and other European languages The thrust of the text was that he was only rectifying past injustice, the seizure of Ingria and Karelia in the Time of Troubles and also Sweden's failure to uphold Russian claims to Livonia, which it had (he argued) recognised in the 1564 truce with Ivan the Terrible. The argument was that Russia, not the dynasty, had claim to all this, and indeed Shafirov even said that the 'Russian empire' (*rossiiskaia imperiia*) had such claims, thus using the term five years before Peter adopted the title of Emperor (*imperator*). In claiming the territory for Russia, Shafirov and Peter did two things. They abandoned the older Russian claims to territory based on patrimonial inheritance: Ivan IV had claimed that Livonia was his personal inherited estate (*votchina*) as a

2 *Rassuzhdenie kakie zakonnye prichiny ego tsarskoe velichestvo Petr pervyi tsar' i povelitel' vserossiiskii . . . k nachatiiu voiny . . . imel* (St Petersburg, 1717); repr. P. P. Shafirov, *A Discourse Concerning the Just Causes of the War between Sweden and Russia: 1700–1721*, ed. W. Butler (Dobbs Ferr, NY: Oceania Publications, 1973).

Riurikovich, as he and his ancestors had also done in the cases of Smolensk and Polotsk. The authors also fit their claims into the then usual definitions of a just war. Samuel Pufendorf, who came to be Peter's favourite European historian and political thinker, alleged two sorts of just war, defence against an attempt against one's life and property (defensive war) and an attempt to recover things lost unjustly in previous conflicts (offensive war) [Pufendorf, *De Officio hominis et civis*, 1682, bk. II, chapter 16.2]. They also followed Pufendorf in pointing to Charles XII's attempt to stir up rebellion in Russia, something both Pufendorf and Grotius had condemned as inflicting more harm on the enemy than humanity in warfare allowed [Pufendorf, *De Officio*, II, 16.12]. The Russians did not, however, follow Pufendorf in all respects. Pufendorf believed in the interests of states, and that these interests were the main motives of their policies, as he described in his history of Europe (translated into Russian in 1710). Peter and Shafirov also got from Pufendorf their idea of Sweden's main motive in the war, to keep Russia ignorant and weak, to prevent it from learning the arts of war of the West. They do not allege any such state interests for Russia, however, perhaps only because the need for a port coincided so neatly with the recovery of unjustly taken territories. It is also the case that European monarchs still preferred to downplay or just plain conceal their own state interests while emphasising those of their opponents. Shafirov's tract followed this example.

In the 1717 tract and elsewhere Peter and his spokesmen also deviated from another norm of earlier Russian justifications for war, the defence of Orthodoxy. In all the wars with Poland and Sweden, but especially in 1653–4, the tsars had made much of this issue, and in 1700 Peter had a good case. The Swedish government did harass and persecute Orthodox peasants, Finnish and Russian alike, after 1619. Stefan Iavorskii, the curator of the patriarchal throne after 1701, did mention this issue in some of his early sermons, but it soon disappeared from Russian official and unofficial pronouncements as well as from the themes of celebrations and other types of propaganda. In a different way, however, Peter retained a religious understanding of his war along with the secular rationale, for he clearly believed that God was on his side. He celebrated his triumphs with liturgy as well as fireworks. In 1724 he decided to correct the liturgy composed by Feofilakt Lopatinskii to celebrate Poltava. He objected to the monk's phrase that Russia had fought for the cross of Christ. The Swedes, he wrote, honour the cross just as we do, 'Sweden was proud, and the war was not about faith, but about measure.'[3] Charles XII, in other words,

3 P. Pekarskii, *Nauka i literatura v Rossii pri Petre Velikom*, 2 vols. (St Petersburg, 1862), vol. II, p. 201.

was proud beyond measure, and God punished him. Peter wanted Feofilakt to quote the Bible, 'Goliath's proud words to David, and David's trusting in the Lord': 'This day will the Lord deliver thee into mine hand, and I will smite thee . . .' (1 Samuel 17: 46).

Many motives made up Peter's decision to start and continue the war with Sweden. He felt that his cause was just, even according to the latest European thinking. He believed that Russia needed a port to maintain its prosperity and power. He thought Sweden was preventing Russia from acquiring the fruits of European civilisation. He also understood the prestige conferred by military victory at home and abroad, and the power that it gave in diplomacy. He wrote to his son Alexis in 1716 that it was through war that 'we had come from darkness out into the light; us, whom no one in the world knew, they now respect . . .'[4]

Thus Peter's dogged determination to bring the war to a victorious close should not be surprising. The success of Charles in deposing Augustus II in 1706 and placing Stanislaw Leszczynski on the Polish throne as a Swedish puppet certainly prompted Peter's proposals for a compromise peace, but when Charles rejected them, Peter continued to fight. At Zólkiew in December, 1706, he chose the basic strategy of withdrawal to the Russian frontier that he pursued for the next two and a half years. Charles was in no hurry, sure as he was that his approach to the Russian border would result in an aristocratic as well as popular revolt against the tsar. Charles's advisers had been telling him for years that Russia was unstable and Peter unloved, and he printed proclamations to circulate in Russia calling for revolt. Indeed many in Europe held the same opinion. As the Swedish king moved east, however, his supplies ran low, and at Lesnaia (28 September/9 October 1708) Peter cut off the relief column. At the Russian frontier there was no revolt, so Charles turned south towards the Ukraine where Hetman Mazepa joined him, but without most of the Ukrainian Cossack host, whose rank and file remained loyal to the tsar. The Swedes managed to survive the winter and laid siege to Poltava, where Peter defeated them (27 June/8 July 1709), his greatest triumph. At Poltava Peter's relentless training, good use of artillery and understanding of his limits gave him victory. Peter built field fortifications and let Charles attack him, realising that his army lacked the precise training and experience for an attack. The steadfast courage of his infantry broke the Swedish assault, not the last battle of this type in Russian history. Even more crushing to Charles's fortunes was

4 N. G. Ustrialov, *Istoriia tsarstvovaniia Petra Velikogo*, 5 vols. in 6 (St Petersburg, 1858–63), vol. VI, p. 347.

the aftermath, for he escaped across the Dnieper to Turkish territory, leaving behind all the troops who had escaped from Poltava. His veterans, dispersed as prisoners through Siberia, could not be replaced in a small country like Sweden.

The rest of the Northern War was a struggle to finish the job. Charles was as stubborn as Peter, and even the loss of all the Swedish German possessions and the Russian conquest of Finland in 1713–14 did not shake his resolve. Instead, Charles spun fantastic plans to conquer Norway, where he perished in 1718. For Russia, the years after Poltava meant coalition warfare in northern Germany and new diplomatic complexities. Denmark was a largely loyal ally until 1720, but too small to be of much use. Hanover and other German states were glad to seize Swedish possessions, but Peter's marriage of his daughter to the Duke of Mecklenburg in 1716 convinced both the Habsburgs in Vienna and King George I of Great Britain and Hanover that Peter had great designs in the Baltic. In fact, the Mecklenburg scheme was part of a desperate attempt to surround Sweden and put enough pressure on Charles to accept defeat and make peace. His death brought a new king and queen to the Swedish throne, who hoped to rely on the British navy to pressure Peter into a peace favourable to Sweden. Their hope was in vain. The British navy was certainly enormously more powerful than Peter's ships of the line with their newly trained crews and foreign officers, but the Russian galley fleet, borrowed from Mediterranean practice to sail in the Baltic skerries, inflicted devastating raids on the Swedish coast with virtual impunity. At Nystad in August, 1721, Peter got all he wanted: Ingria, Karelia, Viborg, Estonia and Livonia. Russia had a port, with a large defensive perimeter around it, and was now a European power, dominant in the north-east.

The final war of Peter's life was in a totally different direction, and seems to have been entirely commercial in inspiration. This was the Persian campaigns. Peter had toyed with the idea of exploiting the internal dissension in Iran for some time, but only with the conclusion of the Northern War was he free to move south. This he did immediately, a difficult series of campaigns overland and by sea, ending in the short-lived Russian occupation of Gilan. Peter's correspondence with Artemii Volynskii and other documents make clear that this was a commercial enterprise. The idea was to seize the silk-producing areas of northern Iran, which had long provided Russia with silk, both for its own needs and for resale to Europe.[5] Peter had learned from the Dutch and

5 S. M. Solov'ev, *Istoriia Rossii s drevneishikh vremen*, 15 vols. (Moscow, 1960–6), vol IX, pp. 366–77.

English that overseas trade backed by military force was the road to wealth and power, and in a small way was determined to imitate them. Ultimately Russia had neither the commercial development nor the type of military forces necessary for such a task, and in 1735 had to return the territories to Iran.

For all Peter's interest in Iran after 1721, Russia's international relations necessarily focused on Europe. Peter had created an entirely new situation in northern and eastern Europe, and needed a new set of alliances and relationships. Most dramatic perhaps was the new relationship to Poland. The return of Peter's erstwhile ally, Augustus II, to the Polish throne after Poltava at first seemed like a great boon to Russia, again giving Russia's former chief antagonist a friendly monarch. Peter continued his earlier policy of supporting Augustus against his magnate opponents in Poland until 1715. As time passed, however, Augustus grew increasingly fearful of Russia's new power, and annoyed that Peter was keeping his conquests in the Baltic provinces. He put out feelers to the Baltic nobility, and began to look for other allies. Peter began to move away from the king and towards his Polish opponents, who proved a constant thorn in the side of the king until his death. Continued royal weakness and magnate rivalries in Poland, to boot a country heavily ruined by the Northern War, gradually changed the relationship. By the end of Peter's life the Russian ambassador in Warsaw was intriguing with the various magnate parties and other ambassadors, keeping the king in check, and operating as if Poland was a Russian protectorate, which in many respects it was until the partitions put a temporary end to its existence as a state.

Sweden also found itself in a wholly new situation. If its economy was in better shape than Poland's, and it gradually recovered from the war, politically there were many analogies. The death of Charles XII in 1718 led to a new constitution, with a weak king and powerful estates, primarily the noble estate. Though the new king had relied on Britain to try to reverse Peter's victories, he signally failed and had to agree to Peter's conditions at the 1721 Treaty of Nystad. The treaty not only ratified Peter's conquests, Ingria, Estonia, Livonia, Karelia and the Viborg district of Finland, it specified that Russia would not interfere with the new Swedish constitution. Peter was perfectly aware that Sweden's 'Age of Freedom' meant the freedom of Russian, French and British ambassadors to bribe the members of the Diet to follow their lead.

For Peter after 1721, the central point of his European policy was to retain his position in the Baltic, which led him to the Holstein alliance and later the 1724 defensive treaty with Sweden. The Holstein alliance gave him a means to pressure Denmark to remove the Sound tolls on Russian shipping, but primarily it gave him a means to influence Swedish politics. At that moment the Swedish estates were resisting King Frederick's attempts to reinforce his position, and thus supported the idea of an eventual Holstein succession (Karl Friedrich of Holstein was the son of Charles XII's sister). The idea seems to have been that Holstein could provide a base for a recovery of the Swedish position in Germany. For Peter, such aims in Sweden meant that Sweden would not be looking to regain his Baltic conquests. Thus Russia assured the leaders of the Swedish estates that she supported the new constitution and the Holstein succession, and the result was a defensive alliance that helped secure Russia's position in the Baltic. Soon afterwards Peter married his daughter Anna to Karl Friedrich. For Peter's lifetime the arrangement brought security, but Russia was to abandon the commitment to Holstein in 1732, as it no longer was needed to restrain Sweden. (The only importance of the whole episode was that it led to the birth of the future Peter III.) In all these manoeuvres around the Baltic Peter avoided taking sides among the larger European powers. Russia would chose Austria for an ally only after his death.

Russia's role in larger European politics was extensive, but should not be exaggerated. Though dominant in north-eastern Europe, Russia did not become a truly Europe-wide power until the Seven Year's War. For the main European rivalry of the time, that of France with the Habsburgs, Holland and Britain, Russia was still peripheral. France did not even bother to send a permanent ambassador until after Nystad, using only low-level commercial agents before. For the Habsburgs, Russia was obviously crucial because of the Ottomans, and Peter's involvement in German affairs brought a sharp reaction. Russian and Austrian ambassadors had complex relations in Warsaw, sometimes antagonistic, sometimes working together. The Dutch and English had commercial relations with Russia, and their stake in the stability of the Baltic and its trade meant that Peter's advances caused great excitement and occasional fear. None of this, however, had much to do with the crucial points of conflict in Flanders, the Rhineland, North America and Asia. Russia remained a major regional power, part of the northern and Balkan systems that overlapped with the conflicts farther west at certain points, but was not part of those conflicts.

* * *

Peter's dreams and Russia's new position demanded not only a better army and navy, it demanded a new diplomatic corps. Most of all this meant permanent Russian ambassadors outside of Russia, in Istanbul as well as Russia's neighbours and the major powers. Before Peter, the Ambassadorial Office (*Posol'skii prikaz*) had been one of the most sophisticated of Russian offices, maintaining detailed records of embassies and negotiations and a broad service of news collecting. European newsletters were obtained in large numbers and translated into Russian to be read in the boyar duma on a regular basis. Russian culture changed rapidly after about 1650, with knowledge of Polish and Latin spreading among the elite and much geographic knowledge in translation as well. None of this, however, could substitute for diplomats on the spot, and in the 1667 treaty with Poland there had been provisions for the exchange of permanent residents. In Moscow by the 1690s the Polish ambassador was part of a group that included emissaries from the Netherlands, Sweden, Denmark and the Holy Roman Emperor, but Russia sent out permanent ambassadors only from 1699. The first two were Andrei Matveev (1699) to the Netherlands (and north-west Europe in general) and Prince Petr Golitsyn to Vienna (1701). These were men with knowledge of (at least) Latin, and some reading on European states, and they also brought their wives and servants. Bringing families was not easy (Princess Golitsyna was very unhappy with high-heeled shoes and stockings), but it meant that Russian diplomats could begin to mix in elite society with greater ease. The new diplomats were men of considerable learning, as Matveev's writings and library demonstrate. He wrote his communications to the Dutch government at first in Latin, but later seems to have learned French. Prince Boris Kurakin, his successor in the Hague and later ambassador to other countries, spoke Italian best of all, a language he learned in Venice. Peter sent him there in 1697 to learn languages and navigation, and he seems to have passed his navigation tests, but learned his Italian also from the famous Venetian courtesans. He found in Venice a justification and ideology of aristocratic government, which he developed in private notes and writings on Russian history and European states, all the time serving the absolute tsar.

Most of the Russian ambassadors were indeed great aristocrats (Matveev the exception here). Kurakin, the Golitsyns, several Dolgorukiis, were all princes and men who could hold their own in contests of honour and pride, as well as political acumen, with their European counterparts. Peter also found foreigners to serve him in this capacity, the unfortunate Patkul but also James Bruce, Heinrich Ostermann, and lesser lights like Johann Baron von Urbich and Johann Baron von Schleinitz. At the centre of this network in Russia was Gavriil Ivanovich Golovkin (1660–1734), who took over foreign policy after the death of Fedor Golovin in 1706. Golovkin came from a noble but not aristocratic family, but he had been part of Peter's household since 1676. He stayed in Moscow in 1697, where Peter wrote to him regularly. His second in command was Petr Pavlovich Shafirov (1669–1739), the son of a converted Jew brought to Moscow in the 1650s. Shafirov was a professional, a translator in the Ambassadorial Office since 1691, serving in that capacity on the Great Embassy. Later he was Fedor Golovin's personal secretary. Golovkin found him indispensable for his knowledge of languages and European politics, though nobody seems to have liked him. He was ambassador to Istanbul in the crucial years after the Prut campaign, and Russia's extrication from that mess owed much to his skill. In court politics Golovkin retained a strict neutrality, as did Shafirov at first. After 1714 he was moving closer to the aristocrats, perhaps out of enmity with Menshikov. Both Golovkin and Shafirov were part of court politics, but they were both lightweights, and both isolated and neutral for most of their careers, Golovkin entirely so and Shafirov until nearly the end of Peter's life. It was their administrative and other talents that kept them where they were, not aristocratic origins or court alliances. They were, however, what Peter needed, knowledgeable executors of his will, good organisers of diplomacy, not policy-makers.

Peter was the policy-maker. In the early years of the reign, Gordon and Lefort seem to have exerted their influence to encourage Peter to return to war with the Ottomans, and after their death the rise of Golovin and Menshikov similarly reflected the new foreign policy. Golovin died in 1706, and by the time of Poltava Peter seems to have made his foreign policy with much consultation with his favourites, but less with the aristocracy. Menshikov certainly had opinions, and as Peter's commander in Germany in 1713 made decisions on his own that Peter did not like, but they were not major changes of direction, and Peter reversed them. Later on there is no information to suggest that Prince V. V. Dolgorukii in his time of favour (1709–18) or Iaguzhinskii, a favourite from about 1710 onwards had any consistent vision of foreign policy or influence over it. The basic factional breakdown at court after 1709 was about the position of the aristocracy, pitting the Dolgorukiis and their allies against Menshikov and his. Legends aside, Peter was not a monarch who refused to consult his ministers and generals, like Charles XII. On campaign he regularly held councils of war and seems to have generally gone with the majority, even when he had doubts, as in the decision not to invade Sweden from Denmark in 1716. Yet his foreign policy was his own, made with the technical assistance of Golovkin, Shafirov, the diplomats and the generals, but not with the great men of the court.

24

Russian foreign policy, 1725–1815

HUGH RAGSDALE

In Russian foreign policy in the era, certain basic generalisations apply: Peter I had dealt remarkably successfully with the Swedish challenge; he had devised a novel and rather satisfactory solution for the Polish problem; but he had failed to resolve satisfactorily the issue of the Ottoman Empire, a challenge for the future. Moreover, these three sensitive areas were so inextricably interdependent in Russian foreign policy that St Petersburg could not isolate them from each other and deal with them separately. A crisis in any one of the three states almost invariably involved complications with the others. The coming of the French Revolution magnified these problems, and the coming of Napoleon Bonaparte to some extent supplanted them by grander geostrategic challenges.

Era of palace revolutions

The first period following Peter's reign was most conspicuous for the instability of the throne and the resultant inconsequence that it inflicted on Russian foreign policy. The diplomatic chancery of the time was not by any means in incompetent hands; it simply lacked the constancy of government support to give it proper effect.

The early post-Petrine era exhibited clear elements of the continuity of Peter's policy in foreign affairs.[1] The most significant such element was the continuation of Russian policy in the experienced hands of Vice-Chancellor

For critical readings and comments I am grateful to Paul Bushkovitch, Claudine Cowen, Anatoly Venediktovich Ignat'ev, Dominic Lieven, Roderick McGrew, Valery Nikolaevich Ponomarev, David Schimmelpenninck and Vladlen Nikolaevich Vinogradov.

1 Considerations of space prohibit entering into all of the issues of the period, in particular the complex marriage alliances that Peter I made in northern Germany. For a clear and authoritative account, see Hans Bagger, 'The Role of the Baltic in Russian Foreign Policy, 1721–1773', in Hugh Ragsdale and Valery N. Ponomarev (eds.), *Imperial Russian Foreign Policy* (Washington and New York: Wilson Center and Cambridge Univerity Presses, 1993), pp. 36–72.

Andrei Ostermann. From the days of the Habsburg-Valois – subsequently Habsburg-Bourbon (1589) – rivalry, France had cultivated the favour of the East European border states hostile to Habsburg Austria, and the rise of Russia naturally threatened these border states and therefore French interests in Eastern Europe. In the circumstances, Ostermann defined Russian policy naturally by forming an Austrian alliance hostile to France.

It was thus natural enough upon the death of King Augustus II of Poland in 1733 that the Russians and the French fielded different candidates for the Polish throne. St Petersburg and Vienna supported the son of Augustus II (Saxon dynasty), while Paris supported former King Stanislaus Leszczynski (1704–9). In the War of Polish Succession (1733–6), Russia and Austria prevailed, and Augustus III became King of Poland (1734–63).

It was equally natural that the Turks perceived in this development a shift of the balance of power against their interests in south-eastern Europe. Border clashes and raiding parties aggravated tension, but the decisive precipitant of conflict was undoubtedly Russian success in the disputed Polish succession. In the Russo-Turkish War (1735–9), Russia and Austria fought a lacklustre campaign, and while Russia re-annexed (Treaty of Belgrade) the territories of Azov and Taganrog (previously annexed in 1700, relinquished in 1711), it surrendered the right to fortify these areas and accepted the humiliating principle of trading on the Black Sea exclusively in Turkish ships.

As the name of the period suggests, discontinuity and volatility were as conspicuous features of the time as was continuity. Ostermann, having served as foreign minister during four transient reigns since 1725, was unseated by a web of intrigues culminating in the palace coup of Elizabeth Petrovna in November 1741. Elizabeth brought a semblance of stability to the throne (1741–62), and she appointed Alexis P. Bestuzhev-Riumin to the office of vice-chancellor and the duties of foreign minister. Bestuzhev was to guide Russian foreign policy during the turbulent and fateful period of the two great European wars of mid-century.

The first challenge to the European order of the time came from the youthful new king of Prussia, Frederick II, who seized the opportunity of the death of Emperor Charles VI in May 1740 to invade and conquer the rich Habsburg province of Silesia, thus precipitating the War of Austrian Succession (1740–8). Europe at once divided into its two traditional warring camps, Prussia and France against Austria and Britain, and Bestuzhev continued the spirit of Ostermann's policy in the form of the Austrian alliance. Thus he naturally listed Prussia among Russia's enemies and Austrian ally Britain among Russia's friends. The bulk of Bestuzhev's activity during this war consisted not of genuine foreign policy, however, but rather of combating the plethora of intrigues mounted by the foreign powers in St Petersburg for the favours of Russian diplomatic and military assistance. In particular, a strong and well-financed French party appealed with some success to the sentiments of Empress Elizabeth, who had as a child entertained romantic illusions, fostered by Peter I, of marrying Louis XV of France. Bestuzhev succeeded in maintaining an independent Russian policy, but the intrigue and counter-intrigue confined that policy largely to an awkward neutrality such that Russia took little part in the war and none in the peace settlement. The only power to profit by the war was Prussia, which maintained its conquest of Silesia (Peace of Aix-la-Chapelle).

Two new factors weighed heavily in the political calculations that followed. The simpler was the conviction of Empress Elizabeth that the newly expanded power of Prussia was dangerous primarily to Russia and hence must be radically diminished or preferably eliminated. The second was the dissatisfaction of all of the major combatants of the previous war with their allies. The British and the French had pursued chiefly their own maritime interests, leaving their continental allies unsupported. What followed, then, was that celebrated reshuffling of the alliance system known as the Diplomatic Revolution. Hence in the wake of the war, the allies changed sides, and the next war found an Anglo-Prussian alliance against a Franco-Austrian alliance. As Russia was already the ally of Austria, and France had now become the antagonist of Prussia, it seemed logical enough for the court of Elizabeth to pursue its own vendetta against Prussia by extending its alliance system to France, which it did in January 1756 (Treaty of Versailles). The consummation of this series of realignments left Prussia as the smallest of the continental great powers – and supported only by maritime Britain – facing the three large continental powers, France, Austria and Russia together. It was a mortal threat, to say the least.

Frederick fought with characteristic genius, exploiting the opportunities that ramshackle coalitions always provide their enemies, but it was an awesome and daunting challenge that he confronted. The Russian army in particular administered him damaging defeats at Gross-Jägersdorf in 1757 and at Zorndorf in 1758, and an Austro-Russian army dealt him another serious blow at Kunersdorf in 1759. The Russians occupied Königsberg and East Prussia in 1758 and Berlin in 1760. Frederick despaired of victory and actually sought an honourable death fighting in the front lines of battle. He was saved, however, by fortunes beyond his influence.

The heir to the Russian throne was Elizabeth's nephew, Grand Duke Peter, Duke of Holstein, an enthusiastic admirer of Frederick. The commanders of the Russian armies all dreaded the consequences of dealing to Frederick's armies a death-blow only to discover on the morrow the demise of Elizabeth, who was well known to be aged and ailing, and the accession to the Russian throne of Frederick's protector, Peter III. Hence they refused to press their campaign with the customary vigour and opportunism. Bestuzhev himself was not above the suspicion of being caught in this net of intrigue, as he was on close terms with some of the Russian field commanders and was necessarily sensitive to opinion at the 'young court'. He was consequently relieved of his duties in 1758. In these circumstances, the war dragged on until Elizabeth's death obliged her enemies in January 1762, and what had been anticipated materialised: Peter III left the coalition and offered Frederick both peace and an alliance. Peter was himself, however, one of those royal transients of the era of palace revolutions. He ruled a mere half year before being overturned and murdered. In the Peace of Hubertusburg, Frederick retained Silesia, and Russia acquired nothing.

Russian foreign policy of the era of palace revolutions, then, had cost the country a good deal and gained it little but unrealised potential influence.

Catherine II

In the eighteenth century, the real sport of kings – of despots enlightened or not – was the aggrandisement of power. Enlightened despotism as a paradigm of modernisation conceived and driven by the state was as unpopular in eighteenth-century Russia as it was imperative. According to a celebrated European witticism of the age, the government of Russia in the era was a despotism tempered by assassination. No idle joke, assassination and the threat of it were a persistent means of intimidating progressive governments all over Europe in the eighteenth century – the age of the nobles' revolt.[2] Catherine II discovered early the force of conservative reaction – it spoiled her Legislative Assembly and her plans to improve the lot of the serfs. Her successor Paul paid for it with his life, and his successor Alexander was made to fear for his own. In the words of Catherine's most ambitious historian, V. A. Bil'basov: 'It is a big mistake to think that there is no public opinion in Russia. Because there are no proper forms of the expression of public opinion,

2 The nobles' revolt took an impressive toll of progressive statesmen of the age. Catherine was merely intimidated. Joseph II was ruined. Frederick II took refuge in cynicism and realpolitik. Friedrich Struensée was brutally executed. Gustav III was assassinated. Gustav Adolf IV was persuaded with a knife at his throat to abdicate. The Marquis de Pombal was tried for treason and banished. Carlos III of Spain sacrificed the Marqués de Esquilache to the demands of the angry crowds; and Louis XVI surrendered Chancellor Maupeou.

it is manifested in improper ways, by fits and starts, solely at crucial historical junctures, with a force that is all the greater and in forms that are all the more peculiar.'[3] The nobles' revolt weighed especially heavily on politics at home, but, as we shall see, foreign policy was not utterly immune to its influence either.

Catherine soon emerged as one of the master diplomats of the time and perhaps, in terms of material achievements, the grand champion of the competition for aggrandisement in her era. Proceeding evidently neither by a blueprint nor without some distinct conception of Russian interests, she was a consummate opportunist, not always without mistakes certainly. All politics, she famously observed, were reduced to three words, 'circumstance, conjecture, and conjuncture',[4] and her diplomacy would be a monument to the principle, if principle is what it was.

If Peter I's achievements in Sweden and Poland had been considerable, there had been some backsliding, some lost ground, in both areas during the era of palace revolutions, and Catherine was to address herself to articulation and repair. In both Poland and Sweden, she would meddle in constitutional questions, as different as they were in the two environments, bribing and supporting political parties in Sweden with money, in Poland supporting or suppressing them with arms. The Turkish challenge she left for the presentation of opportunity.

In the meantime, Catherine evidently appreciated what her neighbouring great powers demonstrably did also, that the geographical position of Russia in Europe enabled it to combine effectively with or against both the weak border states and the more imposing great powers beyond them, while it was difficult for the other powers to bring their strength to bear effectively against Russia. She exploited these advantages artfully.

The first serious issue to arise was Polish. The Polish constitution was notorious for the vulnerability of its vagaries: elective monarchy, liberum veto and the armed confederacies that nourished seemingly perpetual civil war. In this instance, August II was growing old and ill, suggesting a succession crisis. Austria would support a Saxon candidate, because he would be hostile to Prussia. Catherine had her own favourite, a genuine Piast, her own former lover, Stanislaus Poniatowski, acceptable also to Frederick II. Catherine then chose to arrange an alliance with Prussia addressed chiefly to the Polish

3 V. A. Bil'basov, *Istoriia Ekateriny Vtoroi*, 3 vols. (1, 2, 12) (Berlin: Gottgeiner, 1896–1900), vol. I, pp. 473–4.

4 A. V. Khrapovitskii, *Dnevnik* (St Petersburg: Tip. M. M. Stasiulevicha, 1874), p. 4. My thanks to John Alexander for this reference.

issue. When Augustus died in October 1763, Catherine and Frederick signed a treaty to support Poniatowski and to maintain unchanged the anarchical Polish constitutional arrangements (April 1764).

There were gains and losses here. If the gains were obvious, this was the first time that Russia had shared power with a German state in Poland, an area formerly a nearly exclusive Russian sphere of influence. Catherine's chief adviser in foreign policy, Nikita Panin, regarded the arrangement as the foundation of his 'Northern System', a series of alliances in which he intended to include Britain, Sweden and Denmark, a system dedicated to keeping the peace of the North and preventing the intrusion of disturbing influences from the most conspicuous south European system of Austria, France and Spain. The Northern System gave Russia little leverage against the Turks, but so long as Austria was allied with France and France continued to support the Turks, Russian alliance with Austria made little sense. On the other hand, an alliance with Denmark in March 1765 and the manipulation of the triumph of the pro-Russian Cap Party in the Swedish Riksdag at the same time enhanced the Northern System.

Catherine then turned her attention in good Enlightenment fashion to the rights of the religious dissidents in Poland, and in this question she overplayed her hand. She and Panin were willing to countenance limited constitutional reforms in Poland – though Frederick was not – but only in exchange for rights of toleration for religious minorities, while the Poles were largely adamant on the issue of Catholic supremacy, and so the prospects of reform on both issues soon foundered. Orthodox and Catholic confederacies formed, the former supported by Russian military intervention, and the conflict dragged on for years, opening up just such nefarious prospects as the conflict with the Turks that soon ensued.

It was perhaps predictable that a protracted Russian military engagement in Poland would draw into the maelstrom of East European politics a conflict with the other two border states, Turkey and Sweden, as well. The Turks reacted first. Alarmed at the portended shift of the balance of power in their part of the world and encouraged by the powers that shared their fears, the French and the Austrians, they responded to a cross-border raid of Cossack irregulars in summer 1768 and declared war.

The Russian military campaign may be characterised as distinguished and difficult at once. A variety of able commanders, Petr Rumiantsev, Aleksandr Suvorov, Grigorii Potemkin, dealt the Turks serious blows. Meantime, however, the situation grew immensely complicated as a variety of new factors intruded.

The first was Catherine's astonishingly stubborn and ambitious pretentions. She was determined to pursue the campaign to a glorious conclusion, to diminish the Turks if not ruin them and drive them out of Europe. These aspirations could only raise apprehensions elsewhere. The French were naturally committed to the Turks. The Austrians were threatened by Russian successes. The alliance of small and indigent Prussia with St Petersburg required Frederick to pay throughout the war subsidies that he could ill afford. The Swedes naturally found in Russian involvement in two fronts already an opportunity that they could scarcely overlook. In August 1772, the young Gustav III executed a coup d'état to scrap the constitution of 1720, which had placed power in the hands of the four estates of the Riksdag (the Age of Freedom), enabling Russia (and other powers) to manipulate Swedish party politics advantageously. Gustav thus restored constitutional absolutism while Catherine was too engaged elsewhere to do anything about it. In fact, this development portended a new war on yet another front, and Catherine apprehensively deployed troops to deal with it, though it did not actually happen. At the same time, the plague broke out in Moscow (1771), and the stresses and strains of the war in the form of tax and recruitment burdens on the population provoked the infamous Pugachev rebellion (September 1773). This accumulation of liabilities would have undermined the resolve of a pantheon of heroes, but it did not move Catherine, and the longer she persisted, the more the powers of Europe moved to persuade her.

The resolution of what appeared to be an adamantine stalemate of Catherine against Europe was one that had long been bruited about the chanceries of the continent, and it was recommended in this instance by the imaginative covetousness of Frederick: the partition of Poland. The Poles were helpless to resist, their territory would substitute for at least some of the sacrifices that Catherine might demand of the Turks, and the acquisitions that Austria and Prussia would share would reconcile them to Catherine's gains in the south. And so in August 1772 the deal was struck. Meantime, the Russo-Turkish War continued until the Turks, finally exhausted, conceded the essence of defeat and signed with St Petersburg the Treaty of Kuchuk-Kainardzhi (July 1774), one of the most signal Russian military and diplomatic achievements of the era. It stipulated – ominously – the independence of the Crimea; the right of free commercial navigation on the Black Sea and through the straits; a large Turkish indemnity; the right to fortify Azov and Taganrog; annexation of the Black Sea coast between the Dnieper and the Bug; and ill-defined, controversial rights to some kind of protection of Christians in the Ottoman Empire.

The turning of the 1770s to the 1780s marks a watershed in the nature and aspirations of Catherine's foreign policy. The new orientation is explained by several factors; in fact, by several developments of simple good fortune that came Catherine's way quite without any effort on her part.

The first of these was the by-product of the constant rivalry between Austria and Prussia. Joseph II, relentlessly restless, had long harboured the scheme of the so-called Bavarian Exchange. He wished to acquire large parts of Bavaria for Austria, compensating the Bavarian dynasty by the cession of the Austrian Netherlands. Opportunity arose in December 1777, when the Bavarian branch of the Wittelsbach family died without heirs, leaving a complicated and disputed succession. Joseph struck an agreement with the legitimate heir in a cadet branch of the family, the Elector Palatine, and thereupon decided to execute his claims to Bavarian dominions. Naturally, Frederick II objected to uncompensated Austrian aggrandisement, and he called upon his ally Catherine for support and for mediation of the conflict. In the meantime, Joseph similarly called upon his ally in Paris. Catherine was most reluctant to be involved in a war in Germany, as tension with the Turks threatened to renew the conflict in the south of Russia. At the same time, the French, on the verge of entering the American War of Independence, were similarly determined not to be encumbered by a war in Germany. As the crisis played out, the French and the Russians agreed to mediate jointly between the two German powers. The result was the signature of the Treaty of Teschen (May 1779), whereby Joseph acquired modest portions of Bavaria while promising to support comparable Prussian acquisitions elsewhere in Germany. For St Petersburg, the most significant feature of the problem was the acquisition by Russia of the status as guarantor of the German constitution, a serious gain in prestige as well as an instrument for legitimate participation in German politics.

The second such opportunity to come Catherine's way was the American War of Independence. In February 1778, France entered the war in alliance with the rebellious colonies. Virtually simultaneously, then, the two great land powers of Central Europe and the two great maritime powers of Western Europe had entered traditional conflicts with each other such as to divert all their attention away from that increasingly Russian sphere of influence, Eastern Europe. Catherine did not hesitate to see her opportunity or to exploit it.

A British war always entailed the issue of neutral trade, in particular the neutrals' doctrine of 'free ships, free goods'. The British maintained that if trade in neutral ships between a mother country and its colonies was illegal in peacetime – the rules of mercantilism – then it was illegal in wartime. To put the matter another way, London insisted that neutral shipping had no right to deliver a combatant country from the pressure of its enemy's hostilities. The neutrals, on the other hand, invariably attempted to step into the breach that the British navy inflicted on trade between French colonies and the mother country. The American war simply revived an ancient issue.

In these circumstances, the British brought pressure against the Scandinavian neutrals and the Dutch. In this instance, the northern neutrals appealed to Catherine to support their cause. Catherine saw her opportunity and announced first her principles and subsequently the treaties of the League of Armed Neutrality (August–September 1780): no paper blockades; freedom of neutrals to trade along the coasts of belligerents; free ships, free goods; and a narrow definition of contraband. Eventually supported by Prussia and Austria as well, the league brought considerable pressure against British maritime practice. Wherein lay Catherine's advantage? It helped to free Russia from excessive dependence on British shipping. It enabled the neutrals to carry Russian trade formerly carried by British shipping. The force of the League of Armed Neutrality persuaded the British to make serious adjustments for a time in their cherished maritime practices. It won Catherine considerable diplomatic favour all over northern Europe, and in the wake of the lustre of her triumph at Teschen, it enhanced yet more Catherine's and Russia's prestige. It was a victory of considerable significance for Catherine.

These developments enabled Catherine to reorient her foreign policy from the formerly northern European impetus of Panin's system onto the increasingly promising direction of the south. The turn towards the south made a good deal of sense from the viewpoint of the economic development of the empire. Peter I's incorporation of the Baltic coast had paid off in handsome commercial opportunities. In the south, moreover, the land was richer, it was sparsely settled, the growing season was longer, and the ancient Greek ports in the area illustrated clearly enough the commercial possibilities of the region.

In the meantime, a struggle for influence at the Russian court climaxed such as to serve the new orientation of Russian policy. Nikita Panin lost the struggle to Prince Grigorii Potemkin and his associate in Catherine's foreign chancery, A. A. Bezborodko. What the change portended was the abandonment of the Prussian alliance and Panin's favoured Northern System, its emphasis on peace and the status quo, and a turn towards the grander ambitions of Potemkin in south Russia at the expense of the Turks. The project of driving the Turks out of the Balkans was the kind of affair that appealed to Catherine's vanity.

The new outlook was soon embodied in an exchange of notes between Catherine and Joseph II, an exchange that stipulated the notorious grand design known as the 'Greek Project'. It envisioned a partitioning of the Ottoman dominions of the Balkans between Russia and Austria; the establishment of an independent kingdom of Dacia in Romania, presumably for Prince Potemkin; and, in the event of sufficient military success, the complete destruction of Turkey and the restoration of the ancient Byzantine Empire under Catherine's grandson, appropriately named Constantine.

In the wake of the Treaty of Kuchuk-Kainardzhi, the Crimea had degenerated into civil war between the Russian and the Turkish parties. In April 1783, the last native puppet ruler of the territory abdicated in favour of the Russian crown, and the annexation of the territory to Russia was proclaimed. It is possible that Catherine was thus trying to provoke a renewal of the Turkish war, but the Turks prudently held their fire.

The war was nevertheless not long in coming. Catherine's new ally, Joseph II, paid her a visit, and together they took a spectacular and provocative trip to New Russia in the south in summer 1787. By this time a Russian Black Sea fleet graced the harbour of Sebastopol. The visit itself was a tangible symbol of the widely rumoured Greek Project, and it sufficed to provoke a Turkish declaration of war. Swedish and Polish responses to the opportunity were not long in coming. Gustav III of Sweden declared war on Russia in July 1788. Fortunately for Russia, his campaign was handicapped by the revolt of some of his officers, and he was forced to conclude the Treaty of Verelä (August 1790) on the basis of the territorial status quo ante bellum.

The campaign against the Turks was hampered by a revolt in the Austrian Netherlands, the death of Joseph II and the diversion of Austrian attention to the challenge of the French Revolution. Catherine thus had to content herself with much less than her dreams of the Greek Project. The Treaty of Jassy (January 1792) enabled Russia to annex Ochakov and the territory between the Dniester and the Bug and recognised the annexation of the Crimea. Catherine did not, however, surrender the Greek Project, which was written explicitly into the Austro-Russian treaty of January 1795.

Neither had the Poles neglected the opportunity provided by Russian war with both the Turks and the Swedes. Unfortunately for them, they were engaged by the intrigues of King Frederick William II of Prussia in a series of illusions both foreign and domestic. Counting on the support of a new alliance with Prussia, the Poles devoted themselves belatedly to constitutional reform, scrapping elective monarchy, the liberum veto and the practice of confederations alike (the constitution of 3 May 1791). Succession to the throne was settled on a hereditary basis in the House of Saxony. These noble efforts soon fell victim to characteristically Polish ill fortune, however, as the Russians made peace with Sweden and Turkey, and the coming of the French Revolution turned the attention of Prussia and Austria westwards. Catherine had in these circumstances no trouble sponsoring a party of her own in Poland and sent an army to support it. In the face of this challenge, Frederick William shamelessly deserted his new Polish ally and consummated an alliance with Russia for a new partition of Poland (January 1793). The second partition provoked a patriotic revolt led by the hero of the American Revolution, Tadeusz Kosciuszko, but the combined actions of the armies of Russia, Prussia and Austria condemned it to fail, and the third partition consummated the oblivion of Poland (several treaties of 1795–7).

By reference to the standards prevailing in the age, the foreign policy of Catherine was a great success. She conquered 200,000 square miles of new territory and expanded the Russian population from 19,000,000 to 36,000,000.

Yet there is here another element of this story, one taken too little into account. If the opposition of the Russian nobility to the reforming aspirations of the monarchy is well known, its opposition to Russian foreign policy is less familiar.

The Greek Project, for example, provoked dissent even in the inner circle of Catherine's government. As the French ambassador reported in 1786, 'the Russian ministers' loathed the plans of Potemkin.

> Their secret wishes are for peace; war and conquests do not offer them any personal advantage; each of them sees in [war and conquests] . . . complications for their departments [of government] and fatal possibilities for the empire. [Alexander] Vorontsov fears the stagnation of commerce; Bezborodko, numerous obstacles in the course of diplomacy; all of them [fear] the growth of the power of Prince Potemkin, [but] everyone dissimulates his opinions for fear of losing the favor of the empress.[5]

The Austrian ambassador, Louis de Cobenzl, reported the same attitudes in 1795: 'The entire Russian ministry, without exception, disapproves this project of the empress.'[6] The second partition of Poland exhibits the same conflict. The opposition gathered around Alexander Vorontsov, but it was the expansionist party around Potemkin and the Zubovs that triumphed.

In fact, the phenomenon was far older and broader than we have appreciated. We may recall the division of Russian society over Ivan IV's Livonian War or the Dolgorukiis and Golitsyns who transferred the capital briefly back to Moscow in 1727. An English diplomat characterised the nobility's attitude typically in the 1740s:

5 Louis-Philippe de Ségur, *Mémoires*, 3 vols. (Paris: Eymery, 1827), vol. II, pp. 293–4.
6 Cobenzl to Thugut, 5 January 1795; Alfred von Arneth (ed.), 'Thugut und sein politisches System', *Archiv für österreichische Geschichte*, 42 (1870): 442.

> There is not one among [them] who does not wish St Petersburg at the bottom of the sea and all the conquered provinces gone to the devil; then they could all move back to Moscow, where, in the vicinity of their estates, they could all live better and cheaper. Moreover, they are convinced that it would in general be much better for Russia to have no more to do with the affairs of Europe than it formerly did but to limit itself to the defense of its own [traditional] old territories.[7]

The nobility wished in particular to limit the burden of armaments as much as possible.

And yet the remarkable nineteenth-century commercial progress of the newly founded port city of Odessa does speak pointedly to the breadth of Catherine's vision.[8] In any event, Catherine was obviously able to master dissent in foreign policy as she was not able to do in reform at home. And yet, the social dynamic of protest in foreign policy continued. It was clearly present in the reign of Tsar Paul, though it may not have been the chief motivation behind the tragedy of his demise. It was more important, yet still rarely decisive, in the reign of Alexander.

The metamorphosis of the 1790s

The notoriously expansionist nature of Catherine's foreign policy underwent decisive changes in the decade of the 1790s. The new policy was explained in part by alterations in the geopolitical environment.

First, Russian power by the end of Catherine's reign had acquired a secure hold on the Baltic and Black Sea coasts. It thus abutted there on something as nearly like natural frontiers as it is possible to imagine in the circumstances of the time and place. The two seacoasts were of great economic advantage, and as Russia was not a major sea power, it is not easy to imagine its expansion beyond these seas.

7 Robert E. Jones, 'The Nobility and Russian Foreign Policy, 1560–1811', *CMRS* 34 (1993): 159–70, and Robert E. Jones, 'Opposition to War and Expansion in Late Eighteenth Century Russia', *JfGO* 32 (1984): 34–51. Quotation in Walther Mediger, *Moskaus Weg nach Europa: der Aufstieg Russlands zum europäischen Machtstaat im Zeitalter Friedrichs des Grossen* (Braunschweig: Georg Westermann Verlag, 1952), pp. 108, 295.

8 Odessa, founded in 1794, was in 1900 the third largest city in Russia (excluding Warsaw), the conduit of 45 per cent of the foreign trade of the Russian Empire, including 40 per cent of the grain trade. Patricia Herlihy, *Odessa: A History, 1794–1917* (Cambridge, Mass.: Harvard University Press, 1986); I. M. Kulisher, *Ocherk istorii russkoi torgovli* (St Petersburg: Atenei, 1993); S. A. Pokrovskii, *Vneshniaia torgovlia i vneshniaia torgovaia politika Rossii* (Moscow: Mezhdunarodnaia kniga, 1947).

Second, Russia had acquired the bulk of Poland, and the disappearance of an independent Poland both removed a source of instability in East European politics and brought Russia to the frontier of two more stable and more formidable states, Austria and Prussia.

The third factor was the most obvious, the grandest international phenomenon of the age, the ravages of the traditional international order by the French Revolution; or French imperialism in the ideological guise of the war of peoples against kings (the notorious Propaganda Decrees of November and December 1792).

And yet a fourth factor of quite another kind was probably both the most volatile and the most influential. It was simply the personality and values of the new sovereigns, Paul and Alexander.

If Catherine was a masterful opportunist, if her most stable principles were 'circumstance, conjecture, and conjuncture', Paul was her polar opposite. Notoriously motivated by antagonism to his mother and her policies and characterised by some remarkably spastic impulses, Paul was also motivated by the respectable ideas of the age, the ideas of the Panin party, in particular the idea that Russia needed peace, good order and development of its domestic resources. The most basic elements of Paul's unusual personality were moralism and dedication to political and social stability. Even the axiom of legitimacy yielded in his outlook to considerations of political order. In most questions of principle, however, Paul was a literal-minded iconodule.[9]

The contrast with Catherine could not be clearer. Paul said that he regretted the partitions of Poland, and he released Tadeusz Kosciuszko from the Peter and Paul Fortress. He negotiated in 1797 with the French Republic in hopes of persuading it to moderate its foreign policy of conquest – but failed. He extended his protection to the Knights of Malta, whose principles of religion and morality he admired. Similarly, he offered the protection of Russia to the vulnerable German and Italian powers subject to the ravages of the French Revolution. From 1797–9, he three times summoned the powers of Europe to a general peace conference, but there was no response. When Bonaparte invaded Egypt, Paul signed an alliance with the Turks. Eventually convinced that the French Revolution threatened the entire order of Europe, he joined the Second Coalition. Subsequently convinced that the ambitions of his Coalition allies, the Austrians and the British, were as subversive of good order as those of the French, he demonstratively denounced them and left the coalition:

9 The following account is quite contrary to more traditional ones, and I have no space here to elaborate it and document it. See Hugh Ragsdale, 'Russia, Prussia, and Europe in the Policy of Paul I', *JfGO* 31 (1983): 81–118.

> I united with the powers that appealed to me for aid against the common enemy. Guided by honour, I have come to the assistance of humanity . . . But, having taken the decision to destroy the present government of France, I have never wished to tolerate another power's taking its place and becoming in its turn the terror of the neighbouring Princes . . . the revolution of France, having overturned all the equilibrium of Europe, it is essential to re-establish it, but in a common accord.[10]

He added that he sought the pacification of Europe, the general wellbeing, that honour was his only guide. If these documents display a kind of school-marm mentality, was the Alexander of the séances with Julie Krüdener and the Holy Alliance altogether different?

Disappointed in his British allies of the Second Coalition and offended by British naval and commercial policy, he renewed the Armed Neutrality. More ambitiously, he attempted to make it the nucleus of a project that he called the Northern League, designed to include Russia, Prussia, Denmark, Sweden, Saxony and Hanover. The purpose of this constellation of powers was to achieve the pacification of Europe by the instrument of armed mediation. In particular, it was intended to restrain the ambitions of both Austria and France and to preserve the integrity of the German constitution. The Prussians, alas, lacked the heart for so bold a move, and so it failed. The Northern League, then, was reduced to the League of Armed Neutrality, and when the Prussians hesitated to perform Paul's conception of their duty by occupying Hanover, he sent an ultimatum demanding it within twenty-four hours. They complied on 30 March 1801.

By this time, the new First Consul of the French Republic undertook to charm and seduce the reputedly volatile Paul. He dispatched overtures and gifts to St Petersburg, and Paul is supposed to have swooned and fallen prey to Bonaparte's conniving schemes. In fact, Paul was interested in co-operating with any government in France that conducted itself with responsible restraint. Hence he dispatched his terms to Paris: if Bonaparte would respect the legitimate old order in Italy and Germany, then Paul suggested that he should take the crown of France on a hereditary basis 'as the only means of establishing a stable government in France and of transforming the revolutionary principles that have armed all of Europe against her'.[11] This last suggestion was evidently premature, and Bonaparte had no intention of forswearing French

10 D. A. Miliutin, *Istoriia voiny 1799 goda mezhdu Rossieii Frantsiei v tsarstvovanie imperatora Pavla I*, 2nd edn, 3 vols. (St Petersburg: Imperatorskaia akademiia nauk, 1857), vol. II, pp. 553–8, vol. III, pp. 444–5.

11 *Russkii arkhiv*, 1874, no. 2, columns 961–6.

conquests. Paul's antagonism towards London was plain to see, however, and Bonaparte was able to manage the appearance of it sufficiently to create the false impression of a Franco-Russian alliance. As a British fleet entered the Baltic to deal with the Armed Neutrality, a conspiracy of assassins did their work in St Petersburg, and Paris soon faced a quite different government in Russia.

Only one contemporary seems to have understood the foreign policy of Russia in this reign, the Bavarian minister at the court of St Petersburg, the Chevalier François-Gabriel de Bray:

> Russia has no system, the whims of its sovereign are its whole policy . . .
>
> His intentions, however, are always the same. Perhaps no prince has been more constantly occupied with the same idea, more imbued with the same sentiment; and it is . . . not a little extraordinary to see this instability of actions joined so intimately to this constancy of principle.
>
> A scrupulous probity, the sincere desire to see each one come into possession of his own legitimate rights, an innate penchant for despotism, a certain chivalrous turn of spirit, which makes him capable of the most generous resolutions, or the most rash, have constantly guided Paul in his relations with the other powers. He placed himself at the head of the Coalition by sentiment and not by interest . . .
>
> This Monarch wanted to make himself the restorer of Europe, the one to redress all wrongs. He believed that in declaring that he had no designs of ambition, no interests [to pursue], he would prompt the others to do as much . . .[12]

Roderick McGrew comes to similar conclusions. 'Paul was a moralist rather than a politician; it was this which gave a utopian cast to those projects which were nearest to his heart, and a totalitarian tone to the ensemble of his policies.'[13] A good example is his fascination with the Knights of Malta.

> The knights of Malta, reformed and revived . . . were integral to his plans for confronting and defeating revolutionary Jacobinism. He . . . had invited Europe's displaced nobility to come to Russia where he was building a bastion against the destructive forces of the modern world . . . It was for this great enterprise that he was taking over the knights, mobilizing the *émigrés*, and inviting the pope's participation . . . From Paul's perspective, the knights would [also] . . . serve as a model for raising the moral consciousness of the Russian nobility . . . another means to further Paul's moral revolution.[14]

12 F.-G. de Bray, 'La Russie sous Paul I', *Revue d'histoire diplomatique* 23 (1909): 594–6.
13 R. E. McGrew, *Paul I of Russia, 1754–1801* (Oxford: Clarendon, 1992), p. 16.
14 McGrew, *Paul*, pp. 276–7.

McGrew finds – as did the Chevalier de Bray – the fundamental elements of Paul's foreign policy to be stable and consistent. Paul found Russia's vital interests in a stable and lasting peace in Europe. He preferred hereditary monarchy, but the form of government was less important than its behaviour. It was the expansionist policy of the Directory rather than its republican nature that provoked Paul's hostility. Aggressive states were objectionable whether republican or monarchical.

> His principles, in foreign as well as domestic policy, marked out the Russian future . . . he attempted to open new directions in Russian foreign policy. In all of his efforts, he showed himself to be disinterested. He had no territorial claims to make; he offered himself as a mediator and . . . a guardian [of the smaller powers]. The Europe Paul wanted to see was one in which each state would be safe, in which there was justice for the smaller principalities as well as protection . . . The ideas he pursued became the writ of post-Napoleonic Europe; what he failed to create at the end of the eighteenth century, Metternich finally realized between 1815 and 1848.[15]

Alexander I

As Alexander assumed power, the most urgent issue was the approach of the English fleet, which, having left the wreck of Copenhagen (2 April 1801) in its wake, was sailing for St Petersburg. Alexander assured his allies of the Armed Neutrality that he would not forsake them and their common principles, but he warned that these principles were subject to some accommodation with London. In the maritime convention embodying that accommodation, the English surrendered paper blockades, and the Russians surrendered everything else, including the issue of 'free ships, free goods' as well as English rights of search of vessels under convoy. Denmark and Sweden adhered with obvious reluctance to the Anglo-Russian settlement. In the meantime, the British fleet left the Baltic, and Alexander lifted the Russian embargo on British trade.

There was irony in the Russian position in this conflict. According to the observation of a rather canny American diplomat on temporary assignment in Berlin, John Quincy Adams, 'the question whether free ships shall make free goods is to the empire of Russia, *in point of interests*, of the same importance that the question whether the seventh commandment is conformable to the law of Nature would be to the guardian of a Turkish Haram'.[16] Two sovereigns as

15 McGrew, *Paul*, pp. 17, 320.

16 Adams to Secretary of State, 31 January 1801; US National Archives, Record Group 59. Emphasis added (HR).

different as Catherine and Paul had, however, subscribed to the same principle, and as Alexander wrote to his ambassador in Stockholm before the convention was signed, 'The pretensions of the English are absurd . . . their conduct is revolting, the exclusive dominion of the seas to which they presume is an outrage to the sovereigns of the commercial states and an offense to the rights of all peoples.'[17] Alexander was disgusted by the new British attack on Copenhagen, and he would repeat this whole set of attitudes both before and after Tilsit.

Once the crisis of conflict with Britain had passed, Alexander circulated to Russian embassies abroad his first general exposition of foreign policy. In traditionally familiar fashion, he announced the withdrawal of Russia from European affairs as formerly argued by N. I. Panin and represented in Alexander's own reign by V. P. Kochubei. Aggrandisement, Alexander said, was inappropriate for so vast a state as Russia. He wanted no part of the 'intestine dissensions' of Europe and was indifferent to the question of the forms of foreign governments, as Paul obviously had been. His aim, rather, was to give his people the blessing of peace. In other words, he was at this point isolationist, non-interventionist. Yet even here there was a hint of ambivalence. If he took up arms, Alexander said, it would only be to protect his people or the victims of aggrandisement threatening the security of Europe.

As Alexander turned to the next major item of unfinished business inherited from his father, the negotiation with the First Consul, he found that he was, on the one hand, obliged by the treaties and other commitments of the previous reign; and, on the other hand, he was embarrassed by many of them. Though he admitted that his obligations in Italian questions were awkward, Alexander continued to solicit generous treatment for the kingdoms of Naples and Sardinia. In fact, Bonaparte, as soon as he learned of the death of Paul, hastened in both principalities to make pre-emptive arrangements – closing of ports, stationing of French troops in Naples, preparations for annexations in Sardinia – before Alexander could intervene, and Alexander was left with little choice in questions about which at the time he did not seem deeply to care. When the treaty of peace and the accompanying political convention were signed, they reflected French wishes. As in the treaty of Teschen, the two powers would mediate German indemnities. Russia was to mediate French peace with the Turks. Bonaparte engaged himself to maintain the integrity of Naples as stipulated in the treaty that French troops had just imposed on it

17 Alexander to Budberg, 9/21 April 1801; *Vneshniaia politika Rossii XIX i nachala XX veka*, ed. A. L. Narochnitskii et al., 8 vols. (Moscow: Politizdat, 1960–1972), vol. I, p. 19.

(28 March 1801), and French troops were to remain there until the fate of Egypt was settled. The reference to Sardinia was a gossamer gloss leaving the French army fully in charge there.

In the reorganisation of Germany, Alexander's wishes were simple: to alter the German constitution as little as possible and to strengthen Germany such as to avoid revolutionary anarchy and make it more capable of resisting French aggression. What happened here was that Bonaparte was able to use the principle of secularisation of ecclesiastical estates – how many divisions had the pope? – and the proximity and the power of France to reward and seduce the south German states, thus converting them from Russian clients into French satellites.

In the lull of 1801–5 between the two storms of the Second and Third Coalitions, Alexander found a respite for deliberate reflection on the issues of foreign affairs, and here we find a rare and genuinely interesting effort to enunciate something like an official doctrine of Russian foreign policy. The first compelling conception to emerge was the presentation of V. P. Kochubei to the Unofficial Committee in summer 1801. It envisaged a remarkable harmony of domestic and foreign policy, and its basic principles were clear and persuasive.

Russia had two natural enemies, Kochubei maintained, Sweden and Turkey, and two natural rivals, Austria and Prussia. Both Sweden and Turkey were weak, unable to challenge Russia dangerously, and the best policy was simply to maintain them in their present condition, weak enough to be harmless, not so weak as to require the protection of Russia from the designs of another great power. The notorious antagonism of Prussia and Austria required both to solicit the favour of Russia, a state of affairs that easily enabled Russia to preserve a constructive sphere of influence in the German Empire. Russia, Kochubei observed, was sufficiently great both in population and in geographical extent to enjoy extraordinary national security. It had little to fear from other powers so long as it did not interfere in their affairs; yet it had too often entered the quarrels of Europe that affected Russia only indirectly, entailing costly and useless wars. In so far as possible, Russia needed to remain aloof from European alliances and alignments, to establish a long period of peace and prudent administration.

There was, however, even in the midst of these pacific sentiments, one jarring note. It was agreed in a fashion reminiscent of Alexander's foreign-policy manifesto of 17 July 1801 that surrendering the continent to the inordinate ambition of Bonaparte was not an acceptable option.

Unfortunately, the First Consul of the French Republic declined Alexander's pleas for moderation and peace and challenged the order of Europe in a fashion that could not be ignored. Bonaparte annexed Piedmont (April 1801), imposed satellite regimes in the Netherlands (October 1801) and Switzerland (February 1802), made himself First Consul for life (August 1802), then Emperor (May / December 1804), president of the new Italian Republic (February 1802) and subseqently King of Italy (May 1805), manipulated the Imperial Recess to his advantage (1803 ff.), seized the Duc d'Enghien in Baden, the home of the Tsaritsa Elizabeth of Russia, executed him (February 1804) and annexed Genoa (June 1805). The Third Coalition was naturally soon in the making.

By this time, Alexander had come under the influence of a remarkable friendship and the very different foreign-policy ideas that it engendered. As a young man of only nineteen years, Alexander had made the acquaintance of the Polish Prince Adam Jerzy Czartoryski. The two shared a passion for liberal ideas of statecraft and justice, and Alexander confessed emotionally to Czartoryski his embarrassment at his grandmother's partitions of Poland. There were hints of Alexander's intention to rectify the injustice, and it was clearly not a transient idea. In 1812 he was still writing about it to Czartoryski: 'Quel est le moment le plus propre pour prononcer la régénération de la Pologne?'[18] Scarcely any sentiment could have brought the two men more nearly together. As the brief honeymoon of concord with the French Republic dissipated and a new conflict loomed, Czartoryski had become in 1803–4 de facto and then actual minister of foreign affairs. At this point, a new foreign-policy programme was formed.

While V. P. Kochubei had argued that strategic invulnerability *conferred* upon Russia the good fortune of being able to follow an isolationist foreign policy, Czartoryski argued on the contrary that it *imposed* on Russia the obligation to follow an activist policy. Russia, he insisted, would most easily find its own peace by leading the continent to a peaceful condition. Obviously the biggest threat to the peace of Europe at the time was the expansionist policy of France, and that fact made it natural for Great Britain and Russia to seek each other's alliance against the threat. Once French power were curtailed, they agreed, it could best be contained by restoring the independence of the Italian states and forming a confederation of western German states on the French frontier.

18 W. H. Zawadzki, *A Man of Honour: Adam Czartoryski as a Statesman of Russia and Poland, 1795–1831* (Oxford: Clarendon, 1993), p. 36. P. K. Grimsted, *The Foreign Ministers of Alexander I: Political Attitudes and the Conduct of Russian Diplomacy, 1801–1825* (Berkeley: University of California Press, 1969), pp. 44, 46, 47. A. Gielgud (ed.), *Adam Czartoryski: Memoirs and correspondence with Alexander I*, 2 vols. (Orono: Academic International Press, 1968), vol. I, pp. 95–8. Alexander to Czartoryski, 1/13 April 1812; *Vneshniaia politika Rossii*, vol. VI, p. 351.

As Kochubei had also observed, the antagonism of Austria and Prussia would naturally force them to follow Russia's lead. Russia might well undertake a kind of Pan-Slav drive to liberate the Balkan Slavs from the Turks, sharing some of the spoils with Austria if necessary, especially if there were a threat of French imperialism in that area. Moreover, it made sense for Russia to redress the injustice of the Polish partitions, the more so as sharing those spoils with the neighbouring German states worked to Russia's disadvantage. Russia could easily win her Slavic brethren the Poles to her cause by re-establishing the kingdom under Russian Grand Duke Constantine.

> The policy of Russia must be grand, benevolent and disinterested . . . It must assure the tranquillity of all of Europe in order to assure its own and in order not to be distracted from its civilizing concerns [in developing] its own interior. Russia wants each power to have the advantages that justice confers on it, . . . the surest means of assuring the general equilibrium. But it will oppose with force any excessive ambition.[19]

This paper forms the background of the mission of N. N. Novosil'tsev to London in November 1804. Czartoryski drafted Novosil'tsev's instructions. If Russia should overstep the bounds of her own national interests – an important point – and mix in the affairs of Europe, he wrote, it should be for the purpose of establishing a benign and peaceful order of affairs on the continent of Europe, a permanent peace. The ascendancy of Bonaparte in Europe threatened, he said, to supplant all notions of justice, of right, and of morality in international affairs by the triumph of crime and iniquity and thus to suspend the security of the continent in general. Proceeding from these principles, he set out Alexander's particular aims: to return France to its ancient borders; to give it a new government; to liberate Sardinia, Switzerland and the Netherlands; to force the French evacuation of Naples and of Germany; to preserve the Turks – always a volatile and slippery issue – and to form larger states or a federation of states on the French frontiers as a barrier to French expansion.

In order to make success in the war as sure as possible, Alexander contemplated an imitation of Paul's policy of forcing a reluctant Prussia to take part in the coalition (Alexander's so-called *Mordplan*). In the peace to follow, Alexander imagined calling for something like national frontiers drawn along clearly recognisable lines of nationality and/or natural frontiers (a concept which would have disintegrated his own kingdom). Finally,

19 P. K. Grimsted (ed.), 'Czartoryski's System for Russian Foreign Policy: A Memorandum', *California Slavic Studies* 5 (1970): 19–91.

Alexander proposed a kind of concert system to sustain the peace after the war was won. He professed to be motivated by nothing more than the 'general wellbeing'.

Meantime, never mind the fact that Alexander had conspired on war aims and peace terms with the British in advance; he nevertheless represented his plans of 1805 as an armed mediation! That is, he would present to the French and British governments alike the Anglo-Russian terms as those of a coalition of Russia and Austria – and Prussia if possible – in an effort to mediate the conflict between Britain and France.

Here is a most reasonable facsimile of the politics of crazy Paul, who was seeking to use his Russo-Prussian Northern League of the winter of 1800–1 for the same kind of armed mediation between the French on the one hand and the Anglo-Austrian alliance on the other. The idea of the Concert of Europe as it grew out of Vienna is more fully developed than anything that Paul had in mind, but he was notably congress prone. Short of the concert, and with the exception of the extravagances of the last two to three weeks of his life, it is essentially Paul's kind of plan, subject merely to the changes that the course of events had worked in political geography and alliances: that is, Bavaria and Württemberg had been indemnified sufficiently handsomely by Bonaparte to cease to look to Russia for protection, and while Paul had not stipulated in Paris in favour of Switzerland and the Netherlands, he had sent armies to liberate them. About the same time, Alexander renewed Paul's treaty of alliance with the Turks (11/23 September 1805).

Meantime, as implausible as it seems, Alexander did not hesitate, during his negotiations with the British, to urge their evacuation of the island of Malta, and he continued to defend the cause of neutral trade, both of which issues almost cost him the alliance of London. Taking the similarities of the policies of the two sovereigns into account, either Alexander and his allies were under the spell of Paul – a ludicrous suggestion – or there was method in Paul's madness. Or there was something in the context of Russian foreign policy driving very different personalities to similar geopolitical conceptions. That context was very likely the product of the educational values of the Enlightenment and the challenge that the French Revolution posed to conceptions of political order in Europe.

In any event, the awkward alliance – a compromise version of it – was made, and the Austrians adhered to it. War aims stipulated the French evacuation of north Germany (including Hanover), the Netherlands, Switzerland and Piedmont-Sardinia, as well as the augmentation of these territories such as to constitute in future a barrier to French expansion.

Of course, all of these grand plans went terribly awry. The Austro-Russian armies were crushed at the battle of Austerlitz in December 1805, whereupon Austria, deserted briefly by a panicked Alexander, made peace (Pressburg). Prussia, having persisted in the most undignified neutrality since 1795, rallied to the cause too late, and with equal lack of dignity, only to be routed utterly at Jena and Auerstädt in October 1806. Whereupon Russia, after extensive tergiversations, returned to the fray in the most inauspicious circumstances imaginable, carrying on the fight virtually alone until the lost battle of Friedland in June 1807, whereupon it, too, made peace.

By this time, Alexander was thoroughly disgusted with his former allies. As the Baron de Jomini remarked after the costly but indecisive battle of Eylau – February 1807, on the wintry plains of Poland, nearly a thousand miles from Paris – 'Ah, if only I were the Archduke Charles!' In Alexander's opinion, the British were worse than the Austrians. The great wartime prime minister, William Pitt, had died in January 1806, and the Ministry of All the Talents that followed him – Lord Grenville and Charles James Fox – was a vain misnomer. Until the coming of Viscount Castlereagh to the Foreign Office in March 1812, British foreign policy was simply adrift in demoralising, defeatist incompetence, and Alexander's grievances against London were multiple: Russia was bearing a disproportionate burden of the war; the British were niggardly with loans and subsidies; they might have but did not open in Western Europe something like a second front; their navy's enforcement of the British code of maritime commerce was an offence both to Russia and the neutrals. Finally, the Russians had stumbled imprudently into a war with Turkey for fear of Napoleon's designs on the Balkans, and London, always suspicious of the Russians' own designs in the East Mediterranean, stubbornly refused to assist them.

The war had ceased to be popular in Russia, and Alexander's frustration disposed him to a change of front. Here was the celebrated peace of Tilsit and the Franco-Russian alliance attached to it. It recognised the whole of the Napoleonic order of Europe, the Bonaparte dynasty in Naples, the Netherlands and Westphalia; the Grand Duchy of Warsaw; the Confederation of the Rhine; French possession of Cattaro and the Ionian Islands. Russia would mediate peace between France and Britain; France would mediate between Russia and Turkey; and, failing peace, each power would join the other at war. The ancient idea of the partition of the Ottoman Europe was stipulated. Russia would join the Continental System to bar British trade from the continent, and Portugal, Denmark and Sweden would be forced to join it as well.

Of course, this new system, so contrary to Czartoryski's, naturally had to be embodied in a new Russian foreign minister, Count N. P. Rumiantsev. Rumiantsev identified with it naturally, as he was the son of Field Marshal Petr A. Rumiantsev, who had led Catherine's successful campaigns against the Turks. Rumiantsev stood for a division of Europe into eastern/Russian and western/French spheres. Hence he represented one of two traditional variants of Russian foreign policy, the isolationist impulse that we formerly saw in V. P. Kochubei. If the peace was popular in Petersburg, however, the alliance was not. Alexander hoped in vain that the promised partition of the Ottoman Empire and the conquest of Swedish Finland would compensate for the substantial obligations and burdens of the alliance.

And now Alexander turned fondly again to his pet projects of liberal reform at home. This time, his whole 'secret committee' was concentrated in a single person, arguably the most able civil servant in the history of Russia, a priest's son who had married an English woman, Mikhail Speranskii. Alexander asked for the project of a constitution, and Speranskii drafted a prudently progressive document. The French alliance and the Speranskii constitution alike provoked the problem of public opinion again. Napoleon's emissaries carefully monitored the massive Russian discontent with the French alliance. General Savary reported that France had only two friends in Russia, the emperor and his foreign minister. One of Alexander's courtiers allegedly warned him bluntly, 'Take care, Sire, you will finish as your father did!'[20] Speranskii's constitution was naturally never implemented, but the mere drafting of it provoked consternation, and when the war of 1812 approached, Alexander, in deference to the good Russian sentiments that the nation at war would require, dismissed the unpopular Francophile Speranskii and the constitution with him. When another of his intimates questioned the dismissal of so devoted a public servant as Speranskii, Alexander responded, 'You are right, . . . only current circumstances could force me to make this sacrifice to *public opinion*.'[21]

In fact, the arrangements of Tilsit almost predictably contained irreconcilable elements of conflict. The most conspicuous factor here was the unlimited ambition of Napoleon. As Napoleon later remarked after his meeting with Alexander at Erfurt, Alexander expected to be treated as an equal, and it was not Napoleon's habit to deal with others as equals. Particular issues abounded. There was the persistent suspicion of the Grand Duchy of Warsaw. Moreover, Napoleon stubbornly refused to evacuate his troops from the

20 F. Ley, *Alexander I et la Sainte-Alliance* (Paris: Fischbacher, 1975), p. 32.

21 N. K. Shil'der, *Imperator Aleksandr Pervyi: ego zhizn' i tsarstvovanie*, 4 vols. (St Petersburg: Suvorin, 1897–1898), vol. III, pp. 41–2. Emphasis added (HR).

Prussian territory of Alexander's friend, King Frederick William of Prussia. Here were two offensive encroachments on Russian sensitivities in Eastern Europe. In addition, the Continental System was a burden: Britain was a natural commercial ally of Russia; France was not. Finally, Napoleon clearly had no intention of sharing what might have been the most ostentatious Russian benefit of the alliance, the Ottoman possessions of the Balkans. In December 1810, Alexander, thoroughly disillusioned now of the raptures of Tilsit, repudiated the Continental System, and the coming of war was only a matter of time.

The defeat of Napoleon in Russia faced Alexander with a dramatic foreign-policy choice. His commander of the armies, Field Marshal M. I. Kutuzov, stood shoulder to shoulder with Foreign Minister Rumiantsev: Russia was rid of Napoleon, and there was no need to send the armies into Europe. Alexander, however, perhaps predictably, followed the system formerly laid out by Czartoryski.

The Russo-Prussian Treaty of Kalisch (27 February 1813) stipulated an alliance to deliver the nations of the continent from the French yoke and the restoration of Prussia to its possessions of 1806. The Russo-Austro-Prussian Treaty of Toeplitz (9 September 1813) stipulated the restoration of the Austrian Empire, dissolution of Napoleon's Confederation of the Rhine, and an arrangement of the future fate of the Duchy of Warsaw agreeable to the three courts of Russia, Prussia and Austria. This last point, of course, was soon to become a subject of contention. The British joined the coalition in the treaty of Reichenbach (27 June 1813), which stipulated the restoration of Hanover to the British monarchy and, of course, subsidies for the continental powers.

By this time, the outline of the treaties of Vienna was emerging. The treaty of Chaumont (1 March 1814) committed the allies to a German confederation robust enough to sustain its independence; the restoration of an independent Switzerland; independent Italian states between Austria and France; the restoration of Ferdinand VI of Spain; an augmentation of the Netherlands under the sovereignty of the Prince of Orange; the accession of Portugal, Spain, Sweden and the Netherlands to the treaty; and a concert among the powers to maintain these peace terms for twenty years.

The first Treaty of Paris (30 May 1814) recognised Louis XVIII as king of France, reduced France to its frontiers of 1792, restored Malta to Great Britain and stipulated French recognition of the terms of Chaumont. The second Treaty of Paris (20 November 1815) – after Napoleon's return and the battle of Waterloo (18 June) – reduced France to the borders of 1790, assessed an indemnity of 700,000,000 francs and provided an allied army of occupation of 150,000 men supported by France for a period of three to five years.

The treaties of Vienna (9 June 1815) largely ratified the provisions of the preceding treaties with one large exception. By this date, however, Alexander had succumbed, contrary to the stipulations of Kalisch and Toeplitz, to Czartoryski's blandishments on the future of Poland. His wish to restore the Kingdom of Poland under his own auspices and to compensate Prussia for its consequent Polish sacrifices in the Kingdom of Saxony nearly provoked a war with Austria, Britain and France. Alexander compromised, chiefly at the expense of Prussia in Saxony, and peace was made.

Conclusion

One of the grand ironies of the history of Russian foreign policy related here is that foreign-born Catherine exerted herself in foreign affairs for strictly Russian interests, while native-born Paul and Alexander extended Russian protection to the interests of the continent as a whole. This fact is a product of the revolution in foreign-policy outlook that took place in Russia in the 1790s.[22]

In the murky record of Russian foreign-policy programmes and ideas, it is sometimes customary to identify two relatively distinct camps or lobbies. One is known variously as Russian, national, or Eastern; the other, as German, European, or Western.[23] These terms are so poorly documented, especially before the latter part of the nineteenth century, as to make generalisation about them a bit hazardous. Somehow, however, the first party is semi-isolationist. It is sometimes associated with the term *svoboda ruk* – *carte-blanche* more

22 One of the most striking documents on the virtues of Russian foreign policy as well as the continuity of it between 1796 and 1856 was the long instruction for Tsarevich Alexander Nikolaevich composed in 1838 by Nesselrode's assistant, Baron E. P. von Brunnow, an assistant to Foreign Minister Karl Nesselrode, 'Aperçu des principales transactions du Cabinet de Russie sous les règnes de Catherine II, Paul I et Alexander I.' *Sbornik russkago istoricheskago obshchestva*, 148 vols. (St Petersburg: Tip. M. M. Stasiulevicha, 1867–1916), vol. XXXI, pp. 197–416. It is a frank condemnation of the acquisitiveness of Catherine and an endorsement of the moral qualities of the policies of Paul and Alexander. At the other end of the political spectrum of the age was the outlook of Viscount Castlereagh and the British policy that he represented: 'When the Territorial Balance of Europe is disturbed [Great Britain] can interfere with effect, but She is the last Government in Europe, which can be expected, or can venture to commit Herself on any question of an abstract Character. . . . We shall be found in our place when actual danger menaces the System of Europe, but this Country cannot, and will not, act upon abstract and speculative Principles of Precaution' (P. Langford, *Modern British Foreign Policy: The Eighteenth Century, 1688–1815* (New York: St Martin's, 1976), p. 238).

23 For a brief exposition, see Alfred J. Rieber, 'Persistent Factors in Russian Foreign Policy', in Ragsdale and Ponomarev, *Imperial Russian Foreign Policy*, pp. 351–2.

or less.[24] Catherine's policy, whether in the heyday of Panin or in that of the Greek Project, while first in alliance with Prussia and later with Austria, appears to have used these alliances to divide central Europe, and sometimes all of Europe, against itself in order to leave Russia a free hand in imperial enterprise. Her heavily European involvement in the Armed Neutrality of 1780 served this purpose. The policy of Paul and Alexander, on the other hand, one of congress and concert, was distinctly Europhile. They wished to make of Russia the arbiter of the peace of Europe. Some day we may understand these categories, and the way in which they expressed Russian interests, better than we do today. For the moment, they must remain merely intriguing.

If the European extensions of the foreign policy of Paul and Alexander had more benign consequences for the continent than West Europeans realised,[25] their consequences for Russia were less fortunate. As Russian foreign policy adopted a distinctly Europhile outlook, domestic policy just as distinctly repudiated it. Thus the burden of foreign policy increased, while the strength of the empire that supported it succumbed to obsolescence such as to be in the long run unequal to the challenge of supporting the ambitiously conservative task of preserving social and political peace on a continent in the throes of the multiple revolutions of the nineteenth century. The long-term consequences were seen in the First World War. The policy that was good for Europe in 1815 also raised Russia to the pinnacle of its imperial power, but it was in the long run fatal for the empire.

24 The most prominent use of the term *svoboda ruk* is in V. G. Sirotkin, *Duel' dvukh diplomatii* (Moscow: Nauka, 1966), but the authors of the first of five projected volumes to appear in a new and unprecedentedly authoritative history of Russian foreign policy also rely heavily on it (in my opinion excessively and without defining it properly): O. V. Orlik (ed.), *Istoriia vneshnei politiki Rossii: pervaia polovina XIX veka* (Moscow: Mezhdunarodnye otnosheniia, 1995), pp. 27–135 passim.

25 This is the argument of Paul W. Schroeder, *The Transformation of European Politics, 1763–1848* (Oxford: Clarendon, 1994).

25

The imperial army

WILLIAM C. FULLER, JR

It is difficult to exaggerate the centrality of the army to the history of the Russian Empire. After all, it was due to the army that the empire came into existence in the first place. It was the army that conquered the territories of the empire, defended them, policed them and maintained internal security all at the same time. It was the army that transformed Russia into a great power, for it was the army that built the Russian state.

Yet if the army built the state, the state also built the army, and there was a symbiotic relationship between these two processes. By any reckoning the creation of a strong army was an extraordinary achievement, for in the middle of the seventeenth century Russia did not enjoy many advantages when it came to the generation of military power. To be sure, comprising over 15 million square kilometres in the 1680s, Muscovy was extensive in land area, but the population of the country, probably less than 7 million persons, was relatively small, and widely dispersed. Distances were vast, roads were execrable, the climate was insalubrious and much of the soil was of poor agricultural quality. Total state income amounted to a paltry 1.2 million roubles per annum and the country as a whole was undergoverned.[1] Industry was underdeveloped, and Muscovy had to import both iron and firearms.[2] Still worse, Russia lacked any natural, defensible frontiers and was hemmed in from the south, west and north by formidable enemies – the Ottoman Empire, the Khanate of the Crimea, the Polish-Lithuanian Commonwealth and the Kingdom of Sweden.

In view of its numerous weaknesses and vulnerabilities, it is not surprising that Muscovy generally fared poorly in military confrontations with its neighbours during the seventeenth century, enduring defeat after defeat at the

1 A. A. Novosel'skii and N. V. Ustiugov (eds.), *Ocherki istorii SSSR. Period feodalizma. XVIII v.* (Moscow: Izd. AN SSSR, 1955), p. 438.

2 Richard Hellie, *Enserfment and Military Change in Muscovy* (Chicago: University of Chicago Press, 1971), p. 355.

hands of the Swedes, Poles and Tatars. Of course, Russia did manage some successful expansion in this period, such as the acquisition of left-bank Ukraine by the terms of the Truce of Andrusovo (1667). However, this gain owed more to the Cossack rebellions and Swedish invasion that had crippled Poland than it did to any conspicuous Russian military prowess. While Russia did engage in military modernisation during the century, for example by augmenting the traditional cavalry levy with Western-style infantry units, the problem was that the state was capable of mobilising for discrete campaigns only and lacked the resources and stamina necessary for protracted war.

Slightly more than 140 years later, towards the end of the reign of Alexander I, the picture was completely different, for a succession of impressive military victories had resulted in the dramatic expansion in the political influence, population and size of the Russian state. In 1825 Russia's standing army of 750,000 men was the largest in the Western world. By that point Russia's land area had grown to 18.5 million square miles, and her population to 40 million. A full third of that population growth was directly attributable to conquest and annexation.

Understanding Russian military success, 1700–1825

The key element in Russia's transition from military debility to military capability was learning how better to mobilise both material resources and, even more importantly, human beings in the service of the army. This involved a frightening intensification of the coercive exploitation of all classes of people in Russia society from top to bottom. It was Peter the Great who was responsible for inaugurating the change. In 1700 in combination with Saxon and Danish allies, Peter launched what he thought would be a short and easy war against Sweden. In September of that same year, however, King Charles XII of Sweden annihilated Peter's army at Narva, capturing almost its entire artillery park. Over twenty years of war between Russia and Sweden ensued.

Needing to reconstitute his forces under the pressure of military emergency and protracted war, Peter invented a set of institutions to recruit, officer, equip, finance and administer his army that laid the foundation for the upsurge of Russia's military power during the eighteenth century. Although these new arrangements did not operate precisely as intended in Peter's lifetime, in the decades after his death they put down deep roots. There evolved a hybrid military system with both 'Western' and peculiarly 'Russian' characteristics. Partly by design and partly by improvisation, Russia devised a unique military system that represented a brilliant (if costly) adaptation to the realities of warfare in eastern, central and southern Europe.

A reliable source of military manpower was a central feature of that system. In 1705 Peter introduced a new approach to conscription that, with modifications, was to endure until 1874. The country was divided into blocks of twenty peasant households, and in every year each was required to supply a man who was drafted for life into the army's ranks. Serf owners, and in some cases village communities themselves, were to make the selection. Of course, Peter soon ignored the limits that the law of 1705 placed on military reinforcement, and on numerous occasions both arbitrarily raised the numbers of draftees called up and decreed additional special levies in response to the progress of the war.[3] The recruiting procedures laid down in 1705 (as well as the frantic deviations from them) resulted in the induction of over 300,000 men over the next twenty years.[4] Despite its unfair and capricious implementation, this method of recruitment stabilised under Peter's successors. In 1775 Catherine the Great changed the basic unit of conscription to the block of 500 peasant males from which one recruit per year was exacted in peace, but as many as five in wartime. In 1793 she also capped a private soldier's military service at twenty-five years, a measure that produced only a tiny class of retired veterans, as the majority of recruits died or were disabled long before then. The basic concept of the Petrine draft – compelling predetermined units of peasants to replenish the army's ranks on a crudely regular schedule – remained in place. The system worked well enough to furnish the Russian army with more than 2 million soldiers between 1725 and 1801.[5] Because of the dramatic increase in the population of the empire over the century, even larger intakes were possible in times of crisis.

The recruitment system not only made it feasible for Russia to raise a large army but also gave that army some qualities that differentiated it from armies in the West. The first of these was the simple fact that it was wholly conscripted, not partially hired. Until the French Revolution, most of the great European powers maintained armies that included large proportions of highly trained professional mercenaries. And mercenaries, however skilled, manifested an alarming propensity to desert. The military manuals of the day strongly advised against marching forces by night, or moving in the immediate

3 Lindsey Hughes, *Russia in the Age of Peter the Great* (New Haven and London: Yale University Press, 1998), pp. 68–9.

4 William C. Fuller Jr, *Strategy and Power in Russia 1600–1914* (New York: Free Press, 1992), pp. 45–6.

5 John L. H. Keep, *Soldiers of the Tsar: Army and Society in Russia 1462–1874* (Oxford: Oxford University Press, 1985), pp. 145, 165.

vicinity of swamps and dense forests, in order to diminish the risk of mass flight. By contrast, Russia's post-Petrine commanders routinely engaged in all of these manoeuvres, since the rates of desertion from the Russian army were considerably lower than those that obtained in the French, Prussian or Austrian ones.[6]

This ought not to be taken to suggest that military service was popular in rural Russia. Although a serf became legally 'free' when he entered the army, conscription was a species of death. The recruit was torn away from his native village, severed from the company of his family and his friends, and was well aware that the chances were that he would never return to them. Indeed, it became the custom for village women to lament the departure of the recruits with the singing of funeral dirges.[7] Once a soldier had completed his preliminary training and joined his regiment, he entered a milieu in which irregular pay, shortage of supplies, epidemic disease and brutal discipline were all too common.

Yet to enter military service was also in a sense to be reborn, for in the soldier's *artel* the Russian army possessed a powerful instrument for socialising recruits and building group cohesion. Every unit in the army was subdivided into artels, communal associations of eight to ten men who trained, messed, worked and fought together. The artel functioned both as a military and economic organisation, for it held the money its members acquired from plunder, extra pay and hiring themselves out as labourers. In a sense, the artel became a soldier's new family, and it is significant that in the event of his death it was his comrades in the artel, rather than his kinfolk, who inherited his share of the property. Artels, which also functioned at the company and regimental level, were reminiscent of the peasant associations back home with which the recruit was already familiar, and consequently assisted his adjustment to the rigours of his new environment and helped persuade him that the state's military system was legitimate.[8]

The homogeneity of the army also facilitated a soldier's identification with military life. The overwhelming majority of private soldiers in the army were Great Russian by ethnicity and Orthodox by confession. This was so because the bulk of the empire's non-Russian subjects were either excused from service

6 Walter M. Pintner, 'The Burden of Defense in Imperial Russia, 1725–1915', *RR* 43 (1984): 252.

7 Fuller, *Strategy and Power*, pp. 167–73. Elise Kimerling Wirtschafter, *From Serf to Russian Soldier* (Princeton: Princeton University Press, 1990), pp. 110–11.

8 Wirtschafter, *From Serf to Russian Soldier*, pp. 78, 148; Dietrich Beyrau, *Militär und Gesellschaft im Vorrevolutionären Russland* (Cologne and Vienna: Böhlau Verlag, 1984), pp. 347–8.

in exchange for tribute, or organised in special formations of their own. This was another respect in which the Russian army contrasted strikingly with the armies of the West. At various points in the eighteenth century more than half the troops in the service of the kings of Prussia and France were foreign mercenaries. Since ethnic and religious homogeneity promoted cohesion, and cohesion could translate into superior combat performance, contemporary observers understandably viewed the homogeneity of the Russian army as one of its greatest assets. A government commission of 1764 hailed the sense of unity created in the army by a 'common language, faith, set of customs and birth'.[9] Certainly on many occasions Russia's eighteenth-century troops did perform outstandingly in battle, not merely against the forces of the Crimean Khan and Ottoman Sultan, but even when matched against such first-class Western opponents as Prussia. At Zorndorf (August 1758) during the Seven Years War, the Russians killed or wounded over a third of the troops Frederick the Great committed to the field and earned the awed plaudits of an eye-witness for their 'extraordinary steadiness and intrepidity'.[10]

Of course an army must not only be recruited but also led. Peter I initially sought to engage capable military specialists abroad, but soon ordered all males of the gentry estate into permanent service in the army, navy or bureaucracy in his effort to ensure an adequate domestic supply of officers and civil administrators. Moreover, in a series of decrees culminating in the promulgation of the Table of Ranks in 1722, he established the principle that acquisition of an officer's rank conferred nobiliary status even on commoners. Yet the bulk of the officers continued to be drawn from the nobility, and the officer corps became even more 'noble' as the century proceeded, despite the fact that Peter III freed the nobility from the legal obligation to serve in 1762. Over 90 per cent of all officers who fought at Borodino in 1812 were of noble birth.[11] As for the nobles themselves, while the calling of the officer had acquired the cachet of prestige among the wealthy strata of the elite, it was also the case that there were large numbers of impecunious noblemen who had no choice but to rely on government salaries for their livings.

Incompetence, mediocrity, peculation and even sadism were to be met with within Russia's eighteenth-century officer corps. An analysis of military-judicial cases has revealed that the most typical grievances the soldiers voiced

9 Fuller, *Strategy and Power*, p. 171.

10 Christopher Duffy, *Russia's Military Way to the West: Origins and Nature of Russian Military Power 1700–1800* (London: Routledge and Kegan Paul, 1981), pp. 89–90.

11 Keep, *Soldiers of the Tsar*, p. 125; D. G. Tselorungo, *Ofitsery russkoi armii-uchastniki borodinskogo srazheniia. Istoriko-sotsiologicheskoe issledovanie* (Moscow: Kalita, 2002), p. 73.

about their commanders had to do with cruelty in the imposition of corporal punishment on the one hand, and such economic abuses as withholding pay or purloining artel funds on the other.[12] There were, however, also officers who distinguished themselves by their honesty, fairness and paternalistic concern for the wellbeing of their men. In any event, educational standards were low. Certainly, there were the handful of military-technical academies that Peter I had established, as well as some exclusive institutions of later foundation, such as the Noble Land Cadet Corps. But there were not enough places in such schools to accommodate more than a few hundred aspiring officers.

At the highest levels of military authority there was much to criticise, for patronage and court politics were frequently decisive in the bestowal of a general's epaulettes, with predictable results. Yet eighteenth-century Russia also benefited from the masterly leadership of some truly outstanding commanders. Confronted by foreign invasion in 1708–9 and 1812 respectively, Peter I and M. I. Kutuzov figured out how to turn Russia itself, in all its immensity, emptiness and poverty, into a weapon to grind down the enemy. Other figures, including B. C. Münnich, P. A. Rumiantsev, Z. G. Chernyshev and A. V. Suvorov, led the army to impressive victories over Tatars, Turks, Poles, Swedes, Prussians and Frenchmen alike. Münnich smashed the Ottomans at Stavuchany (1739) and was the first Russian commander ever to breech the Tatar defences on the Crimean peninsula. Rumiantsev, a brilliant logistician and tactician, routed the Turks at Kagul (1770) although outnumbered by over four to one. Chernyshev, a talented military administrator no less than a strategist, was instrumental in the capture of Berlin (1760). And in the course of his extraordinary military career, the peerless Suvorov overwhelmed the Turks at Rymnik and Focsani (both 1789), stormed Izmail (1790), forced the surrender of Warsaw (1794) and defeated France's armies in northern Italy (1799). His last great military accomplishment – his fighting retreat through Switzerland – became the capstone of his legend.

Yet even military commanders of genius cannot win wars unless their armies are paid, fed, clothed and supplied. All of this requires money, and money had been a commodity in relatively short supply in seventeenth-century Muscovy. It was once again Peter the Great who devised expedients to extract more cash from his oppressed subjects than ever before by saddling them with all manner of new taxes. Here one of his most important innovations was the poll (or soul) tax of 1718 that required every male peasant as well as most of the male residents of Russia's cities and towns to pay to the state an annual

12 Wirtschafter, *From Serf to Russian Soldier*, p. 123.

sum of 74 (later 70) kopecks. Owing to such fiscal reforms, as well as to the growth in the size of the taxable population during his reign, he was able to push state income up to 8.7 million roubles by the close of his reign. Whereas military outlays had constituted roughly 60 per cent of state expenditure in old Muscovy, under Peter they may have consumed between 70 and 80 per cent of the state budget.[13] The army and navy continued to account for about half of the Russian state's expenses throughout the century until the 1790s, when the empire's territorial, economic and demographic growth combined to whittle this figure down to roughly 35 per cent. By that point, net state revenues exceeded 40 million roubles per annum, although it bears noting that there had been considerable inflation over the previous seventy years.[14]

The Russian army of the eighteenth century, then, evolved into a remarkably effective instrument of state power. It won the overwhelming majority of Russia's wars during the period and was the reliable bulwark of the state against internal disorder, as in 1774 when it was employed to suppress the massive peasant and Cossack insurrection of Emelian Pugachev.

The joists that supported Russian military success in this era were precisely the Russian Empire's political and social backwardness by comparison to Western Europe. Because Russia was an autocracy, and the country lacked an independent Church or an ancient feudal nobility there were few impediments to the ruthless exercise of governmental authority, which could be used to requisition huge quantities of men, money and labour for the military effort despite the meagreness of the resource base. In 1756 the Russian army, if irregulars are included, was larger than the army of France, despite the fact that the revenue of the Empress Elizabeth Petrovna was probably less than one-fifth that of Louis XV.[15] It helped enormously that Russia was a society organised in hereditary orders where institutions like serfdom and peasant bondage of all kinds persisted long after they had been discarded in the West. The subjugation of the peasants made it possible to count, tax and draft them, as well as hold them (or their masters) collectively accountable if they failed to perform any of their obligations. All of this meant that the Russian state could more easily reenforce the ranks of the army with new draftees than could its Western neighbours, particularly as the population of the empire increased. This was no small matter, because Russian military casualties – as a result of combat but even more so from disease – tended to be extremely high. If the

13 Keep, *Soldiers of the Tsar*, p. 137.

14 Arcadius Kahan, *The Plow, the Hammer and the Knout: An Economic History of Eighteenth-Century Russia* (Chicago: University of Chicago Press, 1985), pp. 337, 341.

15 Fuller, *Strategy and Power*, pp. 96, 105.

Russian army was militarily effective, it was not necessarily militarily efficient. Russia may have lost as many as 300,000 men during the Great Northern War and may have taken another quarter of a million casualties during the Seven Years War of 1756–63, a figure equal to two-thirds of the troops who saw service in those years.[16] The military system also enabled the Russian state, in a pinch, to make military efforts that were more robust than its Western rivals. In the later stage of the Seven Years War after 1760, as France, Austria and Prussia began to totter from acute military exhaustion, the growth in size of Russia's field armies in Germany did not abate.[17] And in 1812 a series of extraordinary levies permitted Russia both to make good its losses and even enlarge the forces it pitted against Napoleon. It has been calculated that 1.5 million men, or 4 per cent of the empire's total population, served in the army during the reign of Alexander I.[18] Other than in Prussia, a military participation rate like this one was inconceivable anywhere else in Europe.

For all of its success, however, the Russian military system had some weaknesses, which were already grave by the end of the eighteenth century and became critically so in the next. To begin with, there was the issue of the army's size. Russia's autocrats believed that they had to maintain a large army, not only to support their geopolitical ambitions, but also as a matter of simple security. Russia's borders were longer than those of any other polity, and Russia confronted potential enemies in Asia as well as in Europe. Moreover, there was the question of the internal stability of the empire to consider. It was the army that protected the autocracy from servile rebellion, and the deployment of troops had to take into account domestic threats to the empire, no less than foreign ones. The problem was that the larger the army grew, the harder it became to foot the bill. As the Russian treasury was in constant financial dire straits, tsarist statesmen were always preoccupied with finding economies in the military budget.

One expedient was to make the soldiers themselves responsible for part of their own upkeep. The state supplied the regiments with such materials as leather and woollen cloth and then commanded them to manufacture their own boots, uniforms and other articles of kit. It also authorised the soldiers' artels to engage in 'free work' (that is, paid labour) on nearby estates. Despite the fact that this arrangement diverted the troops away from military

16 A. A. Kersnovskii, *Istoriia russkoi armii*, vol. I (repr., Moscow: Golos, 1992), p. 63; John L. H. Keep, 'The Russian Army in the Seven Years War', in Eric Lohr and Marshall Poe (eds.), *The Military and Society in Russia 1450–1917* (Leiden: Brill, 2002), p. 200.

17 Duffy, *Russia's Military Way*, p. 118.

18 Kersnovskii, *Istoriia*, p. 204.

exercises and opened egregious opportunities for larceny to dishonest regimental colonels, 'self maintenance' (also known as the 'regimental economy') endured within the army in one form or another until 1906.

Another tactic that the state employed to save money concerned housing. In peacetime, for up to eight months of the year the army dispersed and was quartered on the rural peasantry. Since the army therefore only 'stood' during the four months it slept under canvas at summer bivouacs, the government was relieved of the duty to construct (or rent) permanent barracks. This practice naturally led to degeneration in the combat readiness of the armed forces, a situation that was only ameliorated gradually as barracks accommodation became more common in the early nineteenth century.

A final cost-cutting device involved settling a significant proportion of the troops on farms where they would grow their own victuals as well as drill and where their sons could be brought up to join the ranks as soon as they came of military age. Using 'land-militias' to colonise (and thus to secure) dangerous borderlands had long been practised in Russia, as well as in such other European countries as Austria. But Alexander I established an extensive network of *internal* military colonies, which in 1826 were populated by 160,000 soldiers and their families.[19] However, this experiment was an execrable failure: living and working conditions were intolerable, and soldiers hated the harsh and intrusive regimentation of every aspect of their lives. The massive uprisings in the north-western military colonies of 1831 forced the government to institute reforms that (*inter alia*) excused the 'farming soldiers' from the obligation of military training.

A penultimate deficiency in the Russian military system was its inflexibility. The imperial state often found it hard to concentrate its military strength in the most crucial theatre when it went to war. Although the 1830/1 insurrection in Poland assumed the character of a full-blown war, Russia was able to deploy no more than 430,000 of its 850,000 troops there, in view of the magnitude of the other foreign and domestic threats it felt it had to deter.[20] The optimal solution to this problem would have been the introduction of military reserve programme. This would have entailed a deep cut in the recruit's term of military service and a simultaneous increase in the percentage of draft-eligible men taken into the army every year. In that event Russia might have been able to diminish the number of troops it kept on active duty while building up a

19 V. G. Verzhbitskii, *Revoliutsionnoe dvizhenie v russkoi armii 1826–1859* (Moscow: Izd. Sovetskaia Rossiia, 1964), pp. 118–19.

20 Frederick W. Kagan, *The Military Reforms of Nicholas I: The Origins of the Modern Russian Army* (New York: St Martin's Press, 1999), pp. 224–5.

large reservoir of trained reservists on which it could draw in an emergency. Yet the peculiarities of the Russian military system made a proper reserve programme inconceivable. The Russian army had originally been designed as a closed corporation, set apart from Russian society, that swallowed up the peasants inducted into its ranks for good. There was no way in which a civil society defined by hereditary estates and serfdom could have absorbed or even survived an influx of a 100,000 or more juridically free demobilised soldiers every year. Measures to assemble a class of reservists gradually (such as the introduction of 'unlimited furloughs' in 1834) were only palliatives. If serfdom and autocracy were the floor beneath Russian military power, they also constituted its ceiling.

Finally, there is the question of military technology. The logic of the Russian military system presupposed a low rate of military-technical innovation, and the system consequently functioned best in an era when that held true. Over time governmental decrees and entrepreneurial energy had made eighteenth-century Russia mostly self-sufficient in the production of armaments. Russia's rich deposits of minerals were an advantage here, and for several decades in the eighteenth century Russia led Europe in the output of iron. Although improvements were made in the quality and performance of weapons, particularly artillery, during this period, overall the technology of combat remained remarkably stable. The smooth bore musket was the standard infantry arm under Alexander I just as it had been under Peter the Great. The relatively long useful life of muskets – forty years was deemed the norm – obviously made it easier for Russia to bear the cost of equipping its ground forces with them. In fact, in 1800 the Russian state had issued at least some of its regiments with muskets that had been in its arsenals since Peter's time.[21]

By the middle of the nineteenth century, however, the Industrial Revolution was making a major impact on the technology of war. Countries that neglected to invest in the latest weaponry courted military disaster, as Russia herself was to discover during the Crimean War. Unfortunately, Russia was a poor country that could ill afford expensive rearmament drives. Her industrial sector was insufficiently developed to manufacture the new ordnance, rifles and munitions on a large scale. And the social, economic and political institutions generated by autocracy were not particularly hospitable to modern industrial capitalism either.[22]

21 Pintner, 'Burden of Defense', 232.

22 Thomas C. Owen, *Russian Corporate Capitalism from Peter the Great to Perestroika* (New York: Oxford University Press, 1995), pp. 8–9.

Accounting for Russian military failure, 1854–1917

If it was military success that built up the Russian Empire, it was military defeat that helped to bring the empire down. Russia's great victory over Napoleon seemingly validated the military system as it was and had closed the eyes of many to its defects. Nicholas I (r. 1825–55) was personally devoted to the army, desired to impose military order and discipline on his country as a whole, and frequently turned to military officers to fill the most important posts in the civil administration. Yet the army suffered from his neurotic obsession with petty details and his penchant for staging massive parades and reviews, which, though impressive, did little to enhance combat readiness. Nicholas did manage to beat the Persians in 1828, the Ottomans in 1829 and the Poles in 1831. Then, too, his Caucasian Corps fought credibly if unimaginatively and indecisively in its interminable campaigns against the Muslim guerrillas in Chechnia and Daghestan.[23] But when Russia had to battle Britain, France, Sardinia and the Ottoman Empire during the Crimean War of 1853–6 the upshot was a military and political debacle. In its struggle with this powerful coalition, the imperial government fell back on the methods of 1812 and by means of extraordinary levies inundated the 980,000-man regular army with over a million newly mobilised Cossacks, militia and raw recruits. But Russia found it hard to bring more than a fraction of this strength to bear against the enemy since hundreds of thousands of troops were pinned down in Poland, campaigning in the Caucasus, guarding the Baltic frontier or garrisoning the vast expanses of the empire. For much of the time, allied forces on the Crimea peninsula were actually numerically superior to Russia's. Russia's principal Black Sea Fortress, Sebastopol, fell in large measure due to the unremitting pressure of the allies' technologically superior siege artillery. During the conflict, which was the empire's most sanguinary war of the nineteenth century, that of 1812 excepted, 450,000 Russian soldiers and sailors lost their lives.[24] The terms of the Peace of Paris of 1856, with their ban on Russian warships in the Black Sea, were a humiliating infringement of Russia's sovereignty, and left her southern ports and trade perpetual hostages to the French and British fleets. The Crimean War exploded one of the principle justifications for autocracy – its ability to beget military power and security. The Crimean defeat not only discredited the Russian military system but also destroyed confidence in the empire's entire panoply of political, social and economic structures.

23 See Moshe Gammer, *Muslim Resistance to the Tsar: Shamil and the Conquest of Chechnia and Dagestan* (London: Frank Cass, 1994).

24 John Shelton Curtiss, *Russia's Crimean War* (Durham: Duke University Press, 1979), pp. 455, 471.

Under the new emperor Alexander II (r. 1855–81) fundamental domestic reform was complemented by a policy of *recueillement* in foreign affairs. Russia's military leadership took advantage of the respite from major war to attempt an overhaul of the entire military system. However, the army still did have to cope with 'small wars' on the empire's periphery. Although the capture of imam Shamil in 1859 facilitated the eventual pacification of the Caucasus, in 1863 the Poles rose in a serious rebellion that could only be suppressed by brute force. There were also several campaigns in central Asia during the 1860s, 1870s and early 1880s. These solidified the military reputations of such prominent generals as M. G. Cherniaev and M. D. Skobelev and effected the submission to St Petersburg of Kokand, Bukhara, Khiva, Transcaspia and Merv. The motivations behind this central Asian imperialism were complex and confused, and ranged from a desire for more defensible frontiers, to a concern for enlarging Russian trade, to a perceived need to concoct a paper threat against Britain in India.[25] But a great deal of the impetus behind the advance came from Russia's ambitious military commanders there, who often sparked off armed clashes with the Muslims in contravention of their orders.

When Russia's next large-scale war erupted in 1877 against the Ottomans, her military reforms had not yet come to fruition. Yet the protracted eastern crisis that preceded its outbreak did permit the Russian military leadership to develop its mobilisation, concentration and campaign plans with greater than usual care.[26] Although Russia won the war, its military performance was mixed. In the hands of excellent commanders, Russian forces were capable of such magnificent actions as the seizure and defence of Shipka Pass and the astounding Balkan winter offensive that brought the Russian army within fifteen kilometres of Constantinople by January 1879.[27] But these triumphs were to some extent counterbalanced by the failure of the three bloody attempts to storm Plevna, the epidemic of typhus and cholera on the Caucasus front, the total breakdown in army logistics and the appalling dimensions of the butcher's bill. Still worse, the other European powers, led by Germany, colluded to prevent Russia from realising her entire set of war aims.

Germany was already the power that Russia feared the most. Since the establishment of Bismarck's *Reich* at the close of the Franco-Prussian War,

25 Seymour Becker, *Russia's Protectorates in Central Asia. Bukhara and Khiva, 1865–1924* (Cambridge, Mass.: Harvard University Press, 1968), p. 23; Dominic Lieven, *Empire: The Russian Empire and its Rivals* (New Haven: Yale University Press, 2000), p. 211.

26 David Alan Rich, *The Tsar's Colonels: Professionalism, Strategy and Subversion in Late Imperial Russia* (Cambridge, Mass.: Harvard University Press, 1998), pp. 157–8.

27 Bruce W. Menning, *Bayonets Before Bullets: The Imperial Russian Army, 1861–1914* (Bloomington: Indiana University Press, 1992), pp. 77–8.

Russia had been alarmed by the growth in Germany's power and worried that Berlin had designs for European hegemony. How best to defend the empire from an attack by Germany, perhaps supported by Austria, swiftly became the chief preoccupation of Russia's military leadership, and was to remain so until 1914. This was the reason that Russia's venture into east Asian imperialism at the turn of the century so disquieted senior generals. Russia's acquisition of Port Arthur, its lodgement in Manchuria and its intrigues in Korea were attended by the risk of war with Japan. In the view of such influential figures as War Minister A. N. Kuropatkin, Russia did not have either the military budget or the manpower to protect her new acquisitions in the Far East, confronted as she was by a much more dangerous threat to her security in Europe.

When in February 1904 Japan opened hostilities against Russia by launching a surprise attack on Russia's Pacific fleet at Port Arthur, the Russian armed forces in the Far East were caught unprepared. Initially outnumbered, her troops dependent for their reinforcement and supply on the attenuated umbilical cord of the Trans-Siberian railway, Russia endured one military reverse after another in the land war. Port Arthur capitulated to the Japanese in January 1905 after a seven-month siege, and in central Manchuria Russia suffered serious defeats at Liaoyang, the Sha-Ho, Sandepu and Mukden. Nor did the war at sea produce any news more welcome. Dispatched to the Pacific to engage the Japanese in their home waters, Russia's Baltic fleet was spectacularly annihilated in the battle of Tsushima Straits (May 1905). Negotiations resulted in the Peace of Portsmouth, which stripped Russia of Port Arthur, her position in Manchuria and half of Sakhalin island.

Russia's loss of the Japanese war of 1904–5 was not preordained, for she might have won it had she made better operational and strategic decisions during the ground war and had made more offensive use of her naval assets in the Pacific.[28] Indeed, despite all of her flagrant military blunders, arguably Russia *would* have won the war if the revolution of 1905 had not intervened to cripple the military effort. By the time the peace treaty was signed, Russia's forces outnumbered Japan's in Manchuria, while Tokyo had run out of reserves and was precariously close to fiscal collapse besides.

The revolution of 1905–7 brought two dire consequences for the Russian army in its train. First, the contagion of rebellion not only blanketed the towns and villages of the empire but also penetrated into the ranks of the army itself. In late 1905 and throughout 1906 (particularly after April) there occurred over

28 Julian S. Corbett, *Maritime Operations in the Russo-Japanese War 1904–1905*, 2 vols. (Annapolis, Md. and Newport, RI: Naval Institute Press and Naval War College Press, 1994), vol. II, pp. 396–7.

400 military mutinies, in which soldiers defied the orders of their officers and issued economic and political demands.[29] Second, the government answered the mass strikes, protests and agrarian disorders with an unprecedented application of military force: on more than 8,000 occasions between 1905–7 military units were called upon to assist in the restoration of order.[30] Failed war, revolution and repressive service demoralised the army, disrupted its training and made a shambles of the empire's external defence posture. It would take the Russian army considerable time, money and intellectual energy to recover. Military defeat engendered introspection and reform, just as it had after 1856, and although by 1914 the reform process still had some years to run, the Russian army was in good enough condition to wage what most assumed would be a short, general conflict in Europe. But neither the Russian army nor Russian society was up to the strain of the protracted, total, industrial conflict that the First World War quickly became. The War offered conclusive proof that neither the army nor the empire as a whole had adequately modernised since the middle of the nineteenth century.

With respect to the army, one source of inertia was the inherent difficulty of commanding, supplying and managing military units so numerous and so widely dispersed. Centralisation and decentralisation both had administrative advantages and disadvantages, and Russia's military leadership was never able to reconcile the tension among them. One figure who tried to do so was D. A. Miliutin, Russia's most eminent and energetic nineteenth-century military reformer. As war minister for almost the entire reign of Alexander II, Miliutin was responsible for substantive innovation in the army's force structure, schools, hospitals and courts, and presided over the introduction of the breechloading rifle and other up-to-date weapons.[31] But he also sought to streamline the operations of his ministry by creating eight *glavnye upravleniia* (or main administrations), with functional supervision over artillery, cavalry, engineering, intendence (supply and logistics), medicine, law, staff work and so forth. At the same time he divided the empire into fourteen (later fifteen) military districts, each with its own headquarters and staff and sub-departments, that mirrored the organisation of the War Ministry back in St Petersburg. Miliutin's administrative restructuring thus combined the principles of centralisation and decentralisation, for while the various military agencies and

29 John Bushnell, *Mutiny Amid Repression: Russian Soldiers in the Revolution of 1905–08* (Bloomington: Indiana University Press, 1985), pp. 76–7, 173.

30 William C. Fuller, Jr, *Civil–Military Conflict in Imperial Russia, 1881–1914* (Princeton: Princeton University Press, 1985), pp. 129–30.

31 Joseph Bradley, *Guns for the Tsar: American Technology and the Small Arms Industry in Nineteenth-Century Russia* (DeKalb: Northern Illinois University Press, 1990), pp. 126–7.

bureaux at the centre were brought firmly under his thumb, the military district commanders were invested with considerable autonomy. No one denied that this new organisation represented a considerable improvement over its predecessor, for it reduced red tape and permitted the elimination of 1,000 redundant jobs in St Petersburg alone.[32] Yet it had its drawbacks notwithstanding. It has, for example, been argued that perhaps the most important of the main administrations – the Main Staff – was statutorily burdened with so many secondary responsibilities that authentic general staff work suffered in consequence.[33] And the military district system, although a salutary antidote to the rigidity and paralysis of the military administration of the previous decades, led in the end to the fragmentation of intelligence collection and strategic planning.

A second impediment to military progress in the late imperial period was that vital reforms were often inconsistent, incomplete or distorted in implementation. The military conscription reform provides a good illustration. Miliutin clearly saw that Russia's traditional approach to military recruitment had become dangerously obsolete in an era of mass politics and mass armies and had to be scrapped. By dint of arduous political struggle Miliutin and his supporters were able to secure the promulgation in 1874 of a law that instituted a universal military service obligation in Russia. Henceforth the majority of the empire's young men would be eligible to be drafted into the army as private soldiers, regardless of the estate or social class to which they belonged. Miliutin was intent on accomplishing three goals with the statute of 1874. First, since it involved simultaneously widening the pool of prospective draftees and cutting the term of active service, it would give the army the modern system of military reserves that Miliutin regarded as an indispensable precondition for victory in any future European war. Second, Miliutin anticipated that the act would indirectly promote literacy and an elevation in the cultural level of the empire's population, for it also decreased the term of service required of any draftee in accordance with his education. Although the standard period of service was set at seven years, a man with a university degree had to spend only six months with the colours, and a secondary school graduate only a year and a half. Even the most rudimentary primary education shaved three years off the term of active duty. Third, because the law proclaimed military service to be a *universal* obligation, Miliutin hoped that the new system would

32 Menning, *Bayonets Before Bullets*, p. 14.

33 P. A. Zaionchkovskii, *Voennye reformy 1860–1870 godov v Rossii* (Moscow: Izd. MGU, 1952), p. 106. O. R. Airapetov, *Zabytaia kar'era 'russkogo Moltke'. Nikolai Nikolaevich Obruchev (1830–1904)* (St Petersburg: Izd. 'Aleteiia', 1998), p. 98.

eventually produce a culture of citizenship in Russia. The common experience of service was supposed to break down the distinctions of estate, class and rank, thus stimulating dynastic loyalty, unity and patriotism. He strongly believed that an army that evinced those traits would be immeasurably superior to one remarkable chiefly for its bovine obedience.

The statute of 1874, and its subsequent modifications, clearly did ameliorate the Russian Empire's military manpower problem. In 1881 the active army comprised 844,000 troops and in 1904 in excess of a million.[34] By 1914 the active army numbered 1.4 million men and the active reserve 2.6 million, while over 6 million more were enrolled in the various classes of the territorial 'militia' (*opolchenie*). But it nonetheless deserves emphasis that the overwhelming majority of young men in the empire never received military training at all under the 1874 conscription system. The 1874 law had introduced a universal obligation to serve, not universal military service, and contained articles granting exemptions for nationality, profession and family circumstances that were more liberal than those that obtained in any other major European country. There were several reasons for this, but as a partial upshot, while in late-nineteenth-century France four-fifths of those draft eligible passed through the army's ranks, and in Germany, over half, in Russia barely 25 per cent–30 per cent of any given age cohort of 21-year-old males received military training.[35] This meant that in Russia it was impossible for the army to act as a 'school for the nation' in the same way as armies are said to have done elsewhere in Europe. Nor was the concept of equal citizenship well served by the radically reduced length of service awarded to men with educational qualifications. Moreover, when the casualties started to mount in the First World War the empire experienced an authentic military manpower crisis.

It was true that the post-reform army was more heterogeneous than the army of the eighteenth century had ever been, and not just from the standpoint of social class or 'estate'. Despite the 1874 law's grant of exemptions to a variety of national minorities, as time passed the army increasingly became a multiethnic force. In addition to Russians, Jews, Poles, Latvians, Estonians, Germans, Georgians, Baskhirs and Tatars were all represented in its ranks, as were men from the Northern Caucasus and Transcaucasia after 1887. The government tried to mitigate the effects of ethnic dilution by decreeing that

34 P. A. Zaionchkovskii, *Samoderzhavie i russkaia armiia na rubezhe XIX–XX stoletii* (Moscow: Izd. Mysl', 1973), p. 123.

35 David R. Jones, 'Imperial Russia's Forces at War', in Alan R. Millet and Murray Williamson (eds.), *Military Effectiveness*, vol. I: *The First World War* (Boston: Allen and Unwin, 1988), p. 278.

75 per cent of the personnel in the combat unit had to be Great Russians, but that target could not have been met without counting Ukrainians and Belorussians as such.[36] In any event, it is clear that military service in the post-reform era did not build unity across ethnic lines any more successfully than it did across the boundaries of juridical class. Ethnic minorities met with considerable discrimination within the army, and it did not help much when in the 1890s the state adopted a policy of Russification in the borderlands, particularly Poland and Finland.[37] Given the temporary nature of military service, as well as the heterogeneity within the ranks, the soldier's artel could no longer perform the integrative function as well as it had prior to the Crimean War.

A third obstacle to the modernisation of the army in the post-reform era had to do with its leadership. The Russian army consistently experienced more difficulty in attracting and retaining capable non-commissioned officers than did any other first-class army in Europe. In 1882 the army had only 25 per cent of the senior NCOs it needed, and in 1903 there was still a deficit of 54 per cent.[38] With respect to the officer corps, the problem was not so much quantity as quality. Nobles continued to dominate the highest echelons of command, and at the turn of the century over 90 per cent of the empire's generals came from hereditary noble families. Yet of the 42,777 officers then on duty almost half had been born commoners.[39] While this statistic may reveal something about social mobility in late Imperial Russia, it also reflects a much more ominous trend: the relative deterioration in the officer corps' pay, perquisites and status that occurred over the last decades of the *ancien régime*. The salary schedule for regular Russian army officers was set by law in 1859 and changed little over the next forty years, with two unpleasant results. First, the purchasing power of an officer's compensation tended to erode with the passage of time. But second, by the 1890s Russian army officers not only found themselves underpaid by comparison with their counterparts abroad, but also lagging behind civilian bureaucrats at home. In these circumstances, and given the opportunities available in the growing private sector, is it any wonder that the army began to lose out in the competition to recruit the most

36 Zaionchkovskii, *Samoderzhavie i russkaia armiia*, p. 119.

37 One aspect of that policy was the state's effort to dissolve the separate Finnish army, and draft Finns under the same regulations that applied to other groups. This initiative was met with stiff resistance. P. Luntinen, *The Imperial Russian Army and Navy in Finland 1808–1918* (Helsinki: SHS, 1997), pp. 159–70.

38 Zaionchkovskii, *Samoderzhavie i russkaia armiia*, pp. 121–3.

39 A. I. Panov, *Ofitsery v russkoi revoliutsii 1905–07 gg.* (Moscow: Regional'naia obshchestvennaia organizatsiia ofitserov 'Demos', 1996), p. 19.

talented, and best-educated young men for its officer corps? Of course, there still remained wealthy aristocrats for whom a posting to one of the prestigious guard regiments was socially de rigueur. Yet in the non-exclusive regiments, especially those of the army infantry, the proportion of officers who were both humbly born and poorly schooled rose steeply. Of the 1,072 men holding commissions in 1895 whose fathers had been peasants, 997 or over 93 per cent were clustered in the army infantry.[40]

A decline in the prestige of the officer corps accompanied its social dilution and economic distress. But this development was also in part attributable to the burgeoning hostility of the intelligentsia towards the regime and its organs of coercion, the army and the police. Certainly a decay in the image of the officer is observable in the pages of Russian literature. By the late nineteenth and early twentieth centuries, novels, essays and stories by such popular writers as Garshin, Kuprin, Andreev and Korolenko disseminated negative stereotypes of army officers, depicting them as lazy, ignorant, uncouth, homicidal and frequently drunk.[41]

Compounding these woes was the inner factiousness of the officer corps. Imperial army officers were united by their antipathy towards the outer civilian world but by not much else. Officers in one branch of the service typically disdained those who belonged to the others, while the graduates of the most prestigious and specialised military academies were inclined to sneer at all who lacked their educational attainments. This deficiency in cohesion meant that the officer corps as a whole was poorly situated to develop a strong corporate spirit or articulate its collective interests. Naturally enough, the government did make attempts to heal the divisions within the corps by legislation. But such laws as the statute of May 1894 that *required* officers to duel over points of honour or be cashiered were wrongheaded and ineffective remedies.

Nonetheless, the imperial officer corps did contain a thin stratum of military professionals, of whom the majority were so-called 'general staff officers' (GSOs). To gain entry into this prestigious fraternity, an officer had to win admission to the Nicholas Academy of the General Staff, and complete its full academic programme with distinction. Thereafter he was entitled to be known for the rest of his career as an 'officer of the general staff' regardless of actual military assignment. A true intellectual elite, the GSOs occupied the most important staff billets and had a monopoly on intelligence work.

40 Zaionchkovskii, *Samoderzhavie i russkaia armiia*, pp. 204, 225.
41 Fuller, *Civil–Military Conflict*, pp. 143–4.

But they also received a disproportionate share of army commands. Although they constituted no more than 2 per cent of the entire officer corps, in 1913 the GSOs were in command of over a third of the army's infantry regiments and over three-quarters of its infantry divisions.[42]

In the last twenty years of the nineteenth century, Russia's military professionals, including many GSOs, agonised over the declining quality of the officer corps, advocated the raising of standards and tirelessly preached that a young officer's best use of free time was education, rather than dissipation. After the icy shock of the Japanese defeat there were military professionals who concluded that the entire military system had to be regenerated, and that the empire's population had to be militarised and readied for total war. Such people, whom their opponents sometimes labelled 'young turks', argued that the ultimate pledge of future victory would be Russia's transformation into a true 'nation in arms'. Some, like A. A. Neznamov, demanded that Russian adopt a unified military doctrine, that is, a set of binding principles to govern military preparations in peace and the conduct of operations in war. In 1912, however, Emperor Nicholas II announced that 'military doctrine consists in doing everything that I order' and thereby stifled any further discussion.[43]

Nicholas's interference on this occasion may have stemmed from awareness that the vision of a Russian 'nation in arms' profoundly contradicted the political idea of autocracy. Russia was not a nation, but a multinational empire, and the glue that held it together was supposed to be allegiance to the Romanov dynasty, not veneration of some national abstraction. But what this episode also highlights is another chronic problem besetting higher military leadership in the twilight of the old regime: that of imperial meddling. This came in several forms. There were, for example, grand dukes whose positions as heads of army inspectorates permitted them to exert enormous influence on military decision-making, whether they were qualified to do so or not. Yet the most noisome way in which the court retarded military progress had to do with the distribution of promotions and appointments. Russia's last autocrats, and Nicholas II in particular, were often prone to select (and remove) military bureaucrats and field commanders more on the basis of personal loyalty than competence. This lamentable practice occurred even during times of military

42 E. Iu. Sergeev, *'Inaia zemlia, inoe nebo'. Zapad i voennaia elita Rossii 1900–1914* (Moscow: Institut vseobshchei istorii RAN, 2001), pp. 45–6.

43 Menning, *Bayonets Before Bullets*, pp. 211–16; Fuller, *Civil–Military Conflict*, pp. 241–2; Sergeev, *'Inaia zemlia'*, p. 43; J. Sanborn, 'Military Reform, Moral Reform and the End of the Old Regime', in Lohr and Poe, *The Military and Society*, pp. 514, 524.

emergency, such as the First World War. General A. A. Polivanov may have been a ruthless, vindictive opportunist but he was also a masterly administrator who, after taking charge of the War Ministry in the summer of 1915, made immeasurable contributions to the revival of the army after the catastrophic defeats it suffered in Poland that spring. Yet despite this outstanding performance, when Nicholas II became displeased at Polivanov's co-operation with such 'social' organisations as the War Industries Committees, he abruptly dismissed his war minister after barely nine months in office. Polivanov's successor, although honest and straightforward, was considerably his inferior in ability.

A fourth and final drag on the Russian army's capability to adapt to change was financial. Traditionally, the majority of the army's budget had gone to 'subsistence costs' – the expenses of feeding, clothing and housing its troops.[44] But in the second half of the nineteenth century the rapid pace of military-technological change demanded heavy investments in new armaments. Still worse, by the late 1860s it grew apparent to Russia's military elite that a country's transportation infrastructure was indisputably crucial to military power. It was widely believed that Prussia had won the three wars of German unification in large measure owing to her skilful exploitation of railways to mobilise and concentrate her forces. Indeed, victory in future war might hinge entirely on the speed with which an army mobilised, for the war might be decided in its early battles, and the outcome of those would depend on the quantity of troops committed. Russia, however, was a poor country disadvantaged by its enormous size and its relatively sparse railway network.

The Russian Ministry of War consistently applied for extra appropriations to fund both upgrades in weaponry and strategic railway construction, but just as consistently met stiff opposition from the Ministry of Finance, where it was held that solvency and economic growth were only possible if military spending was restrained. Although Miliutin and his brilliant assistant N. N. Obruchev did pry loose enough money to pay for some rearmament, in 1873 Finance Minister Reutern blocked their plan for the development of Russia's western defences on fiscal grounds. Since the Russo-Turkish War left the empire 4.9 billion roubles in debt, there was little sunshine for the army in the state budgets of the 1880s and 1890s. The government did authorise the War Ministry's purchase of magazine rifles in 1888, but the army's share of state expenditures fell below 20 per cent by the mid-1890s and was to remain there for

44 David R. Jones, 'The Soviet Defence Burden through the Prism of History', in Carl Jakobson (ed.), *The Soviet Defence Enigma* (Oxford: Oxford University Press, 1988), p. 161.

almost a decade. The boom in state-subsidised railway construction during this period did not profit the army very much either, because commercial considerations usually trumped strategic ones in decisions about where to lay down track.[45]

Deprived of the wherewithal to build railroads and fortresses to check a German or Austrian attack, the War Ministry redeployed the army so as to concentrate a higher proportion of its active strength close to the western frontiers. By 1892, 45 per cent of the army was billeted in the empire's westernmost military districts. This measure was, however, an inadequate substitute for a thorough technological preparation of the likely theatre of war. The signing of the alliance with France that same year did bring the army some breathing space and rescued the military leadership from the nightmarish prospect of having to fight the Germans solo. Yet new fiscal woes cropped up at the turn of the century, for reckless imperialism in East Asia gave the army new territories to defend and sorely taxed the military budget. Underfunding and overextension produced a situation in which Russia was fully ready for war neither in the East nor in the West. When the Russo-Japanese War began, six of the forts that were supposed to guard Port Arthur from the landward side were still under construction, and none of them boasted any heavy ordnance.

The Japanese war and repressive service in the revolution had drained the strength of the Russian army, and it was imperative that it be reconstituted. The first signs of military recovery manifested themselves in the summer of 1908 when the general staff issued a comprehensive report that detailed ten years' worth of essential reforms and improvements. Some of this plan was actually implemented under the supervision of the controversial V. A. Sukhomlinov (war minister 1909–15). Sukhomlinov reorganised the army, shifted the centre of gravity of its deployment back to the east, introduced a territorial cadre reserve system, augmented Russia's stocks of machine guns and artillery, and purchased the empire's first military aircraft. He was able to pay for these innovations in part because of the enthusiasm of influential Duma politicians for the cause of national security, in part because of the support of the emperor, and in part because of the upsurge in Russian economic growth that began in 1910. The empire's revenues increased by a billion roubles between 1910 and 1914, and the army was a principal beneficiary. In October 1913 Nicholas II approved the 'Big Programme' of extraordinary defence expenditure, which mandated an increase in the size of the peacetime army by nearly 40 per

45 Fuller, *Civil–Military Conflict*, pp. 49, 63–4.

cent.[46] Army appropriations totalled 709 million roubles in 1913, and by that point Russia was spending more on her army than any other state in Europe.

Yet it is important to put these developments in context. Russia's plans for military modernisation may have been impressive, but they were not designed to be complete until 1917 at the earliest and were overtaken by the premature commencement of the general European war. Indeed, there is evidence that one reason Germany chose war in 1914 was the awareness that it would be easier to defeat Russia before her military reforms had taken full effect. Moreover, although the increase in army spending in the last few years of peace was dramatic, it was not ample enough to fund all of the War Ministry's initiatives, including some regarded as urgent. For example, while in 1909 Sukhomlinov made a persuasive case that Russia needed to double the number of heavy artillery pieces in her inventory, he did not succeed in obtaining the 110 million roubles this would have cost. The problem here was the army's resource competition with the navy. Beginning in 1907, the imperial government adopted one expensive and unnecessary naval construction programme after another. The state lavished millions on its fleet primarily for considerations of international prestige, but as subsequent events were to prove, ocean-going dreadnoughts were luxuries that Russia could ill afford.[47]

Conclusion: the World War

The First World War confronted Russia with the full implications of her backwardness. To begin with, her Central Power opponents outclassed her both in transportation infrastructure and in military technology. Germany's railway network was twelve times as dense as Russia's, while even Austria-Hungary's was seven times as dense.[48] Then, too, Russian artillery was inferior to German, and Germany held a crucial advantage over Russia in heavy artillery. By the end of 1914, the unanticipated tempo of combat operations had nearly depleted Russia's pre-war stockpile of artillery shells. This happened in other belligerent countries as well, but most of them were positioned to reorganise their industrial sectors for war production more quickly than Russia could. To be sure, Russia had the fifth largest industrial economy in the world in 1914, but that economy was unevenly developed and not self-sufficient. The chemical

46 Peter Gatrell, *Government, Industry and Rearmament in Russia, 1900–1914: The Last Argument of Tsarism* (Cambridge: Cambridge University Press, 1994), pp. 129–34.

47 K. F. Shatsillo, *Ot portsmutskogo mira k pervoi mirovoi voine. Generaly i politika* (Moscow: Rosspen, 2000), pp. 102, 139, 146, 159, 344.

48 Gatrell, *Government, Industry and Rearmament*, p. 305.

industry was in its infancy, and German imports supplied most of Russia's machine tools prior to the outbreak of the war. Russia did eventually manage to achieve an extraordinary expansion in the military output of her factories, so great in fact that by November of 1917 the provisional government had amassed a reserve of 18 million artillery shells.[49] Most of these, however, were rounds for the army's 3″ field piece, whose utility in trench warfare was severely limited. Russia was never able to manufacture heavy mortars, howitzers and high explosive shell in adequate enough quantities. Despite the growth in war production, the Russian army remained poorly supplied by comparison with its enemies. Germany fired 272 million artillery rounds of all calibre during the war, Austria, 70 million and Russia, only 50 million.[50] For much of the war, the Russian army suffered from a deficiency in *materiel*.

The war also occasioned a military manpower crisis, for the army's losses were unprecedented. Germany virtually destroyed five entire Russian army corps during the battles of August and September 1914. In the same period the forces of the Russian south-west front experienced a casualty rate of 40 per cent. By early 1915, in addition to the dead, there were 1 million Russian troops in enemy captivity or missing in action, and another 4 million who were *hors de combat* owing to sickness or wounds. In the end at least 1.3 million of Russia's soldiers would die in the war; some estimates put the figure at twice that.[51]

Military attrition ground down the officer corps, too. Over 90,000 officers had become casualties by the end of 1916, including a very high proportion of those who had earned their commissions before the war. The War Ministry improvised special short-term training courses to fill officer vacancies, whose graduates streamed to the army in such quantities that the character of military leadership was altered permanently. By 1917 the typical Russian junior officer was a commoner who had completed no more than four years of formal education.[52]

All of this had implications for Russia's military performance. So too did transportation bottlenecks, the excessive independence of front commanders, political turmoil back in Petrograd and sheer command error. The list of Russian defeats in the First World War is a long one and includes Tannenberg

49 Norman Stone, *The Eastern Front 1914–1917* (New York: Charles Scribner's Sons, 1975), p. 211.

50 Shatsillo, *Ot portsmutskogo mira*, p. 340.

51 William C. Fuller, Jr, 'The Eastern Front', in Jay Winter, Geoffrey Parker and Mary R. Habeck, (eds.), *The Great War and the Twentieth Century* (New Haven: Yale University Press, 2000), p. 32.

52 Alan K. Wildman, *The End of the Russian Imperial Army: The Old Army and the Soldiers' Revolt (March–April, 1917)* (Princeton: Princeton University Press, 1980), pp. 96–7.

(1914), the winter battle of Masuria (1915), Gorlice-Tarnow (1915) and Naroch (1916) among other disasters. Yet the operational picture was not unrelievedly bleak, for from 1914 to 1916 the army chalked up some remarkable successes, particularly against the Ottomans and Austrians. The most significant of these was the summer 1916 offensive conducted by General A. A. Brusilov, which inflicted a million casualties on the Austrians and Germans, and overran 576,000 square kilometres of territory before its impetus was spent.

Despite everything, Russia's loss of the First World War was not preordained. It was, after all, the Revolution, not hostile military action that took Russia out of the war. But although Russia's backwardness did not guarantee her defeat in the great war, it nonetheless severely reduced her chances of achieving victory. At the dawn of the imperial era Russia was able to devise a military system that capitalised on backwardness to give rise to military power. By the time of the Crimean War, backwardness was no longer a military blessing, but a curse. The imperial government then endeavoured to reshape the military system and bring it into conformity with the demands of modern war. Success was only partial, for enough vestiges of the old system remained to stymie progress. The Russian army in the late imperial period was therefore something like a butterfly, struggling in vain to free itself completely from its chrysalis. Tsarist military reformers had envisioned an army suitable for an industrial age of mass politics, but it would be up to the Soviets to translate that vision into reality.

26

Russian foreign policy: 1815–1917

DAVID SCHIMMELPENNINCK VAN DER OYE

During the final century of Romanov rule, Russian foreign policy was motivated above all by the need to preserve the empire's hard-won status as a European Great Power.[1] The campaigns and diplomacy of Peter I, Catherine II and the other emperors and empresses of the eighteenth century had raised their realm's prestige to the first rank among the states that mattered in the West. The stunning victories in the French revolutionary wars at the turn of the nineteenth century marked the apogee of tsarist global might. By defeating Napoleon's designs for continental dominion in 1812, Tsar Alexander I won an admiration and respect for Russia unparalleled in any other age. The difficult challenge for his heirs would be to keep Alexander's legacy intact.

Despite a reputation for aggression and adventurism, nineteenth-century tsarist diplomacy was essentially conservative. In the West, Russian territorial appetites were sated. Having recently absorbed most of Poland, one traditional foe, and won Finland from its erstwhile Swedish rival, the empire kept its European borders unchanged until the dynasty's demise in 1917. The imperative here was to protect these frontiers, especially the Polish salient. Surrounded on three sides by the Central European powers of Austria and Prussia, Poland never reconciled itself to Russian rule, and the restive nation seemed particularly vulnerable to foreign military aggression and revolutionary agitation. Maintaining the continental status quo therefore appeared to be the best guarantee for securing Russia's western border. For much of the nineteenth century, the Romanovs would strive to maintain stability in close

1 The five Great Powers of the nineteenth century were Austria, France, Great Britain, Prussia (after 1871, Germany) and Russia. As one standard textbook explains, 'a Power has such rank when acknowledged by others to have it. The fact of a Power belonging in that category makes it what has been called a Power with general interests, meaning by this one which has automatically a voice in all affairs' (R. Albrecht-Carrié, *A Diplomatic History of Europe since the Congress of Vienna* (New York: Harper and Brothers, 1958), pp. 21–2).

partnership with Europe's other leading conservative autocracies, the Prussian Hohenzollerns and the Austrian Habsburgs.

The strategic landscape on Russia's south-western frontier was more unsettled. The neighbour there was Ottoman Turkey, an empire very much in decline by the reign of Alexander I. There were still some lands to be won in this region if the occasion presented itself, especially earlier in the century. At the same time, many Russians sympathised with Orthodox Christians under Ottoman rule in the Balkans. Yet in the main, St Petersburg preferred order to opportunity in Turkey as well. A very basic strategic calculus dictated caution: Ottoman instability might well invite involvement by European rivals, thereby possibly jeopardising the Turkish Straits and the Black Sea, whose waters washed south-western Russia. Tsars did go to war against Turkey four times during the nineteenth century, albeit with increasing reluctance. While the senescent Ottomans could never match the comparatively stronger military of the Romanovs, two such confrontations led to severe humiliations for Russia when other powers intervened to support Turkey.

The only real arena for Russian expansion after 1815 was in Asia. To the east of Turkey, the empire bordered on states of varying cohesion. Like the Ottomans, the ruling dynasties of Persia and China were also well past their prime. Despite growing internal stresses, both of these governments managed to avert territorial disintegration. Nevertheless, St Petersburg benefited from occasional weakness in Tehran and Peking to improve its position in Asia to the latter's detriment. Between Persia and China, Russia's frontier was even less stable. The steppes that lay in this region were peopled by antiquated khanates and fragile nomadic confederations, whose medieval cavalry proved no match for European rifle and artillery. As in Africa and the American West during this era of colonial expansion, these Central Asian lands were ripe for absorption by a more developed power.

To respond to these divergent imperatives along its vast borders, nineteenth-century St Petersburg basically divided the world beyond into three parts and acted with each according to a distinct strategy. To its west, Russia aspired to maintain its dignity as a leading power and therefore championed the status quo. With regard to Turkey, motivated by anxiety over the Straits, tsarist officials jockeyed for position among European rivals. And in Central and East Asia, they pursued a policy of cautious opportunism, occasionally expanding the realm where and when possible. St Petersburg understood that these three regions did not exist in isolation. Developments in Central Asia, for example a conquest near the Afghan border, might well have implications in the West, by straining ties with a European power like Great Britain. Nevertheless, until the turn of the twentieth century tsarist foreign policy maintained this diplomatic trinity with remarkable consistency. Despite two major setbacks, both involving Turkey, the Russian Empire was able to achieve its primary international imperatives along all three lines. However, when Nicholas II acceded to the throne in 1894, unsteadier hands began to guide Russian foreign affairs, with fatal consequences for both dynasty and empire.

From Holy Alliance to Crimean isolation

The Vienna Conference of 1814–15 set the European diplomatic order of the nineteenth century. Summoned in the wake of Napoleon's defeat, statesmen of the leading powers and a host of lesser monarchies assembled in the Austrian capital to rebuild the peace. After a quarter of a century of revolution and war, the victorious allies – Britain, Russia, Austria and Prussia – sought enduring stability rather than revenge. They hoped to achieve this by restoring the map to a semblance of what it had been before the storming of the Bastille in 1789, as well as setting up a mechanism for jointly resolving major disputes. On the whole, the outcome was successful. The four allies, soon rejoined by France, maintained a relative balance of power for the following century, and Europe avoided another major continental conflagration until 1914.

One of the most contentious issues at Vienna was the fate of Poland. Partitioned by Catherine II in the late eighteenth century between her empire, Austria and Prussia, the nation had regained a semblance of independence under Napoleon. Alexander now proposed to join most of Poland to his own realm as a semi-autonomous kingdom. Reflecting his earlier liberal inclinations, the tsar offered to grant his new possession a constitution and other privileges. Despite strong opposition from Austria and Britain,[2] Alexander won the conference's consent. He also convinced the other delegates to join his 'Holy Alliance', a vague, idealistic appeal to all Christian princes to live together in harmony. Bereft of any concrete apparatus to enforce it and scorned by cynical diplomats, this utopian initiative had little lasting effect, serving more as a reflection of the emperor's withdrawal into otherworldly concerns. During the coming years, the diplomatic initiative on the continent was effectively ceded to Austria's conservative foreign minister, Prince Klemens von Metternich.

The disagreement between Russia and Britain in Vienna over Poland augured deeper differences. Both geopolitics and ideology drove this rivalry,

2 In contrast to Prussia, which also took advantage from the Congress of Vienna to make major territorial gains.

which would remain one of the most enduring constants of nineteenth-century tsarist diplomacy. Loyal to its tradition of maintaining a balance of power on the continent, the British Foreign Office inevitably sought to counterpoise the strongest European state. To London, the Russian Empire seemed particularly menacing, since its enormous Eurasian landmass seemed to have the potential to affect British interests both at home and in its colonies overseas. This strategic competition was exacerbated by a strong distaste among many in the British public for the repressive ways of the Romanov autocracy. Meanwhile, the anti-Napoleonic alliance inevitably weakened in the absence of a common foe. Already within seven years of the negotiations at Vienna, the conference system foundered over Britain's reluctance to intervene against revolutions in Europe. This difference of opinion only drove St Petersburg closer to the Habsburgs and the Hohenzollerns, whose conservative politics were more reassuring.

The increasingly reactionary turn of Alexander I's final decade determined Russia's approach to a Greek revolt against Turkish rule in the early 1820s, the first important manifestation of the Eastern Question that would vex Europe's chancelleries with nagging regularity until the Great War. The Eastern Question asked what would happen to the Ottoman sultan's European possessions as his dynasty's grip weakened. Aside from Berlin (until the turn of the twentieth century, at any rate) all of the leading powers considered themselves to be vitally concerned with the fate of the Porte. Vienna, which also ruled over Orthodox minorities in the region, feared that successful emancipation from Turkish dominion of Balkan Christians might contaminate its own Slav subjects with the virus of nationalism. As naval powers, Britain and, to a lesser extent, France worried about the Turkish Straits, the maritime passage from Constantinople to the Dardanelles that linked the Black Sea to the Mediterranean. St Petersburg was similarly concerned about the security of the Straits, 'the key to the Russian house', lest Russia's Black Sea shores become vulnerable to hostile warships. But there were also important elements of Russian opinion that sympathised with the plight of Orthodox co-religionists in European Turkey.

These contradictory elements of tsarist Balkan diplomacy confronted each other during the Greek rising that erupted in spring 1821. Alexander was initially shocked by Turkey's draconian repression of the insurgency, but, with some prodding from Prince Metternich, he gradually became more concerned about maintaining the status quo. Even if it involved a Muslim sultan, the principle of monarchical legitimacy overrode the rights of national minorities. To yield to subversion anywhere, the tsar feared, might open the floodgates to regicide and anarchy throughout the continent, not to mention shattering the post-war alliance system. A mutiny in his own Semenovskii Guards regiment in 1820 had only deepened Alexander's pessimism about a ubiquitous revolutionary 'empire of evil . . . more powerful than the might of Napoleon'.[3] Appeals from the insurgents for support against Turkey fell on deaf ears, and in 1822 the emperor sidelined a leading official in his own Foreign Ministry sympathetic to the revolt, the Ionian Count Ionnes Kapodistrias.

Nicholas I, who inherited the throne in 1825, tended to be equally loyal to the diplomatic status quo, despite some Near Eastern temptations early in his reign. At the same time, he kept on his older brother's foreign minister, Count Karl Nesselrode. More forceful and direct than Alexander and thoroughly immune to any idealistic temptations, Nicholas unambiguously opposed any challenges to the authority of his fellow sovereigns. Such tests were not long in coming. His own reign had begun inauspiciously with the Decembrist revolt, an attempted coup by Guards' officers with constitutionalist aspirations. Five years later, in 1830, a wave of revolutions beginning in France convulsed the continent. When Belgians rose against Dutch rule that year, Nicholas prepared to send troops to support King William I of Orange, who also happened to be his brother-in-law's father. However, such plans were cut short when a separatist revolt erupted in Poland, whose suppression required more immediate attention.

Deeply shaken by these and other disturbances, the tsar resolved to co-operate more closely with the other conservative powers to preserve the political order in Europe. In 1833 he met with the Austrian emperor, Francis II and Prussia's Crown Prince at the Bohemian town of Münchengrätz, where among other matters he signed a treaty on 6 (18) September offering to intervene in support of any sovereign threatened by internal disturbances. It was on the basis of this agreement that Nicholas intervened in Hungary to help the Habsburgs restore their rule in the waning days of a revolt that had begun during the European revolutions of 1848.

At mid-century, Russia still seemed to be the continent's dominant state. Unlike 1830, the disturbances of 1848 had not even touched Nicholas's empire, and his autocratic allies had successfully weathered the recent political storms. The only on-going military challenge was Imam Shamil's lengthy rebellion in the Caucasus Mountains. While it would take nearly another decade to pacify the region, the Islamic insurgency was largely dismissed as a colonial

3 P. K. Grimsted, *The Foreign Ministers of Alexander I* (Berkeley and Los Angeles: University of California Press, 1969), p. 277.

small war by the other powers and hardly diminished Russia's martial reputation. Yet his seeming invincibility began to cloud Nicholas's judgement. At the same time, the zeal of the 'Gendarme of Europe' to root out all enemies of monarchism, wherever they might lurk, earned him the almost universal dislike of his contemporaries abroad. Even the Austrian foreign minister, Prince Felix Schwarzenberg, darkly muttered after Russia's Hungarian intervention that 'Europe would be astonished by the extent of Austria's ingratitude'.[4] When complications arose once again in Turkey in the early 1850s, Nicholas discovered to his cost that Machiavelli's celebrated maxim about the advantages of being feared was not always valid.

The Greek crisis had remained unresolved at the time of Alexander's death in 1825. Although Nicholas shared his brother's distaste for the rising, he negotiated with London and Paris to seek a solution. After a series of clashes, including an Anglo-French naval intervention and a brief, albeit difficult war with Turkey, by 1829 the Eastern Mediterranean was again at peace. According to the Treaty of Adrianople that Nicholas concluded with the sultan on September 2 (14) of that year, the Ottomans formally ceded Georgia, confirmed Greek as well as Serbian autonomy and granted substantial concessions in the Danubian principalities (the core of the future Romania), which became a virtual tsarist satellite. Meanwhile, St Petersburg also won important strategic gains, including control of the Danube River's mouth.

Impressive as they were, Nicholas's gains belied considerable restraint, given the magnitude of the Turkish rout. Although his forces were within striking distance of Constantinople, the tsar refrained from dealing the *coup de grâce*. Order and legitimacy continued to be paramount in his considerations. A commission Nicholas convened that year to consider the Eastern Question unequivocally declared, 'that the advantages of the preservation of the Ottoman Empire in Europe outweigh the disadvantages and that, as a result, its destruction would be contrary to the interests of Russia'.[5]

Preserving the Ottoman Empire in Europe did not necessarily imply foregoing any advantages that St Petersburg might be able to extract from the Porte. Thus four years after Adrianople, Nicholas negotiated an even more favourable pact with the Ottomans, the Treaty of Unkiar-Skelessi on 26 June (8 July) 1833, in return for assistance in putting down a rebellion by the latter's Egyptian vassal. But the tsarist ascent in Turkey led to considerable alarm in

4 In Albrecht-Carrié, *Diplomatic History*, p. 73.
5 In William C. Fuller, *Strategy and Power in Russia 1600–1914* (New York: Free Press, 1992), p. 222.

Britain, which saw a great outburst of Russophobia in the press. Yet another Turkish crisis in 1839 once again invited foreign intervention, now by Russia acting together with Britain and Austria. The outcome of this action was the Straits Convention of 1 (13) June 1841, which forced Russia to backtrack from its demands at Unkiar-Skelessi eight years earlier. For the next decade the Eastern Mediterranean remained relatively calm.

The origins of the Crimean War, Russia's most catastrophic entanglement in the Eastern Question, remain a source of lively controversy. What is clear is that the conflict began, almost innocuously, over a French attempt in 1850 to extend the Catholic Church's rights to maintain the Holy Places, sacred sites of Christendom in Ottoman-ruled Palestine. Motivated by President Louis Napoleon's effort to court domestic political support, the ploy elicited a strong response from Nicholas, who insisted on the prerogatives of the Orthodox Church. Although none of the powers sought war, the tsar's clumsy diplomacy, the intransigence of the sultan and the machinations of Stratford Canning, Britain's Russophobe minister to Constantinople, all helped transform a 'quarrel of monks' into the first major clash among the powers since Waterloo.

The Crimean War itself was more a diplomatic than a military defeat for Russia. The fighting, which eventually focused on the Black Sea naval bastion of Sebastopol, was marked by colossal inefficiency, blunders and incompetence among all combatants. Although Sebastopol eventually fell to the combined forces of Britain, France, Turkey and Sardinia, the siege had taken nearly a year, and logistics made further action against Russia exceedingly difficult. It was only when Austria sided with the allies towards the end of 1855 that St Petersburg was forced to sue for peace.

The moderate terms of the Peace of Paris, which the combatants concluded on 18 (30) March 1856, reflected the relatively inconclusive nature of the Crimean campaign. St Petersburg was forced to return the Danubian region of Bessarabia, annexed in 1812, to the Porte and generally saw its influence in the Balkans decline. More galling were the so-called Black Sea clauses that demilitarised these waters, severely restricting tsarist freedom of action on its south-western frontier. Yet if the allies refrained from exacting a heavy penalty on their foe, Russia's setback in the Crimea was a devastating blow to Romanov prestige. Nicholas's army, feared by many as the mailed fist of Europe's most formidable autocracy, had proven to be a paper tiger. Not for nearly another century, and then under a very different regime, would Russia regain its pre-eminent standing on the continent.

Recueillement

Defeat in the Crimea broke both Nicholas's order and its creator. Profoundly depressed by the humiliations inflicted on his beloved military, the emperor easily succumbed to a cold in February 1855 and was succeeded by his son, Alexander II. The new tsar clearly understood the link between backwardness at home and weakness abroad, and largely withdrew from European affairs to concentrate on reforming his empire. As his foreign minister, Prince Aleksandr Gorchakov, famously put it, 'La Russie ne boude pas, elle se recueille' (Russia is not sulking, it is recovering its strength).[6] Rather than battling the chimera of revolution, Alexander II's diplomacy endeavoured to repair the damage done by the recent war. In Europe, this amounted to ending St Petersburg's isolation and abrogating the distasteful Black Sea clauses.

Recueillement, or the avoidance of foreign complications to focus on domestic renewal, did not apply to all of the empire's frontiers. To the east Alexander II oversaw dramatic advances on the Pacific and in Central Asia. Already in the waning years of Nicholas I's reign, the ambitious governor-general of Eastern Siberia, Count Nikolai Murav'ev, had begun to take advantage of the Qing dynasty's growing infirmity to penetrate its northern Manchurian marches. As would often prove the case in Central Asia during the coming decades, the count was acting on his own, but his master turned a blind eye to his colonial ambitions.

When in 1858 Peking suffered defeat during the Second Opium War with Britain and France, Count Nikolai Ignat'ev, a skilled diplomat who fully shared Murav'ev's enthusiastic imperialism, benefited from the Middle Kingdom's malaise to negotiate vast annexations of the latter's territory. The Treaties of Aigun and Peking, signed on 28 May (9 June) 1858 and 2 (14) November 1860, respectively, ceded the right bank of the Amur River and the area east of the Ussuri River, thereby expanding Russian rule southwards to the north-eastern tip of Korea. Count Murav'ev modestly named a port he founded in his new acquisition Vladivostok (ruler of the East).

Russian gains in Central Asia were no less spectacular. In the early nineteenth century, a string of fortifications, stretching from the northern tip of the Caspian Sea to the fortress of Semipalatinsk on the border with the north-western Chinese territories of Xinjiang, marked the southward extent of Russia's march into Central Asia. The arid plains beyond were ruled by the archaic khanates of Kokand, Khiva and Bokhara. Collectively known to Russians as

6 Constantin de Grunwald, *Trois siècles de diplomatie russe* (Paris: Callman-Lévi, 1945), p. 198.

Turkestan[7] together with the Kazakh Steppe, this troika of Islamic fiefdoms had prospered as transit points for caravans traversing the Great Silk Road in an earlier age. However, they had long since degenerated into internecine strife, and now seemed to derive the bulk of their wealth from raiding overland commerce and taking Russian subjects as slaves.

The final defeat of Shamil in 1859 and the 'pacification' of the Caucasus had freed a large army for action elsewhere. At the same time, martial glory in Central Asia promised to restore some lustre to Russia's badly tarnished military prestige. In 1860 tsarist troops began to engage the Khanate of Kokand. The first major city to fall was Tashkent, which a force led by General Mikhail Cherniaev took in 1865. Three years later General Konstantin von Kaufmann marched through the gates of Tamerlane's fabled capital of Samarkand and within short order Kokand and Bokhara submitted to Russian protection. Finally, in 1873 Kaufmann also subdued the remaining Khanate of Khiva. Rather than being annexed outright, Khiva and Bokhara were made protectorates and retained internal autonomy under their traditional rulers.

During the Central Asian campaigns, Prince Gorchakov sought to reassure the other European powers that his sovereign's Asian policy was largely defensive and aimed primarily to establish a border secure against the restive tribes beyond. In an oft-quoted circular of 1864, Prince Gorchakov stated:

> The position of Russia in Central Asia is that of all civilised states which find themselves in contact with half-savage, nomadic populations . . . In such cases, it always happens that interests of security of borders and of commercial relations demand of the more civilised state that it asserts a certain dominion over others, who with their nomadic and turbulent customs are most uncomfortable neighbours.

He went on to promise that Russia's frontier would be fixed in order to avoid 'the danger of being carried away, as is almost inevitable, by a series of repressive measures and reprisals, into an unlimited extension of territory'.[8]

London remained unconvinced by Gorchakov's logic. Many of its strategists feared that the Russian advance into Central Asia threatened India, and until the early twentieth century, halting what appeared to be Russia's inexorable advance on 'the most splendid appanage of the British Crown'[9] was

7 Not to be confused with Eastern Turkestan, as the Islamic western Chinese region of Xinjiang was then known.

8 A. M. Gorchakov, memorandum, 21 November 1864, in D. C. B. Lieven (ed.), *British Documents on Foreign Affairs: Reports and Papers from the Foreign Office Confidential Print* (University Press of America, 1983–9), part I, series A, I, p. 287.

9 G. N. Curzon, *Russia in Central Asia in 1889 and the Anglo-Russian Question* (London: Longmans, Green and Co., 1889), p. 14.

a prime directive of Whitehall's foreign policy. To the British, this conflict came to be known as the Great Game, whose stakes, in the words of Queen Victoria, were nothing less than 'a question of Russian or British supremacy in the world'.[10] Like the Cold War waged in the latter half of the twentieth century between the United States and the Soviet Union, the Great Game involved very little direct combat between the adversaries. Instead, the conflict was largely waged through proxies and involved considerable intrigue and espionage. Count Nesselrode aptly described the rivalry as a 'tournament of shadows'.[11]

The Pamir Mountains, at the intersection of Turkestan, Afghanistan, British India and Xinjiang, marked Imperial Russia's furthest advance into Central Asia. As long as tsarist territory abutted onto small, independent fiefdoms such as the khanates, Russian armies pressed forward. By the 1890s, its borders had reached those of the more established states of Afghanistan and China. In the case of the former, England's interest in maintaining buffers between Russia and India effectively precluded further advances, and the borders remained fixed.

Alexander II's dramatic conquests in Asia marked the culmination of a process that had begun over three centuries earlier with Ivan IV's storm of the Khanate of Kazan. Because these lands were contiguous to Russia's own territory, because the advance seemed so inexorable and because it was carried out by a somewhat exotic autocracy, Western contemporaries often imputed sinister motives to tsarist expansion. Yet Russian imperialism in Asia was nothing more than a manifestation of the global European drive to impose colonial hegemony over nations with less effective armed forces, a process that had begun in the era of Christopher Columbus.

As with the broader phenomenon of modern imperialism, there have been many explanations for Alexander II's small wars. These include an apocryphal testament by Peter the Great, orthodox Marxist logic involving Central Asian cotton fields, and the German historian Dietrich Geyer's hypothesis about a 'compensatory psychological need' as balm for the wounds inflicted on national pride by the Crimean debacle.[12] Perhaps the most creative conjecture was offered by Interior Minister Petr Valuev in 1865, 'General Cherniaev took Tashkent. No one knows why or to what end . . . There is something erotic

10 D. Fromkin, 'The Great Game in Asia', *Foreign Affairs* (Spring 1980): 951.

11 M. Edwardes, *Playing the Great Game: A Victorian Cold War* (London: Hamish Hamilton, 1975), p. viii.

12 Dietrich Geyer, *Russian Imperialism: The Interaction of Domestic and Foreign Policy, 1860–1914* (New Haven: Yale University Press, 1987), p. 205.

about our goings on at the distant periphery of the empire. On the Amur, the Ussuri, and now Tashkent.'[13]

Whatever its parentage, it is clear that the push into Asia under Alexander II did not follow some nefarious master plan. Much of it was carried out by ambitious officers eager to advance their careers, even to the point of insubordination. When successful, Oriental conquest often brought glory and imperial favour. At the same time, tsarist diplomats remained attentive to the wider international implications of Russia's actions on the frontier. Thus, after a ten-year occupation of the Ili River valley in Xinjiang, ostensibly to help suppress a Muslim rising against Qing rule, Russia returned part of the territory to China according to the Treaty of St Petersburg on 12 (24) February 1881. Meanwhile, the prospect of British aggression, not to mention its increasing economic burden, had already led the emperor to sell his North American colony of Alaska to the United States in 1867.

In Europe, the first priority of Alexander II's diplomacy was to extricate his empire from its Crimean isolation. Even as the Peace of Paris was being negotiated, there were overtures from the French Emperor Napoleon III for a rapprochement with his former combatant. In September 1857 the two sovereigns met in Stuttgart and informally agreed to co-operate on various European questions. The Franco-Russian entente was motivated by mutual antipathy to Austria. Alexander II felt deeply betrayed by Vienna's decision to back his enemies during the Crimean War, while Napoleon III hoped to diminish Habsburg influence in Italy, where that dynasty's possessions were becoming increasingly tenuous. The dalliance came to an abrupt end, however, when the Catholic Second Empire emotionally supported a second Polish revolt against tsarist rule in 1863.

Prussia's Protestant King Wilhelm I, whose subjects also included Poles, harboured no such sympathies for the Catholic insurgents. As the rising gained momentum, he sent a trusted general, Count Albert von Alvensleben-Erxleben, to St Petersburg to offer his kingdom's military co-operation. The resultant Alvensleben Convention of 27 January (8 February) 1863 was not a major factor in restoring order. Yet it provided an important boost to Russian prestige and helped Gorchakov head off efforts by Paris, London and Vienna to intervene in the crisis. Over the coming years, Berlin also proved to be the most stalwart supporter of the foreign minister's efforts to repeal the Black Sea clauses. Prince Gorchakov finally succeeded in this ambition in 1870, during the confusion of the Franco-Prussian War. In return, Russia maintained a

13 Petr Aleksandrovich Valuev, *Dnevnik*, ed. P. A. Zaionchkovskii, 2 vols. (Moscow: Izd. AN SSSR, 1961), vol. II, pp. 60–1.

benevolent neutrality during Prussia's campaigns against Austria of 1866 and France four years later. Tsarist diplomacy thereby helped Wilhelm I realise his dream of uniting Germany into an empire in 1871, a development whose strategic implications soon became apparent to the Russian General Staff.

The two autocracies were bound by more than pure self-interest. Ideology and dynastic ties (Wilhelm I was Alexander II's uncle) also helped foster cordiality between the Romanovs and the Hohenzollerns. As a couple the union was relatively harmonious. The efforts of the new German Empire's Chancellor Otto von Bismarck to establish a *ménage à trois* with the Habsburgs proved less successful. Endeavouring to secure Germany's eastern flank, Bismarck negotiated a *Dreikaiserbund* (three emperors' league) in 1873. Neither an alliance nor a formal treaty, the coalition was nothing more than a vague statement of intent to co-operate along the lines of the old Holy Alliance. Too much had changed in the intervening decades for a full restoration of pre-Crimean solidarity between the three empires. Whereas in the first half of the nineteenth century Russia had been the continent's dominant power, after 1871 Germany had a more valid claim to that distinction. More important, the two junior partners had very divergent aims in the Balkans. When forced to choose, Berlin invariably favoured Teutonic Vienna over Slavic St Petersburg.

Alexander II's reign ended, as it had begun, with a major setback in the Near East. Russia's fourth war with Turkey in the nineteenth century erupted over another anti-Turkish rising among its restive Slavic subjects in 1875. Harsh repression in Bosnia-Herzegovina and Bulgaria horrified the Christian powers, but there was considerable reluctance to become involved once again in a Balkan conflict. For the first time, public opinion in Russia was also making an impact on tsarist policy, as Pan-Slavs noisily agitated in the press for military support to emancipate the sultan's Orthodox subjects. Gorchakov, now close to his eightieth birthday and in failing health, tried to head off a confrontation through the Dreikaiserbund, but more bellicose passions among his compatriots and the Porte's refusal to compromise forced Alexander's hand. Despite some misgivings, the tsar declared war on Turkey on 12 (24) April 1877. After an unexpectedly arduous march through the Bulgarian highlands, in February 1878 Russian troops reached San Stefano, virtually at the gates of Constantinople.

As in 1829, the Ottoman capital was for the taking. However, on this occasion it was the threat of British intervention, underscored by the presence of the Royal Navy's Mediterranean Squadron at anchor in nearby Turkish waters, that discouraged Russian troops from completing their advance. Count Ignat'ev, now ambassador to the Porte, therefore negotiated an end to the conflict with the Treaty of San Stefano on 19 February (3 March) 1878. Although it halted the fighting, the agreement failed to placate London or Vienna. Most alarming to them was the provision of a large Bulgarian state, presumably a Russian satellite, which would dominate the Balkans. Within a few months the European powers met in neutral Germany to negotiate a more acceptable settlement.

The Treaty of Berlin, concluded on 1 (13) July 1878, satisfied none of the signatories, least of all Prince Gorchakov. While the new pact yielded some territorial gains in the Caucasus and in Bessarabia, Russians regarded it as a humiliating setback. Gorchakov declared that Berlin was 'the darkest page of [his] life'.[14] Much like the Congress of Paris twenty-four years earlier, St Petersburg once again found itself diplomatically isolated. But this time there was a different scapegoat. Bismarck, who had hosted the powers as 'honest broker', bore the brunt of Russian resentment because of his failure to support his partner. In the coming years Alexander II would nevertheless instinctively look back to Germany for a new combination, culminating in a secret Three Emperor's Alliance in 1881. But over the longer term the damage to Russo-German relations proved to be irreparable.

Alexander III, who became emperor upon his father's assassination in March 1881, clearly understood the need to keep his realm at peace. A senior diplomat described the priority of the new tsar's foreign policy as 'establishing Russia in an international position that will permit it to restore order at home, to recover from its dreadful injury and then channel all of its strength towards a national restoration'.[15] Under his foreign minister, Nikolai Giers, Alexander III's diplomacy even more steadfastly pursued a course of *recueillement*. Tsarist caution even extended into Central Asia, where the threat of a confrontation in 1885 with Britain at Panjdeh on the Afghan border was quickly defused. Although his contemporaries regarded him as reactionary and unimaginative, Alexander III achieved his goal, and during his thirteen-year reign Russian guns remained at rest.

The most dramatic development of Alexander's comparatively brief rule was a definitive break with Germany in favour of a military alliance with France, which he ratified on 15 (27) December 1893. Despite the tsar's ideological distaste for French republicanism, there were many sound reasons for the new alignment. Relations with the Hohenzollerns had already taken a

14 In David MacKenzie, *The Serbs and Russian Panslavism, 1875–1878* (Ithaca: Cornell University Press, 1967), p. 327.

15 V. N. Lamsdorff, 'Obzor vneshnei politiki Rossii za vremia tsarstvovaniia Aleksandra III', GARF, Fond 568, op. 1, d. 53, l. 1.

distinct turn for the worse in the late 1880s over a German grain tariff and a boycott of Russian bonds. The rift between the two autocracies became inevitable when in 1890 Germany's new Kaiser Wilhelm II offended Alexander by refusing to renew a secret promise of neutrality, the Reinsurance Treaty. There were also dynastic considerations. Whereas Alexander II's fondness for his uncle, Kaiser Wilhelm I, had sustained friendship with Berlin, Alexander III had married a princess of Denmark, which still bore the scars of defeat by Prussia four decades earlier. But the basic reason for the Franco-Russian alliance was geopolitical logic. Russian generals understood that the German Empire, aggressive and militarily powerful, posed the most serious threat to its strategic security. Furthermore, Berlin's growing intimacy with Vienna seriously complicated St Petersburg's position in the Balkans. For its part, France also smarted from its more recent humiliation by German arms. To the Third Republic, alliance with Russia seemed the best guarantee of support in a revanchist war.

When Alexander III died in 1894 (of natural causes), contemporaries commemorated him as the 'Tsar Peacemaker' (*Tsar' mirotvorets*). With the exception of a few short-lived monarchs in the eighteenth century, he was the only Romanov whose reign had been unsullied by war. Alexander was also faithful to a nineteenth-century diplomatic tradition that favoured consistency, caution and stability. Despite setbacks in the Crimea and at Berlin, over the past eighty years St Petersburg had largely steered a steady course in its international relations. During the reign of the last tsar, Nicholas II, the empire entered into distinctly stormier waters.

Decline and fall

Young and relatively unprepared to assume the responsibilities of autocrat, Nicholas was also subject to a much more restless and contradictory temperament than his immediate ancestors. The clearest sign of the unsettled diplomacy that characterised Nicholas's reign is the simple fact that, whereas three foreign ministers had served since 1815, no less than nine men held the post between 1894 and the dynasty's collapse in 1917.[16] However, to be fair

16 Although Nesselrode had held the post jointly with Capodistrias from 1816 to 1822. Nicholas II's foreign ministers were: N. K. Giers (until 1895), Prince Aleksei Borisovich Lobanov-Rostovskii (1895–6), Nikolai Pavlovich Shishkin (acting minister 1896–7), Count Mikhail Nikolaevich Murav'ev (1897–1900), Count Vladimir Nikolaevich Lambsdorff (1900–6), Aleksandr Petrovich Izvol'skii (1906–10), Sergei Dmitrievich Sazonov (1910–1916), Boris Nikolaevich Stürmer (1916), Nikolai Nikolaevich Pokrovskii (1916–17). Of the nine, two, Lobanov-Rostovskii and Murav'ev, died in office.

to this oft-maligned monarch, the turn of the twentieth century was a time of fevered instability throughout much of Europe, ultimately leading to a catastrophic world war that also claimed three other imperial houses.

The first decade of Nicholas II's rule was dominated by events on the Pacific. Much as the continuing decline of Europe's 'sick man', Ottoman Turkey, continued to attract the involvement of more vigorous powers, China, the sick man of Asia, increasingly also became the object of foreign ambitions at century's end. The immediate catalyst was the Qing military's defeat in a war with Japan over Korea during the first year of his reign. After debating the merits of joining Japan in 'slicing the melon' of China or supporting the Middle Kingdom's territorial integrity, Nicholas's ministers opted for the latter. Together with Germany and France, Russia pressed the Japanese into returning the Liaotung (Liaodong) Peninsula, with its strategically important naval base of Port Arthur (Lüshun), near Peking.

The tsarist intervention against Tokyo in 1895 set in motion a chain of events that led to a disastrous war with the Asian empire within a decade. Like the Crimean debacle half a century earlier, confrontation with Japan was neither inevitable nor desired. However, bickering among his councillors, both official and unofficial, severely hampered Nicholas's ability to pursue a coherent policy in the Far East. At first, the tsar benefited from Peking's gratitude by concluding a secret defensive alliance with the Qing on 22 May (3 June) 1896. In August of that year he secured a more concrete reward in the form of a 1,500-kilometre railway concession through Manchuria, which considerably shortened the last stretch of the Trans-Siberian railway then nearing completion. Then, toward the end of 1897 the new foreign minister, Count Mikhail Murav'ev, tricked his master into seizing Port Arthur shortly after the German navy had taken another valuable harbour in northern China, on Kiaochow (Jiaozhou) Bay. While Nicholas's move did not technically violate the previous year's agreement, it effectively killed the friendship with the Middle Kingdom. At the same time, by acquiring the very port that its diplomats had forced Japan to hand back to China in 1895, Russia aroused the unyielding enmity of the Meiji government.

The more immediate cause of the Russo-Japanese War was the tsar's reluctance to evacuate Manchuria, which his troops had occupied in 1900 in concert with an international intervention to suppress the xenophobic 'Boxer' rising in north-east China that summer. Although Russia had formally pledged to withdraw its forces from the region in spring 1902, it failed to live up to the final phase of the agreement, scheduled for autumn 1903. Japan had already become alarmed when Nicholas appointed a viceroy for the Far East two months earlier, an action that seemed to signal a stronger tsarist presence on the Pacific. On 24 January (6 February) 1904, Tokyo recalled its minister to St Petersburg and two days later Japanese torpedo boats launched a surprise nighttime raid on Russia's Pacific Squadron at Port Arthur.

The combat itself eventually became a war of attrition involving increasing numbers of troops in Manchuria. As the fighting wore on, Russian public opinion began to oppose the distant war. An attempt to regain the initiative on the waves by sending the powerful Baltic Fleet around the world to the northern Pacific ended catastrophically when much of it was sunk by the Imperial Japanese Navy in the Straits of Tsushima in May 1905. Humiliated at sea, unable to halt the adversary's advance into the Manchurian interior, financially exhausted and beset by revolutionary unrest on the home front, Nicholas readily accepted an American offer that summer to mediate an end to the conflict. Thanks to the brilliant diplomacy of the former finance minister, Sergei Witte, who headed the tsar's delegation to the peace talks in New Hampshire, Russia's penalty for defeat was comparatively light. Nevertheless, the Treaty of Portsmouth, which was concluded on 23 August (5 September) 1905, marked an end to Nicholas's dreams of Oriental glory.

As in 1855, the consequences of Russian military failure abroad had a major impact on politics at home. Facing mounting opposition from nearly all elements of society, in October 1905 the tsar announced the creation of an elected legislature, the Duma, and broader civil rights. While this concession did not convert the empire into a full parliamentary democracy, it did impose important limitations on the autocracy's prerogatives. More important, Nicholas's October Manifesto appeased many of his critics, thereby bringing his realm much needed domestic quiet.

Over the coming years, Foreign Minister Aleksandr Izvol'skii resolved most of the outstanding quarrels with other powers in East and Inner Asia. Thus on 21 June (4 July) 1907 he authorised an agreement with Japan, which, along with a treaty in 1910, recognised respective spheres of influence on the Pacific. More important, Izvol'skii also responded favourably to a British proposal to negotiate an end to the long-standing Asian rivalry. According to the Anglo-Russian Convention of 18 (31) August 1907, the two signatories accorded London influence over Afghanistan and southern Persia, while St Petersburg won dominance in Persia's more populous north. Although the pact did not entirely end the Great Game, it did much to improve relations between its two players. The convention also facilitated France's goal of forming an anti-German Triple Entente.

Russia's rebuff in the Far East redirected its attention back to the Near East. By now a number of Orthodox monarchies had gained independence from the Ottoman Sultan, while control over his much-diminished European inheritance was becoming increasingly tenuous. Meanwhile, the bacillus of nationalism had also begun to infect Austria-Hungary, whose Slavic minorities were becoming increasingly restive as well. Among the Dual Monarchy's subjects most vulnerable to separatist tendencies were Serbians, Croatians and Slovenes, many of whom yearned to join the Kingdom of Serbia into a 'jugoslav' or South Slavic federation. Belgrade, which was closely aligned with St Petersburg, naturally did little to discourage such aspirations. As a result, relations between Austria-Hungary and Serbia grew increasingly strained in the twentieth century's first decade. By the same token, the Eastern Question continued to be a source of friction between the Habsburgs and the Romanovs.

It was against this backdrop of mutual suspicion that Izvol'skii similarly attempted to fashion a deal with Russia's Balkan antagonist. In September 1908, the tsar's foreign minister secretly met with his Austrian counterpart, Count Alois von Aerenthal, at Buchlau Castle in Moravia. Accounts of the conversation between the two men differ, but their discussion focused on trading Austrian consent in re-opening the Turkish Straits to Russian warships in exchange for Russian recognition of the former's rule over the former Ottoman provinces of Bosnia-Herzegovina. Thinking that he had scored a brilliant diplomatic coup, Izvol'skii instead was horrified when Aerenthal soon publicised his consent to the Bosnian question without mentioning the Straits. Berlin's quick pledge of support for Vienna effectively forced the chastened official to accept the count's fait accompli.

Izvol'skii's 'diplomatic Tsushima' eventually led to his replacement as foreign minister by the relatively ineffectual Sergei Sazonov. But the Bosnian Crisis also had more serious consequences. On the one hand, Austria's absorption of a province with a large Serbian population inflamed nationalist passions in Belgrade. Meanwhile, Aerenthal's apparent duplicity along with German bullying over the matter only further aroused Russian hostility to the Teutonic partners. Along with other growing international stresses and strains, this animosity helped to divide the continent into two mutually hostile coalitions, pitting the Central Powers of Germany and Austria-Hungary against the Triple Entente of France, Britain and Russia. Armed conflict between the two groups was by no means inevitable. Nevertheless, preserving the peace grew increasingly complicated.

Over the next few years, the Balkans would be convulsed by a number of other crises, including two regional wars between 1911 and 1913. Both conflicts were localised as the powers largely kept to the sidelines. But when in June 1914 a Serbian nationalist, Gavrilo Princip, assassinated Archduke Franz-Ferdinand, the heir to the Habsburg throne, during a visit to the Bosnian capital of Sarajevo, Vienna was provoked into drastic measures against Belgrade. Despite determined efforts over the next month among the continent's chancelleries to head off a clash, in late July negotiations gave way to ultimata, mobilisations and finally the outbreak of the First World War.

With the possible exception of Austria-Hungary, which hoped for an isolated campaign to crush Serbia, none of the combatants sought a confrontation in July 1914. Nicholas was particularly reluctant to take up arms. Although his military had largely recovered from the recent defeat in East Asia, he knew that it was still no match for the Central Powers. Nevertheless, the tsar and many of his ministers were even more fearful of the penalty of not supporting Serbia, its partner, against an assault by the Dual Monarchy. Within the past forty years Russia had twice been forced to yield to Austria in the Balkans, at Berlin in 1878 and over the Bosnian question in 1908. A third capitulation might irreparably harm the empire's prestige, with fatal consequences for the Romanovs' standing as a great power.

The start of war did not end tsarist diplomacy. At first, much of Sazonov's attention was directed to securing the agreement of his allies for acquiring German and Austrian territory in a peace settlement. When Turkey entered the conflict on the side of the Central Powers in October 1914, the minister quickly began to focus on the Straits. Already in early 1915 he gained the consent of Britain and France for Russian control of the passage. Of course, to realise its expansive ambitions in Central Europe and the Near East, Russia needed to defeat its enemies. After two Russian armies were routed in East Prussia in August 1914, the likelihood of victory became increasingly remote. And a year later Poland and part of the Baltic provinces were in enemy hands. Although by 1916 tsarist forces had managed to stabilise their positions, once again the home front ultimately decided the outcome of the Russian war effort. Severe economic dislocation in the cities and poor political leadership severely discredited the dynasty, ultimately resulting in Nicholas's abdication in March 1917.

The character of tsarist diplomacy

More than in any other era, between 1815 and 1917 Russia was firmly anchored in the European state system. As one of the founders of the Concert of Europe, St Petersburg fully subscribed to the values that shaped thinking about international relations on the continent. If anything, nineteenth-century Russians were even more scrupulous in their observance of diplomatic protocol than some of the other powers. Fully equating civilisation with Europe, tsarist diplomats and their imperial masters understood that relations among the continent's states were carried out according to a strict code of conduct, which respected honour and the sanctity of national sovereignty.[17]

Despite occasionally being branded as 'Asiatic' in the West, senior officials at the Choristers' Bridge[18] shared an outlook common throughout the European diplomatic corps. Often educated by foreign tutors, speaking French more easily than their native tongue, and sharing the same aristocratic tastes as their colleagues in Paris, Vienna and Berlin, the elite that shaped Russian diplomacy consciously identified with a cosmopolitan European upper strata that often still valued class over nation. Indeed, other Russians occasionally criticised the Foreign Ministry as an alien preserve, and not without reason. Because of the rarefied skills required of an ambassador, most important a familiarity with the social milieu of foreign courts, tsarist diplomats often bore distinctly non-Slavic surnames, such as Cassini, Stackelberg, Tuyll van Serooskerken, Pozzo di Borgo and Mohrenheim.

While Russia was an integral member of the continent's exclusive club of great powers, its foreign policy did exhibit some distinctive features. Contemporary Western observers were often struck by the concentration of authority in the hands of the sovereign. It was not unusual even in parliamentary regimes for the monarch to be closely involved in diplomacy. Great Britain's Queen Victoria was an active player in her kingdom's foreign affairs, while Hohenzollerns and Habsburgs often took an even stronger part in such matters. But right up to the reign of Nicholas II, Russia's tsars saw the relations of their empire with other nations as their exclusive preserve. Even the Fundamental Laws of 1906, which established the Duma, declared, 'Our Sovereign the Emperor is the supreme leader of all external relations of the Russian state with foreign powers. He likewise sets the course of the international policy of the Russian state.' The statute explicitly forbade legislators from debating

17 With respect to the European states, at any rate. Elsewhere, matters could be different. Referring to Central Asia, the Foreign Ministry's legal expert, Fedor Martens, argued that international law did not apply to 'uncivilised peoples'. F. F. Martens, *La Russie et l'Angleterre dans l'Asie Centrale* (Ghent: I. S. van Dooselaere, 1879), pp. 8–19.

18 Because of its location near a bridge that was traditionally used by members of the Imperial Court Choir on their way to sing at the Winter Palace's chapel, the Russian Foreign Ministry was given this nickname.

foreign policy, a provision unknown in any other European constitution at the time.[19]

This did not mean that Romanovs were reluctant to delegate authority to their foreign ministers. When the Choristers' Bridge was headed by a trusted and competent individual, as it was during much of the nineteenth century, that official naturally came to exercise a great deal of influence on tsarist diplomacy. One indication of the minister's prestige was the fact that Russia's highest civil service *chin* (level on the Table of Ranks), chancellor, was typically bestowed on only distinguished holders of that post. Prince Gorchakov once explained, 'in Russia there are only two people who know the politics of the Russian cabinet: The emperor, who sets its course, and I, who prepare and execute it'.[20] Nevertheless, as in many governments, the foreign minister's authority could be eclipsed by others. This was particularly true during Nicholas II's reign, when at various times Finance Minister Sergei Witte or a shadowy group of imperial intimates had a much stronger say in Russian diplomacy.

Even when the Foreign Ministry was firmly in charge of the empire's relations with other states, it did not always speak with one voice. Officials at the Asian Department, which had officially been established in 1819 to deal with Eastern states (including former Ottoman possessions in south-eastern Europe), had a very different outlook on the world than their colleagues who dealt with Western and Central Europe. Unlike the latter, who tended to be well-born, cosmopolitan dilettantes, the Asian Department was largely staffed by ethnic Russians, often with special training in Oriental languages. Caution and aristocratic etiquette were alien to its modus operandi. Acting as a semi-autonomous institution, the Asian Department at times conducted a policy at odds with the broader lines of tsarist diplomacy. This had particularly unfortunate consequences in the Balkans, where more enthusiastic patriots like Count Ignat'ev could frustrate his minister's efforts to defuse tensions.

Despite the autocratic nature of the tsarist regime, by the second half of the nineteenth century public opinion increasingly began to play a role in Russian diplomacy. As throughout Europe, the development of an assertive press and the rise of nationalism began to involve educated Russians in what had hitherto been regarded as the sovereign's exclusive preserve. During Nicholas II's reign, the St Petersburg daily *Novoe vremia* (the New Times) had an authority

19 M. Szeftel, *The Russian Constitution of April 23, 1906* (Brussels: Les éditions de la librairie encyclopédique, 1976), pp. 86, 127.

20 In Baron B. E. Nol'de, *Peterburskaia missiia Bismarka 1859–1862* (Prague: Plamia, 1925), p. 39.

roughly analogous to *The Times*. Read at the Winter Palace and at the Chorister's Bridge, *Novoe Vremia* advocated a pro-entente line, largely reflecting the sentiments of most literate Russians. The creation of the Duma, an elected legislature, in 1907 further involved civil society in foreign policy. Although according to the Fundamental Laws, deputies could not discuss such matters, they nevertheless used their right to approve the Foreign Ministry's annual budget to impose their views on its policies. The relatively liberal Izvol'skii understood the importance of a favourable public and was careful to court the Duma's more moderate members.

But the most dramatic feature of nineteenth-century tsarist diplomacy was its relative success, at least until 1894. During the eight decades that followed the Congress of Vienna, Russian foreign policy displayed a remarkable degree of consistency and, with two major exceptions in the Near East, it achieved the empire's principal geopolitical objectives. It was only under Nicholas II, when impatience and excessive ambition replaced realism, that the achievements of earlier Romanovs came undone.

27

The navy in 1900: imperialism, technology and class war

NIKOLAI AFONIN

At the turn of the twentieth century the Russian navy was in a difficult position. Traditionally, its main theatre of operations was the Baltic Sea. Since the first half of the nineteenth century Russia had been the leading naval power among the countries bordering on this sea. Its main enemy had been the British. The Royal Navy could easily block Russian access to the open ocean by patrolling the Sound, in other words the passage between Denmark and Sweden. As was shown in both the Napoleonic and Crimean wars, not only could it also blockade Russian ports and thereby stop Russia's seaborne trade, it could also mount a realistic threat against Kronstadt and the security of St Petersburg, the imperial capital.[1]

From the early 1880s a new threat emerged on the Baltic Sea as newly united Germany began to build its High Seas Fleet. To some extent this was a worse danger than the British navy had been, since a German fleet enjoying superiority over Russia in the Baltic theatre would be able to operate in conjunction with Europe's most formidable land forces – in other words the German army. Given the right circumstances, joint operations by the German army and fleet could pose a major threat to the security of Russia's capital and her Baltic provinces.[2]

Meanwhile the situation in Russia's second theatre of maritime operations, namely the Black Sea, was also difficult. In the early twentieth century 37 per cent of all Russian exports and the overwhelming majority of her crucially important grain exports went through the Straits at Constantinople. On these exports depended Russia's trade balance, the stability of the rouble, and therefore Russia's credit-worthiness and her ability to attract foreign capital. The Ottoman government could block this trade at any time by closing the Straits.

1 See e.g. on the Crimean War: Andrew Lambert, *The Crimean War: British Naval Grand Strategy 1853–1856* (Manchester: Manchester University Press, 1990).

2 On the early growth of the German navy, see L. Sondhaus, *Preparing for Weltpolitik: German Sea Power before the Tirpitz Era* (Annapolis: Naval Institute Press, 1997).

As was shown in the Crimean War, in alliance with a major naval power the Ottomans could also allow in foreign fleets which could blockade and capture Russia's Black Sea ports. So long as the weak Ottoman regime controlled Constantinople and the Straits it was unlikely to use its geopolitical advantage against Russia except in wartime. But the Ottoman Empire was in steep decline. In the decades before the First World War it was a recurring nightmare for the Russians that a rival great power might come to dominate the Straits either directly or by exercising a dominant influence over the Ottoman government. Should there arise any immediate threat of Ottoman collapse, the Russians were determined at least to seize and fortify the eastern end of the Straits in order to deny access to the Black Sea to the navies of rival great powers.[3]

Faced with these threats, in 1881 the Russian government stated in the prologue to its twenty-year naval construction programme that Russia 'must be able to challenge the enemy beyond the limits of Russian coastal waters both in the Baltic and Black seas'.[4] The financial implications of this decision to build major fleets in both seas to meet possible British or German challenges were daunting. Partly for that reason, in 1885 the twenty-year programme was somewhat reduced. Nevertheless by 1896, fourteen modern battleships and many other vessels were in service or nearing completion in the Baltic and Black Sea fleets. Meanwhile the new 1895–1902 construction programme envisaged the building of still more units. The additional cost just of the ships designated for the Baltic fleet would be almost 149 million roubles. One gains some sense of the enormous pressure of military budgets on Russia's economic development when one compares this sum (devoted to just one fleet of Russia's junior military service) to the 33.6 million roubles which comprised the budget of the Russian Ministry of Education in 1900.

By 1896, however, a new threat and a new potential theatre of naval operations had emerged in the Pacific. In this period competition for empire was reaching its peak. Between 1876 and 1915 roughly one-quarter of the world's land surface was annexed by the European imperialist powers and the United States. The 'Scramble for Africa' was completed in 1899–1902 by the British conquest of the Boer republics. Meanwhile the centre of imperialist competition had moved to East Asia, where the Ching Empire's days seemed clearly

3 On the broader context, see M. S. Anderson, *The Eastern Question* (London: Macmillan, 1966). On Russian plans, see O. R. Airapetov, 'Na Vostochnom napravlenii: Sud'ba Bosforskoi ekspeditsii v pravlenie imperatora Nikolaia II', in O. Airapetov (ed.), *Posledniaia voina imperatorskoi Rossii* (Moscow: Tri kvadrata, 2002), pp. 158–261.

4 V. P. Kostenko, *Na 'Orle' v Tsusime* (Leningrad: Sudpromgiz, 1955), pp. 14–22.

numbered. In 1898 the Americans annexed the Philippines. In 1900 the Boxer rebellion threatened the Ching dynasty's survival and resulted in Great Power military intervention in China.

Russia had a long border with China and was a near neighbour too of Japan, whose military and economic power was growing rapidly. Saint Petersburg neither could nor wished to stand outside imperialist competition in East Asia, on which the whole future global balance of power seemed likely to depend. However, by taking the lead first in 1895 in blocking Japanese annexation of Port Arthur and then three years later in taking the port herself, Russia made herself Japan's potential enemy. The large-scale Japanese 1895 naval programme, funded partly by the proceeds of victory over China in 1894, made clear the potential threat to Russian security. A conference summoned to consider this threat by Nicholas II noted that 'in comparison to 1881 circumstances in the Far East have changed radically and not at all in our favour'. The emperor himself correctly commented that 'our misfortune is that Russia has to build and maintain three independent fleets'.[5]

The main reason why this was the case was the enormous distances between the three theatres in which the Russian navy operated. In addition, however, until the Montreux agreement of 1936 warships had no right of passage through the Straits at Constantinople. The Black Sea fleet was therefore entirely isolated. When Russia wished to send ships even to the Mediterranean they had to come from the Baltic fleet. Russia's Pacific squadron was also made up of ships built in and despatched from the Baltic. Not merely was the voyage to the Far East very long but Russia had no bases between Libau and Port Arthur. This caused difficulties even in peacetime. In wartime, with neutral ports closed, it was a huge problem. Meanwhile the need to create a new infrastructure to sustain the Pacific fleet in Vladivostok and Port Arthur was extremely difficult and expensive, given their geographical remoteness from industrial centres and their dependence on the carrying capacity of the single-track Siberian and East-Chinese railways. Though finances were the main problem surrounding the creation of three independent fleets they were not, however, the only one. The types of ships suitable for war against Germany in the confined coastal waters of the Baltic were wholly unsuitable for long-distance raids against British commerce in the Atlantic or Pacific. A battleship squadron capable of contesting Japanese domination of the Yellow Sea had still other requirements.

The Russian government attempted to prioritise the East Asian theatre. In December 1897 it was decided to limit the Baltic fleet to a purely defensive

5 RGAVMF, Fond 417, op. 1, d. 1728, 13-ob.

role. Though the build-up of the Black Sea fleet was to continue, most of the available naval forces were to be concentrated in the Far East. For this purpose a new construction programme ('For the Requirements of the Far East') was agreed in 1898 in addition to the existing 1895 programme. It aimed to add a further five battleships and numerous smaller ships to the Pacific fleet by 1905.[6]

The new programme was very expensive. In total the navy was allocated 732 million roubles between 1895 and 1903. This was more than three times the Japanese naval budget and it also shifted the share of the navy in overall Russian military expenditure from 17 per cent in 1895 to 25 per cent in 1902.[7]

The Russian Ministry of Finance insisted that the new naval construction programme should be completed in 1905, although the rival Japanese programme was intended to reach fruition significantly earlier. Finance Minister Witte claimed both that it was impossible for Russia to afford such vast sums for shipbuilding in a shorter period and that the Japanese would never be able to finance the completion of their naval programme before 1908. The finance minister proved mistaken. The Japanese programme was completed by 1903.[8] Moreover, awareness that Japan possessed a window of opportunity before the completion of the Russian shipbuilding programme was a major incentive for the Japanese to go to war in 1904. Meanwhile, however, the Russian government was convinced that its build-up of naval forces in the Pacific had checkmated the Japanese. Its attention was returning to Europe and particularly to the Straits, where crisis loomed and the Ottoman regime's survival seemed ever more doubtful. In 1903 a vast new twenty-year naval construction programme was agreed for the Baltic and Black seas. Russia's unexpected involvement in war with Japan changed all these plans.

Within the Naval Ministry responsibility for the design, construction, operation and repair of ships lay with the Naval Technical Committee (MTK), whose basic job was to ensure that the fleet was fully up-to-date in technical terms. However, in the 1890s the committee was too understaffed to do its job properly, which caused much delay and many mismatched and unco-ordinated requirements for new ships. As regards the 1898 programme the MTK only

6 V. Iu. Griboevskii, 'Rossiiskii flot Tikhogo okeana. Istoriia sozdaniia i gibeli 1898–1905', *Briz* (2001), no 3: 2. R. M. Melnikov, *Kreiser Variag* (Leningrad: Sudostroenie, 1975), pp. 17–19.

7 Griboevskii, 'Rossiiskii flot Tikhogo okeana', *Briz* (2001), no. 4: 3.

8 On Japanese preparations for the war, see D. C. Evans and M. R. Peattie, *Kaigun. Strategy, Tactics and Technology in the Imperial Japanese Navy 1887–1941* (Annapolis: Naval Institute Press, 1997).

defined requirements for the draught, speed, cruising range and armament of the new ships. This resulted in ships supposedly of the same class which were built in different factories having significantly different features, which complicated future operations.

The MTK in any case had no control over money: the realisation of all its plans depended on the release of funds by the so-called Chief Administration of Shipbuilding and Supply (GUKiC). Even department chiefs in the GUKiC had no engineering background and little grasp of shipbuilding, however. In the light of spiralling naval budgets, the GUKiC put much effort into enforcing economies in many aspects of naval life. Areas hardest hit included provision of effective modern shells instead of the existing poor explosives; adequate shooting practice; training at sea in order to practise squadron manoeuvres and bring ships and their companies up to a high state of readiness. These economies were a key cause of Russia's defeat in the war against Japan.

Inevitably, the overall economic and technological backwardness of Russia had an impact on the shipbuilding industry. Matters were worsened by the government's reliance on state-owned works (Baltic, Admiralty, Obukhov, Izhorsk, etc.) to build most of its ships. Management of these works at that time was usually very bureaucratic, with little conception of profit, costs or productivity. The naval officers who ran these works also frequently had limited engineering knowledge. As a result, ship-construction in Russia was expensive by international standards and slow.[9] At a time when naval technology was improving rapidly slow construction times were particularly dangerous, since even new ships risked being obsolescent on completion. The MTK itself often introduced changes while construction was already under way. This caused further delay and confusion, and could result in errors in design. One solution to Russia's problems would have been greater reliance on private industry, as occurred after 1906, when the government privatised some works and gave many orders to private firms (especially for non-capital ships), thus attracting large-scale private injection of capital into the Russian shipbuilding industry. Before 1905, however, Russia had only five private works even partially engaged

9 Russian completion rates were very slow by British or German standards, less so by French or Italian ones. See eg. chapter 5 of P. Ropp, *The Development of a Modern Navy: French Naval Policy 1871–1914* (Annapolis: Naval Institute Press, 1987) and the statistics on individual ships in *Conway's All the World's Fighting Ships 1860–1905* (London: Conway Maritime Press, 1979). In 1911 the Naval General Staff reckoned that it cost 1,532 roubles per ton to build a battleship in Russia, 913 in Britain, 846 in Germany, 876 in the United States and 1,090 in Italy: M. A. Petrov, *Podgotovka Rossii k mirovoi voine na more* (Moscow: Gos. voennoe izd., 1926) p. 143. Admittedly, this was at a time when Russia was spending heavily to upgrade construction facilities in order to build dreadnoughts.

in shipbuilding: these firms operated at a loss, partly because when forced to give orders to private firms the naval ministry preferred to place them abroad.[10]

As a result of the naval construction programmes, by the first years of the twentieth century Russia had moved into third place among the world's navies, with 229 ships as against Britain's 460 and France's 391.[11] Many new types of ships were built, including Russia's first submarine, *Delfin*, which was launched in 1903. Among the classes of ships built were armoured coastal defence ships (*Admiral Ushakov* class of 4,127 tons) whose obvious theatre was the Baltic Sea; *Poltava* class battleships (10,960 tons) which followed the normal European model and the three faster battleships of the *Peresvet* class (12,674 tons), designed to operate for long periods at sea. A few battleships were ordered abroad but their design was closely supervised by the MTK and in the case of the *Tsesarevich* (12,912 tons), built in France, served as a model for a class of five battleships subsequently built in Russia (*Borodino* class of 13,516 tons).[12]

During these years a major shift occurred in the design and proposed deployment of armoured cruisers. The earlier cruisers (*Rurik*, *Rossiia* and *Gromoboi*) were designed as long-distance commerce raiders, with British trade as their obvious target. Equal in size to battleships and incorporating many new technologies, they initially aroused exaggerated fears in Britain which resulted in a very expensive class of British armoured cruisers being built to match them.[13] The armoured cruisers of the *Bayan* class (the *Bayan* itself was launched in 1900) were, however, designed to operate in more limited waters and to fight alongside battleships if necessary.[14] Their likeliest enemy was seen as Japan, which had already built a number of similar armoured cruisers. For this reason, in comparison to the earlier commerce-raiders the new cruisers sacrificed long-range cruising capability in order to maximise armour and guns for fleet actions. A similar evolution was evident among Russia's lighter ('protected') cruisers with earlier ships (e.g. the *Diana* class of the 1895 programme) being seen primarily as commerce-raiders and later ships (e.g.

10 K. F. Shatsillo, *Russkii imperialism i razvitie flota* (Moscow: Nauka, 1968), pp. 217, 228–9.

11 L. G. Beskrovnyi, *Armiia i flot Rossii v nachale XXv: Ocherki voenno-ekonomicheskogo potentsiala* (Moscow: Nauka, 1987), p. 187.

12 For good coverage of these ships in English, see S. McLaughlin, *Russian and Soviet Battleships* (Annapolis: Naval Institute Press, 2003).

13 R. M. Melnikov, *Istoriia otechestvennogo sudostroeniia*, 3 vols. General ed., B. N. Malakhov (St Petersburg: Sudostroenie, 1996), vol. II, p. 533. On British fears, see e.g. V. E. Egorev, *Operatsiia vladivostokskikh kreiserov v Russko-iaponskuiu voinu 1904–1905 gg.* (Moscow and Leningrad: V-Morskoe izd., 1939), p. 9; *Conway's*, p. 67.

14 RGAVMF, Fond 421, op. 8, d. 6, l. 356.

Variag, *Askold*, *Bogatyr* and *Novik*) being designed to operate together with the battle-fleet.

The structure and governance of the fleet and the Naval Ministry were defined by the laws of 1885 and 1888. The ministry was comprised of a number of chief administrations (e.g. medical: hydrographic) and committees (e.g. the MTK) but its most important core institution was the Main Naval Staff, which was responsible for the navy's preparedness for war. The Main Naval Staff, however, was swamped in various day-to-day administrative responsibilities. Like many other navies at the time, Russia lacked a true naval general staff, responsible for pre-war strategic planning and overall control of wartime operations. A proposal to establish such a staff was rejected at the end of the nineteenth century and the small (twelve-man) strategic unit established within the Main Naval Staff on the eve of the Japanese war had no chance of seriously affecting wartime operations. The annual war games at the Nicholas Naval Academy had some impact on strategic thinking but although Admiral Makarov had intelligent and aggressive ideas about strategy, the dominant tendency among Russia's senior admirals was defensive – stressing the defence of key positions (e.g. Port Arthur during the war with Japan) and seeing naval assistance to the army largely in terms of the secondment of personnel and weapons. The staffs of the individual fleets saw themselves as mere advisory bodies and showed little initiative.[15]

The prevailing view of tactics was to fight in line ahead or in surprise encounter battles. The squadron's commander was supposed to control movements by flag, semaphore and telegraph from his flagship. The 'two-flag' system was spreading slowly at the turn of the century. S. O. Makarov, N. L. Klado and N. N. Kholodovskii all published useful work on tactics but the point to stress is that the Russian navy had no single and official tactical doctrine which could have provided a common guide for senior officers. The fighting instructions which did exist were either uselessly general (e.g. ship captains should obey the signals of the commanding admiral as much as possible), extremely narrow (e.g. where to keep tubs of sand) or absurdly pedantic (e.g. the requirement for officers to wear swords in combat). Not until the war with Japan had already begun was the first true battle

15 Beskrovnyi, *Armiia i flot*, p. 221. On the question of a naval general staff, see the key publication of A. N. Shcheglov, *Znachenie i rabota shtaba na osnovanii opyta russko-iaponskoi voiny* (St Petersburg: no publ. given, 1905) and the articles by N. Kazimirov entitled 'Morskoi General'nyi Shtab', *Morskoi Sbornik* 372, 9 (Sept. 1912): 55–82; 10 (Oct. 1912): 57–80.

manual for an armoured fleet issued. This was *The Instructions for Campaigns and Battles* written by the new commander of the Pacific fleet, Admiral Makarov.[16]

Peacetime training was organised in accordance with the *Instructions for Preparing Ships for Combat* and with the schedules of individual naval units. It was in general carried out in port and in training sessions devoted to individual, specific tasks. Mine-warfare training units existed in the Baltic and Black sea fleets: the former also trained radio experts. The first wireless stations were set up on ships in the autumn of 1900 and in the course of 1901–2 almost all major ships received them. As the Far Eastern fleet grew in size, the first training schools (for quartermasters – in 1898) and training ships were set up there too. The largest training unit in the Baltic fleet was devoted to gunnery. But the training concentrated on shooting at much shorter ranges than was to be the practice during the Japanese war and was therefore of limited benefit. In 1901 the Technical Commission of gunnery officers in Kronstadt embarked on drawing up new rules for combat. These were completed in 1903, too late to be influential in training gunnery officers and sailors for the Japanese war. On the other hand, the annual training cruises in the Atlantic were of real use in raising preparedness for combat.[17]

Sailors were conscripted on the same basis as soldiers though with longer terms of active service and shorter periods in the first-line reserve (five years in each category). As the fleet grew in the first years of the twentieth century, so did the number of conscripts: between 1900 and 1905 the number of conscripts in the fleet grew from 46,700 to 61,400. There were roughly 15,000 first-line reserves and 40,000 much less well-trained so-called 'naval militia'. In 1905–7 roughly 30 per cent of sailors were said to be of 'working class' background, a far higher proportion than in the army.[18] Given the complexities of warships in the age of steam it made excellent sense to conscript many skilled and literate men into the navy. But with the rapid growth of worker radicalism in the 1890s this carried obvious political dangers.

Men entering the fleet who were inclined to political radicalism were likely to be encouraged in that direction by conditions of service. The five-year term was one source of grievance, as was very low pay and the need to act as 'batmen' for officers. Food was often poor, the most recent Anglophone study of the *Potemkin* mutiny stating that this was yet one more area in which the navy's

16 N. B. Pavlovich, *Razvitie taktiki voenno-morskogo flota* (Moscow: Voenizdat, 1979).
17 Griboevskii, 'Rossiiskii flot', p. 7.
18 Beskrovnyi, *Armiia i flot*, p. 209.

leadership had tried to cut costs in the early twentieth century.[19] Conditions aboard were very cramped. Moreover, partly for reasons of economy but above all because almost all ports were iced up in winter, crews spent the long winter months in barracks ashore. Often ships' crews were split up or diluted, under the command of barracks' commanders and officers whom they barely knew. Under these conditions no sense of solidarity or *esprit de corps* was possible and even supervision was difficult. Even the ships' own officers and priests, however, usually showed little awareness that the increasingly literate, skilled and independent men who were now often being conscripted needed to be trained, led and stimulated in different ways to old-time peasant recruits.[20]

All these factors fed into the wave of mutinies that devastated the navy in the early twentieth century. So too did the impact of defeat by Japan and the unnecessary deaths of thousands of Russian seamen. The first mass protests occurred in 1902. If the June 1905 *Potemkin* affair is the most famous event in this period, the mutinies in the Black Sea in autumn 1905 and in the Baltic in spring 1906 were larger in scale. In 1907 it was the turn for mass mutinies in the Pacific squadron. Although on the surface calm reigned in subsequent years, discontent and revolutionary propaganda was still very real. In 1912 the police pre-empted mass mutiny by large-scale and arbitrary arrests of revolutionary activists among the sailors.

Analysing the reasons for the dramatic conflicts between officers and sailors in 1905–7, one senior admiral saw their basic cause as the deep cultural and mental gulf between Russia's educated elites and the bulk of the population. In a short-service, conscript navy this chasm was bound to be transferred from society as a whole into the armed forces. Traditional suspicion and mutual incomprehension between the two groups had often recently been transformed into strong antagonism by the growth of class conflict and revolutionary agitation. Sailors often saw their officer as a 'lord' and an 'oppressor'. Of course such deep-rooted social and political problems could not be solved by the navy alone but a number of key weaknesses did exacerbate the fleet's difficulties in managing its sailors and winning their allegiance. Of these, the

19 R. Zebrowski, 'The Battleship *Potemkin* and its Discontents', chapter 1 in C. M. Bell and B. A. Elleman (eds.), *Naval Mutinies of the Twentieth Century* (London: Frank Cass, 2003), pp. 9–31.

20 The devastating report of Captain Brusilov, the chief of the Naval General Staff, to Nicholas II in October 1906 implicitly acknowledged this and recommended drafting a new law to define sailors' rights and duties: 'At the basis of this law must be humane principles in accordance with the spirit of the times and the striving to defend the rights of the individual, to the extent of course that this is compatible with the basic principles of military discipline and special circumstances of the naval service' (RGAVMF, Fond 418, op. 1, d. 238, pp. 24–48; the quote is from pp. 42–3).

greatest was the failure to create a strong and numerous group of long-service petty officers, who would be drawn from the ranks and understand the sailors' mentality and needs, while being wholly loyal to the navy and inculcated into its values. Creating such a corps in Russian conditions was difficult, however. In the era before the introduction of short-service conscription there had been few difficulties. Sailors were bound to lifetime service in the fleet and had every incentive to become petty officers. The contemporary conscript in the steam navy, however, had often acquired very marketable skills by the time he finished his term of service in the fleet. Private industry offered pay, conditions and freedom to potential petty officers which the navy could not match.[21]

Naval officers were drawn from a totally different milieu from that of the sailors. The great majority of deck officers were graduates of the Naval Cadet Corps. All the cadets were from the nobility. Though few were aristocrats and very few owned sizeable estates, a great many of these men came from families with strong traditions of service in the fleet. To meet the needs of a rapidly growing fleet, the annual number of midshipmen graduating from the Naval Cadet Corps more than doubled between 1898 and 1911–13, from 52 to 119. Cadets spent one year ashore and then three years mostly at sea on training ships. Meanwhile the Naval Engineering School trained young men drawn from all social backgrounds to be ship engineers. It had two branches – engineering and shipbuilding – which together in 1900 graduated only twenty-eight young men into the navy, though again the numbers increased substantially in subsequent years.

As in many other navies of that time, tensions existed between the traditional caste of deck officers and the new engineer officers, whom they often perceived as their social inferiors. This tension, together with the exclusively noble makeup of the Naval Cadet Corps made it even more difficult to find a sufficient number of young officers to fill the ranks of the growing fleet, though the more attractive pay and conditions often available in civilian employment were an even greater problem. Shortage of officers was an issue during the war with Japan. Even in the war's first month the battleships and cruisers of the Pacific squadron on average were short of four to five officers each. The squadron sent round the world in 1905 to reinforce the Pacific fleet left its Baltic ports with many insufficiently trained younger officers who were promoted

21 Vice-Admiral Prince A. A. Liven, *Dukh i ditsiplina nashego flota* (St Petersburg: Voennaia tip. Ekat. Velikoi, 1914), pp. 86–90. Lieven was at the centre of a group of bright young officers who had done well in the Japanese war and dominated the new Naval General Staff. On the NCO issue and German comparisons, see also P. Burachek, 'Zametki o flote', *Morskoi Sbornik* 365, 7 (1911): 19–50.

to midshipmen without finishing their education, or were drawn from the reserve or in the case of engineers from civilian technical institutes.[22]

The Japanese war revealed a number of defects in the officer corps. Above all, the Naval Cadet Corps had given them little understanding of naval tactics. Nor was this defect corrected even for the minority of officers who subsequently received a higher naval education at the Nicholas Naval Academy. The latter was geared to educating narrow technical specialists in its three core sections – hydrographic, shipbuilding and mechanical. After 1896, alongside these two-year courses, a one-year course in naval tactics was at last established. Only after the war and in the light of its lessons was education in tactics and strategy put on a proper footing. Before 1904 the Naval Academy was unable to fulfil the role of training future staff officers. Similarly, though radio-telegraphy was taught in the officers' mine-warfare class from 1900, no attention was paid to its tactical applications. In fact, though six to seven officers were attached to the army's artillery academy every year, the officers' training even in gunnery was inadequate, in large part because the limited number of instructors were swamped by the sheer scale of gunnery training required by the growing navy.

The regulations introduced in 1885 to govern promotions and appointments had a vicious effect on the navy. They were designed to combat nepotism and to ensure that officers had adequate experience – above all at sea – before being promoted. However, by rigidly requiring specific terms of service at sea before promotion and linking promotion in rank to the availability of specific posts in ships the regulations totally backfired on the navy. To fulfil these requirements officers jumped from ship to ship, in the process weakening the efficient command structures and the sense of solidarity which ought to reign in a ship's crew. This sense of solidarity was already at risk because not just other ranks but also officers spent the long winter months when the ships were ice-bound ashore in barracks. The so-called 'naval regiments' (*ekipazhi*) which were the basic units for shore-time service did not even correspond to the individual ships' companies. Moreover months spent ashore often distracted officers from truly naval training and encouraged attention to drill and other extraneous concerns.[23]

22 *Russko-iaponskaia voina: 1904–1905gg*, 4 vols. (St Petersburg: 1912), vol. I, pp. 150–5.

23 V. Iu. Griboevskii, 'Rossiiskii flot', *Briz* 6 (2001): 9–11. N. Kallistov, 'Petrovskaia, Menshikovskaia i tsenzovaia ideia v voprose o proiskhozhdenii sluzhby ofitserov flota', *Morskoi sbornik*, 369, 3 (1912): 105–18. This issue is usefully seen within the context of the long debate that raged in the Delianov and Peretts special commissions in the 1880s and 1890s on promotions and appointments, the *chin*, and other aspects of Russian civil and military service. The papers are in RGIA, Fond 1200, op. 16ii, ed. khr. 1 and 2. For a discussion of this debate and of the regulations in English, see D. Lieven, *Russia's Rulers under the Old Regime* (London: Yale University Press, 1989), chapter 4.

At the top of the naval hierarchy stood the emperor Nicholas II, who was far from being a mere figurehead where naval matters were concerned. Like his peers, King George V of Britain, Emperor Wilhelm II of Germany and Archduke Francis Ferdinand of Austria, the Russian monarch took a close personal interest in the fleet. This was after all the era of Mahan, when navies were seen as crucial to the struggle for global influence and an essential mark of a great power able to survive in an era of Darwinian imperialist competition. Nicholas II's support was vital for the expansion of the fleet before 1904 and even more crucial in overriding opposition from the army and from civilian ministers to the re-creation of a large high-seas fleet after 1906.

The emperor bore a heavy personal responsibility for Russia's involvement in the war with Japan. Only he could weigh the risks, costs and benefits of Russia's Far Eastern policy in 1895–1904 against the empire's overall needs: this he failed to do. He also failed to co-ordinate Russia's military, naval, diplomatic and financial policy in East Asia, or indeed to ensure co-ordination between the Far Eastern viceroy and the government in Petersburg. Like many of his senior naval advisors, he also overestimated Russian naval power in the theatre and underestimated Japanese strength and determination. Of course, all these failures are more easily revealed in retrospect than at the time. Nor was the emperor mostly responsible for the fleet's sometimes poor performance in the war. Where senior appointments and overall naval preparation for war were concerned, the emperor relied heavily on the advice of his uncle, Grand Duke Alexei, who bears great responsibility for the navy's inadequate performance in 1904–5. So too to a lesser extent did the naval minister until 1903, P. P. Tyrtov, who played the key role in deciding what ships were to be built and where Russian naval forces should be deployed. Though Admiral Alekseev, the Far Eastern viceroy, was subsequently widely blamed for Russia's defeat, he was at least a fine seaman and before the war had stressed the need to strike first rather than leave initiative and surprise to the Japanese.

As regards the actual fleet commanders during the war, many showed inadequate enterprise and offensive spirit.[24] Among them the two outstanding personalities were Admiral S. O. Makarov and Admiral Z. P. Rozhestvenskii. The former commanded the Pacific fleet for only a few weeks from early February 1904 until his death in late March when his flagship hit a mine.

24 Much the best English-language work on the war remains J. S. Corbett, *Maritime Operations in the Russo-Japanese War: 1904–1905*, 2 vols. (Annapolis: Naval Institute Press, 1994).

Makarov was Russia's most brilliant admiral, who had climbed the promotion ladder rapidly and solely on merit. As a young officer in the 1877–8 war with Turkey, he had organised and led torpedo attacks on Ottoman ships, showing great courage and skill. Subsequently he had acquired a worldwide reputation as an expert on strategy, tactics and oceanography. His arrival at Port Arthur to take over command of the Pacific squadron after the surprise Japanese attack galvanised his subordinates. Makarov's death at a moment when he was preparing the fleet for offensive action was a huge loss which possibly had a decisive influence on the outcome of the war. By contrast, Rozhestvenskii was a more equivocal figure. As commander of the Second Pacific Squadron he showed great organisational skill in bringing his ships round the world but at the Battle of Tsushima his passivity contributed to the destruction of his fleet. His rigidly authoritarian and centralised system of command also discouraged his subordinates from showing initiative.

There are very few examples in naval history of defeat more total than that experienced by Russia in the war against Japan. Sixty-nine ships were lost, including almost the entire Pacific fleet and most of the Baltic fleet as well. In October 1908 the Naval General Staff reported to Nicholas II as regards the Baltic fleet that 'our battleships are not a serious force in terms of either their individual quality or their organisation'.[25]

The reasons for Russia's defeat were many. Most basically, having adopted an aggressive policy in the Far East which risked war with Japan, she proved unwilling and unable to deploy the necessary naval and military forces to secure victory. Russian resources were badly overstretched by her Far Eastern policy: this included not just financial resources but also the navy's ability to take on major new strategic commitments and manage the big increase in ships and personnel this required. In addition, never previously had Russia engaged in a war where naval rather than military power was the key to victory. In building and then deploying its naval forces the Russian government failed fully to understand the implications of this fact. Moreover, ships were built in a number of construction programmes with contradictory roles and different enemies in mind. Slow construction times and delays in adopting the latest technology played a role too in an era when naval technology was developing at bewildering and unprecedented speed. Lacking any recent wartime experience, the navy also often failed to appreciate the operational and tactical implications of this new technology.

25 Cited on pp. 223–4 of Beskrovnyi, *Armiia i flot.*

Despite the shattering defeat by Japan and the mutinies which followed, the Russian navy was rebuilt after 1906. Four years after Tsushima the first Russian Dreadnoughts were launched in St Petersburg. The naval minister, Admiral I. M. Dikov wrote that 'as a Great Power Russia needs a fleet and must be able to send her ships wherever state interests demand'.[26] The foreign minister, A. P. Izvol'skii, was equally committed to the re-creation of an imposing high-seas fleet, capable of operating across the globe and not tied to the role as a mere coastal defence force.

The need to regain international prestige and credibility was an important factor in the fleet's rebirth. This was by no means an illegitimate consideration in an era of Darwinian international competition when not just governments but also European public opinion attached huge significance to naval power and when any sign of weakness might well attract the attention of potential bullies and predators. There were also, however, clear strategic reasons to rebuild the fleet. For example, the Ottoman-Italian War of 1911 and the Balkan wars of 1912–13 seemed clear evidence that the long-predicted demise of the Ottoman Empire was nigh. Modernising the Black Sea fleet while sending Baltic fleet squadrons into the Mediterranean in order to deploy maximum Russian power at the Straits seemed vital in these circumstances.

The Naval Ministry achieved a great deal between 1906 and 1914. Many excellent and sometimes genuinely innovative new ships were built or planned. The Russian shipbuilding industry was transformed. A Naval General Staff was created and became the core of a large group of able, younger officers determined to expunge the humiliation of defeat by Japan. The Naval Ministry worked in intelligent co-operation with the Duma (Parliament) and public opinion by 1914, showing political sensitivity and openness to new political currents. Nevertheless, many of the old doubts about Russian naval power remained relevant. The very ambitious plans of the navy's leadership were hugely expensive. The twenty-year construction plan devised by the Naval General Staff was to cost 2.2 billion roubles, more than total state revenue in that year.[27] In the last year of peace Russia spent more on the navy than Germany. Was this the best use of Russia's limited resources? Even these vast sums might not be able to compensate for the poor hand that geography had dealt Russia: for example, even if by some miracle Russia acquired the Straits would it not then simply graduate to the position of Italy, whose admirals

26 Cited by Beskrovnyi, *Armii i flot*, pp. 223–4.

27 On this plan and the covering memo sent to the Duma to justify it, see 'U nashikh protivnikov shirokie plany', *Voenno-istoricheskii Zhurnal* (1996), no. 4: 42–50.

complained that their navy and trade were confined to the Mediterranean and at the mercy of the British fleet, which dominated the Mediterranean Sea and controlled all exits from it to the open oceans? Moreover the arrests of revolutionary sailors in 1912 were a reminder that the Russian state was spending great sums on a weapon which might turn on its creator.

PART VII

★

REFORM, WAR AND REVOLUTION

28

The reign of Alexander II: a watershed?

LARISA ZAKHAROVA

The abolition of serfdom in 1861, under Alexander II, and the reforms which followed (local government reforms, the judicial reform, the abolition of corporal punishment, the reform of the military, public education, censorship and others), were a 'watershed', 'a turning point' in the history of Russia. This is the verdict of the reformers themselves and their opponents, people who lived at the time in Russia as well as beyond its borders, and many researchers. This theme remains crucial for historians. But in particular periods such as during the 1905 Revolution or Gorbachev's perestroika, interest in the history of Alexander II's reforms has acquired a particular topicality and political colouring. At such times instead of the already established term 'the Great Reforms', new terminology emerges particularly in the academic literature for wider audiences such as 'revolution from above', 'a revolutionary break with the past' and 'coup d'etat'.[1]

However, mainstream scholarship still accepts the more subtle term 'the Great Reforms'.[2] If the question of the suitability of the term for designating this epoch is unlikely to evoke serious doubts and disagreements, that is not true of the issues raised in the title of this chapter as well as others (including the personal role of Alexander II in the realisation of the reforms, the interconnection among them, their subsequent fate), on which there is no consensus in the academic literature. It is sufficient to refer to contemporary Western and Russian research whose authors consider the boundary between 'the pre-reforms' of Nicholas I, 'the Great Reforms' of Alexander II and the

1 N. Ia. Eidelman, *'Revoliutsiia sverkhu' v Rossii* (Moscow: Kniga, 1989); T. Emmons, '"Revoliutsiia sverkhu" v Rossii: razmyshleniia o knige N. Eidelmana i o drugom', in *V razdum'iakh o Rossii (XIX vek)* (Moscow: Arkheograficheskii tsentr, 1996), pp. 365–6; B. G. Litvak, *Perevorot 1861 goda v Rossii: pochemu ne realizovalas' reformatorskaia al'ternativa* (Moscow: Politizdat, 1991).

2 L. G. Zakharova, B. Eklof and J. Bushnell (eds.), *Velikie reformi v Rossii, 1856–1874* (Moscow: Izd. MGU, 1992), American version: B. Eklof, J. Bushnell and L. Zakharova (eds.), *Russia's Great Reforms, 1855–1881* (Bloomington: Indiana University Press, 1994). Both books were based on the papers presented at an international conference at Pennsylvania University.

'counter-reforms' of Alexander III relative and even artificial. They present the whole process of reforms as an unbroken continuum spanning the entire nineteenth century.[3] This approach contradicts the other, more traditional one, which views the epoch of the Great Reforms as delimited on the one side by the failure of the Nicholas system with the conclusion of the unsuccessful Crimean War and on the other by the tragic end of the Tsar-liberator on 1 March 1881. There is no doubt that this subject demands further attention and additional research. In this chapter, I will attempt to give my own view of the complex, contested questions that to date remain inadequately addressed in the historiography of the period.

The reasons and preconditions for the abolition of serfdom

Tsar Alexander II himself was the initiator of the transformations in Russia. The question as to what induced the autocratic monarchy to abolish serfdom, which had been its foundation-stone for centuries, has been sufficiently elucidated in the literature. The defeat in the Crimean War (1853–6), which interrupted the one-and-a-half-century-long victorious advance to the Black Sea and was incurred on home territory; the surrender of Sebastopol; the conditions of the Peace of Paris of 18 (30) March 1856, which deprived Russia of its fleet and naval bases on the Black Sea and parts of Bessarabia and shed doubt on Russia's prestige as a great power: all these things exposed the extent to which Russia was lagging behind other European countries. The outdated equipment and system of recruitment for the army, the absence of a railway network and telegraph communications with the south of the country (dispatches from military leaders from the Crimea to the Winter Palace took seven and a half days by courier, whereas telegraph communications about the siege of Sebastopol were coming from Paris, the enemy capital) as well as many other indicators of the country's backwardness left little doubt as to the need for change. 'Sevastopol had an impact on stultified minds.' This pithy expression of V. O. Kliuchevskii referred to every layer of Russian society, including the government. 'The former system had outlived its time' – this was the judgement of one of the former apologists of this system, the historian M. P. Pogodin.[4]

3 G. Freeze, *The Parish Clergy in Nineteenth Century Russia: Crisis, Reform, Counter-reform* (Princeton: Princeton University Press, 1983), p. 350; P. Gatrell, *Znachenie velikikh reform v ekonomike Rossii*, in Zakharova, Eklof and Bushnell, *Velikie reformi v Rossii*, pp. 106–26.

4 M. P. Pogodin, *Istoriko-politicheskie pis'ma i zapiski v prodolzhenie Krymskoi voiny* (Moscow: Izd. V. M. Frish, 1874), p. 315.

Alexander II, who ascended to the throne on 19 February 1855 inherited a difficult legacy.

Later, soon after the abolition of serfdom, the minister of finance M. Kh. Reutern wrote in a report to the tsar: 'If the government after the Crimean War had wished to return to the traditions of the past, it would have encountered insurmountable obstacles, if not openly, then at the very least in the form of passive opposition, which over time may even have shaken the loyalty of the people – the broad foundation, on which the monarchical principle is based in Russia.'[5] But even earlier, in 1856, N. A. Miliutin, the main author of the Great Reforms, acknowledged in a memorandum that the further preservation of serfdom and continued delay of the reforms could lead to an uprising of the peasantry within fifteen years.[6] The explanation for the abolition of serfdom as a response to the rise in peasant disturbances, which dominated Soviet historiography, has now been superseded. In the Western literature, the concept of 'a revolutionary situation' and of the decisive role played by actions taken by the peasantry, which supposedly forced the government to undertake reforms, has been convincingly criticised in the work of Daniel Field, Terence Emmons and Dietrich Beyrau, all of whom spent time at Moscow University under P. A. Zaionchkovskii in the 1960s and 1970s.[7]

Alexander II embarked on the emancipation reforms not because he was a reformer in principle but as a military man who recognised the lessons of the Crimean War, and as an emperor for whom the prestige and greatness of the state took precedence over everything. Particular aspects of his character played a significant role, including his kindness, warmth and receptivity to humane ideas and the effects of his education under the guidance of V. A. Zhukovskii. A. F. Tiutcheva aptly defined this characteristic in Alexander II's nature: 'The instinct of progress was in his heart.' Not a reformer by calling or temperament, Alexander II became a reformer in response to the demands of the time. His character, upbringing and world outlook equipped him with a sufficient understanding of the given situation to take non-traditional decisions. He lacked fanaticism or a rigid conception of politics and this allowed him to pursue new and radical paths, though still within the framework of the

5 RGIA, Fond 560, op. 14, d. 284, l. 1.

6 GARF, Fond. 722, op. 1, d. 230, ll. 1–22.

7 D. Field, *The Reforms of the 1860s: Windows of the Russian Past. Essays on Soviet Historiography since Stalin* (Columbus: Ohio University Press, 1978), pp. 89–104; T. Emmons, 'The Peasant and Emancipation', in W. Vucinich, *The Peasant in Nineteenth-Century Russia* (Stanford: Stanford University Press, 1968), pp. 41–71; D. Beyrau, *Agrarnaia struktura i krest'iianskii protest: k usloviiam osvobozhdeniia krest'iian v 1861 godu: Noveishie podkhody k izucheniiu istorii Rossii i SSSR v sovremennoi zapadnoevropeiskoi istoriografii* (Yaroslavl: Izd. Iaroslavskogo pedagogicheskogo universiteta, 1997), pp. 3–51.

autocratic-monarchical system and while remaining true to his predecessors' traditions.

Speaking in Moscow in front of the leaders of the nobility shortly after the conclusion of the Peace of Paris in 1856, the tsar said: 'There are rumours that I want to announce the emancipation of the peasants. I will not say to you that I am completely against this. We live in such an age that this has to happen in time. I think that you agree with me. Therefore, it is much better that this business be carried out from above, rather than from below.'[8] This short speech tells us much that is important in the history of the 1861 reforms: about the fact that the initiative came from Alexander II himself; that he imposed his will on the nobility; that he recognised the necessity to forestall the initiative of the peasantry, and that he took into account the overall trends of the century. Subsequent events show that Alexander II did not step back from this first declaration about the abolition of serfdom. Some years later in a rather didactic tone he wrote to Napoleon III: 'the true condition of peace in the world lies not in inactivity, which is impossible, and not in dubious political manoeuvrings . . . , but in practical wisdom, which is necessary in order to reconcile history, this unshakeable behest of the past, with progress – the law of the present and the future.[9] These words affirm Alexander II's confidence in the correctness of the course undertaken by him to transform Russia, as do many of his handwritten letters to his brother, the Grand Duke Konstantin Nikolaevich, and to his viceroy in the Caucasus and friend Prince A. I. Bariatinskii.[10] In general the role of Alexander II in the Great Reforms has not been sufficiently explored in the literature.

What were the preconditions of the reform? There is no single opinion on the objective socioeconomic preconditions for the emancipation of the serfs. Soviet historians wrote about the crisis of the feudal-serf system. The majority of Western historians (following P. Struve and A. Gershchenkron) have come to the conclusion that serfdom as an economic system was still fully viable on the eve of the 1861 reforms.[11] This problem clearly needs further research bringing to bear data on macro- and micro-socioeconomic development during the

8 *Golos minuvshego.* 1916, Nos. 5–6, p. 393; L. G. Zakharova, *Aleksandr II, 1855–1881: Romanovy. Istoricheskie portrety* (Moscow: Armada, 1997), pp. 400–90.

9 D. A. Miliutin, *Vospominaniia, 1863–1864* (Moscow: Rosspen, 2003), p. 319.

10 *Perepiska imperatora Aleksandra II s velikim kniazem Konstantinom Nikolaevichem. Dnevnik velikogo kniazia Konstantina Nikolaevicha, 1857–1861* (Moscow: Terra, 1994); A. Rieber, *The Politics of Autocracy: Letters of Alexander II to Prince A. I. Bariatinskii. 1857–1864* (Paris: Rieber, 1966).

11 For sources on the historiography of the question, see P. Gatrell, 'Znachenie velikikh reform v ekonomicheskoi istorii Rossii', in Zakharova, Eklof and Bushnell, *Velikie reformy v Rossii*, pp. 106–26.

pre-reform decades. The effects of the banking crisis at the end of the 1850s on the preparation of the reforms has been convincingly and comprehensively studied in the works of Steven Hoch.[12]

The question of the economic goals and perceptions of the reformers themselves has been illuminated well in the work of Olga Crisp, A. Skerpan and Bruce Lincoln. Economic liberalism and the recognition of the role of private initiative in the development of the economy formed the core of their views. In this light the assertion that the liberal bureaucracy was not aware of the realities of the Russian situation and was only copying the experience of the West looks highly dubious. Rather it can be said that the key reformers took into account the experience of Europe but acted in the awareness of Russian realities and traditions, with which they were very well acquainted. Above all this concerns the Statutes of 19 February. For example, already at the beginning of the 1840s Nikolai Miliutin and A. P. Zablotskii-Desiatovskii carried out detailed on-the-spot studies of serf estates. With this same aim in mind, in the summer of 1860 A.V. Golovnin was sent with Grand Duke Konstantin Nikolaevich to the central provinces. Before he wrote his 1855 memorandum on the emancipation of the peasants, K. D. Kavelin had direct experience with serf-based agriculture.

On the whole, thanks primarily to the work of Bruce Lincoln, it is now clear that a key precondition of the Great Reforms was the existence of cadres, people who were prepared to take upon themselves the massive work of the transformation of Russia, a project which their predecessors in the first half of the nineteenth century had tried to embark on but had not managed. This stratum of progressive, educated people, united in their common views about the forthcoming transformations and the methods for carrying them out, began to take shape in the heart of the bureaucratic apparatus during the reign of Nicholas I in the 1830s and especially in the 1840s. It was characterised by the practically identical conceptions of the 'liberal' or 'enlightened' bureaucracy.[13] Certain ministries (state domains, internal affairs, justice and navy) and the State Chancellery formed its core. The liberal bureaucracy was not shut off from society: it co-operated closely with liberal public figures, academics and

12 S. Hoch, 'Bankovskii krizis, krest'ianskaia reforma i vykupnaia operatsiia v Rossii, 1857–1861', in Zakharova, Eklof and Bushnell, *Velikie reformy v Rossii*, pp. 95–105.

13 The term 'enlightened bureaucracy' has been accepted in the Western literature, 'liberal bureaucracy' in the Russian literature. See W. B. Lincoln, *In the Vanguard of Reform: Russia's Enlightened Bureaucrats, 1825–1861* (DeKalb: Northern Illinois University Press, 1982); R. S. Wortman, *The Development of a Russian Legal Consciousness* (Chicago: Chicago University Press, 1976); L. G. Zakharova, *Samoderzhavie i otmena krepostnogo prava v Rossii 1856–1861* (Moscow: Izd. MGU, 1984).

writers. These links were maintained through personal contacts, interactions in groups and in fashionable salons (especially the salon of Grand Duchess Elena Pavlovna). Iu. F. Samarin, K. D. Kavelin, M. E. Saltykov-Shchedrin, P. N. Mel'nikov (Pecherskii), V. I. Dal' and others were members of the bureaucracy at different times. This collaboration of civil servants (among whom Dmitrii and Nikolai Miliutin stood out particularly) and social and academic figures found an outlet in the Russian Geographical Society which was set up in 1845 under the chairmanship of Grand Duke Konstantin Nikolaevich. Terence Emmons, a leading expert on the 1861 peasant reform, is convinced that the 'bureaucratic "third element"', which had formed during Nicholas's reign 'can undoubtedly be considered one of the preconditions of the 1860 reforms'.[14] Although the study of the enlightened bureaucracy in Russian historiography has far from been exhausted, there is no doubt about the pivotal role it played in the transformations.

Another such precondition was the institutional reforms which were carried out in the reign of Alexander I, including the creation of ministries in which the cadres of the future reformers were trained. It is also important to note the significance of the legacy of M. M. Speranskii. He put large-scale reforms of the state system on the agenda during the reign of Alexander I and during the subsequent reign ordered and codified legislation by producing the Complete Collection of Laws (*Pol'noe sobranie zakonov*) and the Code of Laws of the Russian Empire (*Svod zakonov*). He also did his bit in the education of the future Tsar-liberator (for a year and half Speranskii gave the heir to the throne lectures on law). In addition, the educational reforms in the first half of the nineteenth century created the institutions (universities, School of Law, Tsarskoe Selo Lycee) from which many of the key reformers graduated.[15]

Among the preconditions for the abolition of serfdom, the accumulated experience of discussion and decision-making regarding the peasant problem in the first half of the nineteenth century also played a significant role. The Decree of 1803 on 'Free Agriculturalists' and of 1842 on 'Obligated Peasants', which were not binding on landowners and as a result had little effect, nevertheless meant that ideas about emancipation linked to land-redemption and about the unbreakable link of the peasant with the land had been affirmed in legislation. Local reforms also created models: the abolition of serfdom in the Baltic provinces (Livonia, Kurland and Estonia) in 1816–19 and the introduction of inventories in the south-west of the country (in Kiev, Podolia and Volhynia)

14 Emmons, '"Revoliutsiia sverkhu" v Rossii', p. 380.

15 See F. A. Petrov, *Rossiiskie universitety v pervoi polovine XIX veka i formirovanie sistemy universitetskogo obrazoviniia*, vols. 1–4 (Moscow: Izd. MGU, 1996–2003).

in 1847–8 were obligatory for landowners and provided two models for the solution of the peasant problem which would be taken into account at the time of the preparation of the abolition of serfdom. The reform of the state peasantry, carried out by P. D. Kiselev in 1837 created the model of peasant self-government. The materials from the Secret Committees (particularly of 1835 and 1839), which in 1856 were transferred from the II Department of the Emperor's Personal Chancellery to the Ministry of Internal Affairs, where the preparation of the emancipation of the serfs was started, also received some attention.[16]

How does the legislation of 1861 relate to the preconditions of the reform that were taking shape in the middle of the century? This is the main question of the next section of my work.

The programme and conception of the reformers, the legislation of 19 February 1861 and the other Great Reforms

Terence Emmons rightly observed that 'recently historians have begun to pay particular attention to the interconnections among the reforms of the 1860–1870s'. The view that serfdom was the 'cornerstone' of the state structure (the army, laws, administration), and that it was impossible to leave them unchanged because they simply could not function as before, has been increasingly corroborated in the historiography and is virtually undisputed. However, Emmons stresses that this is only part of the truth and in concentrating too much attention on it we risk losing 'sight of that "ideology" of reforms, which usually unites all large-scale transformations in one epoch and one system'.[17] This important conclusion deserves close attention.

In order to analyse this question we need to consider the ideas of the reformers, their understanding of the aims of the reforms, their views on the interrelationships of all the transformations and the prospects for Russia's development. Without research into this aspect of the history of the Great Reforms, it is impossible to appreciate their depth and scale. One must not forget that the reforms were carried out by an autocratic monarchy, and that the reformers could not clearly and openly state their final aims in the legislation.

16 N. M. Druzhinin, *Gosudarstvennye krest'iane i reforma P. D. Kiseleva* (Moscow: Izd. AN SSSR, 1946–58), vols. I and II; Also his *Russkaia derevnia na perelome 1861–1880 gg.* (Moscow: Nauka, 1978); S. V. Mironenko, *Samoderzhavie i reformy. Politicheskia bor'ba v Rossii v nachale XIX v.* (Moscow: Nauka, 1989), pp. 101–46; also his *Tainye stranitsy istorii samoderzhaviia* (Moscow: Nauka, 1990), p. 238.

17 Emmons, '"Revoliutsiia sverkhu" v Rossii', p. 383.

For this reason many fundamental aspects of the Statutes of 19 February 1861, of the Zemstvo Statute of 1864 and other legislative acts have been somewhat obscured.

Take one of the outstanding leaders of the Great Reforms, the minister of war under Alexander II, the historian, professor and brilliant memoirist D. A. Miliutin. In the middle of the 1880s, in retirement after the death of Alexander II and the change of course, he wrote in his memoirs, '*The Law of 19 February 1861* could not have been a separate, isolated act, it was the *foundation-stone of the restructuring of the entire state system*' (my emphasis). Miliutin considered that in order to understand 'our state regeneration' which happened in the first ten years of the reign of Alexander II, it was necessary to examine 'the course of the three main reforms – the peasant reform, the *zemstvo* reform and the judicial reform.'[18] V. O. Kliuchevskii came to an even broader conclusion about the interconnections of the reforms: 'The peasant reform was the starting point and at the same time the final aim of the whole transformation process. The process of reform had to begin with it, and all the other reforms flowed from it as inevitable consequences and were supposed to ensure that it was carried out successfully. These reforms would find support and justification in the peasant reform's successful realisation.'[19] Finally, in the contemporary research of Steven Hoch and M. D. Dolbilov the preparation of the draft of the redemption scheme in the Editing Commissions is examined in close connection with the work of the Banking Commission.[20]

Apart from memoirs and letters, the ideas of the reformers are most fully and openly revealed in the unofficial chronicle of the Editing Commissions, which prepared the codified drafts of the Statutes of 19 February. This detailed, lively (virtually a stenographic report) record of the journals of the 409 meetings which took place in the nineteen-month existence of this non-traditional institution in the history of autocracy contains the actual words of the participants – their remarks, jokes, quarrels, and the arguments between the sides.[21] This chronicle was created at the initiative of the members of the Editing

18 D. A. Miliutin, *Vospominaniia, 1865–1867* (Moscow: Rosspen, 2005), p. 202.

19 V. O. Kliuchevskii, *Sochineniia v deviati tomakh*, vol. V (Moscow: Sotsekgiz, 1989), p. 430.

20 M. D. Dolbilov, 'Proekty vykupnoi operatsii 1857–1861 gg. K otsenke tvorchestva reformatorskoi komandy', *Otechestvennaia istoria* 1 (2000): 15–33; Hoch, 'Bankovskii Krizis', pp. 95–105.

21 *Osvobozhdenie krest'ian v tsartstvovanie imperatora Alexandra II. Khronika deiatel'nosti Redaktsionnykh komissii po krest'ianskomu delu N. P. Sememova* (henceforth *Khronika H. P. Semenova*) (St Petersburg: 1889–92), vols. I–III. The preparation of the peasant reform in the Editing Commissions has been analysed in the following works: D. Field, *The End of Serfdom: Nobility and Bureaucracy in Russia, 1855–1861* (Cambridge, Mass.: Harvard University Press, 1976); Zakharova, *Samoderzhavie i otmena krepostnogo prava.*

Commissions, who recognised the scale of the tasks that lay before them and their responsibility 'in the eyes of the people', to 'the public' and the nobility of Russia, and in the face of Europe.[22]

The chairman and members of the Editing Commissions often stated that although currently engaged in the transformation of the private serfs' world they were concerned with the fate of all categories of peasants – that is state peasants, appanage peasants and others, who exceeded the numbers of serfs (the peasantry as a whole made up 80 per cent of the population). V. A. Cherkasskii declared that the drafts of the Editing Commissions signified 'a general revolution' in land relations. The Chairman of the Commission Ia. I. Rostovstev formulated the task even more broadly: 'It is our duty to sort out all the questions concerning the peasantry, because the statute on the emancipation of the serfs must change our entire Code of Laws.'[23] N. A. Miliutin, straight after his dismissal on 2 May 1861, wrote to Cherkasskii expressing his concern about the fate of the peasant-reform initiative: 'Now there is no longer that same internal mechanism which led inevitably to the *decisive break* – there are no Editing Commissions, which set the reform on its way' (my emphasis).[24] In general Rostovtsev considered that 'the creation of the Russian *narod* (people, nation) began in 1859'.[25] Here it is worth remembering the task that Speranskii laid down in his list of not yet completed projects at the beginning of the nineteenth century: 'To create our own nation [*of free people* – L.Z.], in order to then give it a form of government.'[26]

The 'General Memorandum Covering the Drafts of the Editing Commissions', written by Samarin and signed by twenty-three members of the Commissions at the last meeting on 10 October 1860, revealed the concept underlying the legislation. These men saw Russia as a special case because it was possible to decide the question of the abolition of serfdom and the future arrangement of land relations in one legislative act – through peasant redemption of plots and the preservation of a significant portion of gentry, that is, noble, landholding. They noted:

> In other states governments followed this path in several stages, and so to speak groped their way because such a reform had never been experienced before in practice, and at the beginning it was impossible to envisage how

22 *Khronika N. P. Semenova*, vol. III, part 1, pp. 487, 119, 183, 273.
23 *Khronika N. P. Semenova*, vol. III, part 1, pp. 487, 208.
24 RGIA, Fond 869, op. 1, d. 1149, l. 246.
25 M. Borodkin, *Istoriia Finliandii. Vremia imperatora Alexandra II* (St Petersburg, 1908), p. 152.
26 M. M. Speranskii, *Proekty i zapiski* (Moscow and Leningrad: Izd. AN SSSR, 1961). M. M. Speranskii, *Zapiski 'O korennykh zakonakh gosudarstva'* (1802).

> the process would end. That is why the sequence of measures leading to the gradual broadening of the rights of the serfs and an improvement in their way of life has virtually everywhere given rise to unforeseen social crises. In this regard, Russia is luckier. By making use of the experience of other countries it has been given the possibility . . . to embrace straightaway the entire path that lies ahead from the first step to the full curtailment of obligatory relations by means of the redemption of land.[27]

It is clear why research on land redemption led B. G. Litvak to the following evaluation of the 1861 reform: 'In fact, this was *a process, at the outset of which the emancipation of the individual from the power of the landowner was proclaimed . . . but whose final stage was the creation of communal and household land-ownership'* (my emphasis).[28]

The legal position of the peasants was transformed radically and consistently in the drafts of the Editing Commissions and in the Statutes of 19 February 1861. Personal dependence of peasants on the nobility ended immediately. The former serfs acquired a civic status, although the peasantry remained subject to certain specific estate (*soslovie*) obligations. Peasant self-government was introduced – at the *volost'* and village level (on the whole on the basis of the *obshchina*) with officials elected by the peasants, with assemblies and a peasant district (*volost'*) court. In this part of the legislation much was borrowed from Kiselev's reform of the state peasantry. Peasant self-governing institutions were placed under the supervision of the local state administration and performed fiscal functions for the government, but they also served to defend the interests of the peasants against the landowners. In addition, they provided the basis for peasant participation in the new institutions for all the *sosloviia* – the *zemstvo* (local elected assembly) and jury courts.

At the same time as the opening of the Editing Commissions in March 1859, a commission for the preparation of the reform of local government under the chairmanship of N. A. Miliutin was set up under the Ministry of Internal Affairs. Its programme was co-ordinated with the peasant reform and laid the foundation for the Zemstvo Statute of 1 January 1864. It was only thanks to this co-ordination that the participation of the peasants in the zemstva was secured, as at the time they were still not landowners and therefore did not have a property qualification. The link with the judicial reform consisted not only of the participation of peasants in juries. The reformers created a completely new institution for the realisation of the peasant reform – the Peace Mediators,

27 *Pervoe izdanie materialov Redaktsionnykh komissii dlia sostavleniia polozhenii o krest'ianakh, vykhodiashchikh iz krepostnoi zavisimosti* (St Petersburg, 1860), part XVIII, pp. 3–6.
28 V. G. Litvak, *Russkaia derevnia v reforme 1861* (Moscow: Nauka, 1972), p. 407.

who were called upon to regulate the relations between the landowner and his former serfs by means of drawing up charters and redemption acts for working out the details of the land settlement on individual estates. Although nobles themselves, the peace mediators were not selected by the noble assemblies but were appointed by the state with the help of the local administration. In 1861 it was proposed that in three years' time they would be selected jointly by the nobility and the free peasantry. And although their exclusively noble status did not correspond to the general ideology of the Great Reforms, other principles surrounding their activity, such as openness and the fact that they could not be removed, ensured their independence from the administration and the noble assemblies and prepared the ground for the introduction of the justice of the peace and the new court system in Russia under the Judicial Statutes of 1864.[29]

If we add to the above the abolition of corporal punishment on 17 April 1863 (Alexander II's birthday), the military service law of 1 January 1874 and the reform of education, it becomes clear that the Great Reforms opened the way to the creation of a civil society (although the reformers did not use this terminology). They were indeed aimed at the development of the people's national and civic consciousness, at instilling in them feelings of dignity and at overcoming traditions of servitude, which had been embedded in generations of Russian peasants.

Solving the land question was more difficult. It depended on gradualism and amendments over time and was complicated by the critical financial situation of the country after the Crimean War. The reformers themselves clung firmly to the idea of the emancipation of the peasants through the redemption of land. This idea was defined in 1855–6 in the memoranda of D. A. and N. A. Miliutin, K. D. Kavelin and Iu. F. Samarin (the last-mentioned held a slightly different position). However, the first public document which began the preparation for the reform – Alexander II's rescript to General-Governor V. I. Nazimov of Vilno of 20 November 1857 – did not contain a definite decision on the land question. It would have been possible to move from it to emancipation based on guaranteed peasant usufract rather than outright property ownership by the peasants. The significance of the rescript was that it made public the government's intention to solve the peasant question, which had been discussed for so long but in secret. Henceforth openness became an independent force on which

29 Here and below when speaking about the resolution of the peasant question in the 1861 reform, material from the following works is drawn on: L. G. Zakharova, *Samoderzhavie i otmena krepostnogo prava*; 'Samoderzhavie, biurokratia i reformy 60-kh godov XIX v. v Rossii', *VI* 10 (1989): 3–24; and 'Samoderzhavie i reformy v Rossii 1861–1874' in Zakharova, Eklof and Bushnell, *Velikie reformy v Rossii*, pp. 24–43.

the reformers relied. In particular, 3,000 copies of the work of the Editing Commissions were immediately published following its meetings.

Throughout 1858 in society, in the periodical press, in the noble provincial committees and in government circles a struggle was waged over different solutions to the peasant question – with land or without land. At the beginning it seemed that the Baltic model (emancipation without land) was winning, the more so because the tsar himself believed in this path which had been tried and tested in the Baltic provinces. However, a series of circumstances (the serious and protracted wave of peasant unrest in the province of Estonia, the rejection by appanage peasants of emancipation without land, the struggles among the fractions in the noble provincial committees) pushed Alexander by the end of 1858 towards the idea of land for the peasants and towards the adoption of the programme of the liberal bureaucracy.[30]

The liberal majority of the Editing Commissions believed that all peasant-farmers must enjoy usufract rights over land from the start of the reform process and ownership rights in time. They projected two types of landholding in Russia's new agrarian sector: large gentry (noble) estates and small peasant holdings. They proposed to attain this goal peacefully, avoiding the revolutionary upheavals that had occurred in the countries of Western and Central Europe, and this was considered one of the principal features of the Russian reform. From the experience of European countries, they pointed to the positive *results* in France (the creation of small private land-ownership), and the *methods* of legislative measures in Prussia and Austria, which consisted of redemption of land by the peasants while preserving gentry landholding, yet avoiding the extremes of the Prussian variant – 'concentration of landed property in the hands of a few great landowners and big farmers' and the proliferation of landless agricultural labourers. As a result, the reform was built on the basis of 'existing realities', that is the preservation of much arable land in the hands of the nobility, and of the pre-reform plots in peasant ownership; the calculation of initial obligations and subsequent redemption payments on the basis of pre-reform dues (with a slight reduction); the participation of the state in the redemption operations in the capacity of creditor. The acquisition of full property rights to their plots through redemption payments by the peasants was seen as the reform's final outcome. Redemption was not obligatory for the gentry landowners. Alexander II said: 'While even one noble is against the redemption of peasant plots, I will not allow compulsory redemption.' At

30 L. G. Zakharova, 'Znachenie krest'ianskikh volnenii v 1858 v Estonii v istorii podgotovki otmeny krepostnogo prava v Rossii', in *Izvestiia Akademii nauk Estonskoi SSR*, no. 33 (Tallinn, 1984): 24–46.

the same time the adoption of 'gradual' and 'voluntary redemption', that is of the principle of the 'self-financing' of redemption operations, was explained by the state's difficult financial situation. The reformers recognised that it was impossible at present for the treasury to subsidise the redemption operation, although the longer-term possibility was recognised.[31] Though they had to accept the limits dictated by the contemporary situation, the Editing Commissions created an internal mechanism for the reform which guaranteed uninterrupted progression toward the projected results. The reform was a process: perpetual peasant usufract at fixed rents quite soon persuaded landowners that redemption was in their own interests.

The peasants too had virtually no choice. Having set the aim of avoiding mass proletarianisation, and recognising at the same time that the economic conditions of emancipation were difficult and that the landowners would strive at all costs to crowd out the peasants, the reformers introduced into the law an article which forbade peasants to repudiate the allotments for nine years (this period was subsequently lengthened). The preservation of the *obshchina* (commune) in its role as a landowner (in addition to its other above-mentioned functions) served the same aim to a significant degree. By preserving the obshchina with its archaic rules about restrictions on peasant land and with joint responsibility for dues, the reformers understood that this would hinder the free development of an independent peasant economy. However, for the start of the reform the preservation of this institution, which was embedded in the organisation of the economy and in the consciousness and everyday life of the peasants, was considered unavoidable. At the same time the idea was not to conserve the obshchina forever. Leaving the obshchina was foreseen under certain conditions and with time this was to be made easier. In the milieu of the Editing Commissions the view predominated that with time obshchina land-ownership would yield to individual ownership, and the administrative functions of the village community would be concentrated in the volost'. Only Iurii Samarin gave his unreserved support to the obshchina. Speaking before the deciding vote about the fate of the obshchina, N. A. Miliutin said that 'by mutual consent it had been decided to leave this question to time and to the peasants themselves, . . . and that the legislation and the government had always rejected the adoption of any artificial or imposed measures for such a transition, and that this decision had been approved by the Emperor himself'.[32]

31 M. D. Dolbilov, 'Proekty vykupnoi operatsii', Hoch 'Bankovskii Krizis', pp. 95–105.
32 P. P. Semenov-Tian-Shanskii, *Memuary: Epokha osvobodzhdeniia krest'ian v Rossii, 1858–1861*, 4 vols. (Petersburg: priv. pub. 1915), vol. III, p. 231.

This conception of the solution to the land question, albeit with several adjustments introduced into the drafts of the Editing Commissions at the Main Committee on the Peasant Question and at the State Council, was embodied in the Statutes of 19 February 1861. As a consequence of the amendments, the peasants' position became more difficult as a result of the reduction in the size of the allotment of land (the so-called 'cut-offs') and the increase in dues, including redemption payments.[33] Emmons rightly considers that 'from the point of view of the state there were in practice no alternatives to this programme'.[34] The reformers understood the burden on the peasants of the economic terms of the emancipation. Even during the course of the preparation of the reform, Miliutin foresaw the land-hunger of the peasants and considered that the state would have to use a portion of the treasury's lands to counter this phenomenon. But for Miliutin the key here was the transformation of the financial system. He tried to take control of three key spheres: the peasant question, local self-government and finance. However, the attempts by his patrons – Grand Duchess Elena Pavlovna and Grand Duke Konstantin Nikolaevich – to get him appointed as minister of finance were not successful. At the beginning of May 1866 when Alexander II considered appointing Miliutin as minister of finance, P. A. Shuvalov managed to convince the monarch to reject this idea, partly by himself threatening to resign.[35]

M. D. Dolbilov in his article about the plans for redemption from 1857 to 1861 plausibly suggested that what the reformers had in mind was the fundamental restructuring of the redemption operation in the not too distant future, at the earliest stage of the implementation of the abolition of serfdom. Valuev's diary supports this interpretation.[36] It is hard now to establish how Nikolai Miliutin conceived of the financial reforms, but his brother and political ally Dmitrii Miliutin, evaluating the financial and economic situation of the country in the 1860s, wrote twenty years later, that it was impossible 'to increase endlessly the burden of taxes which almost exclusively fall on the working, poorest class of the people, who are already impoverished'. He considered that the 'fundamental revision of our whole taxation system was the main task'.[37] At the beginning of the 1880s N. A. Miliutin's colleague N. Kh. Bunge would

33 P. A. Zaionchkovskii, *Otmena krepostnogo prava v Rossii*, 3rd edn (Moscow: Prosveshchenie, 1968), pp. 232–59.

34 Emmons, '"Revoliutsiia sverkhu" v Rossii', p. 381.

35 P. A. Valuev, *Dnevnik*, 2 vols. (Moscow: Izd. AN SSSR, 1961), vol. II; GARF, Fond 583, op. 1, d. 19, l. 173–6 (Material from the manuscript diary of A. A. Polovtsov Das provided by A. V. Mamonov).

36 Dolbilov, *Proekty vykupnoi operatsii*, p. 30; Valuev, *Dnevnik*, vol. I, p. 334.

37 Miliutin, *Vospominaniia, 1865–1867*, p. 440.

begin the reform of the tax system. But this was already in a different era. Peter Gatrell is correct in saying that 'no significant changes took place in taxation policy in the decade following the reform',[38] with the exception of the important excise reform of 1863, which ended the farming-out system for spirits and deprived the nobility of privileges in distillation. At the same time the introduction of excise duty enriched the treasury and encouraged private capital investment in the economy.[39]

The reformers' programme did not envisage transformation of the higher organs of state power, the convocation of an Estates General (*Zemskii sobor*) or of all-Russian representative institutions. At the same time the liberal bureaucrats discussed among themselves those forces that would further advance the reforms. Already in a memorandum of 1856, Nikolai Miliutin pinned his hopes on the monarchy, which, having taken the initiative with the transformations, would find support in the liberal, enlightened nobility. The same hope was mentioned in 'The General Memorandum' of October 1860. The very creation of the Editing Commissions, more than half of whose members were not officials (albeit appointed), an institution directly subordinate through its chairman to Alexander II, was to a certain degree the realisation of the ideas of the reformers about the new role of the autocratic monarchy. Moreover, as P. P. Semenov-Tian-Shanskii has witnessed,

> N. A. Miliutin was in no doubt that with the appropriate development of the activity of the local institutions under the patronage of a strong state power, the sovereign power itself would recognise the need to appeal to representatives of local interests and would share legislative functions with them in order further to develop its reforms, as it had now done for the first time with the convening of local committees and with the summoning of expert-members who were independent of the administrative structures of power.[40]

It is no coincidence that in 1880–1 M. T. Loris-Melikov turned to the experience of the Editing Commissions and to the reforms of local self-government, linking his plans for comprehensive transformations with the experience of the Great Reforms. However, in 1860 the reformers did not succeed in translating all their ideas into legislation. The sudden closure of the Editing Commissions in October 1860, and the dismissal of N. A. Miliutin in April 1861 were testimony to the precariousness of their general calculations.

38 P. Gatrell, 'Znachenie velikikh reform', p. 121.
39 D. Christian, 'Zabytaia reforma: otmena vinnykh otkupov v Rossii', in Zakharova, Eklof and Bushnell, *Velikie reformy v Rossii*, pp. 126–39.
40 P. Semenov-Tian-Shianskii, *Memuary*, vol. IV (1916), vol. 4, pp. 197–8.

The world-view of the reformers was evidently not devoid of a utopian faith in the limitless possibility of the state to direct the course of historical development. Nikolai Miliutin with his characteristic perspicacity instantly understood the emerging danger. In December of that year he wrote to his brother, Dmitrii, the minister of war: 'It is necessary to fashion *opinion*, or perhaps a *middle* party, in parliamentary language "le centre", which we don't have here but the elements of which can evidently be found. Only the government can do this, and it would be the best means of consolidation for the government itself.' In April 1863 in another letter, returning to these thoughts once again, he wrote with alarm: 'There is no greater unhappiness for Russia than letting the initiative slip out of the hands of the government.'[41] The stake placed by the reformers on the initiating role of the monarch and the liberal public turned out to be unreliable, laying bare the enlightened illusions which were characteristic of their generation. But at the time in Russia there were no other guarantees apart from the irreversibility of the legislation that had been adopted.

Legislation and life: the fate of the Great Reforms and the fate of the reformers

The implementation of specific reforms cannot be examined in detail in this chapter.[42] But in order to have an adequate understanding of the problem presented here something must be said about the realisation of the great reforms in general. If one bears in mind the precise meaning of the 1861 legislation, it must be recognised that it did not anticipate the immediate transformation of gentry and peasant farming, let alone an immediate revolution in the economy as a whole. The final goal of the peasant reform was, however, quite definite: the creation of independent small, peasant farming alongside gentry farming. Until very recently, the prevailing view in the literature was that the reform was extortionate towards the peasantry, with inflated redemption payments for reduced plots, which led to land-hunger and ruination of peasant households on a mass scale. Modern methods of statistical analysis of the socioeconomic results of the peasant reform have allowed a number of historians to come to quite different conclusions. In reality, the abolition of serfdom by the terms of the statutes of 19 February led to the creation of self-sufficient peasant farming

41 OR RGB, Fond 169, kart. 69, ed. khr. 11, ll. 9–11.

42 For this the reader should consult the other chapters dealing with the peasantry, the economy, state finances, the legal system, local administration and the army.

and the prospect of the predominance of the peasant family farm in Russian agriculture.[43]

In the legal sphere, the isolation of the peasant estate that was preserved by the statutes of 19 February was overcome to a degree through the implementation of the zemstvo and judicial reforms. The proportion of peasant deputies in the zemstva was significant, although it was exceeded by noble representation (38 and 43 per cent, respectively). In some regions (central-industrial, southern-steppe, and southeastern) representation tended toward predominance by peasants, specifically peasant landowners. Peasant representation was also significant in juries – in the provinces it was even predominant (over 50 per cent). At the same time, the existence of the volost' peasant-estate court created a dualism in the court system, preserving peasant isolation in this respect. This does not, however, justify the general conclusion that the peasant reform retarded the integration of the peasantry into civic life and fortified the schism in Russia between 'traditional' and 'westernized' society.[44] Separate peasant self-administration and the separate volost' court were introduced in the 1861 reform in connection with the termination of the hereditary power of the gentry landowner, which explains their expediency. They were not the final goal of the legislators, only a temporary, inevitable structure on the road to unitary citizenship.

Such an important measure as the abolition of the recruitment system for manning the army militated in the same direction of integrating the peasantry into the new, unitary organisation of Russian society. This last of Alexander II's reforms (the Statute of 1 January 1874) was considerably influenced by the international situation and the experience of European wars. The personal role of Alexander II was great in this reform: he stuck to his decision in the face of strong pressure from the opposition. In all other spheres of state life, reform activity from the 1860s onward continued by inertia, without the previous energy.

Alexander II's own disillusionment with the reforms and a major shift in his own personal state of mind occurred almost simultaneously and for a number of reasons. After the successful introduction of the reforms, the victorious

43 See S. G. Kashchenko, 'Nekotorye voprosy metodiki izucheniia realizatsii reformy 19 fevralia 1861g. v issedovaniiakh P. A. Zaionchkovskogo', *Otechestvennaia istoriia* 4 (2004): 81–92; S. L. Hoch, 'Did Russia's Emancipated Serfs really Pay Too Much for Too Little Land? Statistical Anomalies and Long-tailed Distributions', *SR* 63, 2 (2004): 247–74; D. V. Kovalev, *Agrarnye preobrazovaniia i krestianstvo stolichnogo regiona v pervoi chetverti XIXv.* (Moscow: Rosspen, 2004), pp. 258, 260–5.

44 W. Pintner, 'Reformability in the Age of Reform and Counter-reform', in *Reform in Russia and the USSR* (Urbana: University of Illinois Press, 1989), pp. 83–106.

conclusion in 1864 of the half-century war in the Caucasus, the suppression of the Polish uprising of 1863–4 and the carrying out of the radical agrarian and other transformations in the Polish Kingdom, the establishment of the *Sejm* (assembly) and of the constitutional order in Finland in 1863, the Tsar-liberator came up against some unexpected difficulties and deep personal traumas. The Polish revolutionary response to his efforts at liberalisation was no doubt itself a disappointment. Much more important for Alexander, the Russian nobility, discontented with the emancipation of the serfs, voiced its claims for political rights. The zemstvo assemblies which had just been opened, especially the Petersburg zemstvo, showed a degree of independence which the government disliked.[45] In April 1865 the heir to the throne, Tsarevich Nicholas Alexandrovich, unexpectedly died at the age of twenty-one. A year later Dmitrii Karakozov shot at Alexander II near the gates of the Summer Garden. The news that Karakozov was a Russian shook Alexander II more than the attack itself. The enthusiasm and inspiration which had sustained the emperor in the first, most unclouded and fruitful ten years of his reign was dissipated.

In this depressed state, Alexander II gave in to the pressure from conservative forces. The decree of 13 May 1866 bears witness to the shift towards a conservative course. Karakozov's shot, as one of his contemporaries put it, 'favoured reaction'.[46] In the government the most influential figure became Count Petr Shuvalov, who was appointed head of the gendarmes and given overall responsibility for internal security straight after the attack. Shuvalov was an opponent of the liberal bureaucracy and the reforms carried out by it. The year 1866 was also a turning point in the personal life of the emperor. He was consumed by his passion for the young Princess Ekaterina Dolgorukov, which became stronger over time, often distracting him from affairs of state and at the same time weighing him down with the burden of a double life.[47]

In the Editing Commissions, the reformers had acknowledged that the current legislation would require further development. They hoped that this task would be carried out by an 'enterprising monarchy'. Their hopes were not realised.[48]

45 I. A. Khristoforov, *'Aristokraticheskaia' oppozitsiia Velikim reformam. Konets 1850–seredina 1870kh gg.* (Moscow: Russkoe slovo, 2002), pp. 172–6.
46 Khristoforov, *'Aristokraticheskaia' oppozitsiia*. Prilozhenie, p. 333.
47 L. G. Zakharova, 'Alexander II i mesto Rossii v mire', *Novaia i noveishaia istoriia* 4 (2005): 141.
48 See O. Trubetskaia, Materialy dlia biografii kn. V. A.Cherkasskogo. vol. I. book 2, part 3. V. 1902, p. 43.

Though he accepted the legacy of Nikolai Miliutin in terms of the realisation of the peasant reforms and the preparation and implementation of the zemstvo reform, as minister of internal affairs, P. A. Valuev (Miliutin's irreconcilable opponent) immediately led the attack on the liberal peace mediators – a most important link in the peasant reform.[49] While it was not within his powers to infringe the Statutes of 19 February about the irremoveability and independence of the peace mediators, he began to reduce their number. Valuev's policy transformed the position of peace mediator: from an honourable post, which attracted intelligent and thoughtful people, into a mediocre administrative function. The same phenomenon was observed with the introduction of other institutions created by the reforms – the zemstva and the new courts. From the first independent steps of the zemstva, the government displayed its distrust in them. D. A. Miliutin wrote, 'It was as if the government itself, having just established socially inclusive *(vsesoslovnoe)* self-government, had a sudden rethink – hadn't it taken a rather imprudent step. From the very beginning of the implementation of the new legislation it was considered necessary to follow the new institutions vigilantly, to hold them in check, so to speak.' Already by the end of 1865 in government policy 'instead of the gradual development and broadening of the zemstva, a systematic squeezing and restraining of them began'.[50]

Even more importantly, the peasant question, which demanded special attention and the development of the foundations which had been created in the 1861 reform, found itself by the end of the 1870s on the fringes of government policy. Serious problems which had emerged were not addressed. Already in the middle of the 1860s, M. Kh. Reutern in his reports drew attention to the burden of the dues and redemption payments for the emancipated peasants. But neither the minister of finance himself, nor the government as a whole took any measures to resolve the difficulties that had arisen in the course of the implementation of the peasant reform and to achieve the final goal of the reform – the creation of an independent small peasant economy. The issue of the obshchina was raised but not resolved. After quite a lengthy discussion of the problems of peasant land-ownership the ministers of internal affairs, finance and justice were entrusted with working out a set of measures to ease the departure of peasants from the obshchina, that is the broadening of article 165 of the Statutes of 19 February. The minutes of the Council of Ministers

49 M. F. Ust'iantseva, 'Institut mirovykh posrednikov v krest'ianskoi reforme', in Zakharova, Eklof and Bushnell, *Velikie reformy v Rossii*, pp. 170–1.
50 Miliutin, *Vospominaniia, 1865–1867*, p. 46.

to this effect were approved on 9 March 1874, but the matter was put on hold.[51]

The weakest link in the chain of reforms was finances, and it was only after the war of 1877–8, against a background of financial crisis, social and political discontent, and terrorist acts, that Alexander II and the government acknowledged the need to continue the Great Reforms. This attempt would be undertaken by M. T. Loris-Melikov with the agreement and approval of Alexander II. The most recent research has convincingly shown that Loris-Melikov's programme was not a set of separate measures, but a definite 'scheme', organically linked to those reforms which had been carried out in the first decade of Alexander II's reign. The tsar himself expressed his understanding of this continuity, in particular in his confession to Loris-Melikov that 'there was one person in whom I had full confidence. That was Ia. I. Rostovtsev . . . I have that same confidence in you and perhaps even more.'[52]

As N. A. Miliutin had done in the late 1850s to early 1860s, Loris-Melikov at the end of the 1870s considered it crucial to unite Russian society around a reforming government which rested on the support of public opinion. Without neglecting to strengthen the police, he argued that it was impossible to defeat nihilism by police measures alone. 'Not only did the reforms of the 1860s need to be cleansed from subsequent deviations but their principles had to be developed further.' Loris-Melikov's programme envisaged a whole system of interrelated reforms. Above all it had in mind provincial reform: the reorganisation of the local administrative and social institutions, by removing the antagonism between the zemstva and the state administration, and the transformation of the police in the localities. The improvement of the peasant situation occupied a significant place in the programme: the salt tax was abolished and the tsar's agreement was given to a reduction in redemption payments and a number of other measures. The transformation of the taxation and passport systems was also planned, as was a more flexible policy in the borderlands.

The creation of preparatory commissions along the lines of the Editing Commissions of 1859–60 was proposed in order to facilitate the implementation of this programme. Subsequently, a General Commission attached to the State Council would be created with the participation of representatives of

51 V. G. Chernukha, *Krest'ianskii vopros v pravitel'stvennoi politike Rossii (60-e–70-e gg. XIX v.)* (Leningrad: Nauka, Leningradskoe otdelenie, 1973), pp. 162–3, 170.

52 A. V. Mamonov, 'Graf M. T. Loris-Melikov: k kharakteristike vzgliadov i gosudarstvennoi deiatel'nosti', *Otechestvennaia istoria* 4 (2001): 32–50. This article gives a detailed description of Loris-Melikov's programme.

the zemstva and town self-governments. This was what in the literature has been called the Loris-Melikov 'constitution' and what A.V. Mamonov considers a return to (and development of, I would add) Miliutin's concept of the 'enterprising monarchy'. On 1 March 1881, Alexander II approved the draft government report on the upcoming reforms but died a few hours later. The programme for the further development of the Great Reforms died with him for ever, although certain individual elements of it were realised by N. Kh. Bunge during his time as minister of finance between 1881 and 1886. Bunge's attempts to develop the 1861 peasant reform (he was a believer in independent peasant farming) and modernise the taxation and banking systems only affected limited aspects of state policy, however, and were in any case compromised by the overall programme of counter-reforms carried out in the reign of Alexander III.[53]

By the late nineteenth to early twentieth century, it was understood by the few reformers still alive at the time that the possibility of continuing the reforms that had been decisively and radically begun by the abolition of serfdom had been lost. Russia entered the twentieth century, the century of revolutions and shocks, which they had tried so hard to avoid. In the first months of the 1905 Revolution four elder statesmen gave an independent and realistic appraisal of the Great Reforms and of subsequent government policy. These statesmen – Count K. I. Pahlen, A. A. and P. A. Saburov and A. N. Kulomzin – had experienced the Great Reforms in their early years of service and subsequently participated in their implementation. They produced a memorandum for Nicholas II which stated that the empire's current crisis was rooted in the 'fateful misunderstanding' that the reason for 1 March 1881 (i.e., the assassination of Alexander II) was 'the liberating policy of the tsar-reformer'. They criticised 'the government's endeavour over the last twenty-five years to limit the privileges and advantages which were bestowed on Russia in the epoch of the reforms of Alexander II'.[54]

The revolution wrested from the autocracy the Manifesto of 17 October 1905 and led to the creation of the first Russian parliament (the Duma) and of a true ministerial cabinet and prime minister. The last great reformist statesman of the old regime, P. A. Stolypin, rose on the wave of the revolutionary events and in the struggle with them. While adopting harsh police measures in the struggle with terror, he worked out and began the realisation of

53 See V. L. Stepanov, *N. Kh. Bunge, Sud'ba reformatora* (Moscow: Rosspen, 1998).

54 P. Sh. Ganelin, 'Politicheskie uroki osvoboditel'nogo dvizheniia v otsenke stareishikh tsarskikh biurokratov', in *Osvoboditel'noe dvizhenie v Rossii* (Saratov: 1991), Izd. Saratovskogo universiteta, 14th edn, pp. 122–36.

fundamental changes. In the first place, as in the 1860s, there was agrarian reform, which allowed peasants to leave the obshchina, strengthened peasant property-ownership and aided migration to Russian Asia. It was proposed to combine these paramount reforms with the expansion of local self-government and the extension of the reforms to the empire's borderlands. However, Stolypin's plans were not realised. He was killed in Kiev in 1911, where he had gone for the ceremonial opening of a monument to the Tsar-liberator in connection with the half-century jubilee of the abolition of serfdom. The final possibility for transformations had once again been lost. Russia would soon take part in the First World War and live through a revolution which would sweep away the monarchy and shake the world.

* * *

The Great Reforms, which were organically linked to socioeconomic and political processes in the first half of the nineteenth century, were at the same time a turning point in the history of Russia. While they neither intended nor ensured a simultaneous transformation in all the spheres of public life, they laid the foundations for this turnaround and ruled out the possibility of a restoration of the pre-reform order. As a result of the transformations, 'a basic principle of Russian life was destroyed – the link of progress with serfdom'.[55] The modernisation of Russia continued on a new basis – labour freed from serfdom, the development of private initiative, the origins of civil society. In this context the year 1861 was a watershed, 'the beginning of a new history, a new epoch in Russia' – as many contemporaries understood the abolition of serfdom at the time and as many historians evaluated it later. However, the degree and the depth of the turning point remain to be clarified. In this regard there still remains much for scholars to do.

Among the questions which demand attention are study of the statesmen of the Great Reforms themselves and of the actual circumstances in which they put together their plans. It is probably worth listening more closely to the terms and concepts used by them, their understanding, their perception of reality. For example, it is important to understand how they conceived of 'the new system of agrarian relations', which was supposed to be the result of the implementation of the peasant reform, how they envisaged the coexistence of the landlord and peasant economies. The idea of the reformers about the reforms as a *process* which would necessitate constant modifications by the government also merits attention. Undoubtedly, when studying the Great

55 N. A. Ivnitskii (ed.), *Sud'by rossiiskogo krest'ianstva* (Moscow: Rossiiskii gos. gumanitarnyi universitet, 1996).

Reforms, as well as the counter-reforms, there is the challenge of adopting a differentiated approach to the different stages and 'levels' of the process: to the ideology which lay at the basis of the intended transformations, to the initial draft laws, to the laws as actually adopted (a significant distinction) and finally to how these laws were realised and faced the test of reality.

Such an approach enables one to avoid one-sidedness in the evaluation of the Great Reforms, sometimes observed in the historiography, when either the unbridgeable gulf between epochs or the complete continuity in the gradual advance of the autocracy on the path of reform is emphasised. The undoubted links between the abolition of serfdom and attempts at earlier legislation, the traditions and structures of the pre-reform order, do not contradict the concept of the transformation of various aspects of the country's life begun by the reforms. On the other hand, to acknowledge the inevitability of modifications to the reforms and the presence of pragmatic elements in the legislation of the 1880–90s does not remove the fundamental difference between the Great Reforms and the counter-reforms. For example, it is true that legislative measures were needed to strengthen the system of peasant self-government, and that the volost' court needed to be co-ordinated with the socially inclusive structures of the new court system. In the end, too, and despite the government's original intentions, the Statute of 1890 did not signify a radical change to the zemstvo as created by the reform of 1864. Realities neutralised the conservative amendments which were adopted. But it is impossible to derive from these truths the argument that there were no basic differences between the policies of the 1860s reformers and Loris-Melikov on the one hand, and the instigators of the counter-reforms on the other.

The ideological aims of Count D. A. Tolstoy underlying the revision of the Great Reforms were, for example, far from fully realised in the zemstvo legislation but had a much fuller impact in the spheres of education and censorship, where they created a gulf between the regime and the progressive intelligentsia. The dangerous consequences of this phenomenon were manifest in 1900–6. The co-operation of the liberal bureaucracy and liberal social forces in the eras of Nikolai Miliutin and Loris-Melikov was abandoned, as was their systematic approach to reform. In the 1880s Bunge continued the work of the Great Reforms, and Tolstoi and Pobedonostsev revised it. Thus, if it makes sense to speak of 'the epoch of Great Reforms', there is less reason to speak of 'the epoch of counter-reforms', which would imply co-ordination of the various aspects of internal policy under Alexander III. The course set on preserving the autocracy inviolate, which was proclaimed in the Manifesto of 29 April 1881 and reinforced by the decree of 14 August 1881 on states of emergency, signified the state's loss of initiative in the realisation of large-scale reforms. That initiative would pass to social forces. When Stolypin tried to regain the initiative for the monarchy he did not have the twenty years he asked for. Those twenty years had been lost between 1881 and 1905.

I would like to stress one more problem. Russian and Western historiography has accumulated a rich store of factual material, many valuable conclusions and observations. But these achievements remain disparate and isolated. A comparison of the results of the study of 'institutional' and 'social' history, a comparison of the work on different reforms and a more attentive attitude to the knowledge already established in the historiography, together with a broadening of the range of sources could all yield new approaches and new answers to the question posed in the title of this chapter.

29

Russian workers and revolution

REGINALD E. ZELNIK

'Workers', people who live off their daily labour and the sweat of their brows, have of course been present since the very dawn of Russian history. Depending on the exact time and place, they have included slave labourers (largely extinct by the beginning of the eighteenth century), a wide variety of highly restricted serfs (numerically dominant from the sixteenth century to 1861 if we include peasants whose lord was the state), and free or 'freely-hired' (*vol'nonaemnye*) labourers, but 'free' only in the sense that their obligation to their employer, at least theoretically, was purely contractual, while they remained the bondsmen of their noble lords. Viewed more narrowly, however, defined not simply as people who worked for a living, but only as those employed in manufacturing and paid a wage, workers started to become important to the Russian economy and society mainly in the eighteenth century, beginning with the reign of Peter the Great (1689–1725), who placed a high priority on the country's industrial development. But even under Peter and for many years to come, most workers employed in manufacturing and mining, even if paid in cash or in kind, were unfree labourers, forced to toil long hours either in privately owned enterprises or in factories owned by the government. Among those who experienced the worst conditions in this period of labour-intensive industrialisation were the 'possessional' (*posessionnye*) and 'ascribed' (*pripisannye*) workers – state peasants who, since Peter's time, had been bound to the factory or its owner, and who were compelled to pass this unfortunate status on down to their children.[1] Even those who were 'free' at least in the sense that they were free to negotiate their terms of employment with employers who had no extra-economic, that is, purely coercive controls over them, were almost all *otkhodniki*, the serfs of a

1 See my 'The Peasant and the Factory', in Wayne S. Vucinich (ed.), *The Peasant in Nineteenth Century Russia* (Stanford: Stanford University Press, 1968), from which I draw much of my discussion of the pre-Emancipation period. See also R. E. Zelnik, *Labor and Society in Tsarist Russia: The Factory Workers of St Petersburg, 1855–1870* (Stanford: Stanford University Press, 1971), chapters 1–2.

landowner who controlled their freedom of movement, was given part of their wages as all or part of a quit-rent (*obrok*), and sometimes even negotiated the otkhodniki's terms of employment directly with the owner of the enterprise where they worked, leaving the workers with little or no power to negotiate with their employers. Although the practice of serf owners contracting out their serfs to non-noble manufacturers was outlawed in the early 1820s, the continued coexistence of institutions of (contractually) free and forced labour, often combined in the same individuals, at a time when forced labour (except for convicts) had virtually vanished from the European scene, was a noteworthy and notorious characteristic of Russian society until as late as 1861, when serfdom was abolished and almost all labour except in some military factories was placed on a contractual footing.

The number of freely hired factory workers in Russia expanded considerably in the 1830s and the decades that followed, though mainly in the growing textile sector (especially the spinning and weaving of cotton cloth). One important stimulus was the decision of the British government to lift its ban on the export of cotton-spinning machinery in 1842. Since the manufacture of machinery was perhaps the least developed branch of Russian industry at that time, most Russian factories were still devoid of mechanisation before this shift, and, if we accept the favoured terminology of Soviet Marxist historians, should perhaps be thought of as *manu*factories rather than factories, since they depended on hand labour and outwork, were deficient in steam engines, and were often only minimally centralised.[2] Before the 1840s, those few factories (*fabriki*) that did employ steam-driven machinery, and were therefore likely to bring their workers together under a single roof, had depended to a large extent on the precarious practice of obtaining smuggled British machinery or importing lesser quality machines from Belgium or France. Hence the legalisation of machinery-export by Britain did mark an important stage in the evolution of an industrial landscape in Russia where large numbers of workers, still maintaining the subordinate legal status of serfs, to be sure, were gathered together in large numbers at a central location, most notably

2 This notion, rooted in the writings of Karl Marx and sometimes exaggerated in Soviet historiography, is best exemplified in the title 'Ot manufaktury k fabrike', a widely cited article by the Soviet historian M. F. Zlotnikov published in *Voprosy istorii*, nos. 11–12, 1946. In the discussion that follows, I will ignore the distinctions in Russian between the terms *manufaktura*, *fabrika*, and *zavod* and use the English 'factory' to refer to any physically compact industrial plant. The distinction between *fabrika* and *zavod* and its early origins are complex. Suffice it to say here that in the case of the two most politically sensitive branches of industry, that is, the ones most extensively referenced below, textiles and the machine- and metal-working industries, the former used the term *fabrika*, the latter *zavod*. The term *fabrika* is the one normally used generically when only one term is invoked.

in St Petersburg and in the Central Industrial Region (CIR), especially the provinces of Moscow and Vladimir. The large majority of these were for many years to come the workers of Russia's growing number of cotton-spinning mills, with the mechanisation of weaving following only after some delay and probably not nearing completion until the 1880s. Little wonder, then, that despite ideological imperatives to push Russia's industrial revolution back in time in order to combat the concept of Russia's 'backwardness', serious Soviet economic and social historians have acknowledged the absence of a true proletariat in pre-reform Russia, substituting such compromise concepts as '*pre*-proletariat' (*predproletariat*) and in some cases even arguing that pre-reform Russia was yet to experience a full-fledged industrial revolution, since the presence of a proletariat and a truly free labour market was a necessary sign of that historical phase.[3]

*****

With the abolition of serfdom, the way was open in Russia to new spurts of industrial growth, a modest one in the 1870s and early 1880s, and a major one in the 1890s, during the incumbency of the pro-industrial finance minister Sergei Witte (1892–1903). One can question the extent to which the emancipation as such, meaning its contribution to labour mobility, was a primary stimulus of industrial growth, as contrasted to the state-supported railway construction that followed in its wake and was vigorously pursued in the 1890s, especially the Trans-Siberian line. Surely, despite their emancipation from personal bondage, the peasants' continued attachment to the rural commune (*mir, obshchina*) limited the degree to which conditions after 1861 would remove past restraints on the complete mobility of labour. The omnipresence of the commune prolonged the ties between the urban worker and his or her village, delaying the transformation of the majority of peasant-workers into a permanent, well-trained, urbanised labour force, fully assimilated into modern industrial life, all its bridges to village life having been burned.[4] Sheer numbers of available workers, however, were never an issue. By the 1890s, despite the persistence of communal restraints, and with Russia's industry – including mining, metallurgy and, in the Petersburg region especially, the manufacture

3 The Soviet historian most closely identified with the concept of a *predproletariat* is Anna M. Pankratova, especially in her posthumously published *Formirovanie proletariata v Rossii (XVII–XVIII vv.)* (Moscow: Nauka, 1963). A useful, extensive discussion of the timing of Russia's 'industrial revolution' and related matters is P. G. Ryndziunskii, *Utverzhdenie kapitalizma v Rossii, 1850–1880 g.* (Moscow: Nauka, 1978).

4 The best analysis of industrial workers' continued connection with their villages in the post-reform period is Robert E. Johnson, *Peasant and Proletarian: The Working Class of Moscow in the Late Nineteenth Century* (New Brunswick: Rutgers University Press, 1979).

of machinery, rails, rolling stock, ships and military hardware – expanding at a record pace of 8 per cent per annum, the rapid growth of the land-hungry rural population easily provided factories with a numerically adequate labour pool (while at the same time *reducing* the proportion of workers who were urbanised, literate and self-identified as permanent denizens of the industrial world).

Of course, viewed as a percentage of the overall population, the number of industrial workers was still small at the end of turn of the century. According to the 1897 national census (Russia's first), the empire's population was over 128 million, while the number of industrial workers (an elusive category, to be sure) was only somewhat over 2 million at the turn of the century. However, the social and political importance of these workers became increasingly evident, in part because of their concentration in politically sensitive areas such as St Petersburg (the official capital), Moscow (the old capital and to many contemporaries still Russia's principal city), the ethnically mixed port cities of Baku and Riga, and the industrial regions of Russian-occupied Poland. And to this list should be added the miners of the Urals and the Don basin as well as two groups, the railway workers and the printers, who would become very influential politically – the former because of their rapidly expanding numbers and strategic locations as the empire's railway network expanded from its Moscow hub, the latter because of their special role as an educated middling group located between the industrial working class and the intelligentsia.[5]

The most dramatic manifestation of the workers' social and political importance was their participation in strikes and demonstrations. If a *strike* is loosely understood as any collective work stoppage carried out in defiance of one's employer, then strikes, like other worker actions (most notably flight before the expiration of a contract), certainly took place in the eighteenth and early nineteenth centuries. Dissatisfied workers put down their tools and in some cases fled both the factories and mines of their private employers and those owned by the state. Yet before the 1870s, to the extent that government officials were disturbed by such developments at all – first in the mid-1840s and then again in the early 1860s – they were influenced more by the demonstration effect of developments in Western Europe and the possible destabilising influence of the 1861 Emancipation than by actual labour unrest in Russia. To a great degree, such unrest as there was both before and in the wake of

5 On railway workers, see Henry Reichman, *Railwaymen and Revolution: Russia, 1905* (Berkeley: University of California Press, 1987); on workers in printing, see Mark D. Steinberg, *Moral Communities: The Culture of Class Relations in the Russian Printing Industry, 1867–1907* (Berkeley: University of California Press, 1992).

the Emancipation, much of it confined to railway construction workers and Ural miners, was viewed by the authorities, and not without reason, as an extension of peasant unrest rather than a discrete phenomenon in its own right. Nor was it viewed very differently in the 1860s by Russia's revolutionary youth, whose perception of the workers was limited to the still quite accurate notion that they were peasants who happened to be temporarily employed away from their villages and who, like the young revolutionary populist Petr Kropotkin, sometimes looked askance at the strike as an illusory weapon, one that was bound to end in failure, yet if promoted by *intelligenty*, would implant in workers the false hope that their lot could be improved under the existing system.[6]

Labour unrest among industrial workers began to be taken more seriously by Russian officials, publicists, and political activists of all stripes only in the 1870s, which is when the story of workers in Russia begins to become not only a social but a political narrative. Although it would be foolish to place an exact date on the transition, two events, both involving textile workers – one in 1870, one in 1872 – are particularly relevant.

In 1870 there was a major strike action at what was then St Petersburg's largest textile mill, the Nevsky cotton-spinning factory. Although most of the Petersburg region's larger factories were located at the outskirts of the city, in its industrial suburbs (with some important medium-sized factories located in the city's north-eastern Vyborg District), the Nevsky was exceptional in its location near downtown St Petersburg, at a site that gave it special visibility. In addition, the work stoppage was prolonged and sustained, was followed by a contested, adversarially structured trial of its leaders (made possible by the 1864 judicial reforms), and was widely covered in the press (made possible by the 1865 censorship reforms). In other words, though there had been countless work stoppages in Russian factories before, because it took place in the middle of the Great Reforms this was the first such event in Russia proper to enter the public arena and be incorporated into the new civic discourse that flowered during the reign of Alexander II. Strikes would henceforth be a political issue.[7]

We must, of course, be careful about our use of language. At the time, the workers themselves did not use the term 'strike' – usually *stachka* or *zabastovka* in the Russian of those years, but occasionally *shtreik* – and there

6 Peter Kropotkin, *Memoirs of a Revolutionist*, ed. James Allen Rogers (Garden City: Anchor Books, 1962), pp. 110–13.

7 For a detailed analysis of the Nevsky strike and subsequent trial, see Zelnik, *Labor and Society*, chapter 9.

is no evidence that they thought of themselves as engaging in a new kind of activity, one that charged the participants with the energy that came from partaking in an international workers' movement or even in a pan-European trend. What is significant, however, is that the government authorities, in a sense ahead of the workers' own curve, *did* use such language, as did the contemporary Petersburg press. To be sure, when the authorities spoke of a *stachka*, their emphasis was on the conspiratorial connotation of the term, and at the trial of the leading participants the prosecutors did their best (though with only limited success) to criminalise the workers' action by treating it as a kind of conspiracy against the state. But if official thinking about such phenomena was still quite murky, the views of segments of the press were less so and, as in the case of the paper *Novoe vremia*, which pointedly (and anxiously) described the Nevsky events as a dangerous new phenomenon: 'And a strike has befallen us, and God has not spared us!' Perhaps even more revealing of the shift that was taking place in the press's views of labour unrest was the reaction to much less dramatic work stoppages among some Petersburg clothing workers shortly *before* the Nevsky events. News of these actions had caused the newspaper *Birzhevye vedomosti* to make the questionable claim that this was 'the first example of workers strikes [*stachki rabochikh*]' in Russian history, and to cautiously advance the hope that 'for the moment, they will not give rise to the same kind of difficulties here as in West European countries'.[8]

From this time forth, it would be hard to find a work stoppage of any significant proportions that was not discussed both publicly and in the corridors of government agencies in the context of Russia's possible susceptibility to the European disease of labour unrest and the prophylactic devices that might best be designed to stave off an epidemic. Almost immediately, the government began to move in two divergent directions: on the one hand, harsh police measures, most notably arrest, imprisonment and administrative exile *without trial*, usually imposed by the office of governor, were brought to bear on the leaders of any future strike action, which was to be treated as a criminal conspiracy against the state, and not merely as an economic conflict, between workers and their employers, within civil society. On the other hand, expanding on the work of a mainly abortive commission of the early 1860s, the government created a series of high-level official commissions in the 1870s that, with some participation of and consultation with a narrow segment of the public (mainly manufacturers, but also academic and technical experts),

8 Zelnik, *Labor and Society*, pp. 340–1; *Novoe vremia* quote as cited in Gaston V. Rimlinger, 'The Management of Labor Protest in Tsarist Russia', *International Review of Social History* 5, part 2 (1960): 231.

were intended to devise the kind of factory legislation that might avert the disaffection of workers and discourage them from evolving into a dangerous, 'West European'-type of working class.

The second strike that aroused the fears of both government officials and opinion makers was the prolonged and (unlike the Nevsky strike) ultimately violent clash between textile workers and their employers at Estland Province's Kreenholm Cotton-Spinning and Weaving Factory, the largest textile mill at the time in all of Europe.[9] The dramatic nature of this event – with such striking features as a spectacular setting (a factory less than a hundred miles from St Petersburg, located on a riverine island, its machines powered by a giant waterfall), multiethnic participants on both sides (Russians, Estonians, Germans and a smattering of Finns), death and violence (a collapsed bridge with dozens of women workers drowned, workers hurling stones at soldiers and soldiers almost firing on workers) – magnified the danger (or promise) of worker protest unleashed by the events of 1870, and had the additional effect of propelling a number of disgruntled Kreenholm workers into the ranks of the radical movements that were beginning to arise in St Petersburg at around this time.

From 1872 until the fall of the tsarist regime some forty-five years later, the interaction between workers and members of the radical intelligentsia (*studenty*, as they began to be called by workers whether or not they were actually studying at the time) would be a central element in the evolution of the revolutionary movement in Russia.[10] Out of this often troubled yet often productive relationship would evolve several phases of worker–student political play in two parallel universes dominated by two different kinds of youth: one, the student radicals, formally educated at Russia's leading institutions of higher learning; the other, the politicised workers, self-educated, or formally educated at adult-education centres ('Sunday schools', factory schools, schools of the Imperial Russian Technical Society), or informally educated (or propagandised) in illegal study circles (*kruzhki*) by the studenty themselves.

The political persuasions on the intelligentsia side of this equation would of course vary considerably over time: Populist in the 1870s and much of the

9 R. E. Zelnik, *Law and Disorder on the Narova River: The Kreenholm Strike of 1872* (Berkeley: University of California Press, 1995). In Russian the Estonian 'Kreenholm' was rendered as 'Krengol'm.'

10 These interactions are addressed in detail by the authors of the articles in R. E. Zelnik (ed.), *Workers and Intelligentsia in Late Imperial Russia: Realities, Representations, Reflections* (Berkeley: International and Area Studies, 1999); the same articles and others may be found in Russian in *Rabochie i intelligentsiia Rossii v epokhu reform i revoliutsii, 1861–fevral' 1917* (St Petersburg: Izd. Russko-Baltiiskii informatsionnyi tsentr BLITs, 1997).

1880s, vaguely Marxist in the late 1880s and 1890s (in the 1890s and even earlier Russia's Populists had more than a touch of Marxism and Marxists more than a touch of Populism), and finally evolving into the somewhat more stable groupings of Social Democrats or SDs (as of 1903, both Bolsheviks and Mensheviks) and Socialist-Revolutionaries (SRs) at the start of the new century.[11] Yet the broad structure of the relationship and the conflicts that inhered therein would be surprisingly consistent: radical intelligenty would define themselves as the bearers of the truth that guided and of the intellectual and organisational machinery that drove the revolution, while viewing workers (workers and peasants in the case of Populists and SRs) either as the raw material they would have to forge into a powerful fighting force or as the essential yet still dormant bearers of a revolutionary message, a message that, if most workers were not yet conscious of it, would one day be revealed to them by a combination of experience at the workplace and study with already 'conscious' intelligenty and propagandised workers (sometimes defined as *rabochie-intelligenty*).

Workers, for their part, or at least the ones most politically aware and most attracted to revolutionary ideas, were repeatedly torn between a positive and a negative perception of the studenty, at times appreciating their concentrated, even passionate attention and gaining a higher sense of their own worth as a consequence, but at other times resenting their tutelage and striving to assert their class and even personal independence from their socially more privileged intelligentsia mentors.

*****

By the early twentieth century a fierce and sometimes agonising competition for worker allegiance had begun between radicals of various persuasions (Bolshevik SDs, Menshevik SDs, SRs, and their rough equivalents among many of the non-Russian minorities), liberals, social and religious organisations, and the government, for working-class political support. Indeed, the entire history of the Russian labour movement lends itself to an analysis framed as a competition between the agents of the Left and the agents of the state for the allegiance of the empire's rapidly growing numbers of industrial workers, whose numbers increased by about a million in the course of the 1890s. Certainly by the beginning of the new century, industrial workers – the *proletariat* as they were now often called by those who courted them and those who feared them – were viewed by

11 For the influence of Marxism on Russian Populism, see especially Andrzej Walicki, *The Controversy over Capitalism: Studies in the Social Philosophy of the Russian Populists* (Oxford: Oxford University Press, 1969).

almost all political actors as pivotal players in the on-going struggle for power.[12]

On the government side, as already suggested, there were of course internal divisions, as there were on the Left, as to what strategies were best suited to win this competition with the revolutionaries. If police-driven suppression vied with enlightened, European-model labour legislation as the two main contending models of government action, the latter approach generally held the upper hand from about 1882 to 1900. To be sure, good old-fashioned suppression, sometimes very draconian, was always ready on hand when all else failed, and no labour action, especially violent unrest, would be permitted to attain its goals directly, lest the striking, demonstrating, or rioting workers be encouraged to repeat their successful strategies again and again. Yet in the wake of Russia's most serious strikes of the 1880s and 1890s – the Morozov strike of textile workers in Vladimir Province in 1885 and the great citywide textile strikes in St Petersburg in 1896–7 – new laws were introduced that, building in part on the work of the commissions of the 1870s, were aimed at preventing the abuse and exploitation of industrial workers at the hands of ruthless, inflexible employers.[13]

When this legislation had clearly failed to stem the tide of labour unrest and the on-going, potentially dangerous contacts (often troubled and tense, to be sure) between politicised workers and radical intelligenty, some government officials, most notably Sergei Zubatov of the Ministry of Internal Affairs' Department of Police, began to explore a new and very risky approach.[14] Instead of relying directly on the cruder forms of oppression, but at the same

12 How and why the efforts of *liberals* to win the allegiance of industrial workers had difficulty taking hold is best analysed in William G. Rosenberg, 'Representing Workers and the Liberal Narrative of Modernity', in Zelnik, *Workers and Intelligentsia*, pp. 228–59.

13 The legislation of 1886 was anticipated by laws in 1882 and 1884 that, among other new restrictions, placed limits on the hours worked by women and minors and provided for a permanent corps of factory inspectors (doctors, political economists and others), administered by the Finance Ministry, to see to it that the factory laws were properly enforced. Just how fully they were enforced is an open question, but there is no doubt that there were zealous factory inspectors who took their charge seriously and came into genuine conflict with recalcitrant industrialists. See M. I. Tugan-Baranovsky [Baranovskii], *The Russian Factory in the Nineteenth Century*, trans. Arthur and Claora S. Levin (Homewood, IL: Mysl, 1970), part 2, chapter 2; V. Ia. Laverychev, *Tsarizm i rabochii vopros v Rossii (1861–1917 gg.)* (Moscow: Nauka, 1970), chapter 2; Boris Gorshkov, 'Factory Children: An Overview of Child Industrial Labor and Laws in Imperial Russia, 1840–1914', in M. Melancon and A. K. Pate (eds.), *New Labor History: Worker Identity and Experience in Russia, 1840–1918* (Bloomington, IN: Slavica, 2002), pp. 9–33, esp. pp. 29–32.

14 See Jonathan Daly's chapter on police in this volume. The classical English-language study of Zubatov's programme is Jeremiah Schneiderman, *Sergei Zubatov and Revolutionary Marxism: The Struggle for the Working Class in Tsarist Russia* (Ithaca: Cornell University Press, 1970).

time by-passing the Factory Inspectorate and refusing to allow the workers access to their own, independent labour associations, Zubatov introduced a series of government-sponsored and closely supervised organisations for workers. Often (erroneously) referred to as 'police unions', these organisations were particularly active in Moscow and in the towns of the Jewish Pale of Settlement, most notably Odessa and Minsk. It was Zubatov's aim to divert workers away from socialist agitators, including the so-called 'Bund' (the influential branch of Social Democracy that had been operating successfully among Jewish workers in the Pale since 1897) by providing them with tamer social and intellectual activities such as public lectures, tea rooms and reading rooms, and by expressing enough sympathy for their cause as to give them the impression that it was the government and not the socialists that stood for the attainment of their true interests.[15]

Although Zubatov's efforts began on a successful note, with time his agents, many of them over-zealous, began to lose control of the situation, inadvertently giving the organised workers more rein than they originally intended and, in their efforts to prove that they were pro-labour, encouraging them to defy their employers. When sympathetic Zubatov-sponsored speakers such as the Moscow University political economy professor I. Kh. Ozerov lectured to the workers about the situation of labour in West European countries where labour unions were permitted, this was a signal for some of his listeners to claim the same right to organise that existed by then in England, France and Germany. Factory owners, in turn, complained to the Finance Ministry that Zubatov's activities were poisoning the minds of their employees, complaints that set the stage for conflicts between the two most concerned ministries. In this context it is difficult, however, to assign either ministry with the designation 'pro' or 'anti' labour, since Witte himself, while hostile to Zubatov, began to seriously consider that Russia would be better off with a free labour movement, that is, with workers allowed to organise their own trade unions and even, though only under strictly limited circumstances, to engage in strikes. Though it would take the revolution of 1905 to bring about this concession – a rather feeble 1903 law allowing workers in some factories to elect their own 'elders' (*starosty*) was the only significant labour legislation between 1897 and 1906 – the conflict between the two ministries helped open the door to renewed labour unrest, which was particularly virulent in St Petersburg in the spring of 1901 (the

15 On the Bund (formally, the General Jewish Labour Union in Russia and Poland), see Henry J. Tobias, *The Jewish Bund in Russia: From Its Origins to 1905* (Stanford: Stanford University Press, 1972).

'Obukhov defence') and in Rostov-on-Don and other parts of southern Russia in 1902–3.

The ill-fated Zubatov experiment did have an unforeseen consequence of monumental proportions, the so-called *gaponovshchina*, a series of events that affected the course of Russian history in a manner that took both government officials and revolutionaries completely by surprise. In 1904, as a spin-off to the already discredited project of police-sponsored labour activity in St Petersburg, a charismatic young priest named Father Gapon was encouraged to open tearooms for the workers of that city, social clubs where the inhabitants of the city's various industrial neigbourhoods could safely engage in innocent, non-political sociability, far from the subversive influence of SDs, SRs or other radical intelligenty. An offspring of the *zubatovshchina* (Colonel Zubatov's attempt to control the labour movement by sponsoring police trade unions), this project came at a time when the relations between St Petersburg workers and the SD intelligentsia were in a state of temporary lull. Successful co-operation between Petersburg workers and the Marxist intelligentsia had been visible in the mid-1890s when the Marxist group called the Union of Struggle for the Emancipation of Labour launched the policy of 'agitation' in support of workers' day-to-day grievances, culminating in the basically spontaneous though intelligentsia-assisted strikes of 1896–7. Soon thereafter, however, disagreements between workers and their frequently overweening intelligentsia mentors would lead to repeated conflicts between them, causing many workers (with the support of some 'worker-phile' intelligenty) to be attracted to the kind of worker-centred *ouvriérisme* that was then gathering around the journal *Rabochaia mysl'* (Workers' Thought). These workers, who took seriously the Marxist slogan that the liberation of the working class was the task of the workers themselves, would accept the co-operation of the Marxist intelligentsia on their own terms only, a condition that not only future Bolsheviks like Vladimir Lenin but also future Mensheviks like Iulii Martov, Pavel Aksel'rod and Georgii Plekhanov, the 'father' of Russian Marxism, were unwilling to accept.[16]

16 By far the best treatment of these and related developments are Allan K. Wildman, *The Making of a Workers' Revolution: Russian Social Democracy, 1891–1903* (Chicago: University of Chicago Press, 1967), and Dietrich Geyer, *Lenin in der russischen Sozialdemokratie: Die Arbeiterbewegung im Zarenreich als Organizatsionsproblem der revolutionären Intelligentz, 1890–1903* (Cologne: Böhlau Verlag, 1962). The most useful biographies of the four Marxists mentioned here are by Robert Service (Lenin), Israel Getzler (Martov), Abraham Ascher (Aksel'rod) and Samuel Baron (Plekhanov). All four are also discussed incisively in Leopold Haimson, *The Russian Marxists and the Origins of Bolshevism* (Cambridge, Mass.: Harvard University Press, 1955).

Such conflicts with workers were complicated by other aspects of the SD intelligentsia's troubled situation between 1898 and 1904. Many of their leading cadres were either under arrest in Siberia or other venues or had fled abroad to Paris, Geneva, Zurich or London, with few opportunities for direct personal contact with Russia's workers. The supposed founding congress of the Russian Social Democratic Workers' Party (RSDRP) in Minsk in 1898, poorly attended, and including only one genuine worker, had proved abortive, while the Second Congress (Brussels and London 1903), while well attended, had culminated in the Party's split into Bolshevik and Menshevik factions and the temporary withdrawal of the Jewish Bund from the Party's ranks. Perhaps more to the point, and in a sense underlying all these problems was the SD intelligentsia's difficulty in addressing the issue of how best to relate to the 'spontaneous' labour movement, with its tendency to deviate from the norms of intelligentsia-contrived 'consciousness' at times by spinning off in the allegedly apolitical direction of 'Economism', at other times pulled in the direction of senseless violence and the destructive, self-defeating riot (*bunt*). Although by no means supported by all SD intelligenty, and himself highly critical of those intelligenty who did not share his views, it was Lenin who in his well-known polemical pamphlet *Chto delat'?* (What Is to Be Done?) came closest to openly revealing the deeper problematics of worker–intelligentsia relations and unleashing the painful and divisive issue of spontaneity versus consciousness.[17]

As a result of these circumstances, with the issues of worker autonomy from the intelligentsia now merging with militant workers' emphasis on strikes and other mass actions, the time between the Petersburg textile strikes and the appearance of *What Is to Be Done?* was one of maximum tension between worker-phile (*ouvriériste*) workers and those Marxist intelligenty who were most concerned to retain and expand their leadership role in the movement.

17 For a discussion of Lenin's pamphlet in the broader context of Marxism's unresolved tensions around the leadership role of workers and worker–*intelligenty* relations in Russia see my 'Worry about Workers: Concerns of the Russian Intelligentsia from the 1870s to *What is to Be Done?*', in Marsha Siefert (ed.), *Extending the Borders of Russian History: Essays in Honor of Alfred J. Rieber* (Budapest: Central European University Press, 2003). For more on the intellectual and psychological background to the SD intelligentsia's attitudes see Haimson, *Russian Marxists*. For a rich though regionally restricted discussion of the role of violence in Russia's labour unrest, see Charters Wynn, *Workers, Strikes, and Pogroms: The Donbass-Dnepr Bend in Late Imperial Russia 1870–1905* (Princeton: Princeton University Press, 1992); see also Daniel R. Brower, 'Labor Violence in Russia in the Late Nineteenth Century', *SR* 41, 3 (1982): 417-31; *Vospominaniia Ivana Vasil'evicha Babushkina, 1893–1900* (Moscow: Gospolitizdat, 1955), p. 74. Babushkin's memoir was written in London in 1902 and first published in 1925.

This is not to say that all co-operation between workers and Marxist intelligenty was discontinued, for in the entire period from the mid-1890s to 1905, that thread, while often damaged, was never broken.[18] But it *is* to say that by late 1904, when Father Gapon's leadership of St Petersburg workers had begun to take fire, he found a vacuum of authority among the workers and a hunger for someone to fill the shoes that might otherwise have been filled by revolutionary Social Democrats.

Under Gapon's charismatic leadership, thousands of Petersburg workers were organised into neighbourhood associations centred around local clubhouses, tearooms and libraries that for the first time provided them with venues of social, cultural and eventually political interaction. Gapon himself was influenced and assisted by a small but dedicated group of workers and intelligenty who, having passed through the school of Social Democracy and found it wanting, remained nonetheless dedicated to the workers' cause as they now understood it. As the months went by, it began to dawn on the St Petersburg officials who had begun by supporting Gapon financially that instead of the calming, loyal, religious influence they had hoped for, they had created a sort of Frankenstein monster, sobering (literally) and religious to be sure, but a movement that was rapidly escaping their control. More and more Gapon's 'Assembly of Factory Workers' (*Sobranie russkikh fabrichno-zavodskikh rabochikh*) was being transmogrified into a giant labour union, with pretensions to represent the interests of Petersburg workers against their employers. Hence when three of its members were fired from the giant (*c.* 12,000 workers) Putilov engineering works in late December, precipitating an illegal strike at a plant on which the government heavily relied for its shipbuilding and armaments production, Gapon (after some hesitation) assumed the role of what today might be called 'worker-priest', encouraging the spread of the strike to many other factories and organising a citywide protest demonstration. On 9 January 1905, thanks to nervous, trigger-happy troops and a government that simply did not get the picture, unarmed workers and their families who attempted to march, militantly but without violence, on the Winter Palace were repeatedly fired upon, with over a hundred demonstrators killed and

18 Apposite examples of the numerous militant workers who, despite some painful encounters with intelligenty, continued to identify with the RSDRP and retain their faith in the Marxist intelligentsia are Semen Kanatchikov and Ivan Babushkin; see *A Radical Worker in Tsarist Russia: The Autobiography of Semën Ivanovich Kanatchikov*, ed. and trans. R. E. Zelnik (Berkeley: University of California Press, 1986); *Vospominaniia Ivana Vasil'evicha Babushkina, 1893–1900* (Moscow: Gospolitizdat, 1955).

many more injured. The day has gone down in history as Russia's notorious 'Bloody Sunday', the opening salvo of the revolution of 1905.[19]

Though it was led by a presumably apolitical priest, it would be a mistake to think of the workers' demonstration of 9 January as lacking in political content. The petition to the tsar that was carried by many of the demonstrators was replete not only with the class-centred particularistic demands of industrial labour (including, however, 'economic' demands with strong political connotations such as the eight-hour day and the right to form trade unions), it also contained, though couched in religious rhetoric, something closely resembling the political programme of *Osvobozhdenie* (Liberation), the recently formed organisation that best embodied Russian liberal opinion (regrouped in the form of the Kadet Party some ten months later). These included the demand for a Constituent Assembly elected on the basis of a four-tailed suffrage as well as such basic rights as freedom of speech, assembly and religion. At the same time, the petition included demands – the elimination of redemption payments, for example – that spoke to the interests of the peasantry, the socio-legal group (*soslovie*) to which most workers still belonged and with which many still had genuine economic, familial and personal links. And, though the petitioners had received no direct input from either Bolsheviks or Mensheviks, their language included a hostile reference to the 'capitalist-exploiters of the working class'.[20] Although this and other rhetorical flourishes (including those of a liberal character) may well have reflected the influence of the Assembly of Factory Workers' cohort of disillusioned Marxists, the fact that so many workers appeared to be comfortable with such a seemingly incongruous mix of liberal, radical and traditional discourses – the languages of urban class warfare, 'bourgeois' civic values and 'humble' peasant pleading, accompanied by the visible parading and display of religious icons and portraits of the tsar – speaks volumes of the mixed, labile, internally contradictory state of mind of Russia's most 'advanced' workers as they unwittingly embarked on their and the twentieth century's very first revolution. Little wonder that Lenin craved a party that could provide Russian socialists with the closed continuity

19 The most thorough scholarly account of the *gaponovshchina* is Walter Sablinsky, *The Road to Bloody Sunday: Father Gapon and the St Petersburg Massacre of 1905* (Princeton: Princeton University Press, 1976); see also Gerald D. Surh's insightful essay, 'Petersburg's First Mass Labor Organization: The Assembly of Russian Workers and Father Gapon', parts 1 and 2, *RR* 40, 3/4 (July–October, 1981): 412–41; Sergei I. Potolov, 'Petersburg Workers and Intelligentsia on the Eve of the Revolution of 1905–7: The Assembly of Russian Factory and Mill Workers in the City of St Petersburg', in Zelnik, *Workers and Intelligentsia*, pp. 102–15. See also Gapon's own selective but valuable account, Georgii A. Gapon, *The Story of My Life* (London: Chapman and Hall, 1905).

20 For an English translation of the text of the petition, see Sablinsky, *Road*, pp. 344–9.

of 'consciousness' in the face of such volatile shifts of mood in the class they claimed to represent.[21]

*****

If the revolutionary year began, then, with no clear victor in the struggle between the radical Left and the forces of order for the allegiance of Russia's ideologically still impressionable and unformed labour force, by the end of that year radicals would emerge as the clear winners in this competition, though with no single faction dominating.[22] One way to think of the year 1905 is as an acceleration at hothouse temperatures of the earlier competition for worker allegiance, but this time with a decided advantage on the side of the revolutionaries thanks to the shattering of faith in the tsar precipitated by Bloody Sunday. One observes the government desperately dishing out new proposals to win back the workers but invariably falling behind the curve of disillusionment. Perhaps the most serious government initiative in 1905 (prior to October) was the Shidlovskii Commission, an attempt launched at the end of January to bring the aspirations of volatile St Petersburg workers under control by harnessing them for the first time to an elected body of (male) worker representatives, chosen (in contrast to the feeble and unpopular law on *starostas* of 1903) by workers, without any input from employers (although together with government officials, employers would be represented on the commission itself). With worker representatives chosen via a complex two-stage system of voting based on the size of the factory, the commission was supposed to get at the roots of the workers' discontents and come up with new solutions to their most pressing problems.[23] This was a tacit admission by the government that the traditional notion of a worker population so rooted

21 The degree to which civil and political rights, the rule of law, and related liberal aspirations were part of the workers' value system in this period is carefully analysed in S. A. Smith, 'Workers and Civil Rights in Tsarist Russia, 1899–1917', in Olga Crisp and Linda Edmondson (eds.), *Civil Rights in Imperial Russia* (Oxford: Clarendon Press, 1989), pp. 145–69.

22 Important insights into the role of workers in the 1905 Revolution may be found in: Gerald D. Surh, *1905 in St Petersburg: Labor, Society, and Revolution* (Stanford: Stanford University Press, 1989); Laura Engelstein, *Moscow, 1905: Working-Class Organization and Political Conflict* (Stanford: Stanford University Press, 1982); Robert Weinberg, *The Revolution of 1905 in Odessa* (Bloomington: Indiana University Press, 1994); Solomon M. Schwarz, *The Russian Revolution of 1905: The Workers' Movement and the Formation of Bolshevism and Menshevism*, trans. Gertrude Vakar (Chicago: University of Chicago Press, 1967); Victoria E. Bonnell, *Roots of Rebellion: Workers' Politics and Organizations in St Petersburg and Moscow, 1900–1914* (Berkeley: University of California Press, 1983), part 2; Abraham Ascher, *The Revolution of 1905: Russia in Disarray* (Stanford: Stanford University Press, 1988). See also the books by Reichman and Steinberg cited in note 5, above.

23 Described in detail in Schwarz, *Russian Revolution*, chapter 2, and more concisely in Bonnell, *Roots*, pp. 110–17.

in its peasant traditions as to seek comfort in the goodwill of the tsar, a notion that may still have seemed to be plausible at the dawn of Bloody Sunday, was no longer adequate to the challenge faced by the régime.

Although workers at some St Petersburg factories were sometimes advised by liberal and left-leaning lawyers and other educated well-wishers, revolutionary activists representing the various socialist parties played almost no role in the first-stage elections to the commission that took place in the middle of February. If for a brief moment, it appeared as if the government might have out-manoeuvred the radical Left and recaptured some of its lost ground, however, events were moving too fast and basic distrust was too great for the government to hold on to its advantage. What it *had* succeeded in doing was to promote 'the first basically free elections ever held in Russia by workers',[24] but it then quickly managed to lose control of the process while providing workers with multiple venues where they could nurture their growing political sensitivities and feel the strength and empowerment that comes with open debate, voting and unconstrained political sociability. In one of those unusual sequencings that does seem to distinguish historical processes in modern Russia, workers now found themselves the only social group in the country to have been granted a (relatively) democratic, if ephemeral, franchise under a notoriously autocratic system. Not content to follow the marching orders of the régime that had empowered them, Petersburg workers (from whom workers in other parts of Russia were quickly gaining inspiration) rejected the limitations that the government wished to place upon the new commission, guaranteed its failure by boycotting its meetings and often aired their grievances in language that called the entire political order into question, thereby replicating but also dwarfing the paradoxes of the zubatovshchina.

Instead of becoming a step in the direction of co-optation, the Shidlovskii elections actually contributed to what became the most important revolutionary innovation to emerge from the labour movement in 1905 – the soviet (*sovet*). Although the precise origins of the idea of a citywide representative workers' council are still a matter of some dispute, most historians of 1905 agree that the experience of electing factory delegates in February helped pave the way for Petersburg workers to elect their own representatives to the Petersburg soviet in October. The other important source of the concept was, of course, the citywide strike committee, which was the nuclear body from which the soviet developed, with few participants understanding at first that they were participating in the creation of a historically new

24 Schwarz, *Russian Revolution*, p. 94.

institution. While some Soviet historians have tried to trace the antecedents of the Petersburg soviet a few months further back in time, to the Assembly of Delegates (*Sobranie Upolnomochennykh*) that oversaw the Bolshevik-supported (but not led) multi-factory general strike in Ivanovo-Voznesensk in May and June, Solomon Schwarz has demonstrated that the two institutions were qualitatively different and that the Petersburg soviet was a first of its kind, that is, the first in which the members saw themselves as being not only a local strike committee, but an unauthorised instrument of local self-government, one that dared to substitute itself for the officially constituted authorities.[25]

In fact, the Petersburg soviet was the direct result of the October general strike that was launched on 8 October by Moscow printers and spread by railway workers on the Moscow–St Petersburg line, a strike that, thanks to the railway, soon fanned out into almost all the industrial centres of the Russian Empire. The soviet's origins were 'spontaneous' in the sense that unaffiliated Petersburg workers and not the revolutionary parties launched the initiative, first as a citywide strike committee (not without precedent) and then as a claimant to local, and to some degree, since St Petersburg was the capital city, even *national*, political authority (a phenomenon completely without precedent in Russia, though somewhat analogous to the Paris Commune of 1871). To be sure, all the major revolutionary groups were fairly quick to recognise the importance of the new organisation, though Bolsheviks – still more committed to the tactic of armed uprising and ambivalent about strikes at a time of revolution – more reluctantly so than others. They all – Bolsheviks, Mensheviks, SRs – sought and achieved representation on the soviet's executive committee, with the nominal Menshevik but ultra-radical revolutionary Leon Trotsky, as is well known, playing a very prominent role as the soviet's vice-president.[26]

At least in St Petersburg, the brief period of the October general strike and the soviet's subsequent dominance of the city should be seen as the workers' moment of greatest triumph in 1905. The Petersburg soviet virtually became the governing body of that city for several weeks. However, the bloody suppression of the armed uprising of Moscow workers in December 1905 marked the end of the workers' triumphant period, as those workers who went to the barricades with SD, especially Bolshevik, support were crushed by artillery fire and the onslaught of loyal regiments hurried by train from St Petersburg to Moscow. If the tsar's belated but promising Manifesto of 16 October was

25 Schwarz, *Russian Revolution*, Appendix II.
26 Trotsky's own account of these events, though quite tendentious, still repays reading: Leon Trotsky, *1905*, trans. Anya Bostock (New York: Random House, 1971).

extorted from him by the power of the labour movement, which was supported in diverse ways by radicals and liberals alike, the defeat of the Moscow workers and the near simultaneous arrest of the Petersburg soviet in December placed the government in a much better position to minimise the actual concessions, including workers' rights, projected in the manifesto.

* * * * *

Although labour unrest continued well into 1906,[27] workers would cease to pose a serious threat to the Russian government until the labour movement revived in the wake of the Lena Goldfield massacre of April 1912. Nevertheless, the 1905 Revolution did bear some palpable if limited gains for workers. This included the government's recognition for the first time of their right, albeit within very tight restrictions, to form 'professional' unions and, though only in the private sector, to engage in non-political economic strikes, as well as their right to elect their own delegates to the new Russian parliament, the Duma, though under a very restricted franchise (rendered even narrower after Petr Stolypin's electoral coup of 3 June 1907).[28]

As the country recovered from the throes of revolution, Russian industry, with the aid of a newly energised commercial banking system, began to recover from the setbacks it had undergone in the first few years of the century. By 1910 industry was again experiencing a robust expansion, although at a growth rate of 6 per cent per annum it fell significantly short of the 8 per cent growth rate of the 1890s. As the position of workers in the labour market became more favorable, they grew less and less tolerant of management misconduct and government repression.

Nevertheless, it took the massacre of some one hundred goldminers in the spring of 1912 to resuscitate the still cautious labour movement. If in 1907–11 the labour movement had largely restricted itself to legal, above-ground activities, causing some Bolsheviks to level the exaggerated charge that the trade unions' Menshevik-oriented leaders were acting as 'liquidators' of the underground Party, Lena ushered in a two-year period of militant strike activity and demonstrations, with workers often striking at a significantly higher rate than they had in the revolutionary year 1905. This unrest took place in

27 See Abraham Ascher, *The Revolution of 1905: Authority Restored* (Stanford: Stanford University Press, 1992).

28 See G. R. Swain, 'Freedom of Association and the Trade Unions, 1906–14', in Crisp and Edmonson, *Civil Rights*, pp. 171–90; G. R. Swain, *Russian Social Democracy and the Legal Labour Movement, 1906–1914* (London: Macmillan, 1983); Bonnell, *Roots*, part 3. As Swain points out, the actual restrictions placed on the unions were considerably greater than those that had been contemplated by some government officials in 1905. And in practice, not surprisingly, the unions were subjected to constant persecution by the authorities.

many parts of Russia and among virtually every category of worker, including the unskilled and semi-skilled textile women of the CIR. But once again the movement evolved most dramatically in St Petersburg, though in the summer of 1914 it took on a particularly aggressive form in Baku. Politically, this worker militancy worked to the tactical advantage of the Bolsheviks and, to a lesser extent, the SRs, while working to the disadvantage of the more cautious and to some extent disillusioned Mensheviks, who increasingly feared that workers' irrational passions, which they saw as reflecting their close peasant origins, were moving them in a direction for which Russia's 'objective' conditions was not historically ripe. Those passions, it was felt, had been aroused irresponsibly by the Bolsheviks, and, to a degree that might prove counterproductive or even worse, were threatening to turn back the clock on Russia's progress toward democracy. Some historians, most famously Leopold Haimson, have suggested that Russian industrial centres were on the cusp of a new revolution, or at least of violent, irrepressible conflagration, when the onset of the First World War in the summer of 1914 put a temporary damper on worker unrest. However, it must also be acknowledged, as does Haimson, that labour unrest in the capital was dying down, at least for the moment, shortly before war was declared.[29]

Be that as it may, once the war had begun to go badly for Russia, there were growing signs of the labour movement's revival, especially in 1916. By the middle of February 1917, hungry St Petersburg (now 'Petrograd') workers, their wages lagging far behind a spiralling wartime inflation, were again engaged in significant strike activity. This unrest included women textile workers and, replacing drafted workers, recently recruited woman munitions workers, as well as the traditionally militant, male, metal- and machine-workers. By the last days of the month they were joining with other elements of the urban population, including sections of the military garrison, in increasingly confrontational demonstrations that led directly to the fall of the Romanov dynasty and the tsarist regime.

Almost immediately, Petrograd workers, having played so prominent a role in the overthrow of tsarism, staked out their claim to a numerically

29 L. H. Haimson, 'The Problem of Social Stability in Urban Russia, 1905–1917', *SR* 23, 4 (Dec. 1964): 619–42, and 24, 1 (March 1965): 1–22; for a somewhat different perspective, see Robert B. McKean, *St Petersburg between the Revolutions* (New Haven: Yale University Press, 1990). On the Lena massacre itself, see Michael Melancon, 'The Ninth Circle: The Lena Goldfield Workers and the Massacre of 4 April 1912', *SR* 53, 3 (Sept. 1994): 766–95. For a recent evaluation of the storm over 'Liquidationism', see Alice K. Pate, 'The Liquidationist Controversy: Russian Social Democracy and the Quest for Unity', in Melancon and Pate, *New Labor History*, pp. 95–122.

disproportionate role in determining the character and fate of the new order. Working in co-operation with radical intelligenty among the SD and SR party activists, they resurrected an updated version of the soviets of 1905, but this time with the hot-blooded participation of soldiers from the local garrison, many of whom lived in fear of transfer to the fighting front. Similar soviets quickly mushroomed throughout the empire.

Over the next few months, with the Petrograd soviet sharing 'dual power' with the new, unstable, and insecure Provisional Government, worker militancy escalated rapidly, often following its own trajectory with scant attention to the desires of the left party leaders. Their militancy took many forms – strikes, riots, factory occupations, the creation of increasingly defiant factory committees and, along with soldiers, participation in the organisations and demonstrations of the revolutionary parties, though never in lockstep with those parties. All of this uncontrollable activity added enormously to the difficulties of the Provisional Government, which, even as its composition moved leftward as moderate socialists agreed to assume cabinet positions, was simply unable to satisfy unremitting worker demands under wartime conditions. Hence when the Bolsheviks succeeded in overthrowing the Provisional Government in October 1917 and dispersing the recently elected Constituent Assembly the following January, they would do so with a great deal of working-class support, though not for Bolshevik single-party rule but for a 'soviet' government consisting of a coalition of left parties and supportive of worker democracy within the factory. For workers as for others, the ensuing Civil War of 1918–21 was a period of bloodshed, hunger and, eventually, draconian measures, including the militarisation of labour, the introduction of stringent one-man management and the ending of truly free elections to the workers' soviets, all inflicted upon what had been its own primary constituency by an embattled, often desperate Bolshevik regime. Though indispensable to the 'Reds' in their life-and-death struggle against the 'Whites' in these years of bloody warfare, workers emerged from the Civil War demoralised and, in many cases, thanks to the damage suffered by Russian industry and the consequent shortage of industrial jobs, declassed. Despite flurries of activity and even occasional resistance, workers now ceased to be a major independent force in the country's political life.

30

Police and revolutionaries

JONATHAN W. DALY

Soon after officers of leading noble families rebelled in December 1825, Nicholas I created the Third Section of His Imperial Majesty's Own Chancellery and a uniformed gendarmerie to conduct censorship, oversee the bureaucracy, keep track of the public mood and preserve state security. During the first two decades of its existence, Nicholas's security police were not unpopular. At the end of Nikolai Gogol's *Inspector General* (Revizor, 1836), for example, the gendarme who announces the arrival of the true inspector appears as a symbol of justice. At any given moment during the second quarter of the century, one or two dozen people – mostly officials, society women, writers, journalists and well-connected nobles – provided sporadic, often gossipy information to the Third Section, sometimes quite openly.[1]

Aside from the Polish rebellion of 1830–1, the period from 1826 to 1840 witnessed almost no incidents of political opposition. The intelligentsia was largely preoccupied with literary and philosophical issues. The execution of five Decembrists and the exile to Siberia of over one hundred more in 1826 had surely diverted many from the path of active opposition. As the close association between government and educated public began to break down, in the 1840s, thanks to the expansion of education, increased European influences and the wave of European revolutions in 1848, the police sought to maintain the status quo, driving into internal or external exile prominent intellectuals like Alexander Herzen and Fedor Dostoevsky. The Third Section was beginning to inspire dread but still was not an efficient security police institution. It was generally well informed about the private social gatherings of social elites. It could also make incisive assessments of the public mood, as when in early

1 See Sidney Monas, *The Third Section: Police and Society under Nicholas I* (Cambridge, Mass.: Harvard University Press, 1961); P. S. Squire, *The Third Department: The Establishment and Practice of the Political Police in the Russia of Nicholas I* (Cambridge: Cambridge University Press, 1968).

1855 it warned of war-weariness within the population and urged bringing the Crimean War to a close.[2]

In 1866 in the midst of the Great Reforms, which created an independent judiciary and institutions of local self-government, a terrorist attempt against Alexander II led to minor police reforms: the creation of a forty-man security force (*okhrannaia strazha*) to protect the emperor and of special bureaus for security policing (*Okhrannoe otdelenie*) and regular criminal investigation (*Sysknoe otdelenie*). Although the government appears to have intended earnestly to combat both grave regular and political crime, the robust development of political crime over the next several decades caused the lion's share of resources available for policing to flow to the security bureau. Within a decade and a half, it became the cornerstone of the security police system. Later in the year, the Gendarme Corps was reorganised, its staff increased. Finally, in 1868 a network of twenty-eight 'observation posts' (*nabliudatel'nye punkty*) was created in fourteen provinces.[3]

In 1869, before the onset of anything like systematic government repression, Mikhail Bakunin and S. G. Nechaev, in their 'Revolutionary Catechism', urged gathering rebels and brigands into a violent revolutionary force. Nechaev's People's Revenge group, which advocated the systematic destruction of the established social and political order and the physical annihilation of government officials, attracted many young people, four of whom he persuaded in 1869 to murder a confederate.[4] The Nechaev conspirators were tried and mostly exonerated, prompting the government in 1871 to empower gendarmes to investigate state-crime cases and the justice minister in consultation with the director of the Third Section to propose administrative punishments in these cases. Until 1904, therefore, the majority of state-crime cases were handled administratively.

The next opposition movement was non-violent. In spring and summer 1874, thousands of young idealists, dressed as peasants and some trained in rustic craft and skills, set out to the countryside to bring light to, and learn from, the peasantry. Russian educated youths had 'gone to the people'. Hundreds

2 This chapter draws on my *Autocracy under Siege: Security Police and Opposition in Russia, 1866–1905* (DeKalb: Northern Illinois University Press, 1998) and *The Watchful State: Security Police and Opposition in Russia, 1906–1917* (DeKalb: Northern Illinois University Press, 2004).

3 See I. V. Orzhekhovskii, *Samoderzhavie protiv revoliutsionnoi Rossii (1826–1880)* (Moscow: Mysl', 1982); P. A. Zaionchkovskii, *Krizis samoderzhaviia na rubezhe 1870–1880-kh godov* (Moscow: Izd. MGU, 1964).

4 On all the radical movements of this era, see Franco Venturi, *Roots of Revolution: A History of the Populist and Socialist Movements in Nineteenth-Century Russia*, trans. Francis Haskell (New York: Knopf, 1960).

were arrested and eventually tried, but the defendants won public sympathy. Those who remained committed to political opposition either fled abroad or went 'underground'. Among the latter, some remained covertly in villages; others embraced political terrorism. The first of these terrorist-conspirators, calling themselves Land and Freedom, began in 1877 to carry out acts of violence against senior officials. When a jury acquitted Vera Zasulich, who freely confessed to attempting to murder a prominent official in 1878, the government deprived people accused of committing attacks on government officials of the right to a jury trial. The terrorists countered with more attacks and the government with more emergency measures.[5]

Yet the security police, using primitive methods of surveillance, were no match for the terrorists: only in the 1870s did the police begin to build up a registry of political suspects (the police in Vienna for a half-century had been registering the entire population of the Austrian Empire). Moreover, the terrorists formed a tightly organised, highly disciplined, though small, band of almost religiously devoted crusaders who launched attack after attack. In desperation the police arrested thousands of (mostly non-violent) young radicals, thus alienating the educated public who therefore occasionally abetted the terrorists. After several attempts, their organisation – now called People's Will – assassinated Tsar Alexander II in March 1881.

But the tide was already turning. In August 1880 a centralised police institution subordinated to the Ministry of the Interior, with authority over both political and regular police forces, the Police Department, had replaced the Third Section. Henceforth the security service was just another wheel in the state machine. (The Gendarme Corps remained affiliated with the War Ministry, however.) In October a second security bureau was established in Moscow. Grigorii Sudeikin, chief of the security bureau in St Petersburg and one of a rare breed of professionally sophisticated gendarme officers, penetrated the People's Will with informants and arrested several of its members by early 1881. While he failed to prevent the regicide, over the next two years Sudeikin, his assistant, Petr Rachkovskii, and their key informant, Sergei Degaev, demolished People's Will, which, although using Degaev to help murder Sudeikin, never fully recovered.

Several informants whose identities were discovered by revolutionaries went on to occupy key positions in the police apparatus. In contrast to gendarme officers, men with military training and an abiding sense of hierarchy and authority, erstwhile informants knew the revolutionaries' mentality

5 See Jonathan W. Daly, 'On the Significance of Emergency Legislation in Late Imperial Russia', *SR* 54 (1995): 602–29.

intimately, making them their most dangerous adversaries. Rachkovskii had worked briefly as an informant in 1879, then virtually created a security bureau in Paris, which he headed from 1884 to 1902. Sergei Zubatov, an informant for the Moscow security bureau in 1886–7, rose to head that bureau and transformed it into the heart and soul of the empire's security system. Zubatov, Rachkovskii and several others introduced into the system an inventiveness, a vitality, an enthusiasm, and a spirit of adventure and iconoclasm previously absent from Russia's security service.

The government's apparent inability to deal with the terrible famine of 1890–1 gave rise to underground organisations in the People's Will tradition and broad-based oppositional movements. Radical activists travelled to the famine-stricken areas, where they educated, healed and fed people and agitated for a revolutionary uprising. The peasants largely shunned them, however, driving some in summer 1893 to found the People's Justice party aimed at overthrowing the monarchy. Co-ordinated arrests crushed the organisation.

The number of gendarme inquests into political crimes rose from 56 cases involving 559 people in 1894 to 1,522 cases involving 6,405 people in 1903, an increase of 1,259% and 608%, respectively.[6] Still, until the turn of the century, the security police had revolutionary conspirators well under control. Rachkovskii in Paris with a dozen informants kept abreast of developments among the radical émigrés and occasionally arranged their arrest in collaboration with European police forces. The Police Department co-ordinated the information sent in from provincial gendarme stations, mail interception offices and the security bureaus in the imperial capitals and in Paris. It also recruited informants on an irregular basis. Often this was done without much genuine effort on the police's part. For example, in 1893 Evno Azef, a brilliant informant among leading Socialist-Revolutionaries, voluntarily offered his services.

The Social Democrats enjoyed more success in the late 1890s because the security service focused more on repressing Populists and neo-People's Will groups (though it also harassed the Marxists, especially in Moscow, prompting them to adopt strict methods of secrecy), and thanks to a shift in tactics towards agitation among artisans and workers, articulating their everyday concerns and frustrations in order to incite their anger and channel it towards revolt. This approach formed the core idea of the Union of Struggle for the Liberation of the Working Class, created in St Petersburg in autumn 1895 to unite the

6 A. F. Vovchik, *Politika tsarizma po rabochemu voprosu v predrevoliutsionnyi period (1895–1904)* (Lvov: Izd. L'vovskogo universiteta, 1964), p. 262.

disparate Social Democrat circles.[7] Despite continuous repression, which landed many experienced revolutionaries in exile, the movement helped provoke and organise massive strikes in St Petersburg in 1896 and 1897, leading many manufacturers unilaterally to shorten the regular work day in their factories to eleven and a-half hours. The government extended this concession to the whole country in a law of 2 June 1897. Henceforth, however, the government would deal with strike instigators largely by administrative means, not in the regular courts. The Police Department would also pay far more attention to the labour movement.

Meanwhile, Zubatov was reforming the methods of security policing. Professing a 'profound love for and faith in his cause', he imparted to several of his protégés in the security bureau an ardent commitment rarely encountered in gendarme officers. Zubatov's closest assistant, Evstratii Mednikov, a clever Old Believer of peasant stock, refined the use of plain clothes police agents, called surveillants (*filery*). Before the early 1880s, the gendarmes, despite their easily recognisable blue uniform, were rarely allowed to undertake plain clothes operations. At the Moscow security bureau, surveillants memorised the city's physical layout, including restaurants, bars, factories, taxi stations and tramway routes, as well as streets, alleys and courtyards, to enable them to manoeuvre freely around suspects. During training, experienced agents accompanied fresh recruits and taught them to recognise and commit to memory facial features through systematic study of physiognomy and by poring over photographs of revolutionaries. Finally, the novices learned to employ makeup and disguises. Surveillants jotted down their observations in diaries, tens of thousands of which are preserved in the police archives. They are generally little more than a dull catalogue of pedestrian occurrences in the life of persons under surveillance, yet security bureau clerks used them to prepare a welter of 'finding aids', including weighty name and place registers and complex diagrams of relations among opponents of the government. The number of such trained surveillants in Moscow rose from seventeen in 1881 to fifty in 1902, after which the number fluctuated between fifty and one hundred. (After the turn of the century, the St Petersburg bureau employed slightly more.)

To pursue radical activists out into the provinces, where the majority of provincial gendarme authorities were ineffective, in 1894 a mobile surveillance brigade (*Letuchii otriad filerov*) was created at the Moscow security bureau. As a sort of moveable security bureau, it was designed to uncover distribution

7 See J. L. H. Keep, *The Rise of Social Democracy in Russia* (Oxford: Oxford University Press, 1963).

networks of revolutionary literature, illegal printing presses and propaganda rings. It permitted Zubatov to co-ordinate major operations across the empire – from surveillance to mass arrests. The key to its success was its mobility: those under surveillance were less likely to recognise a surveillant constantly on the move than one permanently stationed in one place. The brigade achieved its success with a staff of only thirty surveillants in 1894 and fifty in January 1901.

More important than surveillants were informants. Zubatov was a master at recruiting and guiding them, winning their confidence and maximising their usefulness. Sometimes he used chance meetings with industrial workers or personnel of important public organisations as opportunities to recruit them as agents. A certain number of informants simply proposed their services. The majority of agents began to work for the police after arrest – and under interrogation. Zubatov questioned political suspects as though leading a radical discussion circle, showering them with attention, offering them food and drink, and arguing passionately that the people never profit from revolutionary violence, that only the emperor was capable of implementing needed reforms in Russia. His enthusiasm and energy were extremely attractive to revolutionaries lacking deep convictions and permitted him to turn some of them away from the paths of political opposition.

Zubatov emphasised that case officers must win their agents' trust, protect them from discovery, assist them in adversity and increase their faith in the Russian monarchy. He urged his officers, according to one of them, to treat their informants as 'a beloved woman with whom you have entered into illicit relations. Look after her like the apple of your eye. One careless move and you will dishonour her . . . Take this to heart: treat these people as I am advising, and they will understand your needs, will trust you, and will work with you honestly and selflessly.'[8]

The number of informants was never great, and before Zubatov they were few indeed. Nikolai Kletochnikov, a revolutionary infiltrator who had access to the security police's most sensitive files in 1879–80, found a record of only 115 permanent informants in the whole empire – at the height of terrorist attacks against the emperor and his officials.[9] Later, part-time police informants worked within nearly every major social group and profession, although even the security bureau in St Petersburg never employed more than 94 informants. The most important ones were students in the 1880s and 1890s and members of the two principal revolutionary parties (the Socialist-Revolutionaries and

8 A. Spiridovich, *Zapiski zhandarma* (Moscow: Izd. 'Proletarii', 1930), p. 50.
9 See Orzhekhovskii, *Samoderzhavie*, p. 122.

Social Democrats) after the turn of the century. People became informants for a variety of reasons. Some agreed to inform in order to take revenge upon their erstwhile comrades (Zubatov claimed this of himself), some sought adventure or took a liking to their case officers, probably all feared punishment and desired material benefits. A few earnestly wished to serve their government in its struggle against the onslaught of revolutionary sedition.[10] Wages ranged from 5–10 roubles to 100–200 roubles (or up to 1,000 for a few 'stars') monthly. (By contrast, surveillants and skilled metalworkers earned 50 roubles per month.) Valuable, long-time informants could hope to receive a solid annual pension (from 1,000 to 3,000 roubles) or a one-time lump-sum subsidy (as much as 5,000 roubles).

Zubatov's development of new police methods, especially the systematic and extensive employment of informants, was undoubtedly the most significant advance in Russian political policing since the creation of the Third Section. It also set him at odds with the majority of Russian security policemen, the gendarmes. Such policemen, even when lacking precise information about criminal activity, sometimes arrested dozens of people in order to discover a few political criminals: that is, not on the basis of evidence of political wrongdoing, but in order to obtain evidence. Zubatov argued, by contrast, that suspects should be arrested or exiled administratively only upon discovery of strong evidence of their involvement in political crime, to avoid creating innocent victims and alienating the population from the government. Zubatov preferred to wait patiently for an underground group to come into possession of incriminating evidence (illegal literature, forged passports, explosives or weapons) or for the arrival of a major revolutionary leader from abroad, before arresting its members. The point was to let the group reveal its purposes in order both to learn more about the broader movement of which it was a part and to catch it in flagrante delicto.

If Zubatov's methods were more effective and fruitful in the long run, they were also more dangerous. By allowing the revolutionaries room to manoeuvre, the police risked letting them perpetrate crimes. Likewise, informants were obliged to participate more fully in the work of the illegal organisations, laying them open to charges of provocation. Given the difficulties and dangers inherent in the new approach, it is hardly surprising that many gendarmes continued to prefer the older, more heavy-handed methods. Yet Zubatov was surely right that by the mid-1890s the security police had to ascend to a higher

10 The best place to start exploring the lives of informants is Leonid Men'shchikov, *Okhrana i revoliutsiia. K istorii tainykh politicheskikh organizatsii v Rossii*, 3 vols. (Moscow: Izd. politkatorzhan, 1925–8).

level of professional sophistication. Whereas the opposition 'movement' had comprised a few dozen members under Nicholas I and only a few thousand under Alexanders II and III, it fell to Nicholas II's lot to rule an empire plagued by mass social discontent. The security system was no longer equipped to punish or otherwise neutralise all such 'suspicious' people in Russia. Furthermore, as a former radical himself, Zubatov was convinced that much popular discontent was justified.

The massive strikes of 1896–7 underscored these points. Moreover, the Social Democrats were enjoying considerable success in spreading their revolutionary theories and agitation among the ranks of the industrial workers. In this context, Zubatov conceived of an astonishing programme: to organise industrial workers on behalf of the government and to strive to improve the material conditions of their life in order to win them away from the revolutionary opposition. He argued that only the absolutist monarchy, an institution above classes and estates, could advance the industrial workers' interests. The revolutionaries, he asserted, wished to use them only to further their own political goals. The patronage of Moscow's powerful governor-general, the emperor's uncle, Grand Duke Serge Aleksandrovich, permitted him to implement this bold policy.[11]

Apparently in response to a coalescing of revolutionary organisations in the late 1890s, in January 1898 the Police Department created a Special Section for co-ordinating security policing operations throughout the empire. The Special Section's staff of five assistants, seven clerks and three typists (1900) were nearly all civilians until 1905, when a few gendarme officers took important positions. The institution was cloaked in secrecy, its offices hidden, and its chief and his assistants, a few of them erstwhile informants, claiming to be professors, writers or merchants. While the actual fighting against the revolutionary opposition was left to Zubatov in Moscow, the Special Section in St Petersburg analysed, classified and interpreted data furnished by police institutions, informants and perlustration; surveyed the various opposition groups and movements and prepared assessments of their strength and significance; compiled, organised and indexed information on social disorders, students, workers and the general mood of the Russian population; and co-ordinated the search for political criminals.

The Social Democrats held their first congress in Minsk on 1–2 March 1898, but the police immediately arrested every delegate – save three whom Zubatov

11 On Zubatov's approach to workers, see Jeremiah Schneiderman, *Sergei Zubatov and Revolutionary Marxism: The Struggle for the Working Class in Tsarist Russia* (Ithaca: Cornell University Press, 1976).

deliberately left at liberty, in the hope that they would lead him to their colleagues in revolution. Both police repression (Vladimir Lenin, Julius Martov and Aleksandr Potresov were exiled to Siberia) and philosophical and programmatic differences among Social Democrats delayed the convocation of a second party congress until 1903. In the meantime, there erupted in February 1899 student disorders that marked the beginning of Russia's revolutionary era. They radicalised the bar by expanding the number of radical law students, stimulated the publication of the Social Democrat newspaper *Iskra* and promoted the formation of the Socialist-Revolutionary party and of the Liberation Movement by awakening Marxists, neo-Populists and left-wing liberals to the immense power available to opponents of the imperial government if only they roused the population against it. The government first overreacted to the student unrest, then relented: it conscripted into the army and expelled hundreds of students from the universities, only to readmit them in the fall.[12] The message was clear: the government was arbitrary and repressive, but not overly to be feared by committed radicals.

The Socialist-Revolutionary party grew up around the newspaper *Revoliutsionnaia Rossiia*, which began publication in late 1900 in Moscow and in early 1901 in Finland. The party evolved from two currents, the People's Will's tradition of political terrorism and a peasant-centred programme of revolutionary propaganda.[13] The party's programme of terrorism received its motor impulse from the assassination in February 1901 of the education minister, Nikolai Bogolepov, whom critics of his handling of the student disorders called 'Mr Absurd' (*Nelepov*). That summer, Zubatov admitted that despite a whole series of successful arrests the revolutionary movement was growing and consolidating itself. Russia's revolutionaries viewed themselves as a kind of holy brotherhood of men and women dedicated to bringing down the imperial government and to putting a more just order in its place. In their quest for right they expected to fall prey to snares and to suffer pain and privations, including arrest, imprisonment and exile. One counted devotion to the cause in terms of jails visited and places of exile known. The Bolshevik Viktor Nogin's tally, for example, reached fifty.[14]

By late 1901 and early 1902, industrial workers and university students joined forces in major demonstrations. In St Petersburg, radical intellectuals also

12 On the student unrest see Samuel D. Kassow, *Students, Professors, and the State in Tsarist Russia* (Berkeley and Los Angeles: University of California Press, 1989).

13 See Manfred Hildermeier, *The Russian Socialist-Revolutionary Party Before the First World War*, English edn (New York: St Martin Press, 2000).

14 'Nogin, Viktor Pavlovich', in *Politicheskie deiateli Rossii. 1917* (Moscow: Bol'shaia Rossiiskaia entsiklopediia, 1993), p. 237.

took part. This seems to have been another important step along the road towards the 1905 Revolution, when students, industrial labourers and liberal and radical intellectuals banded together to launch a united attack on the imperial government. To make matters worse, in spring 1902 massive peasant disorders shook Poltava and Kharkov provinces. It was precisely at this moment that Lenin argued that the revolutionary movement would triumph only if a 'few professionals, *as highly trained and experienced as the imperial security police*, were allowed to organise it'.[15] It seems, however, that the greatest threat to the government was less the revolutionary conspirators, whom the Russian security police generally managed to control, but mass opposition movements.

Neither the provincial gendarme stations, nor the security bureaus, nor even Zubatov's mobile brigade could cope with the growing and diversifying opposition. Few provincial gendarmes were prepared to match wits with anti government activists, and the mobile brigade was now stretched to the limit of its resources. Thus, in mid-1902 Zubatov persuaded the interior minister, Viacheslav Plehve (his predecessor, Dmitrii Sipiagin, was assassinated in April 1902), to authorise the creation of a network of provincial security bureaus staffed by dynamic gendarme officers and surveillants transferred from the mobile brigade. Zubatov was named Special Section chief in August and twenty bureaus were created. The new institutions occupied an ambiguous position within the imperial bureaucracy. In matters affecting 'state security' they were independent and authoritative – being empowered, 'in extreme circumstances', to launch searches or arrests outside their provinces without contacting either local authorities or the Police Department – but in all other affairs they were partially subordinated to the provincial gendarme station chiefs. This was a prescription for disastrous intra-bureaucratic relations, and many gendarme chiefs were justifiably furious. Even so, the new bureaus, especially in Kiev, Odessa, Kharkov and Ekaterinoslav, seemed to deliver impressive results.

Yet within months Russia began its slide towards revolution. In July 1903 massive strikes swept the Black Sea littoral and the Caucasus: a foretaste of the October 1905 general strike.[16] Zubatov urged moderation in dealing with the unrest, the more so as his labour experiment was well entrenched in Odessa. Yet on Plehve's orders, the general strike in that city was brutally crushed in mid-July. Zubatov rebelled. Plehve dismissed and banished him from the

15 V. I. Lenin, *Chto delat'?*, in *Polnoe Sobranie Sochineniia*, vol. 6, pp. 126–7. Italics supplied.
16 See 'K istorii vseobshchei stachki na iuge Rossii v 1903 g.', *KA* 88 (1938): 76–122.

major cities of Russia, depriving the security system of its most talented director. A year later Plehve himself fell before an assassin's bomb. By November Mednikov lamented that the entire security system was crumbling before his eyes.[17] The conciliatory attitude of Plehve's successor, Petr Sviatopolk-Mirskii, merely encouraged oppositional sentiment, which had been building despite government repression, to burst forth into a fever of social militancy exacerbated by Russia's sagging fortunes in its war with Japan. Bloody Sunday (9 January 1905) ignited massive popular unrest and throughout the year the opposition movements grew into a mighty phalanx of anti-government forces – agrarian and urban, educated and illiterate, left-liberal and revolutionary. Officials were continuously threatened by terrorist attacks. From February 1905 to May 1906, 1,075 of them were killed or wounded.[18] Since the security police, by their very nature, were powerless to forestall spontaneous, disorganised outbursts of mass popular discontent, the government would have been less endangered had the regular police apparatus held firm. Yet it did not: under Alexander Bulygin, the entire Interior Ministry was in complete disorganisation by late summer.

The crisis peaked in October 1905 with a general strike that immobilised much of urban Russia and prompted the emperor to issue his October Manifesto, diminishing the power of officialdom and reinforcing the rights of his subjects.[19] Many police officials had no idea how to act or react: in early November the Police Department denied rumours that the security police would be abolished. To make matters worse, terrible agrarian violence broke out in nearly every province of European Russia from late October through December and an armed uprising erupted in Moscow in mid-December. The entire imperial order might have collapsed had not the hardline Petr Nikolaevich Durnovo been appointed interior minister in late October over the indignant protests of nearly all the public figures in Russia. The new interior minister and other proponents of law and order drew three conclusions from the anarchy of late 1905. First, signs of weakness and concessions to the opposition tended to undermine the government. Second, only decisive leadership and timely repression had a prayer of holding the system together. Third, the peasantry and petty urban dwellers could not be relied upon to oppose the radicals. In a word, only a harshly authoritarian state could survive in Russia given the

17 Mednikov to Spiridovich, 7 November 1904, in 'Pis'ma Mednikova Spiridovichu', *KA* 17 (1926), 211.

18 A. M. Zaionchkovskii, 'V gody reaktsii', *KA* 8 (1925): 242.

19 The standard work is Abraham Ascher, *The Revolution of 1905*, 2 vols. (Stanford: Stanford University Press, 1988–92).

strength of the opposition and the complexity of the social and economic problems facing the country. By January 1906, this view held sway within a large portion of officialdom.

The confrontation between government and revolutionaries remained bloody for another two years. The regular and especially military courts heard thousands of state-crime cases beginning in 1906. Whereas 308 alleged political criminals had passed before military judges in 1905, 4,698 did so in 1906.[20] 'Punitive expeditions' restored order along the Trans-Siberian railway, in Ukraine, in the Caucasus and, most notoriously, in the Baltic region. In all perhaps 6,000 people were executed from 1905 to 1907, some 4,600 by court sentence and perhaps 1,400 without trial.[21] Even so, the revolutionary terror did not abate. As many as 1,126 government officials were also killed, and another 1,506 wounded, in 1906. These figures more than doubled the following year; non-official casualties were just as gruesome.[22] Russia was embroiled in a quasi civil war.

At the same time, state and opposition confronted one another uneasily in the State Duma, the new parliament of the Russian Empire. On 26 April, the less despised Petr Arkadievich Stolypin replaced Durnovo as interior minister and was appointed premier on 8 July, the day before the Duma's sudden dissolution. During the inter-parliamentary period that followed, which witnessed massive agrarian unrest and mutinies in key naval bases, Stolypin intended to implement a whole raft of reforms, but his notorious first major act (one week after a terrorist attempt on his life which left twenty-seven people dead) was to institute military field courts for trying persons alleged to have committed violent attacks on state officials or institutions. The field courts, which were obliged to pass judgement in no more than two days and to carry out the sentence (usually death) within one day, operated until April 1907, and executed as many as 1,000 alleged terrorists.[23]

Stolypin is perhaps best known for this official campaign of counter-terror and for his land reforms or 'wager on the strong' peasants, but his administration also reformed the security police system. From December 1906 to

20 N. N. Polianskii, *Tsarskie voennye sudy v bor'be s revoliutsiei, 1905–1907 gg.* (Moscow: Izd. MGU, 1958), p. 33. See also W. C. Fuller, *Civil–Military Conflict in Imperial Russia* (Princeton: Princeton University Press, 1985).

21 Saul Usherovich, *Smertnye kazni v tsarskoi Rossii: K istorii kaznei po politicheskim protsessam s 1824 po 1917 god*, 2nd edn, intro. M. N. Gernet (Kharkov Izd. politkatorzhan, 1933), pp. 493–4.

22 Anna Geifman, *Thou Shalt Kill: Revolutionary Terrorism in Russia, 1894–1917* (Princeton: Princeton University Press, 1993), p. 21.

23 N. I. Faleev, 'Shest' mesiatsev voenno-polevoi iustitsii', *Byloe* 2 (February 1907): 43–81.

January 1907, Stolypin's protégé and director of the Police Department, Maksimilian Trusevich, created eight regional security bureaus, each comprising six to twelve provinces and corresponding roughly to the spheres of activity of the Socialist-Revolutionary party. Their directors were the security bureau chiefs in St Petersburg, Moscow, Kharkov, Kiev, Odessa, Vilno, Riga, and the gendarme station chief in Samara. The directors were supposed to co-ordinate and improve the operations and information-gathering of the several gendarme stations and security bureaus within their jurisdictions but also had the right to order arrest and search operations. This angered gendarme station chiefs who were nearly all of higher rank. To alleviate these tensions and improve operations, Trusevich issued numerous directives and manuals on security police methods and organised periodic summit meetings.

The acrimony between government and public was even more bitter in the second Duma than in the first, and on 3 June 1907 the emperor again peremptorily dissolved the assembly. Expecting massive popular disorders, Stolypin ordered administrative and police authorities to preserve public order at any cost.

Overall, however, a spirit of moderation prevailed among senior police officials. A series of directives rebuked lower administrative and police authorities for taking indiscriminate recourse to administrative exile and for insufficiently strict observance of legal procedure. These strictures were directed primarily at provincial gendarme and security chiefs who often found it difficult to penetrate the revolutionaries' conspiratorial defences. The major security bureaus, by contrast, disposed of well-placed informants permitting them to focus their attention on genuine subversion. This was an extremely important distinction. The police system was able to function within the framework of a legal, constitutional order only in so far as its security police apparatus possessed a reasonably effective intelligence-gathering capability. The efficiency of the security bureaus in the imperial capitals and a few provincial cities permitted them to undermine revolutionary organisations without harassing large numbers of innocent people. Only a really sophisticated police system can distinguish among mere malcontents and genuine subversives.

But perhaps Russia's security men were too sophisticated. The Social Democrat Osip Ermanskii thought so. In his experience, the security men who employed Zubatov's tactic often gave wider latitude than did ordinary gendarme officers to revolutionary activists in the hope that they would incriminate themselves further. Yet, asked Ermanskii, 'who gained more from this policy, the government or the revolutionaries? . . . While the Police Department carefully gathered material and then subjected it to scientific analysis, we were permitted to place a mine beneath the very edifice of absolutism and capitalism whose safeguard and perpetuation that clever [police] system had been designed to ensure.'[24]

Of course, Ermanskii was viewing the system from the point of view of the collapse of the monarchy, an event far from inevitable. Beginning in late 1907 and early 1908, the government gained the upper hand in its struggle against the revolutionaries. One senior official reported in early 1908 that 'Everywhere revolutionary newspapers bitterly complain about the intensification of the "reaction" and about the indifference of the population to the activity of revolutionaries, and this is a good sign of the return to tranquillity of the country.'[25] Indeed, the first issue of a new Socialist-Revolutionary party journal declared in April that 'The autocracy has re-established itself.'[26] Many radical activists remained, but they were driven largely underground, and senior police officials felt sufficiently tranquil over the next two years to return most of the empire to normal law, to issue relatively few death sentences and to seek to prevent excessive use of administrative punishments. The government seemed very much in control, the revolutionaries had been routed and constitutionalism and the rule of law were not entirely jettisoned to accomplish this.

On 7 January 1909, the Socialist-Revolutionary party repudiated one of its most celebrated terrorist leaders, Evno Azef, as a police informant. The perfect 'double agent', he had enjoyed the complete trust of both police and party.[27] Azef's exposure discredited both the Socialist-Revolutionary party, which seemed to be swarming with traitors (some two dozen more informants were unmasked over the next four years), and a government that would make use of assassins to fight assassins. Meanwhile, senior police officials, worried that it would become harder to recruit new informants, reassured existing ones that the Police Department had been able to protect Azef for sixteen years but also warned them that all provocation would be punished severely. It seems, in fact, that the recruitment of police informants did not suffer much from the Azef affair: most of the ninety-four informants employed by the St Petersburg security bureau in 1913 – it had never employed a larger number – had been hired during the previous three years.

24 O. A. Ermanskii, *Iz perezhitogo (1887–1921)* (Moscow: Gos. izd., 1927), pp. 47–9.

25 N. N. Ansimov, 'Okhrannye otdeleniia i mestnaia vlast' tsarskoi Rossii v nachale XX v.', *Sovetskoe gosudarstvo i pravo*, 5 (1991): 123.

26 *Revoliutsionnaia mysl'* 1 (April 1908): 1.

27 On the Azef Affair, see Anna Geifman, *Entangled in Terror: The Azef Affair and the Russian Revolution* (Wilmington, Del.: Scholarly Resources, 2000); L. G. Praisman, *Terroristy i revoliutsionery, okhranniki i provokatory* (Moscow: Rosspen, 2001).

The Police Department's success in devastating the revolutionary organisations did not cause it to become complacent. The Special Section cajoled, provoked, rebuked, encouraged and criticised the directors of both the regional and provincial security bureaus and the gendarme stations with great frequency and vigour. A steady stream of directives urged them to acquire more informants, to study the revolutionary organisations, to train more surveillants, to use conspiratorial methods, to send agents deep into the countryside, to co-operate more effectively, to provide more precise information and to use good judgement before searching suspects. Experienced gendarme officers were sent out to the provinces on inspection tours, a serious training course for gendarme officers was instituted in 1910 and for this purpose Special Section clerks drew up large, multicoloured diagrams of the major revolutionary parties.

The security system was definitely becoming more professional and productive, but its reputation suffered a further blow on 1 September 1911 when an erstwhile police informant, Dmitrii Bogrov, fatally shot Prime Minister Stolypin in Kiev. Public opinion waxed indignant that the security police were still relying on such unsavoury elements as Bogrov, that is, like Azef, a police informant out of control. The reactionary Prince Vladimir Meshcherskii called the security police 'the most harmful, immoral, and dangerous invention in the Russian bureaucratic system', a sort of 'Spanish Inquisition with a slight softening of manners'. Nikolai Gredeskul, a well-known Kadet jurist, admitted that in the face of massive political terror the government had had to adopt secret and underhand methods, but he added that this had led inevitably to the Azef and Bogrov affairs. Since political terrorism had by 1911 come largely to an end, the government, he argued, should put an end to its own covert operations.[28] Curiously, the Kadet was more sympathetic to the government's predicament than was the monarchist. Gredeskul was right: it is essentially impossible to combat a conspiracy without resorting to conspiratorial methods. This was true in the case of both People's Will and the Socialist-Revolutionary terrorists. But once the latter had been disorganised, was it not possible for the police to renounce such methods as Gredeskul urged? Unfortunately, the Socialist-Revolutionaries never officially repudiated the use of terror, and many Social Democrat leaders continued to lay plans to orchestrate the violent overthrow of the imperial order. Thus, in the interest of state security, the imperial security police continued to deploy secret

28 *Grazhdanin*, 36 (18 September 1911): 15–16; N. A. Gredeskul, *Terror i okhrana* (St Petersburg: Tip. 'Obshchestvennaia pol'za', 1912), pp. 28–9.

informants among them, and quite successfully: the major revolutionary parties in 1912 were so disorganised that they could not turn much to their benefit the deep popular outrage provoked by the massacre of 172 striking workers in the Lena Goldfields on 4 April 1912.[29]

Vladimir Fedorovich Dzhunkovskii, appointed deputy interior minister in January 1913, launched a series of reforms of the security police aimed at cutting costs, winning public support for the government and restricting police reliance on informants. In March he prohibited the recruitment of informants in the military, despite a growing perception among senior police officials, expressed at two security conferences in late 1912, that the use of informants should be increased to combat the spread of sedition among enlisted personnel. In May, Dzhunkovskii prohibited deploying informants in secondary schools, which appears to have been an infrequent practice anyway. It might have seemed that he had in mind an all-out assault on the security system, for between May 1913 and February 1914 he abolished most of the provincial and regional security bureaus and transferred their functions to the provincial gendarme chiefs. Although some officials considered the regional bureaus ineffective, senior police officials incessantly criticised most provincial gendarmes, and an authoritative report of December 1912 had attributed the disorganisation of the revolutionary movement to the efficiency of the regional bureaus. In the short term, nevertheless, Dzhunkovskii's reforms seem not to have gravely weakened the security system, and for two reasons: the security bureaus in the imperial capitals remained strong (although Dzhunkovskii dismissed the very able St Petersburg bureau chief, Mikhail von Koten) and the regional bureaus were not abolished until January 1914 when the revolutionary organisations had already been severely weakened.

The logical response to harsh police repression for many revolutionaries lay in developing legal methods of protest and agitation. The Social Democrats founded *Pravda* in April 1912 and *Luch* in September, Bolshevik and Menshevik newspapers, respectively. The police watched them, naturally, seized individual issues and occasionally closed them down, but they repeatedly reopened under different names, a ruse the police were legally powerless to prevent. *Pravda*, for example, was closed down eight times during its two-year pre-revolutionary existence. The police's only recourse was to maintain informants within the editorial board. One informant, Miron Chernomazov, edited *Pravda* from May

29 See Robert B. McKean, *St Petersburg between the Revolutions: Workers and Revolutionaries, June 1907–February 1917* (New Haven and London: Yale University Press, 1990), pp. 88–97.

1913 to February 1914.[30] Similarly, the Bolsheviks participated eagerly in the Fourth Duma, elected in late summer and early autumn 1912. One of the six Bolshevik deputies, Roman Malinovskii, by far the most talented and charismatic, was, in fact, a police informant. In May 1914, however, Dzhunkovskii ordered his dismissal. The rumours attending this event stunned the Bolshevik leadership, as Azef's exposure had disconcerted Socialist-Revolutionary leaders, to the extent that Lenin, still dumfounded, barely reacted to the major political strikes of industrial workers in Petersburg and Moscow in June 1914.[31]

Historians disagree on whether the incidence of labour unrest between April 1912 and June 1914, greater than during the previous years, proves that the government was unstable. All agree, however, that the declaration of war against Germany on 17 July 1914 at least temporarily put an end to this and other popular unrest in Russia. The maintenance of public tranquillity was facilitated by the immediate imposition throughout the empire of a state of either extraordinary security or martial law, which permitted the suppression of legal newspapers, trade unions and educational societies linked to revolutionary groups.[32] The security police also arrested many remaining underground activists and worked to keep Bolsheviks and Mensheviks from uniting. By early 1916 the prospects for revolution seemed to many revolutionary activists very dim.

Yet the imperial system was on the eve of collapse. In September 1916, Aleksandr Protopopov, a favourite of Rasputin and an erratic administrator, became the fifth interior minister in thirteen months. The economic situation, already dismal, worsened throughout 1916. By late November, a court security police report spoke of a 'food crisis', and on 5 February 1917 the Petrograd security bureau warned of coming hunger riots that could lead to 'the most horrible kind of anarchistic revolution'.[33] Large-scale strikes took place on 14 February, but efficient crowd control prevented their getting out of hand. On the night of 25 February the Petrograd Security Bureau arrested a hundred radical activists. The bureau's last report was prepared on the twenty-seventh

30 For a detailed study of government policies toward the radical press in this period, see my 'Pravitel'stvo, pressa i antigosudarstvennaia deiatel'nost' v Rossii, 1906–1917 gg.', *VI* 10 (2001): 25–45.

31 On Malinovskii, see Ralph Carter Elwood, *Roman Malinovskii: A Life Without a Cause* (Newtonville, Mass.: Oriental Research Partners, 1977).

32 Daly, 'Emergency Legislation', 626.

33 Special Section of Court Commandant report, 26 November 1916, GARF, Fond 97, op. 4, d. 117, ll. 93–5; Petrograd security bureau report, 5 February 1917, ibid., ll. 124–124 ob.

amid a general strike, massive troop mutinies and the formation of the Duma's Provisional Committee and the Soviet. That evening crowds sacked and burned the security bureau headquarters in Petrograd.[34] Although Moscow and much of the rest of the empire temporarily remained calm, this concatenation of events marked the end of the imperial government.

On 4 and 10 March, the Provisional Government abolished the security bureaus, the Police Department and the Gendarme Corps; transferred gendarme officers and enlisted men to the regular army; and dismissed all governors and vice-governors. On 18 March it created a bureau for counter-espionage, but against domestic threats to state security the new government left itself nearly defenceless.[35] This was because Russia's new leaders imagined that the collapse of the monarchy would usher in a new form of politics without internal threats to state security. In fact, the dismantling of the imperial police apparatus, as odious as its institutions may have been to many educated Russians, was an invitation to takeover by political conspirators. The imperial security police could not forestall the February Revolution, because it was driven purely by mass discontent; a reasonably sophisticated security police almost certainly could have saved the Provisional Government from the October Bolshevik overthrow, which lacked the sort of mass participation that brought down the imperial dynasty and government in February.

34 The most complete study of the February Revolution is Tsuyoshi Hasegawa, *The February Revolution: Petrograd, 1917* (Seattle and London: University of Washington Press, 1981).
35 Zhurnal zasedanii Vremennogo pravitel'stva, 4, 10 and 18 March 1917, GARF, Fond 1779, op. 2, d. 3, ll. 2, 3 ob., 25, 70.

31

War and revolution, 1914–1917

ERIC LOHR

With the abdication of Tsar Nicholas II on 2 March 1917 in favour of the Grand Duke Michael and the latter's subsequent refusal of the crown, the Romanov dynasty came to an end. The struggle for power and for the definition of the new regime continued through more than four years of revolutionary turmoil and civil war. This chapter outlines Russia's involvement in the First World War, concentrating on the specific ways in which it caused the end of the old regime.

Any attempt to attribute causes must begin with a definition of the event to be explained. When describing 'the end of the old regime', historians are often primarily concerned with the social and national transformations of the revolutionary era that brought the end of the old social order. This chapter focuses on explaining the more specific political end point of regime change when the tsar abdicated and representatives of the national parliament (the Duma), in consultation with representatives of worker and soldier councils, formed a new provisional government. This event marked the end of the Romanov dynasty, the end of Imperial Russia, and the beginning of the social and national revolutions which swept the land through the rest of 1917 and beyond.

The proximate causes of February 1917

The immediate events leading to the abdication began with the confluence of several factors to bring large numbers of people into the Petrograd streets. First, heavy snows in early February 1917 slowed trains, exacerbating chronic wartime problems with flour supply to the cities. Many bakeries temporarily closed due to shortages of flour or fuel. On 19 February, the government announced that bread rationing would be introduced on 1 March, leading to panic-buying and long lines. Fuel shortages led several large factories to close down and the temperature suddenly rose after a long cold spell, both contributing to the number of people in the streets. On 23 February, walk-outs and demonstrations to protest against bread shortages coincided with a small International Women's Day protest march. The next day, these events led to strikes of nearly 200,000 workers. For the first time since 1905, massive demonstrations were held in the centre of the city, on the squares of Nevsky Prospect.

On 25 February, events on the streets remained difficult to classify. Was it another in the series of wartime demonstrations and strikes – which were growing in frequency in late 1916 to early 1917 but still tended to be of short duration because workers preferred not to undermine the troops at the front – or was it the beginning of a revolution? This case exceeded all previous wartime demonstrations and strikes in scale, and people from all walks of life filled the streets, not only protesting against the shortage of bread, but also raising banners calling for the downfall of the monarchy, singing the Marseillaise, cocking their caps to the side and struggling with police for control of public space. In several instances, Cossack soldiers showed their sympathy for the crowd. The proliferation of symbolic acts and the sheer number of people involved already by 25 February gave the sense that a revolution was under way.[1]

But many observers thought that the disorders were primarily focused on the bread shortages and even Aleksandr Shliapnikov, the leading Bolshevik in Petrograd, dismissed the idea that a revolution was at hand on the evening of 25 February. Recent bread riots had eventually run their course, and the commander of the Petrograd garrison, General Sergei Khabalov, thought that the correct course of action would be to continue to avoid confrontation with the crowds.

However, that night the tsar sent the fateful order to Khabalov to use troops to restore order. A small group of the most trusted soldiers was deployed on Sunday morning 26 February. In several places, they fired into the crowds, killing hundreds and invoking parallels to the 1905 Bloody Sunday massacre that had set that revolution in motion. Troops had fired into crowds on other occasions during the war; most seriously when the Moscow garrison was ordered to fire into crowds on the third day of a massive 1915 riot against Germans. That time it succeeded in restoring order; this time it did not.[2]

The bulk of the Petrograd garrison remained in the barracks on 26 February, but heated discussions led to mutinies which spread rapidly through the garrison. By the twenty-seventh, the commanders and loyal officers completely

1 Orlando Figes and Boris Kolonitskii, *Interpreting the Russian Revolution: The Language and Symbols of 1917* (New Haven: Yale University Press, 1999), p. 37.
2 Iu. I. Kir'ianov, '"Maiskie besporiadki" 1915 g. v Moskve', *VI* 12 (1994): 137–50.

lost control of the soldiers, many of whom joined the revolution in the streets. Soldiers freed prisoners, broke into the secret police headquarters and took over government buildings.

For four days, the situation in the capital was uncertain. Power flowed to the soldiers and the authority of the government rapidly melted away. By most accounts, the leaders of socialist parties only began to mobilise and play an active role on the twenty-seventh. A small group of party leaders declared themselves to be an executive committee of the Petrograd Soviet and claimed to speak for the workers and soldiers. It sent an appeal to workers to send representatives to an assembly of the Petrograd Soviet. The process of choosing delegates was extremely informal, resulting in a massive body, two-thirds of which were soldiers. It was such an unwieldy assembly that in practice, the executive committee ended up making nearly all decisions. The executive committee included representatives from a broad array of socialist parties, and they quickly decided not to make an outright bid for power. Some of the party leaders were influenced by the Marxist theory that Russia had to pass through a bourgeois stage (with a presumably bourgeois Duma government) before conditions would be ripe for a proletarian revolution. Many socialists (including the Menshevik defensists, who played a prominent part in these crucial days) feared the anarchy and violence that was already emerging on the streets, and wanted a restoration of order and governmental authority, in order to prevent a collapse of the war effort.

In an all-night negotiation, the executive committee of the Petrograd Soviet worked out a joint programme with the Provisional Committee of the Duma for the creation of a new provisional government. The result, declared early on 2 March, became the basic programme of the revolution. It fulfilled the liberal dream of full equality before the law for all citizens, declaring the immediate abolition of all legal differentiation based on religious, ethnic or social origins. It also granted amnesty for all political prisoners, freedom of speech, assembly, right to strike, and declared elections to organs of local self-government.[3]

While this new polity was forming, the tsar was isolated in Pskov. He remained obstinately opposed to abdication and even refused to make political concessions to the Duma late on 1 March. He changed his mind only when the army command turned against him. A small group of army commanders, in close communication with the president of the Duma, Mikhail Rodzianko, decided early on 2 March that the only solution was abdication.

3 F. Golder (ed.), *Documents of Russian History, 1914–1917* (New York: Century Co., 1927), pp. 308–9.

That morning, the commander-in-chief of the army, Mikhail Alekseev, conducted something close to a *coup d'etat*, sending a circular to the leading army commanders making the case for Nicholas to abdicate and requesting that each send their response directly to the tsar. The commanders of the fronts, including the Grand Duke Nikolai Nikolaevich, unanimously supported abdication. Nicholas consented, insisting only that he abdicate in favour of the Grand Duke Michael rather than his haemophiliac son Alexis. The next day, the Grand Duke Michael met with the Provisional Government leaders and acquiesced to their majority opinion that he should also abdicate. This left government authority solely in their hands until the convocation of a constituent assembly, which was to determine the future governmental system. The promulgation of the two abdication manifestoes marked the formal political end of the old regime.

To reiterate, the immediate chain of events leading to the regime change began with the declaration of bread rationing, followed by the large number of people demonstrating, striking and observing events in the streets. The proximate cause of greatest weight in explaining the end of the monarchy was the mutiny of the Petrograd garrison and, consequently, the pressure applied by the military commanders upon Nicholas to abdicate on 2 March.

Without the mutiny, the demonstrations were probably not sufficient to cause the revolution – as the apparent success of the initial military intervention showed. The mutiny dramatically raised the stakes, radicalising and arming the streets, and making it likely that the only way to preserve the monarchy was to send troops from the front to put down the rebellion forcibly. The tsar was willing to do this up to nearly the last moment, but the army commanders balked. The final crucial factor was the formation of the Provisional Government even before the actual abdication occurred. In a sense, it was stepping into the void left by the absence of the tsar from the capital and the more serious widely shared sense that the tsar and the monarchy had become a barrier to the effective mobilisation of society and industry for the war effort. Recognition of the willingness and ability of the moderate Duma leaders to take over the government in turn helped convince the army commanders to support the revolution.

Relative economic backwardness as a cause?

The first proximate cause, the bread shortage in Petrograd, is inextricably linked to a larger question about the significance of relative Russian economic backwardness as an underlying cause of the revolution. Many memoirs, foreigners' accounts and narratives portray the link between war and revolution in terms of a relatively backward economy unable to hold up under the demands of total war or to produce the shells and weapons needed to compete on the battlefield. But, as Norman Stone has convincingly argued, in many battles, it was not so much a lack of shells, guns or technology that explains Russian defeats as failures of tactics, strategy and command efficiency. He puts the blame on the Russian generals and their strategies, such as the wasteful stockpiling of millions of rounds of ammunition and guns in a massive network of fortresses, which in the end had almost no tactical significance in the fighting. Moreover, old-style social prejudices and outmoded notions of honour contributed to prejudices against the enhanced role of artillery and defensive positioning. As on the western front, a senseless cult of the offensive led to countless wasted lives.[4]

But economic factors also mattered. While the Russian army was superior to the Ottoman army and arguably had a technological edge on the Habsburg army, it was significantly behind the German. At the beginning of the war, the average German division had more than twice the artillery of a Russian division, and Russia was never able to fully close the gap. Unless overwhelmingly outnumbered, technical superiority enabled German troops consistently to defeat Russian troops throughout the entire course of the war. The crucial role of high-powered precision artillery and shells and the drawn-out nature of the fighting behind entrenched defences rapidly turned the war into a production contest.

The mobilisation of Russian industry to increase production for the war effort began slowly and faced many obstacles. Only gradually did the government turn to the kind of aggressive state measures to influence and direct economic activity towards the war that were so successful in Germany. Defence production was further constrained by the relatively poor financial state of the empire. Compared to other countries, Russia had only a very small domestic market for government debt, making it heavily reliant on foreign loans for extraordinary expenditures. This added to the costs and limited the extent of direct state action to expand the output of military products. Moreover, in the decades prior to the war Russia relied heavily on massive yearly inflows of loans and direct investments from abroad. In fact, foreign investment accounted for nearly half of all new capital investment in industry from the 1890s to 1914.[5] The war brought a sharp and sudden end to this key source of industrial growth.

4 N. Stone, *The Eastern Front, 1914–1917* (London: Penguin, 1998).

5 J. P. McKay, *Pioneers for Profit: Foreign Entrepreneurship and Russian Industrialization, 1885–1913* (Chicago: University of Chicago Press, 1970), pp. 28–9.

Germany had been the largest single source of direct investment in the Russian economy. Upon the outbreak of the war, German loans were frozen and by early 1915, the regime embarked on a radical campaign to nationalise businesses and industrial firms owned by enemy citizens. Moreover, from the Ottoman Empire's entry into the war in October 1914, the Straits were closed, leaving only distant Vladivostok and the northern ports of Archangel and Murmansk to receive allied shipments of war matériel. Archangel was frozen half the year and had only a single-track railway line incapable of handling even a portion of the burden. Murmansk had no railway link at all until a wartime project was completed in January 1917. As a result, even when allied shipments finally began to arrive in substantial quantities in mid-1915, many of them simply piled up at their ports of entry. The blockade of Russia was thorough and caused tremendous difficulties for Russian industries and businesses of all kinds by suddenly severing ties to suppliers, engineers, technicians and firms producing specialised items.

These problems were greatly exacerbated by the declaration of prohibition – first of nearly all types of alcoholic beverages during mobilisation, and then of vodka for the duration of the war. On the eve of the war, as throughout its long history, the Russian state had received roughly a quarter of its revenues from alcohol taxes and state sales of vodka. Most studies conclude that prohibition probably curbed some of the traditional drinking bouts as soldiers gathered and travelled to the front, and likely had some positive impacts on health and efficiency in the short run. But the cost to the treasury was immense. Moreover, as the war dragged on, home distilling and illegal markets for alcohol took on a massive scale. The continued sale of wine in elite restaurants added to social resentments, and crowds breaking into alcohol storage facilities contributed to the violence of mobilisation riots, pogroms and the 1915 riot in Moscow. By 1917, the cumulative effects of prohibition were extremely serious. One contemporary financial expert claims the cost reached 2.5 billion roubles by mid-1917, or 10 per cent of all expenditures on the war.[6]

Not least of the impacts of prohibition was that the massive demand for alcohol switched to consumer items and manufactured goods, thereby contributing to inflation – one of the most important links between the war and the revolution. Inflation, of course, had other important sources. Most fundamentally, the lack of a domestic market for government debt, difficulties in acquiring foreign credit and the sharp reduction of exports all combined to

6 Arthur McKey, 'Sukhoi zakon v gody pervoi mirovoi voiny: prichiny, kontseptsiia i posledstviia vvedeniia sukhogo zakona v Rossii, 1914–1917', in V. L. Markov (ed.), *Rossiia i Pervaia Mirovaia Voina* (St Petersburg: RAN, 1999), pp. 147, 154.

leave the government with only one way to pay for its massive defence orders: expansion of the money supply. Russia abandoned the gold standard already on 27 July / 8 August 1914 and by January 1917, the amount of money in circulation had more than quadrupled. Inflation affected the domestic situation in a number of ways. In April 1915, the first significant riots broke out in Moscow over price increases in shops and markets. Inflation riots became an increasingly common and important occurrence on the home front as the problems of the wartime economy accumulated.[7] It also contributed to ethnic violence. The right-wing press and police officials often blamed Jewish, German and foreign shopkeepers and speculators for inflation, especially after the head of the extreme right faction in the State Duma, A. N. Khvostov, was appointed minister of interior in October 1915. Liberals in the Ministry of Agriculture and in co-operatives, *zemstvos* (local elected assemblies) and other public organisations involved in food supply also campaigned against speculators and the market. All co-operated in attempts to require below-market price sales of grain to the army and state and, at the same time, to get rid of the 'middlemen' involved in the pre-war grain market. Both efforts only exacerbated shortages and tensions in the countryside.[8]

Inflation also contributed to the problem of shortages of grain deliveries to the cities. The grain-delivery problem was not the result of an actual shortage of grain. With the blockade, massive exports were entirely shut off, leaving more than enough grain for both the army and for domestic consumption. The problem was the decline in the amount of that grain that was reaching urban markets. Here one of the key problems was that military commanders often used their martial law authority to ban 'exports' of grain from given areas thinking they could thus ensure its delivery to the army at artificially low prices. The civilian administration also tried to regulate prices and work around the commercial grain market. Peasants responded to these kind of administrative measures by waiting for higher grain prices. Unwilling to sell grain to buy industrial products at inflated prices, peasants in increasing numbers chose to store their grain, feed it to their livestock or illicitly convert it into alcohol rather than deliver it to market as inflation accelerated in late 1916 and early 1917.

Despite all the economic problems, Russia managed to increase output for defence, and to do so fairly rapidly. Moreover, by late 1915, Russia's allies

7 Iu. I. Kir'ianov, 'Massovye vystupleniia na pochve dorogovizny v Rossii (1914–fevral' 1917 g.)', *Otechestvennaia istoriia* 1 (1993): 3–18.

8 Lars Lih, *Bread and Authority in Russia, 1914–1921* (Berkeley: University of California Press, 1990), pp. 9–16; Peter Holquist, *Making War, Forging Revolution: Russia's Continuum of Crisis, 1914–1921* (Cambridge, Mass.: Harvard University Press, 2002), pp. 33–4.

were delivering substantial quantities of guns and ammunition. The situation recovered sufficiently that by June 1916, Russia was actually able to fight and win a major offensive on the Habsburg section of the front. The offensive led to nearly a million Austrian casualties and prisoners and forced Germany to send reinforcements to save the Habsburg army from complete collapse. On the eve of February 1917, the Russian army was holding the line. Russia was certainly not losing the war in a military sense. But inflation and the distorted grain market contributed both to the general level of discontent and to the key precipitant cause of the revolution: bread lines in Petrograd.

The rapidity of the wartime industrial expansion caused wrenching social changes. The rapid increases in production by the urban defence industry led to a massive influx of peasants to the cities, increasing the urban population by as much as 6 million by 1917. The institutions and infrastructure of the cities, which could barely cope with the rapid growth of the pre-war years, were simply overwhelmed. In this hothouse growth of the industrial workforce, women entered the workplace in large numbers, breaking down old gender norms. The proportion of women in industry rose from 27 per cent in 1914 to 43 per cent in 1917.[9] In the drive to produce military supplies, the rapidly growing workforce toiled in a dangerous environment where accidents were frequent and long hours the norm. Moreover, shortages of skilled labour and the impossibility of slowing production put many of the most politically active skilled workers in a relatively strong bargaining position. With official recognition on the war industry councils, the skilled workers of Petrograd were in some measure empowered by war conditions. They played an important role in the February crisis by taking control of the working class Viborg district on the twenty-fifth, then engaging in a general strike and crossing over from the working districts to take over the central avenues and squares of the capital. The election of worker councils on 27 and 28 February created a political alternative to the old regime and pressed the Duma leaders to form their own government. But it was the mutiny of the Petrograd garrison which was the turning point in the revolution.

The Petrograd garrison and its mutiny

Why did the Petrograd garrison refuse to follow orders to suppress the demonstrations and strikes? The problem was not a lack of troops. There were roughly

9 J. McDermid and A. Hillyar, *Midwives of Revolution: Female Bolsheviks and Women Workers in 1917* (Athens: Ohio University Press, 1999), p. 128.

180,000 men in Petrograd itself and another 150,000 in the suburbs. In fact, these large numbers were part of the problem. The Russian reserve system used Petrograd and other cities as places to keep troops before sending them to the front. So rather than a manageable force with some preparation for civilian duty, the barracks housed a massive number of some of the least reliable troops in the entire army. Many were new recruits who had almost no training. This reflected larger problems with the military as a whole that were building up as the war ground on. Attrition rates for trained officers and soldiers were high. By the end of 1916, of nearly 15 million men who served in the army, over 2 million had been taken prisoner, over 1.5 million had died and 2 million were seriously ill or injured for a total of 5.5 million casualties.[10] The pointlessness of the endless slaughter makes it perhaps more incumbent upon the historian to explain why mutiny and rebellion did not occur sooner rather than to explain why it occurred when it did.

By 1916 the regime was increasingly desperate for new bodies for the army. Among other things, it abolished exemptions for primary breadwinners; these recruits tended to resent their obligation to serve and were more outspoken than the young. Exemptions previously granted to minorities also came under pressure. Most dramatically, the Kyrgyz in Central Asia rose in a major rebellion to resist their induction in 1916. In the military campaign to suppress the rebellion, thousands were killed. The difficulty in finding reliable men to draft into the army by late 1916 was a problem for the whole army but was particularly acute for the Petrograd garrison, where the Russian reserve system left the least trained and least reliable recent recruits. The Petrograd garrison included disproportionate numbers of convalescent soldiers recovering from injuries and expecting to be forced to return to the front, primary breadwinners and even Petrograd workers who had lost their draft exemptions as punishment for participation in strikes.[11]

Even so, it would be somewhat misleading simply to attribute the causes of the participation of soldiers from the garrison in the revolution to anti-war sentiments. For one thing, many studies of soldier loyalties have found that the key to explaining their behaviour lay in the dynamics of the primary unit. This is a powerful explanation for the occurrence of the first major mutiny in the Russian army well behind the front, where the sense of abandoning fellow

10 A. Wildman, *The End of the Russian Imperial Army*, vol. I: *The Old Army and the Soldiers' Revolt (March–April 1917)* (Princeton: Princeton University Press, 1980), p. 95.

11 J. Sanborn, *Drafting the Russian Nation: Military Conscription, Total War, and Mass Politics, 1905–1925* (DeKalb: Northern Illinois University Press, 2003); Wildman, *The End of the Russian Imperial Army*, p. 157.

soldiers was less direct. Likewise, the mutiny spread most rapidly to sailors of the Baltic fleet (in particular to the crews of the larger warships) – that is, to groups that had not seen action in the war. Police and army reports on the mood of the soldiers often reveal that they expressed their opposition to the tsar and regime along with hatred of the enemy. Among the troops, the notion that the tsar and his government had become the main impediments to the war effort became widespread. This idea took ribald form in the barracks, where rumours ran wild about treason at court and among generals with German names. Respect for the tsar disintegrated so thoroughly by February 1917 that patriotism and mutiny no longer seemed mutually incompatible for many rank-and-file soldiers.

The army command and the February Revolution

Patriotic motives of course much less equivocally lay at the core of an explanation of the actions of the army commanders during the February crisis. At the crucial moment on 1 March, the commander-in-chief of the army, M. V. Alekseev, ordered General Ivanov to halt his march on Petrograd to put down the mutiny, then tried to convince the tsar to abdicate. When the tsar did not immediately agree, Alekseev sent his crucial telegram to all the major military front commanders asking their opinion on the future of the monarchy. The responses came quickly and unanimously argued that Nicholas should abdicate to save the nation and the war effort. In part, Alekseev and the other generals feared that sending frontline troops against the Petrograd garrison and civilians in the Petrograd streets would risk rapidly spreading the revolution to the army at the front. But the unified reaction of the army commanders was also the result of the powerful notion that had long been promoted among military reformers that modern wars could only be won by truly national citizen armies.

Some of the key generals – most importantly General Ruzskii, who was with the tsar on the day of the abdication – had come to believe that the tsar stood in the way of a successful national mobilisation against the enemy well before the February crisis. A key event in the development of this outlook had been the March 1916 removal of the popular war minister A. A. Polivanov, who had worked closely with the Union of Cities and Towns (*Zemgor*), War Industries Councils, and nationalist moderates and liberals. Discussions among military and opposition civilian leaders about the possibility of a *coup d'etat* had begun in earnest already in late 1916. The army command had come to see the tsar and the nation as separate, and even in opposition. As one of the most important generals, A. A. Brusilov, the hero of the successful summer 1916 offensive, reportedly said: 'if it comes to a choice between the tsar and Russia, I will take Russia'.[12]

The formation of the Progressive Bloc and the Provisional Government

One reason the generals thought such a choice could be made in the middle of the war was that a broad-based political opposition that supported the war had firmly established itself as an alternative to the tsar. The crucial turning point in the rise of the political opposition was the abandonment of the 'internal peace' (the pledge of most political and nationality parties to stop all oppositional activities and to stand firmly in support of the tsar) and the creation of a united opposition to the government in the form of the 'Progressive Bloc', a broad coalition of parties in the Duma.

This in turn was a direct result of the German decision to launch a major offensive against Russia in the spring of 1915 in an attempt to force Russian capitulation. Taken by surprise, outnumbered and vastly outgunned, the Russian armies suffered defeat after defeat, retreating in rapid order from April to September 1915 until most of previously occupied Austrian Galicia, all of Russian Poland, Lithuania and much of Latvia had been lost. This 'Great Retreat' had enormous implications for domestic politics. First, it caused a massive wave of refugees to flee the front zones for the Russian interior. Estimates vary widely but likely exceeded 6 million civilians during the war.[13] The refugee crisis was greatly exacerbated by the military command, which had nearly unlimited powers over civilian affairs in a massive zone declared under military rule. While many refugees left of their own volition, the army also conducted targeted mass expulsions of at least a million civilian Jews, Germans and foreigners. Briefly in the summer of 1915 the army turned to a disastrous 'scorched-earth' policy that included driving the entire civilian population of certain regions to the interior. The army did little to stop a wave of dozens of violent pogroms against Jews in the front zones primarily instigated by Cossack army units with substantial participation of local populations. These policies stirred up ethnic tensions both in the predominantly non-Russian areas of refugee creation near the front and in the internal provinces inundated by millions of impoverished displaced people. Not only did inter-ethnic tensions

12 Golder, *Documents of Russian History*, pp. 116–17.

13 P. Gatrell, *A Whole Empire Walking: Refugees in Russia during World War I* (Bloomington: Indiana University Press, 1999), p. 212.

often run high between refugees and native populations, but the refugees put an enormous financial and administrative strain on local governments and administrations throughout the country.

The retreat also caused a great wave of popular anger. The press – on all sides of the political spectrum – turned much more critical of the government. The defeats at the front were in part caused by shortages of key weaponry, and industrialists and Duma members alike began to call on the government to do more to organise and stimulate defence production – above all, to include society more closely in the process. In early June, the tsar made a series of key concessions, replacing conservatives in the Council of Ministers with moderates who were more willing to work with society. In July, the Duma reopened to a series of blistering speeches attacking the government for incompetence in its prosecution of the war. Behind the scenes, negotiations began for the formation of a broad national coalition of parties to form a political opposition. This opposition united nearly three-quarters of the Duma membership in the Progressive Bloc, with representatives from moderate socialists on the left to Russian nationalists on the right. The Progressive Bloc renewed many of the liberal demands of 1905, demanding more powers for the Duma, more legal limitations on the state and military's extraordinary wartime powers in civilian affairs, amnesty for political prisoners, and full equality before the law for all religious and national groups.

The programme was classically liberal, and it expressed the growing sense that the tsar and his government stood in the way of a successful war effort. Only the granting of full civic equality and rights, and the granting of a fully representative government could inspire society and the army to mobilise with true enthusiasm and patriotism for the war effort. Nothing was more instructive of this underlying notion than the negotiations between the notorious right-wing Russian nationalist leader Vasilii Shulgin and Pavel Miliukov, leader of the radical liberal Constitutional Democratic (Kadet) party during the formation of the Progressive Bloc. As Shulgin recalls, he had been deeply suspicious of Miliukov, whom he regarded as an unpatriotic political opponent until he heard Miliukov's ardently patriotic logic based on the idea that only a truly national effort that included society could bring victory.[14] If anything, the leader of the socialist Trudovik faction, Aleksandr Kerenskii (later the head of the Provisional Government), was an even stronger proponent of these ideas than Miliukov.

14 V. V. Shulgin, *The Years: Memoirs of a Member of the Russian Duma, 1906–1917* (New York: Hippocrene, 1984), pp. 241–5.

These moves were followed in the summer of 1915 by the creation of special councils with officials, private entrepreneurs and Duma deputies to deal with the economic crisis and co-ordinate national responses to the war effort. Four special councils – on transport, fuel, grain and, most importantly, war-industry – were created. The war councils included representatives of elected municipal and local government, from private industry, and even worker representatives. It was an important concession to the demands of liberals for a truly national war effort in which society had a significant role to play. The councils made significant contributions to turning around the dire situation in defence production.

At the same time, the government finally dropped its opposition to the formation of a national association to represent local elected bodies, allowing the All-Russian Union of Zemstvo and Municipal Councils (Zemgor) to form. Zemgor took on such tasks as caring for the welfare and needs of the massive wave of refugees that appeared in internal provinces and providing aid and nursing for convalescent soldiers. The special councils and Zemgor together not only helped bring thousands of employees and volunteers directly into the war effort but also gave the leaders of both these national organisations leadership experience and national recognition. They also worked in close co-operation with some of the more progressive branches of the administration such as the food supply administration of the Ministry of Agriculture, assuming what one historian has called 'parastatal' functions.[15] In some measure, liberal society was simply taking over the state.

In 1905 the tsar granted constitutional concessions and appointed strong and competent ministers who accepted the new political realities. Ten years later, the tsar turned in the opposite direction. When the crisis of the German offensive passed, Nicholas misread it as the passing of the larger political crisis. His first move was to take personal command of the army in August 1915. His ministers saw this as a potential disaster. Not only would it create a power vacuum in the capital which they rightly feared might be filled by Alexandra and her favourite Rasputin, but they also saw the replacement of the popular Grand Duke Nicholas with the tsar – who had no real military qualifications for the post – as a move that would directly tie the fate and legitimacy of the monarchy itself to the fortunes of war. But they were unable to convince him to rethink his decision. Within months, the tsar had replaced the competent ministers that he had appointed in June with reactionaries who had no ties to liberal society – perhaps as a result of Empress Alexandra's prodding on

15 Holquist, *Making War, Forging Revolution*, pp. 12–46.

behalf of Rasputin.[16] The most significant change was the replacement of the reasonable N. B. Shcherbatov as minister of interior with Khvostov, leader of the radical Right faction in the Duma, a chauvinist who used every chance to expound on his paranoiac conspiracy theories of Jewish, German and foreign domination of Russians. His repressive policies did much to undermine any remaining spirit of co-operation between the government and society. From late 1915 to February 1917, conflict between the government and society grew more and more intense.

Respect for the tsar continued to decline throughout the following year. Rumours spread throughout society about the pernicious influence and even defeatist or treasonous inclinations of Empress Alexandra and Rasputin, along with ministers and generals with German names. The tsar's rule had always depended to a certain degree upon the respect and dignity of his title and person. By late 1916, the tsar and court had become a laughing-stock. While no solid evidence of treason or even probes for a separate peace by Alexandra, Rasputin or others at court has surfaced, it is clear that they influenced ministerial appointments from late 1915 through the end of 1916 and successfully pushed the wavering tsar to abandon competent moderate ministers willing to work with Zemgor, the War Industries Councils and the Progressive Bloc. The rumours about Alexandra and Rasputin help to explain the sensational response to Miliukov's speech in the Duma in November 1916, in which he directly accused the government of treason. Shortly thereafter, political actors of all persuasions began to take increasingly radical steps against the monarchy in the name of the nation and the war effort. Symbolic of this turn was the assassination of Rasputin by the leader of the extreme Right in the Duma, Vladimir Purishkevich, with the assistance of two relatives of the tsar: F. F. Iusupov and the Grand Duke Dmitrii Pavlovich. By the end of 1916, the monarchy had become fully discredited among liberal and conservative elites alike. At the same time, quasi-governmental organisations headed by liberal politicians had gradually taken over many key elements of the domestic war effort. This dual process – disintegration at the top and the coalescence of opposition from below – drove the politics of the February Revolution and made possible the decisive third step in the revolution, from mutiny to regime change.

The regime change itself was the single most important cause of the series of events that led to the disintegration of the state and the army, the agrarian revolution and the emergence of minority nationalist movements. With the loss of the tsar as the symbolic centre of authority and loyalty, little held the

16 Golder, *Documents of Russian History*, pp. 227–33.

empire together. In creating the new government, the Duma leaders accepted a list of strict conditions imposed upon them by the leaders of the executive committee of the Petrograd Soviet. This compromise dissolved the police and declared elections to positions in local government. This undermined the two most important remaining pillars of authority, the administration and the police. Order No. 1, issued by the Petrograd Soviet on 1 March, called for elections of soldier councils throughout the army and contributed directly to the collapse of authority among army officers. The collapse of the army and the bureaucracy was a complex process that continued through the end of 1917. The disintegration of authority facilitated the agrarian revolution, which swept the land during that year as peasants flooded back to the villages from the army and the city to participate in the expropriation of lands belonging to individual proprietors, gentry and the Church, and then reabsorb them into the commune, which rapidly reasserted its dominance over the countryside.

But the war not only led to the collapse of state authority. As in other countries, it also brought an expansion of the state's activities, in many ways paving the way for the revolutionaries' attempts to transform and shape the population, to watch over it, to cull it of enemies and to manage it more actively. For example, the politics of nationalising both rural and urban property got well under way during the war. The army used its broad powers to requisition, sequester and simply confiscate land, grain, horses and machinery and the civilian government enacted a set of measures to nationalise both lands and businesses belonging to enemy minorities. Likewise, as part of its wartime economic policy, the regime – with the support of public bodies – attempted to overcome 'middlemen' in the grain trade, and in effect the entire domestic grain market. The old regime ended up conducting a massive experiment in a state-administered grain monopoly replete with coercive measures to force grain delivery to the state. These measures can be seen as the first steps in a vicious cycle of increasingly violent interventions in the countryside that continued through the revolutionary era. The First World War not only brought the end of the Russian monarchy but also began the revolutionary creation of a new regime.

Bibliography

I. PRIMARY SOURCES: COLLECTED DOCUMENTS, OFFICIAL HISTORIES, ANTHOLOGIES AND DIRECTORIES

Adres-kalendar'. Obshchaia rospis' nachal'stvuiushchikh i prochikh dolzhnostnykh lits, 135 vols. (St Petersburg: 1765–96; 1802–1916).

Adrianov, S. A., *Ministerstvo vnutrennikh del. Istoricheskii ocherk 1802–1902* (St Petersburg, 1901).

Afanasiev, A., *Russian Fairy Tales Collected by Aleksandr Afanasiev* (New York: Pantheon, 1945).

Arkhiv gosudarstvennogo soveta, 5 vols. (St Petersburg: Tip. II otd., 1869–1904).

Arkhiv vneshnei politiki Rossisskoi imperii (Minneapolis: East View Publications, 1995).

Bartenev, P. (ed.), *Arkhiv kniaz'ia Vorontsova*, 40 vols. (Moscow, 1870–95).

Bezotosnyi, V. M. (ed.), *Otechestvennaia voina 1812 goda. Entsiklopediia* (Moscow: Rosspen, 2004).

Bil'basov, V. A. (ed.), *Arkhiv grafov Mordvinovykh*, 10 vols. (St Petersburg, 1901–3).

Edie, J., Scanlan, J. P., and Zeldin M.-B. (eds.) *Russian Philosophy*, 2 vols. (Chicago: Quadrangle Books, 1965).

Entsiklopedicheskii slovar'. Brokgauz i Efron, 43 vols. (St Petersburg: Brokgauz and Efron, 1890–1906).

Fondy Rossiiskogo gosudarstvennogo voenno-istoricheskogo arkhiva. Kratkii spravochnik (Moscow: Rosspen, 2001).

Golubstov, S. A. (ed.), *Pugachevshchina*, 3 vols. (Moscow: Tsentrarkhiv, 1926–31).

Gosudarstvennaia duma. Stenograficheskie otchoty, 1906–1916, 4 sessions (St Petersburg, 1906–17).

Gosudarstvennyi sovet. Stenograficheskie otchoty, 1906–16, 4 sessions (St Petersburg, 1906–16).

Istoriia Pravitel'stvuiushchego Senata za dvesti let. 1711–1911, 5 vols. (St Petersburg: Senatskaia tip. 1911).

Ivanov, I. S. (ed.), *Ocherki istorii Ministerstva Inostrannykh del Rossii*, 3 vols. (Moscow: OLMA Press, 2002).

Katorga i ssylka, 115 vols. (Moscow: Obshchestvo byvshikh politicheskikh katorzhan, 1921–35).

Kelly, C. (ed. and tr.), *An Anthology of Russian Women's Writing, 1777–1992* (Oxford: Oxford University Press, 1994).

Korkunov, N. M., *Russkoe gosudarstvennoe pravo*, 2 vols. (St Petersburg: Tsinzerling, 1909).

Krasnyi Arkhiv, 106 vols. (Moscow: Tsentrarkhiv, 1922–41).

Leatherbarrow, W., and Offord, D. (eds.), *A Documentary History of Russian Thought from the Enlightenment to Marxism* (Ann Arbor: Ardis, 1987).

Martens, F., *Sobranie traktatov i konventsii, zakliuchennikh Rossiei i inostrannymi derzhavami*, 15 vols. (St Petersburg: Tip. ministerstva put'ei soobshchenniia, 1874–1909).

Mezhdunarodnye otnosheniia v epokhu imperializma. Dokumenty iz arkhivov tsarskogo i vremennogo pravitel'stv, 1878–1917, 2nd series, 6 vols. (Moscow and Leningrad: Gospolitizdat, 1938–40).

Mezhdunarodnye otnosheniia v epokhu imperializma. Dokumenty iz arkhivov tsarskogo i vremennogo pravitel'stv, 1878–1917, 3rd series, 10 vols. (Moscow and Leningrad: Gos. sotsial'no-ekonomicheskoe izd., 1931–8).

Ministerstvo finansov. 1802–1902, 2 vols. (St Petersburg: Expeditsiia zagotovleniia gos. bumag, 1902).

Ministerstvo iustitsii za sto let. 1802–1902. Istoricheskii ocherk (St Petersburg: Senatskaia tip., 1902)

Mironenko, S. V., and Freeze, G. (eds.), *Gosudarstvennyi arkhiv Rossiiskoi Federatsii. Putevoditel'. Fondy Gosudarstvennogo arkhiva Rossiiskoi Federatsii po istorii Rossii XIX–nachala XX vv.*, vol. I (Moscow: Blagovest, 1994).

Padenie tsarskogo rezhima. Stenograficheskie otchoty doprosov i pokazanii, 7 vols. (Leningrad: Gos. izd., 1925).

Pervaia vseobshchaia perepis' naseleniia Rossiiskoi imperii 1897g. (St Petersburg, 1897–1905).

Pis'ma i bumagi Imperatora Petra Velikogo, 11 vols.: vols. I–VII (St Petersburg: Gos. tip., 1887–1918); vols. VIII–XI (Moscow: AN SSSR, 1948–64).

Pol'noe sobranie zakonov Rossiiskoi imperii, 1st series, 45 vols. (St Petersburg: Tip. II otd., 1830).

Pol'noe sobranie zakonov Rossiiskoi imperii, 2nd series, 55 vols. (St Petersburg: Tip. II otd., 1830–84).

Pol'noe sobranie zakonov, 3rd series, 33 vols. (St Petersburg: Senatskaia tip., 1885–1917).

Pravoslavnaia entsiklopediia: Russkaia pravoslavnaia tserkov', in progress, 7 vols. to date (Moscow: Tserkovno-nauchnyi tsentr 'Pravoslavnaia entsiklopediia', 1998–).

Prilozheniia k trudam redaktsionnykh komissii dlia sostavleniia polozhenii o krest'ianakh, vykhodiashchikh iz krepostnoi zavisimosti, 6 vols. (St Petersburg, 1860).

Pypin, A. (ed.), *Sochineniia (Ekateriny II)*, 12 vols. (St Petersburg, 1901).

Rozhdestvenskii, S. V., *Istoricheskii obzor deiatel'nosti ministerstva narodnogo prosveshcheniia. 1802–1902* (St Petersburg: Izd. ministerstva narodnogo prosveshcheniia, 1902).

Russian State Historical Archives: St Petersburg. Annotated Register (St Petersburg: Russian-Baltic Information Center – Blitz, 1994).

Russkaia Starina, 175 vols. (St Petersburg: various publishers, 1870–1918).

Russkii Arkhiv (Moscow: Izd. P. Barteneva, 1863–1917).

Sbornik Imperatortskogo Russkogo istoricheskogo obshchestva, 148 vols. (St Petersburg: Tip. M. M. Stasiulevicha, 1867–1916).

Shilov, D., *Gosudarstvennye deiateli Rossiiskoi imperii. 1802–1917* (St Petersburg: Dmitrii Bulanin, 2001).

Spisok grazhdanskim chinam pervykh chetyrekh klassov po starshinstvu, 1841–1858, 24 vols. (St Petersburg: Senatskaia tip., 1841–58).

Spisok grazhdanskim chinam pervykh chetyrekh klassov, 1876–1916, 80 vols. (St Petersburg: Senatskaia tip., 1876–1916).

Stoletie voennogo ministerstva. 1802–1902, 13 vols. (St Petersburg: various publishers, 1902–14).

Svod zakonov Rossiiskoi imperii, 15 vols. (St Petersburg: Tip. II otd., 1832).

Trudy Vol'nogo Ekonomicheskogo Obshchestva k pooshchreniiu v Rossii zemledeliia i domostroitel'stva, 280 vols. (St Petersburg, 1765–1915).

Ustav dukhovnykh konsistorii (St Petersburg, 1841).

Vernadsky, G. et al (eds.), *A Source Book for Russian History from Ancient Times to 1917*, 3 vols. (New Haven: Yale University Press, 1972).

Vneshnaia politika Rossii XIX i nachala XX veka. Dokumenty rossiiskogo ministerstva inostrannykh del, 1801–1815, 1st series, 8 vols. (Moscow and Leningrad: Gospolitizdat, 1960–72).

Vneshnaia politika Rossii XIX i XX veka. Dokumenty rossiiskogo ministerstva inostrannykh del, 1815–1830, 2nd series, 7 vols. (Moscow and Leningrad: Gospolitizdat, 1974–76).

Zaionchkovskii, P. (ed.), *Istoriia dorevoliutsionnoi Rossii v dnevnikakh i vospominaniiakh*, 19 vols. (Moscow: Kniga, 1976–89).

Spravochniki po istorii dorevoliutsionnoi Rossii. Bibliograficheskii ukazatel', 2nd edn (Moscow: Kniga, 1978).

2. GENERAL HISTORIES: REIGNS AND RULERS: GOVERNMENT

Alexander, J. T., *Catherine the Great: Life and Legend* (New York: Oxford University Press, 1989).

Ananich, B. V., and Ganelin, R. Sh., *Sergei Iulevich Vitte i ego vremia* (St Petersburg: Dmitrii Bulanin, 1999).

Ananich, B. V., Ganelin, R. Sh., and Paneiakh V. M. (eds.), *Vlast' i reformy: ot samoderzhavnoi k Sovetskoi Rossii* (St Petersburg: Dmitrii Bulanin, 1996).

Anisimov, E. V., *Empress Elizabeth: Her Reign and Her Russia*, trans. J. T. Alexander (Gulf Breeze: Academic International Press, 1995).

Vremia petrovskikh reform (Leningrad: Lenizdat, 1989).

Bil'basov, V. A., *Istoriia Ekateriny Vtoroi*, 3 vols. (Berlin: Gottgeiner, 1896–1900).

Bogdanovich, M. I., *Istoriia tsarstvovaniia Imperatora Aleksandra I i Rossiia v ego vremiia*, 6 vols. (St Petersburg: Tip. F. Sushchinskogo, 1869).

Bogoslavskii, M. M., *Petr I: Materialy dlia biografii*, 5 vols. (Moscow: 1940–8).

Bokhanov, A., *Imperator Aleksandr III* (Moscow: Russkoe slovo, 1998).

Bushkovitch, P., *Peter the Great: The Struggle for Power 1671–1725* (Cambridge: Cambridge University Press, 2001).

Byrnes, R., *Pobedonostsev: His Life and Thought* (Bloomington: Indiana University Press, 1968).

Cherniavsky, M., *Tsar and People: Studies in Russian Myths* (New Haven: Yale University Press, 1961).

Crisp, O., and Edmondson, L. (eds.), *Civil Rights in Imperial Russia* (Oxford: Oxford University Press, 1989).

Diakin, V. S., *Burzhuaziia, dvorianstvo i tsarizm v 1911–1914gg: razlozhenie tret'eiun'skoi sistemy* (Leningrad: Nauka, 1988).
Dixon, S., *Catherine the Great* (London: Longman, 2001).
Dzhanshiev, G., *Epokha velikikh reform* (Moscow: Tip. Rassvet, 1896).
Eidel'man, N. Ya. *'Revoliutsiia sverkhu' v Rossii* (Moscow: 1989).
Eklof, B., Bushnell, J., and Zakharova, L. (eds.), *Russia's Great Reforms 1855–1881* (Bloomington: Indiana University Press, 1994).
Emmons, T., *The Formation of Political Parties and the First National Elections in Russia* (Cambridge, Mass.: Harvard University Press, 1983).
Emmons, T., and Vucinich, W. (eds.), *The Zemstvo in Russia: An Experiment in Local Self-Government* (New York: Cambridge University Press, 1982).
Field, D., *Rebels in the Name of the Tsar* (Boston: Houghton Mifflin, 1976).
The End of Serfdom: Nobility and Bureaucracy in Russia, 1855–1861 (Cambridge, Mass.: Harvard University Press, 1976).
Freeze, G., 'The *Soslovie* (Estate) Paradigm in Russian Social History', *AHR* 91 (1986).
Galai, S., *The Liberation Movement in Russia, 1900–1905* (Cambridge: Cambridge University Press, 1973).
Gershenzon, M. O. (ed.), *Epokha Nikolaia* (Moscow: Obozrenie, 1910).
Haimson, L., 'The Problem of Social Stability in Urban Russia, 1905–1917', *SR* 23, 4 (1964): 619–42 and 24, 1 (1965): 1–22.
(ed.), *The Politics of Rural Russia* (Bloomington: Indiana University Press, 1979).
Hamm, M. (ed.), *The City in Late Imperial Russia* (Bloomington: Indiana University Press, 1986).
Hartley, J., *Alexander I* (Harlow: Longman, 1994).
A Social History of the Russian Empire (London: Longman, 1999).
Hosking, G., *The Russian Constitutional Experiment: Government and Duma, 1907–1914* (Cambridge: Cambridge University Press, 1973).
Russia: People and Empire, 1552–1917 (Cambridge, Mass.: Harvard University Press, 1997).
Hughes, L., *Russia in the Age of Peter the Great* (New Haven: Yale University Press, 1998).
(ed.), *Peter the Great and the West: New Perspectives* (Basingstoke: Palgrave, 2000).
Kassow, S., *Students, Professors and the State in Tsarist Russia* (Berkeley: California University Press, 1989).
Klochkov, M., *Ocherki pravitel'stvennoi deiatel'nosti vremeni Pavla i* (Petrograd: Senatskaia tip., 1916).
LeDonne, J., *Ruling Russia: Politics and Administration in the Age of Absolutism, 1762–1796* (Princeton: Princeton University Press, 1984).
Absolutism and the Ruling Class: The Formation of the Russian Political Order, 1700–1825 (New York: Oxford University Press, 1991).
Leonard, C., *Reform and Regicide: The Reign of Peter III of Russia* (Bloomington: Indiana University Press, 1992).
Lieven, D., *Nicholas II: Emperor of all the Russias* (London: John Murray, 1993).
Lincoln, W. B., *Nicholas I: Emperor and Autocrat of all the Russias* (Bloomington: Indiana University Press, 1978).
Lindenmeyr, A., *Poverty is not a Vice: Charity, Society and the State in Imperial Russia* (Princeton: Princeton University Press, 1996).

Litvak, B., *Perevorot 1861 goda v Rossii: pochemu ne realizovalas' reformatorskaia al'ternativa* (Moscow: Izd. politicheskoi literatury, 1991).

Macey, D., *Government and Peasant in Russia, 1861–1917* (DeKalb: Northern Illinois University Press, 1987).

McGrew, R. E., *Paul I of Russia* (Oxford: Oxford University Press, 1992).

Madariaga, I. de, *Russia in the Age of Catherine the Great* (London: Weidenfeld and Nicholson, 1981).

Makarov, S., *Sovet ministrov Rossiiskoi imperii, 1857–1917* (St Petersburg: Izd. SPbU, 2000).

Manning, R. T., *The Crisis of the Old Order in Russia: Gentry and Government* (Princeton: Princeton University Press, 1982).

Mironenko, S., *Samoderzhavie i reformy: politicheskaia bor'ba v Rossii v nachale XIX v.* (Moscow: Nauka, 1989).

Mironov, B., *A Social History of Imperial Russia, 1700–1917*, 2 vols. (Boulder: Westview, 2000).

Montefiore, S., *Prince of Princes: The Life of Potemkin* (London: Weidenfeld and Nicolson, 2000).

Nikolai Mikhailovich, Grand Duke, *Imperator Aleksandr I* (Moscow: Bogorodskii Pechatnik, 1999).

Oldenburg, S. S., *Last Tsar*, 4 vols. (Gulf Breeze: Academic International Press, 1975).

Orlovsky, D., *The Limits of Reform: The Ministry of Internal Affairs in Imperial Russia, 1802–1881* (Cambridge, Mass.: Harvard University Press, 1981).

Pavlenko, N. I., *Petr pervyi* (Moscow: Molodaia gvardiia, 1975).

Pearson, T., *Russian Officialdom in Crisis: Autocracy and Local Self-Government 1861–1900* (Cambridge: Cambridge University Press, 1989).

Peterson, C., *Peter the Great's Administrative and Judicial Reforms: Swedish Antecedents and the Process of Reception* (Stockholm: Rattshistorisk forskning 29, 1979).

Pintner, W., and Rowney, D. (eds.), *Russian Officialdom: The Bureaucratisation of Russian Society from the Seventeenth to the Twentieth Century* (London: Macmillan, 1980).

Pypin, A., *Obshchestvennoe dvizhenie pri Aleksandre I* (Petrograd: Izd. Ogni, 1918).

Raeff, M., *Plans for Political Reform in Imperial Russia* (Englewood Cliffs: Prentice-Hall, 1966).

Imperial Russia 1682–1825 (New York: Knopf, 1971).

The Well-Ordered Police State: Social and Institutional Change through Law in the Germanies and Russia (New Haven: Yale University Press, 1983).

Ragsdale, H. (ed.), *Paul I: A Reassessment of His Life and Reign* (Pittsburgh: Pittsburgh University Press, 1979).

Ransel, D., *The Politics of Catherinian Russia* (New Haven: Yale University Press, 1975).

Riasanovsky, N. V., *Nicholas I and Official Nationality in Russia* (Berkeley: University of California Press, 1959).

A Parting of Ways. Government and the Educated Public in Russia 1801–1855 (Oxford: Clarendon Press, 1976).

The Image of Peter the Great in Russian History and Thought (New York: Oxford University Press, 1985).

Robbins, R., *Famine in Russia, 1891–1892* (New York: Columbia University Press, 1975).

The Tsar's Viceroys: Russian Provincial Governors in the Last Years of Empire (Ithaca: Cornell University Press, 1987).

Ruud, C., *Fighting Words: Imperial Censorship and the Russian Press, 1804–1906* (Toronto: University of Toronto Press, 1982).

Safonov, M., *Problema reform v pravitel'stvennoi politike Rossii na rubezhe XVIII i XIX vv.* (Leningrad: Nauka, 1988).

Seton-Watson, H., *The Russian Empire, 1801–1917* (Oxford: Clarendon Press, 1967).

Shepelev, L., *Tituly, mundiry i ordena Rossiiskoi imperii* (Moscow: Tsentrpoligraph, 2004).

Shil'der, N., *Imperator Aleksandr pervyi: ego zhizn' i tsarstvovanie*, 4 vols. (St Petersburg: Izd. A. S. Suvorin, 1897–98).

Sinel, A., *The Classroom and the Chancellery: State Education Reform in Russia under Count Dmitry Tolstoi* (Cambridge, Mass., Harvard University Press, 1973).

Starr, S. F., *Decentralisation and Self-Government in Russia. 1830–70* (Princeton: Princeton University Press, 1972).

Tatishchev, S. S., *Aleksandr II: ego zhizn' i tsarstvovanie*, 2 vols. (St Petersburg: Izd. A. S. Suvorin, 1903).

Troitskii, S. M., *Russkii absoliutizm i dvorianstvo v XVIIIv: Formirovanie biurokratii* (Moscow: Nauka, 1974).

Verner, A., *The Crisis of Russian Autocracy: Nicholas II and the 1905 Revolution* (Princeton: Princeton University Press, 1990).

Vyskochkov, L., *Imperator Nikolai I* (St Petersburg: Izd. SPbU 2001).

Wcislo, F., *Reforming Rural Russia: State, Local Society and National Politics, 1855–1914* (Princeton: Princeton University Press, 1990).

Whelan, H., *Alexander III and the State Council: Bureaucracy and Counterreform in Late Imperial Russia* (New Brunswick: Rutgers University Press, 1982).

Wittram, R., *Peter I: Czar und Kaiser*, 2 vols. (Göttingen: Vandenhoeck and Ruprecht, 1964).

Wortman, R. S., *Scenarios of Power: Myth and Ceremony in Russian Monarchy*, 2 vols. (Princeton: Princeton University Press, 1995 and 2000).

Yaney, G., *The Systematization of Russian Government: Social Evolution in the Domestic Administration of Imperial Russia* (Urbana: University of Illinois Press, 1973).

Zaionchkovskii, P. A., *Krizis samoderzhaviia na rubezhe 1870–1880-kh godov* (Moscow: Izd. MGU, 1964).

The Russian Autocracy under Alexander III (Gulf Breeze: Academic International Press, 1976).

Pravitel'stvennyi apparat samoderzhavnoi Rossii XIX v. (Moscow: Mysl', 1978).

Zakharova, L. G., *Samoderzhavie i otmena krepostnogo prava v Rossii, 1856–1861* (Moscow: Izd. MGU, 1984).

3. POLITICAL IDEAS

Bakunin, M., *The Confession of Mikhail Bakunin*, trans. R. C. Howes (Ithaca: Cornell University Press, 1977).

Baron, S. H., *Plekhanov: The Father of Russian Marxism* (Stanford: Stanford University Press, 1963).

Barran, T., *Russia Reads Rousseau, 1762–1825* (Evanston: Northwestern University Press, 2002).

Berdyaev, N., *Leontiev* (Orono: Academic International Press, 1968).

Billington, J. H., *Mikhailovsky and Russian Populism* (Oxford: Clarendon Press, 1958).

Blanc, S., *Un disciple de Pierre Le Grand dans la Russie du XVIIIe siècle. V. N. Tatishchev (1686–1750)*, 2 vols. (Paris: Université de Lille III, 1972).

Cahm, C., *Kropotkin and the Rise of Revolutionary Anarchism 1872–1886* (Cambridge: Cambridge University Press, 1989).

Carr, E. H., *Michael Bakunin* (London: Macmillan, 1937).

Crummey, R. O., *The Old Believers and the World of AntiChrist: The Vyg Community and the Russian State 1694–1855* (Madison: University of Wisconsin Press, 1970).

Daniels, R. L., *V. N. Tatishchev: Guardian of the Petrine Revolution* (Philadelphia: Franklin Publishing, 1973).

Danilevskii, N., *Rossiia i Evropa* (St Petersburg: Tip. brat'ev Panteleevykh, 1869).

Durman, K., *The Time of the Thunderer: Mikhail Katkov, Russian Nationalist Extremism and the Failure of the Bismarckian System, 1871–1887* (Boulder: Columbia University Press, 1988).

Eidel'man, N. I., *Poslednii letopisets* (Moscow: Kniga, 1983).

Gleason, W. J., *Moral Idealists, Bureaucracy, and Catherine the Great* (New Brunswick: Rutgers University Press, 1981).

Hamburg, G. M., *Boris Chicherin and Early Russian Liberalism 1828–1866* (Stanford: Stanford University Press, 1992).

Hardy, D., *Petr Tkachev: The Critic as Jacobin* (Seattle: University of Washington Press, 1977).

Jones, W. G., *Nikolay Novikov: Enlightener of Russia* (Cambridge: Cambridge University Press, 1984).

Kelly, A., *Mikhail Bakunin: A Study in the Psychology and Politics of Utopianism* (Oxford: Clarendon Press, 1982).

Kolakowski, L., *Main Currents of Marxism*, 3 vols. (Oxford: Oxford University Press, 1978).

Lampert, E., *Sons against Fathers: Studies in Russian Radicalism and Revolution* (Oxford: Clarendon Press, 1965).

Lang, D. M., *The First Russian Radical: Alexander Radishchev 1749–1802* (London: George Allen and Unwin, 1959).

Lavrov, Peter, *Historical Letters*, trans. J. P. Scanlan (Berkeley: University of California Press, 1967).

Lotman, I. M., *Karamzin* (St Petersburg: Iskusstvo-SPb, 1997).

McConnell, A., *A Russian* Philosophe: *Alexander Radishchev 1749–1802* (The Hague: Martinus Nijhoff, 1964).

Madariaga, I. de, *Politics and Culture in Eighteenth-Century Russia: Collected Essays.* (London: Longman, 1998).

Makushin, A. V., and Tribunskii, P. A., *Pavel Nikolaevich Miliukov: Trudy i dni (1859–1904)* (Riazan, 2001).

Martin, A. M., *Romantics, Reformers, Reactionaries: Russian Conservative Thought and Politics in the Reign of Alexander I* (DeKalb: Northern Illinois University Press, 1997).

Mazour, A. G., *The First Russian Revolution. 1825. The Decembrist Movement: Its Origins, Development, and Significance* (Stanford: Stanford University Press, 1937).

Miller, M., *Kropotkin* (Chicago: University of Chicago Press, 1976).

Pereira, N.G.O., *The Thought and Teachings of N. G. Chernyshevskij* (The Hague and Paris: Mouton, 1975).

Pipes, R., *Karamzin's Memoir on Ancient and Modern Russia: A Translation and Analysis* (New York: Atheneum, 1969).

Struve, Liberal on the Left (Cambridge, Mass.: Harvard University Press, 1970).

Struve, Liberal on the Right (Cambridge, Mass.: Harvard University Press, 1980).

Poe, Marshall, 'What Did Russians Mean When They Called Themselves "Slaves of the Tsar"?' *SR* 57, 3 (Fall 1998): 585–608.

Pomper, P., *Peter Lavrov and the Russian Revolutionary Movement* (Chicago: University of Chicago Press, 1972).

Raeff, M., *The Decembrist Movement* (Englewood Cliffs: Prentice-Hall, 1966).

Reddaway, W. F. (ed.), *Documents of Catherine the Great: The Correspondence with Voltaire and the* Instruction *of 1767 in the English Text of 1768* (Cambridge: Cambridge University Press, 1931).

Rowland, D. 'The Problem of Advice in Muscovite Tales about the Time of Troubles', *Russian History/Histoire russe* 6, 2 (1979): 259–83.

'Did Muscovite Literary Ideology Place Limits on the Power of the Tsar (1540s–1660s)?' *RR* 49 (1990): 125–55.

Shirinianets, A. A., *Russkaia sotsial'no-politicheskaia mysl' XIX–nachala XX veka. N. M. Karamzin* (Moscow: Izd. Vorob'ev A. V., 2001).

Stockdale, M. K., *Paul Miliukov and the Quest for a Liberal Russia, 1880–1918* (Ithaca: Cornell University Press, 1996).

Thaden, E. C., *Conservative Nationalism in Nineteenth-Century Russia* (Seattle: University of Washington Press, 1964).

Walicki, A., *The Controversy over Capitalism: Studies in the Social Philosophy of the Russian Populists* (Oxford: Clarendon Press, 1969).

The Slavophile Controversy: History of a Conservative Utopia in Nineteenth-Century Russian Thought, trans. H. Andrews-Rusiecka (Oxford: Clarendon Press, 1975).

A History of Russian Thought from the Enlightenment to Marxism (Stanford: Stanford University Press, 1979).

Legal Philosophies of Russian Liberalism (Oxford: Clarendon Press, 1987).

Weickhardt, G., 'Political Thought in Seventeenth-Century Russia', *Russian History/Histoire russe* 21, 3 (Fall 1994): 316–37.

Whittaker, C. H., *The Origins of Modern Russian Education: An Intellectual Biography of Count Sergei Uvarov, 1786–1855* (DeKalb: Northern Illinois University Press, 1984).

Wirtschafter, E. K., *The Play of Ideas: Russian Enlightenment Theater* (DeKalb: Northern Illinois University Press, 2003).

Woodcock, G., and Avakumovic, I., *The Anarchist Prince: A Biographical Study of Peter Kropotkin* (London and New York: T. V. Boardman, 1950).

Wortman, R., *The Crisis of Russian Populism* (Cambridge: Cambridge University Press, 1967).

4. CULTURAL HISTORY

Ageeva, O., *Velichaishii i slavneishii bolee vsekh gradov v svete: grad Sviatogo Petra* (St Petersburg: Blits, 1999).

Alekseeva, M. A., *Graviura Petrovskogo vremeni* (Leningrad: Iskusstvo, 1990).
Androsov, S. O., 'Painting and Sculpture in the Petrine Era', in A. G. Cross (ed.), *Russia in the Reign of Peter the Great: Old and New Perspectives* (Cambridge: SGECR, 1998), pp. 161–72.
Zhivopisets Ivan Nikitin (St Petersburg: Dmitrii Bulanin, 1998).
Ital'ianskaia skul'ptura v sobranii Petra Velikogo (St Petersburg: Ermitazh, 1999).
Artem'eva, Iu. V., and Prokhvatikova, S. A. (eds.), *Zodchie Sankt-Peterburga: XVIII vek* (St Petersburg: Lenizdat, 1997).
Bartlett, R. (ed.), *Anton Chekhov: A Life in Letters*, trans. Rosamund Bartlett and Anthony Phillips (London: Penguin, 2004).
Bokhanov, A. N., *Kollektionery i metsenaty v Rossii* (Moscow: Nauka, 1989).
Botkina, A. P., *Tretiakov v zhizni i v iskusstve* (Moscow: Iskusstvo, 1993).
Bowlt, J. E. (ed.), *Russian Art of the Avant-Garde: Theory and Criticism* (London: Thames and Hudson, 1988).
Brown, W. E., *A History of Eighteenth-Century Russian Literature* (Ann Arbor: Ardis, 1980).
Brumfield, W. C., *A History of Russian Architecture* (Cambridge: Cambridge University Press, 1994).
Chrissides, N., 'Creating the New Educational Elite: Learning and Faith in Moscow's Slavo-Greco-Latin Academy, 1685–1694', unpublished PhD thesis, Yale University (2000).
Cracraft, J., *The Petrine Revolution in Russian Architecture* (Chicago: University of Chicago Press, 1990).
The Petrine Revolution in Russian Imagery (Chicago: University of Chicago Press, 1997).
Cross, A. G., *N. M. Karamzin: A Study of his Literary Career, 1783–1803* (Carbondale: Southern Illinois University Press, 1971).
'Catherine the Great and the English Garden', in J. Norman (ed.), *New Perspectives on Russian and Soviet Artistic Culture* (Basingstoke: Macmillan, 1994).
Derzhavina, O. A. (ed.), *Russkaia dramaturgiia poslednei chetverti XVII–nachala XVIIIv.* (Moscow: Nauka, 1972).
Di Salvo, Maria, 'What Did Algarotti See in Moscow?', in R. Bartlett and L. Hughes (eds.), *Russian Society and Culture in the Long Eighteenth Century* (Berlin: LitVerlag, 2004), pp. 72–81.
Dolskaya-Ackerly, Olga, 'Choral Music in the Petrine Era', in A. G. Cross (ed.), *Russia in the Reign of Peter the Great: Old and New Perspectives* (Cambridge: SGECR, 1998), pp. 173–86.
Drage, Charles, *Russian Literature in the Eighteenth Century* (London: published by author, 1978).
Eleonskaia, A. S. (ed.), *P'esy stolichnykh i provintsial'nykh teatrov pervoi poloviny XVIII v.* (Moscow: Nauka, 1975).
Ely, Christopher, *This Meager Nature: Landscape and National Identity in Imperial Russia* (DeKalb: Northern Illinois University Press, 2002).
Figes, Orlando, *Natasha's Dance* (London: Penguin, 2002).
Florovsky, George, 'The Problem of Old Russian Culture', *SR* 21 (1962): 3.
Forbes, I. (ed.), *Catherine the Great: Treasures of Imperial Russia* (Dallas and St Petersburg: State Hermitage, 1990).
Franklin, S., and Widdis, E. (eds.), *National Identity in Russian Culture: An Introduction* (Cambridge: Cambridge University Press, 2004).
Garafola, L., *Diaghilev's Ballets Russes* (New York: Oxford University Press, 1989).

Gasperetti, David, *The Rise of the Russian Novel: Carnival, Stylization and the Mockery of the West* (DeKalb: North Illinois University Press, 1998).

Gray, C., *The Russian Experiment in Art, 1863–1922* (London: Thames and Hudson, 1986).

Gray, Rosalind P., *Russian Genre Painting in the Nineteenth Century* (Oxford: Clarendon Press, 2000).

Hughes, L., 'Peter the Great's Two Weddings: Changing Images of Women in a Transitional Age', in R. Marsh (ed.), *Women in Russia and Ukraine* (Cambridge: Cambridge University Press, 1996), pp. 31–44.

'Restoring Religion to Russian Art', in G. Hosking and R. Service (eds.), *Reinterpreting Russia* (London: Arnold, 1999), pp. 40–53.

'German Specialists in Petrine Russia: Architects, Painters and Thespians', in R. Bartlett and K. Schönwälder (eds.), *The German Lands and Eastern Europe* (Basingstoke: Macmillan, 1999). pp. 72–90.

'Women and the Arts at the Russian Court from the Sixteenth to the Eighteenth Century', in J. Pomeroy and R. Gray (eds.), *An Imperial Collection: Women Artists from the State Hermitage* (Washington DC: National Museum of Women in the Arts, 2003), pp. 19–49.

'From Caftans into Corsets: The Sartorial Transformation of Women during the Reign of Peter the Great', in P. Barta (ed.), *Gender and Sexuality in Russian Civilization* (London: Routledge, 2001), pp. 17–32.

Hughes, L., and di Salvo, M. (eds.), *A Window on Russia: Papers from the Fifth International Conference of SGECR* (Rome: La Fenice edizioni, 1996).

Jones, Gareth, 'Literature in the Eighteenth Century', in Neil Cornwell (ed.), *The Routledge Companion to Russian Literature* (London: Routledge, 2000), pp. 25–35.

Kahn, Andrew (ed.), *Nikolai Karamzin: Letters of a Russian Traveller: A Translation, with an Essay on Karamzin's Discourses of Enlightenment* (Oxford: Voltaire Foundation, 2003).

Kaliazina, N. V. (ed.), *Iz istorii petrovskikh kollektsii. Sbornik nauchnykh trudov* (St Petersburg: Izd. Gos. Ermitazha, 2000).

Kaliazina, N. V., and Komelova, G. N., *Russkoe iskusstvo Petrovskoi epokhi* (Leningrad: Khudozhnik, 1990).

Karlinsky, Simon, *Russian Drama from its Beginnings to the Age of Pushkin* (Berkeley: University of California Press, 1985).

Kean, B. W., *All the Empty Palaces: The Merchant Patrons of Modern Art in Pre-Revolutionary Russia* (London: Barrie and Jenkins, 1983).

Kelly, C., and Shepherd, D. (eds.), *Constructing Russian Culture in the Age of Revolution: 1881–1940* (Oxford: Oxford University Press, 1998).

Kelly, L., *Lermontov: Tragedy in the Caucasus* (London: Robin Clark, 1983).

Kodicek, A. (ed.), *Diaghilev: Creator of the Ballets Russes* (London: Lund Humphries, 1996).

Krasnobaev, B. I. (ed.), *Ocherki istorii russkoi kul'tury vosemnadtsatogo veka* (Moscow: Izd. MGU, 1972).

(ed.), *Ocherki russkoi kul'tury XVIII veka* (Moscow: Izd. MGU, 1985).

Leach, R., and Borovsky, V. (eds.), *A History of Russian Theatre* (Cambridge: Cambridge University Press, 1999).

Levitt, M., *Russian Literary Politics and the Pushkin Celebration of 1880* (Ithaca: Cornell University Press, 1989).

Lotman, Iu. M., and Uspenskii, B. A., 'Binary Models in the Dynamic of Russian Culture to the End of the Eighteenth Century', in A. D. Nakhimovsky and A. S. Nakhimovsky (eds.), *The Semiotics of Russian Cultural History* (Ithaca: Cornell University Press, 1985), pp. 30–66.

Luburkin, D. I., *Russkaia novolatinskaia poeziia: materialy k istorii XVII–pervaia pol. XVIII veka* (Moscow: Rossiiskii gos. gumanitarnyi universitet, 2000).

Luppov, S. P., *Kniga v Rossii v pervoi chetverti XVIII v.* (Leningrad: Nauka, 1973).

McConnell, A., 'Catherine the Great and the Fine Arts', in E. Mendelsohn (ed.), *Imperial Russia 1700–1917: Essays in Honour of Marc Raeff* (DeKalb: Northern Illinois University Press, 1990), pp. 37–57.

Maes, F., *A History of Russian Music from Kamarinskaya to Babi Yar* (Berkeley: California University Press, 2002).

Marker, Gary, *Publishing, Printing, and the Origins of Intellectual Life in Russia, 1700–1800* (Princeton: Princeton University Press, 1985).

Mirsky, D. S., *A History of Russian Literature from its Beginnings to 1900* (New York: Vintage, 1958).

Mishina, E. A., *Russkaia graviura na dereve XVII–XVIII* (St Petersburg: Dmitrii Bulanin, 2000).

Moiseeva, G. (ed.), *Russkie povesti pervoi treti XVIII veka* (Leningrad: Nauka, 1965).

Morris, Marcia A., *The Literature of Roguery in Seventeenth- and Eighteenth-Century Russia* (Evanston: Northwestern University Press, 2000).

Moser, C. (ed.), *The Cambridge History of Russian Literature* (Cambridge: Cambridge University Press, 1982).

Norman, Geraldine, *The Hermitage: The Biography of a Great Museum* (London: Jonathan Cape, 1997).

O'Malley, Lurana, 'How Great *Was* Catherine? Checkpoints at the Border of Russian Theater', *Slavonic and East European Journal*, 43 (1999): 33–48.

Okenfuss, Max, 'The Jesuit Origins of Petrine Education', in J. Garrard (ed.), *The Eighteenth Century in Russia* (Oxford: Oxford University Press, 1973), pp. 106–30.

The Discovery of Childhood in Russia: The Evidence of the Slavic Primer (Newtonville: Academic International Press, 1980).

The Rise and Fall of Latin Humanism in Early Modern Russia (Leiden: Brill, 1995).

Piotrovskii, M. V. (ed.), *Osnovateliu Peterburga. Katalog vystavki* (St Petersburg: Ermitazh, 2003).

Porfir'eva, A. L. (ed.), *Muzykal'nyi Peterburg: entsiklopedicheskii slovar'*, 4 vols. (St Petersburg: Kompozitor, 1996–2001).

Pushkin, A., *Complete Prose Fiction*, trans., intro. and notes Paul Debreczeny (Stanford: Stanford University Press, 1983).

Pyman, A., *A History of Russian Symbolism* (Cambridge: Cambridge University Press, 1994).

Rzhevsky, N. (ed.), *The Cambridge Companion to Modern Russian Culture* (Cambridge: Cambridge University Press, 1998).

Sarabianov, D., *From Neoclassicism to the Avant-Garde: Painting, Sculpture, Architecture* (London: Thames and Hudson, 1990).

Sarabianov, D. *Rossiia i zapad: XVIII–nachalo XX veka* (Moscow: Iskusstvo XXI vek, 1998).

Savinov, A. *Ivan Nikitin 1688–1741* (Moscow: Iskusstvo, 1945).

Segal, H. B. (ed.), *The Literature of Eighteenth-Century Russia*, 2 vols. (New York: E. P. Dixon, 1967).

Shitsgal, A. G. (ed.), *Grazhdanskii shrift pervoi chetverti XVIII veka 1708–1725* (Moscow: Kniga, 1981).

Shvidkovskii, D. O., *The Empress and the Architect: British Gardens and Follies in St Petersburg, 1750–1830* (New Haven and London: Yale University Press, 1996).

Stasov, V., *Selected Essays on Music* (London: Barrie and Rockliff, 1968).

Stavrou, T. G. (ed.), *Art and Culture in Nineteenth-Century Russia* (Bloomington: Indiana University Press, 1983).

Taruskin, R., *Stravinsky and the Russian Traditions*, 2 vols. (Oxford: Oxford University Press, 1966).

Valkenier, E. K., *Russian Realist Art, the State, and Society: The Peredvizhniki and their Tradition* (New York: Columbia University Press, 1989).

Valentin Serov: Portraits of Russia's Silver Age (Evanston: Northwestern University Press, 2001).

Vlasto, A. P., *A Linguistic History of Russia to the End of the Eighteenth Century* (Oxford: Clarendon Press, 1986).

Weiss, P., *Kandinsky and Old Russia* (London: Yale University Press, 1994).

Wigzell, Faith, *Reading Russian Fortunes: Print Culture, Magic and Divination in Russia from 1765* (Cambridge: Cambridge University Press, 1998).

Wirtschafter, Elise Kimerling, *The Play of Ideas in Russian Enlightenment Theater* (DeKalb: Northern Illinois University Press, 2003).

Zhivov, V. M., 'Kul'turnye reformy v sisteme preobrazovaniia Petra I', in A. Koshelev (ed.), *Iz istorii russkoi kul'tury. Tom III. (XVII–nachalo XVIII veka)* (Moscow: Iazyki russkoi kul'tury, 1996), pp. 528–83.

5. LAW

Baberowski, J., 'Rechtsanwälte in Russland, 1866–1914', in C. McClelland and S. Merl (eds.), *Professionen im modernen Europa* (Berlin: Dunckler and Humblot, 1995), pp. 29–59.

'Juden und Antisemiten in der russischen Rechtsanwaltschaft 1864–1917', *JfGO* 43 (1995): 493–518.

Autokratie und Justiz. zum Verhältnis von Rückständigkeit und Rechtsstaatlichkeit im ausgehenden Zarenreich, 1864–1914 (Frankfurt am Main: Vittorio Klostermann, 1996).

'Europa in Russland: Justizreformen im ausgehenden Zarenreich am Beispiel der Geschworenengerichte 1864–1914', in D. Beyrau, and M. Stolleis (eds.), *Reformen im Russland des 19. und 20. Jahrhunderts. Westliche Modelle und russische Erfahrungen* (Frankfurt am Main: Vittorio Klostermann, 1996), pp. 151–74.

'Auf der Suche nach Eindeutigkeit: Kolonialismus und zivilisatorische Mission im Zarenreich und in der Sowjetunion', *JfGO* 47 (1999): 482–504.

Der Feind ist überall. Stalinismus im Kaukasus (Munich: Deutsche Verlags-Anstalt, 2003).

Baranchevich, E. M., *Konokradstvo i mery protiv ego v Rossii. Sudebno-statisticheskii ocherk* (Moscow, 1898).

Berezin, V., *Mirovoi sud v provintsii. Neskol'ko slov o zemskikh i mirovykh uchrezhdeniiakh* (St Petersburg, 1883).

Breitman, G. N., *Prestupnyi mir: ocherki iz byta professional'nykh prestupnikov* (Kiev, 1901)

Brun, M. I., 'Mirovoi sud po sudebnym ustavam Aleksandra II', in *Vybornyi mirovoi sud. Sbornik statei* (St Petersburg, 1898), pp. 1–18.

Burbank, J., 'Discipline and Punish in the Moscow Bar Association', *RR* 54 (1995): 44–64.

Cherniavskii, S., *Narodnyi sud* (Kamenets-Podol'sk, 1901).

Czap. P., 'Peasant Class Courts and Peasant Customary Justice in Russia, 1861–1912', *JSH* 1, 2 (1967/68): 149–78.

Davydov, N. V., and Polianskii, N. N. (eds.), *Sudebnaia reforma*, 2 vols. (Moscow: Ob'edinenie, 1915).

Deitrikh, V. F., 'O sude prisiazhnykh' in *ZMI* 1, 6 (1895): 1–22.

Dingel'shtedt, N. A., 'Musul'manskii sud i sud'i', *ZMI* 4, 6 (1898): 58–81.

Dzhanshiev, G., *Epokha velikikh reform* (St Petersburg: Vol'f, 1907).

Foinitskii, I. Ya., *Kurs ugolovnogo sudoproizvodstva*, new edn, vol. I (St Petersburg: Al'fa, 1996).

Fon-Rezon, A. K., 'O nashem sude prisiazhnykh', *Russkii Vestnik* 182, 3 (1886): 9–70.

Frank, S. P., *Crime, Cultural Conflict, and Justice in Rural Russia, 1856–1914* (Berkeley: University of California Press, 1999).

Frierson, C., 'Crime and Punishment in the Russian Village: Rural Concepts of Criminality at the End of the Nineteenth Century', *SR* 46 (1987): 55–69.

Fuks, V., *Sud i politsiia*, 2 vols. (Moscow, 1889).

Gasman, A. G., 'Sudebnaia reforma v pribaltiiskikh guberniiakh', *ZMI* 20, 9 (1914): 146–69.

Gegidze, M. E., 'K voprosu o reforme ugolovnogo sudoproizvodstva v Zakazvkazskom krae', *ZMI* 2, 8 (1896): 37–61.

Gernet, M. N., *Sud ili samosud* (Moscow: 1917).

Gessen, I. V., *Advokatura, obshchestvo i gosudarstvo 1864–1914. Istoriia russkoi advokatury*, vol. I (Moscow: Izd. Sovetov prisiazhnykh poverennykh, 1914).

Gessen, V. M., *Sudebnaia reforma* (Izd. P. P. Gershunina, 1905).

Gorodyski, I. K., 'Ocherki sudebnoi praktiki v sviazi s eia bytovymi usloviiami', *ZMI* 2, 9 (1896): 45–77; 2, 10 (1896): 27–55.

Hildermeier, M., 'Das Privileg der Rückständigkeit. Anmerkungen zum Wandel einer Interpretationsfigur in der neueren russischen Geschichte', *Historische Zeitschrift* 224 (1987): 557–603.

Iakushkin, E. I., 'Zametki o vliianii religioznykh verovanii i predrassudkov na narodnye iuridicheskie obychai i poniatiia', *Etnograficheskoe obozrenie* (1891), no. 2: 1–19.

Isaev, M., *Podpol'naia advokatura* (Moscow, 1924).

Kaiser, F. B., *Die Russische Justizreform von 1864. Zur Geschichte der russischen Justiz von Katharina II bis 1917* (Leiden: Brill, 1972).

Kapustin, N. S., *Statistika suda prisiazhnykh. Sbornik pravovedeniia i obshchestvennykh znanii*, 3 vols. (St Petersburg, 1894).

Kazantsev, S. M., 'Sudebnaia reforma 1864 goda i reorganizatsiia prokuratury', in *Gosudarstvennoe upravlenie i pravo* (Leningrad: Nauka, 1984), pp. 83–100.

Istoriia tsarskoi prokuratury (St Petersburg: Izd. SPbu, 1993).

Khrulev, S. S., 'O sposobe i poriadke sostavleniia spiskov prisiazhnykh zasedatelei', *Iuridicheskii Vestnik* 16, 5/6 (1884): 196–215.

Kolmakov, N. M., 'Staryi sud', *Russkaia Starina* 52, 12 (1886): 511–44.

Koni, A. F., *Za poslednye gody* (St Petersburg, 1898).

Koni, A. F., *Ottsy i deti sudebnoi reformy. K piatidesiatiletiiu sudebnykh ustavov* (Moscow: Izdanie I. D. Sytina, 1914).

'Novyi sud', *ZMI* 22, 4 (1916): 1–33.

Koni, A. F., *Sobranie sochinenii*, vols. I–II (Moscow: Iuridicheskaia literatura, 1966).

Krasovskii, M. V., 'O nedostatkakh nyneshnago ustroistva mirovykh sudebnykh ustanovlenii', *ZGUP* 18, 4 (1888): 30–57.

Kriukovskii, V. I., 'Sushchestvennyia cherty preobrazovaniia mestnogo suda po zakonu 15 iiuniia 1912 goda', *ZMI* 20, 5 (1914): 117–42.

Kucherov, S., 'Administration of Justice under Nicholas I of Russia', *American Slavonic and East European Review* 7 (1948): 125–38.

Courts, Lawyers and Trials under the Last Three Tsars (New York: Praeger, 1953).

LeDonne, J., 'The Judicial Reform of 1775 in Central Russia', *JfGO* 21 (1973): 29–45.

Levenstim, A. A., 'Konokradstvo s iuridicheskoi i bytovoi storony', *Vestnik prava* 29, 2 (1899): 28–82.

'Sueverie i ugolovnoe pravo. Issledovanie po istorii russkogo prava i kul'tury', *Vestnik prava* (1996), no. 1: 291–343; no. 2: 181–251.

Luhmann, N., *Das Recht der Gesellschaft* (Frankfurt am Main: Suhrkamp, 1995).

Maklakov, V. A., 'Local Justice in Russia', *RR* 2 (1913): 127–46.

Mal'tsev, S. F., 'Kassatsiia opravdatel'nykh prigovorov', *ZMI* 5, 10 (1899): 122–41.

Moshinskii, I., 'Politicheskaia zashchita v dorevoliutsionnykh sudakh', in Vilenskii, V. V. (ed.), *Deviatyi val. K desiatiletiiu osvobozhdeniia iz tsarskoi katorgi i ssylki* (Moscow, 1927), pp. 44–71.

Nabokow, W., 'Das aussergerichtliche Strafverfahren', in J. Melnik (ed.), *Russen über Russland. Ein Sammelwerk* (Frankfurt am Main, 1906), pp. 297–315.

Nos', A. E., *Mirovoi sud v Moskve. Ocherki razbiratel'stva u mirovykh sudei*, vol. I (Moscow: Izd. Cherkesova, 1869).

'O sudebnoi reforme v Turkestanskom krae i Stepnykh oblastiakh', *ZMI* 5, 2 (1899): 63–110.

Okolovich, B. I., 'Ob usloviiakh sledstvennoi sluzhby v okruge Bakinskago suda', *ZMI* 19, 8 (1913): 147–76.

Pearson, Th., 'Russian Law and Rural Justice: Activity and Problems of the Russian Justices of the Peace', *JfGO* 32 (1984): 52–71.

Petrogradskii mirovoi sud za piat'desiat let 1866–1916, 2 vols. (Petrograd, 1916).

Polianskii, N. N., *Epopeia voenno-polevykh sudov 1906–1907 gg.* (Moscow: Izd. Vsesoiuznogo obshchestva politkatorzhan, 1934).

Pomeranz, W. E., 'Justice from Underground: The History of the Underground Advokatura', *RR* 52 (1993): 321–40.

Rawson, D., 'The Death Penalty in Late Tsarist Russia', *RH* 11 (1984): 29–58.

Rennenkampf, N., 'Neskol'ko slov ob usloviiakh sledovatel'skoi deiatel'nosti v Turkestanskom krae', *ZMI* 2, 2 (1896): 212–24.

Schader, A. M., *Languages of the Lash: Corporal Punishment and Identity in Imperial Russia* (DeKalb: Northern Illinois University Press, 2002).

Schmidt, C., *Sozialkontrolle in Moskau. Justiz, Kriminalität und Leibeigenschaft 1649–1785* (Stuttgart: Steiner Verlag, 1996).

Shrag, I. L., 'Krest'ianskie sudy Vladimirskoi i Moskovskoi gubernii', *Iuridcheskii vestnik* (1877), nos. 3–4: 1–48; nos. 5–6: 52–101; nos. 7–8: 58–86; nos. 9–10: 61–99.

Skripilev, E. A. (ed.), *Razvitie russkogo prava vo vtoroi polovine XIX – nachale XX veka* (Moscow: Nauka, 1997).

Sliozberg, G. B., *Dela minuvshikh dnei*, vol. I (Paris: priv. pub., 1933).

Sluchevskii, V. K., 'Iz pervykh let zhizni sudebnykh ustavov', *ZMI* 20, 2 (1914): 181–233.

Spasovich, V. D., *Sochineniia*, 10 vols. (St Petersburg: knizhnii magazin brat'ev Rymovich, 1889–1902).

'Sudebnaia reforma v Sibirii', *ZMI* 2, 6 (1896): 145–60.

Sudebnye ustavy 20 noiabria 1864 goda za piat'desiat let, 2 vols. (Petrograd, 1914).

Svod zamechanii o priminenii na praktike sudebnykh ustavov (1869–1870) (n.p.: n.d.).

Tarnovskii, E. N., 'Otnoshenie chisla opravdannykh k chislu podsudimykh v evropeiskoi Rossii za 1889–1893 gg. (Sravnitel'no-statisticheskii ocherk)', *ZMI* 3, 9 (1897): 169–89.

Tenishev, V. V., *Pravosudie v russkom krest'ianskom bytu* (Briansk, 1907).

Timofeev, N., *Sud prisiazhnykh v Rossii* (Moscow, 1881).

Tsukhanov, 'O nedostatkakh nashego suda prisiazhnykh', *ZGUP* 11, 2 (1882): 81–109; 11, 3 (1882): 133–58.

Tumanov, G. M., *Razboi i reforma suda na kavkaze* (St Petersburg, 1903).

Vilenskii B. V. (ed.), *Sudebnaia reforma. Rossiiskoe zakonodatel'stvo X–XX vekov*, vol. VIII (Moscow: Iuridicheskaia literatura, 1991).

Vinaver, M. M., *Ocherki ob advokature* (St Petersburg: Tip. M. M. Stasiulevicha, 1902).

Vladimirov, L. E., *Advocatus miles. Posobie dlia ugolovnoi zashchity* (St Petersburg: Zakonovedenie, 1911).

Volodimirov, V., 'Mirovoi sud v Peterburge', *ZGUP* 14, 5 (1884): 1–58.

Vysochaishe uchrezhdennaia komissiia dlia peresmotra zakonopolozhenii po sudebnoi chasti. Trudy, 9 vols. (St Petersburg, 1895–9).

Vysochaishe uchrezhdennaia komissiia dlia peresmotra zakonopolozhenii po sudebnoi chasti. Podgotovitel'nye materialy, 12 vols. (St Petersburg, 1894–5).

Wagner, William G., *Marriage, Property, and Law in Late Imperial Russia* (Oxford: Clarendon Press, 1994).

Worobec, C. D., 'Horsethieves and Peasant Justice in Post Emancipation Russia', *Journal of Social History* 21 (1987): 281–93.

Wortman, R., *The Development of a Russian Legal Consciousness* (Chicago: University of Chicago Press, 1976).

Zakrevskii, I. P., 'O zhelatel'nykh izmeneniiach v sudebnykh ustavach', *ZGUP* 11, 2 (1882): 17–57.

Zavadskii, V. R., 'V zale zasedanii s prisiazhnymi zasedateliami. Iz otchetov revizora', *ZMI* 2, 3 (1896): 104–28.

Zviagintsev, A. G., and Orlov, Yu. G., *Pod sen'iu russkogo orla. Rossiiskie prokurory. Vtoraia polovina XIX – nachalo XX v.* (Moscow: Rosspen, 1996).

Zviagintsev, A. G., and Orlov, Iu. G., *V epokhu potriasenii i reform. Rossiiskie prokurory 1906–1907* (Moscow: Rosspen, 1996).

6. NATIONS, NATIONALITIES POLICY, IDENTITIES

Aronson, I. M., *Troubled Waters: The Origins of the 1881 Anti-Jewish Pogroms in Russia* (Pittsburgh: University of Pittsburgh Press, 1990).

Bauer, H., Kappeler, A., and Roth, B. (eds.), *Die Nationalitäten des Russischen Reiches in der Volkszahlung von 1897*, 2 vols. (Stuttgart: Franz Steiner, 1991).

Beauvois, D., *Le Noble, le serf, et le revizor: La noblesse polonaise entre le tsarisme et les masses ukrainiennes (1831–1863)* (Paris: Editions des archives contemporaines, 1985).

La Bataille de la terre en Ukraine, 1863–1914: Les Polonais et les conflits socio-ethniques (Lille: Presses universitaires de Lille, 1993).

Pouvoir russe et noblesse polonaise en Ukraine, 1793–1830 (Paris: CNRS editions, 2003).

Becker, S., *Russia's Protectorates in Central Asia: Bukhara and Khiva, 1865–1924* (Cambridge, Mass.: Harvard University Press, 1968).

Brower, D. R., *Turkestan and the Fate of the Russian Empire* (London: Routledge/Curzon, 2003).

Brower, D. R., and Lazzerini, E. (eds.), *Russia's Orient: Imperial Borderlands and Peoples 1700–1917* (Bloomington: Indiana University Press, 1997).

Bushkovitch, P., 'The Ukraine in Russian Culture', *JfGO* 39, 3 (1991): 339–63.

Carrère d'Encausse, H., *Islam and the Russian Empire: Reform and Revolution in Central Asia* (Berkeley: University of California Press, 1988).

Chmielewski, E., *The Polish Question in the Russian State Duma* (Knoxville: University of Tennessee Press, 1970).

Corssin, S., *Warsaw before the First World War: Poles and Jews in the Third City of the Russian Empire, 1880–1914* (Boulder: Westview, 1989).

Donnelly, A., *The Russian Conquest of Bashkiria 1552–1740: A Case Study in Imperialism* (New Haven: Yale University Press, 1968).

Eisenbach, A., *The Emancipation of the Jews in Poland, 1780–1870* (Oxford: Blackwell, 1991).

Fisher, A. W., *The Crimean Tatars* (Stanford: Hoover, 1978).

Frank, A. J., *Muslim Religious Institutions in Imperial Russia: The Islamic World of Novouzensk District and the Kazakh Inner Horde, 1780–1910* (Leiden: Brill, 2001).

Frankel, J., *Prophecy and Politics: Socialism, Nationalism and the Russian Jews, 1860–1917* (Cambridge: Cambridge University Press, 1981).

Gammer, M., *Muslim Resistance to the Tsar: Shamil and the Conquest of Chechnia and Daghestan.* (London: Frank Cass, 1994).

Gatrell, P., *A Whole Empire Walking: Refugees in Russia during World War I* (Bloomington: Indiana University Press, 1999).

Geiss, P. G., *Pre-Tsarist and Tsarist Central Asia: Communal Commitment and Political Order in Change* (London: Routledge, 2003).

Geraci, R., *Window on the East: National and Imperial Identities in Late Tsarist Russia* (Ithaca: Cornell University Press, 2001).

Geraci, R., and Khodarkovsky, M. (eds.), *Of Religion and Empire: Missions, Conversion and Tolerance in Tsarist Russia* (Ithaca: Cornell University Press, 2001).

Guesnet, F., *Polnische Juden im 19. Jahrhundert: Lebensbedingungen, Rechtsnormen und Organisation im Wandel* (Cologne: Böhlau, 1998).

Haberer, E., *Jews and Revolution in Nineteenth-Century Russia* (Cambridge: Cambridge University Press, 1995).

Haltzel, M., *Der Abbau der deutschen standischen Selbstverwaltung in den Ostseeprovinzen Russlands 1855–1905* (Marburg: Herder-Institut, 1977).

Hamm, M., *Kiev: A Portrait, 1800–1917* (Princeton: Princeton University Press, 1993).

Hrushevsky, M., *A History of Ukraine* (New Haven: Yale University Press, 1941).

Hundert, G., *Jews in Poland-Lithuania in the Eighteenth Century: A Genealogy of Modernity* (Berkeley: University of California Press, 2004).

Isakov, S. G., *Ostzeiskii vopros v russkoi pechati 1860-kh godov* (Tartu: Riikliku Ulikool, 1961).

Jersild, A., *Orientalism and Empire: North Caucasian Mountain Peoples and the Georgian Frontier 1845–1917* (Montreal: McGill-Queen's University Press, 2002).

Kabuzan, V. M., *Izmenenie v razmeshchenii naselenia Rossii v XVIII – pervoi polovine XIXv.* (Moscow: Izd. AN SSSR, 1971).

Narody Rossii v XVIIIv. Chislennost' i etnicheskii sostav (Moscow: Nauka, 1990).

Kappeler, A., *Russlands erste Nationalitäten. Das Zarenreich und die Volker der Mittleren Wolga vom 16 bis 19. Jahrhundert* (Cologne: Böhlau, 1982).

Die Russen: Ihr Nationalbewusstein in Geschichte und Gegenwart (Cologne: Markus, 1990).

The Russian Empire: A Multiethnic History (New York: Pearson Education, 2001).

(ed.), *The Formation of National Elites* (Aldershot: Dartmouth Publishing, 1992).

Katz, M., *Mikhail N. Katkov: A Political Biography, 1818–1887* (The Hague: Nijhoff, 1966).

Kemper, M., *Sufis und Gelehrte in Tatarien und Baschkirien, 1789–1889* (Berlin: Klaus Schwartz verlag, 1998).

Khalid, A., *The Politics of Muslim Cultural Reform: Jadidism in Central Asia* (Berkeley: University of California Press, 1998).

Khodarkovsky, M., *Where Two Worlds Met: The Russian State and the Kalmyk Nomads, 1600–1917* (Ithaca: Cornell University Press, 1992).

Russia's Steppe Frontier: The Making of a Colonial Empire, 1500–1800 (Bloomington: Indiana University Press, 2002).

Kienewicz, S., *The Emancipation of the Polish Peasantry* (Chicago: University of Chicago Press, 1969).

Kirby, D. (ed.), *Finland and Russia 1808–1920. From Autonomy to Independence* (Basingstoke: Macmillan, 1975).

Klier, J., *Russia Gathers her Jews. The Origins of the 'Jewish Question' in Russia, 1772–1825* (DeKalb: Northern. Illinois University Press, 1986).

Imperial Russia's Jewish Question, 1855–1881 (Cambridge: Cambridge University Press, 1995).

Klier, J., and Lambroza, S. (eds.), *Anti-Jewish Violence in Modern Russian History* (Cambridge: Cambridge University Press, 1992).

Kohut, Z., *Russian Centralism and Ukrainian Autonomy: Imperial Absorption of the Hetmanate, 1760s–1830s* (Cambridge, Mass.: Harvard University Press, 1988).

Kostiushkov, I. I., *Krestianskaia reforma 1864 goda v Tsarstve Pol'skom* (Moscow: Izd. AN SSSR, 1962).

Landa, R. G., *Islam v istorii Rossii* (Moscow: Vostochnaia literatura, 1995).

Layton, S., *Russian Literature and Empire: Conquest of the Caucasus from Pushkin to Tolstoy* (Cambridge: Cambridge University Press, 1994).

Lederhendler, E., *The Road to Modern Jewish Politics: Political Tradition and Political Reconstruction in the Jewish Community of Tsarist Russia* (New York: Oxford University Press, 1989).

Leslie, R. F., *Polish Politics and the Revolution of November 1830* (Westport: Greenwood, 1969).

Lohr, E., *Nationalizing the Russian Empire: The Campaign Against Enemy Aliens during World War I* (Cambridge, Mass.: Harvard University Press, 2003).
Lowe, H., *The Tsars and the Jews: Reform, Reaction and Anti-Semitism in Imperial Russia* (New York: Oxford University Press, 1992).
McNeill, R. H., *Tsar and Cossack: 1855–1914* (Houndmills: Macmillan, 1987).
Mendelsohn, E., *Class Struggle in the Pale: The Formative Years of the Jewish Workers' Movement in Tsarist Russia* (Cambridge: Cambridge University Press, 1970).
Nathans, B., *Beyond the Pale: The Jewish Encounter with Late Imperial Russia* (Berkeley: University of California Press, 2002).
Nolde, B. E., *La Formation de l'Empire russe*, 2 vols. (Paris: Institut d'etudes slaves, 1952–53).
Olcott, M. B., *The Kazakhs* (Stanford: Hoover, 1987).
O'Rourke, S., *Warriors and Peasants: The Don Cossacks in Late Imperial Russia* (Houndmills: Macmillan, 2000).
Petrovich, M. B., *The Emergence of Russian Panslavism 1856–1870* (New York: Columbia University Press, 1956).
Pierce, R., *Russia in Central Asia 1867–1917: A Study in Colonial Rule* (Los Angeles: University of California Press, 1960).
Pistohlkors, G. von, *Ritterschaftliche Reformpolitik zwischen Russifizierung und Revolution* (Göttingen: Musterschmidt, 1978).
Porter, B., *When Nationalism Began to Hate: Imagining Modern Politics in Nineteenth-Century Poland* (New York: Oxford University Press, 2000).
Prozorov, S. M. (ed.), *Islam na teritorii byvshei Rossiiskoi imperii* (Moscow: Vostochnaia literatura, 1999).
Rogger, H., *Jewish Policies and Right-Wing Politics in Imperial Russia* (Basingstoke: Macmillan, 1986).
Rorlich, A.-A., *The Volga Tatars: A Profile in National Resilience* (Stanford: Hoover, 1986).
Rywkin, M. (ed.), *Russian Colonial Expansion to 1917* (London: Mansell, 1988).
Saunders, D., *The Ukrainian Impact on Russian Culture 1750–1830* (Edmonton: CIUS, 1985).
Schweitzer, R., *Autonomie und Autokratie. Die Stellung des Grossfurstentums Finnland im russischen Reich in der zweiten Hälfte des 19. Jahrhunderts* (Giessen: Wilhelm Schmitz, 1978).
Slezkine, Y., *Arctic Mirrors: Russia and the Small Peoples of the North* (Ithaca: University of California Press, 1994).
The Jewish Century (Princeton: Princeton University Press, 2004).
Slocum, J. W., 'Who and When were the Inorodtsy? The Evolution of the Category of "Aliens" in Imperial Russia', *RR* 57, 2, (1988): 173–90.
Snyder, T., *Nationalism, Marxism, and Modern Central Europe: A Biography of Kazimierz Kelles-Krauz, 1872–1905* (Cambridge, Mass.: Harvard University Press, 1998).
The Reconstruction of Nations: Poland, Ukraine, Lithuania, Belarus, 1569–1999 (New Haven: Yale University Press, 2003).
Solzhenitsyn, A., *Dvesti let vmeste (1795–1995)*, 2 vols. (Moscow: Russkii put', 2001–2).
Stanislawski, M., *Tsar Nicholas I and the Jews: The Transformation of Jewish Society in Russia, 1825–1855*. (Philadelphia: University of Pennsylvania Press, 1983).
For Whom Do I Toil? Judah Leib Gordon and the Crisis of Russian Jewry (New York: Oxford University Press, 1988).

Subtelny, O., *The Mazepists: Ukrainian Separatism in the Early Eighteenth Century* (New York: Columbia University Press, 1982).

Ukraine: A History (Toronto: University of Toronto Press, 1988).

Suny, R. G., *Looking Towards Ararat: Armenia in Modern History* (Bloomington: Indiana University Press, 1993).

The Making of the Georgian Nation (Bloomington: Indiana University Press, 1994).

(ed.), *Transcaucasia: Nationalism and Social Change* (Ann Arbor: University of Michigan Press, 1983).

Thackeray, F. W., *Antecedants of Revolution: Alexander I and the Polish Kingdom 1815–1825* (Boulder: Westview, 1980).

Thaden, E. C., *Russia's Western Borderlands, 1710–1870* (Princeton: Princeton University Press, 1984).

(ed.), *Russification in the Baltic Provinces and Finland, 1855–1914* (Princeton: Princeton University Press, 1981).

Vital, D., *The Origins of Zionism* (Oxford: Oxford University Press, 1975).

Vucinich, W. S. (ed.), *Russia and Asia: Essays on the Influence of Russia on the Asian Peoples* (Stanford: Stanford University Press, 1971).

Walicki, A., *Philosophy and Romantic Nationalism: The Case of Poland* (Notre Dame: University of Notre Dame Press, 1982).

The Enlightenment and the Birth of Modern Nationhood: Polish Political Thought from Noble Republicanism to Tadeusz Kosciuszko (Notre Dame: University of Notre Dame Press, 1989).

Wandycz, P. S., *The Lands of Partitioned Poland 1795–1918* (Seattle: University of Washington Press, 1974).

Weeks, T. R., *Nation and State in Late Imperial Russia: Nationalism and Russification on the Western Frontier, 1863–1914* (DeKalb: Northern Illinois University Press, 1996).

Werth, P. W., *At the Margins of Orthodoxy: Mission, Governance and Confessional Politics in Russia's Volga-Kama Region 1827–1905* (Ithaca: Cornell University Press, 2002).

Whelan, H. W., *Adapting to Modernity: Family, Caste and Capitalism among the Baltic German Nobility* (Cologne: Böhlau Verlag, 1999).

Wittram, R., *Baltische Geschichte* (Munich: Oldenbourg, 1954).

Zelkina, A., *In Quest for God and Freedom. Sufi Responses to the Russian Advance in the North Caucasus* (London: Hurst, 2000).

Zenkovsky, S. A., *Pan-Turkism and Islam in Russia* (Cambridge, Mass.: Harvard University Press, 1960).

Zipperstein, S., *The Jews of Odessa: A Cultural History, 1794–1881* (Stanford: Stanford University Press, 1986).

Elusive Prophet: Ahad Ha'am and the Origins of Zionism (Berkeley: University of California Press, 1993).

7A: ELITES

Amburger, E., *Geshchichte der Behordenorganisation Russlands von Peter dem Grossen bis 1917* (Leiden: Brill, 1966).

Becker, S., *Nobility and Privilege in Late Imperial Russia* (DeKalb: Northern Illinois University Press, 1985).

Confino, M., *Domaines et seigneurs en Russie vers la fin du XVIIIe siècle. Étude de structures agraires et de mentalites economiques* (Paris: Institut d'etudes slaves, 1963.)

Dolgorukov, P. P., *Rossiiskaia rodoslovnaia kniga*, 4 vols. (St Petersburg, 1854–7).

Emmons, T., *The Russian Landed Gentry and the Peasant Emancipation of 1861* (Cambridge: Cambridge University Press, 1968).

Hamburg, G. M., *Politics of the Russian Nobility 1881–1905* (New Brunswick: Rutgers University Press, 1984).

Ikonnikov, N. I., *La Noblesse de Russie*, 2nd edn, vols. A1–Z2 (Paris: priv. pub. 1958–66).

Jones, R. E., *The Emancipation of the Russian Nobility 1762–1785* (Princeton: Princeton University Press, 1973).

Karnovich, E. P., *Zamechatel'naia bogatstva chastnikh lits v Rossii* (St Petersburg: Suvorin, 1885).

Khristoforov, I. A., *'Aristokraticheskaia' oppozitsiia velikim reformam* (Moscow: Russkoe slovo, 2002).

Korelin, A. P., *Dvorianstvo v poreformennoi Rossii* (Moscow: Nauka, 1979).

LeDonne, J., 'Ruling Families in the Russian Political Order 1689–1825', *CMRS* 3 and 4 (1987): 233–322.

Lieven, D., 'The Russian Civil Service under Nicholas II: Some Variations on the Bureaucratic Theme', *JfGO* 29 (1981): 366–403.

Russia's Rulers under the Old Regime (London: Yale University Press, 1989).

The Aristocracy in Europe 1815–1914 (London: Macmillan, 1992).

Lincoln, B., *In the Vanguard of Reform: Russia's Enlightened Bureaucrats 1825–1861* (DeKalb: Northern Illinois University Press, 1982)

Lotman, Iu. M., *Besedy o russkoi kul'ture: byt i traditsii russkogo dvorianstva (XVIII–nachalo XIX veka)* (St Petersburg: Iskusstvo-SPb, 1994).

Madariaga, I. de, 'The Russian Nobility in the Seventeenth and Eighteenth Centuries', in H. M. Scott (ed.), *The European Nobilities in the Seventeenth and Eighteenth Centuries* (London: Longman, 1995).

Meehan-Waters, B., *Autocracy and Aristocracy: The Russian Service Elite of 1730* (New Brunswick: Rutgers University Press, 1982).

Minarik, L. P., *Ekonomicheskaia kharakteristika krupneishikh sobstvennikov Rossii kontsa XIX–nachala XX vek* (Moscow: Nauka, 1971).

Pintner, W., and Rowney, D. K. (eds.), *Russian Officialdom: The Bureaucratization of Russian Society from the Seventeenth to the Twentieth Century* (London: Macmillan, 1980).

Raeff, M., *Origins of the Russian Intelligentsia* (New York: Harcourt, Brace and World, 1966).

Romanovich-Slavatinskii, A., *Dvorianstvo v Rossii,* new edn. (Moscow: Izd. Kraft, 2003).

Roosevelt, P., *Life on the Russian Country Estate: A Social and Cultural History* (New Haven: Yale University Press, 1995).

Tillander-Godenhielm, U., *The Russian Imperial Award System 1894–1917* (Helsinki: SMYA, 2005).

Torke, H. J., 'Das russische Beamtentum in der ersten Hälfte des 19 Jahrhunderts', *Forschungen zur Geshchichte Osteuropas* 13 (1967): 7–345.

Troitskii, S. M., *Russkii absoliutizm i dvorianstvo v XVIIIv*. (Moscow: Nauka, 1974).

7B: URBAN SOCIETY

Annenskii, N. F., 'Zemskii kadastr i zemskaia statistika', *Trudy pod sektsii statistiki IX s'ezda russkikh estestvoispytatelei i vrachei* (Chernigov, 1894).

Balzer, H. D. (ed.), *Russia's Missing Middle Class: The Professions in Russian History* (Armonk: M. E. Sharpe, 1996).

Brower, Daniel, R., 'The Problem of the Russian Intelligentsia', *SR* 26 (1967): 638–47.

Training the Nihilists: Education and Radicalism in Tsarist Russia (Ithaca: Cornell University Press, 1975).

Burbank, Jane, 'Were the Russian *Intelligenty* Organic Intellectuals?' in L. Fink, S. T. Leonard, and D. M. Reid (eds.), *Intellectuals and Public Life: Between Radicalism and Reform* (Ithaca: Cornell University Press, 1996).

Clowes, E. W., Kassow, S. D., and West, J. L. (eds.), *Between Tsar and People: Educated Society and the Quest for Public Identity in Late Imperial Russia* (Princeton: Princeton University Press, 1991).

Confino, M., 'On Intellectuals and Intellectual Traditions in Eighteenth- and Nineteenth-Century Russia', *Daedalus* 101 (1972): 117–49.

Eklof, Ben, *Russian Peasant Schools: Officialdom, Village Culture, and Popular Pedagogy, 1861–1914* (Berkeley: University of California Press, 1986).

Evtuhov, C., 'Voices from the Provinces: Living and Writing in Nizhnii Novgorod, 1870–1905', *Journal of Popular Culture* 31, 4 (Spring 1998): 33–48.

Farrell, Dianne E., 'Popular Prints in the Cultural History of Eighteenth-Century Russia', unpublished PhD dissertation, University of Wisconsin-Madison (1980).

Frieden, N. M., *Russian Physicians in an Era of Reform and Revolution, 1856–1905* (Princeton: Princeton University Press, 1981).

Frierson, C. A., *Peasant Icons: Representations of Rural People in Late Nineteenth-Century Russia* (New York: Oxford University Press, 1993).

Hellie, R., 'The Stratification of Muscovite Society: The Townsmen', *RH* 5 (1978): 119–75.

Hutchinson, J. F., 'Society, Corporation, or Union? Russian Physicians and the Struggle for Professional Unity (1890–1913)', *JfGO* 30 (1982): 37–53.

Johnson, R. E., *Peasant and Proletarian: The Working Class of Moscow in the Late Nineteenth Century* (New Brunswick: Rutgers University Press, 1979).

Khasanova, S. I., 'K voprosu ob izuchenii intelligentsii dorevoliutsionnoi Rossii', in G. N. Vul'fson (ed.), *Revoliutsionno-osvoboditel'noe dvizhenie v XIX–XX vv. v Povolzh'e i Priural'e* (Kazan: Izd. Kazanskogo Universiteta, 1974).

Laverychev, V. Ia., *Tsarizm i rabochii vopros v Rossii (1861–1917 gg.)* (Moscow: Nauka, 1970).

Leikina-Svirskaia, V. R., 'Formirovanie raznochinskoi intelligentsii v Rossii v 40-kh godakh XIX v.', *Istoriia SSSR*, 1 (1958): 83–104.

Intelligentsiia v Rossii vo vtoroi polovine XIX veka (Moscow: Mysl', 1971)

Marker, Gary, 'The Creation of Journals and the Profession of Letters in the Eighteenth Century', in D. A. Martinsen (ed.), *Literary Journals in Imperial Russia* (Cambridge: Cambridge University Press, 1997).

Melton, James Van Horn, *The Rise of the Public in Enlightenment Europe* (Cambridge: Cambridge University Press, 2001).

Mendelsohn, E., and Shatz, M. (eds.), *Imperial Russia, 1700–1917: State, Society, Opposition. Essays in Honor of Marc Raeff* (DeKalb: Northern Illinois University Press, 1988).

Muller, Otto, *Intelligencija. Untersuchungen zur Geschichte eines politischen Schlagwortes* (Frankfurt: Athenaum, 1971).

Nahirny, Vladimir C., 'The Russian Intelligentsia: From Men of Ideas to Men of Convictions', *Comparative Studies in Society and History* 4 (1962): 403–35.

The Russian Intelligentsia: From Torment to Silence (New Brunswick: Transaction Books, 1983).

Netting, A., 'Russian Liberalism: The Years of Promise', unpublished PhD dissertation, Columbia University (1967).

Pankratova, Anna M., *Formirovanie proletariata v Rossii (XVII–XVIII vv.)* (Moscow: Nauka, 1963).

Pirumova, N. M., *Zemskoe liberal'noe dvizhenie: Sotsial'nye korni i evoliutsiia do nachala XX veka* (Moscow: Nauka, 1977).

Zemskaia intelligentsiia i ee rol' v obshchestvennoi bor'be (Moscow: Nauka, 1986).

Raeff, M., 'Transfiguration and Modernization: The Paradoxes of Social Disciplining, Paedagogical Leadership, and the Enlightenment in Eighteenth-Century Russia', in H. E. Bödeker and E. Hinrichs (eds.), *Alteuropa – Ancien Régime – Frühe Neuzeit: Probleme und Methoden der Forschung* (Stuttgart: Fromann-Holzboog, 1991).

Raleigh, Donald, 'The Impact of World War I on Saratov and its Revolutionary Movement', in R. Wade and S. Seregny (eds.), *Politics and Society in Provincial Russia: Saratov, 1590–1917* (Columbus: Ohio University Press, 1989).

Semenov, A. A., and Khorev, M. M., *A.O. Karelin: tvorcheskoe nasledie* (Nizhnii Novgorod: Volgo-Viatskoe knizhnoe izd. 1990).

Seregny, Scott, *Russian Teachers and Peasant Revolution: The Politics of Education in 1905* (Bloomington: Indiana University Press, 1989).

Shepelev, L. E., *Chinovnyi mir Rossii XVIII–nachalo XX v.* (St Petersburg: Iskusstvo, 1999).

Shmidt, S. O., 'K istorii slova "intelligentsiia"', repr. in *Obshchestvennoe samosoznanie rossiiskogo blagorodnogo sosloviia, XVII-pervaia tret' XIX veka* (Moscow: Nauka, 2002).

Shtrange, M. M., *Demokraticheskaia intelligentsiia Rossii v XVIII veke* (Moscow: Nauka, 1965).

Steinberg, Mark D., *Moral Communities: The Culture of Class Relations in the Russian Printing Industry, 1867–1907* (Berkeley: University of California Press, 1992).

Ulianova, G., 'Entrepreneurs and Philanthropy in Nizhnii Novgorod, from the Nineteenth Century to the Beginning of the Twentieth Century', in W. Brumfield, B. Anan'ich and Iu. Petrov, *Commerce in Russian Urban Culture, 1861–1914* (Washington/Baltimore: Johns Hopkins Press, 2001), pp. 90–107.

Vinogradova, T. P., *Nizhegorodskaia intelligentsiia vokrug N. A. Dobroliubova* (Nizhnii Novgorod: Volgo-Viatskoe knizhnoe izd., 1992).

Wirtschafter, E. K., *Structures of Society: Imperial Russia's 'People of Various Ranks'* (DeKalb: Northern Illinois University Press, 1994).

'Social Misfits: Veterans and Soldiers' Families in Servile Russia', *Journal of Military History* 59 (1995): 215–35.

'Legal Identity and the Possession of Serfs in Imperial Russia', *JMH* 70 (1998): 561–87.

The Play of Ideas in Russian Enlightenment Theater (DeKalb: Northern Illinois University Press, 2003).

Wynn, C., *Workers, Strikes and Pogroms: The Donbass-Dnepr Bend in Late Imperial Russia 1870–1905* (Princeton: Princeton University Press, 1992).

Zelnik, R. E., 'The Peasant and the Factory', in W. S. Vuchinich (ed.), *The Peasant in Nineteenth Century Russia* (Stanford: Stanford University Press, 1968).

Law and Disorder on the Narova River: The Kreenholm Strike of 1872 (Berkeley: University of California Press, 1995).

(ed.), *Workers and Intelligentsia in Late Imperial Russia: Realities, Representations, Reflections* (Berkeley: International and Area Studies, 1999).

(ed.), *Labor and Society in Tsarist Russia: The Factory Workers of St Petersburg, 1855–1870* (Stanford: Stanford University Press, 1971).

7C. ORTHODOX CHURCH AND CLERGY

Belliustin, I. S., *Description of the Rural Clergy*, ed. G. L. Freeze (Ithaca: Cornell University Press, 1985).

Chulos, C. J., *Converging Worlds: Religion and Community in Peasant Russia, 1861–1917* (DeKalb: Northern Illinois University Press, 2003).

Freeze, G. L., *The Russian Levites* (Cambridge, Mass.: Harvard University Press, 1977).

The Parish Clergy in Nineteenth-Century Russia (Princeton: Princeton University Press, 1983).

'Die Laisierung des Archimandriten Feodor (Buchaev) und ihre kirchenpolitischen Hintergründe', *Kirche im Osten* 38 (1985): 26–52.

'Handmaiden of the State? The Church in Imperial Russia Reconsidered', *Journal of Ecclesiastical History* 36 (1985): 82–102.

'Church, State and Society in Catherinian Russia: The Synodal Instruction to the Legislative Commission', in Eberhard Müller (ed.) '*. . . aus der anmuthigen Gelehrsamkeit' Tübinger Studien zum 18. Jahrhundert* (Tübingen: Attempto Verlag, 1988), pp. 155–68.

'A Social Mission for Russian Orthodoxy', in M. Shatz and E. Mendelsohn (eds.), *Imperial Russia, 1700–1917* (DeKalb: Northern Illinois University Press, 1988), pp. 115–35.

'The Orthodox Church and Serfdom in Pre-Reform Russia', *SR* 48 (1989): 361–87.

'Subversive Piety: Religion and the Political Crisis in Late Imperial Russia', *JMH* 68 (1996): 308–50.

'Policing Piety: The Church and Popular Religion in Russia, 1750–1850', in David L. Ransel and Jane Burbank (eds.), *Rethinking Imperial Russia* (Bloomington: Indiana University Press, 1998), pp. 210–49.

'Church and Politics in Late Imperial Russia', in A. Geifman (ed.), *Russia under the Last Tsar* (Oxford: Blackwell, 1999), pp. 269–97.

'"All Power to the Parish"? The Problem and Politics of Church Reform in Late Imperial Russia', in Madhavan Palat (ed.), *Social Identities in Revolutionary Russia* (London: Macmillan, 2001), pp. 174–208.

'Lutheranism and Orthodoxy in Russia: A Critical Reassessment', in Hans Medick and P. Schmidt (eds.), *Luther zwischen Kulturen* (Göttingen: Vandenhoeck and Ruprecht, 2004), pp. 297–317.

'A Pious Folk? Religious Observance in Vladimir Diocese 1900–14', *JfGO* 52 (2004): 323–40.

'Matrimonial Sacrament and Profane Stories: Class, Gender, Confession and the Politics of Divorce in Late Imperial Russia', in M. Steinberg and H. Coleman (eds.), *Sacred Stories* (forthcoming).

Geekie, John H. M., 'The Church and Politics in Russia, 1905–17', unpublished PhD dissertation, University of East Anglia (1976).

Hauptmann, Peter, *Die Katechismen der Russisch-Orthodoxen Kirche. Entstehungsgeschichte und Lehrgehalt* (Göttingen: Vandenhoeck and Ruprecht, 1971).

Herrlinger, K. Page, 'Class, Piety, and Politics: Workers, Orthodoxy, and the Problem of Religious Identity in St Petersburg, 1881–1914', unpublished PhD dissertation, University of California at Berkeley (1996).

Kadson, I. Z., 'Krest'ianskaia voina 1773–5 gg. i tserkov', unpublished candidate dissertation, Leningradskoe otdelenie instituta istorii (1963).

Kartashev, A. V., 'Revoliutsiia i sobor 1917–1918 gg.', *Bogoslovskaia mysl'* 4 (1942): 75–101.

Kenworthy, Scott, 'The Revival of Monasticism in Modern Russia: The Trinity-Sergius Lavra, 1825–1921', unpublished PhD thesis, Brandeis University (2002).

Kivelson, V., and Greene, R. (eds.), *Orthodox Russia: Belief and Practice under the Tsars* (University Park: Penn State University Press, 2003).

Kizenko, N., *A Prodigal Saint: Father John of Kronstadt and the Russian People* (University Park: Penn State University Press, 2000).

Komissarenko, A. I., 'Votchinnoe khoziaistvo dukhovenstva i sekuliarizatsionnaia reforma v Rossii (20–60-gg. XVIII v.)', Unpublished PhD dissertation, Moscow (1984).

Lavrov, A. S., *Koldovstvo i religiia v Rossii* (Moscow: Drevlekharnilishche, 2000).

McLeod, H., *Secularisation in Western Europe, 1848–1914* (New York: St Martin's Press, 2000).

Nichols, R. L., 'The Orthodox Elder *(Startsy)* of Imperial Russia', *Modern Greek Studies Yearbook* 1 (1985): 1–30.

Parfenii (Sopkovskii) and Georgii (Konisskii), *O dolzhnostiakh presviterov prikhodskikh* (St Petersburg: Sinodal'naia tip., 1776).

Pisiotis, A., 'Orthodoxy versus Autocracy: The Orthodox Church and Clerical Political Dissent in Late Imperial Russia, 1905–14', unpublished PhD dissertation, Georgetown University (2000).

Plamper, J., 'The Russian Orthodox Episcopate, 1721–1917: A Prosopography', *JSH* 60 (2001): 5–24.

Pokrovskii, I. M., *Russkie eparkhii v XVI–XIX vv*, 2 vols. (Kazan, 1913).

Polunov, A. Iu., *Pod vlast'iu ober-prokurora* (Moscow: Aero-XX, 1995).

Rozhkov, Vladimir, *Tserkovnye voprosy v Gosudarstvennoi Dume* (Rome: Pontificium institutum orientalium studiorum, 1975).

Shevzov, Vera, *Russian Orthodoxy on the Eve of Revolution* (New York: Oxford University Press, 2004).

Smolitsch, Igor, *Russisches Mönchtum: Entstehung, Entwicklung und Wesen 988–1917* (Würzburg: Augustinus-Verlag, 1953).

Geschichte der russischen Kirche, 2 vols. (Leiden and Berlin: Brill, 1964–91).

Tikhon (Zadonskii), *Nastavlenie o sobstvennykh vsiakogo khristianina dolzhnostiakh* (St Petersburg: Sinodal'naia tip., 1789).

Titlinov, B. V., *Molodezh' i revoliutsiia* (Leningrad: Gosizdat, 1924).

Verkhovskoi, P. V., *Uchrezhdenie dukhovnoi kollegii i dukhovnyi reglament*, 2 vols. (Rostov-on-Don, 1916).

Zav'ialov, A., *Vopros o tserkovnykh imeniiakh pri Imp. Ekateriny II.* (St Petersburg, 1900).

Zyrianov, Pavel N., *Russkie monastyri i monashestvo v XIX i nachale XX veka* (Moscow: Verbum-M, 2002).

7D. WOMEN

Bernstein, L., *Sonia's Daughters: Prostitutes and Their Regulation in Imperial Russia* (Berkeley: University of California Press, 1995).

Black, J. L., 'Educating Women in Eighteenth-Century Russia: Myths and Realities', *Canadian Slavonic Papers* 20, 1 (1978): 23–43.

Curtiss, J. S., 'Russian Sisters of Mercy in the Crimea, 1854–55', *SR* 25, 1 (March 1966): 84–100.

Edmondson, L., *Feminism in Russia, 1900–1917* (Stanford: Stanford University Press, 1984).

Engel, B., 'Women as Revolutionaries: The Case of the Russian Populists', in R. Bridenthal and C. Koonz (eds.), *Becoming Visible: Women in European History*, Ist edn. (Boston: Houghton-Mifflin, 1977), pp. 346–70.

Mothers and Daughters: Women of the Intelligentsia in Nineteenth-Century Russia (New York: Cambridge University Press, 1983).

Between the Fields and the City: Women, Work and Family in Russia, 1861–1914 (New York: Cambridge University Press, 1994).

'Women, Men, and the Languages of Peasant Resistance, 1870–1907', in S. P. Frank and M. D. Steinberg (eds.), *Cultures in Flux: Lower-Class Values, Practices, and Resistance* (Princeton: Princeton University Press, 1994), pp. 34–53.

Women in Russia, 1700–2000 (New York: Cambridge University Press, 2004).

Engelstein, L., 'Gender and the Juridical Subject: Prostitution and Rape in Nineteenth-century Criminal Codes', *JMH* 60 (September 1988): 458–95.

The Keys to Happiness: Sex and the Search for Modernity in Fin-de-siècle Russia (Ithaca: Cornell University Press, 1992).

Freeze, G. L., 'Bringing Order to the Russian Family: Marriage and Divorce in Imperial Russia, 1760–1860', *JMH* 62 (1990): 709–46.

Glagoleva, O., 'Dream and Reality of Russian Provincial Young Ladies, 1700–1850', *The Carl Beck Papers*, no. 1405.

Glickman, R., *Russian Factory Women: Workplace and Society, 1880–1914* (Berkeley: University of California Press, 1984).

Greene, Diana, 'Mid-Nineteenth Century Domestic Ideology in Russia', in R. Marsh (ed.), *Women and Russian Culture: Projections and Self-Perceptions* (New York: Berghahn Books), pp. 78–97.

Hall, C., 'The Sweet Delights of Home', in Michelle Perrot (ed.), *A History of Private Life: From the Fires of Revolution to the Great War*, 5 vols. (Cambridge, Mass.: Harvard University Press, 1990), vol. IV, pp. 47–94.

Johanson, C., *Women's Struggle for Higher Education in Russia, 1855–1900* (Kingston: McGill-Queens University Press, 1987).

Kelly, C., *Refining Russia: Advice Literature, Polite Culture and Gender from Catherine to Yeltsin* (Oxford: Oxford University Press, 2001).

Kollman, N. S., '"What's Love Got to Do with It?": Changing Models of Masculinity in Muscovite and Petrine Russia', in B. Clements, R. Friedman and D. Healey (eds.), *Russian Masculinities in History and Culture* (New York: Palgrave, 2002), pp. 15–32.

Lindenmeyr, A., 'Maternalism and Child Welfare in Late Imperial Russia', *Journal of Women's History* 5 (Fall 1993): 114–25.

'Public Life, Private Virtues: Women in Russian Charity, 1762–1914', *Signs* 18, 3 (Spring 1993): 562–91.

McReynolds, L., 'The "Incomparable" Vial'steva and the Culture of Personality', in H. Goscilo and B. Holmgren (eds.), *Russia. Women. Culture* (Bloomington: Indiana University Press, 1996), pp. 273–91.

Marrese, M., *A Woman's Kingdom: Noblewomen and the Control of Property in Russia, 1700–1861* (Ithaca: Cornell University Press, 2002).

Marsh, R. (ed.), *Women in Russia and Ukraine* (Cambridge: Cambridge University Press, 1996).

Meehan-Waters, B., 'From Contemplative Practice to Charitable Activity: Russian Women's Religious Communities and the Development of Charitable Work, 1861–1917', in K. McCarthy (ed.), *Lady Bountiful Revisited: Women, Philanthropy and Power* (New Brunswick: Rutgers University Press, 1990), pp. 142–56.

Pisarev, S. N., *Uchrezhdenie po priniatiiu i napravleniiu proshenii i zhalob, prinosimykh na Vysochaishee imia, 1810–1910 gg. Istoricheskii ocherk* (St Petersburg: Tovarishchestvo P. Golike i A. Vil'borg, 1909).

Ransel, D., *Mothers of Misery: Child Abandonment in Russia* (Princeton: Princeton University Press, 1988).

Rosslyn, W., *Feats of Agreeable Usefulness: Translations by Russian Women 1763–1825* (London: Ashgate, 2002).

(ed.), *Women and Gender in Eighteenth-century Russia* (London: Ashgate, 2002).

Ruane, C., *Gender, Class and the Professionalization of Russian City Teachers, 1860–1914* (Pittsburgh: University of Pittsburgh Press, 1994).

Sankt-Peterburgskie vysshie zhenskie kursy. Slushatel'nitsy kursov. Po dannym perepisi (ankety), vypolnennoi statisticheskim seminarom v noiabre 1909 g. (St Petersburg, 1912).

Stites, R., *The Women's Liberation Movement in Russia: Feminism, Nihilism and Bolshevism, 1860–1930* (Princeton: Princeton University Press, 1978).

Tishkin, G. A., *Zhenskii vopros v Rossii 50–60-e gody XIX v.* (Leningrad: Izd. LGU, 1984).

Verbitskaya, A., *Keys to Happiness*, ed. and trans. B. Holmgren and H. Goscilo (Bloomington: Indiana University Press, 1999).

Vowles, J., 'The "Feminization" of Russian Literature: Women, Language, and Literature in Eighteenth-Century Russia', in T. Clyman and D. Greene (eds.), *Women Writers in Russian Literature* (Westport: Praeger, 1994), pp. 35–60.

7E PEASANTS AND AGRICULTURE

Aleksandrov, V. A., *Sel'skaia obshchina v Rossii (XVII–nachalo XIX v.)* (Moscow: Nauka, 1976).

Obychnoe pravo krepostnoi derevni Rossii: XVIII–nachalo XIX v. (Moscow: Nauka, 1984).

Anfimov, A. M. (ed.), *Krest'ianstvo Severnogo Kavkaza i Dona v period kapitalizma* (Rostov-on-Don: Izd. Rostovskogo universiteta, 1990).

Atkinson, D., 'Egalitarianism and the Commune', in R. Bartlett (ed.), *Land Commune and Peasant Community in Russia* (Basingstoke: Macmillan, 1990).

Avrich, P., *Russian Rebels, 1600–1800* (New York: Norton, 1972)

Baklanova, E. N., *Krest'ianskii dvor i obshchina na russkom severe: konets XVII–nachalo XVIII v.* (Moscow: Nauka, 1976).

Bohac, R., 'The Mir and the Military Draft', *SR* 47 (1988): 652–66.

'Everyday Forms of Resistance: Serf Opposition to Gentry Exactions, 1800–1861', in E. Kingston-Mann and T. Mixter (eds.), *Peasant Economy, Culture, and Politics of European Russia, 1800–1921* (Princeton: Princeton University Press, 1991).

Brooks, J., *When Russia Learned to Read: Literacy and Popular Literature, 1981–1917* (Princeton: Princeton University Press, 1985).

Burbank, J., 'A Question of Dignity: Peasant Legal Culture in Late Imperial Russia', *Continuity and Change* 10 (1995): 391–404.

Confino, M., *Systèmes agraires et progrès agricole: l'assolement triennal en Russie aux XVIIIe–XIXe siècles* (Paris and The Hague: Mouton, 1969).

Czap, P., 'Marriage and the Peasant Joint Family in the Era of Serfdom', in D. L Ransel (ed.), The Family in Imperial Russia (Urbana: University of Illinois Press, 1978), pp. 103–23.

'"A Large Family: The Peasant's Greatest Wealth": Serf Households in Mishino, Russia, 1814–1858', in R. Wall (ed.), *Family Forms in Historic Europe* (Cambridge: Cambridge University Press, 1983).

Danilova, L.V., *Sel'skaia obshchina v srednevekovoi Rusi* (Moscow: Nauka, 1994).

Dokuchaev, V. V., *Russkii chernozem* (St Petersburg: Deklaron i Evdokimov, 1883).

Dulov, A.V., *Geograficheskaia sreda i istoriia Rossii: konets XV–seredina XIX v.* (Moscow: Nauka, 1983).

Eklof, B., and Frank, S. (eds.), *The World of the Russian Peasant* (Boston: Unwin Hyman, 1990).

Fedorov, V. A., *Pomeshchich'i krest'iane tsentral'no-promyshlennogo raiona Rossii: kontsa XVIII–pervoi poloviny XIX v.* (Moscow: Izd. MGU, 1974).

Figes, O., *Peasant Russia, Civil War: The Volga Countryside in Revolution (1917–1921)* (Oxford: Clarendon Press, 1989).

Frierson, C. A., 'Razdel: The Peasant Family Divided', *RR*, 46 (1987): 35–51.

Gromyko, M. M., *Mir russkoi derevni* (Moscow: Molodaia gvardiia, 1991).

Hoch, S. L., *Serfdom and Social Control in Russia, Petrovskoe, a Village in Tambov* (Chicago: Chicago University Press, 1986)

'On Good Numbers and Bad: Malthus, Population Trends and Peasant Standard of Living in Late Imperial Russia', *SR* 53 (1994): 41–75.

'The Serf Economy and the Social Order in Russia', in M. L. Bush (ed.), *Serfdom and Slavery* (London: Longman, 1996).

Kerans, D., *Mind and Labor on the Farm in Black-Earth Russia, 1861–1914* (Budapest and New York: Central European University Press, 2001)

Khodarkovsky, M., 'The Stepan Razin Uprising: Was it a "Peasant War"?', *JfGO*, 42 (1994): 1–19.

Kolchin, P., *Unfree Labor: American Slavery and Russian Serfdom* (Cambridge: Belknap Press, 1987).

Kotsonis, Y., *Making Peasants Backward: Agricultural Cooperatives and the Agrarian Question in Russia, 1861–1914* (Basingstoke: Macmillan, 1999).

Kozlova, N. V., *Pobegi krest'ian v Rossii v pervoi treti XVIII veka* (Moscow: Izd. MGU, 1983).

Melton, E., 'Proto-industrialization, Serf Agriculture and Agrarian Social Structure: Two Estates in Nineteenth-Century Russia', *Past and Present* 115 (1987): 69–106.

'Household Economies and Communal Conflicts on a Russian Serf Estate, 1800–1817', *JSH* 26 (1993): 559–85.

Milov, L.V., *Velikorusskii pakhar' i osobennosti rossiiskogo istoricheskogo protsessa* (Moscow: Rosspen, 1998).

Minenko, N.A., *Russkaia krest'ianskaia sem'ia v Zapadnoi Sibiri (XVIII–pervoi poloviny XIX veka)* (Novosibirsk: Nauka, 1979).

Mironov, B. N., 'Traditsionnoe demograficheskoe povedenie krest'ian v XIX–nachale XX v.', in A. G. Vishnevskii (ed.), *Brachnost', rozhdaemost', smertnost' v Rossii i v SSSR* (Moscow: Statistika, 1977)

'New Approaches to Old Problems: The Well-Being of the Population of Russia from 1821 to 1910 as Measured by Physical Stature', *SR*, 58 (1999): 1–26.

Moon, D., *Russian Peasants and Tsarist Legislation on the Eve of Reform, 1825–1855* (Basingstoke and London: Macmillan, 1992).

'Peasant Migration and the Settlement of Russia's Frontiers 1550–1897', *Historical Journal* 30 (1997): 859–93.

The Russian Peasantry, 1600–1930 (London and New York: Addison Wesley Longman, 1999).

Pallot, J., *Land Reform in Russia 1906–1917* (Oxford: Clarendon Press, 1999).

Pallot, J., and Shaw, D. J. B., *Landscape and Settlement in Romanov Russia, 1613–1917* (Oxford: Clarendon Press, 1990).

Perrie, M., 'Popular Monarchism: The Myth of the Ruler from Ivan the Terrible to Stalin', in G. Hosking and R. Service (eds.), *Reinterpreting Russia* (London: Arnold, 1999), pp. 156–69.

Popkins, G., 'Peasant Experiences of the Late Tsarist State: District Congresses of Land Captains, Provincial Boards and the Legal Appeals Process, 1891–1917', *SEER* 78 (2000): 90–114.

Raeff, M., 'Pugachev's Rebellion', in R. Forster and J. P., Greene (eds.), *Preconditions of Revolution in Early Modern Europe* (Baltimore: Johns Hopkins Press, 1970).

Robinson, G. T., *Rural Russia under the Old Regime* (Berkeley: University of California Press, 1932).

Rubinshtein, N. L. *Sel'skoe khoziaistvo Rossii vo vtoroi polovine XVIII v.* (Moscow: Gospolitizdat, 1957)

Shapiro, A. L. (ed.), *Agrarnaia istoriia Severo-Zapada Rossii XVII veka* (Leningrad: Nauka, 1989)

Smith, A. K., 'Peasant Agriculture in Pre-Reform Kostroma and Kazan' Provinces', *RH* 26 (1999): 355–424.

Smith, R. E. F., *Peasant Farming in Muscovy* (Cambridge: Cambridge University Press, 1977).

Smith, R. E. F., and Christian, D., *Bread and Salt: A Social and Economic History of Food and Drink in Russia* (Cambridge: Cambridge University Press, 1984).

Vodarskii, Ia. E., *Naselenie Rossii v kontse XVII–nachale XVIII veka* (Moscow: Nauka, 1977).

Worobec, C. D., *Peasant Russia: Family and Community in the Post-Emancipation Period* (Princeton: Princeton University Press, 1991).

8. ECONOMY, FINANCE, TAX

Anan'ich, B.V., *Rossiiskoe samoderzhavie i vyzov kapitalov, 1895–1914* (Leningrad: Nauka, 1957).

Rossiia i mezhdunarodnyi kapital. Ocherki istorii finansovykh otnoshenii (Leningrad: Nauka, 1970).

Bankirskie doma v Rossii. 1860–1914. Ocherki istorii chastnogo predprinimatel'stva (Leningrad: Nauka, 1991).

'Zolotoi standart Finliandii i Rossii: finansovii aspect imperskoi politiki', in *Rossiia na rubezhe XIX–XX vekov. Materialy nauchnykh chtenii pamiati professora V. I. Bovykina*, Moscow, 20 Jan. 1999 (Moscow: Nauka, 1999).

'Stiglitzty – Poslednic pridvornie bankiry v Rossii', in *'Bol'shoe budushchee'. Nemtsy v ekonomicheskoi zhizni Rossii* (Berlin, Bonn, Hessen and Moscow: Mercedes Druk, Berlin, 2000).

Anan'ich, B. V., and Ganelin, P. Sh., *Sergei Iulevich Vitte i ego vremiia* (St Petersburg: Dmitrii Bulanin, 2000).

Anan'ich, B. V., Kalmykov, S. V., and Petrov, Iu. A., *Glavnii bank Rossii. Ot gosudarstvennogo banka Rossiiskoi imperii k tsentral'nomu banku Rossiiskoi Federatsii. 1860–2000* (Moscow: TSPP TSB RPH, 2000).

Anan'ich B. V., and Lebedev S. K., 'Kontora pridvornykh bankirov v Rossii i Evropeiskie denezhnye rynki (1798–1811)', in *Problemy sotsial'no-ekonomicheskoi istorii Rossii* (St Petersburg: Nauka, 1991).

Anan'ich N. I., 'K istorii otmeny podushnoi podati v Rossii', *IZ* 94 (1974): 183–212.

'Materialy lektsionnykh kursov N. Kh. Bunge 60–80x godov XIX veka', *Arkheograficheskii Ezhegodnik za 1977 god* (Moscow: Nauka, 1978), pp. 304–6.

Anfimov, A. M., 'Prodovol'stvennye dolgi kak pokazatel' ekonomicheskogo polozheniia krest'ian dorevolutsionnoi Rossii (konets XIX – nachalo XX veka)', in *Materialy po istorii sel'skogo khoziaistva i krest'ianstva SSSR* (Moscow: Nauka, 1960).

Anisimov, E., *Podatnaia reforma Petra Velikogo* (Leningrad: Nauka, 1982).

Vremia petrovskikh reform (Leningrad: Lenizdat, 1989).

'Rossiia v "epokhu dvortsovykh perevorotov"', in B. V. Anan'ich et al. (eds.), *Vlast' i reformy. Ot samoderzhavnoi k sovetskoi Rossii* (St Petersburg: Dmitrii Bulanin, 1996), pp. 162–3.

Gosudarstvennye preobrazovaniia i samoderzhavie Petra Velikogo v pervoi chetverti XVIII veka (St Petersburg: Dmitrii Bulanin, 1997).

Beliaev, S. G., *P.L. Bark i finansovaia politika Rossii 1914–1917*, (St Petersburg: Izd. SPbu, 2002).

Bowman, L., 'Russia's First Income Taxes: The Effects of Modernized Taxes on Commerce and Industry, 1885–1914', *SR* 52 (1993): 256–82.

Borovoi, S. Ia., *Kredit i banki v Rossii (seredina XVII veka – 1861* (Moscow: 1958).

Bovykin, V. I., *Frantsuzskie banki v Rossii. Konets XIX–nachalo XX vekov* (Moscow: Rosspen, 1999).

Chechulin, N. D., *Ocherki po istorii russkikh finansov v tsarstvovanii Ekateriny II* (St Petersburg: Tip. glavnogo upravleniia udelov, 1906).

Crisp, O., *Studies in the Russian Economy Before 1914* (London: Macmillan, 1976).

Diakin, V. S., *Dengi dlia sel'skogo khoziaistva* (St Petersburg: Izd. SPbu, 1997).

Dokkyu, C., *Rossiia v Koree, 1893–1905* (St Petersburg: Zero, 1996).

Friedman, M., *Kazennaia vinnaia monopoliia* (St Petersburg, 1914).

Gatrell, P., *The Tsarist Economy 1850–1917* (London: Batsford, 1986).

Government, Industry and Rearmament in Russia, 1900–1914: The Last Argument of Tsarism (Cambridge: Cambridge University Press, 1994).

Gerschenkron, A., *Economic Backwardness in Historical Perspective* (Cambridge, Mass.: Harvard University Press, 1962).

Europe in the Russian Mirror: Four Lectures in Economic History (Cambridge: Cambridge University Press, 1970).

Gindin, I. F., *Gosudarstvennyi bank i aktsionernaia politika tsarskogo pravitel'stva (1861–1892)* (Moscow: Gosfinizdat, 1960).

Banki i ekonomicheskaia politika v Rossii (XIX–nachalo XX vekov). Ocherki istorii i tipologii russkikh bankov (Moscow: Nauka, 1997).

Girault, R., *Emprunts russes et investissements français en Russie. 1887–1914* (Paris: Armand Colin, 1973).

Hoch, S. L., 'The Banking Crisis, Peasant Reform and Economic Development in Russia, 1857–1861', *AHR* 96 (1991): 795–820.

Ivanov L. M. (ed.), *Istoriia rabochego klassa Rossii* (Moscow: Nauka, 1972).

Kahan, A., *The Plow, the Hammer and the Knout* (Chicago: University of Chicago Press, 1985).

Kaplan, H., *Russian Overseas Commerce with Great Britain during the reign of Catherine II* (Philadelphia: American Philosophical Society, 1995).

Khromov, P. A., *Ekonomicheskoe razvitie Rossii* (Moscow: Nauka, 1967).

Kitanina, T. M., *Khlebnaia torgovliia Rossii* (Moscow: Nauka, 1978).

Korelin, A., and Stepanov, S., *S. Yu. Vitte – Finansist, politik, diplomat* (Moscow: Terra, 1998).

Laue von, T., *Sergei Witte and the Industrialisation of Russia* (New York and London: Columbia University Press, 1963).

Lebedev, S. K., *S-Peterburgskii mezhdunarodnii kommercheskii bank vo vtoroi polovine XIX veka* (Moscow: Rosspen, 2003).

LeDonne, J., 'Indirect Taxes in Catherine's Russia. I. The Salt Code of 1781', *JfGO* 23 (1975): 161–90.

'Indirect Taxes in Catherine's Russia. II. The Liquor monopoly', *JfGO* 24 (1976): 173–207.

Mendeleev, D. I., 'Fabrichno-zavodskaia promyshlennost' i torgovlia Rossii', in D. I., Mendeleev, *Sochineniia* (Moscow: Izd. AN SSSR, 1952), vol. XXI, p. 190.

Migulin, P. P., *Nasha noveishaia zheleznodorozhnaia politika i zheleznodorozhnie zaimy (1893–1902)* (Kharkov: Tipolitographiia 'Pechatnoe Delo' K. Gagarina, 1903).

Miliukov, P. N. *Gosudarstvennoe khoziaistvo Rossii v pervoi chetverti XVIII veka i reforma Petra Velikogo*, 2nd edition (St Petersburg: Tip. M. M. Stasiulevicha, 1905).

Nifontov, A. S., *1848 v Rossii. Ocherki po istorii 40-kh godov* (Moscow and Leningrad: Sotsial'no-economicheskoe Izd. 1931).

Nikol'skii, B. A., *Frantsiia i Rossiia (k 25-letiu franko-russkogo soiuza)* (Petrograd, 1917).

Owen, T., *Capitalism and Politics in Russia: A Social History of the Moscow Merchants 1855–1905* (Cambridge: Cambridge University Press, 1981).

Petrov, Iu. A., *Kommercheskie banky Moskvy. Konets XIX veka – 1914* (Moscow: Rosspen, 1998).

Moskovskaia burzhuaziia v nachale XX veka: Predprinimatel'stvo i politika (Moscow: Mosgorarchiv, 2002).

Plaggenborg, S., 'Tax Policy and the Question of Peasant Poverty in Tsarist Russia 1881–1905', *CMRS* 36 (1995): 53–69.

Pogrebinskii, A. P., *Ocherki istorii finansov dorevoliutsionnoi Rossii XIX–XX vv.* (Moscow: Gosfinizdat, 1954).

Pokrovskii, V. I., *Sbornik svedenii po istorii i statistike vneshnei torgovli Rossii* (St Petersburg: Departament Tamozhennykh Sborov, 1902).

Pravilova, K., 'Finliandiia i rossiiskaia imperia: politika i finansy', *Istoricheskie zapiski*, 124, 6 (2003): 180–240.

Rieber, A., *Merchants and Entrepreneurs in Imperial Russia* (Chapel Hill: University of North Carolina Press, 1982).

Romanov, B. A., *Ocherki diplomaticheskoi istorii russko-iaponskoi voiny. 1895–1907* (Moscow and Leningrad: Izd. AN SSSR, 1955).

Roosa, R., *Russian Industrialists in an Age of Revolution* (Armonk: M. E. Sharpe, 1997).

Shebaldin, Iu. N., 'Gosudarstvennyi biudzhet tsarskoi Rossii v nachale XX veka (do pervoi mirovoi voiny)', *IZ*, 56 (1959): 163–90.

Shepelev, L. E., *Aktsionernye kompanii v Rossii* (Leningrad: Nauka, 1973).

Shepelev, L. E., *Tsarizm i burzhuaziia vo vtoroi polovine XIX veka. Problemy torgovo-promyshlennoi politiki* (Leningrad: Nauka, 1981).

Tsarizm i burzhuaziia vo vtoroi polovine XIX veka (Leningrad: Nauka 1986).

Tsarizm i burzhuaziia v 1904–1914 (Leningrad: Nauka, 1987).

Shvanebakh, P. A., *Nashe podatnoe delo* (St Petersburg: Tip. M. M. Stasiulevicha, 1903).

Simms, J. Y., 'The Crisis of Russian Agriculture at the End of the Nineteenth Century', *SR* 36 (1977): 378–98.

Simonova, M. S., 'Otmena krugovoi poruki', *IZ*, 83 (1969): 159–95.

Solov'eva, A. N., *Zheleznodorozhnyi transport Rossii vo vtoroi polovine XIX veka* (Moscow: Nauka, 1975).

Stepanov, V. I., *N. Kh. Bunge. Sud'ba reformatora* (Moscow: Rosspen, 1998).

Sud'by Rossii. Doklady i zapiski gosudarstvennykh deiatelei imperatoram o problemakh ekonomicheskogo razvitiia strany (St Petersburg: Liki Rossii, 1999).

Taranovskii, T. (ed.), *Reform in Modern Russian History: Progress or Cycle?* (New York: Woodrow Wilson Center Press and Cambridge University Press, 1995).

Tarnovskii, K. N., *Sovetskaia istoriografiia rossiiskogo imperializma* (Moscow: Nauka, 1964).

Troitskii, S. M., *Finansovaia politika russkogo absoliutizma v XVIII veke* (Moscow: Nauka, 1966).

Tugan Baranovskii, R., *Russkaia fabrika v proshlom i nastoiashchem* (Moscow: Moskovskii rabochii, 1922).

Tvardovskaia, V. A., *Ideologiia poreformennogo samoderzhaviia (M. N. Katkov i ego izdaniia* (Moscow: Nauka, 1978).

Vitchevskii, V., *Torgovaia, tamozhennaia i promyshlennaia politika Rossii* (St Petersburg: Izdanie D. A., Kazitsina i Iu. D. Philipova, 1909).

Witte, S. Iu., *Konspekt lektsii o narodnom i gosudarstvennom khoziastve* (St Petersburg: Fond 'Nachala', 1912).

9. FOREIGN POLICY: ARMED FORCES

Airapetov, O. R., *Zabytaia kar'era 'russkogo Moltke' Nikolai Nikolaevich Obruchev (1830–1904)* (St Petersburg: Izd. 'Aleteiia', 1998).

Aleksandrov, P. A., *Severnaia sistema: opyt issledovaniia idei i khoda vneshnei politiki Rossii v pervuiu polovinu tsarstvovaniia Imperatritsy Ekateriny II* (Moscow: Lomonosov, 1914).

Anderson, M. S., *The Eastern Question, 1774–1923: A Study in International Relations* (New York: St Martin's, 1966).

Anisimov, A. V., *Rossiia v seredine XVIII veka: bor'ba za nasledie Petra* (Moscow: Mysl', 1986).

Bassin, Mark, *Imperial Visions: Nationalist Imagination and Geographical Expansion in the Russian Far East, 1840–1865* (Cambridge: Cambridge University Press, 1999).

Baumann, Robert Fred, 'The Debates over Universal Military Service in Russia, 1870–1874', unpublished PhD dissertation, Yale University (1982).

Beskrovnyi, L. G., *Voprosy voennoi istorii Rossii XVIII i pervaia polovina XIX vekov* (Moscow: Nauka, 1969).

Russkaia armiia i flot v XIX veke. Voenno-ekonomicheskii potentsial Rossii (Moscow: Nauka, 1973).

Armiia i flot Rossii v nachale XX v. Ocherki voenno-ekonmicheskoi potentsiala (Moscow: Nauka, 1986).

Bestuzhev, I. V., *Bor'ba po voprosam vneshnei politiki v Rossii, 1906–1910* (Moscow: Nauka, 1961).

Beyrau, Dietrich, *Militär und Gesellschaft im Vorrevolutionären Russland* (Cologne and Vienna: Böhlau Verlag, 1984).

Bourquin, Maurice, *Histoire de la Sainte Alliance* (Geneva: Georg et Cie., 1954).

Bradley, Joseph, *Guns for the Tsar: American Technology and the Small Arms Industry in Nineteenth-Century Russia* (DeKalb: Northern Illinois University Press, 1990).

Bushnell, John, *Mutiny Amid Repression: Russian Soldiers in the Revolution of 1905–08* (Bloomington: Indiana University Press, 1985).

Chechulin, N. D., *Vneshniaia politika Rossii v nachale tsarstvovaniia Ekateriny II, 1762–1774* (St Petersburg: Glavnoe upravlenie udelov, 1896).

Cherkasov, P. P., 'Frantsiia i russko-turetskaia voina, 1768–1774 gg.', *Novaia i noveishaia istoriia* (1966), no. 1: 50–76.

Corbett, Julian S., *Maritime Operations in the Russo-Japanese War 1904–1905*, 2 vols. (Annapolis: Naval Institute Press, 1994).

Curtiss, J. S., *The Russian Army under Nicholas I* (Durham: Duke University Press, 1965).

Russia's Crimean War (Durham: Duke University Press, 1979).

Davison, Roderic H., '"Russian Skill and Turkish Imbecility": The Treaty of Kuchuk Kainardji Reconsidered', *SR* 35 (1976): 463–83.

Dittmer, Helen Roth-Bergman, 'The Russian Foreign Ministry under Nicholas II', unpublished PhD dissertation, University of Chicago (1977).

Druzhinina, E. I., *Kuchuk-Kainardzhiiskii mir 1774 goda* (Moscow: Izd. AN SSSR, 1955).

Duffy, Christopher, *Russia's Military Way to the West: Origins and Nature of Russian Military Power 1700–1800* (London: Routledge and Kegan Paul, 1981).

Dzhedzhula, K. E., *Rossiia i Velikaia frantsuzskaia burzhuaznaia revoliutsiia kontsa XVIII veka* (Kiev: Izd. Kievskogo universiteta, 1972).

Emets, V. A., *Ocherki vneshnei politiki Rossii 1914–1917* (Moscow: Nauka, 1977).

Feldbæk, Ole, 'The Foreign Policy of Tsar Paul I, 1800–1801: An Interpretation', *JfGO* 30 (1982): 16–36.

Fisher, Alan W., *The Russian Annexation of the Crimea, 1772–1783* (Cambridge: Cambridge University Press, 1970).

Fox, Martynna A., 'The Eastern Question in Russian Politics: Interplay of Diplomacy, Opinion and Interest 1905–1917', unpublished PhD dissertation, Yale University (1993).

Frenkin, M. S., *Russkaia armiia i revoliutsiia 1917–1918* (Munich: Logos, 1978).

Fuller, William C. Jr., *Civil–Military Conflict in Imperial Russia, 1881–1914* (Princeton: Princeton University Press, 1985).

Strategy and Power in Russia 1600–1914 (New York: Free Press, 1992).

'The Eastern Front', in J. Winter, G. Parker and M. R. Habeck (eds.), *The Great War and the Twentieth Century* (New Haven: Yale University Press, 2000), pp. 30–68.

Geisman, Platon A., and Dubovskii, Aleksandr N., *Graf Petr Ivanovich Panin, 1721–1789: istoricheskii ocherk voennoi i gosudarstvennoi deiatel'nosti* (St Petersburg: Vasil'iev, 1897).

Gerhard, Dietrich, *England und der Aufstieg Russlands* (Munich: Oldenbourg, 1933).

Geyer, D., *Russian Imperialism: The Interaction of Domestic and Foreign Policy, 1860–1914* (Leamington Spa: Berg, 1987).

Gillard, D., *The Struggle for Asia 1828–1914: A Study in British and Russian Imperialism* (London: Methuen, 1977).

Girault, R., *Emprunts russes et investissements français en Russie 1887–1914* (Paris: Librairie Armand Colin, 1973).

Glinskii, B. (ed.), *Prolog Russko-Iaponskoi voiny: materialy iz arkhiva Grafa S. Iu. Witte* (Petrograd: Brokgauz and Efron, 1916).

Goldfrank, D., *The Origins of the Crimean War* (London and New York: Longman, 1994).

Golovin, N. N., *The Russian Army in the World War* (New Haven: Yale University Press, 1931).

Griffiths, D., 'Russian Court Politics and the Question of an Expansionist Foreign Policy under Catherine II, 1762–1783', PhD dissertation, Cornell University (1967).

Grimsted, P., *The Foreign Ministers of Alexander I* (Berkeley: University of California Press, 1969).

(ed.), 'Czartoryski's System for Russian Foreign Policy: A Memorandum', *California Slavic Studies* 5 (1970): 19–91.

Grünig, I., *Die russische öffentliche Meinung und ihre Stellung zu den Großmächten 1878–1894* (Berlin: Ost-Europa Verlag, 1929).

Grunwald, C. de, *Trois siècles de diplomatie russe* (Paris: Carlmann-Lévy, 1945).

Hauser, O., *Deutschland und der English-Russische Gegensatz, 1900–1914* (Berlin: Musterschmidt Verlag, 1958).

Hoetzsch, O., *Rußland in Asien. Geschichte einer Expansion* (Stuttgart: Deutsche Verlags-Anstallt, 1966).

Hsü, I., *The Ili Crisis* (Oxford: Oxford University Press, 1965).

Hughes, M., *Diplomacy Before the Russian Revolution: Britain, Russia and the Old Diplomacy, 1894–1917* (Basingstoke: Macmillan, 2000).
Hunczak, Taras (ed.), *Russian Imperialism* (New Brunswick: Rutgers University Press, 1974).
Ignat'ev, A.V., *Vneshniaia politika Rossii 1905–1907* (Moscow: Nauka, 1986).
S. Iu. Vitte – diplomat (Moscow: Mezhdunarodnye otnosheniia, 1989).
Vneshniaia politika Rossii 1907–1914 (Moscow: Nauka, 2000).
Ignat'ev, A. V., Rybachenok, I. S. and Savin, G. A. (eds.), *Rossiiskaia diplomatiia v portretakh* (Moscow: Mezhdunarodnye otnosheniia, 1992).
Ingle, H., *Nesselrode and the Russian Rapprochement with Britain, 1836–1844* (Berkeley: California University Press, 1976).
Jelavich, B., *A Century of Russian Foreign Policy* (Philadelphia: Lippincott, 1964).
The Ottoman Empire, the Great Powers and the Straits Question, 1870–1887 (Bloomington: Indiana University Press, 1973).
Russia's Balkan Entanglements, 1806–1914 (Cambridge: Cambridge University Press, 1991).
Jelavich, C. and Jelavich, B. (eds.), *Russia in the East 1876–1880* (Leiden: E. J. Brill, 1959).
Jones, David R., 'Imperial Russia's Forces at War', in A. R., Millet and W. Murray (eds.), *Military Effectiveness*, vol. I: *The First World War* (Boston: Allen and Unwin, 1988), pp. 249–328.
Jones, Robert E., 'Opposition to War and Expansion in Late Eighteenth Century Russia', *JfGO* 32 (1984): 34–51.
'The Nobility and Russian Foreign Policy, 1560–1811', *CMRS* 34 (1993): 159–70.
Kagan, F. W., *The Military Reforms of Nicholas I: The Origins of the Modern Russian Army* (New York: St Martin's Press, 1999).
Kagan, F. W., and Higham, R. (eds.), *The Military History of Tsarist Russia* (New York: Palgrave, 2002).
Kaplan, H., *The First Partition of Poland* (New York: Columbia University Press, 1962).
Kasatonov, I. V. (ed.), *Tri veka rossiiskogo flota*, 3 vols. (St Petersburg: Logos, 1996).
Kavtaradze, A., 'Iz istorii russkogo general'nogo shtaba', *Voenno-istoricheskii zhurnal* 13, 12 (Dec. 1971): 75–80; 14, 7 (July 1972): 87–92; 16, 12 (Dec. 1974): 80–6.
Kazemzadeh, F., *Russia and Britain in Persia, 1864–1914* (New Haven: Yale University Press, 1968).
Keep, J., *Soldiers of the Tsar: Army and Society in Russia 1462–1874* (Oxford: Oxford University Press, 1985).
'The Russian Army in the Seven Years War', in E. Lohr and M. Poe (eds.), *The Military and Society in Russia 1450–1917* (Leiden: Brill, 2002), pp. 197–220.
Kennan, G., *The Decline of Bismarck's European Order: Franco-Russian Relations, 1875–1890* (Princeton: Princeton University Press, 1979).
The Fateful Alliance (New York: Pantheon Books, 1984).
Kersnovskii, A. A., *Istoriia russkoi armii*, repr. edn, 4 vols. (Moscow: Golos, 1992–6).
Khervrolina, V. M., *Vlast' i obshchestvo: bor'ba v Rossii po voprosam vneshnei politiki 1878–1894 gg.* (Moscow: Institut Rossiiskoi Istorii, 1999).
Kiniapina, N. S., *Vneshniaia politika Rossii vo vtoroi polovine XIX veka* (Moscow: Vysshaia shkola, 1974).
Kiniapina, N. S., et al. (eds.), *Vostochnyi vopros vo vneshnei politike Rossii: konets XVIII–nachalo XX v.* (Moscow: Nauka, 1978).

Klueting, H., *Heinrich Graf Ostermann: von Bochum nach St Petersburg: 1687 bis 1747* (Bochum: Brockmeyer, 1976).

Kochubinskii, A., *Graf Andrei Ivanovich Osterman i razdel Turtsii: iz istorii Vostochnago voprosa.* (Odessa: Odesskii voennyi okrug, 1899).

Koot, J., 'The Asiatic Department of the Russian Foreign Ministry and the Formation of Policy toward the Non-Western World, 1881–1894', unpublished PhD dissertation, Harvard University (1980).

Korostovets, I. I., *Pre-War Diplomacy: The Russo-Japanese Problem* (London: British Periodicals Ltd., 1920).

Rossiia na Dalnem Vostoke (Peking: Vostochnoe Prosveshchenie, 1922).

Kostrikova, E. G., *Russkaia pressa i diplomatiia nakanune pervoi mirovoi voiny* (Moscow: Institut Rossiiskoi Istorii, 1997).

Krüger-Löwenstein, U., *Russland, Frankreich und das Reich, 1801–1805: zur Vorgeschichte der 3. Koalition* (Wiesbaden: Steiner, 1972).

Kudeikin, V. Iu., and Savinkin, A. E. (eds.), *Voennoe zakondatel'stvo Rossiiskoi imperii. Kodeks russkogo voennogo prava* (Moscow: Voennyi universitet, 1996).

Kuropatkin, A. N., *The Russian Army and the Japanese War*, trans. A. B. Lindsay, 2 vols. (New York: E. P. Dutton, 1909).

Kusber, J., *Krieg und Revolution in Russland 1904–06. Das Militär im Verhältnis zu Wirtschaft, Autokratie und Gesellschaft* (Stuttgart: Franz Steiner Verlag, 1997).

Langer, W., *The Franco-Russian Alliance 1890–1914* (Cambridge, Mass.: Harvard University Press, 1929).

European Alliances and Alignments 1871–1890 (New York: Knopf, 1931).

The Diplomacy of Imperialism, 2 vols. (New York: Knopf, 1956).

'The Origins of the Russo-Japanese War', in C. E. Schorske and E. Schorske (eds.), *Explorations in Crisis: Papers on International History* (Cambridge, Mass.: Harvard University Press, 1969), pp. 3–45.

Lebedev, P. S., *Grafy Nikita i Petr Paniny* (St Petersburg: Obshchestvennaia pol'za, 1863).

Lederer, I. J. (ed.), *Russian Foreign Policy* (New Haven: Yale University Press, 1962).

LeDonne, J. P., *The Russian Empire and the World 1700–1917: The Geopolitics of Expansion and Containment* (New York: Oxford University Press, 1997).

Lensen, G., *The Russian Push towards Japan: Russo-Japanese Relations 1697–1875* (Princeton: Princeton University Press, 1959).

Korea and Manchuria between Russia and Japan 1895–1904: The Observations of Sir Ernest Satow (Tallahassee: Diplomatic Press, 1966).

Balance of Intrigue: International Rivalry in Korea and Manchuria, 1884–1899, 2 vols. (Tallahassee: University Press of Florida, 1982).

Ley, F., *Le maréchal de Münnich et la Russie au XVIII siècle* (Paris: Plon, 1959).

Alexander I et la Sainte-Alliance (Paris: Fischbacher, 1975).

Liechtenhan, F.-D., *La Russie entre en Europe: Elisabeth Ire et la succession d'Autriche (1740–1750)* (Paris: CNRS éditions, 1997).

Lieven, D., *Russia and the Origins of the First World War* (London: Macmillan, 1983).

Empire: The Russian Empire and its Rivals (London: John Murray, 2000).

Linke, H. G., *Das zarische Russland und der Erste Weltkrieg* (Munich: Wilhelm Fink Verlag, 1982).

Lobanov-Rostovsky, A., *Russia and Asia* (Ann Arbor: George Wahr, 1951).

Lojek, J., 'Catherine II's Armed Intervention in Poland: Origins of the Political Decisions at the Russian Court in 1791 and 1792', *CASS* 4 (1970): 570–93.

Lord, R. H., *The Second Partition of Poland* (Cambridge, Mass.: Harvard University Press, 1915).

Luntinen, P., *The Imperial Russian Army and Navy in Finland 1808–1918* (Helsinki: SHS, 1997).

McDonald, D. M., *United Government and Foreign Policy in Russia 1900–1914* (Cambridge, Mass.: Harvard University Press, 1992).

Mackenzie, D., *Imperial Dreams, Harsh Realities: Tsarist Russian Foreign Policy, 1815–1917* (Fort Worth: Harcourt Brace, 1994).

Count N. P. Ignat'ev: The Father of all Lies? (Boulder: East European Monographs, 2002).

McLaughlin, S., *Russian and Soviet Battleships* (Annapolis: Naval Institute Press, 2003).

Madariaga, I. de, *Russia, Britain, and the Armed Neutrality of 1780* (New Haven: Yale University Press, 1962).

Malozemoff, Andrew, *Russia's Far Eastern Policy* (Berkeley: University of California Press, 1958).

Marriott, J., *Anglo-Russian Relations 1689–1943* (London: Methuen, 1944).

Martens, F. F., *Le Conflit entre la Russie et la Chine* (Brussels: C. Murquardt, 1880).

Rossiia i Angliia v srednei Azii (St Petersburg: Izd. Garte, 1880).

Mediger, W., *Moskaus Weg nach Europa: der Aufstieg Russlands zum europäischen Machtstaat im Zeitalter Friedrichs des Grossen* (Braunschweig: Goerg Westermann Verlag, 1952).

Mecklenburg, Russland und England-Hannover 1706–1721: Ein Beitrag zur Geschichte des nordishen Krieges, Quellen und Darstellungen zur Geschichte Niedersachsens 70, 2 vols. (Hildesheim: Lax, 1967).

Menning, B., *Bayonets Before Bullets: The Imperial Russian Army, 1861–1914* (Bloomington: Indiana University Press, 1992).

Meyer, K. E., and Brysac, S. B., *Tournament of Shadows: The Race for Empire and the Great Game in Central Asia* (New York: Counterpoint, 1999).

Miliutin, D. A., *Istoriia voiny 1799 goda mezhdu Rossiei i Frantsiei v tsarstvovanii Imperatora Pavla*, 2nd edn, 3 vols. (St Petersburg: Imperatorskaia AN, 1857).

Miller, F., *Dmitrii Miliutin and the Reform Era in Russia* (Charlotte: Vanderbilt University Press, 1968).

Morgan, Gerald, *Anglo-Russian Rivalry in Central Asia: 1810–95* (London: Collins, 1981).

Neilson, Keith, *Britain and the Last Tsar: British Policy and Russia 1894–1917* (Oxford: Oxford University Press, 1995).

Nikolai Mikhailovich, Grand Duke (ed.), *Graf Pavel Aleksandrovich Stroganov (1774–1817)*, 3 vols. (St Petersburg: Ekspeditsiia zagotovleniia gos. bumag, 1903).

Relations diplomatiques de la Russie et de la France d'après les rapports des ambassadeurs d'Alexandre et de Napoléon, 1801–1812, 6 vols. (St Petersburg: Manufacture des papiers de l'état, 1905–8).

Nish, I., *The Origins of the Russo-Japanese War* (London: Longman, 1985).

Nizhinskii, L. N., and Ignat'ev, A.V. (eds.), *Rossiia i chernomorskie prolivy (XVIII–XX stoletiia)* (Moscow: Mezhdunarodnye otnosheniia, 1999).

Nolde, Boris, *L'alliance franco-russe. Les origines du système diplomatique d'avant-guerre* (Paris: Librairie Droz, 1936).

Orlik, O. V., *Rossiia v mezhdunarodnykh otnosheniiakh 1815–1829* (Moscow: Nauka, 1998).

(ed.), *Istoriia vneshnei politiki Rossii: pervaia polovina XIX veka* (Moscow: Mezhdunarodnye otnosheniia, 1995).

Paine, S. C. M., *Imperial Rivals: China, Russia and their Disputed Frontier* (Armonk: M. E. Sharpe, 1996).

Pak Chon Ho, *Russko-iaponskaia voina 1904–1905 gg. i Koreia* (Moscow: Vostochnaia literatura, 1997).

Panov, A. I., *Ofitsery v russkoi revoliutsii 1905–07 gg.* (Moscow: Regional'naia obshchestvennaia organizatsiia ofitserov 'Demos', 1996).

Pintner, Walter M., 'The Burden of Defense in Imperial Russia, 1725–1915', *RR* 43 (1984): 231–59.

Ponomarev, V. N., *Krymskaia voina i russko-amerikanskie otnosheniia* (Moscow: Institut rossiiskoi istorii, 1993).

Popova, A. I., *Griboedov diplomat* (Moscow: Mezhdunarodnye otnosheniia, 1964).

Primakov, E. M. et al. (eds.), *Kantsler A. M. Gorchakov: 200 let so dnia rozhdeniia* (Moscow: Mezhdunarodnye otnosheniia, 1998).

Quested, Rosemary, *The Expansion of Russia in East Asia 1857–1860* (Kuala Lumpur: University of Malaysia Press, 1968).

'Matey' Imperialists? The Tsarist Russians in Manchuria 1895–1917 (Hong Kong: University of Hong Kong, 1982).

Sino-Russian Relations: A Short History (Sydney: George Allen and Unwin, 1984).

Ragsdale, H., *Détente in the Napoleonic Era: Bonaparte and the Russians* (Lawrence : Regents University Press of Kansas, 1980).

'Russia, Prussia, and Europe in the Policy of Paul I', *JfGO* 31 (1983): 81–118.

'Reevaluating Russian Traditions of Aggression: Catherine II and the Greek Project', *SEER* 66 (1988): 75–102.

(ed.), *Imperial Russian Foreign Policy* (Cambridge: Cambridge University Press, 1993).

Rich, D. A., *The Tsar's Colonels. Professionalism, Strategy and Subversion in Late Imperial Russia* (Cambridge, Mass.: Harvard University Press, 1998).

Ritchie, G., 'The Asiatic Department during the Reign of Alexander II 1855–1881', unpublished PhD dissertation, Columbia University (1970).

Romanov, B. A., *Rossiia v Manchzhurii* (Leningrad: Izd. Instituta Dal'nego Vostoka, 1928).

Russia in Manchuria, trans. Susan Wilbur Jones (Ann Arbor: Edwards, 1952).

Rostunov, I. I., *Russkii front pervoi mirovoi voiny* (Moscow: Nauka, 1976).

Istoriia russko-ianponskoi voiny 1904–1905 gg. (Moscow: Nauka, 1977).

Russko-turetskaia voina 1877–1878 (Moscow: Voenizdat, 1977).

(ed.), *Istoriia severnoi voiny: 1700–1721 gg.* (Moscow: Nauka, 1987).

Rybachenok, I. S., *Soiuz s Frantsiei vo vneshnei politike Rossii v kontse XIX v.* (Moscow: Institut istorii SSSR, 1993).

'Rossiia i gaagskaia konferentsiia po razoruzheniiu 1899 g.', *Novaia i noveishaia istoriia*, no. 4 (Apr. 1996): 169–92.

Sakharov, A. N. et al. (eds.), *Istoriia vneshnei politiki Rossii*, 5 vols. (Moscow: Mezhdunarodnye otnosheniia, 1995–9).

Sanborn, J., *Drafting the Russian Nation: Military Conscription, Total War, and Mass Politics 1905–1925* (DeKalb: Northern Illinois University Press, 2003).

Saul, N. E., *Concord and Conflict: The United States and Russia, 1867–1914* (Lawrence: Regents University Press of Kansas, 1996).

Schimmelpenninck van der Oye, D. H., *Toward the Rising Sun: Russian Ideologies of Empire and the Path to War with Japan* (DeKalb: Northern Illinois University Press, 2001).

Schroeder, P. W., *The Transformation of European Politics, 1763–1848* (Oxford: Oxford University Press, 1994).

Scott, H. M., *The Emergence of the Eastern Powers, 1756–1775* (Cambridge: Cambridge University Press, 2001).

Scott, J. B., (ed.) *The Armed Neutralities of 1780 and 1800: A Collection of Official Documents* (New York: Oxford University Press, 1918).

Sergeev, E. Iu., *'Inaia zemlia, inoe nebo' Zapad i voennaia elita Rossii 1900–1914* (Moscow: Institut vseobshchei istorii RAN, 2001).

Shatsillo, K. F., *Ot portsmutskogo mira k peroi mirovoi voine. Generaly i politika* (Moscow: Rosspen, 2000).

Shtrange, M. M., *Russkoe obshchestvo i frantsuzskaia revoliutsiia* (Moscow: Izd. AN SSSR, 1956).

Siegel, Jennifer, *Endgame: Britain, Russia and the Final Struggle for Central Asia* (London: I. B. Tauris, 2002).

Simanskii, P. N., *Sobytiia na Dalnem Vostoke*, 3 vols. (St Petersburg: Voennaia tip., 1910).

Sirotkin, V. G., *Duel' dvukh diplomatii* (Moscow: Nauka, 1966).

Napoleon i Rossiia (Moscow: Olma-Press, 2000).

Stone, N., *The Eastern Front 1914–1917* (New York: Charles Scribner's Sons, 1975).

Sumner, B. H., *Russia and the Ballkans 1870–1880* (Oxford: Oxford University Press, 1937).

Tsardom and Imperialism (Hamden: Archon Books, 1968).

Tarle, E. V., *Severnaia voina i shvedskoe nashestvia na Rossiiu* (Moscow: Izd. sotsial'no-ekonomicheskoi literatury, 1958).

Taube, M., *La politique russe d'avant-guerre* (Paris: Librairie Ernest Leroux, 1928).

Trubetzkoi, Prince G., *Russland als Grossmacht* (Stuttgart: Deutsche Verlags-Anhalt, 1917).

Tselorungo, D. G., *Ofitsery russkoi armii – uchastniki borodinskogo srazheniia. Istoriko-sotsiologicheskoe issledovanie* (Moscow: Kalita, 2002).

Vandal, A., *Napoléon et Alexandre I*, 5th edition, 3 vols. (Paris: Plon and Nourrit, 1898–1903).

Verzhbitskii, V. G., *Revoliutsionnoe dvizhenie v russkoi armii 1826–1859* (Moscow: Izd. Sovetskaia Rossiia, 1964).

Vinogradov, V. N., 'Diplomatiia Ekateriny Velikoi: "My ni za kem khvostom ne tashchimsia"', *Novaia i noveishaia istoriia* (2001), no. 3: 131–50.

'Diplomatiia Ekateriny Velikoi: krymskaia epopeia', *Novaia i noveishaia istoriia* (2001), no. 4: 124–48.

'Diplomatiia Ekateriny Velikoi: Ekateriny II i Frantsuzskaia revoliutsiia', *Novaia i noveishaia istoriia* (2002), no. 6: 109–36.

(ed.), *Vek Ekateriny II: dela balkanskie* (Moscow: Nauka, 2000).

Vozgrin, V. E., *Rossiia i evropeiskie strany v gody Severnoi voiny* (Leningrad: Nauka, 1986).

Wildman, A. K., *The End of the Russian Imperial Army: The Old Army and the Soldiers' Revolt (March–April, 1917)* (Princeton: Princeton University Press, 1980).

Wirtschafter, E. K., *From Serf to Russian Soldier* (Princeton: Princeton University Press, 1990).

Zaionchkovskii, P. A., *Voennye reformy 1860–1870 godov v Rossii* (Moscow: Izd. MGU, 1952).

Samoderzhavie i russkaia armiia na rubezhe XIX–XX stoletii (Moscow: Mysl, 1973).
Zawadzki, W. H., *A Man of Honour: Adam Czartoryski as a Statesman of Russia and Poland, 1795–1831* (Oxford: Clarendon Press, 1993).
Zolotarev, V. A. (ed.), *Istoriia voennoi strategii Rossii* (Moscow: Kuchkovo pole poligrafresursy, 2000).

10. POLICE, SOCIALISTS AND REVOLUTION

Ascher, A., *Pavel Axelrod and the Development of Menshevism* (Cambridge, Mass.: Harvard University Press, 1972).
The Revolution of 1905, 2 vols. (Stanford: Stanford University Press, 1988–92).
Baron, S. H., *Plekhanov: The Father of Russian Marxism* (Stanford: Stanford University Press, 1963).
Billington, J., *Mikhailovsky and Russian Populism* (Oxford: Oxford University Press, 1958).
Bonnell, V., *Roots of Rebellion: Workers' Politics and Organisations in St Petersburg and Moscow, 1900–1914* (Berkeley: University of California Press, 1983).
Daly, Jonathan W., 'On the Significance of Emergency Legislation in Late Imperial Russia', *SR* 54 (1995): 602–29.
Autocracy under Siege: Security Police and Opposition in Russia, 1866–1905 (DeKalb: Northern Illinois University Press, 1998).
The Watchful State: Security Police and Opposition in Russia, 1906–1917 (DeKalb: Northern Illinois University Press, 2004).
Dan, F. I., *The Origins of Bolshevism*, trans. J. Carmichael (New York: Secker and Warburg, 1964).
Elwood, Ralph Carter, *Roman Malinovskii: A Life without a Cause* (Newtonville: Oriental Research Partners, 1977).
Engelstein, L., *Moscow 1905: Working-class Organisation and Political Conflict* (Stanford: Stanford University Press, 1982).
Galai, S., *The Liberation Movement in Russia, 1900–1905* (Cambridge: Cambridge University Press, 1973).
Geifman, Anna., *Thou Shalt Kill: Revolutionary Terrorism in Russia, 1894–1917* (Princeton: Princeton University Press, 1993).
Entangled in Terror: The Azef Affair and the Russian Revolution (Wilmington: Scholarly Resources, 2000).
Getzler, I., *Martov: A Political Biography of a Russian Social Democrat* (London: Cambridge University Press, 1967).
Geyer, D., *Lenin in der russischen Sozialdemokratie: Die Arbeiterbewegung im Zarenreich als Organisationsproblem der revolutionären Intelligentz, 1890–1903* (Cologne: Böhlau Verlag, 1962).
Haimson, L., *The Russian Marxists and the Origins of Bolshevism* (Cambridge, Mass.: Harvard University Press, 1955).
Hasegawa, Tsuyoshi, *The February Revolution: Petrograd, 1917* (Seattle and London: University of Washington Press, 1981).
Hildermeier, Manfred, *The Russian Socialist-Revolutionary Party Before the First World War*, English edn. (New York: St Martin Press, 2000).

Kassow, Samuel D., *Students, Professors, and the State in Tsarist Russia* (Berkeley and Los Angeles: University of California Press, 1989).

Keep, J. L. H., *The Rise of Social Democracy in Russia* (Oxford: Oxford University Press, 1963).

Kindersley, R., *The First Russian Revisionists: A Study of Legal Marxism in Russia* (Oxford: Oxford University Press, 1962).

Knei-Paz, B., *The Social and Political Thought of Leon Trotsky* (Oxford: Oxford University Press, 1978).

Lopukhin, A. A., *Nastoiashchee i budushchee russkoi politsii* (Moscow, 1907).

McKean, Robert B., *St Petersburg Between the Revolutions: Workers and Revolutionaries, June 1907-February 1917* (New Haven and London: Yale University Press, 1990).

Mendel, A. P., *Dilemmas of Progress in Tsarist Russia: Legal Marxism and Legal Populism* (Cambridge, Mass.: Harvard University Press, 1958).

Monas, Sidney, *The Third Section: Police and Society under Nicholas I* (Cambridge, Mass.: Harvard University Press, 1961).

Morrissey, S., *Heralds of Revolution: Russian Students and the Mythologies of Radicalism* (Berkeley: University of California Press, 1999).

Orzhekhovskii, I. V., *Samoderzhavie protiv revoliutsionnoi Rossii (1826–1880)* (Moscow: Mysl', 1982).

Perrie, M., *The Agrarian Policy of the Russian Socialist-Revolutionary Party from its Origins through the Revolution of 1905–1907* (Cambridge: Cambridge University Press, 1976).

Pipes, R., *Social Democracy and the St Petersburg Labor Movement, 1885–1907* (Cambridge, Mass.: Harvard University Press, 1963).

Struve: Liberal on the Left, 1870–1905 (Cambridge, Mass.: Harvard University Press, 1970).

Polianskii, N. N., *Tsarskie voennye sudy v bor'be s revoliutsiei, 1905–1907 gg.* (Moscow: Izd. MGU, 1958).

Politicheskie deiateli Rossii. 1917. (Moscow: Bol'shaia Rossiiskaia entsiklopediia, 1993).

Pomper, P., *Peter Lavrov and the Russian Revolutionary Movement* (Chicago: Chicago University Press, 1972).

Praisman, L. G., *Terroristy i revoliutsionery, okranniki i provokatory* (Moscow: Rosspen, 2001).

Reichman, H., *Railwaymen and Revolution: Russia 1905* (Berkeley: University of California Press, 1987).

Sablinsky, W., *The Road to Bloody Sunday: Father Gapon and the St Petersburg Massacre of 1905* (Princeton: Princeton University Press, 1976).

Schneiderman, Jeremiah, *Sergei Zubatov and Revolutionary Marxism: The Struggle for the Working Class in Tsarist Russia* (Ithaca: Cornell University Press, 1976).

Schwartz, S., *The Russian Reveliution of 1905: The Workers' Movement and the Formation of Bolshevism and Menshevism*, trans: G. Vakar (Chicago: University of Chicago Press, 1967).

Squire, P. S., *The Third Department: The Establishment and Practice of the Political Police in the Russia of Nicholas I* (Cambridge: Cambridge University Press, 1968).

Surh, G., *1905 in St Petersburg: Labor, Society and Revolution* (Stanford: Stanford University Press, 1989).

Theen, R. H., *Lenin: Genesis and Development of a Revolutionary* (Princeton: Princeton University Press, 1973).

Troitskii, N. A., *'Narodnaia volia' pered tsarskim sudom 1880–1894* (Saratov: Izd. Saratovskogo universiteta, 1983).

Tsarskie sudy protiv revoliutsionnoi Rossii (Saratov: Izd. saratovskogo universiteta, 1976).

Venturi, Franco, *Roots of Revolution: A History of the Populist and Socialist Movements in Nineteenth-Century Russia*, trans. Francis Haskell (New York: Knopf, 1960).

Vovchik, A. F., *Politika tsarizma po rabochemu voprosu v predrevoliutsionnyi period (1895–1904)* (Lvov: Izd. L'vovskogo universiteta, 1964).

Wildman, A., *The Making of a Workers' Revolution: Russian Social Democracy, 1891–1903* (Chicago: University of Chicago Press, 1967).

Wortman, R., *The Crisis of Russian Populism* (Cambridge: Cambridge University Press, 1967).

Zaionchkovskii, P. A., *Krizis samoderzhaviia na rubezhe 1870–1880-kh godov* (Moscow: Izd. MGU, 1964).

Zelnik, R. E. (ed.), *A Radical Worker in Tsarist Russia: The Autobiography of Semen Ivanovich Kanatchikov* (Berkeley: University of California Press, 1986).

Index

Abaza, A. A., member of State Council 471
Abdul Hamid II, Ottoman ruler 20
Ablesimov, Aleksandr, playwright 86
abortion 324
About This and That (journal) 86
Abramtsevo estate, artists' colony 105
Adams, John Quincy 519
Adrianople, Treaty of (1829) 559
adultery 309, 336, 339
advertising 320, 324
Aerenthal, Count Alois von, Austrian foreign minister 570
Afanasev, Aleksandr, anthology of folk-tales 98
al-Afgani, Jamal al-Din, Muslim reformer 219
Afghanistan 563, 566, 569
Africa, 'Scramble' for 576
agricultural reforms
  Stolypin's 181, 389, 417, 464, 613
  and vision of social justice 24
agriculture 232, 379, 410
  1870s depression 241
  arable 375
  and environment 373, 390
  expansion southwards 493
  extensive cultivation 374, 375, 387
  harvest fluctuations 375, 381, 478
  Jewish colonies 191
  livestock 376, 380, 387
  long-fallow (two-field) system 375, 379
  and national market 391
  Nizhnii Novgorod 267
  on noble estates 231, 241
  productivity levels 381, 391, 486
  Siberia 387
  three-field system 375, 379–80, 385
Aigun, Treaty of (1858) 561
Aix-la-Chapelle, Peace of (1748) 506
Aksakov, Konstantin Sergeevich, Slavophile writer 127
  Fundamental Principles of Russian History 127
Aksel'rod, Pavel, Menshevik 627
Alash Orda (Loyalty) party, Kazakh 221
Alaska
  Russian settlements in 36
  sold to USA (1867) 564
alcoholism 185, 422, 422n.77
Alekseev, Admiral E. I., Viceroy 586
Alekseev, A. V., army commander-in-chief (1917) 664
Aleksei *see* Alexis
Alexander I, Tsar (1801–25)
  conception of Russian destiny 149
  and conspiracy theories 153
  court
    favourites 152, 438
    liberal advisers 149, 526
  and economy 399–400
  and Europe 149, 520
    'Holy Alliance' 556
  foreign policy 519–28, 554, 556–8
    and Britain 523, 524, 525
    and France 520, 523
  and Jews 190
  monarchy under 151, 240
  and Poland 33, 172
  policy on nationalities 32–4, 149
    Muslims 208
  reforms
    Committee of Ministers 438
    constitutional charter commissioned 124
    and ministerial government system 432, 436, 598
    political reforms 122, 123, 148, 152, 526
    Senate 436

Alexander I, Tsar (*cont.*)
relations with nobility 240
and Russian Bible Society 153, 158
and Treaty of Tilsit 399
Alexander II, Tsar (1855–81)
assassination (1881) 102, 197, 318, 365, 485, 613, 639
attempt on life (1866) 610, 638
culture under 97–102
foreign policy 561–6
government
bureaucracy under 433
Council of Ministers 439–40
and State Council 437, 439
and state finances 480
and imperial army 541
policy towards Muslims 210, 211, 213
and Polish insurrection (1863) 37
reforms
and land reforms 603
and later reform programme 612–13
and law reforms (1864) 344
personal role in Great Reforms 594, 595–6, 609
and selective integration of Jews 194–6
and state secondary schools for girls 314
see also Great Reforms
Alexander III, Tsar (1881–94)
autocracy
and constraints of bureaucracy 361, 443
and counter-reforms 103, 104, 318, 361, 410, 615
culture under 103–7
foreign policy 566–7
policy towards Muslims 211, 213
Alexander Lycée (previously Tsarskoe Selo Lycée), St Petersburg 236
Alexandra, wife of Nicholas II 667, 668
Alexis, Crown Prince (son of Peter I) 117
Alexis, Crown Prince (son of Nicholas II) 658
Alexis, Grand Duke (uncle of Nicholas II) 586
Alexis, Tsar (Aleksei Mikhailovich) 68, 116, 492
court theatre 73
and Ukraine 165
Algeciras conference (1906) 418
Algeria 16
All-Russian Fair, Nizhnii Novgorod (1896) 283
All-Russian Muslim Congress
First (Nizhnii Novgorod) 220
Second (St Petersburg) 221
Third (Nizhnii Novgorod) 221
Fourth (St Petersburg 1914) 221
All-Russian Muslim Ministry 221
All-Russian Teachers Union 260
All-Russian Union for Women's Equality (Women's Union) 322
All-Russian Union of Zemstvo and Municipal Councils (Zemgor) 467, 667
Alvensleben Convention (1863) 564
Alvensleben-Erxleben, Count Albert von 564
Ambassadorial Office (*Posol'skii prikaz*) 501
ambassadors
Peter the Great's 501–3
Peter's use of foreigners 502
American War of Independence 511–12
and League of Armed Neutrality 512
see also United States
Amur river basin, annexation of 53, 60, 561
anarchism 138–40
aristocracy and 240
Andreev, Leonid, writer 547
Andrusovo, Truce of (1667) 531
Andrusovo, Treaty of (1654) 30
Anglo-Russian Convention (1907) 569
Anna, daughter of Peter the Great 71
marriage to Karl Friedrich of Holstein 501
Anna, Tsarina (1730–40) 78
culture under 78–80
and 'debauched' women 312
Her Majesty's Cabinet 435
and Jews 186
and Muslims 204
Anti-Muslim Missionary Division 212, 213
anticlericalism 291
Antokolsky, Mark 105
Antonii (Khrapovitskii), Archbishop 304
Antonovych, Volodymyr, Ukrainian populist 176, 177
'Confessions' (1862) 176
Antropov, Aleksei, painter 79
Arabic language, phonetic teaching of 219
Araja, Francesco, maestro di capella in St Petersburg 79
Arakcheev, Count A. A., review of military expenditure 470
Archangel, port of 395, 400, 493, 660
architects
Catherine the Great's 81
imported by Peter the Great 70
Russian 70, 77
architecture
gothic 82
'Moscow Baroque' 76
neoclassical 81–3
'Petrine' 69

'revivalist' neo-Muscovite 104
wood as commonest building material 76
Arensky, Anton, composer 107
Argunov family (serfs) 83
Argunov, Ivan, painter 84
aristocracy *see* boyars; elites; nobility, hereditary
Armenia 36, 210
Russification policy 41
Armenians, and first Duma (1906) 42
army *see* imperial army; military elite
art
avant-garde 108
democratisation of 101
Futurism 114
independent 89, 105
patronage 77
portrayal of women in 71
prints and engravings 71, 76, 84
rise of National movement 102
sculpture 72, 91
The World of Art journal 110–11
see also ballet; literature; music; paintings; theatre
artists
at Abramtsevo 105
foreign 68, 70, 83
imported by Peter the Great 68, 70
at Kremlin Armoury 69
Russian 71, 77, 79, 83–4, 93
Arts and Crafts movement (European) 105
Ashkhabad, and reformed courts 358
Asia
definition of boundary with Europe 47
Russian civilising mission in 49, 52
see also Central Asia; Russian Empire
assemblies *see* noble assemblies; provincial assemblies; zemstvo assemblies
Assembly of Justices of the Peace 355
Assembly of Russian Factory Workers, Gapon's (St Petersburg) 322, 629, 630
assimiliatsiia (assimilation) 59, 61
Astrakhan, khanate of, conquest of 28, 489
Auerstädt, battle of (1806) 525
Augustus II, King of Poland (1697–1733) 491, 505
deposed 498
and Great Northern War 490, 494
meeting with Peter the Great 168, 490
reinstated 500
Augustus III, King of Poland (1733–63) 505, 508
Augustynowicz, Tomasz 179
Austerlitz, battle of (1805) 525
Austrian Empire (Austria-Hungary) 18, 46, 490
anti-French alliance with 505
and Balkans 14
and Catholicism 20
Central Powers coalition with Germany 570
and Crimean War 560
finances 468
and Franco-Russian Entente (1857) 564
and Great Northern War 499
and Holy League 490
Jewish populations 187
military superiority 551
multiethnic federalism 21
as natural rival 521
and Ottoman Empire 557
and Prussia 511
reconquest of Hungary 490
relations with Serbia 570
and Russia 501, 509, 510, 565, 570–1
summer 1916 offensive against 553
and Third Coalition 524
and Treaty of Toeplitz (1813) 527
War of the Austrian Succession (1740–8) 505
see also Vienna
Austro-German alliance (1879) 14
Austro-Russian treaty (1795) 513
authoritarianism
justified by Napoleonic invasion 146
of Paul I 151
autocracy
and central role of monarch 442, 572
and centralised administration 430, 432, 438–9
and concept of paternalistic monarch 442
defence of 122–3, 132, 409
and development of domestic industry 409
development of 370, 442–6
effect of 1864 law reforms on 344, 607
elite support for 88
fear of 'ministerial despotism' 444, 445
and legality of imperial decrees 437
and Manifesto of 1881 615
and modernisation 447–8
nationalist conception of history and 151
and need for co-ordinating chief minister 443–5
power of 12, 536, 540
relations with bureaucracy 436, 439, 442–3
relationship to State Council 437
and right to initiate legislation 437

autocracy (*cont.*)
as state ideology 34, 94, 124, 150
see also monarchy
Avdeev, A. P., Nizhnii Novgorod citizen 278
Avvakum, archpriest (1620–82) 116
Azat (Muslim newspaper) 222
Azef, Evno, informant 640, 650
Azerbaijan
Musavat (Equality) party 221
see also Baku
Azov 510
capture of (1696) 69, 490
re-annexed (1739) 505
Azov Campaign (1695–6) 494–5
Azov province, Muslim elite conversion (1713) 204
Azov-Don Bank 404

Babushkin, Ivan 267, 629n.18
Baccari, Filippo, dancer 85
Baehr, Karl 266
Bagration family, Georgian origins 234
Bakhchisarai, Muslim reformed school 219
Baku (Azerbaijan)
industrial workers in 620, 635
Muslim press 222
oil production 415
and reformed courts 358
Bakunin, Mikhail Aleksandrovich, anarchist thinker 128, 138, 240
Appeal to the Slavs 130
Confession 130
Federalism, Socialism and Antitheologism 138
'Revolutionary Catechism' 638
The Knouto-German Empire and the Social Revolution 138, 139
The Reaction in Germany 130
Balakirev, Milii, composer 99, 282
Balasoglo, Alexander 52
Balicki, Zygmunt, Polish activist 180
Balkans 14, 523, 541
and Catherine the Great's Greek Project 512
and Ottoman Empire 565–6
unrest (1908–14) 570–1
wars (1912–13) 588
see also Bulgaria; Greece; Hungary; Romania; Serbia
ballet 79, 85
Ballets Russes company 112
Diaghilev's *Saisons russes* in Paris 93, 112
see also music; theatre
Balmont, Konstantin, poet 111
Baltic provinces
1905 revolution in 42, 648
abolition of serfdom (1816–19) 598, 604
absorption of nobility into Russian Empire 29, 35, 231, 234
annexation of 10, 29, 186
land tenure system 384
professional classes 16
reformed courts 356, 358
Russification policies 39
see also Estonia; Finland; Ingria; Latvia; Lithuania; Livonia
Baltic Sea
Russian access to 29, 500–1, 512, 515
Russian navy in 575
Bankal'skii, Petr, writer and businessman in Nizhnii Novgorod 274
Bankovskaia i Torgovaia Zhizn' (journal) 420
banks and banking
court bankers 398
crisis (1850s) 478
Dutch 398, 404, 406
in Europe 394
French support for 419, 421–2
German influence 419
great reforms (1859–60) 402–5
House of Gintsburg private bank 194, 420
joint-stock 404, 419
lending 397
local welfare boards as 461
mutual credit 404
Paper Money (Assignat) Bank (1786) 397, 401
Russian 396
savings banks 401
and *shar'ia* law 416
State Bank (1860) 402
see also credit
Bar, Confederation of 171
Baranov, Nikolai, governor of Nizhnii Novgorod 276
Baranovych, Lazar, Ukrainian cleric 166
'Apollo's Lute' (in Polish) 166
'Spiritual Sword' 165
Barclay de Tolly, Prince Mikhail, Russian army commander 152
Bariatinskii, Prince A. I., viceroy of Caucasus 215, 596
Baring Brothers and Co., London bankers 403, 404
Bark, P. L., minister of finance 422
Barkov, Ivan, novelist 86

Baroque, introduced to Muscovy from Ukraine and Poland 165
Barruel, abbé Augustin 152
Barszczewski, Leon 180
Bashkir, troops 204
Batiushkov, Konstantin, in Nizhnii Novgorod 280
Batum district (Transcaucasia) 216
Baturyn, Cossack capital 169
Bavaria, Prussian acquisition of 511
Bazhenov, Vasilii, architect 82
Beilis, Mendel, trial of 43
Belaia Krinitsa, Old Believer community 278
Belgium, uprising against Dutch (1830) 558
Belgrade, Treaty of (1739) 505
Beliaev, Mitrofan 107
Belinsky, Vissarion Grigor'evich, literary critic and Westerniser 95, 96, 128, 139, 250
  'Letter to N. V. Gogol' 96, 128
  Russia before Peter the Great 128
Belorussia (Belarus) 30, 148
  cultural influence of 69
  cultural Russification in 38
  land tenure system 384
Belosel'sky-Belozersky family, landowners 233
Bely, Andrei 113
  Petersburg (novel) 114
  Silver Dove 278
Bem, Jósef, Polish monarchist 173
Benardaki, D. E., merchant of Nizhnii Novgorod 273
Benckendorff family, Baltic landowners 234
Benckendorff, Count A. Kh., chief of police 94
Bender, Ottoman fort 495
Berendts, Senator E. N. 349
Berlin 189, 506, 535
Berlin, Treaty of (1878) 566
Bernstein, Eduard, and evolutionary socialism 141
Bessarabia
  annexation of 33
  ceded to Turkey 560
Bestuzhev-Riumin, Alexis P., as foreign minister 505, 507
Bestuzhev-Riumin, Konstantin, at Kazan university 279
Bezborodko, A. A. (Bezborod'ko, Oleksandr), in foreign chancery of Catherine the Great 170, 512, 514n.4
Bezborod'ko family 170, 233
Bialoblocki, Jan Andrzej, adviser to Sophia 166
Bil'basov, V. A., historian 507
birth-rates, and infant mortality 192, 374
Birzhevoi artel'shchik (journal) 420
Birzhevye vedomosti (newspaper), on strikes 622
bishops *see* episcopate
Bismarck, Otto von, German Chancellor 565, 566
Black Sea 30
  access to 494, 515, 555, 557
  demilitarised (1856) 560, 594
  free commercial navigation 510
  Russian navy in 575–6
  Turkish Straits 570, 571, 575, 577, 660
Blagoveshchenskii monastery, Nizhnii Novgorod 271, 277
Blinov, Fedor, merchant and miller in Nizhnii Novgorod 273, 277
Blok, Alexander 113
Boborykin, P. B., and inferiority of *raznochintsy* 250
Bobrikov, N. I., Russian governor-general in Helsinki, assassinated (1904) 40
Bogdanov (Aleksandr Aleksandrovich Malinovskii)
  futurologist 140
  Red Star (novel) 143
Bogolepov, Nikolai, minister of education, assassination (1901) 645
Bogrov, Dmitrii, assassin of Stolypin 651
Boguslavsky, General D. N. 212
Bohdanowicz, Karel, Polish geologist 182
Bokhara (Bukhara)
  khanate of 210, 216, 541, 561
  Young Bokharans movement 222
Bolsheviks
  and Fourth Duma 653
  and labour movement 627, 634–5
  and Russian Revolution 636
  and St Petersburg soviet 633
  see also Bogdanov; Lenin
borders
  with China 28
  European 554
  ill-defined 530
  River Dnieper as 490, 494
Borodin, Alexander, composer 99, 109
  Prince Igor 101, 105, 109
Borodino, battle of (1812) 534
Borovikovskii, Vladimir, painter 83
Bortnianskii, D. S., composer 84, 106

Bosnia-Herzegovina 565, 570
Bosnian Crisis (1908) 570
boyars 204, 233
  wealth of 232
Braunstein, Johann Friedrich 70
Bray, Chevalier François-Gabriel, Bavarian minister at St Petersburg 518
bread
  exports 400, 411, 422
  shortage (1916–17) 653, 655, 658, 662
  state regulation of prices 410
  see also grain
bribery, in law courts 465
British Empire 17, 19
  and British identity 20, 58
  and Indian Mutiny 55
  in Ireland 19
  see also Great Britain
Briusov, Valery, poet 110
Bronshtein, Lev Davidovich *see* Trotsky
Brotherhood of Cyril and Methodius 280
Brotherhood of Israel (Agudat Yisrael) 200
Brotherhood of Saint Gurii, Nizhnii Novgorod 278
Bruce, James, as ambassador for Peter the Great 502
Brunnow, Baron E. P., diplomat 229, 528n.22
Brusilov, Captain, chief of Naval General Staff, report (1906) 253, 583n.20
Brusilov, General A. A. 553, 665
Bruyn, Cornelius de 72
Bryullov (Briulov), Karl, painter 95
Bugrov, Nikolai, merchant and miller in Nizhnii Novgorod 273, 281
Bulgakov, S. N. 420
Bulgaria 565, 566
Bulgarin, Tadeusz, Pole and Russian nationalist 175
Bulygin, Aleksandr, minister of interior 647
Bund, the (Jewish labour movement) 199–200, 626, 628
Bunge, N. Kh.
  minister of finance 405, 407–8, 409, 411
  as reformer 613, 615
  and taxation system 481, 485, 606
  and Witte 412
Bunin, Ivan, writer 115
Bunina, Anna, writer 87
bureaucracy
  and empire 12, 15
  as encroachment on autocratic powers 442–3
  formal examinations (1809) 466
  growth of 431
  in local government 465–6
  ministerial 429
  and modernisation 433, 434, 447–8
  professionalisation of 432
  in urban administration 458
bureaucratic elite 227, 234–7
  cadre of liberal reformers 597–8, 615
  competence of 236
  education of 236, 432, 598
  ennoblement of 229
  institutional identity 433
  powers of 361, 433
  relations with aristocracy 240–1, 433
  and rivalry between ministers 443
business class
  ennobled 230
  as sub-elite 228
  see also industrialisation; industry
business organisations, influence of 421
Byzantinism 132

calendar, edict adopting European (1699) 67
Cameron, Charles, architect to Catherine the Great 82
Canning, Stratford, British diplomat in Constantinople 560
capital
  accumulation 394, 396
  Russian worth (1898) 415
capitalism 138, 141
  Lenin's view of 142
  possibility of 'cultured capitalism' in Russia 424
Capodistrias (Kapodistrias), Count Ionnes 247, 558, 567n.16
Caravaque, Louis, painter 70
Carlowitz, Georg Carl von, Polish envoy 495
Castlereagh, Viscount 229, 525, 528n.22
casualties, military 536
  First World War 552, 663
  Russo-Turkish War (1878–9) 541
catechism 121–2, 297, 297n.41
Catherine I, Tsarina (1725–7) 77, 186
  and Senate 435
  Supreme Privy Council 435
Catherine II the Great, Tsarina (1762–96) 13
  abolition of Cossack Hetmanate 169–70
  and bureaucracy 433
  and central administration 436
  and church
    reforms 285, 290
    secularisation of church lands 277, 290
    Toleration to All Faiths edict (1773) 206

and culture
as collector of art 81
golden age 81–8
as playwright 85, 254, 308
and economic development 396–8
foreign policy 507–15, 528
as diplomat 508
'Greek Project' 146, 512–13, 514
and Russia as European power 48
and Jews 31, 187–8
and justice
estate-based justice system 344
Legislative Commission (1767) 121, 151, 169
liberalism
consensus-building monarchy 119–20, 151
Instruction (*Nakaz*) (on importance of liberty) 119–20
local government reform 257, 275, 431, 460
Charter to the Towns (1785) 264, 450, 452, 458
Statute of Provincial Reforms (1775) 431, 450, 460
Manifesto (1783) 206
and Muslims 203, 205–8
and noble assemblies 459
Noble Charter (1785) *see* Charter to the Nobility
and Poland 30–1, 172, 508–9
on Radishchev 87
and state finances 469
Statute on Public Order (1782) 335, 336
and Ukraine 30
and women
education 307
hospitals for 312
Catholic Church
Chaadaev's view of 126
and Habsburg Empire 20
and Holy League 490
land holdings 239
monasteries in Ukraine 176
in Poland 30, 165, 179
and Polish uprising (1863) 178
political influence of 25
Caucasus
1905 revolution in 42
Emergency Laws (1881) 359
expansion into 36, 210
Muslims in 36, 41
Russification policies in 41–2
territorial gains (1878) 566
Transcaucasia
cultural conflicts of law 216, 358
muftiates created (ZMDP) 214
Muslim military administration 214–16
reformed courts 356, 357
Shi'i Muslims in 203, 205
Sufi Islam in 205, 211
see also Orenburg Assembly
viceroyalty of 215
see also Armenia; Baku; Caucasus, north; Georgia
Caucasus, north
annexations in 210
anti-notary uprising (1913) 222
militant Islamic movements 205, 211
Muslim rebellions 41, 211, 215, 217, 541, 558
end of (1864) 210, 610
Muslims in 202, 205
peasant agriculture 387
see also Chechnia; Daghestan
censorship
after 1905 Revolution 108
lack of (under Catherine II) 86
of Polish language 38
Radishchev's attack on 121
relaxation of 97
under Alexander III 103
census, 1897 national (first) 620
Central Asia
cotton production 10
expansion into 36, 49, 53–4, 210, 541, 555, 561–2
Islam in 202, 203
Muslim administrative system 216–17
Muslim political movements 222
Muslim rebellion (1916) 44, 222
Russification policies in 40–1
see also Astrakhan; Bokhara; Kazakh steppe; Kazan
Chaadaev, Petr Iakovlevich 96
Philosophical Letters
on historical insignificance of Russia 126, 127–8
on Russian culture 92, 94, 95
Chaliapin, Fedor, singer 109, 112
chancelleries (*prikazy*) 430
Chancellery (His Imperial Majesty's Own Personal Chancellery) 438–9
First Section 439
Second Section 439
Third Section 439, 441, 455, 637

Chancellery (*cont.*)
  Fifth Section 439
  see also State Chancellery
chancellor, office of 573
charities 281
  women's role in 315, 321
Charles VI, Holy Roman Emperor 505
Charles X, King of Sweden 29
Charles XI, King of Sweden 492
Charles XII, King of Sweden 18, 168, 496, 497
  and battle of Poltava 498
  death (1718) 499, 500
  and deposition of Augustus II of Poland 498
  at Narva (1700) 495, 531
Charter of Ecclesiastical Consistories (1841) 286
Charter to the Nobility (1785) 229, 450, 459
  on property transfers between spouses 334
  on punishment of women 340
Charter to the Towns (1785) 264, 340, 450, 452, 458
Chaumont, Treaty of (1814) 527
Chechens (Muslims) 36
Chechnia
  imamate state 211
  Muslim revolts 205, 217, 540
  Shafi'i Muslims in 203
Chekhov, Anton, playwright 93
  The Cherry Orchard 110
  Ivanov 105
  plays at Moscow Art Theatre 109
  short stories 104
  The Seagull 110
  Three Sisters 110
  Uncle Vanya 110
chemical industry 415
Cherevanskii, V. P., member of State Council 218
Cherkasskii, V. A., on Editing Commissions 601
Cherniaev, General M. G.
  capture of Tashkent 562, 563
  governor-general of Turkestan 218, 541
Chernigov (Chernihiv, Ukraine)
  church of 167
  diocese 166
Chernomazov, Miron, informant 652
Chernyshev, General Z. G. 535
Chernyshevsky, Nikolai, radical critic and novelist 100, 136, 138, 250
  The Aesthetic Relations of Art to Reality 100
  What Is to Be Done? (novel) 100, 136, 316
Chesme, church and palace 82
Chicherin, Boris Nikolaevich
  classical liberal 133–4
  Contemporary Tasks of Russian Life 133
  and mosque-building in Siberia 206
  Philosophy of Law 134
  On Popular Representation 134
  Property and the State 134
  Russia on the Eve of the Twentieth Century 134
Chigirin War (1677–81) 490
child-care institutions 321
children
  of clergy 295
  of convict women 340
  of soldiers 248, 311
  see also foundling hospitals; schools
China
  border with 28
  Boxer rebellion (1900) 568, 577
  imperial bureaucracy 15, 238, 445
  negotiations at Nerchinsk 166
  relations with 49, 555, 561
  Russian ambitions in 568, 576
  secret defensive alliance with (1896) 568
  trade with 395
  war with Japan over Korea 568, 577
  see also Manchuria
chiny see ranks
Chizhevskii (Chyzhevs'kyi), Stepan, first theatrical production in Moscow 165
Chod'sko, Aleksandr, Polish language expert 174
Chod'sko, Józef, Polish topographer 174
cholera 40, 272, 478
Christianity and Christians
  Bakunin's rejection of 130, 138, 139
  and basis of natural law 125
  in Caucasus 36, 41
  Europe as Christian 67
  and individualism 134
  and obedience to unrighteous rulers 116, 118
  in Ottoman Empire 510
  rejection by socialist thinkers 136
  and Russian Bible Society 157–8
  Tatars 40
  Tolstoy's interpretation of 140
  see also Catholic Church; Lutheranism; Orthodox Church; religious toleration
Christology 301
Chulkov, M. D., novelist 86
Cieszkowski, August, Polish Hegelian 174

Circle of Amateurs of Physics and Astronomy (1888), Nizhnii Novgorod 282
civil rights (liberties) 24, 134
  in October Manifesto 42
  proposed 124
  for women 323
civil society
  in cities 280–1, 459
  concept of 129–30, 255–6
  Great Reforms and 603
  institutions of 239, 255, 280
  Jews in 197
  and literary public sphere 256
  movement to promote 125–6
  principle of *grazhdanstvennost'* 56
  and professional classes 259–63
  and provincial assemblies 257
  Russian 256–7
  zemstvo assemblies and 259
Civil War (1918–21) 636
classicism *see* neoclassicism
clergy 288–96
  demand for reform (1905) 303
  education of daughters 312, 313
  education of priests 292–3, 295
  endogamous marriages 294
  episcopate 289–90
  financial support for 294–5
  legal status of offspring 295
  monastic ('black') 290–1
  numbers of 292, 294
  and parish reforms (1860s) 287
  parochial kinship ties 293
  pastoral role 292, 294, 297
  radicalisation of 302
  secular ('white') 292–6
  seminaries to train 266, 277, 286, 292
  social role of 302
  social status of (*dukhovnoe soslovie* hereditary rank) 228, 293–4, 295
  status of Muslim 213, 214
  Ukrainian 165, 182, 289
  use of sermons 121, 297, 297n.38, 300, 302
'clerical liberalism' 296
climate 373
coal, production levels 415, 421
Cobenzl, Louis de, Austrian ambassador 514
Cold War 18
College of Mining and Manufactures 312, 395
colonies 17
  Russian view of Asian provinces 47, 49, 212
Commercial Bank 402
Commission (and Office) for the Affairs of New Converts 205, 206
commissions
  on factory legislation 622
  on law codes 338, 359–61
  on local government 602–3
  on serf emancipation (Editing Commissions) 600–2, 604, 607
  see also Legislative Commission; Shidlovskii Commission;
Committee of Finances 399, 476
  1861 proposals 477
  inconsistent role of 469
  and Reutern's report (1866) 479
  see also Ministry of Finance; state finances
Committee of Ministers 438
  institutional authority of 438
  role of chairman 438
  see also Council of Ministers
communications
  difficulty of 13
  problems of distance 455, 549
communism
  Bakunin's rejection of 138
  Bogdanov's vision of 143
  see also Marxism
Communist Party of Poland 181
Comte, Auguste 135
Concert of Europe 571
Congresses of Representatives of Industry and Trade, Council of 420, 424
conscience court (*sovestnyi sud*) 461
conscription 372, 394
  annual levies 372
  Catherine the Great's modifications (1775) 532
  compulsory military service for Jews 190–1
  effect on household size 382
  exemptions 545
  introduced (1789) 170, 311
  Peter the Great's system (1705) 532
  reformed (1874) 388, 392, 544, 603, 609
  of sailors 582–3
  special levies 532, 537, 540
conservatism, Russian 122–4, 131–3
conspiracy, role in politics 151–3
Constantinople
  Russian advance on (1789) 541
  Russian advance on (1829) 559, 565
Constitutional-Democratic (Kadet) party 58, 135, 220
  and women's suffrage 323
constitutionalism 124–6
consumption
  commercial 324
  by migrant women 320

Copenhagen, battle of (1801) 519
corporal punishment
  abolished (1863) 603
  of women 339, 340–1
corporate institutions 457–60
  and development of corporate identity 467
  noble assemblies 229, 257, 459–60
  urban government 457–9, 463
  see also zemstvo assemblies
corruption, in local government 465
Cossacks 17, 154, 167–8, 175, 183
  Bolotnikov revolt (1606–7) 378
  Hetmanate in eastern Ukraine 167, 168
    abolished 170, 171, 175
  Khmelnyts'kyi rebellion against Poland (1648–54) 165, 169, 491
  military importance of 170
  nobles assimilated into Russian elite 170, 233
  nobles' rights 169, 170
  and Ottoman Empire 167, 168
  peasant rebellions 378
  and Poland 167, 169, 176
  Pugachev revolt (1773–75) 89, 147, 151, 154, 378
  raid on Turkey (1768) 509
  Razin revolt (1670–1) 378
  Society of Notable Military Fellows 169
  under Catherine the Great 169–70
cotton
  industry 400, 421
  production in Central Asia 10
Council of Ministers (1857) 439–40
  collective decision-making 440
  and 'strong minister' role 441
Council of Ministers (1905) 417, 446
  Special Committee 366
Council of Sworn Attorneys 362
Counter-Enlightenment 121–2
courts, local 345, 389, 456, 461
Coxe, Revd William 90
Cracow (Poland) 172
crafts
  concentrated in St Petersburg 76
  Kremlin Armoury workshops 69
  Nizhnii Novgorod 268
  peasant, in towns 453
  traditional 84
  workshops at Abramtsevo 105
credit
  1729 statute on promissory notes 396
  administration of 395
  Catherine credit system 396
  development of commercial 401, 402
  institutions 397
  international state 396
  private 397
  for property market 397, 405
  see also banks and banking
crime
  in cities 352
  distinguished from sin 352
  murder of spouses 339
  political 364, 366, 367, 638, 640
  in rural areas 352, 455
  state-crime 638, 648
  see also criminal law; punishment; terrorism
Crimea 489, 490
  annexation (1783) 186, 397, 513
  campaigns against (1687 and 1689) 490
  and Chigirin War (1677–81) 490
  independence (1774) 510
  jadidism movement 219
  Jewish population in 186
  Melli Firqa (National Party) 221
  Muslim population 205, 206, 214
  Tauride Directorate (TMDP) 209
  war (1736–9) 535
Crimean War (1854–6) 11, 13, 540, 594
  cost of 403, 478, 603
  and need for modernisation 12, 594
  origins of 560
  and Ukraine 176
  and view of empire 53
  women as nurses 314
Criminal Code (1864) 344
criminal law
  age of accountability 339
  development of gender difference in 340, 341–2
  rules of procedure 344
  status of women in 339–42
  see also crime
Croatians 570
Cubism 115
Cui, César, composer 99
cultural life
  middle classes and 256
  in Nizhnii Novgorod 278–83
  in towns 90, 278
culture
  contribution of Russia to global civilisation 10
  Polish influence 31, 68, 69, 165
  Ukrainian influence 68, 165

see also Russian culture
culture, folk, interest in 84, 279
Curie, Marie (née Skodowska) 179
currency
bronze coin 397
and gold standard 410, 413, 417
monetary reform 401, 412
paper money 412, 478, 479
exchange rate 401, 403, 423
introduced (1768) 397
'Siberian rouble' 412
silver coin 397
supply of coin 493
customary law 121, 216, 353
compensation preferred to punishment 352
and dowry rights of peasant women 148, 329n.12
in rural areas 351, 389, 456
and *volost'* courts 456
customs tariffs
1889 410
post-Napoleonic 399
revenue from 482
under Catherine the Great 396
Czartoryski, Prince Adam 149, 152, 173–4
and Alexander I's foreign policy 522–3, 527
Czekanowski, Aleksander 179
Czerski, Jan 179

Dacia (Romania) 513
Dadiani family, Georgian princes 234
Daghestan
administrative system 216
Anti-notary uprising (1913) 222
imamate state 211
Muslim revolts 217, 540
Shafi'i Muslims in 36, 203, 205
Dal', Vladimir, philologist 266, 598
Damaskin, Ioann, Bishop of Nizhnii Novgorod 277
dancing 72, 79
ballet 79, 85, 93, 112
Danilevskii, Nikolai Iakovlevich, Pan-Slav conservative 131
Russia and Europe 61–3, 132
Dannhauer (Tannhauer), Gottfried, painter 70
Danube, River 559
Danzig 491
Darwin, Charles, theory of evolution 108
Dashkova, Princess Catherine, Director of Academy of Sciences 308
De Smeth, Raymond and Theodore, Amsterdam bankers 398
De Velly, J. L., artist 79
deacons 292
Decembrist revolt (1825) 33, 94, 145, 153, 160–1, 558
and formation of secret police 637
Degaev, Sergei, police informant 639
Deitrikh, V. F., public prosecutor 354
Demidov family, merchant aristocrats 233
democracy 19
and introduction of trial by jury 349
liberal 25
and rule of law 362, 367
see also socialism
democratisation
of art 101
of family 313
Denmark
alliance with Russia (1765) 509
and Great Northern War 495, 499
relations with Prussia / Germany 567
treaty with (1699) 491
dervishes, wandering 217
Derzhavin, Gavrila, poet 87
desertion (from army), rates of 533
Desnitskii, S. A., first Russian professor of law 465
Diaghilev, Sergei 93, 110, 111
Ballets Russes company 112
exhibitions 111
and internationalisation of Russian culture 111–12
Digest of Laws (1832) (*Svod zakonov*) 335, 337, 439
on conduct in marriage 337
on duties of husbands 337
see also Law Codes
Dikov, Admiral I. M., naval minister 588
Din we-l-Eleb (Muslim newspaper) 222
Din we-Magyshat (Muslim newspaper) 222
Directorate of Religious Affairs of Foreign Confessions (1810) 208
Discount-Loan Bank of Persia 405, 414
disease *see* cholera; medicine; plague
District Courts 345, 356, 357, 389
districts (*uezd*), noble corporate institutions 229
divorce
church regulation of 286, 309, 335, 336, 342
grounds for 309, 336
and property law 335
and separation 336, 337

divorce (*cont.*)
voluntary (prohibited from 1730) 335
see also marriage
Dmitrii, bishop of Rostov 73
Dmitrii Pavlovich, Grand Duke, and assassination of Rasputin 668
Dmowski, Roman, Polish activist 180, 182
Dnieper, River, Russian border 490, 494
Dniester, River 30
Dobroliubov, Nikolai A., *intelligent* 250, 273, 274
on women's rights 315
Dokuchaev, Vasilii
founder of Nizhnii Novgorod natural history museum 282
study of black earth 390
Dolgorukii family, as ambassadors 502
Dolgorukii, Prince V. V. 503
Dolgorukova, Princess Ekaterina 610
Don, River 494
mining region 620
Dondukov-Korsakov, Prince A. M., Commander in Chief in Caucasus 218, 359
Doroshenko, Hetman 167
Dorpat (Tartu, Estonia) 39, 496
Dostoevsky, Fedor 54, 55, 93
The Brothers Karamazov 103
conservative nationalism of 131, 133
Diary of a Writer 133, 195
exile 97, 637
Notes from Underground 100
and unveiling of Pushkin statue 102
dress
adoption of Western (1700) 67, 90, 306–7
manufactured clothing 319
Russian 90
urban fashions 320
droughts 373
duelling 547
dukhovnost' (spirituality) 51
Dukhovskii, Mikhail, *Statistical Description of Nizhnii Novgorod Province* 279
Dukhovskoi, S. M., governor-general of Turkestan 218
Duma (legislature)
effect of national representation on local government 450
established by October Manifesto 42, 446, 569, 613
first (1906) 42, 220, 648
demand for land expropriation 242
and foreign policy 574
and Provisional Government (1917) 657, 658, 669
second (1907) 649
third (1907–12) 43
church and 303
fourth (1912–17) 303, 653
and formation of 'Progressive Bloc' (1915) 665, 666
workers' delegates 634
Durnovo, Petr Nikolaevich, minister of interior 237, 647
Dvina, River 493
Dzhunkovskii, Vladimir Fedorovich, assistant minister (internal affairs) 652, 653

ecclesiastical law
on divorce 335, 336
influence on civil family law 337
on wife's duty of obedience 300, 333
ecology
Central Eurasian 265
Nizhnii Novgorod 267
see also environment; soils
economic liberalism 25
and goals of reformers 597
see also market economy
economy
backwardness of 12, 369, 394, 401, 493, 530
as factor in 1917 Revolution 658–62
banking and finance reforms (from 1859) 402–5
Catherine system 396–402
crisis (1850s) 478–80
Europeanisation 396
and expansion of empire 10
First World War
in 1916 653
effect of prohibition 660
inflation 660
improvement (1890s) 481
improvement (from 1910) 550
joint-stock companies 406, 423
nature of 423–5
private enterprise 395, 405
in Soviet historiography 424–5
state role in 409–10, 424, 471
under Peter the Great 394–6
world crisis and depression (1900–3) 417, 418, 480
see also state finance
education
army officers 535
of bishops 289

for bureaucratic elite 236, 432, 598
in Congress Kingdom of Poland 174, 179
foreign governesses and tutors 307
and *jadidism* 219
of local officials 465–6
and military service 544
of nobility 94–7, 232, 236, 237, 249, 249n.11
of priests 292–3, 295
primary 262, 464
and *raznochintsy* 249
reforms 598, 603
state funding 473
and state service 248
in Ukraine 176
women 307–8, 323
Alarchinskii courses 317
Liubianskii courses 317
restriction on (1880s) 318, 319
Elagin, Ivan, Imperial Theatre administrator 85
Elbing, Baltic port 491
electoral law 42
revised (1907) 42
electrical industry 415
Elena Pavlovna, Grand Duchess 99, 598, 606
elites, political power of 19, 228
elites, Russian
and 1812 war 148
awareness of social instability 154
civic engagement 154, 256
compared with Asian elites 238
and culture
contempt for native culture 98
Europeanisation 146, 237
as patrons of arts 77, 81, 89
diplomatic 572
effect of 1864 law reforms on 357
Muslim mirzas in 204
perception of empire 22, 147
political 227
relations with tsars 88, 239, 242, 258, 436
revival of interest in Orthodoxy 150
social 227
sub-elites (clergy and business class) 228
Westernisation of 17, 21, 67, 77
see also bureaucratic elite; military elite; nobility, hereditary; ranks; women, elite
Elizabeth, Tsarina (1741–61) 31, 71, 78
and Cossacks 168
culture under 78–9
economic development under 396
foreign policy 505–7
and France 506
and Muslims 186, 204
and Senate 435
and women 340
El'zanowski, Kazimierz, Polish engineer 182
Emancipation Day (1861), Nizhnii Novgorod 270
Emergency Laws (1881) 365–7, 615
Caucasus 359
Emin, F. A., novelist 86
empire (as polity type) 9
and colonial identity 17
maritime compared with land-based 17, 46
means of unification 20–1
and modernity 19
see also Russian Empire
employment
home-working 319
and industrialisation 319
women in 319–20
see also labour; workers
Enikeev family, Muslims 204
Enlightened Absolutism, doctrine of 89
enlightened despotism 507
Enlightenment
French 255
German 88
influence on Russian elite 147, 254
Jewish 189–90, 196
and principles of 1864 law reforms 347
see also modernisation; Russian Enlightenment
entomologists, Polish 179–80
entrepreneurs
peasants as 246
regulation of 247
environment 369, 372–3
impact of peasant agriculture on 373, 390, 393
episcopate 289–90
and 1905 Revolution 303
opposition to reforms 287
origins and education of 289
relations with local clergy 290
volatility of careers 289
Erevan (Armenia) 36
Eriksen, Vigilius, Danish artist 83
Ermak, Cossack commander 28
Ermanskii, Osip, Social Democrat 649
Eropkin, Peter, architect 70
Eshevskii, Stepan, historian of Nizhnii Novgorod 274, 279

Estonia 29, 39, 489
serfdom abolished 598, 604
to Russia (1721) 499
Eternal Peace, Treaty of (1686) 165, 167, 490
ethnicity
and empire 19, 58
and multiethnic federalism 21
see also nationalism; nationalities policy
Europe
absolutist state-building 11
balance of power in 13, 556, 557, 571
before First World War 568, 570
as Christian 67
church lands 239
Diplomatic Revolution (changing alliances) 506
early modern connections with Muscovy 165
experience of land reforms in 604
geographical definition of 26, 47
hereditary privileges of rank 245
industrial growth (1890s) 414
influence on Russia 10, 14, 16, 45–50
Jews in 185, 195
legacy of Napoleonic empire 156, 157
legal traditions 328, 344, 347
military-fiscal state development 11
and peripheral states 18, 23
view of Ottoman Empire 14, 557, 559, 568
and War of the Austrian Succession (1740–48) 505
see also Austrian Empire; France; Germany; Great Britain; Westernisation
Evdoksiia, first wife of Peter the Great 309
evidence, rules of 345
exile, as punishment 339, 341, 366
explorers, Polish 182
exports 397, 400
bread 400, 411, 422
grain 400, 411, 416, 421
increased 411
state monopolies 395
Eylau, battle of (1807) 525

Fabergé, Carl 103
Factory Inspectorate 408, 410
factory legislation 267, 407, 622, 625, 625n.13
famine
1891–2 390, 411, 640
grain distribution 391, 484
harvest fluctuations 375
farmazon (freemason), as pejorative term 153
favourites, court 79, 81, 147, 441
Alexander I's 438
Peter the Great's 503
as unofficial advisers 445
February Manifesto (1903) 288
federalism
multiethnic 21
proposed 124, 125
Fedor Alexeievich, Tsar (1676–82) 166
Fedor Ioanovich, Tsar (1584–98) 204
Ferdinand VI, king of Spain 527
Ferguson, Adam 255
festivals, peasant 386
feudalism 11, 239
Filippov, Mikhail, liberal jurist 315
Filosofova, Anna 315
finance
1850s international crisis 403, 478
1873 stock-market crisis 406
foreign financiers 395
foreign investment 413, 659
and supply of coin 493
see also Committee of Finances; credit; currency; Ministry of Finance; state finance
Finansovoe obozrenie (journal) 420
Finland
annexation of (1808/9) 10, 32, 554
as autonomous province 32
constitutional order (1863) 610
economy 416
Kexholm province 495
Russian conquest (1713–14) 499
Russification policy 39, 235, 546, 546n.37
Socialist Revolutionaries in 645
Finnic peasants 370
First World War 12, 14
blockade of Russia 660
economic effects of 422
German offensive (1915) and 'Great Retreat' 665–6
Habsburg front 662
hunger crisis (1916–17) 653
imperial army and 551–3
inflation 660
and labour unrest 635, 653
and military expenditure 470, 550
military failures 659
and nationalities policies 43–4
Orthodox Church and 304
prohibition (alcohol) 482, 660
and reliance on indirect taxation 482
war councils 667

Flammarion, Camille 282
Focsani, battle of (1789) 535
Foinitskii, Ivan, legal scholar 349
Fokine, Michel, choreographer 112
folk-songs 84
folk-tales 98
  Stravinsky and 112
  used for operas 109
folklore 386
Fonvizin, Denis Ivanovich, playwright 85, 120
  Discourse 120
foreign policy
  from 1815 to Crimean War 556–60
  Alexander I 519–28, 554, 556–8
  Alexander II 561–6
  Alexander III 566–7
  before Peter the Great 489, 490, 494
  Catherine the Great 507–15, 528
    'Greek Project' 146, 512–13, 514
  changes in 1790s 515–19
  character of tsarist diplomacy 571–4
  and Continental System (1807) 526
  defence of Orthodoxy as justification for war 497
  desire for ports 494, 495
  Duma and 574
  era of palace revolutions (1752–62) 504–7
  Europhile 529
  Kochubei's exposition of 521
  Nicholas I 558
  Nicholas II 567–71
  Paul I 516–19
  Peter the Great's ambassadors 501–3
  recueillement (1856–94) 561–7
  role of unofficial advisers to tsar 445
  Russian claims to patrimonial inheritance 496
  Russian national/Eastern (semi-isolationist) (*svoboda ruk*) 528
  strategic position (19th century) 554–6
  and War of the Austrian Succession (1740–48) 505
  see also Great Northern War; Ministry of Foreign Affairs; Russo-Turkish wars
forests
  deforestation 390
  food gathering 376, 380
foundling hospitals 311, 320
  as credit institutions 397
Fox, Charles James 525
France 13, 468
  alliances with 13, 14, 564
    1756 506
    1894 472, 550, 566
    Treaty of Tilsit 525
    Triple Entente 569
  and American war of independence 511
  and Bavarian Exchange 511
  conscription 545
  and Crimean War 560
  expansionism 521, 522
  financial support for Russia 410, 418, 419, 421–2
  Grande Armée 147, 149, 154, 155, 156
  Jewish populations 187
  legacy of Napoleonic empire 156, 157
  nobility 230
  and Polish uprising (1863) 178, 564
  relations with 148, 501, 505
  Tsar Alexander I and 520
  and Turkey 510
  see also French Revolution; Napoleon Bonaparte; Napoleonic invasion of Russia; Napoleonic Wars
Francis II, Holy Roman Emperor 558
Francis Joseph, Emperor of Austria 447
Francis-Ferdinand, Archduke, assassination of 571
Frederick II, King of Prussia 505, 511
  and Poland 30, 508
Frederick, King of Sweden 500
Frederick William III, King of Prussia 513, 527
Fredericks, –, Dutch merchant and banker 398
Free Artists' Co-operative (1863) 100
Free Economic Society 381, 390
Free Music School 99
free speech, privilege of advocates 362
free trade 399
free will 136
Freemasonry 120, 152, 153
French language 34, 572
French Revolution 123, 124, 516
  and conspiracy theories 152
  Tsar Paul and 516
Freud, Sigmund 108
Friedland, battle of (1807) 525
Fundamental Laws (1906) 367, 572
fur trade, Siberia 10, 28
Fürst, Otto, theatre manager 73
Futurism 114
  A Slap in the Face of Public Taste (manifesto) 114
  Victory over the Sun (opera) 114
Fuyuzat (Muslim newspaper) 222

Gagarin family, aristocratic landowners 233, 385
Galicia 181, 665
  eastern 172
Gapon, Father, workers' leader 627, 629
gaponovshchina movement 627
gardens, landscaped 82
Gargarina, Princess 330
Garshin, Vsevolod, writer 547
Gasprinsky (Gaspraly), Ismail Bey, Crimean Tatar 219
Gatsiskii, Aleksandr Serafimovich 272, 274, 276, 281
Gedymin, princely dynasty 233
Gendarme Corps 637, 638, 639, 651
  abolished by Provisional Government (1917) 654
  and political crime inquests 640
  provincial security bureaus 646
  relations with police security bureaus 643, 649
  see also police
General Jewish Workers' Union in Lithuania, Poland and Russia 200
  see also Bund, the
geography of Russia 369, 598
  see also climate; ecology; environment; soils
George I, King of England 499
Georgia
  annexation (1801) 10, 36
  assimilation of nobles into Russian elite 234
  ceded by Turkey (1829) 559
  relations with Russia 42
  southern (Muslim Lazistan), annexation (1878) 210
  see also Tiflis
German Enlightenment 88
Germans, in Russia 43
Germany
  Alexander I and 521
  Alexander III and 566
  aristocracy 232, 239
  banks 406, 419
  Central Powers coalition with Austria 570
  and China 568
  conscription 545
  First World War 43
  investment in Russia 660
  military superiority 551, 567, 659
  as threat to Russia 14, 541, 575
  trade disputes with 566
  unification of 14, 549
  see also Prussia
Gerschenkron, Alexander 424
Gessen, Joseph 196
Giers, N. K., foreign minister 247, 409, 566, 567n.16
Gillet, N. F., artist 79
Gintsburg (Ginzburg), Evzel, Jewish leader 193, 194, 196
Gintsburg (Ginzburg), Horace 194
Gintsburg (Ginzburg), House of, private bank 194, 420
Gippius, Zinaïda 274
Glazunov, Aleksandr, composer 107
Glinka, Mikhail, *A Life for the Tsar* (opera) 95, 96, 109, 150
Glinka, Sergei Nikolaevich, conservative 123
  in Nizhnii Novgorod 280
  Russian Messenger (journal) 123
Godunov family, Muslim origins 204
Gogol, N. V. 96, 170, 250
  Dead Souls 96, 102
  The Government Inspector 95, 455, 637
Golitsyn family, aristocratic landowners 233
Golitsyn, Prince V. V. 490, 494
Golitsyn, Prince G. S., Russian governor in Armenia 42
Golitsyn, Prince Petr, ambassador to Vienna 502
Golovin, Fedor, favourite of Peter the Great 491, 502, 503
Golovkin, Gavriil Ivanovich, and foreign policy under Peter the Great 502
Golovnin, A. V. 597
Gomm, William, English court banker 398
Goncharov Ivan, novelist, *Oblomov* 98
Goncharova, Natalia, artist 113
Gorchakov, Prince Alexander, foreign minister 49, 561, 573
  on policy in Central Asia 562
  and Polish uprising (1863) 564
  and war with Turkey (1877–8) 565, 566
Gordon, General Patrick 490, 503
Goremykin, I. L., prime minister (1914) 422
Gorky, Maxim, playwright 115, 153, 157
  Lower Depths 110
Gorky (city of) *see* Nizhnii Novgorod
Gorlice-Tarnow, battle of (1915) 553
Gorodets, river port 268
government
  and First World War 653, 666
    collapse of (1916–17) 668–9
    war councils (1915) 667

functions and purpose of 124
legal-administrative controls 246, 247
ministerial government system 399, 432–4
and nature of autocracy 442–6
and need for first minister 441, 443
policy-making 429, 431
in ministerial system 432
reaction to 1905 anarchy 647
relations with local administration 450, 451–2
subordinate organs system 430–2
supreme organs (*verkhovnye organy*) 435–41, 448
and workers
attempts to appease 625–7, 631–2
commissions on factory legislation 622
reaction to strikes 622–3
see also autocracy; bureaucracy; Chancellery; Council of Ministers; ministries; State Council; state finances
governors
Nizhnii Novgorod 275
and provincial assemblies 257, 275, 460
relations with local officials 454–5, 466
role in urban affairs 458
and zemstvo assemblies 453–4, 464
governors-general, drawn from aristocracy 235
Grabczewski, Bronisaw 180
grain
exports 400, 411, 416, 421
requisitions by state 391, 484
shortages in First World War 661, 669
trade 268, 423
see also bread
Granovskii, Timofei Nikolaevich, historian and Westerniser 128
grazhdanstvennost' (framework of civil order) 56
Great Apostasy (1866) 217
Great Britain 18
and American War of Independence 511
and Anglo-Russian Convention (1907) 569
and Armed Neutrality 518, 519
English aristocracy and gentry 228, 232, 243
export of textile machinery 618
financial support to Russia 398, 419
and Great Northern War 499
naval power 13, 17, 575
and Poland 556
policy towards Russia 13, 18, 560
and Prussia 506
rivalry with France 13, 522
and Russian threat to India 40, 541, 555, 557, 562–3
and Russo-Turkish War (1878) 565
and Second Coalition 516, 517
and Third Coalition 523, 524, 525
trade with 399, 423, 493, 501
and Treaty of Reichenbach 527
see also British Empire
'Great Game' 18, 563, 569
Great Northern War (with Sweden) (1700–21) 45, 69, 117, 168, 495–9, 531
declaration of 489
effect on commerce and industry 394
Mecklenburg Plan 499
Peter's justification of 496–8
Russian casualties 537
Treaty of Nystad (1721) 499
Great Reforms, under Alexander II 37, 97, 101
and 1905 Revolution 613
aims of reformers 597, 599–602, 608
and bureaucracy 433, 447
and Church 287, 295
and counter-reforms 288, 318, 409, 615
and economic policy 405, 597
Editing Commissions 600–2, 604, 607
and land reforms 604–5
effect on political debate 130
General Memorandum (1860) 607
ideology and programme of 599–608
and Islam 203
and land reform 603–6
and later reform programme 612–13, 615
loss of momentum 609–10
Nizhnii Novgorod 275, 275n.43
and provincial assemblies 257
the reformers 597–8, 614
rise of merchant class 101
role of Peace Mediators 602, 611
as 'watershed' 593–4, 614
see also serfs, emancipation; zemstvo assemblies
Gredeskul, Nikolai, Kadet jurist 651
Greece
and Catherine the Great's 'Greek Project' 146, 512–13, 514
war of independence (1820s) 126, 557, 559
Grenville, Lord 525
Grodekov, General N. I. 212
Gross-Jägersdorf, battle of (1757) 506
Grotius, Hugo 117
Gruzinskii, Prince, marshal of nobility in Nizhnii Novgorod 273, 273n.31

Gubernskie vedomosti (provincial journal), Nizhnii Novgorod 272, 277, 278, 280, 281, 282
Gubin, A. M., mayor of Nizhnii Novgorod 277
guilds
  introduction and regulation of 452
  in provincial administration 275, 281
  St Petersburg 452
Gustav III, king of Sweden 510, 513
Gustavus Adolphus, king of Sweden 491, 492

Habsburg dynasty 13, 14
  see also Austrian Empire
Hamburg, bankers 399
Hanover, and Great Northern War 499
Harman and Company, London bankers 399
Hartung, Mikolaj 179
Hasidism, Jewish mystical-pietist movement 188–9
Haskalah (Jewish Enlightenment) 189–90, 196
Haxthausen, Baron August von 279, 328
Hayat (Muslim newspaper) 222
health care 40
  zemstvos' role in 258, 464
  see also medicine
Hebrew language 187
Hegel, G. W. F. 255
Hegelianism, Polish 174
Herzen, Alexander (Aleksandr Ivanovich), radical writer and Westerniser 128
  Dilettantism in Scholarship 129
  exiled 637
  Letters from France and Italy 129
  On the Development of Revolutionary Ideas in Russia 129
historical determinism 141
Hlukhiv, Cossack capital 169
Hobbes, Thomas 118
Hoffman, Karol 173
Hohenzollern dynasty 13, 14
Holstein, Peter the Great's alliance with 500
Holy League 490
Holy Regiment of the Old Believer Muslims (Vaisov Brotherhood) 210
Hope and Company, Dutch banking house 398, 404, 406
households
  as basis of peasant economy 376
  changes in size and divisions 379, 381–2, 391, 392
  effect of tax changes on size of 382
  gender and generation tensions 383
  Nizhnii Novgorod 274
  in outlying regions 387
  and periodic redistribution of arable land 383–4
  simple 376, 387, 392
  and village communes 385
Hrushevs'kyi, Mykhailo, Ukrainian historian 181
Hubertusburg, Peace of (1763) 507
Hungary
  and 1848 Revolutions 558
  and Habsburg Empire 18, 490
  and liberalism 24
  nobility 230, 243
  see also Austria-Hungary
hunting, game 376
Husainov, Muhammedzhan, Orenburg mufti 210

Iagushinkii, P. I., favourite of Peter the Great 503
Iaokim, Patriarch 166, 285
Iavorskii, Stefan (Iavors'kyi, Stepan) 165, 166, 497
  sermon against Peter I 117
icon processions 298
icons 91
  Pokrova 167, 168
  popularity of 76
  recognised as works of art 113
Idealism, philosophical 126, 129
Ignat'ev, Count A. P., Commission on Emergency Laws 367
Ignat'ev, Count Nikolai 561, 565, 573
illegitimacy 311, 320
  foundling hospitals 311, 320
Il'minskii, Nikolai, professor of Turkic studies 41, 212
Immeritinsky family, Georgian origins 234
Imperial Academy of Arts, training by 89
imperial army
  in 17th century 530
  autocratic power over 536, 540, 548
  deficiencies of 537–9
  failure (1854–1917) 540–51
  and First World War 551–3, 659, 665
  funding and costs 535–6, 549–51
    cost-cutting devices 537–8
    expenditure (1910–14) 470, 550
  manpower 532
    recruitment 532–3, 544, 663
    see also conscription
  minorities in 190–1, 204, 215, 545

and Nicholas II 235, 548–9, 550
demand by commanders for abdication of tsar (1917) 657, 658, 664–5
opposition to, military commanders 664
personal command of army (1915) 667
non-commissioned officers 546
officers
casualties (by 1916) 552, 663
decline in prestige 546–7
drawn from nobility 534, 546
education 230, 535
foreign 230, 492
general staff officers (GSOs) 547
lack of cohesion among 547
quality of 492, 493, 534–5, 546–9
organisation 538
artel units 533, 546
Caucasian Corps 540
elite regiments 233, 547
homogeneity of 533, 545
and reserve system 538, 544, 663
at outbreak of Great Northern War 492
outstanding commanders 535
at Poltava 498
reforms
administrative restructuring 543
after 1905 Revolution 543, 550
military districts 543
under Alexander II 541
under Peter the Great 531–2
size
in 1756 536–7
in 1825 531
by 1914 545
problems of 537–8, 543
success (1700–1825) 531–9
symbiotic relation to state 530
technology
armaments production 551
backwardness 538
improvements 543
investment in 549
under revolutionary control 669
use against internal disorder 536, 543
use of mercenaries 492
see also conscription; military elite; mutinies; soldiers
Imperial Court Chapel 106
Imperial Theatre Administration 85, 105
India, Russian threat to Britain in 40, 541, 555, 557, 562–3
Indian Mutiny (1857) 55
individualism
and Christianity 134
conservative opposition to 133
development of 129
and rationalism 127
rejected by socialists 137
Industrial Revolution, Europe 12, 13
industrialisation 618
conflicting views of 433, 434
Poland 179
and women as factory workers 319
see also industry; workers
industry
aristocratic enterprises 232, 241
and crisis of 1900s 418
domestic production 409, 415
early factories 267, 395, 397, 400, 617, 618n.2
effect of Great Northern War on 394
factory regulation 267, 407, 410, 622, 625, 625n.13
growth (1890s) 414, 619
growth (1910–14) 421, 634
inferiority in 1914 551
and labour force 619
machine building 415
in Muscovy 530
Nizhnii Novgorod 268
policy of forced development 408–17
private enterprise 395, 405
state support for 406, 407
war production 552, 659, 661–2, 666, 667
see also iron and steel; textile industry; workers
infanticide 311
Ingria 495
taken by Russia 496, 499
taken by Sweden 489
inheritance 327–9
gender differences 327, 328, 377
intestate 328
laws of succession revised (1912) 342
peasant customs 377
inorodtsy ('aliens'), category of 34
institutions
all-estate 239, 460–5
of civil society 239, 255, 280
of government 429, 438
Peter the Great and 430
urban 451, 452
welfare 461
see also corporate institutions; government; subordinate organs; supreme organs; zemstvo assemblies

intelligentsia 250–5
  definition of 251–2
  exiled 637
  hostility towards army 547
  interest in peasantry 390
  Jewish 196
  and liberal bureaucracy 615
  myth of 253
  opposition to government 96
  origins 251, 252, 253, 254
  professionals as 259
  provincial 282
  as *raznochintsy* 96, 250–1
  relations with professionals 263
  and secret police 637
  and social identity 252, 254–5
  and workers 623–4, 627, 645
  see also radicals
International Women's Day march (February 1917) 656
International Working Men's Association 138
International Workingmen's Congress (First), and Polish uprising (1863) 178
Iran
  Muslim emigration to 210, 221
  see also Persia
Iranian Revolution (1907–11) 221
Ireland 19, 243
iron and steel industry 268, 401, 415, 421
  cast iron production 415
  Urals 15, 232, 493, 620
Irshad (Muslim newspaper) 222
Irving, Washington 33, 98n.14
Iskra (Social Democrat newspaper) 645
Islam
  Hanafi Muslims 203
  jihad against Russian state 211, 217
  mullahs 204, 214
  in Ottoman Empire 16, 20
  and pan-Islamism 217, 221
  political dimension (from 1905) 203
  qadi (lawyer) 204, 209
  reformism (*jadidism*) 202, 219–20
  Russian oriental studies of 211–13
  Shafi'i Muslims (Daghestan and Chechnia) 203
  shari'a law 207, 208, 359
  Shi'i Muslims (Central Asia and Transcaucasia) 203
  Sufi 208, 209, 211, 217
    in Transcaucasus 205, 211
  traditionalism (*qadimism*) 202
  see also Muslims and Muslim communities; Orenburg Assembly
Islamic institutions 203
Ismail, Usman 206
Istoriia Rusov 175
Italy 23, 527
  landowners 243
  liberalism in 25
  Russian defeat of French in (1799) 535
Ittifaq al-Muslimin (Muslim Union) party 220
Iurev (Tartu, Estonia) 39, 496
Iusupov family, Muslim origins 204
Iusupov, Prince F. F., and assassination of Rasputin 668
Ivan IV, Tsar (the Terrible) 28, 116, 496
Ivan VI, Tsar (1740–1) 78
Ivanov, General 664
Ivanov, Vyacheslav 113
Ivanovo-Voznesensk, strikes (1905) 633
Ivashev, Vasilii, Decembrist 315
Izmail, battle of (1790) 535
Izvol'skii, Aleksandr, foreign minister 247, 567n.16, 569, 570, 574, 588

Jaczewski, Leonard, Polish explorer 182
jadidism (Muslim reform movement) 202, 219–20
  and political parties 220
Jan Kazimierz, King of Poland 167
Jan Sobieski, King of Poland 167, 491
Jankowski, Michal 179
Japan 13, 577
  naval programme (1895) 577, 578
  war with China 568, 577
  see also Russo-Japanese war (1905)
Jaridat Daghestan (Arabic newspaper) 222
Jassy, Treaty of (1792) 513
Jena, battle of (1806) 525
Jewish Enlightenment 189–90, 196
Jewish statute (1804) 32
Jews
  anti-Jewish riots (pogroms) 197, 198–9, 366, 665
  and anti-semitism in Russia 43, 184, 188, 199
    suspected of conspiracies 151, 153
  on Bestushev medical courses for women 318
  compulsory military service 190–1
  conversions to Christianity 186, 190
  cultural separatism 32, 133, 187
  demand for rights and freedoms 193–4, 200
  in Eastern Europe 185–6
  emancipation in Europe 195

emigration of 184, 198
and expansion of Russian empire 31–2, 172, 187
expelled from Kiev 170
and first Duma (1906) 42
and Hasidism 188–9
integration 191
backlash against 197–9
effect on Jewish society 196–7, 200
participation in public life 193–201
policy of selective 194–6
Jewish Committees 190, 191, 193
and *kahal* autonomous community 32, 36, 188–9, 191, 192
labour movement (the Bund) 199–200, 626
as lawyers 196, 363
merchants 186, 187, 193, 402
in Poland 172, 178, 180, 186, 187
corporative autonomy 187, 188
and Polish Uprising (1863) 178
population growth 70, 191, 192n.10, 195
religious education 191
restrictions on 32, 191, 198
excluded from proposed religious toleration 125
Pale of Settlement 32, 184, 188, 402
role in Russian Revolution 184, 196
status
defined as *inorodtsy* 35
meshchane (artisans and petty traders) 31, 187
under Nicholas I 35, 190–1
Zionism 199
Jomini, Baron de 525
Joseph II, emperor of Austria 511, 513
journals *see* literature; press
judges
independence of 345, 346, 360, 364
liberal mission of 362
Judiciary Statutes (1864) 345, 362
jurists
influence of 361, 362
see also lawyers; legal profession
Justice, Ministers of 361
justice of the peace, office of 345, 354–6
abolished 360
appeals from decisions 355
in provinces 358

Kaftal, Handelman & Co., banking house 420
Kagul, battle of (1770) 535
kahal (Jewish autonomous community) 32, 188
abolished 36, 191
decline of influence of 192
threat of Hasidism to authority of 188–9
Kalisch, Treaty of (1813) 527
Kanashevich, Luka, Archbishop of Kazan 205
Kanatchikov, Semen 629n.18
Kandinsky, Vasily 108, 113, 114
Kankrin, Count E. F., minister of finance 400, 478
monetary reform 401
Kantemir, Prince Antiokh, satirist and poet 80
Kara Mustafa pasha, siege of Vienna 490
Karakozov, Dmitri, attempt on life of Alexander II 610
Karamzin, Nikolai, sentimentalist writer 87
on 18th-century Russian culture 88
defence of autocracy 122–3
History of the Russian State 87
in Nizhnii Novgorod 280
on subordinate status of women 338
Karelia, to Russia (1721) 499
Karelin, A. O., photographer in Nizhnii Novgorod 274
Karelina, Vera 322
Karl Friedrich, Duke of Holstein 501
Kars district (Transcaucasia) 216
Katkov, Mikhail Nikiforovich
conservative journalist 131, 359
and Dostoevsky 133
influence on economic reforms 409
Kaufmann, I. I., economist 414
Kaufmann, General Konstantin von 562
Kaufmann, K. P. von, governor-general of Turkestan 217
Kavelin, Konstantin Dmitrievich, jurist and Westerniser 128, 598
Analysis of Juridical Life in Ancient Russia 129
and land reforms 603
memorandum on serf emancipation (1855) 597
on obedience of wives 338
Kazakh steppe 562
mosques 206, 207
Muslim rebellion (1916) 223
schools 212
Kazakhs
Alash Orda (Loyalty) party 221
Islamisation of 206
skirmishes with (1840s) 36
Kazakov, Matvei, architect 82

Kazan 40, 356
Ecclesiastical Academy 212
Muslim elite conversion (1713) 204
Muslim press 222
Kazan, khanate of, conquest of (1551) 28, 266, 489, 563
Kazan, University of
and cultural life in Nizhnii Novgorod 279–80
women at 317
Kazembeg, A. K., professor at Kazan 212, 213
Kelles-Krauz, Kasimierz, Polish Marxist 181
Kerenskii, Aleksandr, leader of Trudovik faction 363, 666
Kexholm province, Russian claims to 495
Khabalov, General Sergei, commander of St Petersburg garrison 656
Khandoshkin, Ivan, violinist 85
Khanykov, N. V. 213
Kharkov
1864 law reforms in 261, 356
peasant disorder (1902) 646
University 175
Kherson, District Court 351, 353
Khiva 40
khanate of 210, 216, 561
Young Khivans movement 222
Khmelnyts'kyi, Bohdan, Hetman 168
Cossack rebellion against Poland (1648–54) 165, 169, 491
Kholodovskii, Admiral N. N. 581
Khomiakov, Aleksei Stepanovich
Slavophile writer 127
The Church is One 127
Khotin, Ottoman fort 495
Khrapovitskii, Antonii, archbishop 304
Khval'kovskii, N. E., Nizhnii Novgorod chief of police 270
Khvoshchinskaia, Nadezhda, *The Boarding School Girl* (novel) 316
Khvostov, A. N., minister of interior 661, 668
Kiaochow (Jiaozhou) Bay 568
Kiev Academy 69, 166
becomes Russian theological school 170
Kiev (Kyiv) 182
annual trade fair 186
courts 356, 357
metropolitanate of 166, 167
and origins of Rus 166
women at university 317
Kiev province 177
Kireevskii, Ivan Vasil'evich, Slavophile thinker 127
'On the Character of European Enlightenment…' 127
Kiselev, Count P. D., reform of state peasantry 476, 599, 602
Kistiakovs'kyi, Bohdan, Ukrainian legal scholar 181
Kitezh, lost city of 264
Kizhi, wooden church of the Transfiguration 76
Klado, Captain N. L. 581
Kletochnikov, Nikolai, revolutionary infiltrator 642
Kliuchevskii, Vasilii
historian 59, 373, 594
on scale of Great Reforms 600
Kniazhevich, A. M., minister of finance 479
Kniazhnin, Iakov, playwright 85
Knights of Malta 516, 518
Kochubei family 170, 233
Kochubei, Prince V. P. 170, 520, 521, 522
Kodiak (Alaska) 36
Kokand, khanate of 210, 541, 561, 562
Kokovtsov, Vladimir, minister of finance 417–22
relations with Nicholas II 447
Koni, Anatolii, jurist 349, 362, 365
Königsberg, Russian occupation (1758) 506
Konstantin Nikolaevich, Grand Duke (brother of Alexander II) 596, 597
and land reforms 606
and Russian Geographical Society 598
Koran
printed in Arabic (1787) 206
translations 212
Korea 542, 561
Sino-Japanese War over 568, 577
Korobov, Ivan, architect 70
Korolenko, Vladimir, writer 547
Korovin, Konstantin 105
Korsh, Fyodor, private theatre 105
Kosciuszko, Tadeusz
Polish uprising (1794) 172, 514
released by Tsar Paul 516
Kositskaia, Liubov, actress of Nizhnii Novgorod 274
Kostroma province, 'women's kingdoms' 383
Koten, Mikhail von, St Petersburg security bureau chief 652
Kotov, Nikolai F. 159
Kovalevskii, M. M. 420
Kraj (Polish language weekly) 39

Kramskoi, Ivan, and Free Artists' Co-operative 100
Kreenholm Cotton-Spinning and Weaving Factory strike (1872) 623
Krivoshein, Alexander, Minister of Agriculture 237
Kronslot (Kronstadt), naval port 496, 582
Kropotkin, Prince Petr, anarchist writer 138, 139–40, 240, 621
  The Conquest of Bread 139
  Mutual Aid 139, 140
  Should We Devote Ourselves to Analyzing the Ideal of the Future Order? 139
Krzemeniec (Ukraine), Polish lycée at 176
Kuchuk-Kainardzhi (Küçük Kaynarca), Treaty of (1774) 30, 510, 513
Kulibin, Ivan, inventor of steam engine 273
Kulomzin, A. N., member of State Council 613
Kunersdorf, battle of (1759) 506
Kunst, Johann-Christian, troupe of actors 73
Kunta-Hajji, Qadiri sheikh 211
Kuprin, Alexander, writer 547
Kurakin, Prince Boris, ambassador in Europe 502
Kurbskii, Prince Andrei Mikhailovich, correspondence with Ivan IV 116
Kurland, serfdom abolished 598
Kuropatkin, Aleksei (A. N.), minister of war 446, 542
al-Kursavi, Abu-l-Nasr 219
Kuskovo estate, Sheremetev family 83
Kustodiev, Boris, painter 115
Kutaisov, Count Pavel, governor of Nizhnii Novgorod 276
Kutuzov, Field Marshal Prince Mikhail 152, 527, 535
Kwieczynski, Andrzej, Polish Jesuit 165
Kyiv *see* Kiev
Kyrgyz
  defined as *inorodtsy* 35
  rebellion against recruitment (1916) 663

labour
  division of 137, 322
  free (in factories) 400
  gendered division of 383
  serf 400
  skills shortages in First World War 662
  and social ownership of means of production 139
  wage 389, 391, 397, 486
  women in employment 319–20
  see also workers
labour mobility 619
labour movement 635–6
  Bolsheviks and 627, 634–5
  the Bund (Jewish) 199–200, 626
labour relations 433, 434
  legislative reforms 625
  unrest (1901–3) 626
  and working conditions 408, 410, 641
  see also strikes
labour service (*barshchina*), owed by peasants 371, 385
Labzina, Anna 147
Lamanskii, Vladimir 62
Lambsdorff, Count Vladimir Nikolaevich, minister of foreign affairs 247, 567n.16
land captains (*zemskie nachal'niki*) (to replace justices of the peace) 360, 410, 455, 466
  as link between villages and zemstvos 463
Land College, and property disputes 331
Land and Freedom movement (1870s) 196, 639
land reform
  and abolition of serfdom 601, 603–6
  demand for (1906) 242
  Poland 178
land tax 371
Landé, Jean-Baptiste, ballet master 79
landowners
  noblewomen as 329
  and peasants 243, 244
  power of provincial 240, 241
  sale of land 241
  size of estates 231
  transformation of estates 82
  Ukraine 176–7
  see also nobility, hereditary; property laws
land-ownership 229, 231, 241, 243
language
  Central Asian 41
  official use of Russian 34, 357, 358
  Russian literary 80
  and Russification policies 38
  see also Arabic; French; Hebrew; Latin; Lithuania; Polish; Turkish; Ukraine
Larionov, Mikhail, artist 113
Latin, status as language of reason 165
Latin America 17
Latvia 29, 39, 665
Lavrov, Petr Lavrovich, populist socialist 136
  Historical Letters 137
  Outlines of a Theory of Personality 136

law
  burden of proof 345
  cassation (annulment of verdicts) 345, 354, 355
  civil law 337, 345
  cultural conflict with local systems 216, 358–9
  estates-based system 344, 357
  Fundamental Laws (1906) 572
  legal dualism in Russia 348, 349, 353
  and principle of separation of powers 345, 355, 357, 367
  role of (as instrument of change) 346
  role of (as substitute constitution) 344, 362–8
  rules of evidence 345
  traditional forms of 121, 262
  use of arbitration 354
  and village communes 385, 456
  volost' system of peasant justice 361, 456, 463, 609
  see also criminal law; customary law; Digest of Laws (1832); ecclesiastical law; Law Codes; lawyers; legal profession; property laws; trial by jury
Law on Assemblies (1718) 72
Law Code, 1649 (*Ulozhenie*) 247, 337
  on ownership of serfs 331, 332
  on property transfers between spouses 334
Law Code, 1832 Digest of Laws 335, 337, 439, 598
Law Code, 1864 reforms 261, 344–8, 362
  criticisms of 359
  failures of 346–8, 368
  and peasants 348–56
  and Russian Empire 356–9
law codes
  1880s commission on 338, 359–61
  1894 commission 361
  see also Legislative Commission (1767)
law courts 261
  bribery in 465
  conscience court (*sovestnyi sud*) 461
  district courts 345, 356, 357, 389
  local 345, 389, 456, 461
  military 648
  Russian language in 357, 358
  Statute of Administration and 456
  street advocacy in 262
  volost' peasant courts 361, 456, 463, 609, 615
  see also lawyers
lawyers
  'candidate' 363
  Jews as 196, 363
  liberalising mission of 363
  as political radicals 363–4
  professional standards of 364
  in reformed justice system 345
  and traditional 'street advocates' 262
  training 465
  'underground' 355
  see also jurists; legal profession
Le Blond, Jean Baptiste, architect 70
League of Armed Neutrality 512, 517, 518, 519, 529
leather industry, Nizhnii Novgorod 268
Lebrun, Elisabeth Vigée 308
Lefort, General François 490, 503
legal profession 261–2
  bar councils 261
  conflict with administration 364–7
  and law reforms (1864) 261
  private attorneys 262
  sworn attorneys 261
  see also lawyers
Legislative Commission (1767) 121, 151, 450
  deputies elected by noble assemblies 459
  and rights of Cossacks 169
  and serf ownership 332
  and status of *raznochintsy* 250
Leibov, Baruch, Jew in St Petersburg 186
Lelewel, Joachim, Polish republican 173
Lena Goldfield, massacre (1912) 634, 652
Lenin (Vladimir Il'ich Ulianov) 140, 141–3
  background in law 363
  Development of Capitalism in Russia 142
  exiled to Siberia 645
  influence of Chernyshevsky on 136, 141
  interpretation of Marxism 141
  on revolutionary movement 646
  State and Revolution 143
  Tasks of Russian Social Democrats 141
  and Trotsky's theory of 'permanent revolution' 143
  What Is to Be Done? 142, 628
  and workers 627
Leont'ev, Konstantin Nikolaevich, conservative and diplomat 131
  Byzantinism and Slavdom 132
Lermontov, Mikhail, poet 96
  'Motherland' (poem) 102
Lesin, G., banking house 420
Lesnaia, battle of (1708) 498
Leszczynski, Stanislaw, king of Poland 498, 505
Levin, Emanuel, secretary to Gintsburg 194

Levinson, Isaac Baer 189
Levitan, Isaak, landscape painter 104
Levitskii, Dmitrii, Ukrainian painter 83
Liadov, Anatol, composer 107
Liaotung (Liaodong) Peninsula 568
Liaoyang, battle of 542
liberal democracy *see* democracy
liberalism
  clerical 296
  economic 25
  national 136
  Russian 131, 133–6
Liberation Movement 630, 645
liberty 130
  Bakunin's defence of 138
  Catherine the Great's defence of 119–20
  individual 134
  natural 119, 121
  political 119, 120, 141
Lieven family, Baltic landowners 234, 234n.20
Lieven, Vice-Admiral Prince A. A. 584n.21
Lilienthal, Dr Max, Jewish educator 35
Lippman and Rosenthal, Amsterdam banking house 406
liquor *see* spirits; vodka
List, Friedrich, German protectionist 56, 412
literacy 262
  among army officers 230
  of conscripts 544
  peasants 318, 392
  in reign of Peter the Great 75
  of women 308, 313, 318
  see also education; schools
literature 79–80, 86, 256
  erotic and pornographic 86
  fiction 74, 86
  journals 80, 86, 103, 281, 420
  non-fiction 74
  poetry 80, 86
  print culture 253
  provincial 281
  religious 74, 75, 297
  in Russian 95
  sentimentalist 87
  short stories 103
  and social reform 100
  translations 80, 86
  under Peter the Great 74–6
  see also press; printing
Lithuania 30, 177
  retreat from (1915) 665
  suppression of Lithuanian language 38
  under Alexander I 173
  see also Poland-Lithuania
Lithuanian Statute 173, 176
Little Russia *see* Ukraine
Liubavskii, M. K., historian 59
Livonia 29, 496
  serfdom abolished 598
  to Russia (1721) 499
Loan Bank (Zaemnyi Bank) (1754) 396, 402
  Bank for the Merchant estate 396
  Bank for the Nobility 396, 397
Lobachevskii, Nikolai, mathematician 279
Lobanov-Rostovskii, Prince Aleksei Borisovich, minister of foreign affairs 247, 567n.16
local government
  Commission on (1859) 602–3
  and crisis relief work 466
  and development of industry 397
  legislation on 450
  and local opinion 450
  and modernisation 449
  participation in 451
  and peasants 449, 450
  professionalisation of 466
  quality of officials 197, 455, 456n.13, 465–6
  reforms 607n.39
    Statute of Provincial Reforms (1775) 257, 275, 431, 450
  relations with centre 450, 451–2
  role of provincial nobles in 257
  western models for 451, 453
  see also urban government; zemstvo assemblies
Locke, John 255
Lomonosov, Mikhail, writer and scientist 48, 80, 118
Lopatinskii, Feofilakt, composer 497
Loris-Melikov, Count M. T. 607, 615
  chief of Supreme Administrative Commission 441
  programme of reforms 612–13
Losenko, Anton, professor of history painting 83
Louis XVIII, as king of France 527
Louis Napoleon *see* Napoleon III
lower land court (*nizhnii zemskii sud*) 461
Luch (Menshevik newspaper) 652
Lutheranism, in Baltic provinces 39
Luxemburg, Rosa, Polish Marxist 181
L'vov, Nikolai, collector of folk songs 84
Lyskovo, river port 268

Lytton, Bulwer 95

Maddox, Michael, theatre impresario 85
Magnitskii, Mikhail Leont'evich, conspiracy 153
Main Society of Russian Railroads 403
Maistre, Joseph de 152
Majewski, Karol, Polish architect 182
Makariev monastery 277
Makarov, Admiral S. O. 581, 586
Malevich, Kasimir, painter 108, 113, 115
 Black Square 115
Malinovskii, Aleksandr Aleksandrovich *see* Bogdanov
Malinovskii, Roman, Bolshevik and informant 653
Malov, Evfimii, teacher 212
Malta 524, 527
Mamontov, Savva, Private Opera 105, 109
Manasein, Nikolai, minister of justice 361
Manchuria 542, 561, 568
Mandelshtam, Max 196
Manifesto 356
 (Catherine the Great)
Manifesto on the Freedom of Conscience (1905) 303
 see also February Manifesto (1903); October Manifesto (1905)
Mansur, Sheikh (Ushurma), Chechen rebel 205
maps, new cartographic projection of Russia 56
al-Marjani, Shihab al-Din 219
market, national 389, 391
market economy 131
 Chicherin's defence of 134
 and civil society 256
market production, peasant 380–1
marriage
 arranged 306, 308, 310
 ban on forced (1722) 309
 church regulation of 286
 of clergy 294
 early (among peasants) 374, 376, 381
 and law on dowries 328, 330, 331, 333, 336, 339
 patriarchal character of 309, 315, 318
 Petrine reforms 308–9
 rules of conduct (1782) 336
 Western views of 310, 336
 see also divorce
marshals of the nobility 454
Martens, Fedor 572n.17
Martov, Iulii, Menshevik 196, 627, 645
Marx, Adolf 281
Marx, Karl 138, 141
 rivalry with Bakunin 138
Marxism 10
 in Poland 180
Marxists
 police repression of 640
 and workers 624, 627–9
masquerades, Empress Elizabeth's passion for 78
Masuria, battle of (1915) 553
materialism 129
Matinskii, M. A., serf playwright 254
Mattarnovy, Georg Johann 70
Matveev, Andrei, painter 79
Matveev, Andrei Artamonovich
 ambassador to Netherlands 502
 on opposition to Peter I 117
Mayakovsky, Vladimir, poet 114
Mazepa, Ivan
 Cossack Hetman 167, 168, 494
 defection to Swedish forces 29, 498
means of production, social ownership of 139
Meck, Nadezhda von 106
medicine
 Bestuzhev medical training courses for women 317, 318, 319
 medical orderlies 262
 as profession 260
 social status of physicians 260
 training for women 316, 317, 318, 319
 village healers 262
 zemstvos' role in health care 464
Mednikov, Evstratii, at Moscow security bureau 641, 647
Medvedev, Sil'vestr, Latin cleric 166
Melli Firqa (National Party), Crimea 221
Melnikov, Pavel Ivanovich (Pecherskii), ethnographer 266, 272, 276, 279, 598
 editor of newspaper in Nizhnii Novgorod 279, 280
Mendeleev, Dmitrii 56, 414
Mensheviks
 and St Petersburg soviet 633, 657
 and trade unions 634
 and workers 627
Menshikov, Prince Alexander, favourite of Peter the Great 70, 73, 233, 491, 503
mercantilism, Peter the Great and 396

mercenaries 492
in European armies 532, 534
Merchant Bank, Moscow 404
merchants
Jewish 186, 193, 194, 402
in Moscow 101
Nizhnii Novgorod 267, 272, 277, 281
as patrons of art 102
in St Petersburg 395, 459
Merezhkovskii, Dmitry, writer 111
Merv 40, 541
meshchane status (artisans and petty traders)
Jews as 31, 187
official urban community 247
Meshcherskii, Prince Nikanor 331
Meshcherskii, Prince Vladimir Petrovich, conservative publicist 133, 651
metallurgy *see* iron and steel industry
meteorology, provincial interest in 282
Metternich, Prince Klemens von 556
and Greek war (1821) 557
Meyerhold, Vsevelod, stage director 115
Michael (Mikhail Aleksandrovich), Grand Duke, offered crown (1917) 655, 658
Michael (Mikhail Nikolaevich), Grand Duke, viceroy in Caucasus (1860–81) 215
Mickiewicz, Adam, Polish Romantic poet 173, 174
Books of the Polish Pilgrimage 30
middle classes
Nizhnii Novgorod 274–5
see also intelligentsia; merchants; professions; *raznochintsy*
migrants *see* peasant migration
Mikhailovskii, Nikolai Konstantinovich, populist socialist 136, 137, 138
Mikhailovskii-Danilevskii, Aleksandr I., *An Account of the War for the Fatherland in 1812* 150
militarism, rise of 159–60
Military Criminal Code, crimes of terrorist violence tried under 365, 648
military elite 227, 535
as bureaucrats 235
ennoblement of 229, 231, 534
opposition to tsar (from 1916) 657, 658, 664–5
professionals 235, 547
view of needs of modern armies 664
see also imperial army; navy
military expenditure 204, 470n.9, 470–1, 486
reviews of 204, 470–1, 471n.11
military power
and empire 9, 369
European model 15, 21
military-technical academies 535
Miliukov, Pavel Nikolaevich, radical liberal 133, 135, 666
on burden of poll tax 483
Essays on the History of Russian Culture 135
History of the Second Russian Revolution 135
Miliutin, Count D. A., war minister 213, 471
on emancipation of serfs 600
and financial reforms 606
and land reforms 603
military reforms 543–5, 549
as reformer 598, 599–602, 611
and training for midwives 317
Miliutin, N. A., reformer 450, 598, 615
and Commission on local government reform (1859) 602
dismissed (1861) 601, 607
and financial reforms 606
and land reforms 603, 605, 606
on need for reforms 595, 607
on serf reforms 597, 601
mining industry
Don basin 620
Urals 620
Ministry of Agriculture 417
Ministry of Communications 471
Ministry of Finance 441
and budget-making 469, 479
competence of officials 236
control over credit 404, 405
and foreign commercial agents 413
foreign financial transactions 399
and industrialisation policy 434
and Pacific fleet shipbuilding programme 578
and St Petersburg business class 228
Special Credit Chancellery 399, 404
and State Bank 402
and state economic policy 405, 414, 417
and war financing 478
see also Committee of Finances; state finances
Ministry of Foreign Affairs 573
Asian Department 573
officials from nobility and gentry 235
see also foreign policy; Gorchakov, Prince; Izvol'skii, Aleksandr; Nesselrode, Count Karl
Ministry of the Imperial Court 204, 479n.34

Ministry of the Interior/Internal Affairs 441
  and local government 450
  and Muslim policy 208, 213, 216, 218, 221
  Police Department (1880) 639
  senior officials 235
  and working conditions 433, 434
Ministry of Justice 346, 361
  and bar associations 364
  budget 472
  and independence of judges 346
  public prosecutors 346
Ministry of Spiritual Affairs and Popular Enlightenment 158, 208
Ministry of Trade and Industry 417
Minkiewicz, Jan 179
Mirsky, D. S., literary critic 95
missionaries
  to Central Asian Muslims 40, 203, 212, 221
  to Volga region 204, 217
missionary schools, Central Asia 41
modernisation 12
  after Great Reforms 101, 614
  agrarian 24
  and enlightened despotism 507
  and local government 449
  and nature of state 19, 433, 434, 447–8
modernism, Russian 110, 114
Mohammed Ali (Dukchi Ishan), Naqshbandi sheikh 217
Mohammed-Hajji, Avar sheikh 217
Molla Nazreddin (Muslim newspaper) 222
Mon Plaisir palace 70
monarchism, Polish 173–4
monarchy
  absolute 97, 118, 119, 256, 256n.29
  consensus-building (under Catherine the Great) 119–20, 151
  early theories of tsarist rule 165
  and Enlightened Absolutism 89
  ideal of virtuous tsar 118
  and moral leadership 120, 122, 300
  nobles' revolt in Europe 229, 507, 507n.2
  obedience and resistance to 116–19
  paternalist 442
  semi-constitutional (after 1905 Revolution) 442, 446
  see also autocracy
monasteries 277, 290, 394
  and anticlericalism 291
  Nizhnii Novgorod 271
  St Alexander Nevskii monastery 70
  Solovetskii monastery 116
  Ukraine (Roman Catholic) 176
Monastery Office, for church taxation 285, 290
monasticism, renaissance of 291
Mongol Empire, collapse of 15
monks
  as bishops 289
  monastic ('black') clergy 290–1
  shortage of 291
monopolies, state 395, 409, 412, 423
Mordovtsev, D. L., publicist 281
Moroccan Crisis (1905–6) 417
Morozewicz, Józef, Polish explorer 182
Morozov, Savva 110
Morozov textile workers' strike (1885) 625
Moscow
  1905 Revolution 633, 647
  as banking centre 404
  bar council 261
  Church of the Resurrection 104
  as cultural centre 79, 102, 108
  District Court 351
  expulsion of Jews from (1891) 198
  fire of (1812) 155
  foundling hospital (1764) 312
  Great Reforms 356, 459
  imperial court at 78
  industry 415, 620
  inflation riots (1915) 661
  Napoleon in 33, 147, 154, 280
  Noble Assembly building 82
  plague (1771) 510
  population 415
  security bureau surveillants 641–2
  theatre(s) 73, 165
    Moscow Art Theatre 109–10
    Petrovskii 85
    Znamenskii 85
  urban class 459
    business elite 228
    merchant industrialists 101
Moscow Academy 69, 73
Moscow Commercial Bank 404
Moscow Conservatoire (1866) 99, 108
Moscow Discount Bank 404
Moscow Higher Women's Courses (Guerrier courses) 317, 319
Moscow International Commercial Bank 404
Moscow Medical School, plays staged by 73
Moscow Merchant Society of Mutual Credit 404
Moscow School of Mathematics and Navigation 75

Moscow University (founded 1755) 80, 82, 236, 249
Moscow-Riazan Bank 404
Moskovskie vedomosti (journal) 359, 409
mosques
  approved designs 209
  construction permitted (1773) 206
  contruction outlawed (1742) 205
  statistics 209
Mukden, battle of 542
Münchengrätz, Treaty of (1833) 558
Municipal Guardianships, for the poor 321
Municipal Statute (1892) 458
Münnich, General B. C. 535
Murav'ev, Count Mikhail Nikolaevich, foreign minister 247, 567n.16, 568
Murav'ev, M. N., sentimentalist writer 87
Murav'ev, Nikita Mikhailovich, political thinker 125
Murav'ev, Count Nikolai, governor-general of Eastern Siberia 561
Murav'ev, Nikolai V., minister of justice 361
Muraviev, Alexander, governor of Nizhnii Novgorod 270, 275
Muridism, Muslim resistance in North Caucasus 211, 216
Murmansk, rail to 660
Musavat (Equality) party, Azerbaijan 221
Muscovy 394, 530
  Belinsky's criticism of 128
  and concept of obedience to grand prince 116–17, 300
  Jewish settlement banned 185
  and Poland 165
  Renaissance and Reformation in 165
museums
  Nizhnii Novgorod natural history 282
  in provincial towns 282
music
  atonality 113
  choral 72, 90, 282
  church 106
  concert 107
  folk-songs 84
  instrumental 72–3
  national style 98–9
  nationalism in 107
  nationalist composers ('the mighty handful') 99, 107
  in Nizhnii Novgorod 281–2
  opera 79
  realism in 100
  under Anna and Elizabeth 79
  under Catherine II 84
  under Nicholas I 94
Muslim identity 203
Muslim Labour Group 220
'Muslim question' (late 19th cent) 217
Muslim Statute (1857) 208
Muslims and Muslim communities 202, 203, 205, 210
  administration 204, 217
    in Caucasus 214–16
    state institutions (muftiates) 207, 214, 218, 223
  anti-mufti movement 210
  in Caucasus 36, 41, 214–16
    emigration from 36, 41
  in Central Asia 28, 40–1, 44
  clergy
    creation of official hierarchy 207–8, 209, 213–15
    role in imperial governance 215
    status of 213, 214
  compulsory registers 208, 214
  connections with Islamic world 203
  elites (mirzas) 204, 206, 209
  emigration 36, 41, 210, 221
  government policy towards 208, 213, 216, 218, 221
  Islamic discourses 210
  and *jadidism* (reform movement) 202, 219–20
  limits on Islamic law 208
  missionaries and conversions 28, 40, 203, 204, 206, 217
  politicisation of (after 1905) 42, 220–3
  press 222
  Tatars 28
  toleration under Peter I 203, 204
  under Alexander II and Nicholas 210–20
  under Catherine the Great 205–8
  Volga-Ural region 202, 209, 217
  see also Caucasus; Central Asia
Mussorgsky, Modest, composer 99, 102, 109
  Boris Gudonov (opera) 101, 112
  Khovanshchina (opera) 101, 278
  The Nursery (song cycle) 100
mutinies
  army 543
  naval 582–4
  Petrograd garrison (1917) 656, 658, 662–4
  Potemkin 582–3
  of Semenovskii Guards (1820) 558

Nabokov, Dmitrii, minister of justice 350, 360, 361
Nabokov, Vladimir, liberal jurist 346
Naples 520
Napoleon I (Napoleon Bonaparte), emperor of France
  and Alexander I 520
  and conspiracy theories 152
  expansionist ambitions of 521, 526
  invasion of Egypt 516
  and Tsar Paul 517
Napoleon III (Louis Napoleon), emperor of France
  and Crimean War 560
  rapprochement 564
Napoleonic invasion of Russia (1812) 33, 145, 147, 154
  and foreign policy 527
  legacy of 157–61
  liberal nationalist view of 145, 150
  popular reaction to 154–5n.19
  religious response to 159
  response of provincial government 154
  and Russian sense of vulnerability 146, 154
  War for the Fatherland 147–8
Napoleonic Wars 32–3, 554
  Continental System 399, 527
  effect on economy 401
  émigré nobles in Russia 518
  foreign loans to fund 399
  and rise of militarism 159
  Russian defeats 148, 152, 154
  Second Coalition 516
  Third Coalition 522–5
  and Treaty of Tilsit 525
Naqshbandiyya order of Muslims 205, 211, 217
Naroch, battle of (1916) 553
Narodnaia volia (terrorist group) 365
Narva, Estonia
  Russian defeat at (1700) 495, 531
  taken by Russia (1704) 496
Naryshkin faction
  and Azov Campaign 494
  under Sophia 490
Naryshkin family, aristocratic landowners 233
Natalia, sister of Peter the Great 73
Natanson, Mark 196
nation-building 56
  in European peripheral states 23
  and Russianisation 58
nationalism 20
  among Austro-Hungarian minorities 570
  and autocracy 151
  and First World War 44
  linguistic 123
  Muslim 222
  Polish Romantic 174
  in Russian culture 96–7, 98–100
  see also patriotism
'nationalities policies', tsarist 27, 32–6
  First World War 43–4
  Lenin's theory of 142
  and October Manifesto (1905) 42, 218
  'Russification' 37–42
  ukaz of (1904) 42
'nationality' (*narodnost'*) 34, 601
Naval Ministry 578–80, 581
  Chief Administration of Shipbuilding and Supply (GUKiC) 579
  Naval Technical Committee (MTK) 578, 579
naval power, need for and cost of 13
Navy
  armament 579
  Baltic fleet 13, 575, 577, 583
    defeat off Japan 542, 569, 587
  Black Sea fleet 13, 513, 575–6, 583
  conscription of sailors 582–3
  construction programmes
    (1895–1902) 576, 578
    (after 1906) 588–9
    (from 1881) 576
  lack of petty officers 584
  Mediterranean fleet 398
  Muslims in 215
  mutinies 582–4
  Naval Cadet Corps 584
  Naval Engineering School 584
  officers
    promotions regulations (1885) 585
    quality of 584–5
    senior 586
  organisation
    Main Naval Staff 581
    Naval General Staff 588
  Pacific fleet 13, 577, 587
    construction programme (1898) 578
  Peter the Great's 490, 493, 499
  ship types and design 577, 580–1, 588
  size
    (1900s) 580
    expansion (from 1907) 551

tactics 581–2
battle manual (1905) 582
Instructions for Preparing Ships for Combat 582
training 581, 582, 585
Nazimov, V. I., governor-general of Vilno 603
Nechaev, Sergei, anarchist, trial of 364, 638
Nektarii, Bishop, of Nizhnii Novgorod 270
Nelidov, A. I., ambassador to France 418
Nemirovich-Danchencko, Vladimir 109
neoclassicism
adoption of 68, 81
in painting 84
in Poland 167
Nerchinsk, Treaty of (1689) 28
Nesselrode, Count Karl, foreign minister 229, 247, 528n.22, 558, 563, 567n.16
Nesterov, Mikhail 105
Taking the Veil 278
Netherlands 527
banks 398, 404, 406
revolt 513
trade with 493, 501
Neva, River 496
newspapers *see* press
Nezhin, annual trade fair 186
Neznamov, A. A., on army reform 548
Nicholas I, Tsar (1825–55) 94, 265
centralisation of power under Chancellery 438–9
and church reform 295
conservatism of 33, 35, 310
and conspiracy theories 153
cultural policy 94, 96
death 561
and Digest of Laws (1832) 337
and family ideals 310
foreign policy 558
growth of bureaucracy 235, 432
and imperial army 540
and industrialisation 12
and Kingdom of Poland 33
and November uprising (1830) 173
policy on nationalities 34–6
policy towards Jews 35, 190–1
policy towards Muslims 208, 211
and Pushkin 96
and security police 637
and state ideology of 'Orthodoxy, autocracy and nationality' 94
Nicholas II, Tsar (1894–1917) 319, 445
abdication (1917) 571, 655, 657–8
as autocrat 442, 446–7, 572
and Bunge 407
culture under 107–15
death of (1918) 184
and economic policies 411, 423
and February 1917 uprising 656
foreign policy 567–71
and imperial army 235, 548–9, 550, 667
intervention in government (1915) 667–8
opposition to 658
among soldiers 664
and loss of popular respect 664, 668
military commanders 664
political 665, 666, 668
personal interest in navy 586
populist preferences 236
and relations with church 288, 303
and religious toleration 218
Nicholas Academy of the General Staff 547
Nicholas Naval Academy 581, 585
Nicholas (Nikolai Aleksandrovich), Tsarevich, death (1865) 610
Nicholas (Nikolai Nikolaevich), Grand Duke 658
Nietzsche, Friedrich 108, 111
nihilists 251
women as 316
Nijinsky, Vaslav, dancer 112
Nikitenko, Aleksandr V. 158, 160
Nikitin, Ivan, painter 71
Niklewicz, Tadeusz, Polish engineer 182
Niva (illustrated weekly) 281
Nixon, Richard, US president 445
Nizhnii Novgorod 264–83
administration and institutions 275–8
Alexander Boys' High School 266
Alexander Nevsky cathedral 264
Alexandrine Fair cathedral 267
Brotherhood of Saint Gurii 278
character 267–71
Church of the Annunciation 266
city duma 266, 277, 280
civic and cultural life 278–83
Moscow literary circles in temporary exile in 280
museum 282–3
music in 281–2
gas lighting 277
gymnasium 279
Kremlin (fortress) 266
modern 264
people 271–5

Nizhnii Novgorod (*cont.*)
middle classes 274–5
population 271–2
post-emancipation workers 273
religions 205, 271
religious holidays 270–1
river port and wharves 267, 268, 269
Rozhdestvenskaia church 267
Sormovo shipyards 273, 274
Theological Seminary 266, 277
topography 264–7
Fair Section 267
houses 265
Il'inka street 267
Kunavino suburb 267, 270
Makariev Section 267
Pecherskaia street 266
Pokrovskaia street 266
trade fairs 268–70
water-supply system 277
zemstvo assembly 276, 280
Nizhnii Novgorod, diocese of 277–8
Nizhnii Novgorod region, Old Believers 264, 271, 278, 283
nobility, hereditary 227, 228, 249
and 1905–6 Revolution 242
absorption of foreign nobles 29, 31, 194, 230, 233
boyar aristocracy 204, 232, 233
as bureaucrats 235
core aristocracy 233–4
and culture 232
differentials of wealth within 231, 232, 241–2, 460
education 94–7, 232, 236, 237, 249, 249n.11
exclusive right to own serfs 229, 231, 247
and Great Reforms 257, 603
hedonism of 147
independent political interest 258
industrial enterprises 232, 241
lack of common identity 231–2
as landowners 82, 229, 231, 241, 243
military service 534, 584
obligatory state service 78, 81, 147, 229, 534
political threats to 242–4
power in provinces 240, 241
and provincial assemblies 229, 257, 459–60
relations with bureaucracy 234, 240–1, 257, 436
relations with tsars 239, 242, 258, 436, 514–15
size of 229, 231
status as *soslovie* 229
and Table of Ranks (1722) 229, 249
view of *raznochintsy* 250
and zemstvo assemblies 258, 463, 464
see also Charter to the Nobility; elites, Russian; noble assemblies
nobility, personal 249
noble assemblies 229, 240, 257, 459–60
political demands of 460
Noble Land Cadet Corps 535
nobles' revolt, against progressive governments in Europe 507, 507n.2
Nogin, Viktor, Bolshevik 645
Nolde, Boris 58
nomads
and conflicts with Russian law 358
displaced by migrant peasants 374
Russian view of 22, 35
north Caucasus *see* Caucasus, north
Northern Bee (journal) 175
Northern League, Tsar Paul's project 517
Northern Messenger (journal)
Northern Society (political movement) 125
'Northern System' (Panin's) 509
Northern War *see* Great Northern War
Notes of the Fatherland (literary journal) 103
November uprising (1830) 34, 150, 173
Novikov, Nikolai Ivanovich
journal editor 86, 120
political satires 120
Novoe vremia (St Petersburg newspaper) 24, 573
on Nevsky cotton-mill strike 622
Novosil'tsev, Nikolai Nikolaevich
mission to London (1804) 523
preparation of constitutional charter 124
Nystad, Treaty of (1721) 499, 500

obrok (service in cash or kind), owed by peasants 371, 475–6
Obruchev, N. N., General, assistant to Miliutin 549
'Obukhov defence' labour unrest (St Petersburg 1901) 626
Ochakov, annexation of 513
October Manifesto (1905) 42, 218, 633, 647
and Constitution of 1906 367, 572
establishment of Duma 42, 446, 569, 613
Odessa 319, 356
as commercial port 399, 400
District Court 353
founded (1794) 10, 30, 515, 515n.8
Jews in 197
municipal government 459
strikes (1903) 646

Odintsov, Aleksei, governor of Nizhnii Novgorod 275
Office of Court Bankers and Commissioners (1798) 398
oil industry 415, 421
  foreign investment 413
Oka, River, at Nizhnii Novgorod 264
Okhotsk, Siberia 28
Old Believers 285, 296, 377
  church campaigns against 277
  and Cossack revolts 378
  and education of girls 313
  monks at Solovetskii monastery 116
  Nizhnii Novgorod region 264, 271, 278, 283
    Melnikov's saga of 272, 278
  Vaisov Brotherhood 210, 211
  view of market economics 417
opera 79, 101, 109
  exported to Paris 112
  Italian company at St Petersburg 94, 101, 105
  private houses 105
Opium War, Second 561
Oranienbaum palace 70
Orbeliani family, Georgian origins 234
Orenburg Assembly, Islamic muftiate 207, 208, 210, 214, 218
  and Muslim military officers 215
  and Tauride Directorate 209, 214
Orientalism
  Russian ideology of 49
  in Russian music 107
  travellers' perception of 90
  view of Islam 202, 211–13
Orlov family, aristocrats 233
Orthodox Church, in Ukraine 166
Orthodox Church, Russian 20, 296
  and 1905–7 Revolution 302, 303
  and 1917 Revolution 305
  administration
    chief procurator (office of) 285, 286
    shortcomings of 284, 287
  administrative colleges 285
  believers 296–300
    numbers of 292
    observance rates 298–300, 304
    popular Orthodoxy 297, 305
  challenges to 298
    enlightenment role for 297
    political weakness 25
  conservatism of 116, 123
  cultural influence 68, 90, 98, 103
    music 72
    religious literature 75
    view of sculpture as 'graven images' 72, 91
  and First World War 304
  Great Reforms and 287
  and Greek War of Independence 126
  hierarchical structure of 132, 289–90
    elderhood (*starchestvo*) 291
  historical
    liturgical reforms (1650s) 284
    medieval 284
    patriarchate (1589) 284
    and Reformation in Muscovy 165
  Holy Synod 103, 285
  institutional changes 284–8
    diocesan administration 285–6, 287
    diocesan assemblies 287
    during Imperial period 284
    parish reforms 287
  lands 371
    secularised 239, 277, 290
  and legacy of 1812 war 158
  in Nizhnii Novgorod 270, 277–8
  Petrine reforms 166, 284, 285, 290, 296, 497
    and adoption of European calendar and dress 67
  and Rasputinism 304
  relations with State 284, 288, 303
  and Russian identity 27
  schism *see* Old Believers
  and serfdom 126, 300–1
  social influence 300–2
    jurisdiction of 457
    relations with laity 298
    suppression of local customs and superstitions 297
    view of marriage and divorce 309, 336
  spirituality of 127
  Synod of 1712 166
  and third Duma 303
  Ukrainian influence in 165, 166, 289
  variations within 296
  see also clergy; episcopate; monasteries; parishes
Ostankino estate, Sheremetev family 83
Ostermann, Andrei, Vice-Chancellor, and foreign policy 505
Ostermann, Heinrich, as ambassador for Peter the Great 502
Ostrovsky, Alexander, playwright 315

Ottoman Empire 13, 30
  and Balkans 565–6
  and Chigirin War (1677–81) 490
  compared with Russian Empire 14–16, 238
  Cossacks and 167, 168, 509
  and Crimea 490, 513
  effect of decline on Muslim populations 16
  European view of 14, 557, 559, 568
  and First World War 43, 571, 660
  independence of Orthodox states 570
  Islam as unifying factor 16, 20
  Jewish populations in 185, 186
  mufti establishment 207
  Muslim emigration to 210, 221
  rights of Christians in 510
  Russian alliance with (1805) 524
  Russian view of 489, 521, 555, 559
  system of government 15
  and threat to Black Sea access 575
  war with Italy (1911) 588
  wars with *see* Crimean War; Russo-Turkish wars
  see also Turkey
Oxenstierna, Count Axel 492
Ozerov, N. Kh. 420
Ozerov, Professor I. Kh., economist 423, 626
Ozvobozhdenie (Liberation) movement 630, 645

Pahlen family, Baltic landowners 234
Pahlen, Count K. I., minister of justice 613
paintings 69, 70–1, 79, 84
  abstract 114
  allegorical 71, 79
  avant-garde 108
  Cubism 115
  'Donkey's Tail' exhibition (1912) 113
  historical 83, 101
  'Jack of Diamonds' exhibition (1910) 113
  Neo-Primitivism 113, 114
  portraits 68, 71, 83
  Russian landscape 102
Palestine 16, 199, 560
pan-Islamism, fear of 217, 221
Panin, Count Nikita, adviser to Catherine the Great 436, 509, 512, 520
Panina, Countess Alexandra 307
Panina, Countess Anna 307
Pan-Slavism 39, 132, 523
  in Balkans 565
  and view of empire 61
  see also Slavophiles; Slavs
Papacy
  and Holy League 490
  see also Catholic Church
Paris
  Diaghilev's *Saisons russes* in 93, 112
  Polish émigré politics in 173–4
  Russian army in (1814) 33, 94
  security bureau in 640
Paris, Peace of (1856) 540, 560, 564, 594
Paris, Treaty of (1814) 527
Paris, Treaty of (1815) 527
parishes 292
  and financial support for clergy 294–5
  funds 299
  parish councils 295, 298
  reforms (1860s) 287
Parliamentary System
  after 1905 Revolution 446
  see also Duma
Paskevich, Field Marshal Prince Igor Fedorovich, viceroy of Poland (to 1856) 34
passports
  internal 394, 408
  for women 337, 343
Patkul, J. R., as ambassador 502
patriotism, war of 1812 and 145, 148, 150, 155, 156
Paul I, Tsar (1796–1801)
  assassination 151, 507, 518
  authoritarianism of 151
  and Bonaparte 517
  and Chancellery 438
  character 516, 518n.11
  economy under 398–9
  forced labour for women 312
  foreign policy 516–19, 524
  and nobility 229, 460
  and rise of militarism 159
Pavlova, Anna, ballerina 112
Pavlova, Karolina K., on 1812 invasion 155
Pavlovo
  choral singing 282
  iron and steel industry 268
Pavlovsk, palace 82
peasant communes 383, 385, 392, 456, 463
  obshchina system of land-ownership 605, 611
  see also households; villages
peasant migration 374–5, 389, 391
  into towns 90, 247, 352, 453
  to cities (First World War) 662
  to outlying regions 387–8
  women 319–21

Peasant Union 323
peasants
  and 1864 judicial system 348–56
  on church lands 371
  contacts with wider society 389–90
  economic self-sufficiency 376
  and effects of 1861 legislation on 608–9
  and environment 372–3
  exploitation of 369, 370, 371, 372, 385
    grievances 379, 392
  and jury duty 349, 350
  and land reform 603–6
    land purchases (redemption schemes) 388, 408, 476, 477, 481, 484
    problems of 605–6, 611
    and reform process 600, 601, 603–6
  and local government 449, 451
    local self-government 602
  on noble estates 371
  obligations
    of military service 372, 382, 532
    to landowners 371, 384
    to state 371, 384, 453
  obrok payments 371, 475–6
  and patriotism in 1812 war 145, 148, 150, 155, 156
  perception of law 351–6
  population growth 369, 373–5, 379, 389
  and reform period 370, 602
  relations with rural landowners 242, 243, 244
  revolts by 377–8, 393, 483
    1902 646
    protests against exploitation 385–6
    threat of rebellion 482–3, 485, 595
  on state lands 371, 388
  supplementary incomes 380, 486
  tax burden on 468, 482–6
  in towns 90, 247, 352
    trading privileges 247
  Ukrainian 177
  way of life 370
    central Russia: late 17th to late 19th century 378–7; to late 17th century 375–8
    customs and practices 378, 381–5, 391–3
    late 19th and early 20th century 388–3
    living standards 386–7, 390–1, 484, 485
    nutrition levels 391
    in outlying regions 387–8
    in paintings 84
    poverty 468, 485
    regional variations 370–1
  women
    consumption patterns 319
    demand for rights 322
    education 318, 319
    in labour market 319–20
  and zemstvos 463, 609
  see also agriculture; households; serfdom; serfs; villages
Pecherskii, Andrei *see* Melnikov, P. I.
Pecherskii monastery, Nizhnii Novgorod 271, 277
Peking, Treaty of (1860) 49, 561
People's Justice Party 640
People's Revenge Group (Nechaev's) 638
People's Will group
  assassination of Tsar Alexander II 639
  infiltrated 639
  women in 318
Pereiaslav, agreement of (1654) 167
Pereire, Isaac and Emile, financiers 402
peripherality 18, 23
Perovskaia, Sofia, and assassination of Alexander II 318
Persia
  relations with 555, 569
  trade with 405, 414, 499
  war with (1820s) 478, 540
  see also Iran
Persian War (1721) 499–500
Pervyi shag, Kazan journal 281
Pestel', Colonel Pavel Ivanovich
  political thinker 125
  Russian Law constitutional plan 125
Peter I, Tsar (the Great) (1689–1725) 11, 46, 72, 166, 309
  building of St Petersburg 69–70
  as collector of art 71
  and Cossack Hetmanate 168
  development of Russian high culture 68–77
  early industrial development 617
  economic reforms 394–6
  edict on calendar (1699) 67
  edict on Western dress (1700) 67, 77, 306–7
  effects of reforms on women 306, 311, 327, 340
  foreign policy
    ambassadors 501–3
    and Azov Campaign 494–5
    and Caucasus 36
    conquest of the Baltic 29, 500–1, 512
    motives for Great Northern War 495–7
    and Persian War (1721) 499–500
    and Poland 168, 500

policy-making 503
and Jews 186
and local government 449, 452
marriage reforms 308–9
and military
annual levies of conscripts 372
as military strategist 535
modernisation of army 492, 531–2, 534
and Muslims 203, 204
incentives for conversion from Islam 204
and *obrok* payments 475
and Orthodox Church 166, 284, 285, 289, 290, 296, 497
political opposition to 117–18
poll tax 371, 394, 473, 483–4, 535
reform of central government 429, 430–1
and Senate 435
and Russian Empire 27, 28, 46, 51, 146
Spiritual Regulation 285, 297
Table of Ranks (1722) 229, 248
and tsarevich affair 117, 166
and the West
first visit (1697–8) 69, 490
and Russian role in Europe 501
Westernisers' admiration for 128
see also Great Northern War
Peter II, Tsar (1727–30) 78, 168, 290
Peter III, Tsar (1761–2) 78, 81, 501
nobles' obligation to state service ended 534
and Prussia 506, 507
Peterhof, palace of 70
Petersburg International Commercial Bank 404, 405
Petersburg Private Bank 404
Petipa, Marius, choreographer 106
petitions, by peasants against exploitation 385
Petrashevskii Circle 97
Petrashevskii, Mikhail 50, 54, 55
Petrograd Soviet 657, 669
and establishment of Provisional Government 669
see also St Petersburg
Petrovskoe estate, Gagarin family 385
Philippines, annexed by USA 577
photography, in Nizhnii Novgorod 274
Physiocrats, influence on Catherine the Great 396
Picart, Peter, engraver 71
Pilsudski, Józef, Polish Socialist Party 181, 182
Pinsker, Yehuda Leib (Lev), Zionist 199
Pirogov, Nikolai, and role of women 314
Pitirim, Bishop, of Nizhnii Novgorod 277
Pitt, William (the Younger) 525
plague, Moscow (1771) 510
Platonov, Sergei, historian 283
Plehve, Viacheslav, minister of interior 646
Plekhanov, Georgii Valentinovich, Marxist and Menshevik 140, 199
as 'father of Russian Marxism' 140, 627
and Lenin 142
Our Differences 141
Socialism and the Political Struggle 141
Pleske, E. D., minister of finance 417
Plevna, assaults on (1879) 541
Pobedonostsev, Konstantin Petrovich, conservative jurist 131
and 1864 law reforms 359
counter-reforms 288, 318, 409, 615
and fear of pan-Islamism 217
on government 429
and parish school movement 278
procurator for the Holy Synod 103
Podolia province (Ukraine) 177, 188
poetry 80, 86, 87
'golden age' 95–6
Symbolist 110, 113
Pogodin, Mikhail (M. P.), historian 51, 53, 55, 594
pogroms 197, 198–9, 366, 665
Pokrovskaia, Maria, feminist 324
Pokrovskii, Nikolai Nikolaevich, foreign minister 247, 567n.16
Poland
1864 law reforms in 356, 358
and 1905 Revolution 42, 181
annexation of 10, 11, 397, 516, 554
Czartoryskii's policy on 522, 523
economy 416
and First World War 43
industrialisation 179, 620
Jews in 172, 180, 186, 187
landless gentry 173
National Democratic movement 180, 182
National League (1893) 180
nobility 230, 234
political activism 180–1
rebellions against Russian rule 22
see also Polish rebellion (1863)
religious dissent in 509
retreat from (1915) 665
Russian embassy in 502
Sejm established (1863) 610
socialism in 180–1

see also Poland, Congress Kingdom of (1815–32); Poland (Polish-Lithuanian Commonwealth); Polish rebellion (1863) (January uprising); Warsaw, Grand Duchy of
Poland, Congress Kingdom of (1815–32) 33, 172, 528, 556–7
autonomy within Russian Empire 33, 172, 556
Catholic Church in 179
defeat of (1831) 540
effect of Napoleonic Wars on relations with 148–50
modern politics in 177
November uprising (1830) 34, 150, 173
'organic statute' (1832) 34, 150, 173
Russian Viceroy imposed (1832) 34
see also Polish rebellion (1863); Western Provinces
Poland, Partitions of 30–1, 148, 186, 510, 514
end of Polish-Lithuanian Commonwealth (1795) 171–3
Poland (Polish-Lithuanian Commonwealth) 30, 166
Catherine the Great and 508–9
Constitution of 3 May 1791 171, 513
Cossacks 167, 169
rebellion (1648) 165, 169, 491
cultural influence 31
on Russia 68, 69, 165
and Great Northern War with Sweden 168, 491, 500
hegemonic power of 31, 489
and Holy League 490
Jews in 31, 185
and Ottoman Empire 166
Renaissance in 165
Russia and 489
science 174–5, 179–80, 182
social and political reform under Stanislaw Poniatowski 171, 508
and Time of Troubles (1612–13) 149
Treaty of Eternal Peace with Muscovy (1686) 165, 167, 490
and Ukraine 166, 167
Uniate Church 173
war of 1653–67 489
War of Polish Succession (1733–36) 505
see also Poland; Poland, Congress Kingdom of (1815–32); Poland, Partitions of; Poles
Polenov, Vasilii 105
Poles
and Decembrist revolt 33
émigré community in Paris 173–4
as explorers 182
and first Duma (1906) 42
Great Emigration from Russia 173
intellectual influence in Russia 182
as scientists 179–80, 182
suspected of conspiracies 151
Poletyka, Hryhorii, Cossack 169
police
provincial forces 197, 454, 456n.12, 465
role in justice system 345
secret (*okhrana*) (Third Section) 361, 439, 441, 455, 637, 638
urban forces 455
see also Gendarme Corps; Police Department (1880)
police chiefs, local (*ispravnik*) 356
Police Department (1880) 639
abolished by Provisional Government (1917) 654
criticism of security police 651
inadequacy of regular 647
methods 643–4, 649
mobile surveillance brigade (for provinces) 641, 646
Moscow bureau surveillants 641–2
reforms 652
relations with Gendarme Corps 643, 646, 649
security bureaus 639–40
regional 649, 652
security during First World War 653–4
Special Section 644, 651
use of informants 640, 642–4, 650, 652
police state (polizeistaat), principles of 208
Polish language
censorship of 38
status as language of reason 165
Polish positivism 179–80
Polish rebellion (1863) (January uprising) 22, 132, 177, 541, 610
Anglo-French intervention 12, 564
financial crisis 403
and 'Russification' 37, 38
and Ukraine 176
Polish Socialist Party 181
political culture
and 1812 war 151–3
pervasiveness of conspiracy theory in 151–3

political opposition 96, 440
  to Peter the Great 117–18
  to Tsar Nicholas II 665, 666, 668
  see also Bolsheviks; Mensheviks; radicals
political parties
  and economic debates 420–1
  Land and Freedom Party 196
  Muslim 221
  Muslim Union 220
  Polish Socialist Party 181
  and Progressive Bloc (1915) 666
  see also Constitutional-Democratic (Kadet) party; Russian Social Democratic Workers' Party (RSDWP)
political thought
  anarchism 138–40
  constitutionalism 124–6
  liberalism 131, 133–6
  nature of monarchy in Russia 116–19
  Polish 173–4
  Polish activism 180–1
  Polish positivism 179–80
  populism 136–8
  republicanism 125
  Russian conservatism 122–4, 131–3
  Russian Enlightenment 119–21
  social democrats 140–4
  socialism 136–44
  Ukrainian influence on 165
  Westerniser / Slavophile debate 126–30
  see also Lenin; Marxism
Polivanov, General A. A. 549
  minister of war 664
poll tax 371, 379, 382, 384, 473–4
  arrears 411
  clergy exemption 293
  impact on peasantry 483–4
  phased out 388, 408, 481
  to finance army 535
Polots'kyi (Polotskii), Symeon, Ukrainian cleric 165
Poltava, battle of (1709) 18, 29, 168, 498
Poltava province, peasant disorder (1902) 646
Poliakov, L. S., Moscow banker 404
Poniatowski, Stanislaw August, last king of Poland 171–2, 508
population
  1897 census 620
  growth 473, 493
  Jewish 70, 191, 192n.10, 195
  Muscovy 530
  Nizhnii Novgorod 271–2
  peasant 369, 373–5, 379, 389
  shift of settlement eastwards 493
  urban 415
populism, women and 317
populist movement 136–8, 181
  and culture 103, 104, 111
  and politicised workers 623
  women and 317–18
Port Arthur (Lüshun) 568
  acquisition 542
  defences 550
  Japanese annexation of 569, 577
  loss of 542
Portsmouth, Peace of (1905) 542, 569
Posen (Poland) 172
Potemkin family, Cossack origins of 233
Potemkin, Prince Grigorii
  favourite of Catherine the Great 81, 509, 512, 514
  opposition to 514
Potemkin mutiny (1905) 582–3
Potresov, Aleksandr, exiled to Siberia 645
poverty 468, 485
  and local government 455
  Municipal Guardianships 321
  Nizhnii Novgorod 272
  rural 390
Prach, Ivan, collector of folk-songs 84
Praskovia, Tsarita 74
Pravda (Bolshevik newspaper) 652
press
  Arabic 222
  commercial 253, 256
  debate on peasant reforms 604
  economic and financial journals 420
  first newspapers 75
  illustrated journals 281
  influence of 573
  Jewish 197
  Muslim 206, 219, 222
  newspapers in Nizhnii Novgorod 281
  provincial 281
  reaction to strikes 622
  revolutionary newspapers 645, 652
  Russian, backlash against Jewish integration 197
  The World of Art journal 110–1
  see also literature; *Novoe vremia*; printing
Pressburg, Peace of (1805) 525
prikazy (chancelleries) 430
Princip, Gavrilo, assassin of Francis-Ferdinand 571
printing
  church control over 76

church script (*kirillitsa*) 75
civil script typeface 75
early 18th century 74
industry 620
state presses 74, 89
prints and engravings 71
lubok wood prints 76, 84
popular 84
Procurator-General of Senate 435, 436
professions and professional classes 259–63
independence 259
and *intelligentsia* 259, 263
law 261–2
medicine 260, 262
politicisation of 260
repression of organisations 261, 263
state training 259
teaching 260, 262
uncertified protoprofessionals and 261, 262
see also bureaucracy; lawyers
'Progressive Bloc', formation of (1915) 665, 666
prohibition, during First World War 482, 660
Prokopovich, Feofan (Prokopovych, Teofan), churchman and writer 74, 75, 118, 165, 166
'Vladimir' (play) 76
proletarian dictatorship, Lenin's theory of 143
property 139
abolition of 136
investments by women 329
property laws 327–9
1753 changes 330, 332
administration of marital property 330
conflict with family law 337, 338
gender difference in 327, 342
and law on dowries 328, 330, 331, 333, 336, 339
ownership of land and serfs by nobility 229
transactions between husband and wife 333–5
Ukraine 176
women's responsibilities 329
women's rights 311, 342
prostitution
among domestic servants 320
regulation of 312
Protasov, Count N. A., chief procurator 286
protectionism 396, 400, 410, 413
Protopopov, Alexander, minister of interior (1916) 653
provinces (*guberniia*) 450
noble assemblies 229, 257
subdivisions (*provintsii*) 450
Provincial Archival Commissions (1883) 283
provincial assemblies
and emancipation of serfs 257
nobility and 257, 275, 460
provincial capitals, administrative structure 275
provincial society 449
Nizhnii Novgorod 278–83
Prus, Boleslaw
The Doll (novel) 179
Pharaoh (novel) 180
Prussia 12
and Austria 511
Jewish populations 187
landowners as political force 241, 242, 243
Napoleon in 527
relations with Russia 506–7, 510, 511, 521, 564–5
and Seven Years' War 506
and Third Coalition 523, 525
and Treaty of Kalisch 527
and Tsar Nicholas I 558
and Tsar Paul's Northern League 517
and unification of Germany 549, 565
see also Germany
Prussia, East, Russian occupation (1758) 506
Przenicki, Andrzej, Polish engineer 182
public opinion, increasing importance of 574, 608, 612
public (social) welfare
boards of 461
role of zemstvos 258, 464
state funding for 472
women's role in 321
public sphere
emergent 256
literary 256
see also civil society
Pufendorf, Samuel 117, 497
Pugachev, Emelian, Cossack 147
Pugachev revolt (1773–75) 89, 147, 151, 154, 483, 510
punishment
administered informally by peasants 352
corporal 339, 340–1
death penalty, for women 339
during states of emergency 366
exile as 339, 341, 366
peasants' view of state 352
use of torture 339
Purishkevich, Vladimir, assassination of Rasputin 668

Pushkin, Alexander 68, 95, 155
Eugene Onegin 95, 96
folk-tales 98
and 'golden age' of Russian poetry 95–6
statue in Moscow to (1880) 102, 133
The Contemporary (journal) 95

Quarenghi, Giacomo, architect 82, 397

Rabochaia mysl' (Workers' Thought) (journal) 627
Rachkovskii, Peter, security chief 639–40
Rachmaninov, Sergei, composer 108, 112
All-Night Vigil 115
radicals 120–1
intellectuals 250–1
lawyers as 363–4
opposition to Alexander II 440
underground organisations 640
and workers 623–4
see also intelligentsia; revolution; terrorism
Radishchev, Alexander Nikolaevich, radical novelist 87, 120–1
Radoszkowski, Oktawiusz, Polish entomologist 180
Raifskii, Aleksei, Orthodox missionary priest 205
railway workers 620
railways 12, 182, 400, 416
bonds issued 406
construction programme 619
credit funding for 403
into Asia 54, 56
into Central Asia 40
national network 388, 391, 549, 551
St Petersburg to Warsaw (1862) 38
state funding for 471
state ownership of 410
to European capitals 108
Trans-Siberian 18, 276, 412, 472, 568
ranks (*chiny*)
and economic function 247
fluctuations in lives of urban workers 272
'honoured citizen' (1832) 249
inorodtsy ('aliens') 34
and legal administration 456
legally defined 194, 229, 245
rights and privileges of 245
Table of (1722) 229, 248, 249n.9
urban 31, 452, 458
see also elites, Russian; *meshchane*; nobility, hereditary; *raznochintsy*; *soslovie*
Rasputin, Grigorii
assassination 668
and Church 304, 305
influence of 667, 668
Rastrelli, Bartholomeo Francesco, architect 78
Rastrelli, Carlo Bartholomeo, sculptor 72
rationalism 127
Raupach, Hermann, maestro di capella in St Petersburg 79
raznochintsy (social category) 246–51
educated commoners as 96, 249
radical intellectuals as 250–1
subgroups 246
and Table of Ranks 249
Razumovskii family, Cossack origins of 233
realism
in literature 97, 100
in music 100
rejected by avant-garde 108
Reformation, and elite landholdings 239
refugees, from German offensive (1915) 665
regionalism, the 'provincial idea' 273
Reichenbach, Treaty of (1813) 527
Reingardt, N. V., on subordination of women 338
Reinke, N., Senator 358
religion
disputation 165
and political theory 118
and unification of empire 20
see also Catholic Church; Christianity; Islam; Orthodox Church
religious holidays, Nizhnii Novgorod 270–1
religious toleration
Catherine the Great's edict (1773) 206
and October Manifesto (1905) 218
principle of 208
proposed 125, 135
under Nicholas II 218
Renny, Aimé, Genoese banking house 398
Repin, Ilya 105
The Volga Barge-Haulers (painting) 101
representative government 124, 129, 130
and civil society 255
flaws of 134
and Great Reforms 607
lack of 240
liberty and 130
and social progress 135
see also Duma; provincial assemblies; zemstvo assemblies
republicanism 125, 157
Rerikh, Nikolai 112

Retusaari Island 496
Reutern, Count M. Kh., minister of finance 405, 479–80, 549
and need for modernisation 595
and problems of peasant redemption scheme 611
Reval (Tallinn) 29
taken by Russia (1710) 496
Revoliutsionnaia Rossiia (Socialist Revolutionary newspaper) 645
revolution of 1905 42–3, 108, 613
and Constitution of 1906 367, 572
effect on army 542–3
effect on economy 417–18
and labour unrest 631–4
Muslims and 220–1
October Manifesto 42, 218, 613, 633
Orthodox Church and 302
Poland and 181
police success against revolutionaries 648, 650
political unrest 645–8
in rural areas 390, 393, 647
and semi-constitutional monarchy 446
Ukraine and 181
and Winter Palace demonstration ('Bloody Sunday') 629, 647
women and 322–5
see also Duma (legislature)
revolution
and conspiracy theories 152
and 'direct action' (violence and terrorism) 135, 242
Marxist theory of 141, 657
popular 129, 130, 138, 139, 243–4
socialist 141
threat of 507
Trotsky's theory of 'permanent' 143
see also Decembrist revolt; French Revolution; Revolution of 1905; Revolutions of 1848; Russian Revolution; terrorism
revolutionaries
assumption of power 669
legal methods of protest 652
Revolutions of 1848 558
Reynolds, Sir Joshua 81
Riga 29, 495
annual trade fair 186
industrial workers in 620
Jewish merchants banned from 186
revenue from tolls 492
taken by Russia (1710) 496
Rimsky-Korsakov, Nikolai 99, 103, 109, 112
Invisible City 278
Scheherazade 107
rivers, characteristics of 265
Rodzianko, Mikhail, president of Duma 657
Romania 513, 559
official discrimination against Jews 70, 184n.1
Romanov, Dmitrii, and Treaty of Peking 49
Romanov dynasty 149, 151
as centre of aristocratic circles 233
desire for recognition 11
instability of in 18th century 147, 151
key positions in government 236
Romanticism
Polish 174
Ukrainian 175
Roslin, Alexander, Swedish artist 83
Rostislavov, Dmitrii, clergyman 312
Rostopchin, Count Fedor V. 151
as governor-general of Moscow 152, 153, 155
Rostov, theatre 73
Rostov-on-Don, labour unrest 627
Rostovstev, Count Ia. I. 612
Chairman of Editing Commission 601
Rothschilds (Paris and London), bankers 403, 406
Rousseau, Jean-Jacques 148
notion of popular sovereignty 131, 134
Rozhestvenskii, Admiral Z. P. 586, 587
Rozumovs'kyi, Kyrylo (Razumovskii, Kyril), Cossack Hetman 168, 169
Rozumovs'kyi, Olekskii (Razumovskii, Aleksei), Ukrainian Cossack 168
Rubinstein, Anton, pianist 98, 282
Rubinstein, Nikolai 99
Rumiantsev, Count N. P., minister of commerce 399, 527
and Continental System 526
Rumiantsev, Field Marshal Count Petr 509, 535
Rumiantseva, Nadezhda 321
Rurik (Riurik), princely dynasty of Rus 233
Rus, origins of 166, 175
Russia
and 1848 European revolutions 558
aspiration to Great Power status 11, 13, 24
and emergent nationalism 22, 23
as European Great Power 554, 571
European influence on 10, 14, 16, 45–50, 54
and Holy League 490
joins Entente (1907) 419
at outbreak of Great Northern War 492–4

Russia (*cont.*)
as peripheral to Europe 23, 501
political instability by 1914 12, 24, 653
prospects for post-Soviet 26
relations with Islam 202, 211, 217
and Seven Years' War 506
territorial gains at partition of Poland 172–3
tsarist system of government 15, 21
see also autocracy
and War of the Austrian Succession (1740–48) 505
see also autocracy; France; Germany; Great Britain; Ottoman Empire; Prussia; Russian culture; Russian Empire
Russian Bank, for foreign trade 404
Russian Bible Society 153
and response to Napoleonic invasion 157–8
Russian culture 27, 34, 68, 89
artists' opposition to state 96
development under Peter the Great 68–7
elite consumption of 89, 253
as European avant-garde 108
and foreign embassies 502
'golden age' under Catherine the Great 81–8
internationalisation of 107
limited independent activity 89, 105
modernism 110
nationalism in 96–7, 98–100, 103
neo-nationalism 112
and origins of intelligentsia 253
Orthodoxy and 41, 68, 90
popular consumption of 84, 253
Populism 103, 104, 111
reputation by early 20th century 92–4
under Alexander II 97–102
under Alexander III 103–7
under Anna and Elizabeth 78–80
under Nicholas I 94–7
under Nicholas II 107–15
see also architecture; art; literature; music; painting; Russian Enlightenment; theatre
Russian Empire 9, 25, 46
as anti-European empire 51–5
civilising mission of 47, 49, 52–3
compared with Ottoman Empire 14–16
and effect of 1864 law reforms 356–9
effect of Europhile foreign policy on 529
and ethnic nationalities 22–3, 28–9, 192n.10
tsarist 'nationalities policy' 27, 32–6
ethnic Russian settlement in Asia 40, 59
as European empire 45–50, 54
expansion of 10, 28–32, 374, 416, 531
effect on economy 397
as inexorable movement eastwards 59
into Central Asia 36, 40, 49, 53–4, 555, 561–2
motivation for 562–4
to East Asia 542, 550, 561
as intermediary between Europe and Asia 50, 62
Jewish populations in 70, 186, 191
metropole-colony distinction 17, 46, 51, 60
Muslim populations within 202, 205
and national consolidation 56, 220
as national empire 55–63
and peasant population growth 374
variations in local administration 450
see also Baltic provinces; Poland; Russian identity; Ukraine
Russian Enlightenment 68, 85
and Counter-Enlightenment 121–2
and origins of intelligentsia 253, 254
political thought 119–21, 256
and religions 207, 297
Russian Geographical Society 598
Russian identity 27, 51, 149
imperial and national 45
political debate on 126
and Russianisation 57
Slavophiles' view of 127–8
Westernisers' view of 128–30
see also Russian nationalism; Russianisation; 'Russification'
Russian language 34, 123
in law courts 357, 358
and Russification policies 38
in schools 38
Russian Museum (state museum of Russian art), St Petersburg 104
Russian Musical Society (founded 1858) 99, 107, 280, 282
Russian nationalism 149
and 1812 war 147–51
as antithesis to Napoleonic France 148
and concept of empire 51–2
and European identity 48
reactionary 146
see also Russian identity; 'Russification'
Russian Revolution (1917) 13, 17, 553
abdication of tsar 571, 655, 657–8
bread shortage (1916–17) 653, 655, 658, 662
demonstrations in St Petersburg 656
and labour movement 635–6

mutiny of Petrograd garrison 656, 658, 662–4
Petrograd Soviet declared 657, 669
Provisional Government 636, 654, 657, 658
proximate causes of abdication 655–8
in rural areas 390, 393, 668
and workers' soviets 636
Russian Social Democratic Workers' Party (RSDWP) 196, 628
and the Bund 200, 626, 628
Russianisation (*obrusenie*) (national homogenisation) 57
'Russification' (after 1863) 27, 37–2, 132
administrative 37
cultural 38, 104
distinct from Russianisation 57
in Finland 39, 235, 546n.36
measures in Poland 178, 546
unplanned 37
Russo-Asian Bank 419
Russo-Chinese Bank 405, 414
Russo-Japanese War (1905) 12, 42, 467, 542, 550, 568–9, 587
economic effects of 405, 417
effect on domestic politics 569
and shipbuilding programmes 578
Russo-Korean Bank 405
Russo-Turkish wars
(1711) 435
(1735–39) 505, 535
(1769–74) 397, 509, 510
(1787–91) 186, 398, 513
(1807) 525
(1829) 478, 540, 559
(1877–78) 210, 471, 541, 565–6
Ruzskii, General 664
Ryabushinskii family, Moscow bankers 417, 420, 424
Ryabushinskii, Stepan 110
Rymnik, battle of (1789) 535

Sablukov, Gordii, teacher 212
Saburov, A. A., jurist 613
Saburov, P. A., ambassador 613
sacristans 292
St Petersburg 10, 13
1864 law reforms in 356
and 1917 Revolution 635, 653
demonstrations (February) 656
garrison mutiny 656, 658, 662–4
and workers' soviet 632–4
Academy of Arts 79, 83, 89, 94, 99, 104
Academy of Sciences 77, 82, 308
ban on marriage of women teachers 321
as banking centre 404, 419
bar council 261
cathedral 70
construction of 69–70, 496
cosmopolitan culture in 107
culture under Peter the Great 68
as economic centre 417
foundling hospital (1764) 312
Imperial Court 72, 78
Jews in 32, 195, 197
jury lists 350
Kremlin Armoury workshops 69
Kunstkamera 70
labour unrest
1901 'Obukhov defence' 626
Assembly of Russian Factory Workers 322, 629, 630
and *gaponovshchina* movement 627, 629
increased militancy 635
and Marxist intelligentsia 627, 645
Nevsky cotton mill strike (1870) 621–2
and Shidlovskii elections 632
strikes (1896–7) 625
as main trading port 395
Medical Surgery Academy, women at 316, 317, 318, 319
municipal reforms (1846) 459
Peter and Paul fortress 70
police security bureau 642
population 415
as Russian capital 394, 395
St Alexander Nevsky monastery 70
School of Law 236
society
business elite 228
industrial workers in 620
social categories 452
tensions between nobles and merchants 459
State Paper Money Bank 397
stock exchange 395
strategic vulnerability 575
Summer Palace 70
symphony concerts 107
and *The World of Art* journal 110
theatres
Bolshoi 85, 105
Hermitage 85
Mariinsky 101, 105, 108
under Anna 78
university 236

St Petersburg (*cont.*)
Winter Palace 78
Women's Medical Institute 319
Zubov's engraving of 72
see also Petrograd Soviet
St Petersburg Cadet Corps 80
St Petersburg Conservatoire (1862) 99, 105
St Petersburg, Treaty of (1881) 564
Saint-Simon, Comte de, and role of credit 402
salt
state monopoly 395
tax on 475
Saltykov-Shchedrin, Mikhail E., reformer and satirist 153, 598
Samarin, Iu. F., reformer 35, 598, 601
and land reforms 603, 605
Samarkand 40, 562
San Stefano, Treaty of (1878) 566
Sandepu, battle of 542
Sandomierz, Confederation of 168
Saratov
1864 law reforms in 356
middle classes 275
Sardinia 520
Sarovskii, Serafim, canonisation of (1903) 288
satire 120
debate on nature of 86
Savary, General, Napoleonic official 526
Savitskii, Petr 62
Sazonov, Sergei Dmitrievich, foreign minister 247, 570, 571, 567n.16
sblizhenie (rapproachment) 57, 61
Schädel, Gottfried Johann 70
Schleinitz, Johann baron von, as ambassador for Peter the Great 502
Schlüter, Andreas, sculptor 70
Schoenebeck, Adriaan, engraver 71
School of Law, St Petersburg 236
schools
church control over 103, 278
and development of Russian literature 80
ecclesiastical 286, 295
girls' 307, 312, 313
boarding 307
primary 312, 318, 464
state secondary (*gimnaziia* and *progimnaziia*) 314, 318
gymnasia 94–7, 249n.11
jadid Muslim reformed 219
Jewish parochial 190
Jewish state 35, 191
Kazakh 212
missionary 41
national 461
primary 103, 278, 312, 318, 464
state high 236, 239, 266, 312
Tatar 212
and use of Russian language 38
village 262, 278, 389
Schwartzenberg, Prince Felix, Austrian foreign minister 559
science
Academy of Sciences 77, 82, 308
Polish 174–5, 179–80
and social development 135
Scott, Sir Walter 95
Scriabin, Alexander 108, 113–14
Mysterium 114
Prometheus 113
sculpture 72
equestrian statue of Peter I 91
wooden relief carving 72
Sebastopol, fall of (1855) 540, 560, 594
Second World War 14
secret societies 160
Seeley, J. R. 58
Sekowski, Józef, Pole and Russian academic 175
self-determination 143
Semenov-Tian-Shanskii, P. P., ethnographer and senior state official 53, 60, 607
seminaries, religious 170, 286, 292
Nizhnii Novgorod 266, 277
Semipalatinsk 561
Senate
administrative supervision by 436
Criminal Cassation Department 345, 354
founded by Peter the Great 435, 450
judicial role of 345, 354, 435
as High Court of Review 436
and law on transactions between spouses 334–5
procurator-general 435
and rulings on serf ownership 331, 332–3
Special tribunal 365
tax collection 435
under Alexander I 436
sentimentalism, vogue for 87
Serbia
autonomy (1829) 559
First World War 571
Slav nationalism in 570
serfdom 369, 370
abolished in Baltic provinces (1816–19) 598

criticism of 94, 96, 120, 121, 124
Decree on Free Agriculturalists (1803) 598
Decree on Obligated Peasants (1842) 598
defence of 123
as economic system 596
flight from 377
inventories (1847–8) 598
Napoleonic Wars and 160
origins 371
serfs
and cultural life on estates 82, 83
exploitation of 16, 17, 21, 128
by non-nobles 247
as factory workers 400, 618
and jury system 349
labour obligations 371, 385
legal emancipation 248, 533
as 'living collateral' 402
married 331
Orthodox Church and 300–1
ownership by (married) women 330–3
participation in local government 451
reform of state peasantry 476, 599
and rights of nobility to ownership 229, 231, 247
scale of ownership 231
and state legal system 456
women as dowry property 331–2
see also peasants
serfs, emancipation (1861) 37, 241, 257, 270, 371, 388, 433
effects of abolition 391, 608–9
first announcement by Alexander II 596
and industrial growth 619
legal changes 602
and local government 450
and *obrok* revenues 476
and Poland 178
and poll tax 474
reasons and preconditions for 594–9
Statute of 19 February 597, 600
and tax revenues 477, 484
see also peasants, and land reform (redemption)
Sergei Aleksandrovich, Grand Duke 644
Serov, V. A. 105
servants, domestic 319
Seven Years' War 506–7, 537
Sha-Ho, battle of 542
Shafirov, Petr Pavlovich 502
Discourse on Swedish war 117, 496, 497
Shakhovskoi, Prince 270
and theatre troupe in Nizhnii Novgorod 279
Shamil, imam in Daghestan and Chechnia 211, 215, 541
defeat of 41, 558, 562
Shchapov, A. P., historian 59, 279
Shcheglovitov, Ivan, minister of justice 43, 361
Shcherbatov, N. B., Prince, minister of interior 668
Shcherbatov, Prince Mikhail Mikhailovich, Counter-Enlightenment thinker 88, 121–2
Journey to the Land of Ophir 121
On Corruption of Morals in Russia 121
Shekhtel, Fedor, architect 110
Sheremetev family, aristocratic landowners 233
Sheremetev, Field Marshal Count Boris 494
Shevchenko, Aleksandr 113
Shevchenko, Taras, Ukrainian Romantic, 'Kobzar' 175
Shibanov, Mikhail, serf painter 84
Shidlovskii Commission, on workers' representation 631–2
shipbuilding 257n.9
20-year programme (from 1881) 576
1895–1902 programme 576
Nizhnii Novgorod 268, 273, 274
Pacific fleet programme (1898) 578
private yards 579
state yards 579
transformation (1906–14) 588
Voronezh yards 69, 490
Shipka Pass, defence of (1878) 541
Shipov, Nikolai, serf entrepreneur 247
Shishkin, Ivan, landscape painter 102
Shishkin, Nikolai Pavlovich, assistant foreign minister 567n.16
Shishkov, Aleksandr Semenovich
and linguistic nationalism 123
and Poland 149
Shliapnikov, Aleksandr, Bolshevik 656
Shmidt, Anna Nikolaevna, journalist in Nizhnii Novgorod 274
Shulgin, Vasilii, nationalist 666
Shuvalov family, aristocratic landowners 233
Shuvalov, Count Ivan, favourite of Elizabeth 79
Shuvalov, Count P. A.
and economic reforms 396, 606
head of gendarmes and security 610

Statute on Public Order (1782)
on conduct in marriage 335, 336, 337
on duties of husbands 337
and obedience of wives 335, 336, 338
Stavuchany, battle of (1739) 535
Stefan, Archbishop of Kursk 304
Stepanova, Afim'ia P. 155
steppe, open, peasant agriculture 387
Steppe region
Muslim administrative area 216, 222
see also Kazakh steppe
steppe, southern
displacement of nomads by peasants 374
expansion into 10, 15
Stieglitz, Alexander, Director of State Bank 402–4
Stieglitz, Ludwig 403
stock exchange, St Petersburg 395
Stolbovo, Treaty of (1619) 489
Stolypin, Petr A. 446, 648
agricultural reforms 181, 389, 417, 464, 613
military field courts 648
and policy towards Muslims 221
prime minister (1907) 42, 182, 237, 616
assassinated (1911) 43, 614, 651
reform of security police system 648–9
use of Emergency Laws 366
Straits Convention (1841) 560
Stravinsky, Igor 108
Firebird 112
Petrushka 112
Rite of Spring (première 1913) 93, 112
Strel'na, palace of 70
strikes 620
1870s 621–3
as extension of peasant unrest 620
general (October 1905) 633, 647
intelligentsia-assisted (1896–7) 625, 627
Ivanovo-Voznesensk (1905) 633
July 1903 646
police measures against 622, 625, 633, 644
as political issue 621–2
women as strikers 322, 635
see also labour relations
Stroganov family, merchant aristocrats 28, 233
Struve, Petr Berngardovich, political thinker and activist 58, 133, 420
Critical Observations on the Economic Development of Russia 141
as Legal Marxist 140
Problems of Idealism 141
Signposts 135
Stupin, A. V., icon painter, Nizhnii Novgorod 274
Sturdza, Aleksandr Skarlatovich, Orthodox conservatism 123
Stürmer, Boris Nikolaevich, senior official and premier 567n.16
subordinate organs (*podchinennye organy*) 430–2
co-ordination of 436, 439, 441
colleges (later ministries) 192, 431n.3, 435
efficiency of 448
and expenditure demands 469, 479
ministerial government system 432–4
Sudeikin, Grigorii, chief of security 639
Sufi Islam 208, 209
Russian measures against 211, 217
in Transcaucasus 205, 211
sugar
industry 399
tax 482
al-Sughuri, Abd al-Rahman, Naqshbandi sheikh 217
Sukhanov, Nikolai 368
Sukhomlinov, V. A., war minister (1909–15) 550, 551
Sukhum district (Transcaucasia) 216
Sumarokov, Aleksandr Petrovich, playwright 80, 119
Sinav i Truvor 119
Supreme Administrative Commission 441
supreme organs (*verkhovnye organy*) 435–41, 448
see also Senate; State Council; Supreme Privy Council
Supreme Privy Council, established by Catherine I 435
Surikov, Vasily, painter 101
Suslova, Nadezhda, first woman doctor in Europe 316
Sutherland, Richard, court financier 398
Suvorov, Alexander (A.V.), Russian commander 509, 535
Sverdlov, Yakov Moiseevich 184, 200
Svetloiar, Lake 264
Sviatopolk-Mirskii, Prince Petr, minister of interior 647
Sweden 29, 510
defensive alliance with Russia (1724) 500
expansion into Estonia 489
hegemonic power of 491
as natural enemy 496, 521
and Northern System 509

at outbreak of Great Northern War 492
persecution of Orthodox peasants 495, 497
and Treaty of Nystad (1721) 500
war with (1656–8) 489
war with (1788–90) 513
see also Great Northern War
Switzerland 527
Symbolism, in Russian literature 98
Symbolist poets 110, 113
Szyma'nski, Adam 179

Table of Ranks (1722) 97, 229, 248
Taganrog 510
re-annexed (1739) 505
T'ai-tsu, first Ming Emperor of China 445
Talashkino estate, artists' colony 110, 112
Tallinn (Estonia) 29, 496
Tannenberg, battle of (1914) 552
Taraqqi (Muslim newspaper) 222
Targowica, Confederations of 171
Tartu (Estonia) (formerly Dorpat) 39, 496
Tashkent 40, 562
cholera riots (1892) 40
Judicial Chamber (1899) 356, 358
Tatars
assimilation into Russian elite 230, 234
Christian (in Kazan) 40
conquest of 489
Lithuanian 206
Muslim 28, 219
peasants 370
Tatishchev, Vasilii Nikitich, governor of Orenburg 47, 118, 205
Tauride Directorate (TMDP), to control Muslim affairs 209
tax
on capital income 408
commerce (on business) 413, 481
excise reforms (1863) 474, 479, 607
on households 371, 382, 384, 473
impact on population 482–6
income 342, 480, 481
increase in indirect 412, 413, 474, 481–2, 485–6
land 371, 382, 463, 481
levied by zemstvos 463, 464
local 453
property-based 408
proposed increases (1861) 477
reforms proposed 477–8, 606
revenues 369, 473–8, 484
sales 388
on salt 475
on sugar 482
on tobacco 482
trade duties 408
and village organisation 384
on wine 398
see also customs tariffs; poll tax; spirits; state finance; tax collection
tax collection
mechanisms 430, 473, 484
supervision by Senate 435
see also tax-farming
tax-farming 193
abolished 474
on liquor sales 474, 479
Tchaikovsky, Peter Ilyich 99, 105–6, 111
ballet music 106
church music 106
Eugene Onegin (opera) 100
orchestral music 106
The Queen of Spades (opera) 105, 108
teachers 260, 262
training courses for women (Guerrier courses) 317, 319
women as 314, 317, 321
telegraph 594
introduction (1860s) 455
Tenishev family, Muslim origins 204
Tenisheva, Princess Maria 110, 112
Tercuman (Muslim weekly newspaper) 219
terrorism 135, 242, 365, 639
and 1905 Revolution 647
casualties among officials 647, 648
Socialist Revolutionary programme of 645, 651
use of military courts to try 648
Teschen, Treaty of (1779) 511
Tevkelev family, Muslims 204
textile industry 399
major strikes (1870s) 621–3
mechanisation 618–19
Morozov strike (1885) 625
St Petersburg strikes (1896–7) 625
women workers 322
theatre 73–4, 85
independent 105
influence of Stanislavsky 93, 109–10
Moscow 73, 85, 109–10, 165
Nizhnii Novgorod 278–9
Russian plays for 80, 85
St Petersburg 85, 101, 105, 108
under Catherine the Great 85
see also ballet

Third Section (of Chancellery), police and intelligence functions 439, 441, 455, 637, 639
Three Emperors' Alliance (*Dreikaiserbund*) 565
Tiflis (Georgia) 214, 356
Tilsit, Treaty of (1807) 32, 399, 525, 526
Time of Troubles (1612–13) 16, 370
 Poland and 148, 149
Tkachev, Petr Nikitich, populist socialist 136, 137–8
tobacco
 state monopoly 395
 tax 482
Tobolsk, Siberia 28
Toeplitz, Treaty of (1813) 527
Tolstoy, Count D. A.
 minister of interior 356
 revisions to Great Reforms 615
Tolstoy, Leo, novelist 93, 102, 113, 138, 140
 Anna Karenina 100
 Childhood 97
 Confession 140
 The Kingdom of God Is within You 140
 War and Peace 100, 145
 What I Believe 140
Tomsk, Siberia 28
Tornau, Baron E.N. 212
torture
 exemption of pregnant women 340
 use of 339
towns and cities
 civic buildings 82
 civic life in 280–1
 cultural life 90, 278
 Jewish populations in 192
 and jury system 349
 justices of the peace 354
 legal categories of inhabitants 31, 452
 migrant women in 320
 migration of peasants into 90, 247, 352, 453, 662
 police force 455
 population growth 415
 and provincial administration 275
 taxes 457, 485
 urban administration
  reforms 450, 456, 458
  structure of 38, 457–9
  under Catherine the Great 151, 264, 458
  under Peter the Great 449, 458
 urban planning 264, 265–7, 458
 and zemstvo assemblies 463
 see also Moscow; Nizhnii Novgorod; St Petersburg
trade 396, 400, 415
 with Asia 414
 with China 395
 and credit 405
 effect of Great Northern War on 394
 and expansion of empire 10
 with Great Britain 399, 423, 493, 501
 growth of 493
 imports 397
 and Napoleonic Wars 399
 with Netherlands 493, 501
 neutral (principle of) 511
 with Persia 405, 414
 and Persian War (1721) 499–500
 protectionism 396, 400, 410, 413
 in towns 247
 see also exports; merchants
trade fairs 186
 Nizhnii Novgorod 268–70
trade unions 626, 634
 lack of rights 24
 police 446
 Shidlovskii Commission proposals 631–2
Transcaspian Province 541
 see also Turkestan
Transcaucasia *see* Caucasus; Caucasus, north
Trediakovskii, Vasilii, writer 80
Trepov, General, governor of St Petersburg 317, 365
Tretiakov, Pavel 101, 104
Trezzini, Domenico, Swiss-Italian architect 69
Trial of the 193, acquittals (1877) 365
trial by jury 345
 acquittal rates 353
 amendments 360
 burden of jury service 349, 350, 609
 complaints to Cassation Department 345, 354
 ignorance of rural jurors 351
 problems in practice 349–51
 in provinces 357–8
trials, public 345
Triple Entente 419, 569, 570
Troshchinskii (Troshschyns'kyi) family 170
Trotsky, Leon (Lev Davidovich Bronshtein)
 internationalist 140, 633
 and Lenin 142
 theory of 'permanent revolution' 143
Trubnikova, Maria 315
Trudovik Party, and women's suffrage 323

Trusevich, Maksimilian, director of Police Department 649
Trzemeski, Józef, Polish explorer 182
Tsaritsyno, gothic palace for Catherine II 82
Tsarskoe Selo, Catherine Palace at 78, 82
Tsederbaum, Alexander 196
Tsiolkovskii, Konstantin, astronomer 282
Tsushima Straits, battle of (1905) 542, 569, 587
Turgenev, Ivan
  A Huntsman's Sketches 97
  Fathers and Sons 97
  and inferiority of *raznochintsy* 250
  and unveiling of Pushkin statue 102
Turkestan 49, 58, 562
  cultural conflicts of law 359
  Muslim administrative system 216–17, 218
  Muslim rebellion (1916) 222
  reformed courts 356, 357
  Russian settlement in 40
Turkestan Spiritual Board 218
Turkey
  genocide in Anatolia 20
  as natural enemy 521
  Russian alliance with (1805) 524
  see also Crimean War; Ottoman Empire
Turkish (Turkic) language 219, 222
Tver
  jury lists 350
  reconstruction of 82
Tyrtov, P. P., naval minister 586

uezdy (provincial divisions) 450
Ufa, Islamic muftiate 207, 214
Ukraine 30, 148
  agricultural reforms 181
  annexation 10, 18
  Commission on National Education 176
  Cossacks in 167–8
  cultural divisions 176
  cultural influence on Russia 68, 165, 182, 289
  elites assimilated into Russia 233
  expansion into (by Catherine the Great) 30
  Jews banned from 186
  land tenure system 384
  'Little Russia' 170, 176
  modern politics in 181
  nationalist movement 22, 181
  Orthodox Church 166
  Reformation in 165–6
  Russian populism 181
  Russian provinces created (1781) 170
  suppression of Ukrainian language 38, 181
  see also Cossacks
Ukraine, eastern (left-bank) 29
  annexation (1667) 10, 18, 186, 489, 490, 531
  history of 175
  Jews in 186
Ukraine, western (right-bank)
  Jewish commercial classes in 176, 177
  peasant uprisings (1905–1907) 177
  and Poland 166, 167
  Polish nobility and landowners in 176–7
  under Russian rule 30, 175
Ukrainians
  and Cossack revolts 378
  influential careers in Russia 170
Ulianov, Vladimir Il'ich *see* Lenin
Ulybyshev, Alexander, musicologist in Nizhnii Novgorod 281
Uniate Church 173, 178
Union of All-Russian Medical Personnel 260
Union of Struggle for the Emancipation of Labour (Marxist) 627, 640
Union of Unions (1905) 260
Union of the United Nobility 229
United States 18, 19, 49
  as economic model 423
  imperialism in East Asia 576
  presidency and bureaucracy 445
  see also American War of Independence
universities 239, 432
  Jews in 195
  Kazan 279–80, 317
  Moscow 80, 82, 236, 249
  Polish 34, 174, 178
  St Petersburg 236
  women in 315, 317
Unkiar-Skelessi, Treaty of (1833) 559
Ural Mountains
  as boundary of Europe and Asia 47, 62
  metallurgical industry 15, 232, 493, 620
urban government
  local-central conflicts 452–3
  structure of 457–9
  under Catherine the Great 151, 264, 458
  under Peter the Great 449, 458
  see also towns and cities
urban planning 458
  Nicholas I's passion for 265
  Nizhnii Novgorod 264, 265–7
Urbich, Johann baron von, as ambassador for Peter the Great 502
Urusov family, Muslim origins 204

Urusov, Prince Mikhail, governor of Nizhnii Novgorod 275
Ushurma (Sheikh Mansur), Chechen rebel 205
Utyz-Imani (al-Bulghari), Abd al-Rahman, Sufi 210
Uvarov, Count Sergei Semenovich, minister of education 35, 124
  on bureaucracy 433
  state ideology of 'Orthodoxy, autocracy and nationality' 34, 94, 124, 150

Vaisov, Baha al-Din, Tatar Sufi 210
Vaisov, Inan al-Din 210
Vaisov Brotherhood 210, 211
Valuev, Count Petr (P. A.), minister of interior 38, 563
  and land redemption scheme 606
  and modification of reforms 611
  proposal for income tax 480
vanguard party, Lenin's theory of 142
Vasilevskii island, Peter the Great's residence on 70
Vasnetsov brothers, Viktor and Apollinari 105
Vaught, Velho, Rally & Co., official court bankers 398
Vedomosti (first newspaper) 75
Velden (Felten), G.-F. 82
Venice, and Holy League 490
Verbitskaia, Anastasia, *The Keys to Happiness* (novel) 324
Verdi, Giuseppe, *La Forza del Destino* 101
Verelä, Treaty of (1790) 513
Vereshchagin, M. N., lynched in Moscow 152, 153, 154
Vernadskii, G. I., historian 59, 62
Vernier, Paris banking house 406
Versailles, Treaty of (1756) 506
Vial'tseva, Anastasia, singer 321
Viborg
  ceded to Russia (1721) 499
  taken by Russia (1710) 496
Victoria, Queen 572
Vienna 93
  Turkish siege of (1683) 490
Vienna, Congress of (1815) 33, 172, 399, 528, 556
  and Alexander's 'Holy Alliance' 556
Vigel, F. F., memoirist 330
villages 377
  arable land held in common 381, 383–5, 410
  commune organisation 383, 385, 392, 456
  festivals 386
  healers 262
  law and order 385
  schools 262, 278, 389
  shared burden of obligations 372, 384, 385
  see also peasant communes
Villuan, V. I., musician 282
Vilno (Vilnius, Wilno, Vilna) 33, 356
  Jews in 35, 197, 199
  lost to Germans (1915) 44
  Polish university in 34, 174
Vinaver, M. M., lawyer 363
Vinogradov, Ioann, priest in Nizhnii Novgorod 273
Virt, Anna, private school 313
virtue
  abstract 122
  civic 120, 121
  private 119, 147
Vishniakov, Ivan, painter 79
Vladimirskii-Budanov, M. F., on legal rights of women 338
Vladivostok 182, 561, 577, 660
vodka 412
  illegal distilling 485
  tax revenues from 472, 474–5
Voiekova, Akulina, lawsuit on serf ownership 331
Volga, River, at Nizhnii Novgorod 264
Volga-Kama Commercial Bank 404
Volga-Kama region, Muslims in 217
Volga-Ural region
  Great Apostasy (1866) 217
  Islam in 202, 204, 209, 217
  jadidism reform movement 219
Volhynia province (Ukraine) 177
Volkonskii family, landowners 233
Volkov, Dmitrii S., provincial goldsmith 151
Volkov, Fedor, actor-manager 80
Volkova, Mariia A. 148
Vologda province, women's association in 315
volost' peasant courts 361, 456, 463, 609, 615
Volotskii, Iosif (1439–1515) 116
Voronezh, shipyards 69, 490
Vorontsov family, aristocrats 233
Vorontsov, Alexander 514
Vorotyn, river port 268
Vrubel, N. A. 105
Vsevolodovich, Prince Georgii (1189–1238), legendary founder of Nizhnii Novgorod 283
Vsevolozhskii, Ivan 106
Vyborg 29

Vyshnegradskii, I. A., minister of finance 405, 409–11, 412, 482

Wagner, Richard 111
Wanderers, the (artists) 101, 103
Wanli, Ming Emperor of China 445
Waqf institutions 203, 208, 209, 216, 217
war, effect on state finances 478
War of the Austrian Succession (1740–48) 505
War for the Fatherland (1812) 147–8
  liberal nationalist view of 145, 150
War Ministry, and Muslims 213, 216, 218
War of Polish Succession (1733–36) 505
Warsaw 171, 178
  Jews in 35, 197
  lost to Germans (1915) 44
  surrendered to Russians (1794) 535
Warsaw, Grand Duchy of (Napoleonic) 149, 172, 525, 526
Waterloo, battle of (1815) 527
Wedgwood, Josiah 81
Weil, G., German orientalist 212
Western Provinces (modern Belarus, Lithuania and western Ukraine) 34, 148
  cultural Russification in 38
  Polish hegemony 31, 37
  see also Belarus; Lithuania; Ukraine
Westernisation
  debate with Slavophiles 126–30
  intellectual opposition to 88
  resistance to Peter the Great's reforms 77
  of Russian elite 17, 21, 67
  see also Europe
Westernisers, view of Russian national identity 128–30
Wielopolski, Aleksander, Polish reformer 178
Wilhelm I, king of Prussia and German Emperor 564
Wilhelm II, emperor of Germany 447, 567
Wilkicki, Andrzej, Polish naval scientist 182
William I, of Orange, king of Netherlands 558
Wilmot, Catherine 328, 331
Wiszniewski, Wincenty, Polish astronomer 174
witchcraft, belief in 353
Witkiewicz, Jan Prosper, Polish scholar 175
Witte, Count Sergei (S. Iu.), minister of finance 56, 221, 237, 405, 411–14, 417
  criticism of Kokovtsov 422
  economic reforms 411
  and expenditure on railways 409, 472
  on inadequacy of state budget 468, 486
  industrialisation policy 241, 434, 619
  influence of 573
  monetary reform (1897) 412
  and Nicholas II 442
  and Russo-Japanese War 569
  and shipbuilding programme 578
Wittelsbach dynasty, Bavaria 511
women 306, 319, 323
  and 1905 Revolution 322–5
  education
    higher 317, 318, 323
    non-elite 312–13, 318
  family responsibilities and ideals 306, 310
  in industry (First World War) 662
  in labour market 319–20
  migrant 319–21
  and modernisation 313–22
    feminist organisations 322
    image of 'new woman' 324–25
    and populist movement 317–18
    rejection of conventions 316
    rights 314–15
    'sexual question' 324
    and socialist ideals 316
  in nunneries 291, 309
  as nurses in Crimean War 314
  peasants
    consumption patterns 319
    gendered division of labour 383
  political rights 322–3
  in public life 321
  in Russian art 71
  soldiers' wives (*soldatka*) 248, 311
  state controls over sexuality 312, 324
  as teachers 314, 317, 321
  in universities 315, 317
  wives' duty of obedience 300, 333, 338
  'woman question' 313–14, 316, 327
  as writers 87, 308
  see also divorce; marriage; women, elite; women, legal status of
women, elite 306, 308, 326
  and criminal law 339, 340
  education 307–8
  and inheritance laws 327–9
  litigation rights 328
  management of estates 329
  and serf ownership 330–3
  and women's rights movement 315
women, legal status of 311, 326–7
  abused wives 334, 335

in criminal law 339–42
and family law 330, 335–9, 341
inheritance laws 327–9
obligation to obey husbands 308, 333, 335, 336, 337–9, 343
and passports 337, 343
presumption of frailty of women 336, 337, 339, 340–1, 343
property transactions between husband and wife 333–5
right to own and manage property 311, 326, 327, 328
and serf ownership 330–3
women's suffrage 323
Women's Union 322, 323
Woolf, Virginia 93
workers 617–18
and 1917 Revolution 635–6
artisans in Nizhnii Novgorod 268, 270
and Civil War 636
on industry councils (First World War) 662
links to communes 619
petition to tsar (1905) 630–1
politicised 24, 623, 634
relations with *intelligentsia* 623–4, 627, 645
and St Petersburg soviet 632–4
serfs as factory workers 400, 618
social and political importance of 620–1, 624–5
state peasants 617
and strikes in 1870s 621–3
urban industrial 619
wage labour 389, 391, 486
women in factories 319
Zubatov's government-sponsored organisations for 625–7, 644
workers' soviets 636
St Petersburg (Petrograd) 632–4, 657, 669
working class
growth of 415
and identity 624
Lenin's view of 142
Nizhnii Novgorod 273
urban 131
working conditions
and labour disputes 433, 434
regulation of 408, 410, 641
World of Art, The (art journal) 110–11

Xinjiang (China) 561, 563, 564

yasak (tribute paid in furs) 28
Yeni Dunai, Turkish fortress 30
Yiddish language 187
Yusupov family, Tatar origins of 234

Zablotskii-Desiatovskii, A. P., survey of serf estates 597
Zachary Zhdanov & Co., banking house 420
Zakataly district (Transcaucasia) 216
Zamoyski, Count Andrzej, Polish nationalist 178
Zaporihizian Sich, free Cossacks in 167, 168, 170
Zarudnyi, S. I., legal reformer 347
Zasulich, Vera, shooting of General Trepov 317, 365, 639
Zavodovs'ky (Zavadovskii, Petr), Petro 171
Zavodovs'kyi (Zavadovskii) family 170
Zeidman, A.I. & Co., banking house 420
Zemgor (All-Russian Union of Zemstvo and Municipal Councils) 667
zemstvo assemblies (from 1864) 259, 275, 388, 450, 461–5
conflicts with central government 453–4, 464, 610, 611
functions of 276, 453
inter-province co-peration 454
and jury lists 350, 609
legislation on 450, 463
Nizhnii Novgorod 276, 280
peasant representation on 609
power of Third Element (employees) 462
property qualifications 462
resistance to Stolypin's land reforms 464
rights of taxation 258, 276, 453, 463
and Statute of 1890 615
Statute (1864) 600, 602
and urban institutions 463
war relief work 454, 466
Zemtsov, Mikhail, architect 70
Zhitomir, Jewish rabbinical institute 35
Zhukovsky, V. V., businessman 420
Zhukovsky, V. A., poet 595
Zhuliakov, Toigil'da, Muslim 205
Zikrism, Sufi movement 211
Zinovev, I. A., ambassador 409
Zionism 199
Zólkiew, battle of (1706) 498
Zorndorf, battle of (1758) 506, 534

Zubatov, Sergei, Moscow Security Bureau 640
and 1903 strikes 646
government organisations for workers 625–7, 644
and growing revolutionary unrest 645
police methods 643–4, 649
use of informants 642–4
use of surveillants 641–2
Zubov family, and Catherine the Great's foreign policy 514
Zubov, Aleksei, engraver 72
Zubov, Ivan, engraver 72
Zybin, S. S., governor of Nizhnii Novgorod 276